CONTENTS

R. Gupta's®

POPULAR MASTER GUIDE

UNIVERSITY OF DELHI

M.Com

Entrance Test

Previous Papers Solved with Explanatory Answers

by

Dr. SIMA KUMARI

RAMESH PUBLISHING HOUSE, NEW DELHI

Published by
O.P. Gupta *for* Ramesh Publishing House

Admin. Office
12-H, New Daryaganj Road, Opp. Officers' Mess
New Delhi-110002 ✆ 23261567, 23275224

E-mail: info@rameshpublishinghouse.com
For Online Shopping: www.rameshpublishinghouse.com

Showroom
- Balaji Market, Nai Sarak, Delhi-6 ✆ 23253720, 23282525
- 4457, Nai Sarak, Delhi-6, ✆ 23918938

Book Code: R-1529

ISBN: 978-93-5012-300-3

HSN Code: 49011010

Price: ₹ 560

Printed at: J.P. Enterprises, Delhi

Previous Paper (Solved)

UNIVERSITY OF DELHI

M.Com., Entrance Exam, 2021 *

1. Rohan Ltd. has bought a piece of machinery. Before ensuring that the machine is a condition of operation for the intended purpose, it operates a trial run. In this trial run, the machine produces 5 units of product @ ₹ 99 per piece. The fair market price of such product, being standard, is ₹ 119 per piece. But these products, bewing extremely sub-standard, are sold in the market @ ₹ 33 per piece. The amount of cost to be added to the machinery for initial recognition is:

A. ₹ 660 B. ₹ 330

C. ₹ 495 D. ₹ 165

2. In the case of a problem based on the insolvency of partners as per Garner V. Murray case, a partner, though solvent, has a credit balance in his capital account on the date of dissolution but has a debit balance in his capital account after sharing the loss on realization. Such a partner should:

A. Neither share the loss of an insolvent partner nor bring in his share of realization loss in cash

B. Only share the loss of an insolvent partner

C. Share the loss of an insolvent partner and also bring in his share of realization loss in cash

D. Only bring the realization loss in cash

3. Standard cost method related to the valuation of inventory of finished goods and work-in-progress is:

A. Only a method of determination of cost for the purpose of valuation of inventory

B. Only a method of valuation of inventory

C. Both a method of determination of cost for the purpose of valuation of inventory and also a method of valuation of inventory

D. Neither a method of determination of cost for the purpose of valuation of inventory nor a method of valuation of inventory

4. As per Accounting Standard (AS) 10 'Property, Plant and Equipment', the costs for regular major inspection for faults as a condition of continuing to operate an item of property, plant and equipment (PPE):

A. Should not be recognized in the carrying amount of that item of PPE even if decided by the management of the entity

B. Should be recognized in the carrying amount of that item of PPE only if decided by the management of the entity

C. Should be charged as an expense in the period in which these costs are incurred

D. Should be recognized in the carrying amount of that item of PPE and additionally, the carrying amount of previous inspection or if the carrying amount of previous inspection is not determinable, the cost thereof should be derecognized

5. Under 'Stock and Debtors' method related to a dependent inland branch, for abnormal loss of stock at branch, besides credit to 'Branch Stock A/c' by 'Branch Profit and Loss A/c' and 'Branch Adjustment A/c':

A. Only cost of abnormal loss is debited to 'Branch Profit and Loss A/c

B. Only loading margin of abnormal loss is debited to 'Branch Adjustment A/c'

C. Neither cost of abnormal loss is debited to 'Branch Profit and Loss A/c' nor is loading margin of abnormal loss debited to 'Branch Adjustment A/c'

*** Exam held on: 26/09/2021.**

D. Cost of abnormal loss is debited to 'Branch Profit and Loss A/c' and loading margin of abnormal loss is debited to 'Branch Adjustment A/c'

6. Unless otherwise stated a Preference Share is always deemed to be:

A. Cumulative, Non-Participating and Non-Convertible.

B. Non-Cumulative, Non-Participating and Non-Convertible.

C. Cumulative, Participating and Non-Convertible.

D. Cumulative, Participating and Convertible.

7. In the Balance Sheet of a company, Reserve Capital:

A. is required to be disclosed under Authorised Capital.

B. is required to be disclosed under Issued Capital.

C. is required to be disclosed under Subscribed Capital.

D. is not required to be disclosed.

8. An item of Income or Expenditure is to be disclosed separately as per The Companies Act, 2013 if its amount exceeds:

A. 1% of the revenue from operations or ₹ 1,00,000, whichever is higher;

B. 1% of the revenue from operations or ₹ 1,00,000, whichever is lower;

C. 1% of the revenue from operations or ₹ 10,00,000, whichever is higher;

D. 1% of the revenue from operations or ₹ 10,00,000, whichever is lower;

9. Net Profits of AATMA Ltd. for the years 2020-2021, 2019-2020, 2018-2019, 2017-2018, 2016-2017 are ₹ 25 crore, ₹ 20 crore, ₹ 15 crore, ₹ 10 crore and ₹ 5 crore respectively. During 2020-2021, the company incurred ₹ 7,00,000 and ₹ 3,00,000 on free education and medical treatment of the employees of the company and their families respectively under CSR projects. State the short fall of expenditure on Corporate Social Responsibility as per The Companies Act, 2013:

A. ₹ 40,00,000 B. ₹ 30,00,000
C. ₹ 20,00,000 D. ₹ 10,00,000

10. On 31st March, 2021, Equity Shares of ₹ 10 each fully paid: ₹ 198 crore, 12% Red Pref. Share Capital: ₹ 42 crore, Securities Premium: ₹ 10 crore, General Reserve: ₹ 200 crore, Infrastructure Development Reserve (Statutory Reserve): ₹ 70 crore, Capital Redemption Reserve: ₹ 30 crore, Plant Revaluation Reserve: ₹ 8 crore. On 1st April, 2021, The company has offered buy back price at 20% over the Market Price. Market Price per share is ₹ 25. Calculate the Maximum permissible number of Equity Shares that can be bought back as per The Companies Act, 2013.

A. 4.95 crores B. 3.75 crores
C. 2.25 crores D. 1.75 crores

11. Under FSN system of inventory control, inventory is classified on the basis of:

A. Volume of material consumption

B. Frequency of usage of items of inventory

C. Criticality of the item of inventory for production

D. Value of items of inventory

12. The repairs and maintenance expenses of a machinery at 6,000 machine hours run is ₹ 1,12,000. If it runs for 9,000 machine hours, it will incur repairs and maintenance cost of ₹ 1,48,000. What will this cost at 12,000 machine hours run?

A. ₹ 2,24,000 B. ₹ 1,94,000
C. ₹ 1,84,000 D. ₹ 1,74,000

13. Controllable variances are best disposed-off by transferring to:

A. Cost of goods sold

B. Inventories of WIP and Finished Goods

C. Cost of goods sold and inventories

D. Costing profit and loss account

14. A material of 7,500 kgs. was introduced in the process and the expected loss is 8% and if the actual output is 7,050 kgs, then there is a:

A. Abnormal Gain of 200 kgs.

B. Abnormal Loss of 150 kgs.

C. Abnormal Gain of 150 kgs.
D. Abnormal Loss of 200 kgs.

15. A company earned a profit of 80,000 on the sales of ₹ 4,00,000 in period 1. It's profit increases by ₹ 20,000 on the sales of ₹ 4,50,000 in period 2. The company will achieve its BEP at:

A. ₹ 1,20,000 B. ₹ 80,000
C. ₹ 1,60,000 D. ₹ 2,00,000

16. Statutory audit is:

A. A certificate as to the correctness of the financial statements
B. An assurance as to the viability of the business of the entity
C. A guarantee that the books of accounts are free from errors and frauds
D. An expression of opinion on the true and fair view of the financial statements

17. Who prepares the Audit Programme for conducting an audit?

A. The Auditor
B. The Client
C. The Institute of Chartered Accountants of India
D. The National Financial Reporting Authority

18. Which of the following is true for Internal Audit in India?

A. Optional for all the companies
B. Compulsory only for the public sector entities
C. Compulsory only for the listed companies
D. Mandatory for all listed companies and other specified companies

19. The objective of 'Vouching' is ______.

A. To ensure that the assets and liabilities of the entity exist on the date of the balance sheet
B. To establish the accuracy and authenticity of the accounting entries in the books of accounts
C. To ensure that the assets and liabilities are in possession of the entity
D. To ensure that assets of the entity are properly valued

20. Who appoints the first auditor of a company (other than a government company)?

A. The Registrar of Companies
B. The National Company Law Tribunal
C. Audit Committee of the company
D. Board of Directors of the company

21. The mean of 15 observations is 40. The mean of first 8th observations is 36 and the mean of last 8th observations is 42. What is the value of the 8th observation?

A. 24 B. 40
C. 48 D. 26

22. Suppose that approximately 15% of the people are left-handed. If two people are selected at random, what is the probability that one is right-handed and the other is left-handed?

A. 0.1275 B. 0.255
C. 0.9775 D. 0.745

23. Which of the following is ***not*** a property of the coefficient of correlation?

A. The coefficient of correlation lies between 1 and +1.
B. The coefficient of correlation depends on the change of scale.
C. The coefficient of correlation is the geometric mean of two regression coefficients.
D. The coefficient of correlation gives the direction of relationship between variables.

24. Which of the following is a relative measure of dispersion?

A. Range
B. Geometric mean
C. Coefficient of variation
D. Quartile deviation

25. In which of the following cases can we use the binomial probability distribution?

A. To calculate the probability of travelling more than 15 kms on 1 litre of petrol.
B. To calculate the probability that students in a class study between 1 hour and 3 hours per day for a certain paper.

C. To calculate the probability that a bulb lasts for a longer time than the advertised figure.

D. To calculate the probability of getting an even number twice on rolling of a dice six times.

26. Prosperity, recession and depression in a business is an example of which of the following:

A. Irregular trend B. Secular trend
C. Cyclical trend D. Seasonal trend

27. If the right tail in a distribution is longer than the left tail, then the distribution is:

A. Positively skewed
B. Negatively skewed
C. Symmetrical
D. Scattered

28. A certain sum of money is invested at 4% p.a. compounded annually. If interest for second year is ₹ 25 interest for 4 year will be ₹.

A. 25 B. 27
C. 26 D. 27.04

29. The demand function of a product is $X = 300 - P^2$. It will have unitary price elasticity of demand at P equal to ₹.

A. 12 B. 9
C. 8 D. 10

30. Marginal cost function of a product is $MC(X) = 3(3X + 4)(-0.5)$ with a fixed cost of ₹ 2.00. Its per unit cost when firm produces 7 units will be ₹.

A. 2 B. 8/7
C. 8/3 D. 8/5

31. A machine costing ₹ C is depreciated at 100 *r* % p.a. using diminishing balance method. Its book value after 2 years will be:

A. $C(1 - r)^2$ B. $C(1 - r^2)$
C. $C(1 - r)$ D. $C(r^2 - 1)$

32. A bill of ₹ 5000 discounted by a customer with his bank due after 3 months. Bank charges discount at 12% p.a. Customer will get ₹.

A. 4800 B. 4900
C. 4850 D. 4950

33. If the price elasticity of demand of a product is unitary at all levels, its demand function will be:

A. $P = X$ B. PX = Constant
C. $P = X^2$ D. $X = P^2$

34. If $A = \begin{bmatrix} 2 & 3 \\ 1 & 4 \end{bmatrix}$ and $B = \begin{bmatrix} 1 & a \\ b & 5 \end{bmatrix}$ and $AB = BA$, then *a* and *b* will be:

A. 2 and 6 B. 6 and 2
C. 4 and 3 D. 3 and 4

35. Mr. X, a non-Government employee, received ₹ 28,00,000 as cash equivalent of leave salary at the time of his retirement on 28 February, 2021. The maximum amount which can be exempt in this case will be:

A. ₹ 3,00,000 B. ₹ 3,50,000
C. ₹ 10,00,000 D. ₹ 20,00,000

36. While computing the value of perquisite in respect of motor car sold by the employer to the employee on 31 January 2021, the following percentage and method will be followed:

A. 10% on straight line method
B. 20% on straight line method
C. 10% on written down value method
D. 20% on written down value method

37. For the assessment year 2021-22, ______ of any sum paid to a National Laboratory with a specific direction that the said sum shall be used for scientific research undertaken under a programme approved in this behalf by the prescribed authority is allowed as deduction under section 35 while computing income under the head Profits and Gains of Business or Profession.

A. 100% B. 125%
C. 175% D. 200%

38. Mr. X, a resident individual, has earned a short term capital gain (covered under section 111A) of ₹ 4,00,000 and business income of ₹ 50,000 during the assessment year 2021-22. He has also invested ₹ 3,00,000 on 29 March, 2021 which is eligible for deduction under section 80C. In this case, the amount of deduction under section 80C for the assessment year 2021-22 will be:

A. Nil B. ₹ 50,000
C. ₹ 1,50,000 D. ₹ 3,00,000

39. Mr. X gifts debentures of a private company of ₹ 10,00,000 to his wife, Mrs. X, without consideration. She earned interest of ₹ 1,00,000 on these debentures which she reinvested and then earned an interest of ₹ 10,000 on this reinvested amount. Assuming the assessment year 2021-22 is applicable, this ₹ 10,000 will be taxable in the hands of:

A. Mr. X
B. Mrs. X
C. Exempt from tax
D. Mr. X or Mrs. X, depending upon the Assessing Officer

40. Mr. X supplies interior designing services to Mr. Y. The location of Mr. X is Tamil Nadu and location of Mr. Y is Canada. In such a situation, the place of supply of service will be determined as per:

A. Section 7 of the CGST Act
B. Section 7 of the IGST Act
C. Section 13 of the CGST Act
D. Section 13 of the IGST Act

41. A goods is subject to periodic increase in supply. Each time supply increases, the supplier finds the total revenue decreasing. Which of the following must be true of the goods?

A. It is an inferior goods
B. It has price inelastic supply
C. It is a superior goods
D. It has price inelastic demand

42. Which of the following sets of commodities are likely to have positive cross elasticity of demand?

A. Aluminium & Plastic.
B. Pencil & Paper.
C. Men's and women's shoes.
D. Jam & Cheese.

43. An increase in the demand for a firm's output:

A. increases the prosperity of the firm but decreases the prosperity of the factors hired by the firm
B. decreases the prosperity of the firm but increases the prosperity of the factors hired by the firm
C. increases the prosperity of both the firm & the factors hired by the firm
D. decreases the prosperity of both the firm & the factors hired by the firm

44. Indifference curve for perfect substitutes are:

A. straight line B. bowed inward
C. bowed outward D. right angles

45. Which of the statement about production function is correct?

A. It shows the minimum output the inputs can produce
B. It relates employment of inputs to output
C. It identifies output cost relationships
D. It identifies the profit maximizing level of output

46. If the average product of labour when 5 workers are employed is 10 and when 6 workers are employed is 12, then:

A. The MP curve lies above the average product curve between 5 and 6 workers
B. The Marginal Product curve lies below the average product curve between 5 and 6 workers
C. The total product curve is decreasing between 5 and 6 workers
D. Marginal product is negative

47. In the long run, the competitive firm's supply curve is the:

A. entire Marginal Cost curve
B. portion of Marginal cost curve that lies above Average total cost curve
C. portion of Marginal cost curve that lies above Average variable total cost curve
D. upward sloping portion of the average variable cost curve

48. Choose the correct combination of economic theory and economist who has contributed to it.

A. Theory of Rent by A.C. Pigou
B. Inflation Rate and Unemployment Rate Trade-off by A.W. Phillips
C. Theory of Absolute Advantage of Trade by David Ricardo
D. Theory of Liquidity Preference by John Williamson

49. Which of the following economic variables is not a flow variable?
A. Profit
B. Wage
C. Exchange Rate
D. Rent

50. Given below are two statements:

Statement I: According to the Keynesian Theory of Income Determination, given all other components of autonomous aggregate demand unchanged, the rise in tax rate leads to rise in equilibrium level of income.

Statement II: According to the Keynesian Theory of Income Determination, given all other components of autonomous aggregate demand unchanged, the rise in Marginal Propensity to Save (MPS) leads to fall in equilibrium level of income.

In light of the above statements, choose the *most appropriate* answer from the options given below:
A. Both Statement I and Statement II are correct.
B. Both Statement I and Statement II are incorrect.
C. Statement I is correct, but Statement II is incorrect.
D. Statement I is incorrect, but Statement II is correct.

51. (*a*) Given all other determinants of money supply constant, the rise in Cash Reserve Ratio (CRR) leads to fall in equilibrium money supply.
(*b*) Given all other determinants of money supply constant, the rise in Currency Deposit Ratio leads to fall in equilibrium money supply.
(*c*) Given all other determinants of money supply constant, the rise in high powered money leads to rise in equilibrium money supply.
(*d*) Given all other determinants of money supply constant, the rise in Cash Reserve Ratio (CRR) leads to rise in equilibrium money supply.

Choose the *correct* answer from the options given below:
A. (*a*), (*b*) and (*d*) only
B. (*a*), (*b*) and (*c*) only
C. (*b*), (*c*) and (*d*) only
D. (*c*) and (*d*) only

52. Given below are two statements

Statement I: According to Quantity Theory of Money, the rise in nominal money supply leads to rise in prices given the velocity of money and real output constant.

Statement II: According to Fisher Equation, rise in nominal money supply leads to rise in real rate of interest.

In the light of the above statements:

Choose the *most appropriate* answer from the options given below:
A. Both Statement I and Statement II are correct
B. Both Statement I and Statement II are incorrect
C. Statement I is correct, but Statement II is incorrect
D. Statement I is incorrect, but Statement II is correct

53. In the national income accounts, all of the following are classified as government purchases except:
A. Payments for procuring military equipments.
B. Cash payments made to the people below poverty line.
C. Salaries paid to parliamentarians.
D. Salaries paid to judicial officers.

54. Monetary policy is linked to fiscal policy when government spending on health infrastructure is financed by:
A. Raising taxes.
B. Borrowing from the domestic market sources.

C. Printing money by the central bank.
D. Cutting down the expenses on purchase of arms equipment.

55. One Nation One Ration Card Scheme announced recently will:
A. Enable migrant workers and their family to access PDS benefits from any fair price shop in the country
B. Enable people below the poverty line to access PDS benefits from any fair price shop in the country
C. Enable people with disabilities to access PDS benefits from any fair price shop in the country
D. Enable small and marginal farmers to access PDS benefits from any fair price shop in the country

56. The National Population Policy of India (NPP) 2000 aims to achieve a stable population by:
A. 2030 B. 2040
C. 2045 D. 2050

57. Liquidity Adjustment Facility (LAF) is used by RBI to bring changes in which of the following:
A. CRR, SLR, Repo and Reverse Repo rates, Bank rate
B. CRR, SLR, Repo and Reverse Repo rates
C. CRR, SLR only
D. Repo and Reverse Repo rates only

58. Which of the following happens because of DBT(Direct Benefit Transfer)?
A. Benefits are given directly to the beneficiary in hand
B. Money is directly given in hand to the beneficiary
C. Money is directly transferred to beneficiaries bank account
D. Money is given by the government official directly

59. Which Indian think tank has been ranked among the top 30 think tanks globally, as per a recent report?
A. Observer Research Foundation (ORF)
B. NITI Aayog
C. Centre for Civil Society (CCS)
D. Centre for National Policy Research (CNPR)

60. Green Revolution was associated with improving the productivity of wheat and other cereals. What is "silver fibre revolution" associated with?
A. Improving Jute production
B. Improving Cotton production
C. Improving egg/poultry production
D. Improving milk production

61. Which of the following characteristics best define matrix structure of organisation?
A. It is a hybrid between functional and divisional structures.
B. A matrix is an array of rows and columns.
C. It is a hybrid between network and virtual organisations.
D. It is inspired from 'The Matrix' series of films.

62. Which of the following represent the twin most cited criteria of managerial performance?
A. Autonomy & Accountability
B. Adverse Selection & Moral Hazard
C. Effectiveness & Efficiency
D. Short Run & Long Run

63. Which of the following is the discriminating factor between the definitions of market value added (MVA) and economic value added (EVA) measures of corporate performance?
A. Net Operating Profit After Tax (NOPAT)
B. Overall Weighted Cost of Capital
C. Value of Debt Capital considered–Book Value versus Market Value
D. Value of Equity Capital considered–Book Value versus Market Value

64. Which of the following is the most correct expression of the two factors in Frederick Herzberg's theory of motivation?
A. Hygiene-Motivation
B. Maintenance-Motivators
C. Satisfiers-Dissatisfiers
D. Lower Order Needs-Higher Order Needs

65. Penalty as provided under the Information and Technology Act, 2000 amounting to upto

INR one crore is not levied if, any individual or group attempts to:

A. Damages a computer system
B. Damages a computer database
C. Disrupts a computer network
D. Disrupts a computer system with permission of the owner of computer system

66. Tampering with Computer Source Document as provided under the Information and Technology Act, 2000, is not applied when a person or group of person:

A. Intentionally conceals a computer source code
B. Destroys a computer source code
C. Knowingly alters a computer source code
D. Unknowingly causes another to conceal a computer source code

67. Hacking a computer system or network as provided under the Information and Technology Act, 2000 is penalized under the Information and Technology Act, 2000 with:

A. Imprisonment of one year and penalty of INR 10,000
B. Imprisonment of upto three years and penalty of INR 100,000
C. Imprisonment of upto three years and penalty of upto INR 200,000
D. Imprisonment of upto three years and penalty of upto INR 200,000 or both

68. The essentials of valid agency, prescribed under the Contract Act, 1872 does not include:

A. Privity of contract
B. Principal be competent to contract
C. Agent must have contractual capacity
D. The principal is bound by the acts of his agent

69. First directors are appointed by the:

A. Shareholders
B. Promoters
C. Underwriters
D. Managing director

70. An alternate director can be appointed by:

A. The shareholders in the annual general meeting
B. The board in board meeting by passing special resolution
C. The shareholders in the annual general meeting by passing a special resolution
D. The board in board meeting by passing resolution

71. Section 2(46) of the Companies Act, 2013, defines the:

A. Subsidiary company
B. Holding company
C. Statutory company
D. Associate company

72. As per the Companies Act 2013, no person shall be eligible to incorporate or become a nominee in more than ______ One Person Company.

A. One B. Two
C. Ten D. Fifteen

73. Which of the following statement is correct?

A. Independent directors are non-executive directors
B. Nominee Directors are independent directors
C. Non-executive directors are independent directors
D. Promoters are non-executive directors

74. Choose the board structure Google Inc follows from the options below:

A. Two-Tier B. One-Tier
C. Hybrid D. Continental

75. Which of the following statement is incorrect?

A. Chief Executive Officer leads the management team
B. In the Anglo-Saxon Model Executive and non-Executive directors sit in different boards
C. In the German Model Executive and Non-Executive directors sit in different boards
D. India has adopted the Unitary model of Corporate Governance

76. Corporate Governance is about:

(*a*) System by which companies are directed and controlled
(*b*) Rules and procedures for making decisions

(c) Distribution of rights and responsibilities among different participants in the corporation

A. (a), (b) & (c) B. (a) only

C. (a) & (c) D. (b) & (a)

77. ______ is one that after implementing a relief package spread over a period not exceeding five years from the commencement of the package, will continue to fulfil its repayment obligations as agreed upon without the help of concessions after the aforesaid period.

A. Corporate debt restructuring
B. Growth company
C. Medium enterprise
D. Potentially viable unit

78. Reconfiguration of existing technology to create process improvement is known as:

A. Breakthrough innovation
B. Discontinuous innovation
C. Dynamically continuous innovation
D. Technological innovation

79. ______ is a highly creative process involving multiple possible solutions to the problem under consideration.

A. Convergent thinking
B. Divergent thinking
C. Lateral thinking
D. Vertical thinking

80. A financial transaction whereby a business entity sells its accounts receivables to a third party at a discount in exchange for immediate money to finance continued business is called ______.

A. Factoring
B. Seed funding
C. Shotgun approach
D. Venture capital

81. Which of the following is not true for capital budgeting?

A. Sunk costs are ignored.
B. Opportunity costs are excluded.
C. International cash flows are considered.
D. Relevant cash flows are considered.

82. In order to find out cost of capital under CAPM, which of the following is not required?

A. Beta factor
B. Market rate of return
C. Market price of equity share.
D. Risk-free rate of return

83. If the fixed cost of production is zero, which one of the following is correct?

A. Operating Leverage is zero.
B. Financial Leverage is zero.
C. Operating Leverage is one.
D. Financial Leverage is one.

84. Dividend irrelevance argument of MM Model is based on:

A. Issue of debentures
B. Issue of bonus shares
C. Arbitrage
D. Hedging

85. If cash discount is offered to customers, then which of the following would increase?

A. Sales
B. Debtors
C. Debt collection period
D. Cost of production

86. Which one of the following is not the objective of Human Resource Management.

A. to identify and satisfy individual and group needs through adequate compensation policy
B. to decide organizational culture and strategy through managerial consensus
C. help attaining organizational goals through proper utilisation of human resource
D. creating congenial work environment through desirable working conditions

87. Compensation Management is ______ function of HRM.

A. Operative B. Managerial

C. Planning D. Controlling

88. Job Description is part of ______ (choose the option from below):

A. Job Specification
B. Job Evaluation
C. Job Enrichment
D. Job Analysis

89. Psychometric Tests are done in order to assess ______ (choose appropriate answer from the following):
A. Technical ability
B. Behavioural adaptability
C. Employee performance
D. Job satisfaction level

90. Which one of the following statements concerning Harvard Framework of Human Resource Management is not TRUE.
A. It identifies stakeholders' interest
B. It targets long-term consequences
C. It avoids situational factors
D. It identifies congruence as one of the HRM outcomes

91. The set of beliefs held about a particular brand is known as:
A. Brand recognition
B. Brand selection
C. Brand image
D. Brand preference

92. The extended Ps of service marketing mix is:
A. People, Product, Place
B. Price, Physical evidence, Promotion
C. People, Process, Physical evidence
D. People, Process, Promotion

93. ______ are fashions adopted quickly by the public but which peak early and decline very fast.
A. Fads
B. Generic products
C. Arts
D. Sporting products

94. ______ involves charging a high price to achieve the highest possible contribution in a short period of time.
A. Penetration pricing
B. Skimming
C. Psychological pricing
D. Transfer pricing

95. Consumer product channels tend to be ______ industrial product channels.
A. shorter than
B. the same length as
C. longer than
D. identical to

96. Which of the following staffing policy requires host country nationals to be recruited to manage subsidiaries, while parent country nationals occupy key positions at corporate headquarters?
A. Geocentric Approach
B. Ethnocentric Approach
C. Polycentric Approach
D. Regiocentric Approach

97. Which of the following theories of International trade assumes 2 × 2 × 2 model for explaining the theory?
A. The Comparative Advantage Theory
B. The Absolute Advantage Theory
C. The Opportunity Cost Theory
D. The Factor-Proportions Theory

98. Which of the following is not a part of Current account of BOP?
A. Export of Goods
B. Export of Services
C. Errors and Omissions
D. Income payments

99. Which of the following is not a feature of Common market under regional integration?
A. Eliminating tariff and non-tariff barriers
B. Unified monitory and fiscal policy
C. Common External Tariff
D. Free movement of product, labour and capital

100. Which of the following is the correct process of stages of internationalization of a company?
A. Domestic company – multinational company – international company – transnational company
B. Domestic company – multinational company – transnational company – international company
C. Domestic company – transnational company – international company – multinational company
D. Domestic company – international company – multinational company – transnational company

ANSWERS

1	2	3	4	5	6	7	8	9	10
B	C	A	D	D	A	D	A	B	B
11	12	13	14	15	16	17	18	19	20
B	C	D	C	D	D	A	D	B	D
21	22	23	24	25	26	27	28	29	30
A	B	B	C	D	C	A	D	D	B
31	32	33	34	35	36	37	38	39	40
A	C	B	B	A	D	A	B	B	D
41	42	43	44	45	46	47	48	49	50
D	A	C	A	B	*	B	B	C	D
51	52	53	54	55	56	57	58	59	60
B	C	B	C	A	C	D	C	A	B
61	62	63	64	65	66	67	68	69	70
A	C	D	A	D	D	D	C	B	D
71	72	73	74	75	76	77	78	79	80
B	A	A	B	B	A	D	C	B	A
81	82	83	84	85	86	87	88	89	90
B	C	C	C	A	B	A	D	B	C
91	92	93	94	95	96	97	98	99	100
C	C	A	B	C	C	D	C	B	D

Previous Years' Paper (Solved)

UNIVERSITY OF DELHI

M. Com., Entrance Test–2020*

1. Under conditions of perfect competition if a particular firm is facing a price which is greater than average variable cost but less than average cost, then

A. The firm is recovering the entire variable costs but not recovering some part of the fixed costs and is facing losses.

B. The firm is recovering the entire fixed costs but not recovering some part of the variable costs and is facing losses.

C. The firm must necessarily shut down operations as it faces losses in the short run.

D. The firm is earning profits as prices are greater than average variable cost.

2. Under the Keynesian Theory of Employment, Interest and Income, the monetary policy shall be less effective if:

A. Interest rates fell

B. Interest rates rose

C. Investment demand is inelastic

D. Investment demand is elastic

3. Oligopoly is a market structure wherein there is:

(*a*) intense competition among few firms in the industry.

(*b*) firms could be producing homogeneous or differentiated products

(*c*) firms recognise interdependence in their decision making

(*d*) firms may enter into overt or tacit cartels.

Choose the correct answer from the options given below:

A. (*a*) and (*d*) only

B. (*a*), (*c*) and (*d*) only

C. (*a*), (*b*) and (*d*) only

D. (*a*), (*b*), (*c*) and (*d*) only

4. Which of the following stakeholders are most financially hurt under conditions of unanticipated inflation?

A. Borrowers with fixed rate loans

B. Borrowers with variable rate loans

C. Creditors

D. Neither borrowers and nor creditors are hurt

5. The production possibility curve is often represented as concave (bowed out) from the origin because of

A. Decreasing opportunity cost

B. Increasing opportunity cost

C. Constant opportunity cost

D. Constant returns to scale

6. One possible cause of Stagflation is:

A. Increase in aggregate supply

B. Increase in aggregate demand

C. Decrease in aggregate supply

D. Decrease in aggregate demand

7. The price of good rises from ₹ 4 to ₹ 5 per unit and the quantity demanded for that good contracts from 100 units to 80 units. The price elasticity of demand for the good (in absolute terms) is:

A. 1   B. 0.8

C. –1   D. –0.8

8. Economic growth will be sluggish when interest rates rise, because;

A. Firms will invest in fewer projects with future payoffs thus limiting growth.

B. Firms will invest in more projects with future payoffs thus limiting growth.

C. Firms will invest the same amount in projects with future payoffs at all interest levels thus leaving growth unaffected.

D. Firms will pay more in dividends and as a result retained earnings will fall.

9. For a monopoly firm, under conditions of short run equilibrium earning just normal profits, the following relationship holds true between price (P) and marginal cost (MC)

A. P > MC

B. P < MC

C. P = MC

D. P and MC are unrelated

* ***Exam held on: 06/09/2020.***

10. A basic assumption of the Classical School of economic thought is:
A. Prices and wages are flexible.
B. Short-run inflation is unlikely to occur.
C. Short-run unemployment is unlikely to occur.
D. Equilibrium will reach equilibrium at any level of output.

11. Existence of external diseconomies of scale shall cause the
A. Long run average cost curve to fall
B. Long run average cost curve to rise
C. Long run average cost curve to shift downwards
D. Long run average cost curve to shift upwards

12. An increase in the long run aggregate supply curve can be caused by
A. An increase in government spending.
B. An increase in literacy levels of the population.
C. An increase in taxes.
D. An increase in interest rates.

13. Which of the following conditions are to be satisfied for a market structure to be termed as monopol?
(*a*) there is only one seller in the market
(*b*) the seller produces a product for which there are no close substitutes
(*c*) there exist strong barriers to entry
(*d*) the monopoly firm has an upward rising supply curve.

Choose the correct answer from the options given below:
A. (*a*), (*b*) and (*c*) only
B. (*a*), (*b*), (*c*) and (*d*)
C. (*a*) only
D. (*a*), (*b*) and (*d*) only

14. An adverse supply shock
A. Can be anticipated and decreases aggregate supply
B. Cannot be anticipated but decreases aggregate supply
C. Can be anticipated and increases aggregate supply
D. Cannot be anticipated but increases aggregate supply

15. What describes the most appropriate relationship between social cost, private cost and external cost in context of "negative externalities of production"?
A. Social Cost = Private Cost – External Cost
B. Social Cost = Private Cost + External Cost
C. Social Cost = (Private Cost) multiplied by (External Cost)
D. Social costs, private costs and external costs are unrelated to each other

16. During the expansionary phase of the business cycle
A. Real GDP declines and inflation rises.
B. Real GDP rises and unemployment rises.
C. Real GDP rises and unemployment falls.
D. Interest rates rise and the number of business failures rise.

17. A monopolistically competitive firm advertises in order to
A. Reduce the industry's barrier to entry
B. Shift the demand curve for its product to the left
C. Make the demand for its product less price elastic
D. Increase its negative externalities

18. Initially, a country is in a no-trade situation and then this country decides to allow imports of a good. This will result in:
A. Domestic consumers lose, domestic producers gain, and the gains outweigh the losses.
B. Domestic consumers gain, domestic producers lose, and the gains outweigh the losses.
C. Domestic consumers gain, domestic producers lose, and the losses outweigh the gains.
D. Domestic consumer gain, but domestic producers lose an equal amount.

19. How much health and educational cess in 2019 has been imposed by the government on all union taxes?
A. 1% B. 4%
C. 3% D. 5%

20. Who recommends the Minimum Support Price (MSP) fixed by the government?
A. Ministry of Finance
B. Empowered group of ministers
C. CACP
D. Minister of Agriculture

21. Identify the correct relationship between Marginal Standing Facility Rate (MSF), Repo Rate (RR) and Reverse Repo Rate (RRR).

A. MSF > RR > RRR
B. MSF < RR < RRR
C. MSF > RRR > RR
D. RRR > MSF > RR

22. The Asset Management Company managing Bharat ETF 22 is
A. Bajaj Allianz B. ICICI Prudential
C. Axis D. DHFL

23. Smart Metering System will be used for measuring
A. Smart Cities in meters
B. Consumption of electric energy
C. Food Intake by Individuals
D. Consumption of Energy fuels

24. Bharat net is related to
A. Connecting the rivers of India
B. Building ports in coastal towns
C. Providing Broad Band Services to Rural areas
D. Building Highways network

25. The 2019 Ease of Doing Business Ranking in India is
A. 60 B. 66
C. 69 D. 63

26. In case of rising prices (inflation), FIFO method will:
A. Provide lowest value of closing stock and profit
B. Provide highest value of closing stock and profit
C. Provide highest value of closing stock but lowest value of profit
D. Provide highest value of profit but lowest value of closing stock

27. Which of the following will cause difference on a trial balance?
A. An invoice omitted from the sale day book
B. An invoice of ₹ 1500 entered in the sale day book as 15000
C. An invoice of ₹ 5000 entered in the sale day book not included in the monthly total
D. A credit note entered to the sales day book

28. International Accounting Standards (IAS) have been developed by:
A. The European commission
B. The International accounting standard committee
C. The financial reporting council
D. All of these

29. How many years' financial statements are required to be annexed to the declaration for initiating voluntary liquidation?
A. Previous 2 years or the period since incorporation whichever is later
B. Previous 2 years or the period since incorporation whichever is prior
C. Previous 3 years or the period since incorporation whichever is later
D. Previous 5 years or the period since incorporation whichever is later

30. Which one of the following item cannot be recorded in the appropriation account in case of partnership accounting?
A. Interest on capital
B. Interest on drawings
C. Rent paid to partners
D. Partners salary

31. In the absence of partnership deed, interest on partners loan is payable by firm
A. 12% p.a B. 6% p.a
C. 10% p.a D. 16% p.a

32. Reserve capital can be called up
A. In an emergency only
B. Any time by passing an ordinary resolution
C. In the event and for the purpose of company being wound–up
D. If all directors agree

33. Stock split is the process of
A. Consolidating the face value of the shares of the company
B. Reducing the capital of the company
C. Restructuring of capital of the company
D. Reducing face value of the shares of the company by dividing one shares into two or more parts

34. Royalties revenue should be recognized
A. On an accrual basis in accordance with the terms of the relevant agreement
B. On cash basis
C. On an actual basis
D. Revenue is recognized on the time proportion basis

35. AS-29 is Applicable only to
A. Provision for valuation adjustment for fixed Assets
B. Provision for Liabilities and charges

C. Provision for valuation adjustment for current assets
D. Furniture

36. Interest paid by other than financial enterprise is shown in the cash flow statement under:
A. Operating activities
B. Investing activities
C. Financing activities
D. Accumulated profit

37. Profit prior to incorporation is
A. Debited to Goodwill Account
B. Credited to General Reserve Account
C. Credited to Capital Reserve Account
D. Credited to Reserve

38. Which is the cost unit is applicable to the bicycle industry?
A. Per part of bicycle
B. Per bicycle
C. Per tonne
D. Per day

39. Stores Ledger is a:
A. Quantitative as well as value wise records of material received, issued and balance
B. Quantitative record of material received, issued and balance
C. Value wise records of material received, issued and balance
D. Record of labour attendance

40. Kaizen costing is applied to a product that is:
A. Produced
B. Under production
C. Targeted to produce
D. Sold to customers

41. Calculate EOQ (approx.) from the following details:
Annual Consumption: 24000 units
Ordering cost: ₹ 10 per order
Purchase price: ₹ 100 per unit
Carrying cost: 5%
A. 310 B. 400
C. 290 D. 300

42. A worker is allowed 60 hours to complete the job but he completes in 50 hours. How much wages will he get under the Halsey Plan?
A. ₹ 720 B. ₹ 540
C. ₹ 600 D. ₹ 660

43. Which of the following is not a reason for an idle time variance?
A. Wage rate increase
B. Machine breakdown
C. Illness or injury to worker
D. Non-availability of material

44. A budget which is prepared in a manner so as to give the budgeted cost for any level of activity is known as:
A. Master budget
B. Zero base budget
C. Functional budget
D. Flexible budget

45. In process costing, if an abnormal loss arises, the process account is generally
A. Debited with the scrap value of the abnormal loss units
B. Debited with the full production cost of the abnormal loss units
C. Credited with the scrap value of the abnormal loss units
D. Credited with the full production cost of the abnormal loss units

46. If sales is ₹ 1,00,000 in 2018 and ₹ 4,00,000 in 2019 and loss ₹ 10,000 in 2018 and profit ₹ 50,000 in 2019, P/V ratio will be
A. 50% B. 20%
C. 30% D. 40%

47. Improvement of profit-volume ratio can be done by
A. Increasing selling price
B. Increasing the variable cost
C. Reducing the fixed cost
D. Increase in sales volume

48. Budget which is directed towards long-term strategic goals is known as
A. Zero-base budget B. Capital budget
C. Rolling budget D. Master budget

49. The two ways to measure the financial performance of an investment centre are
A. ROI and ROE
B. ROI and segment residual income
C. Segment residual income and ROE
D. ROI and leverage ratio

50. Which of the following organisations should not be advised to use service costing?
A. Distribution service
B. Hospitals
C. Maintenance division of a manufacturing company
D. Light engineering company

51. If a curve is more peaked than the normal curve, it is called

A. Mesokurtic B. Platykurtic
C. Leptokurtic D. Asymmetric

52. Two dice are thrown and the side of both dice facing up are observed. Which of the following events are mutually exclusive events?
A. A: Both dice are the same number
B: Both dice are even number
B. A: One of the dice shows a two
B: The sum is greater than 8
C. A: The sum of both dice is even
B: The product of both dice is odd
D. A: The product of both dice is even
B: The sum of both dice is odd

53. Given that the equation for a line is Y = 18 – 10X, which of the following statement is true?
A. The relationship of Y to X is direct and linear.
B. The relationship of Y to X is direct and non-linear.
C. The relationship of Y to X is inverse and linear.
D. The relationship of Y to X is inverse and non-linear.

54. Which of the following is not a property of the binomial distribution?
A. The trials are statistically dependent.
B. Each trial has only two possible outcomes.
C. The probability of the outcomes does not change from trial to trial.
D. The experiment consists of a fixed number of trials '*n*'

55. Which approach to probability would be used to calculate the probability of India winning a match against Australia?
A. Classical approach
B. Subjective approach
C. Relative frequency approach
D. Cluster approach

56. In which of the following case would the Poisson distribution be a good approximation of the binomial distribution?
A. $n = 40, p = 0.32$ B. $n = 40, q = 0.79$
C. $n = 10, p = 0.03$ D. $n = 200, p = 0.02$

57. Under statistical dependence, if we sum up all the probabilities of the joint events in which a certain event A occurs, the result is:
A. Relative probability of A
B. The marginal probability of A
C. The conditional probability of A
D. Bayesian probability of A

58. Which of the following is a measure of dispersion?
A. Standard deviation
B. Median
C. Mode
D. Geometric mean

59. While computing a weighted index, the current period quantities are used in the:
A. Laspeyres method
B. Bayes method
C. Marshall Edgeworth method
D. Paasche's method

60. Which of the following is a continuous random variable?
A. Gender of the customer while selling an automobile.
B. Number of returns containing error in an audit of 100 tax returns.
C. Time between customer arrivals in a bank.
D. Number of employees absent from the first shift during working days.

61. The proportion of total variation in the dependent variable that is explained by the independent variable is measured by
A. Coefficient of determination
B. Coefficient of correlation
C. Coefficient of deviation
D. Coefficient of skewness

62. The difference between 'expected payoff under perfect information' and 'expected payoff under optimal action' is called:
A. Expected payoff
B. Expected value of perfect information
C. Expected regret
D. State of nature

63. Supply function of a product is $X = 4P^2 + 15$. Its price elasticity of supply at P = ₹ 5 will be:
A. 1.50 B. 1.74
C. 1.70 D. 2.00

64. If $\begin{bmatrix} 2X-3Y & Z-W & 3 \\ 5 & X+4Y & 3Z+4W \end{bmatrix} = \begin{bmatrix} 1 & -2 & 3 \\ 5 & 6 & 29 \end{bmatrix}$, then X, Y, Z and W will be equal to:
A. 2, 5, 1, 3 B. 2, 1, 5, 3
C. 2, 1, 3, 5 D. 5, 2, 1, 3

65. Marginal cost function of a product is $MC(X) = 2(2X + 9)^{-1/2}$ and fixed cost is ₹ 4, then per unit cost at X = 8 units will be ₹.
A. 2 B. 3
C. 2.5 D. 1

66. A sum of ₹ 10000 deposited for 10 years at 10% p.a. compounded continuously will amount to ₹.

A. 20,000 B. 21,000
C. 27,183 D. 25,000

67. A linear demand function provides that quantity demanded is NIL at P = ₹ 50 and demand is 100 units if P = 0. Its price elasticity of demand |EP| at P = ₹ 25 will be

A. −2 B. −1.5
C. 1 D. 1.5

68. Marginal revenue function of a product is MR(X) = 2 − 6X. Corresponding demand function will be

A. X = (P − 2)/3 B. X = (2 − P)/3
C. X = 3(P − 2) D. X = 3(2 − P)

69. The average cost function of a product is AC(X) = X + 5 + 36/X. The total cost of producing 10 units will be ₹.

A. 36 B. 85
C. 100 D. 186

70. If $A = \begin{bmatrix} 4 & -2 \\ 1 & 3 \end{bmatrix}$, then A^{-1} will be:

A. $\begin{bmatrix} 3 & -2 \\ 1 & 4 \end{bmatrix}$ B. $\begin{bmatrix} 2/7 & -1/7 \\ 1/14 & 3/14 \end{bmatrix}$

C. $\begin{bmatrix} 3/14 & 1/7 \\ -1/14 & 2/7 \end{bmatrix}$ D. $\begin{bmatrix} -2/7 & -1/7 \\ 1/14 & -3/14 \end{bmatrix}$

71. Profit is maximum when:

A. MR = MC and $\frac{d(MR)}{dx} < \frac{d(MC)}{dx}$

B. MR = MC and $\frac{d(MR)}{dx} > \frac{d(MC)}{dx}$

C. MR = 0

D. MR = MC and $\frac{d(MR)}{dx} = \frac{d(MC)}{dx}$

72. A bill of ₹ 1000 due after 3 months is discounted at 12% p.a, the bank will give ₹.

A. 98 B. 97
C. 99 D. 95

73. The manufacturing cost of a product consists of ₹ 1000 as overheads, material cost ₹ 2 per unit and the labour cost of ₹ $X^2/90$ for X units produced. Its most economic level of output will be:

A. 200 units B. 250 units
C. 300 units D. 350 units

74. If a demand function has unitary price elasticity of demand at all levels, then corresponding demand function will be

A. X = P B. X = Constant/P
C. $X = P^2$ D. X = ln(P)

75. If interest is compounded semi-annually at 12% p.a., then corresponding effective rate will be

A. 12.00% p.a. B. 13.00% p.a.
C. 12.50% p.a. D. 12.36% p.a.

76. Which one of the following statements is not FALSE?

A. Entrepreneurship is a strategy to capture larger market share
B. To a greater extent entrepreneurship promotes concentration of economic power
C. Entrepreneurship does not promote capital formation
D. Entrepreneurship encourages balanced regional growth

77. When was Startup Action Plan launched by the Indian government?

A. 2015 B. 2016
C. 2017 D. 2018

78. Which one of the following statements is not TRUE for an LLP?

A. It is a body corporate
B. It does not have legal entity
C. It has perpetual succession
D. It is an alternative form to run corporate business

79. We have moved to knowledge economy over the last few decades. Who among the following visualised the emergence of Knowledge Worker?

A. Peter Drucker B. Peter Senge
C. CK Prahalad D. Tom Peters

80. As suggested by Robert Katz, the Lower Level Managers need to prioritise different types of skills in this order.

A. Human skills, Technical skills, Conceptual skills
B. Conceptual skills, Human skills, Technical skills
C. Technical skills, Human skills, Conceptual skills
D. Human skills, Conceptual skills, Technical skills

81. For a manufacturing organization, which one of the following shall not be considered business function?
A. Finance
B. Marketing
C. HR
D. Production

82. Which one of the following is least characterised as a quality of a charismatic leader?
A. Personal Risk-taking
B. Sensitivity to follower needs
C. Vision and articulation
D. Conventional behaviour

83. Filtering is considered as a ____ to effective communication.
A. Feedback
B. Barrier
C. Strength
D. Comprehension

84. Which of the following statements is not TRUE?
A. The principle of unity of command leads to a thinking that a subordinate should have one supervisor
B. A simple organizational structure has a low degree of departmentalization and a narrow span of control
C. Divisional structure groups employees into units by product, service, customer, or geographic market area
D. Matrix structure combines functional and product structures

85. Robert Kaplan and David Norton developed Balanced Scorecard to measure strategic organizational performance. Which one of the following is not the part of the scorecard?
A. Financial performance
B. Culture
C. Product
D. Work-life conflict

86. As per Section 22, of the Companies Act 2013, for execution of a bill of exchange
A. A company may or may not have common seal with authorization of Company Secretary
B. A company shall mandatorily have a common seal
C. A company shall not have a common seal
D. A company may or may not have common seal with authorization of company secretary and one director

87. According to Section 2 (92) of the Companies Act, 2013, "unlimited company" means a company.
A. Not having any limit on the liability of its members.
B. Not having any limit on number of members
C. Not having any limit on amount of subscribed capital
D. Not having any limit on amount of creditors

88. The fees payable to the Registrar (ROC) at the time of registration of a new company differs according to the
A. Authorised capital
B. Paid up capital
C. Loan available
D. Number of members

89. A Public Limited Company having share capital, may commence its business activities
A. From the date of its incorporation
B. From the date of submission of documents
C. From the date of online registration of company
D. From the date of Commencement of Business Certificate

90. The offer under the Indian Contract Act 1872 does not stands lapsed
A. By communicating the revocation
B. By lapse of time
C. By failure to accept
D. By accepting the offer

91. In a valid contract under the Indian Contract Act 1872 consideration may not be
A. Past
B. Present
C. Future
D. Adequate

92. An agreement under the Indian Contract Act 1872 is void if having a minor as
A. Beneficiary
B. Offeror
C. Offeree
D. Shareholder

93. Penalty under Information and Technology Act 2000, amounting to upto INR one Crore is not levied if, any individual or group attempts to
A. Introduce any virus
B. Causes to introduce a virus
C. Without permission access a computer system
D. With permission secure access to a computer system or network

94. The essentials of valid agency, prescribed under the Contract Act, 1872 does not include:

A. Privity of contract
B. Principal be competent to contract
C. Agent need not have contractual capacity
D. Agency for Criminal Act

95. Sec 2 (a) of the Information and Technology Act 2000 defines:
A. Addressee
B. Access
C. Adjudicating Officer
D. Appropriate Government

96. Finance Bill 2020 proposed to reduce the rate of Dividend Distribution Tax (DDT) which is applicable on the amount of dividend declared, distributed or paid, by a domestic company, from 15% to:
A. 12.5% B. 10%
C. 5% D. 0%

97. For the assessment year 2020-21, dividend paid by an Indian company outside India is deemed to be:
A. Received in India
B. Accrued in India
C. Received outside India
D. Accrued outside India

98. For the assessment year 2020-21, the parent in whose hands the income of minor child is clubbed can claim an exemption of:
A. ₹ 3,500 in respect of income of two minor children
B. ₹ 3,500 in respect of income of each minor child
C. ₹ 1,500 in respect of income of two minor children
D. ₹ 1,500 in respect of income of each minor child

99. For the assessment year 2020-21, loss from the activity of owning and maintaining race horses can be carried forward to:
A. 4 years
B. 8 years
C. Unlimited number of years
D. Can never be carried forward

100. For the assessment year 2020-21, the deduction under section 80G is respect of donation to National Children's Fund is
A. 50% of the amount donated without any limit on the donated amount
B. 100% of the amount donated without any limit on the donated amount
C. 50% of the amount donated subject to some limits on the donated amount
D. 100% of the amount donated subject to some limits on the donated amount

ANSWERS

1 A	**2** C	**3** D	**4** C	**5** B	**6** C	**7** A	**8** A	**9** A	**10** A
11 D	**12** B	**13** A	**14** B	**15** B	**16** C	**17** C	**18** B	**19** B	**20** C
21 A	**22** B	**23** B	**24** C	**25** D	**26** B	**27** C	**28** B	**29** A	**30** C
31 B	**32** C	**33** D	**34** A	**35** B	**36** C	**37** C	**38** B	**39** A	**40** B
41 A	**42** D	**43** A	**44** D	**45** D	**46** B	**47** A	**48** B	**49** B	**50** D
51 C	**52** B	**53** C	**54** A	**55** C	**56** D	**57** B	**58** A	**59** D	**60** C
61 A	**62** B	**63** B	**64** C	**65** D	**66** C	**67** C	**68** B	**69** D	**70** C
71 A	**72** B	**73** C	**74** B	**75** D	**76** D	**77** B	**78** B	**79** A	**80** C
81 C	**82** D	**83** B	**84** B	**85** D	**86** D	**87** A	**88** A	**89** A	**90** D
91 D	**92** B	**93** D	**94** D	**95** B	**96** D	**97** B	**98** D	**99** A	**100** B

Previous Years' Paper (Solved)

University of Delhi

M.Com, 2019*

1. The accounting department of a manufacturing company is an example of:
A. Cost Centre
B. Profit Centre
C. Investment Centre
D. Contribution Centre

2. Which of the following is incorrect with respect to coefficient of correlation:
A. It is the sum of two regression coefficients
B. It can be zero
C. It can be positive
D. It can be negative

3. Which of the following is most appropriate for marginal rate of technical substitution of L for K ($MRTS_{LK}$)?
A. The amount of K a firm increases by giving up amount of L
B. The amount of K that can be substituted for L
C. The amount of K that firm can give up by increasing the amount of L used by one unit and still remain on same isoquant
D. The amount of L that can be substituted for K

4. Which of the following is not true for Cobb-Douglas production function $Q = AL^{\alpha}K^{\beta}$?
A. $\alpha + \beta = 1$
B. α is the output elasticity of labour
C. Input elasticity of substitution is more than one
D. β is the output elasticity of Capital

5. Which of the following is not a preferential creditors:
A. Amount due under Employees State Insurance Act for 12 months previous to the winding up
B. Amount due to employee under amalgamation or reconstruction
C. All sum due to employee from a provident fund, pension fund, gratuity fund or any other fund maintained for welfare of employee
D. Compensation under Workmen's Compensation Act

6. As per the changes in income tax proposed in the Interim Budget announced on February 1, 2019, if an individual invests in the specified tax savings schemes of the government, the effective income that would be tax-free in a year, would be:
A. ₹ 6,50,000 B. ₹ 5,00,000
C. ₹ 3,00,000 D. ₹ 6,00,000

7. Which form of business does not have perpetual succession?
A. Government Company
B. Partnership Firm
C. Joint Stock Company
D. Limited Liability Partnership

8. When all inputs are increased 5% and output of commodity increases by 10%, the firm is having:
A. Increasing returns to scale
B. Decreasing returns to scale
C. Indeterminant returns to scale
D. Constant returns to scale

9. When budget line shifts parallel towards right, which of the following statement is true?
A. The price of X increases and budget increases
B. The price of Y increases and budget increases
C. The price of X and Y remain constant and the budget increases
D. The price of X decreases and budget increases

* ***Online exam conducted by NTA on 05 July, 2019.***

10. If company changes from offering 40 days credit to 50 days credit, which of the following statement is correct?

A. Cash generated from financing activities will decrease
B. Cash generated from operation will decrease
C. Cash generated from operation will increase
D. There will be no affect on cash flow

11. Raw materials are assigned to a job when:

A. Materials are purchased
B. Materials are issued by the materials store room
C. Materials are received from the vendor
D. Job is sold

12. Examine the two statements and chose the best option:

Statement 1: Higher real wealth stimulates consumer spending and decreases the quantity of goods and services demanded.

Statement 2: The lower interest rate stimulates the investment spending and thus increases the quantity of goods and services demanded.

A. Only statement 2 is correct
B. Only statement 1 is correct
C. Both the statements are correct
D. Both the statements are incorrect

13. Find $\frac{dy}{dx}$ if $\frac{x}{x-y} = \log\left(\frac{a}{(x-y)}\right)$.

A. $x - y$ B. $\frac{1}{(x-y)}$

C. $\frac{x}{y}$ D. $2-\left(\frac{x}{y}\right)$

14. According to an investment proposal, an initial investment of ₹ 1,00,000 is expected to yield a uniform income stream of ₹ 10,000 per annum. If money is worth 8% per annum compounded continuously, what is the expected payback period, *i.e.* after what time, the initial investment will be recovered?

A. 20 years B. 19 years
C. 21 years D. 18 years

15. Strike in a factory which stops production for a few weeks is an example of:

(*i*) Secular trend
(*ii*) Cyclical trend
(*iii*) Irregular trend

A. Only (*iii*)
B. Only (*ii*)
C. Only (*i*)
D. (*i*) and (*ii*) but not (*iii*)

16. A fixed asset originally acquired for ₹ 20,000 is replaced by a new asset costing ₹ 50,000. But the estimated cost of replacement of the original asset is ₹ 30,000. Hence, the capital charge equals.

A. ₹ 50,000 B. ₹ 20,000
C. ₹ 30,000 D. ₹ 40,000

17. In the following problem, find y subject to the given condition $\frac{dy}{dx} = \frac{1}{\left(2\sqrt{x}\right)}$; given that $y = 1$ when $x = 1$:

A. 0 B. 1

C. $\frac{1}{\sqrt{x}}$ D. $\sqrt{x}$

18. Which of the following most appropriately describes classical theory of management?

A. Everyone has desire to be efficient
B. There is only one best of doing the job
C. All of these
D. Money is only motivator

19. The curve or locus point that shows the cost minimizing input combinations for each successive level of output with the input/price ratio held constant is known as:

A. Isocost
B. Isoquant
C. Expansion path
D. Ridge line

20. A firm's demand function is $p = 10\ e^{-x/400}$, where p is the price per unit and x is quantity demanded. Find at what level of output, is the Marginal revenue zero.

A. 800 B. 400
C. 100 D. 200

21. The standard deviation of 30 items in a data set is 5/6. If every item in the data set is multiplied by 6, then the variance of the data set will be:
A. 6 B. 5
C. 8 D. 25

22. The demand D of passenger automobiles is given by D = $0.90\ I^{1.1}\ p^{-0.7}$ where I is the income and p is the price per car. Find the income elasticity of demand.
A. 0.4 B. 1.8
C. 1.1 D. 0.7

23. Decision tree is developed by:
A. Talcott Parson B. Vroom and Yetton
C. Peter Drucker D. Herbert Simon

24. For the assessment year 2019-20, the income tax rate for a domestic company having total turnover up to ₹ 250 crore in the previous year is:
A. 25% B. 35%
C. 28% D. 30%

25. A theory of exchange rate whereby a unit of any given currency should be able to buy the same quantity of goods in all countries is called as:
A. Purchasing power parity theory
B. Exchange rate parity theory
C. Currency rate parity theory
D. Interest rate parity theory

26. John Kotter is mainly known for:
A. human resource development
B. motivational theory
C. change management
D. organizational development

27. The setting of standards is:
A. Preferably set at the ideal level of performance
B. Managerial accounting decision
C. Worker decision
D. Management decision

28. In what case would the Poisson distribution be a good approximation of the binomial distribution?
A. N = 300, q = 0.99
B. N = 18, p = 0.60
C. N = 11, p = 0.30
D. N = 10, p = 0.60

29. A production manager in a manufacturing company would most likely to receive:
A. Despatch department overhead report
B. Income statement
C. Sales report
D. Scrap report

30. If the cross elasticity of demand between X and Y is 0.62, which of the following statement is correct?
A. X and Y are substitutes
B. X and Y are complementary
C. X and Y are not related
D. X and Y are giffen goods

31. The grouping of activities at the top of the organizational structure around two or more activities is:
A. grouping superstructure
B. hybrid superstructure
C. matrix superstructure
D. cross superstructure

32. If A is a singular matrix | A | is __________.
A. 0
B. any positive value
C. 1
D. any negative value

33. A person deposited ₹ 4000 in a bank at 6% compounded continuously. After 3 years, the rate of interest was increased to 7% and after 5 more years, the rate was further increased to 8%. The money was withdrawn at the end of 10 years. Find the amount.
A. 7974.8 B. 8346.7
C. 9212.5 D. 8681.4

34. "People's believe that efforts would be directed toward behaviour" is closely based on:
A. Vroom's theory B. Alderfer's theory
C. Porter's theory D. McClelland's theory

35. A manager faces price elasticity of demand for a product X equal to –0.5. Now manager wishes to increases sales of product X by 15%. By what percentage the price is to be lowered to achieve this objective?

A. –75% B. –45%
C. –7.5% D. –30%

36. A manager of an investment Centre can improve ROI by:
A. Reducing Variable and/or controllable fixed costs.
B. Reducing sales
C. Increasing variable costs
D. Increasing average assets

37. What is the equilibrium level of income, given C = 100 + 0.75Y and I = 25?
A. 500 B. 750
C. 150 D. 250

38. Under compound interest the formula for A is given by __________.
A. A = P*nr*/100 B. A = P (1 + *i*)
C. A = P (1 + *ni*) D. $A = P(1 + i)^n$

39. Given total product of 9 labour units is 2, 5, 9, 12, 14, 15, 15, 14 and 12 respectively. Which unit of labour will produce zero marginal product?
A. 6th B. 7th
C. 8th D. 9th

40. Dave Gilboa has authored a best seller book:
A. Refugee
B. The Efficiency Paradox
C. Factfulness
D. The Third Plate

41. Identify the correct equation:
A. Real interest rate = Nominal interest rate – inflation rate
B. Real interest rate = Nominal interest rate + Inflation rate
C. Real interest rate + Nominal interest rate = Inflation rate
D. Nominal interest rate – Real interest rate = inflation rate

42. The marginal cost function of a product is given by $MC = 2(2x + 9)^{-1/2}$ where x is no. of units produced. Find the average cost of production for 8 units of production, if fixed cost is ₹ 4.
A. 0.5 B. 1.0
C. 2.0 D. 1.5

43. The additional shifts in aggregate demand that result when expansionary fiscal policy increase income and thereby increasing consumer spending is explained by:
A. Multiplier effect
B. Accelerator effect
C. Crowding-out effect
D. Crowding-in effect

44. When a fixed Asset is obtained as a gift, the account to be credited is
A. Capital Reserve A/c
B. Goodwill A/c
C. General Reserve A/c
D. Donor's A/c

45. A company has fixed costs of ₹ 1,50,000 and variable costs of ₹ 9 per unit. If sales price per unit is ₹ 12 per unit, what is the breakeven sales in Rupees.
A. ₹ 2,00,000 B. ₹ 6,00,000
C. ₹ 4,50,000 D. ₹ 4,80,000

46. A firm which has significant influence over another firm but does not actually control the firm or have a dominant influence over the firm's actions would refer to the firm it has influence over as:
A. Subsidiary
B. Holding company
C. Joint Venture
D. Associated undertaking

47. A firm produces two products P_1 and P_2, passing through two machines M_1 and M_2 before completion. M_1 can produce either 10 units of P_1 or 15 units of P_2 per hour. M_2 can produce 15 units of either product per hour. Find daily production of P_1 and P_2, if time available is 12 hours of machine M_1 and 10 hours of M_2 per day using Matrix inversion.
A. 60, 90 B. 50, 75
C. 45, 60 D. 90, 120

48. A firm can hire 10 workers at a wage rate of ₹ 10, but has to pay a wage of ₹ 13 to get the 11th worker. What is the marginal cost of 11th worker?
A. ₹ 33 B. ₹ 10.2
C. ₹ 113 D. ₹ 13

49. In the Interim Budget announced on February 1, 2019, the government has proposed to increase the limit for TDS applicable on interest income (from Post office/Bank deposits) to:

A. ₹ 30,000 per annum
B. ₹ 60,000 per annum
C. ₹ 50,000 per annum
D. ₹ 40,000 per annum

50. For a normal curve with $\mu = 56$ and $\sigma = 10$, how much area will be found under the curve to the left of the value 56?

A. 0.50
B. 0.68
C. 0.32
D. 1

51. "Leaders with strong achievement motivation are likely to have strong concern for task objectives". This statement is largely based on:

A. trait theory
B. contingency theory
C. behavioural theory
D. social theory

52. The essentials of effective budgeting do not include:

A. Top down budgeting
B. Sound organizational structure
C. Research and analysis
D. Management acceptance

53. The essential elements of valid consideration does not include:

A. Consideration need to be adequate
B. Consideration to be furnished by the promise
C. Consideration may be past, present or future
D. Consideration as unlawful act.

54. The essential of a valid acceptance does not include:

A. Acceptance towards completion of unlawful act
B. Acceptance must be unconditional
C. Acceptance must be absolute
D. Acceptance must be communicated

55. Joint probability of two independent events A and B is:

A. P ((A) × P (B))   B. P ((A) / P(B))
C. P ((A) – P(B))   D. P ((A) + P(B))

56. The budgeted income statement is:

A. End product of operating budgets
B. End product of financial budgets
C. Dependent on cash receipts and cash payments
D. Starting point of master budget

57. Income tax is an example of:

A. Proportional tax
B. Regressive tax
C. Progressive tax
D. Indirect tax

58. The Arithmetic Mean of 7 observations is 100 and that of 5 is 70, the combined mean of all the 12 observations will be:

A. 70   B. 80
C. 100   D. 87.5

59. Two variables have correlation coefficient as 0.60, then what percentage of one variable is explained by other variable?

A. 40%   B. 36%
C. 60%   D. 64%

60. Short run aggregate supply curve of Keynes is:

A. Vertical
B. Horizontal
C. Upward sloping from left to right
D. Downward sloping from left to right

61. Fixed production overhead are recognized as:

A. Part of closing inventory costs under both absorption and variable costing
B. Product costs under variable costing
C. Product costs under constant costing
D. Period costs under absorption costing

62. The leadership styles like exploitative, benevolent, consultative, and participative are given by:

A. House
B. Fiedler
C. Likert
D. Blake and Mouton

63. Find w given what that:

$$3\begin{bmatrix} x & y \\ z & w \end{bmatrix} = \begin{bmatrix} x & 6 \\ -1 & 2w \end{bmatrix} + \begin{bmatrix} 4 & z+y \\ z+w & 3 \end{bmatrix}$$

A. 6　　B. 5
C. 3　　D. 4

64. For what value of k the matrix $A = \begin{bmatrix} 2 & k \\ 3 & 5 \end{bmatrix}$ has no inverse?

A. $\frac{3}{10}$　　B. $\frac{10}{3}$
C. 10　　D. 3

65. Accumulated profits include:
A. Workmen's compensation fund
B. Superannuation fund
C. Depreciation fund
D. Provision for doubtful debts

66. If Kurtosis is less than 3 then the curve is:
(*i*) Mesokurtic
(*ii*) Leptokurtic
(*iii*) Platykurtic
A. Only (*iii*)
B. Only (*ii*)
C. Only (*i*)
D. (*i*) and (*ii*) but not (*iii*)

67. The theory which states that, "a asset prices reflect all publicly available information" is known as:
A. Technical analysis
B. Random walk theory
C. Efficient market hypothesis
D. Fundamental analysis

68. Loss on issue of debentures is treated a:
A. Current liability
B. Current asset
C. Miscellaneous expenditure
D. Intangible asset

69. The process by which organizations gain new knowledge and insights that lead to a modification in behaviour and action is:
A. organizational commitment
B. organizational learning
C. learning organization
D. OB modification

70. The process through which people develop beliefs about what is right wrong and just is:
A. judgement　　B. ethics
C. morality　　D. socialization

71. Which of the following is not the reason for shift in aggregate supply curve towards left?
A. Decrease in economy's capital stock
B. An economy experiences decrease in immigration
C. Negative technological growth
D. Technological Progress

72. Which of the following incomes is not taxable under the head "Income from Other Sources"?
A. Ground rent
B. Pension
C. Director's fee
D. Interest on bank deposits

73. Which of the following is an example of relative measure of dispersion?
A. Variance
B. Coefficient of variation
C. Standard deviation
D. Range

74. Which of the following is a disadvantage of incorporating a Limited Liability Partnership (LLP):
A. In certain cases the shield of limited liability may be pierced.
B. Action of single partner can bind the LLP
C. Unlimited members cannot be added
D. Not allowed to raise funds

75. Which of the following is not an example of compressed data?
A. Data array
B. Frequency distribution
C. Histogram
D. Ogive

76. Which of the following is not a deduction from gross total income under section 80C?
A. Life insurance premium
B. Contribution towards an approved superannuation fund
C. Contribution towards statutory provident fund
D. Leave travel concession

77. Which of the following is not a characteristic of an isoquant?
A. Isoquant is convex to the origin
B. Isoquant is downward sloping
C. Isoquant is linear in nature
D. Different combinations of Labour and Capital produce same output on an isoquant

78. Which of the following is True with respect to a Positively Skewed Distribution?
A. Mean > Median > Mode
B. Mode > Median > Mean
C. Mode > Mean > Median
D. Median > Mode > Mean

79. Which of the following is correct?
A. Median is not affected by extreme values
B. Median is affected by extreme values
C. Mean is not affected by extreme values
D. Mode is the middlemost point of a data set

80. Which of the following statement does not hold with respect to incidence of tax?
A. Indian income is always taxable in India irrespective of the residential status of the taxpayer
B. All foreign income is taxable in the hands of resident but not ordinarily resident in India
C. All foreign income is taxable in the hands of resident and ordinarily resident in India
D. All foreign income is not taxable in the hands of non-resident in India

81. Which of the following statement is not true?
A. MC = $\Delta TC/\Delta Q$ B. TC = AFC + AVC
C. AVC = TVC/Q D. AFC = TFC/Q

82. Which of the following statements is false?
A. There is no difference between exemption and deduction
B. Tax rates are not given by the Income Tax Act but by the Finance Act which is passed in the Parliament
C. Income arises either on receipt or accrual basis
D. Deduction can be less than, equal to or more than the amount of income

83. Which of the following statements is false?
A. Debit balance of Bank column of Cash Book is an Asset
B. Credit side total of Discount column of Cash Book is an income
C. Credit balance of Bank Pass Book is an overdraft
D. Debt balance of Cash column of Cash Book is an Asset

84. Which of the following is a flow concept?
A. Mineral resource
B. Capital
C. Forest
D. Income

85. Which of the following items would not form part of the shareholders' equity of a company on the statement of financial position?
A. Ordinary share capital
B. Retained Profit
C. Trade payables
D. Share premium

86. Which of the following is not expressly allowed as deduction while computing business income?
A. Insurance in respect of plant, machinery and furniture used for business purposes
B. Bonus or commission payed to employee
C. Rent and repair expenditure of premises used for the purpose of carrying on business or profession
D. Litigation expenses for registration of shares

87. Which of the following is true for Phillips curve?
A. It shows inverse relationship between rate of unemployment and rate of increase in money wage
B. It shows inverse relationship between rate of unemployment and rate of general price level
C. It shows direct relationship between rate of unemployment and rate of general price level
D. It shows a direct relationship between rate of unemployment and rate of increase in money wage

88. Marginal efficient capital as determinant of private investment does not include the following:
A. Life of the product
B. Supply price of capital
C. Expected yield
D. Propensity to consume

89. Indirect labour is:
A. Raw material cost
B. Non-manufacturing cost
C. Product cost
D. Period cost

90. Aggregate demand curve may shift towards right due to:
A. Government decides to reduce purchase of machinery
B. Availability of investment tax credit to the firm
C. Reduction in exports
D. Increase in savings in economy

91. In make or buy decision, relevant costs:
A. Opportunity costs
B. Purchase price of units
C. Production costs to be saved, purchase price of units, opportunity costs
D. Production costs that will be saved

92. Provision for bad debt is made as per the:
A. Going Concern Concept
B. Entity Concept
C. Conservatism Concept
D. Cost Concept

93. In a company, there are zero units in beginning work in progress, 7000 units started into production and 500 units in ending work in progress 20% completed. The physical units to be accounted for are:
A. 7000 B. 7340
C. 7360 D. 7500

94. While computing income under the head "Salaries", exemption under House Rent Allowance is available to an employee when:
A. the employee pays rent which does not exceed 10% of salary
B. the employee pays rent which exceeds 10% of salary
C. the employee lives in a house for which he does not pay rent
D. the employee lives in his own house

95. Any activity that causes resources to be consumed is called:
A. Cost Driver
B. Non-Value added activity
C. Facility-level activity
D. Just-in-time activity

96. The applicability of the Information and Technology Act, 2000 does not:
A. Applicable on contraventions committed outside India as well
B. Applicable on offenses
C. Apply on Cheques drawn on Indian Bank
D. Extend to whole of India

97. Money without intrinsic value is known as:
A. Commodity money B. Demands deposits
C. Fiat money D. Currency

98. As per section 78 of the Companies Act, amount collected as premium on securities cannot be utilized for:
A. Buy back of its own shares
B. Purchase of fixed assets
C. Writing off preliminary expenses
D. Issuing fully paid bonus shares to the members

99. When price elasticity of demand for chicken is 0.34, which of the following statements is true?
A. The price elasticity of demand for chicken is inelastic.
B. The price elasticity of demand for chicken is elastic.
C. The price elasticity of demand for chicken cannot be determined.
D. The price elasticity of demand for chicken is zero.

100. AS – 14 is not applicable if when transferee company acquires transferor company:
A. Ceases to exist
B. Separate entity is Continue to exist
C. Valuation of inventory
D. Applied in all cases

ANSWERS

1	2	3	4	5	6	7	8	9	10
A	A	C	C	B	A	B	A	C	B
11	**12**	**13**	**14**	**15**	**16**	**17**	**18**	**19**	**20**
B	A	D	A	A	B	D	C	C	B
21	**22**	**23**	**24**	**25**	**26**	**27**	**28**	**29**	**30**
D	C	B	A	A	C	D	A	D	A
31	**32**	**33**	**34**	**35**	**36**	**37**	**38**	**39**	**40**
B	A	A	A	D	A	A	D	B	*
41	**42**	**43**	**44**	**45**	**46**	**47**	**48**	**49**	**50**
*	D	A	A	B	D	A	D	D	A
51	**52**	**53**	**54**	**55**	**56**	**57**	**58**	**59**	**60**
A	A	D	A	A	A	C	D	B	C
61	**62**	**63**	**64**	**65**	**66**	**67**	**68**	**69**	**70**
*	C	C	B	A	A	C	B	B	D
71	**72**	**73**	**74**	**75**	**76**	**77**	**78**	**79**	**80**
A	*	B	A	A	D	C	A	A	B
81	**82**	**83**	**84**	**85**	**86**	**87**	**88**	**89**	**90**
B	*	C	D	C	D	A	D	B	B
91	**92**	**93**	**94**	**95**	**96**	**97**	**98**	**99**	**100**
C	C	A	B	A	C	C	B	A	B

EXPLANATORY ANSWERS

1. A cost centre often represents a department or key function within a company. The manager and employees of a cost center are responsible for costs incurred but are not responsible for revenues or investment decisions that impact the company. As an example, a manufacturer's cost centers include each of its production departments as well as the manufacturing service departments such as the maintenance department or quality control department. Other example of cost centers include the human resource department, the information technology (IT) department, the accounting department, and so on.

Cost centers are usually not limited to departments. There might be several cost centers within a department. For example, each assembly line within a manufacturing company could be assigned a cost center. Even a special production, new product, packaging machine, or media events could have a cost center. Cost centers are usually associated with the topic of decentralization, responsibility accounting, and planning and control.

2. Correlation analysis, is a mean of measuring the strength of 'closeness' of the relationship between two variables. It should be clear that the concept of correlation is very closely linked to regression analysis. If all the paired points (x_i, y_i) lie on a straight line then the correlation between the variables x and y is perfect. Whether the correlation is perfectly positive or negative depends, of course, on whether the straight line through the points has a positive or negative slope.

Correlation analysis provides a numerical summary measure of the degree of correlation between two variables x and y—a *correlation coefficient* denoted by r. This is defined so that its value must be within the range from –1 to +1 so that:

- $r = +1$ denotes perfect positive correlation
- $r = 0$ denotes no correlation,
- $r = -1$ denotes perfect negative correlation.

3. The marginal rate of technical substitution of L for K ($MRTS_{LK}$) refers to the amount of K that a firm can give up by increasing the amount of L used by one unit and still remain on the same isoquant. The $MRTS_{LK}$ is also equal to MP_L/MP_K. As the firm moves down an isoquant, the $MRTS_{LK}$ diminishes.

4. The Cobb-Douglas production function is given by the formula $Q = AL^{\alpha}K^{\beta}$, where A, α and β are positive constants.

In Cobb-Douglas function α and β represent elasticity of output with respect to labour and capital and the sum of two elasticities is equal to elasticity of scale. (This relationship is known as Wicksell Johnson theorem).

Further, marginal production can also be used to derive the marginal rate of substitution R between two factors.

$$R = \frac{\partial Q}{\partial K} / \frac{\partial Q}{\partial L} = \beta\frac{Q}{K} / \alpha\frac{Q}{L} = \frac{\beta}{\alpha} . \frac{L}{K}$$

This can be used in the deviation of elasticity of substitution that is given by

$$\sigma = \frac{d(K/L)/(K/L)}{dR/R}$$

and from the above we have

$$dR = \left(\frac{L}{K}\right) . \left(\frac{\beta}{\alpha}\right)$$

Substitution dR and R in the equation giving α we have

$$\sigma = \frac{d(L/K)(K/L)}{d(L/K)(\beta/\alpha)}\left(\frac{\beta}{\alpha}\right)\left(\frac{L}{K}\right) = 1$$

so that in case of Cobb-Douglas function, elasticity of substitution will always be equal to one.

5. Section 327 of The Companies Act, 2013, provides that subject to the provision of Section 326, following preferential creditors shall be paid in priority to unsecured creditors or creditor having a floating charge:

(*a*) All revenues, taxes, cesses and rates, becoming due and payable by the company within 12 months next before the commencement of the winding up.

(*b*) All wages or salaries (including wages payable for time or piece of work and salary earned wholly or in part by way of commission) of any employee due for the period not exceeding 4 months within 12 months next before commencement of winding up provided the amount payable to one claimant will not exceed such amount as may be notified.

(*c*) All accrued holiday remuneration becoming payable to any employee on termination of employment before winding up order or dissolution of the company.

(*d*) Unless the company is being wound up voluntarily for the purpose of reconstruction, all contributions payable during the 12 months next under the Employees' State Insurance Act, 1948, or any other law for the time being in force.

(*e*) All sums due as compensation to employees under the Workmen's Compensation Act, 1923.

(*f*) All sums due to any employee from a provident fund, pension fund, gratuity fund or any other fund, for the welfare of the employees maintained by the company.

(*g*) The expenses of any investigation held under Section 213 or 216 in so far as they are payable by the company.

All the preferential debts rank equally among themselves and are to be paid in full unless the assets are insufficient, in which case they will abate in equal proportion.

7. According to company law, *perpetual succession* is the continuation of a company's existence despite the death, bankruptcy, insanity, change in membership or an exit from the business of any owner or member, or any transfer of shares. A company ceases to exist only when it is liquidated through a legal process. Therefore, a shareholder can transfer his share to another person without obtaining the consent of the company. Except in rare situations, a company cannot refuse to register the transfer in its record. For a successful company, an investor gets a price higher than his investment, and in the case of failed company, a shareholder gets a price lower than his investment. Return on equity investment is the total of divided and capital appreciation.

8. Returns to scale refers to the returns enjoyed by the firm as a result of change in all the inputs. It explains the behaviour of the returns when the inputs are changed simultaneously. The returns to scale are governed by laws of returns to scale.

Law of Returns to Scale: There are three laws of returns governing production function. They are:

(*a*) **Law of Increasing Returns to Scale:** This law states that the volume of output keeps on increasing with every increase in the inputs. Where a given increase in inputs leads to more than proportionate increase in the output, the law of increasing returns to scale is said to operate. We can introduce division of labour and other technological means to increase production. Hence, the total product increases at an increasing rate.

(*b*) **Law of Constant Returns to Scale:** When the scope for division of labour gets restricted, the rate of increase in the total output remains constant, the law of constant returns to scale is said to operate. This law states that the rate of increase/decrease in volume of output is same to that of rate of increase/decrease in inputs.

(*c*) **Law of Decreasing Returns to Scale:** Where the proportionate increase in the inputs does not lead to equivalent increase in output, the output increases at a decreasing rate, the law of decreasing returns to scale is said to operate. This result in higher average cost per unit.

These laws can be illustrated with an example of agricultural land. Take one acre of land. If you till the land well with adequate bags of fertilisers and sow good quality seeds, the volume of output increases. The following table illustrates further:

Table : *The Laws of Returns to Scale*

Capital (in units)	*Labour (in units)*	*Percentage of Increase in both inputs*	*Output (in units)*	*Percentage of Increase in output*	*Laws applicable*
1	3	–	–	–	
2	6	100	120	140	Law of increasing returns to scale
4	12	100	240	100	Law of constant returns to scale
8	24	100	360	50	Law of decreasing returns to scale

9. The budget line shows the alternative options of commodity combinations available to the consumer given his income and the prices of X and Y.

The budget line is drawn on the basis of the budget equation, given as $M = P_x . Q_x + P_y . Q_y$. Any change in the parameters of the budget equation, viz., M, P_x and P_y, make the budget line shift upward or downward or swivel left or right and up or down. If consumer's income (M) increases, prices remaining constant, the budget line shifts upwards remaining parallel to the original budget line. Income remaining the same, if prices change, the budget line changes its position and slope.

10. Offering a longer credit period to customers will reduce the cash flowing into the business and cash generated from operations will decrease.

12. The aggregate-demand curve shows the total quantity of goods and services demanded in the economy for any price level. There are three reasons the aggregate-demand curve slopes downward:

- *The wealth effect:* A lower price level raises the real value of households' money holdings, which are part of their wealth. Higher real wealth stimulates consumer spending and thus increases the quantity of goods and services demanded.
- *The interest-rate effect:* A lower price level reduces the amount of money people want to hold. As people try to lend out their excess money holdings, the interest rate falls. The lower interest rate stimulates investment spending and thus increases the quantity of goods and services demanded.
- *The exchange-rate effect:* When a lower price level reduces the interest rate, investors move some of their funds overseas in search of higher returns. This movement of funds causes the real value of the domestic currency to fall in the market for foreign-currency exchange. Domestic goods become less expensive relative to foreign goods. This change in the real exchange rate stimulates spending on net exports and thus increases the quantity of goods and services demanded.

These three effects occur simultaneously to increase the quantity of goods and services demanded when the price level falls and to decrease it when the price level rises.

15. Random or Irregular Variations: Random variations are those variations which occur at once or accidentally in a series. The main causes of these variations are strikes, floods, lockouts, wars, earthquakes, etc. There is no regular period or time of their occurrence and that is why they are called random or chance fluctuations. In the words of Freund and Williams, *"Irregular, or erratic, fluctuations of a time series are those variations which are either completely unpredictable or which are caused by such isolated special occurrences as good or bad news, bank failures, elections, floods, earthquakes, strikes and wars."* Thus, by their very nature, irregular variation are unpredictable. Sometimes the fluctuations are so violent that it forces a permanent change on the series and there is a sudden change in the trend. However, since they are irregular in character, so it is difficult to isolate them from the time series completely. Irregular variations are normally short term variations.

16. The difference between the total cost of the entire work and the estimated replacement cost of the old asset in original manner is charged to Capital Account, *i.e.*, capitalised.

Here, Capital Charge = 50,000 – 30,000 = 20,000.

20. The demand function is $P = 10e^{-x/400}$

$\therefore$ Total revenue, $R = px = 10xe^{-x/400}$

$$\therefore \quad R = 10xe^{-x/400} \qquad ...(i)$$

$$\frac{dR}{dx} = 10\left[1.e^{-x/400} + x\left(-\frac{1}{400}\right)e^{-x/400}\right]$$

$$= 10\left(1-\frac{x}{400}\right)e^{-x/400}$$

and $\dfrac{d^2R}{dx^2}$

$$= 10\left(-\frac{1}{400}\right)e^{-x/400} + 10\left(1-\frac{x}{400}\right)\left(-\frac{1}{400}\right)e^{-x/400}$$

$$= -\frac{10}{400}\left(1+1-\frac{x}{400}\right)e^{-x/400}$$

$$= -\frac{1}{40}\left(2-\frac{x}{400}\right)e^{-x/400}$$

$$\frac{dR}{dx} = 0$$

$$\Rightarrow \quad 10\left(1-\frac{x}{400}\right)e^{-x/400} = 0$$

$$\Rightarrow \quad 1-\frac{x}{400} = 0$$

$$\Rightarrow \quad x = 400$$

Also, $$\left.\frac{d^2R}{dx^2}\right|_{x=400} = -\frac{1}{40}\left(2-\frac{400}{400}\right)e^{-1}$$

$$= -\frac{1}{40e} < 0$$

$\therefore$ R is maximum when $x = 400$

$$x = 400$$

$$\Rightarrow \quad P = 10e^{-400/400}$$

$$= \frac{10}{e}$$

$\therefore$ R is maximum when $P = 10/e$ and $x = 400$.

21. As a general rule, the median, mean and quartiles will be changed by adding a constant to each value. However, the range, interquartile range, standard deviation and variance will remain the same. Multiplying every value by a constant, however, will multiply the mean, median, quartiles, range, interquartile range, and standard deviation by that constant, and multiply the variance (which is simply the square of the standard deviation) by the square of the constant.

23. Vroom and his colleagues have developed a model of managerial decision making (a decision tree) in which seven rules specify which of five possible processes is considered feasible. These processes vary from autocratic to participative decision making. The decision rules illustrate a combination of characteristics of the situation and a manager's educated guess at the importance of these characteristics. The decision rules are given in Table. The use of the Vroom and Yetton decision tree provides practical guidelines for managerial behaviour.

Table: *Decision rules:*

1. Is quality required (*e.g.*, is only a specific solution acceptable rather than a number of options)?
2. Is sufficient information available to make a quality decision?
3. Is the problem structured in terms of what information is needed?
4. Is acceptability of the decision to subordinates critical to decision implementation?
5. Is it certain that subordinates would accept the decision if the leader made it on his/her own?
6. Do subordinates have the same goals as the organization in terms of the benefits to be obtained in solving the problem?
7. Is it likely that there would be conflict among subordinates about which is the preferred solution?

24. Income Tax Rates for AY 2019-20/FY 2018-19 for Domestic Company: For the assessment year 2019-20, a domestic company is taxable at 30%. However, the tax rate would be 25% if turnover or gross receipt of the company does not exceed ₹ 250 crore in the previous year 2016-17.

25. Economists have developed many models to explain how exchange rates are determined, each emphasizing just some of the many forces at work. The simplest theory of exchange rates is purchasing-power parity. This theory states that a unit of any given currency should be able to buy the same quantity of goods in all countries. Many economists believe that purchasing-power parity describes the forces that determine exchange rates in the long run.

The theory of purchasing-power parity is based on a principle called the *law of one price.* This law asserts that a good must sell for the same price in all locations. Otherwise, there would be opportunities for profit left unexploited. For example, suppose that coffee beans sold for less in Seattle than in Boston.

A person could buy coffee in Seattle for, say $4 a pound and then sell it in Boston for $5 a pound, making a profit of $1 per pound from the difference in price. The process of taking advantage of price differences for the same item in different markets is called arbitrage. In our example, as people took advantage of this arbitrage opportunity, they would increase the demand for coffee in Seattle and increase the supply in Boston. The price of coffee would rise in Seattle (in response to greater demand) and fall in Boston (in response to greater supply). This process would continue until, eventually, the prices were the same in the two markets.

Now consider how the law of one price applies to the international marketplace. If a dollar (or any other currency) could buy more coffee in the United States than in Japan, international traders could profit by buying coffee in the United States and selling it in Japan. This export of coffee from the United States to Japan would drive up the U.S. price of coffee and drive down the Japanese price. Conversely, if a dollar could buy more coffee in Japan than in the United States, traders could buy coffee in Japan and sell it in the United States. This import of coffee into the Unites States from Japan would drive down the U.S. price of coffee and drive up the Japanese price. In the end, the law of one price tells us that a dollar must buy the same amount of coffee in all countries.

This logic leads us to the theory of purchasing-power parity. According to this theory, a currency must have the same purchasing power in all countries. That is, a U.S. dollar must buy the same quantity of goods in the United States and Japan, and a Japanese yen must buy the same quantity of goods in Japan and the United States.

26. A lot of theories are existed about transforming an organization. The majority of these theories are according to the leadership work and management change guru John P. Kotter. Kotter who is a retired professor expanded his 8-step change model in a book named Leading Change back in 1996. After that he has improved the model and it is used all over the world by a lot of consulting companies. Figure represents the Kotter Model. In continue Kotter Model's steps are briefly explained.

Fig. *Kotter's 8-Step Change Model*

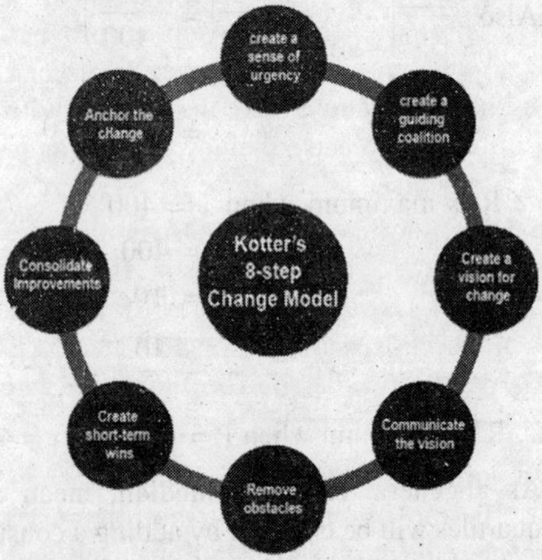

Step 1 : Create a Sense of Urgency—Help others see the need for change and they will be convinced of the importance of acting immediately.

Step 2 : Create the Guiding Coalition–Assemble a group with enough power to lead the change effort, and encourage the group to work as a team.

Step 3 : Create a vision for change—Create a vision to help direct the change effort, and develop strategies for achieving that vision.

Step 4 : Communicate the Vision—Make sure as many as possible understand and accept the vision and the strategy.

Step 5 : Remove obstacles—Remove obstacles, change system or structures that seriously undermine the vision, and encourage risk-taking and nontraditional ideas, activities and actions.

Step 6 : Create Short-term Wins—Plan for achievements that can easily be made visible, follow-through with those achievements and recognize and reward employees who were involved.

Step 7 : Consolidate improvement—Use increased credibility to change systems, structures, and policies that don't fit the vision, also hire, promote, and develop employees who can implement the vision, and finally reinvigorate the process with new projects, themes, and change agents.

Step 8 : Anchor the Changes—Articulate the connections between the new behaviours and organizational success, and develop the means to ensure leadership development and succession.

28. For a large number of observations, *i.e.*, $np \geq 10$, the binomial distribution curve approaches the normal distribution curve, and the properties of the normal distribution may be applied to the binomial distribution. Binomial distribution is not practical to use with large data sets. Poisson distribution is a good approximation of the Binomial distribution to analyze large data sets with rare defects, especially when $n \geq 20$ and $p \leq 0.05$ or $n \geq 100$ and $np \leq 10$.

30. Cross-price elasticity of demand for two goods is positive (XED > 0) when the demand for one goods and the price of the other goods change in the same direction: when the price of one increases, the demand for the other also increases. This occurs when the two goods are *substitutes*.

Substitues: If an increase in the price of one good leads to an increase in the demand for another goods, their cross-price elasticity is positive and the two goods are *substitutes.* For example, an increase in the price of Coke, other things constant, shifts the demand for Pepsi rightward, so the two are substitutes. The cross-price elasticity between Coke and Pepsi has been estimated at about 0.7, indicating that a 10 per cent increase in the price of one increases the demand for the other by 7 per cent.

Complements: If an increase in the price of one goods leads to a decrease in the demand for another, their cross-price elasticity is negative and the goods are *complements.* For example, an increase in the price of gasoline, other things constant, shifts the demand for tires leftward because people drive less and replace their tires less frequently. Gasoline and tires have a negative cross-price elasticity and are complements.

In Summary: The cross-price elasticity of demand is positive for substitutes and negative for complements. Most pairs of goods selected at random are unrelated, so their cross-price elasticity is zero.

32. Singular and Non-singular Matrices: A square matrix A is said to be a *non-singular matrix* if its determinant does not vanish and *singular matrix* if its determinant vanish.

i.e., A is *non-singular* if $|A| \neq 0$ and *singular* if $|A| = 0$.

33. Amount due

$= 4000\ e^{0.06 \times 3} \times e^{0.07 \times 5} \times e^{0.008 \times 2}$

$= 4000 \times e^{0.18} \times e^{0.35} \times e^{0.16}$

$= 4000\ e^{0.18 + 0.35 + 0.16}$

$= 4000\ e^{0.69} = 4000 \times 1.9937$

= ₹ 7974.8.

34. Victor H. Vroom formulated first expectancy theory. The expectancy theory has its roots in the cognitive concepts of Kurt Lewin and Edward Tolman. This theory is based on the idea that work effort is directed towards behaviours that people believe will lead to desired outcomes, as per this thoery the individuals are rational and not impulsive. Through experience, one will develop expectations about whether performance will lead to desired outcomes, and they will direct their efforts towards outcomes that help them to fulfill their needs.

36. Reducing variable or controllable fixed costs will cause the controllable margin to increase, which is one way a manager of an investment center can improve ROI. The other choices are incorrect because increasing average operating assets will lower ROI; reducing sales will cause contribution margin to go down, thereby decreasing controllable margin since there will be less contribution margin to cover controllable fixed costs and resulting in lower ROI; and increasing variable costs will cause the contribution margin to be lower, thereby decreasing controllable margin and resulting in lower ROI.

37. Equilibrium level of National Income (Y)

At Equilibrium, Y = C + I

$[\because AD = AS = Y \text{ and } AD = C + I]$

$[\because C = 100 + 0.75Y]$

Or, $Y = 100 + 0.75\,Y + 25$

$Y(1 - 0.75) = 125$

$0.25\,Y = 125$

$$Y = \frac{125}{0.25} = \frac{12500}{25} = 500.$$

39. Marginal product refers to the additional output produced, when one more unit of variable factor is employed. Calculated as:

MP = Change in output/ Change in input

Here, $MP_{7th} = \frac{15-15}{1} = 0.$

42. Given, $MC = 2(2x + 9)^{-1/2}$, then

$C = \int(MC)dx = \int 2(2x+9)^{-1/2}\,dx$

$= 2.(2x+9)^{1/2} + k$

$= 2\sqrt{2x+9} + k$, where k is constant

Since fixed cost is ₹ 4, then C = 4, when $x = 0$ and hence

$4 = 2\sqrt{2(0)+9} + k$, or $k = 4 - 6 = -2$

Thus, the total cost function is

$C = 2\sqrt{2x+9} - 2$ and the average cost function is $AC = \left[2\sqrt{2x+9} - 2\right]/x$

For $x = 8$,

$AC = \left[2\sqrt{2(8)+9} - 2\right]/8 = [10-2]/8 = 1.$

43. The Multiplier Effect:

- When the government buys a product from a company, the immediate impact of the purchase is to raise profits and employment at that firm.
- As a result, owners and workers at this firm will see an increase in income, and will therefore likely increase their own consumption.
- Thus, total spending rises by more than the increase in government purchases.

The Multiplier Effect:

Definition of multiplier effect: The additional shifts in aggregate demand that result when expansionary fiscal policy increases income and thereby increases consumer spending.

- The multiplier effect goes on and on.
- When consumers spend part of their additional income, it provides additional income for other consumers.
- These consumers then spend some of this additional income, raising the incomes of yet another group of consumers.

45. BEP in sales value

$$= \frac{\text{Fixed costs}}{\text{Contribution margin ratio}}$$

where contribution margin ratio

$$= \frac{\text{Selling price} - \text{Variable cost}}{\text{Selling price}}$$

$$= \frac{12-9}{12} = \frac{3}{12} = \frac{1}{4}$$

$\therefore$ BEP in sales value

$$= \frac{150000}{1/4} = 6{,}00{,}000.$$

46. Indian Accounting Standard (Ind As) 28 deals with accounting for investments in associates. The accounting standard sets out principles and procedures on recognising, in the consolidated financial statements the effect of investment in associates on the financial positions and operating results of the group. An associated company is one in which the investor has significant influence but which is neither a subsidiary nor a joint venture of the investor. Significant influence is the power to participate in the financial and/or operating policy decisions of the investee but not control over those policies. Broadly, it may be state that if the investor holds 20% or more of the voting power, it will have the power to exercise significant influence over the investee company. The interest should be a long-term one-temporary acquistion of shares will not make the investee company an associated company.

47. Time taken to produce one unit of P_1 in machine $M_1 = \frac{10}{10}$ hr

Time taken to produce one unit of P_2 in machine $M_1 = \frac{1}{15}$ hr

Time taken to produce one unit of P_1 in machine $M_2 = \frac{1}{15}$ hr

Time taken to produce one unit of P_2 in machine $M_2 = \frac{1}{15}$ hr

If x unit of P_1 and y units of P_2 are produced

Then, $\frac{x}{10}+\frac{y}{15} = 12$

$\Rightarrow \quad 3x + 2y = 360 \quad ...(i)$

and, $\frac{x}{15}+\frac{y}{15} = 10$

$\Rightarrow \quad x + y = 150 \quad ...(ii)$

Equations (*i*) and (*ii*) can be represented in the matrix from as

$$\begin{bmatrix} 3 & 2 \\ 1 & 1 \end{bmatrix}\begin{bmatrix} x \\ y \end{bmatrix} = \begin{bmatrix} 360 \\ 150 \end{bmatrix}$$

$$\begin{bmatrix} x \\ y \end{bmatrix} = \text{Inverse of } \begin{bmatrix} 3 & 2 \\ 1 & 1 \end{bmatrix} \times \begin{bmatrix} 360 \\ 150 \end{bmatrix}$$

$$= \begin{bmatrix} 1 & -2 \\ -1 & 3 \end{bmatrix}\begin{bmatrix} 360 \\ 150 \end{bmatrix} = \begin{bmatrix} 60 \\ 90 \end{bmatrix}$$

$\Rightarrow \quad x = 60, y = 90.$

48. $MC_n = TC_n - TC_{n-1}$

where, MC_n = Marginal cost of the *n*th labourer

TC_n = Total cost of when '*n*' number of labourers are employed

TC_{n-1} = Total cost of when '*n* – 1' number of labourers are employed

Here, MC of 11th worker = 113 – 100 = 13.

50. Normal (Gaussian) distribution is the distribution with some characteristic properties. The first of all, the mean, the mode and the median are all equal. This mean then the curve is symmetric at the centre (*i.e.*, around the mean, μ) which mean that exactly half of the values are to the left of centre and exactly half the values are to the right.

The curve is sometimes also called the Gaussian curve or the bell curve (because of its shape). The total area under the curve is 1.

51. Traits Theory of Leadership: This theory advocates that leadership qualities and traits are not inborn but can be acquired by an individual through education, training and other forms of learning. Advocates of this theory of leadership are Tead, Schell and others.

Tead holds that there are 10 qualities that are essential for effective leadership, namely, physical and nervous energy, a sense of purpose and direction, enthusiasm, friendliness and affection, integrity, technical mastry, decisiveness, intelligence, teaching skill and faith. It was thought that a successful leader is one who has specific leadership traits that can be acquired. At the development of the traits theory, it was accepted that leadership traits are completely inborn, but also be acquired through learning and experience.

Similarly, in the words of Ralph Stogdill, the leader, to be effective, should have qualities like drive for responsibility, task orientation, vigour and persistence in pursuit of goals, venturesomeness, originality, problem-solving skills, drive to exercise initiative in a social situation, self-confidence, ability to influence other persons, etc.

53. Consideration is one of the essential elements of a valid contract. Technically, it is known as *quid pro quo i.e.,* something in return.

Example: A agrees to sell his car to B for ₹ 1,00,000. A's promise, the car, is B's consideration and B's promise, the price, is A's consideration. So we can conclude that one's promise is the others consideration. Let's take another case: A agrees is sell 100 m of cloth to B in exchange of 50 kg of rice. A has made a promise to give 100 m of cloth to B which is consideration for B. Vice versa B has promised to deliver a 50 kg of rice which is consideration for A.

As per Section 2(d) Consideration is defined as "when at the desire of the Promisor, the promise or any other person has done or abstained from doing, or does or abstains from doing or promises to do or to abstain from doing something, such act or abstinence or promise is called a consideration for the promise.

From the above definition it can be inferred that:

Consideration is doing or not doing something, which the promisor desires to be done or not done:

1. Consideration must be at the desire of the promisor.
2. Consideration may move from one person to any other person.
3. Consideration may be past, present or future and
4. Consideration should be real though not adequate.

55. Joint Probability: The probability of two or more independent events occurring together or in succession is called the joint probability. The joint probability of two or more independent events is equal to the product of their marginal probabilities. In particular, if A and B are independences events, the probability that both A and B will occur is given by

$$P(AB) = P(A \cap B) = P(A) \times P(B) \qquad ...(i)$$

Suppose, we toss a coin twice. The probability that in both the cases the coin will turn up head is given by

$$P(H_1H_2) = P(H_1) \times P(H_2) = \frac{1}{2} \times \frac{1}{2} = \frac{1}{4}$$

The formula (*i*) is applied here because the probability of any outcome is not affected by any preceding outcome, in other words, outcomes are independent.

56. The budgeted income statements is the important end-product of the operating budgets. This budget indicates the expected profitability of operations for the budget period. The budgeted income statements provides the basis for evaluating company performance. Budgeted income statements often act as a call to action. For example, a board member at XM Satellite Radio Holdings felt that budgeted costs were too high relative to budgeted revenues. When management refused to cut its marketing and programming costs, the board member resigned; he felt that without the cuts, the company risked financial crisis.

57. Tax rates can be a flat or proportional percentage, as applied to the economic activity. A sales tax is a flat tax. It is accessed at the same rate regardless of income. A *progressive tax* is a tax rate that increases as the taxable base amount increases. An example is the income tax, where the tax rate increases as a person's income increases. A *regressive tax* is a tax where the rate decreases as the amount of tax paid increases. Regressive taxes place a heavier burden on low-income individuals who have to pay a higher proportional rate for the same public goods. An example of this is the US Social Security tax, which is capped at 6.2% for gross compensation over \$102,000. This structure means that while a comparatively wealthy person may pay significantly more in real taxes, a low-income family will experience a higher burden or impact to their ultimate discretionary income. A proportional tax is a mixture of the two and avoids any penalties or benefits based on income level.

59. The square of the correlation coefficient r, expressed as r^2, is known as the coefficient of determination. It indicates the extent to which variation in one variable is explained by the variation in the other. For example, let two variables, say x and y, be inter-dependent, and variation in x causes variation in y. Here correlation coefficient is 0.60. The coefficient of determination, in this case, is square of 0.60 *i.e.*, 0.36. It implies that 0.36 of 36% of the variation in y is due to variation in x or explained by the variation in x. The remaining 64% (= 100% – 36%) is due to or explained by some other factors. Incidentally, $(1 - r^2)$ is referred to as coefficient of alienation, and gives the percentage of variation in the dependent variable, not explained by the independent variable.

60. The Keynesian model shows the aggregate supply curve is upward sloping because wages and prices are less flexible in the short-run. Under this model, the economy is more likely to be below the full employment level, which means that firms can hire new employees and increase production without raising wages or prices.

65. Accumulated Profits: That portion of profits which is not distributed to the shareholders for more than one year is known as accumulated profits. It is distributed among the shareholders of the company at the time of liquidation of the company. In other words, these are not transferred to the realization account. These are directly transferred to the shareholders' account. Therefore, the student should have a precise knowledge regarding these in order to solve the problems of amalgamation, absorption and reconstruction correctly. The following accounts are treated as accumulated profits–

(*a*) Profit & Loss A/c (credit balance)
(*b*) Revenue Reserve
(*c*) General Reserve
(*d*) Capital Reserve
(*e*) Debenture Redemption Reserve/Sinking Fund A/c
(*f*) Development Rebate Reserve
(*g*) Capital Redemption Reserve
(*h*) Forfeited Shares Account
(*i*) Share Premium Accounts
(*j*) Workmen's Compensation Fund
(*k*) Dividend Equalization Fund
(*l*) Insurance Fund
(*m*) Workmen's Accident Fund.

66. Kurtosis is a statistical measure used for describing the distribution of the data around its mean. It indicates whether the scores are clustered around the mean value. It is measured by β_2. Based on this value, the distribution of data can be classified into any of the three categories; *leptokurtic, mesokurtic* or *platykurtic*. The normal curve is a *mesokurtic* curve whereas the curve which is more peaked than the normal curve is *leptokurtic* and if it is flatter than the normal curve, it is *platykurtic*. Thus, by knowing the value of kurtosis, one can find whether the curve is *mesokurtic* or not. The kurtosis β_2 is computed by

$$\beta_2 = \frac{\mu_4}{\mu_2^2}$$

where μ_r is the rth central moment. For a normal curve, β_2 is 3. The distribution of data is said to be leptokurtic is β_2 is greater than 3 and platykurtic if it is less than 3.

67. The concept of the efficient market was first described by Fama. The *efficient markets* hypothesis is used to describe a market where asset prices fully reflect all available information. There are three types of the efficient markets hypothesis, which are:

- the *weak form*, which describes a situation where market prices reflect only historical data on the asset or security in questions.
- the *semi-strong* form, where prices reflect all publicly reflects all publicly available information;
- the strong form, where prices reflect all known information, whether this information is publicly known or not.

73. There are two types of measures of variation. It may be either absolute or relative. Absolute measure of variation is expressed in the same unit as in the data. For example, if data are given in kilograms or dollars etc., the measures will be in kilograms or dollars. Thus, absolute measure is used only within a series. Such measures are not suitable for comparing the variation of the distributions in which units of measurements are different. In such situations a relative measure of variation is used. A measure of relative variation is the ratio of a measure of absolute variation to an average. It is also called coefficient of variation. Thus, relative measure is used for comparing the variability of two or more series where unit of measurement may be same or different. It is always independent of the unit of measurement.

74. **Limited Liability Partnership (LLP).** A limited *liability partnership*

- is a general partnership that has invoked the limited liability partnership provisions of its governing general partnership statute.
- by filing with a specific public official a specified document (typically called "a statement of qualification" or a "registration")
- thereby becoming a limited liability [general] partnership and eliminating partially or completely the automatic personal liability of each partner for each partnership obligation.

Under some state statues, a limited liability partnership is called a registered limited liability partnership. The term "limited liability partnership" is abbreviated LLP and, except in statutory provisions, the abbreviation is used far more often than the term itself. The term "liability shield" is typically used to refer to the liability protection provided the partners of an LLP. Almost LLP statutes provides a "full shield" for the partners–completely eliminating a partner's liability *qua partner* for the partnership's obligations. A few LLP statutes provide only a "partial shield"–leaving in place some of a partner's automatic liability for partnership obligations.

75. The data array is one of the simplest ways to present data. It arranges values in ascending or descending order.

77. **Characteristics of Isoquants:** Isoquants show the following characteristics:

(*a*) They slope downward to the right.

(*b*) It is convex to origin.

(*c*) It is smooth and continuous.

(*d*) Two isoquants do not intersect.

78. A distribution for which the mean = median = mode, is known as a symmetrical distribution. For an asymetrical distribution, these measures do not coincide. In other words, a distribution which does not satisfy the symmetric property (*i.e,* mean = median = mode), is known as a skewed distribution. Thus, skewness refers lack of symmetry or departure from symmetry. For a positively skewed distribution. A.M. > Median > Mode, and for a negatively skewed distribution, A.M. < Median < Mode. Therefore, the distance between the arithmetic mean and the mode can be used as a measure of skewness.

79.

Measure	**Advantages**	**Drawbacks**
Mean	• Easy to understand • Uses every value • Can be used for further analysis	• Distorted by extreme values • May give as the answer a value not found in the original data
Median	• Easy to understand • Not influenced by extreme values in the data	• Needs the data to be organised • May be unrepresentative with only a few values
Mode	• Easy to understand • Not influenced by extreme values in the data	• Needs the data to be organised • Cannot be used for further mathematical processing

80. Under the Indian Income Tax Act, 1961, incidence of tax on tax payer depends on his residential status and also on the place and time of accrual or receipt of income. Indian Income (*i.e.,* income earned or received in time) always taxable in India irrespective of the residential status of the tax payer. Foreign income (*i.e,* income which is not received or accrued in India) is taxable in the hands of resident (in case of firm, an association of persons, a joint stock company and every other person) or resident and ordinarily resident (in case of an individual and Hindu individual family) in India. Foreign income is not taxable in the hands of non-residents in India (Sec 5 and 9 of the Income Tax Act, 1961).

81. Actual costs of production are the sum of two components:

(*i*) fixed (or overhead) costs which are not directly related to the amount of crop produced on the land resources (they have to be paid whether anything is produced or not and include land rent, land taxes, loan repayments, living expenses);

(*ii*) variable costs, which are directly related to the amount of crop grown and so with the amount of variable inputs used (e.g., weeding, labour, seed, fertiliser). Adding total fixed costs and total variable costs gives the total cost of production.

83. Overdraft balance as per cash book or pass book: Overdraft means the amount overdrawn from the bank. In such cases, the bank makes more payment on our account than the deposits received from us. The word 'overdraft' itself means minus balance whether it is as per cash book or pass book. The credit balance of cash book or the debit balance of pass book both show overdraft balance. Amount over drawn from the bank is always a minus balance.

85. Balance Sheet: The financial statement that present a snapshot of the business's financial position (assets, liabilities, and equity) as of a particular date in time. It's called a *balance sheet* because the things owned by the business (assets) must equal the claims against those assets (liabilities and equity). Sometimes, accountants call this statement the *statement of financial position,* which emphasizes the fact that the amounts presented are a snapshot of a particular point in time.

On a proper balance sheet, the total assets should equal the total liabilities plus the total equity.

87. The Phillips curve is named after A.W. Phillips who, in 1958, presented a study based on the behaviour of wages in the United Kingdom for the time period 1861 to 1957. It shows an inverse relationship or trade-off between the unemployment rate and the rate of increase in money wages or wage inflation. The higher the unemployment rate, the lower is the rate of wage inflation.

According to the Phillips curve, the nominal wages change slowly in conformity with the level of unemployment. Wages have a tendency to increase when employment is high and to decrease when employment is low.

88. MEC is the highest rate of return expected from an additional unit of a capital asset over its cost. It is the expected rate of profitability of a new capital asset. J.M. Keynes has defined MEC as being equal to the rate of discount which would make the present value of the series of annuities given by the returns expected from the capital assets during its life just equal to the supply price. Symbolically, it is expressed as:

$$S_p = \frac{R_1}{(1+i)} + \frac{R_2}{(1+i)^2} + ... + \frac{R_n}{(1+i)^n}$$

Where S_p denotes supply price or replace cost of the asset, R_1, R_2, ... R_n are the prospective annual returns or yield from the capital asset in the year 1, 2 and *n* respectively. *i* is the rate of discount which makes the capital asset exactly equal to the present value of the expected yield from it.

89. Non-manufacturing costs consist of those costs that are incurred outside the plant or factory and typically are categorised as selling and administrative costs. Although non-manufacturing costs are necessarily incurred in running a business, they are not directly incurred in making products. A general rule of thumb is to imagine the product not being made. If a particular cost still occurs, it is generally a non-manufacturing cost. Common examples of non-manufacturing costs include advertising, commissions paid to sales staff, administrative and accounting salaries and office supplies. Non-manufacturing costs also include rent, insurance, taxes, utilities and depreciation equipment when used in selling and administrative activities. Non-manufacturing costs are called period costs. In contrast to manufacturing costs, non-manufacturing costs are expensed on the income statement in the period incurred.

91. Make or buy decisions arise when a company with unused production capacity consider the following alternatives:

(*a*) To buy certain raw materials or subassemblies from outside suppliers.

(*b*) To use available capacity to produce the items within the company.

A make or buy decision is basically one of determining which alternative is economically most desirable and most effectively utilises the firm's resources. These decisions can effect the firm's production methods and capacities, available working capital, cost of borrowing funds, and competitive position. Costs that will be incurred under both alternatives are not relevant to the analysis. The firm should make an analysis of the cost, quality and quantity consideration of the individual make or buy decisions. Differential cost analysis is especially useful if the company has idle capacity and idle workers that can be used to make the tools or parts. Other potential use of available capacity should also be considered; and qualitative factors must be evaluated in the decision process. These considerations include price stability from suppliers, reliability of delivery and quality of the material or component involved. Qualitative factors are not included in differential cost analyses, but they should be used to test the reasonableness of any decision based purely on quantitative cost studies.

92. All financial statements are prepared and presented as per law or conservation not for a specific purpose. That is why it is termed as convention of conservatism. This is well and safest policy. Accordingly all possible losses are taken into account and all (probable) (unrealised) profits/gains are left out. Likewise, stock can be valued either at cost or market price whichever is lower. Similarly, provision for doubtful debts or provision for depreciation can also be arranged as per the convention/principle of conservatism only in case of uncertainties or doubts. This principle of conservatism can be a useful tool in such situations but if it is not used properly, it may lead to unpleasant unforeseen results. For example, if a machine is purchased and the cost of machine is charged as an expense, then profit as well as assets would be under estimated.

Now-a-days conservatism is replaced by prudence which means the principle of conservatism is applied by the accountants only in case of doubts or uncertainties with prudence. The theme of the principle of conservatism is under statement of profit or assets rather than over statement of profit or assets.

94. For most employees, House Rent Allowance (HRA) is a part of their salary structure. Although it is a part of your salary, HRA, unlike basic salary, is not fully taxable. Subject to certain conditions, a part of HRA is exempted under Section 10(13A) of the Income Tax Act, 1961.

The amount of HRA exemption is deductible from the total income before arriving at a taxable income. This helps an employee to save tax. But do keep in mind that the HRA received from your employer, is fully taxable if he does not pay any rent.

Who can avail HRA?

This tax benefit is available only to the salaried individuals who has the HRA component as part of his salary structure and is staying in a rented accommodation. Self-employed professionals cannot avail the deduction.

How much is exempted?

The exemption for HRA benefit is the minimum of:

(*i*) Actual HRA received;

(*ii*) 50% of salary if living in metro cities, or 40% for non-metro cities; and

(*iii*) Excess of rent paid annually over 10% of annual salary.

95. Cost Driver: It is a factor which causes a change in the cost of an activity. There are two types of cost driver.

(*i*) *Resource cost driver:* It is the quantity of resources consumed by an activity. It helps to assign the resource cost to an activity or cost pool.

(*ii*) *Activity cost driver:* It measures the frequency and intensity of demand, placed on activities by cost objects. It helps to assign costs of activity to cost objects.

Examples of cost driver are:

Business activity	Cost driver
1. Customer service	No. of products serviced No. of service calls Hours spent on servicing products
2. Receiving/Inspecting/Quality assurance	Goods Received Note Purchase requisition
3. Production scheduling/machine set-ups/Materials handling	No. of batches
4. Research and Development	Personnel hours on a project No. of research products Technical complexities of projects
5. Stock of raw materials/WTP/Finished goods	Purchase orders, Supplies received, Customers of Finished goods

97. Fiat Money: The money that circulated and was used during the Japanese period had no intrinsic value. This is known as *fiat money.* This kind of money can only be accepted if it is considered as a legal tender. *Legal tender* means the government guarantees the use of the money in all kinds of transactions, like payment of debt and in buying goods and services. During the Japanese occupation, the authorities financed the military and government expenditures by issuing *fiat* money. It was during this period that our country experienced the worst inflation.

98. Issue of Shares at Premium (Under Section 78): When a share is issued at a price higher than the face value, par value or nominal value then it is said that it has been issued at premium. For instance, if a share of ₹ 100 is issued by a company for ₹ 110, ₹ 10 are the premium on share. Premium on issue of shares is the capital profit for the company and the amount to earned has to be credited to a separate account known as share premium account.

Under Section 78 of the Companies Act 1956, the amount of share premium may be used wholly or partly in the following ways:

(*a*) It may be utilized in paying up unissued shares of a company, to be issued to members of the company as fully paid bonus shares, or

(*b*) It may be utilized in writing off the preliminary expenses of the company, or

(*c*) It may be utilized in writing off the expenses of, or the commission paid or discount allowed on any of shares or debentures of the company, or

(*d*) It may be utilized in providing for the premium payable on redemption of any redeemable preference shares or debentures.

Premium on shares maybe collected by a company in a lump sum or in instalments. According to the terms of issue the amount of share premium maybe included in either application money or allotment money or one of call money. Usually, the amount of share premium is to be paid along with application or allotment money. If nothing is mentioned in the problem, it should be assumed that the entire amount of the share premium is to be paid along with allotment money.

99. The Terminology of Elasticity

Description	Numerical value	Total outlay
Infinitely Elastic	equal to infinity ($\eta = \infty$)	Zero for a price rise Infinity for a price fall
Elastic	greater than 1 ($\eta > 1$)	Decreases for a price rise Increases for a price fall
Unit Elastic	equal to 1 ($\eta = 1$)	Remains the same whether price rises or falls
Inelastic	less than 1 ($\eta < 1$)	Increases for a price rise Decreases for a price fall
Zero Elastic	equal to 0 ($\eta = 0$)	Increases for a price rise Decreases for a price fall

100. Standard AS-14, issued by the Institute of Chartered Accountants of India, deals with the accounting for amalgamation and the treatment of any resultant goodwill or reserves.

This standard was issued in 1994. This is mandatory to all companies with effect from the accounting year commencing on or after 1 April, 1995.

According to AS-14, amalgamation means an amalgamation pursuant to the provisions of the Companies Act 1956, or any other statue which may be applicable to companies.

The Standard uses the term "transferor company" for the company which is amalgamated into another company:

The Company selling its business is also called "vendor company".

The Company into which a transferor company is amalgamated is called "transferee company".

The Company which acquires the business is also called the "vendee company".

It is important to note that:

(*i*) The term amalgamation includes "absorption" also

(*ii*) The term amalgamation does not apply to acquisitions in the nature of controlling interest (Because in such cases, the acquired company will not be dissolved and its separate entity will continue to exist).

Previous Paper (Solved)

UNIVERSITY OF DELHI—M.COM Entrance Test-2018*

1. If the probability of A is 0.5 and the probability of B is 0.2 and the probability of the union of A and B is 0.7, then:
A. A and B are dependent
B. A and B are independent
C. A and B are mutually exclusive
D. A and B do have an intersection

2. If the quantity of the commodity demanded remains unchanged as its price changes, the coefficient of price elasticity of demand is:
A. Equal to 1 B. Zero
C. Greater than 1 D. Smaller than 1

3. If the demand function for an article is $p = 35 - 2x - x^2$ and the demand X_0 is 3, then consumer surplus will be:
A. 57 B. 47
C. 37 D. 27

4. If the third moment about mean is zero then distribution is:
A. Positively skewed
B. Mesokurtic
C. Negatively skewed
D. Symmetrical

5. Which of the following statements is correct?
A. Mean is not affected by extreme values
B. Mode is affected by extreme values
C. None of these
D. Median divides the data into two equal parts

6. Which of the following are not true for a bank reconciliation statement
(*i*) Part of double entry system
(*ii*) Not Part of double entry system
(*iii*) Sent by the firm to the bank
(*iv*) Posted to the ledger account
A. (*ii*), (*iii*) and (*iv*) B. (*i*) and (*ii*)
C. (*i*), (*iii*) and (*iv*) D. (*i*), (*ii*) and (*iv*)

7. Which of the following is a trade deficit?
A. Saving < investment
B. Exports < imports
C. Net exports < 0
D. All of these

8. Which of the following changes would not shift the demand curve for a good or service?
A. a change in the price of the good or service
B. a change in the price of a related good or service.
C. a change in income
D. a change in expectations about the future price of the good or service

9. Which of the following is not a reason for an idle time variance?
A. Illness or injury to worker
B. Machine breakdown
C. Wage rate increase
D. Non-availability of material

10. Which of the following events would cause both the equilibrium price and equilibrium quantity of potatoes (assumed as an inferior good) to increase?
A. a decrease in the supply of potatoes
B. a decrease in the incomes of potatoes consumers
C. an increase in the incomes of potatoes consumers
D. an increase in the supply of potatoes

11. Which one of the following statement is not TRUE?
A. Decision making is a part of Planning function

*Exam held on 20/06/2018.

B. Strategy and Plan are one and the same thing
C. Strategic management leads towards achieving long-term goals
D. Strategies focus on gaining competitive advantages

12. Which probability distribution is most likely the appropriate one to use for calculating the probability of the number of autos passing through a tollbooth?
A. Poisson
B. Normal
C. Binomial
D. Insufficient information to decide

13. Given the LM curve, a decrease in taxes shifts the IS curve:
A. Towards right
B. Towards left
C. Any of these
D. Either towards left or right

14. The LAC curve is tangent to the lowest point on the SAC curve when the LAC curve is failing:
A. Sometime B. None of these
C. Always D. Never

15. In inferential statistics, we study:
A. How to draw a sample from a population
B. How to make decisions about mean, median, or mode
C. All of these
D. The methods to make decisions about population based on sample results

16. Calculate the prime cost from the following information:
Direct material purchased: ₹ 1,00,000
Direct material consumed: ₹ 90,000
Direct labour: ₹ 60,000
Direct expenses: ₹ 20,000
Manufacturing overheads: ₹ 30,000
A. ₹ 2,00,000 B. ₹ 2,10,000
C. ₹ 1,80,000 D. ₹ 1,70,000

17. Information concerning A Ltd.'s single product is as follows:
Selling price – ₹ 6 per unit
Variable production cost – ₹ 1.20 per unit
Variable selling cost – ₹ 0.40 per unit
Fix production cost – ₹ 4 per unit
Fix selling cost – ₹ 0.80 per unit
Budgeted production and sales for the year are 10,000 units
What is the company's breakeven point?
A. 10,909 units B. 8,000 units
C. 10,000 units D. 8,333 units

18. The Balance of Sinking fund investment account after the realization of investment is transferred to:
A. Profit and loss account
B. Debenture redemption fund account
C. Debenture account
D. Sinking fund account

19. Following information is available of XYZ Limited for quarter ended June, 2017:
Fixed cost ₹ 5,00,000
Variable cost ₹ 10 per unit
Selling price ₹ 15 per unit
Output level 1,50,000 units
What will be the amount of profit earned during the quarter using the marginal costing technique?
A. ₹ 2,50,000 B. ₹ 7,50,000
C. ₹ 5,00,000 D. ₹ 10,00,000

20. The outflow of funds to acquire an asset that will benefit the business for more than one accounting period is referred to as:
A. Capital Expenditure
B. Deferred Revenue Expenditure
C. Miscellaneous Expenditure
D. Revenue Expenditure

21. Unemployment rate is equal to:
A. Any of these
B. $\frac{\text{Total population}}{\text{Labour force}} \times 100$
C. $\frac{\text{Number of unemployed}}{\text{Labour force}} \times 100$
D. $\frac{\text{Labour force}}{\text{Adult population}} \times 100$

22. When demand for loanable funds is given, tax incentives for saving increase the supply of loanable funds, which in turn?

A. Does not affect interest rate
B. Increases interest rate
C. Decreases interest rate
D. Any of the above

23. When the sales increase from ₹ 40,000 to ₹ 60,000 and profit increases by ₹ 5,000, the P/V ratio is ....

A. 25% B. 20%
C. 30% D. 40%

24. Inter-office-adjustments (net) will appear in the balance sheet of a bank under:

A. both other assets and other liabilities as contra
B. either other liabilities or other assets
C. other liabilities only
D. other assets only

25. Apple and Banana are substitutes, Low snowfall in hill areas sharply reduces the apple harvest, that would:

A. Increase consumer surplus in the market for apple and decrease producer surplus in the market for banana
B. Increase consumer surplus in the market for apple and increase producer surplus in the market for banana
C. Decrease consumer surplus in the market for apple and increase producer surplus in the market for banana
D. Decrease consumer surplus in the market for apple and decrease producer surplus in the market for tea.

26. On consolidation of Balance Sheet if the total of the fair value of assets acquired is less than the whole purchase consideration then the differences should be treated as:

A. Profit on acquisition
B. Goodwill
C. Negative Goodwill
D. Loss on acquisition

27. Deglobalisation implies all of the following except:

A. Reducing interdependence in nation states
B. A borderless world
C. Non-integration of economic activities
D. Reduction in border trade

28. The task of administration of income tax lies with the:

A. Central Board of Indirect Taxes
B. Central Board of Direct Taxes
C. Central Board of Excise and Customs
D. Ministry of Commerce

29. The Government of India launched a campaign in the name of 'Make in India' in the year:

A. 2017 B. 2015
C. 2016 D. 2014

30. A pattern of variation of a time series that repeats every year is called:

A. Cyclical B. None of these
C. Secular D. Seasonal

31. Scientific Management is closely related with:

A. Henry Ford B. Henry Fayol
C. AH Maslow D. Max Weber

32. Money stock M_1 consists of:

A. Demand deposit plus time deposit plus currency
B. Demand deposit plus saving deposit plus currency
C. Demand deposit plus traveller's cheque's plus currency
D. None of these

33. In the long run when aggregate supply curve is horizontal an increase in the aggregate demand leads to:

A. Any of the above
B. Shift in aggregate demand curve downward
C. Shift in aggregate demand curve upward
D. No change in aggregate demand curve

34. Division of labour relates to:

A. Distribution of work as per the ability of the worker
B. Distribution of work as per organizational needs
C. All of these
D. Equal pay for equal work

35. Under floating exchange rate regime a monetary expansion will result in;

A. Increase in income and trade balance but decrease in exchange rate

B. Increase in income and exchange rate but decrease in trade balance
C. Increase in income but decrease in trade balance exchange rate
D. Decrease in income and trade balance but increase in exchange rate

36. Glass ceiling relates to:
A. Equal pay for equal work
B. Discrimination based on caste
C. Whistle blowing
D. Career growth for females

37. Insurance commission received by the assesse is taxable under the head:
A. Capital gains
B. Salaries
C. Income from other sources
D. Profits and gains of business or profession

38. In order to influence spending on goods and services in the short run, monetary policy is directed at directly influencing:
A. Unemployment rates
B. Inflation rates
C. Economic growth rates
D. Interest rates

39. If an accumulated provision for depreciation account is in use then the entries for the year's depreciation would be:
A. Debit Assets Account, Credit Profit and Loss Account
B. None of these
C. Credit Provision for depreciation account, Debit Profit and loss Account
D. Credit Assets Account, Debit Provision for depreciation account

40. A 3 per cent increase in price of a good causes a 10 per cent decrease in quantity demanded. Which of the following statements is most likely applicable to this good?
A. The good is a superior good
B. The good is a giffen good
C. There are many close substitutes for this good
D. The good is a necessity

41. Gross Domestic Product at factor cost plus net property income from abroad minus capital consumption is equal to:
A. Gross national product at factor cost
B. Gross domestic product at market price
C. Net national product at market price
D. Net national product at factor cost

42. Monica deposits money in a bank paying 16% interest rate compounded quarterly. If she wants to have ₹ 15,000 in her account after 5 years. How much should she deposit today?
A. ₹ 7777.77
B. ₹ 8040.50
C. ₹ 6500.00
D. ₹ 6,845.80

43. The weights of students in a college is a:
A. Continuous Variable
B. Discrete Variable
C. Qualitative Variable
D. Any of these

44. A production possibilities frontier shifts outward when:
A. Government increases the amount of money in the economy
B. The economy experiences economic growth
C. The economy abandons inefficient production methods in favour of efficient production methods.
D. The desires of the economy's citizens change

45. In case of rising prices (inflation), FIFO method will:
A. provide highest value of closing stock and profit
B. provide highest value of closing stock but lowest value of profit
C. provide highest value of profit but lowest value of closing stock
D. provide lowest value of closing stock and profit

46. In which of the following cases, clubbing provisions would not be attracted under the income Tax Act?
A. Remuneration received by the spouse of an individual from a concern in which the individual is having substantial interest, and where the spouse has no professional knowledge.

B. Income of a minor child
C. Income from assets transferred to spouse for adequate consideration
D. Transfer of Income without transfer of asset

47. The threshold for deduction of tax at source on interest income for senior citizens has been raised in the Union Budget 2018 to:
A. ₹ 20,000 B. ₹ 40,000
C. ₹ 50.000 D. ₹ 30,000

48. If the order of matrix A is $m \times p$. And the order of B is $p \times n$. Then the order of matrix AB is:
A. $m \times n$ B. $n \times m$
C. $n \times p$ C. $m \times p$

49. AS-6 is not applicable on:
A. All of these
B. Goodwill
C. Forests and plantations
D. Live Stock

50. When the price of a complement of commodity X rises, the demand for X:
A. Remains unchanged
B. All of the above are possible
C. Falls
D. Rises

51. When a tax is imposed on the sellers of a good, the:
A. supply curve shifts upward by less than the amount of the tax
B. supply curve shifts upward by the amount of the tax
C. demand curve shifts downward by the amount of the tax
D. demand curve shifts downward by less than the amount of the tax

52. A key understanding to the relationship between hygiene and motivation factors is:
A. They are interdependent
B. They are positively related
C. They are independent
D. They are additive

53. A company makes a single product and incurs fixed costs of ₹ 30,000 per annum. Variable cost per unit is ₹ 5 and each unit sells for ₹ 15. Annual sales demand is 7,000 units. The breakeven point is:
A. 6,000 units B. 2,000 units
C. 3,000 units D. 4,000 units

54. Process B had no opening inventory. 13,500 units of raw material were transferred in at ₹ 4.50 per unit. Additional material at ₹ 1.25 per unit was added in process. Labour and overheads were ₹ 6.25 per completed unit and ₹ 2.50 per unit incomplete. If 11,750 completed units were transferred out, what was the closing inventory in Process B?
A. ₹ 6562.50 B. ₹ 25,375.00
C. ₹ 14,437.50 D. ₹ 12,250.00

55. A job is budgeted to require 3,300 productive hours including 25% normal idle time. If the total labour cost budgeted for the job is ₹ 36,300, what is the labour cost per hour?
A. ₹ 11.00 B. ₹ 14.67
C. ₹ 8.80 D. ₹ 8.25

56. At equilibrium the slope of the indifference curve is:
A. Equal to the slope of the budget line
B. Smaller than the slope of the budget line
C. Either equal or larger than the budget line
D. Greater than the slope of the budget line

57. Following information is available of P Ltd. For year ended March, 2017: 4,000 units in process, 3,800 units output, 10% of input is normal wastage, ₹ 2.50 per unit is scrap value and ₹ 46,000 incurred towards total process cost then amount on account of abnormal gain to be transferred to Costing P & L will be:
A. ₹ 2,000 B. ₹ 3,500
C. ₹ 2,500 D. ₹ 4,000

58. Social responsibility is:
A. None of these
B. The obligation of an individual to behave in ethical way in society
C. The obligation of an organization to behave in ethical way
D. The obligation of a nation to behave in legitimate way in the interest of the society

59. Section 30 of the Contract Act 1872, provides for the elements of wagering which does not include?

A. None of these
B. There are equal chances of gain or loss
C. No other interest of the parties is involved
D. The agreement is dependent on the occurrence of an event

60. Section 2 (46) of the Companies Act 2013, defines the:

A. Subsidiary company
B. Holding company
C. Statutory company
D. Associate company

61. The sum of squares of deviations is least if measured from:

A. Mean B. Variance
C. Median D. Mode

62. The mean of a distribution is 23, the median is 24, and the mode is 25.5. It is most likely that this distribution is:

A. Positive Skewed
B. Asymptotic
C. Negatively Skewed
D. Symmetrical

63. When Amalgamation is the nature of purchase, the accounting method to be followed is:

A. Consolidated method
B. Purchase Method
C. Equity Method
D. Pooling of interest method

64. .... is a summary of all functional budgets in a capsule form.

A. Flexible Budget
B. Functional Budget
C. Master Budget
D. Long Period Budget

65. The Consumer Price Index is an example of which type of index?

A. None of these B. Simple
C. Multiple D. Composite

Directions: *Answer question 66 and 67 on the basis of following problem:*

66. A small furniture manufacturer produces tables and chairs. Each product must go through three stages of the manufacturing process: assembly, finishing, and inspection. Each table requires 3 hours of assembly, 2 hours of finishing, and 1 hour of inspection. Each chair requires 2 hours of assembly, 2 hours of finishing, and 1 hour of inspection. The profit per table is ₹ 120 while the profit per chair is ₹ 80. Currently, each week there are 200 hours of assembly time available, 180 hours of finishing time, and 40 hours of inspection time. Linear programming is to be used to develop a production schedule. Define the variables as follows:

T-number of tables produced each week

C = number of chairs produced each week

What would the objective function for the above problem be?

A. Minimize 6T + 5C
B. Maximize 120 T + 80 C
C. Maximize 200 T + 200 C
D. Maximize T + C

67. Which of the following would be a necessary constraint in the problem?

A. $T + C \leq 180$
B. $T + C \leq 200$
C. $T + C \leq 40$
D. $120T + 80C \geq 1000$

68. From the following data, determine the total of output to be produced by the concerned two producing sectors of an economy.

Output/Input	Agriculture	Industry
Agriculture	.25	.50
Industry	.30	.40

The final demand for the two producing sectors are 500 and 200 units respectively. If the output coefficient for labour of two industries are respectively, .40 and .60, find the total of labour required.

A. Agriculture sector – 950 units, Industry sector – 1250 units, 1000 hrs.
B. Agriculture sector – 1111 units, Industry sector – 1000 units, 1500 hrs.
C. Agriculture sector – 1333 units, Industry sector – 1000 units, 1133 hrs.
D. Agriculture sector – 1000 units, Industry sector – 1333 units, 1200 hrs.

69. Find the differential coefficient of the function: $e^x \log \times (2x^2 + 3)$

A. $e^x \log x\ (2x^2 + 3x + 2x + 3x^{-1} + 4x)$

B. $e^x \log x\ (2x^2 \log x + 3 \log x + 2x + 3x^{-1} + 4x \log x)$

C. $2ex^2 \log x + 3 \log x + 2x + 3x^{-1} + 4x \log x$

D. $e^x \log x\ (2x^2 \log x + 3 \log x + 2x + 3x^{-1} + 4x)$

70. If MC is above AC and output is rising then:

A. AFC is rising　　B. AVC is failing

C. AVC is rising　　D. ATC is failing

71. Find the effective discount rate when nominal rate of discount is 10% compounded continuously:

A. 9.00%　　B. 9.25%

C. 10%　　D. 9.52%

72. For the Assessment Year 2018-19, the exemption limit for resident individuals aged 60 or above but less than 80 years is:

A. ₹ 2,50,000　　B. ₹ 5,00,000

C. ₹ 3,00,000　　D. ₹ 3,50,000

73. For a monopolist, the demand law is $p = 50 - x^2$ and MC + 1 + x^2. Determine the consumer's surplus at the price which the monopolist would like to fix?

A. 29.7　　B. 30.02

C. 28.58　　D. 26.54

74. Which of the following is not taxable under the head 'Income from other sources'?

A. Dividend

B. Winnings from lotteries

C. Gain from transfer of capital asset

D. Interest on securities

75. Which of the following losses is not deductible from business income?

A. Depreciation of funds kept in foreign currency for capital purposes.

B. Loss of stock-in-trade due to theft.

C. Loss of stock-in-trade due to destruction by fire.

D. Loss of raw material or finished goods in transit.

76. Which of the following statements regarding residential status of a company is not true?

A. An Indian company is resident in India only if the control and management of its affairs is situated wholly or partly in India during the previous year.

B. An Indian company is always resident in India.

C. A foreign company is resident in India if the control and management of its affairs is situated wholly in India during the previous year.

D. A foreign company is non-resident in India if the control and management of its affairs is situated wholly or partly out of India during the previous year.

77. Which of the following statement(s) is/are correct?

A. The value of coefficient of correlation can never be zero.

B. The two regression coefficients must have same sign

C. All of these

D. If coefficient of correlation is 0.80 then 80 per cent of variation in dependent variable is explained by independent variable.

78. Which of the following is not chargeable to tax under the head "Income from House Property"?

A. Rental income received by a tenant from sub-letting

B. Rental income from a shop

C. Rental income in the hands of owner

D. None of these

79. Which one of the following statement is not TRUE concerning Limited Liability Partnership?

A. Low compliance cost

B. Hybrid system of partnership and company

C. Most suitable for SMEs

D. Not suitable for services sector

80. Which one of the following does not drive entrepreneurship?

A. Profitable model　　B. Bilateral relations

C. Innovation　　D. Risk taking

81. Pre-acquisition profit in subsidiary company is considered as:

A. Capital profit B. None of these
C. Goodwill D. Revenue profit

82. Keynes famous three motives for holding money are:

A. Translation motive, precautionary motive and speculative motive
B. Transaction motive, precautionary motive and speculative motive
C. Transaction motive, translation motive and speculative motive
D. Transaction motive, special motive and speculative motive

83. Share capital suspension account is open:

A. When application money is received but balance sheet is prepared before allotment of shares
B. None of these
C. When shares are forfeited
D. When dividend is declared but not paid

84. In 'make or buy' decision, it is profitable to buy from outside only when the supplier's price is below the firm's own ....

A. Fixed Cost B. Prime Cost
C. Total Cost D. Variable Cost

85. A loan of ₹ 20000 is to be repaid in certain equal annual installments of ₹ 2470 each reckoning interest at 4% p.a. compound. Find the number of such installments:

A. 11 B. 10
C. 15 D. 9

86. Fixed cost is a cost:

A. Which do not change in total during a given period despite changes in output
B. Which changes in total in proportion to changes in output
C. Which remains same for each unit of output
D. Which is partly fixed and partly variable in relation to output

87. A person is said to be of unsound mind for the purpose of making a contract, as per sec 12 of the Contract Act, 1872, if, he is:

A. Intoxicated B. Lunatic
C. Idiotic D. All of these

88. A person buys 15 kg of rice, 5 kg of dal and 2 kg of sugar. Rice costs ₹ 10 per kg, dal ₹ 30 per kg, and sugar ₹ 15 per kg. Representing the quantities bought by a row matrix and the prices by a column matrix, determine the total cost of the commodities bought by the person:

A. ₹ 420 B. ₹ 400
C. ₹ 350 D. ₹ 330

89. In a fixed exchange rate regime, fiscal expansion results in:

A. Increase in income, exchange rate and trade balance
B. Increase in income and exchange rate but decrease in trade balance
C. Increase in income and trade balance but no change in exchange rate
D. Increase in income but no change in exchange rate and trade balance

90. According to the Union Budget 2018, the long-term capital gains tax on stocks (in respect of profits exceeding ₹ 1 lakh) has been announced as:

A. 15% B. 12%
C. 10% D. 8%

91. The term "price takers" is a characteristic of which of the following markets?

A. Monopolistic Markets
B. Monopoly
C. Oligopoly
D. Perfectly Competitive Markets

92. The variance of 5 numbers is 10. If each number is divided by 2, then the variance of new numbers is:

A. 5
B. 2.5
C. 20
D. Cannot be determined

93. Economic profit:

A. Is most often equal to accounting profit
B. Will always exceed accounting profit
C. Will never exceed accounting profit
D. Is always at least as large as accounting profit

94. As per the Companies Act 2013, no person shall be eligible to incorporate or become a nominee in more than .... One Person Company.

A. None of these B. One Company
C. Ten Companies D. Two Companies

95. As per the Section 78 of the Companies Act 2013 amount collected as premium on securities cannot be utilized for:

A. Buy back of its own shares
B. Purchase of fixed assets
C. Writing off preliminary expenses
D. Premium payable on redemption of shares

96. Who is the father of Accounting?

A. Al khawarizmy
B. Al Mazendarany
C. Fra luca Picioli
D. Leonardo da vinci

97. Vidya's savings account has a balance of ₹ 2,654.39. The interest rate is 3% compounded monthly. Find the original principal amount deposited two years ago:

A. ₹ 2500 B. ₹ 2550
C. ₹ 2475 D. ₹ 2600

98. Under the sale of Goods Act 1932, the modes of effective delivery includes:

A. Constructive delivery
B. All of these
C. Symbolic delivery
D. Actual delivery

99. Stage II of production begins where the APL begins to decline?

A. Always B. Never
C. None of these D. Sometime

100. The first moment about means is always:

A. Zero B. Positive
C. 1 D. Negative

ANSWERS

1	2	3	4	5	6	7	8	9	10
C	B	D	D	D	C	D	A	C	B
11	12	13	14	15	16	17	18	19	20
B	A	A	C	D	D	A	D	A	A
21	22	23	24	25	26	27	28	29	30
C	C	A	D	C	B	B	B	D	D
31	32	33	34	35	36	37	38	39	40
A	C	C	A	A	D	C	D	C	C
41	42	43	44	45	46	47	48	49	50
D	D	A	B	A	C	C	A	A	C
51	52	53	54	55	56	57	58	59	60
B	C	C	C	A	A	C	C	A	B
61	62	63	64	65	66	67	68	69	70
A	C	B	C	D	B	C	C	B	C
71	72	73	74	75	76	77	78	79	80
D	C	C	C	A	A	B	A	D	B
81	82	83	84	85	86	87	88	89	90
A	B	A	D	B	A	D	D	D	C
91	92	93	94	95	96	97	98	99	100
D	B	C	B	B	C	A	B	A	A

EXPLANATORY ANSWERS

1. We have,

$$P(A) = 0.5$$
$$P(B) = 0.2$$
$$P(A \cup B) = 0.7$$
$$\because \quad P(A \cup B) = P(A) + P(B)$$

$\therefore$ A and B are mutually exclusive.

2. Price elasticity of demand is an economic measure of the change in the quantity demanded or purchased of a product in relation to its price change. Expressed mathematically, it is:

Price Elasticity of Demand = % Change in Quantity Demanded / % Change in Price

Perfectly Inelastic (PED = 0)

When the price elasticity of demand or PED is zero, then the demand is perfectly inelastic. That is, there is no change in the quantity demanded in response to the change in price. The demand curve remains vertical. Demand is completely unresponsive to the change in price.

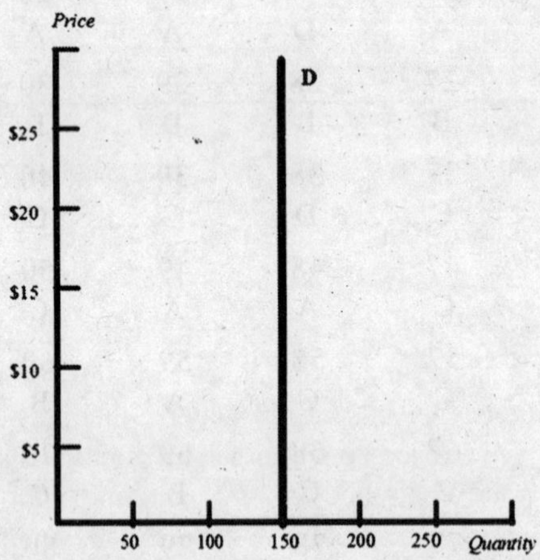

Inelastic (PED is between 0 and 1)

If the percentage of change in demand is less than the percentage of change in price, then the demand is inelastic. For instance, let us say that the price of a chocolate increases from ₹ 10 to ₹ 20 and the associated demand decreases from ten chocolates to five chocolates. So, now the PED will be 50% divided by 100%, which is 0.5. Hence, the demand here is inelastic.

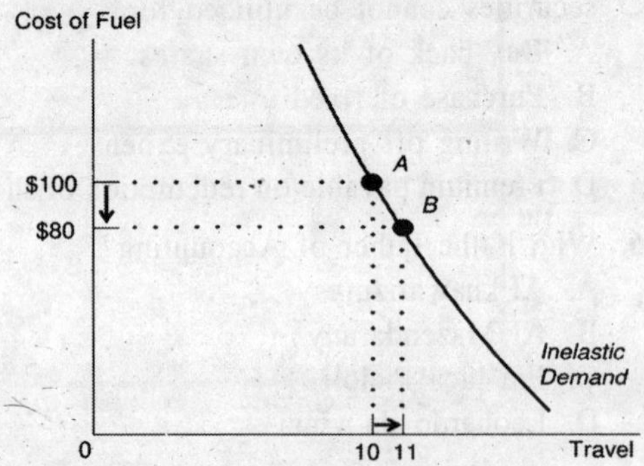

Elastic or Unit Elastic (PED = 1)

When the percentage of change in demand is the same as the percentage of change in price, then the demand is unit elastic. For example, let us say that the price of a candy drops from ₹ 10 to ₹ 5 and the demand increases from 10 candies to 15 candies. Here, the percentage of change in demand is equal to the percentage of change in price (50% divided by 50%, which is 1).

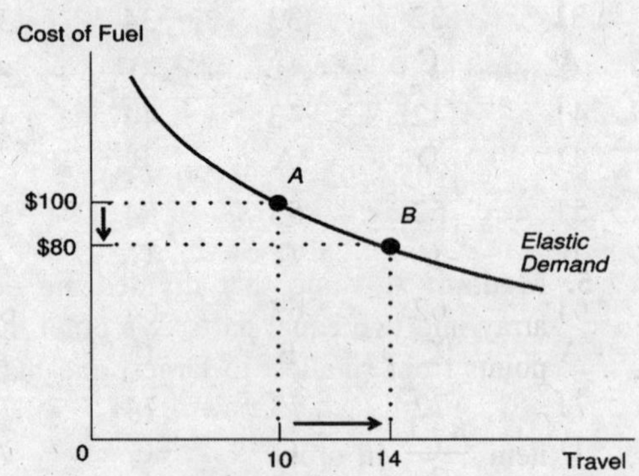

Perfectly Elastic (PED > 1)

If the percentage of change in demand is more than the percentage of change in price, then the demand is perfectly elastic. For instance, if a 10% increase in price causes a 20% drop in demand, then the coefficient of PED is 3, which means that the demand is perfectly elastic.

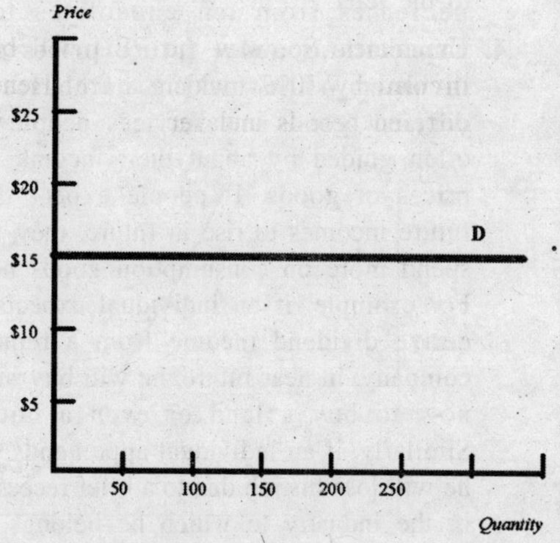

3. $\because$ $P = 35 - 2x - x^2$

$= 35 - 6 - 9$

$= 20$

Consumer surplus

$$= \int_0^3 (35 - 2x - x^2)dx - (20 \times 3)$$

$$= \left[35x - \frac{2x^2}{2} - \frac{x^3}{3}\right]_0^3 - (20 \times 3)$$

$$= \left[\left(35 \times 3 - (3)^2 - \frac{(3)^3}{3}\right) - (0)\right] - (20 \times 3)$$

$= [105 - 9 - 9] - (20 \times 3)$

$= [105 - 78] = 27.$

5. Median: A value that divides the ordered array into two equal parts. We order the data points from smallest to largest and then take item $\frac{n+1}{2}$ in order.

Example.

1\. 1 3 $\underbrace{8}_{\text{median} = 8}$ 13 2000 $\Rightarrow \frac{n+1}{2} = \frac{6}{2} = 3$

2\. 1 5 $\underbrace{8 \quad 11}_{\text{median} = \frac{8+11}{2} = 9.5}$ 13 21 $\Rightarrow \frac{n+1}{2} = \frac{7}{2}$

$= 3.5.$

3\. For our data set with $n = 61$, the median of the ungrouped data is 69.91.

4\. For the grouped data, the median is 60, the 31st element of the set where each data point takes on the value of the midpoint of its class interval. Does this seem like a good measure of central tendency in this case?

Obviously not! When your only source is grouped data, don't put too much confidence in mean and median.

Properties of the Median

1. Uniqueness – as was true with the mean, there is a unique median for a given set of data.
2. Simplicity – the median is easy to calculate.
3. Robustness – it is not as drastically affected by extreme values as is the mean.

7.

Trade Deficit	Balanced Trade	Trade Surplus
Exports < Imports	Exports = Imports	Exports > Imports
Net Exports < 0	Net Exports = 0	Net Exports > 0
Y < C + I + G	Y = C + I + G	Y > C + I + G
Saving < Investment	Saving = Investment	Saving > Investment
Net Capital Outflow < 0	Net Capital Outflow = 0	Net Capital Outflow > 0

8. Demand Shifters

The demand curve shifts when there is a change in any of the determinants of demand such as income of buyers, their tastes and preferences, prices of related goods (substitutes and compliments), expectations about future prices, sociological factors, the numbers of consuming units (buyers) and so on. We may now briefly examine how each of these determinants of demand affects the demand curve.

1. **Income:** The demand for any good or service mainly depends on consumers'

income. The higher the income of a consumer, the larger the volume of goods and services that he can afford to buy at any given price.

2. **Prices of related goods (and services):** Goods which are related to one another are classified into two broad categories: *substitutes* and *compliments*. If the consumption of one good is at the expense of the other, they are called substitutes. Tea and coffee, butter and margarine, wheat and rice are all pairs of substitute goods. Since substitute goods can be used in place of each other, if the price of one rises, the demand for the other will rise, too. If the market price of coffee rises, *ceteris paribus,* the demand for tea will also rise and the demand curve for tea will shift to the right.

   If two goods are used together, or jointly demanded, they are called *complimentary* goods. Pairs of such goods are tea and sugar, motor car and petrol, fountain pen and ink, shoes and socks, shirts and trousers, left shoe and right shoe, cameras and films and so on. If the price of one such good (in a particular pair) rises, the price of the other will automatically rise. If, for example, the price of petrol rises, the demand for motor cars will immediately fall. The reason is obvious. Even if the market price of cars remains unchanged the operating cost of cars will rise. Similarly, if the price of sugar rises, the demand for tea will fall because each cup of tea will now cost more. As the price of sugar rises people buy less sugar, and they tend to buy less tea also. The demand curve for a complimentary good (tea) shifts to the left when the price of the related good (sugar) increases.

3. **Tastes and preferences:** The demand for any good or service depends, to some extent (and in some cases, to a considerable extent), on the people's tastes and preferences. If people suddenly develop a taste for coffee (for whatever reason) they will buy more coffee and less tea and cocoa. In this case the demand curve for coffee will shift to right (and the demand for tea to the left).

4. **Expectations about future prices and income:** While making purchases of different goods and services people are often guided by about their income and prices of goods. If people expect their future incomes to rise in future, they will spend more on consumption goods now. For example, if an individual expects to derive dividend income from a reputed company, in near future, he will buy more now to buy a land or even a house. Similarly, if an individual apprehends that he will lose his job due to a brief recession in the industry to which he belongs, he will curtail his consumption (even when his income remains unchanged) and save as much as he can for the rainy days. Similarly, if people expect the price of a commodity, such as a colour TV set or a refrigerator, to fall in near future they will defer their purchase for the time being. They would prefer to wait and watch. Similarly, rumours that in the next year car prices will rise will increase the demand for cars in the current year. This means that the demand arise for this year's cars will shift to the right. The effect of changed expectations is to shift the demand curve. The demand for a good or service may rise (fall) and the demand curve may shift to the right (left) due to changes in people's income and price expectations. As Boyes and Melvin have succinctly put it: "Expectations about the future can have an effect on demand today. People make purchases today because they expect their income to be a certain amount in the future. A change in expected income can have an effect on today's expenditures."

5. **Number of buyers:** We have noted that market demand consists of the sum of the

demands of all individuals. Thus, the larger the number of buyers with capacity (income) to spend, the higher the market demand is likely to be.

9. Idle Time Variance

Idle time variance occurs when workers are not able to do the work due to some reason during the hours for which they are paid. Idle time can be divided according to causes responsible for creating idle time, *e.g.*, idle time due to breakdown, lack of materials or power failures. Idle time variance will be equivalent to the standard labour cost of the hours during which no work has been done, but for which workers have been paid for unproductive time. Suppose, in a factory 2,000 workers were idle because of a power failure. As a result of this a loss of production of 4,000 units of product A and 8,000 units of product B occurred. Each employee was paid his normal wage (a rate of ₹ 20 per hour). A single standard hour is needed to manufacture four units of product A and eight units of product B. Idle time variance will be computed in the following manner:

Standard hours lost:

$$\text{Product A} = \frac{4{,}000}{4} = 1{,}000 \text{ hr}$$

$$\text{Product A} = \frac{8{,}000}{8} = 1{,}000 \text{ hr}$$

Total hours lost = 2,000 hr

Idle time variance (power failure)

2,000 hours @ ₹ 20 per hour = ₹ 40,000 (Adverse)

12. The Poisson *Distribution*

The Poisson distribution, which is named after the French mathematician Simeon Poisson, is useful for determining the probability that a particular event will occur a certain number of times over a specified period of time or within the space of a particular interval. For example, the number of customer arrivals per hour at a bank or other servicing facility is a random variable with Poisson distribution. Here are some other random variables that may exhibit a Poisson distribution:

1. The number of days in a given year in which a 50-point change occurs in the Dow Jones Industrial Average.
2. The number of defects detected each day by a quality control inspector in a light bulb plant.
3. The number of breakdowns per month that a supercomputer experiences.
4. The number of car accidents that occur per month (or week or day) in the city of Princeton. New Jersey.

The formula for the Poisson probability distribution is

$P(X = x) = e^{-\lambda}\lambda^x/x!$ for $x = 0, 1, 2, 3, \ldots$ and $\lambda > 0$

where X represents the discrete Poisson random variable; x represents the number of rare events in a unit of time, space, or volume; λ is the mean value of x; e is the base of natural logarithms and is approximately equal to 2.71828; and! is the factorial symbol.

13. Shifts of the IS Curve:

As a result of changes in government spending, both income and interest fate respond positively, increase in taxes or reduction in government expenditure or both reduce the level of income and thus shifts the aggregate expenditure curve downwards.

Thus, an increase in taxes shifts to IS curve to the left. National income falls in the commodity market. The demand for money is reduced in the money market and as a consequence to rate of interest falls. So, at the end the rate of interest and the level of income both fall.

Conversely, a reduction in taxes or an increase in government expenditure or both fall. Conversely a reduction in taxes or an increase in government expenditure or both shift the

IS curve to the right (Fig.) and raise both Y and *r*.

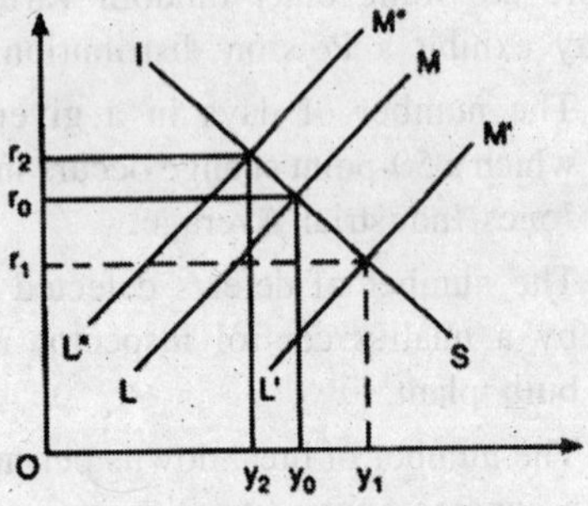

Fig.: *Shift of both IS curve*

15. Inferential Statistics

In statistics, the collection of all elements of interest is called a population. The selection of a few elements from this population is called a sample.

A major portion of statistics deals with making decisions, inferences, predictions and forecasts about populations based on results obtained from samples. For example, we may make some decisions about the political views of all college and university students based on the political views of 1000 students selected from a few colleges and universities. As another example, we may want to find the starting salary of a typical college graduate. To do so, we may select 2000 recent college graduates, find their starting salaries, and make a decision based on this information. The area of statistics that deals with such decision-making procedures is referred to as inferential statistics. This branch of statistics is also called *inductive reasoning* or *inductive statistics.*

Definition

Inferential Statistics: *Inferential statistics* consists of methods that use sample results to help make decisions or predictions about a population.

16. Prime cost = Direct material consumed + Direct labour + Direct expenses
= 90000 + 60000 + 20000 = 170000.

17. Break-even Points in Units

$$= \frac{\text{Total Fixed Costs}}{(\text{Sales price per unit} - \text{Variable cost per unit})}$$

$$= \frac{8000+40000}{6-(1.20+0.40)} = \frac{48000}{6-1.6}$$

$$= \frac{48000}{4.4} = 10909 \text{ units.}$$

18. Where there is Sinking Fund

A sinking fund is a fund created for the repayment of a liability or for the replacement of an asset. It is created by equal periodic instalments in order to accumulate the amount of money required to repay a loan at a set date in the future.

When the debentures are issued for a fixed period, their payment must be made after the expiry of that period. When the debentures are redeemed, the company requires a huge amount of money to pay-off debentureholders. If proper provisions are not made, there will be a strain on working capital and the company will face liquidity crisis, because a lot of money will go out of business.

For collecting funds, a sinking fund is created voluntarily by making a charge against distributable profits. Every year, an equal amount is debited to Profit and Loss Appropriation Account and credited to Sinking Fund Account. The amount so appropriated is invested outside the business in gill-edged securities (debiting investment and crediting cash) and allowed to accumulate at compound interest, so as to produce the amount required to repay the debentureholders on the date of redemption. In the Balance Sheet, Sinking Fund Account is shown on the Liability side and Sinking Fund Investment Account is shown on the Asset side. Other things remaining the same, balances on these two accounts should be equal. In the year of redemption, sinking fund investments will be realised and debentureholders will be paid-off. After redemption, the balance of the Sinking Fund Account is transferred to General Reserve Account.

The creation of a sinking fund is a method of amortisation or extinguishment of a debt (debentures) not yet matured. The establishment of a sinking fund for the redemption is a condition of issuing the debentures. It is as binding on the company as any other provision of the contract.

20. Capital and Revenue Expenditures

Capital expenditure is the outflow of funds to acquire *an asset* that will benefit the business *more than one accounting period.* A capital expenditure takes place when an asset or service is acquired or improvement of a fixed asset is effected. These assets are expected to provide benefits to the business in more than one accounting period and are not intended for resale in the ordinary course of business. In short, it is an expenditure on assets which is not written off completely against income in the accounting period in which it is incurred.

Revenue expenditure is the outflow of funds to meet the running expenses of a business and it will be of benefit for the current period only. A revenue expenditure is incurred to carry on the normal course of business or maintain the capital assets in a good condition.

It may be pointed out here that an expenditure need not necessarily be a payment made to somebody in cash - it may be made by cash, by the exchange of another asset, or by incurring a liability. *Expenditure incurrence and expenditure recognition are distinct phenomena.* Expenditure incurrence refers to the receipt of goods and services, whereas expenditure recognition is a matter to be decided whether the expenditure is of capital or revenue nature, for example, the buying of an asset is a capital expenditure but charging depreciation against profit is a revenue expenditure, over the entire life of that asset. Most of the capital expenditures made by a business become revenue expenditures. On the application of periodicity, accrual and matching concepts, accountants identify all revenue expenditures for a given period for ascertaining profit. An expenditure which cannot be identified to a particular accounting period is considered of capital nature.

The accounting treatment of capital and revenue expenditure are as under:

Revenue expenditures are charged as an expense against profit in the year they are incurred or recognised. Capital expenditures are capitalised-added to an asset account.

21. What is Unemployment

Unemployment occurs when a person who is actively searching for employment is unable to find work. Unemployment is often used as a measure of the health of the economy. The most frequent measure of unemployment is the unemployment rate, which is the number of unemployed people divided by the number of people in the labour force.

Breaking Down Unemployment

While the definition of unemployment is clear, economists divide unemployment into many different categories. The two broadest categories of unemployment are voluntary and involuntary unemployment. When unemployment is voluntary, it means that a person has left his job willingly in search of other employment. When it is involuntary, it means that a person has been fired or laid off and must now look for another job. Digging deeper, unemployment — both voluntary and involuntary — is broken down into three types.

Frictional Unemployment

Frictional unemployment arises when a person is in between jobs. After a person leaves a company, it naturally takes time to find another job, making this type of unemployment short-lived. It is also the least problematic from an economic standpoint. Arizona, for example, has faced rising frictional unemployment in May 2016, due to the fact that unemployment has been historically low for the state. Arizona citizens feel confident leaving their jobs with no safety net in search of better employment.

Cyclical Unemployment

Cyclical unemployment comes around due to the business cycle itself. Cyclical unemployment rises during recessionary periods and declines during periods of economic growth. For example, the number of weekly jobless claims in the United States has slowed in the month of June, as oil prices begin to rise and the economy starts to stabilize, adding jobs to the market.

Structural Unemployment

Structural unemployment comes about through technological advances when people lose their jobs because their skills are outdated. Illinois, for example, after seeing increased unemployment rates in May 2016, sought to implement "structural reforms" that will give people new skills and therefore more job opportunities.

Unemployment Rate Formula

The formula for unemployment rate is: Unemployment Rate = Number of Unemployed Persons / Labour Force. The labour force is the sum of unemployed and employed persons. By dividing the number of individuals whom are unemployed by labour force, you'll find the labour force participation, or unemployment rate.

28. The overall responsibility for administration of Direct Tax Laws lies with Department of Revenue which functions through the Income Tax Department and Central Board of Direct Taxes (Board) at its apex. The Board consists of a Chairman and five members and has several attached and subordinate offices throughout the country. The attached offices function under three Directors General of Income Tax. Viz. Director General of Income Tax (Administration.) Director General of Income Tax (Exemption) and Director General of Income Tax (Training). There are Chief Commissioners of Income Tax, who oversee the work of assessment and collection of direct taxes at regional levels. Besides, there are Directors General of Investigation, who are overall incharge of the investigation machinery on a regional basis to curb tax evasion and to unearth black money. The Chief Commissioners of Income Tax/Directors General of Income Tax oversee the work of the Commissioners/Directors of Income Tax in their respective charges and have also been given certain powers under the Income Tax act, regarding discovery, production of evidence by any person, to requisition books of account, call for information etc. whereby they can issue summons. They are also empowered to authorize search and seizure operations.

29. Prime Minister Narendra Modi launched the Make in India initiative on September 25, 2014, with the primary goal of making India a global manufacturing hub, by encouraging both multinational as well as domestic companies to manufacture their products within the country. Led by the Department of Industrial Policy and Promotion, the initiative aims to raise the contribution of the manufacturing sector to 25% of the Gross Domestic Product (GDP) by the year 2025 from its current 16%. Make in India has introduced multiple new initiatives, promoting foreign direct investment, implementing intellectual property rights and developing the manufacturing sector.

It targets 25 sectors of the economy which range from automobile to Information Technology (IT) & Business Process Management (BPM), the details of each can be viewed on the official site (www.makeinindia.com).

It also seeks to facilitate job creation, foster innovation, enhance skill development and protect intellectual property. The logo of 'Make in India' — a lion made of gear wheels — itself reflects the integral role of manufacturing in government's vision and national development. The initiative is built on four pillars which are as follows:

New Processes: The government is introducing several reforms to create possibilities for getting Foreign Direct Investment (FDI) and foster business partnerships. Some initiatives have already been undertaken to alleviate the business environment from outdated policies and regulations. This reform is also aligned with parameters of World Bank's 'Ease of Doing Business' index to improve India's ranking on it.

30. Variations In Time Series

The term time series are used to refer to any group of statistical information collected at regular intervals of time. There are four kinds of changes, or variations, involved in time series analysis. They are:

(*i*) Secular trend

(*ii*) Cyclical fluctuation

(*iii*) Seasonal variation

(*iv*) Irregular variation

With the secular trend, the value of the variable tends to increase or decrease over a long period of time. The steady increase in the cost of living recorded by the consumer price index is an example of secular trend. From year to year, the cost of living varies a great deal; but, if we consider a long-term period, we see that the trend is towards steady increase. Other examples of secular trend are steady increase of population over a period of time, steady growth of agricultural food production in India over the last ten to fifteen years of time.

The second type of variation that can be observed in a time series is cyclical fluctuation. The most common example of cyclical fluctuation is the business cycle. Over a period of time, there are years when the business cycle has a peak above the trend line, and at other times, the business activity is likely to slump, touching a low point below the trend line. The time between touching peaks or falling to low points is generally 3 to 5 years, but it can be as many as 15 to 20 years.

The third kind of fluctuation that can occur in a time series data is the seasonal variation. Seasonal variation involves patterns of change within a year that tend to be repeated from year to year. For example, sale of umbrellas is on the increase during the months of June and July every year because of the seasonal requirement. Since these are regular patterns, they are useful in forecasting the future production runs.

Irregular variation is the fourth type of change that can be observed in a time series data. These variations may be due to (*i*) random fluctuations: irregular random fluctuations refer to a large number of minute environmental influences (some uplifting, some depressing) operating on a series at any one time — no one of which is significantly important in and of itself to warrant singling out for individual treatment, and (*ii*) non-recurring irregular influences that exert a significant one time impact on the behaviour of a time series and as such must be explicitly recognized. The events included in this category are floods, strikes, wars, and so on, which influence the time series data.

31. *Scientific Management* (1947), Taylor outlined four principles of management:

- the development of a 'science of work' to replace the old rule-of-thumb methods by which working people operated (fulfilling optimum goals would earn higher wages; failure to do so would result in loss of earnings)
- scientific selection and progressive development of the worker, training each to be 'first class' at some task
- bringing together the science of work and the scientifically selected and trained workers for best results
- equal division of work and responsibility between workers and management, cooperating together in closer interdependence.

The car manufacturer Henry Ford was closely associated with this scientific management approach, and consequently the term **Fordism** came to be associated with mass manufacturing organisations producing high-volume output of standardised products with specialist machinery and extensive stocks of spare parts. Ford employed a very strict form of work discipline based on the Theory X approach we have described. Ford's workers were generally better paid than others, but working conditions were very strict and people had to toil. The term 'machine company' is associated with Fordism, because people were treated virtually as part of the machinery, and the organisation operated with machine-like efficiency. Taylor's and Ford's ideas were based heavily on the assumption that good wages are the key motivator.

32. The definitions of M_1 and M_2 differ from one country to another — in some countries there are even M_3 and M_4. In the U.S., M_1 consists of currency in circulation, demand deposits travellers' cheques and other checkable deposits. M_2 is M_1 plus saving deposits and small time deposits.

34. Meaning of Division of Labour

Division of Labour means that the main process of production is split up into many simple parts and each part is taken by different workers who are specialised in the production of that specific part.

Now, a day's production has become so technical and complex that different workers are put to different tasks according to their capacity and ability.

One becomes specialised in the production of those goods for which he or she is best suited.

Different workers perform different parts of production on the basis of their specialisation. The result is that goods come to the final shape with the co-operation of many workers. For example – In a large scale readymade garment factory, a man does cutting of cloth, the second man stitches clothes with machines, the third buttons, the fourth makes folding and packing etc.

This way of doing the work is called division of Labour, because different workers are engaged in performing different parts of production.

36. In the mid-1980s, the phrase "glass ceiling" was coined and has since become an established part of our vocabulary. The glass ceiling refers to an invisible but impermeable barrier that limits the career advancement of women. Since then, terms such as "sticky floors" and "concrete walls" have been used to refer to similar and related obstacles — the difficulties talented women experience in advancing in their careers in medium and large organizations.

During the last two decades, women have made progress. There are now more women in senior-level executive jobs, more women in "clout jobs", more women CEOs, and more women on corporate boards of directors. But real progress has been slow with only modest increases shown at these levels.

37. Specific Incomes Included Under 'Income from other Sources' [Section 56(2)]

There are many incomes which are taxable under the head 'Income from other Sources'. However, Section 56(2) enlists certain specific incomes which shall be chargeable to income tax under the head "Income from other sources' without prejudice to the generality of the provisions of sub-section (1) of Section 56. These are:

(*i*) Dividends.

(*ii*) Winnings from lotteries, crossword puzzles, races including horse races, card games and other games of any sort, or from gambling or betting of any form or nature whatsoever.

(*iii*) Any sum received by the assessee from his employees as contribution to any provident fund, or any other welfare fund for the employees provided it is not taxable under the head profits and gains of business or profession.

(*iv*) Income by way of interest on securities provided the income is not chargeable to income tax under the head profits and gains of business or profession.

(*v*) Income from machinery, plant or furniture belonging to the assessee and let on hire, provided the income is not chargeable to income tax under the head profits and gains of business or profession.

(*vi*) Where the assessee lets on hire, the machinery, plant or furniture belonging to him and also buildings, and letting of buildings, is inseparable from the letting of the said machinery, plant or furniture, the income from such letting, if it is not chargeable to income tax under the head profits and gains of business or profession.

(*vii*) Any sum received under a Keyman Insurance Policy, including the sum allocated by way of bonus on such policy, if such income is not taxable under the head salaries or profits and gains of business or profession.

These are the incomes, which have been specified, in particular, to be chargeable under the head income from other sources.

39. The approach you learnt about is known as the 'one-stage approach'. It was based upon the use of one double entry, a credit to the accumulated provision for depreciation account and a debit to the profit and loss account.

There is another approach which is widely used in practice. It involves using a 'provision for depreciation account', often shortened to 'depreciation account', as well as the 'accumulated provision for depreciation account'. At the end of the period, you calculate the depreciation for the period and make the following double entries:

1. Debit the depreciation account

   Credit the accumulated provision for depreciation account

2. Debit the profit and loss account

   Credit the depreciation account

Compare this two-stage approach to the one-stage approach you learnt earlier:

Debit the profit and loss account

Credit the accumulated provision for depreciation account

40. This impact of a price decrease on quantity demanded is called a substitution effect: The consumer substitutes *toward* the good whose relative price has decreased.

The substitution effect of a price change always moves quantity demanded in the opposite direction to the price change. When the price of a good decreases, the substitution effect works to increase quantity demanded; when price increases, the substitution effect works to decrease quantity demanded.

The substitution effect is a powerful force in the marketplace. For example, while the price of cell phone calls began falling several years ago, the price of pay phone calls remained more or less the same. This fall in the relative price of cell phone calls caused consumers to substitute toward them and away from using regular pay phones. As a result, pay phones have almost disappeared in many areas of the country.

The substitution effect is also important from a theoretical perspective: It is the main factor responsible for the law of demand. Indeed, if the substitution effect were the *only* effect of a price change, the law of demand would be more than a law; it would be a logical necessity. But as we are about to see, a price change has another effect as well.

Type of good	Effect on quantity demanded of a rise in price		
	Substitution effect	Income effect	Total effect
Normal good	Fall	Fall	Fall
Inferior good	Fall	Rise	Fall because substitution effect > income effect
Giffen good	Fall	Rise	Rise because substitution effect < income effect

42. $\because$ Compounded quarterly

$$\therefore \quad R = \frac{16\%}{4} = 4\%$$

$$T = 5 \times 4 = 20 \text{ years}$$

$\because$ Amount after 5 years = ₹ 15000

$$A = P\left(1+\frac{r}{100}\right)^t$$

$$15000 = P\left(1+\frac{4}{100}\right)^{20}$$

$$15000 = P\left(\frac{26}{25}\right)^{20}$$

$$15000 = P(1.04)^{20}$$

$$15000 = P \times 2.19$$

$$\therefore \quad P = \frac{15000}{2.19}$$

$$= ₹\ 6,849.32 \sim ₹\ 6,845.80.$$

48. Order of matrix A = $m \times p$

Order of matrix B = $p \times n$

$\therefore$ Order of matrix AB = $m \times n$.

49. Introduction of Accounting Standard 6 - Depreciation Accounting - AS 6

1. This Statement deals with depreciation accounting and applies to all depreciable assets, except the following items to which special considerations apply:

(*i*) forests, plantations and similar regenerative natural resources;

(*ii*) wasting assets including expenditure on the exploration for and extraction of minerals, oils, natural gas and similar non-regenerative resources;

(*iii*) expenditure on research and development;

(*iv*) goodwill;

(*v*) live stock.

This statement also does not apply to land unless it has a limited useful life for the enterprise.

2. Different accounting policies for depreciation are adopted by different enterprises. Disclosure of accounting policies for depreciation followed by an enterprise is necessary to appreciate the view presented in the financial statements of the enterprise.

50. Complements: Suppose our given good is car. Its complementary good is petrol. Suppose the price of petrol rises. This increases operational cost per kilometer of running a car. This discourages demand for cars. It means that there is inverse relation between the price one complimentary good and demand for the other complementary good. When price of one complementary good falls, demand for the other complementary good rises. If the price of petrol falls, demand for cars rises. This relation is depicted in Figure.

D curve is the cost demend curve. It is downward sloping from left to right indicating inverse relation between price of one complimentary good and demand for the other complementary good.

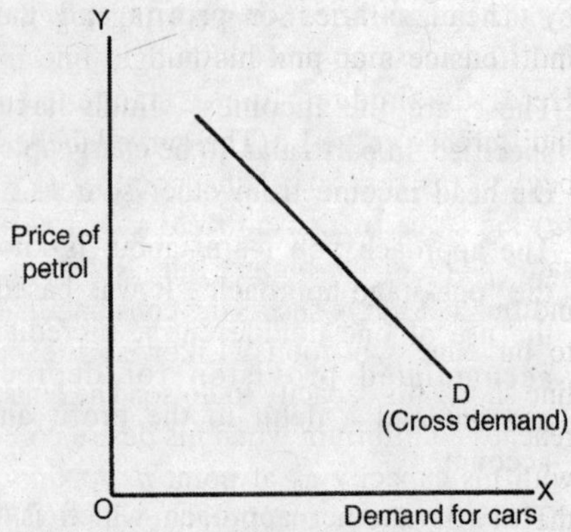

Fig.: *Cross Demand Curve of Two Complementary Goods.*

52. When these hygiene factors are poor or absent, the person complains about "poor supervision," "poor medical benefits," or whatever hygiene factor is poor. Employees experience a deficit and are dissatisfied when the hygiene factors are not present. Many companies have initiated formal flextime policies as a way to reduce dissatisfaction and persuade women leaders to come back to work." Even in the absence of good hygiene factors, employees may still be very motivated to perform their jobs well if the motivation factors are present. Although this may appear to be a paradox, it is not because the motivation and hygiene factors are independent of each other.

56.

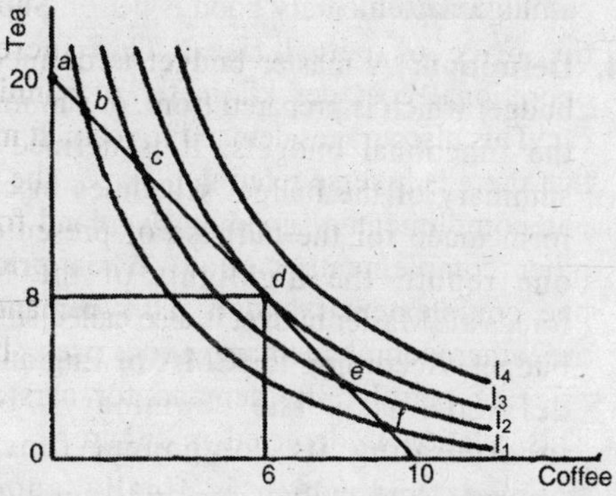

Fig.: *Consumer equilibrium*

A rational consumer, whose objective is utility maximization, would always try to reach the highest attainable indifference curve permitted by the budget line. So, we bring together his indifference map and his budget line in Fig. Here, the budget line is tangent to the indifference curve I_3. (The curve labelled I_4 is beyond his reach.) At the point of tangency (*d*) the slope of the indifference curve is the same slope of the budget line. Recall that the indifference curve shows the consumer's desire to buy the two goods. Likewise the budget line shows his capacity to do so. The consumer reaches equilibrium when his desire coincides with his capacity as at point *d.* At this point the slope of the indifference curve (or the desired rate of consumer substitution) is the same as the slope of the budget line (or the actual rate of substitution). The equilibrium can be formally expressed as follows:

The slope of the indifference curve = the slope of the budget line

or, $$\frac{MU_E}{MU_R} = \frac{P_E}{P_B}$$

i.e., the MRS of tea for coffee is the same as the ratio of the prices of the two goods.

58. The way organizations behave in relationship with their many stakeholders is a good indicator of their underlying ethical characters. When we talk about the "good" and the "bad" in business and society relationships, corporate social responsibility is at issue. Often called "CSR," it is defined as an obligation of the organization to act in ways that serve both its own interests and the interests of its stakeholders, representing society at large.

59. WAGERING AGREEMENTS

Section 30 of the Indian Contract Act, 1872 states that wagering agreements are void. The Section speaks as follows:

"Agreements by way of wager are void; and no suit shall be brought for recovering anything alleged to be won on any wager, or entrusted to any person to abide by result of any game or other uncertain event on which any wager is made."

Section 30 only provides that agreements by way of wager are void, however, it does not define the term, 'wager'. Subba Rao J in the judgement of a leading case quoted Sir William Anson's definition of 'wager' as a promise to give money or money's worth upon the determination or ascertainment of an uncertain event. This definition may be used to bring out the concept of wager declared void by Sec. 30 of the Contract Act. The principle and purpose behind Sec. 30 to treat an agreement by way of wager as void, is to discourage people to enter into games of chance and making money by trying luck instead of spending their time, energy and labour for more fruitful and useful work for themselves, their families and society.

60. Audit of Holding Company

According to section 2(46) of the Companies Act, 2013, a "holding company", in relation to one or more other companies, means a company of which such companies are subsidiary companies. Further, section 2(84) defines a subsidiary company as under:

"Subsidiary company" or "subsidiary", in relation to any other company (that is to say the holding company), means a company in which the holding company:

(i) controls the composition of the Board of Directors; or

(ii) exercises or controls more than one-half of the total share capital either at its own or together with one or more of its subsidiary companies:

Provided that such class or classes of holding companies as may be prescribed shall not have layers of subsidiaries beyond such numbers as may be prescribed.

Explanation— For the purposes of this clause,

(a) a company shall be deemed to be a subsidiary company of the holding company even if the control referred to in sub-clause (i) or sub-clause (ii) is of another subsidiary company or the holding company;

(b) the composition of a company's Board of Directors shall be deemed to be controlled by another company if that other company by exercise of some power exercisable by it at its discretion can appoint or remove all or a majority of the directors.

62.

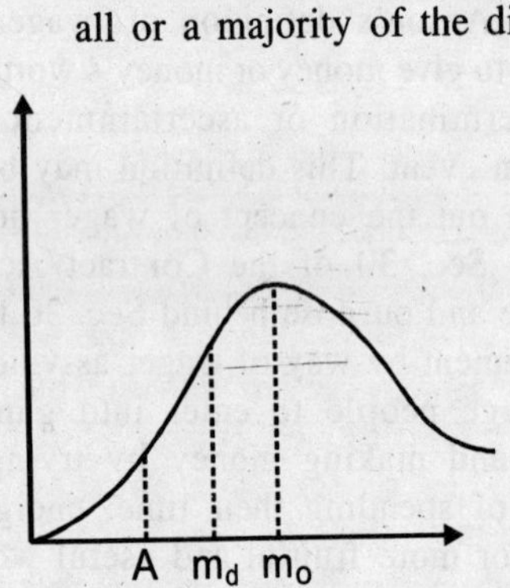

We have,

Mean = 23, median = 24 and mode = 25.5

∵ Mean < median < mode

∴ Distribution is Negative skewness

63. Purchase Method: This method is followed in case of an amalgamation in the nature of purchase. Under this method, the transferee company accounts for the amalgamation either by incorporating the assets and liabilities of the transferor company at their existing carrying amounts or by allocating the consideration to individual identifiable assets and liabilities of the transferor company on the basis of their fair values at the date of amalgamation.

64. Definition: A master budget is defined as a budget which is prepared from, or summarizes, the functional budgets. It is defined as "a summary of the budget schedules in capsule form made for the purpose of presenting, in one report, the highlights of the budget forecast". Master budget is also called summary budget. According to ICMA of England, it is defined as "The summary budget incorporating its component functional budgets and which is finally approved, adopted and employed". It is prepared by the budget committee.

Advantages of a master budget are:

1. A summary of all functional budgets in capsule form is available for reference.
2. This indicates total position of business during the budget period.
3. It tells about the budgeted profit or loss.
4. This highlights on assets and liabilities of business during the budget period.

65. Price Index

The price indexes are of two categories:

(i) Single price index

(ii) Composite price index

The single price index measures the percentage change in the current price per unit of a product to its base period price. To facilitate comparisons with other years, the actual price per unit is converted into a *price relative to* express price per unit in each period as a percentage of price per unit in a base period. Price relatives are helpful to understand and interpret changing economic and business conditions over time.

A composite price index measures the average price change for a group of items taken as a, whole from a base period to the current period. For example, the *wholesale price index* reflects the general price level for a group or items taken as a whole.

The *retail price index* indicates the general changes in the retail prices for a group of items including food, housing, clothing and so on. The consumer price index, a special type of retail price index, is the primary measure of the cost of living in a country. The consumer price index is a weighted average price index with fixed weights. The weightage applied to each item in the basket of items is derived from the urban and rural families.

74. What income is taxed under Income from Other Sources?

All those incomes which are not exempt and are to be taxed and are at the same time not covered in any of the four heads of income namely salary, house property, capital gains and business and profession is included in the head of income from other sources. The income included here is taxable on cash or mercantile basis whichever method assessee follows. There are certain incomes, which are specifically mentioned in section 56 of the income tax act to be included in the head of income from other sources, but there are various other incomes, which are not specified in section 56 of the income tax act but are still included in the income from other sources. The following income shall be chargeable to income tax under the head "Income from other sources", namely:

1. Dividend;
2. Any annuity due or commuted value of any annuity paid under section 280D.
3. Any winning from lotteries, crossword puzzles, races including horse races, card games and other games of any sort or from gambling or betting of any form or nature whatsoever.
4. Any sum, received by the assessee from his employees as contributions to any provident fund or Superannuation fund or any fund set up under the provisions of the Employees State Insurance Act, 1948 (34 of 1948), or any officer fund for the welfare of such employees, if such income is not chargeable to income-tax under the head "Profits and gains of business or profession";
5. Income from machinery, plant or furniture belonging to the assessee and let on hire, if the income is not chargeable to income-tax under the head "Profits and gains of business or profession";
6. Where an assessee lets on hire machinery, plant or furniture belonging to him and also buildings, and the letting of the buildings is inseparable from the letting of the said machinery, plant or furniture, the income from such letting, if it is not chargeable to income tax under the head "Profits and gains of business or profession."
7. Any sum received under a Keyman insurance policy, including the sum allocated by way of bonus on such policy, if such income is not chargeable to income tax under the heads "Profits and gains of business and profession" or under the head "Salaries". (Keyman insurance policy means a life insurance policy taken by a person on the life of another person who is/was the employee of the 1st mentioned person or who is/was connected in any manner whatsoever with the business of the 1st mentioned person.) So, basically "income from other sources" is the residuary head of income, which takes within its ambit any income, which does not specifically fall under any other head of income.

76. *Clause (3) – Residential status of a company*

- To determine the residential status of a company, the following two questions have to be answered:

❑ ***First***: Is the company an Indian company [for definition, *see* section 2(26)]? If the answer is yes, the company is a *resident* (thus, an Indian company cannot be a non-resident). If the answer is no, proceed to question 2.

- ***Second*:** Is the control and management of its affairs situated wholly *in India?* If the answer is yes, the company is *resident.* If no, the company is *non-resident.*

- A company, other than an Indian company, the control and management of the affairs of which is *partly* situated in India and partly outside India, is a *non-resident.*
- A company cannot be a 'resident and ordinarily resident' or a 'resident but not ordinarily resident'. A company can either be a resident or a non-resident.
- *'Control and management'* means the controlling and directive power. It means *actual* or *de facto* control and management. *Mere right* to control and manage does not amount to control and management {*CIT* v. *Nandlal Gandalal* [1960] 40 ITR 1 (SC)}. It means *central* control and management and not the carrying out of routine day-to-day affairs. The place of control and management is situated at a place where the head, the seat and the directive power is situated {*San Paulo (Brazilian) Railway Co.* v. *Carter* [1896] AC 31 (HL)}. It is generally deemed to be situated where meetings of the Board of directors are held (not where the shareholder's meetings are held) {*Narottam & Pereira Ltd.* v. *CIT* [1953] 23 ITR 454 (Bom.)}.
- Burden of proving that a company is resident in India is on the Revenue {*Moosa S Madha & Azam S Madha* v. *CIT* [1973] 89 ITR 65 (SC)}.

78. The following incomes are Taxable under "Income From House Property":

1. Any arrears of rent,
2. Incomes earned by letting-out any farm house or agricultural land from any purpose other than agriculture.
3. Letting of Shops, Complexes, Commercial Buildings.
4. When the property is let-out.

79. Benefits of LLP:

There is no limit on number of owners of LLP

LLP requires minimum 2 partners but there is no limit on maximum number of partners unlike a private limited company wherein there is a restriction of not having more than 200 members.

Lower cost involved in formation of LLP

The cost of registering LLP is low as compared to cost of incorporating a private limited or a public limited company.

No requirement of conducting compulsory Audit in case of LLP

All the companies, whether private or public, irrespective of their share capital, are required to get their accounts audited. But in case of LLP, there is no such mandatory requirement. A Limited Liability Partnership is required to get their accounts audited only if:

(*a*) If the paid up capital of the LLP exceeds ₹ 25 Lakhs, or

(*b*) If the annual turnover of the LLP exceeds ₹ 40 Lakhs.

Lower compliance burden as compared to other forms of business structure

In case of Limited Liability Partnership, the only requirement is to file the Annual Return & a Statement of Accounts & Solvency as compared to other forms of entities which require large number of compliances.

Easy to windup

It is not only easy to start a LLP; it is also easier to wind up the same as compared to other business entities.

80. Characteristics of Entrepreneurship:

Entrepreneurship is characterized by the following features:

1. **Economic and dynamic activity:** Entrepreneurship is an economic activity because it involves the creation and operation of an enterprise with a view to creating value or wealth by ensuring optimum utilisation of scarce resources. Since this value creation activity is performed continuously in the midst of uncertain business environment, therefore, entrepreneurship is regarded as a dynamic force.
2. **Related to innovation:** Entrepreneurship involves a continuous search for new ideas. Entrepreneurship compels an individual to continuously evaluate the existing modes of business operations so that more efficient and effective systems can be evolved and adopted. In other words, entrepreneurship is a continuous effort for synergy (optimization of performance) in organizations.
3. **Profit potential:** "Profit potential is the likely level of return or compensation to the entrepreneur for taking on the risk of developing an idea into an actual business venture." Without profit potential, the efforts of entrepreneurs would remain only an abstract and a theoretical leisure activity.
4. **Risk bearing:** The essence of entrepreneurship is the 'willingness to assume risk' arising out of the creation and implementation of new ideas. New ideas are always tentative and their results may not be instantaneous and positive.

   An entrepreneur has to have patience to see his efforts bear fruit. In the intervening period (time gap between the conception and implementation of an idea and its results), an entrepreneur has to assume risk. If an entrepreneur does not have the willingness to assume risk, entrepreneurship would never succeed.

81. Pre-acquisition Profits and Reserves of Subsidiary Company:

Accumulated profits and reserves which appear in the balance sheet of the subsidiary company up to the date of acquisition of its shares by the holding company are called pre-acquisition profits and reserves. Both the holding company and the minority shareholders will have proportionate share in such profits and reserves. The share of the minority shareholders in such profit and reserves will be added to the amount of minority interest. But the holding company's proportionate share in such profits and reserve should be treated as capital profits and credited to Capital Reserve since the holding company cannot earn any revenue profits from its subsidiary before the shares are acquired in it. While preparing the consolidated balance sheet, this Capital Reserve should be shown on the liabilities side or if there is any Goodwill, it can be shown as a deduction from the Goodwill in the assets side.

82. Keynes's famous three motives for holding money:

- The *transactions motive,* which is the demand for money arising from the use of money in making regular payments.
- The *precautionary motive,* which is the demand for money to meet unforeseen contingencies.
- The *speculative motive,* which arises from uncertainties about the money value of other assets that an individual can hold.

84. Variable cost analysis also helps in make or buy decisions. In such decisions, outside supplier's price should be compared with firm's own variable cost. It is profitable to buy from outside if supplier's price is below firm's own variable cost of manufacture. But before arriving at a final decision, the management should also consider certain non-cost factors, such as assurance of continued supply, quality of the product, etc.

86. Fixed cost – definition

A fixed cost can be defined as:

'A cost which is incurred for an accounting period, and which, within certain output or turnover limits tends to be unaffected by fluctuations in the levels of activity (output or turnover).' *Terminology.*

An alternative term for fixed costs is *period cost.*

The key parts of this definition are that fixed costs are time related and, within limits, are unaffected by changes in the level of activity. This does not mean that fixed costs do not change; rent and rates, for example, change quite frequently. The main point is that the change in the cost is not caused by changes in the volume of activity.

Fixed costs can also be expressed algebraically:

$$\text{Cost} = a$$

where a is a constant. It will be noted that v, the volume of output, does not appear in this expression, so that changes in activity are deemed not to affect the fixed cost.

87. Contract Act 1872 - Person of unsound mind

Person of unsound mind (sec. 12)

1. **Not in sound mind:** A Person is said to be unsound mind for the purpose of making an agreement, if at the time of making the agreement, he is not in sound mind.

2. **Soundness of mind means that:**

   (*a*) **Understand:** He is in a state to understand what he is doing,

   (*b*) **Rational judgement:** He is able to form a rational judgment about the effect of his acts to his interest.

Types of Person of unsound mind

The following types of persons are said to be of unsound mind:

(*i*) **Lunatics:** A person who is mentally deranged. Such person can make a contract when he is mentally stable.

Ex. A patient in a lunatic asylum who is at intervals of sound mind, may contract during those intervals.

(*ii*) **Idiots:** A person who has completely lost his mental powers. Idiocy is permanent where as Lunacy is temporary. An agreement by an Idiot is void.

(*iii*) **Drunken or Intoxicated persons:** A person so drunk or intoxicated that he is not capable of forming a rational judgement during the period of intoxication or drunkenness. Like a Lunatic, a drunken person can make a contract when his condition is stable.

Ex. K a sane man was drunk and cannot understand the terms of the contract entered by him with L. K cannot perform the contract while such drunkenness lasts.

Agreement with Person of unsound mind

(*i*) **Contracts made by Persons of unsound mind:** Contracts made by persons of unsound mind, at the time when they are unsound, are void, but contracts made during the time when he is of sound mind, are valid.

(*ii*) **Estate liable for necessary supplies:** Though the contracts of person of unsound mind is void, their estate is liable for necessary supplies made to support them.

88. $$\begin{bmatrix} \text{Rice} & \text{Pulse} & \text{Sugar} \\ 15\text{ kg} & 5\text{ kg} & 2\text{ kg} \end{bmatrix} \begin{bmatrix} 10 \\ 30 \\ 15 \end{bmatrix} ₹$$

$$\therefore \quad = [15 \quad 5 \quad 2]_{1\times3} \times \begin{bmatrix} 10 \\ 30 \\ 15 \end{bmatrix}_{3\times1}$$

$$= 15 \times 10 + 5 \times 30 + 2 \times 15$$

$$= 150 + 150 + 30$$

$$= ₹\ 330$$

90. Finance Minister Arun Jaitley, in his Union Budget speech, re-introduced LTCG tax on stocks. Investors will have to pay 10 per cent tax on profit exceeding ₹ 1 lakh made from the sale of shares or equity mutual fund schemes held for over one year. Till now, LTCG was exempt from tax. The definition of a long-term investor in stocks for tax purposes is one year. LTCG tax on stocks was scrapped in 2004-05 by then finance minister P Chidambaram.

91. Perfectly competitive markets have four characteristics:

1. The industry is fragmented. It consists of many buyers and sellers. Each buyer's purchases are so small that they have an imperceptible effect on market price. Each seller's output is so small in comparison to market demand that it has an imperceptible impact on the market price. In addition, each seller's *input* purchases are so small that they have an imperceptible impact on *input prices.* The market for fresh-cut roses is an excellent example of a fragmented market. Even the largest producers, such as Nevado Ecuador, are very small in comparison to the overall scale of the market. Buyers that purchase fresh-cut roses from the producers—wholesalers, brokers, and florists—are also small and numerous.
2. Firms produce undifferentiated products. That is, consumers perceive the products to be identical no matter who produces them. When you buy fresh roses from a local flower shop, it probably does not matter to you that they were produced by Nevado Ecuador or one of its competitors. And because this is true for you, it is also true for the flower shops and the wholesalers who buy the roses directly from the growers. If the final consumer sees no difference in the roses grown by the different growers, then florists and wholesalers don't care who they buy roses from either, as long as they get the best price. Roses are thus an example of an undifferentiated product.
3. Consumers have perfect information about prices all sellers in the market charge. This is certainly true in the rose market. The wholesalers and florists that buy roses from the growers are keenly aware of the prevailing prices. These consumers need to be deeply knowledgeable about prices because the price is the main thing they care about when deciding which growers to buy roses from.
4. The industry is characterized by equal access to resources. All firms — those currently in the industry, as well as prospective entrants—have access to the same technology and inputs. Firms can hire inputs, such as labour, capital, and materials, as they need them, and they can release them from their employment when they do not need them. This characteristic is generally true of the fresh-cut rose industry: the technology for growing roses is well understood, and the key inputs necessary to operate a rose-growing firm (land, greenhouses, rose bushes, and labour) are readily available in well-functioning markets.

These characteristics have three implications for how perfectly competitive markets work:

- The first characteristic—the market is fragmented—implies that sellers and buyers act as price takers. That is, a firm takes the market price of the product as given when making an output decision, and a buyer takes the market price as given when making purchase decisions. This characteristic also implies that a firm takes input prices as fixed when making decisions about input quantities.
- The second and third characteristics—firms produce undifferentiated products and consumers have perfect information about prices—implies a law of one price: Transactions between buyers and sellers occur at a single market price. Because the products of all firms are perceived to be identical and the prices of all sellers are known, a consumer will purchase at the lowest price available in the market. No sales can be made at any higher price.
- The fourth characteristic—equal access to resources—implies that the industry is characterized by free entry. That is, if it is profitable for new firms to enter the industry, they will eventually do so. Free entry does not mean that a new firm incurs no cost when it enters the industry, but

rather that it has access to the same technology and inputs that existing firms have.

92. We have,

Variance of 5 numbers = 10

$$\because \quad \text{Variance} = \frac{\Sigma(x_i - \bar{x})^2}{n}$$

$$10 = \frac{\Sigma(x_i - \bar{x})^2}{5}$$

$$\Sigma(x_i - \bar{x})^2 = 50 \quad \text{...(1)}$$

$$\text{Then, New variance} = \frac{\Sigma\left(\frac{x_i}{2} - \frac{\bar{x}}{2}\right)^2}{n}$$

$$= \frac{\Sigma\left(x_i - \bar{x}\right)^2}{4n}$$

$$= \frac{50}{4 \times 5} = \frac{50}{20} = 2.5.$$

94. ***One Person Company (OPC)***

As per Companies Act 2013, a company can be started even by a single person, and such a company is referred to as One Person Company (OPC). Such a company can be started with a minimum capital of ₹ 1 lakh and can be a company limited by shares or company limited by guarantee. One basic pre-requisite for OPC is that it can be started only by a natural person who is an Indian citizen and resident of India. The member has to appoint a nominee. In case of death or any other incapacity, nominee automatically becomes the member. Most important advantage of OPC is that it has limited liability as against sole proprietorship form of business in which liability of owner is unlimited.

Further, No person is eligible to incorporate more than one OPC or become nominee in more than one such company. It is compulsory for OPC to convert itself into public or private company, where the paid up share capital of an OPC exceeds fifty lakh rupees or its average annual turnover during the relevant period exceeds two crore rupees, it shall cease to be entitled to continue as a One Person Company.

95. Under Section 78 of the Act, Securities Premium Reserve may be used wholly or in part for:

(*a*) Issuing fully paid bonus shares to the members.

(*b*) Writing off preliminary expenses.

(*c*) Writing off the expenses of or the commission paid or discount allowed on any issue of shares or debentures of the company.

(*d*) Providing for the premium payable on the redemption of preference shares or debentures of the company.

(*e*) In purchasing its own shares *i.e.*, Buy Back u/s 77 A.

96. In 1494, the first book on double-entry accounting, was published by Luca Pacioli. Since Pacioli was a Franciscan friar, he might be referred to simply as Friar Luca. While Friar Luca is regarded as the "Father of Accounting," he did not invent the system. Instead, he simply described a method used by merchants in Venice during the Italian Renaissance period. His system included most of the accounting cycle as we know it today. The first accounting book actually was one of five sections in Pacioli's mathematics book, titled Summa de Arithmetica, Geometria, Proportioni et Proportionalita (Everything About Arithmetic, Geometry and Proportions). This section on accounting served as the world's only accounting textbook until well into the 16th century. Accounting practitioners in public accounting, industry, and not-for-profit organizations, as well as investors, lending institutions, business firms, and all other users for financial information are indebted to Luca Pacioli for his monumental role in the development of accounting.

Previous Paper (Solved)

UNIVERSITY OF DELHI—M.COM Entrance Test-2017*

1. Assume that a person drinks three glasses of apple juice and then drinks fourth. The marginal utility is equal to:
A. The utility of the third glass
B. The utility of the fourth glass
C. The utility of first three glasses
D. Total utility of four glasses

2. The opportunity cost of an item is:
A. the number of hours needed to earn money to buy the item
B. what you give up to get that item
C. usually less than the dollar value of the item
D. the dollar value of the item

3. Law of diminishing returns refers to an eventual fall in:
A. Total production of all the factors of production
B. Total earnings of the firm
C. Marginal product of the variable factor
D. Average income of the firm

4. When AR is constant, MR is:
A. Equal to AR B. More than AR
C. Less than AR D. Equal to Zero

5. Under perfect competition, firm will be in equilibrium if:
A. MC = MR
B. MC cuts MR from below
C. MC rises when it cuts MR
D. All of the above

6. Value of Marginal Product (VMP) is equal to:
A. MPP × MR B. MPP × Px
C. MPP × APP D. APP × MR

7. If a good is inferior, then an increase in income will result in:
A. an increase in the demand for the good
B. a decrease in the demand for the good
C. a movement down and to the right along the demand curve for the good
D. a movement up and to the left along the demand curve for the good

8. Assume that England and Spain can switch between producing cheese and producing bread at a constant rate:

Labour Hours Needed to Make 1 unit of

	Cheese	Bread
England	1	4
Spain	4	8

Assume that England and Spain each has 40 labour hours available. If each country divides its time equally between the production of cheese and bread, then total production is:
A. 20 units of cheese and 5 units of bread
B. 25 units of cheese and 7.5 units of bread
C. 40 units of cheese and 10 units of bread
D. 50 units of cheese and 15 units of bread

9. Fisher's quantity theory is explained by his famous equation of exchange is given as:
A. MV = PT B. MP = VT
C. MT = PV D. None of these

10. Which of the following is included in Indian GDP?
A. The value of production by a Singaporean working in India
B. The value of production by an Indian working in Singapore

*Exam held on 4-07-2017.

C. Both A and B are correct
D. Neither A nor B is correct

11. The economy's inflation rate is the:
A. Price level in the current period
B. Change in the price level from the previous period
C. Change in the gross domestic product from the previous period
D. Percentage change in the price level from the previous period

12. Which among the following assets is the most liquid?
A. Corporate bonds
B. Fine art
C. Deposits that can be withdrawn using ATMs
D. Shares of stock

13. During a recession the economy experiences:
A. Rising employment and income
B. Rising employment and falling income
C. Rising income and falling employment
D. Falling employment and income

14. Appreciation in domestic currency leads to:
A. No effect on imports
B. No effect on exports
C. Fall in imports
D. Fall in exports

15. Other things the same, as the real interest rate falls:
A. Domestic investment and net capital outflow both rise
B. Domestic investment and net capital outflow both fall
C. Domestic investment rises and net capital outflow falls
D. Domestic investment falls and net capital outflow rises

16. RBI was fully owned by the Government in the year:
A. 1959 B. 1969
C. 1965 D. 1949

17. Narsimham Committee recommended to make banking structure of the country:
A. Two tier B. Three tier
C. Four tier D. Five tier

18. Tenancy reforms include measures like:
A. Regulation of rent
B. Cooperative farming
C. Abolition of intermediaries
D. Redistribution of land

19. Open market operation is a part of:
A. Income policy B. Fiscal policy
C. Credit policy D. Labour policy

20. Current account deficit for the year 2015-16 as a percentage of GDP is:
A. 4.8 B. 3.2
C. 2.5 D. 1.1

21. 8th BRICS summit took place on 15-16 October in:
A. Goa, India B. Ufa, Russia
C. Fortaleza, Brazil D. New Delhi, India

22. Blue revolution is related to:
A. Oil production B. Fish production
C. Grass production D. Food production

23. Which of the following is not the member of SAARC?
A. Nepal B. Afghanistan
C. Myanmar D. Bhutan

24. The Ad-valorem is a tax on the basis of:
A. The value of the commodity
B. The volume of the commodity
C. Value and volume of the commodity
D. None of the above

25. The chairman of NITI Aayog is:
A. Shri Arvind Panagariya
B. Shri Narendra Modi
C. Shri Bibek Debroy
D. Shri V.K. Saraswat

26. Let the probability of event A be 0.3 and the probability of event B be 0.5. Also assume that the two events are independent. Then P(A/B) will be equal to:
A. 0.5 B. 0.3
C. 0.15 D. 0.6

27. The arithmetic mean of a set of 10 numbers is 25. If each number is first multiplied by 3

and then increased by 5, what is the mean of new numbers?
A. 25 B. 30
C. 75 D. 80

28. Which of the following approaches to probability would be used to find out probability of rolling two sixes with two dice?
A. Classical approach
B. Relative frequency approach
C. Subjective approach
D. Independence approach

29. Which of the following is a continuous random variable?
A. The number of questions answered correctly in a 50-question multiple choice exam
B. Gender of the customer while selling an automobile
C. The thickness of a metal sheet used in a production process
D. Number of returns containing error in an audit of 100 tax returns

30. The difference between 'expected payoff under perfect information' and 'expected payoff under optimal action' is called:
A. Expected payoff
B. Expected regret
C. Expected value of perfect information
D. Expected value of regret

31. If the coefficient of determination for a problem involving one dependent variable (Y) and one independent variable (X) is 0.65, it implies which of the following?
A. 65% of the total variation in Y is explained by X
B. 65% of the total variation in X is explained by Y
C. The coefficient of correlation is 0.65
D. The relationship between the two variables is negative

32. To compare the variation/spread of data sets that have different units, we use which of the following?
A. Standard deviation
B. Range
C. Variance
D. Coefficient of variation

33. Which of the following is *not* a property of the normal distribution?
A. Normal distribution is unimodal
B. Mean lies at the centre of the normal curve
C. Mean is twice the value of the median
D. Two tails of the normal distribution never touch the horizontal axis

34. Which of the following indicates the strongest relationship between two variables?
A. $r = 0.08$ B. $r = -0.7$
C. $r^2 = 0.35$ D. $r = 0.6$

35. While computing a weighed index, the current period quantities are used in the:
A. Laspeyre's method
B. Paasche's method
C. Marshall Edgeworth method
D. None of these

36. In time series theory, the shortage of certain consumer goods just before the annual budget will be referred to as:
A. Seasonal variation
B. Cyclical variation
C. Secular trend
D. Irregular variation

37. A numerical value computed from a sample is called:
A. Parameter B. Error
C. Bias D. Statistic

38. Which of the following is a random sampling technique?
A. Convenience sampling
B. Judgment sampling
C. Systematic sampling
D. None of these

39. Which of the following is a special case of LPP:
A. Assignment Model
B. Transportation Model
C. Both A and B
D. None of these

40. The curve

$$y = 2x^3 - 15x^2 - 36x + 16$$

has a local maximum at which value of x

A. $x = \frac{5}{2}$ B. $x = 6$

C. $x = -1$ D. $x = 2$

41. If a young man rides his motorcycle at 25 km/hour, he had to spend ₹ 2 per km on petrol. If he rides at a faster speed of 40 km/hour, the petrol that increases at ₹ 5 per km. He has ₹ 100 to spend on petrol and he wishes to maximise the distance travelled in one hour. What shall be optional combination?

A. (0, 25) B. (40, 0)

C. $\left(\frac{50}{3}, \frac{40}{3}\right)$ D. $\left(\frac{25}{3}, 40\right)$

42. Suppose that the demand equation for a certain product is

$$p = 100 - 0.2x$$

(p is the price and x is the number of items sold at that price) and the cast function is

$$C(x) = 4x + 3000.$$

Find the value of x that maximizes the profit:

A. 96 B. 0.4

C. 24 D. 240

43. Function with general form

$$y = f(x) = \frac{g(x)}{h(x)}$$

is form of function called:

A. Marginal function

B. Rational function

C. Irrational function

D. Polynomial function

44. The demand function of a commodity is given by

$$p = 100 - 8x$$

The consumer's surplus corresponding to $p = 4$ is:

A. 627 B. 575

C. 578 D. 576

45. $f(x) = \sin(x)$ is:

A. Linear function B. Quadratic function

C. Odd function D. Even function

46. If the marginal revenue function of a firm is $R(x) = 10 - 6x$, what shall be total revenue function?

A. $10x + 3x^2$ B. 6

C. $10x - 3x^2$ D. -6

47. Find compound interest (in ₹) on ₹ 7,500 at 4% per annum for 2 years, compounded annually:

A. 312 B. 412

C. 512 D. 612

48. If A is a skew symmetric matrix, then A^t :

A. $-A$ B. A

C. 0 D. Diagonal matrix

49. Accumulated series of deposits as future sum of money is classified as:

A. Marginal fund B. Nominal fund

C. Sinking fund D. Annuity fund

50. If

$$A = \begin{bmatrix} 5 & 3 & 2 \\ 0 & 4 & 1 \\ 0 & 0 & 3 \end{bmatrix}$$

then $|A| = ?$

A. 30 B. 40

C. 50 D. 60

51. Any change in the accounting policy relating to inventories which has an effect in the current or later period should be disclosed. This is in accordance with the Accounting Principle of:

A. Going Concern B. Conservatism

C. Consistency D. Materiality

52. X and Y share profits and losses in the ratio of 2 : 1. They admit Z in the firm with 3/7 share which he gets 2/7 from X and 1/7 from Y. The new profit sharing ratio wouls be:

A. 8 : 4 : 9 B. 7 : 3 : 3

C. 1 : 2 : 3 D. 5 : 2 : 3

53. Accumulated Losses refer to:

A. Profit and Loss Account (Dr. Balance)

B. Preliminary Expenses (to the extent not written off)
C. Discount on issue of shares
D. All of the above

54. A firm has ₹ 40,000 as its annual profits with the rate of normal profit as 10%. The assets of the firm are with ₹ 2,80,000 and liabilities are worth ₹ 1,50,000. Calculate the value of goodwill by capitalisation method:
A. ₹ 1,80,000 B. ₹ 2,70,000
C. ₹ 1,70,000 D. None of these

55. Provision for bad and doubtful debts is created in anticipation of expected bad debts on the basis of:
A. Conservatism principle
B. Going concern principle
C. Disclosure principle
D. None of these

56. From the information given below, calculate the interest to be paid:

Cash price = ₹ 2,00,000

Down Payment = ₹ 20,000

Balance to be paid in three equal instalments of ₹ 60,000 each plus interest @10% p.a.
A. ₹ 36,000 B. ₹ 18,000
C. ₹ 20,000 D. None of these

57. Which of the following is treated as unrecorded liability?
A. A bill discounted with bank dishonoured
B. Payment of outstanding bill
C. Settlement of dispute against the firm
D. None of the above

58. A company may purchase its own shares out of:
A. General reserves and securities premium account
B. Revaluation reserve
C. Debenture redemption reserve
D. None of the above

59. A company purchases from market its own 400, 10% Debentures of ₹ 100 each at ₹ 90 on 31st December, 2015. Calculate the amount paid exclusively for the Debentures if quotations are ex-interest. Debenture interest is paid on 31st March and 30th September every year.
A. ₹ 36,000 B. ₹ 37,000
C. ₹ 38,000 D. None of these

60. Reconstruction Account can be utilized:
A. to write off Provision for doubtful debt
B. to write off Preliminary Expenses
C. to write of Deferred Revenue Expenditure
D. All of the above

61. Financial Ratios are used to:
A. Calculate Profit
B. Determine the Dividend of the Company
C. Calculate relationship between Current Assets and Current Liabilities
D. Assess the financial health of the Company

62. When the liquidation expenses are paid and borne by the transferor the following entry needs to be passed in the books of the transferor company:
A. Realisation Expenses Account Dr
To Bank Account
B. Transferee Company Account Dr
To Bank Account
C. Bank Account Dr
To Transferee Company Account
D. None of the above

63. Issue of shares for purchase of machinery is shown under which heading while preparing Cash Flow Statement as per AS-3?
A. Cash flow from Operating Activity
B. Cash flow from Investing Activity
C. Cash flow from Financing Activity
D. None of the above

64. How much amount will be credited to Capital Reserve Account if 200 shares of ₹ 10 each are forfeited on which ₹ 8 per share has been called and only ₹ 2 per share has been paid, reissued at ₹ 9 per share as fully paid up:
A. ₹ 300 B. ₹ 100
C. ₹ 200 D. ₹ 400

65. Calculate the amount of Current Liability from the following information:

Current Ratio is 2.8 : 1

Acid Test Ratio is 1.5 : 1
Working Capital = ₹ 1,62,000
A. ₹ 70,000 B. ₹ 80,000
C. ₹ 90,000 D. ₹ 96,000

66. Profit under absorption costing will be higher than under marginal costing if:
A. Produced units > Units sold
B. Produced units < Units sold
C. Produced units = Units sold
D. Profit cannot be determined with given statement

67. The FIFO inventory costing method (when using a perpetual inventory system) assumes that the cost of the earliest units purchased is allocated in which of the following ways?
A. First to be allocated to the ending inventory
B. Last to be allocated to the cost of goods sold
C. Last to be allocated to the ending inventory
D. First to be allocated to the cost of goods to sold

68. Standard costing implies:
A. The use of the previous year's actual figure as the Standard
B. The use of pre-determined levels of price and performance as Standard
C. The use of Fixed Budgeting
D. The use of idle costs which are useful to control aid

69. If a company uses a pre-determined rate for absorbing factory overhead, the Volume variance is the:
A. Under applied or over applied variable cost element of factory overhead
B. Under applied or over applied Fixed cost element of factory overhead
C. Difference in Budgeted cost and Actual costs of fixed factory overhead items
D. Difference in Budgeted cost and Actual costs of Variable factory overhead items

70. Which method of accounting for by-product allocates a portion of joint cost to the by-product?
A. Net Realizable Method
B. Reversal Cost Method
C. Both A and B
D. None of the above

71. In Activity Based Costing systems, costs are accumulated by activity using:
A. Cost drivers
B. Cost centres
C. Cost pools
D. Cost benefit analysis

72. A firm previously calculated Product costs using Absorption costing, but now uses activity based costing (ABC). What feature of the product costs calculation remains the same?
A. Overhead Absorption rates for manufacturing overheads
B. Prime cost
C. Overhead absorption rates for support functions
D. The classification of Fixed and Variable costs

73. A department may be used to make and sell a product which will earn a contribution of ₹ 20,000. If it is not used to produce a component for internal use, into which classification should the ₹ 20,000 be categorized?
A. An avoidable cost of the company
B. An opportunity cost of the company
C. An irrelevant cost for decision making
D. An unavoidable positive cash inflow

74. Economic order quantity is that quantity at which cost of ordering and carrying inventory is:
A. Equal
B. Minimum and equal
C. It can be maximum or minimum depending upon case to case
D. Minimum and unequal

75. Which one of the following would *not* be revealed by company cash flow statement?
A. Whether the Company has paid Dividend during the year

B. How the company has managed the working capital over the last financial year
C. Whether the company has exceeded its overdraft limit during the year
D. Whether the company has raised extra long term funding over the year

76. The process of setting goals and deciding how best to achieve them is called:
A. Organizing B. Planning
C. Controlling D. All of these

77. The term leading reflects:
A. Process of influencing others to engage in the work behaviours necessary to reach organizations goals
B. Process of assigning duties to individuals to achieve specified ends effectively
C. Process of centralizing the authority in the hands of an individual to achieve business ends
D. None of the above

78. .... representative of the organizations to reach to conclusion:
A. Manager B. Negotiator
C. Entrepreneur D. All of these

79. .... are skills associated with a manager's ability to work well with others:
A. Human skills
B. Technical skills
C. Conceptual skills
D. None of these

80. Henry Gantt was a close associate of:
A. Henry Fayol B. Peter Drucker
C. FW Taylor D. Elton Mayo

81. The specification of task activities associated with a particular job is known as:
A. Job design
B. Work specialisation
C. Job description
D. All of these

82. A structure that superimposes a horizontal set of divisional reporting relationships onto hierarchical functional structure:
A. Functional Structure
B. Divisional Structure
C. Matrix Structure
D. Hybrid Structure

83. Physiological Needs are as much same as Existence Needs. Who are known for these theories?
A. Maslow and McClelland
B. Maslow and Alderfer
C. McClelland and Alderfer
D. Maslow, Alderfer and McClelland

84. Piece Wage provides:
A. Encouragement to efficient hard workers
B. Discouragement to efficient hard workers
C. Fair compensation to dull employees
D. None of the above

85. Job Analysis should always be done:
A. at the time of placement
B. after recruitment
C. before recruitment
D. None of these

86. In which of the following cases an agreement of a person shall be void?
A. Coercion
B. Fraud
C. Unsoundness of mind
D. Undue influence

87. Which of the following does *not* constitute bailment?
A. Parking car in parking area and giving key to the carataker
B. Placing jewellery in bank locker
C. Handing over goods to an agent for a customer
D. Seizure of goods of a trader by police

88. If before the due date of performance, the promisor refuses to perform the promise, it is known as:
A. ineffective breach of contract
B. contingent breach of contract
C. actual breach of contract
D. anticipatory breach of contract

89. Which of the following is *not* an exception to the rule that an agreement without consideration is void?

A. A promise to compensate for a voluntary act
B. A promise of gift out of natural love and affection
C. A promise of donation in writing
D. A promise to pay a time-barred debt

90. In case of breach of contract, which of the following remedies is *not* available to the aggrieved party?
A. Suit for punishment
B. Suit for damages
C. Suit for specific performance
D. Suit for rescission

91. Which of the following is *true*?
A. If a seller breaks a condition of the contract of sale, the buyer is entitled to cancel the contract
B. A buyer can become the owner of goods without having paid the price
C. If the unpaid seller sells the goods to a third party without serving notice to the first buyer, the sale is valid
D. The subject-matter of the contract of sale of goods, *i.e.*, the goods, must be movable and tangible

92. An unpaid seller of goods cannot exercise which of the following rights upon the buyer's goods:
A. Right of lien
B. Right of resale
C. Right of pledge
D. Right of stoppage in transit

93. A person who is ordered to pay the amount of bill of exchange is known as:
A. drawer B. drawee
C. payee D. acceptor

94. The maximum number of partners now permitted in India under the Limited Liability Partnership Act, 2008:
A. 50 B. 100
C. 20 D. None of these

95. Which of the following can be altered by an ordinary resolution?
A. Articles of association
B. Objects clause
C. Situation clause
D. None of the above

96. As per Sec 2(31) of Income Tax Act a 'Person' includes:
A. An Individual
B. A Hindu Undivided Family (HUF)
C. A Company
D. All of the above

97. Mr. Andrew, an Australian cricketer has been coming to India for 100 days every year since 2002-03. For the Assessment year 2015-16, he is:
A. Resident and ordinarily resident in India
B. Resident but not ordinarily resident in India
C. Non-Resident
D. Both A and B

98. Which income(s) of a minor child is/are not clubbed in the income of parent?
A. Any income of minor child suffering from disability
B. Income which accrue or arise to a minor child on account of application of his skills
C. Both A and B
D. None of the above

99. Which of the following is a non-agricultural income?
A. Income from breeding of livestock
B. Income from growing of flowers and creepers
C. Lease income derived by a lessor from lease of a coconut garden
D. All of the above

100. An assessee who has no income from business or profession will not be required to pay advance tax if the said assessee is a/an:
A. Firm
B. Senior citizen
C. Association of person (AOP)
D. Indian company

ANSWERS

1	2	3	4	5	6	7	8	9	10
B	B	C	A	D	B	B	B	A	A
11	**12**	**13**	**14**	**15**	**16**	**17**	**18**	**19**	**20**
D	C	D	D	A	D	*	A	C	D
21	**22**	**23**	**24**	**25**	**26**	**27**	**28**	**29**	**30**
A	B	C	A	B	B	D	A	C	C
31	**32**	**33**	**34**	**35**	**36**	**37**	**38**	**39**	**40**
A	D	C	B	B	A	D	C	C	C
41	**42**	**43**	**44**	**45**	**46**	**47**	**48**	**49**	**50**
C	D	B	D	C	C	D	A	C	D
51	**52**	**53**	**54**	**55**	**56**	**57**	**58**	**59**	**60**
C	A	A	B	A	A	C	A	B	D
61	**62**	**63**	**64**	**65**	**66**	**67**	**68**	**69**	**70**
D	A	D	C	C	A	D	B	B	C
71	**72**	**73**	**74**	**75**	**76**	**77**	**78**	**79**	**80**
C	B	B	B	C	B	A	B	A	C
81	**82**	**83**	**84**	**85**	**86**	**87**	**88**	**89**	**90**
A	C	B	A	C	C	*	D	*	A
91	**92**	**93**	**94**	**95**	**96**	**97**	**98**	**99**	**100**
D	C	B	D	D	D	B	C	A	B

*** Error in Question Paper.**

EXPLANATORY ANSWERS

1. Total utility is different from marginal utility. Marginal utility is the *additional* utility gained from consuming an additional unit of good *X*. Marginal utility (MU) is the change in total utility (ΔTU) divided by the change in the quantity (ΔQ) consumed of a good:

$$MU = \frac{\Delta TU}{\Delta Q}.$$

2. According to Benham, "The opportunity cost of anything is the next best alternative could be produced instead by the same factors or by an equivalent group of factors, costing the same amount of money." According to W.W. Haynes, "Opportunity cost of a decision means the sacrifice of alternatives required by that decision." Opportunity cost means the cost of foregone opportunities. Opportunity of a product or service means the revenue expected to be earned by the product or service if put to an alternative use. W.W. Haynes has clarified the meaning of the concept of opportunity cost with the help of following examples:

- The opportunity cost of the funds tied up in one's own business in the interest (or profits corrected for differences in risk) that could be earned on those funds in other ventures.
- The opportunity cost of the item one puts into his own business is the salary he could earn in other occupations (with a correction

for the relative 'psychic income' in the two occupations).

- The opportunity cost of using a machine to produce one product is the sacrifice of earnings that would be possible from other products.
- The opportunity cost of using a machine that is useless for any other purpose is nil, since its use requires no sacrifice of other opportunities.

From the above examples, it is clear that opportunity cost requires the measurement of sacrifies. If there is no sacrifice involved by a decision, there will be no opportunity cost. Through the opportunity cost is not recorded in the books of accounts, it is an important consideration in business decisions.

3. Law of diminishing returns refers to a situation in which total output increases at the diminishing rate when more of the variable factor is combined with the fixed factor(s) of production. In such a situation, marginal product of the variable factor must be diminishing.

4. Marginal Revenue is the net addition to the total revenue when an additional unit of a commodity is sold. It is calculated as under:

$$MR = TR_n - TR_{n-1}$$

Relationship: When marginal revenue falls but remains positive, total revenue increases.

- When marginal revenue is zero, total revenue is maximum.
- When marginal revenue becomes negative, total revenue starts declining.
- When AR falls, MR is less than AR.
- When AR is constant, MR is equal to AR.
- When AR rises, MR remains above AR.

AR and MR curves are horizontally straight lines in case of perfect competition. Whereas they are downward sloping curves under imperfect market situations.

AR curve has a steep slope under monopoly. But the firm under monopolistic competition faces an elastic average revenue curve.

5. A firm both under perfect competition and monopoly is in equilibrium at the level of output at which MR equals MC. That is, in both markets, equilibrium is established by the equality of MR and MC.

Since in perfect competition the MR curve is a horizontal straight line, MC curve can cut the MR curve from below only when it (MC curve) is rising. We get the equilibrium point where MC curve cuts the MR curve fulfilling both the conditions of equilibrium, viz., MC = MR and the slope of MC > the slope of MR. This is possible only when MC curve is rising.

But, under monopoly, MR curve is falling downward. MC curve can cut the MR curve from below whether it (MC curve) is rising or horizontal to establish the equilibrium point satisfying both the conditions of equilibrium.

6. **Value of Marginal Product:** VMP is the value of the additional product due to the employment of an additional unit of the variable factor, all other factors remaining the same. We can write VMP = MPP × P_x.

7. **Income Elasticity of Demand:** Income elasticity of demand measures the change in the quantity demanded of a product given a change in income. Income elasticity is calculated as follows:

$$E_i = \frac{\text{Percentage change in quantity demanded}}{\text{Percentage change in income}}$$

The income elasticity of demand can be used to describe the nature of the product. The demand for normal products increases as consumer income increases. For example, the demand for normal goods, such as beefsteaks, increases as consumer income increases. Therefore, E_i for beefsteaks is positive. The demand for inferior goods, such as beans, decreases as income increases, E_i is negative. The demand for inferior goods increases as income declines, because when individuals have less money they substitute these less expensive goods for normal goods.

8. England produces 20 units of cheese from 20 labour hours 5 units of bread from 20 labour hours and Spain produces 5 units of cheese from 20 labour hours and 2.5 units of bread from 20 labour hours.

9. The views of classical economists like Jean Bodin, Richard Cantillon, John Locke, David Hume, Adam Smith and William Petty, are collectively called as the Classical theory of inflation. The cornerstone of the classical theory of inflation is the Classical quantity theory of money.

The first simple version of the classical theory of inflation was propounded by Irving Fisher in his book *The Purchasing Power of Money*, in 1911. According to this theory, the price level depends directly and proportionately on the supply of money. To him, inflation occurs when the quantity of money increases and comes to a halt when the quantity of money becomes stable. This is the quantity theorist's explanation of the inflationary process.

According to Fisher's quantity theory

$$MV = PT$$

and therefore $P = \frac{MV}{T}$.

10. GDP or National Income: GDP means Gross Domestic Product. Growth of a country is decided on the basis of GDP. It is total money value of all final goods and services produced by a country (residents and non-residents) within its geographical boundaries during a given period. GDP is measured at production stage or consumption stage.

11. Economists use the term *inflation* to describe a situation in which the economy's overall price level is rising. The *inflation rate* is the percentage change in the price level from the previous period.

13. A recession is a general slowdown in economic activity spread across the economy, lasting more than a few months. Conventionally, recession is defined as a situation of fall in Gross Domestic Product (GDP) for two quarters in succession, *i.e.*, the economy experiences a negative growth rate for a period of 6 months or more.

During recession various macroeconomic variables like real GDP, real income, employment, investment, incomes of the households, business profit, industrial production and sales, all fall. Aggregate demand falls, and as a result production and employment also fall. A fall in employment leads to fall in personal incomes. Profits fall, resulting in fall in investment. Lower profitability and lower dividends make investment in shares less attractive. As a consequence, share prices fall. In many cases, recession is associated with financial crisis. Financial crisis occurs when households or firms or banks are unable to meet their debts. There is a crisis of confidence and the demand for liquidity (cash) increases all of a sudden.

18. Land reforms are generally defined in the sense of land appropriation and redistribution and other accompanying measures. The scope of land reforms includes:

- Abolition of intermediaries.
- Tenancy reforms which include: (*i*) regulation of rent, (*ii*) security of tenure for tenants, and (*iii*) conferment of ownership on them.
- Ceiling on land holdings.
- Agrarian reorganisation including consolidation of holdings and prevention of sub-division and fragmentation.
- Organisation of cooperative farms.

19. Instruments of Monetary Policy: Roughly we may say that monetary policy is credit control policy. The instruments of credit control can be broadly divided into:

- Quantitative credit control measures; and
- Qualitative credit control measures.

Quantitative credit control instruments include bank rate policy; variation of cash reserve ratios and open market operations.

Bank Rate: The Bank rate is the minimum rate at which the central bank of a country will lend money to all other banks. Suppose, there is too much of money in circulation. Then the central bank should take some money out of circulation. It can do it by increasing the bank rate. When the bank rate goes up, the rates charged by other banks go up. The belief is that if the rate of interest goes up, businessmen will be discouraged to borrow more money and producers will borrow less money for investment. Generally, to control inflation, the central bank will increase the bank rate.

Variation of Cash Reserve Ratios: The ability of a commercial bank to create credit depends upon its cash reserves. The central bank of a country has the power to vary the cash reserve ratios. During inflation, to check the sharp rise in commodity prices and to control credit, the central bank can make use of this weapon.

Open Market Operations: In India, the open market operations have been conducted in Central Government securities and State Government securities. The success of open market operations as a weapon of credit control, depends mainly on (*i*) the possession by the central bank of adequate volume of securities; (*ii*) the presence of well developed bill (securities) market; and (*iii*) stability of cash reserve ratios maintained by commercial banks. These things are missing to a great degree in India. So, open market operations have not become a powerful weapon of credit control in our country. They have been largely used in India more to assist the Government in its borrowing operations rather than controlling credit.

Qualitative Credit Control: The qualitative methods of credit control aim at diverting the bank advances into certain productive functions from unproductive functions. These methods are also known as selective methods of credit control. These methods are as under:

- **Direct Action:** Section 21 of the Banking Regulation Act, 1949 empowers the RBI to issue directives to the banking companies regarding their advances. These directives may relate to:
  - ❑ The purpose for which advances may or may not be made.
  - ❑ The margins to be maintained in respect of secured advances.
  - ❑ The maximum amount of advance to any borrower.
  - ❑ The rate of interest and other terms and conditions for granting advances.
- **Credit Authorisation Scheme:** Under this scheme the commercial banks have to obtain RBI's authorisation before granting any fresh credit of ₹ 1 crore or more to any single party.
- **Moral Suasion:** The RBI periodically sends lettters to the commercial banks to use restraint over their credit policies in general and in respect to certain commodities and unsecured loans in particular.

22. Important Revolutions in Agriculture:

Green Revolution	Agro production
White Revolution	Milk production
Blue Revolution	Fish production
Pink Revolution	Shrimp production
Yellow Revolution	Sunflower and oil seeds resources
Brown Revolution	Non-conventional energy resources
Red Revolution	Tomato production

Silver Revolution	Egg production
Golden Revolution	Fruits production
Rainbow Revolution	Agriculture related wholesome development.

23. The South Asian Association for Regional Cooperation (SAARC) is an organization of South Asian nations, founded in 1985 and dedicated to economic, technological, social, and cultural development emphasizing collective self-reliance. Its seven founding members are Bangladesh, Bhutan, India, the Maldives, Nepal, Pakistan and Sri Lanka. Afghanistan joined the organization in 2007. Meetings of heads of state are usually scheduled annually, meetings of foreign secretaries, twice annually. Headquarters are in Kathmandu, Nepal.

- The concept of SAARC was first adopted by Bangladesh during 1977, under the administration of President Ziaur Rahman.
- Afghanistan was added to the regional grouping on 13 November 2005.
- On 2 August, 2006 the foreign ministers of the SAARC countries agreed in principle to grant observer status to the US, South Korea and the European Union.
- The SAARC Secretariat was established in Kathmandu on 16 January, 1986 and was inaugurated by Late King Birendra Bir Bikram Shah of Nepal.
- The SAARC Secretariat and Member States observe 8 December as the SAARC Charter Day 1.

24. Specific and Ad-valorem Taxes: On the basis of the assessment, taxes on commodities may be classified into two categories, *viz.*, Specific tax and Ad-valorem tax.

- **Specific Tax:** Taxes which are levied on the basis of specific qualities or attributes, such as weight, size, volume, etc., are called specific taxes. For instance, taxes are imposed on sugar according to the weight, and taxes on refrigerators may be imposed on the basis of their size.
- **Ad-valorem Tax:** Taxes which are imposed according to the value of the commodity are known as ad valorem taxes. For instance, the import duty in many cases is levied on the value of goods imported like 20 per cent of the value of goods imported.

25. NITI Aayog Replaces Planning Commission: 65-year-old Planning Commission has been dissolved and a new institution named NITI Aayog has been constituted by the National Democratic Alliance (NDA) government. Like Planning Commission the newly established NITI Aayog will also be chaired by the Prime Minister. NITI Aayog or National Institution for Transforming India will serve as a government think tank and is meant to reflect changes required in India's governance structures and provide a more active role for the state governments in achieving national objectives. The newly constituted institution will provide governments at the central and state levels with strategic and technical advice across the spectrum of policy making. As per official declaration, this institution includes matters of national and international import on the economic front, dissemination of best practices from within the country as well as from other nations, the infusion of new policy ideas and specific issue-based support. NITI Aayog will be headed by the Prime Minister, who will be the chairperson. The Prime Minister will appoint a vice-chairperson and a chief executive officer (CEO). The CEO will be appointed for a fixed tenure; it will be a secretary-level position. The organization will have full-time members and up to two part-time members from leading universities, research organizations and other relevant institutions. It will also have up to four ex-officio members from the Union Council of ministers who will be nominated by the Prime

Minister. While this will be the full-time organizational structure, the new institution will also comprise a governing council which will include state chief ministers and lieutenant governors of Union Territories.

26. Conditional probability: The *conditional probability* of event A given that event B has already occurred is written as P(A|B). Similarly, we may write P (B|A). The vertical bar is read as 'given' and events appearing to the right of the bar are those that have already occurred. To events A and B are said to be independent if and only P(A|B) = P(A) or P(B|A) = P(B). Otherwise, events are said to be dependent.

Here, P(A) = 0.3, P(B) = 0.5

∴ P(A|B) = P(A) = 0.3.

27. If average of some numbers is x and a constant number a

(*a*) Added to each term of the series, then new average = $x + a$

(*b*) Subtracted from each term of the series, then new average = $x - a$

(*c*) Multiplied with each term of the series, then new average = ax

(*d*) Divides each term of the series, then new average = $x \div a$

Mean of New Numbers

$= (25 \times 3) + 5$

$= 75 + 5 = 80.$

28. There are three basic methods for assigning probabilities—they are known as the Classical, Relative Frequency, and Subjective methods. The approach that we use depends on the circumstances of the particular activity we're conducting.

- The *Classical* method applies if we know and can list the possible outcomes of an activity, and we can assume that all basic outcomes share the same likelihood. If there are n equally likely outcomes, then the probability of each outcome is $1/n$. Among other things, the classical method is applicable to games of chance (like card games) and to activities like simple random sampling.
- Computations using classical probabilities often refer to events that can happen in multiple ways. So, for example, when rolling two dice, we can think of the elementary outcomes for each die as being the six distinct faces. In dice games, we sum the spots on the two dice. In the context of the game, the events of interest—rolling a seven, or doubles, or eleven—are not equally likely, but the fundamental outcomes for each die do share the same probability of 1/6.
- The *Relative Frequency* method applies to situations in which we know and can list the possible outcomes, but cannot assume that the outcomes are equally likely. This method relies on empirical observation of a large number of repetitions of the situation, and then computing relative frequencies. Observing dolphin behaviour is one such situation. Other examples include rates of disease incidence, batting averages, and college graduation rates.
- The *Subjective* method applies to situations in which we lack information about possible outcomes or their relative frequency or both. In such instances, expert opinion form the basis for probability assignments. Problems requiring expert opinion are beyound the scope of an introductory course, and will receive no further attention here.

30. The highest expected profits resulting in the presence of perfect predictor is called the expected payoffs of perfect information (EPPI). EPPI is often called the expected value of payoff under certainty. The perfect prediction reduces the opportunity losses due to uncertainty to zero. The highest payoff in the absence of perfect predictor is EP of the optimal action. The difference between EPPI and EP is called the expected value of perfect information (abbreviated EVPI). EVPI represents the maximum amount of money which a decision-maker could spend to obtain additional information regarding the states of nature. It may be noted that EVPI is always equal to the EOL of selecting the optimum action under uncertainty. The identity EP + EOL = EPPI follows from the result EVPI = EPPI – EP.

31. The coefficient of determination r^2 is a measure of the proportion of variation in *y* that is explained by the regression line, using *x* as the explanatory variable. Here $r^2 = 0.65$ is the coefficient of determination. We can say that about 65% of the (variation) behaviour of the *y* variable can be explained by the corresponding (variation) behaviour of the *x* variable if we use the equation of the least-squares line. The remaining 25% of the (variation) behaviour of the *y* variable is due to random chance or to the possibility of lurking variables that influence *y*.

32. Coefficient of Variation Formula: The coefficient of variation, CV, is the ratio of the standard deviation of a set of observations to their mean value:

$$CV = \frac{s}{\overline{X}}$$

Where *s* is the sample standard deviation and $\overline{X}$ is the sample mean.

Expressing the magnitude of variation among observations relative to their average size, the coefficient of variation permits direct comparisons of dispersion across different data sets. Reflecting the correction for scale, the coefficient of variation is a scale-free measure (that is, it has no units of measurement).

33. Characteristic of Normal Distribution: The diagram of a normal distribution is given below. It is called normal curve. It suggests several important properties of the normal distribution.

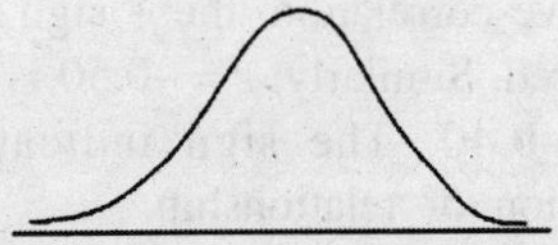

1. The normal distribution is a symmetrical distribution and the graph of the normal distribution is bell shaped.
2. The curve has a single peak point, *i.e.*, the distribution is unimodal.
3. The mean of the normal distribution lies at the centre of normal curve.
4. Because of the symmetry of the normal curve, the median and mode are also at the centre of the normal curve. Hence in a normal distribution the mean, median and mode coincide.
5. The tails of the normal distribution extend indefinitely and never touch the horizontal axes. That is, we say that the normal curve approaches symptotically on either side of its horizontal axes.
6. The normal distribution is a two parameter probability distribution. The parameters mean and standard deviation (μ, σ) completely determine the distribution.

34. Correlation Coefficient: It can be seen that bivariate analysis is a simple (two variable) variant of multivariate analysis (where multiple relations among multiple variables are examined simultaneously). The degree of the relationship between these two variables is presented through a measurement called a *correlation coefficient,* which is represented by *r*. Hence, *r* = +1 symbolizes a perfect positive relationship, *r* = –1 symbolizes a perfect negative relationship, and *r* = 0 indicates the absence of any relationship. Therefore, *r* can vary between –1 and +1, the extremes of a perfect relationship. As the *r* value approaches 0, the strength of the relationship decreases.

The magnitude or strength of a relationship is indicated by its size. For example, *r* = 0.8 denotes a stronger relationship than a value less than 0.80, such as 0.70, 0.60 or 0.50. For positive correlation, the + sign is not always required. Similarly, $r = -0.50$ is stronger than $r = -0.40$. The sign indicates only the direction of relationship.

35. Paasche's Method: This is a method for finding weighted index numbers. In this method, current period quantities (q_1) are used as weights.

If P_{01} is the required index number for the current period, then

$$P_{01} = \frac{\Sigma p_1 q_1}{\Sigma p_0 q_1} \times 100$$

Where p_0, p_1 represents prices per unit of commodities in the base period and current period respectively.

38. A systematic sample is the sampling technique that is closest to simple random sampling in nature. A systematic sample is generally defined as an interval sampling approach.

39. Transportation model: A special case of linear programming which matches sources of supply to destinations on cost or distance considerations. For example, movement of raw materials for different sources to manufacturing plants at different locations based on availability of raw materials at various sources, the requirements at different plants and the cost of transportation involved.

Assignment model: A special case of transportation model where the aim is to assign a number of 'origins' to the same number of destinations at a minimum total cost. For example, assigning of men/machines to same number of jobs/tasks.

40. For maximum

$$\frac{dy}{dx} = 6x^2 - 30x - 36 = 0$$

$$\Rightarrow \quad 6x^2 - (36x - 6x) - 36 = 0$$

$$\Rightarrow \quad 6x(x + 1) - 36(x + 1) = 0$$

$$\Rightarrow \quad (6x - 36)(x + 1) = 0$$

$$\Rightarrow \quad x = 6 \text{ or } -1$$

For maximum

$$\frac{d^2y}{dx^2} < 0$$

$$\therefore \quad 12x - 30 < 0$$

$$\text{At } x = -1, \quad \frac{d^2y}{dx^2} < 0.$$

41. Maximize $z = x + y$, $2x + 5y \leq 100$,

$8x + 5y \leq 200$ Maximum distance = 30 km,

at 25 km/h, $\frac{50}{3}$ km and at 40 km/h $\frac{40}{3}$ km.

42.

$$TR = px = (100 - 0.2x)x$$

$$= 100x - 0.2x^2$$

$$\text{Profit (P)} = TR - TC$$

$$\frac{dP}{dx} = 100x - 0.2x^2 - 4x - 3000$$

$$= 100 - 0.4x - 4 = 0$$

$$96 = 0.4x$$

$$x = \frac{96}{0.4} = \frac{96}{4} \times 10 = 240.$$

46. Given, $\quad MR = 10 - 6x$

$$\text{Then, } \quad \frac{d(TR)}{dx} = 10 - 6x$$

Integrating with sides w.r.t. x, we have

$$TR = \int (10 - 6x)dx$$

$$= 10x - \frac{6x^2}{2}$$

$$= 10x - 3x^2.$$

47.

$$\text{Amount} = ₹\left[7500 \times \left(\frac{1+4}{100}\right)^2\right]$$

$$= ₹\left(7500 \times \frac{26}{25} \times \frac{26}{25}\right)$$

$$= ₹\ (8112 - 7500)$$

$$= ₹\ 612.$$

50. $$A = \begin{bmatrix} 5 & 3 & 2 \\ 0 & 4 & 1 \\ 0 & 0 & 3 \end{bmatrix}$$

$$\therefore |A| = \begin{vmatrix} 5 & 3 & 2 \\ 0 & 4 & 1 \\ 0 & 0 & 3 \end{vmatrix}$$

$$= 5(4 \times 3 - 0) - 3(0 \times 3 - 1 \times 0) + 2(0 \times 0 - 4 \times 0)$$

$$= 5(12) - 3(0) + 2(0) = 60$$

Hence, $|A| = 60$.

51. Consistency is generally accepted as a fundamental accounting assumption. Therefore, any change in the accounting policy relating to inventories (including the basis of comparison of historical cost with net realizable value and the cost formulae used) which has a material effect in the current period or which is reasonably expected to have a material effect in later period should be disclosed.

52. $$\text{X's old share} = \frac{2}{3}$$

$$\text{X's sacrifice for Z} = \frac{2}{7}$$

$$\text{X's new share} = \frac{2}{3} - \frac{2}{7} = \frac{8}{21}$$

$$\text{Y's old share} = \frac{1}{3}$$

$$\text{Y's sacrifice for Z} = \frac{1}{7}$$

$$\text{Y's new share} = \frac{1}{3} - \frac{1}{7} = \frac{4}{21}$$

$$\text{Z's share} = \frac{3}{7} = \frac{2}{7} + \frac{1}{7} = \frac{3}{7} = \frac{9}{21}$$

New profit sharing Ratio among X, Y and Z is 8 : 4 : 9.

53. The losses which have not been distributed among the partners are called Accumulated losses. It is shown in the assets side of the balance sheet as profit & loss account.

54. Good will = Capitalised Value of Profit – Actual Capital Employed

Here, Actual Capital Employed

$$= 2,80,000 - 1,50,000$$
$$= 1,30,000$$

and Capitalised Value Profit

$$= \frac{\text{Profit} \times 100}{\text{Rate of Normal Profit}}$$

$$= \frac{40000 \times 100}{10} = 4,00,000$$

$$\therefore \text{Goodwill} = 4,00,000 - 1,30,000 = 2,70,000.$$

55. ***Convention of conservatism:*** The convention of conservatism means the convention of caution, or the policy of playing safe. The principle of "provide for all expected losses but never for anticipated profits" applies here. This is also known as prudence principle, *i.e.*, judgment about the possible future losses which are to be guarded. This principle requires that in the situation of uncertainty and doubt, the business transactions should be recorded in such a manner that the profits and assets are not overstated and the losses and liabilities are not understated.

The following are a few examples:

- Closing stock is valued at cost price or Net realisable value, whichever is lower
- Provision for doubtful debt is created in anticipation of bad debts
- Joint life insurance policy is shown only at surrender value as against the amount paid
- Provision for pending law suit against the firm, which may either be decided in its favour.

56. Interest at the End of First Year

$$= 180000 \times \frac{10}{100} = 18000$$

Interest at the End of Second Year

$$= 120000 \times \frac{10}{100} = 12000$$

Interest at the end of Third Year

$$= 60000 \times \frac{10}{100} = 6000$$

$\therefore$ Total Interest = 18000 + 12000 + 6000 = 36000.

57. Unrecorded Assets and Liabilities: Sometimes at the time of dissolution, there are some assets and liabilities which do *not* appear in the Balance Sheet. An asset may *not* appear in the Balance Sheet because it may have been fully *written off* but *physically* it may still be present in the business. A liability may not appear in the Balance Sheet because it is either a *contingent liability* (as for example when a *dispute* is going on about a workman's compensation) or because its amount is *not* yet ascertained.

The unrecorded assets and liabilities are dealt with at the time of dissolution as follows:

1. **On sale of unrecorded asset:** Cash/Bank Account is debited and Realisation Account is credited. This is a gain from the point of view of business.
2. **On payment of unrecorded liability:** Realisation Account is debited (as this is a loss) and Cash/Bank Account is credited.

58. A company may buy its own shares from market subject to certain conditions (*Sec.* 77A). *The term buy-back of shares implies the act of purchasing own shares by a company.* Buy-back of equity shares results in the cancellation of share capital and thereby leading to the reduction in the share capital of the company.

Buy-back of its own shares may be made out of the following:

(*a*) Free reserves of the company, *e.g.*, general reserve, reserve fund, credit balance of Profit & Loss A/c.

(*b*) The proceeds of any shares or other specified securities.

(*c*) Securities Premium Account.

A company can buy-back its own shares only when:

(*i*) Its Articles of Association authorise it to do so.

(*ii*) Special resolution to this effect has been passed in general meeting by the shareholders.

(*iii*) All the companies shares are fully paid-up.

(*iv*) The buy-back should not exceed 25% of the total paid-up capital and free reserves of the company.

(*v*) The ratio of the debt owed by the company should not be more than twice the capital and its free reserves after such buy-back.

(*vi*) The buy-back should be completed within 12 months from the date of passing special resolution.

59.

	₹
In case of ex-interest (90 × 400)	36,000
Add interest on ₹ 40,000 @ 10% for 3 months (Ist Oct. to 31st Dec.)	1,000
	37,000

$$\left(40{,}000 \times \frac{10}{100} \times \frac{3}{12} = ₹\,1{,}000\right).$$

60. The primary aim of reconstruction is to show the true value of assets, liabilities and share capital of the company.

61. The relationship between two accounting figures is called a *financial ratio* or simpiy a ratio. Ratios are widely used to assess the financial health (performance) of a company. Since the balance sheet and profit and loss statement include several accountingvariables, there is scope for calculating hundreds of ratios.

63. Investing and financing transactions which do not require use of cash or cash equivalents are not shown in the cash flow statement. Such transactions are–

(*i*) Issue of shares or debentures for a consideration other than cash, *i.e.*, against building, machinery

(*ii*) Conversion of Debentures into shares

(*iii*) Purchase of business by issue of shares/ debentures.

However, AS-3 (Revised) recommends that such transactions may be disclosed under foot note to cash flow statement.

65. Excess of current assets over current liabilities is referred to as working capital.

(1) Current Assets = $\frac{2.8}{1.8} \times$ ₹ 1,62,000

= ₹ 2,52,000

(2) Current Liabilities = $\frac{1}{1.8} \times$ ₹ 1,62,000

= ₹ 90,000

66. Under marginal costing, only variable costs of production (direct material, direct labour and variable manufacturing) are subtracted from sales revenue to determine a balance which is known by different names, such as marginal contribution, marginal income (profit), marginal revenue, marginal balance, profit pick-up, etc. All fixed costs, and variable selling, distribution and administrative costs are deducted from this balance to arrive at the net income. Since fixed manufacturing costs are not charged to products under marginal costing, there can be no volume (capacity) variance. Marginal contribution/marginal income under marginal costing is greater than the gross profit/gross margin under absorption costing.

Under marginal costing, fixed manufacturing overheads are excluded and therefore inventory values are lower than inventory value computed under absorption costing. Income may be higher or lower depending upon whether inventories are built up or liquidated. That is, the income statement under absorption costing may reflect higher profit if the production is more than the normal capacity production and also lower sales have been made. This happens because above normal capacity production has over-absorbed its actual fixed manufacturing overhead.

When inventory of manufactured goods fluctuates from period to period, net income will differ somewhat under the two methods because absorption costing requires that part of the period costs be included in inventory, whereas marginal costing excludes period costs. Therefore:

(*i*) When production exceeds sales (the inventory is increased), the net income reported under absorption costing is higher than that reported under variable costing. This follows because under absorption costing, a portion of the fixed costs budgeted for the period is shifted to the following period in the closing inventories whereas under marginal costing the total fixed costs are charged against income.

(*ii*) When sale exceeds production (the inventories are decreased), marginal costing shows a higher profit because only current period costs are being charged against current revenues, whereas under absorption costing the period costs previously included in inventory are now being charged against current revenues.

Under marginal costing profits always move in the same direction as sales volume. They cannot, of course, increase or decrease in direct proportion because unit fixed costs do not remain constant.

67. First-In, First-Out (FIFO): Under the FIFO method, *the earliest purchases (the first in) are assumed to be the first sold (the first out) and the more recent purchases are in ending inventory.*

68. Standard costing is one of the important tools to control costs. In this system, all costs are pre-determined in advance of production. Such pre-determined costs are then compared with the actual costs. The difference between the actual costs and pre-determined costs are known as variance, and are analysed and investigated on some scientific basis to know their reasons. Variances are reported to management for taking remedial steps so that actual costs may not exceed pre-determined costs. The term 'standard costing' has been defined by different scholars as follows:

1. According to **W.W. Bigg,** "Standard costing discloses the cost of deviations from standard and classifies these as to their causes, so that management is immediately informed of the sphere of operations in which remedial action is necessary."
2. According to **The Institute of Cost and Works Accounts, England,** "Standard costing is the preparation and use of standard costs, their comparison with actual costs and the analysis of variance to their causes and points of incidence."
3. According to **M.C. Shukla** and **T.S. Grewal,** "Standard costing is a system which seeks to control the cost of each unit or batch through determination beforehand of what should be the cost and then its comparison with actual costs."

Therefore, standard costing is a procedure under which pre-determined costs are used to measure the efficiency of production. It refers to the determination of standard cost and their application to managerial problems, particularly those problems relating to product costs, and departmental cost control. Thus, under standard costing system, pre-determined costs are carefully computed which are then compared with actual cost to aid in cost control.

70. When more than one type of output results from a single/common processing operation, it is known as joint products. For purposes of inventory valuation and income measurement, common processing costs should be allocated among the joint products. Among the methods most commonly used as the basis for such allocation are the net realisable value minus normal profit method when products are homogeneous and the weighted average method in the case of heterogeneous products.

When one of the many joint outputs is of relatively small value, it is classified as a by-product. If the by-product is sold at the split-off point, the net realisable value minus normal profit method should be used. For further processing, the reversal cost method is the most appropriate.

71. Activity-based costing (ABC) is a cost system that focuses on activities, determines their costs, and then uses appropriate cost drivers to trace costs to the products based on the activities.

Cost pool: According to CIMA, London, "*cost pool is the point of focus for the costs relating to a particular activity in an activity based cost system*". The concept of cost pool is similar to that of cost centre in traditional cost system. In ABC, a cost pool is created for each activity in which all costs relating to an activity are accumulated. Thus, cost pool is the sum total of all costs assigned to activity. For example, cost pool may be procurement of material in which all costs associated with ordering, receiving, inspecting, etc., would be included.

74. Economic Order Quantity (EOQ): The EOQ is the optimum or the most favourable quantity which should be purchased each time the purchases are to be made. The EOQ is one where the cost of carrying inventory is equal or almost equal to the cost of not carrying inventory (cost of placing orders). Also at EOQ level, the total of these two costs is minimum.

76. Planning: A plan is a forecast for accomplishment. It is a predetermined course of action. It is today's projection for tomorrow's activity. *It is essentially a process to determine and implement actions to achieve organisational objectives.* A plan is nothing but a blueprint for goal achievement. When you make a plan, you make a blueprint for action that describes what you need to do to realize your goals. Planning, simply expressed, is setting goals and deciding how to achieve them.

77. Leading:

- Leading is the management function that involves influencing others to engage in the work behaviours necessary to reach organizational goals.
- Leading includes communicating with others, providing direction and motivating people. This function also includes encouraging the necessary levels of charge and innovation. In the process of leading, a manager strives to match the need of the people with the objectives of the company.
- A leader must also recognize the need for co-operation and combined efforts for surival and growth of the firm. Hence a leader maintains good balance between individual motivation and co-operative efficiency.

79. Human skills: These are skills associated with a manager's ability to work well with others both within a group and as a leader who gets things done through others. Key skills in this area would include the ability to motivate others and skills of leadership and communication.

80. Henry Gantt, an associate of Taylor's, developed the Gantt chart, a bar graph that measures planned and completed work along each stage of production. Based on time instead of quantity, volume, or weight, this visual display chart has been a widely used planning and control tool since its development in 1910.

81. The logical sequence to job analysis is job design. Job analysis, as was explained earlier, provides job-related data as well as the skills and knowledge expected of the incumbent to discharge the job. Job design, then, involves conscious efforts to organise tasks, duties and responsibilities into a unit of work to achieve certain objectives.

Thus, job design involves three steps:

1. The specification of individual tasks,
2. The specification of the method(s) of performing each task, and
3. The combination of tasks into specific jobs to be assigned to individuals.

Steps 1 and 3 determine the content of the job, while Step 2 indicates precisely how the job shall be performed. While designing a job, requirements of the organisation and individual needs of the job holder must be considered. The key to successful job design lies in balancing the requirements of the organisation and the job holder.

82. Every organisation has some goals and objectives and one of the important factors that affect these goals is the organisational structure. The efficiency with which an organisation accomplishes its goals and objectives depends on the structure it adopts. *Departmentation* is the process of grouping activities to achieve organisational goats and objectives, and delegating authority to a manager to supervise the division and guide the staff making him responsible for its results. The process of developing a structure is also referred to as organisation design. There are *four major structural alternatives*—functional structure, divisional structure, hybrid structure, and matrix structure. The *functional structure* is a type of organisation structure which groups positions on the basis of main functional or specialized areas. The *divisional structure* is a type of departmentation based on similarity of products, services or markets. It has three major forms—product division, geographic division, and customer division. The form of *divisional structure* chosen depends on the rationale for divisionalization, A divisional structure can be adopted by organisations that are fairly large and have different products or services, operate in different geographic areas or cater to different customer segments. Many organizations, especially large organizations, adopt hybrid structures in order to incorporate the advantages of both functional and divisional structures. Organizations requiring functional expertise and/or efficiency, and which operate in uncertain environments can adopt a hybrid structure. A *matrix structure* is a type of departmentalization that superimposes a horizontal set of divisional reporting relationships onto a hierarchical functional structure. The essence of a matrix organisation is the combination of functional and product or *project patterns* of departmentation in the same organisation structure.

83. **Alderfer's ERG Theory:** Clayton Alderfer reexamined Maslow's Need Hierarch Theory with the help of empirical research. Thus, he developed another need-based theory called 'Existence, Relatedness and Growth (ERG) Theory.' Alderfer classified all human needs into three broad needs as follows:

1. **Existence Needs:** These are basic material needs for one's existence or survival.
2. **Relatedness Needs:** These refer to desire to establish, maintain, and develop interpersonal relations.
3. **Growth Needs:** These refer to one's intrinsic desire for one's development to the extent one can.

A comparison of Alderfer's Theory with Maslow's Theory reveals the following similarities and dissimilarities between the two:

Similarities: (*i*) Alderfer's 'existence' needs are similar to Maslow's physiological needs.

(*ii*) What is Alderfer's 'relatedness' needs is the same with Maslow's 'social' needs.

Dissimilarities: (*i*) According to Maslow, a person stays at one level of need till it is not satisfied. But as per Alderfer's ERG theory, if (higher level) need is not satisfied, the person's desire to increase a lower need takes place. In other words, frustration due to non-satisfaction of some need may lead to a regression to a lower need. For example, one's inability to satisfy social need might increase the desire for more money to satisfy his/her security need.

(*ii*) Maslow considers that there exists a rigid hierarchy of needs where one can progress to higher need only after the lower level need is fully satisfied. But, Alderfer's ERG theory considers needs as flexible ones. For example, a person can be working on growth needs even though existence or relatedness needs are not satisfied.

84. Commonly used systems for payment of wages are as follows:

1. **Time rate system:** In time rate system, wages are paid to employees based on the duration of work. A definite amount of money for a particular period *viz.*, hourly, weekly or monthly is paid to workers under this system. Incentives are not given to workers under this type of wage system. This type of system is typically implemented in industries where quality of product is given more consideration than quantities to be produced.
2. **Piece rate system:** Under the piece rate system, payment of workers is done as per quantities of work that he completes satisfactorily. Merit is given consideration and thus this system effectively rewards efficient workers. One of the greatest disadvantages of this system is that it does not guarantee a fixed minimum wage to a worker.
3. **Combination of time and piece rate system:** This system takes, into account both time and product into consideration.

Take the case of a worker who is paid on a weekly basis. Minimum weekly wages are guaranteed irrespective of the output given by him during a week. As per rules, he is expected to be present in the organisation for full week. In case, he is absent for some days in a week, wages are proportionately deducted.

85. Job analysis is a second important activity that managers need to undertake prior to recruitment and selection. Job analysis is the process of identifying (1) the tasks, duties, and responsibilities that make up a job (the *job description*) and (2) the knowledge, skills, and abilities needed to perform the job (the *job specifications*). For each job in an organization, a job analysis needs to be done.

88. Discharge by Breach of Contract: Breach of contract means refusal of performance on the part of the parties. That means failure of a party to perform his or her obligation under a contract. Discharge of contract by a breach can be in either of the following ways:

1. Actual breach
2. Anticipatory breach
3. **Actual breach:** Generally, the time of performance of a contract may be determined by the parties, at the time of making a contract. In such a case, the parties must perform their promises within the stipulated time. Failure on the part of the party to perform his promise on the due date is regarded as actual breach of contract. Thus, the actual breach of contract occurs when the party does not perform his promise on the due date, or refuses to perform it on that date. On such a refusal, the other party to the contract is entitled to treat the contract as discharged and can move against the party making breach of contract. A leading case related with this is *Cort* vs. *Ambergate Railway Company* (1851). In this case, Cort contracted with Ambergate Railway Company to supply 3000 tones of railway timber at a certain price to be delivered in instalments. After supplying 1787 tones, the railway company asked Cort not to supply more. It was held that Cort could bring an action for breach of contract.

   Actual breach means breach committed either at the time when the performance of the contract is due or during the performance of the contract.

4. **Anticipatory breach:** When, before due date of performance of a contract, the promisor refuses to perform or disable himself from performing his promise, it is known as anticipatory breach/constructive breach of contract. The promisor either informs the promisee regarding his refusal or may do some act which is inconsistent with the contract or which renders him disabled from keeping his promise. For example, if A agrees to marry B on 1st January and before this date, A gets married to C, then he has disabled himself from getting married to B. This amounts to anticipatory breach of contract.

   Anticipatory or constructive breach of contract may take place because of either of the two causes:

   (*a*) express repudiation of the contract by any party before the date of performance, or

   (*b*) the act of any party making the performance of the contract impossible.

90. Meaning of Remedy: A remedy is the course of action available to an aggrieved party (*i.e.*, the party not at fault) for the enforcement of his right under a contract. *The party committing a breach of contract is called the 'guilty' or 'defaulting' party and the other party is called the 'injured' or 'aggrieved' party.*

Example: Bhushan entered into a contract with Shyam for supply of 500 pens at rupees 5 per pen. On the date of performance, Bhushan attempted to deliver the goods, but

Shyam did not accept the goods. In this case, Shyam is the guilty party or defaulting party and Bhushan is the injured or aggrieved party.

In case of breach of contract, the aggrieved party would have one or more, but not all, of the following remedies against the guilty party. These remedies will be enforced through the Court, if there is no resolution of the conflict between the parties themselves. The remedies are

- Rescission of a contract
- Suit for damages
- Suit for quantum meriut
- Suit for specific performance
- Suit for injunction

92. The rights of the unpaid seller also can be shown diagrammatically as follows :

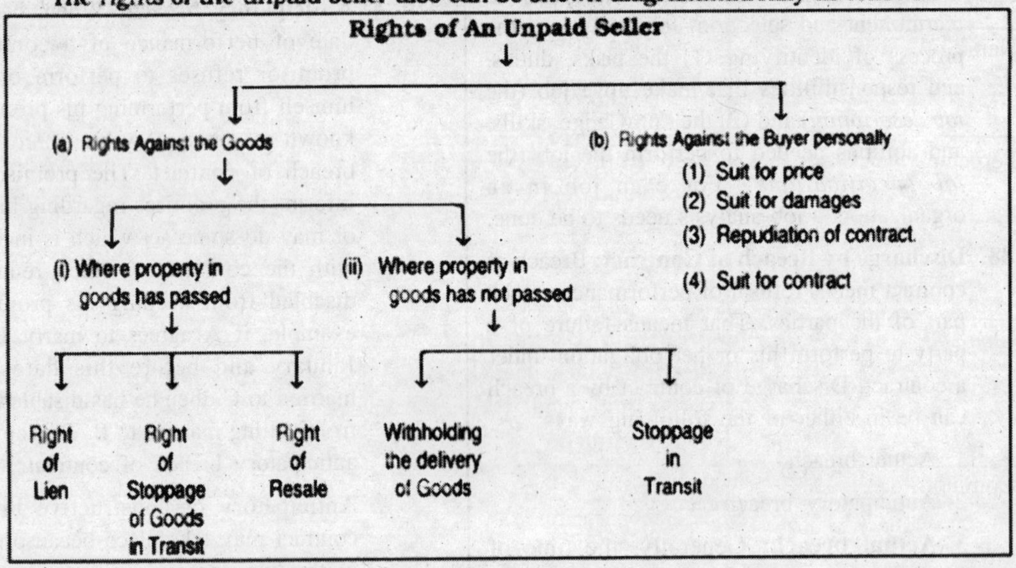

93. Drawee: This is the person on whom the bill is drawn, the person who is ordered to pay the amount of the bill of exchange. When the drawee accepts the bill of exchange (*i.e.*, when he gives his consent to make the payment of the bill on its due date), he becomes the 'acceptor' and liable on it. It may be noted that a bill be negotiated even before its acceptance. If acceptance is refused by the drawee, it becomes dishonoured by non-acceptance.

Payee: This is a person to whom the amount of bill of exchange is payable. The definition of bill states that the bill may be made payable to the payee only. In such a case, it will not remain a negotiable instrument although it shall be a valid bill.

Sometimes, the drawer and the payee may be the same person, *e.g.*, when a person writes a bill of exchange as 'pay to the undersigned or order'. Sometimes, the drawer and the drawee may also be the same person, *e.g.*, a bill of exchange drawn by one branch of a firm on its other branch. In such cases the holder of the bill may treat it, at his option, either as a bill of exchange or as a promissory note.

94. The Limited Liability Partnership Act, 2008 was published in the Official Gazettle of India on January 9, 2009 and has been notified with effect from 31st March 2009. However, the Act has been notified with limited sections only. The rules have been notified in the Official Gazettle on April 1, 2009. The first LLP was incorporated in the first week of April 2009.

COMPARISON BETWEEN EXISTING PARTNERSHIP AND LLP

An Existing Partnership and LLP may be compared as follows:

Basis of Distinction	Partnership	LLP
Regulating Law	It is governed by 'The Indian Partnership Act, 1932'	It is governed by 'The Limited Liability Partnership Act, 2008'.
Registration	Registration is optional.	Registration is compulsory.
Creation	It is created by agreement.	It is created by Law.
Separate Legal Entity	It has no separate legal entity.	It has separate legal entity.
Name of Entity	It can have any name as per choice	Its Name to contain 'Limited Liability Partnership' or 'LLP' as Suffix.
Perpetual Succession	It does not have perpetual succession. The death, insolvency or unsoundness of its members may affect its existence.	It has perpetual succession. The death, insolvency or unsoundness of its members does not affect its existence. Members may come and go but LLP goes forever.
Charter Document	Partnership Deed is a charter of the firm which denotes its scope of operation and rights and duties of the partners	LLP Agreement is a charter of the LLP which denotes its scope of operation and rights and duties of the partners *vis-a-vis* LLP.
Common Seal	There is no concept of common seal in partnership.	It may have its own common seal (*i.e.*, Official Signature) as per its Agreement.
Incorporation Formalities	1. Partnership Deed 2. Form/Affidavit 3. Prescribed Fee. required to be filled with Registrar of Firms.	1. LLP Agreement 2. Various *e* Forms 3. Prescribed Fee. required to be filled with Registrar of LLP.
Time taken to incorporate	It takes 7 days (approx.) to incorporate	It takes 10 days (approx.) to incorporate (inclusive) of time taken to obtain DPIN)
Can it sue third party?	Only registered partnership can sue third party.	An LLP being a legal entity can sue third party.
Can any Foreign National become a partner?	Foreign Nationals can not become a partner in a Partnership Firm in India.	Foreign Nationals can become a Partner in an LLP.
Number of Members	Minimum 2 and Maximum 10 for Banking business & 20 for non-Banking business.	Minimum 2 but there is no limit on maximum number of partners.

Ownership of Assets	Partners have joint ownership of all the assets belonging to partnership firm.	The LLP being a legal entity independent of the partners has ownership of assets.
Rights/Duties/Obligation of the Partners/Managing Partners	Rights/Duties/Obligation of the partners are governed by partnership Deed.	Rights/Duties/Obligation of the partners are governed by LLP Agreement.
Designated Partner	It need not have Designated Partners	It must have at least 2 (two) individuals as Designated Partners, of whom at least one must be resident in India. Each Designated Partner is required to have a DPIN before appointment.
Digital Signature	There is no requirement of Obtaining Digital Signature	Atleast one Designated Partner must have Digital Signatures since *e* forms are filled electronically.
Dissolution	Its Dissolution may take place By Mutual Agreement, Insolvency, Certain Contingencies, and by Court Order.	Its dissolution may take place Voluntarily or by order of National Company Law Tribunal.
Maintenance of Minutes	There is no concept of any minutes.	An LLP by agreement may decide to record the proceedings of meetings of the partners/ Designated partners.

95. There are two kinds of resolutions, ordinary resolutions and special resolutions. The Companies Act requires a special resolution for changing a foundational aspect of the company. The notice indicates whether a resolution is a special resolution or not. For a special resolution to be adopted, the number of votes cast in favour of the resolution should be three times the number of votes cast against it. Any matter, for which a special resolution is not required, can be accomplished through an ordinary resolution, An ordinary resolution requires a simple majority of above 50% of the votes. Some of the issues that require ordinary resolutions are: alteration of authorised capital, declaration of dividends, appointment of auditors and election of directors. Some of the issues that require a special resolution are: an alteration in the object clause of the memorandum of association, shifting of the registered office from one state to another, an alteration in the articles of association, a change in the name of the company, a reduction in the share capital of the company and a merger and/or acquisition. Minutes of the business transacted at the meetings are recorded. Minutes are summaries of all the proceedings of the meeting. A copy of every special resolution has to be forwarded to the Registrar of Companies within 30 days. Thus, the administration stands informed of every vital change in the constitution of the company.

96. Person [Sec. 2(31)]: The definition of a person under the Income-tax Act is very comprehensive and includes both a natural as well as an artificial or a judicial person. The incidence of tax rests on a *person* and only a *person* can be an assessee. The term *person* includes the following:

Individual [Sec. 2(31)(i)]: An individual is a natural person including male, female, major, minor or even a lunatic. However, the income of a minor or a lunatic can only be assessed in the hands of the legal guardian or manager acting as a deemed assessee.

Hindu Undivided Family [Sec. 2(31)(ii)]: The expression "Hindu Undivided Family" is not defined by the income-tax Act and it is understood in the context of the definition of a Joint Hindu Family under the Hindu Law.

Company [Sec. 2(31) (iii) r.w. Sec 2(17) & Sec 2(36)]: In brief, a company means an "Indian Company" incorporated under the Companies Act, 1956, or a corporation established under a Central, State or Provincial Act, or any corporate incorporated under the laws of a foreign country or any institution, association or body, whether incorporated or not, whether Indian or foreign, declared by the Board to be a company.

Firm [Sec. 2(31)(iv) r.w. Sec. 2(23)]: "Firm" has the same meaning assigned to it by the Indian Partnership Act, 1932 (9 of 1932).

Association of Persons (AOP) [Sec. 2(31)(v)]: An "association of person" is the one in which two or more persons join for a common purpose or common action with a view to produce income, profits or gains. The association need not necessarily be on the basis of a contract; consent and understanding may be presumed [CIT *v.* N.V. Shanmugam & Co., (1971) 81 ITR 310 (SC)].

Body of Individuals (BOI) [Sec. 2(31)(v)]: "Body of Individuals" means a conglomeration of individuals who carry on some activity with the object of earning income. The word "body" would require an association for some common purpose or there must be unity under some common tie or occupation. A mere collection of individuals without a common tie or common aim cannot be assumed to be a "body of individuals".

BOI vs. AOP: A "Body of Individuals" is not identical with an "Association of Persons" though they do have some similarities. An association of persons may consist of non-individuals also, but a body of individuals has to be consisted only of individuals, *i.e.*, human beings.

Local Authority [Sec. 2(31)(vi)]: The term 'local' is not defined by the Act. The General Clauses Act, 1897 defines a local authority as a municipal committee, district board, body of port commissioners, or other authority legally entitled to or entrusted by the government.

Other Artificial Judicial Person [Sec. 2(31)(vii)]: It includes every artificial juridical (legal) person, not falling within any of the preceding sub-clauses. This is a residuary clause. An idol, deity, a university, Guru Granth Sahib and trust, etc., are covered under this clause.

99. Following are Non-agricultural income:

(*a*) Income from sale of forests, trees, wild grass, fruit and flowers grown spontaneously and without human effort.

(*b*) Income from salt produced by flooding the land with sea water and then extracting salt therefrom.

(*c*) Income from stone quarries.

(*d*) Income from breeding of livestock.

(*e*) Income from dairy farming, butter and cheese making.

(*f*) Income from poultry farming.

(*g*) Income from fisheries.

(*h*) Preservation of potatoes by refrigeration as it is not a process ordinarily employed by a cultivator.

(*i*) Income from brick making.

(*j*) Income from supplying surplus water to other agriculturists.

(*k*) Interest on arrears of rent in respect of agricultural land.

(*l*) Profit on sale of standing crops/ agricultural produce purchased by the assessee.

(*m*) Income derived from letting out of land/ godowns for storing crops.

(*n*) Royalty income of mines.

(*o*) Annuity payable to vendor of agriculture land or payable to a person giving up his claims to piece of agricultural land.

(*p*) Harvest Crop on purchased land.

(*q*) Compensation/damages paid for loss of agricultural income due to late payment of instalments of the consideration price of rubber plantation site.

(*r*) Registration fee collected from the contractor who is bidding at the auction conducted for sale of plantation is not an agricultural income as such registration fee had no nexus with land.

Previous Paper (Solved)

UNIVERSITY OF DELHI—M.COM Entrance Test-2016*

1. Costs incurred in the past are:
   A. Opportunity cost
   B. Direct and historical costs
   C. Sunk costs
   D. Variable Costs

2. Which of the following is often subject to further processing in order to be salable?

	By-products	Scrap
A.	No	No
B.	No	Yes
C.	Yes	Yes
D.	Yes	No

3. Cost-volume – profit relationships that are curvilinear may be analysed linearly by considering only.
   A. Fixed and semi variable costs
   B. Relevant fixed costs
   C. Relevant variable costs
   D. Relevant range of volume

4. A company has fixed manufacturing overhead costs of ₹ 1,00,000 and variable selling costs of ₹ 80,000. Under variable costing, how should these costs be classified.

	Period costs	Product costs
A.	Zero	1,80,000
B.	80,000	1,00,000
C.	1,00,000	80,000
D.	1,80,000	Zero

5. Accrual basis accounting:
   A. Results in higher income than cash basis accounting
   B. Leads to the reporting of more complete information than does cash basis accounting
   C. Is not acceptable under GAAP
   D. Omits adjusting entries at the end of the period

6. Which of the following is not an account?
   A. Sales revenue
   B. Net sales
   C. Salaries
   D. Supplies expense

7. Accounting conventions include all of the following except:
   A. Periodicity
   B. Materiality
   C. Conservatism
   D. Cost-benefit

8. Which of the following accounts would never be reported in the income statement as an expense?
   A. Depreciation expense
   B. Loss on sale of machinery
   C. Interest expense
   D. Dividends expense

9. A capital reserve is built out of:
   A. Recurring profits
   B. Non-recurring profits
   C. Revenue
   D. Reserve fund

10. With reference to analysis and interpretation of financial statements, the current assets to the current liability ratio is said to be satisfactory, if it is:
    A. 1 : 2
    B. 2 : 1
    C. 1 : 1
    D. 1.5 : 0.5

11. X Ltd. goes into liquidation and an existing company Z Ltd. purchase the business of X Ltd. It is a case of:
    A. Absorption
    B. Exteranational Reconstruction

*Exam held on 22-06-2016.

C. Amalgamation
D. None of the above

12. A and B share profits and losses in the ratio of 2 : 1. C has been admitted with 1/4th share in profits and losses. The new profit-sharing ratio of the partners will be:
A. 2 : 1 : 1 B. 1 : 2 : 1
C. 2 : 1 : 2 D. None of the above

13. The profits made during the year were ₹ 25,000 and there was a decrease in the value of current assets to the extent of ₹ 10,000. However, there was a decrease in the value of current liabilities to the extent of ₹ 5,000. Hence, cash generated from operations equals:
A. ₹ 20,000 B. ₹ 25,000
C. ₹ 30,000 D. None of the above

14. The value of goodwill, according to the simple profit method, is:
A. The product of current year's profits and number of years
B. The product of last year's profits and number of years
C. The Product of average profits of the given years and number of years
D. None of the above

15. In case of inflationary environment:
A. Cost of Goods Sold as per FIFO will be higher than LIFO
B. Cost of Goods Sold as per LIFO will be higher than FIFO
C. Closing inventory as per LIFO will be higher than FIFO
D. None of the above

16. The underlying accounting principle necessitating amortization of Intangible Assets is/are:
A. Cost concept
B. Realization concept
C. Matching concept
D. Both B and C

17. The management decided that depreciation should be charged at 20% on written down basis on the closing balance of each year. Accounting is calendar year. On 1.7.2014 new machine was purchased at a cost of ₹ 50,000. What is the balance in machinery account as on 31.12.2015?
A. ₹ 36,000 B. ₹ 32,000
C. ₹ 18,000 D. ₹ 40,000

18. Preference shares of ₹ 2 lakh are redeemed at par for which fresh equity shares ₹ 80,000 are issued at a premium of 10%. What amount will be transferred to capital Redemption Reserve Account?
A. ₹ 2,00,000 B. ₹ 1,20,000
C. ₹ 1,12,000 D. Nil

19. When debentures are provided as collateral security, interest in paid on:
A. Nominal value of debentures
B. Face value of debentures
C. Discounted value of debentures
D. No interest is paid

20. The following is a non-current account:
A. Inventory
B. Plant and Machinery
C. Debtors
D. Account Receivable

21. Unit matrix written in format of square matrix is also called as:
A. Identity matrix
B. Unidentified matrix
C. Direction matrix
D. Dimension matrix

22. At a maximum turning point:
A. $\frac{dy}{dx} = 0$ and $\frac{d^2y}{dx^2} < 0$
B. $\frac{dy}{dx} < 0$ and $\frac{d^2y}{dx^2} = 0$
C. $\frac{dy}{dx} = 0$ and $\frac{d^2y}{dx^2} > 0$
D. $\frac{dy}{dx} > 0$ and $\frac{d^2y}{dx^2} = 0$

23. $y = 48x - 2x^2$
Where y = total revenue

x = output

At what output is total revenue a maximum?

A. 48 B. 12

C. 2 D. 14

24. Function f is defined by:

$$f(x) = -2x^2 + 6x - 3$$

Find $f(-2)$

A. 23 B. −23

C. 27 D. None of the above

25. For a new product, a manufacturer spends ₹ 1,00,000 on the infrastructure and the variable cost is estimated as ₹ 150 per unit of the product. The sale price per unit was fixed at ₹ 200. Find the break-even point.

A. 500 B. 1000

C. 1500 D. 2000

26. The cost function of a firm is given by $C = 2x^2 + x - 5$. Find the marginal cost, when $x = 4$.

A. 17 B. 18

C. 19 D. 20

27. Interest rate per year is 16 and compounding occurs every quarter then interest rate per compounding period is:

A. 0.4 B. 0.04

C. 40 D. 0.004

28. A sum fetched a total simple interest of ₹ 4016.25 at the rate of 9 p.c.p.a. in 5 years. What is the sum?

A. ₹ 4462.50 B. ₹ 8032.50

C. ₹ 8900 D. ₹ 8925

29. The difference between simple interest and compound on ₹ 1200 for one year at 10% per annum reckoned half-yearly is:

A. ₹ 2.50 B. ₹ 3

C. ₹ 3.75 D. ₹ 4

30. The effective annual rate of interest corresponding to a nominal rate of 6% per annum payable half-yearly is:

A. 6.06% B. 6.07%

C. 6.08% D. 6.09%

31. Which of the following is used to represent a known value for the population variance?

A. S B. σ

C. σ^2 D. s^2

32. If Spearman's co-efficient of rank correlation is equal to one, then:

A. The rankings of the two variables totally agree

B. The rankings of the two variables is totally different

C. All the 'total vairation' is 'explained' by the regression line

D. The rankings of the two variables partially agree

33. This index measures the change from month to month in the cost of a representative 'basket' of goods and services of the type bought by a typical household:

A. Retail Price Index

B. Laspeyres Price Index

C. Financial times Index

D. Paasche Price Index

34. If we first subtract the trend value (T) for each quarter from the original value (Y), then average the values for a given quarter over successive years, then for short-term data we get:

A. Unseasonal data

B. Cyclical component

C. Deseasonalised data

D. Seasonal component

35. Discrete probability distribution in which outcome is very small with a very small period of time is classified as:

A. Posterior distribution

B. Cumulative distribution

C. Normal distribution

D. Poisson distribution

36. If the value of $r^2 = 0.64$, then what is the coefficient of correlation:

A. 0.40 B. 0.04

C. 0.80 D. 0.08

37. fpc stands for:

A. Finite parameter correction

B. Finite population coefficient

C. Finite parameter coefficient

D. Finite population correction

38. .... is a measure of lack of symmetry of data.
A. Kurtosis B. Skewness
C. Mean D. None of the above

39. The null hypothesis (H_0) is a statement about a population parameter:
A. That is assumed to be true
B. That is assumed to be false
C. That is assumed to be unknown
D. None of the above

40. Two regression lines are perpendicular to each other when:
A. $r = 0$ B. $r = \frac{1}{3}$
C. $r = -\frac{1}{2}$ D. $r = +1$

41. A binomial distribution may be approximated by a Poisson distribution provided ....
A. n is small and p is large
B. n is large and p is small
C. n is large and p is large
D. n is small and p is small

42. The first two moments of a distribution about the value 5 of the variable are 2 and 20. The value of variance:
A. 16 B. 18
C. 20 D. None of the above

43. What is the probability that a leap year, selected at random will have 53 Sundays?
A. $\frac{1}{7}$ B. $\frac{2}{7}$
C. $\frac{3}{7}$ D. $\frac{4}{7}$

44. The demand and supply function under perfect condition are: $Y = 16 - X^2$ and $Y = 2X^2 + 4$ respectively. Find the producers surplus:
A. 5 B. 11
C. $\frac{11}{5}$ D. $\frac{5}{11}$

45. Find the sum of the first 8 terms of the geometric sequence 1, 2, 4, 8, ...
A. 255 B. 16
C. −256 D. 128

46. Find the common ratio of the geometric sequence 4, 2, 1....
A. 2 B. $\frac{1}{2}$
C. 4 D. $\sqrt{2}$

47. Identify the top most goal of management:
A. Legal compliance
B. Competitive edge
C. Productivity
D. Work force adaptability

48. Which of the following match is incorrect?
A. McGregor – theory X & Y
B. McClelland – Expectancy theory
C. Ouchi – theory Z
D. Hersey-Blanchard – Situational Leadership

49. An organization structure is effective if it enables individuals to contribute to the objectives of the enterprise. This is known as:
A. Scalar principle
B. Principle of functional definition
C. Principle of unity of objectives
D. None of the above

50. "Learning" and "motivation" which are influencing factors in a person's buying choice are part of the:
A. Social factors
B. Personal factors
C. Psychological factors
D. Cultural factors

51. Span of management may be larger in the case of:
A. Hard working subordinates
B. Loyal subordinates
C. Centralised works and less responsibility
D. Repetitive work and clear responsibility

52. Leadership is a function of all the following factors except:
A. Work group
B. Product or service
C. Leader
D. Situation

53. Which one of the following defines Co-ordination?

A. Actuating force which inspires a person to put his best for the fulfillment of a task

B. Orderly arrangement of group effort to provide unity of action in the pursuit of a common purpose

C. Process of transmitting information from one person to another or from one unit to another

D. Process of determining what is to be accomplished and what has been accomplished and if necessary applying corrective measures

54. Consider the following basic steps involved in the process of control:

1. Identifying the strategic control points
2. Establishing the standards
3. Measuring performance against standards
4. Correcting deviations from the standards

The correct sequence of the above steps in the process of control is:

A. 1, 4, 3, 2 B. 4, 3, 2, 1

C. 2, 1, 4, 3 D. 2, 3, 1, 4

55. Match List-I with List-II and select the correct answer using the codes given below the lists:

List-I (Management Thinkers)	List-II (Contribution/ work)
(*a*) Elton Mayo	1. Importance of integrating the company's and employees' goal
(*b*) Frederick W. Taylor	2. Social Problems of Industrial Civilization
(*c*) Henri Fayol	3. General and Industrial Management
(*d*) Mary Parker Follet	4. Principles of Scientific Management

	(*a*)	(*b*)	(*c*)	(*d*)
A.	1	4	3	2
B.	4	3	2	1
C.	2	4	3	1
D.	3	4	1	2

56. Which one of the following order indicates the correct logical order of managerial functions?

A. Organizing, planning, directing, staffing, coordination and control

B. Planning, organizing, staffing, directing, Coordination and control

C. Planning, direction, organizing, staffing, control and coordination

D. Organizing, planning, staffing, directing, control and coordination

57. A person, who is usually of unsound mind, but occasionally of sound mind:

A. May make a contract

B. May make a contract when he is of sound mind

C. May not make a contract

D. None of the above

58. Which one of the following is not considered to be coercion under Section 15 of the Indian Contract Act, 1872?

A. A threat to commit suicide

B. Committing and Act forbidden by law

C. An act done to obtain the consent of the party

D. None of the above

59. Sale as defined under the provisions of the Sale of Goods Act, 1930 is an:

A. Executed contract

B. Executory contract

C. Executive contract

D. None of the above

60. There is always existing debt in case of:

A. Contract of Indemnity

B. Contract of Guarantee

C. Both the above

D. None of the above

61. The intentional relinquishment of a claim or privilege is:

A. Remission

B. Rescission

C. Waiver

D. None of the above

62. The liability of indemnifier arises:

A. Only before the occurrence of loss

B. Only on the occurrence of any loss to the indemnity-holder

C. When the indemnity holder compel the indemnifier to make good his loss even before he has suffered actual loss by paying off the claim
D. None of the above

63. Sec 2(92) of the Companies Act 2013, provides that unlimited company means:
A. A company not having any limit on the number of members
B. A company not having any limit on the liability of the company
C. A company not having any limit on the liability of its members
D. None of the above

64. Associate Company in relation to another company means a company in which that:
A. The other company has a significant influence
B. The other company has a significant influence, but which is not the subsidiary company
C. The other company does not have a significant influence, but which is not the subsidiary company
D. None of the above

65. An individual, at one point of time, can be appointed as a Whole time Director in:
A. Any number of companies
B. Only ten companies
C. Only five companies
D. Only one company

66. The Companies Act 2013, prescribes that the following matters shall not to be dealt in a meeting through video conferencing:
A. The approval of financial statements
B. The approval of board's report
C. The approval of prospectus
D. All of the above

67. The directors participating in a board meeting through video conferencing:
A. Shall constitute quorum
B. Shall not constitute quorum
C. Shall constitute with 3/4th members present
D. All of the above

68. Which of the following is not correct in respect of Income tax rules applicable for the AY 2016-17?
A. Deduction u/s 80C is ₹ 1,50,000
B. Deduction on account of interest on loan from house property is ₹ 2,00,000
C. Surcharge is levied at the rate of 10% on Individuals, HUF, AOP etc having income exceeding ₹ 1 crore
D. Deduction u/s 80D on health insurance premium is ₹ 25,000

69. Which of the following is not a Direct tax?
A. Value added Tax
B. Income tax
C. Corporate tax
D. None of the above

70. Which of the following incomes are Taxable in the hands of a Resident but Not Ordinary resident?
A. Income received or deemed to be received in India, whether earned in India or elsewhere
B. Income which accrue or arise or deemed to accrue or arise in India during the previous year whether received in India or elsewhere
C. Income which accrue or arise outside India and received outside India from a business controlled from India
D. All of the above

71. For FY 2015-16, the rates of Short term capital gain and Long term capital gain for equity shares are:
A. 15% and Nil respectively
B. Nil and 15% respectively
C. 15% and 10% respectively
D. Nil and Nil respectively

72. Which of the following income are exempt from tax u/s 10 of Income Tax Act 1961?
A. Income from a house property
B. Share of income from the firm
C. Interest paid to a Resident
D. All of the above

73. If the quantity of a commodity demanded remains unchanged as its price changes, the coefficient of price elasticity of demand is:

A. Greater than 1 B. Equal to 1
C. Smaller than 1 D. Zero

74. If the income elasticity of demand is greater than 1, the commodity is:
A. A necessity B. A luxury
C. An inferior good D. Non-related good

75. The substitution effect for a fall in the price of a commodity is given by:
A. A movement up a given indifference curve
B. A movement from a higher to a lower indifference curve
C. A movement down a given indifference curve
D. Any of the above

76. The elasticity of technical substitution is measured by:
A. The slope of isoquant
B. The change in the slope of the isoquant
C. The ratio factor inputs
D. None of the above

77. If we have constant returns to scale and we increase the quantity of labour used per unit of time by 10% but keep the amount of capital constant, output will:
A. Increase by 10%
B. Decrease by 10%
C. Increase by more than 10%
D. Increase by less than 10%

78. An entrepreneur running a business takes out ₹ 20,000/year as "salary" from the total receipts of the firm. The implicit cost of this entrepreneur is:
A. ₹ 20,000/year
B. More than ₹ 20,000/year
C. Less than ₹ 20,000/year
D. Any one of the above is possible

79. The output elasticity of labour measure:
A. $\Delta Q/\Delta L$ B. $\%\Delta Q/\%\Delta L$
C. $\Delta L/\Delta Q$ D. $\%\Delta L/\%\Delta Q$

80. The best, or equilibrium level of output for a perfectly competitive firm is given by the point where:
A. MR = AC
B. MR = MC
C. MR exceeds MC by the greatest amount
D. MR = MC and MC is rising

81. The short run supply curve of the perfectly competitive firm is given by:
A. The rising portion of its MC curve over and above the shut down point
B. The rising portion of its MC curve over and above the breakeven point
C. The rising portion of its MC curve over and above the AC curve
D. The rising portion of its MC curve

82. If the factor prices and factor quantities move in the same direction, we have:
A. A constant cost industry
B. An increasing cost industry
C. A decreasing cost industry
D. Any of the above

83. At the best, or optimum, level of output for the pure monopolist:
A. MR = SMC B. P = SMC
C. P = lowest SAC D. P is the highest

84. If the monopolist incurs losses in the short run, then in the long run:
A. The monopolist will go out of business
B. The monopolist will stay in business
C. The monopolist will break even
D. Any of the above is possible

85. In both the Chamberlin and kinked demand curve models, the oligopolists:
A. Recognize the interdependence
B. Do not collude
C. Tend to keep prices constant
D. All of the abvoe

86. The period of the business cycle in which real GDP is increasing is called:
A. Expansion B. Peak
C. Recession D. Trough

87. An increase in the money supply causes:
A. Interest rates to fall, investment spending to rise, and aggregate demand to rise
B. Interest rates to rise, investment spending to rise, and aggregate demand to rise
C. Interest rates to rise, investment spending to fall, and aggregate demand to fall

D. Interest rates to fall, investment spending to fall, and aggregate demand to fall

88. Cash reserve ratio is:
A. Ratio of deposits commercial banks has to keep with Central Bank
B. Ratio of deposits commercial banks has to keep with themselves
C. Ratio of deposits Central Bank has to keep with commercial banks
D. Ratio of deposits Central Bank has to keep with themselves

89. The difference between Export of Import of goods is called:
A. Balance of payment
B. Balance of trade
C. Balance of invisible trade
D. None of the above

90. Zero primary deficits indicates that in a government budget:
A. Interest payments are equal to fiscal deficit
B. Interest payments are less than fiscal deficit
C. Fiscal deficit and budget deficit are equal
D. There is no interest payment

91. Which of the following is not related to capital account of BOP?
A. Foreign direct investment
B. Purchase of land abroad
C. Investment in share abroad
D. Scholarship from abroad

92. Problem of double counting can be avoided by using:
A. Final output approach
B. Production method
C. Value added method
D. All of the above

93. A decrease in the interest rate will increase the level of investment since:
A. The cost of borrowing will decrease
B. The value of government bonds will decrease
C. The return on private saving will decrease
D. All of the above

94. The three approaches to measure economic activity are:
A. Cost, income and expenditure approach
B. Product, income and expenditure approach
C. Consumer, business and government approach
D. Private, public and international approach

95. The Phillips curve describes the relationship between:
A. The budget deficit and the trade deficit
B. Savings and investment
C. The unemployment rate and the inflation rate
D. Marginal tax rates and tax revenue

96. Depreciation in domestic currency leads:
A. Rise in Exports B. Fall in Exports
C. Rise in Imports D. No effect

97. Which of these is a direct tax?
A. VAT
B. Custom Duty
C. Income Tax
D. Excise Duty

98. If money demand becomes less sensitive to interest rate changes, the LM-curve will:
A. Shift to the right B. Become flatter
C. Become steeper D. Remain unaffected

99. Which of the following telecom company has launched "Project Leap" that will provide a transparent view of coverage of voice and high speed broadband services?
A. Idea B. Airtel
C. Vodafone D. Reliance

100. What was the presented State Budget estimate of Madhya Pradesh for the 2016-17?
A. 1.56 lakh crores B. 2.56 lakh crores
C. 1.58 lakh crores D. 2.58 lakh crores

101. President Pranab Mukherjee has declared which of the following Indian state as the first digital state of the country?
A. Karnataka B. Kerala
C. Gujarat D. Goa

102. Devaluation of currency will be more beneficial if:
A. Prices of exports remain constant
B. Prices of domestic goods remain constant
C. Prices of imports remains constant
D. Prices of exports rise proportionately

103. The annual yield from which of the following Union Government taxes is the highest?

A. Custom duties
B. Excise duties
C. Corporation tax and income tax
D. Inheritance tax, wealth tax, interest tax and gift tax

104. In India, inflation is measured by the:

A. Consumers Price Index for urban non-manual workers
B. Consumers Price Index for agricultural workers
C. Wholesale Price Index number
D. National Income Deflation

105. In India, rural incomes are generally than the urban incomes, which of the following reasons account for this?

I. A large number of farmers are illiterate and know little about scientific agriculture.
II. Prices of primary products are lower than those of manufactured products.
III. Investment in agriculture has been low when compared to investment in industry.

Select the correct option

A. I and II B. I, II and III
C. I and III D. II and III

106. .... includes current account and capital account.

A. Customer Stock
B. Credit
C. Balance of Trade
D. Balance of Payment

107. Who was recently got appointed as Partner and CEO of KPMG India?

A. Sameer Chadha B. Vivek Malhotra
C. Sabeer Bhatia D. Muneesh Pal

108. The government has recently set up a committee to prepare a blueprint for doubling farmers' income by 2022. This committee is headed by:

A. Ashok Dalwai B. Ashok Kamdar
C. Brijesh Dalwai D. Brijesh Kamdar

109. Maharashtra accounts for .... % of total sugar production in India.

A. 69% B. 57%
C. 48% D. 32%

110. Piyush Goyal, Minister of State (IC) for Power, Coal and New & Renewable Energy launched Deep e-Bidding & e-Reverse Auction portal for procurement of short term power by DISCOMs. What does abbreviation 'DEEP' stand for?

A. Dependable and Efficient Electricity Price
B. Detailed and Efficient Electricity Price
C. Discovery of Efficient Electricity Price
D. Discovery of Estimated Electricity Price

111. Satyanand Munjal who passed away in April 2016, was a co-founder of which business group?

A. TVS Group B. Mahindra Group
C. Hero Group D. Ashok Leyland

112. An indent house is one which:

A. Packs and forwards the goods
B. Guarantees the payments for good
C. Serves as middleman between importer and exporter of goods for getting orders
D. Performs custom formalities on behalf of importer

113. A letter of credit (L/C) is furnished by:

A. An importer
B. An exporter
C. Custom authorities
D. Shipping & Logistics company

114. The currency convertibility concept in its original form originated in:

A. Taylors Agreement
B. Wells Agreement
C. Bretton Woods Agreement
D. None of the above

115. In the Union Budget 2015-16 Fiscal deficit was estimated at .... of GDP in 2015/16?

A. 3.9% B. 4.7%
C. 5.2% D. 5.9%

116. Non-development expenditure involves:

I. Interest payments
II. Subsidies
III. Defense
IV. Irrigation

Select the correct option:

A. I and II B. I only

C. II, III, IV D. I, II, III

117. Which of the following statements is/are correct?

I. Internal control includes quality control.

II. Internal control is compulsory for all forms of business organizations.

III. Internal control helps external auditor to design suitable audit programme for client's organization.

Select the correct option:

A. I only B. II only

C. III only D. I and III

118. India has set up bilateral mechanism for sharing information for tracking movements of satellites with which of the following country?

A. United States B. Afganistan

C. Canada D. Australia

119. Which of the following agencies related to the United Nation was in existence before the Second World War?

A. Food and Agricultural Organization

B. World Health Organization

C. International Monetary Fund

D. International Labour Organization

120. The headquarters of World Intellectual Property Organization (WIPO) is located in:

A. Paris B. Geneva

C. Madrid D. New York

121. Where is the Headquarter of Organization of the Petroleum Exporting Countries (OPEC)?

A. Riyadh, Saudi Arabia

B. Dubai, United Arab Emirates

C. Vienna, Austria

D. Baghdad, Iraq

122. 'Earth Day' is celebrated on 22nd April every year. What was the 2016 theme for 'Earth Day'?

A. Clean Earth Green Earth

B. Trees for the Earth

C. Do Your Part, Be Smart

D. Give Back to the Planet

123. Recently in April 2016, Union Government allotted ₹ 800 Cr. to clean up polluted lakes of .... city?

A. Jaipur B. Kochi

C. Nagpur D. Bengaluru

124. Union Government has appointed .... as the Chairman of Rubber Board.

A. V Venkat Rao

B. A. Ajith Kumar

C. Chetan Nayak

D. Kumar Vishvajeet

125. In behavioural analysis, costs are divided into:

A. Production and non-production costs

B. Controllable and non-controllable costs

C. Di ect and indirect costs

D. Fixed and variable costs

126. Sharing of a percentage of value added is done under:

A. Emerson's differential pay plan

B. Rucker plan

C. Tyler's plan

D. Rowan plan

127. The scope of inventory control is:

A. Related to maintaining the correct level of inventory at all times

B. Related to fixation of stock levels for various items

C. To locate the slow and non-moving items

D. All the above

128. The following factor is an avoidable cause for labour turnover:

A. Lower wages

B. Resignation

C. Retirement

D. Worker's moving nature

129. Which of the following should not be considered in a make or buy decision?

A. Potential use of manufacturing capacity

B. Variable costs of production

C. Potential rental income from space occupied by production area

D. Unchanged fixed cost

130. If sales is of ₹ 5,00,000 and variable cost per unit is ₹ 50. If fixed cost is ₹ 1,00,000 and break-even is reached at 1,000 units, sale price is:

A. 50 B. 100

C. 150 D. 200

ANSWERS

1	2	3	4	5	6	7	8	9	10
C	D	*	*	B	B	A	D	B	B
11	**12**	**13**	**14**	**15**	**16**	**17**	**18**	**19**	**20**
*	A	C	C	B	C	A	B	D	B
21	**22**	**23**	**24**	**25**	**26**	**27**	**28**	**29**	**30**
A	A	B	B	D	A	B	D	B	D
31	**32**	**33**	**34**	**35**	**36**	**37**	**38**	**39**	**40**
C	A	A	D	D	C	D	B	A	A
41	**42**	**43**	**44**	**45**	**46**	**47**	**48**	**49**	**50**
B	A	B	B	A	B	C	B	C	C
51	**52**	**53**	**54**	**55**	**56**	**57**	**58**	**59**	**60**
C	B	B	D	C	B	*	D	A	B
61	**62**	**63**	**64**	**65**	**66**	**67**	**68**	**69**	**70**
C	*	C	D	D	D	A	*	A	D
71	**72**	**73**	**74**	**75**	**76**	**77**	**78**	**79**	**80**
A	B	D	B	C	D	D	D	B	D
81	**82**	**83**	**84**	**85**	**86**	**87**	**88**	**89**	**90**
A	B	A	D	D	A	A	A	B	A
91	**92**	**93**	**94**	**95**	**96**	**97**	**98**	**99**	**100**
D	A	A	B	C	A	C	C	B	C
101	**102**	**103**	**104**	**105**	**106**	**107**	**108**	**109**	**110**
B	A	B	C	B	D	A	A	D	C
111	**112**	**113**	**114**	**115**	**116**	**117**	**118**	**119**	**120**
C	C	A	C	A	D	D	A	D	B
121	**122**	**123**	**124**	**125**	**126**	**127**	**128**	**129**	**130**
C	B	D	B	D	B	D	A	D	C

* These questions were removed by Department of Commerce (University of Delhi).

EXPLANATORY ANSWERS

1. **Sunk Costs:** These are the historical or past costs incurred by a past decision. Since sunk costs can not be changed by later decision, these are not relevant for decision-making.
2. By-products are those products of limited sales value produced simultaneously with products of greater sales value, known as main or joint products. Main products are generally produced in much greater quantity than by-products. By-products are an incidental result of producing main products. By-products may result from the cleansing of main products or the preparing of raw materials before they are used to manufacture main products, or they may be the leftovers after main products are processed.

   After they have emerged along with joint products at the split-off point, by-products either may be sold in the same form as originally produced or they may undergo further processing before sale.

Occasionally there is a problem of whether to classify a product as a by-product or as scrap. The basic difference between the two is that by-products have a greater sales value than scrap. Also, scrap is generally sold immediately, whereas by-products quite often must undergo further processing after the split-off point in order to be salable.

The classification of products as joint products, by-products, or scrap may change as new uses of the products are discovered or old ones abandoned. Because of technological discoveries, a product may change from a by-product to a joint product. For example, in the petroleum industry, gasoline was originally a by-product of the main product, kerosene. After the invention of the automobile, however, gasoline became the main product and kerosene the by-product. In many cases, uses have even been found for products formerly considered waste. For example, many sewage plants have found ways to convert their waste into fertilizer.

5. There are two basic ways to do accounting:
- Cash basis
- Accrual basis

The cash basis of accounting records only cash transactions—cash receipts, cash payments, and the balance of cash on hand. By contrast, the accrual basis records all transactions and their effects on a company. The basic defect of cash-basis accounting is that the cash basis ignores important information. That makes the financial statements incomplete. People using the statements make bad decisions. For example, investors may be led to believe a company is better than it really is; they buy the stock and lose their money. Managers make wrong predictions about the results of their actions.

Accrual Accounting is more complex—and more complete—than cash-basis accounting. Accrual accounting records cash transactions, including:
- Collecting from customers
- Borrowing money
- Receiving cash from interest earned
- Paying off loans
- Paying salaries, rent, and other expenses
- Issuing stock.

Accrual accounting also records non-cash transactions, such as:
- Purchases of inventory on account
- Depreciation expense
- Sales on account
- Usage of prepaid rent, insurance, and supplies
- Accrual of expenses incurred but not yet paid.

7. Financial statements are based largely on estimates and the application of accounting rules for recognition and allocation. To facilitate interpretation, accountants depend on five conventions, or rules of thumb, in recording transactions and preparing financial statements; comparability and consistency, materiality, conservatism, full disclosure, and cost-benefit.

8. A dividend paid by a corporation is a distribution of previously earned net income (profits). A dividend is not an expense or a loss. Therefore, dividends declared and/or paid are not part of the computation of net income that is presented on the income statement.

Dividends declared by corporations are reported in their statements of changes in Retained Earnings and Stockholders' Equity.

9. **Capital Reserve:** It is created out of capital profits. Capital profit arises out of non-recurring (*i.e.*, occasional) transactions. For example, capital reserve created out of profit made on sale of fixed asset, say plant and machinery which is the excess of sale price over the cost of that fixed asset. Capital profit can be converted into capital reserve. But, with regard to companies, the following are some of the examples or capital reserve.

(*a*) Pre-incorporation profits
(*b*) Premium received on issue of shares
(*c*) Premium received on issue of debentures
(*d*) Profit on cancellation of own debentures

Features of Capital Reserve

1. Capital reserve is appropriated out of profit and loss appropriation account.
2. It is not meant to cover up liability, contingency, commitment or reduction in the value of an asset.
3. It is meant to meet prospective losses or liabilities.
4. It is not ordinarily, distributed as dividend to share holder certain restrictions are imposed.
5. Certain provisions of Companies Act, 1956 has to be followed to use.

10. Current ratios are the most common ratio for measurement of liquidity. Current ratio is the ratio of total current assets to total current liabilities. It is calculated by dividing current assets by current liabilities.

$$\text{Current Ratio} = \frac{\text{Current Assets}}{\text{Current Liabilities}}$$

Current ratio indicates rupees of current assets available for each rupee of current liability. Higher the current ratio, larger the amount available per rupee of current liability. It indicates the high liquidity. A ratio of 2 : 1 (Two times of current assets to current liabilities) is considered satisfactory as rule of thumb.

12. Let total profits = 1

$$\text{C's share} = \frac{1}{4}$$

$$\text{Remaining share} = 1 - \frac{1}{4} = \frac{3}{4}$$

$$\text{A's share} = \frac{2}{3} \text{ of } \frac{3}{4} = \frac{6}{12}$$

$$\text{B's share} = \frac{1}{3} \text{ of } \frac{3}{4} = \frac{3}{12}$$

$$\text{C's share} = \frac{1}{4} = \frac{3}{12}$$

Thus, the new ratio among A, B & C is

$$\frac{6}{12} : \frac{3}{12} : \frac{3}{12} = 2 : 1 : 1.$$

13. Cash generated from operations
= Profits + Decrease in current assets – Decrease in current liabilities
= 25,000 + 10,000 – 5000 = 30,000.

14. Simple Profit Method: This is a very simple method. Goodwill is calculated on the basis of the no. of past years profits. Because past profits indicate as to what profits are likely to accrue in the future. Therefore, past profits are averaged. Average of such profits is multiplied by the agreed no. of years to find out the value of goodwill.

Value of Goodwill = Average Profit × Number of Years of Purchase

Some adjustment should be done while calculating the average profit:

- Abnormal income of a year should be deducted out of the net profit of that year.
- Abnormal loss of a year should be added back to the net profit of that year.
- Income from investments should be deducted out of the net profit of that year.

15. Under the last-in, first-out (LIFO) method, the item purchased most recently is assumed to be the first item sold. In an inflationary environment, LIFO COGS will be higher than FIFO COGS, and earnings will be lower. Lower earnings translate into lower income taxes, which increase cash flow. Under LIFO, ending inventory on the balance sheet is valued using the earliest costs. Therefore, in an inflationary environment, LIFO ending inventory is less than current cost.

Under the LIFO method, the item purchased most recently is assumed to be the first item sold. In an inflationary environment, LIFO COGS will be higher than FIFO COGS, and earnings will be lower. Lower earnings translate into lower income taxes, which increase the operating cash flow. Under LIFO, ending inventory on the balance sheet is valued using the earliest costs. Therefore, in an inflationary environment, LIFO ending inventory is less than current cost.

16. Amortization of intangible assets means charging a reasonable portion of the asset on a product basis to the revenue of that year. This is done as per the Matching Concept. Matching Concept states that all expenses matched with the revenue of that period should only be taken into consideration.

Amortization is treated as an expense of that particular year. In the financial statements of the organization if any revenue is recognized then expenses related to earn that revenue should also be recognized.

17. Cost of the Asset = ₹ 50,000

⇒ Annual Depreciation = 20%

⇒ Year 1 Depreciation = 20% of 50,000

= 10,000

⇒ Year 1 WDV = ₹ 40,000

⇒ 6 months Depreciation

$= \frac{1}{2}$[20% of ₹ 40,000]

= ₹ 4,000

⇒ Balance in Machinery Account

= ₹ 40,000 – 4,000

= ₹ 36,000

18. Amount of transfer to Capital redemption reserve = Nominal value of preference shares redeemed – Nominal value of fresh issue of shares made.

In the given case,

Nominal value of shares redeemed

= ₹ 2,00,000

Nominal values of shares issued = ₹ 80,000

Transfer to CRR (2,00,000 – 80,000)

= ₹ 1,20,000

19. Collateral security means additional security, *i.e.,* in addition to the principal security. This security is treated as subsidiary or secondary security. Hence, collateral security is to be realised when the principal security fails to payoff the loan.

Sometimes a company issues its own debentures as a collateral security against a loan taken from bank or any other party. The company incurs no liability against such debentures (since they are in the nature of a contingent liability). On repayment of the loan, it can take its debentures back. If the company fails to payoff the loan as per agreement or in the event of liquidation, such debentures become actual liability.

The following points should be remembered in connection with debentures issued as collateral security:

1. Lender will simply be the custodian of these debentures.
2. No interest is payable on the debentures as collateral security because interest on loan is being paid.
3. The liability of the company is for the amount of loan and not for the face value of debentures issued.

20. Table: Non-current Accounts

Sl. No.	Non-Current or Permanent Liabilities	Non-Current or Permanent Assets
1.	Equity Share Capital	Goodwill
2.	Preference Share Capital	Land
3.	Debentures	Building
4.	Long-term Loans	Plant and Machinery
5.	Share Premium	Furniture and Fittings
6.	Share Forfeited	Trade Marks
7.	Profit and Loss Account	Parent Rights
8.	Capital Reserve	Long-term Investments
9.	Capital Redemption Reserve	Discount on Issue of Shares and Debentures
10.		Preliminary Expenses
11.		Other Deferred Expenses

21. Unit Matrix: A square matrix in which every non-diagonal element is zero and every diagonal element is 1, is called a unit matrix or an identity matrix. Thus, a square matrix A $= [a_{ij}]_{n \times n}$ is a unit matrix if

$$a_{ij} = \begin{cases} 0 \text{ when } i \neq j \\ 1 \text{ when } i = j \end{cases}$$

A unit matrix of order n is denoted by I_n or I. For example,

$$I_2 = \begin{bmatrix} 1 & 0 \\ 0 & 1 \end{bmatrix} \text{ and } I_3 = \begin{bmatrix} 1 & 0 & 0 \\ 0 & 1 & 0 \\ 0 & 0 & 1 \end{bmatrix}$$ are unit matrices of order 2 and 3 respectively.

22. Turning points

⇒ The graph of $g(y) = f(x)$ will have turning point(s)

1. If $\boxed{\frac{dy}{dx} = 0}$, it is classified as:

- a maximum *stationary turning point* if $\frac{d^2y}{dx^2} < 0,$

- a minimum *stationary turning point* if $\frac{d^2y}{dx^2} > 0$, and
- a point-of-inflexion *stationary turning point* if $\frac{d^2y}{dx^2} = 0$, with respect to the *x-axis*.

2. If $\boxed{\frac{dx}{dy} = 0}$, it is classified similarly as 1, except it is turning with respect to the y-axis.

3. If $\frac{dx}{dy} \neq 0$, but $\boxed{\frac{d^2y}{dx^2} = 0}$, then it is a non-stationary point-of-inflexion.

23. $\frac{dy}{dx} = 0$ and $\frac{d^2y}{dx^2} < 0$

For Maximum Value

Here, $y = 48x - 2x^2$

$\therefore \quad \frac{dy}{dx} = 48 - 4x = 0$

$\Rightarrow \quad x = 12$

At $\quad x = 12$

$\frac{d^2y}{dx^2} = -4 < 0$

At $x = 12$, Total Revenue is maximum.

25. (*i*) Let x be the number of units produced and sold,

then cost function $C(x)$

$= \text{Fixed cost} + \text{Variable cost}$

$= 1,00,000 + 150x$

(*ii*) Revenue function $= p.x = 200x$

(*iii*) Profit function $P(x) = R(x) - C(x)$

$= 200x - (100,000 + 150x)$

$= 50x - 100,000$

(*iv*) At Break-Even point $P(x) = 0$

$50x - 100,000 = 0$

$x = \frac{100,000}{50} = 2000$

Hence $x = 2000$ is the break even point.

i.e., When 2000 units of the product are produced and sold, there will be no profit or loss.

26. $AC = \frac{C}{x} = \frac{2x^2 + x - 5}{x}$

$= 2x + 1 - \frac{5}{x}$

At, $\quad x = 4,\ AC = 2(4) + 1 - \frac{5}{4}$

$= 9 - 1.25 = 7.75$

$\therefore \quad MC = \frac{d}{dx}(C) = 4x + 1$

$\therefore$ MC at $x = 4 = 4(4) + 1 = 16 + 1 = 17$

27. Interest rate per compounding period

$= \frac{.16}{4} = 0.04.$

28. Principal $= ₹\left(\frac{100 \times 4016.25}{9 \times 5}\right)$

$= ₹\left(\frac{401625}{45}\right) = ₹\ 8925.$

29. Interest is reckoned half yearly.

$\therefore \quad S.I. = \frac{1200 \times 5 \times 2}{100} = ₹\ 120$

$C.I. = 1200\left[\left(1 + \frac{5^2}{100}\right) - 1\right]$

$= 1200\left(\frac{441 - 400}{400}\right)$

$= 1200 \times \frac{41}{400} = ₹\ 123$

$\therefore$ Required difference

$= ₹\ (123 - 120) = ₹\ 3.$

30. Amount of ₹ 100 for 1 year when compounded half-yearly

$= ₹\ 100\left(1 + \frac{3}{100}\right)^2 = ₹\ 106.09$

$\therefore$ Effective rate $= (106.09 - 100)\%$

$= 6.09\%.$

32. The Spearman co-efficient of rank correlation indicates whether the respective rankings of two variables agree or disagree. If the value of this co-efficient is 1, then the rank-order is the same whichever variable is used.

33. There are at least four commonly used measures of price increases. These are the Consumer Price Index (CPI), the Retail Price Index (RPI), the Wholesale Price Index (WPI), and the Stock Price Index (SPI).

The *Consumer Price Index* is the most popular and the most used measure as it reflects what happens to the living standards of most of us, the consumers. The *Retail Price Index* is designed to measure monthly changes of the prices at which retailers dispose of their goods to consumers and end-users. The *Wholesale Price Index* measures monthly changes in the general price level of commodities that flow into wholesale trade intermediaries in Metro Manila; hence, it measures price changes during trade turnover. The *Stock Price Index* serves as a measure of the changes in, and to trace the movement of the average prices of company shares of stocks traded in the Makati and Manila Stock Exchanges.

34. If we first subtract the trend value (T) for each quarter from the original value (Y), then average the values for a given quarter over successive years, then for short-term data we get:

Your Answer: Seasonal component

Y = T + S + I for each quarter

Y – T = S + I for each quarter

Averaging values over different years for that quarter eliminates the irregular component (I), leaving us with the seasonal component (S). For shot-term data, there is no cyclical factor.

35. Poisson distribution is named after the French mathematician S. Poisson (1781-1840). The Poisson process measures the number of occurrences of a particular outcome of a discrete random variable in a *pre-determined time interval, space, or volume,* for which an *average number* of occurrences of the outcome is known or can be determined. In the Poisson process, the random variable values need counting. Such a count might be (*i*) number of telephone calls per hour coming into the switchboard, (*ii*) number of fatal traffic accidents per week in a city/state, (*iii*) number of patients arriving at a health centre every hour, (*iv*) number of organisms per unit volume of some fluid, (*v*) number of cars waiting for service in a workshop, (*vi*) number of flaws per unit length of some wire, and so on. The Poisson probability distribution provides a simple, easy-to compute and accurate approximation to a binomial distribution when the probability of success, p is very small and n is large, so that $\mu = np$ is small, preferably $np > 7$. It is often called the *'law of improbable'* events meaning that the probability, p, of a particular event's happening is very small. As mentioned above Position distribution occurs in business situations in which there are a few successes against a large number of failures or vice-versa (*i.e.*, few successes in an interval) and has single independent events that are mutually exclusive. Because of this, the probability of success, p is very small in relation to the number on trials n, so we consider only the probability of success.

Conditions for Poisson Process: The use of Poisson distribution to compute the probability of the occurrence of an outcome during a specific time period is based on the following conditions:

(*i*) The outcomes within any interval occur randomly and independently of one another.

(*ii*) The probability of one occurrence in a small time interval is proportional to the length of the interval and independent of the specific time interval.

36. ∵ Coefficient of dctermination

$$= r^2 = 0.64$$

∴ Coefficient of correlation $= \sqrt{r^2}$

$$= \sqrt{0.64}$$

$$= 0.80.$$

37. Finite Population Correction (*FPC*) Factor

When the population is infinite, the standard error is given by $\sigma_{\bar{x}} = \dfrac{\sigma}{\sqrt{n}}$, that is, when a sample is selected from a finite population with replacement. However, when the population is finite, then the standard case needs a correction factor to be multiplied.

$$\therefore \quad \sigma_{\bar{x}} = \frac{\sigma}{\sqrt{n}}\sqrt{\frac{N-n}{N-1}}$$

Where N is the size of the population. This term which is multiplied to $\frac{\sigma}{\sqrt{n}}$ is called *fpc* factor.

38. The measure of central tendency and variation alone do not reveal all the characteristics of a given set of data. For example, 2 distributions may have the same mean and standard deviation, but may differ widely in the shape of their distribution. Either the distribution of the data is symmetrical or it is not. The term symmetry is described as the balance between the right and left halves of the curve. That is, if we draw a vertical line through the centre of the distribution then it should look the same on both sides. This is also known as normal distribution and is characterised in the form of a bell-shaped curve. In a symmetrical distribution, the majority of the scores lie around the central value. If the distribution of data is not symmetrical, it is called 'asymmetrical' or 'skewed'. Thus, skewness refers to the lack of symmetry of a distribution. A simple method of detecting the direction of skewness is to consider the tails of the distribution.

39. Hypothesis Testing

Hypothesis testing is a branch of statistics in which the researcher states statistical hypotheses and subsequently tests whether the collected data support those hypotheses. Statistical hypotheses are central to hypothesis testing and are referred to as the *null hypothesis* and the *alternative hypothesis.* The null hypothesis, H_0, is a statistical statement about a population parameter that is assumed to be true. By convention, H_0 states that no difference or relationship exists in the population and this hypothesis is tested using the collected data. In fact, for this reason, many statistical texts refer to hypothesis testing as *null hypothesis significance testing.*

The alternative hypothesis, H_1, is also a statistical statement about a population parameter, but in this case, it states that the population parameter is some value other than the value stated in H_0. Also by convention, we state H_0 and H_1 together, and since they both cannot be true, the collected data can either support H_0 as being tenable or support H_1 as being tenable.

40. If r = 0, the two Regression Lines are perpendicular to each other

The equations of two regression lines are

$$Y-\bar{Y} = b_{YX}(X-\bar{X})$$
$$= r\frac{\sigma_Y}{\sigma_X}(X-\bar{X})$$

and
$$X-\bar{X} = b_{XY}(Y-\bar{Y})$$
$$= r\frac{\sigma_X}{\sigma_Y}(Y-\bar{Y})$$

If r = 0, the two equations become

$$Y-\bar{Y} = 0 \text{ or } Y=\bar{Y}$$

and $X-\bar{X} = 0$ or $X=\bar{X}$

From the graph it is clear that $Y=\bar{Y}$ and $X=\bar{X}$ are perpendicular to each other.

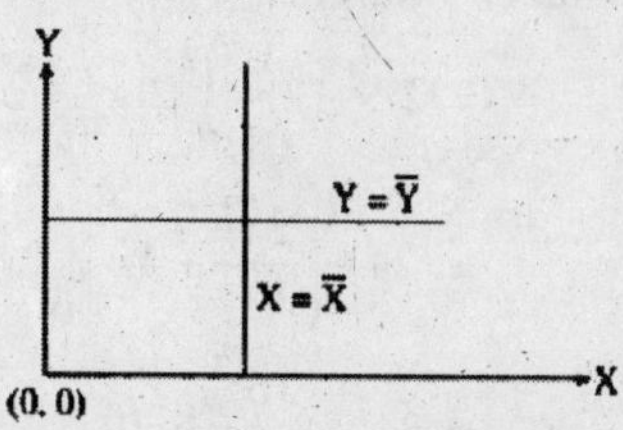

41. The Poisson and binomial distributions have a useful relationship. A binomial distribution with sample size n and probability p can be approximated by a Poisson distribution with parameter $\lambda = np$, if n is large and p is small, with the approximation improving as $n \to \infty$ and $p \to 0$.

42. Given that A = 5, $\mu_1' = 2$, $\mu_2' = 20$

$$\text{Mean} = A + \mu_1' = 5 + 2 = 7$$

$$\text{Variance } (\sigma^2) = \mu_2' - (\mu_1')^2 = 20 - (2)^2 = 20 - 4 = 16.$$

43. In a leap year, there are 366 days. For every consecutive 7 days we have a Sunday. So, in any leap year, there are at least $\left[\frac{366}{7}\right] = 52$ Sundays. Now, a year can start on any of the seven days in a week and an extra Sunday would be available if the year starts on Saturday or Sunday. Thus, out of 7 elementary events that are equally likely, 2 are favourable for the event in questions.

Hence, The required probability $= \frac{2}{7}$.

44. Under perfect competition market price is: demand = supply *i.e.*,

$$16 - x^2 - 2x^2 - 4 = 0$$

or, $$-3x^2 + 12 = 0$$

or, $$-3x^2 = -12$$

$$\therefore \quad x^2 = \frac{12}{3}$$

$$x = \sqrt{\frac{12}{3}} = 2 \text{ units}$$

$$Y = 2x^2 + 4 = 12$$

Market price = 12

$\therefore$ Producer's Surplus

$$= 2 \times 12 - \int_0^2 2(x^2 + 2)dx$$

$$= 24 - \left[\frac{2x^3}{3} + 4x\right]_0^2$$

$$= 24 - \frac{16}{3} - 8 - 0$$

$$= 24 - \frac{16}{3} - 8$$

$$= \frac{32}{3}.$$

45. To find the sum of the first S_n terms of a geometric sequence use the formula

$$S_n = \frac{a_1(1 - r^n)}{1 - r}$$

Where n is the number of terms, a_1 is the first term and r is the common ratio.

$$\therefore \quad S_n = \frac{1(1 - 2^8)}{1 - 2} = \frac{-255}{-1} = 255.$$

46. A sequence is geometric when the ratios of consecutive terms are the same. So, the sequence $a_1, a_2, a_3, a_4, ..., a_n, ...$ is geometric when there is a number r such that

$$\frac{a_2}{a_1} = \frac{a_3}{a_2} = \frac{a_4}{a_3} = ... = r, \; r \neq 0.$$

The number r is the common ratio of the geometric sequence.

Here, Common Ratio $(r) = \frac{2}{4} = \frac{1}{2}$.

48. Vroom's Expectancy Theory: Victor Vroom's expectancy theory examines motivation through the perception of what a person believes will happen. According to the expectancy theory, human motivation is affected by anticipated rewards and costs. An employee will be motivated to work toward a particular goal if it is perceived that a personal need will be satisfied. The employee's desire for a goal (valence) multiplied by what the organization expects (expectancy) will equal satisfaction and motivation.

49. According to Koontz et al. (1984) the purpose of organizing is summarized by the following general truths: (*a*) "principle of unity of objective" and (*b*) "principle of efficiency." The "principle of unity of objective" concludes that an organization structure is effective if it facilitates the contributions of individuals in the attainment of the organization's objectives (Koontz et.al.). "This principle implies that there is an existence of formulated and understood goals of the organization that people within the organization strive to achieve".

The other general truth of the purpose of organizing is the "principle of efficiency." As described by Koontz et al. (1984), "an effective organization is one that is structured to aid in the accomplishment of objectives with the minimum of unsought consequences or costs". The effectiveness of a structure should be judged by how it contributes to the attainment of objectives or goals. The principles of organizing imply the existence of formulated and understood organizational and goals.

50. **Psychological Factors:** There are four major psychological factors that influence buying choices. These factors are—motivation, learning, and beliefs and attitudes.

53. Coordination means harmonising, synchronising and unifying individual efforts towards the common objectives. According to Fayol, to coordinate is to harmonise all the activities of an organisation so as to facilitate its working and its success.

Coordinating is the process of integrating and harmonising the activities of different individuals and departments for the accomplishment of organisational goals.

'Coordination is the orderly arrangement of group efforts to provide unity of action in the pursuit of a common purpose.'

—***Mooney and Railey***

'Coordination is the process whereby an executive develops an orderly pattern of group efforts among his subordinates and secures unity of action in the pursuit of common purpose.' —***Dalton E. McFarland***

'Coordination is the orderly synchronisation of the efforts of the subordinates to provide the proper amount, timing and quality of execution so that unified efforts lead to the stated objective, namely, the common purpose of enterprise.' —***Theo Haimann***

54. Controlling is the last function of the management process. But it is closely related to the first function of management, *i.e.*, planning. Some writers on management think that planning and controlling are the blades of a pair of scissors. Without objectives and plans control is not possible, because performance has to be compared against some established criteria. Similarly, without controlling planning may be meaningless.

The basic control process: Control systems and techniques are same for all types of activities. The basic control process, wherever it is found and whatever is being controlled, involves three steps: (1) establishing standards, (2) measuring performance against these standards, and (3) correcting variations from standards.

56. There is no unanimity among management scholars about management functions. They have given different classifications. Among those, who tried to analyse the functions or process of management, Henri Fayol's name comes first. He has classified managerial functions into five parts, viz., planning, organizing, command, coordination and control. This classification is widely accepted in management world.

Lyndall Urwick divides management functions into six categories, viz., Forecasting, Planning, Organizing, Command, Coordination and Control. Besides these, he considers investigation (or research) and communication as important functions of management. Luther Gulick coined the word POSDCORB to indicate the principal functions of management. The POSDCORB stands for Planning (P), Organizing (O), Staffing (S), Directing (D), Coordinating (CO), Reporting (R), and Budgeting (B). Of these, Reporting is covered by the controlling function and budgeting represents both planning and controlling.

R.C. Davis has identified only three functions of management. *i.e.*, Planning, Organizing and Controlling Command and Coordination, according to him facilitate control and should, therefore, be considered a part of it.

Newman and Summer identified management functions into (*i*) Organizing, (*ii*) Planning, (*iii*) Reading, and (*iv*) Measuring and Controlling.

J.L. Massie classifies management functions into (*i*) Decision-making, (*ii*) Organizing, (*iii*) Staffing, (*iv*) Planning, (*v*) Controlling, (*vi*) Communicating, and (*vii*) Directing.

Koontz and O'donnel classify the managing process into (*i*) Planning, (*ii*) Organizing, (*iii*) Staffing, (*iv*) Directing, and (*v*) Controlling.

58. Coercion means forcibly compelling a person to enter into a contract. Coercion is a threat or force used by one party against the other for making him to enter into an agreement. Sec. 15 of the Act defines:

"Coercion is the committing or threatening to commit, any act forbidden by the Indian Penal Code, or the unlawful detaining, or threatening to detain, any property, to the prejudice of any person whatever, with the intention of causing any person to enter into an agreement."

Coercion implies a committing or threatening to commit some act which is contrary to law. According to the above definition of coercion, it may be in any of the following acts:

1. To commit an act forbidden by the Indian Penal code; or
2. The threat to commit an act forbidden by the Indian Penal Code; or
3. Unlawful detention of any property; or
4. The threat to unlawful detention of any property.

However, it is necessary that

(*i*) The act, amounting to coercion, must have been done with the intention of causing any person to enter into an agreement, and

(*ii*) It does not matter, whether the Indian Penal Code is or is not in force at the place where coercion is employed.

Examples: 1. ***Renganayakamma Vs. Alwar Chetty (1889)***

A young widow of 13 years was forced to agree to adopt a boy to her husband under the threats of preventing the dead body of her husband from being removed for cremation. The widow adopted the boy and subsequently applied for cancellation of the adoption. Because her consent was not free but induced by coercion. It was held that coercion was employed as any person who obstructed a dead body from being removed would be guilty of an offence under Sec. 197 of the Indian Penal Code.

2. ***Muthiah Chettiar Vs. Karuppen Chetty (1927)***
An agent refused to hand over the account books of a business to the new agent unless the principal released him from liability in respect of all the past transactions. It was held by the Madras High Court that the release deed was avoidable at the option of the principal as it was given under coercion.

3. ***Bansraj Vs. the Secretary of State (1939)***
The Government gave a threat of attachment against the property of A, for the recovery of a fine due from B, the son of A, A paid the fine. Held, the payment of fine was induced by coercion and, therefore, A was entitled to recover the money paid to remove wrongful attachment.

Threat to File a Suit

To threaten a criminal or civil prosecution does not constitute coercion because it is not an act forbidden by the Indian Penal Code. But a threat to file a suit on a false charge constitutes coercion, for such an act is forbidden by the Indian Penal Code.

Threat to Commit Suicide

Sometimes, by threat to commit suicide, a person obtains the consent of the other. The doubt arises because suicide though forbidden by the Indian Panel code is for obvious reasons not punishable. A dead person cannot be punished. But, since Section 15 declares that committing or threatening to commit suicide should obviously be so regarded (suicide being forbidden).

Example: ***Chikkam Ammiraju Vs. Chikkam Seshamma (1918)***

In this case a person, by threat to commit suicide, induced his wife and son to execute a release deed in favour of his brother in respect of certain properties which they claimed as their own. The transaction was set aside on the grounds of coercion. It was stated by the majority of judges that though 'a threat to commit suicide' was not punishable under the Indian Penal Code, it must be deemed to be forbidden by that Code, as 'an attempt to commit suicide' was punishable under Sec. 309 of that Code. Their Lordships observed: "The term 'any act forbidden by the Indian Penal Code' is wider than the term 'punishable by the Indian Penal Code'. Simply because a man escapes punishment, it does not follow that the act is not forbidden by the Penal Code. For example, a lunatic or a minor may not be punished. This does not show that their criminal acts are not forbidden by the Penal Code."

Effect of Coercion

The effect of coercion is that it makes the contract voidable at the option of the party whose consent is obtained by coercion, that is, such party can put an end to the contract if he so chooses. The burden of proof that coercion was used lies on the party who wants to set aside the contract on the plea of coercion. The effect of coercion is emphasised in Sections 19 and 72 of Indian Contract Act.

Section 19 states: "When consent to an agreement is caused by coercion, the agreement is a contract voidable at the option of the party whose consent was so caused."

Section 72 states: "A person to whom money has been paid or anything delivered under coercion, must repay or return it."

59. A contract of sale includes both sale and agreement to sell. In sale, the ownership is transferred immediately. The term Sale is defined in the Section 4(3) of the Sale of Goods Act, 1930 as – "*where under a contract of sale the property in the goods is transferred from the seller to the buyer, the contract is called a sale.*"

In an agreement to sell the ownership of the goods is not transferred immediately. It is intending to transfer at a future date upon the completion of certain conditions thereon. The term is defined in Section 4(3) of the Sale of Goods Act, 1930, which is as follows – "*where under a contract of sale the transfer of the property in the goods is to take place at a future time or subject to some condition thereafter to be fulfilled, the contract is called an agreement to sell.*"

Sale	Agreement to sell
Ownership of the goods is transferred immediately.	Ownership of the goods is transferred on a future date after the fulfilment of certain conditions.
The risk of the goods lies with the buyer.	The risk of the goods lies with the seller.
It is an executed contract.	It is an executory contract.
The seller can in case of breach sue for the whole price.	The aggrieved party can sue only for damages. He can claim price only if it was payable at a stated date.
Breach on the part of the seller gives the buyer a double remedy; a suit for damages against the seller and a proprietary claim over the goods.	The seller still being the owner of the goods, the buyer only has a remedy to file a suit for the recovery of damages.

60. Distinction between a Contract of Indemnity and a Contract of Guarantee

The following are the points of distinction between the two:

1. Number of parties: In a contract of indemnity, there are two parties — the indemnifier and the indemnity-holder. In a contract of guarantee, there are three parties — the creditor, the principal debtor and the surety.

2. Object or purpose: A contract of indemnity is for the reimbursement of loss, whereas a contract of guarantee is for the security of a debt or good conduct of an employee.

3. Number of contracts: In indemnity, there is only one contract between the indemnifier and the indemnified, while in guarantee, there are three contracts—one between the principal debtor and the creditor, the second between the creditor and the surety, and the third between the surety and the principal debtor.

4. Nature of liability: In a contract of indemnity, the liability of the indemnifier is primary in nature. In a contract of guarantee, the liability of the surety is secondary, *i.e.,* the surety is liable only on default of the principal debtor. (If the principal debtor fulfils his obligation, the question of surety's liability does not arise.)

5. Request by the debtor: In a contract of indemnity, the indemnifier acts independently without any request of the debtor of the third party, whereas in a contract of guarantee it is necessary that the surety should give the guarantee at the request of the debtor.

6. Existing debt or duty: In a contract of indemnity, in most cases there is no existing debt or duty, whereas in a contract of guarantee there is an existing debt or duty, the performance of which is guaranteed by the surety.

7. Right to sue: In a contract of guarantee, the surety, after he discharges the debt owing to the creditor, can proceed against the principal debtor in his own right. But in the case of a contract of indemnity the indemnifier cannot sue the third party for loss in his own name, because there is no privity of contract. He can do so only, if there is an assignment in his favour, otherwise he must bring the suit (against the third party) in the name of the indemnified.

61. Waiver is the intentional relinquishment of a right or claim. It is when one party agrees to "give up" an existing, or in some cases, future right. A waiver could apply to a right a party has under a contract or it could apply to a right the party has as a matter of law.

63. Unlimited Companies:

- Sec2(92) "unlimited company" means a company not having any limit on the liability of its members.
- The members will be liable for all the debts of the company like partners in a Partnership firm.
- The Articles must state the number of members with which the company is to be registered.
- It is a contingent liability of the members which will fall due only on the winding up of the company.
- The Unlimited Company can be re-registered as Limited Company through appropriate alterations in Liability Clause of MOA and alterations in AOA.

64. Section 2 Sub-section (6) "associate company", in relation to another company, means a company in which that other company has a significant influence, but which is not a subsidiary company of the company having such influence and includes a joint venture company.

Explanation—For the purposes of this clause, "significant influence" means control of at least twenty per cent of total share capital, or of business decisions under an agreement.

65. As per section 203(3) of the Companies Act, 2013, a Whole-time KMP of a company shall not hold office in more than one company except in its subsidiary company. This section restricts a person to hold office in more than one company, while at the same time enables a person to hold office in its subsidiary company and ideally he may be appointed in only one subsidiary.

67. Quorum for meetings of Board (Section 174 of the Companies Act, 2013)

A quorum is the minimum number of qualified persons who must attend in order to transact business at a duly convened Board meeting. A meeting shall not be deemed to have been properly held unless the quorum was present at that meeting.

A new section 174 of the Companies Act, 2013 came into force from 1st April, 2014 which provides for Quorum for meetings of Board. According to this section:

(*i*) The quorum for a Board Meeting shall be one-third of its total strength or two directors, whichever is higher.

(*ii*) The directors who participate by video conferencing or by other audio visual means shall also be counted for the purpose of determining the quorum at the meeting.

Further, the explanation as given in *the Companies (Meetings of Board and its*

Powers) Rules, 2014 provides that a director participating in a meeting through video conferencing or other audio visual means shall be counted for the purpose of quorum, unless he is to be excluded for any items of business under any provisions of the Act or the rules.

69. Indirect tax: Indirect tax is usually levied on consumer goods. Some examples are:
- Value Added Tax (VAT);
- Excise Duty (on cigarettes and alcohol); and
- Import Tax (on articles that are imported).

72. Under the provisions of Section 10(2A), in the case of a person being a partner of a firm which is separately assessed as such, his share in the total income of the firm is completely exempt from income tax since AY 1993-94.

For this purpose, the share of a partner in the total income of a firm separately assessed as such would be an amount which bears to the total income of the firm the same share as the amount of the share in the profits of the firm in accordance with the partnership deed bears to such profits.

73. Perfectly Inelastic Demand: A perfectly inelastic demand is one in which a change in price produces no change in the quantity demanded. In other words, despite a considerable change in price there is no change in demand. In Figure, it is shown perfectly inelastic demand curve. DD demand curve is parallel to OY-axis. It means that when price is ₹ 2 demand is for 4 units. When price rises to ₹ 4.00 or ₹ 6.00 demand remains the same *i.e.*, 4 units. Thus, change in price causes no change in demand. In this case, elasticity of demand is zero or $E_d = 0$ (zero).

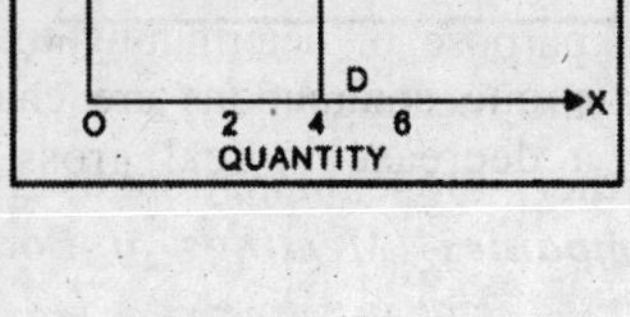

74. Income Elasticity of Demand

The coefficient of *income elasticity of demand* (e_M) measures the percentage change in the amount of a commodity purchased per unit time (ΔQ/Q) resulting from a given percentage change in a consumer's income (ΔM/M). Thus,

$$e_M = \frac{\Delta Q / Q}{\Delta M / M} = \frac{\Delta Q}{\Delta M} \cdot \frac{M}{Q}$$

When e_M is negative, the goods is inferior. If e_M is positive, the goods is normal. A normal goods is usually a *luxury* if its $e_M > 1$, otherwise it is a *necessity.* Depending on the level of the consumer's income, e_M for a goods is likely to vary considerably. Thus, a goods may be a luxury at "low" levels of income, a necessity at "intermediate" levels of income and an inferior goods at "high" levels of income.

76. The $MRTS_{LK}$, the change in the $MRTS_{LK}$, the K/L ratio, and the change in the K/L ratio are all components of the coefficient of elasticity of technical substitution but cannot individually give us that coefficient.

77. Under constant returns to scale, if we increase both labour and capital by 10%, output will also increase by 10%. Since we are increasing only labour by 10%, output will increase by less than 10% (if we are operating *within* stage II of production).

78. The implicit cost of this entrepreneur depends on how much labour and other factors that person owns and uses in the enterprise could earn collectively in their best alternative use.

79. Given the production function Q = Q(L, K), the labour elasticity of output (e_l) is the proportional change in output, resulting from a given proportional change in labour input, L, the input capital, K, being held constant. Similarly, the capital elasticity of output (e_n) is the proportional change in output, resulting from a given proportional change in capital K, the input labour, L, being held constant.

Like demand elasticities, input elasticities can be expressed as follows:

$$e_L = \frac{\%\partial Q}{\%\partial L} = \frac{\partial Q / Q}{\partial L / L}$$

$$e_l = \frac{\partial Q}{\partial L} \times \frac{L}{Q} = \frac{\partial Q / \partial L}{Q / L} = \frac{MP_L}{AP_L}$$

$$e_K = \frac{\%\partial Q}{\%\partial K} = \frac{\partial Q / Q}{\partial K / K}$$

$$e_k = \frac{\partial Q}{\partial K} \times \frac{K}{Q} = \frac{\partial Q / \partial K}{Q / K} = \frac{MP_k}{AP_k}$$

Thus, the input elasticity of output turns out to be a ratio of the input's marginal product and average product. In general, marginal and average products vary as the input ratios change. Hence, the Input elasticities change as well.

80. Under MR – MC approach, a producer is in equilibrium, (*i.e.*, maximises profits) at that level of output where (*i*) MR = MC and (*ii*) MC is rising.

Conditions of Producer's Equilibrium under Perfect Competition

In a perfectly competitive market, the marginal revenue and average revenue of a producer coincide and is equal to market price, *i.e.*, AR = WR = P. A competitive producer's equilibrium is established at that level of output where,

(*i*) P = MC, (*ii*) MC is rising and (*iii*) P ≥ AVC in short-run and P ≥ AC in the long-run. In a situation of equilibrium, a producer may be earning maximum profit, break-even or shut-down.

A competitive producer always choose that level of output which lies on the rising portion of the MC curve. He will never produce on the decreasing portion of the MC curve. MC curve gives the supply curve of the firm.

81. The short-run supply curve of the perfectly competitive firm is that portion of its marginal cost curve that lies above the point where it intersects the average (short-run) variable cost curve—that is, above the minimum level of AVC. If price falls below this level, the firm's quantity supplied drops to zero.

82. **Increasing cost industry:** An industry is said to be increasing cost industry if the prices of the factors of production employed increase as the industry output expands. In other words, production costs rise with the output. Shifts in supply fail to match those in demand.

83. The short-run equilibrium level of output for the monopolist is the output at which MR = SMC *and the slope of the* MR *curve is smaller than the slope of the* SMC *curve* (provided that at this output P ≥ AVC).

84. In the long run, a monopolist will remain in business only if he or she can make a profit (or at least break even) by producing the best level of output with the most appropriate scale of plant. The best level of output in the long run is given by the point where the LMC curve intersects the MR curve from below. The most appropriate scale of plant is the one whose SAC curve is tangent to the LAC curve at the best level of output.

85. In both these models, the oligopolists do recognize their mutual dependence (which makes these models better than the Cournot, Bertrand, and Edgeworth models) but act without collusion.

86. **Business Cycles**

1. A business cycle is a fluctuation in aggregate economic output that lasts for several years. Business cycles are recurring but vary in terms of both length and intensity. They are depicted as a series of peaks and troughs. A peak marks the end of a period of economic expansion and the beginning of a recession (contraction) while a trough marks the end of a recession and the beginning of an economic recovery (expansion). The chart below illustrates the nature of the business cycle.

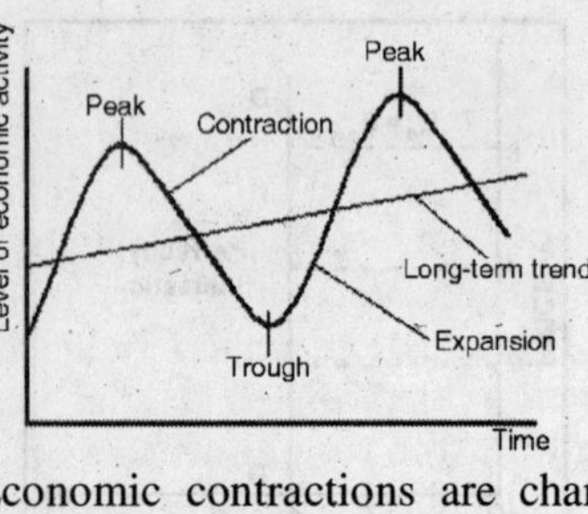

2. Economic contractions are characterized by a decrease in real gross domestic

product (GDP) due to reduced spending. In a period of expansion, real GDP is increasing. At the peak real GDP generally surpasses potential GDP causing a scarcity of labour and materials. These shortages generally cause inflation.

88. Cash Reserve Ratio: Cash reserve ratio implies that every commercial bank is required to keep a certain percentage of its total deposits as cash reserve with the central bank of the country. The credit creation power of the commercial banks depends upon the amount of cash reserve ratio kept by them. There is an inverse relationship between the cash reserve ratio and the volume of credit created by the banks. If the cash reserve ratio is large, the smaller will be the volume of credit created by the banks and if the cash reserve ratio is small, the larger will be the volume of credit created by the banks. Thus, if the commercial banks lend more, the cash reserve ratio will fall.

89. Balance of Trade: The difference between the value of a country's exports and the value of its imports during a specific time is the country's balance of trade. A country that exports more than it imports is said to have a *favourable* balance of trade, called a trade surplus. A country that imports more than it exports is said to have an *unfavourable* balance of trade, or a trade deficit. When imports exceed exports, more money from trade flows out of the country than flows into it.

90. Primary Deficit: One of the major components of government expenditure is interest payment. Though interest payments in the current period are obligatory, they are on the outstanding public debt that is an outcome of past policies. In any given period, though the government may be following the policy of fiscal contraction and consolidation, the amount of interest payment may be large due to a substantial amount of outstanding public debt Fiscal deficit, which is the difference between total receipt and total expenditure including the expenditure on interest payments, hence, does not reflect on the current fiscal stance. It is unable to reflect on the extent to which the current discrepancy in fiscal operations improves or worsens the government's net indebtedness. Hence, the concept of primary deficit, which is the fiscal deficit net of interest payment is estimated. The primary deficit can be estimated as:

Primary deficit = Gross fiscal deficit – Interest payment
= (Revenue expenditure + Capital expenditure) – (Revenue receipts + Capital grants + Recovery of loans + Disinvestment proceeds) – (Interest payments)

92. To avoid double counting, two methods are used: (*i*) Final Output Method, and (*ii*) Value Added Method.

(*i*) Final Output Method: According to this method, the value of intermediate goods is deducted from the value of output. In other words, the value of final goods and services only is included in national income. In the above example, the bread sold to the consumers is the final output. Only the value of final output *i.e.*, ₹ 900 will be included in national income. The value of wheat, flour and baking-breed *i.e.*, ₹ 400, ₹ 600 and ₹ 800 = ₹ 1,800 are the values of intermediate goods. The value of the final output can be calculated by deducting the value of intermediate goods from the value of output. In other words,

Value of Final Output = Value of Output – Value of Intermediate Goods = ₹ 2,700 – ₹ 1,800 = ₹ 900.

(*ii*) Value Added Method: Value Added refers to the difference between value of output and the value of intermediate consumption of each producing unit in the country. Sum total of value added by all the producing units within the domestic territory of the country is equal to Domestic Product.

93. Lower interest rates make it cheaper to borrow. This tends to encourage spending and investment. This leads to higher aggregate demand (AD) and economic growth. This increase in AD may also cause inflationary pressures.

94. A measure of the money value of the goods and services becoming available to the nation from economic activity. There are three approaches to measuring this; (1) Income Approach, (2) Expenditure Approach, (3) Product Approach. First, as a sum of the incomes derived from economic activity, these broadly divide into incomes from *profits* and incomes from employment; second, as the sum of expenditures with the main distinction being between expenditure on *consumption* and expenditures which add to the capital stock *(investment);* finally, as the sum of the products of the various industries of the nation.

95. The Phillips Curve: In a celebrated article published in 1958. Australian economist A. W. Phillips of the London School of Economics plotted data on unemployment rates and the rate of change in wage rates between 1861 and 1957 in the United Kingdom. Phillips showed there was a remarkably stable inverse relationship between changes in money wages and the unemployment rate. Economists have since extended this concept to the following definition of the Phillips curve. The Phillips curve is a curve showing an inverse relationship between the inflation rate and the unemployment rate. The reason it is acceptable to use the inflation rate, rather than the change in wages, is that wages are the main component of prices. At low rates of unemployment, labour has the market power to push up wages and, in turn, prices. When many workers are pounding the pavement eager for jobs, labour lacks bargaining power to ask for raises. As a result, the upward pressure on prices eases.

96. Depreciation in a country's currency increases the prices of imports in terms of domestic currency. The increase in prices of imports may reduce the quantity of imports. However, if price elasticity of demand is inelastic for imported goods, the higher prices of imports may result in a higher value of imports. In other words, depreciation in the home currency may deteriorate the country's balance of trade. But depreciation in domestic currency makes exports cheaper in terms of foreign currency and this will increase the volume of exports. The value of exports thus increases with the increased quantity of exports. However, if the export demand is price inelastic, then depreciation in the home currency may not cause an increase in the volume of exports.

98. The LM-curve shows all combinations of the interest rate and level of output such that the money sector is in equilibrium, that is, the demand for real money balances is equal to the supply of real money balances. An increase in income will increase the demand for real money balances. Given a fixed real money supply, this will lead to an increase in interest rates, which will then reduce the quantity of real money balances demanded until the money sector is again in equilibrium. In other words, the LM-curve is upward sloping.

If money demand is less interest sensitive, then the LM-curve is steeper and monetary policy changes have a stronger effect on equilibrium income. If money supply is changed to a new fixed level, the adjustment to a new equilibrium in the money sector has to come solely through changes in money demand. If money demand is less interest sensitive, any increase in money supply requires a larger increase in income and a larger decrease in the interest rate in order to bring the money sector into a new equilibrium.

102. The effect of devaluation on the balance of payments will be favourable if the price level remains constant in the devaluing economy. After devaluation, exports increase and imports decrease resulting in shortage of goods within the domestic market. As a result, the price level rises in the domestic economy. After price rise of domestic products, prices of imported products and domestic products will be almost same *i.e.*, the imported goods will not be dearer as was expected after devaluation. So the imports will not decline. Similarly, the price level of export goods will also increase on account of increased cost of inputs in the domestic economy. Hence, export goods will not remain cheaper for the foreign buyer. So, our exports will not increase even after devaluation.

103. The central excise duty, leviable on the production or manufacture of goods, is the single most important source of revenue, accounting for about one-third of consolidated (the Central, State and Union Territory Government) tax revenues and about one-fourth of current revenues.

104. The Wholesale Price Index (WPI) is the most widely used price index in India and is an indicator of movement in wholesale prices of 676 commodities in all trade and transaction. WPI is the only price index in India, which is available on a weekly basis with shortest time lag of two weeks. It is due to these attributes that it is widely used in business and industry circle and by government and is generally taken as an indicator of the rate of inflation in the economy.

106. Balance of payment record of a country has two accounts (*a*) Current Account, (*b*) Capital Account. While Current account in the balance of payment record consists of mainly exports and imports, Capital account refers to financial investments, deposits and loans, However, current account includes invisible items viz, receipts and payments for services such as travel, insurance, transportation etc.

111. The co-founder of Hero Cycles group Satyanand Munjal passed away in Ludhiana, Punjab. He was 99. He was popularly known as 'mahatma'. Satyanand Munjal for being devoted to several social causes related to the Arya Samaj.

112. **Indent Firms:** There are firms of importing and exporting agents at every important port town. These firms are known as "Indent Firms". The indent firms serve as middlemen between the exporters and the importers. They purchase goods for foreign traders at the lowest available prices and arrange for their shipment abroad. They also undertake purchase of goods in foreign market on behalf of the home traders and then import into their country. They charge a small commission for their services. These indent firms are also called commission agents.

113. Letter of credit assume great importance in international trade. The letter of credit assures payment to exporters soon after he parts with the goods and enables the importers to make payment only after he receives the goods or the documents of title to goods.

Letter of credit may be defined as a letter issued by the importer's bank in favour of the exporter authorising him to draw bills upto an amount specified in it and assuring him of payment against the delivery of the prescribed documents in his own country.

The letter of credit is a sort of a guarantee to the exporter that his draft will be honoured by a specified bank upto a certain amount as per the specified terms.

Parties to the Letter of Credit

The various parties connected with the letter of credit are:

1. **Opener:** The opener is the buyer (the importer). The buyer who makes the application and on whose behalf the credit is 'opened' is called opener of the letter of credit.
2. **Issuer:** The issuer is also called as the opening or issuing bank in the importing country; which establishes the letter of credit on behalf of the opener.
3. **Beneficiary:** The beneficiary is the person in whose favour the credit is opened, normally, the seller or exporter.
4. **Negotiating bank:** Usually beneficiary's bank through which the documents are normally negotiated. In other words, negotiating bank is the bank that pays or accepts the drafts of the exporter. It is also called as the paying bank.

114. The postwar international economic system was mapped out at a landmark meeting in July 1944, when economists and government leaders from both sides of the Atlantic gathered at the Mount Washington Hotel, set in the forested hills of Bretton Woods, New Hampshire. There they laid down the principles of what became known as the Breatton Woods system: the convertibility of currencies, free trade, non-discrimination, and stable rates of exchange.

116. Non-development expenditure does not really entail the production of any good or service and is a plain transfer payment, made by the government to certain sections of society. At the same time, it is essential for both economic and political reasons.

There are mainly three sub-headings here. These are — interest payments, subsidies and defense expenditure.

120. The World Intellectual Property Organization (WIPO) is an international organization that protects intellectual property rights in the global economy. Intellectual property, broadly defined, includes human endeavours that reach beyond existing accomplishments in the realms of science, technology, and artistic expression. The Convention Establishing the World Intellectual Property Organization was signed in Stockholm, Sweden, on July 14, 1967, and the provisions of the agreement went into force in 1970. In the WIPO Convention, contracting parties expressed a desire "to encourage creative activity, to promote the protection of intellectual property throughout the world." WIPO was established as an autonomous specialized agency within the United Nations system. In 2005, WIPO consisted of 182 member states and administered twenty-three international intellectual property treaties. WIPO membership is open to countries within the United Nations System and to countries invited to join by the WIPO General Assembly. WIPO's headquarters is located in Geneva, Switzerland.

121. The Organization of the Petroleum Exporting Countries (OPEC) is a permanent, inter-governmental Organization, created at the Baghdad Conference on September 10-14, 1960, by Iran, Iraq, Kuwait, Saudi Arabia and Venezuela. The five Founding Members were later joined by nine other Members: Qatar (1961); Indonesia (1962) – suspended its membership from January 2009-December 2015; Libya (1962); United Arab Emirates (1967); Algeria (1969); Nigeria (1971); Ecuador (1973) – suspended its membership from December 1992 – October 2007; Angola (2007) and Gabon (1975-1994). OPEC had its headquarters in Geneva, Switzerland, in the first five years of its existence. This was moved to Vienna, Austria, on September 1, 1965.

125. Cost behaviour can be defined as the manner in which costs changes due to changes in volume or activity. In relation to cost behaviour analysis, fixed and variable cost classifications are generally found. A proper analysis of cost behaviour patterns is the basis of all profit planning and cost control.

126. **Rucker plan:** A type of *gain sharing* scheme that is concerned with the value added by labour. The Rucker plan was developed in the 1950s by Allen Rucker. A typical Rucker plan includes a suggestion scheme, a committee system, and a bonus formula, based on *value added*. It assesses the relationship between the value added to goods as they pass through the manufacturing process, and the total labour costs. Bonuses are earned when the current ratio is better than the base ratio over a given time period. A Rucker plan usually has a far less elaborate structure than the similar *Scanlon plan*.

127. Inventory control is a part of material control. The term inventory refers to the sum of raw material, packing material, fuels, lubricants, spare parts, maintenance consumables, semi-processed items and finished goods. Inventories are kept to ensure smooth flow of business operations. The scope of inventory control related to maintaining the correct level of inventory at all times. This can be ensured through fixation of stock levels for various items, and fixation of buying quantities and buying schedules.

128. A minimum value of labour turnover is common and is good for all industries. But excessive or high labour turnover is dangerous. Excessive labour turnover may occur due to the following reasons:

1. **Avoidable causes:** Low wages and allowances, dissatisfaction with the job, poor working conditions, odd working hours, poor interpersonal relationships, poor welfare facilities, unfair methods of product promotion.
2. **Unavoidable causes:** Retirement, death while in service, accident, illness, dismissals and marriages in case of women.

Previous Paper (Solved)

UNIVERSITY OF DELHI—M.COM Entrance Test-2015

1. In a contract by post, acceptance is:
   A. Required
   B. Not required
   C. Acceptance should be only in writing
   D. None of the above
2. Which of the following statements is correct?
   A. Minor's agreements are valid
   B. Minor's agreements are void
   C. Minor's agreements are absolutely void
   D. Minor's agreements are voidable
3. Director's Identification number is mandatory for:
   A. All directors
   B. Only executive directors
   C. External directors
   D. Independent director
4. Indian Contract Act was enacted in the year:
   A. 1832 B. 1852
   C. 1872 D. None of these
5. A threat to commit an act forbidden by the Indian Penal Code amounts to:
   A. Fraud B. Misrepresentation
   C. Coercion D. None of these
6. Every agreement and promise enforceable by law is a ....
   A. Contract B. Offer
   C. Consideration D. None of these
7. Which one of the following is essential for a valid contract?
   A. Mutual consent
   B. Legal obligation
   C. Free consent
   D. All of the above
8. Indian Contract Act classifies the Quasi Contract into five categories under:
   A. Section 68 to 72
   B. Section 69 to 73
   C. Section 65 to 70
   D. None of them
9. A .... is the delivery of goods by one person to another for some purpose, upon a contract that they shall, when the purpose is accomplished, be returned or otherwise disposed of according to the directions of the person delivering them.
   A. Bailment B. Pledge
   C. Lien D. None of these
10. In a bailment contract the right to terminate the contract lies with the ....
    A. Bailee B. Bailer
    C. Wager D. None of these
11. The Bailor is also called as .... in a pledge.
    A. Pawnor B. Pawnee
    C. Wager D. None of these
12. The right of lien remains with the .... under the Sale of Goods Act, 1930.
    A. Unpaid seller against the goods
    B. Unpaid seller against the buyer
    C. Unpaid seller against the finder of goods
    D. None of the above
13. In the Limited Liability Partnership (LLP):
    A. Partnership Act 1932 applies
    B. Only selective provisions of Partnership Act 1932 apply
    C. Partnership Act 1932 does not apply
    D. None of the above

14. Every Limited Liability Partnership has at least ....
   A. Two designated partners
   B. Three designated partners
   C. Four designated partners
   D. None of the above

15. The regulatory mechanism of a Limited Liability Partnership lies with the:
   A. Registrar of Companies
   B. Tribunal
   C. Central Government
   D. All of the above

16. A Limited Liability Partnership is not subject to .... , however a .... is applicable.
   A. Dividend Distribution Tax, Minimum Alternate Tax
   B. Minimum Alternate Tax, Dividend Distribution Tax
   C. Surcharge, Cess
   D. None of the above

17. The Information Technology Act 2000 is not applicable on:
   A. A power of attorney as defined under the Powers of Attorney Act, 1882
   B. A trust as defined in the Indian Trusts Act, 1882
   C. A Will as defined under the Indian Succession Act, 1925
   D. All of the above

18. The provision laid down under Sec 4 of the Information Technology Act, 2000 makes:
   A. An email as a valid admissible evidence
   B. An email as an invalid evidence
   C. An email as a valid admissible evidence till it is in consonance with the provision of Sec 65B (2) of the Indian Evidence Act, 1872
   D. None of the above

19. The Information Technology Act, 2000 entails a punishment for sending offensive messages by means of computer resource or a communication device for:
   A. An imprisonment which may extend to three years and with fine
   B. An imprisonment which may extend to five years and with fine
   C. An imprisonment which may extend to three years and without fine
   D. An imprisonment which may extend to five years and without fine

20. Which of the following statements is true in case of an Unlimited Company?
   A. Unlimited company may or may not have a share capital
   B. Unlimited company is not subjected to any restrictions regarding purchase of its own shares
   C. A company registered as unlimited company may subsequently convert itself into a limited company
   D. All of the above

21. The provisions of Section 153 to 159 of the Companies Act 2013 requires the director to intimate his DIN to the company or all companies in:
   A. DIN form 1 B. DIN form 2
   C. DIN form 3 D. DIN form 4

22. A company may change its registered office from the local limit of one place to another within the same town, city or village by passing a:
   A. Special resolution
   B. Ordinary resolution
   C. Board resolution
   D. Resolution by special majority

23. In case of Doctrine of Constructive Notice the .... is protected from the ....
   A. Company, outsider
   B. Outsider, company
   C. Insider, company
   D. Company, insider

24. As per Sec 25 of the Companies Act 2013, a document containing offer of securities for sale is:
   A. Shelf prospectus
   B. Deemed prospectus
   C. Abridged prospectus
   D. None of the above

25. The first directors are appointed by the:
A. Promoters
B. Shareholders
C. Registrar
D. Central government

26. Casual director may be appointed by the company to fill a vacancy occurred due to:
A. Death of a director
B. Disqualification of a director
C. Removal of a director
D. All of the above

27. As per Companies Act 2013, every director shall hold .... shares as qualification shares.
A. One B. Two
C. Ten D. None

28. Sec 165 of the Companies Act 2013 provides that no person shall hold the office of director in more than:
A. Ten companies
B. Fifteen companies
C. Twenty companies
D. None of the above

29. Annual general meeting may be called by giving not less than clear .... notice.
A. 14 days B. 21 days
C. 23 days D. None of these

30. The Companies Act 2013 requires a listed company to inform the stock exchange .... in advance of closing the register of members for payment of dividend declared at the annual general meeting for determining the names of shareholders entitled to dividend declared at the annual general meeting for determining the names of shareholders entitled to dividend.
A. 22 days
B. 21 days
C. 20 days
D. None of the above

31. Which of the following consists of planning and decision-making?
A. Organising communication
B. Directing traditional management
C. Controlling network
D. None of the above

32. .... entails supervising, disciplining, evaluating, and managing the change of the four managerial resources.
A. Controlling B. Organising
C. Directing D. Planning

33. Management theory propounded by Taylor emphasise on ....
A. Unity of command
B. Unity of direction
C. Division of labour
D. Selecting right people for the job

34. .... is associated with participative management context.
A. Lewin B. Likert
C. Ericc D. Leavitt

35. Change may bring some potential .... to the organizational power to some people.
A. Barrier B. Opportunity
C. Threat D. None of these

36. Motivational concepts that focus on the perceived internal needs and outcomes of individuals are referred to as:
A. Process theories
B. Motivational theories
C. Content theories
D. Internal theories

37. Who is credited with having developed the concept of a priority or hierarchy of needs?
A. F.W. Taylor B. F.U. Herzberg
C. A.H. Maslow D. None of these

38. Following incomes are taxable for resident and ordinarily resident in India:
A. Business income from United States
B. Rental income from house property in United Kingdom
C. Interest from State Bank of India
D. All of the above

39. Interest payable by the Government of India to the non residents always deemed to accrue or arise in India:
A. True
B. False
C. Only in select cases
D. None of the above

40. The rate of tax that is leviable on the short-term capital gain arising of equity shares of a company or units of mutual funds is:

A. 10% B. 15%
C. 20% D. Tax free

41. Which National Park has been accorded approval as India's 48th Tiger Reserve by the National Tiger Conservation Authority (NTCA) in April, 2015?

A. Kanha Tiger Reserve
B. Rajaji National Park
C. Ranthambore National Park
D. Dudhwa National Park

42. Which South Korean steel company is facing problems regarding allocation of mines in Odisha due to the newly passed Mines and Minerals (Development and Regulation) Act, 2015?

A. Arcelor Mittal B. Ansteel
C. Nippon Steel D. POSCO

43. Who has been conferred with the prestigious Dinanath Mangeshkar Award on 25th April, 2015?

A. Shreya Goshal B. Anil Kapoor
C. Arijit Singh D. Shah Rukh Khan

44. Which day has been declared the International Yoga Day by the United Nations General Assembly?

A. June 21 B. May 13
C. January 18 D. December 20

45. Which company has Nokia acquired in April 2015 that will be now called the Nokia Corporation?

A. Broadcom B. Mobilink
C. Alcatel-Lucent D. Hutchinson Essar

46. Which country has been named the, world's happiest country according to the latest *World Happiness Report* published by United Nations?

A. Switzerland B. Australia
C. France D. Argentina

47. Which of the following Indian sportsperson has *not* won a medal at the 2012 Olympics held in London?

A. Saina Nehwal B. Mary Kom
C. Vijender Singh D. Sushil Kumar

48. Who has been appointed the CEO of Infosys?

A. Vishal Sikka B. Satya Nadella
C. Bill Gates D. Indra Nooyi

49. Prime Minister Narendra Modi recently signed an important agreement with France regarding purchase of which fighter jets?

A. P51 Mustang B. Rafale
C. Mig 21 D. F18 Super Hornet

50. Which of the following is not an agreement under WTO?

A. Agriculture Agreement
B. Sanitary and Phytosanitary measures (SPS)
C. General Agreement on Trade in Services (GATS)
D. Industry Agreement

51. Which company did Flipkart acquire in 2014 making it one of the biggest e-commerce acquisitions?

A. Myntra.com B. Yepme.com
C. Aerolife.com D. Snapdeal

52. The rate of growth of the Indian economy in the first three decades after Independence was also referred to as:

A. Indian rate of growth
B. Hindu rate of growth
C. Colonial rate of growth
D. None of the above

53. Which of the following came into existence in 2010 through an Act of Parliament and has been created as a revival of an ancient centre of learning?

A. Osmania University
B. Indian Institute of Science
C. Nalanda University
D. University of Hyderabad

54. Where will the 2016 Olympic games be held?

A. Beijing B. London
C. South Korea D. Rio de Janeiro

55. Which of the following is a person of Indian origin who has recently been elected to the British Parliament?

A. Kiran Shaw B. Piyush Gupta
C. Rishi Sunak D. Anshu Jain

56. Which of the following is not an Indian pharmaceutical company?
A. Dr. Reddy's Laboratories Limited
B. Novartis
C. Cadila Healthcare
D. Cipla

57. Which of the following sectors has the largest share in India's GDP?
A. Industry B. Agriculture
C. Services D. Textile

58. The foothills of Himalayas are also known, as the:
A. Satpuras B. Vindhayas
C. Nilgiri D. Sivalik hills

59. Who has been appointed the Head of the BRICS New Development Bank?
A. K.V. Kamath
B. Chanda Kochhar
C. Aditya Puri
D. Arundhati Bhattacharya

60. Which of the following is not permitted under Islamic banking?
A. Loan B. Interest
C. Deposits D. Profits

61. India is the largest producer in the world of which of the following:
A. Milk B. Dry fruits
C. Fish D. Coffee

62. The FDI ceiling in India's defence sector has been raised to:
A. 26% B. 49%
C. 51% D. 75%

63. Which of the following political systems is the basis of China's economy?
A. Democracy
B. Communism
C. Theocratic totalitarianism
D. None of the above

64. Which of the following countries was *not* a participant in the 2015 Cricket World Cup?
A. Afghanistan
B. Scotland
C. Denmark
D. United Arab Emirates

65. Which city is known as the Silicon Valley of India?
A. Hyderabad B. Bengaluru
C. Pune D. Delhi

66. The state having the largest area of forest cover in India is:
A. Assam B. Maharashtra
C. Kerala D. Madhya Pradesh

67. Which of the following is a tax reform related to sales taxes in India?
A. Direct Tax Code (DTC)
B. Wealth-Tax
C. Goods and Service Tax (GST)
D. Specific Anti-Avoidance Rules (SAAR)

68. Which Act was replaced with the introduction of Competition Act, 2002?
A. Monopolies and Restrictive Trade Practices Act
B. Foreign Exchange Management Act
C. Foreign Exchange Regulation Act
D. Industrial Disputes Act

69. Which institution has replaced Planning Commission in India?
A. Central Information Commission
B. National Knowledge Commission
C. NITI Aayog
D. Finance Commission

70. The Second Five Year Plan of India was based on which of the following models?
A. Mahalanobis model
B. Wage-goods model
C. Theocratic model
D. EPRG framework

71. Which of the following bodies/authorities deals with the auditing of receipts and expenditures of the Central government and State governments?
A. Office of the Chief Secretary
B. Reserve Bank of India
C. Department of Income Tax
D. Comptroller and Auditor General of India

72. The 2013 Ministerial Conference of WTO was held in:
A. Geneva B. Bali
C. Honk Kong D. Seattle

73. The National Stock Exchange of India has its headquarters in:
A. Delhi B. Mumbai
C. Chennai D. Bengaluru

74. Olympic medal winner Gagan Narang belongs to which of these sports?
A. Shooting B. Wrestling
C. Boxing D. Badminton

75. In terms of FDI inflows, which is the top investing country in India?
A. USA B. Singapore
C. UK D. Mauritius

76. Which of the following Indian authors is a winner of the coveted Booker Prize?
A. Aravind Adiga B. Chetan Bhagat
C. Jyoti Singh D. Shobhit Agarwal

77. Which of the following is associated with the development of the Human Development Index?
A. David Ricardo B. Michael Porter
C. Amartya Sen D. John Dunning

78. Who is the present Secretary General of the United Nations?
A. Kofi Annan B. Warren Buffet
C. Pascal Lamy D. Ban Ki-moon

79. The autobiography of India's former President A.P.J. Abdul Kalam is also known as:
A. Wings of Fire
B. Playing it my Way
C. One Life is not Enough
D. Courage and Conviction

80. Which of the following is the highest civilian award of India?
A. Padma Shree B. Padma Bhushan
C. Padma Vibhushan D. Bharat Ratna

81. Which of the following is not correct?
A. With the nominal level, the data are sorted into categories with no particular order to the categories
B. The ordinal level of measurement presumes that one classification is ranked higher than another
C. The interval level of measurement has the ranking characteristics of the ordinal level of measurement plus the characteristic that the ratio between two values is meaningful
D. The ration level of measurement has all the characteristics of the interval scale, plus there is 0 point.

82. Geometric mean is:
A. Greater than arithmetic mean
B. Less than or equal to arithmetic mean
C. Less than arithmetic mean
D. Always equal to arithmetic mean

83. Which of the following is not correct statement?
A. Normal distribution is symmetrical about mean
B. Poisson distribution is formed by counting
C. Normal distribution is bell shaped because it falls off smoothly in either direction from the central value
D. In a Poisson distribution intervals do not overlap and are independent

84. Which of the following is not included in definition of statistic?
A. Collecting B. Organizing
C. Selling D. Interpreting

85. A useful measure to observe lack of symmetry in a set of data is called:
A. Coefficient of skewness
B. Coefficient of normalcy
C. Coefficient of variation
D. Variance

86. A coefficient of determination was computed to be .38 in a problem involving one independent and one dependent variable. The result means:
A. The relationship between two variables is negative
B. The correlation coefficient is 38
C. 38 per cent of the total variation is explained by the independent variable
D. There is 38 per cent variation in the data set

87. An index number is:
A. Actually a per cent but per cent sign is omitted

B. Useful for comparing data with different units
C. Useful for evaluating the change in very large numbers
D. All of the above

88. If the occurrence of one or more event means that the other cannot happen, the events are:
A. Independent
B. Mutually exclusive
C. Bayesian
D. Empirical

89. The collection of one or more outcomes for an experiment is called a/an:
A. Event B. Probability
C. Random variable D. Z value

90. A joint probability is:
A. The likelihood of two events happening
B. The likelihood of an event happening given another event has already happened
C. Based on two mutually exclusive events
D. Also called prior probability

91. Which of the following is *not* the condition of binomial distribution:
A. Only 2 possible outcomes
B. Constant probability of success
C. Must have at least 3 trials
D. Independent trials

92. Which one of the following is correct statement related to a regression model?
A. Scatter diagram depicts variation in the variables around mean
B. Dummy variable assumes only zero value
C. Standard error of estimate measures dispersion of the actual Y values about the regression line
D. The variable that is depended upon for prediction is a dependent variable

93. Multicollinarity exists when:
A. Independent variables are correlated less than –.70 or more than .70
B. Independent variable is strongly associated with dependent variable
C. There is only one independent variable
D. The relationship between independent and dependent variable is non-linear

94. A summary of the data measured on two nominal variables is called:
A. Scatter diagram
B. Contingency table
C. Frequency distribution
D. Histogram

95. The ages of sample of tourists flying from Delhi to Kathmandu were: 32, 21, 60, 47, 54, 17, 72, 55, 33 and 41. The mean deviation is:
A. 24.4 B. 10.4
C. 14.4 D. 14

96. The probabilities of the event A and B are .20 and .30 respectively. The probability that both A and B occur is .15. The probability that either A or B occur is:
A. .35 B. .34
C. .36 D. .06

97. In a management trainee programme, 80% of trainees are females and 20% male. Ninety per cent of the female attended college and 78% of the males attended college. A management trainee is selected at random. The selected female person who did not attend college is a case of:
A. Conditional probability
B. Priori probability
C. Joint probability
D. Posterior probability

98. A study of Human Resource Department of a Medical Centre revealed the following information on the number of absences last month for housekeeping employees.

Days absent	No. of Employees
0	20
1	35
2	90
3	40
4	10
5 or more	5

The probability that an employee selected at random was absent for less than 3 days is:
A. .70 B. .725
C. .71 D. .75

99. A sample of 10 families in Delhi reveal the following figures for family size and amount spent on food per week:

Family size	Amount spent on food ($)
3	99
6	104
5	151
6	129
6	142
3	111
4	74
4	91
5	119
3	91

R value 0.589 suggests that:

A. Family size is the only determining factor of spend on food

B. Family size does not affect food spend

C. Larger families spend more on food explaining nearly 35% variation in food spend

D. Can't say

100. A recent survey by the American Association revealed 23% of the students graduating with a major in accounting select public accounting. Suppose we select a sample of 15 students, the probability that two students select public accounting is:

A. 0.1858 B. 0.1897

C. 0.1822 D. 0.1901

101. For a square matrix $A = \begin{bmatrix} 1 & 1 & 1 \\ 1 & 2 & -3 \\ 2 & -1 & 3 \end{bmatrix}$

the adj. A is:

A. $\begin{bmatrix} 3 & -4 & -5 \\ -9 & 1 & 4 \\ -5 & 3 & 1 \end{bmatrix}$ B. $\begin{bmatrix} 3 & 4 & 5 \\ -9 & 1 & 4 \\ -5 & 3 & 1 \end{bmatrix}$

C. $\begin{bmatrix} 3 & -4 & -5 \\ -9 & -1 & -4 \\ -5 & 3 & 1 \end{bmatrix}$ D. $\begin{bmatrix} 3 & -4 & -5 \\ -9 & -1 & 4 \\ -5 & -3 & -1 \end{bmatrix}$

102. Which of the following statements is not true?

A. Inverse of the inverse of original matrix is a matrix itself

B. Inverse of a matrix is unique

C. A non-singular matrix has unique inverse

D. $(A B)^{-1} = A^{-1} B^{-1}$

103. Which of the following is not the assumption of Leontief Input Output model?

A. Economy decomposed into '*n*' number of interdependent sectors

B. Output of an industry is either used for production or final consumption

C. Production level of an industry is determined on the basis of certain optimality criteria

D. Technical coefficients do not change as there is change in industry output

104. Simon-Hawkins condition for the viability of the input-output model implies that:

A. Determinant of Leontief matrix (I–A) must always be positive and a_{ij} for $i = j$ should be equal to one.

B. Determinant of Leontief matrix (I–A) must not equal to zero and a_{ij} for $i = j$ should be equal to one.

C. Determinant of Leontief matrix (I–A) must always be negative and a_{ij} for $i = j$ should be equal to one.

D. Determinant of Leontief matrix (I–A) must always be positive and a_{ij} for $i = j$ should be equal to zero.

105. Given a demand function $q = ap^{\alpha}$, where a and α are the constants. If $\alpha < -1$, total revenue will:

A. Decrease B. Increase

C. Be constant D. Equal to 1

106. The demand function $p = xe^{1/2}$ is:

A. Perfectly elastic when $x = 1$

B. Perfectly inelastic when $x = 1$

C. Unit elastic when $x = 1$

D. Elastic when $x = 1$

107. For the cost function $C = 4{,}860 + 7{,}50{,}000q + 15q^2$, AC is minimum at:

A. $q = 18$ B. $q = 15$

C. $q = 19$ D. $q = 14$

108. For discriminating monopolist, elasticity of demand in market I = 11/10 and in market II = 27/23. The price charged in market I can be:

A. More than price charged in market II
B. Less than price charged in market II
C. Same as in market II
D. According to customer capacity

109. For the production function given by $x = f(l, k) = (al^4 + bk^4)^{1/2}$, the reward to factors of production as per their marginal productivities will be:

A. Half of total output
B. Double of total output
C. Equal to total output
D. Having no relation with total output

110. The CEO of which of the following companies is NOT an Indian or Person of Indian Origin?

A. Arcelor-Mittal B. PepsiCo
C. Reckitt Benckiser D. None of these

111. Third Nuclear Security Summit 2014 was held at:

A. Netherlands B. Canada
C. UAE D. Japan

112. India's largest solar power plant was launched in March 2014 in which of the following states:

A. Rajasthan B. Gujarat
C. Madhya Pradesh D. Maharashtra

113. Which of the following statements is True about "El Nino"?

A. It is the name given to unusual warming of waters in the central and eastern equatorial Pacific, which is linked to changes in the wind patterns and anomalous weather in many parts of the globe.
B. It results in extended and heavy monsoon in all parts of the globe.
C. There is a high probability of developing this phenomenon in the next few months.
D. A and C

114. A constraint in an LPP restricts:

A. Value of an objective function
B. Value of decision variable
C. Use of available resources
D. Uncertainty of optimum value

115. Which of the following is correct statement?

A. Variables cannot be unrestricted in the context of an LPP.
B. For LPP having 'n' decision variables, there must be equal number of constraints.
C. Objective function specifies the dependent relationship between decision variables and the objective function.
D. Linear programming is probabilistic in nature.

116. At any iteration of the usual Simplex method, if there is at least one basic variable at zero level and all Zj – Cj³ 0, the current solution is:

A. Infeasible B. Unbounded
C. Non-degenerate D. Degenerate

117. 'No feasible solution' case in maximization LPP occurs when:

A. All d_{ij}'s are negative or zero
B. At least one artificial variable is in the basis, but not at zero level, and all Zj – Cj ≤ 0.
C. One of the basic variables is zero
D. Number of variables ≠ number of constraints

118. If dual has an unbounded solution, primal has:

A. An unbounded solution
B. An infeasible solution
C. A feasible solution
D. None of the above

119. Which of the following is not correct statement?

A. Associated with every LPP, there is always another LPP which is based on same data and having same solution
B. Given LPP is called *primal* while the associated LPP is called its *dual.*
C. It is always necessary to convert inequality constraint into equality constraint for writing dual of an LPP.
D. Dual of the dual is primal.

120. For any primal and its dual:
A. Optimum value of the objective function is same
B. Both primal and dual cannot be feasible
C. Primal will have optimum solution if and only if dual does too
D. All of the above

121. Suppose for a consumer tea is a substitute of coffee and milk is a complement of coffee. Suppose prices of both tea and milk rise simultaneously. The demand for coffee will:
A. Rise
B. Fall
C. Remains unchanged
D. All of the above are possible

122. Given the individual demand function $Qdx = 50 - 2Px$, what is the maximum quantity the individual will ever demand of the good X?
A. 100
B. 25
C. 50
D. Cannot be derived without further information

123. A consumer spends her entire income on two goods, X and Y. Her cross elasticity of demand for good X with respect to price of Y is less than zero. Then we can infer that X is:
A. A substitute of Y
B. A complement of Y
C. An inferior commodity
D. Cannot say

124. If the price of a good decreases, the substitution effect ....
A. Shows the increase in the quantity of the good demanded, holding income constant
B. Must be greater than the income effect
C. Shows the increase in the quantity of the good demanded, holding utility constant
D. Can increase or decrease the quantity of the good demanded

125. The rate at which a consumer is willing to substitute one good for another is measured by the:
A. Slope of the tangent to the indifference curve
B. Slope of the budget line
C. Indifference map
D. Consumer's real income

126. A consumer's budget line is presently defined by income = ₹ 100, price of X = ₹ 1, price of Y = ₹ 2.

The consumer's budget line would have exactly the same position if:
A. Income = ₹ 100, price of X = ₹ 2, price of Y = ₹ 1
B. Income = ₹ 200, price of X = ₹ 2, price of Y = ₹ 4
C. Income = ₹ 50, price of X = ₹ 1, price of Y = ₹ 2
D. Income = ₹ 200, price of X = ₹ 1, price of Y = ₹ 2

127. If the $MRTS_{L,K} = 1/3$, then the MP_K/MP_L is:
A. 3 B. 1/3
C. 6 D. 2/3

128. If only a part of the labour force employed by a firm can be dismissed at any time and without pay, the total wages and salaries paid out by the firm must be considered as:
A. A fixed cost
B. A variable cost
C. A sunk cost
D. Partly a fixed cost and partly a variable cost

129. When is the LAC curve tangent to the lowest point on the SAC, if the LAC curve is falling?
A. Always
B. Never
C. Sometimes
D. Cannot say without further information

130. The short-run supply curve of a perfectly competitive firm is given by:
A. The rising portion of its SMC curve over and above the shut-down point
B. The rising portion of its SMC curve over and above the break-even point
C. The rising portion of its SMC curve over and above its SAC curve
D. The rising portion of its SMC curve

131. If in response to an increase in the demand for inputs, the inputs become more expensive, then the long run supply curve of a perfectly competitive industry will be:
A. Downward sloping from left to right
B. Upward sloping from left to right
C. Horizontal
D. L-shaped

132. Monopsony exists in a market when:
A. There is a single buyer and a single seller of the product
B. There is a single seller and large number of buyers
C. There is a single buyer and large number of sellers
D. Any of the above

133. A monopoly will never operate in the inelastic portion of its demand curve because:
A. Average revenue is negative
B. Total revenue is declining
C. Total revenue is rising
D. None of the above

134. In the kinked demand curve model, the oligopolists:
A. Recognize their interdependence
B. Do not collude
C. Tend to keep prices constant
D. All of the above

135. Factor productivity remaining constant, if the product price increases:
A. The firm moves down the Value of Marginal Product (VMP) curve of the factor
B. The firm moves up the VMP curve of the factor
C. The VMP curve of the factor shifts to the left
D. The VMP curve of the factor shifts to the right

136. Macro-economics is concerned with:
A. The level of output of goods and services
B. The general level of prices
C. The growth of real output
D. All of the above

137. An expansive monetary and fiscal policy shifts:
A. Aggregate demand to the right
B. Aggregate demand to the left
C. Aggregate supply to the right
D. Aggregate supply to the left

138. A rightward shift of aggregate demand, with no change in the aggregate supply schedule, results in an increase in:
A. Real output and no change in the price level when aggregate supply is upward sloping
B. Real output and no change in the price level when aggregate supply is horizontal
C. The price level and no change in real output when aggregate supply is upward sloping
D. The price level and no change in real output when aggregate supply is horizontal

139. The equation C = \$20 + 0.90 Yd predicts that consumption is:
A. \$90 when disposable income is \$100
B. \$100 when disposable income is \$90
C. \$110 when disposable income is \$100
D. \$180 when disposable income is \$200

140. *Ceteris paribus* means that:
A. Other factors are held constant
B. No other variable affects the dependent variable
C. No other model can explain the dependent variable
D. The model is logical

141. Which of the following statements is correct?
A. A variable is endogenous when its value is determined by forces outside the model
B. A change in exogenous variable is classified as an autonomous change
C. A variable is an exogenous when its value is determined by forces within the model
D. A variable is autonomous when its value is determined by forces within the model

142. Which of the following will not result in an increase in the level of income?
A. An increase in autonomous spending

B. A decrease in autonomous taxes
C. An increase in autonomous transfers
D. An increase in net tax revenues

143. When an increase in government spending is matched by an equal decrease in government transfers, the income level will:
A. Stay the same B. Increase
C. Decrease D. None of these

144. Suppose the net export function is NX = X – mY and the net export balance is zero. An increase in autonomous investment spending will:
A. Increase the net export balance and the income level
B. Increase the income level but make the net export balance negative
C. Increase the income level and have no effect upon the net export balance
D. Have no effect upon the income level but cause the net export balance to become negative

145. An increase in the marginal propensity to import:
A. Has the same effect upon the multipliers as an increase in the MFC
B. Has no effect upon the multipliers
C. Increase the value of the multipliers
D. Decrease the value of the multipliers

146. IS curve is:
A. Downward sloping
B. Relates to goods market
C. Y-800-20I
D. All of the above

147. LM curve is:
A. Relates to money market
B. Upward sloping
C. Y = 800 + 20I
D. All of the above

148. Suppose there is full employment and aggregate supply is vertical. A decrease in taxes:
A. Increases the price level and real output
B. Increases the price level but has no effect on real output
C. Increases real output but has no effect on the price level
D. Has no effect on the price level or real output

149. Suppose there is full employment and a vertical aggregate supply schedule. An increase in the nominal money supply:
A. Causes the real money supply to increase, which changes the consumption of output
B. Has no effect on the real money supply or the consumption of output
C. Causes a proportional increase in real output
D. Reduces the rate of interest and changes the consumption of output

150. When aggregate supply is positively sloped and there is a decrease in the markup on variable cost, aggregate supply shifts to the:
A. Right, the price level falls, and the real output increases
B. Left, the price level falls, and the real output increases
C. Right, the price level falls, and the real output decreases
D. Left, the price level falls, and the real output decreases

151. First nationalization of commercial banks took place in the year:
A. 1969 B. 1970
C. 1968 D. 1971

152. Malhotra Committee recommendations were for:
A. Banking
B. Insurance
C. Mutual funds
D. Non-banking financial corporations

153. First Five Year Plan stressed on:
A. Agriculture B. Industry
C. Services D. Export

154. Micro finance is:
A. Credit to poor
B. Loan without collateral
C. Based on social capital
D. All of the above

155. Global financial crisis was exported to India from:
A. Germany B. U.S.A.
C. Russia D. UK

156. VAT is:
A. Value added tax
B. Value augmenting tax
C. Value addition tax
D. Value augmented tax

157. New Companies Act was passed in the year:
A. 2013 B. 2014
C. 2015 D. 2009

158. RBI was established in:
A. 1935 B. 1940
C. 1947 D. 1950

159. A major corporate governance scam in recent years related to:
A. L & T B. Infosys
C. Satyam D. House of Tatas

160. Recently Indian agriculture was in the news because of:
A. Suicide by farmers
B. Loan mela for farmers
C. Massive investment by state
D. High export prices for agricultural products

161. Which of the following items would most likely be classified as an operating activity?
A. Issuance of debt
B. Acquisition of a competitor
C. Sale of automobiles by an automobile dealer
D. Issuance of equity shares

162. Which of the following elements represents an economic resource?
A. Asset
B. Liability
C. Owner's equity
D. Retained earnings

163. Which of the following is most likely not any objective of financial statements?
A. To provide information about the performance of an entity
B. To provide information about the financial position of entity
C. To provide information about the users of an entity's financial statements
D. To provide information about cash flows

164. The assumption that an entity will continue to operate for the foreseeable future is called:
A. Accrual basis B. Comparability
C. Going concern D. Consistency

165. The assumption that the effects of transactions and other events are recognized when they occur, not when the cash flows occur, is called:
A. Relevance B. Accrual basis
C. Going concern D. Cash basis

166. A company had the following income statement information:

Revenue	₹ 40,00,000
Cost of goods sold	₹ 30,00,000
Other operating expenses	₹ 5,00,000
Interest expense	₹ 1,00,000
Tax expense	₹ 1,20,000

The company's gross profit is equal to:
A. ₹ 2,80,000 B. ₹ 5,00,000
C. ₹ 10,00,000 D. ₹ 15,00,000

167. Money receiving from customers for products to be delivered in the future is recorded as:
A. Revenue and an asset
B. An asset and a liability
C. Revenue and a liability
D. Neither revenue nor liability

168. The initial measurement of goodwill is most likely affected by:
A. An acquisition's purchase price
B. Acquired company's book value
C. Fair value of the acquirer's assets and liabilities
D. Market value of assets and liabilities

169. An investor concerned with whether a company can meet its near term obligation is most likely to calculate:
A. Current ratio
B. Return total capital
C. Financial leverage ratio
D. Asset turnover ratio

170. The sale of a building for cash would be classified as what type of activity on cash flow statement?
A. Operating B. Investing
C. Financing D. Not considered

171. Comparison of a company's financial results to other peer companies for the same period is called:
A. Technical analysis
B. Time series analysis
C. Cross-sectional analysis
D. Fundamental analysis

172. In order to assess a company's ability to fulfil its long-term obligations, an analyst would most likely examine:
A. Activity ratios B. Liquidity ratios
C. Solvency ratios D. Debt equity ratio

173. A company uses the FIFO method and B company uses the LIFO method. Compared to the cost of replacing the inventory, during periods of rising prices, the cost of sales reported by:
A. A company is too low
B. B company is too low
C. B company is too high
D. A company is too high

174. Intangible assets with finite useful lives mostly differ from intangible lives with respect to accounting:
A. Revaluation B. Impairment
C. Amortisation D. Valuation

175. Why do accountants record transactions in the journal?
A. To ensure that all transactions are posted to the ledger
B. To ensure that total debits equal total credits
C. To have a chronological record of all transactions
D. To help prepare the financial statements

176. Under the revenue principle, revenue is recorded:
A. At the earliest acceptable time
B. At the latest acceptable time
C. After it has been earned, but not before
D. At the end of the accounting period

177. A capital reserve is built out of:
A. Recurring profits
B. Non-recurring profits
C. Revenue
D. Reserve fund

178. Transfer to capital redemption reserve is not allowed from:
A. General reserve
B. Profit prior to incorporation
C. Reserve fund
D. Net profit

179. When interest on own debentures becomes due, it will be credited to:
A. Profit and loss account
B. Own Debentures Account
C. Debentures Interest Account
D. Interest on own Debentures Account

180. Once an accounting policy is adopted by a company, it:
A. Must never be changed
B. Must be changed on an annual basis
C. Can be changed if another policy is more appropriate
D. Can only be changed with the government's approval

181. Cost-volume-profit analysis is based on several assumptions. Which of the following is not one of the assumptions?
A. A salesmix of the product is constant
B. Inventory quantity changes during the year
C. Behaviour of both revenues and cost is linear throughout the relevant range
D. Factor prices, for example, material prices and wage rates remain unchanged

182. Which of the following should not be considered in a make or buy decision?
A. Potential use of manufacturing capacity
B. Variable cost of production
C. Potential rental income from space occupied by production area
D. Unchanged fixed cost

183. The cost per unit of a product manufactured amounts to ₹ 160 (75% variable) when production is 10,000 units. What will be the cost of production per unit if production increases by 25%?

A. ₹ 145 B. ₹ 152
C. ₹ 150 D. ₹ 140

184. A company has net working capital of ₹ 3 lakh, current ratio of 1.8 and liquid ratio of 1.6. Its value of stock is:

A. ₹ 55,000 B. ₹ 65,000
C. ₹ 75,000 D. ₹ 85,000

185. A company has margin of safety of ₹ 40 lakhs and earns an annual profit of ₹ 10 lakhs. If the fixed costs amount to ₹ 20 lakhs, annual sales will be:

A. ₹ 160 lakhs B. ₹ 140 lakhs
C. ₹ 120 lakhs D. ₹ 200 lakhs

186. If actual output is lower than budgeted output, which of the following costs would you expect to be lower than the original budget?

A. Total variable costs
B. Total fixed costs
C. Variable cost per unit
D. Fixed cost per unit

187. The salary a student foregoes while in college is an example of:

A. Opportunity cost B. Direct cost
C. Sunk cost D. Variable cost

188. In developing a predetermined factory overhead application rate for use in a process costing system, which of the following could be used in the numerator and denominator?

	Numerator	Denominator
A.	Actual factory overhead	Actual machine hours
B.	Actual factory overhead	Estimated machine hours
C.	Estimated factory overhead	Actual machine hours
D.	Estimated factory overhead	Estimated machine hours

189. Units of production is an appropriate method of assigning overhead when:

A. Several well-differentiated products are manufactured
B. Direct labour costs are low
C. Only one product is manufactured
D. Manufacturing process is complex

190. Which of the following is not included in (changed to) factory overhead?

A. Factory depreciation and supplies
B. Cost of service departments
C. Cost of marketing departments
D. Cost of maintenance departments

191. During a period, Hindustan Ltd. Co. experienced scarp, normal spoilage and abnormal spoilage units manufacturing process. The cost of units produced includes:

A. Scrap, but not spoilage
B. Normal spoilage, but neither scrap nor abnormal spoilage
C. Scrap and normal spoilage but not abnormal spoilage
D. Scrap, normal spoilage and abnormal spoilage

192. A true process costing system could make use of each of the following except:

A. Standard costing
B. Individual lots
C. Variable costing
D. Responsibility accounting

193. In computation of manufacturing cost per equivalent unit, the weighted average method of process costing considers:

A. Current cost only
B. Current cost plus cost of beginning work-in-process inventory
C. Current cost plus cost of ending work-in-process inventory
D. Current cost minus cost of beginning work-in-process inventory

194. A company produces one product with a standard direct manufacturing labour cost of four hours at ₹ 12 per hour. During a period 1000 units were produced using 4100 hours at ₹ 12.20 per hour. The unfavourable direct labour effect every variance was:

A. ₹ 1220 B. ₹ 1200
C. ₹ 820 D. ₹ 400

195. Cost volume profit relationships that are currilinear may be analysed linearly by considering only:
A. Fixed and semivariable costs
B. Relevant fixed costs
C. Relevant variable costs
D. A relevant range of volume

196. Which department is customarily held responsible for an unfavourable materials usage variance?
A. Quality control B. Purchasing
C. Engineering D. Production

197. Which of the following is normally included in the financial budget of a firm:
A. Direct materials budget
B. Selling expense budget
C. Budgeted balance sheet
D. Sales budget

198. Payment of royalties is:
A. Direct expenses
B. Factory overhead
C. Charged to P and L account
D. Administration cost

199. An increase in fixed cost will result into:
A. Decrease in P/V ratio
B. Decrease in contribution per unit
C. Increase in Breakeven level
D. Increase in P/V ratio

200. A company wants to sell 1,00,000 units at ₹ 12 each. Fixed costs are ₹ 2,80,000. In order to earn a profit of ₹ 2,00,000, the variable cost should be:
A. ₹ 4,80,000
B. ₹ 7,20,000
C. ₹ 9,00,000
D. ₹ 9,20,000

ANSWERS

1	2	3	4	5	6	7	8	9	10
A	*	A	C	C	A	D	A	A	B
11	**12**	**13**	**14**	**15**	**16**	**17**	**18**	**19**	**20**
A	A	C	A	D	A	D	C	A	D
21	**22**	**23**	**24**	**25**	**26**	**27**	**28**	**29**	**30**
B	C	A	B	A	D	D	C	B	B
31	**32**	**33**	**34**	**35**	**36**	**37**	**38**	**39**	**40**
B	A	D	B	C	C	C	D	A	B
41	**42**	**43**	**44**	**45**	**46**	**47**	**48**	**49**	**50**
B	D	B	A	C	A	C	A	B	D
51	**52**	**53**	**54**	**55**	**56**	**57**	**58**	**59**	**60**
A	B	C	D	C	B	C	D	A	B
61	**62**	**63**	**64**	**65**	**66**	**67**	**68**	**69**	**70**
A	B	B	C	B	D	C	A	C	A
71	**72**	**73**	**74**	**75**	**76**	**77**	**78**	**79**	**80**
D	B	B	A	D	A	C	D	A	D
81	**82**	**83**	**84**	**85**	**86**	**87**	**88**	**89**	**90**
C	B	C	C	D	C	D	B	A	A
91	**92**	**93**	**94**	**95**	**96**	**97**	**98**	**99**	**100**
C	C	A	B	C	A	C	B	C	A
101	**102**	**103**	**104**	**105**	**106**	**107**	**108**	**109**	**110**
A	D	C	*	B	C	A	A	B	D

111	112	113	114	115	116	117	118	119	120
A	C	D	C	C	*	B	B	C	A
121	122	123	124	125	126	127	128	129	130
D	C	B	C	A	B	A	D	B	*
131	132	133	134	135	136	137	138	139	140
B	C	B	D	D	D	A	B	C	A
141	142	143	144	145	146	147	148	149	150
B	D	B	B	D	D	D	B	*	D
151	152	153	154	155	156	157	158	159	160
A	B	A	D	B	A	A	A	C	A
161	162	163	164	165	166	167	168	169	170
C	A	C	C	B	C	B	A	A	B
171	172	173	174	175	176	177	178	179	180
C	C	*	C	C	C	B	B	C	C
181	182	183	184	185	186	187	188	189	190
B	D	B	C	C	A	A	D	C	C
191	192	193	194	195	196	197	198	199	200
C	B	B	B	D	D	C	*	C	B

SOME SELECTED EXPLANATORY ANSWERS

3. Director Identity Number (DIN): Amending the Section 253 of the Companies Act, 1956 in May 2006 and inserting new Sections 266 A to G to the Act have made DIN possible. The Amendment Act provides for the allotment of mandatory Director Identification Number (DIN) for all existing and future directors on company boards. Only a single DIN is required for an individual irrespective of number of directorships held by him. DIN is also mandatory for directors of Indian companies who are not citizens of India (foreigner). But, DIN is not mandatory for directors of foreign company having branch offices in India. Every director is to intimate his/her DIN in form DIN-2 to all companies where he/she is a director and all companies are required to inform the DIN's of its directors to the Registrar of Companies (ROC).

5. Coercion means compelling a person to enter into a contract under a pressure or a threat. According to Section 15, a contract is said to be caused by coercion when it is obtained by—

(*a*) committing any act which is forbidden by the Indian Penal Code; or

(*b*) threatening to commit any act which is forbidden by the Indian Penal Code; or

(*c*) unlawful detaining of any property; or

(*d*) threatening to detain any property.

Example I : X beats Y and compels him to sell his car for Rs 50,000. Here, Y's consent has been obtained by coercion because beating someone is an offence under the Indian Penal Code.

Example II : A Hindu widow of 13 years was forced to adopt a boy under threat that her husband's dead body would not be allowed to be removed if she does not adopt the boy. She adopted the boy. Here, widow's consent has been obtained by coercion because preventing the dead body from being removed for cremation is an offence under Section 297 of the Indian Penal Code.

6. In the words of Pollock, 'every agreement and promises enforceable by law is contract'.

Section 2(*h*) of the Indian Contract Act, 1872 states that 'an agreement enforceable by law is contract'. This definition gives us two ingredients—an agreement and 'enforceable by law'. We can summarize it as under.

Contract = An agreement + enforceable by law.

7. **Essential Elements of a Contract**

Section 10 of the Contract Act, 1872 provides for the essential elements of a valid contract. To constitute a valid contract, following elements are essential–

1. Offer and acceptance.
2. Intention to create legal relationship.
3. Parties must be competent to contract.
4. Lawful consideration is a must.
5. There must be free consent of the parties entering into contract.
6. The object of contract must be lawful.
7. Agreement must not be expressly declared void by the Contract Act itself or by the other laws.

8. **Quasi contract :** There are certain dealings which are not, strictly speaking, contracts, though the parties act as if there is a contract. The Contract Act specifies the various situations which come within what is called quasi contract. Sections 68-72 deal with the quasi contract. Quasi contract is also called *constructive contract.* The cases grouped under this type of contracts have little or no affinity with contract. Such a contract does not arise by virtue of any agreement (i.e., express or implied) between the parties, but the law infers a contract under special circumstances.

Examples: The obligation of the finder of the lost goods to return them to the true owner or the liability of the person to whom money is paid by mistake to repay it back cannot be said to arise out of a contract even in its remotest sense, as there is neither offer and acceptance nor consent, but these are very much covered under quasi contracts as per Sections 71 and 72, respectively.

A quasi contract is based upon the equitable principle that a person shall not be allowed to gain unjust benefit at the expense of another. It is an obligation which the law creates in the absence of any agreement, but based on equitable principle.

A quasi contract is a contract in which there is no intention on either side to make a contract, but the law imposes a contract. In such a contract, rights and obligations arise not by any agreement between the parties but by operations of law.

9. "Bailment" is defined in Section 148 of the Indian Contract Act in the following terms:

A 'Bailment' is the delivery of goods by one person to another for some purpose, upon contract that they shall, when the purpose is accomplished, be returned or otherwise disposed of according to the directions of the person delivering them.

The person who delivers the goods is called the 'bailor' and the person to whom they are delivered is called the 'bailee'.

11. A pledge has been defined under Section 172 of the Indian Contract Act 1872 as under: *"The bailment of goods as security for payment of a debt or performance of a promise is called 'pledge'. The bailer is in this case called "pawner'. The bailee is called 'pawnee'."*

12. **Rights of unpaid seller against goods**

'Lien' means a right which a creditor has to retain possession of goods until payment of the price. Lien depends on actual possession, and not on title. 'Unpaid seller's lien' is the right of the unpaid seller of goods who is in possession of them until payment or tender of the price, *i.e.,* it is a possessory lien as well as a particular lien.

14. Designated Partner means any partner designated as such in Section No. 7 of the Act. According to Section 7(1), every LLP must have two designated partners who are individuals. Out of the two designated partners, at least one of them must be a

resident in India. Resident means a person who has stayed in India for not less than 182 days during the preceding one year. In case of an LLP in which all the partners are bodies corporate or in which one or more partners are individuals and bodies corporate, at least two individuals who are partners of such LLP or nominees of such bodies corporate shall act as designated partners.

Every designated partner of a LLP shall obtain a Designated Partner Identification Number (DPIN) from the Central Government and the provisions of Sections 266A to 266G of the Companies Act, 1956 shall apply mutatis mutandis for the said purpose.

If an LLP contravenes the provision of Section 7(1), then the LLP and its every partner shall be punishable with of fine, which is not less than ₹ 10,000 but not more than ₹ 500,000.

Responsibilities of designated partners: The designated partner is responsible for all acts to be performed under the LLP Act like filing of documents, returns, statements, those mentioned in the LLP Agreement and penalties for non-compliance.

17. The Information Technology Act 2000 extends to the whole of India. It shall also apply to any violation or contravention of the provisions of the Act done by any person any where in the world. The Act is not applicable to:

(*a*) A negotiable instrument as defined in Section 13 of the Negotiable Instruments Act, 1881;

(*b*) A power-of-attorney as defined in Section 1A of the Powers-of-Attorney Act, 1882;

(*c*) A trust as defined in Section 3 of the Indian Trusts Act, 1882;

(*d*) A will as defined in clause (h) of Section 2 of the Indian Succession Act, 1925, including any other testamentary disposition by whatever name called;

(*e*) Any contract for the sale or conveyance of immovable property or any interest in such property;

(*f*) Any such class of documents or transactions as may be notified by the Central Government in the Official Gazette.

21. Section 156 stipulated that Every existing director shall intimate his DIN to the company or all companies wherein he is a director within 1 month of the receipt of DIN from the Central Government.

Every existing director shall, within one month of the receipt of DIN, intimate his DIN to the company or all companies, wherein he is a director, in Form No DIN-2.

24. Sec 25: Document containing offer of securities for sale is deemed to be prospectus: When a company allots securities to the public based on an offer that has been made, then any document through which such an offer is made is considered to be a prospectus and it has to fulfil all the requirements of a prospectus.

Securities to be offered for sale to the public

- Within 6 months after the allotment or agreement to allot or
- At the date when the allotment was made and the whole of the consideration was received.

28. Section 165 : (1) No person, after the commencement of this Act, shall hold office as a director, including any alternate directorship, in more than twenty companies at the same time:

Provided that the maximum number of public companies in which a person can be appointed as a director shall not exceed ten.

***Explanation*—**For reckoning the limit of public companies in which a person can be appointed as director, directorship in private companies that are either holding or subsidiary company of a public company shall be included.

(2) Subject to the provisions of sub-section (1), the members of a company may, by special resolution, specify any lesser number of companies in which a director of the company may act as directors.

33. Management Theory Propounded by Taylor

Taylor's approach	Relevance to modern industry
Economic man	Some managers still believe that money is the only way to motivate staff. However, the more general view is that workers have a wide range of needs – not just money – that can be met, in part at least, from work.
Select the right people for each job	Before Taylor there had been few attempts to identify the principles of staff selection. The importance he gave to this is still reflected in the significance given to careful staff selection in nearly all businesses.
Observe and record the performance of staff	This was widely adopted and became known as 'time and motion study'. Regarded with suspicion by workers as a may of making them work harder, it is still employed as a technique but often with the cooperation and involvement of staff.
Establish the best method of doing a job-method study	Again, this is still accepted as being important as efficiency depends on the best ways of working being adopted. However, the Taylor approach of management giving instructions to workers with no discussion or feedback is considered to be undesirable. Worker participation in devising best work practices is now encouraged.
Piece-work payment systems	This is not now a widely used payment system. Quality may be sacrificed in the search for quantity – workers will vary output according to their financial needs at different times of year and it discourages them from accepting changes at work in case they lose some pay. In most of modern industry, especially service industries, it has become very difficult to identify the output of individual workers.

34. One of the best-known proponents of participative management was the social scientist Rensis Likert, who was director of the Institute for Social Research at the University of Michigan. It was Likert's conviction, based on years of research in organizations, that better decisions come out of participation and the people who make those decisions are more highly committed to carrying them out than those not involved in the process. He published his research in two books—*New Patterns of Management* (1961) and *The Human Organization* (1967)—where he defined four management systems: (1) Exploitative Autnoritative, (2) Benevolent Authoritative, (3) Consultative, and (4) Participative Group.

35. Resistance to Change : Resistance to change may be of two types: individual and organizational. Individuals resist to change due to fear of losing jobs, obsolescence of skills, change in the equations in the social relationships, etc. The organizations may also resist to change due to resource crunch, difficulty to bring in the change in the set operational methods and sometimes simply due to the fear of the unknown.

Individual resistance to change : Change leads to insecurity among the employees because of its unknown consequences.

Employees do not know for certain whether the change will bring in better prospects. For example, because of technological change people may feel threatened due to the fear of obsolescence of skills, less wages and losing the job. Change sometimes leads to new dimensions of work relationships. Due to organizational redesign, the employees may have to work with other set of people than their existing co-workers with whom they have direct relationship, and it is generally not welcome by most of the employees.

Organizational resistance to change : Change may bring some potential threat to the organizational power to some people. Therefore, people try to resist change. The structural inertia in the bureaucratic organizations also hinders change. Furthermore, resource constraints play a vital role in resistance to change.

36. Content Theories of Motivation: These theories focus on identifying internal factors such as instincts, needs, satisfaction and job characteristics that energise employee motivation. These theories do not explain how motivation is influenced by the dynamic interaction between an individual and the environment he works in.

Content theories of motivation are based upon the assumption that an employee's needs influence motivation. Needs are physiological or psychological deficiencies that arouse behaviour. They can be strong or weak and are influenced by environmental factors and so they vary over time and place. The basic idea behind the need theories of motivation is that unmet needs motivate people to satisfy them. Therefore, people are motivated to pursue the unsatisfied need. There are four popular theories of motivation:

(*a*) Maslow's Need Hierarchy Theory

(*b*) Alderfer's ERG Theory

(*c*) Herzberg's Motivator-Hygiene Model

(*d*) McClelland's Need Theory

Comparison of the Four Content Theories

Each of these theories is based on a different perspective but all of them provide the need for an understanding of individual behaviour of employees. The crucial aspect of the content theories is that unmet or deprived needs motivate individuals to act to fulfil those needs and get satisfaction. Smart managers need to look at the positive and negative aspects of all the theories in order to get maximum benefit of these approaches.

37. Maslow's Hierarchy of Human Needs

Abraham Maslow (1868-1954) developed a hierarchy of human needs. In this theory he assigned priorities to basic needs. This hierarchy of human needs arranged the basic human needs in five level of priority as follows.

1. Physiological needs.
2. Safety and security needs.
3. Love and belonging needs (social affiliation).
4. Self esteem needs.
5. Self actualization needs.

39. As per section 9(1) (v) interest payable by Govt. of India is always deemed to accrue or arise in India whether the loan is used in India or outside India. (2) Since source of interest income is loan which in India, therefore income is deemed to accrue or arise in India and therefore taxable.

40. Income-tax is leviable on gains arising from sale of capital Assets other than agricultural land, excluding personal effects like car etc., but inclusive of jewellery.

Short-term Capital Assets is an asset held for 12 months or less in case of shares / units of Unit Trust of India and approved Mutual Funds and 36 months or less in case of others.

Long-term Capital Assets are assets held for more than 12 months in case of shares / units of Unit Trust of India and approved Mutual Funds and 36 months for others.

Short-term Capital Gain tax on security transactions is to be taxed at 15% on sale of shares or units of equity oriented mutual funds.

Long-term Capital Gain is taxable at 20% in case of individuals, HUF and Companies for assets other than shares. No long-term capital gains tax on listed equities. Transfer of house under reverse mortgage No capital gain tax.

44. International day of yoga is also called as the World Yoga Day. United Nations General Assembly has declared 21st of June as an International Yoga Day on 11th of December in 2014. Yoga in India is considered to be around 5,000 years old mental, physical and spiritual practice. Yoga was originated in India in ancient time when people were used of meditation to transform their body and mind. Launching a particular date of practicing yoga all across the world and celebrating as yoga day was initiated by the Indian Prime Minister to the United Nations General Assembly.

49. India and France signed 20 Memorandum of Understandings (MoUs) and Agreements on 10 April 2015 to give new impetus to bilateral co-operation between the two nations.

The two nations signed agreements covering the fields of Defence and Nuclear Energy, Space, Economic relations, Railways, Energy, Tourism, Science and Technology, Skill Development and Ayurveda.

The MoUs and Agreements were signed during visit of Prime Minister Narendra Modi to France between 9 April and 12 April 2015.

52. India's economic growth performance during the first three decades since it achieved independence in 1947 was christened the "Hindu" rate of growth by the late Professor Raj Krishna of the Delhi School of Economics.

53. Nalanda University was established in November 2010. The University came into being by a special Act of the Indian Parliament – a testimony to the important status that Nalanda University occupies in the Indian intellectual landscape.

56. Novartis (NYSE : NVS) is a world leader in the research and development of products to protect and improve health and well-being. The company has core businesses in pharmaceuticals, vaccines, consumer health, generics, eye care and animal health.

Headquartered at Basel, Switzerland, Novartis employs nearly 115,000 people in over 140 countries worldwide to help save lives and improve the quality of life. The Group is present in India through Novartis India Limited, listed on the Mumbai Stock Exchange and its wholly owned subsidiaries Novartis Healthcare Private Limited, Sandoz Private Limited and Chiron Behring Vaccines Private Limited.

57. Services form the largest share of India's GDP, which is indicative of the changing structure of the economy in favour of more value added activities. It also reflects that India is moving towards a more advanced stage of development.

62. FDI ceiling in the sensitive defence sector has been hiked from current 26 per cent, with the condition that the company seeking permission of the government for FDI up to 49 per cent should be an Indian company owned and controlled by Indians.

65. The Silicon Valley of India is a nickname of Bengaluru. The name signifies Bengaluru's status as a hub for information technology (IT) companies in India and is a comparative reference to the original Silicon Valley, based around Santa Clara Valley, California, a major hub for IT companies in the United States. Bengaluru, however, is located on a plateau and not in a valley; the use of the term in reference to Bengaluru is not truly toponymous. One of earliest mentions of this sobriquet occurred in late 1980s in the Indian Express. The more prevalent application of the nickname Bengaluru began in the 1990s based on a concentration of firms specialising in Research and Development (R&D), electronics and software production.

68. Competition Act, 2002 has been framed to replace MRTP Act, 1969. With the enactment of this Act, MRTP Act has been repealed. Keeping in view the widespread economic reforms and rapid economic development of the nation, the focus of the government was shifted from curbing monopolies to promoting competition in line with the international environment. In 1999, government of India appointed a committee on 'Competition Policy and Law' under the chairmanship of Sh. S.V.S. Raghavan.

This committee submitted its report in year 2000. On the basis of recommendations of this committee, the Competition Act 2002 was passed. The Act was enforced on 13th January, 2003. The Competition Act extends to whole of India except the state of Jammu and Kashmir. This Act has replaced the Monopolies and Restrictive Trade Practices Act, 1969 (MRTP Act). The Competition Act has set up Competition Commission of India (CCI) and it has taken over Monopolies and Restrictive Trade Practices Commission (MRTPC).

69. **National Institution for Transforming India (NITI) Aayog replaced Planning Commission:** The Government of India has scrapped its 65-year old Planning Commission, replacing it with the National Institution for Transforming India (NITI) Aayog. The new National Institution for Transforming India (NITI) will act more like a think tank or forum, say its supporters, in contrast with the Commission which imposed five-year-plans and allocated resources to hit set economic targets.

70. The Second Five-Year Plan (1956-57 to 1960-61) was based on a theoretical model developed by P.C. Mahalanobis, a member of the NPC and a noted statistician who had earlier founded the Indian Statistical Institute (ISI). Mahalanobis's model was similar to the model of the Soviet economist Feldman, whom Mahalanobis may have known, as the ISI collaborated with Soviet academicians. The Mahalanobis model suggested that if a country wants to reach a high level of consumption rapidly, the best strategy is to invest first in building the capacity to produce capital goods for some years. After accumulating enough of such capacity, the country can use the capital goods to augment its capacity to produce consumer goods. Thus, the emphasis on heavy industries and capital goods was theoretically justified and formed the basis of the Second Plan.

73. **National Stock Exchange (NSE)**

- It is the biggest stock exchange of India.
- In 1991, Pheswani Committee recommended the establishment of National Stock Exchange.
- NSE was established in Nov. 1992 and it started trading operation from June 30, 1994.
- NSE is ranked 3rd in the world stock exchange ranking based on the total transaction held, NASDAQ is ranked first while New York Stock Exchange is ranked second.

76. Arvind Adiga, the 33-year old, Chennai-born author won the £ 50,000 Man Booker Prize 2008 for his debut novel, "The White Tiger". This is the English-speaking world's most important award. His novel has been hailed by the judges as an "Extraordinary portrait of modern India." Adiga is the fourth Indian to win a Booker after Salman Rushdie, Arundhati Roy and Kiran Desai. Adiga was the youngest among the six shortlisted writers.

78. Ban Ki-moon is the eighth Secretary-General of the United Nations. Mr. Ban took office on 1 January 2007. On 21 June 2011, he was unanimously re-elected by the General Assembly and will continue to serve until 31 December 2016.

80. Bharat Ratna : The highest civilian award of the country, the Bharat Ratna is conferred for exceptional service to the nation in any field such as science, arts, literature, and "in recognition of public service of the highest order".

Chakravarti Rajagopalachari, Sarvepalli Radhakrishnan, and Chandrasekhara Venkata Raman were the first recipients of the award in 1954.

Cast in bronze, the decoration is designed as a pipal *(Ficus religiosa)* leaf with a sunburst in the centre and "Bharat Ratna" inscribed beneath it. On the reverse are embossed the national emblem (the lion capital of Sarnath) and the motto (*Satyamev Jayate*, "only truth shall prevail"). The decoration is worn around the neck suspended on a white ribbon.

82. Important Relationships Between the Arithmetic Mean and Geometric Mean

- The geometric mean is always less than, or equal to the arithmetic mean.
- The geometric mean equals the arithmetic mean only when all the observations are identical.
- The difference between the geometric and arithmetic mean increases as the dispersion in observed values increases.

84. *Statistics* is a field or discipline of study. A basic definition of *statistics* is the method of collecting, organizing, analyzing, presenting, and interpreting numerical data. Statistical methods help us make scientific and intelligent decisions based on the data collected. Decisions made on the basis of scientific methods are called *educated guesses,* whereas those made without such methods are *pure guesses* and may prove to be unreliable. Reasonable decisions and valid conclusions may be drawn based on the analysis of statistical data. Statistics therefore involves both numbers and the techniques and procedures to be followed in collecting, organizing, analyzing, interpreting, and presenting information in a numerical form. Although the term *statistics* is a broad term, it is narrowed and defined by its representative data, such as accident statistics, hospital statistics, employment statistics, vital statistics, and several other descriptors.

85. Coefficient of skewness: A measure of the lack of symmetry in a distribution. For a symmetric distribution there is no skewness, so the coefficient of skewness is zero. Otherwise, it is either positive or negative, with the limits of ± 3.0.

86. The concept of coefficient of determination is used for the interpretation of coefficient of correlation and comparing the two or more correlation coefficients. The coefficient of determination is defined as the square of the coefficient of correlation. It is denoted by r^2. The coefficient of determination explains the percentage variation in the dependent variable Y that can be explained in terms of the independent variable X. If coefficient of determination (r^2) is 0.38 which implies that 38% of the total variations in the dependent variable (Y) occurs due to the independent variable (X). The remaining 19% variation occurs due to outside or external factors. Thus, the coefficient of determination is defined as the ratio of the explained variance to the total variance. In terms of formula:

Coefficient of Determination (r^2)

$$= \frac{\text{Explained Variance}}{\text{Total Variance}}.$$

88. Mutually exclusive events: Two events resulting from the same random experiment are said to be *mutually exclusive* or *disjoint* or *incompatible* if they cannot occur simultaneously in a single outcome. For example, if a coin is tossed, there are only two possible outcomes viz. a head or a tail. Since both events cannot occur on the same toss, they are mutually exclusive.

89. Two fundamental components necessary to describe the probability of an occurrence are (1) a *random experiment* and (2) an *event.* A random experiment is a process that produces an identifiable *outcome* not predetermined by the investigator. An event is a collection of one or more distinct possible outcomes. An event occurs if the observed outcome of the experiment is contained in the collection of outcomes defining the event. For example, in tossing a coin one usually thinks of only two possible outcomes—'heads' and 'tails'. Here, the experiment is the toss of a coin, and an event might be that the coin comes up heads. A qualitatively similar situation occurs with the administration of a specific therapy to a patient with a certain disease. Here, the random experiment is application of treatment, with possible events being "patient cured" or "patient not cured"; not that "not cured" may be defined in terms of combinations of simple outcomes such as blood pressure reading or amount of inflammation.

90. A *joint probability* is the likelihood of two (or more) events happening at the same time. The joint probability of Events A and B occurring is written $p(A, B)$. Note that this is different from the conditional probability.

91. **Binomial probability distribution** is a widely used probability distribution for a discrete random variable. This distribution describes discrete data resulting from an experiment called a *Bernoulli process* (named after Jacob Bernoulli, 1654-1705, the first of the Bernoulli family of Swiss mathematicians). For each trial of an experiment, *there are only two possible complementary (mutually exclusive)* outcomes such as, defective or good, head or tail, zero or one, boy or girls

93. **Multicollinearity:** The extent to which independent variables are related to each other. Independent variables that are highly related to each other can produce unreliable regression coefficients, including dramatic changes in the direction of a relationship. Relatively uncommon in most survey-based studies, multicollinearity can be mitigated by removing one or more highly correlated independent variables from the equation or combining such variables into a scale or index.

94. **Contingency table :** A table used to classify observations according to two or more nominal characteristics. Deciles Values of an ordered (minimum to maximum) data set that divide the data into ten intervals of approximately equal frequencies.

95. $MD = \frac{144}{10} = 14.4$; Where $\bar{X} = 43.2$

$$\because \quad MD = \frac{\sum |X - \bar{X}|}{N}.$$

96.
$$\begin{aligned} P(A \text{ or } B) &= P(A) + P(B) - P(A \text{ and } B) \\ &= 0.20 + 0.30 - 0.15 \\ &= 0.50 - 0.15 = 0.35. \end{aligned}$$

97. A joint probability is a probability that measures the likelihood that two or more events will happen concurrently.

99. $r = 0.589$

$$r^2 = (0.589)^2 = 0.3469$$

H_0 : $\rho \le 0$;

H_1 : $\rho > 0$.

Reject H_0 if $t > 1.860$.

$$t = \frac{0.589\sqrt{10-2}}{\sqrt{1-(.589)^2}} = 2.062$$

H_0 is rejected. There is a positive association between family size and the amount spent on food.

101. We know that if,

$$A = \begin{bmatrix} a_{11} & a_{12} & a_{13} \\ a_{21} & a_{22} & a_{23} \\ a_{31} & a_{32} & a_{33} \end{bmatrix}, \text{ then}$$

$$\text{Adj } A = \begin{bmatrix} c_{11} & c_{21} & c_{31} \\ c_{12} & c_{22} & c_{32} \\ c_{13} & c_{23} & c_{33} \end{bmatrix}$$

Given, Matrix $A = \begin{bmatrix} 1 & 1 & 1 \\ 1 & 2 & -3 \\ 2 & -1 & 3 \end{bmatrix}$

$$c_{11} = \begin{vmatrix} 2 & -3 \\ -1 & 3 \end{vmatrix} = 2 \times 3 - (-1) \times (-3) = 3$$

$$c_{12} = \begin{vmatrix} -3 & 1 \\ 3 & 2 \end{vmatrix} = -3 \times 2 - 1 \times 3 = -9$$

$$c_{13} = \begin{vmatrix} 1 & 2 \\ 2 & -1 \end{vmatrix} = 1 \times (-1) - 2 \times 2 = -5$$

$$c_{21} = \begin{vmatrix} -1 & 3 \\ 1 & 1 \end{vmatrix} = -1 \times 1 - 3 \times 1 = -4$$

$$c_{22} = \begin{vmatrix} 1 & 1 \\ 2 & 3 \end{vmatrix} = 1 \times 3 - 2 \times 1 = 1$$

$$c_{23} = \begin{vmatrix} 2 & -1 \\ 1 & 1 \end{vmatrix} = 2 \times 1 - (-1) \times 1 = 3$$

$$c_{31} = \begin{vmatrix} 1 & 1 \\ 2 & -3 \end{vmatrix} = 1 \times (-3) - 1 \times 2 = -5$$

$$c_{32} = \begin{vmatrix} 1 & 1 \\ -3 & 1 \end{vmatrix} = 1 \times 1 - 1 \times (-3) = 4$$

$$c_{33} = \begin{vmatrix} 1 & 1 \\ 1 & 2 \end{vmatrix} = 1 \times 2 - 1 \times 1 = 1$$

$$\therefore \quad \text{Adj } A = \begin{vmatrix} 3 & -4 & -5 \\ -9 & 1 & 4 \\ -5 & 3 & 1 \end{vmatrix}.$$

105. We have, $q = ap^{\alpha}$

Taking log on both sides, we have,

$$\log q = \log a + \alpha \log p$$

Differentiating both sides w.r.t. p, we get

$$\frac{1}{q} \cdot \frac{dq}{dp} = \frac{\alpha}{p}$$

or $$\frac{p}{q} \cdot \frac{dq}{dp} = \alpha \qquad ...(i)$$

or $$\eta_d = \alpha \text{ (constant).}$$

Hence, elasticity of given demand curve is constant. Now R and MR are given by

$$R = p.q = p.ap^{\alpha} = a.p^{\alpha+1}$$

$$MR = \frac{dR}{dq} = \frac{d}{dq}(ap^{\alpha+1})$$

$$= a(\alpha+1)p^{\alpha}\frac{dp}{dq}$$

$$= q(\alpha+1)\frac{p}{\alpha.q}$$

Since, $\dfrac{dq}{dp} = \dfrac{\alpha q}{p}$

and $q = ap^{\alpha}$

$$= p\left(\frac{\alpha+1}{\alpha}\right) = p\left(1+\frac{1}{\alpha}\right)$$

Since $p > 0$, the sign of MR will depend upon the sign of $\left(1+\dfrac{1}{\alpha}\right)$.

(*i*) If $\alpha < -1$ or $1/\alpha < 0$, therefore $\left(1+\dfrac{1}{\alpha}\right) > 0$. Thus, R decreases with decrease in q or increase in p. In this case demand is elastic.

(*ii*) If $-1 < \alpha < 0$, or $0 < \alpha + 1 < 1$, therefore $\left(1+\dfrac{1}{\alpha}\right) < 0$. Thus, R increases with decrease in q or increase in p. In this case demand is inelastic.

(*iii*) If $\alpha = -1$ or $\alpha + 1 = 0$, therefore R is independent of q. In this case demand is unitary.

107. $$AC = \frac{TC}{q} = \frac{4860}{q} + 750000 + 15q$$

$$\Rightarrow \quad AC' = \frac{-4860}{q^2} + 15 = 0$$

$$\Rightarrow \quad \frac{-4860}{q^2} = -15$$

$$\Rightarrow \quad 4860 = 15q^2$$

$$q^2 = 324$$

$$q = 18$$

AC is minimum at $q = 18$.

108. Price discrimination is possible when elasticity of demand will be different in different markets. The monopolist will fix higher price per unit in the market where demand is *inelastic* and lower price per unit in the market where demand is *elastic.* In this way alone he can increase his total revenue. There will be no fear of any change in demand. If elasticity of demand is the same in different markets, then price discrimination will either not be possible or will be detrimental.

114. Basic Requirements of Linear Programming

(*i*) There must be a well defined *objective* to achieve (to maximize or minimize).

(*ii*) There must be *limited availability of the resources i.e.,* there are *constraints* or restrictions on the usage/allocation of limited resources amongst the competing activities.

(*iii*) There are a *finite* number of *decision variables* (*activities* or *products*) and a finite number of constraints.

(*iv*) All the elements of an L.P.P. should be *quantifiable.*

(*v*) Both the objective function and constraints must be expressed in terms of *linear* equations or inequations.

(*vi*) Programming/planning requires that these must be *alternative courses of line of action i.e.,* there are alternatives available to which resources can be put.

(*vii*) All decision variables should assume non-negative values.

117. If all $Z_j - C_j \le 0$ and then at least one artificial variable appears in the optimum basis at non zero level the LPP does not possess any solution.

118. Statement of Duality Theorems

The following duality theorems are helpful in solving a LPP:

Theorem I : The dual of the dual problem is the primal problem.

Theorem II (Fundamental Duality Theorem) : When either the primal or the dual problem has a solution, then the other also has a solution and the optimum values of the objective functions of the two are the same.

Theorem III : When either the primal or the dual problem has an unbounded solution, then the solution to the other problem is infeasible (i.e., no solution)

Theorem IV : When any one of the primal or dual problem has only as infeasible solution, then the value of the objective function of the other is unbounded.

Theorem V : When the primal problem has a feasible solution but the dual problem does not has feasible soution, then the primal problem will not have a finite optimum solution and vice versa.

120. The following two properties of primal-dual should be understood.

Primal-Dual Property 1 : If feasible solution exists for both primal and dual problems, then both problems have an optimal solution for which the objective function values are equal. A peripheral relationship is that, if one problem has an unbounded solution, its dual has no feasible solution.

Primal-Dual Property 2 : The optimal values for decision variables in one problem are read from row (0) of the optimal table for the other problem. The following steps are involved in reading the solution values for the primal from the optimal solution table of the dual:

Step I : The slack-surplus variables in the dual problem are associated with the basic variables of the primal in the optimal solution. Hence, these slack-surplus variables have to be identified in the dual problem.

Step II : Optimal value of basic primal variables can be directly read from the elements in the index row corresponding to the columns of the slack-surplus variables with changed signs.

Step III : Values of the slack variables of the primal can be read from the index row under the non-basic variables of the dual solution with changed signs.

Step IV : Value of the objective function is same for primal and dual problems.

122. The maximum quantity of this commodity that the individual will ever demand per unit of time is 50 units. This occurs at a zero price. This is called *the saturation point* for the individual. Additional units of X result in a storage and disposal problem for the individual.

125. The slope of an indifference curve at a particular point measures the marginal rate of substitution (MRS), the rate at which the consumer is willing to trade one good to gain one more unit of another good.

126. Multiplying money income by some constant λ, and simultaneously multiplying all money prices by λ, leaves the buget line unaffected and hence leaves consumer purchases unaffected.

127. $$MRTS_{L,K} = \frac{MP_L}{MP_K} = \frac{1}{3}$$

$$\Rightarrow \quad \frac{MP_K}{MP_L} = 3.$$

129. **Holland** has aptly said, "The lowest point on each SAC curve, however, may not be the point of tangency with the LAC curve. The lowest point on an SAC curve is tangent to the LAC curve only at the lowest point of the LAC curve.

132. ***Monopsony*** is the mirror image of monopoly. While *monopoly* refers to the single seller of a commodity, *monopsony* refers to the single buyer of a commodity. *Monopsony* can be defined as a *situation where there is a single buyer who is not in competition with other buyers for the products which he purchases, and in which the entry into the market by other buyers is impossible.* Thus, *monopsony* refers to a situation when there is a single buyer of a commodity or service. It applies to any situation in which there is a monopoly element in buying. The single buyer is called a monopsonist.

135. The Value of Marginal Productivity (VMP) of a factor is derived by multiplying the marginal physical productivity (MPP) of the factor with the price (AR) of the product. According to Prof. Ferguson, *"The value of marginal productivity of a variable factor is equal to its marginal product being multiplied by the market price of the commodity in question."*

Therefore, VMP = MPP × AR.

137. Monetary and fiscal policy as described above shift the aggregate demand curve right or left. Loose monetary policy, lower interest rates, increases the demand for goods and services at each price level, shifting the aggregate demand curve to the right. Loose fiscal policy, increases in government expenditures and/or tax cuts, also increases the demand for goods and services at each price level and shifts the demand curve to the right.

Tight monetary policy, higher interest rates, and tight fiscal policy, reductions in government expenditures and/or tax increases, reduce the aggregate demand for goods and services at each price level and shift the aggregage demand curve to the left.

139. $C = 20 + 0.90\ Yd$

when $Yd = 100$

Then $C = 20 + .9 \times 100$

$= 20 + 90$

$= 100.$

141. Endogenous and Exogeneous Variables : A variable is *endogeneous* if its value is determined within the model and *exogenous* if its value is determined by forces outside the model. A change in an exogenous variable is noted as an *autonomous* change.

145. Foreign trade multiplier is also known as export multiplier. As exports increase, there is an increase in the incomes of all persons associated with the export industries. This, in turn, creates demand for goods. This will continue and national income will increase by the value of foreign trade multiplier. The value of foreign trade multiplier. The value of foreign trade multiplier is determined by (*i*) marginal propensity to save (mps) and (*ii*) marginal propensity to import (mpm). The smaller these two marginal propensities, the larger will be the value of multiplier.

$$\text{Foreign Trade Multiplier} = \frac{1}{\text{mps} + \text{mpm}}.$$

148. *A classical aggregate supply curve* is a vertical line at the full-employment level of output. *A Keynesian aggregate supply curve* has output increasing without any change in the price level until the economy reaches full employment, at which time aggregate supply becomes positively sloped. According to a Keynesian aggregate supply curve, output can be increased from a point within the production possibility frontier to a point on the production-possibility frontier without any increase in the price level. Output beyond the normal full-employment level (outside the production-possibility frontier) is achieved only by increases in the price level.

150. Aggregate Supply : Aggregate supply is the real value of output (real GDP) producers are willing and able to bring to the market at alternative price levels, *ceteris paribus.* The upward slope of the aggregate supply curve reflects both profit effects (the lure of widening profit margins) and cost effects (increasing cost pressures).

152. In the year 1993, the Central Government set up a committee under the chairmanship of R.N. Malhotra, the former insurance secretary and RBI governor, to examine the present working of the insurance sector and recommend its future course of action.

The committee submitted its report in 1994 with the following recommendations:

1. The central and zonal offices of LIC should be restructured and reorganised. The central office should concentrate on policy formulation, review, evaluation, product development and pricing, actuary valuation, investments, personnel policies, systems development, etc. The zonal offices should look after the insurance business and related matters.
2. The government should bring down its stake in the insurance companies to 50%.
3. GIC should cease to be a holding company. The government should take over holdings of GIC and its subsidiaries so that they can act as independent corporations. GIC should function exclusively as a reinsurance company.
4. Private companies with a minimum paid-up capital of ₹ 100 crore should be allowed to enter the insurance industry.

154. Microfinance is the provision of small loans and savings facilities to people otherwise excluded from formal financial systems. From its beginnings in the 1970s, microfinance has become one of the most lauded development interventions. In 2005 the United Nations celebrated its first International Year for Microfinance, and in 2006 the Grameen Bank and its founder, Muhammad Yunus were awarded the Nobel Peace Prize for 'their efforts to create economic and social development from below.

156. Value added tax or VAT is an indirect tax, which is imposed on goods and services at each stage of production, starting from raw materials to final product. VAT is levied on the value additions at different stages of production. VAT is widely applied in the European countries. However, now a number of countries across the globe have adopted this tax system.

VAT was first introduced in France as *taxe sur la valeur ajoutee* or *TVA*. In 1954, the French economist, Maurice Laure, the joint director of the French tax authority, the Direction generale des impost, initiated the concept of VAT, which came into effect on April 10, 1954. Initially introduced for large businesses of France, with the passage of time, VAT was employed for all business sectors of the country. In France, value added tax is considered to be one of the major sources state finance.

157. The Companies Act, 2013 passed by the Parliament, received the assent of the President of India on 29th August, 2013 and replaced the 57-year-old Companies Act, 1956.

158. The Reserve Bank of India (RBI) is the central bank of the country. The origins of the RBI can be traced to 1926, when the Royal Commission on Indian Currency and Finance (also known as the Hilton-Young Commission) recommended the creation of a central bank in India. It recommended that the control of currency and credit be made separate from the Government and that banking facilities be enhanced in the country. The RBI was established on April 1, 1935 under the Reserve Bank of India Act, 1934, which provides the statutory basis for its functioning. When the RBI was established, it took over the functions of currency issue from the Government of India and the power of credit control from the then Imperial Bank of India. Since then, the Reserve Bank's role and functions have undergone numerous changes as the nature of the Indian economy and financial sector changed.

Important highlights of the evolution of the RBI

Year	Events
1913	The Royal Commission on Indian Finance and Currency (Chamberlain Commission) underlined the need for a Central Bank for India.
1926	Hilton Young Commission recommended the establishment of a Central Bank in India, to be named as Reserve Bank of India.
January 1927	The Government introduced "The Gold Standard and Reserve Bank of India" in the legislature.
March 1927	The Bill was referred to a joint Committee to resolve some of the controversial clauses.
January 1928	Government of India published the "New Gold Standard and Reserve Bank Bill", as amended by the Joint Committee.
February 1929	Government clarified that it did not intend to bring the Reserve Bank Bill before the legislature in the near future.
1931	Report of the Indian Central Banking Enquiry Committee released, strongly recommending the establishment of the Reserve Bank.

Year	Events
March 1933	Report of the India Office Committee released, recommending establishment of Reserve Bank of India as a private shareholders' bank.
July 1933	London Committee, which was set up after the India Office Committee, adopted the 1928 Reserve Bank Bill as the basis and proposed certain amendments to the Bill.
September 1933	Reserve Bank of India Bill, drafted on the basis of London Committee recommendations, introduced in the Legislative Assembly.
December 1933	Reserve Bank of India Bill passed by the Assembly.
February 1934	Reserve Bank of India Bill was passed by the Council of States.
March 1934	Reserve Bank of India Bill received the assent of the Governor-General.
April 1935	The Reserve Bank of India was created as a private shareholder's bank. Sir Osborne smith was appointed the first Governor of the Reserve Bank of India.
July 1937	Sir James Braid Taylor assumed office of the Governor.
March 1937	The Reserve Bank acted as banker to the Government of Burma and was also responsible for note issue in Burma as per the Burma Monetary Arrangements Order.
January 1938	The Reserve Bank issued its own bank notes.
September 1939	Introduction of Exchange Controls in India under Defence of India Rules.
1939	Indian Bank Act to bring bank within the ambit of the Reserve Bank.
March 1940	The Reserve Bank's accounting year changed from January-December to July-June.
1940	The silver rupee replaced by the quaternary alloy rupee. One Rupee Note reintroduced. This note had the status of a rupee coin and represented the introduction of official fiat money in India.
August 1943	Sir C.D. Deshmukh took over as Governor.
1944	The Public Debt Act passed by the Government enabled the consoldiation of laws relating to Government securities and management of public debt by the Reserve Bank.
February 1945	Non-scheduled banks were allowed to open accounts with the Reserve Bank.
1945	Establishment of Department of Banking Operations and Development and Research and Statistics Department in the Reserve Bank.
January 1946	High Denomination Bank Notes of ₹ 500, ₹ 1,000 and 10,000 were demonetised to curb unaccounted money.
1946	Interim arrangements for bank supervision were put in place by an ordinance.
March 1947	The Reserve Bank ceased to function as Central Bank of Burma.

Year	Events
1947	Foreign Exchange Regulation Act was passed.
1948	Foreign Finance Corporation of India was established on the recommendation of the Central Board of the Reserve Bank.
June 1948	The Reserve Bank ceased to function as Central of Pakistan.
January 1949	The Reserve Bank was nationalised.
March 1949	Banking Companies Act, 1949 came into force, replacing the earlier interim arrangements. This formed the statutory basis of bank regulation and supervision in India.
July 1949	Sir Benegal Rama Rau assumed office as Governor.

161. Operations activities transform inputs into final products or services. For example, motor vehicle assembly line activities convert raw materials into a finished car.

162. The accounting equation shows the relationship between the economic resources of a business and the claims against those resources. At all times, the following relationship holds:

Economic resources = Claims

Economic resources are assets. The claims consist of creditors' claims or *liabilities.* and owners' claims or *equity.*

The accounting equation may now be modified as follows:

Assets = Liabilities + Equity

We can analyze any business transaction in terms of its effect on the accounting equation, regardless of its size and complexity. The balance sheet shows the position of assets, liabilities and equity.

164. Going Concern Assumption : It is also known as *continuity assumption.* According to this assumption, the enterprise is normally viewed as a going concern, that is, continuing in operation for the foreseeable future. It is assumed that the enterprise has *neither* the intention *nor* the necessity of liquidation or of curtailing materially the scale of its operations. It is because of the going concern assumptions:

(*i*) that the assets are classified as *current assets* and *fixed assets.*

(*ii*) the liabilities are classified as *short-term liabilities* and *long-term liabilities.*

(*iii*) the unused resources are shown as *unutilised costs (or unexpired costs)* as against the break-up values as in case of liquidating enterprise. Accordingly, the earning power and not the break-up value evaluates the continuing enterprise.

According to Accounting Standard (1) issued by the Institute of Chartered Accountants of India, if this concept is followed, this fact need not be disclosed in the financial statements since its acceptance and use are assumed. In case this concept is not followed, the fact should be disclosed in the financial statement together with reasons.

It may be noted that if there are good reasons to believe that the business, or some part of it, is going to be liquidated or that it will cease to operate (say within a year or two), then the resources could be reported at their current values (or liquidation values).

165. Accrual Basis : When financial statements are prepared on the *accrual basis of accounting,* the effects of transactions and other events are recognized *when they occur* (as opposed to when cash or its equivalent is received or paid), and they are recorded in the accounting records and reported in the financial statements of the periods to which they relate.

The accrual basis assumption is also addressed in IAS 1, *Presentation of Financial Statements,* which clarifies that when the accrual basis of accounting is used, items are recognized as assets, liabilities, equity, income, and expenses (the elements of financial statements) when they satisfy the definitions and recognition criteria for those elements in the *Framework.*

166. Gross Profit = Revenue – Cost of goods sold

= 40,00,000 – 30,00,000 = 10,00,000.

167. Assets : Assets refer to the resources which a business has and can use to carry out its activities. Thus, cash, equipment, furniture and buildings are assets because they are resources which can be used for running the business. Assets also include unused office supplies and stock (goods available for sale).

In addition to assets which have physical forms like buildings and furniture, assets include money owing to a business. This is because the business can expect to receive payment in future from its debtors (those who owe money). An example is trade debtors which refer to money owing to the business by customers for goods or services provided on credit.

Liabilities : Liabilities consist mainly of money owing by the business to others. An example is trade creditors, which refer to money owing to suppliers for the purchase of goods or services on credit. Other liabilities include loans, which refer to money borrowed by a business. An example is bank loans.

Liabilities also include business obligations to provide goods or services in the future. Sometimes, a business may have received money from customers for goods which are not yet delivered to them at the given date. At that date, such money received in advance from customers is regarded as liabilities called **'prepaid revenue'.** This is because a business 'owes' its customers the goods which it has to deliver in the future.

168. Goodwill : When one company acquires another, the purchase price is allocated to all the identifiable assets (tangible and intangible) and liabilities acquired, based on fair value. If the purchase price is greater than the acquirer's interest in the fair value of the identifiable assets and liabilities acquired, the excess is described as goodwill and is recognized as an asset. To understand why an acquirer would pay more to purchase a company than the fair value of the target company's identifiable assets and liabilities, consider the following three observations. First, as noted, certain items not recognized in a company's own financial statements (e.g., its reputation, established distribution system, trained employees) have value. Second, a target company's expenditures in research and development may not have resulted in a separately identifiable asset that meets the criteria for recognition but nonetheless may have created some value. Third, part of the value of an acquisition may arise from strategic positioning versus a competitor or from perceived synergies. The purchase price might not pertain solely to the separately identifiable assets and liabilities acquired and thus may exceed the value of those net assets due to the acquisition's role in protecting the value of all of the acquirer's existing assets or to cost savings and benefits from combining the companies.

The subject of recognizing goodwill in financial statement has found both proponents and opponents among professionals. The proponents of goodwill recognition assert that goodwill is the present value of excess returns that a company is able to earn. This group claims that determining the present value of these excess returns is analogous to determining the present value of future cash flows associated with other assets and projects. Opponents of goodwill recognition claim that the prices paid for acquisitions often turn out to be based on unrealistic expectations, thereby leading to future write-offs of goodwill.

169. The current ratio measures a firm's ability to pay their current obligations. The greater the extent to which current assets exceed current liabilities, the easier a company can meet its short-term obligations.

$$\text{Current Ratio} = \frac{\text{Current Assets}}{\text{Current Liabilities}}$$

After calculating the current ratio for a company, you should compare it with other companies in the same industry. A ratio lower than that of the industry average suggests that the company may have liquidity problems.

171. Potential investors and creditors typically restate financial statements into percentage terms to facilitate comparison to other companies and previous years. Techniques such as horizontal analysis, vertical analysis, and ratio analysis use percentages for comparison purposes. A comparison of a company's performance in one time period with its performance in different time periods is called time series, or trend analysis, When the performance of a company is compared with similar companies, in either current or past periods, it is referred to as cross sectional analysis. These comparisons are useful because very few analysis techniques involve comparison with an absolute standard that can be applied to a large variety of companies for multiple periods.

172. Solvency ratios measure the ability of a company to meet long-term obligations. Major solvency ratios include debt ratios (including the debt-to-assets ratio, debt-to-capital ratio, debt-to-equity ratio and financial leverage ratio) and coverage ratios (including interest coverage and fixed charge coverage).

174. Under acquisition accounting, if the purchase price of an acquisition exceeds the sum of the amounts that can be allocated to individual identifiable assets and liabilities, the excess is recorded as goodwill.

The capitalized costs of long-lived tangible assets and of intangible assets with finite useful lives are allocated to expense in subsequent periods over their useful lives. For tangible assets, this process is referred to as depreciation, and for intangible assets, it is referred to as amortization.

176. In most business transactions, cash is paid after the product or service has been delivered. In some cases, cash is paid before delivery. You have probably paid for magazines that you will receive at some time in the future. The publisher collects money for your subscription in advance, before the magazine is published. When a company collects cash before the related revenue has been earned, the cash is called deferred revenues or unearned revenues.

Under the revenue principle, revenue cannot be recorded until it has been earned. Deferred revenues are reported as a liability because cash has been collected but the related revenue has not been earned by the end of the accounting period. The obligation to provide services or goods in the future still exists. These obligations are classified as current or long term, depending on when they must be satisfied.

177. **Capital Reserve :** It is created out of capital profits. Capital profit arises out of non-recurring (i.e., occasional) transactions. For example, capital reserve created out of profit made on sale of fixed asset, say plant and machinery which is the excess of sale price over the cost of that fixed asset. Capital profit can be converted into capital resrve. But, with regard to companies, the following are some of the examples of capital reserve.

(*a*) Pre-incorporation profits.

(*b*) Premium received on issue of shares.

(*c*) Premium received on issue of debentures.

(*d*) Profit on cancellation of own debentures.

179. Interest on Own Debentures

Debentures purchased by a company, if not cancelled immediately, are retained as investment (popularly known as own debentures). These are deemed to be outstanding. Interest will be due on the total debentures (including the retained debentures by the company as investment). However, interest will be paid only on those debentures that are held by outsiders and interest on own debentures will be retained by the company itself and will be transferred to interest on own debentures account.

181. Assumptions of Cost-Volume-Profit Analysis

Cost-volume-profit analysis depends on several assumptions. The primary assumptions are as follows:

1. Total sales and total costs can be represented by straight lines.
2. Within the relevant range of operating activity, the efficiency of operations does not change.
3. Costs can be divided into fixed and variable components.
4. The sales mix is constant.
5. There is no change in the inventory quantities during the period.

These assumptions simplify cost-volume-profit analysis, Since they are often valid for the relevant range of operations, cost-volume-profit analysis is useful for decision making.

183. Variable Cost per unit = ₹ 160 × 0.75 = ₹ 120

Fixed Cost per unit = (160 – 120) = ₹ 40

Total fixed Cost = 10,000 × 40 = ₹ 4,00,000

Total Cost per unit when production is 12,500 units (10,000 × 1.25)

$$= 120+\frac{4,00,000}{12,500} = 120 + 32 = ₹\ 152.$$

184. $\frac{CA}{CL} = 1.8\ CA = 1.8\ CL$

$$CA - CL = \text{Working Capital} = ₹\ 3\ \text{lakh}$$

$$1.8\ CL - CL = 3 \text{ or } CL = ₹\ 3.75\ \text{lakh}$$

$$CA = 1.8 \times 3.75 = ₹\ 6.75\ \text{lakh}$$

$$\text{Liquid ratio} = \frac{LA}{CL} = \frac{CA - \text{Stock}}{CL} = 1.6$$

Hence, $\text{stock} = 6.75 - 1.6 \times 3.75 = 0.75\ \text{lakh} = ₹\ 75{,}000.$

185. $\text{P/V Ratio} = \frac{10}{40} = 0.25$

$$\text{BEP} = \frac{20}{0.25} = 80$$

Sales = Margin of Safety + BEP

Sales = 80 + 40 = 120.

190. Factory (manufacturing) overhead normally includes indirect manufacturing labour costs, supplies cost, and other production facility costs such as plant depreciation, taxes, etc. It is comprised of all manufacturing costs that are not direct materials or direct manufacturing labour.

191. The cost of spoiled units not resulting from ordinary manufacturing process is called abnormal spoilage and this is not included in the computation of the cost of good units produced. Scrap and normal spoilage are the results of normal manufacturing process, thus they should be included in the computation of the cost of good units produced.

193. Cost per Equivalent Unit–Weighted-Average Method : In the weighted-average method, the cost per equivalent unit is computed as follows:

Cost per equivalent unit

$$= \frac{\text{Cost of beginning work to process inventory} + \text{Cost added during the period}}{\text{Equivalent units of proudction}}$$

194. The solutions approach to compute the direct manufacturing labour efficiency variances is to set up a diagram as follows:

AH × SR	SH × SR
(4,100 × ₹ 12)	(4,100 × ₹ 12)
₹ 49,200	₹ 48,000

?

Efficiency variance

₹ 1,200 unfavourable

Note: To compute the Standard Hours (SH), multiply the Standard Hours allowed per unit produced (4) by the number of units produced (1,000).

197. The Financial Budget : The financial budget presents the plans for financing the operating activities of the firm. The financial budget is made up of the budgeted balance sheet and the budgeted statement of cash flows, each providing essential financial information.

Budgeted Balance Sheet : The budgeted balance sheet for the coming accounting periods is derived from the *actual* balance sheet at the beginning of the current budget period and the *expected* changes in the account balances of the operating, capital-expenditure, and cash budgets.

The budgeted balance sheet is more than a collection of residual balances resulting from other budget estimates. Undesirable projected balances and account relationships may cause management to change the operating plan. For instance, if a lending institution requires a firm to maintain a certain relationship between current assets and current liabilities, the budget must reflect these requirements. If it does not, the operating plan must be changed until the agreed requirements are met.

200. Total Sales = Variable Costs + Fixes Costs + Desired Profit

12,00,000 = Variable Costs + 2,80,000 + 2,00,000

⇒ Variable costs = 12,00,000 − 2,80,000 − 2,00,000 = 7,20,000.

Previous Paper (Solved)

DELHI UNIVERSITY—M.COM ENTRANCE TEST-2014*

1. The system of simultaneous equations is found inconsistent when:
   A. The system has no unique solution
   B. The system has its determinant value, |A| equal to zero
   C. Two equations are linearly dependent
   D. The system has its determinant, *i.e.*, |A| = 0 and (adj A) B is not equal to zero

2. The system of equation is expressed below in matrix form:

$$\begin{bmatrix} 1 & 1 & -1 \\ 1 & -2 & 1 \\ 3 & 6 & -5 \end{bmatrix}\begin{bmatrix} x \\ y \\ z \end{bmatrix} = \begin{bmatrix} 0 \\ 0 \\ 0 \end{bmatrix}$$

   The given system has:
   A. Infinite set of solutions
   B. Infinite many non-trivial solutions
   C. Only one non-trivial solution
   D. Only one trivial solution

3. The viability of input-output system is ensured when:
   A. $|I - A| \neq 0$ and for $i = j$ $(1 - a_{ij}) \neq 0$
   B. $|I - A| \neq 0$ and for $i = j$ $(1 - a_{ij}) > 0$
   C. $|I - A| > 0$ and for $i = j$ $(1 - a_{ij}) > 0$
   D. $|I - A| > 0$ and for $i = j$ $(1 - a_{ij}) < 0$

4. The solution to a linear programming problem is infeasible when:
   A. There is no point of optimality in the feasible region
   B. There is no single point of tangency between feasible region and iso-profit or iso-cost line
   C. One of the constraint is redundant in the problem
   D. The constraints are inconsistent and feasible region does not exist

5. In a simplex table, the variables constituting an identity matrix are called.
   A. Decision variables B. Slack variables
   C. Surplus variables D. Basic variables

6. Choose the correct statement from the following:
   A. Solution by a simplex method requires that all the constraint of a given LPP have none of the constants of the constraints with negative sign
   B. In improving a non-optimal solution, the key element may be positive, negative or zero
   C. The multiple soultion to a given LPP implies the same objective function value and consumption of same amount of resources
   D. When there is tie between $c_j - z_j$ values, it leads to the case of degeneracy

7. The function $f(x)$ defined by $f(x)$

$$= \begin{cases} 2x & \text{when } 0 \le x < 1 \\ 3 & \text{when } x = 1 \\ 4x & \text{when } 1 < x \le 2 \end{cases}$$ is discontinuous at:

   A. $x = 2$ B. $x = 1$
   C. $x = 0$ D. None of the point

8. Choose an appropriate term to fill in the blank. When $0 < e_d < 1$, demand is said to be ....
   A. Elastic B. Unit elastic
   C. Inelastic D. Perfectly inelastic

9. For the given cost function $c = \frac{x^2}{4} + 3x + 400$, average cost minimum occurs at:
   A. $x = 30$ B. $x = 40$
   C. $x = 35$ D. $x = 50$

*Exam held on 22-06-2014.

10. The function $z = \dfrac{x^2 + y^2}{x^3 + y^3}$ is:

A. Homogenous function
B. Non-homogenous function
C. Homogenous function of degree1
D. Homogenous function of degree 'n'

11. The two productions are complementary in nature, when:

A. Both cross partial elasticities are positive
B. Both cross partial elasticities are negative
C. Both cross partial elasticities are zero
D. Both cross partial elasticities are equal

12. An annuity is an .... annuity when the first annuity is paid at the end of first payment interval.

A. Ordinary. B. Annuity due
C. Annuity certain D. Contingent annuity

13. The effective rate of discount 'd_e' corresponding to nominal rate of discount 'd' convertiable 'm' times a year is:

A. $d_e = \left(1 - \dfrac{d}{m}\right)^m$

B. $1 - d_e = \left(\dfrac{d}{m} - 1\right)^m$

C. $1 - d_e = \left(1 - \dfrac{d}{m}\right)^m$

D. $1 - d_e = \left(1 - \dfrac{d}{m}\right)^t$

14. At the equilibrium of demand and supply functions given respectively as: $\rho_d = 18 - 2x - x^2$ and $\rho_s = 2x - 3$, the size of consumer surplus is:

A. 30 B. 27
C. 28 D. 32

15. For a monopolist discriminating in two markets, if $e_1 > e_2$:

A. $P_1 > P_2$ B. $P_1 < P_2$
C. $P_1 = P_2$ D. $P_1 \le P_2$

16. Elasticity of substitution between labour and capital as factors of production, measures:

A. Ratio of proportionate change in factor ratio to the proportionate change in MRTS
B. Ratio of proportionate change in MRTS to proportionate change in factor ratio
C. Ratio of change in factor ratio to MRTS
D. Ratio of change in factors of production

17. Choose the statement which is true:

A. Constant product curves are concave to origin
B. Constant product curves are equi-distant
C. Constant product curves are upward sloping
D. Constant product curves downward sloping and convex to origin

18. Classical EOQ model is based on the assumption of:

A. Constant and uniform demand with positive lead time
B. Uncertain demand with zero dead time
C. Certain and uniform demand with zero lead time
D. Certain and uniform demand with variable cost structure

19. Choose an incorrect statement from the following:

A. Elasticity of total cost is ratio of percentage change in total cost to a given percentage in output
B. Elasticity of total cost is related to elasticity of average cost, *i.e.*, elasticity of average cost equals elasticity of total cost minus one
C. Elasticity of total cost is related to elasticity of average cost, *i.e.*, elasticity of average cost equals elasticity of total cost plus one
D. Elasticity of total cost is expressed as $e_c = \dfrac{x}{c} \cdot \dfrac{dc}{dx}$

20. The linear programming problem is said to be degenerated when:

A. Basis cannot be improved
B. Basic variable has value equal to zero
C. Basis has either slack or surplus variables
D. Basis has artificial variable

21. Cost-volume-profit analysis is based on several assumptions. Which of the following is not one of these assumptions.
A. The sales mix of products is constant the year
B. Inventory quantities change during the year
C. The behaviour of both revenues and cost is linear throughout the relevant range
D. Factor prices, for example, material prices and wage rates remain unchanged

22. Which of the following should not be considered in a make or buy decision?
A. Potential use of manufacturing capacity
B. Variable costs of production
C. Potential rental income from space occupied by production area
D. Unchanged fixed cost

23. A company uses several types of materials to manufacture its product. The result of combining these materials in proportion different from standard proportion is the:
A. Material price variance
B. Material usage variance
C. Material mix variance
D. Material yield variance

24. In two consecutive periods, sales and profit were ₹ 1,60,000 and 8,000 respectively in the first period and ₹ 1,80,000 and ₹ 14,000 respectively during the second period. If there is no change in fixed cost between the two periods, then P/V ratio must be:
A. 20% B. 25%
C. 30% D. 40%

25. ABC company having its net working capital of ₹ 3 lakhs, has the current ratio 1.8 and liquid ratio 1.6. Its value of stock is:
A. ₹ 55,000 B. ₹ 65,000
C. ₹ 75,000 D. ₹ 85,000

26. If the provision for bad debts account has a debit balance of ₹ 84 and provision is ₹ 462, the charge against the profit and loss account is:
A. ₹ 546 B. ₹ 462
C. ₹ 378 D. ₹ 84

27. The item, closing inventory, is shown in balance sheet under:
A. Fixed assets
B. Current assets
C. Current liabilities
D. Miscellaneous expenditure

28. Which of the following is an important reason for studying accounting?
A. The information provided by accounting is useful in making many economic decisions
B. Accounting plays an important role in society
C. The study of accounting could lead to a challenging career
D. All of the above are important reasons

29. Economic events that affect the financial position of a business are called:
A. Separate entities
B. Business transactions
C. Money measures
D. Financial actions

30. Which of the following types of accountants should be completely independent of the firm or organisation whose financial data is being examined?
A. Controller
B. Chartered accountant
C. Internal auditor
D. Firm's budget director

31. The immediate recognition of loss is supported by the underlying principle of:
A. Matching B. Consistency
C. Judgement D. Conservation

32. Generally Accepted Accounting principles:
A. Define accounting practice at a time
B. Are similar in nature to the principles of chemistry or physics
C. Are rarely changed
D. Are not affected by changes in the way business operates

33. The valuation of a promise to receive cash in the future at present value on the financial statement of a business entity is valid by virtue of which accounting postulate or principle.

A. Entity B. Materiality
C. Matching D. Going Concern

34. A debit may signify:
A. An increase in an asset account
B. A decrease in an asset account
C. An increase in a liability account
D. An increase in the capital account

35. Which of the following is not true of a trial balance?
A. It proves that the total debts equals total credit, if it balances.
B. It facilitates preparation of financial statements.
C. It proves that no errors have been made in recording transactions, if it balances.
D. It will not detect an error where the accounts debited in recording a particular transaction.

36. Deciding whether an expenditure for a desk is properly recorded as store equipment or office equipment is an example of:
A. Recognition problem
B. Valuation problem
C. Classification problem
D. Communication problem

37. As generally applied to accounting, what is depreciation?
A. It is a process of asset valuation for balance sheet purposes.
B. It applies only to long lived intangible assets.
C. It is used to indicate a decline in market value of long lived assets.
D. It is an accounting process which allocates long lived assets cost to accounting periods.

38. The initial cost of a plant asset is equal to the asset's implied cash price and:
A. Interest paid on debt incurred to finance the asset's purchase.
B. Market value of any non-cash asset given up to acquire the plant asset.
C. Reasonable and necessary costs incurred to prepare the asset for use.
D. Asset's estimated salvage value.

39. If a unit of inventory has declined in value in original cost, but the market value exceeds net reasonable value, the amount to be used for purpose of inventory valuation is:
A. Net realisable value
B. Original cost
C. Market value
D. Net realisable value less a normal profit margin

40. An inventory pricing procedure in which the oldest costs incurred rarely have an effect on the ending inventory valuation is:
A. FIFO B. LIFO
C. Weighted average D. Simple average

41. The amount of share premium can be used wholly or in part for:
A. Writing off preliminary expenses
B. Writing off goodwill
C. Writing of advertising expenses
D. Purchasing fixed assets

42. The profit made on reissue of forfeited shares is transferred to:
A. Capital reserve
B. Capital redemption reserve
C. General reserve
D. Profit and loss account

43. Discount on the issue of debentures is written off:
A. Before redemption of debentures
B. After redemption of debentures
C. In any period selected by the company
D. In no case later than the date of redemption

44. Dividend by a company can be paid from:
A. Profit of the current year
B. Undistributed profits of previous years
C. Money provided by central govt. or any state govt. for the payment of dividend
D. All of the above

45. Which of the following items is included on statement of changes in financial position only because of the total financial resources concept?
A. Depreciation

B. Issue of equity capital
C. Purchase of govt. securities
D. Retirement of long term debt by issue of preferred capital

46. A manufacturer used 400 units of a component every month and he buys them entirely from an outside supplier @ ₹ 40 per unit. The order placing and receiving cost is ₹ 100 and storage and carrying cost is 15% of the value of stock. EOQ will be:
A. 300 units B. 400 units
C. 450 units D. 500 units

47. A company has margin of safety of ₹ 40 lakhs and earns an annual profit of ₹ 10 lakhs. If the fixed costs amount to ₹ 20 lakhs, annual sales will be :
A. ₹ 160 lakhs B. ₹ 140 lakhs
C. ₹ 120 lakhs D. ₹ 200 lakhs

48. A company maintains a margin of safety of 25% on its current sales and earns a profit of ₹ 30 lakhs per annum. If the company has a profit volume ratio of 40%, its current sales amount to:
A. ₹ 200 lakhs B. ₹ 300 lakhs
C. ₹ 325 lakhs D. None of the above

49. If actual output is lower than budgeted output, which of the following costs would you expect to be lower than the original budget.
A. Total variable costs
B. Total fixed costs
C. Variable costs per unit
D. Fixed costs per unit

50. Fixed costs are conveniently deemed to be:
A. Constant per unit of output
B. Constant in total when production volume changes
C. Outside the control of management
D. Those unaffected by inflation

51. Costs incurred in the past are:
A. Opportunity costs B. Direct cost
C. Sunk costs D. Variable cost

52. In a job cost system, manufacturing overhead is:

	Indirect cost	Product cost
A.	No	Yes
B.	No	No
C.	Yes	Yes
D.	Yes	No

53. Unit of production is an appropriate method of assigning overhead when:
A. Several well-differentiated products are manufactured
B. Direct labour costs are low
C. Only one product is manufactured
D. Manufacturing process is complex

54. Spoilage from a manufacturing process was discovered during an inspection of work-in-process. In a process costing system, the cost of spoilage is added to the cost of the good units produced if the spolage is:

	Abnormal	Normal
A.	No	Yes
B.	No	No
C.	Yes	Yes
D.	Yes	No

55. In the computation of manufacturing cost per equivalent unit the weighted average method of process costing considers:
A. Current costs only
B. Current costs plus cost of beginning work-in-process inventory
C. Current cost plus cost of ending work-in-process inventory
D. Current costs minus cost of beginning work-in-process inventory

56. A company manufactures one product with a standard direct manufacturing labour cost of four hours at ₹ 12 per hour. During June, 1000 units were produced using 4100 hours at ₹ 12.20 per hour. The unfavourable direct labour efficiency is:
A. ₹ 1220 B. ₹ 1200
C. ₹ 820 D. ₹ 400

57. Which of the following is normally included in the financial budget of a firm?
A. Direct materials budget
B. Selling expense budget

C. Budgeted balance sheet
D. Sales budget

58. Which department is customarily held responsible for an unfavourable materials usage variance?
A. Quality control B. Purchasing
C. Engineering D. Production

59. Bad debts are treated as:
A. Direct expenses
B. Cost of production
C. Selling overheads
D. Distribution overheads

60. The following factor is an avoidable cause for labour turnover:
A. Lower wages
B. Resignation
C. Retirement
D. Workers' moving nature

61. When an individual's income rises, that person's demand for a normal good:
A. Rises B. Falls
C. Remains the same D. Any of the above

62. If the quantity of a commodity demanded remains unchanged as its price changes, the coefficient of price elasticity of demand is:
A. Greater than 1 B. Equal to 1
C. Smaller than 1 D. Zero

63. A fall in the price of a commodity who's demand curve is a rectangular hyperbola cause total expenditures on the commodity to:
A. Rise B. Fall
C. Remain the same D. All of the above

64. The instruments of monetary policy are:
A. Open market operations
B. Reserve requirements
C. Bank rate
D. All of the above

65. The Engle curve for a Giffen good is:
A. Negatively sloped
B. Positively sloped
C. Vertical
D. Horizontal

66. The substitution effect for a fall in the price of a commmodity is given by:
A. Movement up a given indifference curve
B. A movement from a higher to a lower indifference curve
C. A movement down a given indifference curve
D. None of the above

67. The Engel curve for a normal good is:
A. Negatively sloped
B. Positively sloped
C. Vertical
D. Horizontal

68. When the marginal productivity of land is negative it is in:
A. Stage for land
B. Stage 3 for labour
C. Stage 2 for land
D. None of the above

69. At the point of producer equilibrium:
A. Isoquant is tangent to the isocost
B. The $MRTS_{lk}$ equals $\frac{pl}{pk}$
C. $\frac{MP_l}{P_l} = \frac{MP_k}{P_k}$
D. All of the above

70. If there are constant returns to scale and if the quantity of labour used per unit of time is increased by 10% but the amount of capital remains constant then output will:
A. Increase by 10%
B. Decrease by 10%
C. Increase by more than 10%
D. Increase by less than 10%

71. When the law of diminishing returns begins to operate, the TVC curve begins to:
A. Fall at an increasing rate
B. Rise at a decreasing rate
C. Fall at a decreasing rate
D. Rise at an increasing rate

72. Marginal cost is given by:
A. Slope of the TFC curve
B. Slope of the TVC curve but not by the slope of TC curve

C. Slope of the TC curve but not by the slope of the TVC curve
D. Either the slope of TVC curve or the slope of TC curve

73. The LAC curve falls as output expands, this is due to:
A. Economies of scale
B. The law of diminishing returns
C. Diseconomies of scale
D. Any of the above

74. Given the supply of a commodity in the market period, the price of the commodity is determined by:
A. The market demand curve alone
B. The market supply curve alone
C. The market demand curve and market supply curve
D. None of the above

75. The optimum level of output for a perfectly competitive firm is given by the point where:
A. MR = AC
B. MR = MC
C. MR exceeds MC by the greatest amount
D. MR = MC and MC is rising

76. In the short run the monopolist:
A. Breaks even B. Incurs a loss
C. Makes a profit D. Any of the above

77. In the long run equilibrium the pure monopolist can make pure profits because of:
A. Blocked entry B. High selling prices
C. The low LAC D. Advertising

78. If input A is the only variable input for a perfectly competitive firm in the product market the firms demand curve for input A is given by its:
A. VMP curve B. MP curve
C. MRC curve D. None of the above

79. When VMP is greater than MRP and MRP is greater than P:
A. We have monopolistic exploitation
B. Monopsonistic exploitation
C. Both monopolistic and monopsonistic exploitation
D. None of the above

80. In an economy of two commodities X and Y and two factors L and K, General equilibrium of production is reached when:
A. MRTSlk = Pl/Pk
B. MRTSlk = MRSxy
C. MRTxy = MRSxy
D. (MRTSlk)x = (MRTSlk)y

81. The balance budget is:
A. Government expenditure is equal to tax revenue
B. Government expenditure is greater than tax revenue
C. Government expenditure is lesser than tax revenue
D. None of the above

82. The government expenditure multiplier is:
A. 1/c B. 1-c
C. 1/1-c D. None of the above

83. The demand for loanable fund is equal to:
A. Investment + demand for foreign investment
B. Investment
C. Demand for foreign investment
D. None of the above

84. When total utility increases marginal utility is:
A. Negative & increasing
B. Negative & decreasing
C. Zero
D. Positive & decreasing

85. The total demand for money is due to:
A. Transaction motive
B. Precautionary motive
C. Speculative motive
D. All of the above

86. The Fisher's Equation is given by:
A. MV = PT B. M/P = KY
C. M/P = YR D. None of the above

87. The APS + APC is equal to:
A. 1 B. 2
C. 0.1 D. 1.5

88. The Fisher equation shows the following linkage:

A. Consumption and interest linkage
B. Saving and interest linkage
C. Inflation and interest linkage
D. None of the above

89. Expansionary fiscal policy implies:
A. Increase in aggregate demand
B. Decrease in aggregate demand
C. Increase in savings
D. None of the above

90. The credit multiplier is equal to:
A. $\frac{1}{c}$ B. $\frac{1}{r}$
C. $\frac{1-r}{c+r}$ D. $\frac{1}{c+r}$

91. Economic development implies:
A. Rise in output
B. Technological changes
C. Institutional organization of production
D. All of the above

92. The foreign exchange crises in India occurred in:
A. 1990 B. 1980
C. 1985 D. 1991

93. The macroeconomic reforms in India started in:
A. 1990 B. 1991
C. 1992 D. 1993

94. The service sector consist of:
A. Agriculture B. Industry
C. Manufacturing D. None of the above

95. Over the recent years, India's growth has occurred the most in:
A. Agriculture B. Industries
C. Services D. Manufacturing

96. The high growth phase of 2004-08 was in:
A. Export B. Imports
C. Capital inflows D. All of the above

97. Land reform measures includes:
A. Abolition intermediaries
B. Tenancy reforms
C. Ceiling on land holdings
D. All of the above

98. The service sector consist of:
A. Financing B. Trade
C. Hotels D. All of the above

99. Food management implies:
A. Procurement of food
B. Distribution of food
C. Maintenance of food buffers
D. All of the above

100. Structural reforms were broadly in the area of:
A. Industrial licensing
B. Foreign trade
C. Financial sector
D. All of the above

101. Who among the following is NOT one of the recipients of Nobel Prize 2013 in Economics?
A. Eugene Fama B. Peter Hansen
C. Robert Shiller D. Michael Levitt

102. "Heartbleed" term which is being reported recently in newspapers is a:
A. New heart related disease
B. Social media site
C. Software bug
D. Fruit

103. Which among the following is the first country to sign a civil nuclear agreement with India?
A. Russia B. Namibia
C. France D. U.K.

104. As per the revised Direct Tax Code, the proposed tax slab for individuals having income more than ₹ 10 crore is:
A. 10% B. 15%
C. 25% D. 35%

105. Which of the following is an experimental, decentralised digital currency that enables instant payments to anyone, anywhere in the world?
A. All Time Money B. Bitcoin
C. Moncoin D. Cointime

106. Which of the following Global Drug major announced a multi-billion dollar revamp plan on April 2014, under which it will swap assets with Glaxo Smith Kline (GSK) and will sell some business to Eli Lily?

A. Pfizer Ltd. B. Novartis
C. Daiichi Sankyo D. Lupin

107. Which airline flew Boeing 777 Plane powered by biofuel on 19th Jan. 2014?
A. Air India B. Ethihad Airways
C. US'Airways D. British Airways

108. Name the country that won the final of Hero Hockey World League 2014:
A. Netherlands B. Argentina
C. Spain D. New Zealand

109. Which of the following is a credit rating agency in India?
A. CRISIL
B. CARE
C. India Ratings and Research
D. All of the above

110. The CEO of which of the following companies is NOT an Indian or Person of Indian Origin?
A. Arcelor-Mittal B. PepsiCo
C. Reckitt Benckiser D. None of the above

111. Third Nuclear Security Summit 2014 was held at:
A. Netherlands B. Canada
C. UAE D. Japan

112. India's largest solar power plant was launched in March 2014 in which of the following states:
A. Rajasthan B. Gujarat
C. Madhya Pradesh D. Maharashtra

113. Which of the following statements is True about "El Nino"?
A. It is the name given to unusual warming of waters in the central and eastern equatorial Pacific, which is linked to changes in the wind patterns and anomalous weather in many parts of the globe.
B. It results in extended and heavy monsoon in all parts of the globe.
C. There is a high probability of developing this phenomenon in the next few months.
D. A and C

114. Which among the following is not one of the so called "Fragile Five" countries?
A. India B. Greece
C. South Africa D. Brazil

115. The Committee on New Bank Licenses which recently submitted its report to RBI is headed by:
A. C. Rangarajan
B. Bimal Jalan
C. Montek Singh Ahluwalia
D. Jagdish Bhagwati

116. Which among the following industries contributes maximum excise revenue to the Indian exchequer?
A. Automobiles B. Oil and Gas
C. Steel D. Cement

117. Who is the CEO of Microsoft?
A. Satya Nadela B. John Thompson
C. Bill Gates D. Indra Nooyi

118. Which company has acquired mobile messaging service WhatsApp as announced in Feb 2014?
A. Twitter B. Microsoft
C. Facebook D. Google

119. RBI constituted a committee in Feb 2014 to examine the recommendations of Financial Sector Legislative Reforms Commission (FSLRC) relating to capacity building in the banking sector. Who is heading this committee?
A. R. Gandhi B. G. Gopalkrishna
C. V.S. Malhotra D. Urjit R. Patel

120. As per companies Act 2013, every company having net worth of ₹ .... crore or more, or turnover of ₹ .... crore or more, or a net profit of ₹ .... crore or more during any financial year shall constitute a CSR committee of the Board. Choose the correct option to fill in the blanks.
A. 500, 1000, 5 B. 1000, 500, 5
C. 5, 500, 1000 D. 5, 1000, 500

121. Sachin Tendulakar retired from cricket recently after his 200th Test. Sachin played his first test against which team in 1989:

A. England B. West Indies
C. Pakistan D. Sri Lanka

122. Which of the following statements are correct?
(*i*) Foreign Investment Promotion Board (FIPB) has given green signal to Singapore Airlines' proposal to start an aviation venture with Tata Sons.
(*ii*) The venture called, Tata SIA Airlines Ltd. entails an initial foreign investment of $ 49 million.
(*iii*) In the new venture, Tata Sons would hold 51% stake and Singapore Airlines (SIA) 49% stake.
A. (*i*) and (*ii*) B. (*i*) and (*iii*)
C. (*ii*) and (*iii*) D. All (*i*), (*ii*) and (*iii*)

123. Microsoft has recently developed a new cost effective sign language translator known as:
A. KINECT B. CONNECT
C. KOMNET D. KABOL

124. The Montreal Protocol is a multilateral environment agreement aimed at restoring:
A. Ozone layer B. Wetlands
C. Glaciers D. Soil productivity

125. What is the name of the company of legendry investor Warren Buffet?
A. Goldman Sach
B. Morgan Stanely
C. Berkshire Hathways
D. United Investments

126. Recently launched Central Public Sector Enterprises (CPSE) ETE scheme is managed by:
A. RBI
B. Bombay Stock Exchange
C. National Stock exchange
D. Goldman Sachs India

127. Which among the following companies emerged as the only Indian entities in the 2014 list of World's most ethical companies?
A. Wipro and Infosys
B. Infosys and Tata Power
C. Wipro and Tata power
D. TCS and Infosys

128. India's first all women bank is:
A. Bharatiya Mahila Bank
B. Women Bank of India
C. Bharatiya Stree Bank
D. Stree Shakti Bank

129. Which of the following organisations publishes the "World Investment Report" annually?
A. WTO B. UNCTAD
C. World Bank D. IMF

130. Recently, which of the following countries has been given final approval to join Eurozone, becoming it's 18th member:
A. Poland B. Romania
C. Latvia D. Lithuania

131. In the 61st National Film Awards announced in April 2014, which film bagged the Best Film award?
A. Shahid B. Bhag Milkha Bhag
C. Fandry D. Ship of Theseus

132. Which of the following is an Index of green companies in Bombay Stock Exchange?
A. ESG India Index B. GREENEX
C. NIFTY JUNIOR D. DOLLAX

133. Basel III deadline is extended to which of the following dates:
A. 31st March 2016 B. 31st March 2017
C. 31st March 2018 D. 31st March 2019

134. According to Global Information Technology Report 2014, which country was placed first in terms of leveraging information and communication technology (ICT) .
A. Finland B. Germany
C. USA D. New Zealand

135. As per Interim Union Budget 2014-15, fiscal deficit target for FY 2015 is:
A. 4.6% B. 4.1%
C. 4% D. 3.5%

136. Who is the author of "Imagining India"?
A. Khushwant Singh B. Nandan Nilekani
C. APJ Abdul Kalam D. Chetan Bhagat

137. Which of the following pairs are correctly matched?

(*i*) SHENZHEN-CHINA
(*ii*) NASDAQ-USA
(*iii*) SGX-SINGAPORE
(*iv*) DAX-ITALY

A. (*i*) and (*ii*) B. (*ii*) and (*iii*)
C. (*i*), (*ii*) and (*iii*) D. (*i*), (*ii*), (*iii*) and (*iv*)

138. "Nalanda Project" is launched by:
A. Ministry of HRD
B. Ministry of External Affairs
C. Ministry of Minority affairs
D. Ministry of Culture

139. Cadbury India Ltd. has changed its name to:
A. Mondelez India Foods Ltd.
B. Nestle India Ltd.
C. Confectionery India Ltd.
D. None of the above

140. Which country has pulled out from hosting 2019 Asian Games citing economic recession and lack of preparedness?
A. Indonesia B. Thailand
C. Philippines D. Vietnam

141. Trading on equity means:
A. Using borrowed funds to enhance the return to the owners
B. Using owned funds to enhance the return to the owners
C. Buying and selling of equity shares
D. None of the above

142. Which of the following is *not* a characteristic of a business system?
A. Purposeful B. Creative
C. Outside-regulated D. Synergistic

143. To make a business socially responsible, the theory of trusteeship was developed by:
A. Pt. Jawahar Lal Nehru
B. Dr. Rajendra Prasad
C. Mahatma Gandhi
D. Mrs. Indira Gandhi

144. Decentralisation of authority:
A. Increases the importance of superiors
B. Decreases the importance of superiors
C. Increases the importance of subordinates
D. Decreases the importance of subordinates

145. Advertising in print is:
A. Personal paid form of communication
B. A non-personal paid form of communication
C. Using coupons to obtain discounts
D. Sending publicity material to named respondents

146. 'Grapevine' refers to:
A. Informal channels of communication
B. Formal channels of communication
C. Both (A) and (B)
D. Neither (A) nor (B)

147. '50-50' wage incentive plan is a popular name of :
A. Rowan Premium Plan
B. Halsey Premium Plan
C. Gantt Premium Plan
D. Emerson Premium Plan

148. In 'Line and Staff' organisation, the authority lies with:
A. Line
B. Staff
C. Both Line and Staff
D. Neither Line nor Staff

149. According to whom, the decision - making power in modern organisation rests with the "technostructure"?
A. Peter F. Drucker
B. Joel Dean
C. John K. Galbraith
D. None of the above

150. Integration of two or more business operating at the same stage of the production-marketing chain is called:
A. Horizontal integration
B. Vertical integration
C. Lateral integration
D. Diagonal integration

151. The entrepreneurs, who try to be successful by delaying adoption of changes, are called:
A. Imitative entrepreneurs
B. Fabian entrepreneurs
C. Dronish entrepreneurs
D. Innovative entrepreneurs

152. Gilt-edged securities are:
A. Government Securities
B. Shares in a company with very little risk
C. Shares in a company with greater risk of loss
D. None of the above

153. The arrangement of facilities and equipment in groups according to the functions performed is called:
A. Process Layout
B. Product Layout
C. Static product Layout
D. None of the above

154. Price is what you pay for what you get. Which of the following is *not* a price?
A. Rent B. Interest
C. Salary D. Movie

155. The process of studying and collecting information relating to the operations and responsibilities of a specific job is called:
A. Job evaluation B. Job design
C. Job analysis D. Job specification

156. For the Assessment Year 2014-15, a surcharge of 10% of the income tax is applicable where total taxable income is more than:
A. 10 lakh B. 50 lakh
C. 1 crore D. 5 crores

157. Which of the following statements is *false*?
A. Exemption can never exceed the amount of income
B. Exemption may be more than the amount of income
C. Deduction is given from income chargeable to tax
D. There is a difference between exemption and deduction

158. Salary is taxable when:
A. It is accrued
B. It is received
C. It is due
D. It is received or due, whichever is earlier

159. ABC Ltd. is a company registered in Singapore. The control and management of its affairs is situated wholly in India. What is the residential status of ABC Ltd. in India?
A. Non-Resident
B. Resident
C. Resident but not ordinarily resident
D. Resident and ordinarily resident

160. Mr. A, a chartered accountant, is employed as an internal auditor with X Ltd. He requests the employer to call his remuneration as internal audit fee. Mr. A shall be chargeable to tax for such fee under the head:
A. Salaries
B. Income from other sources
C. Profits and gains of business or profession
D. Capital Gains

161. A "company limited by shares" means a company having the liability of its members limited ...., if any, unpaid on the shares respectively held by them.
A. By the articles to the amount
B. Unlimited
C. By the memorandum to the amount
D. None of the above

162. The definition of "promoter" does not include a person:
A. Who has been named as such in a prospectus or is identified by the company in the annual return referred to in section 92.
B. Who has control over the affairs of the company, directly or indirectly whether as a shareholder, director or otherwise.
C. In accordance with whose advice, directions or instructions the Board of Directors of the company is accustomed to act.
D. Person who is acting merely in a professional capacity.

163. As per the provisions of the Indian Companies Act, 2013, which one of the following meetings can be held more than once in a calendar year:
A. Extra ordinary general meeting
B. Statutory meeting
C. Annual general meeting
D. None of the above

164. The "related party", with reference to a company, does not include:
A. A key managerial personnel or his relative;
B. A firm, in which a director, manager or his relative is a partner;
C. A private company in which a director or manager is a member or
D. None of the above

165. "Special Notice" in the context of resolution implies:
A. Notice by the company only
B. Notice by proposer of resolution only
C. Notice by Proposer of specified resolutions to the company and by company to members in turn
D. None of the above

166. A special resolution is passed with ....
A. Simple majority
B. 2/3rd majority
C. 3/4th majority
D. Vote casted in favour are three times than votes casted against

167. The non rotational directors:
A. Do not retire at all
B. Retire after 20 years
C. Retire after 30 years
D. None of the above

168. Every company shall, within .... of the receipt of intimation under section 156, furnish the Director Identification Number of all its directors to the Registrar or any other officer or authority as may be specified by the Central Government.
A. 30 days B. 45 days
C. 15 days D. None of the above

169. A board meeting can be called by giving a notice of:
A. 21 days B. 15 days
C. 07 days D. None of the above

170. A cost auditor makes his report to:
A. The member of a company
B. The director of a company
C. The registrar
D. The Central Government

171. As per the Indian Contract Act, 1872, a proposal when accepted, becomes a:
A. Promise B. Agreement
C. Contract D. None of the above

172. As per the Indian Contract Act, 1872, which of the following is not an essential of a valid contract?
A. Offer and Acceptance
B. Legal obligation
C. Lawful object
D. Incompetent Parties

173. As per the Indian Contract Act, 1872, an agreement enforceable by law is a ....
A. Promise B. Contract
C. Valid offer D. None of the above

174. According to Section 2 (ha) of the Information Technology Act (Amendment), 2000, "Communication devise" does not include:
A. Cell Phones
B. Personal Digital Assistance
C. Laptops
D. Keyboard

175. For a Limited Liability Partnership (LLP) to be incorporated, ... associated for carrying on a lawful business with a view to profit subscribe their names to an incorporation document.
A. Two or more B. Three or more
C. Ten or more D. Five or more

176. The .... may direct a Limited Liability Partnership (LLP) to change its name under section 17, and the LLP shall comply with the said direction within 3 months after the date of such direction or any other time specified.
A. Central Government
B. Registrar
C. Ministry of Corporate Affairs
D. None of the above

177. Every LLP shall file an annual return duly authenticated with the Registrar within .... of closure of its financial year in such form and manner and accompanied by such fee as may be prescribed.

A. 30 days B. 45 days
C. 60 days D. 90 days

178. An agreement to sale under the Sale of Goods Act, 1930 is a contract that defines a .... sale.

A. Future B. Past
C. Completed D. None of the above

179. Which of the following is not a mode of making contract of sale under the Sale of Goods Act, 1930?

A. There may be immediate delivery of goods and immediate payment of price.
B. There may be immediate payment of price, but it may be agreed that the delivery is to be made at some future date.
C. There may be delivery or payment or both to be made at some future date.
D. There may be delivery or payment or both not to be made.

180. In which of the following case the implied condition and warranties may be treated as excluded?

A. The implied condition or warranty has been negated or varied with an expressed agreement
B. The implied condition or warranty has not been negated or varied with an expressed agreement
C. The course of dealings between the parties may also negate the implied condition or warranty
D. The customs or trade usage may also exclude the implied condition or warranty from a contract

181. Choose a correct statement from the following:

A. Median is the middle position in the data set
B. Mean and median identify the centre of the data around which the observations are located
C. Weighted mean is calculated on the basis of frequency of observations
D. The data set is always unimodal

182. The variance (r^2) of the given data set of observations, *i.e.*, 110, 145, 125, 95 and 150 is:

A. 450 B. 350
C. 400 D. 425

183. Choose an incorrect statement from the following:

A. Mean Deviation is based on each and every item of the data set
B. Change in the value of any item would change the value of mean deviation
C. Value of extreme items affects mean deviation more as compared to standard deviation
D. Mean deviation is non-algebric method

184. For a symmetrical distribution, which one of the following does not hold true?

A. Mean $\pm 1\sigma$ covers 68.27% of the items
B. Mean $\pm 2\sigma$ covers 90.45% of the items
C. Mean $\pm 3\sigma$ covers 99.73% of the items
D. Mean $\pm 2\sigma$ covers 95.45% of the items

185. If difference between two quartiles = 8, sum of two quartiles = 22, and median = 10.5, the coefficient of skewness is:

A. 0.5 B. −0.5
C. 0.125 D. −0.125

186. Which one of the following statement does not hold true as assumption of Karl Pearson's coefficient of correlation?

A. There is linearity of relationship between the variables
B. The two variables under study are influenced by a large number of independent causes
C. There is cause and effect relationship between the factors affecting the distribution of items in the two series
D. Only first two statements hold true

187. Which one of the following statements is not the point of difference between correlation and regression?

A. Correlation is a degree of covariability between two variables, and regression is the study of nature of relationship between variables.

B. Correlation does not suggest about cause and effect relationship, in regression analysis one variable is taken as dependent while other, as independent.
C. Correlation analysis is a measure of degree of linear relationship only, and it is symmetric. In regression analysis, it is both the measure of degree and direction and is non-symmetric.
D. There may be nonsense correlation due to chance between two variables, but there is nothing like nonsense regression.

188. Which one of the following statement does not relate to standard error of estimate?
A. It measures dispersion in the data set
B. It indicates the extent of inaccuracy in prediction
C. Smaller the value of standard error of estimate, the closer will be the dots to the regression line
D. The zero value of standard error of estimate implies perfect correlation

189. Time series contains:
A. Secular trend and seasonal variations
B. Seasonal variation and cyclical trend
C. Four components: secular, seasonal, cyclical and irregular
D. At the most any three variations

190. Homoscedasticity means:
A. Error term $\in$ is a normally distributed random variable
B. Variance in the Y values are the same at all values of X
C. Error terms are independent of each other
D. None of the above

191. Which of the following statement is not true for OLS?
A. It is a method to calculate b_0 and b_1
B. It produces the line that extends through the middle of scatter diagram and comes closer to all the data points than any other line
C. Given the sums of squares and cross products the regression coefficient, *i.e.*, $b_1 = \frac{SSxy}{SSx}$
D. The vertical intercept of regression line *i.e.*, $b_0 = \overline{y} + b_1\overline{x}$

192. A committee comprises of 5 persons of distinct age groups and gender. There are: Male aged 40 years; Male aged 43 years; female aged 38 years; female aged 27 years; and male aged 65 years. The probability of selecting a chairperson, either female or over 30 years of age, is:
A. $\frac{3}{5}$
B. $\frac{2}{5}$
C. 1
D. $\frac{1}{5}$

193. The joint probability of three independent events A, B and C is:
A. P(ABC) = P(A) × P(B) × P(C)
B. P(ABC) = P(A) × P(B) × P(C/AB)
C. P(ABC) = P(A) × P(B/A) × P(C/AB)
D. P(ABC) = P(A) × P(A/B) × P(A/C)

194. Choose an incorrect statement from the following:
A. Priori probability is an unconditional probability
B. Bayes' theorem asks the probability of the sample or experimental result given the state value
C. Posterior probability is the conditional probability
D. Bayesian information is based on prior information alone

195. Which one of the following is not continuous random variable?
A. The revenue earned by a shopkeeper
B. Weight of spring water in a container
C. Height of students in a class
D. Number of vehicles arriving at Petrol Pump

196. The situations like: number of arrivals of customers per hour, the number of industrial accidents each month, the number of defective electrical connections per mile of wiring in a city's power system, fulfills the assumptions of:

A. Poisson Distribution
B. Binomial Distribution
C. Exponential Distribution
D. Uniform Distribution

197. Which one of the following statements is true?
A. When the value of coefficient β_2 is less than 3, the curve is more peaked than the normal curve
B. Normal curve and other curves with $\beta_2 = 3$ are called mesokurtic
C. Sign of skewness depends upon value of μ_2
D. A Curve more flat topped than the normal curve, is called leptokurtic

198. Quartile deviation is:
A. Inter quartile range
B. Semi-quartile range
C. Distance from median value
D. Absolute measure of dispersion

199. In a class of 50 students, 10 have failed and their average of marks is 2.5. Total marks secured by the class were 281. The average marks of those who have passed is:
A. 6 B. 6.5
C. 6.4 D. 6.3

200. The rate of a certain commodity in first week of a month is 0.4 kg per rupee, 0.6 kg per rupee in second week and 0.5 kg per rupee in third week. The average price is:
A. 0.5 kg per rupee
B. 0.486 kg per rupee
C. 0.49 kg per rupee
D. 0.51 kg per rupee

ANSWERS

1	2	3	4	5	6	7	8	9	10
D	B	C	D	D	A	B	C	B	D
11	**12**	**13**	**14**	**15**	**16**	**17**	**18**	**19**	**20**
B	A	C	B	B	A	D	C	C	B
21	**22**	**23**	**24**	**25**	**26**	**27**	**28**	**29**	**30**
B	D	C	C	C	A	B	D	B	B
31	**32**	**33**	**34**	**35**	**36**	**37**	**38**	**39**	**40**
D	A	D	A	C	C	D	C	A	A
41	**42**	**43**	**44**	**45**	**46**	**47**	**48**	**49**	**50**
A	A	D	D	D	B	C	B	A	B
51	**52**	**53**	**54**	**55**	**56**	**57**	**58**	**59**	**60**
C	C	C	A	B	B	C	D	C	A
61	**62**	**63**	**64**	**65**	**66**	**67**	**68**	**69**	**70**
A	D	C	D	A	C	B	*	D	*
71	**72**	**73**	**74**	**75**	**76**	**77**	**78**	**79**	**80**
D	D	A	A	D	D	A	A	*	D
81	**82**	**83**	**84**	**85**	**86**	**87**	**88**	**89**	**90**
A	*	A	D	D	A	A	C	A	C
91	**92**	**93**	**94**	**95**	**96**	**97**	**98**	**99**	**100**
D	D	B	D	C	D	D	D	D	D
101	**102**	**103**	**104**	**105**	**106**	**107**	**108**	**109**	**110**
D	C	C	D	B	B	B	A	D	D
111	**112**	**113**	**114**	**115**	**116**	**117**	**118**	**119**	**120**
A	C	D	B	B	B	A	C	B	A

121	122	123	124	125	126	127	128	129	130
C	D	A	A	C	D	C	A	B	C
131	**132**	**133**	**134**	**135**	**136**	**137**	**138**	**139**	**140**
D	B	D	A	B	B	C	C	A	D
141	**142**	**143**	**144**	**145**	**146**	**147**	**148**	**149**	**150**
A	C	C	C	B	A	B	A	C	*
151	**152**	**153**	**154**	**155**	**156**	**157**	**158**	**159**	**160**
B	A	A	D	C	C	B	D	B	A
161	**162**	**163**	**164**	**165**	**166**	**167**	**168**	**169**	**170**
C	D	A	D	C	D	D	C	*	D
171	**172**	**173**	**174**	**175**	**176**	**177**	**178**	**179**	**180**
A	D	B	D	A	A	C	A	D	B
181	**182**	**183**	**184**	**185**	**186**	**187**	**188**	**189**	**190**
*	*	C	B	C	*	C	A	C	B
191	**192**	**193**	**194**	**195**	**196**	**197**	**198**	**199**	**200**
D	C	A	B	D	A	B	D	C	*

SOME SELECTED EXPLANATORY ANSWERS

1. Criterion of Consistency of a System of Linear Equations

(*i*) The non-homogeneous system AX = B, B ≠ 0 has unique solution if |A| ≠ 0 and the unique solution is given by $X = A^{-1}B$.

(*ii*) **Cramer's Rule:** If |A| ≠ 0 and $X = (x_1, x_2, \ldots, x_n)$ then for each $i = 1, 2, 3, \ldots, n$;

$x_i = \frac{|A_i|}{|A|}$ where A_i is the matrix obtained from A by replacing the *i*th column with B.

(*iii*) If |A| = 0 and (adj. A)B = O, then the system AX = B is consistent and has infinitely many solutions.

(*iv*) If |A| = 0 and (adj. A)B ≠ O, then the system AX = B is inconsistent.

(*v*) If |A| ≠ 0, then the homogeneous system AX = O has only null solution or trivial solution (*i.e.*, $x_1 = 0, x_2 = 0, \ldots, x_n = 0$).

(*vi*) If |A| = 0, then the system AX = O has a non-null solution.

3. Hawkins-Simon conditions have been developed to ensure that the solution of the input-output model does not contain negative output. Negative output means that more quantity is used as input than what is got as output. For example, if more than one quintal of seed is required to produce one quintal of wheat, then we get negative output and clearly such a situation is economically non-viable. Hawkins-Simon conditions are developed to ensure that the system is economically viable.

Hawkins and Simon prescribe two conditions for viability of the system. These are:

1. Determinant of (I – A) *i.e.*, |I – A| is positive, and
2. The diagonal elements of [I – A] matrix should all be positive, *i.e.*, $(1 - a_{11}) > 0$, $(1 - a_{22}) > 0$, ... $(1 - a_{nn}) > 0$. When translated in term of technology matrix, it would mean that $a_{11} < 1$, $a_{22} < 1$, ..., $a_{nn} < 1$. It implies that 1 unit of output of any sector should not use more than 1 unit of its own output as input. (The condition of economic viability).

4. Infeasible Solution: Infeasibility is a condition that arises when constraints are inconsistent (mutually exclusive), *i.e.*, no value of the variables satisfy all of the constraint simultaneously. This means, there is no unique (single) feasible region. Such a problem arises due to wrong model formulation with conflicting constraints.

5. The variables corresponding to the columns of the identity matrix are called *basic variables* and the remaining ones are *non-basic variables.* In general, if an LP model has n variables and $m(< n)$ constraints, then m variables would be basic and $n - m$ variables non-basic.

7. A function $f(x)$ is continuous at a if the following three conditions hold:
   1. $f(x)$ is defined at a
   2. $\lim_{x \to a} f(x)$ exists
   3. $\lim_{x \to a} f(x) = f(a)$

   We can summarize these three 4conditions by writing

$$\lim_{x \to a} f(x) = f\left(\lim_{x \to a} x\right) = f(a)$$

   If $f(x)$ does not satisfy these conditions, then $f(x)$ is said to be discontinuous at a.

9. Total cost function

$$C(x) = \frac{x^2}{4} + 3x + 400$$

$$\therefore \quad AC = \frac{x}{4} + 3 + \frac{400}{x}$$

$$\text{Now,} \quad \frac{d(AC)}{dx} = \frac{1}{4} + \left(-\frac{400}{x^2}\right)$$

$$= \frac{1}{4} - \frac{400}{x^2}$$

$$\therefore \quad \frac{d(AC)}{dx} = 0 \Rightarrow \frac{1}{4} - \frac{400}{x^2} = 0$$

$$\Rightarrow \quad \frac{400}{x^2} = \frac{1}{4}$$

$$\Rightarrow \quad x^2 = 1600$$

$$x = 40$$

$$\frac{d^2(AC)}{dx^2} = \frac{800}{x^3} > 0 \text{ at } x = 40.$$

11. Cross elasticity of demand is the degree to which the quantity demanded of one commodity responds to a change in the price of another commodity.

   The formula for measuring the coefficient of cross-elasticity of demand is:

$$E_l = \frac{\text{Proportionate change in quantity demanded of } a}{\text{Proportionate change in price of } b}$$

   Cross elasticity may be positive or negative, depending on the relationship between the two commodities. If the commodities are substitutes, cross elasticity will be positive, *i.e.*, a rise in the price of the first commodity will cause an increase in the demand for the other commodity. If the commodities are complements, cross elasticity will be negative, *i.e.*, a rise in the price of one commodity will cause a fall in the demand for the other. For example, if the price of sugar rises, less sugar will be bought and there will be a fall in the demand for coffee also.

12. Annuities may be classified into two main classes:

   (*i*) Ordinary annuities and

   (*ii*) Deferred annuities.

   In the case of *ordinary annuities* the first payment to be made is due in the first period of the term of the annuity. Ordinary annuities are again divided into two sub-classes:

   (*a*) Ordinary annuities certain and

   (*b*) Ordinary annuities due.

   Deferred annuities refer to annuities where the first payment is made at some future period later than the end of the first interest period. A common example of a deferred annuity is where a trust fund is specifically instructed to pay the beneficiary a regular instalment from some future date, *e.g.* after the beneficiary turns 18 years of age.

14. At equilibrium, $pd = ps$

$$\Rightarrow 18 - 2x - x^2 = 2x - 3$$

$$\Rightarrow x^2 + 4x - 21 = 0$$

$$\Rightarrow x^2 + 7x - 3x - 21 = 3$$

$$\Rightarrow x(x + 7) - 3(x + 7)$$

$$\Rightarrow \text{Either } (x - 3) = 0 \text{ or } x + 7 = 0$$

$$\therefore x = 3, x = -7 \text{ Rejecting the negative values}$$

$$\therefore x = 3$$

At $x = 3$, $p = 18 - 2 \times 3 - 9$
$= 118 - 6 - 9 = 3$

$$CS = \int_0^x pdx - px = \int_0^3 (18 - 2x - x^2)dx - 3 \times 3$$

$$= \left[18x - \frac{2x^2}{2} - \frac{x^3}{3}\right]_0^3 - 9$$

$$= \left[\left(18 \times 3 - 9 - \frac{27}{3}\right) - (0 - 0 - 0)\right] - 9$$

$= [(54 - 9 - 9) - (0 - 0 - 0)] - 9$
$= 36 - 9 = 27$
$\therefore$ C.S. = 27.

18. In order to establish the classical popularly known as EOQ model, we make certain assumptions. The assumptions are as follows:
1. Cost of one item and ordering cost per order remains constant over a period of time—pre-defined or pre-fixed. (Generally one year).
2. Demand rate is pre-known and remains fixed over a period of time.
3. Lead time is known and remains constant over a period of time. The demand during the lead time remains the same as the current demand rate.
   Alternatively, if the lead time is zero, the demand rate is instantaneous and infinite.
4. Annual demand is known and remains constant.
5. Supply rate is instantaneous of infinite. [as per the requirement of an order size]

20. Basic feasible solutions are of two types:
(*a*) *Degenerate:* A basic feasible solution is called degenerate if value of at least one basic variable is zero.
(*b*) *Non-degenerate:* A basic feasible solution is called non-degenerate if values all *m* basic variables are non-zero and positive.

23. **'Material Mix'** refers to the condition, where the product in question is manufactured, by using more than one type or grade of raw materials, or their combinations/mix in the required proportion. The 'Material Mix Sub-Variance' refers to the extent of deviation from the pre-determined standard ratio or mix of the raw materials. This may occur due to various reasons, some of which are given hereunder:
(*i*) Insufficient supply, or non-availability of, one or more types/grades of the required raw materials;
(*ii*) A subsequent rise in the price of some of the pre-specified raw materials, making the use of the same (identical) one rather uneconomical and hence avoidable, and necessitating a more economical substitution, resulting in the sub-variance of the 'material mix'.
(*iii*) Availability of the substitutes for one or more of the materials, of the same or similar quality, at a relatively lesser price (or even of a better quality, but at the same price), making it a better business sense to go for the same, instead, etc.

24. $\frac{\text{Change in profit}}{\text{Change in sales}} = \text{P/V ratio}$

$$= \frac{14{,}000 - 8{,}000}{1{,}80{,}000 - 1{,}60{,}000}$$

$$= \frac{6{,}000}{20{,}000} = 0.30 \text{ or } 30\%.$$

25. $\frac{\text{CA}}{\text{CL}} = 1.8 = \text{Current ratio}$

$\Rightarrow$ CA = 1.8 CL
$\Rightarrow$ CA – CL = working capital = 3 Lakh
1.8 CL – CL = 3
$\Rightarrow$ CL = 3.75 lakh
and CA = 1.8 × 3.75 = 6.75 Lakh

$$\text{Liquid Ratio} = \frac{\text{CA} - \text{stock}}{\text{CL}}$$

$\Rightarrow$ 1.6 × 3.75 = CA – stock
$\Rightarrow$ 6 = 6.75 – stock
$\Rightarrow$ stock = 6.75 – 6 = 75,000

27. **Current assets** (working capital), which are always listed first in a balance sheet, include those assets that are relatively liquid—that is, assets that can be converted into cash relatively quickly. Current assets primarily include cash, accounts receivable, and inventory.

31. **Principle of Conservation or Prudence:** The firm should not consider the profit if it depends on probability of any transaction or event but the firm should recognize all the possible losses.

33. To receive cash in future takes into account the future operating possibility of the business which is depicted by going concern concept.

39. **Net Realisable Value (NRV):** Net realisable value is the estimated selling price, in the ordinary course of business, less cost of completion, and the estimated cost necessary to make the sale.

40. **First-in-first-out (FIFO):** This method of inventory valuation assumes that the cost of items sold in a period consists of the oldest inventory cost just prior to sales. By charging the oldest costs in inventory to the sale, FIFO assumes that inventory at the end of the period consists of the most recent costs incurred. The rationale behind FIFO is that it reflects the fact that companies generally use the oldest items is inventory first so that they can continually turn over stock and prevent deterioration or obsolescence. FIFO is widely used in times of stable pricing.

42. Reissue of forfeited shares is not an allotment of fresh shares but resale of forfeited shares and therefore, the company do not required to file any return of allotment with the Registrar regarding these shares. Forfeited shares become the property of the company only for disposal and they may be reissued at any price fixed by the company. It is to be noted here that the amount collected at the time of reissue plus the amount already collected from the ex-shareholder (default shareholder) is not less than the amount credited as paid-up share capital at the time of reissue.

If out of the forfeited shares, only a portion is reissued, then profit on reissue on that part is to be transferred to Capital Reserve Account and the remaining amount in Share Forfeited Account is to be kept intact (*i.e.* the actual amount collected from the forfeited shares is not reissued).

If shares are originally issued at a discount before forfeiture, but are reissued at a discount, then the amount of old is to be reinstated at the time of reissue. If more discounts are allowed than that of the old amount, then the excess amount of the discount is to be adjusted by debiting Share Forfeited Account. If the shares are reissued at a price more than the face value, then the excess must be transferred to the Securities Premium Account.

44. Some of the important statutory provisions regarding the declaration and payment of dividend are as follows:

1. Dividends can be paid only out of profits and can never be paid out of the capital of the company.
2. Dividends can be paid out of profits or undistributed profits of previous years or money provided by the Government.
3. Dividends are to be paid in cash only.
4. The dividend shall be paid to the holder of the shares whose name appears in the register of members or to his banker.
5. The dividends should be paid within 42 days from the date of declaration.
6. Before any dividend is declared or paid out of the profits of the current year, certain percentage of profits, not exceeding 10%, will have to be transferred to the reserves of the company.
7. Arrears of depreciation for prior years, if any, should be set off against the profits out of which dividend is to be paid.
8. The dividends can be declared only by a resolution of the shareholders at the general meeting.
9. Generally, the dividend is declared at the annual general meeting of the members.

10. If authorized by the Articles of Association, the directors can also declare an interim dividend at any time between the two annual general meeting.
11. Once a dividend is declared, it becomes a debt due from the company to its shareholders.
12. Once a dividend is declared at the annual general meeting, the company cannot declare a further dividend.

46. $$\text{EOQ} = \sqrt{\frac{2 \times \text{Annual Demand} \times \text{Ordering Cost}}{\text{Storage Cost}}}$$

$$= \sqrt{\frac{2 \times 400 \times 12 \times 100}{15\% \text{ of } 40}}$$

$$= \sqrt{\frac{2 \times 400 \times 12 \times 100}{6}}$$

$$= \sqrt{400 \times 4 \times 100}$$

$$= \sqrt{40000 \times 4} = 400 \text{ units.}$$

47. ∵ Margin of Safety = Total Sale – Breakeven sale

⇒ Total sale = Margin of Safety + Breakeven sale

and $$\text{Margin of Safety} = \frac{\text{Profit}}{\text{P/V}}$$

$$\Rightarrow \quad 40 = \frac{10}{\text{P/V}}$$

$$\Rightarrow \quad \text{P/V} = \frac{10}{40} = \frac{1}{4}$$

and $$\text{Breakeven sale} = \frac{\text{Fixed Cost}}{\text{P/V}}$$

$$= \frac{20}{1/4} = 80$$

∴ Total sale = 40 + 80 = 120 lakhs.

48. $$\text{Margin of Safety} = \frac{\text{Profit}}{\text{P/V}}$$

$$= \frac{30}{0.40} = ₹\ 75 \text{ lakhs}$$

0.25 of sales = ₹ 75 lakhs

Hence, $$\text{Sales} = \frac{75}{0.25} = ₹\ 300 \text{ lakhs}$$

51. Sunk Costs: Sunk costs are costs incurred in the past. They are the results of past decisions and cannot be changed by future decisions. Since they do not influence future decision-making, they are irrelevant costs. They are unavoidable and irrecoverable historical costs.

53. Units of Production: Under this method the charge per unit is calculated by dividing total estimated factory overhead by total estimated units. This is the most direct and simplest method used for the assignment of factory overhead to units produced. The overhead absorption rate is calculated as under:

$$\frac{\text{Estimated factory overhead in the budget period}}{\text{Estimated units of production (at normal capacity)}}$$

The unit of production method is suitable when a company produces only one product. However, if a company produces many products and they are similar or closely related (their difference being only in volume, weight etc), this method can be used by the conversion of physical units into equivalent units.

56. The direct labour efficiency variance is that portion of the flexible budget variance attributable entirely to a difference in the number of hours required to generate a unit of output. It is calculated by multiplying the actual hours used in production, times the difference between the standard and actual hours per unit of output, times the standard hourly rate [AQ × (SI/O – AI/O) × SP]. The actual hours consumed per unit of output were 4.1 (4,100 hours ÷ 1,000 outputs). Thus, efficiency variance is ₹ 1,200 unfavourable [1,000 × (4 – 4.1) × ₹ 12.00].

57. The financial budget presents the plans for financing the operating activities of the firm. The financial budget is made up of the budgeted balance sheet and the budgeted statement of cash flows, each of which provides essential financial information.

The budgeted balance sheet is derived from the budgeted balance sheet at the beginning of the budget period and the expected changes in the account balances reflected in the operating budget, capital expenditure budget and cash budget. It is necessary to use a budgeted balance sheet for the beginning of the period because the new budget is prepared before the previous accounting period has ended.

59. Bad debt: There are two approaches for treating bad debt in cost accounts. One view is that bad debt is a financial loss only and should be excluded from cost accounts. The other view is that bad debt is similar to other expenses and should not be excluded from cost accounts. Accordingly, bad debt is considered an item of selling overhead. Abnormally high bad debts and bad debts of exceptional nature should be excluded from cost accounts. They should be charged to the profit and loss account.

62. A perfectly inelastic demand is one is which the quantity demanded is totally insensitive to any change in price. In this case, $e_D = 0$ and the demand curve is vertical (parallel to y-axis). If the product is absolutely essential like demand for a rare medicine, then its demand is perfectly inelastic.

64. To achieve the objectives of monetary policy there exist various instruments, which can be divided into two categories; quantitative or general measures and qualitative or selective measures.

Quantitative or general measures of monetary policy controls the total volume of credit and the cost of credit in the economy and thus the supply of money. They include open market operations, variations in reserve requirements, statutory liquidity requirement, bank rate policy, repo rate and reverse repo rate.

Qualitative or selective measures of monetary policy control the direction and distribution of credit in the economy. They include rationing of credit, change in margin requirements, moral suasion and direct action.

67. The Engel curve for a commodity records the relationship between the quantities demanded of the good and the total income, with all prices being held constant. That is, it is a graphical representation of the demand for the good as a function of income, keeping all prices constant. The Engel curves are not necessarily straight lines. The demand for some luxury goods may increase more proportionately than income, whereas the demand for necessities may grow less proportionately than income. It is clear that for an inferior good, the Engel curve is negatively sloped and for a normal good the curve is positively sloped.

73. In the long run there are no fixed inputs, and the shape of the LAC curve is determined by economies and diseconomies of scale. That is, as output expands from very low levels, increasing returns to scale cause the LAC curve to decline initially. But as output becomes greater and greater, diseconomies of scale may become prevalent, causing the LAC curve to start rising.

75. The marginal approach tells us that the perfectly competitive firm maximizes its short-run total profits at the output level, where MR or P equals marginal cost (MC) and MC is rising.

78. A profit-maximizing firm will employ an input as long as the extra income from the sale of the output produced by the input is larger than the extra cost of hiring the input. If input A is the only variable input used by the firm to produce commodity X, the extra income or *marginal revenue product* of input A (MRP_a) is given by the marginal product of input A (MP_a) times the marginal revenue of the firm (MR_x). That is, $MRP_a = MP_a \times MR_x$.

If the firm is a perfect competitor in the product market, $MR_x = P_x$ and $MRP_a = VMP_a$ (the value of the marginal product of input A). That is, $VMP_a = MP_a \times P_x = MP_a \times P_x = MRP_a$. As more units of input A are hired, the

MP_a, and thus the MRP_a, eventually decline. The declining portion of the MRP_a schedule is the firm's demand schedule for input A.

83. The demand for loanable funds comes from domestic investment (I) and net foreign investment (NFI).

86. Equation of Exchange: Fisher explained the Quantity Theory of Money algebraically. The Equation of Exchange was developed by Irving Fisher as is given below:

$$MV = PT$$

where M = Quantity of money in circulation.

V = Velocity of money in circulation.

It indicates average turnover of a unit of money in change hands.

P = Price Level

T = Total Volume of transactions of goods and services during a given period of time.

87. Relationship between APC and APS

APC + APS = 1

Following relationships show how APC + APS = 1.

We know that,

C + S = Y (Income is either saved or consumed)

Dividing both sides of the equation by Y, we get, $\frac{C}{Y} + \frac{S}{Y} = \frac{Y}{Y}$

or APC + APS = 1

or APC = 1 – APS

or APS = 1 – APC

[As, $\frac{C}{Y}$ = APC, and $\frac{S}{Y}$ = APS]

90. Credit Multiplier: This is a concept, which is akin to the deposit multiplier. The credit multiplier is the ratio of the change in the amount of credit to the change in reserves. Thus,

$$C_m = \frac{\Delta C_r}{\Delta R}$$

where, ΔC_r = change in credit

ΔR = change in reserves

Thus, we have

Credit Multiplier, $C_m = \frac{1-r}{c+r}$

In our example, as c is 0.5 and r is 0.1, the value of the deposit multiplier will be.

98. Every economy consists of three sectors. They are primary sector (extraction such as mining, agriculture and fishing), secondary sector (manufacturing) and the tertiary sector (service sector).

The service sector consists of the soft parts of the economy such as insurance, government, tourism, banking, retail, education, and social services. In soft-sector employment, people use time to deploy knowledge assets, collaboration assets, and process-engagement to create productivity, effectiveness, performance improvement potential and sustainability. Service industry involves the provision of services to businesses as well as final consumers. Services may involve transport, distribution and sale of goods from producer to a consumer as may happen in wholesaling and retailing, or may involve the provision of a service, such as in pest control or entertainment. Goods may be transformed in the process of providing a service, as happens in the restaurant industry or in equipment repair.

101. The Royal Swedish Academy of Sciences on 14 October 2013 decided to award— The Sveriges Riksbank Prize (Nobel Price) in Economic Sciences in Memory of Alfred Nobel for 2013 to Eugene F. Fama, Lars Peter Hansen and Robert J. Shiller for their empirical analysis of asset prices.

114. Five emerging markets, India, Brazil, Turkey, South Africa and Indonesia, have become known to the world in 2013 as the 'Fragile Five', a term coined by analysts at Morgan Stanley. This term refers to those five emerging economies that were considered most vulnerable to the winding down of the US Federal Reserve's quantitative easing program (bond-buying program) as capital inflows dried up, or, in fact reversed. The five countries were assessed as risky due to their twin fiscal and current-account deficits, slowing economic growth and high inflation.

120. Section 135 of the 2013 Act states that every company having:

- net worth of ₹ 500 crore or more, or
- turnover of ₹ 1000 crore or more, or
- net profit of ₹ 5 crore or more during any financial year

shall constitute a Corporate Social Responsibility Committee of the Board

126. Goldman Sachs Asset Management India Ltd has launched a new exchange-traded fund (ETF), called Central Public Sector Enterprises Exchange Traded Fund (CPSE ETF). This is a passively-managed scheme that will invest its entire corpus in the National Stock Exchange's (NSE) CPSE index and in the same proportion as they lie in the index. This index consists of 10 state-owned companies such as Oil and Natural Gas Corp. Ltd, GAIL (India) Ltd, Coal India Ltd, and so on, where the Government of India intends to divest some of its stake.

129. The World Investment Report has been published annually since 1991 by United Nations Conference on Trade and Development (UNCTAD). The World Investment Report focuses on trends in foreign direct investment (FDI) worldwide, at the regional and country levels and emerging measures to improve its contribution to development.

132. In a new development, the BSE has launched the Green Index called Greenex. This is India's first carbon-efficient live index. The index has been developed by the BSE in collaboration with IIM Ahmedabad. It is the second thematic index launched by BSE. BSE Greenex will measure the performances of companies in terms of carbon emissions. The index will target socially-aware investors. There are many investors willing to pay a premium for green investments in companies to get better returns.

The new index will comprise 20 stocks based on a minimum carbon footprint, market capitalisation and turnover. The BSE Greenex will assess the energy efficiency of firms, based on energy and financial data.

133. The Reserve Bank of India has extended the timeline for full implementation of the Basel III capital regulations by a year to March 31, 2019.

136. Nilekani, Nandan (2008). Imagining India: Ideas for the New Century: The Penguin Books India.

137. Major Financial Centres and their Stock Exchanges

Shanghai Stock Exchange (SSE) — China
Shenzhen Stock Exchange (SZSE) — China
Singapore Exchange (SGX) — Singapore
NSX National Stock Exchange of Australia — Australia
Australian Securities Exchange (ASX) — Australia
Canadian National Stock Exchange (CNSX) — Canada
London Stock Exchange (LSE) — UK
Dubai Stock Exchange (DIFX) — Dubai
Boston Stock Exchange (NASDAQ OMX BX) —USA
Chicago Stock Exchange (CSE) — USA
The New York Stock Exchange (NYSE) — USA

141. Trading on Equity refers to the practice of using borrowed funds, carrying a fixed charge, to obtain a higher return to the Equity Shareholders.

With a larger proportion of the debt in the financial structure, the earnings, available to the owners would increase more than the proportionately with an increase in the operating profits of the firm.

This is because the debt carries a fixed rate of return and if the firm is able to earn, on the borrowed funds, a rate higher than the fixed charges on loans, the benefit will go the shareholders. This is referred to as "Trading on Equity".

143. Gandhiji was against centralization of economic power in the hands of the state. Also he was very anxious to prevent misuse of property of private owners. For a solution of this he evolved the theory of Trusteeship.

Foundation of Trusteeship: Gandhiji evolved his theory of trusteeship in 1903, while in South Africa.

145. "Advertising is non-personal form of communication conducted through paid media under clear sponsorship."

— *Philip Kotler*

146. **The grapevine:** The grapevine is a universal method of transmitting messages of unofficial means. One informal organizational communication network along which information flows quickly if not always accurately is the grapevine. The grapevine is an informal network along which unofficial information flows. Every organization has its grapevine. This is a perfectly natural activity since it fulfills the employees' desires to know the latest information and to socialize with other people. The grapevine offers members of an organization an outlet for their imaginations and an opportunity to express their apprehensions in the form of rumors.

147. **Halsey premium plan:** This plan was introduced by F.A. Halsey, an American engineer, in 1891. In this plan time rate is guaranteed and a worker who takes the same time or more than allowed time receives his time rate. If the job is completed in less than allowed time the worker is paid a fixed percentage of the saving in time.

This percentage varies from 30 to 70 per cent of time saved, the most usual percentage being 50, the remainder 50% represents the employer's share.

149. Technostructure is a term coined by the economist John Kenneth Galbraith in The New Industrial State (1967) to describe the group of technicians within an enterprise (or an administrative body) with considerable influence and control on its economy. It usually refers to managerial capitalism where the managers and other company leading administrators, scientists, or lawyers retain more power and influence than the shareholders in the decisional and directional process.

151. **Fabian entrepreneurs:** Entrepreneurs of this type are very cautious and skeptical while practicing any change. They have neither the will to introduce new changes nor the desire to adopt new methods innovated by the most enterprising entrepreneurs. Such entrepreneurs are shy and lazy. Their dealings are determined by custom, religion, tradition and past practices. They are not much interested in taking risk and they try to follow the footsteps of their predecessors.

153. **Process or functional layout:** It is an arrangement of facilities and equipment in groups according to functions. Different orders follow different paths due to flexibility needed for a large variety of products and services, low volume of orders with no standardization of components and parts. When the product variety is large, and the quantity per product is low and the type of operation is unique for each type of product, the process layout is resorted to as an effective and efficient type of plant layout. Frequent changes in the setting of the machines involves a high degree of changes with low production volume. This is also known as the job shop type of production. The machines are general purpose machines or GPMs. This type of plant layout has total flexibility in terms of accommodating the variety of product design, small quantity in each product type, frequent machine setting and routing or process flexibility.

155. According to Edwin B. Flippo: "Job analysis is the process of studying and collecting information relating to the operations and responsibilities of a specific job."

158. The salary is taxable either on due basis or receipt basis, whichever matures earlier.

(*i*) **Due basis:** When it is earned even if it is not received in the previous year.

(*ii*) **Receipt basis:** When it is received even if it is not earned in the previous year.

(*iii*) **Arrears of salary:** Which were not due and received earlier are taxable when due or received, whichever is earlier.

159. Residential Status of a Company: As per Section 6(3), an Indian company is always resident in India. A foreign company is resident in India only if, during the previous year, control and management of its affairs is situated wholly in India. However, a foreign company is treated as non-resident if, during the previous year, control and management of its affairs is either wholly or partly situated out of India.

161. Companies Limited by Shares: According to Section 12(2)(a) of the Companies Act, "a company having the liability of its members limited by the memorandum of association to the amount, if any unpaid on the shares respectively held by them is termed as a company limited by shares." Such a company is commonly known as Limited Liability Company as the liability of the members is limited up to the face value of the shares held. Most of the companies established in India are limited by shares.

164. The Companies Act: The Companies Act 2013 contains the definition of related party, as follows:

"Related party", with reference to a company, means:

(*i*) a director or his relative;

(*ii*) a key managerial personnel or his relative;

(*iii*) a firm, in which a director, manager or his relative is a partner;

(*iv*) a private company in which a director or manager is a member or director;

(*v*) a public company in which a director or manager is a director or holds along with his relatives, more than two per cent, of its paid-up share capital;

(*vi*) anybody corporate whose Board of Directors, managing director or manager is accustomed to act in accordance with the advice, directions or instructions of a director or manager;

(*vii*) any person on whose advice, directions or instructions a director or manager is accustomed to act:

"Provided that nothing in sub-clauses (*vi*) and (*vii*) shall apply to the advice, directions or instructions given in a professional capacity.

(*viii*) any company which is:

(*a*) a holding, subsidiary or an associate company of such company; or

(*b*) a subsidiary of a holding company to which it is also a subsidiary;

(*ix*) such other person as may be prescribed".

165. Resolution Requiring a Special Notice: There are certain matters specified in the Companies Act, 1956 which may be discussed at a general meeting, only if a special notice is given regarding the proposal to discuss these matters at a meeting.

A special notice enables the members to be prepared on the matter to be discussed and gives them time to indicate their views on the resolution.

In case a special notice of resolution is required by the Companies Act, 1956 or by the articles of a company, the intention to propose such a resolution must be notified to the company at least 14 days before the meeting. The company must within 7 days before the meeting, give the notice of the proposed resolution to its members.

The notice of the resolution is required to be given in the same way in which the notice of a meeting is given or if that is not practicable, the company may give notice by advertisement in a newspaper having an appropriate circulation or in any other manner allowed by the articles, not less than seven days before the meeting.

166. **Special resolution:** A resolution which in its notice expressly states that the resolution to be moved is a special resolution and which is passed by a three-fourths majority of the members voting by shown of hands or on poll either in person or by proxy is called as a special resolution. The number of votes cast in favour of the resolution is to be three times the number cast against it. A 21 day prior notice has to be given duly for calling the meeting. Matters which are discussed and passed in special resolutions are:

1. Alteration of Memorandum.
2. Shifting or registered office within the state.
3. Change of name of the company with the consent of the Central Government.
4. Alteration of the Articles of the company.

170. Under section 233B of the Companies Act, the cost auditor has to submit his report to the central government in the prescribed form and simultaneously send a copy of the report to the company.

171. **What is Promise:** According to Section 2*b* of the Indian Contract Act, 1872, when a person to whom the proposal is made signifies his assent thereto, the proposal is said to be accepted. A proposal when accepted, becomes a promise. It can be said that for promise, the proposal is said to be accepted, or there should be proposal and acceptance.

Proposal + Acceptance = Promise

172. In terms of Section 10 of the Act, "all agreements are contracts if they are made by the free consent of the parties competent to contract, for a lawful consideration and with a lawful object and are not expressly declared to be void".

Thus, in order to create a valid contract, the following elements should be present:

1. Intention to create legal obligation through offer and acceptance should be present.
2. Free consent of the parties is necessary.
3. Competency or capacity of parties to enter into contract must be ensured.
4. Lawful consideration & lawful object should be present, and
5. Agreement not expressely declared to be void.

174. According to section 2 (ha) "Communication device" means cell phones personal digital assistance or combination of both or any other device used to communicate, send or transmit any text, video, audio or image.

178. The basic distinction between sale and agreement to sell is stated by Section 4(3) of the Sale of Goods Act, 1930 in the following words:

"where under a contract of sale the property in the goods is transferred from seller to the buyer, the contract is called a sale, but where the transfer of the property in the goods is to take place at a future time or subject to some condition thereafter to be fulfilled, the contract is called an agreement to sell".

182. Mean $= \dfrac{110+145+125+95+150}{5} = 125$

$\therefore$ Variance (r^2)

$$= \frac{(110-125)^2 + (145-125)^2 + (125-125)^2 + (95-125)^2 + (150-125)^2}{5}$$

$= 430.$

185. Coefficient of Skewness $= \dfrac{(Q_3 + Q_1 - 2M)}{Q_3 - Q_1}$

$$= \frac{22 - 2 \times 10.5}{8} = 0.125.$$

189. A time series may contain one of more of the following four components:

1. Secular trend
2. Seasonal variation
3. Cyclical variation
4. Irregular variation

It is ordinarily assumed that there is a multiplicative relationship amongst these four components. In symbols this can be written as

$$Y = T \times S \times C \times I$$

where, Y is the result of the four components, T = trend, S = seasonal variation, C = cyclical variation and I = irregular variation. An alternative approach is to assume that the relationship amongst these components is additive, that is,

$$Y = T + S + C + I$$

192. P(Female or Over 30)

= P(Female) + P (Over 30) – P(Female and Over 30)

$$= \frac{2}{5}+\frac{4}{5}-\frac{1}{5} = \frac{5}{5} = 1.$$

193. Multiplication Rule: For calculating *joint* probability that two events will occur while the events are *independent* (the outcome of any previous trial has no effect on the following trial), the following equation, also referred to as the equation of joint probability, can be used.

$$P(AB) = P(A \text{ and } B) = P(A) \times P(B)$$

For more than two independent events, the above equation becomes

$$P(ABC \dots N) = P(A \text{ and } B \text{ and } C \dots \text{ and } N)$$
$$= P(A) \times P(B) \times P(C) \times \dots \times P(N)$$

198. Dispersion is a measure of the nature of spread of the observations. There are two types of measures of dispersion. They are:

1. Absolute measure of dispersion
2. Relative measure of dispersion

There are 4 different measure of absolute measures of dispersion.

They are:

1. Range
2. Quartile deviation
3. Mean deviation
4. Standard deviation

There are four different relative measures of dispersion. They are:

1. Coefficient of range
2. Coefficient of quartile deviation or quartile coefficient of dispersion
3. Coefficient of mean deviation
4. Coefficient of variation.

199. N = 50, Failed = 10

Mean marks of those who failed = 2.5

Total marks of 10 students who failed

= 2.5 × 10 = 25

Total marks secured by entire class = 281

Total marks obtained by those who passed

= 281 – 25 = 250

Average marks obtained by those who passed

$$= \frac{256}{40} = 6.4.$$

Previous Paper (Solved)

DELHI UNIVERSITY—M.COM ENTRANCE TEST-2013*

1. Which inventory pricing method reflects the most recently incurred purchase costs in the ending inventory:
A. FIFO B. LIFO
C. Simple average D. Weighted average

2. 'Lower of cost or market rule' is an example of which concept?
A. Consistency B. Conservatism
C. Realisation D. Matching

3. X Co. Ltd. forfeited shares of ₹10 each on which ₹4 per share was paid. The company issued 40 shares @ ₹8 per share as fully paid. Amount transferred to capital reserve will be:
A. ₹400 B. ₹160
C. ₹240 D. ₹80

4. To the extent preference shares have been redeemed out of profits, amount equal to the face value of preference shares redeemed should be transferred to:
A. Development Rebate Reserve
B. General reserve
C. Sinking fund
D. Capital redemption reserve

5. The amount of share premium can be used wholly or in part for:
A. Writing off the preliminary expenses
B. Writing off goodwill
C. Writing off advertising expenses
D. Purchasing fixed assets

6. Indian companies are required to maintain their accounts on:
A. Cash basis
B. Accrual basis
C. Accrual basis and double entry system
D. Double entry system

7. The credit balance of profit and loss appropriation account in the case of a company is transferred to:
A. Capital account
B. Current account
C. Reserve and surplus
D. None of the above

8. Calls-in-advance is a:
A. Long term liability
B. Current liability
C. Contingent liability
D. None of the above

9. Which of the following does not describe accounting?
A. Language of business
B. Is an end rather than a means to an end
C. Useful for decision-making
D. Used by business, government, non-profit organisations and individuals

10. Sale of goods has:
A. Only revenue effect
B. Only expense effect
C. Both A and B
D. None of the above

11. AS–6 is related to:
A. Valuation of inventories
B. Accounting for construction contracts
C. Cash flow statement
D. Depreciation accounting

12. In two consecutive periods, sales and profit were ₹1,60,000 and ₹8,000 respectively in the first period and ₹1,80,000 and ₹14,000 respectively during the second period. If there is no change in fixed costs between the two periods, then P/V ratio must be:
A. 20% B. 25%
C. 30% D. 40%

*Exam held on 23-06-2013.

13. A manufacturer used 400 units of a component every month and he buys them entirely from an outside supplier @₹40 per unit. The order placing and receiving cost is ₹100 and storage and carrying cost is 15% of the value of stock. EOQ will be:

A. 300 units B. 400 units
C. 450 units D. 500 units

14. The current ratio of a company is 2 : 1 while quick ratio is 1.80 : 1. If the current liabilities are ₹40,000, they value of stock will be:

A. ₹6,400 B. ₹8,000
C. ₹10,000 D. ₹12,000

15. A company maintains a margin of safely of 25% on its current sales and earns a profit of ₹30 lakhs per annum. If the company has a profit volume (p/v) ratio of 40%, its current sales amount to:

A. ₹200 lakhs B. ₹300 lakhs
C. ₹325 lakhs D. None of the above

16. In a job costing system, manufacturing overhead is:

	An indirect cost of jobs	A necessary element in production
A.	No	Yes
B.	No	No
C.	Yes	Yes
D.	Yes	No

17. Units of production is an appropriate method of assigning overhead when?

A. Several well differentiated products are manufactured
B. Direct labour costs are low
C. Only one product is manufactured
D. The manufacturing process is complex

18. Many companies recognize three major categories of costs of manufacturing a product. These are direct materials, direct labour and overhead. Which of the following is an overhead cost in the production of an automobile?

A. Cost of small tools used in mounting tyres on each automobile
B. Cost of tyres on each automobile
C. Cost of labourers who place tyres on each automobile
D. Delivery costs for the tyres on each automobile

19. In the computation of manufacturing cost per equivalent unit, the weighted average method of process costing considers:

A. Current costs only
B. Current costs plus cost of beginning work-in-process inventory
C. Current costs plus cost of ending work-in-process inventory
D. Current costs minus cost of beginning work-in-process inventory

20. The budgeted fixed overheads amounted to ₹84,000. The budgeted and actual production amounted to 20,000 units and 24,000 units respectively. This means there will be:

A. Under-absorption of ₹16,800
B. Under-absorption of ₹14,000
C. Over-absorption of ₹16,800
D. Over-absorption of ₹14,000

21. Which of the following is not an indirect cost?

A. Wages of production department machine operator
B. Wages of a production department cleaner
C. Materials used for machine maintenance in the production department
D. Materials used to clean the production department floor

22. In order to identity costs that relate to a specific product, an allocation base should be chosen that:

A. does not have a cause and effect relationship
B. has a cause and effect relationship
C. considers variable costs but not fixed costs
D. considers direct materials and direct labour but not factory overhead

23. The types of costs presented to management for a non-routine decision should be limited to:

A. Relevant costs B. Standard costs
C. Controllable costs D. Conversion costs

24. Other things remaining the same, ideal product mix is determined in terms of:
A. Sales
B. Variable costs
C. Total cost
D. Contribution margin

25. A cost incurred in the past and hence irrelevant for current decision-making is:
A. Fixed cost
B. Discretionary cost
C. Sunk cost
D. Direct cost

26. If a company follows a practice of isolating variances at the earliest point in time, what would be the appropriate time to calculate a material price variance?
A. When material is issued
B. When material is purchased
C. When material is used in production
D. When purchase order is originated

27. Material usage variances are normally charged to which department?
A. Production
B. Purchasing
C. Finished goods department
D. Materials storage

28. Flexible budgets are useful for:
A. Planning purposes only
B. Control of performance only
C. Planning, performance evaluation and feedback control
D. Nothing at all

29. The budgeted standard hours of a factory is 12,000. The capacity utilization ratio for April 2013 stood at 90% while the efficiency ratio for the month came to 120%. The actual production in standard hours for April 2013 is:
A. 10,800 B. 12,960
C. 14,400 D. 12,800

30. Fixed costs are conveniently deemed to be:
A. Constant per unit of output
B. Constant in total when production volume changes
C. Outside the control of management
D. Those unaffected by inflation

31. Which of the following is not a characteristic of the geometric mean as a measure of central tendency?
A. It is equal to the mean if the data are skewed to the right
B. It mitigates the effects of large data values
C. It is useful in business data to calculate average growth rates
D. It cannot be calculated when the data contain negative or zero values

32. Which of the following is a correct statement about median?
A. In a left-skewed distribution, we expect that the median will exceed the mean
B. The sum of the deviations around the median is equal to zero
C. The median is always one of the observed data values in any data set
D. The median always lies halfway between Q_1 and Q_3

33. Which is not a characteristic of standard deviation?
A. Its physical interpretation is not as easy as that of the mean deviation
B. It can be calculated even when the data contain negative or zero values
C. It is not applicable when data are continuous
D. It is always equal to square root of the variance

34. In a population having normal distribution with $\mu = 100$ and $\sigma = 10$, we expect:
A. About 95 per cent of the data to be within 70 and 130
B. Nearly one-half the data to exceed 75
C. Nearly all the data within 80 and 120
D. About 68 per cent of the data within 90 and 110

35. Consider the following data : 6, 7, 17, 51, 3, 17, 23 and 69. The range and the median are:
A. 69 and 17.5 B. 66 and 17.5
C. 66 and 17 D. 69 and 17

36. Histograms are best used to:
A. Reveal the inter-quartile range of the data set
B. Assess the shape of the given distribution
C. Show the lower and upper quartiles of the data set
D. Provide a visual estimate of the standard deviation

37. The 25th percentile for waiting time at a doctor's clinic is 19 minutes. The 75th percentile is 31 minutes. The semi inter-quartile range is:
A. 12 minutes
B. 6 minutes
C. 25 minutes
D. Impossible to determine without knowing n

38. In a positively skewed distribution, the percentage of observations that fall below the median is:
A. About 50 per cent
B. Less than 50 per cent
C. More than 50 per cent
D. Can't tell without knowing n

39. Mark the wrong statement:
A. A decision tree is also known as decision flow diagram
B. A decision tree is a graphic representation of the sequences of action-event combinations available to a decision maker
C. A decision cannot be used where costs are involved as pay-offs
D. A square in a decision tree represents a decision fork while a circle represents a chance fork at which events are branched out

40. The values in one of the series in a bivariate data set are multiplied by a constant k. Which of the following would change as a result of this?
A. Karl Pearson's coefficient of correlation
B. Rank correlation coefficient
C. Covariance between the variables
D. None of the above

41. From the following statements related to Karl Pearson's coefficient of correlation (r) and Spearman's coefficient of rank correlation (ρ), mark the correct one:
A. r and ρ can both vary between ± 1
B. r can assume positive or negative values but ρ can only be positive
C. For a given set of bivariate data, r and ρ would both be equal
D. r and ρ would both change if the largest value of each of the series of a bivariate data is increased by a constant, say 20

42. If various points in a scatter diagram fall on a straight line which is parallel to the X-axis, it indicates:
A. Perfect positive correlation
B. Perfect negative correlation
C. No correlation
D. Very low degree of positive correlation

43. Mark the wrong statement:
A. When the lower quartile is located at a smaller distance from median than the upper quartile is from it, the distribution has negative skewness
B. For a positively skewed distribution, $Q_3 + Q_1 \neq 2$ Median
C. A right-tailed distribution is a positively skewed distribution
D. A negatively skewed distribution has longer tail to the left

44. A coin and a pair of dice are tossed together. The total number of possible outcomes for this experiment is:
A. 14 B. 72
C. 24 D. 36

45. The chances of occurrence of event A and non-occurrence of event B are 0.4 and 0.3 respectively. If A and B are independent, what is the chance that they both do not occur?
A. 0.12 B. 0.72
C. 0.18 D. 0.28

46. Mark the incorrect statement:
A. If event A precludes the happening of event B, they are mutually exclusive events

B. The union of complementary events is the sample space
C. $P(A \cup B \cup C)$ gives the probability that at least one of A, B or C will occur
D. Overlapping events cannot be independent

47. Which of these is not true about normal distribution?
A. The mean, median and mode are identical
B. The mean deviation is nearly 4/5th of the standard deviation
C. It may or may not be moderately skewed
D. It is mesokurtic

48. Mark the wrong statement:
A. A Poisson distribution involves a discrete variable
B. There is no upper limit to the number of successes in a Poisson distribution
C. The mean of a Poisson distribution cannot have a value smaller than 1
D. The mean and variance of a Poisson distribution are equal in value

49. Mark the incorrect statement:
A. Index numbers are a part of descriptive analysis of past data
B. Index numbers are calculated for time series data
C. For any set of index numbers, the base period is always fixed
D. Index numbers are used to measure and reflect changes in a single or a group of related variables over a period of time

50. Mark the wrong statement:
A. For shifting the origin of a second-degree parabolic trend equation, we have, $Y_t = a + b(X \pm k) + c(X \pm k)^2$
B. If the origin of a trend equation is to be shifted forward, then k is positive and if it is to be shifted backward, then k is negative.
C. The rate of change of slope in a second-degree parabola is equal to $2c$.
D. The slope of an exponential trend equation $Y_t = ab^x$ is given by b.

51. When applying LP to diet problems, the objective function is usually designed to:
A. Maximize profits from blends of nutrients
B. Maximize ingredient blends
C. Minimize production losses
D. Minimize the costs of nutrient blends

52. If in the optimal tableau of an LP problem an artificial variable is present in the solution mix, this implies:
A. Infeasibility
B. Unboundedness
C. Degeneracy
D. Alternate optimal solution

53. An iso-profit line represents
A. An infinite number of solutions all of which yield the same profit
B. An infinite number of solutions all of which yield the same costs
C. A border of the area of the feasible solutions
D. An infinite number of optimal solutions

54. How is the variable which will be replaced in the next simplex solution determined?
A. By choosing the variable with the largest $C_j - Z_j$ value
B. By choosing the variable with the smallest $C_j - Z_j$ value
C. By choosing the variable which yields the minimum positive ratio of quantity to substitute rate in the key column
D. It can be chosen arbitrarily

55. The maximum number of units which can be transferred along the closed path is equal to:
A. The minimum quantity chosen from among the cells
B. The minimum quantity chosen from among the cells bearing negative sign
C. The maximum quantity chosen from the table
D. The minimum quantity chosen from among the cells bearing a negative sign on the closed path

56. In using the assignment problem algorithm, if you have five employees and six machines, you:
A. Arbitrarily forget one of those machines

B. Select a slow machine to omit and then solve the problems using a 5 × 5 matrix
C. Create a dummy employee
D. None of the above

57. In finding the opportunity cost table in the assignment problem:
A. Part of the first step is to subtract the smallest column value from each cell value in the column
B. Part of the first step is to subtract the smallest row value from each cell value in the row
C. You are finding the relative penalty associated with making a particular assignment as compared to making another assignment
D. All of the above

58. The total cost C(x) of a firm is:
$C(x) = 1500 + 30x + x^2$
Where x is the output. Determine the marginal cost when 20 units are produced.
A. 70 B. 71
C. 72 D. 73

59. For the supply curve $p = \frac{e^x}{x}$, the elasticity of supply is:
A. $\frac{1}{x}$ B. $\frac{1}{x-1}$
C. $\frac{1}{1-x}$ D. $-\frac{1}{x}$

60. The production function $x = f(l, k) = (al^4 + bk^4)^{1/2}$ (where x, l and k are the units of output, labour and capital respectively) gives:
A. Constant returns to scale
B. Increasing returns to scale
C. Decreasing returns to scale
D. None of the above

61. Let (a, b) be a critical point of a function $z = f(x, y)$. If $A = f_{xx}(a, b)$, $B = f_{xy}(a, b)$ and $C = f_{yy}(a, b)$, then f has a saddle point at (a, b) when:
A. $AC - B^2 > 0$
B. $AC - B^2 < 0$
C. $AC - B^2 = 0$
D. $AC - B^2 > 0$ and $A < 0$

62. The supply function for a commodity is $p = 4 + x$. Determine producer's surplus if 12 units of goods are sold:
A. 192 B. 120
C. 72 D. 312

63. The effective rate equivalent to a nominal rate of 6% compounded semi annually is given by:
A. 6.09% B. 6.13%
C. 6.16% D. 6.18%

64. An annuity due is an annuity:
A. Whose payments continue forever
B. The first payment of which is made at the end of the first payment interval
C. The first payment of which is made at the beginning of the first payment interval
D. None of the above

65. How much money is needed to endure a series of lectures costing ₹2500 at the beginning of each year indefinitely, if money is worth 5% compounded annually?
A. ₹50,000
B. ₹52,500
C. ₹1,00,000
D. ₹1,02,500

66. The multiplicative inverse of the matrix $A = \begin{bmatrix} -4 & -1 \\ 3 & 1 \end{bmatrix}$ is:
A. $\begin{bmatrix} 1 & 1 \\ -3 & -4 \end{bmatrix}$ B. $\begin{bmatrix} 4 & 1 \\ -3 & -1 \end{bmatrix}$
C. $\begin{bmatrix} -1 & -1 \\ 3 & 4 \end{bmatrix}$ D. $\begin{bmatrix} -4 & 3 \\ -1 & 1 \end{bmatrix}$

67. The marginal cost of a product is MC = 2 $e^{0.001x}$. Find the total cost function if fixed cost is ₹2,000:
A. $C = 2000\, e^{0.001x}$
B. $C = 2000\, e^{0.001x} + 2000$
C. $C = 2\, e^{0.001x} + 2000$
D. $C = e^{0.001x} + 2000$

68. In a two sector economy, it is known that industry I uses 10 paise worth of its own product and 60 paise worth of commodity II to produce a rupee worth of commodity I; industry II uses 30 paise worth of its own product and 50 paise worth of commodity I in producing a rupee worth of commodity II. Determine the technology matrix:

A. $\begin{bmatrix} 0.10 & 0.60 \\ 0.30 & 0.50 \end{bmatrix}$ B. $\begin{bmatrix} 0.10 & 0.60 \\ 0.50 & 0.30 \end{bmatrix}$

C. $\begin{bmatrix} 0.10 & 0.30 \\ 0.60 & 0.50 \end{bmatrix}$ D. $\begin{bmatrix} 0.10 & 0.50 \\ 0.60 & 0.30 \end{bmatrix}$

69. The amount of an ordinary annuity consisting of n payments of ₹ R each at the rate i per period is given by:

A. $R\left[\frac{1-(1+i)^{-n}}{i}\right]$ B. $R\left[\frac{(1+i)^{n}-1}{i}\right]$

C. $R+\frac{R}{i}$ D. $\frac{R}{i}$

70. The function $f(x) = e^x$ is always:
A. increasing and convex from above
B. increasing and convex from below
C. decreasing and convex from above
D. decreasing and convex from below

71. Manufacturing industry creates:
A. Place utility B. Time utility
C. Form utility D. All of the above

72. To what category of industries can sugar mill or oil refinery be put?
A. Primary B. Secondary
C. Tertiary D. None of the above

73. Co-operative society is called a democratic organization because of:
A. One share one vote
B. One member one vote
C. No voting rights of members
D. All of the above

74. Which of the following statement is not true?
A. The sole aim of business is to earn profit by fair or foul means
B. There is a strong case for the business to fulfil its social obligations
C. Ethics is good business
D. Black marketing of goods is an unethical practice

75. Commercial banks cannot engage in:
A. Trading in goods and services
B. Accepting deposits from the public
C. Lending money to traders
D. Remittance of funds

76. In case of life insurance, insurable interest must exist at the time of:
A. Taking the policy
B. Death
C. Both (A) & (B)
D. Neither (A) nor (B)

77. Name the document containing the guarantee or assurance by the importer's bank to honour bills drawn on it by the exporter:
A. Bill of Exchange
B. Bill of Lading
C. Letter of Credit
D. None of the above

78. Which of the following policies can be surrendered?
A. Theft insurance policy
B. Marine insurance policy
C. Fire insurance policy
D. Life insurance policy

79. Classical organization theory is an amalgamation of
A. Scientific Management Approach
B. Management Process Approach
C. Bureaucratic Approach
D. All of the above

80. Which is not an assumption of Theory Y?
A. Work is as natural as play
B. Motivation occurs at the social, esteem and self actualizing levels as well as physiological and security levels
C. Most people have little capacity and creativity in solving organizational problems
D. People are self-directed and creative at work

81. Vroom's theory of motivation states that motivation results from:
A. Valance + Expectancy
B. Valance – Expectancy
C. Valance × Expectancy
D. None of the above

82. Likert's System 1 suggests:
A. Exploitative Autocratic Leadership
B. Benevolent Autocratic Leadership
C. Participative Leadership
D. None of the above

83. Chris Argyris' maturity-immaturity continuum states that the number of dimensions of personality are:
A. 5 B. 7
C. 9 D. 10

84. The main drawback of functional organization developed by Taylor is that it fails to recognise the:
A. Scalar principle
B. Principle of scientific and training
C. Principle of unity of command
D. Principle of division of work

85. The democratic leadership style goes with:
A. Theory X B. Theory Y
C. Theory Z D. All of the above

86. The term 'ERG' stands for:
A. Existence, Relatedness, Growth
B. Economic, Relationship, Growth
C. Existence, Relationship, Goal
D. Economic, Relationship, Goal

87. Which company's shares can be freely transferable?
A. Private Company B. Public Company
C. Both (A) & (B) D. None of the above

88. Maximum no. of members in case of private company is:
A. 50 B. 100
C. 150 D. 200

89. Under which section a private company can be automatically converted into a public company......... :
A. 34 B. 43
C. 53 D. 35

90. Central Government permission is required in case of.........conversion:
A. Private company to public
B. Public company to private
C. Both (A) & (B)
D. None of the above

91. Within how many days prospectus or statement in lieu of prospectus should be filed with ROC?
A. 30 B. 40
C. 20 D. 50

92. One of the following persons can enter a valid contract:
A. A minor
B. A person of sound mind
C. An alien enemy
D. An insolvent

93. Consent will be said to be free when there is:
A. Quid pro quo
B. Consensus ad-idem
C. Coercion
D. Mistake

94. Where both the parties to an agreement are under a mistake of fact, the contract is:
A. Valid B. Voidable
C. Void D. None of the above

95. An agreement is .... because of inadequate consideration.
A. void B. voidable
C. unlawful D. illegal

96. One of the following is not an unsound person:
A. Idiot B. Lunatic
C. Drunken D. Sane person

97. One of the following elements does not vitiate free consent:
A. Coercion B. Due influence
C. Fraud D. Mistake

98. Foreign Limited Liability Partnership under the Limited Liability Partnership Act, 2008 means:
A. A Limited Liability Partnership formed, incorporated or registered in that country to which the partners belong

B. A Limited Liability Partnership formed, incorporated and registered under Economic Council of UNO
C. A Limited Liability Partnership formed, incorporated and registered in Indian territory
D. A Limited Liability Partnership formed, incorporated or registered outside India which established a place of business in India

99. Every Limited Liability Partnership as per the Limited Liability Partnership Act, 2008 shall have at least two Designated Partners (DPs) who are individuals and:
A. At least one among them shall be resident in India
B. Both of them shall belong to one family residing in India
C. Both of them should be non-resident Indians (NRI's)
D. Both of them should belong to a single country outside India

100. The doctrine of indoor management is an .... to the doctrine of constructive notice.
A. exception B. extension
C. alternative D. None of these

101. Minimum no. of Directors in case of private company is .... :
A. 1 B. 2
C. 3 D. 4

102. Age limit of Directors in case of public company is .... :
A. 65 B. 70
C. 75 D. 80

103. Mr. A, a foreign national visited India during previous year 2012-13 for 170 days. He has never visited India before this. In India, what is the residential status of Mr. X in this case?
A. Resident and ordinarily resident
B. Resident and not ordinarily resident
C. Non-resident
D. None of the above

104. For the financial year 2013-14, the maximum marginal rate of income tax applies on which of the following slabs?
A. Above ₹5,00,000
B. Above ₹8,00,000
C. Above ₹10,00,000
D. Above ₹12,00,000

105. While computing income under the head 'Salaries', which of the following does not come under the category of 'perquisites?'
A. Rent-free accommodation
B. Transport facility provided to employee
C. Leave travel salary reimbursed to employee
D. Gratuity

106. Clubbing provisions under Section 60 of the Income Tax Act, 1961 deals with:
A. Remuneration of spouse
B. Transfer of income without transfer of assets
C. Assets transferred to spouse
D. Income of a minor child

107. In case an assessee is engaged in the business of plying, hiring or leasing goods carriage, scheme of presumptive tax under section 44AE is applicable if the assessee owns not more than:
A. 10 goods carriages
B. 8 goods carriages
C. 6 goods carriages
D. 12 goods carriages

108. Which of the following is a capital asset for the purpose of Income Tax Act, 1961?
A. Stock-in-trade
B. Jewellery
C. Furniture for personal use
D. Gold bonds

109. The price at which a parent firm (MNC) sells its products, services and technology to its subsidiaries in other countries is known as:
A. Transfer price B. Market price
C. Transaction price D. Source price

110. Which of the following is Indian income?
A. Income received or deemed to be received in India
B. Income accrues or arises in India
C. Income deemed to accrue or arise in India
D. All of the above

111. Parliament on May 5, 2010 passed the payment of Gratuity (Amendment) Bill 2010 which increases the gratuity limit for employees from ₹3.5 lakh to:

A. ₹ 5 lakh B. ₹ 7.5 lakh
C. ₹ 10 lakh D. ₹ 12.5 lakh

112. Who is the Chairperson of Identification Authority of India (UIA)?

A. Dr. M.S. Swaminathan
B. Nandan Nilekani
C. E. Shreedharan
D. M.N. Bush

113. The Finance Minister has proposed replacement of the Income Tax Act by:

A. The Finance Act, 2008
B. The Direct Tax Act
C. The Indian Taxation Code
D. The Direct Taxes Code

114. Discussions till now on the Financial Sector Legislative Reforms Commission's (FSLRC) report submitted recently have centered around its recommendations. What is the most important point of discussions? Find out from the following:

A. Recommendations are potential game changer
B. Recommendation are out of touch with Indian reality
C. There were several dissenting views even among its members
D. Recommendation to setup a monetary policy committee which, rather than the RBI governor will decide on policy rates and to appoint the Finance Minister as head of the Financial Stability and Development Council (FSDC)

115. Credit Information Bureau India Ltd. is an independent organization meant to assist banks. What services does it render?

A. It is a storehouse of information about credit facilities availed of by bank clients
B. It provides credit reports on individual borrowers
C. It maintains credit history about all bank borrowers for use by its member banks
D. It decides whether loan should be granted or not

116. Many banks are presently recruiting large numbers of business correspondents in terms of RBI instruction. What would be their nature of work?

A. These persons would approach customer for large business
B. Business correspondents would cover rural areas for generating business
C. Business correspondents would provide basic banking services to the rural population
D. Persons recruited would do market survey in rural areas to explore business potential

117. The 'Oil India Ltd.' has become:

A. The 20th Navratna Company
B. The 21st Navratna Company
C. The 19th Navratna Company
D. The 18th Navratna Company

118. The highest density of population is found in:

A. Bangladesh B. India
C. Pakistan D. Sri Lanka

119. Which of the following chemicals has been recently allowed by the government of India to be mixed with petrol?

A. Methanol B. Ethanol
C. Kerosene D. Butanol

120. Which is the first Asian country to host the Commonwealth Games?

A. South Korea B. Japan
C. Malaysia D. China

121. Public Interest Litigation (PIL) may be linked with:

A. Judicial review
B. Judicial activism
C. Judicial intervention
D. Judicial sanctity

122. Which state is the leading producer of Soyabean in India?

A. Maharashtra B. Punjab
C. Kerala D. Madhya Pradesh

123. The best coking coal is mostly obtained from:

A. Neyveli B. Raniganj
C. Singrauli D. Jharia

124. Scheme of Mid-day meals is not concerned with:
A. Educational Advancement
B. Social Equity
C. Right to Food
D. Child Nutrition

125. World Environment Day is observed on:
A. June 1 B. June 5
C. June 15 D. June 22

126. For National Manufacturing and Investment Zones (NMIZ), Special Economic Zones (SEZs) and EOUs (Exports-Oriented Units), which of the following statement is true?
A. NMIZs and EOUs will be located within SEZs
B. SEZs and EOUs will be located within NMIZs
C. NMIZs are independent of SEZs and EOUs
D. NMIZs and SEZs will be competitors in nature

127. Which of the countries recently passed the historic healthcare bill?
A. Russia B. Germany
C. U.S.A. D. France

128. BRIC (Brazil, Russia, India and China) recently adopted Moscow Declaration regarding:
A. Agriculture
B. Regional Security
C. Terrorism
D. Cultural Cooperation

129. Which one of the following is a Human Right as well as a Fundamental Right under the Constitution of India?
A. Right to Information
B. Right to Education
C. Right to Work
D. Right to Housing

130. Which of the following courts in India is/are known as the Court(s) of Records?
A. The High Courts only
B. The Supreme Court only
C. The High Courts and the Supreme Court
D. The District Courts

131. The process of 'Artificial Application of Water to the soil usually for assisting in growing crops' is technically know as:
A. Water harvesting B. Irrigation
C. Water recharging D. Percolation

132. The census in India is done after a gap of every:
A. 5 years B. 10 years.
C. 12 years D. 20 years

133. Who has the power to constitute a new state in the Union of India?
A. President of India
B. Parliament of India
C. State Assembly
D. Supreme Court of India

134. One among the following is the Chairman of the 14th Finance Commission:
A. Dr. C. Rangarajan
B. Dr. Vijay Kelkar
C. Dr. S. Acharya
D. Dr. Y.V. Reddy

135. In which State of India is *Nathula* Pass located?
A. Sikkim B. Uttarakhand
C. Uttar Pradesh D. Himachal Pradesh

136. Which of the following nations is considered the originator of the concept of Micro Finance?
A. India B. Bangladesh
C. South Africa D. USA

137. Which engineering and construction company, on 1 April, 2013 announced that it bagged the order worth ₹5689 crore from Rajasthan Rajya Vidyut Utpadan Nigam Ltd. in order to set up super critical thermal power project in Rajasthan?
A. Punj Lloyd Group
B. Lanco Infratech Limited
C. Larsen and Toubro Ltd.
D. IVRCL Infrastructures & Projects Ltd.

138. Who on 1 April, 2013 was appointed as CEO of Dr. Reddy's Laboratories?
A. Satish Reddy B. Anji Reddy
C. Kallam Reddy D. G.V. Prasad

139. China emerged as the world's second largest economy in 2012 overtaking........... :

A. France B. Britain
C. Germany D. Japan

140. Mahatma Gandhi National Rural Employment Guarantee Act (MGNREGA) completed how many years of operation recently?

A. 3 years B. 4 years
C. 5 years D. 7 years

141. Indian Commerce and Industry minister has recently said that India is committed to take the Doha round to a successful conclusion. What is Doha round about?

A. Trade negotiations
B. Nuclear treaty
C. Oil accord
D. Peace negotiations

142. The 2014 Shooting World Championship will be held in:

A. Granada in Spain
B. New Delhi in India
C. Toronto in Canada
D. Melbourne in Australia

143. Life Time Achievement Award 2012 was conferred to an Indian by Ernst & Young. Name the person who was conferred with the award?

A. Azim Premji
B. Aditya Vikram Birla
C. Gautam Thapar
D. Ratan Tata

144. World cancer day was observed on 4 February, 2013 in order to raise awareness about this illness as well as to promote the measures, early detection, prevention and treatment of the disease. What was the theme for World Cencer Day, 2013?

A. Global burden of cancer
B. Cancer–Did you know?
C. Together it is possible
D. Teach children and teenagers to avoid UV exposure by being 'sun smart'

145. May 11th of every year is celebrated as:

A. National Technology Day
B. National Human Day
C. National Rights Day
D. National Nutrition Day

146. Recently, University of Delhi was very predominantly reported in various national dailies, because:

A. New academic session is to start in July 2013
B. Results of school examinations of various boards were notified and prospective students were very anxious for their admissions to the colleges of Delhi
C. Final examinations of semester system were being conducted
D. Academic reform in the form of Four-Year Under Graduate Programme (FYUP) is expected to roll out by July 2013

147. A high level sub-committee set up to revisit the criteria for deciding backwardness of states is headed by:

A. Raghuram Rajan
B. Subir Gokaran
C. C. Rangarajan
D. Montek Singh Ahluwalia

148. Who is the Prime Minister of Pakistan?

A. Raja Parvez Ashraf
B. Imran Khan
C. Asfandyar Wali Khan
D. Nawaz Sharif

149. Which State in India registered decline in its population as per India's Census of 2011?

A. Kerala B. Manipur
C. Nagaland D. Goa

150. In what context Supreme Court said that "The job of the agency was not to interact with the government officials but to interrogate them and find out the truth"?

A. 2 G Scam B. Railgate Scam
C. Toilet Scam D. Coalgate Scam

151. If the demand were to decrease and supply were to increase, it would result in:

A. A fall in price and a decrease in quantity
B. A fall in price and an increase in quantity
C. A fall in price and no change in quantity
D. All of the above alternatives are possible

152. A fall in the price of commodity X and an increase in the demand for Y imply that:
A. X and Y are substitute goods
B. X and Y are complimentary goods
C. The law of demand is violated
D. None of the above is possible

153. A fall in price of a commodity accompanied by a decrease in revenue from its sale implies that:
A. The commodity's demand is price inelastic
B. The commodity's demand is unit price elastic
C. The commodity's demand is price elastic
D. The commodity's demand is price perfectly (infinitely) elastic

154. As labour is substituted in place of capital along an isoquant:
A. The marginal product of capital diminishes
B. The marginal product of labour increases
C. The amount of capital that can be substituted by labour decreases
D. The amount of capital that can be substituted by labour increases

155. The short run AC (average cost) is U shaped because:
A. The average variable cost is U shaped
B. The average fixed cost is U shaped
C. The marginal cost cuts the average fixed cost at its lowest point
D. None of the above

156. Is it possible for the elasticity of demand for food to be less than one and the elasticity of demand for a food item such as a particular brand of high quality tea to be more than one?
A. Sometimes
B. Only if tea is a habit forming drink
C. No
D. Yes

157. Under perfect competition, the long run supply curve is horizontal for:
A. An increasing cost industry
B. A constant cost industry
C. A decreasing cost industry
D. An industry which at first experiences decreasing costs then constant costs and finally increasing costs

158. Under Monopolistic competition in the long run:
A. A firm will make no economic profits or losses
B. A firm will make economic profits that are smaller than in the case of monopoly
C. Some firms in a product group may make profits
D. Some firms may make losses

159. Under third degree price discrimination the price of the product will be higher:
A. In the market where the marginal revenue is higher
B. In the market where the marginal revenue is lower
C. In the more elastic market
D. In the less elastic market

160. The earnings of any factor consist entirely of rent if the supply of that factor is:
A. Elastic B. Unit elastic
C. Inelastic D. Perfectly inelastic

161. When the rate of interest ensures that the demand for loanable funds equals the supply of loanable funds, it aslo ensures that:
A. Investment is equal to public saving
B. Investment is equal to private saving
C. Aggregate demand equals aggregate supply
D. Aggregate demand is less than aggregate supply

162. In the short period the total output of final goods will be at its equilibrium level, when:
A. Inventories are increasing
B. There is no change in inventories
C. Inventories are decreasing
D. Inventories are zero

163. If marginal propensity to consume out of disposable income were to be 0.8 and the rate of proportional tax were to be .25, the value of the multiplier would be:
A. 2.5 B. 5
C. 4 D. 1.05

164. The greater the value of the multiplier and greater the sensitivity of Investment with respect to the rate of interest:
A. Greater the upward slope of the IS curve
B. Lesser the upward slope of the IS curve
C. Greater the downward slope of the IS curve
D. Lesser the downward slope of the IS curve

165. An increase in money supply causes:
A. Fall in the interest rate in the short run
B. Increase in output in the short run
C. No change in either the rate of interest or output in the long run, only an increase in the price level
D. All of the above

166. The sacrifice ratio is the:
A. Ratio of the cumulative loss of output to the reduction in the rate of inflation
B. Ratio of the cumulative loss of tax revenue to reduction of output
C. Ratio of the loss of purchasing power of rupee to the rate of inflation
D. Ratio of the cumulative rise in inflation to the increase in money supply

167. The transaction demand for money is a function of:
A. Income only B. Interest rate only
C. Both A and B D. None of the above

168. In a small open economy with freely mobile capital flows, the domestic rate of interest is:
A. Less than the world rate of interest
B. Equal to the world rate of interest
C. Greater than the world rate of interest
D. Independent of the world rate of interest

169. According to the Mundell-Fleming model, a small open economy with perfectly mobile capital flows and flexible exchange rates will find:
A. Fiscal policy to be effective
B. Monetary policy to be effective
C. Both A and B
D. Neither A nor B

170. If capital stock is at its optimum level at the existing rate of interest, the level of net investment will be:
A. Equal to zero
B. Equal to the level of depreciation
C. Equal to the level of output
D. Equal to the rate of interest

171. Economic development implies:
A. Rise in output
B. Technological changes
C. Institutional organization of production
D. All of the above

172. The core values of development are:
A. Sustenance
B. Self esteem
C. Freedom from servitude
D. All of the above

173. The macroeconomic reforms in India started in:
A. 1990 B. 1991
C. 1992 D. 1993

174. The service sector consists of:
A. Agriculture B. Industry
C. Manufacturing D. None of the above

175. Over the years India's growth occurred maximum in:
A. agriculture B. industries
C. services D. None of the above

176. The high growth phase of 2004-08 was in:
A. exports B. imports
C. capital inflows D. All of the above

177. Land reform measures include:
A. abolition of intermediaries
B. tenancy reforms
C. ceiling on land holdings
D. All of the above

178. Mahalanobis model was used in:
A. first 5-year plan B. second 5-year plan
C. third 5-year plan D. None of the above

179. Food management implies:
A. procurement of food
B. distribution of food
C. maintenance of food buffers
D. All of the above

180. In the long run equilibrium the pure monopolist can make pure profits because of:
A. Blocked entry B. High selling prices
C. The low LAC D. Advertising

181. When an individual's income rises, that person's demand for a normal good:

A. Rises B. Falls
C. Remains the same D. Any of the above

182. If the quantity of a commodity demanded remains unchanged as its price changes, the coefficient of price elasticity of demand is:
A. Greater than 1 B. Equal to 1
C. Smaller than 1 D. Zero

183. A fall in the price of a commodity whose demand curve is a rectangular hyperbola causes total expenditures on the commodity to:
A. Rise B. Fall
C. Remain the same D. All of the above

184. When total utility increases, marginal utility is:
A. Negative & increasing
B. Negative & decreasing
C. Zero
D. Positive & decreasing

185. The Engel curve for a Giffen good is:
A. Negatively sloped B. Positively sloped
C. Vertical D. Horizontal

186. The substitution effect for a fall in the price of a commodity is given by:
A. Movement up a given indifference curve
B. A movement from a higher to a lower indifference curve
C. A movement down a given indifference curve
D. None of the above

187. For a fall in price, the price consumption curve for a Giffen good is:
A. Positively sloped B. Negatively sloped
C. Vertical D. Horizontal

188. When the marginal productivity of land is negative it is in:
A. Stage 1 for land B. Stage 3 for labour
C. Stage 2 for land D. None of the above

189. At the point of producer equilibrium:
A. Isoquant is tangent to the isocost
B. The $MRTS_{lk}$ equals P_l/P_k
C. $MP_l/P_l = MP_k/P_k$
D. All of the above

190. If there are constant returns to scale and if the quantity of labour used per unit of time is increased by 10% but the amount of capital remains constant, then output will:
A. Increase by 10%
B. Decrease by 10%
C. Increase by more than 10%
D. Increase by less than 10%

191. Which of the following is an important reason for studying accounting?
A. The information provided by accounting is useful in making economic decisions
B. Accounting plays an important role in society
C. The study of accounting could lead to a challenging career
D. All of the above are important reasons

192. Which of the following groups uses accounting information for planning a company's profitability?
A. Investors B. Creditors
C. Management D. Regulatory agencies

193. The payment of liability will:
A. Increase both assets and liabilities
B. Increase assets and decrease liabilities
C. Decrease assets and increase liabilities
D. Decrease assets and decrease liabilities

194. The accounting principle of matching is best demonstrated by:
A. Not recognising any expense unless some revenue is realised
B. Associating effort (cost) with accomplishment (revenue)
C. Recognising prepaid rent received as revenue
D. Establishing a reserve for possible future market decline in inventory account

195. Which of the following cost items would be matched with current revenues on a basis other than association of cause and effect?
A. Goodwill
B. Sales commission
C. Cost of goods sold
D. Purchases on credit

196. The valuation of a promise to receive cash in the future at present value on the financial statements of a business entity is valid by virtue of which accounting postulate or principle?
A. Entity B. Materiality
C. Matching D. Going concern

197. Payment for a two year insurance policy requires a debit to:
A. Prepaid Insurance B. Insurance Expense
C. Cash D. Accounts payable

198. Which of the following is not true of a trial balance?
A. It proves that the total debits equal total credits, if it balances
B. It facilitates preparation of financial statements
C. It proves that no errors have been made in recording transactions, if it balances
D. It will not detect any error where the accounts debited and credited are reversed in recording a particular transaction

199. As generally applied to accounting, what is depreciation?
A. It is a process of asset valuation for balance sheet purposes
B. It applies only to long lived intangible assets
C. It is used to indicate a decline in market value of long lived asset
D. It is an accounting process which allocates long lived asset cost to accounting periods

200. Which of the following reasons provides the best theoretical support for accelerated depreciation?
A. Assets are more efficient in early years and initially generate more revenue
B. Expenses should be allocated in a manner that smoothens earnings result
C. Repairs and maintenance costs will probably increase in later period so depreciation should be decline
D. Accelerated depreciation provides easier replacement because of the time value of money

ANSWERS

1	2	3	4	5	6	7	8	9	10
A	B	D	D	A	C	C	B	B	C
11	12	13	14	15	16	17	18	19	20
D	C	B	B	B	C	C	A	B	A
21	22	23	24	25	26	27	28	29	30
A	B	A	D	C	B	A	C	B	B
31	32	33	34	35	36	37	38	39	40
A	A	C	D	C	B	B	A	C	C
41	42	43	44	45	46	47	48	49	50
A	C	A	B	C	D	C	C	C	D
51	52	53	54	55	56	57	58	59	60
D	A	A	C	D	C	D	A	B	B
61	62	63	64	65	66	67	68	69	70
B	C	A	C	B	C	B	D	B	B
71	72	73	74	75	76	77	78	79	80
C	B	B	A	A	A	C	D	D	C
81	82	83	84	85	86	87	88	89	90
C	A	B	C	B	A	A	A	B	B
91	92	93	94	95	96	97	98	99	100
A	B	B	C	A	D	D	D	A	B
101	102	103	104	105	106	107	108	109	110
B	A	*	C	D	B	A	B	A	D

111	112	113	114	115	116	117	118	119	120
C	B	D	D	C	C	A	A	C	B
121	**122**	**123**	**124**	**125**	**126**	**127**	**128**	**129**	**130**
B	D	D	C	B	B	C	A	B	C
131	**132**	**133**	**134**	**135**	**136**	**137**	**138**	**139**	**140**
B	B	B	D	A	B	C	D	D	D
141	**142**	**143**	**144**	**145**	**146**	**147**	**148**	**149**	**150**
A	A	D	B	A	D	A	D	C	D
151	**152**	**153**	**154**	**155**	**156**	**157**	**158**	**159**	**160**
D	B	A	C	A	B	B	A	D	C
161	**162**	**163**	**164**	**165**	**166**	**167**	**168**	**169**	**170**
C	B	A	D	D	A	C	B	B	A
171	**172**	**173**	**174**	**175**	**176**	**177**	**178**	**179**	**180**
D	D	B	D	C	D	D	B	D	A
181	**182**	**183**	**184**	**185**	**186**	**187**	**188**	**189**	**190**
A	D	C	D	A	C	A	D	D	D
191	**192**	**193**	**194**	**195**	**196**	**197**	**198**	**199**	**200**
D	C	D	B	A	D	A	C	D	A

SOME SELECTED EXPLANATORY ANSWERS

2. Conservatism refers to the manner in which accountants deal with uncertainty regarding economic situations. When accountants are faced with uncertainty about how to account for or report a particular transaction or situation, conservatism dictates that they use the accounting that is least likely to overstate the company's assets and revenues or to understate the company's liabilities and expenses. A common example of conservatism in action is the lower-of-cost-or-market rule for inventory. According to this rule, inventory must be recorded and reported at the lower of its cost or its current market value. This ensures that the value of inventory is not overstated. Other applications of conservatism will be discussed in subsequent chapters.

4. When shares are redeemed by utilising distributable profit, an amount equal to the face value of shares redeemed is transferred to Capital Redemption Reserve Account. Sometimes, bonus shares are issued by utilising this capital redemption reserve and other reserves. In that case, the entries will be as follows:

Capital Redemption Reserve Account Dr.
Other Reserve Account Dr.
To Bonus to Shareholders Account
(Being the amount appropriated for issue of bonus shares).

Bonus to Shareholders Account Dr.
To Equity Share Capital Account
(Being the utilisation of bonus dividend for issue of equity shares)

Logic Behind the Creation of a Capital Redemption Reserve: Capital Redemption Reserve is created for the following reasons:

(*a*) The most important purpose for the creation of a Capital Redemption Reserve is to maintain the capital intact. Emphasis has been put on the '*capital maintenance*' aspect to safeguard the '*scale of capital*' to which the company was geared just before redemption. The very fact that the company had recourse to Preference Share Capital once, would indicate that it had faced some kind of financial crisis by way of shortage of capital required for doing business at a certain budgeted level of activities. The crisis was overcome by issuing preference shares, obviously the company realised that the investing public was reluctant to subscribe to its equity share capital. The willingness of the company to redeem its preference shares would suggest the company's period of convalescence was over. But shortage-of-capital oriented problems may reappear following the repayment of the preference shares. The Government would not like to take chances. Hence, Section 80 of the Companies Act, 1956 ensures, first, the maintenance of the capital which had helped the company to overcome the financial crisis (shortage capital by issuing the necessary number of preference shares. But has this been achieved? Surely, by giving only two statutory methods for redemption of preference shares, namely, either out of the proceeds of a fresh issue or creating the required Capital Redemption Reserve out of certain specified profits only. The utilisation was further restricted to issuance of fully paid-up bonus shares only, to complete the picture of capitalisation.

(*b*) The another reason for the creation of a capital redemption is for the protection of the company's creditors, since the directors of the company may distribute divisible profits by way of dividend.

5. When a share is issued at a price which is above its face value, it is said to be issue of share at premium. For example, a share having a face value of ₹ 10 is issued for ₹ 15; ₹ 5 (15 – 100) is the premium on the share. The Companies Act does not impose any restrictions on issue of shares at a premium. However, only successful companies, whose shares are in great demand, offer shares at a premium.

Share premium should not be treated as revenue profits because it is a capital receipt. According to the provisions of Companies Act, when a company issues shares at a premium, whether received in cash or otherwise, must be credited to a separate account called "Securities Premium Account". Securities Premium Account is shown in the Balance Sheet under the heading "Reserves and Surplus."

Under Section 78 of the Companies Act, the Securities Premium Account may be used wholly or in part for:

(*i*) issuing fully paid bonus shares to the members;

(*ii*) writing off preliminary expenses of the company;

(*iii*) writing off the expenses of or the commission paid or discount allowed on any issue of shares or debentures of the company; or

(*iv*) providing for the premium payable on the redemption of any redeemable preference shares or of any debentures of the company.

If a company uses securities premium account for any other purpose, it is treated as reduction of paid-up capital which is not permitted because reduction of capital will require the compliance of the provisions contained in Section 100 of the Companies Act.

6. It has been made compulsory, through the Companies (Amendment) Act, 1988, that the Companies shall maintain their books on accrual basis and according to double entry system of account.

7. The net profit of a company is disclosed by the Profit and Loss Account. When Profit and Loss Account is prepared (without dividing into Trading Account, Profit and Loss Account; and Profit and Loss Appropriation Account), the net profit or loss is transferred to the opposite side of the Profit and Loss Account 'below the line'. All entries, relating to (*i*) disposal or distribution of profit; and (*ii*) adjustment relating to previous years, etc. are made on that section.

When Profit and Loss Account is prepared by dividing into (*a*) Trading Account, (*b*) Profit and Loss Account, and (*c*) Profit and Loss Appropriation Account, all "below the line" entries are made in the Profit and Loss Appropriation Account. The entries appear as follows:

Profit and Loss Appropriation Account

Dr.			Cr.
Particulars	₹	Particulars	₹
To General Reserve To Interim Dividend To Preference Dividend To Proposed Dividend To Balance c/d		By Balance b/d By Net profit (current year) By Provision for taxation (excess of previous year)	

Credit balance of Profit and Loss Appropriation Account is shown in the Balance Sheet under the head 'Reserves and Surplus'. Debit balance is shown in the Balance Sheet under 'Miscellaneous Expenditures'.

8. Distinction between Calls-in-Arrears & Calls-in-Advance

Calls-in-arrears differ from Calis-in-advance in the following respects:

Basis of Distinction	*Calls-in-arrears*	*Calls-in-advance*
1. Meaning	It refers to the amount called up by the company which has not yet been paid by the shareholders till the last day fixed for payment thereof.	It refers to the amount paid by the shareholders in excess of the amount due from them.
2. Authority under Articles	There is no question of any authority under Articles.	A company may accept Calls-in-advance only if Articles authorise to do so.
3. Interest	Interest is charged on Calls-in-arrears.	Interest is allowed on Calls-in-advance.
4. Disclosure	The amount of Calls-in-arrears is shown by way of deduction from the called-up capital in the Balance Sheet.	The amount of Calls-in-advance is shown as a separate item under the head 'Share Capital' (but is not added to the amount of paid up capital) or 'Current Liabilities'.

11. The Institute of Chartered Accountants of India (ICAI) has issued Accounting standard-6 (AS-6) on *Depreciation Accounting. AS*-6 lays down the accounting treatment of depreciation under different situations and the disclosure requirements. Depreciation is defined as '*a measure of the wearing out, consumption or other loss of value of a depreciable asset arising from use, effluxion of time or obsolescence through technology and market changes.*' Depreciation is charged on the historical cost of the depreciable assets or other amounts substituted for the historical cost in the financial statements, less the estimated residual value. The term 'depreciable assets' refers to tangible fixed assets. Intangible assets (assets having no physical existence, the value of which is limited by the rights and anticipated benefits that possession confers upon the owner) also lose value over time, but they are 'amortised' (and not depreciated). Amortisation is charging off a part of the cost of an intangible asset in the income statement. Such amortisation amount is arrived at on the basis of the useful life of the asset. No fixed rates are prescribed.

The historical cost of a depreciable asset comprises its purchase price, including import duties and other non-refundable dues, taxes or levies, and any directly attributable cost of bringing the asset to its working condition for its intended use; any trade discount and rebate are also deducted in arriving at the purchase price. However, the cost of a depreciable asset may undergo changes subsequent to its acquisition or construction on account of exchange fluctuations, price adjustments, etc. Financing costs relating to deferred credits attributable to construction or acquisition of depreciable assets for the period up to the completion of construction or acquisition of fixed assets are included in the cost.

12. When two periods profits and sales are given, P/V ratio can be computed as given below:

$$\text{P/V Ratio} = \frac{\text{Change in Profit}}{\text{Change in Sales}} \times 100$$

Here change in Profit

$$= 14000 - 8000 = 6000$$

$$\text{P/V Ratio} = \frac{6000}{20,000} \times 100 = 30$$

and change in Sales

$$= 180000 - 160000$$
$$= 20000$$

13.
$$\text{EOQ} = \sqrt{\frac{2 \times \text{D} \times \text{O}}{\text{S}}}$$

$$\text{D} = 400 \times 12 = 4800$$

$$\text{O} = ₹\ \frac{100}{\text{Order}}$$

$$\text{S} = \frac{15 \times 40}{100} = 6$$

$$\text{EOQ} = \sqrt{\frac{2 \times 4800 \times 100}{6}}$$

$$= \sqrt{160000} = 400.$$

15. Margin of safely = 25% of x

x = current sales amount

$$\because \text{Margin of safely} = \frac{\text{Profit}}{\text{P/V Ratio}}$$

$$\frac{25}{100} \times x = \frac{30,00,000}{40\%}$$

$$\frac{25}{100} \times x \times \frac{40}{100} = 30,00,000$$

$$\frac{x}{10} = 30,00,000$$

$\therefore$ x = 3,00,00,000 thousand only

17. Units of Production: Under this method the charge per unit is calculated by dividing total estimated factory overhead by total estimated units. This is the most direct and simplest method used for the assignment of factory overhead to units produced. The overhead absorption rate is calculated as under:

$$\frac{\text{Estimated factory overhead in the budget period}}{\text{Estimated units of production (at normal capacity)}}$$

The unit of production method is suitable when a company produces only one product. However, if a company produces many products and they are similar or closely related (their difference being only in volume, weight etc), this method can be used by the conversion of physical units into equivalent units. This is none by using 'points' or 'weights'. It is likely to be arbitrary.

19. In computing a current-period unit cost for a department, two approaches have evolved for dealing with the prior-period output and prior-period costs found in BWIP: the weighted average method and the FIFO method.

The weighted average costing method combines beginning inventory costs and work done with current-period costs and work to calculate this period's unit cost. In essence, the costs and work carried over from the prior period are counted as if they belong to the current period. Thus, beginning inventory work and costs are pooled with current work and costs, and an average unit cost is computed and applied to both units transferred out and units remaining in ending inventory.

The FIFO costing method, on the other hand, separates work and costs of the equivalent units in beginning inventory from work and costs of the equivalent units produced during the current period. Only current work and costs are used to calculate this period's unit cost. It is assumed that units from beginning inventory are completed first and transferred out. The costs of these units include the costs of the work done in the prior period as well as the current-period costs necessary to complete the units.

20. Volume variance = SR (AQ – BQ)

$$= \frac{BFO}{BQ} \times (AQ - BQ)$$

Here BFO = 84000
AQ = 24000
BQ = 20000

∴ Volume variance

$$= \frac{84000}{20000} \times (24000 - 20000)$$

$$= \frac{84}{20} \times 4000 = 16800$$

23. Relevant and Irrelevant Costs: Cost which is influenced by a decision is a relevant cost and hence, is important for decision-makers. Cost which is not affected by a decision is irrelevant cost, that is, it will be the same regardless of the choice that is made. As a result, such a cost is of no relevance to decision-makers. Therefore, it should be ignored while taking decisions. Committed fixed costs are irrelevant costs. However, it should not be taken to mean that relevant costs are equivalent to variable costs. In situations where additional fixed costs are to be incurred as a result of a decision, fixed costs are as much the relevant costs as the variable costs are. As an illustration, if the company wants to make a component hitherto purchased from the outside suppliers, the relevant costs will be: (*i*) Cost of material and direct labour (variable cost) and (*ii*) Fixed costs (required for creating new facilities so that the manufacturing process of making a component can start). Thus, relevant costs, truly speaking, are incremental costs, fixed and variable classification notwithstanding.

24. Product Mix Decisions: Managers might be tempted to produce the products with the highest contribution margins or unit sales. *Contribution margin* is the amount each product contributes to profits and overhead; no fixed costs are considered when making the product mix decision. We call this approach the *traditional method.* The problem with this approach is that the firm's actual throughput and overall profitability depend more upon the contribution margin generated at the bottleneck than by the contribution margin of each individual product produced. We call this latter approach the *bottleneck method.*

25. Sunk costs are costs which have already been incurred and would not require current cash expenditure.

27. The material usage variance is normally controllable by the manager of the appropriate production responsibility centre. Common causes of material usage variances include the careless handling of materials by production personnel, the purchase of inferior quality materials, pilferage, changes in quality control requirements, or changes in methods of production. Separate material usage variances should be calculated for each type of material used and allocated to each responsibility centre.

32. Skew: A property of a statistical distribution indicating lack of symmetry; a distribution is said to be skewed to the right or left if observations are concentrated to the left or right of the mean, respectively. A distribution is skewed right (positive skew) when the mean is greater than the median and is skewed to the left (negative skew) when the mean is less than the median.

34. Area Property: One of the most fundamental properties of the normal probability curve between the ordinates at $x = \mu - \sigma$ and $x = \mu - \sigma$ is 0.6826. In other words the range $\mu \pm \sigma$ covers 68.26% of the observation.

∴ $x = 100 - 10 = 90$
$x = 100 + 10 = 110$

∴ About 68% of the data within 90 and 110.

35. Given data in ascending order are
3, 6, 7, 17, 17, 23, 51, 69

∴ Median = Arithmetic Mean of two Middle term

$$= \frac{17+17}{2} = 17$$

and, Range is the difference between the greatest and the smallest observation of the distributing, this

Range = $X_{max} - X_{min}$
$= 69 - 3 = 66.$

37. Quartile deviation or Semi Inter Quartile Range is obtained from inter-quartile range on dividing by 2.

Thus, Semi Inter Quartile Range

$$= \frac{\text{Inter Quartile Range}}{2}$$

$$= \frac{Q_3 - Q_1}{2} = \frac{31-19}{2} = 6$$

44. The coin has 2 possible outcomes, and the single die has 6 possible outcomes. Therefore total number of possible outcomes for a coin and a pair of dice is 2 × 6 × 6 = 72.

45. Probability that both (A and B) do not occur is

$$P(\bar{A} \cap \bar{B}) = P(\bar{A}) \cdot P(\bar{B})$$

then $P(\bar{A}) = 1 - P(A)$
$= 1 - 0.4 = 0.6$

and $P(\bar{B}) = 0.3$

$\therefore$ $P(\bar{A} \cap \bar{B}) = 0.6 \times 0.3 = 0.18.$

51. The diet problem, one of the earliest applications of LP, was originally used by hospitals to determine the most economical diet for patients. Known in agricultural applications as the feed mix problem, the diet problem involves specifying a food or feed ingredient combination that satisfies stated nutritional requirements at a minimum cost level.

53. Iso-profit Line: In the graphical method, all points in the feasible region represent feasible decision alternatives but they are not all meeting our desired objectives. Some provide a greater profit contribution or lower total cost than others. In other words, we seek to obtain the feasible solution which optimizes. It therefore, requires adding one more line to the graph which is called Iso-profit or constant profit line. A straight line representing all non-negative combinations of X_1 and X_2 for a particular profit level. As the name implies, all the points on an iso-profit line yield the same profit.

58. $\because$ $TC = 1500 + 30x + x^2$

$$\therefore \quad MC = \frac{d(TC)}{dx} = 30 + 2x$$

Since $x = 20$ units

$\therefore$ $MC = 30 + 2 \times 20 = 70$

60. A firm has increasing returns to scale if, when it increases all inputs by X%, output goes up by more than X%. What increases as the firm makes its scale larger is the ratio of output to inputs. One reason for increasing returns to scale is that many physical production processes require a large scale to be run efficiently.

A second reason is that a larger scale of operation may afford certain economies not available to smaller firms. A larger firm can have managers, staff, and workers performing specialized tasks to the degree that they become expert in doing them. This division of labour makes these personnel more efficient at what they are doing.

62. Producer surplus

$$= p_e \times x_e - \int_0^{x_e} S(x)dx$$

Here $x_e = 12$
$p_e = 16$

$$\therefore \quad PS = 12 \times 16 - \int_0^{12} (4+x)dx$$

$$= 192 - \left| 4x + \frac{x^2}{2} \right|_0^{12}$$

$= 192 - 120 = 72.$

63. $$\text{Effective Rate} = \left(1+\frac{r}{n}\right)^n - 1$$

Here, $r = 6\% = 0.06$
$n = 2$

$$\therefore \quad ER = \left(1+\frac{0.06}{2}\right)^2 - 1$$

$$= \left(\frac{2+0.06}{2}\right)^2 - 1$$

$$= \left(\frac{2.06}{2}\right)^2 - 1 = (1.03)^2 - 1$$

$= 1.0609 - 1 = .0609$
$= 6.09\%.$

65. The present value of a perpetuity of ₹ A payable at the beginning of each interest period with money worth i per period is given by

$$P = A + \frac{A}{(1+i)} + \frac{A}{(1+i)^2} + \frac{A}{(1+i)^3} \ldots$$

$$= A + \frac{A}{i} = \frac{A(1+i)}{i}$$

Hence, $i = 0.05$

$A = 2500$

$$\therefore \quad P = \frac{2500(1.05)}{0.05} = 52500.$$

66. Method for finding inverse of a 2 × 2 square matrix

We know that for a square $A = \begin{bmatrix} a & b \\ c & d \end{bmatrix}$,

$$A^{-1} = \frac{1}{ad-bc}\begin{pmatrix} d & -b \\ -c & a \end{pmatrix} = \frac{1}{|A|}\begin{pmatrix} d & -b \\ -c & a \end{pmatrix}.$$

From this formula we can find A^{-1} using the following steps:

1. Find whether $|A| = 0$ or not. If $|A| = 0$, then the given matrix is singular, so A^{-1} doesn't exist. If $|A| \neq 0$, then the matrix has a multiplicative inverse and can be found by the following steps (2), (3) and (4).
2. Interchange the elements of principal diagonal.
3. Multiply the other two elements by −1.
4. Multiply each element of the matrix by $\frac{1}{|A|}$.

67. $MC = 2 \times e^{0.001x}$

On Integration, we get

$$= \int 2 \cdot e^{0.001x}$$

$$= \frac{2}{0.001} e^{0.001x} + C$$

$$= 2000 \cdot e^{0.001x} + C$$

Given that C = 2000

$\therefore$ Answer $= 2000 \cdot e^{0.001x} + 2000.$

77. A letter of credit, abbreviated L/C, is an instrument issued by a bank at the request of an importer, in which the bank promises to pay a beneficiary upon presentation of documents specified in the L/C. In international trade an L/C is sometimes called a *commercial letter of credit,* a *documentary letter of credit* or simply a *credit.* An L/C reduces the risk of noncompletion because the bank agrees to pay against documents rather than actual merchandise.

A typical transaction is as follows. An importer and exporter agree on a transaction and the importer applies to its local bank for the issuance of an L/C. Based on its assessment of the importer's creditworthiness, the bank may require a cash deposit or other collateral from the importer and issues the L/C. The bank wants to know the type of transaction, the amount of money and currency involved and which documents must accompany the draft that will be drawn against the L/C. Examples of such documents are a commercial invoice, a packing list issued by the beneficiary, an insurance certificate and a full set of original shipped "on board" ocean bills of lading issued by the shipping company. At this point in time the credit of the importer's bank has been substituted for that of the importer and the L/C becomes a financial contract between the importer's bank and the designated beneficiary, the exporter. This financial contract is a separate transaction from the sale of the goods. If the terms of the L/C are met, any payment problems that develop at a later date are of concern only to the importer and the issuing bank. All other parties to the transaction may rely on the bank's credit without concern about the financial status of the importer.

81. Vroom's Expectancy Theory: In 1964, Victor Vroom made a significant contibution to our understanding of motivation through his Expectancy Theory, though it has its critics, most of the research evidence supports this theory.

Vroom's expectancy theory can be classified as a process theory in contrast to the content theory primarily because it attempts to identify relationships among variable in a dynamic state as they affect individual behaviour. This systems orientation is in direct contrast to the content theories which have attempted largely to specify correlates of motivated behaviour. In the expectancy theory, it is the relationship among inputs that is the basic focal point rather than the inputs themselves.

Vroom has developed his motivation model around the concepts of value, expectancy and force. His basic assumption is "the choice made by a person among alternative course of action is lawfully related to psychological events occurring contemporaneously with the behaviour". In this theory the concept of force is equivalent to motivation and can be shown as the algebraic sum of the products of valences multiplied by expectancies. According to Vroom:

Motivation (Force) = Valency × Expectancy

82. The theory of leadership proposed by Likert (1959a) suggests that the management of human resources is the most important task of a leader. The effectiveness of leader depends on his location on the 'Organisationals Style Scale'. This scale is divided into four segments (systems). These systems are as follows.

System 1 refers to a purely authoritarian, exploitative, hierarchical approach.

System 2 is less exploitative but still authoritarian.

System 3 refers to a more consultative approach.

System 4 is a total participative approach.

83. Chris Argyris (Personality and Organization): It is a theory of maturity of personality. Argyris states that the organization is an open system, full of dynamic activities and it includes formal and informal behaviour. These behaviours include three fold processes: (*a*) socializing process, (*b*) personalising process, and (*c*) fusion process.

Argyris identifies specific dimensions of human personality at different stages of development. His seven dimension continuum of maturity immaturity model of personality is more pertinent to the study of organizational behaviour. He has presented a unifying personality theory.

The maturity immaturity continuum theory developed by Argyris may be summarized under the following tables:

Immaturity characteristics	Maturity characteristics
Passivity	Activity
Dependence	Independence
Few ways of behaving	Divers behaviour
Shallow interest	Long term perspectives
Subordinate position	Superordinate position
Lack of self awareness	Self awareness and control

According to Argyris, human personality progresses along a continuum from immaturity at the childhood to maturity at adulthood. Human personality does not necessarily pass through all these stages. Much depends upon individual's perception, self concept, adaptation and adjustment. The organization should strive at promoting mature characteristics. As there is apprehension of participants being frustrated in a mature organization, the organization shuld impart sensitivity training. He feels that aspirations of the individuals should be taken into account while bringing out change in the organization.

85. Comparison of Theory X and Theory Y

Theory X	*Theory Y*
• Autocratic (Leadership style)	• Democratic (Leadership style)
• Close Supervision	• Liberal supervision
• Stick approach	• Carrot approach
• Emphasis on coercion and punishment	• Emphasis on freedom and liberty
• People are lazy	• People enjoy work
• People like to be directed	• People have self-direction
• People are motivated by economic considerations	• People are motivated by self-development
• Managers are result oriented	• Managers are welfare oriented
• People are immature	• People are mature

86. ERG theory, developed by Clayton Alderfer, condenses the five needs proposed by Maslow into three and ERG stands for existence, relatedness and growth. The existence needs are roughly comparable to physiological and safety needs of Maslow's model and are satisfied primarily by material incentives. Relatedness needs roughly correspond to social and self-esteem needs and finally, the growth needs are similar to primarily self-actualisation needs and partially to esteem needs.

93. The consent means an act of assenting to an offer. *According to Section 13,* "Two or more persons are said to consent when they agree upon the same thing in the same sense." Thus, consent involves identity of minds in respect of the subject matter of the contract. In English Law, this is called '*consensus-ad-idem.*'

Free consent is one of the essential elements of a valid contract as it is evidenced by Section 10 which provides that all agreements are contracts if they are made by the free consent of the parties...

According to Section 14, "Consent is said to be free when it is not caused by (*a*) coercion, or (*b*) undue influence, or (*c*) fraud, or (*d*) misrepresentation, or (*e*) mistake".

95. According to Section 25 of the Indian Contract Act. An agreement made without consideration is void, unless:

1. It is expressed in writing and registered under the law for the time being in force for the registration of documents, and is made on account of natural love and affection between parties standing in a near relation to each other, or unless.
2. It is promise to compensate, wholly or in part, a person who has already voluntarily done something for the promisor, or something which the promisor was legally compellable to do, or unless.
3. It is a promise, made in writing and signed by the person to be charged therewith or by his agent generally or specifically authorized in that behalf, to pay wholly or in part a debt of which the creditor might have enforced payment but for the law for the limitation of suits.

In any other case such an agreement is a contract.

100. Doctrines of constructive notice and indoor management: In consequences of the registration of the memorandum and articles of association of the company with the Registrar of Companies, a person dealing with the company is deemed to have constructive notice of their contents. This is because these documents are construed as "public document" under Section 610 of the Companies Act, 1956. Accordingly if a person deals with a company in a manner incompatible with the provisions of the aforesaid documents or enters into transaction, which is ultra vires, *these documents,* he must do so at his peril. However, the doctrine of constructive notice is not a positive one but a negative one like that of estoppel of which it forms parts. It operates only against the person who has been dealing with the company but not against the company itself; consequently he is prevented form alleging that he did not know that the constitution of the company rendered a particular act or a particular delegation of authority *ultra vires.* Thus, the doctrine is a "cloud" for the strangers.

One limitation to the doctrine of constructive notice of the memorandum and articles of a company is the doctrine of indoor management. According to the doctrine of indoor management, the outsider, dealing with the company are entitled to assume that as far as the internal proceedings of the company are concerned, everything has been regularly done. They are bound to lend the registered documents and to see that the proposed dealing is not inconsistent therewith, but they are not bound to do more, they need not inquire into the regularity of the internal proceedings as required by the memorandum and articles. This limitation of the doctrine of constructive notice is known as the 'Doctrine of Indoor Management', popularly known as rule in *Royal British Bank v. Turquand.* Thus the doctrine of indoor management aims to protect outsiders against the company.

The following are the circumstances in which doctrines of indoor management is inapplicable:

1. *Knowledge of irregularity:* Where a person dealing with a company has actual or constructive notice of the irregularity as regards internal management, he cannot claim the benefit under the rule of indoor management.
2. *Negligence:* Where a person dealing with a company could discover the irregularity if he had made proper inquiries, he cannot claim the benefit of the rule of indoor management. The protection of the rule is also not available where the circumstances surrounding the contract are so suspicious as to invite inquiry, and the outsider dealing with the company does not make proper inquiry.
3. *Act void ab initio and forgery:* Where the acts done in the name of a company are void ab initio, the doctrine of indoor management does not apply. The doctrine applies only to irregularities that otherwise might affect a genuine transaction. It does not apply to a forgery. A Company can never he held liable for forgeries committed by its officers.
4. *Acts outside the scope of apparent authority:* If an officer of a company enters into a contract with a third party and if the act of the officer is beyond the scope of his authority, the company is not bound.
5. A person having no knowledge of Articles cannot seek protection under Indoor Management.

106. Sometimes an individual is taxed in respect of others income. The income legally belongs to somebody else but it is clubbed with the income of some other person in some special circumstances. These provisions are contained in Sections 60 to 64.

Section 60 & 61 contains provisions when income from an asset is transferred without transferring the asset or transferring an asset but the transfer is revocable. In both the situations income from such assets is treated as income of the transferor.

Transfer or income without transfer of asset [Section 60]

(*i*) If any person transfers the income from any asset without transferring the asset itself, such income is to be included in the total income of the transferor.

(*ii*) It is immaterial whether the transfer is revocable or irrevocable and whether it was made before the commencement of this Act or after its commencement.

(*iii*) For example, Mr. X confers the right to receive rent in respect of his house property on his wife, Mrs. X, without transferring the house itself to her. In this case, the rent received by Mrs. X will be clubbed with the income of Mr. X.

109. Transfer pricing: Transfer pricing is the price at which services or products are bought and sold across international borders between related parties. As an example, if a US parent company purchases products from its French subsidiary, a transfer price must be established for the products. Because the transfer price affects the parent and subsidiary's net income, it affects the taxes that the firm pays in the US and France. Multinational companies can minimize their overall tax burden by using transfer prices to minimize net income in jurisdictions with higher income tax rates, and maximizing net income in jurisdictions with lower income tax rates. However, many governments have established tax regulations that are designed to help ensure that transfer prices estimate market prices.

113. The Direct Taxes Code Bill, 2010 consolidates and integrates all direct tax laws and replaces both the Income-tax Act, 1961 and the Wealth-tax Act, 1957 by a single legislation. The provisions applicable to a taxpayer are in the main clauses while complex computations and exceptions have been placed in Schedules.

The proposed DTC Bill, 2010 comprises of
(*i*) 22 Chapters
(*ii*) 319 Clauses
(*iii*) 22 Schedules

115. CIBIL is the country's credit information bureau owned by banks and other lending institutions. It collects commercial and consumer credit-related data and collates such data to create and distribute credit reports to members. Accessing to such data is crucial for lenders to assess the credit worthiness of a borrower. CIBIL gets information from its members only and supplements it with public domain information to create a comprehensive snapshot of an entity's financial track record. The RTI Act, 2005 is not applicable to CIBIL and it can't provide credit information report to credit providers in other countries.

117. In 1997, the Government of India, had identified Nine Public sector enterprises (PSES) as potential and prestigious having authority to compete as a global giant in the global market. The number of Navaratna was raised from Nine to thirty twenty.

The term Navaratna means nine gems ornament or a talisman in old days in the courts of King Vikramaditya and the Mughal emperor Akbar, Navaratna were a group of nine extra ordinary men in their respective courts. In case of Public sector enterprises, company which enhances its economical and operational capacity and invest up to ₹ 1000 crore of 15% of their net worth on a single project without seeking governments approvals, are offered with the status of Navaratna.

128. BRICS is the acronym for an association of five major emerging national economies: Brazil, Russia, India, China and South Africa. The grouping was originally known as "BRIC" before the inclusion of South Africa in 2010. The BRICS members are all developing or newly industrialised countries, but they are distinguished by their large, fast-growing economies and significant influence on regional and global affairs; all five are G-20 members.

133. Article 2 empowers the Parliament to 'admit into the Union of India, or establish, new states on such terms and conditions as it thinks fit'. Thus, Article 2 grants two powers to the Parliament: (*a*) the power to admit into the Union of India new states; and (*b*) the power to establish new states. The first refers to the admission of states which are already in existence while the second refers to the establishment of states which were not in existence before. Notably, Article 2 relates to the admission or establishment of new states that are not part of the Union of India. Article 3, on the other hand, relates to the formation of or changes in the existing states of the Union of India. In other words, Article 3 deals with the internal re-adjustment *inter* se of the territories of the constituent states of the Union of India.

135. Nathula Pass is a pass on the Indo-China (Tibet) border in the state of Sikkim. The pass forms part of an offshoot of the ancient Silk Route. Nathula Pass is located at an elevation of 4,310 m (14,200 feet) above mean sea level. The route leading up to the pass is one of the world's highest navigable roads, and is maintained by the Border Roads Organisation, a wing of the Indian Army.

140. *National Rural Employment Guarantee Act (NREGA):* It was introduced in February 2006, in all 596 rural districts in India, with the assistance of Central Government with the provision of ₹ 16000 crore. This is renamed as Mahatma Gandhi National Rural Employment Guarantee Act from October 2009.

142. The city of Changwon in Korea has been awarded the shooting World Championship of 2018 by the International Shooting Sport Federation (ISSF).

The last World Championship was held in Munich, Germany, in 2010 and the next championship will be held in Granada, Spain, in 2014.

145. National Technology Day was celebrated on 11 May 2013 as a symbol of quest for scientific inquiry, technological creativity and the translation of that quest in the integration of Science, Society and Industry. This day is also celebrated to honour technological innovations and their successful commercialization which makes fruits of research reach people at large. This year's function is centered on the Theme Innovation-Making a Difference.

On 11 May 1998 India achieved a major technological breakthrough by successfully carrying out nuclear tests at Pokhran. Also first, indigenous aircraft Hansa-3 was test flown at Bangalore on this day and India also performed successful test firing of the Trishul missile on the same day.

Considering above technological achievements on a particular date *i.e.* 11 May, the day of 11 May was chosen to be commemorated as National Technology Day.

147. The committee headed by the former Chief Economic Advisor Raghuram Rajan submitted its report on 26 September, 2013 to the Union Government. The committee was appointed by the Union Government of India to decide the criteria for granting special category status to states.

According the criteria given by the report Odisha, Bihar least developed states and Goa and Kerala are most developed states.

149. The percentage decadal growth during 2001-2011 has a registered the sharpest decline since independence. For 2001-2011, this decadal growth has become 17.64 percent, a decrease of 3.9 percentage points from 21.54 percent for the period 1999-2001.

Nagaland led the states with the lowest population growth rate at –0.47 percent whereas Meghalaya showed the highest growth rate at 27.82 percent.

152. Complementary goods are those that are used with some other goods, such as — ink is complementary to pen, refill is complementary to a ball-point pen, petrol is complementary to moped, scooter, motor cycle and car etc. The demand of complementary goods is derived from the demand of main goods. If the demand of main goods increases, the demand of complementary goods will also increases. If the demand of main goods decreases, the demand of complementary goods will also decrease. Elasticity of demand of complementary goods is negative in relation to price. If the price of main goods increases, demand of complementary goods will increase because the demand of main goods will also increase.

154. Iso-quants are negatively sloped, the logic being the principle of diminishing marginal rate of technical substitution. In order to maintain a given level of output, a reduction in the use of one input must be offset by an increase in the use of another input.

155. Short-run average cost curve is 'U'-shaped. It means that at first this curve falls and after reaching the minimum point it begins to rise. The following are the main causes for the 'U' shape of Average Cost Curve.

(*i*) Basis of Average Fixed Cost and Average Variable Cost: As we know, Average cost is the summation of average fixed cost and average variable cost, *i.e.*,

$$AC = AFC + AVC$$

With every increase in output average fixed cost continue to fall. The average variable cost continues to fall in the beginning, till it reaches the minimum point. Then it begins to rise. Thus AC tends to decrease initially, stabilises subsequently, and rises finally. It finally rises because at later stages of output fixed cost is over-shadowed by the variable cost.

(*ii*) Basis of the Laws of Variable Proportions: Initially, when variable factors are combined with a fixed factor, then the fixed factor is more efficiently used. Consequently, average cost begins to diminish. After the fixed factors have been optimally used, then due to excess use of variable factors, the ratio between them and the fixed factor begins to fall. This results into decline in the efficiency of the variable factors and accordingly production increases at a diminishing rate. This signifies the operation of Law of Diminishing Returns to factor or Law of Increasing Costs. That is why, average cost curve begins to rise.

157. In the long run, the industry supplies various quantities at a constant price. This means that: the long run supply curve of a constant-cost industry is horizontal (perfectly elastic) at the minimum average total cost.

159. Third-degree price discrimination is where consumers are grouped into two or more independent markets and a separate price is charged in each market. Examples include different-priced seats on buses for adults and children, and different prices charged for the same product in different countries. Third-degree price discrimination is much more common than first- or second-degree discrimination.

Conditions necessary for price discrimination to operate

There are three conditions that must be met:

1. The firm must be able to set its price. Thus price discrimination will be impossible under perfect competition, where firms are price takers.
2. The markets must be separate. Consumers in the low-priced market must not be able to resell the high-priced market. For example, children must not be able to resell a half-priced child's cinema ticket for use by an adult.
3. Demand elasticity must differ in each market. The firm will charge the higher price in the market where demand is less elastic, and thus less sensitive to a price rise.

160. When the supply of the factor is perfectly inelastic: In this case, elasticity of supply of the factor is equal to zero. It means that the factor cannot be transferred from its present employment. Thus, the supply curve of the factor, SS, is the vertical line parallel to Y-axis as shown in figure A. It shows that OQ units of factors are supplied irrespective of price. Given the demand curve DD, price of the factor is determined by the intersection of the demand curve and the supply curve. The factors will receive the price equal to OP per unit and the total earnings are equal to OPEQ.

Now, economic rent is the difference between the actual earnings and the transfer earnings. Since, the factor cannot be transferred from its present occupation, its transfer earnings are zero. Therefore, economic rent is equal to the actual earnings.

Economic rent = Actual earnings – Transfer earnings

Economic rent = OPEQ – zero

Economic rent = OPEQ

Few examples of the factors whose supply is perfectly inelastic are rare painting, rare stamp, antique statue etc.

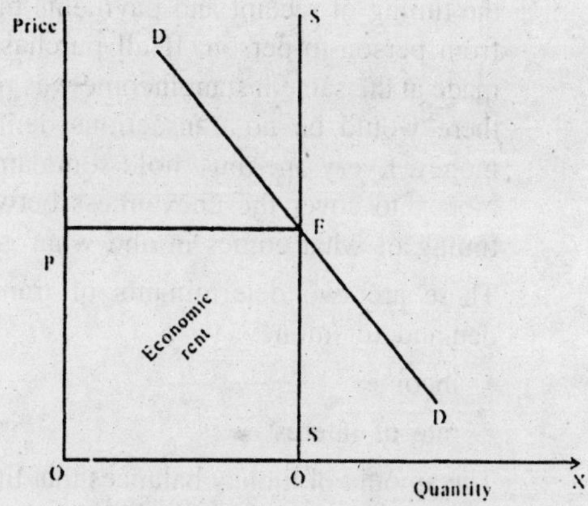

Fig A: *All the earnings of the factor are economic rent*

163. Value of multiplier

$$= \frac{1}{1-\text{MPC}(1-\text{Tax})}$$

$$= \frac{1}{1-0.8(1-0.25)}$$

$$= \frac{1}{1-0.8\times 0.75}$$

$$= \frac{1}{1-0.6} = 2.5$$

166. Sacrifice ratio is defined as the ratio of the cumulative percentage loss of output to the actual reduction in inflation. In other words, sacrifice ratio is the cost of disinflation. Economists calculate sacrifice ratio of the disinflation policy before implementing the policy.

Factors that lead to less costly disinflation or sacrifice ratio (as given by IMF study paper) are:

1. Announcement of policy in advance.
2. Gradual fall in inflation.
3. More credibility of the policy.
4. Greater relative importance of expected inflation in determining current inflation.
5. Greater responsiveness of prices and wages to demand conditions.

167. The Transactions Demand for Money: Daily transactions require some money. However, the timing of receipt and payments may vary from person-to-person, If all purchases were made at the same instant income was received, there would be no transactions demand for money. Every one must hold some amount of money to cover the unevenness between the timing of what comes in and what goes out.

There are two determinants of transactions demand for money:

- income
- rate of interest

The amount of money balances that the public as a whole wishes to hold for transactions purposes depends directly on the level of income. It is possible to expect the amount of money demanded for transactions purposes to vary directly with the level of income. Similarly, it is possible to expect it to vary inversely with the rate of interest.

$$\text{Transaction Demand} \propto \text{income}$$

$$\text{Transaction Demand} \propto \frac{1}{\text{Rate of interest}}$$

169. On of the major conclusions of the Mundell-Fleming model is that the relative effectiveness of monetary and fiscal policies depends on both the existing exchange rate regime and the degree of international capital mobility. Mundell (1963) analyzes the case of perfect capital mobility under both fixed and flexible exchange rates. Under a fixed exchange rate system, an increase in the money supply through open market operations creates excess liquidity and exerts downward pressure on interest rates, causing a capital outflow. To prevent the exchange rate from depreciating, central banks intervene in the market, selling foreign exchange and buying domestic money until the money supply is restored to its original level. Thus, monetary policy has no sustainable effect on the level of income, but it does lead to a change in international reserves. An expansionary fiscal policy, conversely, has a multiplier effect on income and no effect on international reserves. The increase in income increases saving, taxes, and imports. The need for higher liquidity in the private sector leads to a capital inflow that offsets the deterioration in the trade balance, so that the balance of payments remains unchanged.

Under a flexible exchange rate system, a monetary expansion has a strong effect on the levels of income and employment, not because it lowers the rate of interest but because it induces a capital outflow, depreciates the exchange rate, and (normally) improves the trade balance.

An expansionary fiscal policy, conversely, causes the trade balance to deteriorate without affecting domestic output or employment. In this case, the increase in the demand for goods raises the demand for money (hence the interest rate) and attracts a capital inflow, resulting in an appreciation of the exchange rate and in turn depressing income.

172. There core values of development as given by Prof. Goulet are.

(*a*) Life sustenance

(*b*) Self esteem

(*c*) Freedom from servitude

174. In India's National Accounts Statistics, the service sector consists of the following economic activities: wholesale and retail trade, hotels and restaurants, transport services, storage services, communication services, financial services, real estate, ownership of dwellings and renting services, business services and other social, community and personal services. This is broadly similar to the classification of services sector activity in the UN International Ṣtandard Industrial Classification (ISIC), but there is one important point of distinction. In contrast to the UN ISIC, India's National Accounts Statistics consider electricity, gas and water supply and construction activity to be part of the industrial sector rather than the services sector (CSO, 2008).

178. The second Fine-year Plan has also been called the Nehru-Mahalanobis strategy of development as it articulated Nehru's vision and P.C. Mahalanobis happened to be its chief architect. The central idea underlying this strategy is we conveyed by recalling the following statement from the plan document—"If industrialisation is to be rapid enough, the country must aim at developing basic industries and industries which make machines to make the machines needed for further development".

The Mahalanobis model showed that, given certain assumptions, the higher the allocation of investment in the investment goods sector, the higher the investment rate at the margin, which would load to a higher rate of growth of output. The emphasis was on expanding the productive ability or power of the system, through forging strong industrial linkages, as rapidly as possible.

180. A monopolist sells a product with no close substitutes. Short-run economic profit earned by a monopolist can persist in the long run only if the entry of new firms is blocked. Three barriers to entry are (*a*) legal restrictions, such as patents and operating licenses; (*b*) economies of scale over a broad range of output: and (*c*) control over a key resource.

182. The coefficient of *price elasticity of demand* (*e*) measures the percentage change in the quantity of a commodity demanded per unit of time resulting from a given percentage change in the price of the commodity. Since price and quantity are inversely related, the coefficient of price elasticity of demand is a negative number. In order to avoid dealing with negative values, a minus sign is often introduced into the formula for *e*. Letting ΔQ represent the change in the quantity demanded of a commodity resulting from a given change in its price (ΔP), we have

$$e = -\frac{\Delta Q / Q}{\Delta P / P} = -\frac{\Delta Q}{\Delta P}\frac{P}{Q}$$

Demand is said to be *elastic* if $e > 1$, *inelastic* if $e < 1$ and *unitary elastic* if $e = 1$.

183. Point elasticity and total expenditures: A straight-line demand curve (extended to both axes) is elastic above its midpoint, has unitary elasticity at the midpoint, and is inelastic below its midpoint. There are no such generalizations for curvilinear demand curves. In the special case when a demand curve takes the shape of a rectangular hyperbola, $e = 1$ at every point on it.

Regardless of the shape of the demand curve, as the price of a commodity falls, the total expenditures of consumers on the commodity (P times Q) rise when $e > 1$, remain unchanged when $e = 1$, and fall when $e < 1$.

184. Marginal utility is defined as the change in total utility resulting from a one unit change in consumption of the commodity per unit of time. In other words, marginal utility is the additional utility which a person derives from a small addition to his stock of the commodity X is the difference between the total utility of *n* units and the total utility of *n* – 1 units of the commodity. Symbolically,

$$MUn = TUn - TUn - 1$$

where MUn = Marginal utility of *n* units

TUn = Total utility of *n* units

$TUn - 1$ = Total utility of *n* – 1 units

The marginal utility of any quantity can also be stated as the slope of the total utility curve for the same quantity. Mathematically,

$$MU = \frac{d(TU)}{dX} = \text{Slope of total utility curve}$$

Since marginal utility defined as an increase in the total utility due to the consumption of an additional unit of a commodity, total utility will increase till the marginal utility demands positive of $\frac{d(TU)}{dX} > 0$. When marginal utility becomes negative, or $\frac{d(TU)}{dX} < 0$, total utility will decrease. When marginal utility is equal to zero, or $\frac{d(TU)}{dX} = 0$, total utility becomes maximum.

185. Ernst Engel was a 19th-century German statistician who analyzed consumer expenditure data. He found that food purchases increased as income rose, but at a decreasing rate. This became known as *Engel's Law.* A graph of demand for a good as a function of income, ceteris paribus, is called an *Engel Curve.*

The slope of the Engel Curve reveals whether the good is normal or inferior. A *normal* good, has a positively sloped Engel Curve: when income rises, so does optimal consumption. An *inferior* good has a negatively sloped Engel Curve: increases in income lead to decreases in optimal consumption of the good.

189. The producer's equilibrium refers to the situation in which a producer maximises his profits. In other words the producer is producing given amount of output with least cost combination of factors. The least cost combination of factor is also called optimum combination of the factors.

Condition of Optimum Combination of Factors or Least Cost Combination

1. The following are the conditions of optimum combination of factors (least cost combination) or producer's equilibrium. At the point of equilibrium the isocost line must be tangent to isoquant curve. And, at the point of tangency the slope of both Isoquant curve and Isocost line should be equal. The slope of the isocost line is the ratio of the prices of the inputs. The slope of the isoquants is the ratio of the marginal products. It is also called the marginal rate of technical substitution.
2. At point of tangency, *i.e.*, E the isoquant curve is convex to the origin or $MRTS_{LK}$ is diminishing.

We can thus state the conditions of optimum combination of factors as follows:

1. Slope of Isoquant Curve = Slope of Isocost Curve

$$MRTS_{LK} = \frac{\Delta K}{\Delta L} = \frac{MP_L}{MP_K} = \frac{P_L}{P_K}$$

2. At point of tangency Isoquant curve is convex of $MRTS_{LK}$ is diminishing.

196. All financial statements are prepared on the basis of the concept of a 'Going Concern' which means that the business entity will continue its operation in the foreseeable future, and will also continue to generate profits.

In is important to be assured that the enterprise has neither the intention not the necessity of liquidation nor of curtailing materially the scale of operation.

197. When the insurance policy was initially purchased, the entire balance was debited to a prepaid asset account (*i.e.*, prepaid insurance).

199. Depreciation is the accounting process of allocating the cost of long-lived tangible assets to expense in a systematic and rational manner to those periods expected to benefit from the use of the asset.

Identify the factors involved in the depreciation process. Three factors involved in the depreciation process are: (1) determining the depreciation base for the asset. (2) estimating the service life, and (3) selecting a method of cost apportionment (depreciation).

Previous Paper (Solved)

DELHI UNIVERSITY—M.COM ENTRANCE TEST-2012*

1. Upon forfeiture of shares, share capital account is debited by:
   A. Paid-up amount
   B. Calls-in-arrears
   C. Nominal value of such shares
   D. Called-up amounts

2. When valuing inventory at lower of cost or market, what is the meaning of the term market?
   A. Net realizable value
   B. Net realizable value less a normal profit margin
   C. Current replacement cost
   D. Discounted present value

3. Which method of inventory pricing best approximates specific identification of the actual flow of cost and units in most situation?
   A. Average cost
   B. LIFO
   C. FIFO
   D. Specific identification

4. As generally applied to accounting, what is depreciation?
   A. It is a process of asset valuation for balance sheet purposes
   B. It appears only to long lived intangible assets
   C. It is used to indicate a decline in market value of long lived asset
   D. It is an accounting process which allocates long lived asset cost to accounting periods

5. Which of the following reasons provides the best theoretical support for accelerated depreciation?
   A. Assets are more efficient in early years and initially generates more revenue-
   B. Expenses should be allocated in a manner that smooth earnings result
   C. Repairs and maintenance costs will probably increase in later periods so depreciation should decline
   D. Accelerated depreciation provides easier replacement because of the time value of money

6. Provision for bad debts is made to:
   A. Prevent bad debts arising
   B. Obtain a true debtor's figure for the balance sheet
   C. Even out actual bad debts incurring
   D. Encourage prompt payment of debts by debtors

7. The accounting principle of matching is best demonstrated by:
   A. Not recognizing any expenses unless some revenue is realized
   B. Associating effort (cost) with accomplishment (revenue)
   C. Recognizing prepaid rent received as revenue
   D. Establishing a reserve for possible future market decline in inventory account

8. Generally accepted accounting principles:
   A. Define accounting practice at a point in time
   B. Are similar in nature to the principles of Chemistry or Physics?
   C. Are rarely changed?
   D. Are not affected by changes in the way business operates?

9. Cost volume profit analysis is based on several assumptions. Which of the following is not one of these assumptions?

*Exam held on 17-06-2012.

A. Sales mix of the products is constant
B. Inventory quantities change during the year
C. Behaviour of both revenues and cost is linear throughout the relevant range
D. Material prices and wage rates remain unchanged

10. Which of the following should not be considered in a make or buy decision?
A. Potential use of manufacturing capacity
B. Variable costs of production
C. Potential rental income from space occupied by production area
D. Unchanged fixed cost

11. A company uses several types of materials to manufacture its products. The result of combining these materials in proportions different from standard proportion is the:
A. Material price variance
B. Material usage variance
C. Material mix variance
D. Material yield variance

12. The cost per unit of a product manufactured in a factory amounts to ₹ 160 (75% variable) when production is 10,000 units. When production increases by 25%, the cost of production per unit will be:
A. ₹ 145/- B. ₹ 152/-
C. ₹ 150/- D. ₹ 140/-

13. A manufacturer used 400 units of a component every month and he buys them entirely from an outside supplier @ ₹40 per unit. The order placing and receiving cost is ₹100/- and storage costs and carrying costs is 15% of the value of stock. EOQ will be:
A. 300 units B. 400 units
C. 450 units D. 500 units

14. A company has margin of safety of ₹ 40 lakhs and earns an annual profit of ₹ 10 lakhs. If the fixed costs amount to ₹ 20 lakhs, annual sales will be:
A. ₹ 160 lakhs B. ₹ 140 lakhs
C. ₹ 120 lakhs D. ₹ 200 lakhs

15. The current ratio of a company is 2:1 while quick ratio is 1.80. If the current liabilities are ₹40,000/- the value of stock will be:
A. ₹ 6,400/- B. ₹ 8,000/-
C. ₹ 10,000/- D. ₹ 12,000/-

16. Prime cost is:
A. All costs incurred in manufacturing a product
B. Total of direct costs
C. Material cost of product
D. Cost of operating a department

17. The salary a student foregoes while in a college is an example of:
A. Opportunity cost B. Direct cost
C. Sunk cost D. Variable cost

18. Costs are accumulated by responsibility centre for control purposes when using

	Job order costing	Process costing
A.	Yes	Yes
B.	Yes	No
C.	No	No
D.	No	Yes

19. Companies characterized by the production of heterogeneous products will most likely use which of the following methods for the purpose of averaging costs and providing management with unit cost data.
A. Process costing B. Job order costing
C. Direct costing D. Absorption costing

20. Many companies recognize three major categories of costs of manufacturing a product. These are direct materials, direct labour and overhead. Which of the following is an overhead cost in the production of an automobile?
A. Cost of small tools used in mounting tyres on each automobile
B. Cost of tyres on each automobile
C. Cost of labourers who place tyres on each automobile
D. Delivery cost for the tyres on each automobile

21. During a month, a company experienced scrap, normal spoilage and abnormal spoilage units manufacturing process. The cost of units produced includes
A. Scrap, but not spoilage

B. Normal spoilage, but neither scrap nor abnormal spoilage
C. Scrap and normal spoilage, but not abnormal spoilage
D. Scrap, normal spoilage and abnormal spoilage

22. In the computation of manufacturing cost per equivalent unit, the weighted average method of process costing considers:
A. Current costs only
B. Current costs plus cost of beginning work-in-process inventory
C. Current costs plus cost of ending work-in-process inventory
D. Current costs minus cost of beginning work-in-process inventory

23. Which of the following is/are often subject to further processing in order to be saleable?

	By-products	Scrap
A.	No	No
B.	No	Yes
C.	Yes	Yes
D.	Yes	No

24. One of the purposes of standard cost is to:
A. Simplify costing procedures and expedite costs reports
B. Replace budgets and budgeting
C. Serve as a basis for product costing for external reporting purposes
D. Eliminate accounting for under or over applied factory overhead at the end of the period

25. Production of a special order will increase gross profit when the additional revenue from the special order is greater than:
A. Direct material and labour costs in producing the order
B. Fixed costs incurred in producing the order
C. Indirect costs of producing the order
D. Marginal costs of producing the order

26. A company has fixed manufacturing overhead costs totalled ₹1,00,000 and variable selling costs ₹80,000. Under variable costing, how should these costs be classified?

	Period Costs	Product Costs
A.	₹ Nil	₹ 1,80,000/-
B.	₹ 80,000/-	₹ 1,00,000/-
C.	₹ 1,00,000/-	₹ 80,000/-
D.	₹ 1,80,000/-	₹ Nil

27. The scarce factor of production is known as:
A. Key factor B. Limiting factor
C. Critical factor D. All of the above

28. If a company follows a practice of isolating variances at the earliest point in time, what would be the appropriate time to isolate and calculate a material price variance?
A. When material is issued
B. When material is purchased
C. When material is used in production
D. When purchase order is originated

29. Relevant costs are:
A. Future costs B. Standard costs
C. Controllable costs D. Historical costs

30. What costs are treated as product costs under variable costing?
A. Only direct costs
B. Only variable production costs
C. All variable costs
D. All variable and fixed manufacturing costs

31. Which of the following describes a linear relationship?
A. $\hat{y} = b_0 + b_1x + b_2x^2$
B. $\hat{y} = b_0 + b_1x$
C. $\hat{y} = b_0 + b_1x^2$
D. None of the above

32. If a curve is more peaked than the normal curve, it is called:
A. Mesokurtic B. Leptokurtic
C. Platykurtic D. Asymmetric

33. In which of the following case would Poisson distribution be a good approximation of the binomial distribution?
A. $n = 40, p = 0.32$ B. $n = 40, q = 0.79$
C. $n = 200, p = 0.02$ D. $n = 10, p = 0.03$

34. Let the probability of event A be 0.2 and the probability of event B be 0.5. Also suppose that the two events are independent. Then P(A/B) will be:

A. 0.2 B. 0.5
C. 0.4 D. 0.1

35. Which of the following components will not be present in a time series of annual data?
A. Secular trend
B. Cyclical fluctuations
C. Seasonal variations
D. All of the above

36. Which of the following is a parameter?
A. Sample mean
B. Sample standard deviation
C. Population mean
D. None of the above

37. In decision theory, events beyond the control of the decision maker are called:
A. Opportunity cost B. Marginal events
C. Expected value D. States of nature

38. A medical treatment has a success rate of 0.8. Two patients will be treated with this treatment. Assuming the results are independent for the two patients, what is the probability that neither one of them will be successfully cured?
A. 0.49 B. 0.09
C. 0.04 D. 0.6

39. Which of the following is *not* a measure of central tendency?
A. Geometric mean B. Standard deviation
C. Median D. Mode

40. Suppose data are normally distributed with a mean of 120 and a standard deviation of 30. Between what two values will approximately 68% of the data fall?
A. 90 and 150 B. 60 and 180
C. 30 and 210 D. 105 and 135

41. Suppose, for a particular estimating line with one independent variable, the value of intercept is 8 and the value of slope is 2. If the independent variable has a value of 6, what value should be expected for the dependent variable?
A. 50 B. 12
C. –4 D. 20

42. The middle value of an ordered array of numbers is the:
A. Mean B. Median
C. Mode D. Kurtosis

43. The ratio of the standard deviation of a distribution to the mean of that distribution is referred to as:
A. Probability distribution
B. Expected return
C. Standard error
D. Coefficient of variation

44. Which of the following situations could ***not*** be described by a binomial distribution?
A. The number of defective parts produced by an assembly process
B. The amount of water used daily by a single household
C. The number of people in a class who can answer this question correctly
D. The number of customers who like a restaurant

45. Which probability approach would be used to determine the probability of India winning the next cricket match with England?
A. Classical approach
B. Subjective approach
C. Relative frequency approach
D. Judgemental approach

46. Given the following set of data, what is the range? [12, 23, 34, 54, 21, 8, 9, 67]
A. 59 B. 55
C. 8 D. 56

47. Two cards are drawn from a well-shuffled pack of 52 cards. Find the probaility that they are both aces if the first is replaced.
A. $\frac{1}{169}$ B. $\frac{2}{52}$
C. $\frac{1}{221}$ D. None of these

48. Two dice are thrown and the side of both dice facing up is observed. Which of the following events are *mutually exclusive events*?
A. 1. Both dice are the same number
2. Both dice are even number
B. 1. The sum of both dice is even
2. The product of both dice is odd

C. 1. One of the dice shows a two
2. The sum is greater than 8

D. 1. The product of both dice is even
2. The sum of both dice is odd

49. Which of the following is ***not*** a property of the coefficient of correlation?
A. The coefficient of correlation lies between −1 and +1
B. The coefficient of correlation is the geometric mean of two regression coefficients.
C. The coefficient of correlation gives the direction of relationship between variables
D. The coefficient of correlation depends on the change of scale

50. Which of the following values could not represent a correlation coefficient?
A. $r = 0.99$ B. $r = 1.09$
C. $r = 0.73$ D. $r = -1.0$

51. Which of the following is not correct?
A. A non-binding constraint is a redundant constraint.
B. An infeasible solution exists, when there is no feasible solution.
C. Feasible region of an LPP must be a convex set.
D. A possible solution on the graph corresponds to every point (x,y)

52. If dual has an unbounded solution, primal has:
A. An unbounded solution
B. An infeasible solution
C. A feasible solution
D. None of the above

53. Shadow prices are:
A. Imputed value of the resources
B. Prices of non-binding constraints
C. Marginal profitablility of the products
D. None of these

54. For $A = \begin{pmatrix} 1 & 1 \\ 0 & 0 \end{pmatrix}$, and $B = \begin{pmatrix} 1 & 0 \\ 0 & 0 \end{pmatrix}$

A. AB = BA B. AB = BA = 0
C. AB ≠ BA D. None of these

55. Multiple solutions to an LPP exists when:
A. Feasible region is a convex set
B. Iso-cost line coincides with a constraint line
C. There are more number of constraints
D. Two constraints have same slope

56. The solution to a transportation problem with m-sources and n-destinations is feasible, if the number of allocations are:
A. $m + n - 1$ B. $m + n + 1$
C. $m + n$ D. $m \times n$

57. Degeneracy in transportation problem means that:
A. Total supply equal total demand
B. The solution so obtained is not feasible
C. A few allocations become negative
D. There is no solution to the problem

58. If there are n workers and n jobs, there would be:
A. n solutions B. $n!$ solutions
C. $(n-1)!$ solutions D. $(n)^n$ solutions

59. Total cost function

$$TC(x) = \begin{cases} 3x, \text{ if } 0 \le x \le 100 \\ 100 + 2x, \text{ if } 100 < x \le 500 \\ 500 + x, \text{ if } x > 500 \end{cases}$$ is continuous at

A. 0 B. 500
C. 100 D. None of these

60. For the demand curve $p = ae^{-kx}$ where p is the price and x is the quantity demanded, the elasticity of demand is:
A. kx B. k
C. $\frac{1}{k}$ D. $\frac{1}{kx}$

61. The function $x^3 + 3x^2y - xy^2 - y^3$ is a homogeneous function of degree:
A. 2 and has constant returns to scale
B. 2 and has increasing returns to scale
C. 3 and has increasing returns to scale
D. 3 and has decreasing returns to scale

62. If x is the number of units produced, and the total cost of production is given by

$$TC = \frac{1}{3}x^3 - x^2 + 5x + 3, \text{ at } x = \frac{3}{2}$$

A. Total cost is minimum
B. Average cost is minimum
C. Average variable cost is minimum
D. None of these

63. The total cost function of a product is given by:
$C(x) = x^3 - 315x^2 + 27{,}000x + 20{,}000$;
Where x is the number of units produced. Determined the number of units that should be produced to minimize the total cost.
A. 350 B. 150
C. 450 D. 250

64. For a production function
$Z = f(x, y)$
If $A = f_{xx}(a, b)$, $B = f_{xy}(a, b)$, $C = f_{yy}(a, b)$ and a, b are the critical points. The function has saddle point when:
A. $AC - B^2 > 0$
B. $AC - B^2 < 0$
C. $AC - B^2 = 0$
D. $AC - B^2 > 0$ and $A < 0$

65. Two products are competitive in relationship when:
A. e_{11} and e_{22} are negative, and e_{12} and e_{21} positive
B. e_{11} and e_{22} are negative, and e_{12} and e_{21} negative
C. e_{11} and e_{22} are positive, and e_{12} and e_{21} positive
D. e_{11} and e_{12} are negative, and e_{22} and e_{21} positive

66. The expression $S = Pe^{rt}$ is the compounded value when:
A. Compounding is semi-annual
B. Compounding is quarterly
C. Compounding is monthly
D. Compounding is continuous

67. For the expression $d_e = 1 - e^{-d}$, force of discount is:
A. d_e B. e^{-d}
C. d D. $-d$

68. Perpetuity is:
A. Principal P earns fixed interest forever
B. Annuity of size P continues forever
C. Principal of size P earns interest at different rates
D. None of these

69. A Money-lender charges 'interest' at the rate of 5 rupees per 100 rupees per quarter, payable in advance. What effective rate of interest does he charge per annum?
A. 22.7% B. 20.7%
C. 18.7% D. 21.7%

70. The possibility of entering a non-basic variable into the basis arises when:
A. $C_j - Z_j > 0$ B. $C_j - Z_j < 0$
C. $C_j - Z_j = 0$ D. None of these

71. What do you mean by commerce?
A. Industry
B. Selling and buying of goods
C. Business
D. Selling and buying of goods and all activities that facilitate trade

72. Identify the extractive industry out of the following:
A. Hunting B. Flour mills
C. Cattle breeding D. Forest cultivation

73. Which of the following factors is the most important determinant of the form of business organization?
A. Type of business
B. Expected volume of business
C. Area of operations
D. Financial requirements

74. How many partners can a firm carrying on banking business have at the most?
A. 7 B. 10
C. 20 D. 50

75. Leadership is a function of all following except:
A. Work group B. Product or service
C. Leader D. Situation

76. In e-commerce what is C2B situation:
A. Consumer to buyer
B. Buyer to consumer
C. Consumer to business
D. Customer to buyer

77. Planning and policy making are essentially functions of:
A. Top management
B. Middle management
C. Lower management
D. Entire staff

78. The voting rights of members in a cooperative organization are:
A. In proportion to the capital held
B. Equal, irrespective of capital contribution
C. Dependent on their popularity among the members
D. Proportionate to the capital held and loans given by members

79. Consider the following basic steps involved in the process of control:
1. Identifying the strategic control points
2. Establishing the standards
3. Measuring performance against standards
4. Correcting deviations from the standards

The correct sequence of the above steps in the process of control is:
A. 1, 4, 3, 2 B. 4, 3, 2, 1
C. 2, 1, 4, 3 D. 2, 3, 1, 4

80. Match List-I with List-II and select the correct answer using the codes given below the lists.

List-I	List-II
(*a*) Forecasting	1. Controlling
(*b*) Communication	2. Planning
(*c*) Selection of managers	3. Leading
(*d*) Establishing performance standards	4. Staffing

Codes:

	(*a*)	(*b*)	(*c*)	(*d*)
A.	2	3	4	1
B.	1	2	4	3
C.	2	4	3	1
D.	1	3	4	2

81. Indian Contract Act was enacted in the year:
A. 1832 B. 1852
C. 1872 D. None of the above

82. Which of the following statements is correct?
A. A contract without consideration is void
B. A contract without consideration is voidable
C. A contract without consideration is illegal
D. A contract without consideration has no value in the eyes of law

83. In a contract by post, acceptance is:
A. Required
B. Not required
C. Acceptance should be only in writing
D. None of the above

84. Which of the following statements is correct?
A. Minor's agreements are valid
B. Minor's agreements are illegal
C. Minor's agreements are absolutely void
D. Minor's agreements are voidable

85. In the Limited Liability Partnership (LLP):
A. Partnership Act, 1932 applies
B. Only selective provisions of Partnership Act, 1932 apply
C. Partnership Act, 1932 does not apply
D. None of the above

86. Producer Company can be formed by:
A. Only partnership firms
B. Only institutional members
C. Only individuals
D. By both individuals and institutional members

87. Dividend is paid with:
A. 42 days B. 40 days
C. 30 days D. 20 days

88. Company is to file secretarial compliance report if it has capital above:
A. 2 lakhs B. 7 lakhs
C. 10 lakhs D. 5 crore

89. Director's identification number is mandatory for:
A. All directors
B. Only executive directors

C. External directors
D. Independent directors

90. Buy back of shares was introduced in the year:
A. 1985 B. 1988
C. 1999 D. 2000

91. Quorum of general meeting for public company is:
A. 100 or 1/3rd whichever is lower
B. 100 or 1/3rd whichever is higher
C. 5 members
D. None of these

92. AGM may be held:
A. Anywhere in the country
B. Outside the country
C. Only in the city, town where the registered office is situated
D. None of these

93. A shareholder can
A. Chair a board meeting
B. Chair a shareholder meeting
C. Cannot chair a shareholder meeting
D. None of these

94. Proxy must be received at the registered office within:
A. 24 hours
B. 48 hours
C. 72 hours
D. None of these

95. For a board meeting:
A. Notice is a must
B. 7 days notice is a must
C. 14 days notice is a must
D. None of these

96. Minutes may be recorded in:
A. Loose leaves
B. In a register signed by the chairman
C. In a soft copy
D. None of these

97. Online filing in the case of companies is:
A. Optional
B. Mandatory
C. Required only in the case of special business
D. Required only in the case of business requiring special notice

98. Manager and managing director:
A. May be appointed simultaneously
B. May not be appointed simultaneously
C. May be apppointed simultaneously after court's approval
D. None of the above

99. Sarbanes-Oxley (SOX) Act, 2002 was enacted in:
A. USA B. UK
C. France D. Germany

100. Audit committee is a committee of:
A. Internal auditors
B. External auditors
C. Mix of auditors and directors
D. Directors

101. Which of the following statements regarding residential status of a company is not true?
A. An Indian company is always resident in India
B. An Indian company is resident in India if the control and management of its affairs is situated wholly or partly in India during the previous year
C. A foreign company is resident in India if the control and management of its affairs is situated wholly in India during the previous year
D. A foreign company is non-resident in India if the control and management of its affairs is situated wholly or partly out of India during the previous year

102. A person has two house properties. Both are self-occupied. The annual value of:
A. Both houses shall be nil
B. One house shall be nil
C. None of the houses shall be nil
D. None of the above

103. The rate of MAT (Minimum Alternate Tax) for the financial year 2012-13 is:
A. 15% B. 16.5%
C. 17% D. 18.5%

104. Fair and equitable distribution of tax burden among taxpayers is referred to as:
A. Tax efficiency B. Tax equity
C. Tax buoyancy D. Tax elasticity

105. Which of the following is allowed as a deduction from the gross total income of the assesse under the Income Tax Act?
A. Life Insurance Premium
B. Contribution to Provident Fund
C. Medical Insurance Premium
D. All of the above

106. Mr. A has a substantial interest in XYZ Ltd. Mrs. A, his wife is employed by XYZ Ltd. without any technical or professional qualification to justify the remuneration. In this case, the salary income of Mrs. A will be taxable in the hands of:
A. Mr. A
B. Mrs. A
C. Both Mr. A and Mrs. A
D. XYZ Ltd.

107. What is the exemption limit for women for personal income tax for the financial year 2012-13?
A. ₹ 1,60,000/- B. ₹ 1,90,000/-
C. ₹ 2,00,000/- D. ₹ 2,40,000/-

108. Which of the following statements is true for a regressive tax structure?
A. It increases the absolute gap but reduces the relative gap between two taxpayers
B. It reduces the absolute gap but increase the relative gap between two taxpayers
C. In increase the absolute gap but does not change the relative gap between two taxpayers
D. It does not change the absolute gap but increase the relative gap between two taxpayers

109. Which of the following transactions would not be regarded as transfer of capital asset under Sec. 2(47) of the Income Tax Act, 1961?
A. Relinquishment of the asset
B. Transfer under a gift
C. Compulsory acquisition of the asset under any law
D. Conversion of capital assets into stock-in-trade

110. Insurance commission is taxable under the head:
A. Salaries
B. Profits and gains of business or profession
C. Capital gains
D. Income from other sources

111. What is the common name for Aurora Australialis?
A. Northern lights B. Southern lights
C. Rainbow D. Meteor

112. What is a beavers home called?
A. A lodge B. Dam
C. Sty D. Pen

113. What is the larynx used for in the human body?
A. Smell B. Speech
C. Hearing D. Locomotion

114. Whose palace is located at Mcleodganj?
A. Dalai Lama
B. Raja Ravi Varma
C. Vasundhara Raje
D. Yudhvir Singh Parmar

115. Where is the European Parliament located?
A. Brussels B. Paris
C. Hague D. Vienna

116. Yanam, which belongs to Union Territory of Puducherry, is situated in:
A. Tamil Nadu B. Karnataka
C. Andhra Pradesh D. Goa

117. To which country does the Port of Aden belong:
A. Yemen B. Saudi Arabia
C. UK D. France

118. Which is the "City of Seven Hills"?
A. Rome B. Udaipur
C. Geneva D. Shimla

119. Which is the "City of Dreaming Spires"?
A. Salzburg B. Bonn
C. Brussels D. Oxford

120. Which is the "City of Palaces"?
A. Kolkata B. Jaipur
C. Milan D. Florence

121. Which is the "City of Golden Gate"?
A. San Francisco B. Columbia
C. Benaras D. Belur

122. Which is the 'City of Magnificent Buildings'?
A. Paris B. Hamburg
C. Washington D.C. D. Vienna

123. Which is the "Cockpit of Europe"?
A. Belgium B. Germany
C. Amsterdam D. Berlin

124. Which is the "Land of Midnight Sun"?
A. Finland B. Sweden
C. Denmark D. Norway

125. Land of Thousand Elephants is:
A. Thailand B. India
C. Laos D. Kampuchea

126. The name of Kunjarani Devi is associated with:
A. Weight lifting B. Target shooting
C. Athletics D. Swimming

127. 'Dronacharya Award' is given to:
A. Sportsmen B. Coaches
C. Umpires D. Sports editors

128. SEBI (Securities and Exchange Board of India) was initially constituted on:
A. April 12, 1988 B. March 25, 1991
C. April 1, 1993 D. March 12, 1990

129. Which Indian State has the minimum population density?
A. Arunachal Pradesh B. Mizoram
C. Sikkim D. J&K

130. Which is the smallest Indian State in terms of population?
A. Goa B. Nagaland
C. Mizoram D. Sikkim

131. Which Indian State has the maximum literacy rate?
A. Maharashtra B. Mizoram
C. Kerala D. Goa

132. Which Indian State has the maximum female literacy rate?
A. Meghalaya B. Mizoram
C. Kerala D. Delhi

133. Which Indian State has the maximum percentage of urban population?
A. Tamil Nadu B. Maharashtra
C. Goa D. Gujarat

134. Which Indian State has the maximum percentage of tribal population?
A. Mizoram B. Meghalaya
C. Manipur D. Nagaland

135. When did Swami Vivekanand Address the World Parliament of Religions at Chicago?
A. 1901 B. 1893
C. 1922 D. 1897

136. Who is the author of 'Ignited Minds: The Power of Youth'?
A. S. Radhakrishnan B. Rajendra Prasad
C. A.P.J. Abdul Kalam D. Jawahar Lal Nehru

137. Who was the physicist who received Bharat Ratna in 1954?
A. Homi Bhabha
B. Hargobind Khurana
C. Vikram Sarabhai
D. C.V. Raman

138. In which year was A.P.J. Abdul Kalam awarded Bharat Ratna?
A. 1996 B. 1997
C. 2000 D. 2002

139. The team of Indian scientists reached the South Pole in a record time of:
A. Seven Days B. Ten Days
C. Six Days D. Eight Days

140. The Sri Krishna Report was about:
A. Telangana separatist movement
B. Mumbai attack
C. Post Godhra riots
D. Ram Janma Bhoomi

141. In the Union Budget 2012, the exemption limit for personal income tax was raised by:
A. ₹ 30,000/- B. ₹ 10,000/-
C. ₹ 20,000/- D. ₹ 25,000/-

142. In the Union Budget 2012, the qualifying age for senior citizens is:
A. 62 years B. 60 years
C. 65 years D. None of the above

143. In the Union Budget 2012, the surcharge on domestic companies was reduced from:
A. 8 to 6 per cent B. 7.5 to 5 per cent
C. 7 to 5 per cent D. 5 to 3 per cent

144. In the Union Budget 2012 the peak rate of customs duty was maintained at:
A. 8 per cent B. 15 per cent
C. 10 per cent D. 12 per cent

145. In 2011-2012, the disinvestment was seen at:
A. 400 billion rupees B. 450 billion rupees
C. 420 billion rupees D. 410 billion rupees

146. Development expenditure of the Central government does not include:
A. Defence expenditure
B. Expenditure on economic services
C. Expenditure on social and community services
D. Grant to states

147. Gilt-edged market means:
A. Bullion market
B. Market of Government securities
C. Market of weapons
D. Market of imported metals

148. Which of the following are not associated with United Nations?
A. ILO B. WHO
C. FAO D. ASEAN

149. Which of the following is not a chief organ of the United Nations Organizations?
A. ILO
B. Security Council
C. International Court of Justice
D. General Assembly

150. Permanent Secretariat to coordinate the implementation of SAARC programme is located at:
A. Dhaka B. New Delhi
C. Colombo D. Kathmandu

151. When an individual's income rise, that person's demand for a normal good:
A. Rises B. Falls
C. Remains the same D. Any of the above

152. If the quantity of a commodity demanded remains unchanged as its price changes, the coefficient of price elasticity of demand is:
A. Greater than 1 B. Equal to 1
C. Smaller than 1 D. Zero

153. A fall in the price of a commodity who's demand curve is a rectangular hyperbola cause total expenditures on the commodity to:
A. Rises B. Falls
C. Remains the same D. Any of the above

154. When total utility increases marginal utility is:
A. Negative & increasing
B. Negative & decreasing
C. Zero
D. Positive & decreasing

155. The Engel curve for a Giffen good is:
A. Negatively sloped B. Positively sloped
C. Vertical D. Horizontal

156. The substitution effect for a fall in the price of a commodity is given by:
A. Movement up a given indifference curve
B. A movement from a higher to a lower indifference curve
C. A movement down a given indifference curve
D. None of the above

157. When returns to a factor are diminishing, the returns to scale are:
A. Constant B. Decreasing
C. Increasing D. Any of the above

158. When the marginal productivity of land is negative it is in:
A. Stage one for land B. Stage 3 for labour
C. Stage 2 for land D. None of the above

159. At the point of producer equilibrium:
A. Isoquant is tangent to isocost
B. The $MRTS_{lk}$ equals pl/pk
C. $MP_l/P_l = MP_k/P_k$
D. All of the above

160. If there are constant returns to scale and if the quantity of labour used per unit of time is increased by 10% but the amount of capital remains constant then output will:
A. Increase by 10%
B. Decrease by 10%
C. Increase by more than 10%
D. Increase by less than 10%

161. When the law of diminishing returns begins to operate, the TVC curve begins to:
A. Fall at an increasing rate
B. Rise at a decreasing rate
C. Fall at a decreasing rate
D. Rise at an increasing rate

162. Marginal cost is given by:
A. Slope of the TFC curve
B. Slope of the TVC curve but not by the slope of the TC curve
C. Slope of the TC curve but not by the slope of the TVC curve
D. Either the slope of TVC curve or the slope of the TC curve

163. The LAC curve falls as output expands, this is due to:
A. Economies of scale
B. The law of diminishing returns
C. Diseconomies of scale
D. Any of the above

164. Given the supply of a commodity in the market period, the price of the commodity is determined by:
A. The market demand curve alone
B. The market supply curve alone
C. The market demand curve and market supply curve
D. None of the above

165. The optimum level of output for a perfectly competitive firm is given by the point where:
A. MR = AC
B. MR = MC
C. MR exceeds MC by the greatest amount
D. MR = MC and MC is rising

166. In the short run the monopolist:
A. Breaks even B. Incurs a loss
C. Makes a profit D. Any of the above

167. In the long run equilibrium, the pure monopolist can make pure profits because of:
A. Blocked entry B. High selling prices
C. The low LAC D. Advertising

168. If input A is the only variable input for a perfectly competitive firm in the product market, the firms demand curve for input A is given by its:
A. VMP curve B. MP curve
C. MRC curve D. None of the above

169. When VMP is greater than MRP and MRP is greater than P:
A. We have a monopolistic exploitation
B. Monopsonistic exploitation
C. Both A and B exploitation
D. None of the above

170. In an economy of two commodities X and Y and two factors L and K. General equilibrium in off production is reached when:
A. MRTSlk = PL/Pk
B. MRTSlk = MRSxy
C. MRTxy = MRSxy
D. (MRTSlk)x = (MRTSlk)y

171. If inflation rate is 4% and nominal interest rate is 10% the real interest rate is:
A. 6% B. 5%
C. 7% D. 8%

172. The aps + apc is equal to:
A. 1 B. 2
C. 1.5 D. Cannot say

173. The fisher equation shows the following linkage:
A. Consumption and interest linkage
B. Saving and interest linkage
C. Inflation and interest linkage
D. None of the above

174. Expansionary fiscal policy implies:
A. Increase in aggregate demand
B. Decrease in aggregate demand
C. Increase in savings
D. None of the above

175. The credit multiplier is equal to:
A. l/c B. l/r
C. (l – r)/(c + r) D. l/(c + r)

176. The narrow measure of money that is M_1 is equal to:
A. Currency + demand deposits
B. Currency + savings account
C. Currency + money market mutual funds
D. None of the above

177. Inflation due to increase in the cost of production is known as:

A. Cost push inflation
B. Demand pull inflation
C. Stagflation
D. None of the above

178. Deflation is a situation of:
A. Falling prices B. Rising prices
C. Constant prices D. None of the above

179. Large increase in the price level leads to:
A. Maintain the value of money
B. Lower the purchasing power of money
C. Increases the purchasing power of money
D. None of the above

180. A situation where the economy experiences unemployment along with the high rate of inflation is known as:
A. Deflation B. Disinflation
C. Stagflation D. None of the above

181. Inflation is caused by:
A. Increase in money supply
B. Increase in money supply and fall in production
C. Decrease in money supply and a fall in production
D. Fall in production

182. A liquidity effect occurs when:
A. Reduction in Government spending lowers the rate of interest
B. A money supply increase lowers the rate of interest
C. An increase in Government spending increases the rate of interest
D. A money supply increase raises the rate of interest

183. Which of the following will not result in an increase in the level of income
A. An increase in autonomous spending
B. A decrease in autonomous taxes
C. An increase in autonomous transfers
D. An increase in net tax revenues

184. For controlling inflation the central bank should:
A. Buy the Government security in the open markets
B. Raise the bank rate
C. Raise the CRR
D. Both B and C

185. When there is excess demand in the economy, the price level:
A. Increases B. Decreases
C. Remains constant D. None of the above

186. Credit creation is function of:
A. Central Bank
B. Central Government
C. Monetary Authority
D. Commercial Banks

187. The second phase of banking sector reforms were initiated in India in the year:
A. 1998 B. 1995
C. 1951 D. 1985

188. Fiscal policy refers to the policy relating to:
A. Taxation B. Public expenditure
C. Public debt D. All of the above

189. Economic reforms have failed to:
A. Fully deregularize
B. Fully open the economy to trade
C. Achieve fiscal discipline
D. All of the above

190. Globalisation means .... economic policy on foreign trade and investment:
A. Common B. Liberal
C. Restrictive D. None of the above

191. The payment of an account payable (or any other liability) will:
A. Increase one asset and decrease another asset
B. Decrease an asset and decrease owner's equity
C. Decrease an asset and decrease a liability
D. Increase an asset and increase a liability

192. Which account causes the main difference between a merchandiser's adjusting and closing process and that of a service business?
A. Advertising expenses
B. Interest revenue
C. Inventory
D. Accounts receivable

193. The purpose of an accounting system include all of the following except:
A. Interpret and record the effects of business transactions
B. Classify the effects of transactions to facilitate the preparation of reports
C. Summarize and communicate information to decision makers
D. Dictate the specific types of business transactions that the enterprise may engage in

194. Financial accounting information is characterized by all of the following except.
A. It is historical in nature
B. It sometimes results from inexact and approximate measures
C. It is factual, so it does not require judgement to prepare
D. It is enhanced by management's explanation

195. Which of the following financial statements is generally prepared first?
A. Income statement
B. Balance sheet
C. Statement of retained earnings
D. Statement of cash flows

196. Brand value for a business is:
A. Capital B. Asset
C. Profit D. Liability

197. Joint venture account is a:
A. Nominal account
B. Real account
C. Artificial personal account
D. Representative personal account

198. Goods purchased from Mr. Ajay for ₹10,000/- passed through the sales book. The rectification will result in:
A. Increase in gross profit
B. Decrease in gross profit
C. No effect on gross profit
D. Either A or B

199. Indian companies are required to maintain their accounts on:
A. Cash basis
B. Accrual basis
C. Accrual basis and double entry system
D. Double entry system

200. Dividend by a company can be paid from:
A. Profit of the current year
B. Undistributed profits of the previous year
C. Money provided by Central Government or any State Government for the payment of dividend
D. All of the above

ANSWERS

1	2	3	4	5	6	7	8	9	10
D	C	C	C	C	B	B	A	B	D
11	12	13	14	15	16	17	18	19	20
C	B	B	C	B	B	A	A	B	A
21	22	23	24	25	26	27	28	29	30
C	B	D	A	A	B	D	B	A	B
31	32	33	34	35	36	37	38	39	40
B	B	C	A	D	A	D	C	B	A
41	42	43	44	45	46	47	48	49	50
D	B	D	D	C	A	A	C	D	B
51	52	53	54	55	56	57	58	59	60
A	B	A	C	B	A	B	B	C	D

61	62	63	64	65	66	67	68	69	70
C	D	B	B	C	D	A	B	A	A
71	72	73	74	75	76	77	78	79	80
D	A	D	B	B	C	A	B	D	A
81	82	83	84	85	86	87	88	89	90
C	A	C	C	C	D	C	C	A	C
91	92	93	94	95	96	97	98	99	100
C	C	B	B	B	B	C	B	A	D
101	102	103	104	105	106	107	108	109	110
B	B	D	B	D	B	B	C	B	D
111	112	113	114	115	116	117	118	119	120
B	A	B	A	A	C	A	A	D	A
121	122	123	124	125	126	127	128	129	130
A	C	A	D	C	A	B	A	A	D
131	132	133	134	135	136	137	138	139	140
C	C	C	A	B	C	D	B	D	A
141	142	143	144	145	146	147	148	149	150
C	B	B	C	A	A	B	D	A	D
151	152	153	154	155	156	157	158	159	160
A	D	C	D	A	C	B	A	D	A
161	162	163	164	165	166	167	168	169	170
D	D	A	A	D	D	C	A	B	C
171	172	173	174	175	176	177	178	179	180
A	A	C	A	A	A	A	A	B	C
181	182	183	184	185	186	187	188	189	190
B	B	B	D	A	D	A	D	D	B
191	192	193	194	195	196	197	198	199	200
C	C	D	C	A	B	A	B	C	D

SOME SELECTED EXPLANATORY ANSWERS

11. Material Mix variance has been defined as– That portion of the direct material usage which is due to difference between the standard and actual composition of a mixture. In other words, where two or more than two materials are used in the manufacture of a product, the difference between the standard composition and the central compostion of material mix is the material mix variance. The mix variance situation arises in industries like textile, rubber, chemical etc, were different materials in standard ratios or quantities are mixed to produce a product.

13. $\text{EOQ} = \sqrt{\dfrac{2 \times \text{Annual demand} \times \text{ordering cost}}{\text{Storage cost}}}$

$= \dfrac{2 \times 400 \times 12 \times 100}{15\% \text{ of } 40}$

$= \sqrt{\dfrac{9,60,000}{6}} = 400 \text{ units}$

14. Current ratio being 2 : 1

and current liabilities (CL) being ₹ 40,000

Current Assets = 2 × 40,000

= ₹ 80,000

$$\text{Now, Quick ratio} = \frac{(\text{Current Assets} - \text{Stock})}{\text{CL}}$$

$$1.80 = \frac{80{,}000\text{–Stock}}{40{,}000}$$

$$\text{Stock} = ₹\ 8{,}000$$

16. Prime cost is the total of direct materials, direct labour and direct expenses. These are all costs or expenses incurred directly to produce product or service. Prime cost excludes overhead expenses. The formula to compute prime cost is below:

Prime cost = Direct Materials Cost
+
Direct Labour Cost
+
Direct Expenses.

17. The value of benefits foregone, when one decision alternative is selected over another, are opportunity costs.

18. A responsibility center is any point within an organisation where control exists over cost incurrence, revenue generation, and/or the use of investment funds.

A responsibility center can be an operation, a department, a division or even an individual. The key point to not for this question is that no matter what product costing method is used, the responsibility center is always used for control purposes. In job order costing, costs are accumulated by responsibility centre and then assigned to specific jobs or orders through the use of a job cost sheet. Even though the job cost sheet will usually reflect the efforts of a number of responsibility centres, it will not be used for control purposes. Any needed cost control will be handled on the responsibility center level. In process costing, costs are accumulated by the responsibility center and recorded on a production cost report that will be used to develop a product's cost. Since the production cost report shows the efforts of only one responsibility center, it is used for both product costing and control purposes. Thus, for control purposes, costs are accumulated by responsibility center for both job order and process costing.

19. Job order costing or job costing is a system for assigning manufacutring costs to an individual product or batches of products. Generally, the job order costing system is used only when the products manufactured are sufficiently different from each other. When products are identical or nearly identical, the process costing system will likely be used.

20. The Cost of small tools used in mounting tyres cannot be identified solely with the manufacture of a specific automobile. This cost should be treated as factory overhead because. It is identifiable with the production process.

24. A Standard cost system differentiates the standard cost from the actual cost, thus identifying deviations from expected (attainable) results on a routine basis.

26. Product costs are those costs which are identified with the product and included in inventory values. In other words the costs, that are included in the cost of manufacturing a product are called product cost. In a manufacturing concern, it is composed of four elements:

(*i*) direct materials
(*ii*) direct labour
(*iii*) direct expenses
(*iv*) manufacturing overhead.

Period costs are the costs which are not identified with product or job and are dedicated as expenses during the period in which they are incurred. There costs are necessary to generate revenues but they cannot be directly associated with units of product. Selling and administrative expenses are period costs.

30. Under Variable costing, only those manufacturing costs that vary with output are treated as product costs. This includes direct materials, variable overhead, and direct labour.

32. If a curve is peaked like a normal curve it is called Mesokurtic. If the curve of a distribution is more peaked than normal curve, it is called Leptokurtic and if it has flat top than normal curve, it is called Platykurtic.

33. The Poisson distribution is a good approximation of the binomial distribution when $n \geq 20$ and $p \leq 0.05$ and an excellent approximation when $n \geq 100$ and $np \leq 10$.

34. If A and B are independent so that the probability of occurrence or non-occurrence of A is not affected by the occurence or non-occurrence of B, we have

P(A/B) = P(A) and P(B/A) = P(B)

36. The statistical constants of the population like mean variance, skewness, kurtosis, moments, correlation coefficient etc, are known as parameters.

37. State of nature : A possible future condition (consequence or event) resulting from the choice of a decision alternative depends upon certain factors beyond the control of the decision maker. These factors are called states of nature (future). For example, if the decision is to carry an umbrella or not, the consequence (get wet or do not) depends on what action nature takes.

The states of nature are mutually exclusive and collectively exhaustive with respect to any decision problem.

39. Measures of central tendency are numbers that tend to cluster around the middle of a set of values. Three such middle numbers are the mean, the median, and the mode.

40. 68% of the data fall within 1 standard deviation of the mean. Therefore, 68% of the data will fall between 120 – 30 and 120 + 30, or betwen 90 and 150.

41. Predicted Value of y (Dependent Variable) = y axis intercept (The constant) + Predicted increased y for 1 increase in x (The slope or coefficient) × Multiply value of x (Independent variable)

42. The median is the middle value in an ordered array of numbers. For an array with an odd number of terms, the median is the middle number. For an array with an even number of terms, the median is the average of the two middle numbers.

46. Range = Largest Value – Smallest Value

∴ Range of the Given data

$$= 67 - 8$$
$$= 59$$

48. Two events are mutually exclusive if they cannot occur at the same time. Another word that means mutually exclusive is disjoint. If two events are disjoint, then the probability of them both occurring at the same time is 0.

49. Correlation coefficient is independent of the change of origin and scale.

50. Correlation coefficient cannot exceed 1 numericelly. In other words, it lies between –1 and +1. Symbolically $-1 \leq r \leq 1$.

52. If the primal is feasible, then the dual is bounded. Also, if the primal is infeasible, the dual is unbounded.

53. Shadow pricing system was very common in the socialist economics, where price mechanism did not exist or if at all it existed, it was for name's sake. It happened to be a state-controlled market, where prices were determined by the planning council rather than by the market forces of demand and supply. Prices so fixed were called shadow or accounting prices. They are also used to find the implicit values in social cost benefit analysis. In business and inclusing it is used to estimate the implicit value of a scarce resource used by a company. Shadow prices are the measurement of implicit or imputed value of a scarce resource. It is also called the intrinsic value.

54. $A = \begin{bmatrix} 1 & 1 \\ 0 & 0 \end{bmatrix}, \; B = \begin{bmatrix} 1 & 0 \\ 0 & 0 \end{bmatrix}$

$$\therefore AB = \begin{bmatrix} 1 & 0 \\ 0 & 0 \end{bmatrix} \begin{bmatrix} 1 & 0 \\ 0 & 0 \end{bmatrix}$$

$$= \begin{bmatrix} 1\times1+1\times0 & 1\times0+1\times0 \\ 0\times1+0\times0 & 0\times0+0\times0 \end{bmatrix} = \begin{bmatrix} 1 & 0 \\ 0 & 0 \end{bmatrix}$$

BA =

$$\begin{bmatrix}1 & 0\\0 & 0\end{bmatrix}\begin{bmatrix}1 & 1\\0 & 0\end{bmatrix}=\begin{bmatrix}1\times1+0\times0 & 1\times1+0\times0\\0\times1+0\times0 & 0\times1+0\times0\end{bmatrix}$$

$$=\begin{bmatrix}1 & 1\\0 & 0\end{bmatrix}$$

$\therefore$ AB $\neq$ BA.

55. Multiple solutions of a linear programming problem are solutions each of which maximize or minimize the objective functions. Under graphical method, the existence of multiple solution is indicated by a situation under which the objective function line coincides with one of the half planes generated by a constraint. In other words, where both the objective function line and one of constraint lines have the same slope.

59. A function $y = f(x)$ is said to be continuous at $x = c$ if

(*i*) $f(c)$ exists, *i.e.*, f is defined at $x = c$

(*ii*) $\lim_{x\to c} f(x)$ exists and is finite.

(*iii*) $\lim_{x\to c} f(x) = f(c)$, *i.e.*, limit of function equals functions value.

60. Differentiating $p = ae^{-kx}$ w.r.t. p we get

$$1=(-ak\,e^{-kx})\frac{dx}{dp}$$

$$\Rightarrow \frac{dx}{dp}=\frac{1}{-ake^{-kx}}$$

$\therefore$ Elasticity of Demand

$$= \frac{p}{x}\cdot\frac{dx}{dp}$$

$$= -\frac{ae^{-kx}}{x}\cdot\frac{1}{-(ake^{-kx})}$$

$$= \frac{1}{kx}.$$

61. Let Z $= x^3 + 3x^2y - xy^2 - y^3 = f(x, y)$, then

$$f(Kx, Ky) = K^3x^3 + 3K^2x^2.Ky - Kx.K^2y^2 - K^3y^3$$

$$= K^3(x^3 + 3x^2y - xy^2 - y^3)$$

$$= K^3 f(x, y)$$

$\therefore$ Z is a homgeneous function of degree 3.

62. Condition for minimum value:

1. First order condition (Necessary condition) $f'(x) = 0$
2. Second order condition (Sufficient condition) $f''(x) > 0$

64. If $f_{xx} f_{yy} - (f_{xy})^2 < 0$ then function has saddle point.

66. If a principal P is invested at an annual interest rate of r compounded continuously, then the amount of investment S after t years in given by $S = Pe^{rt}$

68. Perpetuity is an annuity whose payments are made on a fixed date and continue forever.

72. Industrial activities which deal in finding out wealth from soil, sea and other parts of nature is known as extractive industry.

Mining, Fishing, Hunting, Forestry, Farming are all extractive industry.

74. In partnership, there can be at least two partners and at the most 10 partners in case of a form carrying on a banking business and 20 partners in a firm carrying on other kind of business, but in the Companies Act, There is no restriction on the maximum number of shareholders.

76. Consumer-to-business (C2B) is a business model in which consumers create value and firms consume this value.

78. The main characteristics of co-operative organisation are as follows :

1. Volumtary Association
2. Equal Voting Rights
3. Separate Legal Entity
4. Service Motive
5. Distribution of Surplus
6. Democratic Management
7. Capital

84. An agreement with a minor is not voidable but absolutely void *ab initio*. The Privy

Council while interpreting the provisions of Section 11 of the Indian Contract Act stated in the famous case of Mohori Bibi Vs. Dharmodas Ghose that a contract with a minor is void and not voidable.

86. Producer Company can be formed by

1. Any 10 or more individual producers or
2. Two or more producer institutions or
3. A combination of both 1 and 2

91. The general rule is that at least two directors or one-third of the total number of directors, whichever is higher should be present in order to constitute a quorum of a meeting of the Board and for a General Meeting, at least five members of a company should be personally present in the case of public company (other than a public company which has become such by virtue of section 43A) and atleast two members should be personally present in the case of any other company.

95. The notice for the Board meeting shall be given at least 7 days before the date of the meeting. A shorter notice may be given provided the reasons thereof are recorded in writing by the Board.

96. A company shall not appoint or employ at the same time both a managing director and a manager. Section 197A makes prohibition in appointment or employment of certain different categories of managerial personnel at the same time. The prohibition is applied to both a public company and a private company.

100. The audit committee of the company consitituted by the Board, comprises of two independent part time directors and one Govt. nominee part time director.

101. As per section 6(3), and Indian Company is always resident in India. A foreign company is resident in India only if, during the previous year, control and management of its affairs were situated wholly in India.

116. Yanam is situated on the east coast of the Indian Peninsula bounded on all sides by the East Godavari district of Andhra Pradesh state.

119. Oxford is known as the city of 'dreaming spires' a term coind by poet Matthew Arnold in reference to the harmonious architecture of oxford's university buildings.

128. The Securities Exchange Board of India (SEBI) was established on April 12, 1988 through an administrative order, but it became a statutory and really powerful organisation only in 1992.

141. In the Union Budget 2012-13 the exemption limit for income tax was raised by ₹ 20,000 from ₹ 1,80,000 to ₹ 2 Lakhs.

143. In the Union Budget 2012-13, the surcharge on domestic companies has been reduced to 5% from 7.5%.

147. The Gilt-edged Market is the market for Government and semi-government securities, which carry fixed interest rates and backed by RBI. The securities traded in this market are stable in value and are much sought after by banks and other institutions.

152. Price elasticity of demand is a measure of the relative change in quantity purchased of a good in response to a relative change in its price.

$$\text{Price Elasticity} = \frac{\text{Percentage change in quantity}}{\text{Percentage change in price}}$$

153. The graph of unit elasticity demand is rectangular hyperbola. And when price elasticity of demand is equal to unit ($e_p = 1$), the total expenditure remains the same with the fall or rise in price.

155. Engel Curve for a Giffen good

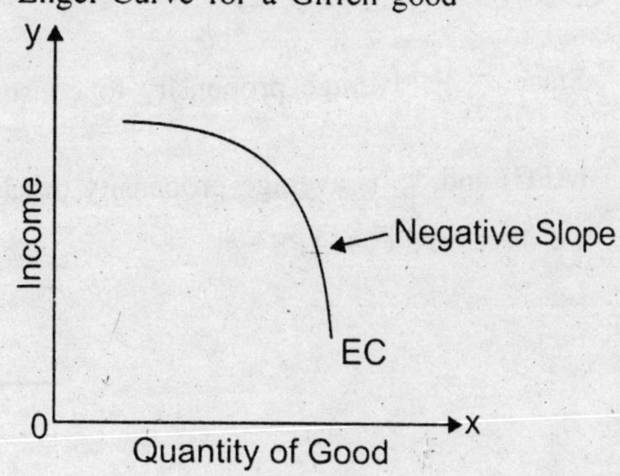

158. During Stage 3, Marginal productivity of factor of production is negative.

162. Graphically, the MC is the slope of the TC curve (which of course is the same at any point as the slope of the TVC). The slope of a curve at any one of its points is the slope of the tangent at that point with an inverse-S-shape of the TC (and TVC) the MC curve will be U-shaped.

164. The market period is very short period in which the supply is fixed, that is, no adjustment can take place in supply conditions. In this period more goods cannot be produced in response to an increase in demand.

165. The optimum level of output for a perfectly competitive firm is given by the point where
1. MR = MC
2. (Slope of MC) > (Slope of MR)
[MC curve must be rising at the point of equilibrium].

166. Monopoly is a market structure in which there is a single seller, there are no close substitutes for the commodity it produces and there are barriers to entry.

169. If firms have monopolisitc power, the factor is paid its MRP which is smaller than the VMP. This effect has been called monopolistic exploitation by Joan Robinson.

172. $y = c + s$

Dividing with sides by disposable income y we have

$$\frac{c}{y} = \frac{s}{y} = \frac{y}{y} \qquad \Rightarrow \frac{c}{y} + \frac{s}{y} = 1$$

Since $\frac{c}{y}$ is average propensity to consume (APC) and $\frac{s}{y}$ is average propensity to save, we have APC + APS = 1

175. Credit multiplier refers to the ratio of increase in total deposits to increase in primary deposits.

$$\text{Credit Multiplier} = \frac{1}{\text{Cash Reserve Ratio}}$$

176. M_1 = Currency with the public + demand deposits of the public

M_1 is also known as narrow money.

180. The stagflation refers to a situation when a high rate of inflation occurs simultaneously with a high rate of unemployment.

186. Credit creation is one of the important functions of a commercial banks. It consititutes the major component of money supply in the economy. Commercial banks differs from other financial institutions in this aspect.

188. Fiscal policy relates to the governmental decision making with respect to
1. taxation
2. government spending
3. government borrowing
4. the management of the goverment debt.

195. The four financial statements are prepared in the following order:
1. Income Statement
2. Statement of changes in shareholder's equity
3. Balance sheet
4. Statement of cash flows

197. A joint venture account is a nominal account prepared by the co-venturers involved in the joint ventures.

199. The companies (Amedment) Act, 1988 has amended section 209 of the Companies Act, 1956, with effect from 15th June, 1988, making it obligatory on all companies to maintain their accounts on accrual basis and according to the double entry system of accounting.

Previous Paper (Solved)

DELHI UNIVERSITY—M.COM ENTRANCE TEST-2011*

1. As per Accounting Standard-14, purchase consideration means the amount payable by the Transferee Co. to the Transferor Co. for :
   A. The shareholders plus liquidation expenses
   B. The shareholders
   C. The shareholders and secured creditors
   D. The shareholders and secured debentures
2. In case of amalgmation in the nature of purchase, the excess of purchase consideration over the net assets is debited to :
   A. Profit and Loss A/c
   B. General Reserve A/c
   C. Goodwill A/c
   D. Amalgamation Adjustment A/c
3. X Ltd. forfeited 200 shares of Rs. 10 each on which Rs. 6 per share were paid. The company reissued 150 shares as fully paid up on a payment of Rs. 4 per share. What amount will be transferred to Capital Reserve A/c?
   A. Rs. 1,200 B. Rs. NIL
   C. Rs. 300 D. Rs. 900
4. Which among the following is *not* a condition for Buy-back of Equity Shares?
   A. Buy-back is authorised by Articles of Association of the Company
   B. A special resolution for buy-back of shares is passed in the general meeting
   C. Only partly paid-up shares can be bought-back
   D. SEBI guidelines relating to buy-back are to be followed
5. If the rate of dividend declared by a company exceeds 20%, then the compulsory transfer of reserves out of the current year profit shall be :
   A. 2.5% of profit after tax
   B. 5% of profit after tax
   C. 7.5% of profit after tax
   D. 10% of profit after tax
6. In the Balance Sheet of a Company, the assets are arranged in the order of their:
   A. Book-value B. Liquidity
   C. Permanence D. Market value
7. Which one of the following will lead to under-statement of profits?
   A. Creation of general reserve
   B. Treating revenue expenditure as capital expenditure
   C. Amortization of fictitious assets
   D. Treating capital expenditure as revenue expenditure
8. Which of the following is *not* a current liability?
   A. Bank Overdraft
   B. Bills Payable
   C. Unclaimed Dividend
   D. Minority Interest
9. What is the 'Prescribed Form of the Balance Sheet' of a Limited Company?
   A. Horizontal form only
   B. Vertical form only
   C. No form is prescribed under the Companies Act
   D. Both A and B
10. Premium on issue of securities can be used for :
   A. Payment of dividend
   B. Payment of interest on debentures
   C. Transfer to Capital Redemption Reserve
   D. Issue of fully paid bonus shares

*Exam held on 01-07-2011.

11. Which of the following methods is used to describe a process for describing an inventory management process that attempts to minimise the money invested in inventory?
A. CFM B. TQM
C. JIT D. ABC

12. Which of the following product cost is both a prime cost and conversion cost?
A. Direct Material
B. Direct Labour
C. Manufacturing overhead
D. All of these

13. Manufacturing costs are known as product costs. Which of the following best describes those costs. Which are considered to be manufacturing costs?
A. Direct Material, Direct Labour and Factory overheads
B. Direct Material and Direct Labour only
C. Direct Labour and Factory overheads
D. Direct Material, Direct Labour Factory overheads and Administrative overheads

14. Opening 'work-in-process' of inventory can be calculated as under:
A. FIFO and Simple Average Price method
B. LIFO and Simple Average Price method
C. LIFO and FIFO methods
D. None of the above

15. Incremental costs are same as :
A. Standard Cost B. Differential Cost
C. Prime Cost D. None of these

16. The distinction between fixed costs and variable costs depends on :
A. Opinion of the Cost Accountant
B. Cost behaviour
C. Policy of the Management
D. The amount of expenditure incurred

17. The most important purpose of standard costing is to :
A. Estimate cost B. Control cost
C. Both A and B D. None of these

18. Which one of the following centres is responsible to earn sales revenue?
A. Cost centre B. Investment centre
C. Revenue centre D. Profit centre

19. An unfavourable material price variance occurs because of :
A. Price increase of raw material
B. Price decrease of raw material
C. Wastage of raw material less than the anticipated normal wastage in the manufacturing process
D. None of the above

20. When sales revenue increases from Rs. 2,00,000 to Rs. 2,60,000 and profit increases by Rs. 36,000, the P/V ratio would be :
A. 40%
B. 60%
C. 50%
D. Cannot be computed

21. If sales are Rs. 15,00,000; fixed cost is Rs. 5,00,000 and P/V ratio is 40%, what would be the profit?
A. Rs. 1,00,000 B. Rs. 2,50,000
C. Rs. 2,00,000 D. Rs. 3,00,000

22. If the direct labour is Rs. 36,000 and fixed overhead is 40% of conversion cost, what would be the amount of fixed overhead?
A. Rs. 14,400 B. Rs. 24,000
C. Rs. 21,600 D. Rs. 60,000

23. If material cost variance is Rs. 5,000, favourable and material price variance is Rs. 3,000 Adverse, then material usage variance should be :
A. Rs. 2,000 Adverse
B. Rs. 2,000 Favourable
C. Rs. 8,000 Favourable
D. Rs. 8,000 Adverse

24. If profit is Rs. 20,000; margin of safety is 20% and P/V ratio is 50%, the sales value would be :
A. Rs. 20,000 B. Rs. 2,00,000
C. Rs. 40,000 D. Rs. 4,00,000

25. If margin of safety is 40% of sales, find out fixed cost when profit is Rs. 2,00,000 :
A. Rs. 30,000 B. Rs. 3,00,000
C. Rs. 40,000 D. Rs. 4,00,000

26. For which one of the following industry, would you recommend a job order costing system :

A. Tyre Manufacturing
B. Oil Exploration
C. Ship Making
D. Beverage Production

27. Which of the following represents a Cost-Volume Proft Equation?
A. Sales = Contribution + Fixed Cost + Profit
B. Sales = Variable Cost + Fixed Cost + Profit
C. Sales = Variable Cost – Fixed Cost + Profit
D. Sales = Contribution – Fixed Cost + Profit

28. An increase in fixed cost results in :
A. Increase in P/V ratio
B. Increase in Contribution
C. Increase in Margin of Safety
D. Increase in Break-even Point

29. Semi-variable costs are segregated into fixed and variable costs with the help of :
A. Scatter diagram
B. Method of least square
C. High and low points method
D. All of the above

30. Contribution is :
A. Fixed Cost + Profit
B. Sales – Variable Cost
C. Fixed Cost – Loss
D. All of these

31. If A and B are two matrices of the same order and A + B = B + A, it implies matrix addition is :
A. Commutative B. Additive inverse
C. Associative D. Additive identity

32. If the manufacturer's cost function is $C = 0.1x^2 + 3$ (where 'C' is total cost and 'x' is output), the marginal cost function will be:
A. $0.5x$ B. $0.8x$
C. $0.4x$ D. $0.2x$

33. If the manufacturer's cost function is $C = 0.005x^3 - 0.02x^2 - 30x + 5000$ (where 'C' is total cost and 'x' is output), the marginal average cost function will be :
A. $0.01 - 0.02x - (5000/x)$
B. $0.015x - 0.02 - (5000/x^2)$
C. $0.02x - 0.02x - (5000/x^2)$
D. $0.01x - 0.02 - (5000/x^2)$

34. A firm knows that the demand function for one of its product is linear. It also knows that it can sell 1000 units when the price is Rs. 4 per unit, and it can sell 1500 units when the price is Rs. 2 per unit. The marginal revenue function of the firm will be given as :
A. $10 - (x/125)$ B. $8 - (x/125)$
C. $8 - (x/250)$ D. $4 - (x/125)$

35. If the demand function is $p = 4 - 5x$ (where 'p' is price and 'x' is output), the value of x at which demand will have unit elasticity is :
A. (2/5) B. (5/2)
C. (3/5) D. None of these

36. The average cost per repair of a car is found to be Rs. 320 and number of repairs is given by $0.5t^{3/2}$, where t is time in months since the purchase of the car. The replacement cost is estimated to be Rs. 80,000. The optimum replacement period will be :
A. 100 years B. 1000 months
C. 10 years D. 100 months.

37. A manufacturer of a product finds that the first 500 units that are produced and sold, the profit is Rs. 50 per unit. The profit on each of the units beyond 500 is decreased by 0.10 times the number of additional units produced. The level of output at which profit is maximum will be :
A. 250 units B. 500 units
C. 750 units D. None of these

38. The demand function for two commodities X and Y are given by :
$x = (100/p^2q)$ and $y = (50/pq^2)$
respectively, where x and y are the quantities demanded for X and Y respectively, and p and q are their respective prices. The commodities are :
A. Complementary
B. Not related
C. Competitive
D. Cannot be determined

39. A production function is given by :
$$Q = AL^{1/3} K^{1/3}$$
(where 'Q' is total production, 'A' is constant and 'L' and 'K' represent labour and capital respectively)

The return to scale for the production function will be :

A. decreasing

B. constant

C. increasing

D. Cannot be determined

40. If C is the total cost of an output x, it is known that the marginal cost MC always equals average cost AC. Therefore, total cost C is a constant multiple of :

A. x^2 B. x^3

C. x D. $2x^2$

41. A manufacturer's marginal cost function is $MC = 4 - 2x + x^2$ (where x is output). The total cost function, given that the fixed cost is Rs. 100, will be given as :

A. $C = 4x - 2x^2 + (x^3/3) + 100$

B. $C = 4x - x^2 + (2x^3/3) + 100$

C. $C = 4x - x^2 + (x^3/3) + 100$

D. $C = 4x - x^2 + (x^3/3) + 1000$

42. A manufacturer's marginal revenue function is $MR = 2 - 6x$ (where 'x' is output). The demand law will be :

A. $p = 2 - 8x$ B. $p = 2 - 3x$

C. $x = 2 - 3p$ D. $p = 8 - 3x$

43. The rate of change of revenue and cost of a company with respect to time are given as $R'(t) = 9 - t^{1/3}$ and $C'(t) = 1 + 3t^{1/3}$ respectively (where t is measured in years and R and C measured in million of rupees). Determine how long the operation should continue and the profit that can be generated during the period :

A. 8 years, 16 million rupees

B. 16 years, 8 million rupees

C. 8 years, 20 million rupees

D. 16 years, 16 million rupees

44. The price elasticity of demand for a commodity is p/x^3 (where 'p' is price and 'x' is output). The demand function, if the demand is 3 when the price is 2, will be given as :

A. $p = 11 - (2x^3/3)$ B. $p = 10 - (x^3/3)$

C. $p = 11 - (4x^3/3)$ D. $p = 11 - (x^3/3)$

45. The demand function for a commodity is given by $p = 100 - 8x$ (where 'p' is price and 'x' is output). The consumer surplus corresponding to $p = 4$ will be :

A. 546 B. 456

C. 526 D. 576

46. At what rate of interest will Rs. 3,000 yield Rs. 120 in simple interest in 6 months?

A. 16% B. 8%

C. 12% D. 6%

47. A certain sum of money is invested at 4% compounded annually. The interest for the second year is Rs. 25. The interest for the third year will be :

A. Rs. 24 B. Rs. 28

C. Rs. 29 D. None of these

48. Which of the following is *not* an essential part of Linear programming problem?

A. Linear constraints

B. A subjective function

C. Non-negative restrictions

D. An objective function

49. An existence of slack variable in the final simplex table indicates that the :

A. solution is not feasible

B. resource is not fully utilized

C. solution is multiple optimal

D. resource has been optimally utilized

50. In the final simplex table, a zero entry in the index row for a non-basic variable indicates that the probelm is :

A. multiple optimal B. redundant

C. not optimal D. degenerate

51. If arithmetic mean and geometric mean of two values are 10 and 8 respectively, the two values are :

A. 16 and 4 B. 6 and 4

C. 6 and 14 D. 16 and 14

52. The daily sales of a store were Rs. 2,750 for the month of February, 2010 (assume 28 days). During the month the highest and the lowest sales were Rs. 8,950 and Rs. 580 respectively. The average daily sales if the highest and the lowest sales are not taken into account is :

A. Rs. 2,500 B. Rs. 2,550

C. Rs. 2,595 D. Rs. 2,695

53. If first, second and third quartile are 20, 30 and 40 respectively, the coefficient of quartile deviation will be :

A. 1 B. 5.33
C. 10 D. 0.33

54. A symmetrical distribution has standard deviation of 30. The quartile deviation of the distribution will be approximately :

A. 20 B. 30
C. 12 D. 24

55. If the first quartile is 142 and the semi-interquartile range is 18, the median of the distribution (assuming the distribution to be symmetrical) will be :

A. 160 B. 178
C. 150 D. 142

56. The elasticity of cost is given by $\frac{9x}{2(9x+16)}$.

Find the totat cost function, given that the fixed cost is Rs. 16.

A. $4\sqrt{9x+16}$ B. $5\sqrt{3x+17}$
C. $\sqrt{9x+16}$ D. None of these

57. If the co-variance between X and Y variable is 6 and the variance of X and Y are 16 and 9 respectively, the coefficient of correlation will be :

A. 0.25 B. 0.5
C. 0.33 D. 1

58. If the value of coefficient of correlation is less than ...., the value of coefficient of correlation is not at all significant.

A. probable error B. one
C. standard error D. standard deviation

59. If one of the coefficient of regression has positive sign, the other co-efficient of regression shall have ....

A. positive sign
B. any value less than zero
C. negative sign
D. no specific requirement

60. If the standard deviation of X and Y are 4 and 3 respectively and coefficient of regression of X on Y is 0.6, the co-efficient of correlation between X and Y will be :

A. 0.75 B. 0.80
C. 0.45 D. 0.90

61. Mr. X was getting Rs. 2,400 as salary when the cost of living index was 100. If the cost of living index is currently at 325, what extra allowance be paid to Mr. X so that he can maintain same standard of living?

A. Rs. 7,800 B. Rs. 8,000
C. Rs. 3,500 D. Rs. 5,500

62. If the fixed base index number of the current year and previous year are 196 and 188 respectively, the chain base index of the current year wil be :

A. 368.48 B. 104.26
C. 110 D. 95.91

63. The process of converting two indices into a continuous series is called :

A. Deflating B. Shifting
C. Splicing D. Base shifting

64. The sales for the current quarter (Q1) is Rs. 15,000. If the sales of the next quarter (Q2) are expected to rise by 4% and seasonal index of the same quarter (Q2) is 85, the estimated stock based on seasonal index shall be :

A. Rs. 13,260 B. Rs. 14,260
C. Rs. 15,600 D. Rs. 15,685

65. Given trend equation Y = 110 + 2X (origin 2005, time unit 1 year). If the origin is shifted to 2009, the new equation will be :

A. Y = 118 + 2X B. Y = 110 + 7X
C. Y = 110 + 6X D. Y = 120 + 7X

66. A speaks the truth 2 out of 3 times and B speaks truth 4 out of 5 times. They agree that from a bag containing 6 balls of different colours, a black ball has been drawn. The probability that the statement is true will be :

A. 8/9 B. 16/30
C. 15/27 D. 40/41

67. The odds are 3 to 2 against a person aged 50 years living till he is 70 and 3 to 4 against a person aged 40 years living till he is 60. The probability that at least one of them will be alive after 20 years will be :

A. 124/190 B. 124/196
C. 114/196 D. 22/35

68. In a given binomial distribution, the mean and standard deviation are 4 and $\sqrt{2}$ respectively. The total number of trials (n) will be :

A. 20 B. 8

C. 6 D. 16

69. The height of the normal curve is maximum at :

A. Mode B. Mean

C. Median D. All of these

70. The result of combining prior information and the sampling information is the new probability distribution on the states of nature called the :

A. Uniform distribution

B. Normal distribution

C. Posterior distribution

D. Binomial distribution

71. What do you understand by the term business?

A. Commerce

B. Services and commerce

C. Industry and commerce

D. Selling and buying of goods

72. The term Industry includes :

A. Construction of buildings

B. Banking companies

C. Insurance companies

D. Transport companies

73. Which of the following is *not* an essential condition for an activity to be termed a business?

A. There should be an exchange or transfer of goods or services

B. Continuity of dealings

C. The profit motive

D. Certainty of profit

74. Fish-culture should be classified as :

A. Manufacturing industry

B. Genetic industry

C. Pharmaceutical industry

D. Extractive industry

75. The oldest form of business organization is :

A. Partnership

B. Joint-stock Company

C. Co-operative undertaking

D. Sole proprietorship

76. How many partners can a firm carrying on banking business have at the most?

A. 7 B. 10

C. 20 D. 50

77. Which of the following Act has specified the maximum number of partners in a firm?

A. The Partnership Act, 1932

B. The Contract Act, 1872

C. The Companies Act, 1956

D. None of these

78. A manager with a share in the profits :

A. is still only an employee of the firm

B. becomes a partner by law

C. becomes a partner by implied agreement

D. becomes a partner from status

79. Leadership is a function of all the following *except* :

A. Work group B. Product or service

C. Leader D. Situation

80. Delegation of authority is linked to :

A. planning B. organising

C. directing D. controlling

81. In e-commerce what is C2B situation?

A. Consumer to buyer

B. Buyer to consumer

C. Consumer to business

D. Customer to buyer

82. Expectancy theory of motivation is given by :

A. Victor Vroom

B. Herzberg

C. Porter and Lawler

D. McClleland

83. Match List-I with List-II and select the *correct* answer using the codes given below the Lists :

List-I	List-II
1. Span of control	I. The superior helps, through continuous guidance, the subordinate to react his goals
2. M.B.O.	II. Numerical limit of subordinates to be supervised by an Executive

3. M.B.E.	III.	Subordinate remains accountable to his superior and the superior has the authority to demand accountability from his subordinate
4. Delegation of authority	IV.	The management will concern itself and confine its activities to those areas and operations where the actual performance is short of the target

Codes:

	1	2	3	4
A.	I	II	III	IV
B.	I	II	IV	III
C.	II	I	III	IV
D.	II	I	IV	III

84. Consider the following basic steps involved in the process of control :

I. Identifying the strategic control points
II. Establishing the standards
III. Measuring performance against standards
IV. Correcting deviations from the standards

The *correct* sequence of the above steps in the process of control is :

A. I, IV, III, II   B. IV, III, II, I
C. II, I, IV, III   D. II, III, I, IV

85. Match List-I with List-II and select the *correct* answer using the codes given below the Lists :

List-I (Management Thinkers)	List-II (Contribution/Work)
1. Elton Mayo	I. Importance of integrating the company's and employees goal
2. Frederick W. Taylor	II. Social problems of Industrial civilization
3. Henry Fayol	III. General and Industrial Management
4. Mary Parker Follet	IV. Principles of Scientific Management

Codes:

	1	2	3	4
A.	I	IV	III	II
B.	IV	III	II	I
C.	II	IV	III	I
D.	III	IV	I	II

86. Indian Contract Act was enacted in the year :

A. 1832   B. 1852
C. 1872   D. None of these

87. Which of the following statements is *correct*?

A. Minor's agreements are valid
B. Minor's agreements are void
C. Minor's agreements are absolutely void
D. Minor's agreements are voidable

88. In the Limited Liability Partnership (LLP) :

A. Partnership Act, 1932 applies
B. Only selective provisions of Partnership Act, 1932 apply
C. Partnership Act, 1932 does not apply
D. None of the above

89. Producer Company can be formed by :

A. Only co-operative societies
B. Only institutional members
C. Only individuals
D. By both individiuals and institutional members

90. Dividend is paid within :

A. 42 days   B. 40 days
C. 30 days   D. 20 days

91. Company is to file secretarial compliance report if it has capital above :

A. 2 lakhs   B. 7 lakhs
C. 10 lakhs   D. 2 crores

92. Director's Identification number is mandatory for :

A. All directors
B. Only executive directors
C. External directors
D. Independent directors

93. Buy back of shares was introduced in the year :

A. 1985   B. 1988
C. 1999   D. 2000

94. General meeting quorum for public company is :
A. 100 or 1/3rd whichever is lower
B. 100 or 1/3rd whichever is higher
C. 5 members
D. None of the above

95. AGM may be held :
A. Anywhere in the country
B. Outside the country
C. Only in the city, town where the registered office is situated
D. None of the above

96. Proxy must be received at the registered office within :
A. 24 hours B. 48 hours
C. 72 hours D. None of these

97. For a board meeting :
A. Notice is a must
B. 7 days notice is a must
C. 14 days notice is a must
D. None of these

98. Online filing in the case of companies is :
A. Optional
B. Mandatory
C. Required only in the case of special business
D. Required only in the case of business requiring special notice

99. Manager and Managing Director :
A. May be appointed simultaneously
B. May not be appointed simultaneously
C. May be appointed simultaneously after Court's approval
D. None of the above

100. Sarbanes-Oxley (SOX) Act, 2002 was enacted in :
A. USA B. UK
C. France D. Germany

101. X Ltd. is registered in Japan. The control and management of its affairs is situated wholly in India. X Ltd. shall be :
A. Resident in India
B. Non-resident
C. Not ordinarily resident in India
D. None of the above

102. Which of the following is a capital asset for the purpose of Income Tax Act, 1961?
A. Stock-in-trade
B. Jewellery
C. Furniture for personal use
D. Gold bonds

103. Mr. A, a chartered accountant, is employed as an internal auditor with XYZ Ltd. He requests the employer to call his remuneration as internal audit fee. Mr. A shall be chargeable to tax for such fee under the head :
A. Salaries
B. Income from other sources
C. Profits and gains of business or profession
D. Capital gains

104. Which of the following losses is *not* deductible from business income?
A. Loss of stock-in-trade due to destruction by fire
B. Loss of stock-in-trade due to theft
C. Depreciation of funds kept in foreign currency for capital purposes
D. Loss from sale of securities held in the regular course of business

105. In order to be entitled to depreciation allowance, which of the following conditions needs to be satisfied?
A. Asset must be owned by the assessee
B. Asset must be used for the purpose of business or profession
C. It should be used during the relevant previous year
D. All of the above

106. Which of the following incomes is *not* taxable under the head 'Income from other sources'?
A. Pension
B. Dividend
C. Interest on bank deposit
D. Insurance commission

107. In which of the following cases, income of other persons is included in assessee's total income?
A. Transfer of income without transfer of assets
B. Revocable transfer of assets

C. Income from assets transferred to spouse
D. All of the above

108. Deduction under Section 80C (in respect of life insurance premia, Provident Fund contribution etc.) is available to :
A. All assessees
B. An individual
C. An individual or Hindu Undivided Family
D. All assessees except company

109. Which of the following is a Direct tax?
A. Import duty B. Excise duty
C. Property tax D. Sales tax

110. A tax system that places a relatively large tax burden on the higher income group and relatively low tax burden on the lower income group is called a :
A. Progressive tax system
B. Proportional tax system
C. Regressive tax system
D. Specific tax system

111. Mr. U.K. Sinha is the Chairman of :
A. RBI
B. SEBI
C. IRDA
D. Planning Commission

112. What is the current interest rate on EPF deposits?
A. 8% B. 8.50%
C. 9% D. 9.50%

113. BRICS Summit, 2011 concluded recently in :
A. India B. Brazil
C. China D. Russia

114. RBI increased repo rate recently in May, 2011 by :
A. 75 basis points B. 50 basis points
C. 25 basis points D. None of these

115. Which statement is *true* in case of Vodafone-Essar?
A. Essar's remaining stake in Vodafone-Essar goes to Vodafone
B. Vodafone's remaining stake in Vodafone-Essar goes to Essar
C. Essar has sold 10% of its stake to Vodafone
D. Vodafone has sold 10% of its stake to Essar

116. Who won the Swiss open Grand Prix Gold title in March, 2011?
A. Lionel Messi B. Cheng Li
C. Hyun Sung D. Saina Nehwal

117. The five year plan effective from the year 2012 will be :
A. 10th Five Year Plan
B. 11th Five Year Plan
C. 12th Five Year Plan
D. 14th Five Year Plan

118. The novel "White Tiger" which won the Booker Prize, 2008 is authored by :
A. Arundhati Roy B. V.S. Naipal
C. Kiran Desai D. Arvind Adiga

119. Who is appointed as the new Chairman of Infosys?
A. Nanadan Nilekani
B. K.V. Kamath
C. S. Subramaniam
D. Sudha Murthy

120. With which company Kiran Majumadar Shaw is associated with?
A. Biocon Ltd. B. Bio-tech Ltd.
C. Ranbaxy Ltd. D. ICICI Bank

121. Who is the Minister of Environment in India?
A. Anand Sharma B. Dayanidhi Maran
C. Sachin Pilot D. Jairam Ramesh

122. The major component in LPG is :
A. Butane B. Methane
C. Ethane D. Propane

123. Planning Commission has given a forecast of India's GDP growth rate for 2010-11 at :
A. 8% B. 8.9%
C. 9% D. 9.5%

124. 1 MB is equivalent to :
A. 2^{10} Bytes B. 2^{20} Bytes
C. 2^{50} Bytes D. 2^{100} Bytes

125. Which type of financial derivatives are available in India?
A. Index futures and options
B. Stock futures and options
C. Currency futures and options
D. All of the above

126. Which country has recently banned wearing Burqa in public?
A. France B. Germany
C. Polland D. UK

127. Who was the captain of Indian Cricket Team which won World Cup in 1983?
A. M.S. Dhoni B. Kapil Dev
C. Ravi Shastri D. Sunil Gavaskar

128. On which of the commodities ETFs are available in India?
A. Gold B. Grains
C. Silver D. All of these

129. The men's singles champion of Wimbledon 2010 "Rafael Nadal" is of which country?
A. Portugal B. Spain
C. Australia D. US

130. Mark Zuckerburg is the founder of :
A. Facebook B. Orkut
C. Twitter D. Linked in

131. Schengen Visa is applicable for which of the following countries?
A. UK
B. USA
C. European Union countries
D. China

132. Which of the companies is involved in 2G scam?
A. Airtel B. Vodafone
C. Etisalat D. Idea

133. India's largest and only listed microfinance institution is :
A. SRS Microfinance Ltd.
B. Grameen Bank Ltd.
C. SKS Microfinance Ltd.
D. None of these

134. Who is the Minister of Commerce and Industry in India?
A. Salman Khursheed
B. Kamal Nath
C. Prafulla Patel
D. Anand Sharma

135. The Chief of International Monetary Fund (IMF), who resigned recently is :
A. Shashi Tharoor
B. Dominique Strauss-Kahn
C. Dominique Clark
D. Ben Bernanke

136. Recently, Tsunami in Japan affected nuclear plants at which of these places?
A. Fukushima B. Hiroshima
C. Tokyo D. None of these

137. Osama Bin Laden was killed by US special forces at :
A. Allahabad B. Islamabad
C. Karachi D. Abbottabad

138. Which is the company of Warren Buffett?
A. Berkshire Hathaway
B. Blackstone
C. Warren Investments
D. Royal Funds

139. Who is the Governer of RBI at present?
A. D. Subbarao
B. Y.V. Reddy
C. Bimal Jalan
D. Montek Singh Ahluwalia

140. Who was the last Chief Minister of West Bengal from Communist Party of India-Marxist (CPM)?
A. Jyoti Basu
B. Prakash Karat
C. Buddhadeb Bhattacharya
D. Somnath Chatterjee

141. Which company has recently announced to acquire "Skype"?
A. Microsoft B. IBM
C. HP D. Dell

142. The Financial Sector Legislative Reforms Commission (FSLRC) has been set up by the Union Govt. to rewrite and clean up financial laws in India. It is headed by :
A. Justice P.N. Bhagwati
B. Justice B.N. Srikrishna
C. Justice S. Bhushan
D. Justice J.S. Subramaniam

143. Who is the Prime Minister of Pakistan?
A. Mohammad Gilani
B. Yusuf Raza Gilani
C. Parvez Musharaf
D. None of theses

144. In May 2011, European Union finance ministers approved a 78 billion euro bailout package for :

A. Greece B. Ireland
C. Austria D. Portugal

145. What is the name of NASA's Space Shuttle which successfully launched from the Kennedy Space Center in the U.S. State of Florida on its final mission?

A. Endeavour B. Excellent
C. Elevator D. Empower

146. The ousted Egyptian President is :

A. Hamid Mubarak B. Suzanne Mubarak
C. Hosni Mubarak D. None of these

147. In terms of Nominal GDP, what is the rank of the economy of India?

A. 7th B. 10th
C. 13th D. 15th

148. The population of India as per provisional figures of census 2011 is :

A. 1111.11 million B. 1210.19 million
C. 1260.19 million D. 1310.19 million

149. Which of the following is the smallest paper size?

A. A2 B. A3
C. A4 D. A5

150. The Skoda car company is based at which country?

A. Uzbekistan B. Hungary
C. Czech Republic D. Japan

151. An excise tax levied on each unit of X consumed :

A. Would reduce consumption of X and lower expenditure on X
B. Would rotate the budget line outward along the X axis and allow the consumer to reach a higher indifference curve
C. Would place the consumer on a lower indifference curve
D. Cause the consumer to reduce consumption of the taxed good and other non-taxed goods equally

152. The elasticity of demand for colour TV is reported to be –0.7 with respect to price and 3.0 with respect to income of buyers. Therefore, one would expect that a 1% increase in income and a 1% increase in price would :

A. Increase demand by 3.7%
B. Increase demand by 2.3%
C. Increase demand by 1%
D. Decrease demand by 2.3%

153. The slope of the total product curve measures :

A. The marginal rate of technical substitution
B. Average product
C. The maximum output
D. Marginal product

154. Which of the following may explain why decreasing returns to scale occur?

A. Diminishing marginal rate of technical substitution
B. The law of diminishing marginal returns
C. Managerial diseconomies
D. All of the above

155. The short run total cost can never be less than long term total cost :

A. Always true B. Often true
C. Rarely true D. Never true

156. A firm that is making zero economic profit in the long run will have incentive to :

A. Shut down
B. Relocate to another industry
C. Expand production
D. Continue to operate as it is

157. The supply curve is very elastic. A change in demand will bring about relatively :

A. Larger change in price and a smaller change in quantity supplied
B. Larger change in price and also larger change in quantity supplied
C. Smaller change in price and a larger change in quantity supplied
D. Smaller change in price and also a smaller change in quantity supplied

158. The demand function is given by Q = 500 – P. When the current quantity is Q = 200, the price elasticity of demand is :

A. –1.5 B. –5.0
C. –50 D. None of these

159. Of the following which one is a cause of 'cost-push' inflation?
A. Increased consumption expenditure
B. A reduction in taxation
C. Increase in demand
D. Increase in wages and salaries

160. By depreciation of a currency we mean :
A. A fall in the domestic value of the currency
B. A fall in the external value of a currency caused by market forces
C. A fall in the external value of a currency caused by the government action
D. Any of the above

161. If there is a balance of payments deficit then in a floating exchange rate system :
A. The external value of the currency would tend to fall
B. The external value of the currency would tend to rise
C. The injections from trade are greater than the withdrawals
D. Aggregate demand is increasing

162. Tobin tax is a tax on :
A. Exports
B. Imports
C. Sales
D. Transactions in foreign exchange

163. When the Federal Reserve Bank lowers the reserve requirement,
A. Investors will purchase "open market" bonds
B. Banks must hold less money
C. People will deposit more money
D. Banks will create more money

164. Fiscal drag occurs when :
A. Tax bands do not increase with inflation
B. Tax rates move inversely with inflation
C. Government spending falls to reduce aggregate demand
D. Tax bands increase with inflation

165. As an economy grows :
A. The government's budget position should automatically improve
B. The government's budget position should automatically worsen
C. This will have no effect on the government's budget position
D. This will reduce the government's tax revenue

166. An outward shift in the demand for money, other things being equal should lead to :
A. A lower interest rate but the same quantity of money
B. A higher interest rate but the same quantity of money
C. A higher quantity of money but lower interest rates
D. A higher quantity of money but the same interest rate

167. Under the flexible exchange system, the exchange rate is determined by :
A. The nation's monetary authorities
B. The price of gold
C. The forces of demand and supply in the foreign exchange market
D. Exchange arbitrage

168. Increased unemployment benefits and less incentive to work would :
A. Shift aggregate supply to the right
B. Shift aggregate supply to the left
C. Shift aggregate demand to the right
D. Shift aggregate demand to the left

169. In a regressive tax system :
A. The amount of tax paid increases with income
B. The marginal rate of tax decreases with more income
C. The average rate of tax falls as income increases
D. The average rate of tax is constant as income increases

170. For a firm with TC = 45000 + 500Q – $5Q^2$ + $0.2Q^3$, the marginal cost when Q = 10 is :
A. 360 B. 560
C. 460 D. 660

171. Incremental Capital-Output Ratio (ICOR) is defined as :
A. Increment in output/increment in capital
B. Increment in capital/increment in output
C. Increment in income/increment in consumption

D. Increment in saving/increment in consumption

172. Who has suggested the utilisation of "disguised unemployment" as a source of savings potential in underdeveloped countries?

A. Ragnar Nurkse B. W.A. Lewis
C. K.K. Kurihara D. G. Myrdal

173. Ricardo's law of comparative advantage is based on :

A. The opportunity cost theory
B. The law of diminishing returns
C. The labour theory of value
D. All of the above

174. Stagflation refers to a situation which is characterized by :

A. Deflation and rising unemployment
B. Inflation and deflation
C. Sustained price-rise and rising unemployment
D. Stagnant employment and deflation

175. Economy rent earned by any factor will be the highest if its elasticity of supply is :

A. Zero
B. Between zero and one
C. Equal to one
D. Infinity

176. In the Keynesian theory, the liquidity preferences and the rate of interest are :

A. Directly related B. Inversely related
C. Not at all related D. None of these

177. When the Central Bank sells securities, then :

A. The cash resources at the disposal of the commercial banks increase
B. The cash resources at the disposal of the commercial banks get diminished
C. The cash resources of the commercial banks remain unchanged
D. None of the above

178. Who finally approves the draft of the Five-Year Plans?

A. Parliament and State Legislatures
B. National Developmet Council
C. Planning Commission
D. The President

179. Capital formation means :

A. Addition to the stock of capital goods
B. Replacement of capital goods used in the process of production
C. Employment of the capital goods in the process of production
D. Consumption of fixed capital

180. Which one of the following taxes/duties is *not* levied by the Central Government?

A. Income tax
B. Stamp duties
C. Estate duty
D. Union excise duties

181. If the consumption function arises from the origin :

A. APC = MPC B. APC > MPC
C. APC = 1 D. MPC = 1

182. In the Classical range the elasticity of the LM function is :

A. Equal to one B. Equal to zero
C. Less than one D. Equal to infinity

183. Government expenditure multiplier is :

A. Greater than Keynesian multiplier
B. Less than Keynesian multiplier
C. Equal to Keynesian multiplier
D. None of the above

184. Precautionary demand for holding money is :

A. Not dependent on rate of interest
B. Not dependent on income
C. Not a straight line
D. None of the above

185. The total liquidity preference for money is always :

A. Perfectly elastic
B. Interest inelastic
C. Sometimes interest elastic
D. Has zero elasticity

186. Keynesian multiplier is :

A. Inversely related to MPS
B. Inversely related to MPC
C. Inversely related to APC
D. Directly related to APC

187. Crowding-out effect is due to :

A. Rise in income
B. Rise in interest rate

C. Fall in government expenditure
D. None of the above

188. Phillips' curve shows the trade-off between :
A. Real wage and unemployment
B. Nominal wage and unemployment
C. Price inflation and unemployment
D. Change in nominal wage and unemployment rate

189. Which of the following is *true*?
A. MEI is a straight line MEC is a curve
B. MEC is a straight line MEI is a curve
C. Both are staight lines
D. Both are curves

190. Liquidity preference curve becomes flat due to :
A. Precautionary demand for money
B. Money supply
C. Transactions demand
D. Speculative demand

191. What is the *correct* sequence of the following steps required for the preparation of final accounts?
I. Preparation of Trial Balance
II. Balancing of accounts
III. Preparation of annual financial statements
IV. Making adjustment entries
A. IV, II, I, III B. II, IV, III, I
C. II, I, III, IV D. IV, II, III, I

'. A contingent liability is shown due to :
A. Convention of full disclosure
B. Convention of conservatism
C. Convention of materiality
D. Dual aspect concept

Which of the following is *not* a fundamental accounting assumption according to Accounting Standard-1 :
A. Going concern B. Business entity
C. Consistency D. Accrual

Which item of revenue of the following is covered by Accounting Standard-9?
A. Revenue arising from construction contracts
B. Revenue arising from hire-purchase agreements
. Revenue arising from Govt. grants
. Revenue arising from sale of goods and rendering of services

195. An asset is purchased for Rs. 1,00,000 on which depreciation is to be provided annually according to the straight line method. The useful life of the asset is 10 years and the scrap value is Rs. 20,000. The rate of depreciation is :
A. 20% B. 18%
C. 10% D. 8%

196. First-in First-out (FIFO) method of inventory valuation is advisable in case of :
A. Rising prices B. Falling prices
C. Constant prices D. Fluctuating prices

197. The cash price of a music system was Rs. 5,000 and its Hire Purchase Price was Rs. 6,000. There was no down payment. The payment was to be made in four equal instalments of Rs. 1,500 each payable at the end of each year. The amount of interest included in the first instalment was :
A. Rs. 250 B. Rs. 400
C. Rs. 300 D. None of these

198. In the absence of any agreement to the contrary, the deficiency of an insolvent partner's capital account (debit balance) must be borne by the other solvent partners in :
A. Profit and loss sharing ratio
B. Equal proportion
C. Capital ratio which stood prior to dissolution
D. Capital ratio which stood after the dissolution of the firm

199. Donation received by a Not-for-profit organisation for a specific purpose is a :
A. Liability B. Asset
C. Capital receipt D. Revenue receipt

200. Financial Accounting is primarily concerned with :
A. Recording of financial information relating to activities of business
B. Providing financial information to assist the management in decision-making
C. Reporting financial information for external users of accounting reports
D. Interpretation of financial statements

ANSWERS

1	2	3	4	5	6	7	8	9	10
B	C	C	C	D	C	D	D	D	D
11	12	13	14	15	16	17	18	19	20
D	D	A	A	B	D	B	C	A	B
21	22	23	24	25	26	27	28	29	30
A	A	B	B	B	C	B	D	D	D
31	32	33	34	35	36	37	38	39	40
A	D	D	B	A	D	C	A	A	C
41	42	43	44	45	46	47	48	49	50
C	B	A	D	D	B	D	B	B	D
51	52	53	54	55	56	57	58	59	60
A	C	D	A	A	A	B	A	A	C
61	62	63	64	65	66	67	68	69	70
C	B	C	A	A	D	D	B	B	C
71	72	73	74	75	76	77	78	79	80
C	A	D	B	D	B	C	A	B	B
81	82	83	84	85	86	87	88	89	90
C	A	D	C	C	C	B	D	D	C
91	92	93	94	95	96	97	98	99	100
C	A	C	C	C	B	B	D	B	A
101	102	103	104	105	106	107	108	109	110
B	B	A	D	D	B	D	C	C	A
111	112	113	114	115	116	117	118	119	120
B	D	C	B	A	D	C	D	B	A
121	122	123	124	125	126	127	128	129	130
D	D	A	B	D	A	B	A	B	A
131	132	133	134	135	136	137	138	139	140
C	C	C	D	B	A	D	A	A	C
141	142	143	144	145	146	147	148	149	150
A	B	B	D	A	C	B	B	D	C
151	152	153	154	155	156	157	158	159	160
C	B	D	D	A	D	C	D	D	B
161	162	163	164	165	166	167	168	169	170
A	D	D	A	A	B	C	B	C	C
171	172	173	174	175	176	177	178	179	180
B	A	C	C	A	B	B	B	A	B
181	182	183	184	185	186	187	188	189	190
A	B	A	D	C	A	B	D	C	D
191	192	193	194	195	196	197	198	199	200
C	A	B	D	D	B	B	C	C	C

SOME SELECTED EXPLANATORY ANSWERS

31. Properties of matrix addition

(i) Matrix addition is commutative *i.e.* A + B = B + A

(ii) Matrix addition is associative *i.e.* (A + B) + C = A + (B + C)

(iii) Existence of additive identity: Null matrix is the identity w.r.t. addition of matrices

Given a matrix $A = [a_{ij}]_{m \times n}$ there will be a corresponding null matrix O of same order such that

$$A + O = O + A = A$$

(iv) The existence of additive inverse

Let $A = [a_{ij}]_{m \times n}$ be any matrix, then there exists another matrix

$$-A = -[a_{ij}]_{m \times n}$$

Such that

$$A + (-A) = (-A) + A = 0.$$

32. Marginal Cost $= \dfrac{dc}{dx}$

$$= \frac{d}{dx}(0.1x^2 + 3) = 0.2x.$$

33. Since total cost function is

$$TC = 0.005\,x^3 - 0.02x^2 - 30x + 5000$$

where 'x' is output

∴ Average cost function is

$$AC = \frac{TC}{x}$$

$$= \frac{0.005x^3 - 0.02x^2 - 30x + 5000}{x}$$

$$= 0.005x^2 - 0.02x - 30 + \frac{5000}{x}$$

∴ Marginal Average Cost $= \dfrac{d(AC)}{dx}$

$$= \frac{d}{dx}\left(0.005x^2 - 0.02x - 30 + \frac{5000}{x}\right)$$

$$= 0.01x - 0.02 - \frac{5000}{x^2}.$$

34. Let demand function is

$$P = ax + b \qquad ...(1)$$

(where P is price, x is quantity and 'a' and 'b' are constant)

When P = Rs. 4 and $x = 1000$

∴ $4 = 1000a + b$ (from equation 1)

and when

P = Rs. 2 and $x = 1500$

then $2 = 1500a + b$ (from equation 1)

Solving equations

$$4 = 1000a + b$$

and $$2 = 1500a + b$$

We get $a = -\dfrac{1}{250}$ and $b = 8$

∴ Demand function is expressed as

$$P = 8 - \frac{x}{250}$$

∴ Total Revenue (TR) = P.x

$$= \left(8 - \frac{x}{250}\right)x$$

$$= 8x - \frac{x^2}{250}$$

$$\therefore \quad MR = \frac{d(TR)}{dx} = 8 - 2 \times \frac{x}{250}$$

$$= 8 - \frac{x}{125}.$$

35. Since Demand Elasticity $= -\dfrac{p}{x}.\dfrac{dx}{dp}$

Given that $p = 4 - 5x$

$$\therefore \quad \frac{dp}{dx} = -5$$

$$\therefore \quad \text{Elasticity} = -\frac{p}{x}.\frac{dx}{dp}$$

$$1 = -\frac{4 - 5x}{x}.\frac{1}{-5}$$

(given that elasticity is one)

$$\Rightarrow \quad 1 = \frac{4-5x}{5x}$$

$$\Rightarrow \quad 5x = 4 - 5x$$

$$\Rightarrow \quad x = \frac{4}{10} = \frac{2}{5}.$$

36. Average repair cost per month

$$= \frac{\text{Average number of repairs}}{\text{Month}} \times \text{Average cost per repair}$$

$$= \left(\frac{0.5t^{3/2}}{t}\right) 320 = 160t^{1/2}$$

and average replacement cost $= \dfrac{80000}{t}$

First and second order conditions for minimum AC are

$$\frac{dy}{dt} = 0 \quad \text{and} \quad \frac{d^2y}{dt^2} > 0$$

Now $\dfrac{dy}{dt} = 80t^{-1/2} - \dfrac{80000}{t^2} = 0$

$$\Rightarrow \quad 80t^{-1/2} = \frac{80000}{t^2}$$

$$\Rightarrow \quad t^{3/2} = 1000 = 10^3$$

$$\therefore \quad t = 100$$

Also $\dfrac{d^2y}{dt^2} = \dfrac{40}{t^{3/2}} + \dfrac{160000}{t^3} > 0,$

when $t = 100$

Hence the optimum replacement period is $t = 100$ months.

38. The two commodities are complementary if and only both $\left(\dfrac{dx}{dq}\right)$ and $\left(\dfrac{dy}{dp}\right)$ are both negative.

And two commodities are substitutes (or competitive) if and only if $\left(\dfrac{dx}{dq}\right)$ and $\left(\dfrac{dy}{dp}\right)$ are both positive.

39. The mathematical representation of Cobb-Douglas production function is given as

$$Q = AL^{\alpha} K^{\beta}$$

A, $\alpha, \beta > 0$, where L is level of labour and K is the level of the captial. The return of scale of Cobb-Douglas production function is dependent of sum of α and β.

⇒ If $\alpha + \beta > 1$, then return to scale is increasing.

⇒ If $\alpha + \beta = 1$, then return to scale is constant.

⇒ If $\alpha + \beta < 1$, then return to scale is decreasing.

41. Given that

$$MC = 4 - 2x + x^2$$

$$\therefore \quad TC = \int (MC)dx + K$$

$$= \int (4 - 2x + x^2)dx + K$$

$$= 4x - x^2 + \frac{x^3}{3} + K$$

Given the fixed cost = 100

$$\therefore \quad TC = 4x - x^2 + \frac{x^3}{3} + 100.$$

42. Given that MR = $2 - 6x$

$$\therefore \quad TR = \int (MR)dx + K$$

$$= \int (2 - 6x)dx + K$$

$$= 2x - \frac{6x^2}{2} + K$$

$$= 2x - 3x^2 + K$$

Since TR = 0, when $x = 0$, K = 0

$$\therefore \quad TR = 2x - 3x^2$$

$$\because \quad TR = px$$

$$\therefore \quad p = \frac{TR}{x}$$

$$= \frac{2x - 3x^2}{x}$$

$$= 2 - 3x.$$

43. Use of the machine will be profitable as long as the rate at which revenue is generated is greater than the rate at which costs accumulate, *i.e.*, until

$$R'(t) = C'(t)$$

$$\Rightarrow \quad 9 - t^{1/2} = 1 + 3t^{1/3}$$

$$\Rightarrow \quad 8 = 4t^{1/3}$$

$$\Rightarrow \quad t^{1/3} = 2 \Rightarrow t = 8 \text{ years}$$

Thus, operation of machine should continue for 8 years and the net earnings (or profit) for next 8 years are represented by the definite integral:

$$\int_0^8 R'(t) - C'(t)dt$$

$$= \int_0^8 \left[(9 - t^{1/3}) - (1 + 3t^{1/3})\right]dt$$

$$= \int_0^8 (8 - 4t^{1/3})dt$$

$$= \left| 8t - 4\frac{t^{4/3}}{4/3} \right|_0^8$$

$$= \left[8 \times 8 - \frac{4 \times 3}{4} \times 8^{4/3} \right]$$

$$= 64 - 3 \times 2^4$$

$$= 64 - 48$$

$$= 16 \text{ million rupees.}$$

45. If $p = 4$

then $p = 100 - 8x$

$$\Rightarrow \quad 4 = 100 - 8x$$

$$\Rightarrow \quad 8x = 96$$

$$\Rightarrow \quad x = \frac{96}{8} = 12 \text{ units}$$

$\therefore$ Consumer Surplus (CS)

$$= \int_0^{12} (100 - 8x)dx - 12 \times 4$$

$$= \left| 100x - 4x^2 \right|_0^{12} - 48$$

$$= 1200 - 576 - 48$$

$$= 576.$$

46. Simple Interest

$$I = \frac{P \times r \times t}{100}$$

$$120 = \frac{3000 \times r \times 0.5}{100}$$

$$r = \frac{120 \times 10 \times 100}{3000 \times 5}$$

$$= \frac{12}{150} \times 100 = 8\%.$$

51. Let the numbers be a and b

Since A.M. between a and b is 10.

$$\therefore \quad \frac{a+b}{2} = 10 \Rightarrow a + b = 20 \quad \text{...(1)}$$

Since G.M. between a and b is 8.

$$\therefore \quad \sqrt{ab} = 8 \Rightarrow ab = 64$$

We know that

$$(a - b)^2 = (a + b)^2 - 4ab$$

$$= (20)^2 - 4 \times 64$$

$$= 144$$

$$\therefore \quad a - b = 12 \quad \text{...(2)}$$

Adding (1) and (2), we get $2a = 32$

$$\therefore \quad a = 16$$

and $b = 16 - 12 = 4$.

52. Average daily sale

$$= \frac{2750 \times 28 - (8950 + 580)}{28 - 2}$$

$$= \frac{77000 - 9530}{26}$$

$$= 2595.$$

53. Coefficient of quartile deviation

$$= \frac{Q_3 - Q_1}{Q_3 + Q_1}$$

54. Quartile Deviation

$$= \frac{2}{3} \text{ Standard deviation.}$$

56. Given: $\eta_c = \frac{9x}{2(9x+16)}$

$$\Rightarrow \quad \frac{x}{C} \cdot \frac{dC}{dx} = \frac{9x}{2(9x+16)}$$

$$\Rightarrow \quad \frac{dC}{C} = \frac{9}{2(9x+16)} dx.$$

Integrating both sides, we get

$$\log C = \frac{9}{2} \int \frac{1}{9x+16} dx$$

$$= \frac{9}{2} \cdot \frac{\log(9x+16)}{9} + \log k$$

$$= \log\left[\sqrt{9x+16} \cdot k\right]$$

$$\therefore \quad C(x) = k\sqrt{9x+16}$$

When $x = 0$, C = 16

so that $16 = k\sqrt{9 \times 0 + 16} = 4k$

or $k = 4$

Hence, $C(x) = 4\sqrt{9x+16}$, is the required total cost function.

57. Karl Pearson's coefficient of correlation

$$r = \frac{\text{Cov.}(x, y)}{\sigma_x \sigma_y}$$

where Cov.(x, y) = Co-variance between X and Y

σ_x = S.D. of X

σ_y = S.D. of Y

∴ Coefficient of correlation

$$r = \frac{6}{\sqrt{16} \times \sqrt{9}}$$

[∵ Variance is square of S.D.]

$$= \frac{6}{4 \times 3} = \frac{6}{12} = \frac{1}{2}$$

$= 0.5.$

60. The co-efficient of correlation between X and Y will be

$$r = \frac{\sigma y \cdot bxy}{\sigma x}$$

where bxy = co-efficient of X on Y

σx = standard deviation of X

σy = standard deviation of Y

$$\therefore \quad r = \frac{3 \times 0.6}{4} = \frac{3 \times 3}{4 \times 5}$$

$$= \frac{9}{20} = 0.45.$$

62. Current Year Fixed Base Index (F.B.I.)

$$= \frac{\text{Current Year Chain Base Index (C.B.I.)} \times \text{Previous Year F.B.I.}}{100}$$

$$\therefore \text{ C.B.I. of the current year} = \frac{196 \times 100}{188}$$

$$= 104.26.$$

65. The new trend equation is obtained on changing the value of X to (X + 4). Since change in the origin is 2009 - 2005 = 4 years.

∴ The new trend equation becomes

$$Y = 110 + 2(X + 4)$$

$$= 100 + 2X + 8$$

$$= 118 + 2X$$

66. The probability of drawing a red ball = $\frac{1}{6}$.

⇒ The probability of drawing a non-red ball

$$= \frac{5}{6}$$

P{A says red ball to red ball} = $\frac{2}{3}$

P{B says red ball to red ball} = $\frac{4}{5}$

If a red ball has been drawn, the probability that both A and B agree in asserting that it is red is given by compound probability theorem as:

$$\frac{1}{6}\times\frac{2}{3}\times\frac{4}{5} = \frac{4}{45}$$

The probability that A asserts falsely that a certain ball is red = $\left(1-\frac{2}{3}\right)\times\frac{1}{5}=\frac{1}{15}$, because there are 5 balls of different colours, other than red.

Similarly, the probability that B asserts falsely that a certain ball is red = $\left(1-\frac{4}{5}\right)\times\frac{1}{5}=\frac{1}{25}$

Hence, if a non-red ball is drawn, the probability that both A and B agree in asserting that it is red is

$$\frac{5}{6}\times\frac{1}{15}\times\frac{1}{25}=\frac{1}{450}$$

After a ball is drawn the probability that both agree in saying truth to the probability that both say false is

$$\frac{4}{45}:\frac{1}{450}$$

∴ Required probability that the statement is true is:

$$\frac{\frac{4}{45}}{\frac{4}{45}+\frac{1}{450}}=\frac{40}{41}.$$

68. Mean of Binomial distribution = np

and S.D. of Binomial distribution = $\sqrt{npq}$

$\because \quad np = 4 \quad$ ...(1)

and $\quad \sqrt{npq} = \sqrt{2}$

$\Rightarrow \quad npq = 2 \quad$ ...(2)

Divide (1) by (2)

$$\frac{np}{npq} = \frac{4}{2}$$

$$\Rightarrow \quad \frac{1}{q} = 2 \quad \Rightarrow \quad q = \frac{1}{2}$$

$$\therefore \quad p = \frac{1}{2}$$

From equation (1)

$$np = 4$$

$$\Rightarrow \quad n\times\frac{1}{2} = 4$$

$$n = 8.$$

170. $TC = 45000 + 500Q - 5Q^2 + 0.2Q^3$

$$\therefore \quad MC = \frac{d(TC)}{dx} = 500 - 10Q + 0.6Q^2$$

If $\quad Q = 10$

$$MC = 500 - 100 + 60$$

$$= 460.$$

ECONOMICS

Including

- ☞ Micro Economics
- ☞ Macro Economics
- ☞ Indian Economy

Micro Economics

DEMAND AND SUPPLY ANALYSIS

DEMAND

Demand is a function of price, income, price of related goods and tastes and is expressed as

$$D = f(p, y, pr, t).$$

When income, prices of related goods and tastes are given, the demand function is

$$D = f(p).$$

Types of Demand

Three kinds of demands may be distinguished :

(a) Price Demand
(b) Income Demand
(c) Cross Demand

Price Demand : Price demand refers to the various quantities of a commodity or service that a consumer or service that a consumer would purchase at a given time in a market at various hypothetical prices. It is assumed that other things, such as consumer's income, his tastes and prices of inter-related goods, remain unchanged.

Income Demand : The income demand refers to the various qualities of goods and services which would be purchased by the consumers at various levels of incomes. Here we assume that the price of the commodity or service as well as the prices of inter-related goods and the tastes and desires of consumers do not change.

Cross Demand : The cross demand means the quantities of a good or service which will be purchase with reference to change in price not of this good but of other inter-related goods. These goods are either substitutes or complementary goods. A change in the price of tea, for instance, will affect the demand for coffee.

Law of Demand

This law expresses a relationship between the quantity demanded and its price. It may be defined in Marshall's words as "the amount demanded increase with a fall in price, and diminishes with a rise in price." Thus it expresses an inverse relation between price and demand. The inverse price-demand relationship is based on **other things remaining equal.**

Exceptions to the Law of Demand

As we have said above, generally the demand curve slopes downward to the left. But some times, the demand curve, instead of sloping downward, will rise upwards. In other words, some time people will buy more when the price rises. This can be represented only by a rising demand curve. These were first investigated by **Sir Robert Giffen.** The **Giffen Paradox** holds that the demand is strengthened with a rise or weakened with a fall in price.

Many causes are attributed to an upward sloping demand curve :

1. War
2. Depression

3. Giffen Paradox
4. Demonstration Effect
5. Speculation

Increase and Decrease Vs. Extensive and Contraction of Demand

When the demand changes merely because the price has changed, it is a case of **extension** or **contraction.** If the change in demand is due to a factor other than the price, it is known as **increase** or **decrease** in demand.

Various Concepts of Demand Elasticity

Demand for a good is determined by its price, incomes of the people, prices of related goods etc. Quantity demanded of a good will change as a result of a change in the size of any of these determinants of demand. The concept of elasticity of demand therefore refers to the **degree of responsiveness** of quantity demanded of a good to a change in its price, income or prices of related goods. Accordingly, there are three kinds of demand elasticity–

1. Price Elasticity
2. Income Elasticity
3. Cross Elasticity

Price Elasticity of Demand

Price elasticity means the degree of **responsiveness** or **sensitiveness** of quantity demanded of a good to a changes in its prices.

Thus

$$\text{Price Elasticity} = -\frac{\text{Percentage change in quantity}}{\text{Percentage change in price}}$$

$$= -\frac{\text{Change in quantity demanded / Quantity demanded}}{\text{Change in price / Price}}$$

or, in symbolic terms

$$e_P = -\frac{\Delta q/q}{\Delta P/P}$$

$$= -\frac{\Delta q}{q} \times \frac{P}{\Delta P}$$

Price Elasticity : Measures, Meaning and Nomenclature

Numerical measure of elasticity	*Verbal description*	*Terminology*
* Zero	Quantity demanded does not change as price changes	Perfectly inelastic
* Greater than Zero, but less than one	Quantity demanded changes by a smaller percentage than does price.	Inelastic
* One	Quantity demanded changes by exactly the same percentage as does price.	Unit elasticity
* Greater than one, but less than infinity	Quantity demanded changes by a larger percentage than does price	Elastic
* Infinity	Purchasers are prepared to buy all they can obtain at some price and none at all at an even slightly higher price	Perfectly elastic

Price Elasticity and Changes in Total Expenditure

1. When Price elasticity of demand is equal to unit ($e_P = 1$), the total expenditure remains the same with the fall or rise in price.
2. When Price elasticity of demand is greater than one ($e_p > 1$), the total expenditure will increase with the fall in price and will decrease with the rise in price.
3. When Price elasticity of demand is less than one ($e_P < 1$), the total expenditure will decrease with the fall in price and will increase with the rise in price.

Cross Elasticity of Demand

The change in the demand for one good in response to the change in price of the other good represents the cross elasticity of demand of one good for the other. In other words, the cross elasticity of demand is the relation between percentage change in the quantity demanded of a good to the percentage in the price of a related good.

Coefficients of cross elasticity of demand of x for y

$$= \frac{\text{Percentage change in the quantity demanded of } x}{\text{Percentage change in the price of } y}$$

or,

$$e_c = \frac{\Delta q_x / q_x}{\Delta p_y / p_y}$$

$$= \frac{\Delta q_x}{q_x} \div \frac{\Delta p_y}{p_y}$$

$$= \frac{\Delta q_x}{q_x} \times \frac{p_y}{\Delta p_y}$$

$$= \frac{\Delta q_x}{\Delta p_y} \times \frac{p_y}{q_x}$$

Income Elasticity

The responsiveness of demand to changes in income is termed **income elasticity of demand.**

Income Elasticity

$$= \frac{\text{Percentage change in quantity demanded}}{\text{Percentage change in income}}$$

Income Elasticity : Measures and Meaning

Numerical Value of Income Elasticity	*Verbal description*
• Negative	Demand for the commodity falls as income rises
• Zero	Demand for the commodity does not change as income changes
• Greater than Zero but less than one	Demand for the commodity rises less than in proportion to the rise in income
• Unity	Demand for the commodity rises in the same proportion as the rise in income
• Greater than Unity	Demand for the commodity rises more than in proportion to the rise in income

THE ELASTICITY OF SUBSTITUTION

Elasticity of substitution is defined as the proportionate change in the ratios of goods X and Y to the proportionate change in their price ratio. Its numerical coefficient is

$$e_s = \frac{\text{Proportionate change in the ratio of } x \text{ and } y}{\text{Proportionate change in their price ratios}}$$

Algebraically

$$e_s = \frac{\Delta\left(\frac{x}{y}\right) \Big/ \frac{x}{y}}{\Delta\left(\frac{P_x}{P_y}\right) \Big/ \frac{P_x}{P_y}}$$

Factors Affecting Price Elasticity of Demand

1. Nature of the Commodity
2. Existence of Substitutes
3. Several Uses
4. Deferred Consumption
5. Habits
6. Income Groups
7. Proportion of Income Spent
8. Level of Prices
9. Time Factor

ELASTICITY OF SUPPLY

Elasticity of supply refers to the sensitiveness or **responsiveness** of the supply to changes in price. In other words, the elasticity of supply is defined as the percentage change in quantity supplied divided by the percentage change in price, and it is a measure of the degree to which the quantity supplied responds to price changes. Thus,

Elasticity of Supply

$$= \frac{\text{Percentage change in quantity supplied}}{\text{Percentage change in price}}$$

CONCEPT OF REVENUE

The term 'revenue' refers to the receipts obtained by a firm from the sale of certain quantities of a commodity at various prices. The revenue concept relates to total revenue, average revenue and marginal revenue.

Total Revenue : Total revenue refers to the total amount of money that the firm receives from the sale of its products. Thus, the total revenue is obviously equal to the quantity sold multiplied by the selling price of the commodity, *i.e.,*

$$TR = P.Q$$

where

TR = total revenue

P = price per unit

Q = quantity

Average Revenue : Average revenue can be obtained by dividing by the total revenue by the number of units sold. Thus,

$$\text{average revenue} = \frac{\text{total revenue}}{\text{total output sold}}$$

$$\text{or,} \quad AR = \frac{TR}{Q} = \frac{P.Q}{Q} = P$$

Thus, average revenue is the price of commodity. It follows from this that the curve which relates average revenue to output is identical with the demand curve that relates price to output.

Marginal Revenue : Marginal revenue is the net revenue earned by selling on additional unit of the product. In other words, marginal revenue is the addition made to the total revenue by selling one more unit of the good. Putting it in algebraic expression marginal revenue is the addition made to total revenue by selling n units of a product instead of $(n - 1)$ where n is any given number. Therefore,

Marginal Revenue = difference in total revenue in increasing sales from $(n - 1)$ units to n units

$$MR_n = TR_n - TR_{n-1}$$

If TR stands for total revenue and Q stands for output, then marginal revenue (MR) can be expressed as follows :

$$MR = \frac{d(TR)}{dQ}$$

$\frac{d(TR)}{dQ}$ indicates the slope of the total revenue curve. Thus if the total revenue curve is given to us, we can find out marginal revenue at various levels of output by measuring the slopes at the corresponding points on the total revenue curve.

Relationship among Total Revenue, Average Revenue and Marginal Revenue

In the price theory we are more interested in relationship between average revenue and marginal revenue. We can say that :

1. So long as average revenue is falling, marginal revenue (MR) will be lower than the AR
2. Marginal revenue falls more sharply than average revenue (AR)
3. So long as marginal revenue (MR) is positive, total revenue will be increased.
4. When marginal revenue is zero, total revenue is maximum.
5. When marginal revenue is negative then total revenue begins to fall.

Relationship among Price Elasticity of Demand, Marginal Revenue and Total Revenue

The revenue schedule brings out the relationship between different revenues and elasticity of demand. This can be done in terms of elasticity of demand. The relationship between revenue and elasticity may be stated more precisely by as :

$$E = \frac{AR}{AR - MR}$$

where E stands for elasticity of demand.

From this equation we can derive the following two equations :

$$(i) \quad AR = MR\left(\frac{E}{E-1}\right)$$

$$(ii) \quad MR = AR\left(\frac{E-1}{E}\right)$$

It follows that if we have known elasticity of demand, we can calculate marginal revenue at different prices. For example, if demand for a product is highly elastic, a small percentage change in prices will lead to a much higher percentage change in demand. Marginal revenue, *i.e.*, the revenue derived from the sale of an additional unit, shall be very close to the average revenue. We can sum up these relationships as :

1. So long as the average revenue is falling, marginal revenue (MR) will be lower than the average revenue (AR).
2. MR falls more sharply than AR.
3. So long as MR is positive, total revenue will be increasing.
4. Where MR is zero, total revenue is maximum.
5. Where MR is negative, the total revenue begins to fall.

The relationship among price elasticity, average revenue and marginal revenue can be stated as :

$$e = \frac{AR}{AR - MR}$$

$$\Rightarrow AR = MR\left(\frac{e}{e-1}\right)$$

$$\Rightarrow MR = AR\left(\frac{e-1}{e}\right)$$

Here, e = Price elasticity of demand
AR = Average revenue
MR = Marginal revenue.

CONSUMER BEHAVIOUR

INDIFFERENCE CURVES

An indifference curve is the locus of points-particular combinations or bundles of goods-which yields the same utility (level of satisfaction) to the consumer, so that he is indifferent as to the particular combination he consumes. In other words, all combinations of the goods lying on a consumer's indifference curve are equally desirable to or equally preferred by him.

MARGINAL RATE OF SUBSTITUTION

The concept of marginal rate of substitution is an important tool of indifference curve analysis of demand. Marginal rate of substitution of x for y (MRS_{xy}) represents the amount of y which the consumer has to give up for the gain of one additional unit of x so that his level of satisfaction remains the same.

The negative of the slope of an indifference curve at any one point is called the marginal rate of substitution of the two commodities (MRS_{xy}). In other words, the MRS_{xy} is in fact the slope of the curve at a point on the indifference curve. Thus

$$\text{Slope of indifference curve} = -\frac{\Delta Y}{\Delta X} = MRS_{xy}$$

Note

* If the MRS_{xy} is diminishing, the indifference curve must be **convex** to the origin.
* If MRS_{xy} is constant, the indifference curve will be **straight line** sloping downwards to the right.
* If MRS_{xy} is increasing, the indifference curve will be **concave** to the origin.
* In the case of perfect complementaries the MRS_{xy} is zero and the indifference curve will be L shaped.

PROPERTIES OF INDIFFERENCE CURVES

1. Indifference Curves slope downward to the right
2. Indifference Curves are Convex to the Origin
3. Indifference Curves cannot Intersect each other
4. Indifference Curves are not necessarily parallel to each other
5. A Higher Indifference Curve represents Higher Level of Satisfaction than the Lower Indifference Curve
6. An Indifference Curve cannot Touch either Axis

Slope of the Budget Line

The slope of the budget line is equal to the ratio of the prices of two goods.

The two determinants of the price line or budget line are :

1. The prices of goods.
2. The consumer's income to be spent on the goods.

CONSUMER'S EQUILIBRIUM

A consumer is in equilibrium when given his tastes, and prices of the two goods, he spends a given money income on the purchase of two goods in such a way as to get the maximum satisfaction.

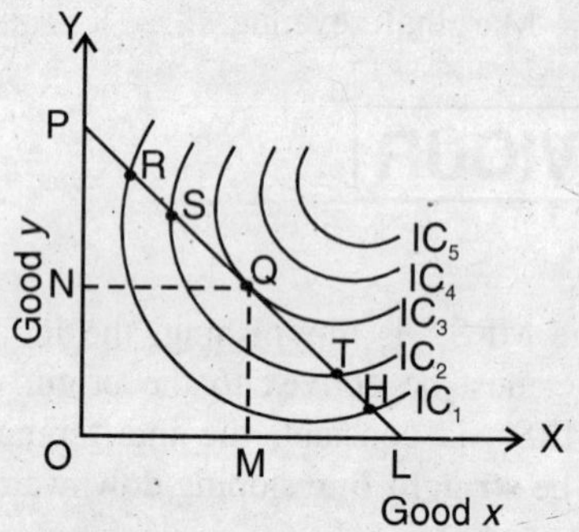

Fig.: *Consumer's Equilibrium*

With the given money expenditure and the given prices of the goods as shown by PL (Budget Line) the consumer will obtain maximum possible satisfaction and will therefore be in equilibrium position at point Q at which the rate budget line PL is tangent to the indifference curve IC_3. In this equilibrium position at Q the consumer will buy OM amount of good X and ON amount of good Y.

At the tangency point Q, the slopes of the price line PL and indifference curve IC_3 are equal. Slope of the indifference curve shows the marginal rate of substitution of X for Y (MRS_{xy}), while the slope of the price line indicates the ratio between the price of two goods (p_x/p_y). Thus at the equilibrium point Q,

$$MRS_{xy} = \frac{MU_x}{MU_y} = \frac{P_x}{P_y}$$

This is a necessary but not sufficient condition for equilibrium. The **second condition** is that the indifference curves be convex to the origin, or to put it in another way, the MRS_{xy} must be falling at the point of equilibrium.

INCOME EFFECT

Income effect is the effect on the quantity demanded exclusively as a result of change in money income, all prices remaining constant.

Income effect can either be **positive** or **negative.** Income effect for good is said to be **positive** when with the increase in income of the consumer, his consumption of the good also increases. This is the normal case.

Income effect for a good is said to be **negative** when with the increase in his income, the consumer reduces his consumption of the good. Such goods for which income effect is negative are called **Inferior Goods.**

SUBSTITUTION EFFECT

Substitution effect means the change in the purchases of a good as a consequence of a change in relative prices alone, real income remaining constant.

Now, two slightly different concepts of substitution effect have been developed, one by Hicks and Allen and the other by Slutsky.

In **Hicks-Allen Substitution effect** price change is accompanied by so much change in money income that the consumer is neither better or nor worse off than before. In other words, money income of the consumer is changed by an amount which keeps the consumer on the same indifference curve on which he was before the change in the price. Thus **Hick-Allen substitution effect takes place on the same indifference curve.**

ENGEL CURVE

Engel curve shows the quantities of a good which the consumer will purchase at various income levels, given his tastes, preferences and the price of the good in question. Engel curve of **normal goods** is upward sloping which shows that as income increases consumer buys more of a commodity.

PRICE EFFECT

When the price of a good changes, the consumer would be either better off or worse off them before, depending upon whether the price falls or rises. In other words, as a result of change in price of the good, his equilibrium position would lie at a higher indifference curve in case of the fall in price and at a lower indifference curve in case of the rise in price.

Suppose, with a certain fixed income and given market prices of the two goods X and Y represented by the Price line ML_1, the consumer is in equilibrium at point P_1 in Figure.

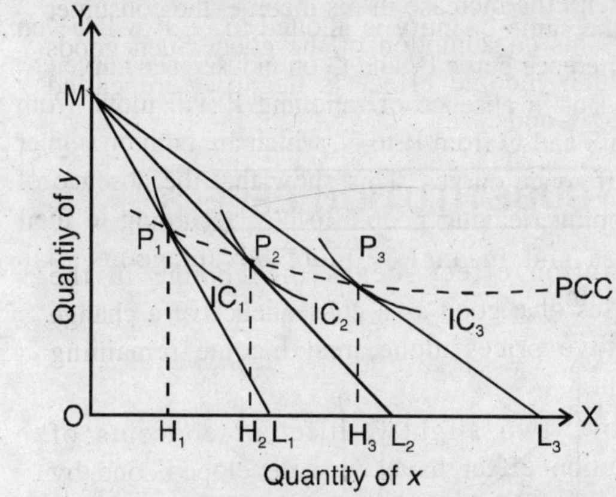

Fig.: *Price Effect*

Suppose the price of X falls, income and price of Y remaining unchanged, so that new price line becomes ML_2, the consumer will be in equilibrium at point P_2 on the higher indifference curve IC_2. In this position, he will be buying OH_2 of commodity X.

If the price of X falls further, so that the relevant price line is ML_3 the consumer will be in equilibrium at point P_3 and will be buying OH_3 of commodity X. In the same way, we can discover other points of equilibrium for every other price at which X-might be sold. When all the points such as P_1, P_2, P_3 are joined together we have the price consumption curve of the consumer for good X. This shows the price effect. It shows how the consumption of commodity X changes, as its price changes, the consumer's income and price of Y remaining the same.

Consumer's Surplus

Concept of consumer's surplus is a very important concept in economic theory especially in welfare economics. The concept of consumer's surplus was first of all evolved by **Dr. Alfred Marshall,** who maintained that it can be measured in monetary units, and is equal to the difference between the amount of money that a consumer actually pays to buy a certain quantity of a commodity X, and the amount that he would be willing to pay for this quantity rather than do without it.

Consumer's Surplus = What a consumer is prepared to pay minus what he actually pays.

$= \sum MU -$ (Price × Number of units purchased)

SOME APPLICATIONS OF INDIFFERENCE CURVE ANALYSIS

The indifference curve technique is not merely a tool of theoretical analysis. It can also be put to practical use in several economic spheres. As such, or occupies an important place in applied economics. Indifference curves have been used to explain the concept of consumer's surplus, substitutability and complementarily, supply curve of labour of taxation, index number problem and several other things. We shall explain here only few of the applications.

TAXATION : DIRECT VS. INDIRECT TAXES

An important application of indifference curve is to judge the welfare effects of direct and indirect taxes on the individuals. In the other words, if the Government wants to raise a given amount of revenue whether it wil be better to do so levying a direct tax or indirect tax from the view point of welfare of the individuals. Consider Figure where on the X-axis, good X and on the Y-axis money are measured. With a given income of the individual and the given price of good X, the price line is PL_1 which is tangent to indifference curve IC_3 on point Q_0 where the individual is in equilibrium position.

Suppose now that Government levies an excise duty (indirect tax) on good X. With the imposition of excise duty, the price of good X will rise. As a result of the rise in price of good X, the price line will rotate to a new position PL_2 which is tangent to indifference curve IC_1 at point Q_1. It is thus clear that as a result of the imposition of excise duty, the individual has shifted from a higher indifference curve IC_3 to a lower one IC_1, that is, his level of satisfaction or welfare has declined. It should be further noted that at point Q_1 (that is, after the imposition of excise duty), the individual is purchasing ON amount of good X and has paid PM amount of money for it. At the old price (before the excise duty was imposed), he could purchase ON quantity of good X for PT amount of money. Thus, the difference TM (or KQ_1) between the two is the excise duty which the individual is paying.

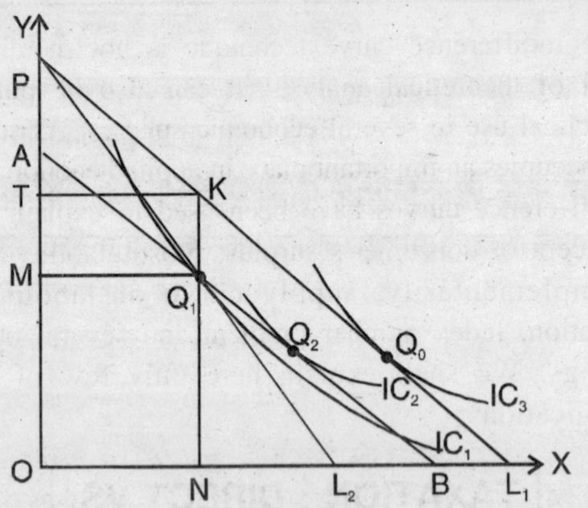

Fig.

Now, suppose that instead of excise duty, Government levies income tax on the individual when the individual is initially at point Q_0 on indifference curve IC_3. With the imposition of income tax, the price line will shift below but will be parallel to the original price line PL_1. Further, if the same amount of revenue is to be raised through income tax as with excise duty, then the new price line AB should be drawn at such a distance from the original price line PL_1 that it passes through the point Q_1. So, it will be seen in Figure that with the imposition of income tax, we have drawn the price line AB which is passing through the point Q_1. However, with AB as the price line, individual is in equilibrium at point Q_2 on indifference curve IC_2 which lies at a higher level that IC_1. In other words at point Q_2 individual's level of welfare is higher than at Q_1. Income tax has reduced the individual's welfare less than that by the excise duty. Thus, indirect tax (excise duty) causes an excess burden on the individual.

RATIONING

Rationing is another field in which the indifference curve technique can be applied. Suppose in **non-price rationing,** an equal quantity of the rationed commodity is allotted to each individual. Take two individuals P and Q (Fig.). X_0 is alloted to P and Y_0 the same quantity is allotted to Q. P will be on indifference curve P_1 and Q on indifference curve Q_1.

But in absence of rationing P will move from R to S and Q from R to N, which are both on higher indifference curves. This show that the absence of rationing (leaving people to buy according to their tastes and means) is more advantageous than rationing.

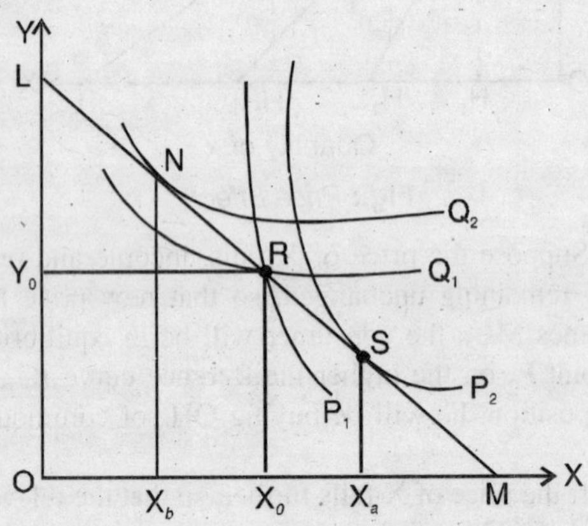

Fig.

COST OF LIVING INDEX

The cost of living depends on the collection of goods and services consumed by the household. The standard of living consists of the various combinations of goods yielding equal satisfaction. Such combinations can be represented by points on the same indifference curve. If the combinations of goods purchased in two successive years are plotted on the indifference curve, it can be shown whether the standard of living has risen or fallen according as the most preferable combination is on a higher or lower indifference curve touching the respective price lines.

EFFECT OF SUBSIDIES TO CONSUMERS

Another important application of indifference curve is to analyse with its aid the effect of subsidies to the consumers. Let us take the case of food subsidy which is given by the Government to help the needy families. Suppose that under food-subsidy programme, the needed families are entitled to purchase food at half the market price, the other half of the market price is paid by the Government as subsidy. The effect of this subsidy on consumer's welfare and money value of this subsidy to the consumer is illustrated in Figure where the quantity of food is measured on the X-axis and money on the Y-axis.

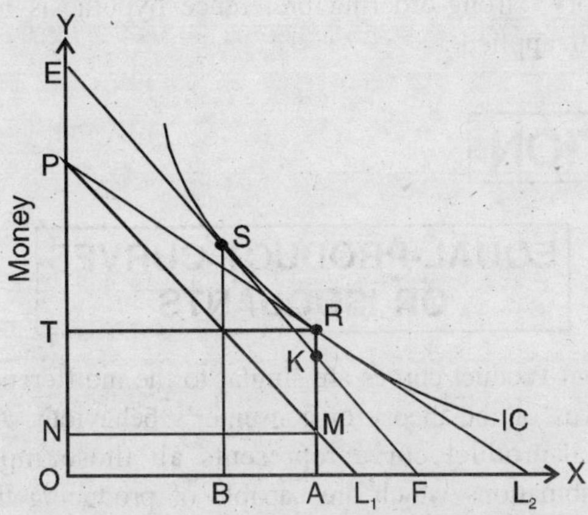

Fig. : *Effect of Subsidies to Consumer*

Let us suppose that the individual has OP money income. Given this money income and given the market price of food, the price line is PL_1. Since we are assuming that subsidy paid by the Government is half the market price of food, the consumer would pay half the market price. Therefore, with subsidy the individual will face the price line PL_2 where $OL_1 = L_1L_2$. With price line PL_2, the individual is in equilibrium at point R on the indifference curve IC at which he is purchasing OA quantity of food. By purchasing OA quantity of food, the individual is spending PT amount of money.

Now, if no food subsidy was given and therefore the price line was PL_1, then for buying OA quantity of food, the individual would have spent PN amount of money. In other words, PN is the market price of OA quantity of food. Since PT amount of money paid by the individual himself, the remaining amount TN or RM is paid by the Governments as food subsidy for the individual.

The important question is what is the money value of this food subsidy (RM) to the individual. When no food subsidy is paid, the individual faces the price line PL_1. In other to find the money value of the subsidy to the individual, draw a line EF parallel to PL_1 so that it touches the same indifference curve IC where the individual comes to be in equilibrium when subsidy is paid. It will be seen in figure that price line EF touches the indifference curve IC at a point S and is buying OB quantity of food. This means that if individuals is paid PE amount of money, he reaches the same indifference curve IC (same level of welfare) at which he is when subsidy is paid by the Government. Thus, PE, is money value of the subsidy to the individual. It will be seen in Figure that PE is less than RM which is the amount of money paid by the Government as subsidy. In our figure PE = MK and RM is greater than MK. Therefore, RM is also greater than PE. It follows that PE is less than RM. If instead of giving RM as subsidy on food, Government pays the individual cash money equal to PE, the individual will reach the same level of welfare as he does with RM subsidy. Thus, the money equivalent of the subsidy to the individual is less than the cost of the subsidy to the Government.

Professor Scitovsky remarks, "The value of the subsidy to the subsidised person is smaller than the cost of subsidy to the Government. The common sense interpretation of this result is that one can make a man happier by giving him cash and letting him spend it as he thinks best than by forcing him take all his relief in the form of one commodity. Hence, relief payments in cash are preferable to a food subsidy because they are economically more efficient, giving the relief receipts either a greater gain at the same cost to the Government or the same gain at a lower cost."

But the above principle regarding the programme of subsidised food, subsidised housing etc. cannot always be validly applied to the Government subsidy programme since the above principle based upon the **subjective benefits to the individuals** which is not always the correct criteria to judge the desirability of Government subsidy programme.

For instance, the aim of Government's food subsidy programme may be that the needy families should consume more food so that their health and efficiency may be improved. It will be seen in figure that with food subsidy RM, the individual is having OA amount of food, whereas with equivalent cash payment of PE the individual purchases OB amount of food which is less than OA. Thus the food subsidy has induced the individual to consume move food than in case of cash payment. Similarly, if a country has food surplus and want to dispose of them then the food subsidy to the needy families will be the ideal measure to increase the consumption of foodgrains and thereby to dispose of the food surpluses.

REVEALED PREFERENCE THEORY

Samuelson introduced the term **'revealed preference'** into economics in 1938. Since then the literature in this field has proliferated, Revealed preference theory is called the behaviourist ordinal-utility theory.

Assumptions

1. Rationality
2. Consistency
3. Transitivity
4. The Revealed Preference Axiom
5. Positive Income-Elasticity of Demand

Prof. Samuelson's revealed preference theory is based upon the **strong form of preference hypothesis.** In other words, in revealed preference theory, strong-ordering preference hypothesis has been applied.

PRODUCTION

PRODUCTION FUNCTION

The production function expresses a functional relationship between quantities of inputs and outputs. It shows how and to what extent output changes with variations in inputs during a specified period of time. Algebraically, it may be expressed in the form of an equation as

$$Y = f(L, K, R, S)$$

where

Y = output

L = labour input

K = capital input

R = raw materials

S = land input

EQUAL-PRODUCT CURVES OR ISOQUANTS

Equal-Product curves are similar to the indifference curves of the theory of consumer's behaviour. An equal-product curve represents all those input combinations which are capable of producing the same level of output. These equal-product curves are also known as isoquants and iso-product curves.

Properties of Isoquants

The following are the important properties of equal product curves.

1. Isoquants are negatively inclined.
2. An isoquant lying above and to the right of another represents a higher output level.

3. No two iso-quants can intersect each other.
4. No isoquant can touch either axis.
5. Isoquant are convex to the origin.

MARGINAL RATE OF TECHNICAL SUBSTITUTION

The principle of marginal rate of technical substitution (MRTS) is based on the production function where two inputs can be substituted in variable proportions in such a way as to produce constant level of output.

Thus, marginal rate of technical substitution

$$MRTS_{xy} = -\frac{dY}{dX}$$

An important point to be noted about the marginal rate of technical substitution is that it is equal to the ratio of the marginal products of two factors.

MARGINAL PRODUCTS OF THE FACTORS

The marginal product of a factor is defined as the change in output resulting from a (very small) change of this factor, keeping all other factors constant.

Mathematically the marginal product of each factor is the partial derivative of the production function with respect to this factor. Thus

$$MP_L = \frac{dQ}{dL}$$

and $$MP_K = \frac{dQ}{dK}$$

where

MP_L = marginal product of labour

MP_K = marginal product of capital

RIDGE LINES

The locus of points of isoquants where the marginal products of the factors are zero form the ridge lines. The upper ridge line implies that the MP **of capital is zero.** The lower ridge line implies that the MP **of labour is zero.** Production techniques are only (technically) efficient inside the ridge lines. Outside the ridge lines the marginal products of factors are negative and the methods of production are inefficient, since they require more quality of both factors for producing a given level of output. Such inefficient methods are not considered by the theory of production, since they imply irrational behaviour of the firm.

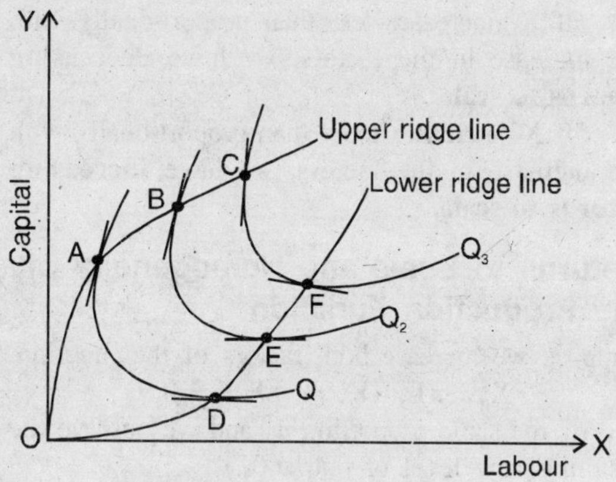

Fig. : *Ridge Lines*

Laws of Production

The laws of production describe the technically possible ways of increasing the level of production. Output may increase in various ways.

Output can be increased by changing all factors or production. Clearly this is possible only in the long-run. Thus **the laws of returns to scale** refer to the long-run analysis of production.

In the short run output may be increased by using more of the variable factor, while capital (and possibly other factors as well) are kept constant. The marginal product of the variable factor will decline eventually as more and more quantities of this factor are combined with the other constant factors. The expansion of output with one factor constant is described by the **law of diminishing returns** of the variable factor, which is often referred to as the **law of variable proportions.**

The term 'return to scale' refers to the changes in output as all factors change by the same proportion.

Suppose we start from an initial level of inputs and output

$X_0 = f(L, K)$

and we increase all the factors by the same proportion *m*. We will clearly obtain a new level of output X^*, higher than the original level X_0,

$X^* = f(mL, mK)$

*If X^* increases by the same proportion *m* as the inputs, we say that there are **constant returns to scale.**

*If X^* increases less than proportionally with the increase in the factors, we have **decreasing returns to scale.**

*If X^* increases more than proportionally with the increase in the factors, we have **increasing returns to scale.**

Returns to Scale and Homogeneity of the Production Function

Suppose we increase both factors of the function

$X_0 = f(L, K)$

by the same proportion *m*, and we observe the resulting new level of output X^*

$X^* = f(mL, mK)$

If *m* can be factored out, then the new level of output X^* can be expressed as a function of *m* (to any power *a*) and the initial level of output

$X^* = m^a f(L, K)$

or $X^* = m^a X_0$

and the production function is called **homogeneous.** If *m* cannot be factored out, the production function is non-homogeneous. The power *a* of *m* is called the **degree of homogeneity** of the function and is a measure of the returns to scale :

*If $a = 1$, we have constant returns to scale. Thus production function is something called **linear homogeneous.**

*If $a <$ a, we have decreasing returns to scale.

*If $a > 1$, we have increasing returns to scale.

The Law of Variable Proportions : Short Run Analysis of Production

Law of variable proportions occupies an important place in economic theory. This law examines the production function with one factor variable, keeping the quantities of other factors fixed. In other words, it refers to the input-output relation when the output is increased by varying the quantity of one input.

Three Stages of the Law of Variable Proportions

The behaviour of output when the varying quantity of one factor is combined with a fixed quantity of the other can be divided into three distinct stages.

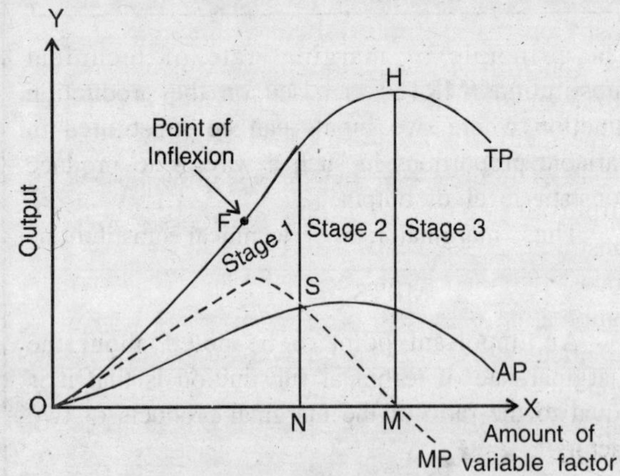

Fig. : *Three Stages of the Law of Variable Proportions*

In order to understand these three stages it is better to graphically illustrate the production function with one factor variable. This is done in Figure. In this figure, on the X-axis is measured the quantity of the variable factor and on the Y-axis are measured the total product, average product and the marginal product. The total product curve TP goes on increasing to a point and after that it starts declining. Average and marginal product curves also rise and then decline, marginal product curve starts declining earlier than the average product curve. The behaviour of these total, average and marginal products of the variable factor consequent on the increase in its amount is generally divided into three stages.

Iso Cost Line

The isocost line is the locus of all combinations of factors the firm can purchase with a given monetary cost outlay. There is a close analogy between the consumer's price line and firm's isocost line.

The slope of the isocost line is equal to the ratio of the prices of the factors of production. Thus,

Slope of isocost line = $\frac{w}{r}$

$= \frac{\text{Price of Labour}}{\text{Price of Capital}}$

Case 1 : Maximisation of output Subject to a Cost Constraint (financial constraint)

The firm is in equilibrium when it maximizes its output given its total cost outlay and the prices of the factors, *w* and *r*.

In figure we see that the maximum level of output the firm can produce, given the cost constraint, is X_2 defined by the tangency of the isocost line, and the highest isoquant. The optimal combination of factors of production is K_2 and L_2, for price *w* and *r*. Higher levels of output (to the right of *e*) are desirable but not attainable due to the cost constraint. Other points on AB or below it lie on a lower isoquant than X_2. Hence X_2 is the maximum output possible under the above assumptions (of given cost outlay, given production function, and given factor prices). At the point of tangency (*e*) the slope of the isocost line (*w/r*) is equal to the slope of the isoquant (MP_L/MP_K). This constitutes the first condition for equilibrium. The second condition is that the isoquant be convex to the origin. **In summary : the conditions for equilibrium of the firm are :**

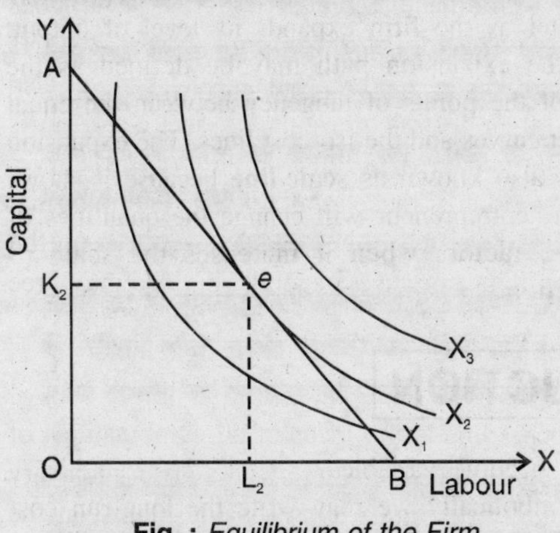

Fig. : *Equilibrium of the Firm*

(*a*) Slope of Isoquant = Slope of Isocost line

or $\quad \frac{w}{r} = \frac{MP_L}{MP_K}$

$$\frac{w}{r} = \frac{dX/dL}{dX/dK}$$

$$\frac{w}{r} = MRS_{LK}$$

(*b*) The isoquants must be convex to the origin. If the isoquant is concave the point of tangency of the isocost and the isoquant curves does not define an equilibrium position (figure).

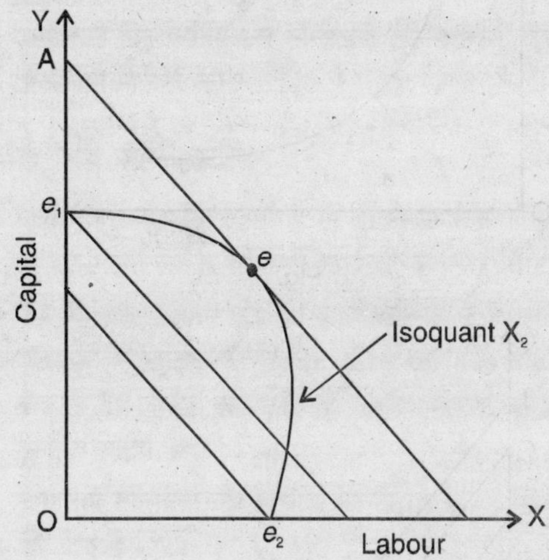

Fig. : *Concave Isoquant*

Output X_2 (depicted by the concave isoquant) can be produced with lower cost at e_2 which lies on a lower isocost curve than *e* **With a concave isoquant we have *a* 'corner solution'.**

Case 2 : Minimisation of Cost for a given Level of Output

The conditions for equilibrium of the firm are formally the same as in case 1. That is, there must be tangency of the (given) isoquant and the lowest possible isocost curve, and the isoquant must be convex. However, the problem is conceptually different in case of cost minimisation. The entrepreneur wants to produce a given output (for example, a bridge, a building, or $\overline{X}$ tons of a commodity) with the minimum cost outlay.

In this case we have a single isoquant (figure) which denotes the desired level of output, but we have a set of isocost curves (figure). Curves closer to the origin show a lower total cost outlay. The isocost lines are parallel because they are drawn on the assumption of constant prices of factors. Since w and r do not change, all the isocost curves have the same slope w/r.

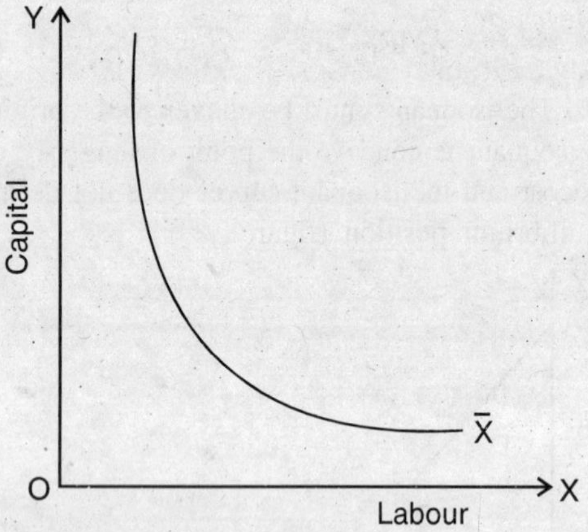

Fig.

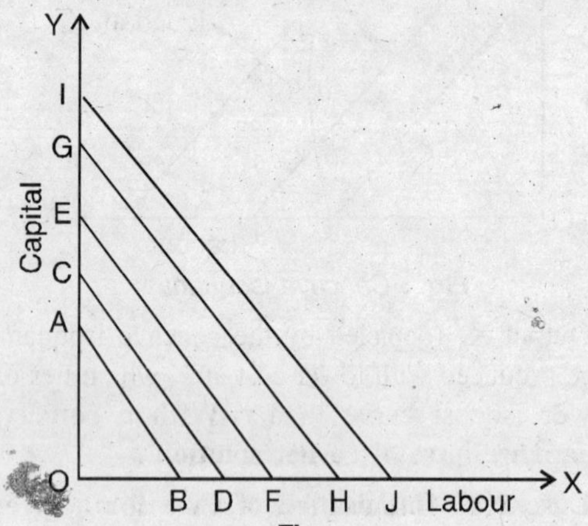

Fig.

The firm minimises its costs by employing the combination of K and L determined by the point of tangency of the $\bar{X}$ isoquant with the lowest isocost line (figure). Points below e are desirable because they show lower cost but are not attainable for output $\bar{X}$. Points above e show higher costs. Hence point e is the **least-cost point,** the point denoting the **least-cost combination** of the factors K and L for producing $\bar{X}$.

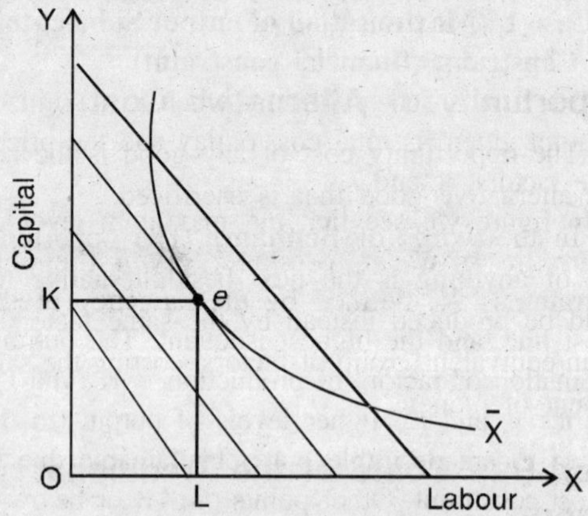

Fig. : *Least-Cost Combination*

Clearly the conditions for equilibrium (least cost) are the same as in case 1, that is, equality of the slopes of isoquant and the isocost curves, and convexity of the isoquant.

Expansion Path

The line joining the minimum cost combinations is called the **expansion path** because it shows how the factor combination with which the firm produces will alter as the firm expands its level of output. Thus the expansion path may be defined as the locus of the points of tangency between the equal product curves and the iso-cost lines. The expansion path is also known as **scale-line** because it shows how the entrepreneur will change the quantities of the two factors when it increases the scale of production.

COST OF PRODUCTION

Economic theory distinguishes between short-run costs and long-run costs. **Short-run costs** are the costs over a period during which some factors of production are fixed. The **long-run costs** are the costs over a period long enough to permit the change of all factors of production. In the long run all factors become variable.

Symbolically we may write the long-run cost function as

$$C = f(X, T, P_f)$$

and the short-run cost function as

$$C = f(X, T, P_f, \bar{K})$$

where

C = total cost

X = output

T = technology

P_f = prices of factors

$\overline{K}$ = fixed factors

Opportunity or Alternative Cost

The opportunity cost of any good is the next best alternative good that is sacrificed.

In the words of **Benham,** "The opportunity cost of anything is the next best alternative that could be produced instead by the same factors or by an equivalent group of factors, costing the same amount of money''.

Short-Run Costs of the Traditional Theory

In the traditional theory of the firm total costs are split into two groups : **total fixed costs and total variable costs.**

$$TC = TFC + TVC$$

where

TC = total cost

TFC = total fixed cost

TVC = total variable cost

The **fixed costs include :**

(a) salaries of administrative staff

(b) depreciation of machinery

(c) expenses for building depreciation and repairs

(d) expenses for land maintenance

The **variable costs include :**

(a) the raw materials

(b) the cost of direct labour

(c) the running expenses of fixed capital, such as fuel, ordinary repairs and routine maintenance.

The average fixed cost is found by dividing TFC by the level of output. Thus

$$AFC = \frac{TFC}{X}$$

Graphically the AFC is a **rectangular hyperbola.**

The average variable cost is similarly obtained by dividing the TVC with the corresponding level of output :

$$AVC = \frac{TVC}{X}$$

The ATC is obtained by dividing the TC by the corresponding level of output.

$$ATC = \frac{TC}{X}$$

$$= \frac{TFC+TVC}{X} = AFC + AVC$$

Marginal Cost

The marginal cost if defined as the change in TC which results from a unit change in output. In other words, marginal cost is the addition to the total cost of producing *n* units instead of (*n* – 1) units where *n* is say any given number. In symbols :

$$MC_n = TC_n - TC_{n-1}$$

Mathematically the marginal cost is the first derivative of the TC function. Denoting total cost by TC and output by X we have

$$MC = \frac{dTC}{dX}$$

The independence of the marginal cost from the fixed cost can be proved algebraically as follows:

$$\begin{aligned} MC_n &= TC_n - TC_{n-1} \\ &= (TVC_n + TFC) - (TVC_{n-1} + TFC) \\ &= TVC_n + TFC - TVC_{n-1} - TFC \\ &= TVC_n - TVC_{n-1} \end{aligned}$$

Hence marginal cost is the addition to the total variable costs when output is increased from *n* – 1 units to *n* units of output.

Long-Run Costs of the Traditional Theory : The 'Envelope' Curve

In the long run all factors are assumed to become variable. We said that the long-run cost curve is a **planning curve,** in the sense that it is a guide to the entrepreneur in his decision to plan the future expansion of his output.

The long run average-cost is derived from short-run cost curves. Each point on the LAC corresponds to a point on a shout-run cost curve, which is tangent to the LAC at that point.

Long-run average cost curve depicts the least possible average cost for producing all possible levels of output.

In the traditional theory of the firm the LAC-curve is U-shaped and it is often called the **'envelope curve'** because it **'envelopes'** the SRC-curve (figure).

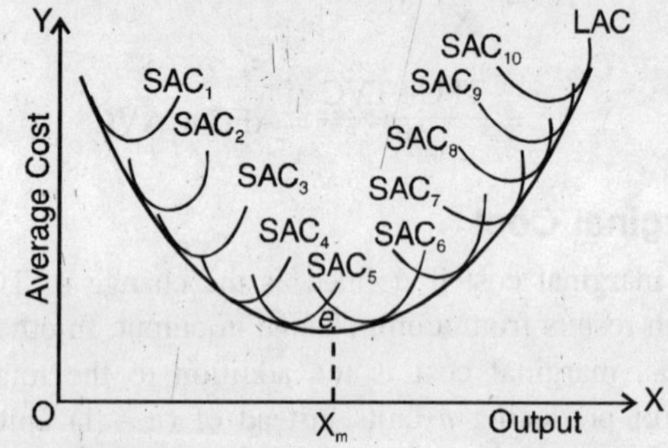

Fig. : *Long Average Cost Curve*

Empirical Evidence And L-Shaped Long-Run Average Cost Curve

Some economists argue on the basis of empirical evidence that the long-run average cost curve is

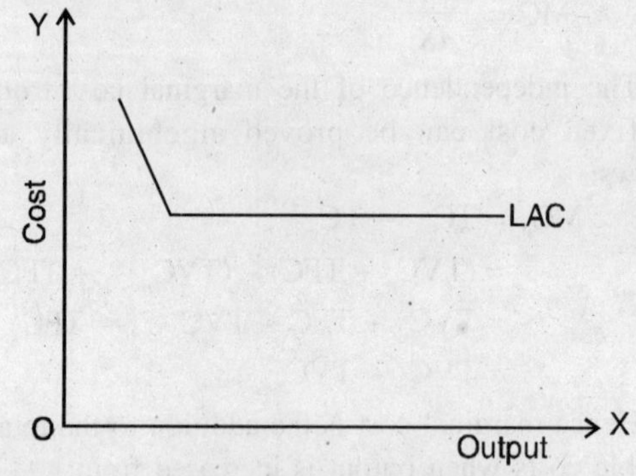

Fig. : *Flat LAC Curve*

L-shaped, rather than U-shaped, as in figure. The L-shaped curve shows a rapid fall in the beginning but after a point "the curve remains flat, or may slope gently downwards, at its right-hand end." The difference between L-shaped LAC and the U-shaped LAC is that there is no rising portion in the former.

External Economies and Diseconomies and Cost Curves

We have explained above that the long-run average cost curve falls downward in the beginning because of economies of scale, namely, the use of greater degree of division of labour and the specialised machinery at higher levels of output. The uses of greater degree of division of labour and the specialised machinery at higher levels of output are the internal economies. They are internal in the sense that they accrue to the firm when its own output or scale increases. Besides internal economies, Marshall introduce the concept of external economies which play an important role in Marshall's partial equilibrium theory of value, especially in his analysis of equilibrium problem under conditions of increasing returns or decreasing cost.

Costs of a firm depend not only on its output level but also on the output level of the industry as a whole. External economies and diseconomies are those economies and diseconomies which accrue to the firms as a result of the expansion in the output of the whole industry and they are not dependent on the output level of individual firms. They are external in the sense that they accrue to the firms not out of its internal situation but from outside it *i.e.,* the output of the industry.

PERFECT COMPETITION

Perfect competition is a market structure characterised by a complete absence of rivalry among the individual firms. In other words, perfect competition implies no rivalry among firms.

Assumptions

The model of perfect competition is based on the following assumptions:

1. There are a large number of firms producing and selling a product.

2. The product of all firms is homogeneous.

The assumptions of large numbers of sellers and of product homogeneity imply that the individual firm in perfect competition is a **price-taker :** Its demand curve is infinitely elastic, indicating that the firm can sell any amount of output at the prevailing market price (figure). The demand curve of the individual firm is also its average revenue curve and its marginal revenue curve.

3. Both the sellers and buyers have perfect information about the prevailing price in the market.

4. Entry into and exit from the industry is free for the firms.

5. No government regulation.

6. Perfect mobility of factors of production.

Equilibrium of the Firm : By Curves of Marginal Revenue and Marginal Cost.

The twin conditions of firms equilibrium under perfect competition are :

1. MC = MR = Price
2. (Slope of MC) > (Slope of MR)

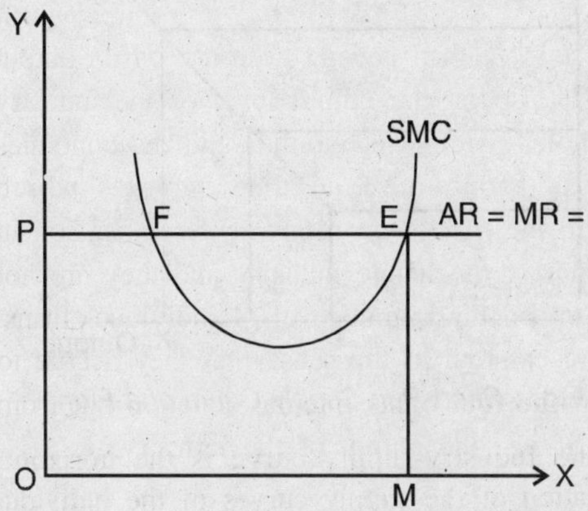

Fig. : *Firm's Equilibrium Under Perfect Competition*

But the fulfilment of the above two conditions does not guarantee that the profits will be earned by the firm. Whether the firm makes excess profits or losses depends on the level of the ATC at the short-run equilibrium. If the ATC is below the price at equilibrium the firm earns excess profits. If, however, the ATC is above the price the firm makes a loss (equal to the area FPEC). In the latter case the firm will continue to produce only if it covers its variable costs. Otherwise, it will close down, since by discontinuing its operations the firm is better off: it minimises its losses. The point at which the firm covers its variable costs is called 'the closing-down point.'

LONG-RUN EQUILIBRIUM OF THE FIRM

In the long run firms are in equilibrium when they have adjusted their plant so as to produce at the minimum point of their long-run AC curve, which is tangent (at this point) to the demand curve defined by the market price. In the long-run the firms will be earning just normal profits, which are included in the LAC.

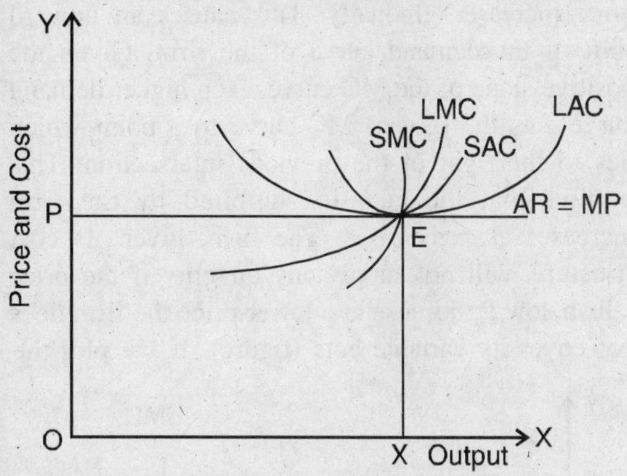

Fig. : *Long-Run Equilibrium of the firm*

The condition for long-run equilibrium of firm can be written as :

SMC = SAC = LMC = LAC = MR = Price

It is clear from above that long-run equilibrium of the firm under perfect competition is established at the minimum point of the long-run average cost curve. Operating at the minimum point of the long-run average cost curve signifies that the firm is of optimum size, that is, it is producing output at the lowest possible cost.

A Classification of Market Forms

Forms of Market Structure	*Number of Firms*	*Price Elasticity of Demand for an individual firms*	*Degree of Control over price*
(a) **Perfect Competition**	A large number of firms	Infinite	None
(b) **Imperfect Competition**	A large number of firms	Large	Some
(i) **Monopolistic Competition**	—	Large	Some
(ii) **Pure Oligopoly** (Oligopoly without Product Differentiation)	Few firms	Small	Some
(iii) **Differentiated Oligopoly** (Oligopoly with product differentiation)	Few firms	Small	Some
(c) **Monopoly**	One	Very Small	Considerable

The Supply Curve of the Firm and the Industry

The supply curve of the firm may be derived by the points of intersection of its MC curve with successive demand curves. Assume that the market price increases gradually. This causes an upward shift of the demand curve of the firm. Given the positive slope of the MC curve, each higher demand curve cuts the (given) MC curve to a point which lies to the right of the previous intersection. This implies that the quantity supplied by the firm increases as price rises. The firm, given its cost structure, will not supply any quantity if the price falls below P, because at a lower price the firm does not cover its variable cots (figure). If we plot the successive points of intersection of MC and the demand curves on a separate graph we observe that the supply curve of the individual firm is identical to its MC curve to the right of the closing-down point (above AVC) M. Below P the quantity supplied by the firm is zero. As price rises above P the quantity supplied increases. The supply curve of the firm is shown in figure.

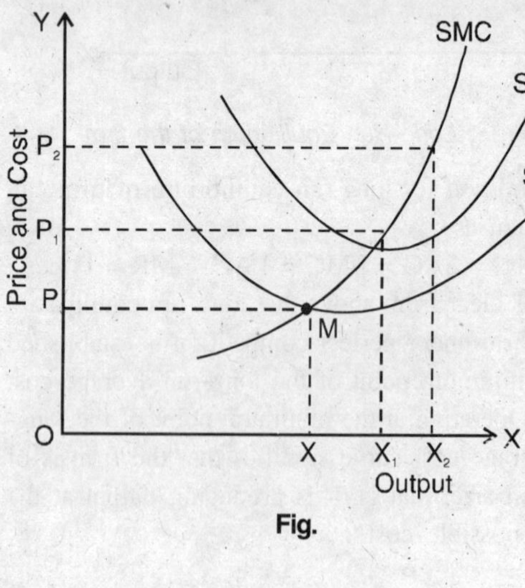

Fig.

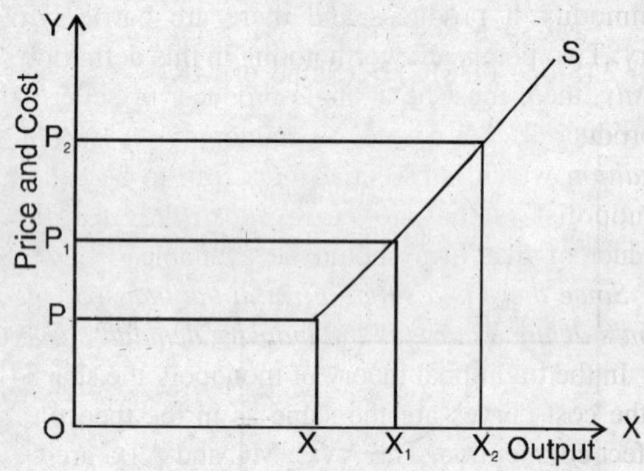

Fig. : ***Short-Run Supply Curve of a Firm***

The Industry-supply curve is the horizontal summation of the supply curves of the individual firms. It is assumed that the factor prices and the technology are given and that the number of firms is very large. Under these conditions the total quantity supplied in the market at each price is the sum of the quantities supplied by all firms at that price. In figure we show the industry supply as a straight line with a positive slope. It should,

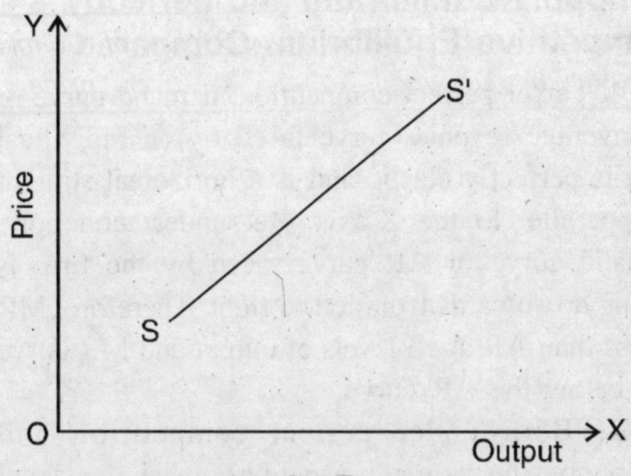

Fig. : *Short-Run Industry Supply Curve*

however, be noted that the particular shape of the market-supply curve depends on the technology and on factors prices, as well as the size distribution of the firms in the industry. All firms are not usually of the same size. The particular size of each firm in perfect competition depends on the entrepreneurial efficiency of the businessman, which is traditionally considered as a random attribute.

Marshall's Time Analysis and Price

Marshall, who propounded the theory that price is determined by both demand and supply, also gave a great importance to the **time element** in the determination of price.

Marshall divided time into following three periods on the basis of response of supply to a given and permanent change in demand.

1. Market Period
2. Short Run
3. Long Run

MONOPOLY MARKET STRUCTURE

Monopoly is a market structure in which there is a single seller, there are no close substitutes for the commodity it produces and there are barriers to entry. Two points are worth noting in this definition. *Firstly*, there must be a single producer or seller of a product if there is to be monopoly. A *second condition* which is essential for a firm to be called monopolist is that no *close substitutes* for the product of that firm should be available.

Since there is a single Firm in the industry, the Firm's demand curve is the industry demand curve.

In the traditional theory of monopoly the shapes of the cost curves are the same as in the theory of perfect competition. The AVC, MC and ATC are U-shaped, while the AFC is a *rectangular hyperbola.*

One point should be stressed here. *The MC curve is not the supply curve of the monopolist, as is the case in perfect competition.* In monopoly there is no unique relationship betwen price and the quantity supplied.

EQUILIBRIUM OF THE MONOPOLIST

A. Short-Run Equilibrium

The monopolist maximises his short-run profits if the following two conditions are fulfilled :

1. MC = MR

2. The slope of MC is greater than the slope of the MR at the point of the intersection.

In Figure the equilibrium of the monopolist is defined by point E, at which the MC intersects the MR curve from below. Thus both cundtions for equilibrium are fulfilled. Price is P and the quantity is X. The monopolist realises excess profits equal to the shaded area APCB. Note that the price is higher than the MR.

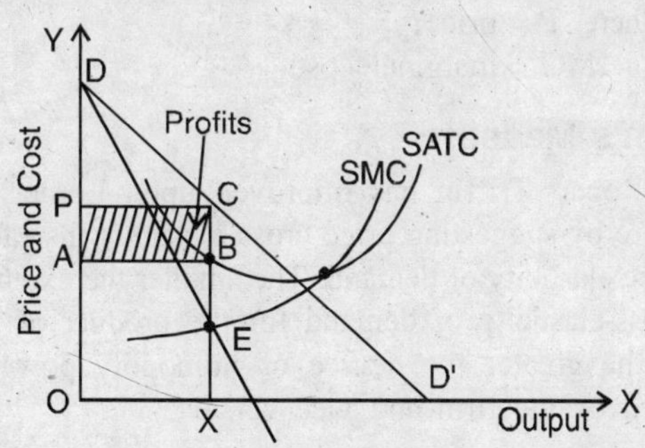

Fig. : *Short-Run Equilibrium Under Monopoly*

It is generally thought that monopolists always earn profits and therefore in layman's mind profits are generally associated with monopoly. But this is a wrong notion.

In the short-run, monopolist can make losses also. If demand is inadequate, the complete absence of competition is of little benefit to the seller. In the short-run, monopolist will continue working so long as price is above the average variable cost. If the price falls below average variable cost, the monopolist would shut down even in the short-run.

In perfect competition the Firm is a price-taker, so that its only decision is output determination. The monopolist is faced by two decisions : setting his price and his output. However, given the downward-sloping demand curve, the two decisions are interdependent. The monopolist will either set his price and sell the amount that the market will take at it, or he will produce the output defined by the intersection of MC and MR, which will be sold at the corresponding price, P.

MEASUREMENT OF THE DEGREE OF MONOPOLY POWER

Monopoly power indicates the degree of control which a producer of seller wields over the price and output to his product.

Lerner's Measure

One of the earliest methods' to measure monopoly power is expressed by Prof. A.P. Lerner in terms of the bargaining strength. The difference between price and marginal cost is the measure of the degree of monopoly power.

$$\text{Degree of monopoly power} = \frac{P - MC}{P}$$

where P = price

MC = marginal cost

Triffin's Measure

Prof. Robert Triffin has improved upon Lerner's measure by suggesting price cross-elasticity instead of price elasticity of demand. The smaller the extent of cross-elasticity of demand for the product of a firm, the greater the degree of monopoly power enjoyed by the firm and vice versa.

Bain's Measure

Prof. J.S. Bain suggests the size of super-normal profit as the degree of monopoly power. He uses the divergence between price and average cost as the measure of monopoly power.

Monopoly Equilibrium and Perfectly Competitive Equilibrium Compared

1. Under perfect competition, demand curve or the average revenue curve faced by an individual firm is perfectly elastic and is a horizontal straight line parallel to the X-axis. But under monopoly, demand curve or AR curve faced by the firm is falling downwards from left to right. Therefore, MR is less than AR at all levels of output and MR curve lies below the AR curve.

2. Both under perfect competition and monopoly, the firm is in equilibrium at that level of output where MC is equal to MR. But in perfect competition since MR is equal to AR or price, therefore, MC, when equal to MR in equilibrium condition, is also equal to price or AR. This is not true in case of a monopoly.

Under perfect competition

$$MC = MR = AR = \text{Price}.$$

But under monopoly

$$MC = MR < AR = \text{Price}$$

3. Another significant difference between the two is that whereas a perfectly competitive firm is in long-run equilibrium at the minimum point of the long-run average cost curve, monopolistic firm is generally in equilibrium at the level of output where average cost is still declining and has yet not reached its minimum point.

4. Another important difference between monopoly equilibrium and perfectly competitive equilibrium is that under monopoly price is higher and output smaller than under perfect competition, assuming cost conditions in the two cases to be the same.

5. Another difference between the two is that while under perfect competition, equilibrium is possible only when marginal cost is rising at the point of equilibrium, but monopoly equilibrium can be realised whether MC is rising, remaining constant or falling at the equilibrium output.

6. Another difference between monopoly and perfect competition may be noted. A monopolist can charge discriminatory prices for his goods but a firm operating under perfect competition cannot.

MONOPOLISTIC COMPETITION AND OLIGOPOLY

The concept of monopolistic competition put forth by *Prof. Chamberlin* was a true revolutionary as well as more realistic than either pure competition or pure monopoly.

Chamberlin's concept of monopolistic competition is a blending of competition and monopoly. The distinguishing feature of monopolistic competition which makes it as a blending of competition and monopoly is the *differentiation of the product*. This means that the products of various firms are not homogeneous but different though they are closely related to each other.

Cost Curves and Selling Cost

Chamberlin, in his model of monopolistic competition has assumed the traditional U-shaped cost-curves—AC, AVC and MC. In addition he has introduced a new cost, i.e., *Selling Cost*. "Selling Costs are defined as costs incurred in order to alter the position or the shape of the demand curve for a product." Selling costs include all the expenses that are intended to promote the sales, including cost of advertisement, salesman's salaries, expenses of sales department, margins granted to dealers, wholesalers and retailers, window displays and demonstration of new goods.

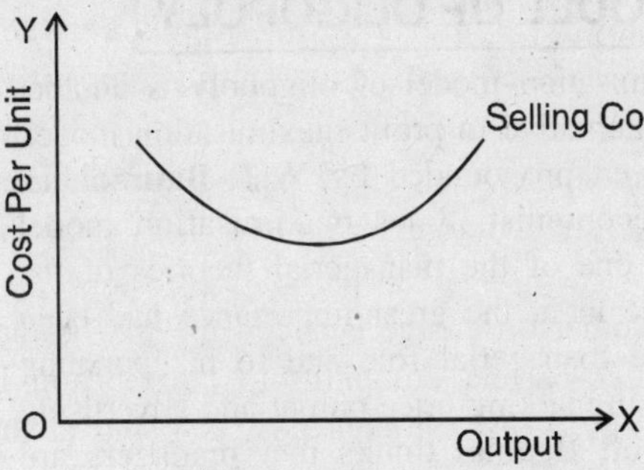

Fig. : *Selling Costs Curve*

EQUILIBRIUM UNDER MONOPOLISTIC COMPETITION

The demand curve for the product of an individual Firm, as noted above, is downward sloping. Since the various Firms under monopolistic competition produce products which are close substitutes of each others, the position and elasticity of the demand curve for the product of any of them depend upon the availability of the competiting substitutes and their prices. Therefore, the equilibrium adjustment of an individual firm cannot be defined in isolation to the general field of which it is a part. However, for sake of simplicity in analysis, conditions regarding the availability of substitute products produced by the rival firms and prices charged for them are held constant while the equilibrium adjustment of an individual firm is considered in isolation. Since close substitutes for his products are available in the market, the demand curve for the product of an individual firm working under conditions of monopolistic competition is fairly elastic thus, although a firm under monopolistic competition has a monopolistic control over his variety of the product but his control is tempered by the fact that there are close substitutes available in the market and that if he sets too high a price for his product, many of his customers will shift to the rival products.

OLIGOPOLY

Oligopoly is said to prevail when there are few firms or sellers in the market producing or selling a product. In other words, when there are two or more than two, but not many, producers or sellers of a product, oligopoly is said to exist. Oligopoly is also often referred to as "Competition among the Few."

COURNOT'S DUOPOLY MODEL

The earliest duopoly model was developed in **1838** by the French economist **Augustin Cournot.**

Cournot assumed that there are two firms each owning a mineral well and operating with zero costs. They sell their output in a market with a straight line demand curve. Each firm acts on the assumption that its competition will not change its output, and decides its own output so as to maximise profit.

STACKELBERG'S DUOPOLY MODEL

This model was developed by the German economist Heinrich von stackelberg and is an extension of Cournot's model. Stackelberg assumes that one of the duopolist (Say A) is sophisticated enough to play the role of a leader and the other (Say B) acts as a follower. The leading duopolist A recognises that his rival seller B has a definite reaction function which A uses into his own profit function and maximises his profits. In summary, if only one firm is sophisticated, it will emerge as the leader, and a stable equilibrium will emerge, since the naive firm will act as a follower.

KINKY DEMAND CURVE

The Kinked demand curve hypothesis was put forward by **Paul M. Sweezy.** In explaining price and output especially under oligopoly with product differentiation economists often use the kinked demand curve hypothesis. This is because when under oligopoly products are differentiated, it is unlikely that when a firm raises its price, all customers would leave it because some customers are intimately attached to it due to product differentiation. As a result, demand curve facing a firm under differentiated oligopoly is not perfectly elastic.

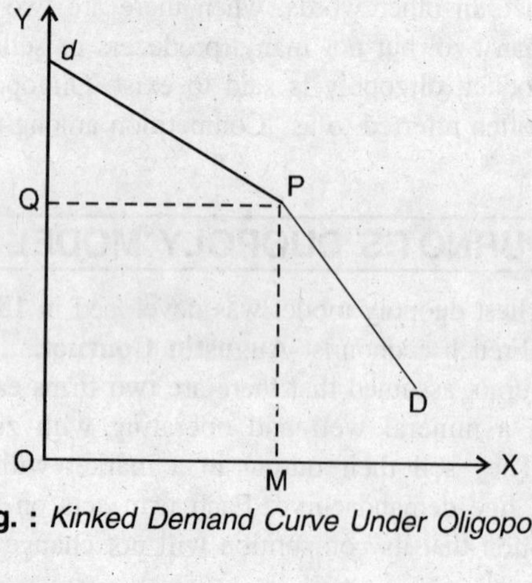

Fig. : *Kinked Demand Curve Under Oligopoly.*

The competitive reaction pattern assumed by the kinky oligopoly demand curve theory is as follows:

Each oligopolist believes that if he lowers the price below the prevailing level his competitors will follow him and will accordingly lower their prices, whereas if he raises the price above the prevailing level his competitors will not follow his increase in price.

COLLUSIVE OLIGOPOLY

There are at least three major factors which bring collusion between the oligopolistic firms. Firsts, collusion reduces the degree of competition between the firms and helps them act monopolistically in their effort of profit maximisation. Second, collusion reduces the oligopolistic uncertainty surrounding the market since cartel members, are not supposed to act independently and in the manner that is detrimental to the interest of other firms. Third, collusion forms a kind of barrier to the entry of new firms.

Collusion between oligopoly firms may take many forms depending on their relative strength, their objective and whether collusion is legal or illegal. There are however two main types of collusion:

(i) Cartels *(ii)* Price leadership

SALES MAXIMISATION MODEL OF OLIGOPOLY

Sales maximisation model of oligopoly is another important alternative to profit maximisation model. This has been propounded by **W.J. Baumol,** an American economist. Sales maximisation model represented one of the managerial theories of the firm because in it, the great importance had been given to the managerial role and to his pursuing self-interest in marking price output and advertising policies. Prof. Baumol thinks that managers are more interested in maximising sales than profits.

It should be noted that by sales maximisation Baumol does not mean the maximisation of the physical volume of sales but the maximisation of total revenue from sales, that is, the dollar value of the sales made. Therefore, his theory is also known as revenue maximisation model.

MARKET FOR FACTOR INPUTS

(*a*) In perfectly competitive markets the factor is paid its VMP.

(*b*) If the firm has monopolistic power in the product market but no power in the input market, the factor is paid its MRP < VMP.

(*c*) If the firm has both monopolistic power in the product market and monopsonistic power in input market the factor is paid a price which is even lower than its MRP. This is the basic characteristic of monopsonistic exploitation.

ROLE OF COLLECTIVE BARGAINING BY TRADE UNIONS IN RAISING WAGES

First. If the firm-buyers have no monopsonistic power, labour unions can attain an increase in the wage rate at the expense of a lower employment. Whether this result is beneficial to all the members of the union depends on the elasticity of demand for labour and the distribution policies of the union.

Second. If the firm-buyers have monopsonistic power, the union's actions can eliminate one part of the monopsonistic exploitation, namely the part that is solely attributable to the monopsonistic power of the firms. However, the other portion of the monopsonistic exploitation, that which is due to the monopoly power of firms in the product market, cannot be eliminated by trade union action.

Third. If the firm-buyers have monopsonistic power, trade unions can increase the total wage bill in cases, by either increasing employment, or the wage rate, or both. Only if the demand for labour is elastic can the union harm its members, if it sets the wage rate above the maximum level for the initial (pre-union) level of employment.

If each factor is rewarded equal to its marginal product, the total product should be disposed of without any surplus or deficit. The problem of proving that the total product will be just exhausted if all factors are paid rewards equal to their marginal products has been called "Adding-up-Problem" or Product Exhaustion Problem.

RICARDIAN THEORY OF RENT

David Ricardo was a brilliant 19th century economist of England who propounded a systematic theory of rent which is in many ways the basis of the modern concept of rent.

Ricardo defined rent as: "Rent is that portion of the produce of earth which is paid to the land lord for the use of the original and indestructible powers of the soil." It should be noticed that land rent, according to Ricardian definition, is a payment for the use of only land and is different from contractual rent.

- According to Ricardo, marginal land earns no rent.
- In Ricardian Theory, rent is not price determining. In fact, in this theory rent is price determined, that is, it is price which determines rent. To quote Ricardo, "Corn is not high because a rent is paid, but a rent is paid because corn is high."

MODERN THEORY OF RENT

Modern theory of rent does not confine itself to the determination of the reward of only land as a factor of production. Rent according to the modern sense can arise in respect of any factor of production. It is a surplus payment in excess of transfer earnings of that factor. Transfer earnings means the amount of money which any particular unit of a factor could earn in its next best alternative use. In other words, economic rent in such a case is the difference between the present earnings and transfer earnings. In Joan Robinson's words, "The essence of the conception of rent is the conception of a surplus earned by a particular part of a factor of production over and above the minimum earnings necessary to induce it to its work."

QUASI-RENT

The doctrine of quasi-rent was introduced into economic literature by **Marshall** who extended Ricardo's theory of land-rent to other factors fixed in supply during the short-run.

Quasi-Rent = TFC + Excess Profit

or

Excess Profit = Quasi-Rent – TFC

Macro Economics

Circular Flow of Income

The circular flow of income is explained with a simplest model consisting business (firms or producers) and public (households or consumers). The public own the productive resources (*i.e.,* factors of production namely land, labour and capital). Business sector or producers employ the factors of production to produce the goods and services. Such goods and services are bought by the public. Thus, public own the factors of production and provide them to producers. The producers employ the factor *inputs* to produce *output* of goods and services, which is bought by the consumers (public). For the employment of factor services, the public receive the factor *income* namely rent (for land), wages (for labour) and interest (for capital). This *income* flows back from the public to the business sector as consumption *expenditure* to buy the goods and services.

Thus, the flow chart consist two segments – real flow and money flow. As the outer flow in given figure shows the flow of *input* (factors viz. land, labour, capital and organisation) and *output* (goods and services), they represent the real economy (or real flow). The inner flow shows the money received as factor *income* (rent, wage, interest and profit) and it goes to the producer as consumption *expenditure* (commodity price) to buy the goods and services. As this flow chart involves only income received and expenditure made in terms of money, it represents the money economy (or money flow).

The most important point to be noted for the computation of national income is that income (Y) received is equal to the consumption expenditure (C) made by the consumers, *i.e.,* Y = C. This simple circular flow model is explained without the other components of national income namely savings or investment (I), public expenditure by government (G) and expenditure on net exports (X-M). If we include all the above components of national income Y = C will become

$$Y = C + I + G + (X\text{-}M)$$

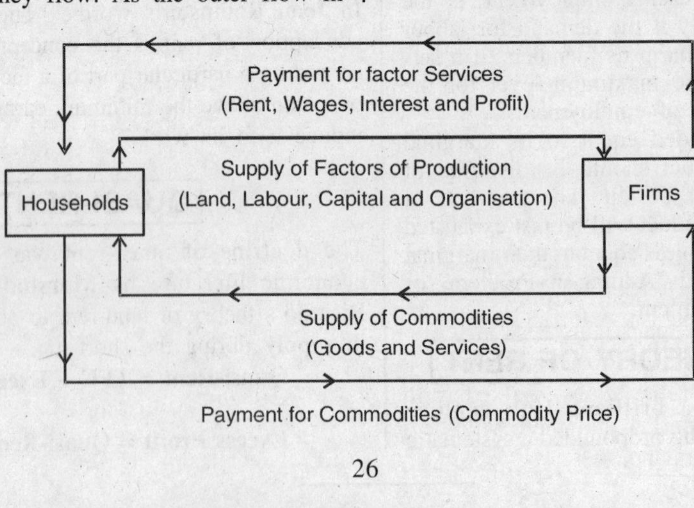

Thus, national income is the aggregate summation of income or expenditure made through these four components, consumers (C), investors (I), government (G) and foreign trade (Exports [X] – Imports [M])

Methods of Calculating National Income

There are three different methods of calculating national income. They are :

1. Product or Output Method
2. Income Method
3. Expenditure Method

The following are some of the national income identities:

1. NNP = GNP - Depreciation
2. NNI = NNP - Indirect taxes
3. PI = NNI - Retained earnings, corporate taxes and interest on public debt
4. PDI = PI - Personal taxes.

Where, GNP - Gross National Product
NNP - Net National Product
NNI - Net National Income
PI - Personal Income
PDI - Personal Disposable Income

CLASSICAL THEORY OF EMPLOYMENT

The classical theory assumes the existence of full employment without inflation. Given wage-price flexibility, there are automatic forces in the economic system that tend to maintain full employment, and produce output at that level. Thus full employment is ragarded as a normal situation and any deviation from this level is something abnormal which automatically tends towards full employment.

Say's Law and Classical Theory

According to J. B. Say's law, **"Supply creates its own demand"**. This implies that every increase in production made possible by the increase in the productive capacity or the stock of fixed capital will be sold in the market and there will be no problem of lack of demand.

Concept of Effective Demand

The principle of 'effective demand' is basic to Keynes analysis of income, output and employment. It was Keynes, who for the first time, put forward a systematic and convincing theory of employment based on the **"Principle of Effective Demand."**

Meaning of Effective Demand

Effective demand represents the money actually spent by people on the products of industry. Keynes used the term 'effective demand' to denote the total demand for goods and services at various levels of employment. Different levels of employment represent different levels of aggregate demand. But there can be a level of employment where aggregate demand equals aggregate supply. This is the point of effective demand.

Determinants of Effective Demands

The determinants of effective demand are the aggregate demand function and the aggregate supply function.

Aggregate Supply

At any given level of employment of labour, aggregate supply price is the total amount of money which all the entrepreneurs in the economy taken together must expect to receive from the sale of the output produced by the given number of labourers employed. In other words, the aggregate supply price is the total cost of production incurred by employing a certain given number of labourers.

Aggregate Demand

Aggregate demand price at any level of employment is the amount of total money or price (proceeds) which all the firms or entrepreneurs in the economy **actually expect** to receive from the sale of output produced by a given number of men employed. In other words, aggregate demand price represents the amount of expenditure expected by the entrepreneurs when a given number of men are employed to produce goods and services. Like the aggregate supply price, aggregate demand price also varies at different levels of employment.

Aggregate demand is determined by consumption demand and investment demand. Therefore,

Aggregate Demand = Consumption Demand + Investment Demand

$$AD = C + I$$

Where AD = aggregate demand
C = consumption demand
I = investment demand

Equilibrium Level of Income : Equality of Aggregate Demand and Aggregate Supply

The equilibrium level of national income is determined at a point where the aggregate demand function intersects the aggregate supply function.

The Keynesian theory may also be presented in a tabular form as under:

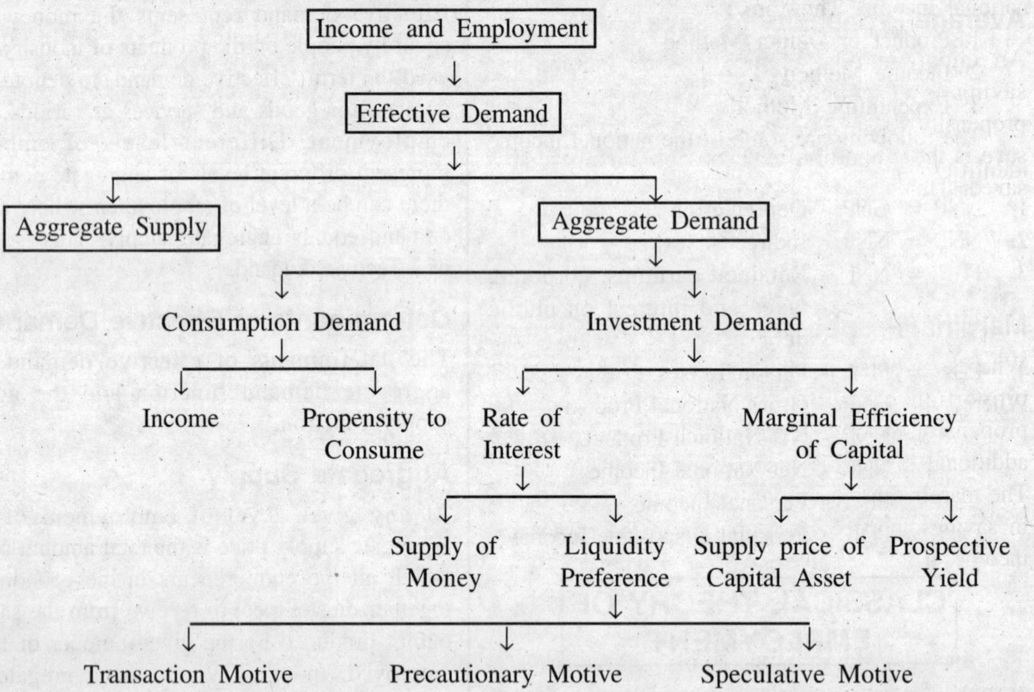

CONSUMPTION FUNCTION

Consumption function can be defined as the schedule detailing the relationship between aggragate consumption expenditures and income, Therefore

$$C = f(Y)$$

The consumption function has two technical attributes or properties:

1. The average propensity to consume
2. The marginal propensity to consume

The Average Propensity to Consume

Average propensity to consume is the ratio of the amount of consumption to total income. Therefore, average propensity to consume is calculated by dividing the amount of consumption by the total income. Thus,

$$APC = \frac{C}{Y}$$

Where
APC = average propensity to consume
C = amount of consumption
Y = level of income

Marginal Propensity to Consume

The marginal propensity to consume (MPC) measures the change in consumption resulting from a change in income. In other words, marginal propensity to consume may be defined as the ratio of the change in consumption to the change in income or as the rate of change in the average propensity to consume as income changes. Thus,

$$MPC = \frac{\Delta C}{\Delta Y}$$

Where

MPC = marginal propensity to consume

ΔC = change in consumption

ΔY = change in income

Average Propensity to Save (APS)

An important relationship between income and saving is described by the concept of average propensity to save (APS). Average propensity to save is the proportion of disposable income that is saved. Thus,

$$APS = \frac{\text{Saving}}{\text{Income}} = \frac{S}{Y}$$

Marginal Propensity to Save (MPS)

Whereas average propensity to save indicates the proportion of income that is saved, marginal propensity to save represents how much of the additional disposable income is devoted to saving. The marginal propensity to save is therefore change in savings induced by a change in the disposable income. Thus,

$$MPS = \frac{\Delta S}{\Delta Y}$$

Since the additional income is either consumed or saved, the sum of marginal propensity to consume and marginal propensity to save is equal to one.

$$MPC + MPS = 1$$

KEYNES'S PSYCHOLOGICAL LAW OF CONSUMPTION

Keynes propounded a basic law about the consumption function. This has been described as psychological law of consumption by **Prof. Kurihara.** According to this law of consumption, when the aggregate income increases, consumption expenditure will increase but by a somewhat smaller amount. It means that out of the increment in income, a part is saved and not consumed. In other words, marginal propensity to consume is less than one.

THE CONCEPT OF MULTIPLIER

The concept of multiplier was first developed by **Richard F. Kahn** in 1931. Kahn's multiplier was the 'employment multiplier.' Keynes took the idea from Kahn and developed the Investment Multiplier.

Derivation of the Multiplier

The size of the multiplier depends upon the size of the MPC. The two are closely related. Given the MPC, the multiplier can be easily derived. Keynes has expressed it by the symbol K. 'K' can be found out from the formula

$$K = \frac{1}{1 - MPC} \quad \text{or} \quad K = \frac{1}{MPC}$$

The multiplier is derived as follows:

$$\Delta Y = K.\Delta I$$

$$K = \frac{\Delta Y}{\Delta I}$$

THE PRINCIPLE OF ACCELERATION

The term "**acceleration principle**" was first introduced into economics by **J.M. Clark** in 1917. It was further developed by Hicks, Samuelson, and Harrod in relation to the business cycles.

The principle of acceleration is based on the fact that the demand for capital goods is derived from the demand for consumer goods which the former help to produce. The acceleration principle explains the process by which an increase (or decrease) in the demand for consumption goods leads to an increase (or decrease) in investment on capital goods.

DEMAND FOR MONEY

The demand for money arises from two important functions of money. The first is that money act as a medium of exchange and the second is that it is a store of value. Thus, individuals and businesses wish to hold money partly in cash and partly in the form of assets.

THE KEYNESIAN APPROACH : LIQUIDITY PREFERENCE

What is known as the Keynesian theory of the demand for money was first formulated by **Keynes** in his well-known book, *The General Theory of Employment, Interest and Money (1936)*. It has been developed further by other economists of Keynesian persuasion. Keynes suggested three motives which led to the demand for money in an economy :

1. The Transactions Demand
2. The Precautionary Demand
3. The Speculative Demand

The transactions demand for money arises from the medium of exchange function of money in making regular payments for goods and services.

The transactions demand for money is directly proportional and positive function of the level of income, and is expressed as

$$L_t = K.Y$$

where L_t is the transactions demand for money, K is the proportional of income which is kept for transactions purposes, and Y is the income.

In recent years, two post-Keynesian economists **W.J. Baumol** and **James Tobin** have shown that the rate of interest is an important determinant to transactions demand for money.

Precautionary Demand for Money

Precautionary motive for holding money refers to the desire of the people to hold cash balances for unforeseen contingencies.

Keynes held that the precautionary demand for the money, like transactions demand, was a function of the level of income. But the post-Keynesian economists believe that like transactions demand, it is inversely related to high interest rates.

Speculative Demand For Money

The speculative motive of the people relates to the desire to hold one's resources in liquid form in order to take advantage of market movements regarding the future changes in the rate of interest (or bond prices).

The demand for money under speculative motive is a function of the current rate of interests increasing as the interest rate falls and decreasing as the interest rate rises. Thus, *demand for money under this motive is a decreasing function of the rate of interest.*

The demand for money under speculative motive is a function of the current rate of interests increasing as the interest rate falls and decreasing as the interest rate rises. Thus, *demand for money under this motive is a decreasing function of the rate of interest.* This is shown in Figure. Along OX is represented the speculative demand for money and along OY the current rate of interest. The liquidity preference curve LP is a downward sloping towards the right signifying the higher the rate of interest, the lower the demand for money for speculative motive, and vice versa.

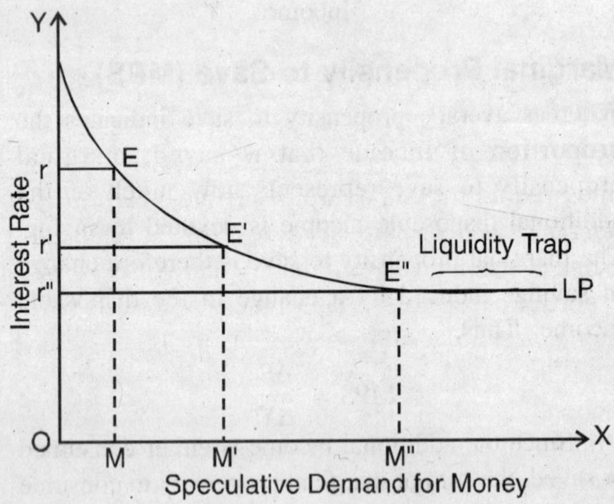

Fig. : *Demand for Money for Speculative Motive*

Liquidity Trap

At very low rate of interest, such as *r"* in Figure the LP curve becomes *perfectly elastic* and the speculative demand for money is infinitely elastic. This perfectly elastic portion of liquidity preference curve indicates the position of *absolute liquidity preference* of the people. That is, at a very low rate of interest people will hold with them as inactive balances any amount of money they come to have. This portion of liquidity preference curve with absolute liquidity preference is called *liquidity trap* by the economists.

Baumol's Inventory Theoretic Approach

The inventory theoretic approach to the demand for money is associated with the name of **W. Baumol**. The most famous result of Baumol is the **Square-root-law** of the demand for money. William Baumol has made an important addition to the Keynesian transactions demand for money.

In this inventory theory of the demand for money, Baumol emphasises that the demand for money is a demand for real balances. Therefore demand for real balances for transactions purposes becomes.

$$M_d = \frac{1}{2}\sqrt{\frac{2b.Y}{r}} \times P$$

Where

M_d = demand for money

P = price level

Tobin's Portfolio Selection Model : The Risk Aversion Theory of Liquidity Preference

James Tobin in his famous article "*Liquidity Preference as Behaviour Towards Risk*" Formulated the risk aversion theory of liquidity preference based on portfolio selection. This theory removes two major defects of the Keynesian theory of liquidity preference. One, Keynes's liquidity preference function depends on the inelasticity of expectations of future interest rates; and two, individuals hold either money or bonds. Tobin has removed both the defects. His theory does not depend on the elasticity of expectations of future interest rates but proceeds on the assumption that the expected value of capital gain or loss from holding interest -bearing assets is always zero.

Moreover, it explains that an individual's portfolio holds both money and bonds rather than only one at a time.

Fisher's Cash Transactions Approach

In the words of **Fisher,** "Other things remaining unchanged, as the quantity of money in circulation increases, the price level also increases in direct proportion and the value of money decreases and vice versa." If the quantity of money is doubled, the price level will also double and the value of money will be one half. On the other hand, if the quantity of money is reduced by one half, the price level will also be reduced by one half and the value of money will be twice.

Fisher has explained his theory in terms of his equation of exchange :

$$PT = MV + M'V'$$

FOUR CONCEPTS OF MONEY SUPPLY

From April 1977, the Reserve Bank has adopted four concepts of money supply in its analysis of the quantum of and variations in money supply. These four concepts of measures of money supply are explained below:

1. Money supply M_1 or Narrow Money

This is the narrow measure of money supply as defined above and is composed of the following items:

$$M_1 = C + DD + OD$$

where

C = Currency with the public

DD = Demand deposits of banks,

OD = Other deposits of the RBI.

2. Money supply M_2

In addition to the three items of M_1, the concept of money supply M_2 includes savings deposits with the post office saving banks. Thus,

$M_2 = M_1$ + saving deposits with the post office saving bank.

3. Money supply M_3

This is also called **broad money.** Besides the items of M_1 the net time deposits of the banks are also included in M_3. In the terminology of money supply employed by the RBI till April 1977, this M_3 was called **Aggregate Monetary Resources**(AMR). Thus

M_3 + Net time deposits of the banks.

4. Money Supply M_4

The measure M_4 of money supply includes not only all the items of M_3 described above but also the total deposits with the post office savings organisation. However, this excludes contributions made by the public to the national savings certificates. Thus,

$M_4 = M_3$ + Total Deposits of post office saving organistion.

HIGH POWERED MONEY

High powered money or what is also called **reserve money** or **monetary base** consists of currency issued both by Government and Reserve Bank of India. It is important to note that a part of currency issued is held by the public and a part is held by Banks as reserves. Accordingly, the high powered money can be obtained as sum of currency held by the public and the part held by the banks as reserves.Thus

$$H = C + R$$

Where

H = The amount of high powered money,

C = Currency held by the public,

R = Cash reserves of currency with the banks.

INFLATION AND DEFLATION

DEMAND–PUSH INFLATION

Basically, inflation represents a situation where by the pressure of aggregate demand for goods and services exceeds the available supply of output. In such a situation, the rise in price level is the natural consequence. Now this excess of aggregate demand over supply may be the result of more than one force at work. As we know, aggregate demand is the sum of consumers' spending on goods and services, government spending on goods and services and net investment being contemplated by the entrepreneurs. Inflation is thus caused when aggregate demand for all purposes—consumption, investment and government expenditure, exceeds the supply of goods at current prices. This is demand-push inflation.

COST–PUSH INFLATION

We can visualise a situtation where, even though there is no increase in aggregate demands, prices may still rise. This may happen if costs, particularly the wage costs, go on rising. Now as the level of employment rises, the demand for workers also rises so that the bargaining position of the workers becomes stronger. To exploit this situation, they may ask for an increase in wage rates which are not justifiable on grounds either of a prior rise of productivity or of cost of living.

The employers in a situation of high demand and employment are more agreeable to concede these wage claims; because they hope to pass on these rises in costs to the consumers in the shape of rise in prices. If this happens, we have another inflationary factor at work and the inflation thus caused is called the **wage–induced** or **cost–push inflation.**

STAGFLATION

The word "Stagflation" is the combination of stag plus flation, taking 'stag' from stagnation and 'flation' from inflation. Thus it is a paradoxical situation where the economy experiences stagnation or unemployment alongwith a high rate of inflation. It is, therefore, also called **inflationary recession**. In other words, the stagflation refers to a situation when a high rate of inflation occurs simultaneously with a high rate of unemployment.

PHILLIPS CURVE

Professor Phillips urged there was a close link between the level of unemployment and the rate of wage increase. Phillips curve expresses an inverse relationship between the rate of unemployment and the rate of increase in money wages.

The Phillips curve depicts the **trade off** betweeen unemployment and money wages. It relates percentage change in money wages on the vertical axis with percentage of labour force unemployment on the horizontal axis, as shown in figure.

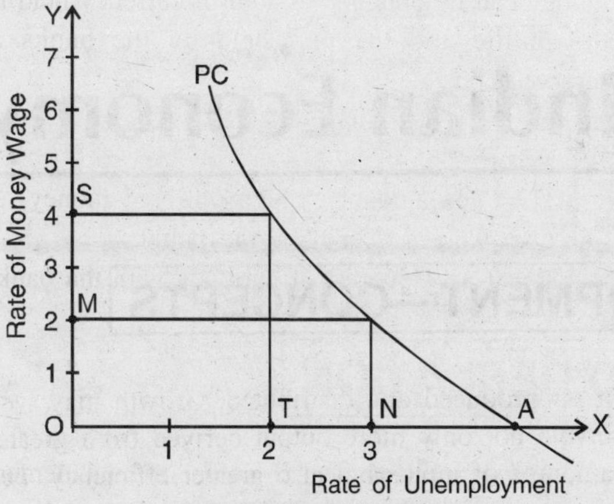

Fig. : *Phillips Curve*

Samuelson and Solow extended the Phillip's analysis to the **trade off** between the level of unemployment and the rate of change in the level of prices. Thus, the Phillips curve suggests that unemployment can always be reduced by having more inflation and that the inflation rate can also be reduced by having more unemployment.

IS AND LM FUNCTIONS : GENERAL EQUILIBRIUM OF PRODUCT AND MONEY MARKETS

The term IS is the shorthand expression of the equality of investment and saving which represents the product market equilibrium. On the other hand, the term LM is the shorthand expression of the equality of money demand and money supply and representy the money market equilibrium.

General Equilibrium of Product and Money Market

Now we study how these markets are brought into simultaneous equilibrium. It is only when the equilibrium pairs of interest rate and income of the IS curve equals the equilibrium pairs of interest rate and income of the LM curve that the general equilibrium is established. In other words, when there is a single pair of interest rate and income level in the product and money markets that the two markets are in equilibrium.

Such an equilibrium position is shown in figure where the IS and LM curves intersect each other at point E relating Y level of income to R interest rate. This pair of income level and interest rate leads to simultaneous equilibrium in the real or goods (saving investment) market and the money (demand and supply of money) market.

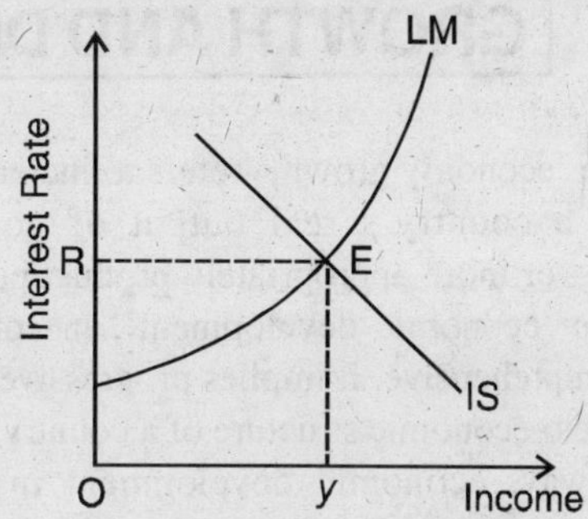

Fig.

This general equilibrium position persists at a point of time, given the price level. If there is any deviation from this equilibrium position, certain forces will act and react in such a manner that the equilibrium will be restored.

Effectiveness of Monetary and Fiscal Policies

The relative effectiveness of monetary and fiscal policy depends upon the shape of the IS and LM curves and the economy's initial position. If the economy is in the Keynesian range, monetary policy is in effective and fiscal policy is highly effective. On the other hand, in the classical range, monetary policy is effective and fiscal policy is ineffective. But in the intermediate range both monetary and fiscal policies are effective. In fact, in the intermediate range, the effectiveness of monetary and fiscal policies depends largely on the elasticities of the IS curve. If the IS curve is inelastic, fiscal policy is more effective than monetary policy. On the other hand, if the IS curve is elastic, monetary policy is more effective than fiscal policy.

Indian Economy

GROWTH AND DEVELOPMENT—CONCEPTS

The term 'economy growth' refers to increases over time in a country's real output of goods and services—or more appropriately product per capita. The term 'economic development', in contrast, is more comprehensive. It implies progressive changes in the socio-economic structure of a country. Viewed in this way, economic development involves a steady decline in agriculture's share in GNP and a corresponding increase in the share of industries, trade, banking, construction and services. This transformation in economic structure is invariably accompanied by a shift in the occupational structure of the labour force and an improvement in its skill and productivity.

In fact, the terms 'development' and 'growth' have nothing to do with the type of economy. The distinction between the two relates to the nature and causes of change. *Schumpeter* makes the distinction clearer when defines development as a discontinuous and spontaneous change in the stationary state which forever alters and displaces the equilibrium state previously existing; while growth is a gradual and steady change in the long run which comes about by a gradual increase in the rate of savings and population. This view of Schumpeter has been widely accepted and elaborataed by the majority of economists. According to *Kindleberger*, "Economic growth means more output, while econmic develop-ment implies both more output and changes in the technical and institutional arrangements by which it is produced and distributed. Growth may well invole not only more output derived from greater amounts of inputs but also greater efficiency, *i.e.*, an increase in output per unit of input. Development goes beyond this to imply changes in the composition of output and in the allocation of inputs by sectors."

Friedman defines growth as an expansion of the system in one or more dimensions without a change in its structure, and development as an innovative process leading to the structural transformation of social systems.

Thus economic growth is related to a quantitative sustained increase in the country's per capita output or income accompanied by expansion in its labour force, consumption, capital and volume of trade. On the other hand, economic development is a wider term. It is related to qualitative change in economic wants, goods incentives and institutions.

CHARACTERISTICS OF AN UNDER DEVELOPED COUNTRY

1. General Poverty
2. Agriculture, the Main Occupation
3. A Dualistic Economy
4. Underdeveloped Natural Resources
5. Demographic Features
6. Unemployment and Disguised Unemployment
7. Economic Backwardness

8. Lack of Enterprise and Initiative
9. Insufficient Capital Equipment
10. Technological Backwardness
11. Foreign Trade Orientation

Sectoral Composition of National Income

National income is derived from many sectors. We generally classify them into three major sectors namely primary, (agriculture), secondary (manufacturing) and tertiary (services). During the initial stage of development, share of primary sector in the national income will be high. But this will decline during the course of development and share of industry will be greater. At very high level of development, the share of service sector in the national income will be more.

Sectoral Contribution in GVA New Series (At Constant 2011-12 Prices)

Sector	*2016-17*	*2019-20*	*2020-21*
Primary	15.2	18.4	20.2
Secondary	23.1	26.6	25.9
Tertiary	61.7	55.0	53.9
	100.0	**100.0**	**100.0**

Population Growth 1901-2011

Census years	*Decadal Growth*		
	Population	*Absolute*	*Per cent*
1901	23,83,96,327	–	–
1911	25,20,93,390	1,36,97,063	5.75
1921	25,13,21,213	–7,72,177	–0.31
1931	27,89,77,238	2,76,56,025	11.00
1941	31,86,60,580	3,96,83,342	14.22
1951	36,10,88,090	4,24,27,510	13.31
1961	43,92,34,771	7,81,46,681	21.64
1971	54,81,59,652	10,89,24,881	24.80
1981	68,33,29,097	13,51,69,445	24.66
1991	84,64,21,039	16,30,91,942	23.87
2001	1,02,87,37,436	18,23,16,397	21.54
2011	1,21,08,54,977	18,14,55,986	17.70

State Wise Population 2011

SL.No.	*India/State/ Union territory*	*Total Population*		
		Persons	*Males*	*Females*
	India	**1,21,08,54,977**	**62,32,70,258**	**58,75,84,719**
1.	Jammu and Kashmir	1,25,41,302	66,40,662	59,00,640
2.	Himachal Pradesh	68,64,602	34,81,873	33,82,729
3.	Punjab	2,77,43,338	1,46,39,465	1,31,03,873
4.	Chandigarh	10,55,450	5,80,663	4,74,784
5.	Uttarakhand	1,00,86,292	51,37,773	49,48,519
6.	Haryana	2,53,51,462	1,34,94,734	1,18,56,728
7.	Delhi	1,67,87,941	89,87,326	78,00,615
8.	Rajasthan	6,85,48,437	3,55,50,997	3,29,97,440
9.	Uttar Pradesh	19,98,12,341	10,44,80,510	9,53,31,831
10.	Bihar	10,40,99,452	5,42,78,157	4,98,21,295
11.	Sikkim	6,10,577	3,23,070	2,87,507
12.	Arunachal Pradesh	13,83,727	7,13,912	6,69,815
13.	Nagaland	19,78,502	10,24,649	9,53,853
14.	Manipur	28,55,794	14,38,586	14,17,208
15.	Mizoram	10,97,206	5,55,339	5,41,867
16.	Tripura	36,73,917	18,74,376	17,99,541
17.	Meghalaya	29,66,889	14,91,832	14,75,057

SL No.	India/State/ Union territory	Total Population		
		Person	Males	Females
18.	Assam	3,12,05,576	1,59,39,443	1,52,66,133
19.	West Bengal	9,12,76,115	4,68,09,027	4,44,67,088
20.	Jharkhand	3,29,88,134	1,69,30,315	1,60,57,819
21.	Odisha	4,19,74,218	2,12,12,136	2,07,62,082
22.	Chhattisgarh	2,55,45,198	1,28,32,895	1,27,12,303
23.	Madhya Pradesh	7,26,26,809	3,76,12,306	3,50,14,503
24.	Gujarat	6,04,39,692	3,14,91,260	2,89,48,432
25.	Daman and Diu	2,43,247	1,50,301	92,946
26.	Dadra and Nagar Haveli	3,43,709	1,93,760	1,49,949
27.	Maharashtra	11,23,74,333	5,82,43,056	5,41,31,277
28.	Andhra Pradesh	4,93,86,799	2,47,38,068	2,46,48,731
29.	Karnataka	6,10,95,297	3,09,66,657	3,01,28,640
30.	Goa	14,58,545	7,39,140	7,19,405
31.	Lakshadweep	64,473	33,123	31,350
32.	Kerala	3,34,06,061	1,60,27,412	1,73,78,649
33.	Tamilnadu	7,21,47,030	3,61,37,975	3,60,09,055
34.	Puducherry	12,47,953	6,12,511	6,35,442
35.	Andaman and Nicobar Island	3,80,581	2,02,871	1,77,710
36.	Telangana	3,51,93,978	1,77,04,078	1,74,89,900

Census Report – 2011

States and Union Territories by Density

Sl No.	State/Union Territories	Density	
		2001	2011
1.	Delhi	9,340	11,320
2.	Chandigarh	7,900	9,258
3.	Puducherry	2,034	2,547
4.	Lakshadweep	1,895	2,149
5.	Daman and Diu	1,413	2,191
6.	West Bengal	903	1,028
7.	Bihar	881	1,106
8.	Kerala	819	860
9.	Uttar Pradesh	690	829
10.	Punjab	484	551
11.	Tamilnadu	480	555
12.	Haryana	478	573
13.	Dadra and Nagar Haveli	449	700
14.	Goa	364	394
15.	Assam	340	398
16.	Jharkhand	338	414
17.	Maharashtra	315	365
18.	Tripura	305	350

Sl No.	State/Union Territories	Density	
		2001	2011
19.	Andhra Pradesh	277	308
20.	Karnataka	276	319
21.	Gujarat	258	308
22.	Telangana	—	307
23.	Odisha	236	270
24.	Madhya Pradesh	196	236
25.	Rajasthan	165	200
26.	Uttarakhand	159	189
27.	Chhattisgarh	154	189
28.	Nagaland	120	119
29.	Himachal Pradesh	109	123
30.	Manipur	111	115
31.	Meghalaya	103	132
32.	Jammu and Kashmir	100	124
33.	Sikkim	76	86
34.	Andaman and Nicobar	43	46
35.	Mizoram	42	52
36.	Arunachal Pradesh	13	17

Sex Ratio: 1901-2011

Census Year	*Sex Ratio (Females Per 1,000 Males)*
1901	972
1911	964
1921	955
1931	950
1941	945
1951	946
1961	941
1971	930
1981	934
1991	926
2001	933
2011	943

Literacy Rate : 1951-2011

Census Year	*Persons*	*Males*	*Females*
1951	18.33	27.16	8.86
1961	28.3	40.40	15.35
1971	34.45	45.96	21.97
1981	43.57	56.38	29.76
1991	52.21	64.13	39.29
2001	64.84	75.26	53.67
2011	73.00	80.90	64.60

Rural and Urban Population

Census Year	*Population (Million)*		*Percentage of total population*	
	Rural	*Urban*	*Rural*	*Urban*
1901	213	26	89.2	10.8
1911	226	26	89.7	10.3
1921	223	28	88.8	11.2
1931	246	33	88.0	12.0
1941	275	44	86.1	13.9
1951	299	62	82.7	17.3
1961	360	79	82.0	18.0
1971	439	109	80.1	19.9
1981	524	159	76.7	23.3
1991	629	218	74.3	25.7
2001	743	286	72.2	27.8
2011	833	377	68.84	31.20

Birth Rate and Death Rate in India

(Per Thousand Population)

Year	*Birth Rate*	*Death Rate*
2008-09	22.8	7.4
2009-10	22.5	7.3
2010-11	22.1	7.2
2011-12	21.6	7.0
2012-13	21.4	7.0
2013-14	21.0	6.7
2014-15	20.8	6.5
2015-16	20.4	6.4
2016-17	20.2	6.3
2017-18	20.0	6.2
2018-19	19.7	6.0
2019-20	18.2	7.0

PLANNING IN INDIA

In India, the planned economic development began in 1951 with the inception of the First Five Year Plan. The theoretical efforts for economic development in Indian economy had already begun before independence. In the year 1934, Sir M. Visheshvraya wrote a book named *'Planned Economy for India'*, which was the first attempt in this direction. In 1938, the Indian National Congress, under the leadership of Pt. Jawaharlal Nehru, made a National Planning Committee. Its recommendations could not be implemented due to the beginning of the Second World War and changes in the Indian political situation. In 1944, eight industrialists of Bombay presented a well organised plan called '**The Bombay Plan**', which could not be brought into action due to various reasons. In August 1944, the Indian Government inaugurated a separate department called 'The Planning and Development Department' and appointed Sir Ardishar Dalal, the Controller of Bombay Plan, as its acting member. Inspired by the economic views of Mahatma Gandhi, Shri Sriman Narayan constructed a plan in 1944 which is known as

'Gandhian Plan'. Mr. M.N. Rao, chairman of post-war Reconstruction Committee of Indian Trade Union, introduced a 'People's Plan' in April 1945. This plan introduced before independence again could not be implemented due to various reasons. In 1946, the Interim Government was formed in India. This Government established a High Level Advisory Planning Board in order to study the problems of planning and developments in the country. The Board studied all the problems very deeply and gave recommendations to establish a stable planning commission at the central level which could continuously work for the planning and development of the country. In January 1950, Shri Jai Prakash Narayan published a plan called **'Sarvodaya Plan'**. The Government did not accept the entire plan and adopted only a few parts of it. The Planning Commission was constituted on 15th March, 1950, by the Government of India.

Uptil now, the Planning Commission has made ten Five Year Plans and Seven Annual Plans. One of the special features of economic planning in our country is that during the planning period the investment made in Private Sector has been more than that of the Public Sector.

NITI Aayog

The National Institution for Transforming India, also called NITI Aayog, was formed via a resolution of the Union Cabinet on January 1, 2015. NITI Aayog is the premier policy 'Think Tank' of the Government of India, providing both directional and policy inputs. While designing strategic and long term policies and programmes for the Government of India, NITI Aayog also provides relevant technical advice to the Centre and States. The Government of India, in keeping with its reform agenda, constituted the NITI Aayog to replace the Planning Commission instituted in 1950. This was done in order to better serve the needs and aspirations of the people of India. An important evolutionary change from the past, NITI Aayog acts as the quintessential platform of the Government of India to bring States to act together in national interest, and thereby fosters Cooperative Federalism.

At the core of NITI Aayog's creation are two hubs—**Team India Hub** and the **Knowledge and Innovation Hub**. The Team India Hub leads the engagement of states with the Central government, while the Knowledge and Innovation Hub builds NITI's think-tank capabilities. These hubs reflect the two key tasks of the Aayog.

NITI Aayog is also developing itself as a State of the Art Resource Centre, with the necessary resources, knowledge and skills, that will enable it to act with speed, promote research and innovation, provide strategic policy vision for the government, and deal with contingent issues.

National Development Council (NDC)

National Development Council is a non-statutory body which was constituted to build co-operation between the states and the Planning Commission for economic planning. The National Development Council was constituted on 6th August, 1952, by a proposal of the Government. The Prime Minister is the Chairman and the Secretary of the Planning Commission remains its secretary. In the beginning, only the Chief Ministers of the states were its members, but after 1967 all the Ministers of the Central Cabinet, Administrators of the States ruled by the Centre and all the members of the Planning Commission were included as members of this body.

Growth Performance in Various Plan

(in % per annum)

Plans	*Target*	*Actual*
1. First Plan	2.1	3.6
2. Second Plan	4.5	4.21
3. Third Plan	5.6	2.72
4. Fourth Plan	5.7	2.05
5. Fifth Plan	4.4	4.83
6. Sixth Plan	5.2	5.54
7. Seventh Plan	5.0	6.02
8. Eighth Plan	5.6	6.68
9. Ninth Plan	6.5	5.55
10. Tenth Plan	8.0	7.7
11. Eleventh Plan	8.1	7.9
12. Twelfth Plan	8.0	—

Various Employment Programmes in India—At a Glance

S. N.	Programme	Year of beginning	Objective
1.	Community Development Programme (CDP)	1952	Overall development of rural areas with people's participation.
2.	Green Revolution	1966-67	To increase the foodgrains, specially wheat production.
3.	Drought-Prone Area Programme (DPAP)	1973	To try an expedient for protection from drought by achieving environmental balance and by developing the ground water.
4.	Command Area Development Programme (CADP)	1974-75	To ensure better and rapid utilisation of irrigation capacities of medium and large projects.
5.	Twenty Point Programme (TPP)	1975	Poverty eradication and raising the standard of living.
6.	Antyodaya Yojana	1977-78	To make the poorest families of the village economically independent (only in Rajasthan State).
7.	Training Rural Youth for Self-Employment (TRYSEM)	Aug., 15, 1979	Programme of training rural youth for self-employment.
8.	Integrated Rural Development Programme (IRDP)	Oct., 2, 1980	All-round development of the rural poor through a programme of asset endowment for self-employment.
9.	National Rural Employment Programme (NREP)	1980	To provide profitable employment opportunities to the rural poor.
10.	Development of Women and Children in Rural Areas (DWCRA)	Sept. 1982	To provide suitable opportunities of self-employment to the women belonging to the rural families who are living below the poverty line.
11.	Comprehensive Crop Insurance Scheme	Aprl 1, 1985	For insurance of agricultural crops.
12.	Council for Advancement of People's Action and Rural Technology (CAPART)	Sept. 1, 1986	To provide assistance for rural prosperity.
13.	Jawahar Rozgar Yojana	April 1989	For providing employment to rural unemployed.
14.	Nehru Rozgar Yojana	Oct. 1989	For providing employment to urban unemployed.
15.	Supply of Improved Toolkits to Rural Artisans	July 1992	To supply modern toolkits to the rural craftsmen except the weavers, tailors, embroiders and tobacco labourers who are living below the poverty line.
16.	Employment Assurance Scheme (EAS)	Oct., 2, 1993	To provide employment of at least 100 days in a year in villages.

S. N.	Programme	Year of beginning	Objective
17.	District Rural Development Agency (DRDA)	1993	To provide financial assistance for rural development.
18.	Mahila Samridhi Yojana	2 Oct., 1993	To encourage the rural women to deposit in Post-office Saving Account.
19.	Ganga Kalyan Yojana	1997-98	To provide financial assistance to farmers for exploring and developing ground and surface water resources.
20.	Kasturba Gandhi Education Scheme	Aug., 15, 1997	To establish girls schools in districts having low female literacy rate.
21.	Swarna Jayanti Shahari Rozgar Yojana (SJSRY)	Dec., 1997	To provide gainful employment to urban un-employed and under-employed poor through self-employment or wage-employment.
22.	Bhagya Shree Bal Kalyan Policy	Oct., 19, 1998	To uplift the girls conditions.
23.	Rajrajeshwari Mahila Kalyan Yojana	Oct., 19, 1998	To provide insurance protection to women.
24.	Swarna Jayanti Gram Swarozgar Yojana	April 1999	For eliminating Rural poverty and unemploy-ment and promoting self-employment.
25.	Jan Shree Bima Yojana	Aug., 10, 2000	Providing Insurance Security to people living below poverty line.
26.	Antyodaya Anna Yojana	Dec., 25, 2000	To provide food security to poor.
27.	Ashraya Bima Yojana	June 2001	To provide compensation to labourers who have lost their employment.
28.	Pradhan Mantri Gram Sadak Yojana (PMGSY)	Dec., 25, 2000	To line all villages with Pacca Road.
29.	Mahatma Gandhi National Rural Employment Guarantee Act (MNREGA)	Feb., 2, 2006	To provide at least 100 days wage-employment in rural areas.
30.	Pradhan Mantri Kaushal Vikas Yojana	March 2015	To Provide skill training to youth.
31.	Pradhan Mantri Jeevan Jyoti Bima Yojana	2015-16	Renewable one year life cover of ₹ 2 lakh to all savings bank account holders in the age group of 18-50 years covering death due to any reason for a premium of ₹ 330 per annum per sub-scriber.
32.	Pradhan Mantri Suraksha Bima Yojana	2015-16	Renewable one year accidental death cum disability to all savings bank account holders in the age group of 18-70 years for a premium of ₹ 12 per annum per subscriber.
33.	Atal Pension Yojana	2015-16	Pension to the labourers of unorganized sector
34.	Deen Dayal Upadhyay Grameen Kaushlya Yojana	Sep. 24, 2015	Skill development of rural youth.
35.	Atal Innovation Mission	2015-16	Atal Innovation Mission and Self Employement and Talent Utilisation.

S. N.	Programme	Year of beginning	Objective
36.	Swachh Bharat Mission	Oct. 2, 2014	Providing access to clean toilet to all rural households and initiating solid and liquid waste management activities in all gram panchayats.
37.	Pandit Deen Dayal Upadhyay Shramev Jayate Scheme	Oct. 16, 2014	To improve employability, skill development and other conveniences for labour.
38.	Shyama Prasad Mukherjee Rurban Mission	Sept. 16, 2015	Setting up 300 village clusters by 2019-20 across the country with all possible urban amenities.
39.	'Housing for all by 2022'	June 18, 2015	Providing affordable housing in Urban Areas.
40.	Pradhan Mantri Awas Yojana	June 25, 2015	Providing housing facilities in rural areas.
41.	Startup India, Standup India	16 Jan., 2016	To provide Support to all start-up businesses in all aspects of doing business in India.
42.	Pradhan Mantri Ujjwala Yojana	May 1, 2016	Launched to Provide free LPG connection to women from below poverty line families.
43.	Urja Ganga Yojana (UGY)	Oct. 24, 2016	To provide the accessibility of approx, 5 Lakh LPG gas cylinders within next 5 years.
44.	Pradhan Mantri Vittiya Saksharta Abhiyan (PMVSA)	Dec. 1, 2016	To go for cashless transaction and payment modes like using credit or debit cards or the payment wallets to reduce the malpractice in the country.
45.	Pradhan Mantri Garib Kalyan Yojana (PMGKY)	Dec. 2016	To improve the financial position of the poor people.
46.	Atal Amrit Abhiyan (AAA)	Dec. 25, 2016	To provide health insurance against 437 illnesses including 5 critical diseases.
47.	Pradhan Mantri Sahaj Bijli Har Ghar Yojana "Saubhagya"	Sep. 25, 2017	The objective of the 'Saubhagya' is to Provide energy access to all by last mile connectivity and electricity connections to all remaining un-electrified households in rural as well as urban areas to achieve universal household electrification in the country.
48.	Ayushman Bharat Yojana (AB PM-JAY)	2018	Ayushman Bharat National Health Protection Scheme (AB-NHPS) aims to provide free access to healthcare for 50 crore people in the country. By July 2021 Ayushman cards issued numbered 16.14 crore.
49.	PM Kisan Samman Nidhi	2019	Income support of ₹ 6,000 per year to eligible farmers through Direct Benefit Transfer.
50.	Garib Kalyan Rojgar Abhiyaan	2020	Employment campaign for the poor following coronavirus pandemic covering 12 ministries and 6 states. Launched on 20 June 2020 and ended on 22 October 2020.

AGRICULTURAL GROWTH DURING PLANNING PERIOD

In a developing country like India, agriculture sector and rural economy have a significant role in providing livelihoods, ensuring food security and providing impetus to the growth of industries and service sectors. The process of development inter alia results in declining share of agriculture in Gross Value Added (GVA), which is being witnessed in India too. However, the declining share does not undermine the significance of the sector for employment, livelihood and food security. With structural changes in agriculture, there is greater scope to broaden the range of activities related to agriculture to improve productivity and make way for sustainable growth.

The growth rates of agriculture & allied sectors have been fluctuating at 1.5 per cent in 2012-13, 5.6 per cent in 2013-14, (–) 0.2 per cent in 2014-15, 0.7 per cent in 2015-16 and 3.6 per cent in 2020-21. The uncertainties in growth in agriculture are explained by the fact that more than 50 per cent of agriculture in India is rainfall dependent which aggravate the production risks.

Production of Crops

As per Fourth Advance Estimates for 2020-21, total foodgrain production in the country is estimated at a record 308.65 million tonnes which is 11.15 million tonnes higher than that during 2019-20. The production of rice, wheat and coarse cereals has increased at compound annual growth rates (CAGR) of 2.7, 2.9 and 4.8 per cent respectively during last six years i.e. 2015-16 to 2020-21. The CAGR for pulses, oilseeds and cotton has been 7.9, 6.1 and 2.8 per cent, respectively during the same period. Figure 6 depicts the trend in agricultural production over the past six years.

As per the First Advance Estimates for 2021-22 (kharif only), total foodgrain production in the country is estimated at a record level of 150.50 million tonnes which is higher by 0.94 million tonnes than kharif foodgrain production of 2020-21.

Establishment years of major financial institutions in India

Institutions	*Establishment Year*
1. Reserve Bank of India	April 1, 1935
2. Industrial Finance Corporation of India (IFCI)	1948
3. ICICI	Jan. 1955
4. State Bank of India	July 1, 1955
5. Unit Trust of India	Feb. 1, 1964
6. IDBI	July 1964
7. NABARD	July 12, 1982
8. SIDBI	1990
9. EXIM Bank	Jan. 1, 1982
10. National Housing Bank	July 1988
11. Life Insurance Corporation (LIC)	Sept. 1956
12. General Insurance Corporation (GIC)	Nov. 1972
13. Regional Rural Banks	Oct. 2, 1975
14. Housing Development Finance Corporation Ltd (HDFC)	1977

PUBLIC FINANCE

Finance Commission

Finance Commission is constituted to define financial relations between the Centre and the States. Under the provision of Article 280 of the constitution, the President appoints a Finance Commission for the specific purpose of devolution of non-plan revenue resources. The functions of the commission are to make recommendations to the President in respect of:

1. The distribution of net proceeds of taxes to be shared between the union and the states and the allocation of share of such proceeds among the states.

2. The principles which should govern the payment of grants-in-aid by the centre to the states.
3. Any other matter concerning financial relations between the centre and the states.

Finance Commission	*Chairman*	*Operational Duration*
I	K.C. Niyogi	1952-57
II	K. Santhanam	1957-62
III	A.K. Chanda	1962-66
IV	P.V. Rajamannar	1966-69
V	Mahaveer Tyagi	1969-74
VI	Brahma Nand Reddy	1974-79
VII	J.M. Shellet	1979-84
VIII	Y.B. Chawan	1984-89
IX	N.K.P. Salve	1989-95
X	K.C. Pant	1995-00
XI	A.M. Khusro	2000-05
XII	Dr. C. Rangrajan	2005-10
XIII	V.L. Kelkar	2010-15
XIV	Y.B. Reddy	2015-20
XV	N.K. Singh	2021-26

New Industrial Policy 1991: An Overview

***(A) Main Features** (Objectives)*

- To maintain a sustained growth in productivity.
- To enhance gainful employment.
- To achieve optimum utilisation of human resources.
- To attain international competitiveness.
- To transform India into a major partner and players in the global arena.

(B) Main Focus on

- Deregulating Indian industry.
- Allowing the industry freedom & flexibility in responding to market forces and
- Providing a policy regime which facilitates and fosters growth of Indian industry.

(C) Policy Measures

(*i*) Liberalisation of Industrial Licensing Policy.
(*ii*) Introduction of Industrial Entrepreneur's Memorandum (*i.e.,* no industrial approval is required for industries not requiring compulsory licensing).
(*iii*) Liberalisation of Locational Policy.
(*iv*) Liberalised Policy for Small Scale Sectors.
(*v*) Non-Resident Indians Scheme (NRIs are allowed to invest upto 100% equity on non-repatriation basis in all activities except for a small negative list).
(*vi*) Electronic Hardware Technology Park (EHTP)/ Software Technology Park (STP) Scheme for building up strong electronic industry to enhance exports.
(*vii*) Liberalised policy for Foreign Direct Investment (FDI).

List of Industries Requiring Compulsory Licence

With the introduction of New Industrial Policy in 1991, a substantial programme of deregulation has been undertaken. Industrial licensing has been abolished for all items except for a short list of five industries related to security, strategic or environmental concerns. These are:

1. Distillation and brewing of alcoholic drinks.
2. Cigar, Cigarettes and other substitutes of prepared tobacco.
3. Electronic, Aerospace and all types of defence equipment.
4. Industrial Explosives including match boxes.
5. Hazardous chemicals.

Areas Reserved for the Public Sector

The areas reserved for the public sector are—(a) atomic energy; (b) the substances specified in the schedule to the notification of the Government of India in the department of Atomic Energy dated the 15 March, 1995 and (c) railway transport.

Multiple Choice Questions

1. The revealed preference theory of consumer's behaviour is based on
   A. Consistency
   B. Strong Ordering
   C. Positive income elasticity of demand
   D. All the above

2. An individual's supply curve for labour will bend backwards when
   A. The substitution effect of wage rate increase is higher than income effect.
   B. The income effect of wage rate increase is negative and higher than the substitution effect.
   C. Leisure is a Giffen good.
   D. The substitution and income effect of wage rate increase reinforce each other.

3. The short run supply curve of a firm under perfect competition is the same as the
   A. marginal cost curve
   B. marginal cost curve above the average variable cost curve
   C. average variable cost curve
   D. average total cost curve

4. Match **List-I** with **List-II** and select the correct answer from the codes given below:

List-I	List-II
(*a*) Quasi rent	1. Hicks
(*b*) Elasticity of substitution	2. Chamberlin
(*c*) Monopolistic competition	3. Neumann and Morgenstern
(*d*) Theory of Games	4. Marshall

Codes:

	(*a*)	(*b*)	(*c*)	(*d*)
A.	4	1	3	2
B.	2	1	4	3
C.	2	1	3	4
D.	4	1	2	3

5. The difference between the value of marginal product and the marginal revenue product arises only if
   A. Average revenue is not equal to marginal revenue.
   B. Average cost is not equal to marginal cost.
   C. Total revenue is not equal to total cost.
   D. Average cost is not equal to average revenue.

6. Inventory-theoretic approach to transactions demand for money has been given by
   A. J. M. Keynes
   B. Milton Friedman
   C. Don Patinkin
   D. W.J. Baumol

7. Liquidity trap is a situation when demand for money is
   A. Zero elastic
   B. Unit elastic
   C. Relatively more elastic
   D. Perfectly elastic

8. Which of the following is not an indicator of Globalization ?
   A. Opening of the economy for unrestricted imports and exports.
   B. Allowing free capital movement among nations.
   C. Free movement of technology among nations.
   D. Achieving exchange rate stability.

9. Which one of the following is an indicator of poverty?
A. Head-count index
B. Poverty-gap ratio
C. Poverty-square gap ratio
D. All of the above

10. Various trade reforms after 1991 in India were implemented by
A. Manmohan Singh
B. C.N. Vakil
C. P.R. Brahmananda
D. Jagdish Bhagwati

11. Which one of the following is not the objective of monetary policy in India?
A. To accelerate economic development
B. To achieve price stability
C. To regulate foreign trade
D. To stabilise exchange rate

12. The continuous deficit in the balance of payments of India is due to
A. Continued rise in imports
B. Slow rise in exports
C. Exchange rate volatility
D. All of the above

13. Match **List-I** with **List-II** and select the answer using the codes given below:

List-I (Institution)	**List-II (Year of establishment)**
(*a*) R.B.I.	1. 1935
(*b*) N.A.B.A.R.D.	2. 1982
(*c*) Planning Commission	3. 1950
(*d*) F.C.I.	4. 1964

Codes :

	(*a*)	(*b*)	(*c*)	(*d*)
A.	1	2	3	4
B.	3	4	2	1
C.	4	2	1	3
D.	2	1	3	4

14. Which one of the following is not correctly matched in the case of India ?
A. Revenue expenditure : Revenue receipts + Revenue deficit
B. Primary deficit : Revenue deficit – interest payments
C. Total receipts : Revenue receipts + capital receipts
D. Revenue receipts : Tax revenue + non-tax revenue

15. The incidence of sales tax is on the seller when the demand curve
A. for the product is a rectangular hyperbola
B. for the product is perfectly elastic
C. for the product is perfectly inelastic
D. for the product is moderately elastic

16. A progressive income tax implies that
A. the amount of tax falls with a rise in income
B. the rate of tax rises with a rise in income
C. both (A) and (B)
D. the rate of tax decreases with a rise in income

17. Under which Article of the Constitution of India is the Finance Commission is appointed by President of India?
A. 279 B. 280
C. 281 D. 282

18. Marshallian Theory of consumer's behaviour is based on
A. Hypothesis of additive utilities
B. Hypothesis of independent utilities
C. Both A and B
D. Weak ordering

19. Consider the following statements:
(*i*) Income effect is positive in case of normal goods
(*ii*) Income effect is zero in the case of superior goods
(*iii*) All Giffen goods are inferior goods, but not all inferior goods are Giffen goods
(*iv*) Income effect is negative in case of inferior goods
Which of the above is/are correct?
A. (*i*) only B. (*ii*) only
C. (*iii*) & (*iv*) D. (*i*), (*iii*) and (*iv*)

20. A profit maximising firm will stop production in the short run if price is
A. less than the average variable cost
B. less than the marginal cost

C. less than the average total cost
D. equal to the average total cost

21. Consider the following statements:
(*i*) When MC curve is below the AC curve, then the AC curve must be rising
(*ii*) When MC curve is above AC curve, then AC curve must be falling
(*iii*) MC curve intersects AC curve at the point where AC is constant
Which of the above statement(s) is/are correct?
A. (*iii*) only
B. (*i*) and (*ii*)
C. (*i*), (*ii*) and (*iii*)
D. (*i*) and (*iii*)

22. With which of the following is the doctrine of excess capacity in the long run associated?
A. Monopoly
B. Oligopoly
C. Monopolistic competition
D. Perfect competition

23. To derive the demand curve for a firm for one of the several variable factors, the following must be considered:
A. The external effect of the change in the factor price
B. The internal effect of the change in factor price
C. Monopolistic exploitation
D. Monopsonistic exploitation

24. In case of Keynes' Psychological Law of Consumption Function, which one of the following statements is incorrect?
A. As disposal income increases, consumption also increases, but less than proportionately.
B. Marginal propensity to consume is positive but less than unity.
C. As disposable income increases, average propensity to consume falls, and vice versa.
D. Average propensity to consume equals marginal propensity to consume at all levels of income.

25. Given that C = Currency with the public, DD = Demand Deposits, TD = Time Deposits and R = Cash balances with the Commercial Banks, then high powered money is defined as
A. C + DD B. C + R
C. C + TD D. C + DD + TD

26. The premise that there exists inverse relationship between money wage inflation and unemployment was originally given by
A. A.W. Phillips B. Milton Friedman
C. Philip Cagan D. Robert Lucas

27. Which of the following statements is incorrect?
A. Monetary Policy is relatively ineffective, when the interest elasticity of investment is low (IS curve is steep)
B. Monetary Policy is relatively ineffective, when the interest elasticity of demand for money is high (LM curve is flat)
C. Fiscal policy is relatively ineffective, when interest elasticity of demand for money is low (LM curve is steep)
D. Fiscal policy is ineffective, when interest rate elasticity of investment is low (IS curve is steep)

28. The Human Development Index was first developed by
A. UNDP B. IMF
C. UNICEF D. UNCTAD

29. Which one of the following is not an instrument of fiscal policy?
A. Public Revenue
B. Public Expenditure
C. Public Borrowing
D. Cash Reserve Ratio

30. The role of the State under globalization is
A. zero B. maximum
C. minimum D. neutral

31. Which one of the following is the most important source of revenue of State Governments in India?
A. Land Revenue
B. Sales Tax

C. Stamps and Registration Fees
D. State Excise Duties

32. Marginal cost of a pure public good is
A. zero or close to zero
B. one
C. A and B both
D. very high

33. The demand for labour by a firms is a derived demand because it depends upon
A. The demand for goods and services that labour helps to produce
B. The degree of substiution between labour and other factors of production
C. The elasticity of demand for labour
D. The demand for other factors of production.

34. Shift in LM curve takes place due to
A. Increase in autonomous investment
B. Increase in money supply
C. Increase in consumption
D. Increase in saving rate

35. The Phillips Curve shows the relation between
A. Income and consumption
B. Income and price level
C. Income and investment
D. Inflation and unemployment

36. Rolling Plan Concept was propounded by
A. Gunnar Myrdal
B. J.K. Galbraith
C. Paul A. Samuelson
D. A.K. Sen

37. The difference between the export and import of services is called
A. Balance of Trade
B. Balance of Invisibles
C. Balance of Current account
D. Balance of Capital account

38. The Cobb-Douglas Production Function assumes that the elasticity of substitution is:
A. One B. Two
C. Three D. Four

39. A consumer attains his/her equilibrium at the point where:
A. Total Utility = Price
B. Marginal Utility > Price
C. Marginal Utility < Price
D. Marginal Utility = Price

40. According to Say's Law, unemployment can be removed by:
A. Rise in wages
B. Fall in wages
C. Taxing wages
D. Subsidising wages

41. Which of the following is generally referred to as a '*broader measure of money supply*'?
A. M_1 B. M_2
C. M_3 D. M_4

42. The concept of consumers surplus was coined by:
A. Ricardo B. Fisher
C. Marshall D. Pigou

43. For complementary goods the indifference curve takes the shape of:
A. a straight line
B. a downward sloping line
C. a right angle
D. a negatively sloped curve

44. PAUL M SWEEZY used kinked demand curve to explain:
A. Price determination in oligopoly
B. Price rigidity in oligopoly
C. Profit maximisation in oligopoly
D. Price output determination in oligopoly

45. According to Phillips curve when rate of inflation increases, then rate of:
A. unemployment also increases
B. unemployment decreases
C. unemployment will remain constant
D. Full employment will prevail

46. According to Milton Friedman quantity theory of money is the theory of:
A. Prices
B. Income
C. Demand for money
D. Supply of money

47. Which of the following feature is not a universally observed in under developed countries?

A. Low per capita income
B. High density of population
C. Higher share of agriculture in G.D.P.
D. Low literacy rate

48. For the first time in India zero base budgeting was implemented in the finance ministership of:
A. P. Chidambaram
B. Manmohan Singh
C. V. P. Singh
D. Jaswant Singh

49. Gadgil formula is applicable to:
A. Grants given by planning commission
B. Grants given by Finance commission
C. Grants given by RBI
D. Grants given by Foreign Countries

50. One of the important factors in trade reforms is to:
A. increase export duties
B. reduce import duties
C. keep export duties constant
D. keep import duties constant

51. Chamberlin introduced the concept of cost known as:
A. Fixed cost B. Floating cost
C. Selling cost D. Variable cost

52. If commodities are perfect complements indifference curve becomes a:
A. Downward sloping curve
B. straight line with negative slope
C. Right angle
D. Rectangular hyperbola

53. C E S Production function is associated with the name of one of the following:
A. Joan Robinson
B. B. S. Minhas
C. Manmohan Singh
D. A. K. Sen

54. Natural rate of unemployment is the rate of unemployment at which:
A. Rate of inflation is stable
B. Rate of inflation is unstable
C. Rate of inflation is falling
D. Rate of inflation is rising

55. Revealed preference theory can be used:
A. to prove convexity of an indifference curve
B. to break price effect
C. to prove basic proposition of law of demand
D. all of the above

56. In case of perfect substitutes indifference curve is
A. right angled
B. linear upward sloping
C. linear downward sloping
D. concave to origin

57. A ridgeline is a locus of such points where marginal productivity of a factor input is:
A. equal to zero B. greater than zero
C. negative D. equal to one

58. When the negative income effect outweighs the substitution effect, the concerned good is:
A. a Giffin good
B. an inferior good
C. a normal good
D. none of the above

59. Attempts to force inflation below non-accelerating inflation rate of unemployment (NAIRU) will cause:
A. inflation to accelerate without any change in employment or output
B. Inflation to decelerate with rising employment and output
C. inflation to decelerate with employment and output remaining the same
D. inflation to remain unchanged with fall in employment and output.

60. Square root formula for money demand was developed by some of the following:
(*i*) Milton Friedman
(*ii*) James Tobin
(*iii*) A. C. Pigou
(*iv*) William Baumol

Of the above, select correct answer from the code given below:

Code:
A. (*i*) and (*ii*) are correct
B. (*i*) and (*iii*) are correct
C. (*ii*) and (*iv*) are correct
D. (*ii*) and (*iii*) are correct

61. Disposable income in National Accounts is calculated as:
A. GDP + Net income from abroad + Transfer Payments – Taxes – undistributed profit
B. GNP + Net income from abroad + Transfer Payments – Taxes + undistributed profit
C. GDP – Net income from abroad + Transfer Payments – Taxes + undistributed profit
D. GNP – Net income from abroad + Transfer Payments – Taxes + undistributed profit

62. Physical Quality of Life Index (PQLI) was calculated by:
A. Mahboobul Haq B. Meier G.M.
C. Morris D. D. None of the above

63. The base year for estimating GDP in India at constant prices at present is:
A. 1993-94 B. 1996-97
C. 2004-05 D. 2001-02

64. If demand curve assumes the shape of a rectangular hyperbola, price elasticity is equal to:
A. zero B. less than one
C. greater than one D. one

65. Let the consumption function be C = Rs. 30 + 0.80 Y and investment spending be I = Rs. 70 – 2 i, where i is the rate of interest. Then an increase in autonomous investment by Rs. 30 would shift the IS curve:
A. To the left by Rs. 150
B. To the right by Rs. 150
C. To the right by Rs. 30
D. To the left by Rs. 30

66. The concept of Multiplier was introduced for the first time by:
A. R. F. Kahn B. J. M. Keynes
C. R. F. Harrod D. V.K.R.V. Rao

67. Sustainable development addresses to:
A. the needs of the present generation.
B. the needs of the future generation.
C. the needs of the present generation without compromising the needs of the future generations.
D. the needs of the future generations, without compromising on the needs of the present generation.

68. Sen's measure of poverty includes:
A. The Head Count ratio.
B. The Head Count ratio and the poverty-gap ratio.
C. The poverty-gap ratio and the distribution of income among the poor.
D. The Head Count ratio, the poverty-gap ratio, and the distribution of income among the poor.

69. From April 1999, Jawahar Rojgar Yojana has been renamed as:
A. Jawahar Gram Samriddhi Yojana
B. Jawahar Swarna Jayanthi Yojana
C. Jawahar Samriddhi Yojana
D. Jawahar Rural Development Yojana

70. In case of public goods market demand is derived by vertical summation because public goods are:
A. Free goods
B. Unlimited in supply
C. Non-rival in consumption
D. Owned by public sector

71. Marshallian demand curve can be derived with the use of revealed preference theory if one of the following is ignored:
A. Price effect
B. Income effect
C. Substitution effect
D. Demand effect

72. If the two goods are bad substitutes, indifference curve will:
A. be a straight line
B. approach a straight line
C. approach a right angle
D. slope upwards

73. A given total outlay on factor inputs available at given prices is reflected by:
A. iso-revenue line

B. iso-cost line
C. iso-quant
D. production possibility curve

74. In Stackelberg's model of duopoly, if both sellers act as followers, we then have:
A. Cournot solution
B. A price war between sellers
C. A situation of disequilibrium
D. Collusion between sellers

75. The merit of revealed preference theory over earlier theories is that it explain consumer behaviour without reference to:
A. Utility
B. Consumer's income
C. Consumer's preferences
D. Rationality assumption

76. Utility function for a consumer is monotonically increasing in the quantities consumed of a single available commodity. Such a utility function is always:
A. a concave function
B. a strictly quasi-concave function
C. a strictly concave function
D. a linear function

77. Laffer curve studies the relationship between:
A. tax rate and tax revenue
B. tax rate and expenditure
C. tax rate and consumption
D. tax rate and welfare

78. The five year plans in India are finalised after the approval of:
A. The President and the Prime Minister
B. The Rajya Sabha
C. National Development Council
D. The Lok Sabha

79. In India national income is estimated by:
A. Finance Commission
B. Central Statistical Organisation
C. Planning Commission
D. Finance Ministry

80. Poverty line for rural areas in India is determined on the basis of minimum average daily consumption of calories which is:
A. 2000 B. 2700
C. 2500 D. 2400

81. Indian Planning Commission is a:
A. A parliamentary body
B. Ad hoc body
C. Non-statutory body
D. constitutional body

82. Which state in India has the highest HDI?
A. Andhra Pradesh B. Delhi
C. Kerala D. Uttar Pradesh

83. The goods which are non-rival in consumption are called:
A. Private goods
B. Free goods
C. Public goods
D. Non-economic goods

84. A competitive firm achieves long-run equilibrium in the product market when:
A. AR = MR B. MR = AC
C. MR = MC D. Price = AR

85. In the Sweezy model of Oligopoly, an increase in demand will make upper portion of the demand curve:
A. More elastic B. Less elastic
C. Unitary elastic D. None of the above

86. Which of the following factors does not stall the entry of other firms in an Oligopolistic industry:
A. huge advertising expenditure incurred by existing firms
B. economies of scale
C. technology
D. increase in demand

87. Which of the following is not an element of selling cost:
A. salary of the salesmen
B. expenses incurred in advertising
C. transportation cost
D. costs incurred on window displays

88. The most comprehensive measure of the aggregate price level is the:
A. consumer price index
B. producer price index
C. GNP deflator
D. wholesale price index

89. A person who left the job to find another job would be classified as:
A. fractionally unemployed
B. structurally unemployed
C. cyclically unemployed
D. no longer in the labour force

90. Vicious Circle of Poverty was proposed by:
A. A. Marshall B. J.M. Keynes
C. Ragner Nurkse D. M. Friedman

91. Second Five Year plan was based on a model developed by:
A. C.H. Hanumantha Rao
B. P.C. Mahalanobis
C. A.K. Sen
D. K.N. Raj

92. 'Pump priming' should be resorted to at a time of:
A. Inflation B. Deflation
C. Reflation D. None of the above

93. VAT is imposed:
A. on final stage of production
B. on first stage of production
C. directly on consumers
D. at every stage between production and consumption

94. New Agricultural Strategy (Green Revolution) was introduced in India in the year:
A. 1969 B. 1966
C. 1970 D. 1960

95. New Economic Policy in India was introduced in:
A. 1981 B. 1971
C. 1991 D. 2001

96. Barometric price leadership implies leadership of:
A. Low cost firm
B. High cost firm
C. Most experienced firm
D. Least experienced firm

97. For substitute, cross-elasticity of demand is:
A. Positive B. Negative
C. Zero D. Infinite

98. According to Keynes, level of employment depends on:
A. Aggregate demand
B. Aggregate supply
C. Demand and supply equilibrium
D. Effective demand

99. Under whose chairmanship was the first Finance Commission of India appointed?
A. K.C. Niyogi B. K. Santhanam
C. A.K. Chanda D. C. Rangarajan

100. The law of Demand refers to
A. Price-supply relationship
B. Price-cost relationship
C. Price-demand relationship
D. Price-income relationship

101. In a typical demand schedule, quantity demanded
A. Varies directly with price
B. Varies proportionately with price
C. Varies inversely with price
D. Is independent of price

102. The demand curve for a commodity is generally drawn on the assumption that
A. The commodity has no substitutes
B. Tastes, income and all other prices remain constant
C. The average house hold consists of two persons
D. Purchases of the commodity are made by a free market.

103. When the law of demand operates the demand curve
A. Slopes downward from left to right
B. Slopes upward from left to right
C. Slopes upward from right to left
D. Parallel to horizontal axis

104. 'Ceteris paribus' clause in the Law of Demand does not mean
A. The price of the commodity does not change
B. The price of its substitutes does not change
C. The income of the consumer does not change
D. The price of complementary goods does not change

105. Which of the following could provide an example of exceptional demand curves?

I. Demand for "Giffen goods"
II. Demand based on fears of a future rise in prices
III. Demand for second-hand clothes
IV. Demand for daily newspapers

A. I only B. I and II
C. II and III D. I, II, III and IV

106. Bread and butter, lamb and mint sauce, illustrate the type of inter related demand known as

A. Rival demand
B. Composite demand
C. Competitive demand
D. Joint demand

107. When an individual's income falls (while everything else remains the same), his demand for an inferior goods:

A. Increases
B. Decreases
C. Remains unchanged
D. We cannot say without additional information

108. An income-demand curve for a "Luxury commodity" slopes:

A. Upwards to the right from the origin
B. Vertically
C. Upwards from left to right only beyond a certain level of consumer's income
D. Horizontally

109. An income demand curve for inferior commodity always slopes

A. Upwards to the right
B. Backwards to the left
C. Downwards to the right
D. Horizontally

110. 'Change in quantity demanded' refers to

A. Upward shift of the demand curve
B. Downward shift of the demand curve
C. Movement on the same demand curve
D. None of these

111. Cross demand is the change in the quantity demanded to a given commodity in response to the

A. Change in the utility of another commodity
B. Change in the price of another commodity
C. Change in the nature of another commodity
D. Change in the size of another commodity

112. To calculate the elasticity of demand which of the following formula is used

A. $\dfrac{\text{Percentage change in demand}}{\text{Original demand}}$

B. $\dfrac{\text{Proportionate change in demand}}{\text{Proportionate change in price}}$

C. $\dfrac{\text{Change in demand}}{\text{Change in price}} \div \dfrac{\text{original demand}}{\text{original price}}$

D. $\dfrac{\text{Change in demand}}{\text{Change in price}}$

113. Market demand is

A. The sum of all individual demands
B. Demand at prevailing average prices
C. Ability to pay the price asked
D. Demand in a perfectly free market

114. Extension and contraction of demand are results of

A. Change in consumer's income
B. Change in consumer's tastes
C. Change in price
D. None of these

115. Giffen goods are those goods—

A. For which demand increases as price increases
B. Which have a high income elasticity of demand
C. Which are in very short supply
D. None of these

116. In measuring price-elasticity

A. Price is a dependent variable and quantity is an independent variable
B. Price is a independent variable and quantity is a dependent variable
C. Price and quantity both are independent variables
D. Price and quantity both are dependent variables

117. Income-Elasticity of demand will be zero when a given change in income brings about

A. A less than proportionate change in quantity demanded

B. A more than proportionate change in quantity demanded

C. The same proportionate change in demand

D. No change in demand

118. A straight line, downward-sloping demand curve implies that, as price falls, the elasticity of demand

A. Increases

B. Decreases

C. Remains the same

D. is zero

119. Which of the following does not have a uniform elasticity of demand at all points—

A. A downward sloping demand curve

B. A vertical demand curve

C. A rectangular hyperbola demand curve

D. A horizontal demand curve

120. Match the following

1. Responsiveness of demand to change in price	*(i)* Income elasticity of demand
2. Responsiveness of demand to change in tastes	*(ii)* Price elasticity of demand
3. Responsiveness of demand to change in income	*(iii)* Cross elasticity of demand
4. Responsiveness of demand to change in price of related goods.	*(iv)* Taste elasticity of demand

	1	2	3	4
A.	*i*	*ii*	*iii*	*iv*
B.	*iv*	*iii*	*i*	*ii*
C.	*iii*	*iv*	*ii*	*i*
D.	*ii*	*iv*	*i*	*iii*

121. A monopolist charging high price operates on

A. The elastic part of a demand curve

B. The inelastic part of a demand curve

C. The constant elastic part of a demand curve

D. Ignores elasticity of demand altogether

122. Elasticity of demand in the following figure at point Q_1 is

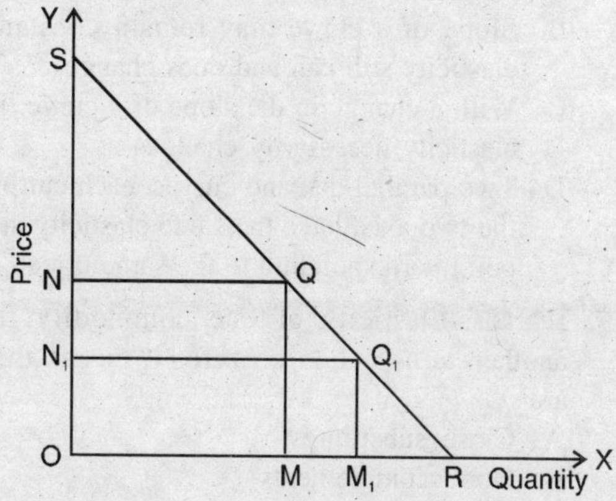

A. $\frac{RQ_1}{SQ_1}$ B. $\frac{Q_1N_1}{OS}$

C. $\frac{Q_1F}{RQ_1}$ D. $\frac{RQ}{RQ_1}$

123. If two commodities are substitutes a change in the price of one, ceteris paribus, causes a change in the quantity purchased of the other

A. In the same direction

B. In the opposite direction

C. In an insignificant manner

D. Cannot be known

124. Income elasticity of demand is expressed as

A. $\frac{\text{Percentage change in quantity demanded}}{\text{Percentage change in income}}$

B. $\frac{\text{Percentage change in income}}{\text{Change in quantity demanded}}$

C. Change in quantity demanded $\times \frac{\text{Change in marginal income}}{100}$

D. $\frac{\text{Change in income}}{100 \times \text{change in quantity demanded}}$

125. Pick out the correct formula for arc elasticity

A. $\frac{\Delta q}{\Delta P} \cdot \frac{P_1 + P_2}{q_1 + q_2}$ B. $\frac{\Delta P}{\Delta q} \cdot \frac{P_1 + P_2}{q_1 + q_2}$

C. $\frac{\Delta P}{\Delta q} \cdot \frac{100}{q_1 + P_1}$ D. $\frac{\Delta q \times 100}{P}$

126. Which of the following statements is correct?
A. Slope of a curve and its elasticity are one and the same thing
B. Slope of a curve may remain constant; elasticity still can and does change
C. With a change in the slope of a curve, its elasticity necessarily changes
D. Two parallel demand curves, each cutting the two axis, have the same elasticity at a point corresponding to the same price

127. If cross-elasticity of one commodity for another turns out to be zero, it means they are
A. Close substitutes
B. Good complements
C. Completely unrelated
D. None of these

128. The vertical demand curve for a commodity shows that its demand is
A. Highly elastic B. Perfectly inelastic
C. Fairly elastic D. Moderately elastic

129. Utility may be defined as
A. The power of a commodity to satisfy wants
B. The usefulness of a commodity
C. The level of satisfaction given by a commodity
D. The desire for a commodity

130. The law of Equi-Marginal utility states
A. $MU_x.P_x = MU_y . P_y = MU_z . P_z$
B. $\frac{MU_x}{P_x} = \frac{MU_y}{P_y} = \frac{MU_z}{P_z} = MU_m$
C. $\frac{MU_x}{P_x} > \frac{MU_y}{P_y} > \frac{MU_z}{P_z} > MU_m$
D. $\frac{MU_x}{P_x} < \frac{MU_y}{P_y} < \frac{MU_z}{P_z} < MU_m$

131. A consumer's demand curve can be obtained from
A. Income-consumption curve
B. Engel's curve
C. Price-consumption curve
D. None of these

132. A falling MU curve illustrates
A. The principle of diminishing marginal utility
B. The principle of diminishing marginal rate of substitution
C. The principle of equi-marginal utility
D. None of these

133. Which of the following is called as the Gossen's First Law?
A. Law of substitution
B. The Law of equi-marginal utility
C. The Law of diminishing utility
D. The Law of indifference

134. A stable equilibrium position is one in which
A. There are never any departures from the equilibrium position
B. There are only two forces influencing equilibrium
C. Any departure from the equilibrium position calls into play forces which end to restore that position
D. There are endless oscillations

135. Ordinal approach is based on
A. Law of maximum satisfaction
B. Utility could not be measured in cardinal numbers
C. Utility could not be measured in ordinal numbers
D. Utility can be measured

136. Gossen's second law states that—
A. When the income increases the money value or real income will decrease
B. The consumers consume only when $\frac{P_x}{P_y} = MU_m$
C. Once a person has spent his entire income he would have maximised his total pleasure from it only if the satisfaction gained from the last item of each commodity bought was the same
D. None of these

137. Economists associated with the development of indifference curve analysis are
A. Hicks and Allen

B. Hicks and Robbins
C. Marshall and Hicks
D. Hicks and Walras

138. An indifference curve is always
A. Concave to the origin
B. Convex to the origin
C. A vertical straight line
D. A horizontal straight line

139. The indifference curve which is 'L' shape represents
A. Perfect complementarity
B. Perfect substitutability
C. No substitutability
D. Non Complementarity

140. All the points on a budget line represent
A. Increasing total expenditure
B. Decreasing total expenditure
C. The same total expenditure
D. None of the above

141. The total effect of a price change of a commodity is
A. Substitution effect + Price effect
B. Substitution effect + Income effect
C. Substitution effect + Demonstration effect
D. Substitution effect – Income effect

142. The Doctrine of consumer's surplus is based on
A. Indifference curve analysis
B. Revealed preference theory
C. Law of substitution
D. The law of diminishing marginal utility

143. The Revealed Preference Theory was formulated by
A. Lionel Robbins B. Paul Samuelson
C. Joan Robinson D. Alfred Marshall

144. Consumer's surplus is the highest in the case of
A. Necessities
B. Comforts
C. Luxuries
D. Conventional necessities

145. The Revealed Preference Theory is based on
A. The assumption of indifference
B. Utility and demand
C. Introspection
D. Observed consumer behaviour

146. A rightwards shifte in supply curve indicates
A. A decrease in supply
B. An increase in quantity supplied
C. An increase in supply
D. None of the above

147. External economies are witnessed in
A. A rising supply curve
B. A rising demand curve
C. A falling supply curve
D. A falling demand curve

148. Supply of a commodity is a
A. Stock concept
B. A flow concept
C. Both stock and flow concept
D. None of these

149. "Production" may be defined as an act of—
A. Creating utility
B. Earning profit
C. Destroying utility
D. Providing services

150. In general, most of the production functions measure
A. The productivity of factors of production
B. The relation between the factors of production
C. The economies of scale
D. The relations between change in physical inputs and physical output

151. When average product increases, the marginal product is
A. Less than the average product
B. More than the average product
C. Equal to the average product
D. None of the above

152. In short run the law of variable proportions is also known as the
A. Law of increasing returns
B. Law of diminishing returns
C. Law of constant returns
D. Law of return to scale

153. The Law of variable proportions comes into being when

A. There are only two variable factors
B. There is a fixed factor and a variable factor
C. All factors are variable
D. Variable factors yield less

154. Which of the stages is relevant for a firm which aims at maximum economic efficiency in the following diagram—

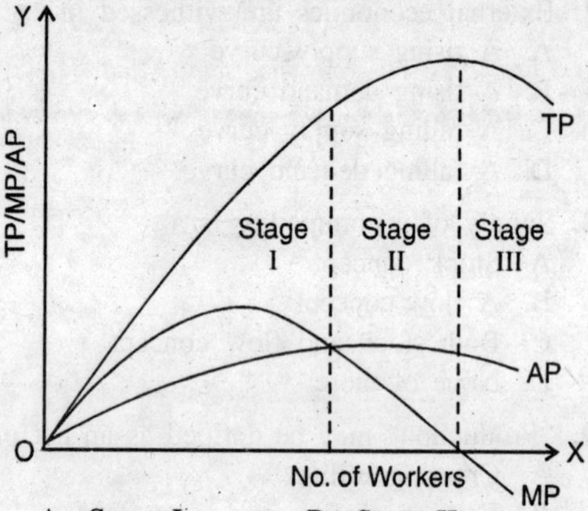

A. Stage I B. Stage II
C. Stage III D. Stage IV

155. Isoquant refers to
A. Another name of indifference curve
B. The production Indifference curve
C. An equal quantity curve of a consumer
D. An equal cost curve of a producer

156. If, by increasing the quantity of labour used by one unit, the firm can give up 2 units of capital and still produce the same output, then the $MRTS_{LK}$ is:
A. $\frac{1}{2}$ B. 2
C. 1 D. 4

157. The marginal product curve is above the average product curve when the average product is—
A. Decreasing
B. Increasing
C. Becomes constant
D. None of the above

158. When the AP_L is positive but declining, the MP_L could be —
A. Declining B. Zero
C. Negative D. Any of the above

159. If the $MRTS_{LK}$ equals 2, then the MP_K/MP_L is—
A. 2 B. 1
C. ½ D. 4

160. The following Table shows the various combinations of labour (L) and capital (K) and the resulting outputs—

Combination	*Output (Units)*
1L + 1K	200
2L + 2K	400
3L + 3K	600
4L + 4K	800
5L + 5K	1000

This Table shows the
A. Constant returns to scale
B. Diminishing returns to scale
C. Increasing returns to scale
D. None of the above

161. The slope of the iso-cost line is determined by
A. Prices of the two factors
B. Productivity of the two factors
C. Degree of substitutability of two factors
D. None of these

162. Rectangular hyperbola is the shape of
A. TFC B. AFC
C. FC D. MC

163. Marginal cost curve always cuts the average cost curve
A. From below on the falling portion of the AC curve
B. From below on the rising portion of the AC curve
C. From below at the minimum point of the AC curve
D. From below at any point on the AC curve

164. Which is an inverted 'U' shaped curve?
A. AC B. MP
C. TC D. FC

165. If the total cost curve is plotted, marginal cost can be illustrated by—
A. A U-shaped curve cutting the total cost curve at its lowest point
B. The slope of a tangent to the curve at any given output

C. A straight line from the origin to the mid-point of the curve
D. A straight line cutting the curve at its lowest point

166. 'The price which is necessary to retain a given unit of a factor in a certain industry may be called its transfer earnings or transfer price.' Defined by
A. Prof. Lipsey B. Alfred Marshall
C. Robertson D. Joan Robinson

167. The prime cost may be considered as
A. Variable cost B. Direct cost
C. Sunk cost D. Fixed cost

168. Why the average fixed cost curve does not touch the output axis—

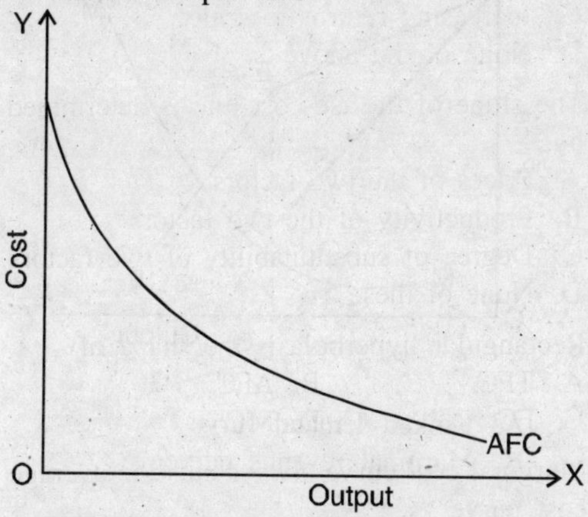

A. Because AFC cannot be negative
B. Because AFC cannot be zero
C. Because AFC cannot be less than one
D. None of these

169. An Iso-cost line represents—
A. Combinations of two inputs which yield the same amount of output
B. Combinations of two inputs which cost the same amount to a firm
C. Combinations of two inputs which yields varying amounts of output
D. Combinations of two inputs which cost different amounts of outlay to a firm

170. The MP of a factor—
A. Is always positive
B. Is always either positive or zero
C. Can be positive, negative or zero
D. Is always negative

171. The LAC curve is tangent to the lowest point on the SAC curves when the LAC curve is
A. Falling
B. Rising
C. At its minimum
D. None of the above

172. Average fixed cost can be obtained through
A. $AFC = \frac{TFC}{TC}$
B. $AFC = \frac{TFC}{MC}$
C. AFC = TC + TVC
D. AFC = MC + TVC

173. The advertisement cost is included in—
A. Fixed cost
B. Some times in fixed cost sometimes in variable cost
C. Always in variable cost
D. Never included in variable cost

174. All of the following curves are U-shaped except—
A. The AVC curve B. The AFC curve
C. The AC curve D. The MC curve

175. Opportunity costs are also known as—
A. Spill-over costs
B. Money costs
C. Alternative costs
D. External costs

176. Which of the following formula explain the term average revenue?
A. $AR = \frac{\text{Total units produced}}{\text{Total Revenue}}$
B. $AR = \frac{\text{Total Revenue}}{\text{Number of units produced}}$
C. AR = MR × No. of units produced
D. AR = TR – MR

177. The relationship between elasticity of demand (*e*), Average Revenue (AR) and Marginal Revenue (MR) is shown by the following formula

A. $e = \dfrac{AR}{AR - MR}$ B. $e = \dfrac{MR}{AR - MR}$

C. $e = \dfrac{TR}{AR - MR}$ D. $e = \dfrac{AR}{MR}$

178. The following figure gives the cost of a firm

1.	No. of units produced	10
2.	Total variable cost	200
3.	Total average cost	30

The average fixed cost is

A. 30 B. 10
C. 20 D. Data is not sufficient

179. In the following diagram of a competitive firm T point include

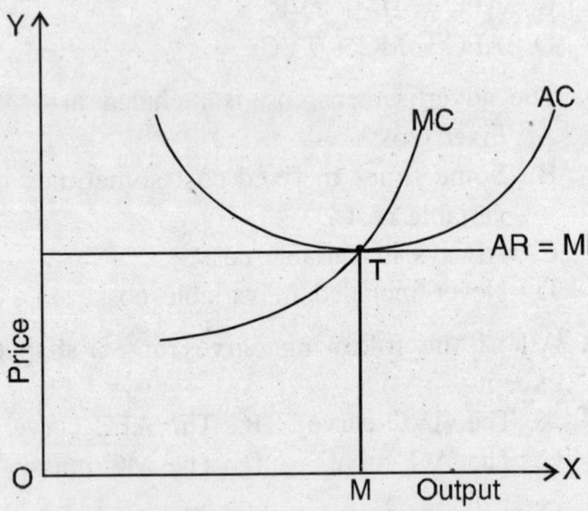

A. No profit B. Abnormal profit
C. Normal profit D. Heavy loss

180. By "normal profits" is meant

A. The profit made by the marginal entrepreneur in a normal year
B. The payment made to the marginal entrepreneur for his abilities
C. The surplus profit made by the least efficient firms
D. The payment needed to keep an entrepreneur in an industry

181. Under price discrimination price will be higher in the market where demand is—

A. Unitary elastic B. Highly elastic
C. Less elastic D. None of the above

182. From the resource allocation view point, perfect competition is preferable because

A. The firms operate at excess capacity levels
B. There is a whole variety of output produced
C. There is no restriction on entry and exit of firms
D. There is no idle capacity

183. Excess capacity is not found under

A. Monopoly
B. Monopolistic competition
C. Perfect competition
D. Oligopoly

184. The line ACDG represents

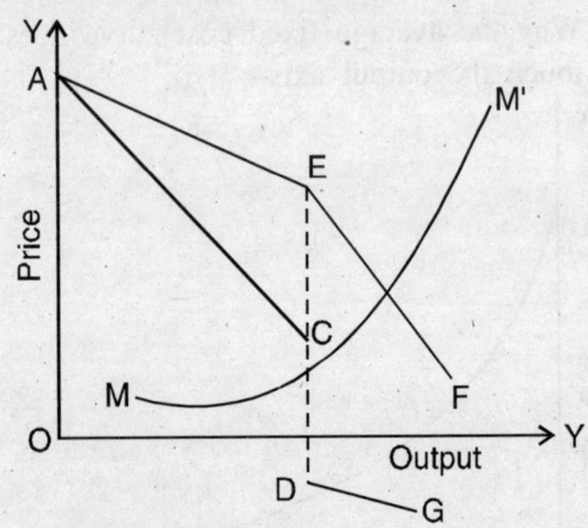

A. Kinked-demand curve
B. Marginal revenue curve
C. Cost curve
D. Marginal cost curve

185. OPEC is an example of the type of producer's organization known as a

A. Marketing board
B. Producer's cooperative
C. Trust
D. Cartel

186. In monopoly, the relationship between average revenue and marginal revenue curves is as follows—

A. Average revenue curve lies above the MR curve
B. AR curve coincides with the MR-curve
C. AR curve lies below the MR-curve
D. AR curve is parallel to the MR-curve

187. A firm practising price discrimination will be—

A. Charging different prices for different qualities of a product
B. Buying in the cheapest and selling in he dearest markets
C. Charging different prices in different markets for a product
D. Buying only from firms selling in bulk at a distance

188. Equilibrium of a discriminating monopolist requires the fulfilment of which one of the following conditions—
A. It must be profitable for him to sell output in more than one market
B. MR in both markets must be the same
C. MR in both markets must also be equal to the marginal cost of producing the monopolist's aggregate output
D. All the above

189. The hypothesis that the firms seek to maximise their sales revenue own its origin to
A. W.J. Baumol B. J.S. Baumol
C. W.J. Hicks D. J.W. Baumol

190. Price discrimination is possible
A. Only under monopoly situation
B. Under any market form
C. Only under monopolistic competition
D. Only under perfect competition

191. The degree of monopoly power can be measured by the formula

A. $\frac{P - MC}{P}$ B. $\frac{AR}{AR - MR}$

C. $\frac{MR}{AR - MR}$ D. $\frac{AR - MR}{MR}$

192. Bilateral monopoly means
A. Two rival sellers only
B. Two rival buyers only
C. A monopoly seller buying his input from many suppliers
D. A monopolist facing a monopsonist

193. The equilibrium level of output for the pure monopolist is where
A. MR = MC B. MR > MC
C. MR < MC D. P < AC

194. Modern theories of imperfect competition were inspired by
A. Joan Robinson B. Sraffa
C. Cournot D. Chamberlin

195. Monopolistic can fix
A. Both price and output
B. Either price or output
C. Neither price nor output
D. None

196. Monopolistic competition differs from perfect competition due to
A. Large number of firms and heterogeneous product
B. Large number of firms and homogeneous product
C. Small number of firms and differentiated products
D. Only a few firms and similar products

197. In the case of price leadership by the dominant firm, when all the firms in the purely oligopolistic industry will produce their best level of output?
A. Always B. Often
C. Never D. None of these

198. Which of the following used the kinked demand curve only to explain why oligopoly prices are 'sticky'?
A. P.M. Sweezy B. Chamberlin
C. Hall and Hitch D. Stigler

199. In the following diagram the total consumer's surplus is measured by—

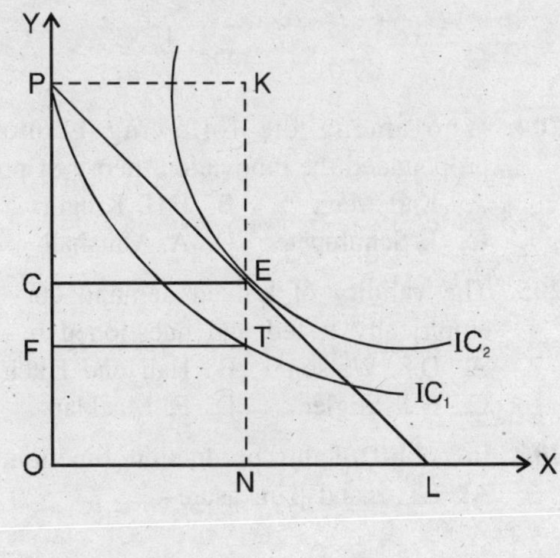

A. CF B. PC
C. CFTE D. PKE

200. Each seller assumes his rival's output as constant in the model of—
A. Cournot B. Edgeworth
C. Bertrand D. Price-leadership

201. Which of the following statements are true regarding the Cobb-Douglas production function—
1. It is long period production function
2. It is short period production function
3. It assumes increasing returns to scale
4. Out-put elasticities with respect to factors are constant

Choose the correct answer from the code given below
A. 1 and 3 B. 1 and 4
C. 2 and 3 D. 3 and 4

202. In Edgeworth's box diagram, the curve showing the equilibrium of two consumers is known as—
A. Income-consumption curve
B. Ridge lines
C. Expansion path
D. Contract curve

203. As a result of increase in the price of tea from Rs. 40 to Rs. 50 per pound, the demand for coffee increases from 600 pound to 720 pounds. The cross elasticity of demand is—
A. $\frac{1}{2}$ B. $\frac{2}{3}$
C. $\frac{3}{4}$ D. $\frac{4}{5}$

204. Who among the following Economists propounded the innovation theory of profit—
A. Karl Marx B. F.H. Kinght
C. J. Schumpeter D. A. Marshall

205. The validity of kinked demand curve was empirically tested and questioned by—
A. D.S. Watson B. Hall and Hitch
C. G.J. Stigler D. F. Maeklap

206. In cobb-Douglas production function, $Q = Ak^{\alpha}L^{\beta}$, α and β measure—
A. Elasticity of substitution
B. Input shares
C. Output elasticities of inputs
D. Technological condition

207. Classical writers could not resolve the 'water-diamond' paradox because they could not distinguish between
A. AU and MU B. MU and TU
C. AU and TU D. MU and MC

Where AU = average utility
MU = marginal utility
TU = total utility
MC = marginal cost

208. Expansion path in the theory of production corresponds to
A. Engel's curve
B. Price consumption curve
C. Income consumption curve
D. Budget constraint

209. Consider the following combinations of inputs and outputs—

Labour	*Capital*	*Output*
5	10	1
6	12	2
7	14	3
8	16	4
9	18	5
10	20	6

This production technology satisfies
A. Increasing returns to scale
B. Diminishing returns to scale
C. Constant returns to scale
D. Increasing returns initially, followed by decreasing returns to scale

210. In the linearly homogeneous Cobb-Douglas production function with two inputs, the elasticity of substitution between the inputs is
A. Zero B. Greater than one
C. One D. Less than one

211. Suppose that there are two goods, x and y, facing a consumer. The price are P_x = Rs. 4 and P_y = Rs. 5. He has Rs. 110 to spend on these goods. Suppose, he is currently buying 15 units of good x (with marginal utility

equal to 40) and 10 units of good y (with marginal utility equal to 45).
In the above context, which one of the following statements is correct?
A. His total utility will increase if he reallocates his spending towards more of good x and less of good y
B. His total utility will increase if he spends more on good y and less on good x
C. His total utility will increase if he spends less on both the goods
D. His total utility is being maximized subject to the budget constraint he is facing

212. Given the demand function $Q = \frac{20}{P}$, where P = Price of product and Q = quantity of product, the elasticity of demand at P = 10 would be
A. 0 B. –1
C. –2 D. ∞

213. A consumer spends all his income of Rs. 500 equally on two goods x and y by purchasing 50 units of x at Rs. 5 per unit and 25 units of y at Rs 10 per unit. Because of recession, prices of x and y fall by 50% and his employer reduces his salary from Rs. 500 to Rs. 250. In this situation he is expected to
A. increase the purchase of both x an y as they are now cheaper
B. decrease the purchase of both x and y as his income goes down
C. leave the purchase basket unaltered at 50 of x and 25 of y
D. alter his purchase in an uncertain way

214. Assume a production function $y = L^{\alpha}K^{1-\alpha}$ (Y = output, L = labour and K = capital) for a firm in a purely competitive market. Which one of the following would measure the share of labour in output?
A. α B. L(α)
C. L^{α} D. $\frac{\alpha}{L}$

215. The **Adding Up Theorem** under constant returns to scale holds when the factors of production are paid according to their
A. Marginal productivities
B. Average productivities
C. Total productivities
D. Ration of marginal productivities to average productivities

216. Rent earned by a factor of production equals
A. What this factor can earn in its next best use
B. the sum of what this factor earns in its current use and what is can earn in its next best use
C. its current earnings
D. the difference between what this factor is currently earning and what it can earn in its next best use

217. We say of the demand for a factor that it is a "derived demand", because
A. It is derived from the entrepreneur's need for profit
B. It stems from government policy relating to labour
C. It emerges from the demand for the final product
D. It is derived from long period expectations

218. The price elasticity of demand in demand function $q = ap^b$ is
A. a B. 1
C. b D. ab

219. A fall in the price of fish will have comparatively little effect on demand for meat, whereas a fall in the price of chicken will have a far greater effect on the demand for mutton, because
A. Chicken is a much better substitute for mutton than fish for meat
B. Chicken and fish are complementary goods
C. meat and fish are substitutes
D. meat is a better substitute to fish than to chicken

220. If the price elasticity of demand is 0.5, a 10 percent increase in price leads to—
A. 5% increase in demand
B. 5% decrease in demand
C. 0.5 units decrease in demand
D. 0.5 units increase in demand

221. In order to get a Pareto-optimal distribution the goods must be distributed in a fashion such that—
A. MRS between any two goods is different for different individuals
B. MRS between any two goods of individual is greater than those of others
C. MRS between any two goods is the same for all individuals
D. MRS between any two goods of one individual is less than those of others

222. According to the Modern theory, rent is the difference between
A. Actual earning and transfer earning
B. A land's produce and B land's produce
C. Reward of marginal and sub marginal units of a factor
D. All of these

223. The Modern Theory of Rent has been developed by—
A. J.M. Kynes B. Alfred Marshall
C. Joan Robinson D. D.H. Robertson

224. Transfer earnings are
A. The maximum payment necessary to retain the factor in its employment
B. The level of earnings required to tempt factors to take up less remunerative employment
C. That part of a factor's earnings classed as Economic Rent
D. Payments made to labour during periods of retraining

225. According to the Ricardian Theory, rent is
A. Difference of product of superior land and interior land
B. Difference of income between smaller formers and bigger farmers
C. Surplus of product of all categories of land above the marginal land
D. None of these

226. With perfect competition in the labour market and monopoly in the product market the monopolistic exploitation of labour is equal to the difference between
A. MU and AW B. MRP and AW
C. VMP and MRP D. MRP and ARP

227. When there is monopsony in the labour market and monopoly in the product market, total of monopsonistic and monopolistic exploitation is the difference between
A. VMP and AW B. VMP and MW
C. MRP and MW D. ARP and AW

228. A negatively sloped supply curve of labour of an individual indicates that the substitution effect of an increase in the wage rate is
A. Equal to income effect
B. Weaker than income effect
C. Stronger than income effect
D. Either (B) or (C) depending upon his income level

229. Which of the following statements is not true? A trade union is likely to be successful in obtaining a wage increase when—
A. The demand for the product made by the labour is inelastic
B. There is full employment
C. The supply of labour saving equipment is elastic
D. Labour costs form a small proportion of total cost

230. The demand curve for labour is also its
A. Average revenue productivity curve
B. Marginal revenue productivity curve
C. Total revenue productivity curve
D. Total utility curve

231. According to the subsistence theory of wages, the long run supply curve of labour is—
A. Perfectly elastic
B. Perfectly inelastic
C. A straight line sloping up towards right passing through the origin
D. A straight line sloping up towards right cutting and intercept on *y*-axis

232. The subsistence wage theory is due to—
A. T. R. Malthus B. David Ricardo
C. Adam Smith D. J. S. Mill

233. Which one of the following is not true in the wage fund theory?
A. Wages depend upon the wage-fund set aside for the purchase of labour

B. Wages depend upon the number of workers seeking employment
C. Wage could rise only by a reduction in the number of workers
D. Trade unions and collective bargaining can raise the wages for labour class as a whole

234. Collective bargaining refers to—
A. Inter-union discussions aimed at resolving an industrial dispute
B. Negotiation between employer's associations and worker's unions
C. The determination of factor prices in a collective economy
D. Government trade union decisions on industrial legislation

235. In the IS-LM model of income determination, an increase in the propensity to save leads to a—
A. right ward shift of the LM curve
B. right ward shift of the IS curve
C. left ward shift of the LM curve
D. left ward shift of the IS curve

236. Neutrality of money implies that a given increase in the money supply will—
A. increase all prices in the same proportion
B. increase all prices in different proportions
C. decrease all prices in the same proportion
D. not change prices at all.

237. The theory that the transactions demand for money also depends on the rate of interests, was put forward by—
A. Keynes and Pigou
B. Bumal and Tobin
C. Hicks and Solow
D. Samuelson and Meada

238. The quantity theory of money implies that an increase in the price level will be associated with—
A. an increase in out put
B. an increase in money supply
C. a decrease in money supply
D. both (A) and (B)

239. High powered money is—
A. Bank's reserves at the Central Bank
B. all loans and advances of banks
C. money held by banks
D. currency held by public and reserves with the Central Bank

240. If the investment multiplier is 4, the relevant consumption function is given by—
A. $c = 28 + 0.75y$ B. $c = -28 + 0.78y$
C. $c = 28 + 0.70y$ D. $c = 28 + 0.40y$

241. Which of the following is consistent with the cross-sectional consumption function ?
A. APC = MPC B. MPC = O
C. APC > MPC D. APC = O

242. The speculative demand for money depends on—
A. interest rate B. income
C. profit D. out put

243. Liquidity preference curve slopes down ward to right because—
A. as rate of interest rises, the opportunity cost of holding money falls.
B. as rate of interest rises, the opportunity cost of holding money rises.
C. as rate of interest falls, the opportunity cost of holding money does not change.
D. when the rate of interest is low, the central banks reduces the supply of money.

244. Quantity theory of money should be regarded as a theory of demand for money. This view has been given by—
A. D.H. Robertson B. J.M. Keynes
C. A.C. Pigou D. M. Friedman

245. Inflation is unjust and deflation is inexpedient. of the two, deflation is worse. Who made this statement—
A. J.M. Keynes B. G. Crowther
C. A. Marshall D. A.H. Hansen

246. The quantity theory of money was first propounded by—
A. D. Ricardo B. Davanzatti
C. D. Hume D. J. Mill

247. Who among the following Economists, was the first to mention effective demand as a determinant of the level of economic activity—

A. D. Ricardo B. T.R. Malthus
C. A. Marshall D. J.M. Keynes

248. Who among the following Economists introduced the concept of permanent income as a determination of consumption function—
A. M. Friedman
B. J.M. Keynes
C. J.S. Duesenberry
D. N. Kaldor

249. An increase in money supply leads to—
A. rightward shift of IS curve
B. leftward shift of IS curve
C. leftward shift of LM curve
D. rightward shift of LM curve

250. According to the IS-LM model, given by Hicks-Hansen there is simultaneous equilibrium between—
A. income level and rate of interest
B. income level and consumption
C. inflation and unemployment
D. demand and supply of money

251. Okun's law postulates a—
A. positive relationship between unemployment and real gross domestic product.
B. negative relationship between enemployment and real gross domestic product.
C positive relationship between money supply and price level.
D. negative relationship between money supply and rate of interest.

252. The speculative demand for money depends only on the expected prices of bonds. This view has been held by—
A. J.M. Keynes B. K. Wickscell
C. D.H. Robertson D. M. Friedman

253. When income falls, what happens to the liquidity preference curve?
A. It does not shift
B. It shifts to the left
C. It shifts to the right
D. It becomes parallel to the vertical axis

254. Stagflation refers to situation which is characterised by—
A. deflation and rising unemployment
B. inflation and rising employment
C. inflation and rising unemployment
D. stagnant employment and deflation

255. The elasticity in respect of speculative demand for money under the liquidity trap condition is
A. zero
B. one
C. greater than one
D. infinite

256. When the intrinsic value of money and its face value are equal, it is called
A. token money B. full-bodied money
C. quasi-money D. fiat money

257. Which one of the following factors affects velocity of circulation ?
A. Time unit of income receipts
B. Frequency of transaction
C. Liquidity preference
D. All of the above

258. The speculative demand for money, according to Keynes, is a function of—
A. Rate of interest
B. Level of income
C. Level of savings
D. Level of output

259. M_2, money supply measure in india, constitutes
A. M_1 + all post-office deposits
B. M_1 + time deposits of cummercial banks
C. M_1 + post-office saving deposits
D. M_3 + all post-office deposits

260. Investment multiplier can be obtained from (symbols have the usual meaning)
A. $\dfrac{1}{1-\dfrac{\Delta c}{\Delta s}}$ B. $\dfrac{1}{1-\dfrac{\Delta c}{\Delta y}}$
C. $\dfrac{1}{1+\dfrac{\Delta c}{\Delta s}}$ D. $\dfrac{1}{1+\dfrac{\Delta c}{\Delta y}}$

261. According to Keynes, marginal propensity to consume
A. can never exceed unity
B. may exceed unity when dissaving occurs

C. can never exceed the average propensity to consume
D. is the reciprocal of the marginal propensity to save

262. Super multiplier refers to
A. interaction of the Multiplier and the Accelerator
B. reciprocal of the marginal propensity to consume
C. capital output ratio
D. budget maltiplier

263. Liquidity preference refers to—
A. the extent to which investors prefer to keep their assets in money
B. RBI's share holdings in other financial institutions
C. community's preference for gold
D. community's effective demand for capital goods

264. The IS-LM model has been formulated by—
A. J.R. Hicks B. F. Modigliane
C. P.A. Samuelson D. J.M. Keynes

265. Portfolio theory of the demand for money assumes that the individual—
A. disregards risk B. is risk neutral
C. is risk lover D. is risk averse

266. The National income is equal to
A. GNP – Subsides – Taxes
B. NNP – Indirect Taxes + Subsidies
C. NNP – Direct Taxes + Subsides
D. GNP – Subsidies + Taxes

267. An example of double counting in national income would be
A. Wages of bus and train drivers
B. Cotton output and cotton cloth output
C. Electricity output and water output
D. Tax receipts and earnings of inland revenue officials

268. Which one of the following is a transfer income?
A. The salary of an M.P.
B. Company dividends to share holders
C. Rents from house property
D. Unemployment allowance

269. The 'Hindu rate of growth'
A. refers to growth of Hindu population
B. is the term used by Raj Krishna to represent the nature of the growth of the Indian economy at around 3.5 percent per year
C. is the term used by Amartya sen to represent the nature of the growth of the Indian economy at around 3.5 percent per year
D. is the term used by V.K.R.V. Rao to decide the nature of the growth of the Indian economy at around 4 Percent

270 Value added means value of
A. output at market prices
B. goods and services less depreciation
C. goods and services less cost of intermediate goods and services
D. output at factor cost

271. National Income is the—
A. Net National Product at market price
B. Net National Product at factor cost
C. Net Domestic Product at market price
D. Net Domestic Product at factor cost

272. The implicit national income deflator represents a price index number of the type known as
A. Laspeyre's index number
B. Fisher's index number
C. Paasche's index number
D. Marshall-Edgeworth's index number

273. Human Development Index (HDI) is a composite index of
A. Health, literacy and employment
B. National income, size of population and the general price level
C. National income, per capita income and per capita consumption
D. Physical resources, monetary resources and populatoin size

274. Which one of the following is **NOT** a source of the state tax revenue?
A. Land revenue
B. Motor vehicles tax
C. Entertainment tax
D. Corporate tax

275. Tobin tax is a tax on
A. exports
B. imports
C. transactions in foreign exchange
D. sales

276. Which one of the following is **NOT** a source of the 'Union Tax revenue'?
A. Property taxes B. Wealth tax
C. Corporate taxes D. Customs duties

277. If supply is perfectly inelastic, then the short run impact of a specific sales tax would be to shift the tax burden
A. entirely on to the consumers
B. entirely on to the producers
C. equally between the producers and the consumers
D. on the other goods where the supply condition may be more elastic

278. Octrio is levied and collected by:
A. Centre B. State Government
C. Local bodies D. All the above

279. The One Rupee currency note bears the signature of the
A. Governor, Reserve Bank of India
B. The Minister for Finance
C. Chair man, State Bank of India
D. None of the above

280. Stagflation means
A. Inflation with recession
B. Recession and stagnation
C. Inflation galloping like a stag
D. Inflation and increasing output

281. All the revenues received, loans raised and money received in repayment of loans by the Union government go into
A. Consolidated Fund of India
B. Contingency Fund of India
C. Public Account of India
D. Prime Minister's Relief Fund

282. In India, the states get maximum income from
A. Sales Tax
B. Land Revenue
C. Agricultures income tax
D. State excise duties

283. MODVAT means
A. Modified Value Added Tax
B. Moderate Value Added Tax
C. Modest Value Added Tax
D. Modern Value added Tax

284. Who appoints the Finance Commission
A. President of India
B. Prime Minister of India
C. Chairman of the Rajya Sabha
D. Speaker of the Lok Sabha

285. Which of the following is not a direct tax?
A. Income Tax
B. Wealth Tax
C. Expenditure Tax
D. Entertainment Tax

286. The incidence of which of the following will entirely be on the monopolist—
A. lump-sum tax
B. specific tax
C. regulated monopoly pricing
D. none of the above

287. The concept of Zero-Based-Budget (ZBB) was given by
A. R.A. Musgrave B. J.M. Keynes
C. Peter A. Pyhr D. A.H. Hansen

288. The tax which is not shared by states is—
A. Sales tax B. Income tax
C. Corporation tax D. Central Excise duty

289. Agricultural income tax is a source of revenue to—
A. Central Government
B. State Government
C. Local Administration
D. Central and State Government

290. It is generally believed that a rise in the tax rate would normally lead to a rise in the revenue. But there is also a view the reduced rates on income tax would lead to a significant rise in income tax revenue. This later view has been attributed to
A. Arthur Laffer B. Robert Lucas
C. Herbert Simon D. J.B. Say

291. The whole burden of a tax will be borne by the sellers, if

A. the demand for a commodity is inelastic and supply is perfectly elastic
B. the elasticity of demand for a commodity is same as the elasticity of supply of the commodity
C. the demand for a commodity is perfectly elastic and supply is inelastic
D. the elasticity of demand for a commodity is less than the elasticity of supply of that commodity

292. In the Indian context deficit financing means
A. An excess of government's revenue over expenditure
B. An excess of government's current expenditure over its current revenue
C. An excess of government's total expenditure over its total revenue
D. None of these

293. Debt-Service Ratio is a ratio of—
A. GDP which is to be paid as debt
B. Total debt which is to be paid in the form of interest burden
C. Export earnings which are to be paid by way of interest and principal
D. None of these

294. The relationship between tax collections and tax rates has been expressed by
A. Lorenz Curve B. Engel's Law
C. Laffer Curve D. Indifference Curve

295. Ad Valorom means—
A. According to value
B. According to weight
C. According to size
D. According to advertisement costs

296. The devaluation according to Marshall and Learner conditions will not be helpful, if the sum of the elasticities of exports and imports is
A. equal to unity B. greater than unity
C. less than unity D. zero

297. In a flexible exchange-rate system, an increase in the domestic interest rate would tend to
A. improve the current account and worsen the capital account.
B. improve both the current and capital accounts.
C. worsen both the accounts.
D. worsen the current account and improve the capital account.

298. In the current international monetary system the Indian rupee is pegged to
A. U.S. dollar
B. U.K. pound
C. Euro
D. A basket of currencies

299. The terms of trade refer to—
A. the excess of import expenditures over export earnings.
B. trade agreements.
C. the ratio between export prices and import prices.
D. the terms and conditions on which a country is offered loan in the event of balance of payments difficulties.

300. Special Drawing Rights (SDRs) is the currency of IMF. This is in the form of
A. paper currency
B. gold
C. silver and gold both
D. book-keeping entry only

301. A deficit in a country's balance of payments refers to the difference between
A. autonomous receipts and autonomous payments.
B. accommodating receipts and autonomous payment.
C. accommodating receipts and accommodating payments.
D. autonomous receipts and accommodating payments.

302. In Heckscher-Ohlin theory of international trade, the most important source of difference in relative commodity prices between nations is a differnce in
A. factor endowments
B. technology
C. tastes
D. demand conditions

303. For a closed economy having no foreign trade which one of the following is correct?
A. GDP = GNP B. GDP > GNP
C. GDP < GNP D. None of these

304. Dumping aims at flooding a foreign country with
A. high-priced commodities
B. low-priced commodities
C. commodities with similar prices
D. commodities with fluctuating prices

305. Which one of the following is the major characteristic of foreign direct investment (FDI)?
A. It is non-debt creating capital flow.
B. It is portfolio investment in stock market.
C. It is that investment which involves debt servicing.
D. It is investment made by foreign institutional investors in government securities.

306. Hot money refers to the
A. Short-term capital movements from one country to another seeking either a higher rate of interest or safety of capital irrespective of the rate of interest.
B. Long-term capital movements from one country to another seeking higher rate of interest.
C. medium-term capital movements from one country to another.
D. Currency which is very much in demand in the foreign exchange market.

307. Which institution is known as 'soft loan window' of World Bank?
A. IFC
B. IDA
C. IMF
D. Indian Development Forum

308. 'Backwash Effect' was firstly introduced by—
A. Gunnar Myrdal B. Peter Suderland
C. Arthur Dunkel D. Kindelberger

309. Finance Commission is appointed by the President under Article—
A. 256 of constitution
B. 280 of constitution
C. 293 of constitution
D. 356 of constitution

310. National Income estimates in India is prepared by—
A. Planning Commission
B. RBI
C. Finance Ministry
D. C.S.O.

311. Scheduled bank is that bank which is—
A. Nationalised
B. Not–nationalised
C. Based at foreign country
D. Included in the second schedule of R.B.F

312. According to 2011 census the state having highest urban population is—
A. U.P. B. Maharashtra
C. Tamil Nadu D. Kerala

313. The base year of the present Wholesale Price Index (WPI) is—
A. 2011-12 B. 1991-92
C. 1980-81 D. 2004-05

314. CAPART is related with—
A. Assisting and evaluating rural welfare programmes
B. Computer hardware
C. Consultant service of export promotion
D. Controlling pollution in big industries

315. 15th Finance Commission has been constituted under the chairmanship of—
A. C. Rangrajan B. N.K. Singh
C. K.C. Pant D. None of these

316. SEBI was established in—
A. 1993 B. 1992
C. 1988 D. 1990

317. Which statement of the following is true for IMF?
A. It is not an agency of UNO
B. It can grant loan to any country of the world
C. It can grant loan to state Govt. of a country
D. It grants loan only to member nations

318. 'Closed Economy' is that economy in which—

A. Only export takes place
B. Money supply is fully controlled
C. Deficit financing takes place
D. Neither export nor import takes place

319. The Headquarter of World Bank is situated at—
A. Manila B. Washington D.C.
C. New York D. Geneva

320. As per the N.S.S. 61st round, poverty ratio in India for the year 2004-05 is estimated at—
A. 23.6 per cent B. 32.4 per cent
C. 27.5 per cent D. 16.0 per cent

321. Which of the rate is not determined of RBI?
A. Bank Rate B. CRR
C. SLR D. PLR

322. Who is the Chairman of NDC?
A. Finance Minister
B. Prime Minister
C. Planning Minister
D. Lok Sabha Speaker

323. Which of the following represents the correct combination of sex-ratio in India in 1951 and 2011?
A. 941, 933 B. 946, 940
C. 946, 927 D. 972, 933

324. Population Density means—
A. No. of persons living per sq. km.
B. No. of persons living per kilometre
C. Ratio of population living below poverty line to total population
D. No. of persons in a village

325. The Headquarter of IMF is in—
A. New York B. Washington D.C.
C. London D. Manila

326. Mixed Economy means—
A. Co-existence of small and large industries
B. Promoting both Agriculture and Industries in the economy
C. Co-existence of public and private sectors
D. Co-existence of rich and poor

327. Which state has the lowest women literary rate in India (2011 census)?
A. Bihar B. Jharkhand
C. U.P. D. Rajasthan

328. According to Banking Regulation Act, RBI can fix SLR upto the ceiling of—
A. 40% B. 50%
C. 30% D. 45%

329. The First Finance Commission was constituted in the year—
A. 1947 B. 1950
C. 1951 D. 1952

330. NABARD was established in—
A. Fourth Plan B. Fifth Plan
C. Sixth Plan D. Eighth Plan

331. The headquarter of SIDBI is in—
A. Lucknow B. New Delhi
C. Mumbai D. Bangalore

332. LIC of India was established in—
A. 1897 B. 1950
C. 1956 D. 1965

333. According to 2011 census, per 1000 male female number is—
A. 939 B. 959
C. 943 D. 927

334. Which plan was suspended one year before the time schedule?
A. First Plan (1951-56)
B. Third Plan (1966-71)
C. Sixth Plan (1980-85)
D. Fifth Plan (1974-79)

335. The Headquarter of Asian Development Bank (ADB) is at—
A. Singapore B. Manila
C. Hong Kong D. Tokyo

336. Which one of the following pairs is not correctly matched?
A. EXIT policy — Import controls
B. EXIM scrips — Export subsidy
C. LERMS — Rupee convertibility
D. EPZ — Export promotion

337. Which one of the following is not correctly matched?
A. Rural Credit : NABARD
B. Industrial Finance : SIDBI
C. Rural poverty : SJSRY
D. Disguised unemployment : Subsistence agriculture

338. Bank Rate is the rate :
- A. which is reference rate in all countries for interest structure.
- B. at which the central bank rediscounts the first class gilt edged securities of the banks.
- C. the rate which is given to the depositors of money with bank.
- D. the rate which is charged on loans given by banks.

339. Statutory liquidity ratio (SLR) of commercial banks means—
- A. the percentage of cash that banks keep with them under rules
- B. the bank rate which is reference rate also
- C. the ratio of government and other gilt-edged securities to liquid liabilities
- D. the "reserve money"

340. If banks want to increase credit creation.
- A. they should increase interest rate to have more deposits
- B. they should reduce the rate of interest
- C. they should have high cash reserves with them
- D. they should force investors to create demand for loans

341. Which combination represents the IS curve?
- A. High interest rate and high income level
- B. High interest rate and low income level
- C. High interest rate and low saving level
- D. High interest rate and high investment level

342. The time-preference theory of interest is mainly associated with
- A. J.M. Keynes
- B. I. Fisher
- C. K. Wicksell
- D. M. Friedman

343. Open market operations refers to :
- A. borrowing by scheduled banks from the RBI
- B. lending by commercial banks to industry and trade
- C. purchase and sale of government securities by the RBI
- D. deposit mobilisation

344. The objectiv^ of selective credit controls is mainly to
- A. selectively allocate credit to commercial banks
- B. selectively allocate credit among borrowers
- C. regulate the quantity of demand deposits created by commercial banks
- D. regulate the quantity of credit created by commercial banks

345. Under the 'liquidity trap' situation the liquidity preference curve
- A. is perfectly inelastic
- B. is perfectly elastic
- C. intersects the horizontal axis
- D. interests the vertical axix

346. IS–LM model relates to
- A. Rent
- B. Interest
- C. Wages
- D. Profits

347. The IS–curve shows
- A. a positive relationship between rate of interest and the level of income
- B. a negative relationship between rate of interest and the level of income
- C. a positive relationship between rate of interest and the level of autonomous investment
- D. a negative relationship between rate of interest and level of autonomous investment

348. Grasham's law relates to :
- A. money supply
- B. money and prices
- C. real output
- D. employment

349. 'Misery Index' represents
- A. Sum of rate of inflation and rate of unemployment
- B. Product of rate of inflätion and rate of unemployment
- C. Proportion of very poor to poor living below the poverty line
- D. Both the above B and C

350. Banking Sector will fall under which of the following sectors?
- A. Agricultural Sector
- B. Service Sector
- C. Manufacturing
- D. Industrial Sector

ANSWERS

1	2	3	4	5	6	7	8	9	10
D	A	B	D	A	D	D	D	D	A
11	12	13	14	15	16	17	18	19	20
C	D	A	A	B	B	B	C	D	A
21	22	23	24	25	26	27	28	29	30
A	C	A	D	B	A	C	A	D	C
31	32	33	34	35	36	37	38	39	40
B	A	A	B	D	A	B	A	D	B
41	42	43	44	45	46	47	48	49	50
C	C	C	B	B	C	B	C	A	B
51	52	53	54	55	56	57	58	59	60
C	C	B	A	C	C	A	A	A	C
61	62	63	64	65	66	67	68	69	70
A	C	C	D	C	A	C	D	A	C
71	72	73	74	75	76	77	78	79	80
B	C	C	B	A	D	A	C	B	D
81	82	83	84	85	86	87	88	89	90
C	C	C	B	B	D	C	D	A	C
91	92	93	94	95	96	97	98	99	100
B	B	D	A	C	C	A	D	A	C
101	102	103	104	105	106	107	108	109	110
C	B	A	A	B	D	A	C	B	C
111	112	113	114	115	116	117	118	119	120
B	B	A	C	A	B	D	B	C	D
121	122	123	124	125	126	127	128	129	130
B	A	A	A	A	C	C	B	A	B
131	132	133	134	135	136	137	138	139	140
C	A	C	C	B	C	C	B	A	C
141	142	143	144	145	146	147	148	149	150
B	D	B	A	D	C	C	B	A	D
151	152	153	154	155	156	157	158	159	160
B	B	B	B	B	B	B	D	C	A
161	162	163	164	165	166	167	168	169	170
A	B	C	B	B	B	B	B	B	C
171	172	173	174	175	176	177	178	179	180
C	A	D	B	C	B	A	B	C	D

181	182	183	184	185	186	187	188	189	190
C	D	C	B	D	A	C	D	A	A
191	**192**	**193**	**194**	**195**	**196**	**197**	**198**	**199**	**200**
A	D	A	B	B	C	A	C	A	A
201	**202**	**203**	**204**	**205**	**206**	**207**	**208**	**209**	**210**
B	D	D	C	C	C	B	B	C	C
211	**212**	**213**	**214**	**215**	**216**	**217**	**218**	**219**	**220**
D	B	C	A	A	D	C	C	A	B
221	**222**	**223**	**224**	**225**	**226**	**227**	**228**	**229**	**230**
C	A	C	A	C	C	A	D	C	B
231	**232**	**233**	**234**	**235**	**236**	**237**	**238**	**239**	**240**
A	A	D	B	D	D	B	B	D	A
241	**242**	**243**	**244**	**245**	**246**	**247**	**248**	**249**	**250**
A	A	B	D	A	B	B	A	D	A
251	**252**	**253**	**254**	**255**	**256**	**257**	**258**	**259**	**260**
B	A	B	C	D	B	D	A	C	B
261	**262**	**263**	**264**	**265**	**266**	**267**	**268**	**269**	**270**
A	A	A	A	C	B	B	D	B	C
271	**272**	**273**	**274**	**275**	**276**	**277**	**278**	**279**	**280**
B	A	A	D	C	A	B	C	D	A
281	**282**	**283**	**284**	**285**	**286**	**287**	**288**	**289**	**290**
A	A	A	A	D	A	C	C	B	A
291	**292**	**293**	**294**	**295**	**296**	**297**	**298**	**299**	**300**
C	C	B	C	A	C	D	D	C	D
301	**302**	**303**	**304**	**305**	**306**	**307**	**308**	**309**	**310**
A	A	A	B	A	A	B	A	B	D
311	**312**	**313**	**314**	**315**	**316**	**317**	**318**	**319**	**320**
D	B	A	A	B	C	D	D	B	C
321	**322**	**323**	**324**	**325**	**326**	**327**	**328**	**329**	**330**
D	B	B	A	B	C	A	A	C	C
331	**332**	**333**	**334**	**335**	**336**	**337**	**338**	**339**	**340**
A	C	C	D	B	A	C	B	C	A
341	**342**	**343**	**344**	**345**	**346**	**347**	**348**	**349**	**350**
B	B	C	B	B	B	B	A	A	B

ACCOUNTING

Including

- Accounting
- Process of Accounting
- Accounting for Depreciation
- Accounting of Joint Stock Companies
- Financial Statement Analysis
- Fund Flow and Cash Flow Statement
- Cost Accounting
- Management Accounting

Chapter 1
Accounting

Definition of Accounting

Accounting is defined as "the art of recording, classifying, and summarising in terms of money transactions and events of a financial character and interpreting the results thereof".

Objectives of Accounting

The objectives of the term 'accounting' can be stated as follows:

(a) To maintain records of a business
(b) Calculation of profit or loss
(c) Depiction of financial position, and
(d) To make information available to various groups and users.

Functions of Accounting

Accounting embraces the following functions:

1. Keeping systematic records
2. Protecting properties of the business
3. Communicating the results
4. Meeting legal requirements

CONCEPTS OF ACCOUNTANCY

Accounting is the language of business. The financial transactions are recorded and reported by means of financial statements to a number of interested parties. In the absence of systematic approach, accountants may use their own language and whatever they will be writing, will not be understood necessarily in the same sense by others concerned. Thus, the uniformity in understanding of accounting records is possible only when some standard language is used. With a view to make the accounting language a standard language, certain accounting principles or concepts have been developed.

Accounting principles or rules or concepts are general guidelines for sound accounting practices. Their usefulness depend on general acceptability rather than individual acceptability. These are known as 'generally accepted accounting principles' having been formalised on the basis of usage, reason, and experience. As stated by the AICPA (American Institute of Certified Public Accountants):

"Generally accepted accounting principles incorporate the consensus at any time as to which economic resources and obligations should be recorded as assets and liabilities, which changes in them should be recorded, when these changes should be recorded, how the recorded assets and liabilities and changes in them should be measured, what information should be disclosed and how should it be disclosed, and which financial statements should be prepared." Thus, generally accepted accounting principles (GAAP) comprises a set of rules, concepts and guidelines used in preparing financial accounting reports.

Following is a list of accounting concepts agreed to by accountants:

1. Business entity concept
2. Dual aspect concept
3. Going concern concept
4. Accounting period concept
5. Money measurement concept
6. Cost concept
7. Periodic matching of cost and revenue concept
8. Verifiable objective evidence concept
9. Realisation concept
10. Accrual concept

11. Disclosure concept
12. Materiality concept
13. Consistency concept
14. Conservatism concept

1. Business Entity Concept : According to this concept, 'business is treated as a unit or entity apart from its owner, creditor, managers and others'. This concept is applicable to all forms of business organisations.

2. Dual Aspect Concept: According to this principle of accounting, every transaction has a dual aspect, i.e., two fold effect. Every receiver is also a giver and every giver is also a receiver.

Receiving and giving aspects are the two aspects of every business transaction. This principle is called double entry system of book-keeping. As per dual aspect, total assets and total liabilities must be equal. This equality is called 'Balance sheet equation or accounting equation. It can be stated as:

Liabilities = Assets

or

Capital + Liabilities (outside) = Assets

or

Capital = Assets – Liabilities.

3. Going Concern Concept: According to Kohler's Dictionary for Accountants, a going concern is defined as "any enterprise which is expected to continue operating indefinitely in the future".

This concept assumes that a business entity will continue to operate in definitely. Indefinitely existence means that the business enterprise will not be wound up within the foreseable future and therefore would be able to meet its contractual obligations and use its resources according to the plans and predetermined goals. This concept forms the basis for depreciation.

4. Accounting Period Concepts: Life of business is indefinitely, so, the measurement of income is not possible for a very, very long period. At frequent intervals properietor has to know "how things are going". Therefore, accountants choose some shorter and convenient time for the measurement of income. Normally, twelve month period is adopted for this purpose. The time interval is called "Accounting period."

5. Money Measurement Concept: The money measurement concept underlines the fact that is terms of money. A fact or a happening which cannot be expressed in terms of money is not recorded in the account book. As general health condition of the chairman of the company quality of products introduced by the enterprise etc. cannot be expressed in terms of money and thus are not recorded in the books.

As per this concept a transaction is recorded at its money value on the date of occurrence and the subsequent changes in the money value are ignored. Here, correct fact cannot be recorded in the book.

6. Cost Concept: The idea of cost assumption in that:

(i) asset is recorded at the price paid to acquire it-that is, at cost;

(ii) this cost is the basis for all subsequent accounting for the asset.

The cost concept implies that if nothing has been paid for acquiring something, it not be shown is the accounting books as an asset.

7. Periodic Matching of cost and Revenue concept: To compare profit or loss of an accounting period., it is necessary to match all expenses incurred in an accounting period with the revenue earned during that year.

Net income = Revenues – Expenses

8. Verifiable Objective Evidence Concept: This concept means that all accounting transactions should be evidenced and supported by business documents. These supporting documents (invoices, vouchers etc) provide the basis for making accounting entries and for later verification by auditors.

9. Realisation Concept: Kohler defines realisation concept as follows:

(i) A concept which gives accounting recognition to an exchange transaction, such as sale of goods or services only, when an inflow or outflow of cash equivalent results.

(ii) The realisation principle holds that revenue should be recognised with accompanying gains or losses at the point of sale in an arm's length transaction if the earning process is virtually complete.

10. Accrual Concept: Accrual means the recognition of events and conditions as they occur, rather than in the period of their incurrence, receipts or payments. Also the partial recognition of an item of revenue or expense and its related asset or liability: the result of the lack of coincidence of the accounting period and the contractual or benefit period.

11. Disclosure Concept: The disclosure principle implies that accounts must be prepared honestly, and all material information must be disclosed therein.

12. Materiality Concept: American Accounting Association (AAA) defines the term materiality as "An item should be regarded as material if there is reason to believe that knowledge if it would influence the decision of informed investor". It should be noted that an item material for one concern may be immaterial for another.

13. Consistency Concept: The principle of consistency plays its role when alternative accounting method is equally accepted.

14. Conservatism Concept: This is the policy of' Playing safe. It takes into consideration all prospective losses but leaves all prospective profit. Kohler defines 'Conservatism' as "a guidelines which chooses between acceptable accounting alternatives for recording events or transactions so that the least faveurable immediate effect on assets, income and owner's equity is reported." Following are the examples of this concept:

(*a*) Making the provision for doubtful debts and discount on debtors in anticipation of actual bad debts and discount.

(*b*) Valuing the stock-in-trade at market price or cost price whichever is less.

INCOME MEASUREMENT

The main purpose of accounting is to measure the income of a business because the business is started with the sole aim of organizing the various factors of production for the purpose of increasing its wealths.

Definition of Income : Income can be defined as the amount of change (favourable) in wealth which results from business activities.

The AAA Committee has defined the term 'Income' as "the realised net income of an enterprise measures its effectiveness as an operating unit and is the change in its net assets arising out of:

(*a*) the excess or deficiency of revenue compared with related expired cost, and

(*b*) Other gains or losses to the enterprise from sales, exchanges or other conventions of assets ..." The measurement of income is influenced by many concepts: Conservatism, consistancy, the entity business, the periodicity, the cost basis, and the realisation principles.

Conservatism

The approach of conservatism in the measurment of income, although shifts the income from one period to another, has been defended on the argument that the risk of understatement of income under the concept of conservatism cannot be equated with the danger of its over statement. The later approach to measurement of income may prove more disastrous for the business. The measurement of stock at cost or market price whichever is lower, the principle of amortization of intangible assets not recognizing the appreciation in the value of assets, are the examples of concepts of conservatism as applied to the measurement of income. But the concept of conservatism does not and must not lead towards bais for understatement of income by providing excessive depreciation, excessive reserves etc.

Consistency

To facilitate the comparison of performance of one year with that of another, it is essential that basis of measurement of income should remain the same from year to year. Therefore, the measurement of income in any particular year depends upon the basis followed in the previous year (s).

The Entity

The entity concept maintains that business should be regarded as an institution separate and distinct from its legal owners. Thus any measurement of income is to be done from the business point of view and not from the proprietor's point of view. The interest on the capital of partners, though income to individual partners, is considered as an expense of measuring income of a business.

The Accounting Period

It should be appreciated that income of an enterprise can precisely be determied only at the termination of entity's life. But inderterminable life-span of the entity makes the period so long and uncertain that no business can wait that long for finding out the fruit of hard work put in carrying the business. Moreover, if unfortunately, at that time it is found that results are unfavourable, it will be too late to correct the decision. It is thus essential for correct decision that interim progress of the business must be calculated. The satisfactory period for measuring income is either the calender year or a natural business year.

The Accrual Concept

With the choosing of calender year or natural business year as a period for reporting income, the continuous process of business does not come to standstill simply because the accounting period has ended. The flow of entity transactions does not confirm exactly to the prescribed time interval. Instead, there will be quantities unsold, goods-in-transit, accounts and bills to be collected, contract for services in the various stages of completion. This period convention has given rise to the accrual basis of accounting. This entails the necessity of recognising the revenue with the preiod in which it was realised and the application of costs to the period benefiting from services. For example, revenue from sales will be considered in the year in which shipment takes place regardless of when the payment is received. Rent, insurance, interest, salary etc., paid in advance will be prorated between successive years according to the specific period covered by the payments.

The Going Concern

Since the termination of business at the end of accounting period is a fiction and since life span of the business is indefinite, the determination of profits by means of assets appraisal is not considered proper. Any valuation of accounting income on the basis of appraisal of its assets on market value is much influenced by excessive emphasis on the liquidation rather than continuity.

EXPIRED COST AND INCOME MEASUREMENT

It has already been stated in the definition of income given by AAA that it is "... the excess or deficiency of revenue compared with related expired cost...". Thus any attempt to measure accounting income will be futile unless the correct measurement of the expired cost is available.

The costs which helps income determination may be direct cost or indirect cost, may be fixed cost or variable cost. The cost may be inclusive of purchase discount. Costs may be historical or standard. In order to have a more precise idea about the cost and its influence on the determination of income, it is studied under the following major heads:

(*a*) **Cost of property and its expiration:** Property is constructed or acquired to provide a source of revenue and so long as it helps in providing revenue, each revenue increment derived from its usage should bear its proportionate share of the total actual cost of the property. As to what part of the cost of asset should go to determine income would much depend upon the determination of cost of asset itself.
The determination of the cost of asset, is a dificult process. The allocation of various overheads makes the cost of asset an intelligent expression of estimates if not an arbitrary one. Determination of life expectancy and scrap value of the asset pose a serious problem. The calculation of cost expiration for measuring income cannot be very accurate.

(*b*) **Inventory Costs:** Inventory costs include costs of those *(i)* which are held for resale, *(ii)* are in the process of production for sale, and *(iii)* are those which are currently consumed in the production of goods.
Determination of income depends much upon the determination of cost inventory as an expired cost. The calculation of inventory cost depends upon the direct cost, indirect cost efficiency on allocating costs between joint costs, by product costs, and so-on.

(*c*) **Intangible Costs:** The calculation of expiration costs of intangible assets like patent rights leasehold rights, goodwill, development expenses, advertisement, etc. is also in the way of determining correct income. But these intangible assets pose a serious problem because their useful life is absolutely unknown.

(*d*) **Imputed Cost:** In determining accounting income, besides taking same explicit or actual costs, some implicit or imputed costs like interest on capital, salary of a partner or proprietor, rent of the building owned by the proprietor are considered. The imputed costs are carved to facilitate comparison and management decision.

THE REALISATION PRINCIPLE AND INCOME MEASUREMENT

The definition of accounting concept of income by AAA lays emphasis on the realisation aspect of income. It aims at comparing the realised revenue with the corresponding expired cost. Thus in order to calculate proper amount of income it is essential and imperative to have a proper recognition of revenue.

The recognition of revenue leads to the problem of determination of precise point of time in income producing cycle when its realisation can be considered to be worthwhile and acceptable to standards. This leads to the consideration of following point :

(*a*) The sale as a basis of revenue recognition.
(*b*) The asset as a basis of revenue recognition, i.e., cash vs. mercantile system.
(*c*) Completed production as the basis of revenue recognition
(*d*) Recognition of revenue prior to productive completion, and
(*e*) Appreciation as the basis of revenue recognition.

(*a*) **The sale as a basis of revenue recognition:** The sale completes the transaction and receives the primary objective of manufacturing or purchasing goods, it provides a satisfactory measure of recognition of revenue. The sale also denotes the expiration of all proportionate costs and permits their comparison with revenue for measuring income. It eliminates all future speculation as to whether they will be selling or not and also to their prices at which they will be selling. From legal point of view also, sale point recognition is justified.

(*b*) **Asset received as a basis of revenue recognition:** The advocates of this principle want to postpone the recognition of revenue till its actual relisation in cash.

Cash vs. Accrual or Mercantile Basis of Accounting : According to cash basis, the actual receipts and payment in cash is the real basis of recording transaction in the accounting period. The revenue will be considered in a particular accounting period only when it is realised in cash. Similarly, an expense will be considered only when it is paid in actual cash in the accounting period.

(*c*) **Completed production as the basis of revenue recognition:** Where there are compelling reasons for the maintenance of large inventory for any purpose whatsoever, the revenue is recognised even before the sale takes place. The main purpose of holding the inventory in such business houses is to push up the sale price. The retention of goods in such industries serves the purpose of getting the revenues. The production basis of revenue recognition has its utility in agriculture, extractive industries (oil, gold, silver, other metals), etc.

(*d*) **Recognition of Revenue prior to productive completion:** In long-term contracts, the basis of recognition of revenue is discarded in as much as this will result in the postponement of income for a very long period. When all of a sudden heavy amount of revenue will be recognised. This type of procedure will bring frustration to shareholders during the period it is not recognised and also will attract high rate of income tax when it is recognised.

(*e*) **Appreciation as the basis of revenue recognition:** The value of an asset sometimes appreciates due to change in general price. Any increment in the value of asset due to above mentioned reasons, is treated as fictitious increment. It does not add to the source of revenue. It is more an expression of original cost into the currency as per the changed index number.

CONCLUSION

The calculation of income is an important affair in as much as its correct calculation determines the divident policy, acts as an important tool for measuring the effective use of money and managerial proficiency. It determines the future policy of the concern. But its determination is a difficult process as it is affected by:

(a) Various concepts and conventions
(b) Correct calculation of expired cost and
(c) Correct recognition of revenue

The concepts and conventions affecting the calculation of income are numerous, the calculation of expired cost is a difficult process and recognition of revenue is affected by various considerations. The job of measuring income is not an easy one.

Important Accounting Standards

Accounting standards may be defined as codified or written statements of uniform accounting rules and guidelines for preparing financial statements in a uniform and consistent manner and for their disclosures to the user of financial information. Accounting standards constitute a structural framework with the help of which credible financial statements can be prepared.

Accounting standards are prepared by the ICAI and are mandatory to be followed by the companies. So far, the ICAI has issued a number of standards. But, all of them are not equally important for the purpose of the examination. So, here we explain the important points of some standards which are important from the examination. point of view and the rest are summarized in one. Also, for the reference, is given the list of all the standards so far issued. The list is as below :

AS1 Disclosure of Accounting Policies
AS2 Valuation of Inventories
AS3 Cash Flow Statements
AS4 Contingencies and Events Occurring after the Balance Sheet Date
AS5 Net Profit or Loss for the period, Prior Period and Extraordinary Items and Changes in Accounting Policies
AS6 Depreciation Accounting
AS7 Construction Contracts (revised 2003)
AS8 Accounting for Research and Development
AS9 Revenue Recognition
AS10 Accounting for Fixed Assets
AS11 Accounting for the Effects of Changes in Foreign Exchange Rates
AS12 Accounting for Government Grants
AS13 Accounting for Investments
AS14 Accounting for Amalgamations
AS15 Accounting for Retirement Benefits in the Financial Statement of Employers
AS16 Borrowing Costs
AS17 Segment Reporting
AS18 Related Party Disclosures
AS19 Leases
AS20 Earnings Per Share
AS21 Consolidated Financial Statements
AS22 Accounting for taxes on income.
AS23 Accounting for Investments in Associates in Consolidated Financial Statements
AS24 Discontinuing Operations
AS25 Interim Financial Reporting
AS26 Intangible Assets
AS27 Financial Reporting of Interests in Joint Ventures
AS28 Impairment of Assets
AS29 Provisions, Contingent Liabilities and Contingent Assets

APPLICABILITY OF STANDARDS

For the purpose of applicability of Accounting Standards, enterprises are classified into three categories, viz., Level I, Level II and Level III. Level II and Level III enterprises are considered as SMEs (Small and Medium Enterprises).

— Level I enterprises are required to comply fully with all the accounting standards.
— It has been decided that no relaxation should be given to Level II and Level III enterprises in respect of recognition and measurement principles. Relaxations are provided with regard to disclosure requirements. Accordingly, the applicability of various standards on them is as below :

Accounting Standards not applicable to Level II and Level III enterprises in their entirety:

I. AS3 Cash Flow Statements
II. AS17 Segment Reporting

III. AS18 Related Party Disclosures
IV. AS24 Discontinuing Operations.

(B) Accounting Standards not applicable to Level II and Level III enterprises since the relevant Regulators require compliance with them only by certain Level I enterprises:

(*a*) AS21 Consolidated Financial Statements
(*b*) AS23 Accounting for Investments in Associates in Consolidated Financial Statements
(*c*) AS 27, Financial Reporting of Interests in Joint Ventures (to the extent of requirements relating to consolidated financial statements)

(C) Accounting Standards in respect of which relaxations from certain disclosure requirements have been given to Level II and Level III enterprises:

(*a*) AS19 Leases
(*b*) AS20 Earnings Per Share
(*c*) AS29 Provisions, Contingent Liabilities and Contingent Assets

(D) Accounting Standard applicability of which is deferred for Level II and Level III enterprises:

AS 28, Impairment of Assets - For Level I Enterprises applicable from 1-4-2004

For Level II Enterprises applicable from 1-4-2006

For Level III Enterprises applicable from 1-4-2008

The important provisions of some of the standards are explained in points as under :

(A) AS1 Disclosure of Accounting Policies

1. All significant accounting policies adopted in the preparation and presentation of financial statements should be disclosed.
2. The disclosure of the significant accounting policies as such should form part of the financial statements and the significant accounting policies should normally be disclosed in one place.
3. Any change in the accounting policies which has a material effect in the current period or which is reasonably expected to have a material effect in later periods should be disclosed. In the case of a change in accounting policies which has a material effect in the current period, the amount by which any item in the financial statements is affected by such change should also be disclosed to the extent ascertainable. Where such amount is not ascertainable, wholly or in part, the fact should be indicated.
4. If the fundamental accounting assumptions, viz. Going Concern, Consistency and Accrual are followed in financial statements, specific disclosure is not required. If a fundamental accounting assumption is not followed, the fact should be disclosed.

(B) AS2 Valuation of Inventory

(*a*) Net realisable value is the estimated selling price in the ordinary course of business less the estimated costs of completion and the estimated costs necessary to make the sale.
(*b*) Inventories should be valued at the lower of cost and net realisable value.
(*c*) The cost of inventories should comprise all costs of purchase, costs of conversion and other costs incurred in bringing the inventories to their present location and condition.
(*d*) Interest and other borrowing costs are usually considered as not relating to bringing the inventories to their present location and condition and are, therefore, usually not included in the cost of inventories.
(e) In determining the cost of inventories, it is appropriate to exclude certain costs and recognize them as expenses in the period in which they are incurred. Examples of such costs are: Abnormal amounts of wasted materials, labour, or other production costs; storage costs, unless those costs are necessary in the production process prior to a further production stage; administrative overheads that do not contribute to bringing the inventories to their present location and condition; and selling and distribution costs.
(*f*) The cost of inventories should be assigned by using the First-in First-out (FIFO), or weighted average cost formula.

(C) AS6 Depreciation Accounting

(1) This standard applies to all depreciable assets, except items to which special considerations apply like forests, plantations and similar

regenerative natural resources; wasting assets including expenditure on the exploration for and extraction of minerals, oils, natural gas and similar non-regenerative resources; expenditure on research and development; goodwill; live stock.

(2) This standard also does not apply to land unless it has a limited useful life for the enterprise.

(3) Depreciation is a measure of the wearing out, consumption or other loss of value of a depreciable asset arising from use, effluxion of time or obsolescence through technology and market changes. Depreciation is allocated so as to charge a fair proportion of the depreciable amount in each accounting period during the expected useful life of the asset. Depreciation includes amortization of assets whose useful life is predetermined.

(4) Depreciable assets are assets which are expected to be used during more than one accounting period, have a limited useful life and are held by an enterprise for use in the production or supply of goods and services.

(5) Useful life is either (*i*) the period over which a depreciable asset is expected to be used by the enterprise; or (*ii*) the number of production or similar units expected to be obtained from the use of the asset by the enterprise.

(6) Depreciable amount of a depreciable asset is its historical cost, or other amount substituted for historical cost in the financial statements, less the estimated residual value.

(7) A change from one method of providing depreciation to another is made only if the adoption of the new method is required by statute or for compliance with an accounting standard or if it is considered that the change would result in a more appropriate preparation or presentation of the financial statements of the enterprise. When such a change in the method of depreciation is made, depreciation is recalculated in accordance with the new method from the date of the asset coming into use. The deficiency or surplus arising from retrospective re-computation of depreciation in accordance with the new method is adjusted in the accounts in the year in which the method of depreciation is changed. In case the change in the method results in deficiency in depreciation in respect of past years, the deficiency is charged in the statement of profit and loss. In case the change in the method results in surplus, the surplus is credited to the statement of profit and loss.

(D) AS7 Accounting for Construction Contracts

(*a*) The principal problem relating to accounting for construction contracts is the allocation of revenues and related costs to accounting periods over the duration of the contract.

(*b*) Construction contracts are formulated in two basic types: Fixed price contracts in which the contractor agrees to a fixed contract price, or rate, in some cases subject to cost escalation clauses; and Cost plus contracts where the contractor is reimbursed for allowable or otherwise defined costs, and is also allowed a percentage of these costs or a fixed fee.

(*c*) Two methods of accounting for contracts commonly followed by contractors are the Percentage of completion method and the Completed contract method.

(*d*) Under the percentage of completion method, revenue is recognized as the contract activity progresses based on the stage of completion reached. The costs incurred in reaching the stage of completion are matched with this revenue.

(*e*) Under the completed contract method, revenue is recognized only when the contract is completed or substantially completed. Costs and progress payments received are accumulated during the course of the contract but revenue is not recognized until the contract activity is substantially completed.

(*f*) Costs attributable to a contract include expected warranty costs. Warranty costs are provided for when such costs can be reasonably estimated.

(*g*) The selection of a method of accounting for a construction contract depends on various considerations. The contractor may use both methods simultaneously for different contracts depending upon circumstances.

(*h*) When current estimates of total contract costs and revenues indicate a loss, provision is made for the entire loss on the contract irrespective of the amount of work done and the method of accounting followed.

(*i*) Progress payments and advances received from customers in respect of construction contracts in relation to the work performed thereon are disclosed in financial statements either as a liability or shown as a deduction from the amount of contract-work-in-progress

(E) AS9 Revenue Recognition

(*a*) This standard deals with the issue as to when a business organization should recognize in the books of accounts that it has earned the revenue under various business conditions.

(*b*) Revenue can be recognized on the basis of one of the following methods i.e. Completed service contract method which recognizes revenue in the statement of profit and loss only when the rendering of services under a contract is completed or substantially completed and Proportionate completion method is a method of accounting which recognizes revenue in the statement of profit and loss proportionately with the degree of completion of services under a contract.

(*c*) Criterion for determining when to recognize revenue from a transaction involving the sale of goods is that the seller has transferred the property in the goods to the buyer for a consideration.

(*d*) Revenue from service transactions is usually recognized as the service is performed, either by the proportionate completion method or by the completed service contract method.

(*e*) Interest accrues, in most circumstances, on the time basis determined by the principal amount outstanding and the rate applicable.

(*f*) Royalties accrue in accordance with the terms of the relevant agreement and are usually recognized on that basis unless, having regard to the substance of the transactions, it is more appropriate to recognize revenue on some other systematic and rational basis.

(*g*) Dividends from investments in shares are not recognized in the statement of profit and loss until a right to receive payment is established.

(*h*) Where the ability to assess the ultimate collection with reasonable certainty is lacking at the time of raising any claim, e.g., for escalation of price, export incentives, interest etc., revenue recognition is postponed to the extent of uncertainty involved.

(*i*) When goods are sold on approval or return basis, revenue should not be recognized until the goods have been formally accepted by the buyer or the buyer has done an act adopting the transaction or the time period for rejection has elapsed or where no time has been fixed, a reasonable time has elapsed.

(*j*) When the consideration is receivable in instalments, revenue attributable to the sales price exclusive of interest should be recognized at the date of sale. The interest element should be recognized as revenue, proportionately to the unpaid balance due to the seller.

(*k*) In cases where installation fees are other than incidental to the sale of a product, they should be recognized as revenue only when the equipment is installed and accepted by the customer.

(*l*) If the membership fee permits only membership and all other services or products are paid for separately, or if there is a separate annual subscription, the fee should be recognized when received. If the membership fee entitles the member to services or publications to be provided during the year, it should be recognized on a systematic and rational basis having regard to the timing and nature of all services provided.

(F) AS10 Accounting for Fixed Assets

1. Fixed asset is an asset held with the intention of being used for the purpose of producing or providing goods or services and is not held for sale in the normal course of business.
2. The cost of an item of fixed asset comprises its purchase price, including import duties and other non-refundable taxes or levies and any directly attributable cost of bringing the asset to its working condition for its intended use;

any trade discounts and rebates are deducted in arriving at the purchase price.

3. The expenditure incurred on start-up and commissioning of the project, including the expenditure incurred on test runs and experimental production, is usually capitalised as an indirect element of the construction cost.
4. Subsequent expenditures related to an item of fixed asset should be added to its book value only if they increase the future benefits from the existing asset beyond its previously assessed standard of performance.
5. When a fixed asset is acquired in exchange for another asset, its cost is usually determined by reference to the fair market value of the consideration given.
6. An increase in net book value arising on revaluation of fixed assets is normally credited directly to owner's interests (capital) under the heading of revaluation reserves and is regarded as not available for distribution of dividends.
7. Gains or losses arising on disposal are generally recognized in the profit and loss statement.
8. Goodwill, in general, is recorded in the books only when some consideration in money or money's worth has been paid for it.

(G) Other Accounting Standards

As regards other accounting standards, the following points are important :

(*a*) Cash flows arising from taxes on income should be separately disclosed and should be classified as cash flows from operating activities unless they can be specifically identified with financing and investing activities.

(*b*) The existence and amount of guarantees, obligations arising from discounted bills of exchange and similar obligations undertaken by an enterprise are generally disclosed in financial statements by way of note.

(*c*) The amount of a contingent loss should be provided for by a charge in the statement of profit and loss if it is probable that future events will confirm that, after taking into account any related probable recovery, an asset has been impaired or a liability has been incurred as at the balance sheet date, and a reasonable estimate of the amount of the resulting loss can be made.

(*d*) Contingent gains should not be recognized in the financial statements.

(*e*) Assets and liabilities should be adjusted for events occurring after the balance sheet date that provide additional evidence to assist the estimation of amounts relating to conditions existing at the balance sheet date or indicate that the fundamental accounting assumption of going concern (i.e., the continuance of existence or substratum of the enterprise) is not appropriate.

(*f*) Research and development costs are usually charged to expense in the period in which they are incurred. If it can be demonstrated, however, that the product or process is technically and commercially feasible and that the enterprise has adequate resources to enable the product or process to be marketed, it may be appropriate to defer the costs of related research and development to future periods.

(*g*) Exchange differences arising on foreign currency transactions should be recognized as income or as expense in the period in which they arise.

(*h*) Exchange differences arising on repayment of liabilities incurred for the purpose of acquiring fixed assets, which are carried in terms of historical cost, should be adjusted in the carrying amount (book value) of the respective fixed assets.

(*i*) The cost of an investment should include acquisition charges such as brokerage, fees and duties.

(*j*) Extraordinary items should be disclosed in the statement of profit and loss as a part of net profit or loss for the period. The nature and the amount of each extraordinary item should be separately disclosed in the statement of profit and loss in a manner that its impact on current profit or loss can be perceived.

❑ ❑ ❑

Chapter 2

Process of Accounting

DOUBLE ENTRY SYSTEM

Rules of Debit and Credit : The transactions in the Journal are recorded on the basis of the rules of debit and credit. The rules are made according to the type of accounts as explained above. The rules are as under :

For Personal Accounts,

"DEBIT THE RECEIVER AND CREDIT THE GIVER"

For Real accounts,

"DEBIT WHAT COMES IN AND CREDIT WHAT GOES OUT"

For Nominal accounts,

"DEBIT ALL EXPENSES AND LOSSES AND CREDIT ALL INCOMES AND GAINS"

Fundamental Accounting Equation

The fundamental accounting equation is based on the division of all types of accounts into only three categories:

(*a*) Assets, (*b*) Liabilities, (*c*) Equity

The equation is

Assets = Liabilities + Capital

This equation represents that what the company owes to outsides is equal to what the company has received from outsiders. Here, for the company, even the owners are outsiders and are a liability for the company which is shown separately as capital. Whenever, a firm enters into any transaction, this equation gets affected. But as per the double entry system, this equation will always hold true. This is explained with the help of following illustration:

Illustration 1 : Mr. Kothari starts a new business with a cash of Rs. 50,000.

Assets	=	Liabilities	+	Capital
(Cash – Rs. 50,000)		NIL		(Owner's capital – Rs. 50,000)

Now, he purchases building of Rs. 10,000 and stock worth Rs. 8,000 on credit.

Assets	=	Liabilities	+	Capital
(Cash – Rs. 40,000 Building – Rs. 10,000 Stock – Rs. 8,000)		(Creditors – Rs. 8,000)		(Capital – Rs. 50,000)

This accounting equation is fundamental in accounting as the double entry system is based on this equation. It is very necessary to understand this equation for proper learning of accounts. Like any other equation, this equation called also be presented in many ways like:

Assets – Liabilities = Capital

Assets – Capital = Liabilities

Records and Terms in Accounting

In an accounting system, various kinds of records are maintained and various terms are used. As a student of commerce, you must have learnt them. But, as a revision, these records and terms are explained hereunder:

1. Voucher : The basic record of any accounting system is 'Voucher'. A voucher is a documentary evidence in support of a transaction. For example, a cash memo showing cash sale, invoice showing credit sale etc.

2. Cash Book : It is meant to record all the cash transactions of the firm. Cash book can be single column, two column or three column. In one column cash book, only cash account is maintained. In two column cash book, the bank account is also maintained. Sometimes, cash is deposited in bank or withdrawn from the bank. In this case, entry is made on both the sides of the cash book. Such transactions are known as 'Contra' transactions or **'Contra Entry'**. Some firms also maintain a three-column cash book which apart from the above two accounts also maintains cash discount received and paid account. In case of cash and bank accounts, their closing balances are found out and carried forward but cash discount column is only totalled and not balanced.

3. Journal : It is the basic book of accounts which records all the transactions of a firm. In case the firm is maintaining the subsidiary books of accounts then the transactions which do not appear in those books, find their place in the journal.

4. Purchase and Sales Book : They constitute the bulk of the transactions of a trading firm. Since, most of the firms make sales and purchases on credit basis, they need to know the extent of it. For this purpose, these two subsidiary books are maintained. Only credit purchases and sales of goods in which the firm deals in are recorded in these books. The purchases are evidenced by credit bills received from the supplier whereas sales are supported by the invoice made out against the customer. With this, many firms also maintain separate books for goods returned to the suppliers and goods returned by the customers, which are known as 'Return Books'.

5. Debit and Credit Notes : A debit note is issued to a party for raising a debit against that party for various reasons like return of goods, availing some discounts etc. When the debit note is issued, the issuing firm debits the account of the person to whom it is issued and the person receiving it credits the sending firm. The reverse is for the credit note.

6. Ledger : The book which contains all accounts is known as the ledger. Since final information pertaining to the final accounts emerges only from accounts, the ledger is also called 'Principal book'. Other books like purchase or sales book, journal etc. merely facilitates the preparation of accounts or the ledger, they are known as subsidiary books or books of original entry. The cash book has unique position. It is a subsidiary book because cash entries are first entered here and then other accounts are prepared. But, it also contains the accounts of bank and cash itself and hence is a part of ledger. So, it is a book of original entry as well as the Principal book.

7. Operating Expenses : These are expenses of the business connected with the basic or day to day functioning of the enterprise. These include production, administration as well as selling expenses. Similarly, operating incomes are income from business activities.

8. Non-Operating Expenses : These are expenses not directly associated with the main activity of the enterprise like interest payment. Similarly, non-operating incomes are not associated with the principal activity of the business like dividend on investments.

9. Trade and Cash Discount : Trade discount is given by the seller at the time of sale of product which is deducted from price of product. The bill is raised by seller after deducting trade discount. Cash discount is provided to the buyer for making payment earlier than scheduled time. No journal entry for trade discount is made whereas cash discount is loss for seller and income for buyer.

10. Current Assets : These are assets of the enterprise which are expected to be converted into cash within the normal operating cycle of the business which is one year.

11. Current Liabilities : Such liabilities which will become due for payment within one year and are normally paid out of current assets.

12. Working Capital : It refers to the investment made by the enterprise in the business to keep the business going on smoothly. It is represented as the difference between the current assets and current liabilities. Sometimes, it is also referred as Net Working Capital. In such a case, Gross Working Capital is equal to the current assets.

TRIAL BALANCE

Trial balance is a statement containing the ledger balances of all the accounts on a particular date. It has two sides viz., debit and credit to show the balance of a particular account. As under the double entry system, every transaction has two sides, *i.e.*, credit and debit which are equal. Therefore, when we take the balances of all the accounts, the total of accounts with debit balance should match with the total of accounts with credit balance. The following are the objectives of preparing the trial balance :

1. Checking the arithmetic accuracy of the accounting entries and their postings.
2. It gives a bird's eye view of the balances in various accounts.
3. It is a useful basis for the preparation of P&L account and Balance Sheet.
4. If the total of debit and credit side of Trial balance matches, it gives reasonable assurance of accuracy of accounts. But, still there can be some mistakes. This has been explained later.

GENERALLY ACCEPTED PRINCIPLES OF ACCOUNTING

The practice of accounting is influenced and guided by certain conventions, concepts and principles which from experience are proved acceptable and useful. The term 'Concept' is used to connote accounting assumptions or conditions upon which accounting is based. On the other hand, 'Convention' is used to signify customs or traditions as a guide to the preparation of accounting statements. While concepts have logical thinking and rationality at their base, the conventions are established by the practicability and use over a long period of time.

Conventions of Accounting

The following are treated as basic conventions of accounting :

(A) Consistency : The principle of consistency implies that the same accounting procedure and method should be continuously followed by a firm from year to year. They should not be changed frequently.

This principle helps in making the statements comparable over a period of time. This principle applies more to items like depreciation, valuation of closing stock, deferred revenue expenditure etc. where a number of methods are available to accountant for valuation.

According to this convention, whatever method suitable to the organization, once applied, should be applied every year.

If at all, any change in the accounting procedure or method is considered necessary, then such changes giving due explanation made and its effect should be clearly stated in the accounts.

(B) Conservatism : This is one of the most recognized and widely practiced accounting conventions. It recognizes the natural human behaviour of playing safe. According to this principle, all future losses and expenses are to be recognized whereas all future incomes and profits should be ignored. It is on this basis, the value of closing stock is taken at the cost or market price, whichever is lower. Some other examples of convention of conservatism are the provision for bad and doubtful debts and provision for fluctuation in the value of investment, showing joint life policy at surrender value, not providing for discount on creditors etc.

But, there are certain drawbacks of this convention. Excessive application of this concept leads to creation of secret reserves. It is contrary to the policy of full disclosure and consistency. Moreover, it conflicts with the concept of matching of revenues and costs. Therefore, it should be cautiously followed.

(C) Materiality : It implies that the accountant need not record events which are trivial considering the size of organisation and the work of recording them is not justified by the usefulness of the results. For example expenditure of Rs. 1,30,000.05 may be written as Rs. 1,30,000. Also, many small events can be clubbed under one accounting head instead of showing each of them separately. For example, many small expenses on different stationary items are clubbed under one head or certain petty expenses are clubbed as 'Sundry expenses'.

Materiality is a relative concept. What is material for one firm may be immaterial for another. Moreover, materiality is related not only to the monetary value but also with the importance of the item. An item is considered material if it is large enough to influence the judgement or decision based on accounting reports.

(D) Disclosure : The term disclosure suggests that all accounting statements should be honest and full disclosure of all significant information should be made. However, it does not mean that all information like sale price, details of customers should be disclosed but a sufficient disclosure of an information which is of material interest to proprietors, creditors and investors and affect their decision making should be made. This principle has more to do with the disclosures regarding the accounting policies and significant events of the firm. The accounting statements should conform to the generally accepted accounting principles. Moreover, where an important change has been made in presentation of information, as compared to preceding accounting periods, the nature of such change should be clearly indicated.

CONCEPTS OR ASSUMPTIONS OF ACCOUNTING

Of all the concepts and conventions, certain fundamental accounting assumptions underlie the preparation and presentation of financial statements. They are usually not specifically stated because their acceptance and use are assumed. Disclosure is necessary if they are not followed. The following have been generally accepted as fundamental accounting assumptions:-

(1) The Going Concern Concept : This concept is based on the assumption that the business will continue for the indefinite period or a sufficiently long period. Except the undertaking of a particular venture, it is assumed that business will last for a long time. It is due to this assumption that the fixed assets are usually stated in the balance sheet at the acquisition cost less provision for depreciation without any regard to the actual market value of the asset. The transactions are so recorded that the benefits likely to accrue in future of the money spent now are also taken into account.

For example, when a machine (expected to last for 10 years) is acquired, the total cost of the machine is not treated as an expense in the year in which it is acquired. Only a part of its cost is charged to profit and loss account every year in the name of depreciation. Similarly, the Contingent liabilities are shown at the footnote of the balance sheet with the assumption that the business is going to continue for a long time.

(2) Business Entity Concepts : According to this concept, business is considered as a distinct entity from its owners, managers and employees. In the accounting, the business has a separate personality and accountant must take note of the transactions between the business entity and its owners or employees just like the transactions with the third parties.

It should be remembered that companies and co-operative societies have legal existence or entity for all purposes but there is no separate legal entity for a sole proprietor or partnership. However, accounting will distinguish the business from the owners in all cases. So, even a sole proprietorship and partnership firm has a separate accounting entity though not separate legal entities.

Accordingly, all the transactions of the business are recorded in the books of the business from the viewpoint of the business entity and the owner is treated as a creditor to the extent of his capital. This is clear from the fact that capital is shown as a liability in the balance sheet. Any personal expense of the owner done from the money of the business is considered as reduction in capital (Drawings). If any expenditure does not involve the money of the business, it does not appear in the accounts.

(3) Money Measurement Concept : As per this concept, only such transactions and events which can be expressed in terms of money are recorded. In other words, the transactions and events on which money value cannot be put will not be recorded in the books of account even though the events may be extremely important. For example, if the chairman of the company dies in a plane crash, though the event may be a great loss to the company, it will not be recorded in the books of account, as it has no money value.

The main advantage of expressing events in monetary terms is that money provides a common denominator by means of which heterogeneous facts of the business can be expressed in one single object. It also avoids the subjective judgement about the importance of an event.

(4) Accounting Period Concept : Net income for the entire life of an organization is relatively easy to measure. It is the difference between the investments and returns. But, generally businesses run for several years. According to going concern concept, they are assumed to continue for indefinite period. Therefore, it is imperative for the management of the organization to know the results of their business at regular intervals. This leads to the Accounting period concept. It measures the activities of the organization for a period of time, called accounting period. Generally, it is one year since it is assumed that during this period, most of the kinds of business transactions does take place one or more times.

(5) Cost Concept : Under this concept, in accounting all transactions and events are recorded at their monetary cost of acquisition, *i.e.,* actual amount of money paid for the acquisition of the asset or for receiving the goods or services. Accounting should make a record of the transactions on the objective basis. The personal views of the people regarding the actual value of the asset are not considered.

Elaborating the concept, it means that if an asset does not cost anything, then such transaction would not be recorded in the books of account. Thus the knowledge and skill that is built up as business operates, the teamwork within the organization, managerial competence, a favourable location etc. in spite of being valuable assets do not appear in the books of account. However, if a tangible asset is acquired at free of cost, then the transaction is recorded at a nominal value of Re. 1 so that the record of the asset is available, according to convention of disclosure.

BASIC ACCOUNTING PRINCIPLES

Basic accounting principles are the general rules which are used as a guide in accounting and as a basis of practice. These principles are based upon logic and practical experience. These principles are flexible and are modified from time to time to meet the changing needs of business. These basic accounting principles are as follows:

(1) The Realisation Principle : According to this principle, revenue is deemed to be realised earned when the goods have been transferred or the services have been rendered to a customer. In the realisation of revenue, the receipt of cash is not significant. If a firm sells goods in April and receives cash in June, revenue will be considered as realised in April when the goods were sold.

Similarly, expenses are recognised not when the cash is paid but when the assets or services are used to produce revenue. For example, rent for January 1, 2001 to 31 March, 2001, though unpaid, will be recognised during the accounting year 2000-2001. Likewise, cost of goods lost by fire is immediately recognised in the year of loss.

(2) Maching Principle : According to Matching principle, the revenues or income and the expenses incurred to earn that income should be matched so that net income of the business operation is available in respect of a particular period. This principle has led to formation of rules regarding recognition of income as well as matching the expenses to that income.

This concept implies two principles. The first is that when revenue or sale is recognized to be earned, then all costs incurred to produce or sell must be considered. And secondly, that when the cost is incurred but sale or service is likely to be earned in the future, then such cost should not be considered during the current period. The result is that the figures shown in P&L Account are mutually interrelated and the resultant profit or loss is arrived at only after considering relevant revenue and relevant cost.

(*a*) When an item of revenue is included in the profit and loss account, all expenses incurred on it whether paid or not, should be included in the profit and loss account. Outstanding expenses are debited in the profit and loss account on this basis.

(*b*) If an amount is spent, but revenue from it will be earned in the next year, the amount should be carried down as an asset and should be shown as an expense next year. Prepaid expenses (e.g., prepaid insurance) are shown as assets in the balance sheet on this basis.

(*c*) Cost of goods remaining unsold at the end of the year together with expenses incurred on them must be carried forward to the next year. Therefore, closing stock is carried over to the next year as opening stock.

(*d*) Incomes received in advance must be treated as a liability, while income earned but not received should be recognised as revenue.

There is an exception to matching principle. In case of losses against which no revenue is earned or expected to earn, are debited to the P&L Account in the year in which they are incurred. For example, loss due to fire or theft.

(3) Accrual Principle : Accrual concept is very much related to the Matching principle. The mercantile system of accounting is based on accrual concept only. Under this, revenue is recognized when it accrues, whether received in cash or not. Accrual of income or expense arises when the right to receive income or the obligation to pay for the expenses is fixed.

According to this concept, as the income or expenses accrue, they are recorded in the books of account as outstanding income or expense, if cash is not received or paid at the same time. Whenever the cash is received or paid, the transaction is recorded again and the outstanding balance is cleared. Extending the concept, if any income is received or expense is paid in advance (i.e. not accrued), it is not taken into P&L Account, but is shown in the balance sheet as an asset or liability, as the case may be.

(4) The Dual Aspect Principle : The economic resources of an entity are called assets. The claims of various parties against these assets are called liabilities. Liabilities are of two types: Outside liabilities (or simply liabilities) and Capital (liability towards the owner). Since all types of assets of a business are claimed by someone and business does not have anything of its own, the total of these claims cannot exceed the amount of assets to be claimed, it follows that

ASSETS = LIABILITIES

As already explained, liabilities are of two types. So, the above equation can be rewritten as below:

ASSETS = OUTSIDE LIABILITIES + CAPITAL

This is the Fundamental Accounting Equation, which is the formal expression of the dual aspect concept. As per this concept, every transaction has a dual impact on the accounting records and this equation holds true all the time, as already explained earlier.

(5) The Principle of Full Disclosure : According to this principle, there should be complete and understandable reporting on the financial statements of all significant information relating to the economic affairs of the firm. To meet the requirements of this method of depreciation or method of valuation of stock, market value of investments and contingent liability are shown in foot notes. For example, change in the method of depreciation or method of valuation of stock, market value of investments and contingent liability are shown in footnotes. The Companies Act has prescribed the proforma and contents of Balance Sheet and Profit and Loss Account to ensure full disclosure of financial information.

(6) The Principle of Vertifiable Objective : This principle requires that all transactions recorded in the books of accounts must be evidenced and supported by business documents, such as cash memos invoices, vouchers, etc. These supporting documents provide the basis for making entries and for audit. Objectivity principle also requires that the accounting records must be free from the personal bias of the owners and managers.

ACCOUNTING CONVENTIONS OR MODIFYING PRINCIPLES

These principle are exceptions to the basic accounting principles stated above. These modifying principles are as under :

1. Principle of Materiality : This principle is

an exception to the principle of full disclosure. According to this principle, items having an insignificant effect or irrelevant to the user need not be disclosed. American Accounting Association defines materiality as, "An item should be regarded as material if there is reason to believe that knowledge of it would influence decision of informed investor". Materiality of an item depends on its nature and amount. It should be noted that what is material for one firm may be immaterial for another. For example, the cost of small tools may be material for a small repair workshop but may be immaterial for TELCO. Therefore, the accountant should judge the importance of each transaction or event to determine its materiality.

2. Principle of Consistency : This principle states that accounting procedures and methods should remain consistent from one year to another. These should not be changed from year to year as otherwise the net profits of different years will not be comparable. For example, a firm can choose any one of the several methods of depreciation. But the method once chosen should be followed consistently year after year. However, change may be made to adopt improved techniques of accounting, to keep accounting flexible and to ensure better disclosure of financial information. In case a change becomes necessary, the change and its effect should be stated clearly.

3. Principle of Conservatism or Prudence : According to this principle record all anticipated losses but ignore all anticipated gains. Conservatism is thus, the policy of playing safe. Some examples of the application of this principle are :

(*a*) Closing stock is valued at cost price or market price whichever is less.

(*b*) Provision for doubtful debts is created in anticipation of actual bad debts.

(*c*) Joint life insurance policy is shown at surrender value as against the premiums paid.

The principle of conservatism should be applied carefully. Otherwise it may result in the creation of secret reserves which is against the principle of full disclosure.

4. Principle of Timeliness : Financial statements provide useful information on the basis of which users take important decisions. If the statements contain old and late information they are of little use. Therefore, this principle states that the financial statements should be prepared quickly at the end of the accounting period. They should be made available to the users at the earliest possible time. To ensure timely information, the Companies At requires companies to report quarterly results of their operations.

5. Principle of Industry Practice : Sometimes, the peculiar nature of an industry may required departure from the basic accounting principles. Three may be a long standing accounting practice in an industry. For example, a particular method of valuation of stock may be prevailing in an industry. While preparing its financial statements every firm in that industry must follow the prevailing accounting practice of that industry. Otherwise the results of the firm will not be comparable to those of other firms.

ERRORS IN ACCOUNTING

During the recording or summarizing the transactions, the accountant may make certain mistakes which leads to errors in the accounting The first major check to find out the errors is Trial Balance. If the trial balance does not tally, it means that there is some error in the accounting. But, even if the trial balance tallies, the accounts may have some errors. Before we understand that, errors are classified mainly into four types:

1. Errors of Omission - When the transaction is completely or partly omitted from the books of account
2. Errors of Commission - When transaction is recorded with wrong amount or in wrong account or error in casting totals.
3. Error of Principle - When the amount received or spent is not properly allocated between revenue and capital
4. Compensating errors - When two errors compensate each other in such a way that it does not affect the trial balance

Of the above, the error of complete omission, errors of principle and compensating errors do not affect the matching of trial balance and hence may be present even if the trial balance is matched.

Suspense Account : On knowing that there is some error in the accounts, the accountant should try to find it out and correct it. In case, he cannot find it and he is in hurry to close the books of account, he may transfer the difference between the credit and debit side of the trial balance to an account called 'Suspense account'. On location of the errors in the next year, the correct accounting entry is passed with the help of suspense account and the suspense account is closed.

Rectification of Errors : For rectification of errors, the following rules are observed.

(1) If the error is located at the trial balance stage, and it affects only one account, no Journal entry is passed. A correction is made in the ledger and explanation is given. If the error affects two or more accounts, those accounts are rectified by passing a journal entry.

(2) If the accountant fails to locate the errors at Trial Balance stage and it is important to prepare the Final accounts, the balance amount is transferred to Suspense Account. When the errors are located at subsequent stage, journal entry is passed by posting correct amount in the correct account and the second entry is made in suspense account.

(3) If the error comes to notice in the subsequent year, the Profit & Loss Adjustment A/c is opened and all the transactions where a revenue account is involved, instead to making entry in that account, P&L Adjustment account is used. The other entry is made in the concerned account and if no other account is involved, it is made to suspense account. The balance in P&L adjustment A/c is transferred to Capital account. This is done with an objective that due to the errors of previous year, the Profit & Loss A/c of current year should not be affected.

Illustration 2 : The following are certain illustrations regarding rectification of errors :

(1) Total of debit side of Salary account has been cast in excess by Rs. 100.

(2) One purchase of Rs. 25 has been posted from day book to the ledger as Rs. 250.

(3) A cheque of Rs. 10,000 issued to Suresh for his past dues has been wrongly debited to the purchase account.

(4) Expenditure of Rs. 5000 incurred for trial run of the machine has been debited to the expenditure account.

(5) Expenditure of Rs. 250 was wrongly credited in the ledger as Rs. 520.

(6) Payment of Rs. 1100 received from Kamal was credited in the cash book.

(7) Purchase of Rs. 4500 from Rajan was entered in the Sales day book.

(8) Sale of Rs. 1500 to Surendra on credit was omitted from the day book.

(9) Sale of Furniture for Rs. 500 was entered in the Sales day book.

(10) Rent of office paid in advance Rs. 1200 was debited to the Rent account.

(11) Goods returned to Sunita valued Rs. 750 was debited to Anita's account.

(12) Rs. 1000 being purchase returns was posted to the Purchase day book.

(13) A sale of Rs. 1000 to Sanjay was entered in the Purchase day book from where the account of Sanjay was debited by Rs. 100.

No.	Particulars		Debit	Credit
1.	Suspense A/c To Salary A/c	Dr.	100	100
2.	Creditor's A/c To Suspense A/c	Dr.	225	225
3.	Suspense A/c To Purchase A/c	Dr.	10,000	10,000

4.	Machine A/c	Dr.	5,000	
	To Expenditure A/c			5,000
5.	Expenditure A/c	Dr.	770	
	To Suspense A/c			770
6.	Cash A/c	Dr.	2,200	
	To Kamal A/c			2,200
7.	Purchase A/c	Dr.	4,500	
	Sales A/c	Dr.	4,500	
	To Rajan A/c			9,000
8.	Surendra A/c	Dr.	1,500	
	To Sales A/c			1,500
9.	Sales A/c	Dr.	500	
	To Furniture A/c			500
10.	Advance Rent A/c	Dr.	1,200	
	To Rent A/c			1,200
11.	Sunita A/c	Dr.	750	
	To Anita A/c			750
12.	Creditor's A/c	Dr.	2,000	
	To Purchase Return A/c			1,000
	To Purchase A/c			1,000
13.	Suspense A/c	Dr.	1,100	
	Sanjay A/c	Dr.	900	
	To Purchase A/c			1,000
	To Sales A/c			1,000

❑ ❑ ❑

Chapter 3

Accounting for Depreciation

DEPRECIATION

Depreciation means a permanent and continuing fall in the value of the asset. According to the Institute of Chartered Accountants of England, "Depreciation is that part of the cost of a fixed asset to its owner which is not recoverable when the asset is finally put out of use by him. Provision against this loss of capital is an integral cost of conducting the business during the effective commercial life of the asset and is not dependant upon the amount of profit earned." The term depreciation is used only in respect of fixed assets. Any diminution in the value of current assets is taken care of by valuing them for Balance sheet purpose 'at cost or market price whichever is less'. Depreciation is a charge against profit and hence is debited to P&L account but it is a non-cash expenditure as no cash is paid for it.

Causes of Depreciation

Depreciation may occur due to various reasons which are listed as below :

(*a*) Wear and tear (normal use of the asset)

(*b*) Exhaustion (in case of mineral mines, oil wells etc.)

(*c*) Obsolescence (due to change in the technology)

(*d*) Efflux of time (for patents, copyright, lease assets etc.)

(*e*) Accidents

Depletion and Amortization : These two terms are used interchangeably with depreciation but are different from depreciation. Depletion implies removal of an available but irreplaceable resource such as extracting coal from a coal mine or oil out of oil well.

Amortization is the process of writing off intangible assets. Intangible assets like patent, copyright, leasehold etc. have limited useful life after which they cease to be of any value to the owner. Therefore, the cost of acquiring them must be written off over the useful life of the concerned asset.

Methods for Providing Depreciation

The purpose of providing depreciation in the accounts is to show the true value of the assets of the firm, to ascertain the true profits of the firm earned during the year and make arrangement for the replacement of the asset after the end of its useful life. There are various methods of providing depreciation on assets. The important among them are as follows :

(1) **Straight Line Method :** Under this methods, depreciation remains same throughout the life of the asset. The total amount of depreciation is allocated to the useful life of the asset in equal proportion. This is most simple and widely used method of depreciation.

(2) **Reducing Balance Method :** Also, known as Written Down Value method, the depreciation is high in the initial years and less in the subsequent years. Since the maintenance expenditure is low in initial years and high in later years, this method leads to more or less uniform expenditure on depreciation and maintenance taken together, throughout the life of the asset. Though, the calculation of percentage of depreciation is complex, it is widely used and even for Income Tax purposes, only this method is used to calculate depreciation. In this method the value of the asset never becomes zero.

(3) **Annuity Method :** In this method, the depreciation is calculated based on the annuity table, considering the amount to be required to replace the asset at the end of the useful life of the asset. Here also, the amount of depreciation remains same in all the years.

(4) **Depreciation Fund Method :** It is actually not a method of calculating depreciation but a method of providing depreciation in the books. In this method, the depreciation amount is calculated using the straight line or annuity method. The annual depreciation amount is set aside in an account called Depreciation Fund account and it is invested in safe and liquid securities. The annual depreciation amount is decided in such a way that the total amount accumulated from the depreciation and the income from the investments is nearly equal to the amount required to replace the assets at the end of the useful life. The journal entries are similar to the debenture redemption fund method, which is explained in the chapter of company accounts.

(5) **Depletion Method :** It is used for peculiar assets like mines, quarries etc. where an estimate of total quantity of output by the asset can be fairly known. The depreciation per unit of the asset is calculated based on the availability of total units. Each year depreciation is calculated according to the number of units extracted out of the asset.

(6) **Sum of Years Digit Method :** The amount of depreciation to be charged goes on decreasing every year. The following formula is used to calculate depreciation :

Remaining life of asset (including current year)

$$\text{Depreciation} = \frac{\text{Remaining life of asset (including current year)}}{\text{Sum of all digits of the life of asset in years}} \times \text{Original cost}$$

Sum of all digits of the life of asset in years

(7) **Machine Hour Rate Method :** This method is used when the life of the asset can be fairly known in terms of its usage in number of hours. In this method depreciation is calculated as below:

$$\begin{matrix}\text{Depreciation}\\ \text{(Per machine hour)}\end{matrix} = \frac{\text{Original cost of asset - Scrap value}}{\text{Life of asset in hours}}$$

(8) **Revaluation Method :** This method is used for items like loose tools, jigs etc. and cattle. At the end of the year, the market value of the assets on hand is calculated. Depreciation is taken as the difference between the value of assets at the beginning of the year and at the end of the year.

Apart from above, the following practices are followed in respect of various assets :

(*a*) No depreciation is charged on the Goodwill. It is generally written off over a number of years.

(*b*) In case of Freehold Land also, no depreciation is charged.

FINAL ACCOUNTS

Preparation of final accounts is the final step in the accounting cycle. Final accounts are prepared to achieve the objectives of accountancy. In order to know the profit or loss earned by a firm "Trading and Profit and Loss Account" i.e. income statement is prepared. Balance sheet of financial position statement will show the financial condition of the firm on a particular date. Under Section 210 of the Companies Act it has been made compulsory for companies to prepare their final accounts and present the same before the share holders for their approval, at every annual general meeting of the company.

Types of Final Accounts

Every firm prepares final account to know the results of its operations as well as to know the current financial position of the firm. The following accounts are prepared for this purpose :

(1) Manufacturing Account (only manufacturing firms)

(2) Trading Account

(3) Profit & Loss Account

(4) Balance Sheet

(1) Manufacturing Account. It is prepared only by the manufacturing concerns. This account is prepared by the manufacturer to know the cost of production. So, all the expenses related to the manufacturing are debited to this account. The cost of production ascertained is then transferred to the Trading account.

(2) Trading Account. This account gives the overall result of trading i.e. purchase and sell of goods. Trading account may be defined as an account which is prepared to ascertain the gross profit or gross loss of business concern for a given time period. It compares the cost of goods sold (which includes all the expenses on purchasing the goods) and sales price of goods. The difference between the two is called 'Gross Profit' or loss. Cost of goods sold can be defined as

Cost of goods sold = Opening stock + Net Purchases + Exp. on purchases – Closing Stock

Expenses on purchases include Wages, Customs and import duty, Freight, Carriage and cartage, Royalty, Gas, Electricity, Fuel etc., Packing materials and other similar items.

(3) Profit and Loss Account. Profit and Loss account is the account which is prepared to calculate the net profit or net loss of the business for a given accounting period. It may be defined as a financial statement that matches the gross profit and indirect revenues with the indirect expenses during an accounting period to show the net profit or net loss earned by a business firm. After knowing the gross profit, the owner is interested in finding out the net result of the operations of business. This is done with the help of P&L account. In this account, all the expenses other than those taken into trading account, are debited. These expenditures are related to the administration of the business as well as selling of the goods. Gross profit and other incomes of the business are credited. This also includes all incomes and expenses whether related to normal course of business or not. The net amount is 'Net Profit or Loss' of the business for the year.

(4) Balance Sheet. Balance Sheet is a statement (not an account) of the assets and liabilities of the business concern. It shows the financial position of the business. Also, the trading and P&L accounts are prepared for a particular period (say a year) but balance sheet is prepared for a particular point of time (say a day) in business.

Form of Balance Sheet. Balance sheet means a financial statement which sets out the assets and liabilities of a trading or non-trading organisation as at a certain date.

There is no prescribed form of balance sheet for the sole proprietorship firm or partnership firm. The form of balance sheet for companies is contained in Schedule VI of Companies Act, 1956. but even for sole proprietorship and partnership firms the items of the balance sheet are shown in an orderly fashion. The order may be any of the following :

(*a*) Order of Permanence

(*b*) Order of Liquidity

These orders classify the assets in the order in which the expected time within which the asset can be converted into cash. Generally companies and manufacturing concerns use the order of permanence, which is mandated by the Schedule VI of Companies Act. In this order, the asset, which is

LIABILITIES	AMOUNT	ASSETS	AMOUNT
Capital		Goodwill	
Long Term Loans		Land	
		Building	
Sundry Creditors		Plant & Machinery	
Bills Payable		Furniture	
Outstanding Expenses		Closing Stock :	
Bank Overdraft		Raw material	
		Work in progress	
		Finished goods	
		Sundry Debtors	
		Bills Receivable	
		Prepaid Expenses	
		Cash at Bank	
		Cash in Hand	

most difficult to liquidate, is shown first and the asset, which is most liquid, is shown last. Hence, goodwill appears on the top (as goodwill is sold only after all other assets are sold) and cash on hand appears last. The reverse is the order when balance sheet is presented in the order of liquidity. The detailed explanation of order of permanence is given in the chapter relating to company accounts.

The following is the mode of a balance sheet prepared according to Permanency Order.

NOTE :

(*a*) Wages are debited to the Trading account whereas Salaries are debited to P&L account.

(*b*) Trading expenses are expenses related to trading but Trade expenses are petty or miscellaneous expenses which are debited to P&L account.

(*c*) Deferred revenue expenditure to the extent not written off appears on the asset side in the balance, but they are not represented by actual asset and hence are known as Fictitious Assets.

(*d*) Closing stock of raw material and work in progress appear in Manufacturing account, but stock of finished goods appears in trading account only.

(*e*) Freight, Carriage and Cartage are taken as direct expenses incurred on purchase of goods and hence they appear on the debit side of Trading account.

(*f*) Royalty is a direct expense, as it is paid on the production of goods. Hence it appears in the manufacturing account as a direct manufacturing expense. It royalty is paid on sales and not manufacturing, it is debited to Trading account.

(*g*) Treatment of packing material depends on the actual circumstances. Expenditure on packing to convert goods into saleable items are direct expenses and hence appear in the Trading account whereas packing expenses to make the goods look attractive for marketing is considered as marketing expense and hence should be debited to Profit & Loss account.

CLOSING ENTRIES

Final accounts i.e. Trading and P&L account and Balance Sheet are prepared by the accountant at the end of the year based on all the transaction of the year. At the end of the year, the accountant may know of certain adjustments to be made in the books of accounts to give a true picture of the performance of the business which is not taken into account till the stage of preparing Trial balance. These adjustments pertain to valuation of closing stock, annual interests on capital, provision for bad debts and discounts, depreciation, outstanding incomes and expenses, prepaid incomes and expenses, rectification of mistakes etc. Treatment of some important closing entries have been explained hereunder :

(1) Provision for Bad Debts. In business, generally a part of the credit sales do not materialize in cash and has to be foregone by the firm. This is known as bad debts. It is a loss of the business. Moreover, every year while preparing the final accounts, the businessman estimates the amount of bad debts that may occur in the subsequent year and considers it as a loss of this year because the debts belong to this year. For this purpose he debits the profit and loss account and creates a liability on the business by crediting Bad Debt Reserve account. This amount is shown as a deduction from the debtors in the balance sheet. The following is the format of showing bad debts and bad debt reserves in the P&L account and in the balance sheet.

PROFIT AND LOSS ACCOUNT

To Bad debts (old)	____			
Add :				
Bad debts (new)	____			
Bad debts Reserve(new)	____			
Less :				
Bad debts Reserve (old)	____	____		

BALANCE SHEET

			Debtors	______	
			Less :		
			Bad debts(new)	______	
			Bad debts		
			Reserve(new)	______	______

Here, bad debts new refer to the bad debts given in the adjustment to be recognized while preparing the final accounts. Bad debts reserve (old) represents the balance in the account in the last year. Bad debts reserve (new) is the amount to be set aside out of the profits for the next year. It should be remembered that when bad debts reserve is to be created as a certain percentage of debtors it should always be calculated on the amount of debtors as reduced by the new bad debts. Next year when the actual bad debts happen, it is debited to the bad debt reserve account and not the profit and loss account. Similar treatment is given in case of discount and Discount Reserve on Debtors and Creditors. The only thing to remember is that new provision for discount on debtors is calculated on the net balance, *i.e.,* after deducting the Bad debt reserve, if any.

Illustration 1: In a trial balance, debtors are appearing at Rs. 1,08,000. a provision is to be made for doubtful debtors @5% on the debtors after considering following information:

1. An amount of Rs. 1,000 is included in debtors who is bankrupt and his estate is expected to realise 50 paise in a rupee.
2. Debtors include an amount of Rs. 5,000 for goods supplied to proprietor.
3. Bills receivable include a bill of Rs. 3,000, which is dishonoured.
4. Goods sold on 'Sale or return' basis amounting to Rs. 5,000 have been included in debtors.
5. Debtors include an amount of Rs. 1,000 from a customer whose financial position is doubtful.

The total provision to be made will be calculated as follows:

Debtors (Balance given)	1,08,000
Less : Debtor who is bankrupt	(1,000)
[As the amount to be received and loss is certain]	
Less : Goods supplied to proprietor	(5,000)
[This amount needs to be debited to drawings]	
Add : Dishonoured bill	3,000
[After dishonour of bill, he is now again a debtor]	
Less : Goods on 'Sale or return' basis	(5,000)
[This amount cannot be considered as sale]	
Amount on which provision is to be made1,00,000	
So, the provision to be made is	Rs. 5,000

(2) Closing Stock. As already explained, closing stock is valued at cost or market price, whichever is lower. Since closing stock is calculated on the last day of the year, it is taken as closing adjustment entry. Therefore, the value of closing stock appears at two places viz. credit side of Trading account and under Current assets in the Balance sheet. But, if the closing stock is given in the trial balance, it means that closing stock has been valued before preparation of trial balance and hence the accounting entry for closing stock has been made. The balance appearing in trial balance, therefore, is asset and will go to the asset side of balance sheet.

(3) Outstanding Expenses. Outstanding expenses mean those expenses, which are due to be paid by the firm, but they are still not paid in cash. Examples are outstanding salary, outstanding rent, Insurance premium etc. The following entry is made for outstanding expenses:

Expense A/c Dr.
To Outstanding Expense A/c

This will result in adding the outstanding amount to the amount appearing in the trial balance and showing the outstanding expense account as current liability in the balance sheet.

(4) Prepaid Expenses. Prepaid expenses are those which will become due for payment in the next year or the part of payment made belongs to the next year but the whole payment is made in the current year. Example are: Prepaid insurance, salary, commission etc. The following accounting entry is made for prepaid expenses:

Prepaid Expense A/c Dr.
To Expense A/c

This will result in reducing the account of the expense by the amount prepaid and showing the prepaid expense account as current asset in the balance sheet.

Illustration 2 : Trial balance as on 31-3-2005 shows Debit of Insurance premium account Rs. 6,000. But, Insurance premium paid Rs. 4,000 was for period from 1-1-2005 to 31-12-2005.

Here, Rs. 4000 were paid for the period from 1-1-2005 to 31-12-2005 out of which only 3 months, *i.e.,* 1-1-2005 to 31-3-2005 belongs to the current financial year. Rest 9 months' premium has been paid in advance.

So, the pre paid premium will be 4,000 * 9/12 = Rs. 3,000

The accounting entry to be passed is
Prepaid Insurance A/c Dr. 3,000
To Insurance A/c 3,000

(5) Outstanding Income. It refers to the incomes accrued to the firm but not received in cash. It may be commission, rent receivable etc. The accounting entry for outstanding income is:

Outstanding Income A/c Dr.
To Income A/c

Outstanding income will appear in the balance sheet as current asset.

(6) Income Received in Advance. Many a times, the firm may receive certain income in the current year which is due to it in the next financial year. Such receipt is known as income received in advance. The accounting entry will be:

Income A/c Dr.
To Income Received in Advance A/c

(7) Hidden Entries. Sometimes, some closing entries are hidden in the question which the reader is expected to notice. For example, the trial balance may give two figures : 6% Debentures : Rs, 50,000; Interest on debentures : Rs. 1,500. As one can notice that the total interest due for payment on these debentures was Rs. 3,000 for the year. But only Rs. 1,500 has entered the books. This means that the rest 1,500 is due but not paid and no accounting entry for this has been passed. Therefore, closing entry will be passed debiting the P&L account by Rs. 1,500 as Interest on debentures due but not paid and showing the same amount as current liability in the balance sheet.

(8) Commission Problem. A common type of question sometimes asked is about the calculation of commission of Manager, Director etc. In such questions, the wordings of the question are very important. For example, suppose, the net profit(before commission) of the firm is Rs. 11,000. The manager is entitled to get a commission of 10% on net profit. Now, since the net profit can be decided only after deducting the manager's commission, this profit involves the net profit as well as the manager's commission. So, if the net profit is say, 100 then after adding 10% commission, the profit before commission should be 110. So, in this case, the manager's commission will be (11000 * 10/110) = 1000 and net profit will be Rs. 10,000. In this way manager's commission is now 10% of the net profit.

But, there is catch. This procedure should be adopted only if the expenditure is to be deducted from the revenues for finding out the net profit. If any appropriation of profit is to be made, flat calculation should be made. For example, in the above case, if 10% of net profit is to be reserved for contingency, then the reserve amount will be (11000 * 10/100) = Rs. 1100. This is because reserve is created after calculating the net profit unlike the manager's commission which is calculated before finding net profit.

FINAL ACCOUNTS OF PARTNERSHIP

Final accounts of partnership firm are prepared in the same way i.e. Trading and Profit and loss accounts are prepared along with the balance sheet. Apart from these accounts, partnership firms also prepare an additional account i.e. Profit and Loss Appropriation account. This account is prepared to show the appropriation of the net profit and distributing the profit among the partners in their profit sharing ratio. Also, instead of preparing one capital account, separate capital account is prepared for each partner. The following is the format of profit and loss appropriation account:

Dr. **Profit and Loss Appropriation A/c** **Cr.**

Particulars	Amount	Particulars	Amount
To Transfer to general reserve		By Net profit for the year	
To Transfer to sinking fund			
To Transfer to capital accounts			
A's Capital account			
B's Capital account			
C's Capital account			

Nature of Non-profit Organisation

Charitable institutions like clubs, hospitals, schools etc. do not carry on trading and hence do not earn profit. They do not prepare a trading and profit and loss account. But they also want to know whether their incomes are sufficient to meet current expenses and what is their financial position at the end of the accounting period. Therefore, they prepare two types of accounts viz.,

1. Income and Expenditure A/c and
2. Receipt and Payment A/c

Apart from it, they also prepare Balance sheet like a trading firm.

Income and Expenditure Account. This account is very similar to the Profit and Loss Account. The difference between the revenues and expenses is not treated as profit or loss but considered as Surplus (excess of revenue over expenditure) or Deficit (excess of expenditure over revenue). This account contains all the incomes and revenues for the current year only whether received or paid in cash or accrued.

Receipts and Payment Account. Receipts and payments account is a summary of cash transactions appearing in the cash book. To keep a note of daily transactions of the organization, such organizations prepare receipts and payment account. It is like a cash or bank account. All the receipts and payments whether of the current year or any other year, whether capital or revenue gets recorded in this account. Accordingly, the closing balance of this account does not mean that income for the year has exceeded the expenditure by an amount equal to the balance in hand.

BALANCE SHEET

Balance sheet in case of a non-trading concern is prepared in the usual way and contains particulars of all assets and liabilities of the institution. The excess of assets over liabilities is termed as **'Capital Fund'**. The capital fund is made up of excess of income over expenditure and other incomes or surplus which might have been capitalized by the institution form time to time.

Distinction Between R/P Account and I/E Account

RECEIPTS AND PAYMENT A/C	INCOME AND EXPENDITURE A/C
It is a real account	It is a nominal account
It is like cash account of a business entity	It is like Profit and Loss account of a business entity
It has opening and closing balance of cash in hand and bank	It has no opening balance. The difference between credit and debit is transferred to balance sheet as excess of income over expenditure or vice-versa.
Receipts and payments relating to any accounting period are recorded in the year of receipt or payment	Income and expenditure of an accounting period gets recorded in the income and expenditure account of respective period only
It includes both capital and revenue receipts and payments	It includes only revenue incomes and expenditures
Balance sheet need not accompany this account	Balance sheet must accompany this account
Debit side of this account records receipts and the credit side records payments during the year.	Debit side of this account records expenses and the credit side records incomes for the year.

TREATMENT OF CERTAIN PECULIAR ITEMS

The treatment of certain peculiar receipts and payments in such organizations is as below:

(*a*) Any money received by such organizations for performing a specific activity in future like sports is called Endowment fund. It is capital receipt and figures only in the Receipt and Payment Account.

(*b*) General Donations received from time to time may be added to the Capital Fund or be treated as revenue receipts depending on the nature of the enterprise and the amount. But, in case of charitable institutions, they are treated as income.

(*c*) Specific Donations received for special purposes are to be used only for that activity. So, this amount is shown on the liability side of balance sheet and expenses done out of that fund are shown as deductions from the fund.

(*d*) Legacy is a sum received at the wish of a deceased person and should be treated as capital receipt.

(*e*) The Membership Fee or Entrance Fee should be treated as revenue receipt if it is received every year. If received once in the life time, it should be capitalized.

(*f*) Capitation Fee is collected by the educational institutions in a lump sum from the students seeking admission in a school or a college. This amount is quite heavy and is meant for development of the institution or incurring some capital expenditure. This amount is taken to balance sheet either as separate item or added to the Capital fund.

METHODOLOGY OF ANSWER

In the examination paper, generally the questions give figure appearing in one account i.e. either Income and Expenditure account or Receipt and payment account. With this certain additional information is also given. With the help of these, it is required to arrive at a figure which should appear in the other account. While solving such question, one should keep in mind the differences in the two accounts, the key among them are:

1. Receipts and payment account records receipts and payments relating to any year happening in the current year. But, income and expenditure account records income and expenditure relating to current year only

irrespective of the year in which it was received.

2. Receipts and payment account records revenue as well as capital receipts and payments whereas Income and expenditure account records only revenue incomes and expenditures.

Receipt and payment account to Income and expenditure account : If, in the question, the income appearing in the Receipts and payment account is given, the following steps should be followed to arrive at the income which should appear in the Income and expenditure account:

Step 1 : Take the income appearing in the Receipt and Payment account

Step 2 : Deduct the incomes which belongs to the year preceding and succeeding the current year but received in the current year.

Step 3 : Add the incomes received in the preceding or succeeding year but belonging to the current year.

This will give you the figure which should appear in the Income and Expenditure account. Same process should be followed for the expenditures. But, in case the figure given in the question belongs to Income and expenditure account, to arrive at the figure of Receipt and payment account the above steps should be reversed i.e. deduct will become add and add will be come deduct.

Income and Expenditure Account of Professionals

Professionals like Doctors, lawyers etc. have a peculiar distinction from other organizations. Professionals prepare their accounts on the cash basis and therefore, they ignore outstanding incomes. They do take into account outstanding expenses but not income that has not yet been received. This is because they do not file suits for recovery of their dues. Hence they prepare **Receipt and Expenditure Account** which means that all incomes are considered on the receipt i.e. cash basis and all expenditures are considered on accrual basis. To reflect this, on one hand, they add the outstanding income to the corresponding income head, and on the other hand they debit the Receipt and Expenditure account with the outstanding income as reserve. This nullifies the effect of crediting the outstanding income.

PARTNERSHIP ACCOUNTS

Introduction

Partnership has been defined in the Indian Partnership Act, 1932. According to it, 'Partnership is the relation between two or more persons who have agreed to share profits of a business carried on by all or any of them acting for all'. It is voluntary for a partnership firm to register. But, the law provides certain benefits to the partnership firms which are registered. The partners may or may not have a written agreement. In absence of any agreement to the contrary, the following rules apply:

(*a*) Every partner is entitled to share the profits or losses equally.

(*b*) No partner is entitled to any interest on his capital nor interest is charged on drawings.

(*c*) A partner is not entitled to any salary from the firm for his work as a partner.

(*d*) A partner is entitled to interest @6% p.a. for any loans given by him to the firm.

Partnership Deed

Partnership is created by an agreement but it is not necessary that the agreement should be in writing. But to avoid future disputes, it is always better to have it in writing. The document containing the important terms of partnership as agreed by the partners between themselves is called 'Partnership Deed'. It contains all the details regarding salary to be paid to any partner, interest on capital and drawings, duration of the firm, rules regarding operation of bank accounts, management of the firm etc. In the absence of any agreement in writing, the rights and duties of partners will be those as given in the Partnership Act, 1932.

Rights of Partners

Every partner in a partnership firm has the following rights, according to the Indian Partnership Act:

1. Right to take part in the conduct and management of business.

2. Right to be consulted and heard in all matters affecting the business of the partnership.
3. Right of free access to all records, books and accounts of the business, and also to examine and copy them.
4. Right of share in profits equally, in absence of any agreement
5. Partner is entitled to be indemnified by the firm for all the acts done by him in the course of the partnership business, for all payments made by him in respect of partnership debts or liabilities and for expenses and disbursements made by him in an emergency for protecting the firm from the loss.
6. Every partner is a joint owner of the partnership property. He is entitled to have the partnership property used exclusively for the purposes of the partnership.
7. Every partner is entitled to prevent the introduction of a new partner into the firm without his consent.
8. Every partner has a right to retire according to the agreement or with the consent of the other partners. If the partnership is at will, he can retire merely by giving notice to other partners.
9. A retiring partner or the heirs of the deceased partner are entitled to share in the profits earned with the aid of the proportion of assets belonging to such outgoing partner until the accounts are finally settled.

Duties of Partners

(*a*) Every partner is bound to diligently carry on the business of the firm to the greatest common advantage.

(*b*) A partner is bound to keep and render true, proper and correct accounts of the partnership.

(*c*) A partner is bound to indemnify the firm for any loss caused by his willful neglect or fraud in the conduct of the business.

(*d*) A partner must not carry on a competing business, nor use the property of the firm for his private purposes.

(*e*) Every partner is bound to share the losses equally with the others.

(*f*) A partner is bound to act within the scope of his authority.

(*g*) No partner can assign or transfer his partnership interest to any other person so as to make him a partner in the business, without consent of other partners.

Kinds of Partners

Besides the usual partners who contribute to the capital of the firm and take part in its business who are known as Active Partners, the following types of partners may also exist :

(1) Sleeping Partner : A Sleeping partner does not take part in the day today activities of the business. He merely contributes capital and shares profit or losses. But, he is liable to outsiders for debts of the firm.

(2) Nominal Partner : A Nominal partner merely lends his name to the firm to be used as a partner but neither contributes capital not shares the profit/losses. But, he is liable to those third parties who give credit to the firm on the strength of his being a partner.

(3) Partner in Profit Only : As the name implies, this kind of partner shares only profit and not the losses of business. But, in case of insolvency of firm, his liability to outsider for the payment of debts of the firm is similar to those of other partners.

(4) Partner by Estoppel and Holding Out : Partner by Estoppel is one who without really being a partner, so conducts himself as to lead others to believe him to be a partner. Similarly, if one is declared to be a partner in a firm and does not disclaim the partnership, he is treated as partner by Holding out. Such persons are also liable to third parties who give credit to the firm on the belief of his being a partner.

(5) Sub-Partner : A Sub-partner gets a share of profits of the firm from one of the partners. He has no rights against the firm and he is not liable to its debts also.

(6) Minor Partner : A minor can be admitted to the benefits of an existing partnership with the consent of all the partners. His position is peculiar in the firm. He is not personally liable for the debts of the firm like other partners, only his share in the partnership property and profits of the firm are liable. He can sue the firm for the accounts and his share when he wants to severe his connections with the firm but not otherwise. After attaining majority, within 6 months he has to decide whether he wants to become a regular partner in the firm or wants to withdraw from the firm.

Capital Account

Partners may maintain their capital accounts in either of two systems :

1. Fixed Capital System
2. Fluctuating Capital system

In Fixed Capital System a Capital A/c and Current A/c is opened for each partner. The initial capital brought by the partner is credited to the capital a/c. The adjustments regarding salary, interest, drawings, profit etc. are made in the current accounts of the partners. In the *Fluctuating Capital System,* only one Capital account is maintained and all the transactions related to the capital are recorded in this account.

To transfer the net profit of the firm between the partners, the firm prepares an account called "Profit and Loss Appropriation A/c" which contains all the appropriations out of the net profits including the reserves and distribution of profit to the partners.

Joint Life Policy

A partnership firm may decide to take a joint life insurance policy on the lives of all partners. The firm pays the premium and the amount of policy is payable to the firm in the event of death of any partner or on maturity of the policy. The objective is to minimize the financial hardship to the firm in the event of payment of a large sum to the legal representative of a deceased partner. The premium paid is treated as the revenue expenditure of the firm and debited to the P&L account. On maturity of the policy, the amount is received by the firm and is credited to all the partners' capital account in the profit sharing ratio.

Certain firms treat the insurance premium as capital expenditure. In that case a 'Joint Life Insurance Policy' account is opened and the premium paid is debited to this account. The surrender value of the policy is credited to this account as the balance to be carried forward to the next year. The difference between the premium paid and the surrender value is debited to P&L account as loss. Surrender Value remains to be shown on the asset side of the balance sheet till the maturity. On maturity of the policy the amount realized is credited to this account and final balance is distributed between all the partners in the profit sharing ratio.

Admission of a Partner

Sometimes, the firm may introduce a new partner to add to the capital of the business or associate with a renowned businessman or for any other purpose. But a new partner cannot be admitted without the consent of all the partners unless otherwise agreed upon. This admission of a new partner raises various issues.

(A) Legal Position. From admission of a new partner, the following legal consequences arise:

1. On admission of new partner, legally the old partnership is considered to be dissolved. However, the partnership firm is not dissolved. Profit sharing ratio of old partners is changed and partnership relation between all the partners (including the new one) comes into existence.
2. The new partner becomes liable for all future acts of the firm i.e., he becomes liable jointly and severally in respect of all liabilities created after his admission. However, he is not liable for liabilities created by the firm before he was admitted as a partner.
3. Old partners are liable for all the debts of the firm existing on the date of new partner's admission.

(B) Revaluation of Assets and Liabilities. To determine the share of the new partner as well as how much he should bring as capital and goodwill to be entitled to his share of profit, the true value of the firm as on the date of admission of the partner has to be calculated. For that purpose, all the assets and liabilities of the firm are revalued and the net value of the firm is found out.

This is done through an intermediary account called "Profit and Loss Adjustment Account" or "Revaluation Account". Any increase or decease in the asset or liability of the firm is shown in the revaluation account and the final balance of this account is transferred to the old partners in the old profit sharing ratio.

Sometimes, the partners decide that even though the assets and liabilities are revalued, the value in the books of account should not be changed. In such a situation, 'Memorandum Revaluation Account' is prepared. In this account the assets and liabilities are revalued and the resulting profit/loss is distributed between the old partners. Then again the assets and liabilities are brought to the original book values and the resultant profit and loss is shared by the new partners. In this process the net treatment in the old partners' capital account is in the Sacrifice ratio. An example of Memorandum revaluation account is shown as below :

MEMORANDUM REVALUATION ACCOUNT

Particulars	Amount	Particulars	Amount
To Furniture	500	By Land & Building	5,000
To Stock	1,000		
To Provision for bad debts	300		
To Machinery	2,000		
To Profit transferred to old Partners			
A 300			
B 400			
C 500	1,200		
	5,000		5,000
To Reverse entry for increase in value of L & B	5,000	By Reverse entry for decrease in value of assets	3,800
		By Loss transferred to new partners	
		A 300	
		B 300	
		C 300	
		D 300	1,200
	5,000		5,000

The Journal Entries for revaluation of assets and liabilities are as follow :

(a) Increase in the market value of the asset

Asset A/c Dr.

To Revaluation A/c

(b) Decrease in the value of an asset

Revaluation A/c Dr.

To Asset A/c

(c) To reduce the debtors, new Bad Debts Reserve is created

Revaluation A/c Dr.

To Bad Debt Reserve A/c

(d) If any liability is to be brought to the books of account or increase in the liability

Revaluation A/c Dr.

To Liability A/c

(e) When a liability is cancelled or reduced by settlement

Liability A/c Dr.

To Revaluation A/c

(f) For recording income due but not received or prepaid expenses

Income Receivable A/c	Dr.
Prepaid Expenses A/c	Dr.
To Revaluation A/c	

(g) To transfer the balance of the revaluation account to the partners' capital account (if Profit)

Revaluation A/c	Dr.
To Old Partners' Capital A/c	

If there is any Loss, reverse entry is passed.

(h) To transfer any balance in the Reserves account to the old partners

Reserve Fund A/c	Dr.
To, Old Partners' Capital A/c	

(C) New Profit Sharing Ratio of Partners after Admission. After the admission of new partner, the new profit sharing ratio of all the partners has to be determined for sharing future profits. For this purpose, the new partner may either get a fixed share in the firm's profits or he gets from the share of the old partners (purchase of share). In both the ways, the old partners have to sacrifice some part of their share in the profits in favour of the new partner. The proportion in which the old partners' contribute towards the share of the new partner is known as the **'Sacrifice Ratio'.**

(D) Capital of the New Partner. When the new partner is admitted to the firm, he generally brings capital to the firm. This capital may be brought in cash or in form of some asset. The amount of capital is determined by all the partners based on the value of the firm and the share of profit proposed to be given to the new partner. Sometimes, the new partner in his personal capacity may have given loan to the firm which is converted into his capital on being admitted as the partner. Moreover, it is not compulsory for the new partner to bring capital. For example, a manager of the firm may be made partner without bringing any capital to the firm.

(E) Distribution of Accumulated Profit. When a new partner is admitted, there may be existing accumulated profit in the firm. It may be in the name of Reserve Fund or credit balance of Profit and Loss Account. There may also be accumulated losses in the form of debit balance of Profit and Loss Account. This accumulated profit or loss belongs to the old partners and must be distributed among the old partners in the old profit sharing ratio before the new partner is admitted. The journal entry for this purpose is as below :

Reserve Fund A/c	Dr.
Capital Reserve A/c	Dr.
Profit & Loss A/c	Dr.
To Old Partners' Capital A/cs	

For accumulated losses, the entry will be reverse.

But, if there are specific reserves against assets in the books of the firm like Bad Debt Reserve, Depreciation Fund, Investment Fluctuation Fund etc., they are not free reserves and cannot be distributed among the partners.

(F) Treatment of Goodwill. On admission, the new partner has to pay some compensation, other than the capital, to acquire a share in the future profits of the firm, which is termed as goodwill. Goodwill is nothing but a possibility that the old customers will stick to the old firm.

The main base for calculation of goodwill is its profit earning capacity and hence past profits are taken into account for its calculation. There are many factors which determine the earning capacity of the business such as place of business, personal skills, control over raw material, latest technology, trade mark etc. In the following circumstances, the calculation of goodwill is necessary in the partnership firm :

(1) When a new partner is admitted into the firm

(2) When a partner retires or dies

(3) When firm is dissolved

(4) When Profit sharing ratio of partners is changed

(5) When method of computation of Profit is changed

Valuation of Goodwill

There are various methods of calculation of goodwill. Some of them are explained here :

(1) Simple Average Profit Method. In this method, Goodwill is computed on the basis of 3 to 5 years' profit of the firm depending on the estimated period up to which the benefit of goodwill will be available. By taking average profit, the effect of fluctuation in the profits is eliminated. For example, if the average profit of the firm for last 5 years is Rs. 20,000 and goodwill is to be valued at 3 times the average profit of last 5 years, the value of goodwill will be Rs. 60,000.

(2) Weighted Average Profit Method. This method is similar to the earlier one. The difference is that in this method, higher weightage is given to the profits earned in the recent period based upon assumption that the recent trend is likely to continue in the future. So, weights are given to all the years whose average is taken. The formula for weighted average profit is :

$$\text{Weighted Average Profit} = \frac{\text{Total Weighted Profit}}{\text{Total Weights}}$$

For example,

Year	Profits	Weights	Weighted Profits
1999	12,000	1	12,000
2000	18,000	2	36,000
2001	26,000	3	78,000
2002	31,000	4	1,24,000
2003	40,000	5	2,00,000
Total		15	4,50,000

Weighted Average Profit = 4,50,000 / 15 = 30,000

Value of goodwill = 30,000 × 3 = Rs. 90,000

(3) Capitalisation Method. In this method, based on the current profits of the firm the capitalization is found out and it is compared with the present capitalization of the firm. The difference between the two is treated as goodwill. For example, the average profits of the firm for last 5 years are Rs. 16,000. The capitalization factor is 8%. So, the present capitalization of the firm is (16,000 *100 / 8) = 2,00,000. If the capital required to earn this much profit as per the market conditions is Rs. 2,50,000 then the goodwill of the firm is Rs. 50,000.

Treatment of Goodwill in the Books on Admission of Partner

Goodwill is an asset of the old firm and the old partners. So, when the new partner brings in goodwill, it is transferred to the old partners. The recording of goodwill in the books depends on how the partners wish to treat goodwill. In following different circumstances, the recording of goodwill in the books of account will be different:

(a) **When the new partner pays the old partners goodwill in cash outside the firm :** In this case no record is made in the books of the firm. The amount is paid to partners outside the firm. So, the question of making any entry in the books of the firm does not arise.

(b) **When goodwill is brought in cash and retained in the business :** In such a case, only two entries are made. The first is for bringing goodwill in cash, *i.e.,*

Cash A/c Dr.
To Goodwill A/c

Then this amount of goodwill is transferred to the old partners' capital account in the proportion of Sacrifice Ratio.

Goodwill A/c Dr.
To Old Partners' Capital A/c

(*c*) **When goodwill is brought in cash and withdrawn by partners :** Here, first, the above two entries will be passed. In addition, one more entry will be passed as below:

Old Partners' Capital A/c Dr.
To Cash A/c

Here also, the goodwill is credited to the old partners in the sacrifice ratio.

Note : It should be remembered that in all the above methods, the goodwill does not remain in the books. If the partners wish it to appear in the balance sheet, then the goodwill account is debited and the new partners' account is credited in the new profit sharing ratio. Moreover, if any old goodwill is already appearing in the books of the old firm, the same is to be written off to the old partners' capital account.

(*d*) **Revaluation Method :** In this case, the new partner does not bring goodwill in cash. Instead, the goodwill of the firm is valued and the old partners are given credit according to their sacrifice ratio. Here also, if the firm wishes the value of goodwill to appear in the books of account then only the following entry is passed :

Goodwill A/c Dr.
To, Old Partners' Capital A/c
(Old Profit sharing Ratio)

And if the firm does not want goodwill to appear in the books then after passing the above entry the following additional entry is passed :

All Partners' Capital A/c Dr.
(New Profit sharing ratio)
To Goodwill A/c

Retirement/Death of a Partner

When any partner retires from the partnership or if he dies, the following important points arise again:

(1) Treatment of Goodwill and New Profit Sharing Ratio. In this case, since the future profits will be shared only by the remaining partners, they stand to gain. So, they have to compensate the outgoing partner for this. This compensation is made by the remaining partners in the **'Gaining Ratio'.** The gaining ratio is decided based on what proportion of profit share of the outgoing partner is taken by which partner. So, it is again a difference between the old and new profit sharing ratios. On retirement, the treatment of goodwill may be done in any of the following ways :

(*a*) Goodwill may be raised in the books as an asset and credited to all the partners including the retiring partner in the old profit sharing ratio.

(*b*) After raising the goodwill as above, it is written off between the remaining partners in the new profit sharing ratio.

(*c*) Retiring partner's share of goodwill may be adjusted in the capital accounts of the continuing partners in the gaining ratio without opening the goodwill account.

The following is an example of treatment of goodwill in method (c) as above :

(2) Revaluation of Assets and Liabilities. On death or retirement of a partner, a Revaluation account or P&L adjustment account is prepared to find out the profit or loss on the revaluation of assets. As in the case of admission of partner, here also all the profits or losses on revaluation are taken into account in the P&L adjustment account. The net profit or loss on revaluation is transferred to all the old partners (including the retired or deceased partner) in their old profit sharing ratio.

(3) Distribution of Accumulated Profits and Reserves. As in the case of admission of partner, here also, all the existing accumulated profits and reserves of the firm are transferred to old partners' capital account (including the retiring or deceased partner) in the old profit sharing ratio. Many a times, firm may only transfer the share of the retiring or the deceased partner to his capital account. This can be used only when the profit sharing ratio of the remaining partners remains unchanged.

(4) Amount due to the Retiring Partner. The retiring partner's capital account is credited with his share of goodwill, profit on revaluation of assets, past profits and reserves etc. and is debited by drawings or accumulated losses etc. The balance in the capital account represents the amount due to him by the firm. This amount is transferred to the Partner's Loan account until it is paid off.

Dissolution of Partnership

When a partnership ceases to exist, it is said to be dissolved. The dissolution may take place with the consent between the partners or by the decision of court in certain circumstances. The following issues arise on dissolution of the partnership.

(A) Realisation Account. A new account, called Realisation account is opened for arriving at the profit or loss made by the firm while dissolving the firm. All assets, other than cash and bank, are transferred to Realisation account at their book values. Similarly, all the liabilities other than capital and reserves are transferred to this account. The payments made for the liabilities are debited to the account and similarly the amounts realized from the assets are credited to this account. The expenses of dissolution are also debited to Realisation account.

The balance of Realisation account, profit or loss, is transferred to the capital accounts of the partners. Balances in the reserve account or P&L account are transferred to the partners' capital accounts in the profit sharing ratio. Partner's current accounts are also transferred to the Capital account. The balance in the capital account is their dues from the firm.

(B) Treatment of Goodwill. It is treated like any other asset in the balance sheet. Any balance appearing in the goodwill account is transferred to the Realisation account. Since, goodwill is not sold separately, generally no cash is realized against goodwill. It is reflected in the higher selling price of other assets.

(C) Insolvency of a Partner. When a partner is adjudicated as insolvent and he owes a sum of money to the firm, the uncollected portion of his dues is a loss to the firm. The question arises as to the distribution of this loss to the existing partners whether it should be divided into the capital accounts balance proportion or in the profit sharing ratio.

The decision in this regard was given by the court in the case of **Garner V/s Murray**. Court made a distinction between ordinary loss due to realization of assets and extraordinary loss due to insolvency of a partner. According to it, the following rules are observed for sharing the loss arising due to insolvency of a partner :

1. The solvent partners should bring in cash to make up their share of realization account loss.
2. The loss due to insolvency of a partner should be arrived at after transferring all the balances in the P&L A/c and reserves to all the partners in the profit sharing ratio.
3. The loss due to the insolvency of the partner is divided among the other partners in the fixed capital ratio, if the capital is fixed or in the ratio of capital balances after transferring any transferable balances appearing in the balance sheet but before adjusting profit or loss on the realisation, if the capital is fluctuating.
4. If any solvent partner has negative balance (debit) in the capital account, he will not share the loss arising due to insolvency of a partner. This will happen only in case of fluctuating capital account system. In fixed capital system, all the partners will have credit balance.

(D) When All Partners are Insolvent. When all partners are insolvent, the creditors of the firm will suffer as they cannot be repaid in full. In such a situation, the balance in the creditors' account should not be transferred to the Realisation account. A separate account should be opened for creditors. They should be paid whatever can be recovered from the private assets of the partners after paying the realisation expenses. The balance in the creditors' account should be transferred to the partners' capital account in the profit sharing ratio and the books of the firm are closed.

Piecemeal Distribution of Assets

In practice, when a firm is dissolved, all the assets are not sold on a single day. They are realized gradually and the liabilities are discharged as and when the cash is available. In this sequence, the liabilities to the third parties are first paid out, then the partners' loans, if any, and finally the partners' capital is returned. Here the question arises as to the basis of distribution of cash to the partners for their capital balances (when capital ratio is different from profit sharing ratio), after paying outside liabilities. For this purpose one of the following two methods may be adopted :

(1) Proportionate or Surplus Capital Method. In this method, the partners' capitals are arranged according to the profit sharing ratio by taking the least capital for one share as the base. If there is any surplus, the least surplus is eliminated and the extra surplus is determined. The extra surplus is first paid to the concerned partners in their due proportion. This results in equal ratio of capital and profit sharing. Now, the balance amount is distributed in this ratio.

(2) Maximum Loss Method. Under this method, it is assumed that every realization of assets is the final realization and according to that the loss is arrived at and divided among the partners in their profit sharing ratio. Any debit balance in the capital account will be transferred to other partners in the capital account ratio. Now, all the partners' balance will be equal to the available cash in hand and will be distributed to them according to their respective balances. This process will continue till the last asset is realized.

❑ ❑ ❑

Chapter 4

Accounting of Joint Stock Companies

Before going through this chapter, it is advisable to go through the salient features of the companies as well as the Companies Act (both explained in this book in detail) to get a full idea of the functioning of the companies and its salient features.

SHARE CAPITAL

A company is a legal entity separate from its owners. But as far as the accounting is concerned, the basic rules are same whether it is a company or a firm. Though there are some peculiarities in the company accounts which we shall discuss as we go along, the basic difference is that unlike in the partnership where there are few owners, in companies the owners may run into thousands. All of them hold share in the company. The various divisions of share capital are as follows :

Authorized or Nominal Capital : It is the capital mentioned in the Capital clause of the Memorandum of Association of the company with which the company is registered. The company cannot issue shares more than the authorized capital unless Capital clause is altered.

Issued Capital : It is that portion of authorized capital which is offered to the public for subscription. The remaining part of the Authorized capital is known as the 'Unissued Capital' which can be issued later on..

Subscribed Capital : Out of the issued capital, the portion for which public subscribe to the shares of the company is called subscribed capital.

Called up Capital : It is that portion of the subscribed capital which has been called up by the company from the shareholders. Capital is generally called on allotment as well as through various instalments known as 'Calls'.

Paid up Capital : It represents that portion of the Called up capital with regard to which the company has received call money from the shareholders.

Reserve Capital : According to Section 99 of the Companies Act a company may, by a special resolution determine that a portion of its uncalled capital should not be called up, except in the event of winding up of the company.

ISSUE OF SHARES

When the company issues shares to the public, the journal entries in respect of various transactions are explained as below :

TRANSACTION	ACCOUNTING ENTRY	
	DEBIT	CREDIT
(1) Receipt of application money	Bank A/c	Share Application A/c
(2) Application money in respect of shares allotted	Share Application A/c	Share Capital A/c
(3) Refund for rejected applications	Share Application A/c	Bank A/c
(4) Adjustment of excess application money towards allotment	Share Application A/c	Share Allotment A/c
(5) Adjustment of excess application money towards calls-in-advance	Share Application A/c	Calls-in-advance A/c
(6) When allotment is made and money is due	Share Allotment A/c	Share Capital A/c
(7) Receipt of allotment money	Bank A/c	Share Allotment A/c
(8) Where a call is made for the call money due	Share Call A/c	Share Capital A/c
(9) Adjustment of money in calls-in-advance towards the call account	Calls-in-advance A/c	Share Call A/c
(10) Receipt of call money	Bank A/c	Share Call A/c

When the company receives applications for shares more than it wants to issue, it gives pro-rata allotment to the applicants. For example, if the company wants to allot 1000 shares and number of shares applied are 3000, the company will allot only 1/3rd of the shares applied by the applicants. The balance amount on application is either adjusted as calls in advance or is refunded to the applicants.

CALLS-IN-ADVANCE AND ARREARS

When the applicant sends more money than required, the excess money is called calls-in-advance. Such a calls-in-advance can be accepted only when the company is so authorized by its Articles of Association. If the company has adopted Table A, then it is required to pay 6% interest on such amount. The shareholder is not entitled to any dividend on the amount paid as calls-in-advance.

On the other hand, if shareholder makes default in sending call money according to conditions, then money not so sent is called calls-in-arrear. It is a liability of the shareholder and default to pay this may lead to forfeiture of shares.

ISSUE OF SHARES FOR CONSIDERATION OTHER THAN CASH

Shares are sometimes issued to certain persons for consideration other than cash. For example issue of shares to a vendor who sells some asset to the company or to the promoters for their services. In the first case, the treatment is simple. In place of making payment by cheque, the payment is made in the form of shares and hence the share capital account will be credited in place of bank account. But, when the shares are issued to the promoters, the following accounting entry is made :

Goodwill A/c Dr.

To Share Capital A/c

The amount is debited to Goodwill account because it is considered that without the work of the promoters, it would not have been possible to create the company.

ISSUE OF SHARES AT PREMIUM

When a share is issued at a price which is above its face value, then it is said that it has been issued at premium. Share premium is often charged by the company at the time of allotment of shares. As per the Companies Act, 1956, such premium whether received in cash of in kind must be credited to a separate account called "Share Premium Account". Under Section 78 of Companies Act, the amount to the credit of this account may be used wholly or in part for following purposes :

1. Paying up un-issued shares of the company to be issued to members of the company as fully paid bonus shares.
2. Writing off the preliminary expenses of the company.
3. Writing off the expenses of, or the commission paid or discount allowed on any shares or of any debentures of the company.
4. Providing for the premium payable on the redemption of any redeemable preference shares or of any debentures of the company.

ISSUE OF SHARES AT DISCOUNT

When a share is issued at a price which is less than its face value then it is said that it has been issued at discount. A Company can issue share at discount on fulfilling the conditions of Section 79 of the Companies Act. Discount on issue of shares being a loss of capital nature, is shown on the asset side of the balance sheet and is amortised (written off) over a period of time decided by the company.

FORFEITURE OF SHARES

In case a member fails to pay any call on the day appointed for payment, the directors may, either by the adoption of Table A or by an express provision in its Articles, proceed to forfeit the shares held by such a defaulting shareholder. On forfeiture, the name of the shareholder is removed from the register of the company. But, before forfeiting shares, a proper notice requiring payment of the calls with interest should be served to the shareholder.

It may be noted that share capital account, on forfeiture, is debited with the called up amount(excluding the share premium called and paid by the shareholder) and not with the face value of the share.

FORFEITURE OF SHARES ISSUED AT PREMIUM / DISCOUNT

When shares issued at premium are forfeited, the share premium which was due and not paid by the shareholder should be cancelled by giving a debit entry to the share premium account. But, the share premium which was due and paid by the shareholder should not be cancelled. This is according to Sec. 78 of Companies Act that share premium once collected cannot be cancelled even if the shares are forfeited.

On the other hand, discount on issue of shares is a loss and is debited at the time of issue of shares. When these shares are forfeited, the discount on issue of shares account is credited to cancel the effect of earlier debit entry.

RE-ISSUE OF FORFEITED SHARES

Shares forfeited on the non-payment of calls can be re-issued by the company as and when company finds it suitable and convenient. But, the amount collected on re-issue together with the amount already paid before the share were forfeited should not be less than the amount credited as paid up on re-issue of shares. When the shares forfeited are re-issued at a discount, such discount is to be debited to forfeited shares account. After setting off the amount earlier received on shares, if still there is some balance, it should be transferred to Capital Reserve Account. The accounting entries on re-issue of shares are similar to those at the time of issue of fresh shares.

VALUE OF RIGHT SHARE

In case a company makes a further issue of shares to its existing shareholders, it is known as a Right Issue. The existing shareholders may accept or reject the offer of shares. They can even sell these right shares in the market. In such a situation it is important to know the value of the share being offered by the company as right. The following method is employed.

ISSUE OF BONUS SHARES

Bonus shares are those shares which are allotted to the existing equity shareholders of the company without any consideration, either in cash or in kind. In other words, these are free shares issued by the company to the existing shareholders in some ratio of their existing shareholding. Bonus shares can be issued subject to the provisions of the Articles of Association and the Companies Act, 1956. Issue of bonus shares result into the capitalization of profits and reserves of the company. According to the SEBI guidelines, following conditions must be observed while making any bonus issue :

1. Bonus issue should be made out of free reserves built out of genuine profits or share premium collected in cash only.
2. Reserves created out of revaluation of fixed assets should not be capitalized.
3. The bonus issue cannot be made unless the partly paid shares, if any, are made fully paid up.
4. The company has not defaulted in payment of interest or principal in respect of fixed deposits or debentures.
5. Consequent to the issue of bonus shares, if the subscribed and paid up capital exceeds the authorized share capital, resolution shall be passed by the company at its general meeting for increasing the authorized capital.

BROKERAGE

Brokerage is merely the act of procuring subscriptions for shares or debentures without any responsibility. The company pays brokerage to the broker on the shares subscribed through him and he has no obligation to take up the shares that may remain unsold.

REDEMPTION OF PREFERENCE SHARES

According to Section 80, the following are the rules for redemption of preference shares :

(*a*) The shares to be redeemed should be fully paid up.

(*b*) They can be redeemed either out of the profits of the company which would otherwise be available for dividend or out of the proceeds of a fresh issue of shares (may be equity but not debentures) made for the purpose of redemption.

(*c*) The premium payable on redemption must be provided either out of accumulated profits of the company or the Share Premium account before the shares are redeemed.

(*d*) When the shares are redeemed out of the profits, an amount equal to the nominal value of the shares so redeemed should be transferred from the profits to a reserve account called **Capital Redemption Reserve** account which may be used in issuing the fully paid bonus shares by the company.

(*e*) Redemption of preference shares does not amount to reduction in the authorized capital of the company.

It is to be noted that in "Proceeds of fresh issue of shares" as mentioned above, only the nominal value of shares issued should be considered for determining the amount to be credited to Capital Redemption Reserve Account. It means that any premium received on issue of shares should be disregarded. But if the shares are issued at discount, the actual proceeds of the issue (Discounted price of shares) should be deducted from the face value of preference shares to be redeemed to arrive at the amount to be transferred to CRR A/c. The following journal entries are passed by the company on redemption of preference shares :

(*a*) If the company makes fresh issue of shares

Bank A/c Dr.

To Share Capital A/c

To Share Premium Account

(if issued on premium)

(*b*) When preference shares are redeemed at premium

Share Premium A/c Dr.

Profit and Loss A/c Dr.

To Premium on Redemption A/c

(*c*) Transferring the Amount to the CRR A/c

Profit & Loss A/c Dr.

General Reserve A/c Dr.

To CRR A/c

(Face value of shares to be redeemed - Face value of fresh issue of shares)

(*d*) Transferring the capital to the shareholders A/c

Preference Shares A/c Dr.

Premium on Redemption A/c Dr.

To Preference Shareholders A/c

(*e*) When payment is made to the shareholders

Preference Shareholders A/c Dr.

To Bank A/c

Illustration 1 : A company has to redeem 1,000 preference shares of Rs. 100 each at Rs. 103. For this purpose, it issues 500 equity shares of Rs. 100 each at a premium of 10%. The following figures will be important :

Total amount to be redeemed (105 * 1000)	1,03,000
Share premium on equity shares (10 * 500)	5,000
Amount to be transferred to CRR A/c (1,00,000-50,000)	50,000

The premium to be paid on redemption will be adjusted against the premium received from the new issue. The balance amount of premium by the new issue will not be considered for determining the amount to be transferred to the CRR A/c. If the fresh issue of shares is to be determined according to the divisible profit available with the company, the minimum possible number of shares to be issued has to be determined. This can be arrived at by applying the following equation:

Face value of preference shares + Premium on redemption = Share Premium account in the balance sheet + Divisible profit available (including reserves) + Fresh shares to be issued (say 'X') + Premium on issue of fresh shares.

Illustration 2 : Preference shares of Rs. 20,000 are to be redeemed at 10% premium and the Balance of Profit and Loss account and General Reserves is Rs. 4,000 and Rs. 6000 respectively. Share premium accounts balance is Rs. 1,000. Fresh issue of shares is to be made at 10% premium.

Applying the formula, the company needs to issue shares of Rs. 10,000.

ISSUE AND REDEMPTION OF DEBENTURES

The accounting entries for issue of debentures are same as that of equity shares. The only difference is that after the issue of debentures, the company has to make regular payment of interest to the debenture holders. It should be kept in mind that the amount of interest payable to the debenture holders is calculated at the rate of interest those debentures are carrying multiplying it with the face value of debentures irrespective of the fact that the debentures may have been issued at par, or at premium or at discount. Also first interest is payable from the date of issue of debentures to the date of payment of interest (quarterly, half yearly or yearly).

Illustration 3 : A company has issued 1000, 8% debentures of Rs. 100 each at Rs. 95 to be repayable at Rs. 105 each to be repayable after 5 years. The interest is payable half yearly. The interest to be paid at the end of each half year will be

$$1000 \times 100 \times \frac{8}{100} \Big/ 2 = 4{,}000.$$

Another point is that if the debentures are issued at discount and to be redeemed at premium, the total loss on discount as well as the premium is booked at the time of issue itself by debiting the total amount to 'Loss on issue of debentures' A/c. This loss is considered as Deferred Revenue expenditure and is written off over the period of tenure of the debentures equally. If the debentures are repayable in installments, the amount is written off based on the proportion of the debentures outstanding at the end of each year.

Illustration 4 : In the above example, the total loss on issue of debentures is Rs. 10,000 (1,000 * 10). This loss will be written off over a period of 5 years i.e. Rs. 2,000 per year. If the debentures are to be redeemed in 5 installments starting from the end of the first year, the use of funds in 5 years will be Rs. 1,00,000, 80,000, 60,000, 40,000 and 20,000 respectively. So, the loss of Rs. 10,000 will be written off in the ratio of 5:4:3:2:1.

CUM-INTEREST AND EX-INTEREST PURCHASE OF DEBENTURES

Debentures may be purchased either on cum-interest basis or on ex-interest basis. If the debentures are purchased on cum-interest basis, it means that the price of the debenture includes the next installment of interest payable by the company. So, the purchaser of the debentures is entitled to the interest from the date of purchase. On the other hand, in ex-interest purchase, the next interest installment is received by the seller only and thereafter all the interests are received by the purchaser. So, ex-interest price of debentures is always lower than the cum-interest price.

MANNER OF REDEMPTION OF DEBENTURES

The debentures can be redeemed in any of the following ways :

(1) One time payment on maturity

(2) Payment in Instalments

(3) Purchase of debentures in open market

As regards, the first two manners, the accounting entries are simple. Complications arise in case debentures are redeemed by way of purchase in open market. Under this method also, the debentures may be purchased for two purposes :

(*a*) Purchase of debentures for redemption

(*b*) Purchase of debentures for investment

PURCHASE OF DEBENTURES FOR REDEMPTION

In this case, the company purchases debentures in the open market some time before the debentures are due for redemption. The purchased debentures are redeemed once the due date arrives and hence no payment need be made to the outsiders. In this case, the debentures may be purchased cum-interest or ex-interest.

Illustration 5: A company buys on 1-10-2004 own debentures of Rs. 10,000 of Rs. 100 each at Rs. 98 ex-interest for cancellation. Interest is payable @6% on 30th June and 31st December. The accounting entry will be

6% Debentures A/c	Dr.	10,000	
Interest on Debentures A/c	Dr.	150	
To Bank A/c			9950
To Profit on Redemption A/c			200

(Since the debentures were purchased ex-interest, original holder is entitled to the interest for the whole 6 months. On 31st December, since the debentures are held by the company, no interest will be paid. So, the interest will be paid to the original debenture holder for 3 months at the time of purchase and rest 3 months' interest is included in the purchase price. So interest will be debited only for 3 months instead of 6 months.)

In the same case, had the debentures been purchased on cum-interest, the company would have got the benefit of interest from October to December and hence the purchase price would have been only Rs. 98 and consequently, the profit would have been Rs. 350.

PURCHASE OF DEBENTURES AS INVESTMENT

Often, companies buy their own debentures as investment to save the interest which would otherwise have been payable. Such debentures are kept alive and can be disposed off again in the market. The accounting treatment is done like any other investment. When a company buys its own debentures as investment, an account called 'Own Debentures Account' will be debited with the amount actually paid, disregarding the nominal value of debentures purchased. When own debentures are bought and kept as investment, the interest on such debentures should be credited to the P&L account, the debit being given to the Interest on debentures account. In this manner, the interest on debentures account will show the full amount due on outstanding debentures. The credit to the P&L account shows the gain made by the purchase of own debentures.

The profit made by the company on redemption through open market purchase is a capital profit(which is considered when the debentures are cancelled). Any loss on issue of debentures may be written off against such profit. The balance of profit, if any should be transferred to Capital Reserve A/c.

Illustration 6 : A company issued 1000, 6% debentures of Rs. 1000 each. Interest is paid half yearly on 30th Sept. and 31st March. On February 1, 2004, the company purchased 20 of its own debentures as investment at Rs. 970. The journal entry will be as below:

		Dr.	Cr.
Own Debentures A/c	Dr.	19,400	
Interest on Debentures A/c	Dr.	400	
To Bank A/c			19,800

(Debentures purchased ex-interest, interest for 4 months being payable extra)

OR

		Dr.	Cr.
Own Debentures A/c	Dr.	19,000	
Interest on Debentures A/c	Dr.	400	
To Bank A/c			19,400

(Debentures purchased cum -interest, interest for 4 months included in the price)

		Dr.	Cr.
Interest on Debentures A/c	Dr.	200	
To Profit & Loss A/c			200

(Being the interest on debentures held by the company for 2 months)

		Dr.	Cr.
6% Debentures A/c	Dr.	20,000	
To Own Debentures A/c			19,400
To Profit on Redemption A/c			600

(Being the cancellation of the debentures purchased ex-interest. In case of cum-interest debentures, profit would be Rs. 1000)

REDEMPTION AT PREMIUM OF DEBENTURES ISSUED AT DISCOUNT

Sometimes, to attract the investors, the company may issue the debentures on the discount and in addition promise to redeem the debentures at premium. In such a case, since both the losses are known at the time of issue of debentures, they are taken into the accounts and is written off over a period of time.

DEBENTURE REDEMPTION RESERVE/ SINKING FUND

When debentures are to be redeemed, the company has to arrange a large amount of cash for payment. This may affect the company's working capital. To avoid such a situation and to pay the debentures out of the profits, the company creates Debenture

Redemption Reserve. Every year, the company transfers some part of its profit to this account and this amount is invested by the company in some liquid assets. The transfer made every year and the income on such investments keeps on accumulating and when the debentures are to be redeemed, the company sells this investment and repays the debentures. The following journal entries are made in this respect :

(1) When amount is transferred to the reserve
P&L Appropriation A/c Dr.
To Debenture Redemption Reserve A/c

(2) When the amount is invested
DRR Investment A/c Dr.
To Bank A/c

(3) Interest on investment is received
Bank A/c Dr.
To DRR A/c

(4) When investing the total amount including the interest received
DRR Investment A/c Dr.
To Bank A/c

(5) On sale of investment
Bank A/c Dr.
To DRR Investment A/c

(6) Transferring the loss/profit on sale of investment
DRR Investment A/c (if Profit) Dr.
To DRR A/c

(7) Transfer of balance in DRR A/c
DRR A/c Dr.
To General Reserve A/c

Note : The above entries are similar to those made for creation of sinking fund for replacement of a fixed asset.

FORM OF BALANCE SHEET

Every company has to follow the form of balance sheet as given in Schedule VI of Companies Act which has been reproduced as below :

Balance Sheet of XYZ Ltd. as at 31st March, 2008

PARTICULARS	AMT.	PARTICULARS	AMT.
SHARE CAPITAL Authorised shares of Rs------each Issued: (distinguishing between various classes of capital) ----- shares of Rs. ------ each Subscribed : ------- shares of Rs. ------ each Of the above shares, ----- shares are allotted as fully paid up pursuant to a contract without payment being received in cash. Of the above shares,-----shares are allotted as fully paid up by way of bonus shares. *Less :* Calls unpaid : (*a*) My managing agent or secretaries (*b*) By Directors (*c*) By others. Add :Forfeited shares (amount originally paid up) (any capital profit on reissue of forfeited shares should be transferred to Capital Reserve)		**FIXED ASSETS** Distinguishing expenditure upon : (*a*) Goodwill (*b*) Land (*c*) Buildings (*d*) Leaseholds (*e*) Plant and Machinery (*f*) Furniture and fittings (*g*) Patents, trademarks, and design (*h*) Livestock (*i*) Vehicles Under each of the assets, the original cost, additions and deductions during the year and total depreciation provided should be mentioned. If any amount is written off on reduction of capital, the balance sheet for the first 5 years after reduction shall also show the amount of reduction made.	

PARTICULARS	AMT.	PARTICULARS	AMT.
RESERVES AND SURPLUS (1) Capital Reserves (2) Capital Redemption Reserve (3) Share Premium Account (4) Other Reserves specifying the nature of each reserve and the amount in respect thereof. *Less :* Debit balance in profit and loss account (if any) (5) Surpluses i.e. balance in profit and loss account (6) Proposed additions to reserves (7) Sinking Funds. (The word 'Fund' in relation to any reserve should be used only where such reserve is specifically represented by earmarked investments) **SECURED LOANS :** (*a*) Debentures (*b*) Loans and advances from bank (*c*) Loans and advances from subsidiaries (*d*) Other loans and advances (Loans from directors, secretaries, manager should be shown separately)(In case of debenture, terms of redemption or conversion is to be stated with the earliest date of redemption or conversion) ***UNSECURED LOANS :*** (1) Fixed Deposits (2) Loans and advances from subsidiaries (3) Short term loans from : (*a*) Banks (*b*) Others (Short term loans include those which are due for not more than 1 year as at the date of balance sheet) Other loans and advances **CURRENT LIABILITIES AND PROVISIONS:** **CURRENT LIABILITIES** (*a*) Acceptances (Bills Payable)		**INVESTMENTS** (1) Investment in Govt. or trust securities (2) Investment in shares, debentures etc. (3) Immovable properties (4) Inv. In capital of partnership firm Aggregate amount of the company's quoted investments and also the market value thereof shall be shown. **CURRENT ASSETS, LOANS AND ADVANCES** **(A) Current Assets** (*a*) Interest accrued on investment (*b*) Stores and spare parts (*c*) Loose tools (*d*) Stock in trade (*e*) Work in progress (*f*) Sundry debtors (less : provision) Debts outstanding for more than 6 months should be stated separately. (*g*) Cash balance in hand (*h*) Bank balance **(B) Loans and Advances** (1) Advances and loans to subsidiaries (2) Bills of exchange ***MISCELLANEOUS EXPENDITURE AND LOSSES NOT WRITTEN OFF*** (*a*) Preliminary expenses (*b*) Expenses of commission or underwriting on issue of shares and debentures (*c*) Discount allowed on the issue of shares and debentures (*d*) Interest paid out of capital during construction (*e*) Development expenditure not adjusted (*f*) Debit balance of Profit and Loss account	

PARTICULARS	AMT.	PARTICULARS	AMT.
(*b*) Sundry Creditors (*c*) Subsidiary Companies (*d*) Advance payments and unexpired discounts for the portion for which value has still to be given (*e*) Unclaimed Dividends (*f*) Other liabilities (*g*) Interest accrued but not due on loans **PROVISIONS** (1) Provision for Taxation (2) Proposed dividends (3) For Contingencies (4) For Provident Fund scheme (5) For insurance, pension and other benefits (6) Other provisions. A foot note to the balance sheet may be added to show separately: (*a*) Claims against the company not acknowledged as debts (*b*) Uncalled liability on shares partly paid (*c*) Arrears of fixed cumulative dividends (*d*) Estimated amount of contracts remaining to be executed on capital account (*e*) Other moneys for which the company is contingently liable			

Note : Now the companies have to disclose the names of all small scale industrial undertakings to whom the company owes any sum together with interest outstanding for more than 30 days in the balance sheet under the heading 'Current Liabilities and Provisions'.

❑ ❑ ❑

Chapter 5

Financial Statement Analysis

FINANCIAL STATEMENTS

Any business organization prepares various statements for different information and purposes. The income statement report what has actually happened to earnings during the given period. The balance sheet presents a summary of financial position of the company at a given point of time. Both of them are known as financial statements.

The analysis and interpretation of these statements is the job of a manager. This can be done in many ways. The important methods of analysis and interpretation of financial statements are as below :

(*a*) Comparative statement
(*b*) Common size statement
(*c*) Ratio analysis
(*d*) Funds flow analysis
(*e*) Cash flow analysis

COMPARATIVE STATEMENT

A financial statement gives a lot of information about the entity. But, the information is more useful and more clear to a lay man if it is given in a comparative form. The data of the current year is compared with that of last year or last few years. This can be done by showing the figures for more than one year for all items in the balance sheet or profit and loss account side by side. It can also be done by showing the actual figure for the current year and giving the difference from the previous year in rupees or in percentage. The following is an illustration of comparative profit and loss account and balance sheet.

Illustration 1 :

Comparative Balance Sheet

Particulars	For the period		Increase / Decrease	
	2007	2008	Absolute	Percentage
Share Capital	1,00,000	1,00,000	Nil	-----
Debentures	2,00,000	1,50,000	(–) 50,000	(–) 25%
Sundry Creditors	60,000	72,000	12,000	20%
TOTAL LIABILITIES	3,60,000	3,22,000	(–) 38,000	(–) 10.5%
Plants and Machinery	1,00,000	1,50,000	50,000	50%
Investments	80,000	72,000	(–) 8,000	(–) 10%
Sundry Debtors	80,000	70,000	(–) 10,000	(–) 12.33%
Cash-at-hand	1,00,000	30,000	(–) 70,000	(–) 70%
TOTAL ASSETS	3,60,000	3,22,000	(–) 38,000	(–) 10.5%

Comparative Income Statement

Particulars	For the period		Increase / Decrease	
	2007	2008	Absolute	Percentage
Sales	12,00,000	15,00,000	3,00,000	25%
Purchases	8,00,000	9,60,000	1,60,000	20%
Closing Stock	30,000	25,000	(–) 5,000	(–) 16.67%
GROSS PROFIT	2, 45,000	3,50,000	1,05,000	43%
Operating Expenses	1,00,000	1,50,000	50,000	50%
Non-operating Expenses	80,000	72,000	(–) 8,000	(–) 10%
NET PROFIT	65,000	1,28,000	63,000	98%

BENEFITS OF COMPARATIVE STATEMENTS

Comparative statements are very useful for the financial statement analysis in the following ways:

(*a*) It reveals trend of the item concerned

(*b*) It helps the management to know the inefficiency in any part of the operations, if any

(*c*) It shows how the business has performed with respect to the last year

(*d*) It is also useful for comparing performance in the same year as compared to other firms placed similarly.

COMMON SIZE STATEMENTS

It is a method in which various items of a financial statement are compared to each other in terms of their weightage in the concerned financial statement. In this method, one figure of the statement is taken as base figure which is assumed as 100%. All other figures are then arrived at in percentage as a portion of the base figure. For example, in balance sheet the total of the statement is taken as 100 and all the assets and liabilities are expressed as a percentage with respect to total. Similarly, in profit and loss account, the base figure is taken as Sales. This is called 'Vertical analysis' and when the same type of statement is prepared for a number of years to show the trend, it is called 'Horizontal analysis'.

Illustration 2 : Taking the above figures, the common size statements may also be prepared :

Comparative Balance Sheet

Particulars	2007		2008	
	Amount	% of Total	Amount	% of Total
Share Capital	1,00,000	27.8%	1,00,000	31.06%
Debentures	2,00,000	55.6%	1,50,000	46.58%
Sundry Creditors	60,000	16.6%	72,000	22.36%
TOTAL LIABILITIES	3,60,000	100%	3,22,000	100%
Plants and Machinery	1,00,000	27.8%	1,50,000	46.58%
Investments	80,000	22.2%	72,000	22.36%
Sundry Debtors	80,000	22.2%	70,000	21.74%
Cash-at-hand	1,00,000	27.8%	30,000	09.32%
TOTAL ASSETS	3,60,000	100%	3,22,000	100%

Comparative Balance Sheet

Particulars	2007		2008	
	Amount	% of Total	Amount	% of Total
Sales	12,00,000	100%	15,00,000	100%
Purchases	8,00,000	67%	9,60,000	64%
Closing Stock	30,000	2.5%	25,000	01.67%
GROSS PROFIT	2, 45,000	20.42%	3,50,000	23.33%
Operating Expenses	1,00,000	08.33%	1,50,000	10.0%
Non-operating Expenses	80,000	06.7%	72,000	04.8%
NET PROFIT	65,000	05.42%	1,28,000	08.53%

Now, it is easy for a lay man also to analyse that the gross profit margin has increased due to reduction in the cost of purchases. Also, thought there is an increase in the operating expenses, due to reduction in non-operating expenses the net profit margin has increased.

While preparing the above statement, the figures are expressed in terms of percentage of the base figure like to find the percentage of cash for 2007 we took

1,00,000 / 3,60,000 × 100 = 27.8%

Similarly, to find the percentage for purchases in 2008

9,60,000 / 15,00,000 × 100 = 64%

RATIO ANALYSIS

Ratio analysis is a very powerful analytical tool for measuring performance of an organization. The ratio analysis concentrates on the inter-relationship among the figures appearing in the above mentioned and various other statements. It helps the management to analyze the past performance of the firm and to make further projections. Ratio analysis allows interested parties like shareholders, investors, creditors, government and analysts to make an evaluation of certain aspects of a firm's performance.

The calculation of ratios is a relatively easy and simple task but the proper analysis and interpretation of ratios can be made only by skilled analyst. While interpreting the financial information, the analyst has to be careful about limitations imposed by the accounting concepts and methods of valuation. Information of non-financial nature will also be taken into consideration before a meaningful analysis is made. Ratio analysis pinpoints the strengths and weaknesses of the business mainly in two ways. Firstly, by comparing current performance with that of past and secondly by comparing the performance of the business with that of the industry as whole or other firms in the industry.

INTERPRETATION OF RATIO

A ratio may be interpreted in many ways depending upon the purpose of the ratio.

1. It may be interpreted individually or as a stand alone ratio. For example, a ratio of 20% net profit on the sales shows a good margin in itself.
2. It may be interpreted by doing comparison between the ratio over a period of time. For example, if the same ratio is compared with the last year which was 30%, it means that margin have fallen this year.
3. It may also be interpreted by comparing with similar firms in the same industry. If the same ratio of a comparable firm is 16%, the margins of company under consideration is very good.
4. It may be interpreted by taking it together with other ratios. For example, in this case the margins are good but the return on capital employed is only 5%. It means the sales is very less but margins are high because of higher prices.

TYPES OF RATIOS

There are various ratios used in analysis. For the convenience of understanding, they can be divided into the following broad categories :

A. Long Term Solvency Ratios
B. Short Term Solvency Ratios
C. Turnover Ratios
D. Profitability Ratios
E. Operating Ratios
F. Market Test Ratios

We shall discuss various ratios under all the above categories.

A. Long Term Solvency Ratios

The long term financial stability of the firm may be considered as dependent upon its ability to meet all its liabilities, including those not currently payable. The following are important ratios measuring the long term solvency :

(1) Debt-Equity Ratio : Capital is derived from two sources : shares and loans. Every company has to raise equity capital. The effect of raising loan is to introduce an element of gearing or leverage into the capital structure of the company.

$$\text{Debt-Equity ratio} = \frac{\text{Long term debt}}{\text{Shareholders' Fund}}$$

Shareholders' fund is equal to the share capital plus reserves and surpluses less preliminary expenses, if any. This ratio indicates the relationship between loan funds and net worth of the company, which is known as gearing. A debt-equity ratio of 2:1 is accepted norm. Higher the ratio, higher is the gearing and higher is the risk of long term insolvency. As a general rule, gearing should be low in those industries where demand is volatile and profits are subject to fluctuations. Usually, in calculating the ratio, the preference share capital is excluded from debt, but if the ratio is to show effect of use of fixed interest sources on earnings available to the shareholders then it is to be included. On the other hand, if the ratio is to examine financial solvency, then preference shares shall form part of the capital.

The ratio may also be calculated as below :

$$\text{Debt-Equity ratio} = \frac{\text{Long term debt}}{\text{Shareholders' Fund} + \text{Long term Debt}}$$

(2) Capital Gearing Ratio : It is the proportion of fixed interest bearing funds to equity shareholders' funds.

$$\text{Capital Gearing Ratio} = \frac{\text{Fixed Interest Bearing Funds}}{\text{Equity Shareholders' Funds}}$$

The fixed interest bearing funds include debentures, long term loans, and preference share capital. This ratio indicates the degree of vulnerability of earnings available for equity shareholders.

(3) Fixed Assets To Long Term Funds Ratio

$$\text{F/A to L/T Funds Ratio} = \frac{\text{Fixed Assets}}{\text{Long Term Funds}}$$

Fixed assets represent the gross fixed assets minus depreciation till the date of calculation. The closeness of the ratio to 1 indicates that fixed assets are financed by long term funds. If the ratio is significantly less than 1, it means that long term funds are being used to finance current assets also. A very high ratio is dangerous for short term solvency as it implies that short term funds are also used to finance long term assets.

(4) Proprietary Ratio : It expresses the relationship between net worth and total assets.

$$\text{Proprietary Ratio} = \frac{\text{Net Worth}}{\text{Total Assets}}$$

Net worth = equity capital + Preference share capital + Reserves − Fictitious assets

Total assets = Fixed assets + Current assets

Reserves earmarked specifically for a particular purpose should not be included in calculation of net worth. A high proprietary ratio is indicative of strong financial position of the business.

(5) Dividend Cover

$$\text{Dividend Cover} = \frac{\text{Net Profit after Tax}}{\text{Dividend}}$$

This ratio indicates the number of times the dividends are covered by net profit. This highlights the amount retained by a company for financing of future operations.

(6) Interest Cover

Interest Cover

$$= \frac{\text{Profit before Interest, Depreciation and Tax (PBDIT)}}{\text{Interest}}$$

It shows how many times interest charges are covered by funds that are available for payment of interest. Here, PBDIT is used because interest is paid before payment of tax and depreciation is non-cash expense. In the dividend cover ratio as shown above, since the dividend is paid on PAT, PAT is in numerator. A high interest cover indicates that the firm is conservative in using debt and a very low ratio indicates excessive use of debt.

(7) Debt Service Coverage Ratio : It indicates whether the business is earning sufficient profits to pay not only the interest charges, but also the installments due to the 'principal' amount. This ratio is widely used by banks for analyzing the profitability of a project before financing it.

$$\text{DSCR} = \frac{\text{Profit before Interest and Tax}}{\text{Interest} + \text{Loan Installments}}$$

B. Short Term Solvency Ratios

These ratios measure the liquidity of the firm and its ability to meet its maturing short term obligations. Liquidity is defined as the ability to realise value in money, which is the most liquid of all assets. It refers to the ability to pay in cash, the obligations that are due. Excess liquidity, though a guarantor of solvency would reflect lower profitability. On the other hand, too little liquidity may lead to risk of insolvency. The important ratios to measure short term solvency are :

(1) Current Ratio

Current ratio

$$= \frac{\text{Current Assets (including loans and advanced}}{\text{Current Liabilities (including Provision)}}$$

The ratio measures the solvency of the company in the short term. Current assets are those assets which can be converted into cash within a year. Current liabilities are those liabilities that are payable within a year. A current ratio of 1.33:1 is considered good. A very high ratio will have adverse impact on the profitability of the organization. To know the reason of high current ratio the next ratio is used.

(2) Quick Ratio/Liquid Ratio

This ratio shows whether high current ratio is due to piling up of inventory. If the difference between current ratio and quick ratio is significant, then the organization is carrying high inventory.

Quick ratio =

$$\frac{\text{Quick Assets (Current Assets } - \text{ Inventories } - \text{ Prepaid Expenses)}}{\text{Quick Liabilities (Current Liabilities } - \text{ Bank Overdraft)}}$$

It is also known as Acid-test ratio. It is used along with the current ratio.

(3) Absolute Liquidity Ratio

$$\text{Absolute Liquidity Ratio} = \frac{\text{Cash + Marketable Securities}}{\text{Current Liabilities}}$$

Absolute liquidity ratio is a subsequent innovation in ratio analysis. It eliminates uncertainty of receipts attached to the bills receivables. Therefore, this ratio excludes bills receivables also. The Absolute Liquidity Ratio only tests short-term liquidity in terms of cash and marketable securities.

C. Turnover Ratios

Turnover or activity ratios measure how effectively the firm employs its resources. These ratios involve comparison between the level of sales and investment in various assets - inventories, debtors, fixed assets etc. Activity ratios are used to measure the speed with which various accounts are converted into sales or cash. The following activity ratios are important:

(1) Inventory Turnover Ratio

$$\text{Inventory turnover ratio} = \frac{\text{Cost of goods sold}}{\text{Average Inventory}}$$

Average inventory is average of opening and closing stock. If the cost of goods sold is not available, sales figure is used. It shows how many times the company's inventory has been sold during the year. Higher the ratio, higher is the efficiency of the business.

(2) Debtor Turnover Ratio

$$\text{Debtor turnover ratio} = \frac{\text{Total Credit Sales}}{\text{Average Debtors}}$$

This ratio indicates the number of times of sales as compared to debtors. In other words, it shows the duration of credit given to debtors. The inverse of this ratio is Average collection period.

$$ACP = \frac{\text{Average Debtors}}{\text{Total Credit Sales}} \times 365$$

It shows in how many days the company receives payment for its credit sales. The actual collection period can be compared with the stated terms of the company. Higher this ratio(or lower the turnover ratio), lower is the efficiency in collection.

(3) Creditors Turnover Ratio : Similar to above ratios, the Creditor's turnover ratio or the Average payment period is :

Creditors' Turnover ratio

$$= \frac{\text{Total Credit Purcases}}{\text{Average Creditors}}$$

Average Payment Period

$$= \frac{\text{Average Creditors}}{\text{Credit Purchases}} \times 365$$

(4) Fixed Asset Turnover Ratio

$$\text{F/A turnover ratio} = \frac{\text{Sales}}{\text{Fixed Assets}}$$

This measures the company's ability to generate sales revenue in relation to the size of the investment. A high ratio indicates efficient utilization of fixed assets in generating sales and a low ratio indicates otherwise.

D. Profitability Ratios

The purpose of study and analysis of profitability ratios are to help assess the adequacy of profits earned by the company and also to discover whether profitability is increasing or declining. These ratios show the combined effects of liquidity, asset management and debt management. They are measured with reference to various items as below:

(1) Return On Capital Employed: ROCE or Return on Investment (ROI) is one of the fundamental ratios.

$$ROI = \frac{\text{Net Profit before interest and tax}}{\text{Capital Employed}} \times 100$$

Here, capital employed is equal to capital of the company (equity plus loan) less any fictitious assets and debit balance of Profit and Loss Account. This ratio encourages managers to obtain assets that will provide a satisfactory return on investment and to dispose of assets that are not providing an acceptable return.

(2) Earning Per Share (EPS) : It is one of the most widely used ratios to determine the market value of the firm.

$$EPS = \frac{\text{Profit after Tax - Preference dividend}}{\text{No. of equity shares}}$$

Higher EPS means better capital productivity. Growth in EPS is more relevant than the absolute value for pricing of share. It should be kept in mind that higher EPS does not necessarily lead to higher dividend payout.

(3) Gross Profit Margin:

G/P Ratio

$$= \frac{\text{Gross profit (Sales-Cost of goods sold)}}{\text{Sales}} \times 100$$

Gross profit, as shown is calculated before taking into consideration the administrative and marketing expenses. It measures, the company's manufacturing or trading efficiency.

(4) Net Profit Margin: It is calculated as above after deducting the administrative and marketing expenses but before deducting interest and taxes.

$$\text{N/P Ratio} = \frac{\text{Net Profit after Tax (PAT)}}{\text{Sales}} \times 100$$

(5) Return On Net Worth:

Return on Net worth

$$= \frac{\text{Net Profit after Tax}}{\text{Net worth}} \times 100$$

This ratio indicates the efficiency of utilization of assets in generating revenue.

E. Operating Ratios

The ratios of all operating expenses (material, labour, factory overheads, administration and selling expenses) to sales is the operating ratio. A comparison of the operating ratio would indicate whether the cost content is high or low in the figure of sales. If the annual comparison shows that the ratio has increased, the management would be naturally interested to know as to which element of the cost has gone up. It is not necessary that the management should be concerned only when the operating ratio goes up. If the operating ratio has fallen, though the unit selling price has remained the same, still the position needs analysis as it may be the sum total of efficiency in certain departments and inefficiency in others. An effective management is interested in making a complete analysis. It is therefore, necessary to break up the operating ratio into various cost ratios. They are :

$$\text{Material cost ratio} = \frac{\text{Material consumed}}{\text{Sales}} \times 100$$

$$\text{Labour cost ratio} = \frac{\text{Labour cost}}{\text{Sales}} \times 100$$

Factory overheads ratio

$$= \frac{\text{Factory Expenses}}{\text{Sales}} \times 100$$

Administrative expenses ratio

$$= \frac{\text{Administrative Expenses}}{\text{Sales}} \times 100$$

Selling and Distribution Overhead ratio

$$= \frac{\text{Selling and Distribution Expenses}}{\text{Sales}} \times 100$$

$$\text{Operating ratio} = \frac{\text{Cost of Goods Sold}}{\text{Sales}} \times 100$$

F. Market Test Ratios

These ratios relate to the firm's stock price to its earnings and book value. They give management an indication of what investors think of the company's past performance and future prospectus. Market test ratios are as follows:

(1) Dividend Payout Ratio : Dividend payout

$$\text{ratio} = \frac{\text{Dividend per share}}{\text{Earnings per share (EPS)}}$$

This ratio indicates the extent of the net profits distributed to the shareholders as dividend. A high payout signifies a liberal distribution policy and a low payout reflects conservative distribution policy.

(2) Dividend Yield : Dividend Yield

$$= \frac{\text{Dividend per share}}{\text{Market price of share}} \times 100$$

This ratio reflects the percentage yield that an investor receives on his investment at the current market price of the share.

(3) Book Value : Book value

$$= \frac{\text{Net Worth}}{\text{No. of equity shares}}$$

This ratio indicates the net worth per equity share. It is reflection of past earning and distribution policy of the company. A high book value indicates that the company has huge reserves and is a potential candidate for issue of bonus. Book value is considered as less relevant for market price as compared to EPS.

(4) Price Earning (P/E) Ratio : P/E ratio

$$= \frac{\text{Market Price of Share}}{\text{EPS}}$$

This ratio indicates the number of times the earnings of the latest year at which the share price of a company is quoted. A low P/E ratio as compared to industry reflects under valuation of the price of the share. It is considered as barometer of market sentiment.

IMPORTANCE OF THE RATE OF RETURN ON INVESTMENT

Return on investment (R0I) is one of the most important ratios used by managers while making an investment. As already explained,

$$\text{ROI} = \frac{\text{Net Profit before Interst and Tax}}{\text{Capital Employed}} \times 100$$

But, there is no unanimity over the use of capital employed or the profit taken. Managers may take net profit after tax, net profit before interest and tax, net profit after interest but before tax etc. For the purpose of simplicity, it is often taken as

$$\text{ROI} = \frac{\text{Net Profit}}{\text{Capital Employed}}$$

American company DuPont has given a chart which shows how the Return on investment can be broken into various ratio and form this one ratio the whole analysis of the performance of the organization can be done. The chart is as below :

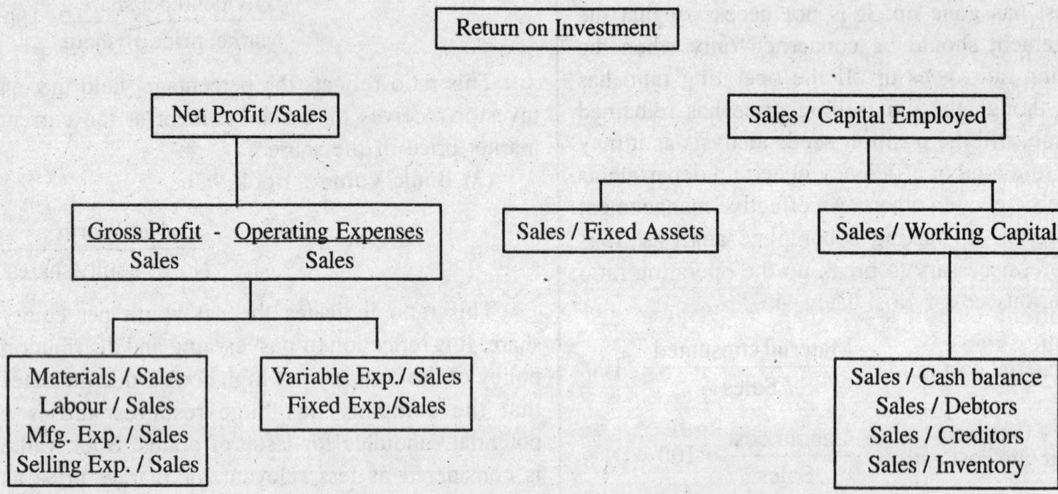

As the above chart shows that one single ratio may give a broad picture of the performance of the organization. Here, capital employed can be taken as Fixed assets and Net working capital, and operating expenses can be broken into various expenses. In the above chart, Sales/Capital employed is also known as 'Capital Turnover Ratio'.

Illustration 3 : From the following P&L A/c and Balance Sheet calculate various ratios.

To opening Stock	10000	By Sales	100000
To Purchases	55000	By Closing Stock	15000
To Gross Profit	50000		
	115000		115000
To Administration expenses	15000	By Gross profit	50000
To Interest	3000		
To Selling expenses	12000		
To Net profit	20000		
	50000		50000

Balance Sheet

Capital	100000	Land and Building	50000
Profit and Loss A/c	20000	Plant and Machinery	30000
Creditors	25000	Stock	15000
Bills payable	15000	Debtors	15000
		Furniture	20000
		Bills receivable	12500
		Cash at bank	17500
	160000		160000

(1) Inventory Turnover Ratio = Cost of goods sold / Average Stock
Average Stock = Opening Stock + Closing stock / 2 = 10000 + 15000 / 2 = 12500
Cost of goods sold = Opening stock + Purchases – Closing stock = 10000 + 55000 – 15000 = 50000
Stock / Inventory Turnover ratio = 50000 / 12500 = 4 times

(2) Current Ratio = Current Assets / Current Liabilities
Current assets = 60000 (Stock, Debtors, Bills and Cash)
Current Liabilities = 40000 (Creditors and Bills)
So, Current Ratio = 60000 / 40000 = 1.5 : 1

(3) Net Profit Margin/Ratio = $\frac{\text{Net Profit}}{\text{Net Sales}} \times 100$;

$$\frac{2000 \times 100}{100000} \times 100 = 20\%$$

(4) Liquid Ratio = Liquid Assets / Current Liabilities
Liquid Assets = 45000 (Current assets - Stock)
Current Liabilities = 40000
Liquid Ratio = 45000 / 40000 = 1.125 : 1

(5) Proprietary Ratio = $\frac{\text{Shareholders' Funds}}{\text{Total Assets}} \times 100$;

$$\frac{120000\,(\text{Capital} + \text{Profit})}{160000} \times 100 = 75\%$$

Illustration 4 :

Current Ratio 2.5 Bank Overdraft 10000
Liquid Ratio 1.5 Working Capital 60000

From the above information, find out the value of inventory and creditors

If current ratio is 2.5, means Current assets and Current liabilities are in the ratio of 2.5 : 1

Working capital = Current assets – Current liabilities

So, 60000 = 2.5 Current Liabilities – Current Liabilities (since C/A = 2.5 C/L)

60000 = 1.5 Current Liabilities
Current Liabilities = 40000

Since, no information is given, it is considered that current liabilities comprise only Bank overdraft and creditors.

So, Creditors = 40000 – 10000 = 30000
Current Assets = 2.5 (40000) = 100000

Liquid Ratio is 1.5 and liquid liability is only creditors, *i.e.,* 30000

Therefore, Liquid Assets = 1.5 (30000) = 45000
Inventory = Current Assets – Liquid Assets
= 100000 – 45000 = 55000

LIMITATIONS OF RATIO ANALYSIS

(1) It is based on financial statements which are themselves subject to severe limitations. Therefore, any ratio analysis based on a mis-statement suffers from the similar limitations.

(2) In case of inter-firm comparison, no two firms are similar in age, size and product unit. Therefore, any comparison of ratios of two such firms must take these factors into account.

(3) Both, the inter-period and inter-firm comparisons are affected by price level changes. A change in the price level can affect the validity of ratios calculated for different time periods.

(4) The ambiguity in defining terms like gross profit, capital employed, operating profit, current assets etc. also leads to distortions in the ratio analysis and ratios based on different concepts can be misleading.

(5) Any decision cannot be taken based on a single ratio. The analyst has to use various ratios and other forms of accounting analysis before taking any decision.

(6) Conclusions from analysis of statements are not sure indicators of bad or good management.

(7) Ratio analysis is only a tool and is helpful to spot out the symptoms. The analyst has to carry out further investigations and exercise his judgement in arriving at a correct diagnosis.

❑ ❑ ❑

Chapter 6

Fund Flow and Cash Flow Statement

CONCEPT OF FLOW STATEMENT

A balance sheet is a snapshot view of the status of a firm's funds at one instance of time. But it does not give a picutre of from where the funds have come and how funds from various sources wree received and utilised during the year. A flow statement explains the changes that took place in a balance sheet account or group of accounts during the period between the dates of two balance sheets. Income statement is also a flow statement. Similarly two flow statements cash flow and fund flow are widely used. It contains all the details of the financial resources which have become available during an accounting period and the ways in which those resources have been used up.

The term fund has been defined differently be different authors. But, in general, it means 'working capital' which is excess of current assets over current liabilities.

PREPARATION OF FUNDS FLOW STATEMENT

The funds flow statement is not prepared alone. To take a holistic view, three statements are prepared:

(*i*) Funds flow statement
(*ii*) Statement of changes in working capital
(*iii*) Adjusted profit and loss account

(i) Funds Flow Statement. It is also known as Statement of Sources and Application of funds. This statement summarizes all the areas from which funds were received and the areas in which funds were used. The format of the statement is as below:

Sources	Amount	Application	Amount
Funds from Operations (Adjusted P&L A/c)		Funds lost in Operations	
Issue of share capital Issue of Debentures		Redemption of preference shares/Debentures	
Raising Long term loans		Repayment of long term loans	
Receipt of calls on shares		Purchase of fixed assets/Investments	
Sale of Fixed assets or Investments		Non-trading payments like dividends/Tax	
Decrease in Working capital		Net increase in working capital	
Non-trading receipts like dividends			

This statement is like Cash account. All the receipts are considered as sources and all the payments are considered as application of funds.

(ii) Statement of Changes in Working Capital. The primary purpose of this statement is to determine the net changes in the working capital and that figure appears in the Funds flow statement as shown above. In this statement, all current assets and liabilities are individually listed. The acquisition of current assets and repayment of current liabilities will result into application of funds or increase in working capital. On the other hand, decrease in current assets and increase in current liabilities results in decrease in working capital and hence sources of funds.

(iii) Adjusted Profit and Loss Account. This is also called as Statement showing Funds generated from Operations. In this statement, we start with the profit/loss as shown in the profit and loss account. Then we exclude all the revenues and expenditures which do not pertain to the basic operations of the firm or are incidental losses and revenue. We add all the non-operational expenses and deduct all the non-operational revenues. The items are : Depreciation, Amortisation of fictitious assets, Appropriation of retained earnings, Loss/profit on sale of fixed assets, Payment or receipt of dividend, Taxation, Appreciation in value of fixed assets etc.

FUNDS FROM OPERATIONS

Funds from operations show the amount generated by the business activities. It is important to note that net profit as shown by the P&L account does not always mean the funds from operation. For this purpose only, adjusted P&L account is prepared as shown in the above example. The reasons for difference in net profit and funds from operations are many. One of them is there are certain expenses for which no payment is made like depreciation which does not affect the working capital. So, to arrive at the funds generated from operations, the following adjustments are made in the Profit and Loss Account.

ADD : Following items are added to the Net Profit as shown in P&L account :

(1) Depreciation on fixed assets

(2) Written off fictitious and intangible items like goodwill, preliminary expenses, discount on issue of shares etc.

(3) Loss on sale of fixed assets

(4) Appropriation of profits like transfer to general reserve or sinking funds.

(5) Dividend on shares

DEDUCT : Following items are deducted from net profit :

(*a*) Profit on sale of fixed assets

(*b*) Profit on revaluation of fixed assets

(*c*) Non-operating incomes like dividend, interest on investment, ret received etc.

In case there is net loss in the profit and loss account, the first set of items are deducted and the second set of items are added to the net loss to arrive at the figure of funds from operations.

Illustration 1 : Calculate funds from operations from the following P&L account :

To Expenses paid and outstanding	1,50,000	By Gross Profit	2,25,000
To Depreciation	35,000	By Gain on sale of land	30,000
To Loss on sale of machine	2,000		
To Discount	100		
To Goodwill written off	10,000		
To Net Profit	57,900		
	2,55,000		2,55,000

Calculation of funds from operations :

Net Profit (as given)		57,900
Add : Non-operating items debited to P&L A/c		
Depreciation	35,000	
Loss on sale of machine	2,000	
Goodwill written off	10,000	47,000
		1,04,900
Less : Non-operating items credited to P&L A/c		
Gain on sale of land	30,000	30,000
FUNDS FROM OPERATIONS		74,900

TREATMENT OF SPECIFIC ITEMS

There are certain accounts which need specific treatment while calculating the funds flow.

(1) Provision For Taxation. While preparing funds flow statement, the provision for taxation may be treated either as appropriation of profit or as current liability. If it is treated as current liability, it is considered while preparing the statement of changes in working capital and showing it as current liability. If it is treated as appropriation of profit, no effect will be given on funds flow when the provision is made. But, the payment of tax is shown as application of funds. The amount of tax paid is calculated by opening Provision for Taxation account as follow :

To Bank A/c (Tax paid, *i.e.,* application of money) To Closing balance	By Opening balance By P&L Appropriation A/c (Provision made during the year)

(2) Proposed Dividend. This account can also be treated either as current liability or as appropriation of profit. When treated as current liability, like provision of taxation, it is also taken as current liability in the preparation of statement of changes in the working capital. In case it is treated as the appropriation of profit, the proposed dividend for the year is added back to the profit and proposed dividend for the last year is deducted form the profit while calculating the funds form operations.

(3) Interim Dividend. Interim dividend paid is shown as an application of fund in the funds flow statement. It is also added back in the net profit for calculating the funds from operations, if it has already been debited to P&L account.

Illustration 2 : From the following balance sheet, prepare funds flow statement :

Liabilities	2007	2008	Assets	2007	2008
Share Capital	30,000	40,000	Goodwill	11,500	9,000
Preference Shares	15,000	10,000	Land & Building	20,000	17,000
General Reserve	4,000	7,000	Plant	8,000	20,000
Profit and Loss A/c	3,000	4,800	Debtors	16,000	20,000
Proposed Dividend	4,200	5,000	Stock	7,700	10,900
Creditors	5,500	8,300	Bills Receivable	2,000	3,000
Bills Payable	2,000	1,600	Cash-in-hand	1,500	1,000
Provision for Taxation	4,000	5,000	Cash-at-bank	1,000	800
	67,700	81,700		67,700	81,700

1. Depreciation of Rs. 2,000 on L&B and Rs. 1,000 on Plant has been charged in 2008.
2. Interim Dividend of Rs. 2,000 has been paid in 2008.
3. Income tax of Rs. 3,500 has been paid during the year 2008.

Statement of Changes in Working Capital

Particulars	2007	2008	Effect (+/–) on Working capital
CURRENT ASSETS			
Debtors	16,000	20,000	(+) 4,000
Stock	7,700	10,900	(+) 3,200
Bills receivable	2,000	3,000	(+) 1,000
Cash-in-hand	1,500	1,000	(–) 500
Cash-at-bank	1,000	800	(–) 200
TOTAL CURRENT ASSETS	28,200	35,700	
CURRENT LIABILITIES			
Creditors	5,500	8,300	(–) 2,800
Bills payable	2,000	1,600	(+) 400
Provision for taxation	4,000	5,000	(–) 1,000
Proposed dividend	4,200	5,000	(–) 800
TOTAL CURRENT LIABILITIES	15,700	19,900	
NET WORKING CAPITAL (Application of Funds)	12,500	15,800	(+) 3,300

Adjusted Profit and Loss Account

Particulars	Amount	Particulars	Amount
To Depreciation on		By Opening balance	3,000
Plant	1,000	By Funds from Operations	12,300
Building	2,000	(Balance figure)	
To Goodwill Written off	2,500		
To Transfer to G.R.	3,000		
To Interim dividend	2,000		
To Closing balance	4,800		
	15,300		15,300

Funds Flow Statement

Sources of Funds	Amount	Application of Funds	Amount
Issue of Equity shares	10,000	Redemption of Preference shares	5,000
Sale of building	1,000	Purchase of plant	13,000
Funds from operations	12,300	Dividend paid	2,000
		Net increase in working capital	3,300
	23,300		23,300

Note :

1. Sale of building figure has been calculated as (20,000 – 2,000 – 17,000 = 1,000)
2. Purchase of plant has been calculated as (1,000 + 20,000 – 8,000 = 13,000)

CASH FLOW ANALYSIS

It is very similar to Funds flow analysis. The major difference between the two is that cash flow statement analyses the receipts and application of cash only (which is a part of working capital) whereas funds flow statement analyses movement in the funds as a whole. According to SEBI guidelines, are listed companies have to present their cash flow statement in the Annual Report of the company. Cash flow statement during a period is classified into three categories

A. Operating activities
B. Investing activities
C. Financing activities

Operating activities are defined as all transactions that are not investing or financing activities. These transactions include the cash inflows associated with sales, interest and dividend revenues and outflows associated with purchases, operating expenses, interest, taxes etc. In nutshell, if we consider the format of the balance sheet, transactions occurring in current assets and current liabilities and transaction of profit and loss account fall under this category. While calculating cash from operations, all non-cash as well as non-operating incomes and expenditures are excluded.

Investing activities include acquiring or disposing off long term assets such as plants and equipments, securities, lending money etc. Increase or decrease in accounts receivables and inventory are not treated as investment activities; they are included in operating activities. In this category falls the transaction under the heads Fixed assets and Investments.

Financing activities include the borrowing of funds and issue of securities, their repayments etc. Transaction coming under the heads Capital and Reserves and surplus, Secured and Unsecured loans are financing activities.

BENEFITS OF CASH FLOW STATEMENT

A cash flow statement, when used in conjunction with the other financial statements, provides information that enables users to evaluate the changes in net assets of an enterprise, its financial structure, including solvency and liquidity, and its ability to affect the amount and timing of cash flows in order to adapt to changing circumstances and opportunities. Cash flow information is useful in assessing the ability of the enterprise to generate cash and cash equivalents and enable users to develop models to assess and compare the present value of the future cash flows of different enterprises. It also enhances the comparability of the reporting of operating performance by different enterprises because it eliminates the effects of using different accounting treatments for the same transactions and events.

CASH FROM OPERATIONS

Finding out cash from operations is similar to that finding out funds from operations with one change. In funds flow analysis, we prepare three statement viz., Adjusted P&L account, Statement of changes in working capital account and Funds flow account. But in cash flow analysis only two accounts are prepared, *i.e.*, Adjusted P&L account and Cash from operations.

So, while finding out the cash from operations, the adjustment regarding changes in the working capital is also made. Hence, to find out cash from operations, two steps are followed :

1. Find out the funds from operations as shown before
2. Add or deduct the net changes in working capital.

FUNDS FLOW ANALYSIS v/s CASH FLOW ANALYSIS

(*a*) Funds flow statement is based on accrual system while in preparing cash flow statement, only cash or cash equivalent items are considered.

(*b*) Funds flow analysis is more useful for long range financial planning. Cash flow analysis is more useful for identifying and correcting the current liquidity problem of the firm.

(*c*) Funds flow statement is a broader concept as cash itself is part of funds.

(*d*) Funds flow statement tallies the funds generated from various sources with various uses to which they are put. Cash flow statement starts with the opening balance of cash and reach to the closing balance of cash by proceeding through sources and uses.

(*e*) Cash flow statement is to be presented with the annual report of a company statutorily.

Preparation of funds flow statement is not legally binding.

(*f*) In cash flow statement, the changes in the working capital are incorporated in the cash flow from operating activities.

Illustration 3 : From the following information, calculate cash from operations.

Particulars	**2008**	**2008**
Debtors	50,000	47,000
Bills Receivable	10,000	12,500
Creditors	20,000	25,000
Bills Payable	8,000	6,000
Outstanding Expenses	1,000	1,200
Prepaid Expenses	800	700
Accrued Income	600	750
Income received in Advance	300	2,501
Profit made during the year		1,30,000

Cash from Operations :

Profit made during the year				1,30,000	
Add :	Decrease in Debtors			3,000	
	Increase in Creditors			5,000	
	Increase in outstanding expenses				200
	Decrease in Prepaid expenses			100	
				1,38,300	
Less :	Increase in Bills receivable	2,500			
	Increase in accrued Income	150			
	Decrease in Bills payable		2,000		
	Decrease in Income received in Advance		50		4,700
Cash from Operations				1,33,600	

Illustration 4 :

From following information prepare the cash flow statement for the year 2008. (Amounts in '000)

Net Profit	25,000	Interest Expenses	10,000
Dividend paid	8,535	Interest paid during the year	10,520
Provision for Income-tax	5,000	Increase in Working capital (except cash)	56,075
Income tax paid during the year	4,248	Purchase of Fixed asset	14,560
Loss on sale of asset	40	Investment in Joint Venture	3,850
Book value of asset sold	185	Expenditure on work-in-progress	34,740
Depreciation	20,000	Proceeds from calls in arrear	2
Amortisation of capital grant	6	Receipt of grant for capital project	12
Profit on sale of investment	100	Receipt from long term borrowings	25,980
Book value of investment sold	27,765	Receipt from short term borrowings	20,575
Interest income on investment	2,506	Opening cash balance	5,003
Closing cash balance	6,988		

Cash Flow Statement for the Year 2008

CASH FLOW FROM OPERATING ACTIVITIES		
Net profit before taxation (25000 + 5000)	30,000	
Adjustment for :		
Depreciation	20,000	
Loss on sale of asset	40	
Amortisation of capital grant	(6)	
Profit on sale of investment	(100)	
Interest income on investment	(2506)	
Interest expenses	10,000	
Operating profit before working capital changes	57,428	
Changes in working capital (Increase)	(56075)	
Cash generated from Operations	1,353	
Income tax paid	(4248)	
Net cash used in operating activities		(2,895)
CASH FLOW FROM INVESTING ACTIVITIES		
Sale of assets	145	
Sale of investments (27765 + 100)	27,865	
Interest income from investments	2,506	
Purchase of fixed assets	(14560)	
Investment in Joint Venture	(3850)	
Expenditure on work-in-progress	(34740)	
Net cash used in Investing activities		(22,634)
CASH FLOW FROM FINANCING ACTIVITIES		
Proceeds from calls in arrear	2	
Receipt of grant for capital project	12	
Receipt from long term borrowings	25,980	
Receipt from short term borrowings	20,575	
Interest paid	(10520)	
Dividend paid	(8535)	
Net cash from financing activities		27,514
Net increase in cash and cash equivalent	1,985	
Cash balance at the beginning of the period	5,003	
Cash balance at the end of the period	6,988	

❑ ❑ ❑

Chapter 7

Cost Accounting

PROCEDURES INVOLVED IN COST ACCOUNTING

Cost accounting is an art because it involves costing techniques and methods, such as those of differential costing, marginal costing, standard costing etc. The application of these techniques helps the cost accountant in deciding how to control costs, whether to go for replacement of the existing plant by a new one or not etc.

The main objectives of cost accounting are :

(i) Determining selling price

(ii) Measuring and increasing efficiency

(iii) Facilitating preparation of financial and other statements

(iv) Providing basis for operating policy

In general 'cost' means "the amount of expenditure incurred on, or attribute to, a given thing."

ELEMENTS OF COST ACCOUNTING

- Materials
- Labour
- Expenses

There are two main methods used to determine costs :–

1. The job cost method
2. The process cost method.

It is possible to ascertain the costs under each of the above methods by two different systems:

1. *Historical costing,* 2. *Standard costing*

1. Historical Costing

Historical costing (conventional or orthodoc costing) is the determination of cost by actuals.

It may be in the nature of *(i)* Post costing or *(ii)* Continuous costing

(i) **Post costing :** It means ascertainment of cost after the production is completed. This is done by analysing the financial accounts at the end of the period in such a way as to disclose the cost of the units which have been produced. For instance, if the cost of product 'A' is to be calculated on this basis, one must wait till the materials are actually purchased and used labour actually paid, and overhead expenditure actually incurred. This system is useful only for ascertaining the costs but not useful for exercising my control over cost, as one comes to know of things after they had taken palce. It can serve as a guidance for future production only when conditions in future continue to be the same.

(ii) **Continuous costing:** In case of this system, cost is ascertain as soon as the job is completed or even when the job is in progress. This is done usually by charging the job or product with actual expenditure on materials and wages and estimated share of overheads. Hence, the figure of cost ascertained in this case is not exact. But it has an advantage of providing cost information to the management promptly there by enabling it to take the necessary corrective action in time. However, it neither provides any standard for judging current efficiency nor does it disclose what the cost of the job ought to have been.

2. Standard Costing

Standard costing is a system under which the cost of the product is ascertained in advance on the basis of certain pre-determined standards. Taking the above example, the cost of product 'A' can be calculated in advance if one is in a position to estimate in advance the material, labour and overhead costs that should be incurred over the product. All this requires an efficient system of cost accounting. However, this system will not be useful if a vigorous system of controlling cost and keeping it upto standard cost is not in force.

Standard costing is becoming more and more popular now-a-days.

Marginal Costing

The Charted Institute of management Accountants, London defines the term marginal cost as "the amount at any given volume of output by which aggregate costs are changed if the volume of output is increased or decreased by one unit."

Marginal cost is, the total variable cost because within the capacity of the organisation, an increase of one unit in production will cause an increase invariable cost only. The variable cost consists of direct materials, direct labour, variable direct expenses and all variable overheads. The term "all variable overheads" include variable overheads plus the variable portion contained in semi-variable overheads.

The Accountant's concept of marginal cost differs from the Economist's concept of marginal cost. According to economists, the cost of producing one additional unit of output is the marginal cost of production.

Marginal cost = Direct material cost + Direct Labour cost + other variable costs

or

Total cost – Fixed cost

Marginal Costing and Direct Costing

Marginal costing and Direct costing are used by some accountants as synonymous terms since they take all "direct cost as variable cost".

Marginal costing and Differential costing : Marginal costing is sometimes confused with 'different costing'. Differential costing is the net increase or decrease in total cost resulting from a variation in production.

Marginal costing and Absorption costing : Marginal costing differs from absorption or traditional costing. Under absorption costing, full costs are charged to production. *i.e.,* all fixed and variable costs are recovered from production.

While, under marginal costing, only variables are charged to production. Fixed costs are ignored. There are two main differences between the absorption costing system and the marginal costing system :—

1. Valuation of stocks : Stocks of work-in-progress and finished goods are valued at works cost (including fixed works overheads) and total cost of production (including fixed works overheads and office overheads) respectively under absorption costing system. The two stocks are valued at marginal cost under marginal costing system.

2. Absorption of overheads : There can be under-recovery of overheads under marginal costing system as only variable overheads are absorbed to production. In marginal costing actual fixed overheads are wholly transferred to costing Profit and Loss Account, while in absorption costing, the over or under-recovery of overheads can be transferred to costing Profit and Loss Account.

On account of the above differences, the treatment of costs and profit differ under marginal costing and absorption costing systems. Since marginal costing system lays stress on *contribution i.e., sales minus variable cost,* any increase in contribution mean increase in profit, since fixed costs remain constant for all levels of production. Profit is arrived at after deducting fixed costs from the contribution fund. Under absorption costing, all the costs are first charged to products and then total costs are deducted from sales to arrive at the figure of profit. This would be clear from the following illustration.

Illustration: 1 from the following data prepare statements of cost according to both absorption costing and marginal costing systems :

	Product A	*Product B*	*Product C*
	Rs.	*Rs.*	*Rs.*
Sales	30,000	60,000	80,000
Direct Material	12,000	25,000	36,000
Direct Labour	8,000	10,000	14,000
Factors overheads :	6,000	8,000	6,000
Fixed variable	2,000	3,000	5,000
Administrative overheads	1,000	2,000	2,000
Fixed selling overheads	2,000	2,000	3,000
Fixed variable	1,000	3,000	3,000

Solution:

Statement of Cost
(under absorption costing system)

Particulars	*Total* *Rs.*	*Product A* *Rs.*	*Product B* *Rs.*	*Product C* *Rs.*
Sales	1,70,000	30,000	60,000	80,000
Less: cost of sales:				
Direct Material	73,000	12,000	25,000	36,000
Direct Labour	32,000	8,000	10,000	14,000
Factory over-heads	30,000	8,000	11,000	11,000
Administrative overheads	5,000	1,000	2,000	2,000
selling over-heads	14,000	3,000	5,000	6,000
Total	1,54,000	32,000	53,000	69,000
Profit	16,000	(–)2000	7,000	11,000

Statement of Cost
(under marginal costing system)

Particulars	*Total* *Rs.*	*Product A* *Rs.*	*Product B* *Rs.*	*Product C* *Rs.*
Sales	1,70,000	30,000	60,000	80,000
Less: Marginal costs of sales				
Direct Materials	73,000	12,000	25,000	36,000
Direct Labour	32,000	8,000	10,000	14,000
Variable factory overheads	10,000	2,000	3,000	5,000
Variable selling overheads	7,000	1,000	3,000	3,000
Total	1,22,000	23,000	41,000	58,000
Contribution Margin	48,000	7,000	19,000	22,000
Less: fixed costs (factory administration & selling)	32,000	9,000	12,000	11,000
Profit	16,000	(–)2,000	7,000	11,000

Contribution

The difference between selling price and variable cost (*i.e.,* the marginal cost) is known as 'contribution' or 'Gross Margin' or 'Contribution Margin'. In other words, fixed costs plus the amount of profit is equivalent to contribution. It can be expressed as

Contribution = Selling price – Variable cost
or = Fixed cost + Profit

We can derive from it that profit can not result unless contribution exceeds fixed costs. In other word, the point of 'no profit no loss' shall be arrived at where contribution is equal to fixed costs. We can see in the following example :

Variable cost = Rs. 50,000
Fixed cost = Rs. 20,000
Selling Price = Rs. 80,000
Contribution = Selling Price – Variable cost
= Rs. 80,000 – Rs. 50,000
= Rs. 30,000
Profit = Contribution – Fixed cost
= Rs. 30,000 – Rs. 20,000
= 10,000

Profit/Volume Ratio

This term is important for studying the profitability of operations of a business. Profit volume ratio establishes a relationship between the contribution and the sales value. The ratio can be shown in the form of percentage also. The formula can be expressed thus:–

$$\text{P/V Ratio} = \frac{\text{Contribution}}{\text{sales}}$$

$$= \frac{\text{Sales variable costs}}{\text{sales}}$$

This ratio can also be called as 'contribution/sales' ratio. This ratio can also be known by comparing the change in contribution to change in sales or change in profit to change in sales. Any increase in contribution would mean increase in profit only because fixed costs are assumed to be constant at all levels of production. Thus,

$$\text{P/V Ratio} = \frac{\text{change in contribution}}{\text{change in sales}}$$

$$= \frac{\text{change in Profit}}{\text{change in sales}}$$

This ratio would remain constant at different levels of production since variable costs as a proportion to sales remain constant at various levels.

Example

	Rs.
Sales	2,00,000
variable costs	1,20,000
Fixed costs	40,000

$$\text{P/V ratio} = \frac{\text{Rs.}2,00,000 - \text{Rs.}1,20,000}{\text{Rs.}2,00,000}$$

$$= 0.4 \text{ or } 40\%$$

The ratio is useful for the determination of the desired level of output or profit and for the calculation of variable costs for any volume of sales. The variable costs can be expressed as under:

V.C = s(1 – P/V ratio)

Variable Cost = sales (1 – P/V ratio)

In the above example

If we know the P/V ratio and sales before hand, the variable costs can be computed as follows:

Variable costs = 1 – 0.4 = 0.6, *i.e.,* 60% of sales = Rs. 1,20,000 (60% of Rs. 2,00,000)

Alternatively by the formula:

$$\text{P/V Ratio} = \frac{S-V}{S}, \therefore S - V = S \times \text{P/V Ratio}$$

$$V = S - S \times \text{ P/V Ratio}$$

$$= S(1 - \text{P/V Ratio})$$

Comparison of difference P/V Ratios is usually made by the management to find out which product is most profitable. Management tries to increase the value of the ratio by reducing the variable costs or by increasing the selling prices.

Key factor

"Key factor" is that factor which is the most important one for taking decisions about profitability of a product. the extent of its influence must be assessed first so as to maximize the profits.

Cost Volume Profit Analysis

Cost volume profit (CVP) analysis is an important tool of profit planning. It provides information about the followng matters :

1. The behaviour of cost in relation to volume
2. Volume of production or sales, where the business will break even.
3. Sensitivity of profits due to variation in output
4. Amount of profit for a projected sales volume.
5. Quantity of production and sales for a target profit level.

Cost volume profit analysis may therefore be defined as a managerial tool showing the relationship between various ingredients of profit planning, viz, cost (both fixed and variable), selling price and volume of activity, etc.

Such an analysis is useful to the Finance Manager in the following respects:

(i) It helps him in forecasting the profit fairly accurately

(ii) It helps in setting up flexible budgets, since on the basis of this relationship, he can ascertain the costs, sales and profits at different levels of activity.

(iii) It also assits him in performance evalution for purposes of management control.

(iv) It helps in formulating price policy by projecting the effect which different price structures will have on cost and profits.

(v) It helps in determining the amount of overhead cost to be charged at various levels of operation, since overhead rates are generally pre-determined on the basis of a selected volume of production.

Thus , cost-volume profit analysis is an important media through which the management can have insight into effects on profit on account of variation in costs (both fixed and variable) and sales (both volume and value) and take appropriate decisions.

BUDGETARY CONTROL

The budgetary control is an essential tool of the management for controlling costs and maximising profits.

Meaning of Budget

A budget is a detailed plan of operations for some specific future period. It is an estimate prepared in advance of the period to which it applies. It acts as a business barometer as it is complete programme of activities of the business for the period covered. The chartered Institute of Management Accountants, London, defines a budget as "a financial and/or quantitative statement, prepared prior to defined period of time, of the policy to be pursued during that period for the purpose of attaining a given objective". Thus, the essentials of a budget are :

(a) It is prepared in advance and is based on a future plane of actions

(b) It relates to a future period and is based on objective to be attained

(c) It is a statement expressed in monetary and/ or physical units prepared for the implementation of policy formulated by the management.

Meaning of Budgetary control: The chartered Institute of Management Accountants, London, defines budgetary control as "the establishment of budget relating to the responsibilities of executives to the requirements of a policy, and the continuous comparison of actual with budget results, either to secure by individual action the objective of that policy or to provide a basis for its revision." According to J.A. Scot "It is the system of management control and accounting in which all operations are forecasted and planned so far as possible ahead and the actual results compared with the forecasted and planned ones." Thus the budgetary control involves–

(a) establishment of budgets

(b) continuous comparison of actual with budgets for achievement of targets and placing the responsibility for failure to achieve the budget figures.

(c) revision of budgets in the light of changed circumstances.

The difference between budget, budgeting and budgetary control has been stated thus:

"Budgets are the individual objectives of a department, etc. whereas Budgeting may be said to be the act of building budgets. Budgetary control embraces all this and in addition includes the science of planning the budgets themselves and the utilisation of such budgets to effect an overall management tool for the business planning and control."

Advantages of Budgetary Control

It is a useful management tool for comparing the current items with pre-planned items with a view to attain equilibrium between ends and means, output and effort. It corrects the deviations from planned path through the media of observation, research, planning, control and decision making and thus helps in performance of future activities in an orderly way. It acts as a friends, philosopher and guide to the management. Its major advantages are given here below :–

1. It brings efficiency and economy in the working of the business enterprises. Even though a monetary reward is not offered, the budget becomes a game—a goal to achieve or a target to shoot at—and hence it is more likely to be achieved or hit than if there was no predetermined goal or target.
2. It establishes divisional and departmental responsibility. It thus prevents alibis and "buck-passing" when the budget figures are not met.
3. It co-ordinates the various divisions of a business, namely, the production, marketing, financial and administrative divisions. It "forces executives to think, and think as a group."
4. It guards against undue optimism leading to over-expansion because the targets are fixed by the executives after cool and careful thought.
5. It acts as a safety signal for the management. It shows when to proceed cautiously and when manufacturing or merchandising expansion can be safety undertaken. It serves as an automatic check on the judgement of the executives as losses are revealed in time which is a caution to the management to stop wastages.
6. Uniform policy without the disadvantages of a military type of business organisation can be pursued by all divisions of the business by means of centralisation of budgetary control.
7. Seasonal variation in production can be reduced by developing new "fill in" products. This results in decreasing the cost of production by increasing volume of output.
8. The use of budget figures as measures of operating performance and financial position makes possible the adoption of the standard

cost principle in divisions other than the production division.

9. It helps management in obtaining the most profitable combination of different factors of production. This results in a more economical use of capital.
10. Management which have developed a well-ordered budget plan and which operate accordingly, receive greater favour from credit Agencies.
11. It is the only means of predetermining when and to what extent financing will be necessary avoiding the possibility of both over and under-capitalisation.

Limitation to Budgetary Control

1. **Opposition against the very spirit of budgeting :** There will always be active and passive resistance to budgetary control as it points out at the efficiency or inefficeincy of individuals. The opposition is also due to human nature–the tendency to ressist change.
2. **Budgeting and changing economy :** The preparation of a 'budget which gives a realistic position of the firm' affairs under inflationary pressure and changing Government policies is really dificult. Thus, the accurate position of the business cannot be estimated.
3. **Time factor :** Accuracy in budgeting comes through experience. Management must not expect to much during the development period.
4. **Not a substitute for management :** Budget is only a management tool. It can not substitute management. Besides that no budgetary programme can be successful unless adequate arrangements are made for supervision and administration.
5. **Co-operation required :** The success of the budgetary control depends upon willing co-operation and teamwork. Budget officer must get co-operation from all departmental managers. These managers must feel the responsibility for achieving or bettering departmental goals laid down in the budgets.

Steps in Budgetary control

I. Organising Budgeting

II. Responsibility of Budgeting

1. Budget controller
2. Budget committee
3. Fixation of the budget period.

III. Budget procedure

1. Determination of key factor
2. Making of forecasts
3. Consideration of alternative combination of forecasts
4. Prepration of budgets

TYPES OF BUDGETS

I. Sales Budget

For the sales budget following factors should take into consideration:

(a) Past sales figures and trend
(b) Salesman's estimates
(c) Plant capacity
(d) General trade prospects
(e) Orders or hand
(f) Proposed expansion of discontinuance of products
(g) Seasonal fluctuations
(h) Potential market
(i) Availability of material and supply
(j) Financial aspect
(k) Other factors :–
   (i) The nature and degree of competition within the industry
   (ii) Cost of distributing goods
   (iii) Government control, rules and regulations related to the industry, and
   (iv) Political situation-national and international as it may have an influence upon the market.

II. Production Budget

This budget provides an estimate of the total volume of production productwise with the scheduling of operations by days, weeks and months a forecast of the closing finished product inventory. The responsibility of the total production budget lies with works manager and that of Departmental Production Budgets lies with Departmental Works Manager.

III. Performance Budgeting

Performance budgeting involves evaluation of the performance of an organisation in the context of both specific as well as over all objectives of the organisation. This requires the complete clarity about both the short-term and long-term organisational objectives.

The features of Performance Budgeting are given here below:–

1. The budget is prepared for each managerial level.
2. The jurisdiction of the authority and responsibility for different costs controllable by the executive concerned is fixed up.
3. The concerned executive is vested with the requisite authority required for the responsibility intrusted to him.

IV. Zero Base Budgeting

ZBB is a new technique designed to revitalise budgeting. A company should not only make decisions about the proposed new programmes but it should also from time to time review the appropriateness of the existing programmes.

Zero base budgeting as the term suggests, examines a programme or function be allowed. The manager proposing the activity has, therefore, to prove that the activity is essential and the various amounts asked for are really reasonable taking into account the volume of activity.

Standard Costing

Standard costing is a specialised technique of costing under which standard costs are predetermined, actual costs are compared with such predetermined costs, the variations between the two are noted and analysed as to their causes so that corrective measures may be taken to control the factors leading to unfavourable variations. The system of standard costing, thus, involves various steps—from the setting up of stndards to finally exercising control over costs. It aims at assessing or prefixing the costs of a product, process or operation under standard operating conditions. It serves as an effective tool in the hands of the management for planning, co-ordination and control of various activities of the business. There is a continuous process of growth effected in business through the help of standard costing technique since the standard costs set in are realistic, capable of being attained and are revised from time to time according to needs and requirements of the business enterprise. This technique, if implemented in conjunction with the system of budgetary control, provides better and more successful functions of the business.

Definition of Standard Costing

According to the Chartered Institute of Management Accountants. London Standard Costing is "the preparation and use of standards costs, their comparison with actual costs and the analysis of the variances to their causes and points of incidents". The definition given by W.W. Biggs makes concept of standard costing more clear. According to him, "Standard Costing discloses the costs of deviations from standard and classifies these as to their causes, so that management is immediately informed of the sphere of operations in which remedial action is necessary."

Thus, standard costing is a method of ascertaining costs where by statistics are prepared to show :

(a) the standard cost;
(b) the actual cost;
(c) the difference between these costs which is termed as variance.

Standard costs are determined for each element of cost—direct materials, direct labour, overheads (fixed and variable)—separately and then variations from actual costs are computed in respect of each element distinctly so as to detect which part of the costs needs control and to which department, process or operation, the responsibility may be placed. The standard costs are organised to uncover and report off-standard conditions. The management should strive for the attainment of standard costs because they are attainable ideal costs and are practical from the point of view of business.

Application of the Technique of Standard Costing

Standard costing is not a method of costing just as process or job or unit costing. It is a system or technique of cost accounting which can be used in conjuction with process, job or operating costing without any difficulty, whatsoever. Industries where standard costing is more suitable can be categorised as under :

1. Process industries where the method of production and nature of output are the same. The examples of such industries are chemical industries, distilleries, paper-making and metal processing etc.
2. Industries where the methods of manufacture are repetitive and products are more or less homogeneous, *e.g.*, agricultural and food products.
3. Service industries where operation costing is also applicable like transport, gas and water, electricity etc.
4. Engineering and textile industries where large range of products are manufactured.
5. Extraction industries such as coal, oil and timber.

Where the work is not repetitive, *e.g.*, construction work, contract work, ship-building and erection work etc., it is difficult to set standards and, therefore, standard costing would not be suitable. But in certain cases it can be applied partially though not fully, at least to some advantage of the concerns.

Advantages of Standard Costing

It is imperative for management to have prior knowledge of costs so that decision making can be effective. Management can control costs on information being provided to it immediately for comparison of results. The advantages of standard costing can thus be listed as follows :

1. **Formulation of price and production policies:** Standard costing acts as a valuable guide to management in the formulation of price and production policies. It assists management in the field of inventory pricing, product pricing, profit-planning and also further reporting to higher levels.
2. **Comparison and analysis of data:** Standard costing provides a stable and sound basis for comparison of actual costs with standard costs according to different elements separately. It brings out clearly the impact of external factors and internal causes on the cost and performance of the concern. Thus, it indicates places where remedial action in necessary and how far improvement is possible in the long run.
3. **Cost consciousness:** An atmosphere of cost consciousness is created among the staff, managerial as well as workmen, of the business. Standard costing also provides incentives to workers and middle and top executive personnel for efficient work.
4. **Better capacity to anticipate:** A tighter, more accurate and effective budget can be formulated for the coming years by once knowing the deviations of actual costs from standard costs. Data are available at an early stage and the capacity to anticipate about charging conditions is developed.
5. **Delegation of authority and fixation of responsibility:** The net profit is analysed and responsibility can be placed on the person incharge, for any variations from the standards. The sphere of operation of adverse variations is disclosed and particular production department or centre can be held accountable for it. Thus, delegation of authority and fixation of responsibility can be done by management to control the affairs in different departments.
6. **Management by 'exception':** The principle "management by exception" can be made applicable in the business. This helps the management in concentrating its attention on cases which are off-standard *i.e.,* below or above the standard set in. The trend of costs is portrayed and therefore, a pattern is provided for the elimination of undesirable factors causing damage to the business.
7. **Better economy, efficiency and productivity:** Managerial review of costs is more effective as the operations are scrutinised carefully and inefficiencies are disclosed. Men, machines and materials are more effectively utilised and thus economies can be effected in business together with increased productivity. Besides

it, a lot of clerical labour is also saved and economy is attained in calculations and computations.

Limitations of Standard Costing

1. Fixation of standards may be costly and may require high order of skill and competency. Small concerns, therefore, feel difficulty in the operation of such system.
2. The industries which deal with non-standardised products and the jobs, which change according to customer's specifications, may find the system of standard costing unsuitable and costly.
3. Responsibility can be delegated upon a particular person, process or production only when the controllable and non-controllable factors are distinctly known—and this is a very hard nut to crack.

Pre-Requisites for installation of standard costing system

Installation of standard costing system for accomplishing the desired objectives require existence of certain pre-requisities. These pre-requisties can be put as follows:

1. Acceptance of the system: The standard costing system can have the desired effects only when the system is acceptable both to the management as well as to the workers. The management should take sufficient interest in the system to make it effective. Similarly the workers should also believe that in the long run, the system would be beneficial to all of them. This is possible by fixing the standards in a way that they are capable of being achieved by an average worker.

2. Judicious setting of standards: The standards should be fixed after a careful study of all technical processes and operations of the business. They should be fixed judiciously and should not be ideal but capable of being achieved. Setting of standards at too high a level will create resentment among the workers and depress their performance while setting of standards at too low a level will have adverse effects on personal initiative and costs. It will be appropriate to fix the responsibility of setting standards on a committee consisting of important persons such as Production Controller, Purchase Manager, Personal Manager Cost Accountant, etc.

3. Reasonable size: The system of standard costing can be introduced with advantage in concerns which are of a reasonable size. The system may not be suitable for small concerns since in their case careful scheduling of production may not be possible. For example, in a small concern a worker may be handling different machines and at times he may be called to handle different jobs and therefore, it may not be possible to correctly fix the standard time for different jobs or different operations handled by him. Moreover the system of standard, costing requires specialisation of jobs and processes which may not be possible in a small concern.

4. Competent staff: The successful operation of standard costing system requires existence of well qualified and trained staff for fixing the standards, measuring performance and reporting variances to different levels of management. The reports submitted help the management in applying the principle of "management by exception" which means that the management pays attention only to those cases where performance is below or above the standard.

5. Existence of budgetary control system: Existence of budgetary control system is a pre-requisite for the standard costing system. Budgets fix the targets which the executives have to achieve. They create a sense of discipline, financial or otherwise, among employees at different levels. Budgets are the projections for the future and therefore they are of great use to the effective functioning of the standard costing system.

6. Proper delegation of authority and responsibility: Standard costing system requires proper delegation of authority and responsibility at different levels. This is possible by drawing an organisation chart clearly laying down the authority and responsibility of different executives in the organisation.

7. Efficient accounting system: An efficient accounting system is also an essential requisite for successful operation of the standard costing system.

The accounting information supplied should not only be accurate but also be complete and up to date. The system of coding may be used for speedy recording and analysing the accounting information. Appropriate cost centres should also be set up in the organisation.

MEANING OF STANDARD COSTS

Ideal costs

These are costs which should be there under ideal working conditions, ideal management and ideal plant capacity. Such an ideal is a myth, far from reality. Such a flight of imagination does not have any material significance in the eyes of practical manager who is aware of certain limitations which exist in spite of every possible check, control, care and caution. Perfection can never be achieved when one has to deal with men, materials and machines; and not simply figures. Perfection is not possible, even in biological and mathematical sciences, what to talk of management science which involves handling of man in particular whose behaviour is totally unpredictable at any given time. Sometimes, miraculous results are achieved due to certain abnormal conditions but we concern ourselves not with such abnormalities but with whatever is feasible if strived for. When the plant is working maximum capacity or even at more than its capacity level, perfection is a far cry and hence ideal costs cannot be regarded as standard costs for managerial control.

Normal costs

Such costs can be determined on the basis of the prevailing conditions of the business or industry. Thus, here it is assumed that plant is working at normal level of capacity and efficiency, workers are engaged in production activities performing their normal functions and the normal efficiency operations are being carried out. The cost shall thus be an average standard cost which is normally there in the business. Then, where would the management need control? How would the business progress and brighten its prospects, broaden and widen its field of activities and achieve prominence and success in the competitive market? Besides that, the meaning of 'normal' differs from one business to another. This suggests that normal levels of workmanship, efficiency, capacity and managerial operations are not significant and of worth for practical planning and control of costs.

Cost based on 'average of past performance'

If past is any guide for future action, as it popularly regarded the average of past performance should serve as the best ground for the ascertainment of standard costs. The costs which have been incurred during the past 3 or 5 years, for instance, as the case may be, are averaged out and same may be taken as standard costs for the following period. This, again, would not be a correct basis for the computation of standard cost because it is not logical and rational to assume that past trend will continue in future without any changes or reservation, whatsoever. No doubt, past results have a significant role to play in shaping the standards, yet they are not enough and self-sufficient to constitute standards. Several errors, wastes, ineconomies and inefficiencies of plant and business are comprised therein. The circumstances in the present set-up might have altogether changed; plant capacity might have increased or diminished, market conditions also might be adverse or more favourable. Besides that, different trends and tendencies might be foresighted. It is imperativge to take a record of all these factors and, therefore, historical costs cannot serve the purpose of standards costing.

Current costs

The costs which are currently or presently being incurred are also not a useful guide for standard costs since they are neither in rhythm with past trends nor are inclusive of factors and conditions to follow. Present is always required to be adjusted for past as well as future. Current costs have even a weaker ground for being regarded as a suitable basis for treatment as standards.

Current actual costs are, in one way, the costs which are more accurate to be assumed as standards if the conditions remain static and circumstances do not change. But this is seldom true in business and moreover we need cost control, the scope of which is absent if we adopt the current costs as standards.

Expected or anticipated costs

The costs which are expected to be incurred during a forthcoming period are costs which closely follow the pattern of present costs, though adjusted according to past behavioural pattern as well as future tendencies. But such costs would be an estimate of what the actual costs shall be in respect of the period for which the estimates have been prepared. As pointed out while distinguishing estimated costing from standard costing, such estimated costs do not provide any basis for comparison and control. Estimated cost is just a prediction of the actual costs; it is, in a way, better than what the cost is or what the cost shall be under normal conditions. A standard should be fixed assuming somewhat higher level of efficiency than what is reflected under simple estimation of actual costs.

Reasonably attainable costs

Costs which can be attained reasonably if the management tries for them, *i.e.,* it makes a sincere and concerned effort to achieve the targets set in, can be regarded as a satisfactory yardstick or benchmark for standards. Here, we assume a level of operation which is certainly above the normal level of efficiency. It neither means perfection (an ideal) not the current conditions nor even the normal conditions. The management by fixing costs at such a level can make wholehearted effort to bring down the actual costs to the level of standard and can achieve better efficiency in business operations. It is argued that reasonably attainable standards cannot be regarded as standards for our purpose because it is difficult to set a level in between actual costs and ideal costs. But, as a matter of fact, it is not at all difficult to set in such standards because we assume an efficiency level better than what is prevailing at present or even what shall prevail in the period for which standards are being fixed.

Standard Cost and Budgeted Cost

There is no conceptual difference between the terms "Standard cost" and "budgeted cost", expect that the term 'standard cost' is a unit concept while the term "budgeted cost" is a total concept. It other words, cost per unit, if carefully predetermined is termed as standard cost while total cost carefully predetermined is termed as budgeted costs.

Preliminaries to Setting of Standards

Certain factors are to be borne in mind while fixing the standards :

Period of use

The first important criterion for establishment of standard costs is the length of the operation period for which standards are to be used. Long-term as well as short-term standards may be fixed ranging for different periods. For long-term planning and growth standards for a longer duration, say 3 to 5 years, may be justified while for planning and budgeting for the accounting period short term standards for a year or so are beneficial. For measuring the performance and exercising control over costs short-term standards are most suited. The standards according to length of time may be categorised as—

(a) **Basic standards:** These are not alerted over a long period of time; revisions are not frequent and there is a stability and stagnancy in standards fixed. These 'basic' or 'bogey' standards remain constants for a very long time and are applied in industries where only a *small range of products* are manufactured and *long-term planning* is required. But since the conditions do not remain static in this dynamic world. The standards become obsolete and require overhauling and, therefore, the long-term basic standards are not realistic.

(b) **Current standards:** Short-term standards are known as current standards. These are more suitable for business since they take into account the current conditions and are related to the budget period.

In business, it will be useful to set both—long term as well short term standards. This will help in finding out the variations in respect of both these standards in advance of actual production.

Setting of standards

The standard cost is determined for each and every element of cost distinctly. The elements can be divided under the following categories :

(i) Direct Material; *(ii)* Direct Labour; *(iii)* Overheads—*(a)* Fixed Overheads and *(b)* Variable Overheads.

Standards for direct material cost

The direct material cost is found out by multiplying the quantity of materials to be purchased with the rate or price at which they are available and hence the standards are to be set for both quantity and rate, separately, for the determination of standard cost of direct materials.

(i) **Quantity standards.** To know, 'how much materials is required' is a task which can be performed with the help of —

(a) records of past experience *i.e.,* historical data;
(b) mathematical or scientific computations and engineering specifications;
(c) test runs and experiments; or
(d) standard bills of materials.

(ii) **Price standards.** The material price standards can be set on the basis of either :

(a) prices paid in the past taking into account the anticipated trends of rise or fall of prices in the market during the period for which standards are to be determined; or
(b) average of the prices paid during the past period, *i.e.,* average or normal price; or
(c) 'basic' or 'bogey' prices which are static or fixed in nature. Market fluctuations are not incorporated while deciding such prices.

Standards for direct labour cost

Just as for direct materials the standards are fixed separately for quantity and rate, similarly for direct labour also the standards are determined separately for quantum of labour to be employed in production and the rate of wages to be paid to them. The standard direct labour cost can be arrived at by multiplying the standard quantity with the standard rate. The quantity of labour can be fixed in terms of time required for performing the various operations involved in production. The standards regarding time and rate have been discussed below:

(i) **Standard time:** The time to be consumed by labourers can be measured by time, motion and fatigue studies. Works and methods analysis can be adopted and operation time for every activity noted down. The total time required is further adjusted for wastages.

(ii) **Standard rate:** The type of labour required for performing a specific job or activity would be the most important factor for deciding the rate of wage to be paid to the workers. Efficient and skilled workers having technical knowledge might have to be employed for certain types of technical jobs and therefore, the wages paid to such workers will be higher than those for unskilled and non-technical workers. Where the work requires some knowledge of art or science, specialisation in certain fields like product design or priduct specifications, engineerig etc. would be basically responsible for disparity in the rates of wages. Besides, production of certain commodities may requiere experienced workers-they also will have to be paid more. Then, if the management wants to provide some incentives to workers the rates of payment should be higher than what are expected by the workers. Again, the rates may be fixed according to look done, *i.e.,* piece rates or according to fixed hours of work, *i.e.,* time rates. The type of wage system to be followed is important in this respect.

The wages rates can be determined on the basis of one or more of the above considerations. Therefore, the standard may be set by computing the average of past figures and adjusting it further on the assumption that normal working conditions will continue. Estimates may be made on the grounds of judgement, intuition, guess or scientific calculations also.

Standards for Overheads

Overheads may be classified as manufacturing, administration, selling and distribution overheads. They may also be categories as fixed and variable. Before setting the standards in respects of overheads, the following points should be carefully gone through:

1. What level of activity has been taken as standard level? Does it represent current, or normal or reasonably attainable level?
2. The overheads would have to be classified into two broad categories— fixed and variable, because different standards are required to be fixed for them.
3. Quantum of expenses to be incurred on each item, according to each department for every process or operation will have to be determined. Flexible budgeting may be helpful in this connection.

Fixed Overhead Standards

Fixed overheads are not affected by the volume of production and therefore, fixation of standards for fixed overhead is relatively easy. The past figures shall be the best guide in this reference. In case the plant capacity is increased or business is carried on in more shifts, the fixed overheads might be more than what they were in the preceding period. A reasonable budgeted estimate of the same would be incorporated while determining fixed overhead standards. Normally, the fixed overhead rate per unit of output or per hour is determined so as to know the recovery of fixed overheads for the actual output or for actual time taken (as the case may be).

Variable Overhead Standard

The volume of production multiplied by the cost of overhead per unit of output would determine the total variable overhead cost for a period. The per unit variable cost is fixed and, therefore, it also depends to a large extent on the past data.

Manufacturing overhead standard

Indirect costs like indirect material cost, indirect labour cost and other manufacturing costs can be estimated with the help of the material and labour standards. The burden of overheads per hour can be determined. This standard overhead rate is to be applied for calculating standard cost for the total hours taken.

Office and administration overhead standard

The standards in respect of such overheads will depend upon the number of persons employed on the clerical and managerial staff, the hours of their work, the quantum of production, and the amount of control and vigilance exercised by the executives in this respect.

Selling and distribution overheads standard

The indirect selling expenses depend on the sale promotion efforts, channels of distribution, nature of the product, transportation and other difficulties for distribution of goods to different areas etc. A decision is to be taken in this regard and finally the total of such overheads is to be computed.

After fixing the standards for direct material cost, direct labour cost and overhead cost separately, the total standard cost of manufacturing a product or taking up a specific operation can be known by just aggregating the different costs.

Standard cost of standard output

When the standard quantity which shall be manufactured during a particular period has been decided upon, the standard cost of standard production can be computed by a simple multiplication of the standard units to be produced by the standard per unit cost of production.

Standards of sales

Standards are to laid down both for the probable quantity of sales and the selling price, so as to know the standard value of sales. The budgeted estimate of the expected volume of sales and the selling price can be made by the management. The deviations of actual volume of sales and the price at which the goods are actually sold are also important for effecting managerial control over costs.

Standards for profit

The excess of standard sales over standard costs is the standard profit. Sometimes standards for profit are determined at a fixed percentage on cost or on selling price, keeping in view the minimum return expected on investment. This helps in determining standards for sales also.

Revision of standards

The standards set in are required to be revised from time to time according to change in circumstances. Any alterations effected in standards should represent the changed conditions of work, increased plant capacity, market contditions etc. If a new range of products is to be manufactured or some operations turn out to be unprofitable due consideration would have to be given to such factors in fixation of standards. Normally, there should not be frequent changes in standards, otherwise the very purpose of determination of standards shall be defeated. If variations from actuals occur in practice, they may be due to controllable or non-controllable causes.

❑ ❑ ❑

Chapter **8**

Management Accounting

Introduction

The term management accounting refers to accounting for the management. Management accounting provides necessary information to assist the management in the creation of policy and in the day-to-day operations. It enables the management to discharge all its functions *i.e.*, planning, organization, staffing, direction and control efficiently with the help of accounting information.

Definitions

"Management accounting is concerned with accounting information that is useful to management". —*R.N. Anthony.*

"Management accounting is the presentation of accounting information is such a way as to assist management in the creation of policy and in the day-to-day operations of an undertaking".

—*Anglo American Council of Productivity.*

Objectives of Management Accounting

The objectives of management accounting are:

(1) to assist the management in promoting efficiency. Efficiency includes best possible services to the customers, investors and employees.

(2) to prepare budget covering all functions of a business (i.e. production, sales, research and finance).

(3) to analysis monetary and non-monetary transactions.

(4) to compare the actual performance with plan for identifying deviations and their causes.

(5) to interpret financial statements to enable the management to formulate future policies.

(6) to submit to the management at frequent intervals operating statements and short-term financial statements.

(7) to arrange for the systematic allocation of responsibilities.

(8) to provide a suitable organization for discharging the responsibilities.

In short, the objective of management accounting is to help the management in making decisions and implementing them efficiently.

Scope of Management Accounting

Management accounting has various facets. The field of management accounting is very wide. The main purpose of management accounting is to provide information to the management to perform its functions of planning directing and controlling. Management accounting includes various areas of specialization to render effective service to the management.

Financial Accounting : Financial Accounting deals with financial aspects by preparation of Profit and Loss Account and Balance Sheet. Management accounting rearranges and uses the financial statements. Therefore management accounting does not exclusively maintain factual data for itself. It is closely related and connected with financial accounting. Thus, management accounting is dependent on financial accounting which limits its scope.

Cost Accounting : Cost accounting is an essential part of management accounting. Cost accounting, through its various techniques, reveals efficiency of various divisions, departments and products. It also provides information regarding cost of products process and jobs through different methods of costing. Management accounting makes use of all this data by focusing it towards managerial decisions.

Budgeting and Forecasting : Budgeting is setting targets by estimating expenditure and revenue for a given period. Forecasting is prediction of what will happen as a result of a given set of circumstances. Targets are fixed for various departments and responsibility is pinpointed for achieving the targets. Actual results are compared with preset targets and performance is evaluated.

Inventory Control : This includes, planning, coordinating and control of inventory from the time of acquisition to the stage of disposal. This is done through various techniques of inventory control like stock levels, ABC and VED analysis physical stock verification, etc.

Statistical Analysis : In order to make the information more useful statistical tools are applied. These tools include charts, graphs, diagrams index numbers, etc. For the purpose of forecasting, other tools such as time series regression analysis and sampling techniques are used.

Analysis of Data : Financial statements are analysed and compared with past statements, compared with those of other firms and with standards set. The analysis and interpretation results in drawing reports and presentation to the management.

Internal Audit : Internal audit helps the management in fixing individual responsibility for internal control.

Tax Accounting : Tax liability is ascertained from income statements. Tax planning in done by following the various tax incentives offered by the Central and State Governments. Knowledge of tax provisions helps the management in meeting the tax liabilities and complying with other legislations like Sales tax, Companies Act and MRTP Act.

Methods and Procedures : In includes keeping of efficient system for data processing and effective reporting of required data in time.

Functions of Management Accounting

Main objective of management accounting is to help the management in performing its functions efficiently. The major functions of management are planning, organizing, directing and controlling. Management accounting helps the management in performing these functions effectively.

Presentation of Data : Traditional Profit and Loss Account and the Balance Sheet are not analytical for decision making. Management accounting modifies and rearranges data as per the requirements for decision making through various techniques.

Aid to Planning and Forecasting : Management accounting is helpful to the management in the process of planning through the techniques of budgetary control and standard costing. Forecasting is extensively used in preparing budgets and setting standards.

Decision Making : Management accounting provides comparative data for analysis and interpretation for effective decision making and policy formulation.

Communication of Management Policies : Management accounting conveys the policies of the management downward to the personnel effectively for proper implementation.

Effective Control : Standard costing and budgetary control are integral part of management accounting. These techniques lay down targets, compare actual with standards and budgets to evaluate the performance and control the deviations.

Incorporation of non-financial information : Management accounting considers both financial and non-financial information for developing alternative courses of action which leads to effective and accurate decisions.

Co-ordination : The targets of different departments are communicated to them and their performance is reported to the management from time to time. This continual reporting helps the management in co-ordinating various activities to improve the overall performance.

Advantages of Management Accounting

The advantages of management accounting are summarized below:

Helps in Decision Making : Management accounting helps in decision making such as pricing, make or buy, acceptance of additional orders, selection of suitable product mix etc. These important decision are taken with the help of marginal costing technique.

Helps in Planning : Planning includes profit planning, preparation of budgets, programmes of capital investment and financing. Management accounting assists in planning through budgetary control, capital budgeting and cost-volume-profit analysis.

Helps in Organizing : Management accounting uses various tools and techniques like budgeting, responsibility accounting and standard costing. A sound organizational structure is developed to facilitate the use of these techniques.

Facilitates Communication : Management is provided with up-to-date information through periodical reports. These reports assist the management in the evaluation of performance and control.

Helps in Co-ordinating : The functional budgets (purchase budget, sales budget, and overhead budget etc.) are integrated into one known as master budget. This facilitates clear definition of department goals and coordination of their activities.

Evaluation and Control of Performance : Management accounting is a convenient tool for evaluation of performance. With the help of ratios and variance analysis, the efficiency of departments can be measured. Management accounting assists the management in the location of weak spots and in taking corrective actions.

Interpretation of Financial Information : Management accounting presents information in a simple and purposeful manner. This facilitates quick decision making.

Economic Appraisal : Management accounting includes appraisal of social and economic forces and government policies. This appraisal helps the management in assessing their impact on the business.

Limitations of Management Accounting

Management accounting suffers from the following limitations:

Based on Accounting Information : Management accounting derives information from past financial accounting and cost accounting records. If the past records are not reliable, it will affect the effectiveness of management accounting.

Wide Scope : Management accounting has a very wide scope incorporating many disciplines. This results in inaccuracy and other practical difficulties.

Costly : The installation of management accounting system requires a large organization. Hence, it is very costly and only big concerns can afford to adopt it.

Evolutionary Stage : Management accounting is still in its initial stages. Tools and techniques are not fully developed. This creates doubts about the utility of management accounting.

Opposition to Change : Introduction of management accounting system requires a number of changes in the organization structure, rules and regulations. This rearrangement is not generally liked by the people involved.

Intuitive Decisions : Management accounting helps in scientific decision making. Yet, because of simplicity and personal factors the management has a tendency to arrive at decisions by intuition.

Not an Alternative to Management : Management accounting will not replace the management and administration. It is a tool of the management. Decisions are of the management and not of the management accountant.

Distinguish Between Management Accounting and Cost Accounting

Cost accounting and Management accounting are two modern branches of accounting. Both the systems involve presentation of accounting data for the purpose of decision making and control of day-to-day activities. Cost accounting is concerned not only with cost ascertainment, but also cost control and managerial decision making. Management accounting makes use of the cost accounting concepts, techniques and data. The functions of cost accounting and management accounting are complimentary. In cost accounting the emphasis is on cost determination while management accounting considers both the cost and revenue. Though it appears that there is overlapping of areas between cost and management accounting, the following are the differences between the two systems.

Purpose : The main objective of cost accounting is to ascertain and control the cost of products or services. The function of management accounting is to provide information to management for efficiently performing the functions of planning, directing, and controlling.

Emphasis : Cost accounting is based on both historical and present data, whereas management according deals with future projections on the basis of historical and present cost data.

Principles and Procedures : Established procedures and practices are followed in cost accounting. No such prescribed practices are followed in Management accounting. The analysis is made and the resulting conclusions are presented in reports as per the requirements of the management.

Data Used : Cost accounting uses only quantitative information whereas management accounting uses both qualitative and quantitative information.

Scope : Management accounting includes, financial accounting, cost accounting, budgeting, tax planning and reporting to management, whereas Cost accounting is concerned mainly with cost ascertainment and control.

Distinguish Between Management Accounting and Financial Accounting

The following are the main differences between financial accounting and management accounting.

Objective : The main objective of financial accounting is to supply information in the form of profit and loss account and balance sheet to outside parties like shareholders, creditors, government etc. But the objective of management accounting is to provide information for the internal use of management.

Performance Analysis : Financial accounting is concerned with the overall performance of the business. On the other hand management accounting is concerned with the departments or divisions. It report about the performance and profitability of each of them.

Data Used : Financial accounting is mainly concerned with the recording of past events whereas management accounting is concerned with future plans and policies.

Nature : Financial accounting is based on measurement while management accounting is based on judgement. Because of this, financial accounting is more objective and management accounting is more subjective.

Accuracy : Accuracy is an important factor in financial accounting. But approximations are widely used in management accounting. This is because most of the information is related to the future and intended for internal use.

Legal Compulsion : Financial accounting is compulsory for all joint stock companies but management accounting is only optional.

Monetary Transactions : Financial accounting records only those transactions which can be expressed in terms of money. On the other hand, management accounting records not only monetary transactions but also non-monetary events, namely technical changes, government policies etc.

Control : Financial accounting will not reveal whether plans are properly implemented. Management accounting will reveal the deviations of actual performance from plans. It will also indicate the causes for such deviations.

Distinguish Between Cost Accounting and Financial Accounting

Differences between Cost Accounts and Financial Accounts are listed below:

Objective : The main objective of cost accounting is to provide cost information to management for decision making. The main objective of financial accounting is to prepare Profit and Loss A/c and Balance Sheet to report to owners and outsiders.

Legal Requirement : Cost accounts are maintained to fulfil the internal requirements of the management as per conventional guideline. Financial records are maintained as per the requirement of Companies Act and Income Tax Act.

Classification of Transactions : Cost accounting records and analyses expenditure in an objective manner viz., according to purpose for which costs are incurred. Financial accounting classifies records and analyses transactions in a subjective manner i.e., according to nature of expenses.

Stock Valuation : In cost accounts stocks are valued at cost. In financial accounts, stocks are valued at cost or realisable value, whichever is lesser.

Analysis of Profit and Cost : Cost accounts reveal Profit of Loss of different products, departments separately. In financial accounts, the Profit or Loss of the entire enterprise is disclosed into.

Accounting period : Cost report are continuous process and are prepared as per the requirements of managements, may be daily, weekly, monthly, quarterly, or annually. Financial reports are prepared annually.

Emphasis : Cost accounting lays emphasis on ascertainment of cost and cost control. Financial accounts emphasis is laid on the recording of transactions and control aspect is not given importance.

Nature : Cost accounts lay emphasis on both historical and predetermined costs. Financial accounts are maintained on the basis of historical records.

❑ ❑ ❑

Multiple Choice Questions

1. Profits can be frauduletly inflated by
(*a*) Suppression of sales returns
(*b*) Treating capital expenditure as revenue
(*c*) Overestimation of liabilities
(*d*) Omission of prepaid expenses

2. A credit sale of goods to shivendra should be debited to
(*a*) Sales Account (*b*) Goods Account
(*c*) Shivendra Account (*d*) Purchase Account

3. Which of the following assets does not depreciate?
(*a*) Machinery and equipment
(*b*) Patents
(*c*) Land
(*d*) Furniture

4. Valuing the stock in trade at market price or cost price which is less is an example of the convention of
(*a*) consistency (*b*) disclosure
(*c*) knowing the value (*d*) none of these

5. Double entry principle means
(*a*) Having debit for every credit and similarly credit for each debit.
(*b*) Writing all the entries twice in the book.
(*c*) Maintaining the double account for all busness transactions.
(*d*) Writing two times the same entry.

6. A sale of goods to Vaibhav Deep for cash should be debited to
(*a*) Vaibhav's A/C (*b*) Cash A/C
(*c*) Sale of goods A/C (*d*) None of these

7. A withdrawal of cash from business by the proprietor of the firm should be credited to
(*a*) Capital Account
(*b*) Cash Account
(*c*) Drawing Account
(*d*) Proprietor's Account

8. The preparation of a trial balance helps in
(*a*) Locating errors of principle
(*b*) Locating errors of ommission
(*c*) Locating clerical errors
(*d*) Locating compensatory errors

9. A cheque received and deposited in the bank on the same day is recorded in the
(*a*) Cash column of the cash book
(*b*) Bank column of the cash book
(*c*) Credited in the cash book
(*d*) Debited in the cash book

10. Petty cash may be used to pay
(*a*) the expenses relating to postages and conveyance
(*b*) salaries and wages to the final staff
(*c*) for the purchase of furniture and fittings
(*d*) none of these

11. A reserve is charge against
(*a*) Trading account
(*b*) Profit and loss account
(*c*) Profit and loss appropriation account
(*d*) None of these

12. The payment side of cash book is under cost by Rs 200 when over draft as per pass book is the starting point
(*a*) Rs. 200 will be deducted
(*b*) Rs. 200 will be added
(*c*) No effect will be in the pass book
(*d*) None of these.

13. An amount of Rs. 300 is debited twice in the pass book when overdraft as per the cash book is the starting point
(*a*) Rs. 600 will be added
(*b*) Rs. 500 will be deducted
(*c*) No effect will be in the cash book
(*d*) None of these

14. Expenditure incurred by a publisher for acquiring copy rights is a
(*a*) Capital expenditure
(*b*) Revenue expenditure
(*c*) Deferred revenue expenditure
(*d*) None of these.

15. Immediately after purchasing a new truck Rs. 1,000 is paid to have the name of the company and other advertising material painted on the truck this Rs.1,000 is a
(*a*) Capitalexpenditure
(*b*) Deferred revenue expenditure
(*c*) Revenue expenditure
(*d*) None of these

16. A return Inwards book is kept to record
(*a*) return of goods sold
(*b*) returns of anything purchased
(*c*) returns of goods purchased
(*d*) returns of anything sold

17. Bill Receivable Book is a part of the
(*a*) Ledger
(*b*) Balancesheet
(*c*) Journal
(*d*) Profit and Loss Account

18. A sales of Rs. 2000 wrongly entered in the purchase book
(*a*) decreases the gross profit by Rs. 2000
(*b*) increases the gross profit by Rs. 2000
(*c*) increases the gross profit by Rs. 4000
(*d*) none of these.

19. Which of the following are current assets?
(*a*) Bank loan for three years
(*b*) Account receivable
(*c*) Long-term investments
(*d*) Debentures sinking fund investments

20. Insurance unexpires accounts is a
(*a*) Real account (*b*) Personal account
(*c*) Nominal account (*d*) None of these.

21. Goodwill account is a
(*a*) Nominal Account (*b*) Real Account
(*c*) Personal Account (*d*) None of these.

22. Bank overdraft account is a
(*a*) Personal Account (*b*) Real Account
(*c*) Nominal Account (*d*) All of these.

23. Contingent liability is shocon due to
(*a*) Convention of full disclosure.
(*b*) Convention of conservatism.
(*c*) Convention of materiality.
(*d*) Dual aspect concept.

24. Which item is shown on the debit side of a trial balance?
(*a*) Rent outstanding
(*b*) Prepaid Expenses
(*c*) Purchases
(*d*) Excess of income over expenses by the firm

25. Purchase for office furniture on account is recorded in
(*a*) General Journal (*b*) Cash book
(*c*) Purchase book (*d*) Sales book

26. Sales on account is recorded in
(*a*) Cash book (*b*) Journal
(*c*) Sales book (*d*) General Journal

27. The credit balance in the bank account is
(*a*) Capital (*b*) a liability
(*c*) an asset (*d*) an expense

28. Cash sales are recorded in
(*a*) Sales book (*b*) Cash book
(*c*) Journal (*d*) Purchase book

29. Error of commission do not permit
(*a*) The trial balance to agree
(*b*) Correct the total of balance sheet
(*c*) Correct totalling of trial balance
(*d*) None of these

30. An item of Rs.72 has been debited to a personal account as Rs. 27, is an error of
(*a*) Commission (*b*) Omission
(*c*) Principle (*d*) None of these

31. Sales to shyam of Rs. 500 not recorded in the books would affect
(*a*) Shyam's account (*b*) Sales account
(*c*) Sales account (*d*) Cash account

32. Which of the following accounts is increased by credit entries?
(*a*) Bank Overdraft
(*b*) Purchases Account
(*c*) Goodwill Account
(*d*) Sales Returns Account

33. Profit and loss account of business shows the
(*a*) Net profit earned
(*b*) Gross profit earned
(*c*) Balance of all accounts
(*d*) Capital employed in business

34. If a receipt of Rs. 200 from Rajesh out debtor has not been recorded in the books the profit would show
(*a*) an increase of Rs. 200
(*b*) a decrease of Rs. 200
(*c*) neither an increase nor a decrease
(*d*) none of these

35. Closing stock is valued at
(*a*) Market price
(*b*) Cost price
(*c*) Cost price or market price whichever is lower
(*d*) Cost price or market price whichever is higher

36. Unearned income account is
(*a*) an asset (*b*) a liability
(*c*) an expernse (*d*) an income

37. Depreciation is provided on
(*a*) Current Assets (*b*) Liquid Assets
(*c*) Fictitious Assets (*d*) Fixed Assets

38. A bill of exchange is drawn by a
(*a*) Creditor (*b*) Debtor
(*c*) Shareholder (*d*) Debentureholder

39. Bills receivable account is
(*a*) an expense Account
(*b*) an asset Account
(*c*) a liability Account
(*d*) a revenue Account

40. When goods are purchased for the joint venture out of joint bank A/C the amount is debited to
(*a*) Joint bank A/C
(*b*) Joint venture A/C
(*c*) Purchases account
(*d*) None of these

41. Bills receivable endorsed are debited to
(*a*) Debtor's Account
(*b*) Creditor's Account
(*c*) Bills payable Account
(*d*) Bills receivable Account

42. Subscription received during the year were Rs. 800 for the current year. Rs.100 for the previous year and Rs. 100 for the next year. In the receipts and payments account the receipts from subscriptions would appear at
(*a*) Rs. 700 (*b*) Rs. 800
(*c*) Rs. 900 (*d*) Rs. 1000

43. Any donation received for a specific purpose is a
(*a*) Liability
(*b*) Assets
(*c*) Revenue receipts
(*d*) Capital receipts

44. The convention of conservatism will have the effect of
(*a*) Over statement of assets
(*b*) Under statement of assets
(*c*) Under statement of liabilities
(*d*) Under statement of provision for bad and doubtful debts

45. An accountant is mainly concerned with
(*a*) Audit work
(*b*) Preparation of budget for his employees
(*c*) Management Constancy Services
(*d*) Filling tax returns

46. Expenses incurred on research and development is an example of
(*a*) Capital expenditure
(*b*) Revenue expenditure
(*c*) Deferred revenue expenditure
(*d*) None of these

47. Amount spent on increasing the seating capacity in a cinema hall is
(*a*) Capital expenditure
(*b*) Revenue expenditure
(*c*) Deferred revenue expenditure
(*d*) None of these

48. Which of the following is not capital expenditure?
(*a*) Cost of issuing shares and debentures
(*b*) Wages paid for construction of building
(*c*) Repairs on a second-hand machinery newly purchased
(*d*) Purchase of new spark plug at a cost of Rs. 8.50 for a two-year old car

49. Window dressing is prohibited due to
(*a*) Convention of conservatism
(*b*) Convention of disclosure
(*c*) Convention of materiality
(*d*) Accrual concept

50. Quantitative transactions are not recorded in accounts due to
(*a*) dual concept
(*b*) accrual concept
(*c*) money measurement concept
(*d*) none of these

51. Concept of Realisation implies
(*a*) When cash is received from debtors
(*b*) When goods are delivered to customer
(*c*) When order is received
(*d*) None of these

52. Which of the following are not current liabilities?
(*a*) Bank overdraft
(*b*) Redeemable debentures
(*c*) Provision for doubtful debts
(*d*) Accounts payable

53. Provision for doubtful debts account is a
(*a*) Personal account (*b*) Real account
(*c*) Nominal account (*d*) None of these

54. LIFO inventory method was used in year I, FIFO in year II and weighted average in year III. Which accounting principle is violated?
(*a*) Cost principle
(*b*) Consistency
(*c*) Materiality
(*d*) No principle of accounting is violated

55. Land was reported at its selling price which is substantially higher than its cost. The increase in value was included in the income statement, which accounting principle is violated ?
(*a*) Cost principle
(*b*) Going concern concept
(*c*) Entity concept
(*d*) Conservatism

56. The cost of three small files (of Rs. 4 each) was charged to expenses when purchased even though they had a useful life of several years. This was done according to the
(*a*) Cost principle
(*b*) Conservatism principle
(*c*) Full disclosure
(*d*) Materiality

57. The amount spent on unsuccessful patent rights is a
(*a*) Capital expenditure
(*b*) Deferred revenue expenditure (if the amount is large)
(*c*) Revenue expenditure (even though the amount is large)
(*d*) None of these

58. Double entry system of bookkeeping refers to a system where
(*a*) the number of accounts with a debit balance must agree with the number of accounts with the credit balance
(*b*) each transaction is recorded twice, once in journal and then in legder
(*c*) equal debit and credit entries are made for each transaction
(*d*) each transaction is recorded in two set of account books

59. An entry of Rs. 500 was wrongly posted to wages account instead of machinery account, as wages are to be capitalised. It is an error of
(*a*) Commission
(*b*) Omission
(*c*) Principle
(*d*) Clerical error

60. Which of the following statements best explains the relationship between journal and ledger?
(*a*) First recording in journal and then posting to ledger completes the double entry of the transaction.
(*b*) The journal is the book of original entry where as the ledger is the book of second entry.
(*c*) The journal is the book for analytical record and ledger is the book for chronological record.
(*d*) The process of recording, in the journal is called journalising, the process of recording in the ledger is called posting.

61. In order to determine the amount of sales, to which of the following records one should refer?
(*a*) Sales book
(*b*) Sales account
(*c*) Journal
(*d*) Total debtors account

62. Which of the following errors is revealed by trial balance?
(*a*) Wrong amount entered in the book of original entry
(*b*) Wrong amount entered in a ledger account
(*c*) Complete omission of an entry from the book of original entry
(*d*) All of these

63. Which of the following errors are revealed by trial balance?
(*a*) Omission of an amount from the trial balance
(*b*) Posting of the wrong amount
(*c*) Wrong totalling of the book of original entry
(*d*) None of these

64. Which of the following errors will cause the trial balance to be out of balance?
(*a*) The total of the purchase book is Rs. 1000 short
(*b*) Goods received back from mahesh, Rs. 250 have not been entered in the Returns inward book
(*c*) Office furniture purchased from Ravi and Co. Rs. 950 has been entered in the purchase book
(*d*) A purchase of Rs. 251 from Gopal and Co. has been entered in the purchase book as Rs. 215.

65. Which of the following errors will not cause the trial balance to be out of order?
(*a*) Rs. 590 received from P. Das has been debited to (*b*) Rs. 10 Das
(*b*) A purchase of Rs. 258 from Lekhi has been debited to his account as Rs. 285
(*c*) The total of the discount columm of the cash book (cr.) is Rs. 20 short
(*d*) An invoice for Rs. 460 is entered in the sales book as Rs. 640

66. Which of the following errors will not cause the trial balance to be out of balance?
(*a*) Rs. 310 for goods sold, was posted to the credit of charges
(*b*) Purchases returns book for December 1978 was overcast by Rs. 220
(*c*) Sales book carried forward Rs. 2400 instead of Rs. 2004
(*d*) All of these

67. An invoice of Rs. 560 is entered in the sales book as Rs. 650. The total of the debit side of the trial balance is Rs. 21,440. Assuming no other error what is the total of the credit side of the trial balance?
(*a*) Rs. 21,240 (*b*) Rs. 21,350
(*c*) Rs. 21,330 (*d*) None of these

68. Which of the following books should be used to record purchase of a type writer on account?
(*a*) Cash books (*b*) Purchase book
(*c*) Sales book (*d*) Journal

69. Which of the following books should be used to record purchase of merchandise an account?
(*a*) Cash book (*b*) Purchase book
(*c*) Sales book (*d*) Journal

70. Agreement of the trial balance may not indicate that
(*a*) no error remains undetected
(*b*) double entry has been completed
(*c*) arithmetic accuracy is reasonably proved
(*d*) all ledger accounts have been correctly posted

71. Use of subsidary books can be made by
(*a*) Only large business concerns
(*b*) Only small business concerns
(*c*) Only medium size business concerns
(*d*) All of these

72. Petty cash system is designed
(*a*) to meet the needs of small businesses
(*b*) to cover small and miscellaneous income
(*c*) to cover the small expenditure to be paid in cash
(*d*) to cover both small incomes and expenditures

73. The term "Imprest system" is used in relation to
(*a*) Purchase book (*b*) Sales book
(*c*) Cash book (*d*) Petty cash book

74. Trial balance is a proof that
(*a*) every transaction is recorded twice
(*b*) no error remains in the books of accounts
(*c*) books are authentically and correctly written
(*d*) none of these

75. Which of the following is an error of commission?
(*a*) A sale of Rs. 560 ommitted to be recorded
(*b*) A purchase of Rs. 840 was wrongly posted
(*c*) Treating charges as addition to asset
(*d*) Sales book over cost by Rs. 600 and purchase book was under cost by the same amount

76. Which of the following errors is disclosed by trial balance?
(*a*) Error of principle
(*b*) Wrong amount posted in ledger account
(*c*) Non-recording of a transaction in the book of original entry
(*d*) None of these

77. 'Bank over draft' should be classified as
(*a*) Current asset (*b*) Current liability
(*c*) Intengible asset (*d*) Intangible asset

78. Assets appearing in the book but having no value are known as
(*a*) Wasting assets (*b*) Intangible assets
(*c*) Current assets (*d*) Fictitious assets

79. Which of the following is an accounting equation
(*a*) Capital – Assets – Liabilities
(*b*) Capital – Assets – Liabilities
(*c*) Assets – Liabilities – Capital
(*d*) Liabilities – Assets – Capital

80. Which of the following is an equation?
(*a*) Assets = Equities
(*b*) Assets = Liabilities – Capital
(*c*) Assets = Liabilities – Equities
(*d*) Assets = Equities + Liabilities

81. The capital in a business on Jan. 1 and Jan. 31 is Rs. 17,000 and Rs. 17,200 respectively. Investment by owner and withdrawal by owner during Jan amount to Rs. 1,000 and Rs.700 respectively. What is the net income for January?
(*a*) Rs. 100 (Loss) (*b*) Rs. 300
(*c*) Rs. 200 (*d*) Rs. 500

82. Which of the following transactions will result in decrease in assets and decrease in liabilities?
(*a*) Payment of a promissory note with cash
(*b*) Materials returned to supplier on account
(*c*) Redemption of debentures
(*d*) All of these

83. Cost of goods sold – Rs. 13,300, Gross Profit –Rs. 3,200, Netprofit – Rs. 700, what is the amount of sales?
(*a*) Rs. 14,000 (*b*) Rs. 10,100
(*c*) Rs. 16,500 (*d*) Rs. 17,200

84. Select the correct amount of purchases, given the following information :
Cost of goods sold – Rs. 1,20,000;
Carriage in wards – Rs. 1,890;
Opening stock – Rs. 43,640;
Closing stock – Rs. 38,500;
Purchase returns – Rs. 2,150;
Sales – Rs. 2,82,650
(*a*) Rs. 1,15,120 (*b*) Rs. 62,650
(*c*) Rs. 1,10,420 (*d*) None of these

85. Depreciation is appearing in the trial balance of a company. While making final accounts, it should be shown in
(*a*) the profit and loss account
(*b*) the balance sheet as a deduction from the asset concerned
(*c*) the profit and loss account and balance sheet
(*d*) the profit and loss account or balance sheet

86. From the following find out the correct equation
I. A represents opening stock
II. B represents purchases
III. C represents closing stock
IV. D represents cost of goods sold
(*a*) A - C = D - B (*b*) A + B = D - C
(*c*) D - A = B + C (*d*) None of these

87. While assertaining profit in single entry system the amount of additional capital introduced is
(*a*) added to the capital in the beginning
(*b*) deducted from the capital in the beginning
(*c*) added to the capital at the end
(*d*) deducted from the capital at the end

88. When capital at the end is Rs. 21,500 drawings Rs. 4,300 and capital in the begining Rs.19,400, what is the amount of profit or loss?
(*a*) Rs. 2,200 (profit) (*b*) Rs. 2,200 (loss)
(*c*) Rs. 6,400 (profit) (*d*) Rs. 6,400 (loss)

89. Generally, under single entry system
(*a*) only personal accounts are maintained
(*b*) only personal, cash and bank accounts are maintained
(*c*) all accounts are maintained
(*d*) no account is maintained

90. Opening debtors Rs.12,000,closing debtors Rs.15,000 cash received from debtors Rs. 25,000 what is the amount for sales?
(*a*) Rs. 22,000 (*b*) Rs. 28,000
(*c*) Rs. 2,000 (*d*) None of these

91. If the rate of gross profit on sales is 25% and the cost of goods sold is Rs. 75,000, then the amount of total sales will be
(*a*) Rs. 1,00,000 (*b*) Rs. 93,750
(*c*) Rs. 92,150 (*d*) Cannot be known

92. Total debtors account will be affected by
(*a*) Cash sales (*b*) Credit sales
(*c*) B/R closing balance (*d*) All of these

93. If the cost of goods sold is Rs. 1,20,000 and the rate of gross loss is 1/4 on sales,the amount of sales is
(*a*) Rs. 1,20,000 (*b*) Rs. 90,000
(*c*) Rs. 80,000 (*d*) Rs. 96,000

94. Cost of goods sold is Rs.1,00,000 rate of gross profit on sales is 20%. What is the amount of sales?
(*a*) Rs. 1,20,000 (*b*) Rs. 80,000
(*c*) Rs. 1,25,000 (*d*) None of these

95. The single entry system is defective because
I. only one account is maintained
II. the trial balance cannot be prepared
III. the net profit cannot be accurately calculated
IV. the possibility of fraud and misappropriation is great
Select the correct answer from the following:
(*a*) I, III and IV (*b*) I and II
(*c*) II, III and IV (*d*) I only

96. Assets in the beginning of the year Rs. 10,000, Assets at the end of the year Rs. 18,000 Drawing during the year Rs. 2,000. Therefore the profit is
(*a*) Rs. 6,000 (*b*) Rs. 8,000
(*c*) Rs. 10,000 (*d*) None of these

97. Depreciation, as the term is used in accounting, means
(*a*) physical deterioration of a fixed asset
(*b*) decline in the market value of an asset
(*c*) allocation of the cost of fixed asset over its useful life
(*d*) making a provision for the replacement of the fixed asset

98. The term depletion is used in relation to
(*a*) Fixed assets (*b*) Wasting assets
(*c*) Current assets (*d*) Intangible assets

99. Under the annuity method the amount of total depreciation is determined by
(*a*) deducting the scrap value from the cost of the asset
(*b*) deducting the amount of interest from the cost of the asset
(*c*) adding the cost of the assets and interest there on
(*d*) adding the cost of the assets and expected cost of maintenance

100. Which method of depreciation is suggested for coal mines?
(*a*) Dimishing balance
(*b*) Fixed instalment method
(*c*) Sum of years' digits method
(*d*) Depletion method

101. Which one of the following accounting conventions stipulates that contingent assets appear as a foot note in the balancesheet?
(*a*) Materiality (*b*) Consistency
(*c*) Disclosure (*d*) Conservatism

102. Which one of the following is not related to the convention of conservatism?
(*a*) Making provision for doubtful debts and discount on debtors in anticipation of actual bad debts and discount
(*b*) Valuation of stock at market price or cost price whichever is higher
(*c*) Charging of small capital items as Revenue
(*d*) Adopting written-down value method of depreciation as against straight–line method

103. Match List I (Standards issued by ICAI) with List II (Objects/areas covered) and select the correct answer using the codes given below the lists:

List I	List II
I. AS-1	(A) Valuation of Inventories
II. AS-2	(B) Cash flow Statement
III. AS-3	(C) Revenue Recognition
IV. AS-9	(D) Disclosure of Accounting Policies

Codes:
(*a*) I-D, II-A, III-B, IV-C
(*b*) I-D, II-A, III-C, IV-B
(*c*) I-A, II-D, III-C, IV-B
(*d*) I-A, II-D, III-B, IV-C

104. On March 31, 2001, the closing stock of X Ltd. was Rs. 3,45,000 was destroyed by fire. The company closes its account on March 31. If the balance sheet of the company on March 31, 2001 was finalised on April 25, 2001, then the balance sheet will show the closing stock at
(*a*) Rs. 3,45,000 with no mention of fire
(*b*) Rs. 1,20,000 with no mention of fire
(*c*) Rs. 3,45,000 showing loss by fire in foot note
(*d*) Rs. 1,20,000 showing loss by fire in foot note

105. Consider the following
The investment port folio of a business man as on 31-12-2000 stood as follows :
I. 8% Debentures of X Co. Ltd. (Rs. 6,000). Interest payable on March 31 and Sept. 30
II. 7% Debentures of Y Co. Ltd. (Rs. 4,000). Interest payable on June 30 and Dec. 31
III. 10% Debentures of Z Co. Ltd. (Rs. 9,000). Interest payable on June 1 and Dec. 1
Amount of interest accrued on the closing data will be
(*a*) Rs. 335 (*b*) Rs. 1,025
(*c*) Rs. 195 (*d*) Rs. 830

106. Which one of the following is correct with respect to going concern convention
(*a*) The enterprise is not going to terminate its operations in the period a head
(*b*) The enterprise may go out of business in the next accounting period
(*c*) The enterprise may not divest or diversify its operational spheres
(*d*) The enterprise may not revalue its assets during the current accounting period?

107. Consider the following statements:
Continuous evaluation of the relevance of generally accepted accounting principles is required, because
I. They are the everlasting operating realiries
II. The environment, in which business operates, under goes constant change
III. The business enterprises can develop financial statements of value to the end-users
IV. Realities of social,economic and legal frame work have to be considered by professional accountants
Which of the above statements are correct ?
(*a*) I, II and III
(*b*) I, II and IV
(*c*) III and IV
(*d*) I and IV

108. Which one of the following will lead to under statement of net profit?
(*a*) Amortisation of fictitous Assets
(*b*) Treating capital expenditure as revenue expenditure
(*c*) Treating revenue expenditure as capital expenditure
(*d*) Creation of general reserve

109. Which one of the following items is considered revenue expenditure ?
(*a*) Expenditure by way of maintenance that has increased productivity
(*b*) Repair of a gear box in a car that has enhanced its operational life
(*c*) Complete over haul of a machines pending around 20% of its value
(*d*) Changing a small component of a machine to maintain its operating efficiency

110. After the construction of their new factory building M/s XYZ Co. shifted to it. During this process Rs. 20,000 were spend on pulling down the old structure and Rs.2,000 weres spent on shifting the stocks to new building. This expenditures are to be classified as
(*a*) Capital expenditure
(*b*) Revenue expenditure
(*c*) Capital and revenue expenditure respectively
(*d*) Deferred revenue expenditure

111. Match List I with List II select the correct answer :

List I	List II
I. Reducing capital	A. Contribution margin
II. Sales > variable cost	B. Reorganisation
III. Sales > Break even sales	C. Absorption
IV. Take–over of firm	D. Margin of safety

Codes:
(*a*) I-B, II-A, III-C, IV-D
(*b*) I-A, II-B, III-C, IV-D
(*c*) I-A, II-B, III-D, IV-C
(*d*) I-B, II-A, III-D, IV-C

112. Preparation of Trial Balance helps, mainly, in
(*a*) summarising business transactions
(*b*) verifying that 'generally accepted accounting principles' have been observed
(*c*) finalising the 'sources and uses of funds' statement
(*d*) locating errors if any in books of accounts

113. Match List I with List II select the correct answer:

List I	List II
I. Goodwill	A. Current liability
II. Over-draft	B. Fixed assets
III. Preliminary expenses	C. Reserves and surpluses
IV. Premium on issue of shares	D. Fictitious assets

Codes:
(*a*) I-B, II-A, III-D, IV-C
(*b*) I-A, II-B, III-D, IV-C
(*c*) I-A, II-B, III-C, IV-D
(*d*) I-B, II-A, III-C, IV-D

114. If opening stock = Rs. 2,45,000, purchases = Rs. 15,00,000, sales = Rs. 17,40,000 and rate of gross profit = 20% on cost of goods sold, the closing stock would be at
(*a*) Rs. 3,53,000 (*b*) Rs. 2,95,000
(*c*) Rs. 2,45,000 (*d*) Rs. 1,95,000

115. Match List I (Items) with List II (Recorded in) and select the correct answer :

List I	List II
I. Wrapping material	A. Trading account
II. Wages and salaries	B. Profit and loss account
III. Prepaid expenses	C. Balance sheet
IV. Opening stock	

Codes:
(*a*) I-B, II-A, III-A, IV-C
(*b*) I-B, II-A, III-C, IV-A
(*c*) I-C, II-B, III-B, IV-A
(*d*) I-C, II-B, III-A, IV-C

116. The basis adopted for piecemeal distribution of cash among the partners should be such that amounts finally left unpaid are in the ratio in which
(*a*) Capital stands on the data of dissolution
(*b*) Profit and losses are shared
(*c*) Capital balance stood at the beginning of partnership
(*d*) Private assets appear on the date of dissolution

117. The capital of a firm is Rs. 80,000. The reasonable return in the industry is 7.5 per cent. If the profit earned by the firm during past five years was Rs. 8,000; Rs. 9,000; Rs. 7,000; Rs. 8,500 and Rs. 10,000; then the super profit of the firm will be
(*a*) Rs. 2,000 (*b*) Rs. 2,500
(*c*) Rs. 3,000 (*d*) Rs. 3,500

118. Consider the following :
A football club has received the following subscriptions during the year ending March 31, 2001:

	31-3-2000	31-3-2001
Out standing Subscription	19,500	25,500
Subscription	12,800	9,500

Subscription received during the year 2000-01: Rs. 2,45,000. The subscription income of the club for the year 2000-01 was
(*a*) Rs. 2,63,800
(*b*) Rs. 2,80,000
(*c*) Rs. 2,47,700
(*d*) Rs. 2,84,000

119. 'A' and 'B' are partners in a firm sharing profits and losses in the ratio of 2:3 'C' a new partner is admitted for 1/4 th share. 'A' and 'B' old partners share C's profit into their profit sharing ratio. The new profit sharing ratio of 'A', 'B' and 'C' would be.
(*a*) 1 : 1 : 1 (*b*) 2 : 3 : 4
(*c*) 1 : 2 : 2 (*d*) 6 : 9 : 5

120. Consider the following statements with respect to the sinking-fund method of depreciation :
I. Depreciation is smaller than the assets' annual depreciable cost
II. Amount of interest constantly declines due to assets' reducing balance
III. Amount net incidence on profit and loss account remains constant due to changing fixed depreciation
IV. Periodic depreciation is recorded through the asset account
Which of the above statements are correct
(*a*) II and III (*b*) I and III
(*c*) I, II and IV (*d*) II, III and IV

121. The following information about share capital is required to be disclosed in the balance sheet of a Ltd. company.
I. Issues, subscribed and paid-up capital
II. Add forfeited shares
III. Less calls in arrear from directors
IV. Less calls in arrear from others
The chronological order of their disclosure under the head'share capital, in the balance sheet would be
(*a*) I, II, III ,IV (*b*) I, III, IV, II
(*c*) I, IV, III, II (*d*) I, II, IV, III

122. Match List I (Fund) with List II (Purpose of fund) and select the correct answer :

List I	List II
I. Sinking fund	A. Maintaining stable rate of dividend
II. Capital redemption reserve fund	B. Periodical of debentures redemption
III. Dividend equalisation fund	C. Strengthening financial position
IV. General reserve fund	D. Redeeming preference shares

Codes:
(*a*) I-C, II-B, III-A, IV-C
(*b*) I-B, II-D, III-C, IV-A
(*c*) I-D, II-B, III-C, IV-A
(*d*) I-B, II-D, III-A, IV-C

123. Provisions are amounts set a side out of profits and other surpluses for
(*a*) meeting a liability, the amount of which can be determined with exact figure
(*b*) any known liability of which the amount cannot be determined with substantial accuracy
(*c*) meeting an eventuality arising out of revaluation of assets in ordinary course of business
(*d*) meeting a liability arising out of arbitration

124. A trader does not keep a complete set of books and gives the following information :
He started business with Rs. 10,000 on June 1, 2000.

He drew at the rate of Rs. 500 per month for the last six months. He also introduced further capital of Rs. 2,000 in the business during the year.

His total assets on Dec. 31, 2000 were Rs. 23,700 and his creditors were Rs. 3,000 on the same date. Outstanding expenses on Dec. 31, 2000, were Rs. 500. His net profit during the year would be

(*a*) Rs. 11,200 (*b*) Rs. 11,500
(*c*) Rs. 13,000 (*d*) Rs. 14,200

125. X who holds 100 shares of Rs. 10 each, fails to pay a final call of 2 Rs. The directors forfeited all the shares and subsequently reissued 50 shares of Rs. 6 each as fully paid. The amount to be transferred to Capital Reserve A/C would be

(*a*) Rs. 200 (*b*) Rs. 300
(*c*) Rs. 400 (*d*) Rs. 800

126. A Ltd. company issues 3000,15% debentures of Rs. 100 each at a discount of 7.5% repayable at a premium of 5% at the end of 5 years. The loss on issue of debentures will be

(*a*) Rs. 22,500 (*b*) Rs. 30,000
(*c*) Rs. 37,500 (*d*) Rs. 45,000

127. Match List I with List II and select the correct answer

List I	List II
I. Technique of cash management	A. Fund flow Analysis
II. Technique of working capital management	B. Economic order quantity
III. Technique of inventory management	C. Common size balancesheets
IV. Technique of Analysis of financial statement	D. Cash flow Analysis

Codes:

(*a*) I-A, II-D, III-B, IV-C
(*b*) I-A, II-D, III-C, IV-B
(*c*) I-D, II-A, III-C, IV-B
(*d*) I-D, II-A, III-B, IV-C

128. Match List I (Transactions) with List II (Impact on current ratio) and select the correct answer using the codes given below the lists:

List I	List II
I. Goods sold at profit	A. Improvement
II. Creditors paid	B. Deterioration
III. Debts realised	C. No change
IV. Materials purchased on credit	

Codes:

(*a*) I-A, II-C, III-B, IV-B
(*b*) I-B, II-C, III-A, IV-C
(*c*) I-A, II-A, III-C, IV-B
(*d*) I-B, II-A, III-C, IV-C

129. The following information had been made available from the profit and loss account for the year ending on March 31, 200 :

Gross profit...................... Rs. 2,00,000
Gross profit margin.......... 20%
Stock velocity.................. 4

If, in current year, the sales are expected to increase by 50 %, then the average inventory required would be

(*a*) Rs. 2,00,000 (*b*) Rs. 2,50,000
(*c*) Rs. 3,00,000 (*d*) Rs. 3,50,000

130. X Ltd. has current ratio of 2 :1 and quick ratio of 1.5:1. If its current liabilities are Rs. 80,000, then the value of stock would be

(*a*) Rs. 1,60,000 (*b*) Rs. 1,20,000
(*c*) Rs. 40,000 (*d*) Rs. 80,000

131. If earning per share of a company is Rs.5 and the price earning ratio of other similar companies is 4,then the market value of the share of the company would be

(*a*) Rs. 0.80 (*b*) Rs. 1.25
(*c*) Rs. 9 (*d*) Rs. 20

132. If the cost of goods sold is Rs. 1,00,000 the value of opening stock is Rs. 20,000 and the value of closing stock is Rs. 80,000. Then the stock turnover ratio would be

(*a*) 5 times (*b*) 4 times
(*c*) 2 times (*d*) 1 time

133. Match List I with List II and select the correct answer using the codes given below the lists:

List-I	List-II
I. Current ratio	A. Sufficiency of EBIT to cover interest charges
II. Debt equity ratio	B. Short term solvency
III. Net profit margin ratio	C. Exposure to financial risk
IV. Interest coverage ratio	D. Earnings left for share holders

Codes:
(*a*) I-B, II-C, III-A, IV-D
(*b*) I-C, II-B, III-A, IV-D
(*c*) I-C, II-B, III-D, IV-A
(*d*) I-B, II-C, III-D, IV-A

134. Match List I with List II and select the correct answer :

List I	List II
I. Leverage ratio	A. Short-term solvency
II. Liquid ratio	B. Earning capacity
III. Turn-over ratio	C. Relationship of debt and Equity
IV. Profitability ratio	D. Efficiency of Assets management

Codes:
(*a*) I-B, II-A, III-D, IV-C
(*b*) I-C, II-B, III-A, IV-D
(*c*) I-D, II-C, III-A, IV-B
(*d*) I-C, II-A, III-D, IV-B

135. PEPs is calculated as

(*a*) $\frac{\text{EBIT Equity shares}}{\text{Equity Shares}}$

(*b*) $\frac{\text{EBIT - Preference Dividend}}{\text{Equity Shares}}$

(*c*) $\frac{\text{EAT}}{\text{Equity Shares}}$

(*d*) $\frac{\text{EAT-Preference Dividend}}{\text{Equity Shares}}$

136. Consider the following information provided by XY Ltd. :

Net profit before depreciation and taxes .... Rs. 44,000
Depreciation for the year .... Rs. 8,000
Goodwill written off during the year.. Rs. 10,000
Rate of tax.................................... Rs. 50%

The cash flow of XY Ltd. form perations will be
(*a*) Rs. 36,000 (*b*) Rs. 28,000
(*c*) Rs. 26,000 (*d*) Rs. 13,000

137. If profit made during the year Rs.10,000; increase and decrease in the current assets is Rs. 5,000 and Rs. 4,000 respectively, then the cash from operation equals
(*a*) Rs. 9,000 (*b*) Rs. 10,000
(*c*) Rs. 11,000 (*d*) Rs. 19,000

138. Match List I with List II select and the correct answer :

List I	List II
I. Interest on capital in construction works	A. Performance and propriety
II. Management Audit	B. Capilal expenditure
III. Financial Audit	C. Authorisation of expenditure
IV. Valuation in balance sheet	D. Critical review by management
	E. Entity concept

Codes:
(*a*) I-B, II-D, III-E, IV-C
(*b*) I-D, II-A, III-B, IV-E
(*c*) I-B, II-A, III-C, IV-E
(*d*) I-D, II-B, III-C, IV-A

139. Consider the following with regard to furniture and fixtures:
I. Valuation with reference to bills and invoices
II. Authorisation of expenditure and its capitalisation
III. Adequate provison of depreciation
IV. Whether furniture is mortgaged or free from any mortgage

The correct sequence to be adopted by the auditor during the course of analytical review, vouching and examination of documents, would be
Codes:
(*a*) I, II, III, IV (*b*) II, III, I, IV
(*c*) III, IV, II, I (*d*) IV, I, II, III

140. Match List I with List II and select the correct answer using the codes given below the lists:

List I	List II
I. Public limited company	A. One man one vote

II. Partnership firm	B. Can make public issue
III. Cooperative society	C. Restricted membership
IV. Private limited company	D. Unlimited liability
	E. Direct supervision

Codes:

(*a*) I-E, II-D, III-B, IV-C
(*b*) I-B, II-D, III-A, IV-C
(*c*) I-E, II-C, III-B, IV-A
(*d*) I-B, II-C, III-A, IV-D

141. Networking capital of a firm is the
(*a*) Effective capital of the company when the business is in full swing.
(*b*) Capital borrowed from banks.
(*c*) Difference between the current assets and current liabilities.
(*d*) Capital provided by shares holders only.

142. If sales are Rs. 60,000; gross profit 1/3 on cost. Purchases are Rs. 49,000 and the closing stock is Rs. 9,000 the opening stock will be
(*a*) Nil (*b*) Rs. 5,000
(*c*) Rs. 20,000 (*d*) Rs. 49,000

143. A company has inadvertently overstated its ending inventory. This will
(*a*) Increase the income of the succeeding year.
(*b*) Decrease the income of the current year.
(*c*) Have no effect on the income of the succeeding year.
(*d*) Decrease the income of the succeeding year.

144. Modern Leasing Co. Ltd. has debt equity ratio 8:1. It has decided to issue bonus shares in the ratio of 1 : 1. The debt-equity ratio after the issue would be
(*a*) 8 : 1 (*b*) 4 : 1
(*c*) 1 : 8 (*d*) 1 : 4

145. How is current ratio calculated?
(*a*) $\frac{\text{Current Liabilities}}{\text{Current Assets}}$ (*b*) $\frac{\text{Current Assets}}{\text{Current Liabilities}}$
(*c*) $\frac{\text{Fixed Assets}}{\text{Current Liabilities}}$ (*d*) $\frac{\text{Current Assets}}{\text{Stock}}$

146. To test the liquidity of a concern which of the following ratios are useful
(*a*) Acid test ratio.
(*b*) Capital turnover ratio.
(*c*) Bad debts to sales ratio.
(*d*) Inventory turnover ratio.

147. A low inventory turnover ratio may be the result of
I. obsolescence of some of the stock.
II. Slow moving inventory.
III. Frequent stock-outs.
IV. Fast moving inventory.
of these statements
(*a*) I and II are correct.
(*b*) II alone is correct.
(*c*) IV alone is correct.
(*d*) II and III are correct.

148. If earning per share of X limited is Rs 15 and the price-earnings ratio of other similar companies is Rs.10 then the market value of the share of Rs. X Ltd. will be
(*a*) Rs. 300
(*b*) Rs. 150
(*c*) Rs. 75
(*d*) Rs. 25

149. Which one of the following is least suited for measuring return on investment?
(*a*) Income invested capital.
(*b*) Net operating income before interest and taxes verage total assets.
(*c*) Operating income ratio total assets turnover.
(*d*) Net income after interest but before taxes average total share holder equity.

150. Given in the following table is data for various companies in the same industry

	A	B	C	D
Current Assets	150	140	100	120
A/C Receivable	60	50	50	70
Turnover Ratio	6.5	5.0	5.5	5.0
Current Liabilities	100	120	80	130

The two firms which appear to be having better liquidity position are
(*a*) A and B (*b*) B and C
(*c*) A and C (*d*) B and D

151. While calculating the Net Present Value under discounted cash flow method of return on Investment analysis the operations involved are
I. cash out flow
II. discounted net cash flow
III. cash inflow
IV. net present value
The correct sequence of these operations is
(*a*) I, II, III, IV
(*b*) I, III, II, IV
(*c*) IV, I, III, II
(*d*) III, I, IV, II

152. Rate of return on investment is meaningful to
I. Shareholder
II. Creditors
III. Management
of the statements given above
(*a*) I alone is true.
(*b*) I and III are true.
(*c*) II and III are true.
(*d*) I, II and III are true.

153. Purchase of machinery and equipment for cash by firm
(*a*) Increases the total assets.
(*b*) Keeps total assets unchanged.
(*c*) Decreases the total assets.
(*d*) Increases the liability of the firm.

154. Which of the following is an operating expense?
(*a*) Depreciation of plant.
(*b*) Expired insurance.
(*c*) None of the above.
(*d*) Both (*a*) and (*b*)

155. Which of the following are current assets?
(*a*) Bank loan for three years.
(*b*) Account Receivable.
(*c*) Long-term investments.
(*d*) Debentures sinking fund investments.
(e) All of these.

156. Purchase of office equipments results in
(*a*) Decrease in liability.
(*b*) Decrease in capital.
(*c*) Increase in capital.
(*d*) Increase in fixed assets.

157. Payment of a liability results in
(*a*) Increase in total Assets.
(*b*) Decrease in total Assets.
(*c*) No change in total Assets.
(*d*) None of these.

158. Which one of the following is correct about 'marg – in of safety' ratio?
(*a*) Capital employ/net worth.
(*b*) Contribution/sales volume.
(*c*) Operating profit/contribution.
(*d*) Contribution/sales of BEP.

159. If the profit is 25% of the cost price then it is
(*a*) 20% of the sale price.
(*b*) 25% of the sale price.
(*c*) 30% of the sale price.
(*d*) 33% of the sale price.

160. Repayment of loan results into
(*a*) Source of fund.
(*b*) Application of fund.
(*c*) No flow of fund.
(*d*) All of these.

161. Sale of building results into
(*a*) Source of fund. (*b*) No flow of fund.
(*c*) Application of fund (*d*) None of these.

162. The term 'funds' as used in'funds flow statement means
(*a*) Cash
(*b*) Current assets
(*c*) Current liabilities
(*d*) Current Assets minus current liabilities

163. Payment of interim dividend is a
(*a*) Source of fund
(*b*) Application of fund
(*c*) No flow of fund
(*d*) All of these

164. If the rate of gross profit is 25% on cost of goods sold and the sales are Rs. 200000 the amount of profit will be
(*a*) Rs. 50000 (*b*) Rs. 40000
(*c*) Rs. 45000 (*d*) None of these

165. Quick ratio is a good indicator of the liquid position of a concern. The ideal quick ratio is
(*a*) 2 : 1 (*b*) 1 : 1
(*c*) 3 : 1 (*d*) 4 : 1

166. When current ratio is 4 : 1 and the amount of current liabilities Rs. 12,000. What is the amount assets?
(*a*) Rs. 12,000 (*b*) Rs. 4,000
(*c*) Rs. 48,000 (*d*) Rs. 60,000

167. Which of the following is a non–operating income
(*a*) Profit on the sale of used plant in manufact- uring company.
(*b*) Revenue from sales in a trading concern.
(*c*) Dividends received by an investment company.
(*d*) Premiums received by an insurance company.

168. Which of the following is correct?
(*a*) Cost of goods sold + closing stock – opening stock = Purchases
(*b*) Cost of goods sold – closing stock + opening stock = Purchases
(*c*) Opening stock + closing stock – cost of goods sold = Purchases
(*d*) Closing stock – cost of goods sold + opening stock = Purchases
(e) None of these

169. Which of the following is not correct?
(*a*) Purchases + Opening stock – Cost of goods sold = Closing stock
(*b*) Opening stock + Purchases – Closing stock = Cost of goods sold
(*c*) Closing stock + Cost of goods sold – Purchase = Opening stock
(*d*) Cost of goods sold–Closing stock – Purchases = Opening stock

170. The equation for the Debt Equity Ratio is?
(*a*) Long-term debt/Equity share capital.
(*b*) Liquid Assets/current liability.
(*c*) Current Assets/current liabilities.
(*d*) Net profits/net sales.

171. Opening stock – Rs. 15,000, Purchases – Rs. 40,000; cost of goods sold – Rs. 52,000 ; Sales – Rs. 57,000 what is the amount of gross profit or loss ?
(*a*) Rs. 12,000 (*b*) Rs. 5,000
(*c*) Rs. 5,000 (Loss) (*d*) Rs. 7,000

172. Sales returns – 2,500; Sales – Rs. 12,800; Purchases – Rs. 8,400; Gross profit Rs. 2,100 *What is the amount of cost of goods sold ?*
(*a*) Rs. 10,700 (*b*) Rs. 10,500
(*c*) Rs. 8,200 (*d*) Rs. 6,300

173. For the purpose of final accounts, stock is valued according to
(*a*) Cost or market value whichever is less.
(*b*) First–in first–out basis.
(*c*) Last–in first–out basis.
(*d*) Base stock method.
(e) Any of these.

174. The work manager gets commission of 10% on the profits after charging such commission. If the profit is Rs. 2, 200 what is the amount of his commission
(*a*) Rs. 220 (*b*) Rs. 200
(*c*) Rs. 240 (*d*) Rs. 244.44

175. If profits are 25% of selling price,what is the percentage of profit to cost?
(*a*) 20% (*b*) 25%
(*c*) 30% (*d*) 33%

176. In which of the following methods, inventory is valued at the latest prices prevailing in the market?
(*a*) Last-in first-out (LIFO).
(*b*) First-in first-out (FIFO).
(*c*) Replacement price method.
(*d*) Weighted average method.

177. In ABC Analysis,which category represents those items which are used in largest quantity but their value is not high ?
(*a*) 'A' items (*b*) 'B' items
(*c*) 'C' items (*d*) None of these

178. FIFO is advisable in case of
(*a*) Rising prices (*b*) Falling prices
(*c*) Canstant prices (*d*) All of these

179. Which of the following methods results in lower valuation of inventory and lower income when prices are rising ?
(*a*) FIFO
(*b*) LIFO
(*c*) Simple average
(*d*) Weighted average

180. When current ratio is 2:1, an equal increase in current assets and current liabilities would
(*a*) Increase the current ratio.
(*b*) Decrease the current ratio.
(*c*) Not change the current ratio.
(*d*) Will affect some other ratio.

181. When the current ratio is 2:5, and the amount of current liabilities is Rs. 25,000 what is the amount of current assets
(*a*) Rs. 62,500 (*b*) Rs. 12,500
(*c*) Rs. 10,000 (*d*) None of these

182. When quick ratio is 1.5 : 1 and the amount of quick assets Rs.30,000 what is the amount of quick liabilities
(*a*) Rs. 20,000 (*b*) Rs. 50,000
(*c*) Rs. 45,000 (*d*) Rs. 30,000

183. Which of the following items is not taken into account while computing current ratio
(*a*) Sundry creditors (*b*) Sundry debtors
(*c*) Furniture (*d*) Bank over draft

184. Which of the following items is not an operating expense?
(*a*) Advertising
(*b*) Depreciation of office equipment
(*c*) General management salaries
(*d*) Power consumed

185. When net sales for the year are Rs. 2,50,000 and debtors Rs. 50,000, the average collection period is (assuming year of 360 days)
(*a*) 60 days (*b*) 45 days
(*c*) 42 days (*d*) 72 days

186. Given-fixed long term liabilities Rs. 5,50,000, fixed assets Rs. 12,00,000 capital Rs. 8,50,000 current liabilities Rs. 2,50,000,current assets Rs. 4,00,000, solvency ratio is
(*a*) 5:12 (*b*) 8:16
(*c*) 15:17 (*d*) 10:15

187. If the cost of goods sold is Rs. 1 lakh, the value of opening and closing stock is Rs.20,000 and Rs. 30,000 respectively, the stock turnover ratio will be
(*a*) 3.3 times (*b*) 4 times
(*c*) 5 times (*d*) 6 times

188. Dividing net sales by average debtors would yield
(*a*) Acid test ratio.
(*b*) Return on sales ratio.
(*c*) Debtors turnover ratio.
(*d*) None of these.

189. Which of the following transactions change the current ratio?
(*a*) Purchase of goods for cash.
(*b*) Plant acquired on account.
(*c*) Sold goods on credit.
(*d*) Debentures converted into equity capital.

190. When the operating ratio is 91.5, the ratio of operating profit to sales
(*a*) Will be 91.5%.
(*b*) Will be 8.5%.
(*c*) Cannot be known from the given information.
(*d*) None of these.

191. In setting the accounts of a firm after its dissolution the assets of the firm shall be applied first in paying
(*a*) Each partner proportionately what is due to him on account of loans advanced by him
(*b*) Each partner proportionately what is due to him on account of capital
(*c*) Each partner proportionately what is due to him on account of past profits
(*d*) The debts of the firm to third parties

192. Capital employed in a business is Rs. 1,50,000, profits are Rs. 50,000 and the normal rate of profit is 20%. The amount of goodwill as per capitalisation method would be
(*a*) Rs. 1,00,000 (*b*) Rs. 1,50,000
(*c*) Rs. 2,00,000 (*d*) Rs. 3,00,000

193. 'A' and 'B' are sharing profits and losses in the ratio of 4 : 1 'C' is admitted as a new partner for 1/3rd share of profits for which he pays Rs. 30,000 as goodwill. If 'A' and 'B' agree to share future profits equally, then the amount of goodwill to be credited to 'A' would be
(*a*) Rs. 30,000 (*b*) Rs. 90,000
(*c*) Rs. 48,000 (*d*) Rs. 42,000

194. Assertion (A) : Share premium amount can be refunded in cash to equity share holders

Reason (R) : Share premium is usually collected when the market price of the shares is higher than the face value of the share

In the context of the above two statements, which one of the following is correct?

(*a*) Both A and R are true,but R is the correct explanation of A
(*b*) Both A and R are true,but R is NOT correct explanation of A
(*c*) A is true,but R is false
(*d*) A is false,but R is true

195. Match List I with List II and select the correct answer from the codes given bolow the lists :

List I (Item)	List II (Nature of Item)
I. Cash	A. Share holder's equity
II. Profits	B. Fixed assets
III. Discount on issue of shares	C. Current assets
IV. Plant and machinery	D. Fictitious assets
	E. Intangible assets

Codes :

(*a*) I-B, II-E, III-A, IV-C
(*b*) I-C, II-A, III-D, IV-B
(*c*) I-C, II-D, III-D, IV-E
(*d*) I-A, II-C, III-D, IV-B

196. When a goodwill account is raised at the time of admission of a new partner, credit is given to old partners in their

(*a*) New profit sharing ratio
(*b*) Old profit sharing ratio
(*c*) Ratio of sacrifice
(*d*) Capital ratio

197. A and B were equal partners in a firm on 1.1.1982, they admitted C on the following conditions:

C should bring Rs. 10,000 as capital, and Rs. 5,000 as goodwill. In future A, B and C would share profits and losses in the ratio of 2: 1:2. A and B will share the goodwill in the ratio of

(*a*) 1 : 1 (*b*) 3 : 1
(*c*) 1 : 3 (*d*) 2 : 1

198. On 31st December 1982, the assets and liabilities of a firm were Rs. 40,000 and Rs. 30,000 respectively

The firm was dissolved and a sum of 60 paise in a rupee was paid to the creditors. What was the loss on realisation?

(*a*) Rs. 10,000 (*b*) Rs. 12,000
(*c*) Rs. 18,000 (*d*) Rs. 22,000

199. When an incoming partner purchases his share from one of the existing partners

(*a*) The total assets of the firm do not change.
(*b*) The assets of the firm will be augmented to the extent of the payment received from the new partner.
(*c*) The assets of the firm will be augmented to the extent of the payment received from the new partner and existing partner with draws the share surrendered.
(*d*) The changes in the total assets of the firm will depend upon the structure of the assets.

200. While preparing the final accounts from incomplete records, the capital is to be taken as equal to the

(*a*) Value of fixed assets.
(*b*) Total assets.
(*c*) Difference between the current assets and current liabilities.
(*d*) Net assets.

201. Profit on reissue of forfeited shares is transferred to

(*a*) Profit and loss A/c
(*b*) Capital reserve A/c
(*c*) Share capital A/c
(*d*) General reserve A/c

202. Consider the following items which appear under "Reserves and Surplus" of balance sheet of a company

I. Profit and loss Account
II. Capital Redemption Reserve
III. Share Premium
IV. Capital Reserve

The correct sequence of these items is

(*a*) IV, II, III, I (*b*) IV, III, II, I
(*c*) I, II, III, IV (*d*) II, IV, III, I

203. The term current assets does not include
(*a*) Stock (*b*) Cash
(*c*) Advance payment (*d*) Furniture

204. Bonus share are issued by the companies because
(*a*) Surplus cash is available.
(*b*) There are heavy accumulated general reserves.
(*c*) There is heavy competition from similar companies.
(*d*) They have high gross profit ratio.

205. Profit can be fraudulently inflated by
(*a*) Suppression of sales returns.
(*b*) Treating capital expenditure as revenue.
(*c*) Overestimation of liabilities.
(*d*) Omission of prepaid expenses.

206. The trial balance of a manufacturing concern at the close of its financial year showed the following revenue balances Rs.

Raw materials and stores consumed	2,00,000
Salaries and wages	50,000
Other manufacturing expenses	1,00,000
Sales	3,00,000

The closing stock at selling rates amounted to Rs. 80,000. The management wants to change the basis of valuation of closing stock from selling rates to cost or market price, whichever is lower. Besides the figures given above, no other data are available
The closing stock value is
(*a*) Rs. 83,674.30 (*b*) Rs. 75,933.50
(*c*) Rs. 73,684.22 (*d*) Rs. 64,385.40

207. What is the correct sequence in which the capital of a company is raised?
(*a*) Issued, Nominal, Subscribed, Called-up.
(*b*) Issued, Nominal, Calledup, Subscribed.
(*c*) Nominal, Issued, Called-up, Subscribed.
(*d*) Nominal, Issued, Subscribed, Called-up.

208. Secret reserves may result by
(*a*) Creating general reserve.
(*b*) Providing excessive depreciation.
(*c*) Over valuation of stocks.
(*d*) Under valuation of liabilities.

209. Which of the following is not a capital reserve?
(*a*) Profits prior to incorporation.
(*b*) Dividend equalisation reserve.
(*c*) Profit on sale of fixed assets.
(*d*) All of these.

210. Which of the following is created by debiting the Profit and Loss Account?
(*a*) Provision
(*b*) Sinking fund for redemption of debentures
(*c*) Dividend equalisation fund
(*d*) All of these.

211. Any reserve which is not apparent on the face of the balance sheet is known as
(*a*) Secret reserve. (*b*) Hidden reserve.
(*c*) Inner reserve. (*d*) Any of these.

212. A provision is a
(*a*) General reserve. (*b*) Specific reserve.
(*c*) Capital reserve. (*d*) None of these.

213. If a company issues 1000 equity shares of Rs. 10 each will be legally all right if it asks an application.
(*a*) Rs. 2.50 (*b*) Rs. 3.50
(*c*) Rs. 4.50 (*d*) Rs. 5.00

214. If a share of Rs. 10 issued at a premium of Re.1, on which Rs. 9 (including premium) have been called and Rs. 7 (including premium) paid is forfeited the capital account should be debited by
(*a*) Rs. 8 (*b*) Rs. 9
(*c*) Rs. 7 (*d*) Rs. 6

215. A partnership firm is compulsorily dissolved when its business becomes illegal is described in which section of Partnership Act.
(*a*) Section 42 (*b*) Section 43
(*c*) Section 41 (*d*) Section 44

216. If vendors are issued fully paid shares of Rs. 1,00,000 in consideration of Net Assets of Rs. 1,20,000, the balance of Rs. 20,000 will be credited to
(*a*) Goodwill Account.
(*b*) Capital Reserve Account.
(*c*) Profit and Loss Account.
(*d*) Vendor's Account.
(e) None of these.

217. Partner's salaries to be debited to
(*a*) Profit and loss Account.
(*b*) Trading Account.
(*c*) Profit and Loss Appropriation Account.
(*d*) None of these.

218. In the absence of any partnership deed, interest on partner's loan will be allowed at the rate of
(*a*) 5 % (*b*) 6 %
(*c*) 9 % (*d*) 12 %

219. If A and B who are sharing profit in the ratio of 3:1. They admit C to one profits, the profit sharing ratio shall be
(*a*) A : 9/16; B: 3/16; C: 4/16
(*b*) A: 10/16; B: 2/16; C: 4/16
(*c*) A: 8/16; B: 4/16; C: 4/16
(*d*) A: 7/16; B: 5/16; C: 4/16

220. On the admission of a new partner the decrease in the value of Assets is debited to
(*a*) Revaluation Account.
(*b*) Old partner's capital Account.
(*c*) New partner's capital Account.
(*d*) Assets Account.

221. X, Y and Z are partners in the ratio of 1/2: 2/5 : 1/10, what will be the new ratio of the remaining partners if X retires?
(*a*) 2 : 1 (*b*) 4 : 1
(*c*) 5 : 1 (*d*) 3 : 1

222. Goodwill of a firm of A and B is valued at Rs. 30,000. It is appearing in the books at Rs. 12,000 C is admitted for 1/4 share. What amount he is supposed to bring for goodwill?
(*a*) Rs. 3,000 (*b*) Rs. 4,500
(*c*) Rs. 7,500 (*d*) Rs. 10,500

223. A and B are partners in the ratio of 2:1. They admit C for 1/4 share who contributes for Rs. 3,000 for his share of goodwill. The total value of good will of the firm is
(*a*) Rs. 3,000 (*b*) Rs. 9,000
(*c*) Rs. 12,000 (*d*) Rs. 15,000

224. When a firm is dissolved, profit or loss on realisation is shared by the partners
(*a*) Equal
(*b*) In the ratio of their capital balances.
(*c*) In the profit sharing ratio.
(*d*) In the ratio laid down in Garner V. Murray.

225. C and D are equal partners. Their capital balances on dissolution of the firm are C– Rs. 25000 and D–Rs. 15,000
Total cash available is Rs. 30,000
How should this cash be distributed between C and D?
(*a*) Rs. 15,000 each.
(*b*) Rs. 20,000 to C and Rs. 10,000 to D.
(*c*) Rs. 18,750 to C and 11,250 to D.
(*d*) According to decision in Garner V. Murray.

226. At the time of dissolution, an unrecorded asset taken by Mr. X, a partner should be debited to
(*a*) Mr. X's capital A/c. (*b*) Realisation A/c.
(*c*) Assets A/c. (*d*) None of these.

227. The term fixed assets include
(*a*) Bank balance.
(*b*) Stock of finished goods.
(*c*) Goodwill.
(*b*) Loose tools.

228. Secret reserves serve the purpose of
(*a*) Enabling the directors to tide over unfavour- able times.
(*b*) Meeting exceptional losses.
(*c*) Increasing the working capital.
(*d*) None of these.

229. In *Garner V. Murray* the deficiency of the insolvent partners is borne by other partner in the
(*a*) Profit sharing ratio.
(*b*) Ratio of their capitals.
(*c*) Equal share by each.
(*d*) None of these.

230. The remuneration payable to a whole-time director of the company should not exceed
(*a*) 5% of the net profits.
(*b*) 6% of the net profits.
(*c*) 7% of the net profits.
(*d*) 10% of the net profits.

231. In what order the following items are shown on the liability side of the balance sheet?
I. Share capital
II. Debentures
III. Sundry creditors

IV. Proposed dividends

Codes:

(*a*) I, II, III, IV
(*b*) I, III, II, IV
(*c*) II, III, IV, I
(*d*) I, IV, II, III

232. If on a share of Rs. 100 and called -up capital Rs.90 while the company received Rs.80, the capital account should be credited with

(*a*) Rs. 100 (*b*) Rs. 90
(*c*) Rs. 80 (*d*) Rs. 70

233. Unclaimed dividend is shown in the balance sheet under the heading as

(*a*) Current liabilities.
(*b*) Unsecured loans.
(*c*) Reserves and surplus.
(*d*) None of these.

234. Contingent liability is shown due to

(*a*) Convention of full disclosure.
(*b*) Convention of conservatism.
(*c*) Convention of materiality.
(*d*) Dual aspect concept.

235. Assets of a business are Rs. 21,315 and liabilities Rs. 4,120. What is the amount of owner's equity?

(*a*) Rs. 21,315 (*b*) Rs. 17,195
(*c*) Rs. 25,435 (*d*) Rs. 4,120

236. Which of the following transactions will increase an asset and also decrease an asset?

(*a*) Stores purchased on account.
(*b*) Stores purchased on cash.
(*c*) Payment of a promissory note with cash.
(*d*) Declaration of a dividend.

237. Which of the following transactions results in decrease in owner's equity and increase in liabilities?

(*a*) Declaration of a dividend, payable in cash next month
(*b*) Shares forfeited, on which call money is not paid
(*c*) Reduction in the par value of shares, from Rs. 10 to Rs. 5
(*d*) Reduction in the paid-up value of shares, from Rs. 5 to Rs. 3

238. "A three year permium paid on a fire insurance policy" should be classified as

(*a*) Accrued asset (*b*) Accrued liability
(*c*) Unearned revenue (*d*) Prepaid expense

239. "Wages outstanding" is appearing in the trial balance of a company while preparing Income statement and balance sheet, wages outstanding should appear in

(*a*) The balance sheet only.
(*b*) Income statement only.
(*c*) Both income statement as well as balance sheet.
(*d*) Either income statement or balance sheet.

240. The income statement reports the

(*a*) Net effect of income generating activities.
(*b*) Net effect of profit generating activities.
(*c*) The financial position of business.
(*d*) The overall effect on funds.

241. An example of an intangible asset is

(*a*) Goodwill.
(*b*) Debit balance of Profit and Loss A/c.
(*c*) Preliminary expenses.
(*d*) Deferred revenue expenditure.

242. How the following liabilities are to be shown on the liability side of the balance sheet in the order of permanence

I. Current liabilities and provisions
II. Secured loans
III. Share capital
IV. Unsecured loans
V. Reserves and surplus

Codes:

(*a*) III, V, II, IV, I (*b*) III, II, I, IV, V
(*c*) I, IV, II, V, III (*d*) V, IV, III, II, I

243. How shou'd the following items shown in the balance sheet in the liquidity order?

I. Cash at bank
II. Cash in hand
III. Plant and machinery
IV. Sundry debtors
V. Goodwill

Codes:

(*a*) I, II, IV, V, III
(*b*) I, II, III, IV, V
(*c*) II, I, III, IV, V
(*d*) II, I, IV, III, V

244. On an equity share of Rs. 100, the minimum amount of application money under the laws should be
(*a*) Rs. 2 (*b*) Rs. 5
(*c*) Rs. 10 (*d*) Rs. 50

245. Rights shares mean the shares which are
(*a*) Issued to the directors of the company.
(*b*) First offered to the debenture-holders
(*c*) First offered to the existing shareholders.
(*d*) Issued by a newly formed company

246. For which of the following purposes, share premium can be used?
(*a*) In writing off the discount on debentures of the company.
(*b*) In writting off the preliminary expenses of the company.
(*c*) Issuing bonus shares.
(*d*) In providing for the premium payable on the redemption of preference shares.

247. Issue of shares at a discount of 10% or less must be
(*a*) Authorised by the central government
(*b*) Authorised by the court.
(*c*) Authorised by the resolution passed by the company general meeting
(*d*) Authorised by the resolution passed by the company in general meeting and sanctioned by company Law Board.

248. In case the shares have been issued at a premium and the amount of premium has been received, then at the time of forfeiture of such shares.
(*a*) Share premium account should be debited.
(*b*) Share premium account should be credited.
(*c*) Share premium account should be neither debited no credited.
(*d*) It should be written off.

249. X Ltd. forfeited 30 shares of Rs. 10 each fully called-up for non- payment of allotment money of Rs. 3 per share and call money of Rs. 4 per share. These share are re-issued for Rs. 8 per share fully paid. What is the amount to be trans- ferred to capital reserve account?
(*a*) Rs. 300 (*b*) Rs, 60
(*c*) Rs. 30 (*d*) Rs. 90

250. X Ltd. forfeited 20 shares of Rs. 10 each, Rs. 8 called-up, on which John had paid application and allotment money of Rs. 5 per share of these, 15 shares were re-issued to parker as fully paid-up for Rs. 6 per share. What is the balance in the share forfeiture account after the relevant amount has been transferred to capital Reserve Amount.
(*a*) Nil (*b*) Rs. 5
(*c*) Rs. 25 (*d*) Rs. 100

251. A Ltd. issued a prospectus inviting applications for 2,000 shares. Applications were received for 3,000 shares and pro rata allotment was made on the application for 2, 400 shares. If white had been alloted 40 shares, how many shares he must have applied for?
(*a*) 40 (*b*) 44
(*c*) 48 (*d*) 52

252. X Ltd. forfeited 20 shares of Rs. 10 each and on which Rs. 4 per share were paid, what minimum price company must charge if the forfeited shares are re-issued as Rs. 8 per share paid-up?
(*a*) Rs. 2 per share. (*b*) Rs. 4 per share.
(*c*) Rs. 8 per share. (*d*) Rs. 10 per share.

253. Which of the following may be utilised by a limited company for the redemption of redeemable perference shares?
(*a*) General Reserve.
(*b*) Dividend Equilisation Fund.
(*c*) Profit and loss account balance.
(*d*) All of these.

254. If preference share are redeemed at premium, then such premium may be provided out of the
(*a*) Share premium account.
(*b*) Proceeds of a fresh issue of shares.
(*c*) Share forfeiture account.
(*d*) Capital redemption reserve account.

255. "Capital Redemption Reserve Account" is created
(*a*) voluntarily to accumulated funds to redeem preference shares in future.
(*b*) to meet legal requirements regarding redemption of preference shares.

(c) out of share premium account to redeem preference shares.
(d) out of share forfeiture account to redeem pre-ference shares.

256. Redeemable preference shares of Rs. 2,00,000 are redeemed at par for which purpose fresh equity capital of Rs. 80, 000 is issued at par. What amount should be transferred to capital Redemption Reserve Account?
(a) Nil (b) Rs. 80,000
(c) Rs. 1,20,000 (d) Rs. 2,00,000

257. Redeemable preference shares of Rs. 2,00,000 are redeemed at par for which purpose fresh equity capital of Rs. 80,000 is issued at a discount of 10%. What amount should be transferred to capital Redemption Reserve Account?
(a) Rs. 1,20,000 (b) Rs. 1,28,000
(c) Rs. 2,00,000 (d) Rs. 72,000

258. X Ltd. purchased land and building worth Rs. 28,80,000 and in lieu issued debentures of Rs. 100 each at a discount of 4%. What is the number of debentures issued?
(a) 28,800 (b) 30,000
(c) 32,000 (d) 32,000

259. When shares are forfeited, capital account is debited by
(a) Nominal value of shares.
(b) Paid-up amount on shares.
(c) Called-up amount on shares.
(d) Forfeited amount.

260. When all the debentures are redeemed, the balance left in the 'Debenture Sinking Fund account's is transferred to
(a) General Reserve.
(b) Sinking Fund Investment A/c.
(c) Debentures A/c.
(d) Capital Redemption Reserve.

261. The Balance sheet of a company
(a) Must be prepared in the form set by law
(b) May be prepared in any form
(c) Should be prepared in any form so as to give a true and fair picture of the state of affairs of the company.
(d) Items should be shown in order of perfor-mance.

262. Share forfeited Account is shown on the liability side of the balance sheet.
(a) Under the heading "Reserves and Surplus".
(b) By adding to the paid-up capital.
(c) Under the heading "current liabilities and provisions".
(d) Under the heading "Miscellaneous".

263. The profit or loss disclosed by the accounts of a company is
(a) Transferred to share capital account.
(b) Shown in the column of "Current liabilities and provisions".
(c) Shown in the column of 'Reserves and surp- lus' under a separate account.
(d) Transferred to General Reserve.

264. Unclaimed dividends is shown on the liability side of the balance sheet under the heading.
(a) Reserve and Surplus
(b) Provisions
(c) Current Liabilities
(d) Miscellaneous items

265. The remuneration payable to a whole time director of the company should not exceed
(a) 5% of the net profits.
(b) 6% of the net profits.
(c) 7% of the net profits.
(d) 10% of the net profits.

266. Which of the following is not required to be made under statutes?
(a) Profit & Loss
(b) Funds Flow Statement.
(c) Balance Sheet
(d) None of these.

267. 6% Debentures A/c Rs. 3,00,000; Debenture Interest Rs. 6,000
What amount should be shown in P and L A/c ?
(a) Rs. 6,000 (b) Rs. 12,000
(c) Rs. 18,000 (d) None of these

268. ' Non-convertible' debentures refers to
(a) Owners' capital.
(b) Loan capital.
(c) Short-trem debts.
(d) All of these.

269. The authorised capital of a company is Rs. 5 lakhs, issued capital Rs. 3 lakhs and subscribed capital Rs. 2 lakhs. It has received Rs.5 per Share on application and allotment and Rs.2 per share on first-call except on 2,500 shares. Share capital is credited with.
(*a*) Rs. 3,00,000
(*b*) Rs. 2,00,000
(*c*) Rs. 1,40,000
(*d*) Rs. 1,35,000

270. Which of the following is not a current liability?
(*a*) Unclaimed dividends
(*b*) Minority interest
(*c*) Bills payable
(*d*) Bank overdraft

271. A company has a share capital of Rs. 1,00,000 and general reserve of Rs. 1,20,000. It proposes to issue shares out of general reserve in such a way that after issue of shares the remaining balance in General Reserve should be equal to 25% of the total capital (new). Find the remaining reserve from the following:
(*a*) Rs. 25,000
(*b*) Rs. 30,000
(*c*) Rs. 44,000
(*d*) Rs. 70,000

272. 30 shares of a company on which application money of Rs. 3 per share has been duly paid are forfeited for non-payment of allotment money of Rs. 3 each and first and find call of Rs. 4 each. These shares are then re-issued at Rs. 8 per share fully paid. How much money should be transferred to Capital Reserve?
(*a*) Rs. 30
(*b*) Rs. 60
(*c*) Rs. 90
(*d*) Rs. 120

273. Which of the following is current liability?
(*a*) Outstanding wages (*b*) Debentures
(*c*) Long-term loans (*d*) Share capital

274. Account books for how many proceeding years should be preserved in good condition?
(*a*) 5 (*b*) 8
(*c*) 10 (*d*) 13

275. Provision for discount on debtors shall be made on
(*a*) Book debts before incurring bad debt and before providing for bad debt.
(*b*) Book debts after incurring bad debt and after providing for bad debt.
(*c*) Book debts before incurring bad debt but after providing for bad debt.
(*d*) Book debts after incurring bad debt but before providing for bad debt.

276. Closing stock appearing in trial balance will be taken to
(*a*) Trading Account only.
(*b*) Balance Sheet only.
(*c*) Trading Account and Balance Sheet.
(*d*) Profit and Loss Account only.

277. In a trial balance, debtors appear at Rs. 45,00. Provision for doubtful debts at 5% is to be made after considering the following adjustments.
I. An amount of Rs. 1,000 is included in debtor who is bankrupt and his estate is expected to realise 50 (fifty) paise in the rupee.
II. Debtors include an account of Rs. 2, 000 for goods supplied to proprietor.
III. Bill receivable include a dishonoured bill for Rs. 1,000.
IV. Goods sold in 'Sale of Return' basis not approval by the customer for Rs.5,000 recorded as sale.
V. Debtor includes as amount of Rs. 500 from a customer whose financial position is doubtful. The total provision to be made for doubtful debts is
(*a*) Rs. 1,900
(*b*) Rs. 2,250
(*c*) Rs. 2,425
(*d*) None of these.

278. In the event of dissolution of a firm, the partners' personal assets are first applied for payment of
(*a*) the personal liabilities.
(*b*) the firm's liabilities.
(*c*) both the personal and firm's liabilities.
(*d*) the preferential and tax liabilities.

279. 'A'and 'B' are partners in a business sharing profits in the ratio of 5:3. They admit 'C' as a partner with 1/4 share in the profits. Which he acquires 3/4 from 'A' and 1/4 from 'B'. He pays Rs. 4, 000 as his share of goodwill. 'A' and 'B' will be credited by
(*a*) Rs. 2,500 and Rs. 1,500 respectively
(*b*) Rs. 200 each
(*c*) Rs. 1,000 and Rs. 300 respectively
(*d*) Rs. 3,000 and Rs. 1,000 respectively

280. 'A' and 'B' who are partners, share profits in the ratio of 7:3. 'C' is admitted as a new partner. 'A' surrenders 1/7 of his share and 'B' surrenders 1/3 of his share in favour of 'C'. The new profit sharing ratio will be
(*a*) 6:2:2 (*b*) 4:1:1
(*c*) 3:2:2 (*d*) None of these.

281. 'A' and 'B' are two partners of a firm having capitals of Rs. 15,000 and Rs. 5, 000 respectively, sharing profit and loss in the ratio of 2:1. On dissolution of the firm the assets realised is:

1st instalment	Rs. 3,000
2nd instalment	Rs. 5,000

Under Proportionate capital Method, the loss to 'B' will be
(*a*) Rs. 100
(*b*) Rs. 2,100
(*c*) Rs. 3,000
(*d*) Rs. 4,000

282. A, B, C, D are partners sharing profits and losses in the ratio 3:3:2:1. The partnership is dissolved and D becomes insolvent. C brings only his share of loss and shows his inability to contribute anything towards D's deficiency. According to Garner vs. Murray ruling, D's deficiency in the total will be shared by
(*a*) A and B in their capital ratio.
(*b*) A, B and C in their profit sharing ratio.
(*c*) A, B and C in their capital ratio.
(*d*) A, B and C equally.

283. According to companies Act, a "reserve capital" is created
(*a*) For a specific purpose at anytime during its working life.
(*b*) For issue to the existing shareholders as rights issue of shares.
(*c*) As the uncalled portion of share capital of a limited company to be called only in the event of winding up.
(*d*) For conversion of FCDS into equity shares.

284. Match List I with List II and select the correct answer using the codes given below the Lists:

List I (Items of balance sheets of company)	**List II** (Headings of balancesheet)
I. Profit prior to Incorporation	A. Provisions
II. Proposed dividend	B. Miscellaneous expenditure.
III. Interest paid out of capital	C. Current liabilities
IV. Unclaimed dividend	D. Reserves and surplus

Codes :
(*a*) I-D, II-A, III-C, IV-B
(*b*) I-D, II-A, III-B, IV-C
(*c*) I-A, II-D, III-B, IV-C
(*d*) I-A, II-D, III-C, IV-B

285. Amount set a part to meet probable losses on account of bad debts is a
(*a*) Liability
(*b*) Reserve
(*c*) Provision
(*d*) Contingent liability

286. *Consider the following statements.*
Redeemable preference shares can be redeemed out of
I. sale proceeds of the new issue of shares.
II. sale proceeds of the new issue of debentures.
III. profits available for dividends.
IV. sales proceeds of the assets of the company.
Of these statements:
(*a*) I and III are correct.
(*b*) I alone is correct.
(*c*) II, III, and IV are correct.
(*d*) I, II, III and IV are correct.

287. Match List I with List II and select he correct answer using the codes given below the Lists:

List I	List II
I. Balance of Debenture Redemption Fund Account	A. Realisation Account
II. Balance of Sinking Fund Account for replacement of an asset.	B. Funds-flow Statement.
III. On dissolution of a firm, the provisions made for doubtful debts appearing in Balance Sheet.	C. General Reserve
IV. Financial Consequences of business operations	D. Asset Account

Codes:

(*a*) I-A, II-B, III-C, IV-D
(*b*) I-C, II-D, III-A, IV-B
(*c*) I-A, II-B, III-D, IV-C
(*d*) I-C, II-D, III-B, IV-A

288. A company issue 10,000 shares of Rs. 10 each at a discount of 10% payable as follows:

on application Rs. 2.50
on allotment Rs. 3.00
on first and final call Rs. 3.50

A holder of 100 shares did not pay the final call and his shares were forfeited. Share capital A/c will be debited by

(*a*) Rs. 650 (*b*) Rs. 1,000
(*c*) Rs. 850 (*d*) Rs. 900

289. Owner's equity stands for

(*a*) Fixed Assets minus Fixed Liabilities.
(*b*) Fixed Assets minus Current Liabilities.
(*c*) Current Assets minus Fixed Liabilities.
(*d*) Total Assets minus Total Liabilities.

290. Which one of the following is an intangible asset?

(*a*) Furniture
(*b*) Patent right
(*c*) Investment in shares
(*d*) Losse tools.

291. XYZ Ltd. incurs a net loss of Rs. 5,000 during an accounting year. Depreciation for the relevant year amounts Rs. 1,000, preliminary expenses written off during the accounting year is Rs. 3,000 and a loss of Rs.4,000 is due to sale of plant and machinery. Based on this data, funds from operations would amount to

(*a*) Rs. 3,000 (*b*) Rs. 2,000
(*c*) Rs. 5,000 (*d*) Rs. 4,000

292. One of the consequences of non-registration of a partnership firm is that

(*a*) A partner cannot sue the other partner to enforce a right arising from a contract.
(*b*) The partner of such a firm cannot sue third parties.
(*c*) Third parties cannot sue the firm for claims exceeding Rs.100
(*d*) The official Assignee or Receiver will have no power on the property, of the dissolved firm.

293. Consider the following rights:

I. Right to take part in the business.
II. Right to share profits.
III. Right to interest on advances in excess of capital.
IV. Right to expel a non-cooperative partner

Codes:

(*a*) I and II
(*b*) II and IV
(*c*) I, I and III
(*d*) I, III and IV

294. Match List I with List II and select the correct answer using the codes given below the lists:

List I (Type of combinations)	List II (Illustrations)
I. Association	A. Cartel
II. Federation	B. Chamber of commerce and industry.
III. Partial consolidation	C. Holding company.
IV. Complete consolidation	D. Amalgamation.

Codes :

(*a*) I-B, II-A, III-C, IV-D
(*b*) I-A, II-B, III-C, IV-D
(*c*) I-B, II-A, III-D, IV-C
(*d*) I-A, II-B, III-D, IV-C

295. Which one of the following is an example of a company incorproated by a special Act of parliament?
(*a*) Life Insurance Corporation of India
(*b*) Indian Oil Corporation.
(*c*) State Trading Corporation of India.
(*d*) Bharat Heavy Electricals Limited.

296. Match List I (Activity) with List II (Associated organisation) and select the correct answer by using the codes given below the lists:

List I	List II
I. Mutual fund	A. Stock exchange
II. Public issue of capital	B. Assets management company
III. Forward trading	C. Merchant banking
IV. Option pricing	D. Forex market.

Codes :
(*a*) I-C, II-B, III-D, IV-A
(*b*) I-C, II-B, III-A, IV-D
(*c*) I-B, II-C, III-A, IV-D
(*d*) I-B, II-C, III-D, IV-A

297. In the context of foreign trade, the CIF cost may be obtained by
(*a*) Adding freight and marine insurance premium to the FOB price.
(*b*) Deducting freight and marine insurance premium to the FOB price.
(*c*) Adding customs duties, freight and marine insurance premium to the cost.
(*d*) Deducting customs duties, freight and marine insurance premium from the price.

298. Paid-up value is payable on a life insurance policy
(*a*) On the maturity of the policy.
(*b*) When the policy lapses.
(*c*) When the policy is surrendered.
(*d*) On maturity or death which ever is earlier.

299. An important aspect of control is that the
(*a*) Manager motivates his subordinates to give better performance.
(*b*) Manager sets as effective management information system.
(*c*) Plans are checked before implementation against predetermined measures of performance.
(*d*) Performance is checked against predetermined standards.

300. Consider the following steps:
(*a*) Analysis of variances.
(*b*) Initiating corrective action.
(*c*) Measurement of actual performance.
(*d*) Establishment of standards.
What is the sequence of steps?
(*a*) I, II, III, IV (*b*) II, III, I, IV
(*c*) III, I, II, IV (*d*) IV, III, I, II

301. Rights issue refers to the shares issued to
(*a*) Employees
(*b*) Public
(*c*) Existing directors
(*d*) None of these.

302. Social obligation of accounting refers to
(*a*) The completion of journal entires.
(*b*) The preparation of final accounts.
(*c*) Cost recording.
(*d*) Servicing the needs of various stakeholders.

303. An asset is purchased for Rs. 50,000 on which depreciation is to be provided annually according to the straight line method. The useful life of the asset is 10 years and the residual value is Rs. 10,000. The rate of depreciation is
(*a*) 20% (*b*) 18%
(*c*) 10% (*d*) 8%

304. Bonus shares can be issued by a company
(*a*) Out of the Reserves created by revaluation of fixed assets.
(*b*) Out of share premium not collected in cash
(*c*) Without any provision for it in the Articles of Association of the company.
(*d*) Out of free Reserves built of genuine profits.

305. During a period of declining prices,which one of the following inventory pricing methods will result in lower cost of goods sold?
(*a*) F I F O.
(*b*) L I F O.
(*c*) Simple average method.
(*d*) Inflated price method.

ANSWERS

1	2	3	4	5	6	7	8	9	10
A	C	C	D	A	B	B	C	B	A
11	**12**	**13**	**14**	**15**	**16**	**17**	**18**	**19**	**20**
C	B	B	A	C	A	C	D	B	B
21	**22**	**23**	**24**	**25**	**26**	**27**	**28**	**29**	**30**
B	B	A	B	A	C	C	B	A	A
31	**32**	**33**	**34**	**35**	**36**	**37**	**38**	**39**	**40**
C	A	A	C	C	B	D	A	B	B
41	**42**	**43**	**44**	**45**	**46**	**47**	**48**	**49**	**50**
B	D	D	B	A	C	A	D	B	C
51	**52**	**53**	**54**	**55**	**56**	**57**	**58**	**59**	**60**
B	B	B	B	A	D	C	C	C	D
61	**62**	**63**	**64**	**65**	**66**	**67**	**68**	**69**	**70**
C	B	C	A	D	D	B	D	B	D
71	**72**	**73**	**74**	**75**	**76**	**77**	**78**	**79**	**80**
D	C	D	A	B	B	B	D	B	D
81	**82**	**83**	**84**	**85**	**86**	**87**	**88**	**89**	**90**
A	D	C	D	A	A	D	C	B	B
91	**92**	**93**	**94**	**95**	**96**	**97**	**98**	**99**	**100**
A	B	C	C	C	C	C	B	C	D
101	**102**	**103**	**104**	**105**	**106**	**107**	**108**	**109**	**110**
D	B	A	C	C	A	B	B	D	A
111	**112**	**113**	**114**	**115**	**116**	**117**	**118**	**119**	**120**
D	D	A	B	B	B	B	D	D	B
121	**122**	**123**	**124**	**125**	**126**	**127**	**128**	**129**	**130**
B	D	B	A	A	C	D	C	C	A
131	**132**	**133**	**134**	**135**	**136**	**137**	**138**	**139**	**140**
B	C	D	D	D	B	A	A	B	B
141	**142**	**143**	**144**	**145**	**146**	**147**	**148**	**149**	**150**
C	B	D	B	B	A	A	B	C	C
151	**152**	**153**	**154**	**155**	**156**	**157**	**158**	**159**	**160**
B	B	B	B	B	D	B	D	A	B
161	**162**	**163**	**164**	**165**	**166**	**167**	**168**	**169**	**170**
A	D	B	B	B	C	A	A	D	A
171	**172**	**173**	**174**	**175**	**176**	**177**	**178**	**179**	**180**
B	C	E	B	A	C	C	A	B	B
181	**182**	**183**	**184**	**185**	**186**	**187**	**188**	**189**	**190**
C	A	C	B	D	B	B	C	B	B

191	192	193	194	195	196	197	198	199	200
D	A	D	D	B	B	C	D	C	D
201	202	203	204	205	206	207	208	209	210
B	A	D	B	A	C	D	B	B	D
211	212	213	214	215	216	217	218	219	220
A	B	A	A	C	B	C	B	A	A
221	222	223	224	225	226	227	228	229	230
B	B	C	C	B	A	C	A	B	A
231	232	233	234	235	236	237	238	239	240
A	B	A	A	B	B	A	D	C	B
241	242	243	244	245	246	247	248	249	250
A	A	D	B	C	C	D	C	C	C
251	252	253	254	255	256	257	258	259	260
C	B	D	A	B	C	B	B	C	A
261	262	263	264	265	266	267	268	269	270
A	B	C	C	A	B	A	B	C	B
271	272	273	274	275	276	277	278	279	280
C	A	A	B	B	C	A	A	D	A
281	282	283	284	285	286	287	288	289	290
D	C	C	B	C	A	C	C	D	B
291	292	293	294	295	296	297	298	299	300
A	B	C	B	A	D	C	D	D	D
301	302	303	304	305					
C	D	D	D	C					

❑ ❑ ❑

BUSINESS STATISTICS & BUSINESS MATHEMATICS

Business Statistics

MEASURES OF CENTRAL TENDENCY OR STATISTICAL AVERAGES

There are five alternative measures of central tendency. They are:

1. Arithmetic Mean (A.M.)
2. Median
3. Mode
4. Geometric Mean (G.M.)
5. Harmonic Mean (H.M.)

ARITHMETIC MEAN

Arithmetic mean of given set of observations is their sum divided by the number of observations. For example, the arithmetic mean of 5, 8, 10, 15, 24 and 28 is

$$\frac{5+8+10+15+24+28}{6}=\frac{90}{6}=15$$

Calculation

Arithmetic mean can be calculated in the following manner:

A. Arithmetic Average in Individual Series

Direct method

$$\overline{X}=\frac{\Sigma X}{N}$$

where

$\overline{X}$ = Arithmetic Average or Mean

Σ = Sum of values and read as summation

X = Values of variable X

N = Number of items

B. Arithmetic Average in Discrete Series

Direct Method $\overline{X}=\dfrac{\Sigma fx}{N}$

where

Σfx = Total of products of the frequencies (f) and the variable X

N = Total of frequencies, *i.e.*, $N=\Sigma f$

C. Arithmetic Average in Continuous Series

Direct Method

$$\overline{X}=A+\frac{\Sigma fm}{N}$$

where

M = Mid-point

Σfm = Total of products of frequencies (f) and the mid-point (m)

Mathematical Properties of Arithmetic Mean

Property–1

The algebraic sum of the deviations of the given set of observations from their arithmetic mean is zero.

Property–2

If n_1 and n_2 are the sizes and $\overline{X}_1, \overline{X}_2$ are the respective means of two series then the mean $\overline{X}$ of the combined series of size $n_1 + n_2$ is given by :

$$\overline{X}=\frac{n_1\overline{X}_1+n_2\overline{X}_2}{n_1+n_2}$$

Property–3

The sum of the squares of deviations of the given set of observations is minimum when taken from the arithmetic mean.

Property–4

If all the observations of a series are added, subtracted, multiplied or divided by a constant, the mean is also added, subtracted, multiplied or divided by the same constant.

Property–5

The weighted arithmetic mean of first n natural numbers whose weights are equal to the corresponding numbers is equal to

$$\left(\frac{2n+1}{3}\right)$$

Property–6

The arithmetic mean of first n natural numbers is equal to the arithmetic mean of its first and last term.

$$\overline{X} = \frac{1+2+3+.....+n}{n}$$

$$= \frac{n(n+1)}{2} \cdot \frac{1}{n} = \frac{n+1}{2}$$

MEDIAN

Median is the central value of the variable when the values are arranged in *ascending* or *descending* order of magnitude.

Calculation: Median may be, calculated in the following manner:

1. Calculation of Median in Individual Series

$$M = \text{Size of } \left(\frac{N+1}{2}\right) \text{th item}$$

where

M = Median
N = Number of items

2. Calculation of Median in Discrete Series

$$M = \text{Size of } \left(\frac{N+1}{2}\right) \text{the item}$$

where

M = Median
N = Total of frequencies

3. Calculation of Median in Continuous Series

$$M = \text{Size of } \left(\frac{N}{2}\right) \text{th item}$$

$$M = L_1 + \frac{i}{f}(m-c)$$

where

L = Lower limit of median group
i = Difference of lower and upper limit of median group
f = Frequency of median group
m = Median number = $\left(\frac{N}{2}\right)$ th item
c = Cumulative frequency of the group preceding the median group

If data are arranged in descending order then we apply the following formula:

$$M = L_2 - \frac{i}{f}\left(\frac{N}{2} - c\right)$$

where

L_2 = Upper limit of the median group

PARTITION VALUES

The values which divide the series into a number of equal parts are called the *partition values.* Thus, median may be regarded as a particular partition value which divides the given data into two equal parts.

QUARTILES

The values which divide the given data into four equal parts are known as *quartiles* obviously there will be three such points θ_1, θ_2 and θ_3 such that $\theta_1 \leq \theta_2 \leq \theta_3$, termed as the three quartiles. θ_1, known as the lower or *first quartile* is the value which has 25% of the items of the distribution below it and consequently 75% of the items are greater than it. θ_2, known as the *second quartile,* coincides with the median and has an equal number of observations above it and below it θ_3, known as the upper or *third quartile,* has 75% of the observations below it and consequently 25% of the observations above it.

To compute θ_1, the following steps are required:

(i) Find $\frac{N}{4}$ where N = Σf

(ii) See the cumulative frequency *(c.f.)* just greater than N/4

(iii) The corresponding value of x and observation gives the value of θ_1. In case of continuous frequency distribution, the corresponding class contains θ_1 and the value of θ_1 is obtained by the interpolation formula:

$$\theta_1 = l + \frac{h}{f}\left(\frac{N}{4} - C\right)$$

where

l = lower limit of the class containing θ_1
f = frequency of the class containing θ_1
h = magnitude of the class containing θ_1
c = cumulative frequency (*c.f.*) of the class preceding the class containing θ_1

Similarly to compute θ_3, see the *c.f.* just greater than $\frac{3N}{4}$. The corresponding value of items gives θ_3. In case of continuous frequency distribution, the corresponding class contains θ_3 and value of θ_3 is given by the formula:

$$\theta_3 = l + \frac{h}{f}\left(\frac{3N}{4} - C\right)$$

where

l = lower limit of the class containing θ_3
h= magnitude of the class containing θ_3
f = frequency of the class containing θ_3
c= *c.f.* of the class preceding the class containing θ_3

DECILES

Deciles are the values which divide the series into ten equal parts. Obviously, there are nine deciles D_1, D_2, D_3, ..., D_9 such that $D_1 \le D_2 \le ...... \ge D_9$. Incidentally D_5 coincides with the median.

The method of computing the deciles D_i, *(i = 1, 2,...9)* is the same as discussed for θ_3 and θ_3. To compute the *i*th decile D*i*, (*i* = 1, 2, 3, ..., 9). See the *c.f.* just greater than $\frac{iXN}{10}$. The corresponding value of item is D*i*. In case of continuous frequency distribution, the corresponding class contains D*i* and its value is obtained by the formula

$$Di = l + \frac{h}{f}\left(\frac{i \times N}{10} - C\right)$$

$$i = 1, 2, 3, ..., 9$$

where

l = lower limit of the class containing D*i*
f= frequency of the class containing D*i*
h= magnitude of the class containing D*i*
c= *c.f.* of the class preceding the class containing D*i*

PERCENTILES

Percentiles are the values which divide the series into 100 equal parts. Obviously, there are 99 percentiles P_1, P_2, ...P_{99} such that $P_1 \le P_2 \le .... \le P_{99}$. The *i*th percentile P*i*, (*i* = 1, 2, ...99) is the value of item corresponding to *c.f.* just greater than $\frac{i \times N}{100}$. In case of continuous frequency distribution, the corresponding class contains P*i* and its value is obtained by the formula

$$Pi = l + \frac{h}{f}\left(\frac{i \times N}{100} - C\right)$$

$$i = 1, 2, 3, ...99$$

where

l = lower limit of the class containing P*i*
h= magnitude of the class containing P*i*
f= frequency of the class containing P*i*
c= *c.f.* of the class preceding the class containing P*i*

In particular, we shall have:

$$P_{25} = Q_1$$
$$P_{50} = D_5$$
$$P_{75} = Q_3$$
$$D_1 = P_{10}, D_2 = P_{20}, D_3 = P_{30}, ...D_9 = P_{90}$$

MODE

Mode is the value which occurs frequently in a set of observations and around which the other items of the set cluster densely. In other words, mode is the value of a series which is predominant in it. In the words of Croxton and Cowden, "The mode of a distribution is value at the point around which the items tend to be most heavily concentrated. It may be regarded as too most typical of a series of values."

Computation of Mode

The value of mode is obtained by the following formula:

$$\text{Mode} = L_1 + \frac{f_1 - f_0}{2f_1 - f_0 - f_2} \times i$$

where

L = lower limit of the modal class

f_1 = frequency of the modal class

f_0 = frequency of the class preceding the modal class

f_2 = frequency of the class succeeding the modal class

i = class interval of modal class

When mode is ill-defined the value of mode may be calculated with the help of following formula:

Mode = 3 Median – 2 Mean

Empirical Relation Between Mean (M), Median (M_d) and Mode (M_0)

In case of a *symmetrical distribution* mean, median and mode, coincide. Thus

Mean = Median = Mode

However, for a *moderately asymmetrical (non-symmetrical or Skewed)* distribution, mean and mode usually lie on the two ends and median lies in between than and they obey the following important empirical relationships given by Prof. Karl Pearson.

Mode = Mean – 3(Mean – Median) ...(1)

$\Rightarrow$ Mean – Mode = 3(Mean – Median)

$\Rightarrow$ Mean – Median = $\frac{1}{3}$ (Mean – Mode)

Thus we see that the difference between mean and mode is three times the difference between mean and median. In other words, median is closer to mean than mode. The above relation between mean (M), median (M_d) and mode (M_0) can be exhibited diagrammatically as follows:

Relationship Between Arithmetic Mean, Median and Mode

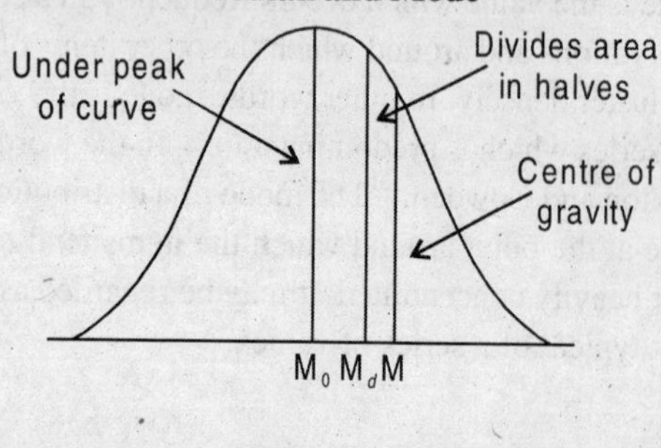

Remarks

1. Equation (1) may be rewritten to give:
   Mode = Mean – 3 Mean + 3 Median
   Mode = 3 Median – 2 Mean ...(2)
   This formula is specially useful to determine the value of mode in case of bimodal or multimodal distributions.
2. If we know any two of the three values M, M_d and M_0 the third can be estimated by using the formula (2).
3. For a positively Skewed distribution, mean will be greater than median and median will be greater than mode *i.e.*

$$M > M_d > M_0 \Rightarrow M_0 < M_d < M$$

However, in a negatively Skewed distribution the order of the magnitudes of the three averages will be reversed *i.e.,* for negatively Skewed distribution we have

$$M_0 > M_d > M \Rightarrow M < M_d < M_0$$

GEOMETRIC MEAN

The geometric mean (usually abbreviated as G.M.) of a set of n observations is the nth root of their product. Thus if X_1, X_2, ...,X_n are the given n observations then their G.M. is given by

$$\text{G.M.} = \sqrt[n]{X_1.X_2.X_3.........X_n}$$

$$= (X_1.X_2.X_3.........X_n)^{1/n} \quad ...(3)$$

If n = 2, *i.e.,* if we are dealing with two observations only then G.M. can be computed by taking the square root of their product. For example, G.M. of 4 and 16 is

$$\text{G.M.} = \sqrt{4 \times 16} = \sqrt{64} = 8$$

But if the number of observations is greater than 2, then the computation of the nth root is very tedious. In such a case, the calculations are facilitated by making use of the logarithms. Taking logarithm of both sides in (3), we get

$$\log(\text{G.M.}) = \frac{1}{n} \log (X_1.X_2......X_3)$$

$$= \frac{1}{n} (\log X_1 + \log X_2 + ...\log X_n)$$

$$= \frac{1}{n} \Sigma \log X \quad ...(4)$$

Thus, we see that the logarithm of the G.M. of a set observations is the arithmetic mean of their logarithms.

Taking Antilog of both sides in (4) we finally obtain,

$$\text{G.M.} = \text{Antilog}\left[\frac{1}{n}\Sigma \log X\right]$$

HARMONIC MEAN

If $X_1, X_2, ...X_n$ is a given set of n observations, then their harmonic mean affreviated as H.M. or simply it is given by:

$$H = \frac{1}{\frac{1}{n}\left[\frac{1}{X_1}+\frac{1}{X_2}+.....+\frac{1}{X_n}\right]}$$

$$= \frac{1}{\frac{1}{n}\left[\Sigma\left(\frac{1}{X}\right)\right]} = \frac{n}{\Sigma\left(\frac{1}{X}\right)}$$

In other words, Harmonic Mean is the reciprocal of the arithmetic mean of the reciprocals of the given observations.

Relation Between Arithmetic Mean, Geometric Mean and Harmonic Mean

The arithmetic mean (A.M.), the geometric mean (G.M.) and the harmonic mean (H.M.) of a series of n observations are connected by the relation

$$\text{A.M.} \geq \text{G.M.} \geq \text{H.M.} \qquad \ldots(1)$$

the sign of equality holding if and only if all the n observations are equal.

DISPERSION

According to Connor, "Dispersion is the measure of the extent to which the individual items vary".

Measures of Dispersion

The various measures of dispersion are

1. Range
2. Quartile deviation or Semi-Interquartile range
3. Mean deviation
4. Standard deviation
5. Lorenz curve

RANGE

The range is defined as the difference between the highest and lowest values in the series. This is the simplest method of measuring dispersion. Thus,

$$\text{Range} = L - S$$

where

L = Largest value
S = Smallest value

Absolute and Relative Measures of Range

Range as defined above is an absolute measure of dispersion and depends upon the units of measurement. Thus, if want to compare the variability of two or more distributions with the same units of measurement, we may use the above formula. However, to compare the variability of the distributions given in difference units of measurement we cannot use the above formula but we need a relative measure which is independent of the units of measurement. This relative measure, called the *coefficient of range,* is defined as follows:

$$\text{Coefficient of Range} = \frac{L-S}{L+S}$$

In other words, coefficient of range is the ratio of the difference between two extreme observations (biggest and smallest) of the distribution to their sum.

QUARTILE DEVIATION OR SEMI INTER QUARTILE RANGE

Quartile deviation is obtained by dividing the difference of third quartile and first quartile ($Q_3 - Q_2$) by 2. Thus

$$\text{Quartile Deviation (Q.D.)} = \frac{Q_3 - Q_1}{2}$$

where

Q_3 = Third Quartile or Upper Quartile
Q_1 = First Quartile or Lower Quartile

Q.D. as defined obove is only an absolute measure of dispersion. For comparative studies of variability of two distributions we need a relative measure which is known as coefficient of Quartile Deviation and is given by

$$\text{Coefficient of Q.D.} = \frac{Q_3 - Q_1}{Q_3 + Q_1}$$

Remarks

The Quartile deviation gives the average amount by which the two quartiles differ from median. For a *symmetrical distribution*, we have

$$Q_3 - Q_d = M_d - Q_1$$

$$\Rightarrow \quad M_d = \frac{Q_3 + Q_1}{2} \quad \text{... (1)}$$

i.e., median lies half way on the scale from Q_1 to Q_3. Thus , for a symmetrical distribution, we have

$$\text{Q.D.} + Q_1 = \frac{Q_3 - Q_1}{2} + Q_1$$

$$= \frac{Q_3 + Q_1}{2} = M_d \text{ [From (1)]}$$

$$\text{and} \quad Q_3 - \text{Q.D.} = Q_3 - \frac{Q_3 - Q_1}{2}$$

$$= \frac{Q_3 + Q_1}{2} = M_d \text{ [From(1)]}$$

In other words, for a symmetrical distribution, we have

$$Q_1 = M_d - \text{Q.D.}$$

$$\text{and} \quad Q_3 = M_d + \text{Q.D.} \quad \text{... (2)}$$

Since in a distribution 25% of the observations lie below Q_1 and 25% observations lie above Q_3, 50% of the observations lie between Q_1 and Q_3. Therefore, using (2) we conclude that for a symmetrical distribution

$M_d \pm$ Q.D. covers exactly 50% of the observations.

It may also be pointed out here that the word symmetrical distribution used in above connection refers to symmetry in the central 50% of the distribution and may be asymmetrical (Skewed) at the tail ends.

PERCENTILE RANGE

This is a measure of dispersion based on the difference between certain percentiles. It P_i is the ith percentile and P_j is the Jth percentile then the so-called i-j percentile range is given by

$$i\text{-}j \text{ Percentile Range} = P_j - P_i \ (i < j)$$

$$\text{and } i\text{-}j \text{ Semi Percentile Range} = \frac{P_j - P_i}{2} \ (i < j)$$

The above measures are absolute measures only. The relative measure of variability based on percentiles is given by

$$\text{Coefficient of } i - j \text{ percentile} = \frac{P_j - P_i}{P_j + P_i}$$

MEAN DEVIATION

Mean deviation is defined as the arithmetic average of the deviations of various items from a measure of central tendency, may it be, mean, median or mode. Generally, mean deviations is calculated either from mean or from median. Mode is usually not considered as its value is indeterminate. Between mean and median, the median is supposed to be better than the mean because the sum of the deviations from the median is less than the sum of the deviations from the mean. It is also known as first moment of dispersion.

Computation of Mean Deviation

If $X_1, X_2, \ldots\ldots, X_n$ are n given observations then the mean deviation (M.D.) about an average A, say, is given by $\text{M.D.} = \frac{1}{n}\Sigma|X - A| = \frac{1}{n}\Sigma|D|$

where $|D| = |X - A|$ read as mod (X – A) is the modulus value or absolute value of the deviation (after ignoring the negative sign) $d = X - A$ and $\Sigma|d|$ is the sum of these absolute deviations and A is any one of the averages mean (M), median (M_d) and mode (M_0).

In the case of frequency distribution or grouped or continuous frequency distribution, mean deviation about an average A is given by

$$\text{M.D.} = \frac{1}{N}\Sigma f\,|X - A|$$

where

X = value of the variable or mid-value of the class interval

N = Σf

A = Mean/Median/Mode

Remarks

1. Usually, we obtain the mean deviation (M.D.) about any one of the three averages mean (M), median (M_d) or mode (M_0). Thus,

$$\text{M.D. (about mean)} = \frac{1}{N}\Sigma f|X - M|$$

$$\text{M.D. (about median)} = \frac{1}{N}\Sigma f|M - D_d|$$

$$\text{M.D. (about mode)} = \frac{1}{N}\Sigma f|X - M_0|$$

2. The sum of the absolute deviations (after ignoring the signs) of a given set of observations is minimum when taken about median.
3. For a symmetrical distribution the range Mean ± M.D. (about mean) or M_d ± M.D. (about median), [$\because M = M_d$ for a symmetrical distribution] covers 57.5% of the observations of the distribution. If the distribution is mode rately (Skewed) the range will cover approximately 57.5% of the observations. Thus, a small value of mean deviation would imply that the distribution is uniform since in this case a small interval around the average will contain more than 50% of the observations of the series.

Relative Measures of Mean

The relative measure of dispersion, called the coefficient of mean deviation is given by

Co-efficient of M.D.

$$= \frac{\text{Mean Deviation}}{\text{Average about which it is calculated}}$$

Thus

$$\text{Co-efficient of M.D. about mean} = \frac{\text{M.D.}}{\text{Mean}}$$

$$\text{Co-efficient of M.D. about median} = \frac{\text{M.D.}}{\text{Median}}$$

The co-efficients of mean deviation defined above are pure numbers independent of the units of measurement and are useful for comparing the variability of different distributions.

STANDARD DEVIATION

Standard deviation, usually denoted by the letter σ (sigma) of the Greek alphabet was first suggested by *Karl Pearson* as a measure of dispersion in 1893. It is defined as the positive square root of the arithmetic mean of the squares of the deviations of the given observations from their arithmetic mean. Thus, if $X_1, X_2, ..., X_n$ is a set of n observations then its standard deviation is given by

$$\sigma = \sqrt{\frac{1}{n}\Sigma(X - \overline{X})^2}$$

where

$$\overline{X} = \frac{\Sigma X}{n} = \text{arithmetic mean of the given values}$$

Computation of Standard Deviation in Case of Frequency Distribution

In case of frequency distribution, the standard deviation is given by

$$\sigma = \frac{1}{N}\sqrt{\Sigma f(X - \overline{X})^2}$$

where X is the value of the variable or the mid-value of the class (in case of grouped or continuous frequency distribution); f is the corresponding frequency of the value X; N = Σf, is the total frequency and

$$\overline{X} = \frac{1}{N}\Sigma fX$$

is the arithmetic mean of the distribution.

Remarks

1. It may be pointed out that although mean deviation could be calculated about any one of the averages (M, M_d or M_0), standard deviation is always computed about arithmetic mean.
2. The value of the *s.d.* depends on the numerical value of the deviations $(X_1 - \overline{X}), (X_2 - \overline{X})...,$ $(X_n - \overline{X})$. Thus, the value of σ will be greater if the values of X are scattered widely away

from the mean. Thus, a small value of σ will imply that the distribution is *homogeneous* and a large value of σ will imply that it is heterogeneous. In particular *s.d.* is zero if each of the deviations is zero *i.e.*, σ = 0 if and only if,

$$X_1 - \overline{X} = 0,\ X_2 - \overline{X} = 0, \ldots\ldots X_n - \overline{X} = 0$$

$$\Rightarrow\ X_1 = X_2 = X_3 + \ldots X_n = \overline{X}$$

which is the case if the variable assumes the constant value *i.e.*,

$\sigma = 0$

if $X_1 = X_2 = X_3 = \ldots\ldots X_n = K$ (constant)

VARIANCE

Variance is the square of the a standard deviation and is denoted by σ^2. For a frequency distribution variance is given by

$$\text{variance} = \sigma^2 = \frac{1}{N}\Sigma f(X - \overline{X})^2$$

Remark

Variance or standard deviation is independent of the change of origin but not of the scale.

CO-EFFICIENT OF VARIATION

Standard deviation is only an absolute measure of dispersion, depending upon the units of measurement. The relative measure of dispersion based on standard deviation is called the coefficient of standard deviation and is given by

$$\text{Coefficient of Standard Deviation} = \frac{\sigma}{\overline{X}}$$

This is a pure number independent of the units of measurement and thus, is suitable for comparing the variability, homogeneity or uniformity of two or more distributions.

We have already discussed the relative measures of dispersion based on range, quartile deviation and mean deviation. Since standard deviation is by for the best measure of dispersion, for comparing the homogeneity or heterogeneity of two or more distributions we generally compute the coefficient of standard deviation asked otherwise.

100 times the coefficient of dispersion based on standard deviation is called the *coefficient of variation,* abbreviated as C.V. Thus,

$$\text{C.V.} = 100 \times \frac{\sigma}{\overline{X}}$$

For comparing the variability of two distributions we compute the 'coefficient of variation' for each distribution. A distribution with smaller C.V. is said to be more homogeneous or uniform or less variable than the other and the series with greater C.V. is said to be more heterogeneous or more variable than the other.

RELATION BETWEEN VARIOUS MEASURES OF DISPERSION

For a Normal Distribution we have the following relations between the different measures of dispersion:

1. Mean ± Q.D. covers 50% of the observation of the distribution.
2. Mean ± M.D. covers 57.5% of the observations.
3. Mean ±σ includes 68.27% of the observations.
4. Mean ±2 σ includes 95.45% of the observations
5. Mean ± σ includes 99.73% of the observations.
6. $\text{Q.D.} = \frac{2}{3}\text{S.D.}$ (approximately)
7. $\text{M.D.} = \frac{4}{5}\text{S.D.}$ (approximately)
8. $\text{Q.D.} = \frac{5}{6}\text{S.D.}$ (approximately)

   Combining the results (6), (7) and (8) we get approximately:

   $$3\,\text{Q.D.} = 2\,\text{S.D.}$$
   $$5\,\text{M.D.} = 4\,\text{S.D.}$$
   $$6\,\text{Q.D.} = 5\,\text{M.D.}$$
   $$\Rightarrow\quad 4\,\text{D.S.} = 5\,\text{M.D.} = 6\,\text{Q.D.}$$

   Thus we see that standard deviation ensures the highest degree of reliability and Q.D. the lowest.

9. We have:

   $$\text{Q.D.} : \text{M.D.} : \text{S.D.} :: \frac{2}{3}\sigma : \frac{4}{5}\sigma : \sigma$$

   $\Rightarrow$ Q.D. : M.D. : S.D. ::10 :12: 15.
10. Range = 6 S.D. = 6σ.

LORENZ CURVE

This is the graphic method of measuring dispersion between two series. It was designed by Dr. Lorenz for measuring in equalities in the distribution of wealth. It is a cumulative percentage curve.

A very distinctive feature of the Lorenz curve consists in dealing with the cumulative values of the variable and the cumulative frequencies rather than its absolute values and the given frequencies.

GINNI'S COEFFICIENT OF CONCENTRATION

Ginni's coefficient of concentration, also known as concentration Ratio is based on his coefficient of mean difference and is defined as:

$$G = \frac{\Delta_1}{2\overline{X}}$$

where

G = Ginni's coefficient of concentration

Δ_1 = Ginni's coefficient of mean difference

$\overline{X}$ = Mean of the given distribution

Ginni's Coefficient of concentration G is a pure number independent of units of measurement and lies between O and 1. G is equal to O in *equal distribution* and its value goes up with increase in the inequality.

In fact, Ginni's coefficient is the ratio of area of concentration to the total area of lower triangle below the line of equal distribution.

SKEWNESS AND KURTOSIS

Two distributions may have the same mean and standard deviation but may differ widely in their overall appearance. It is this difference which shows the presence of Skewness. The *Skewness* refers to '*lack of symmetry*'. It means when a distribution is asymmetrical (not symmetrical) it is known as a Skewed distribution. Measures of Skewness help us to distinguish between various types of distribution.

In a symmetrical frequency distribution which is unimodal, if the frequency curve or histogram is folded about the ordinate at the mean, the two halves so obtained will coincide with each other. In other words, in a symmetrical distribution equal distances on either side of the central value will have same frequencies and consequently both the tails, (left and right), of the curve would also be equal in shape and length.

A distribution is said to be Skewed if;

The frequency curve of the distribution is not a symmetric bell shaped curve but it is stretched more to one side than to the other. In other words, it has a longer tail to one side (left or right) than to the other. A frequency distribution for which the curve has a longer tail towards the right is said to be positively Skewed and if the longer tail lies towards the left, it is said to be negatively Skewed.

MEASURES OF SKEWNESS

Absolute Measure of Skewness

a. Skewness = Mean – Mode = $M - M_0$

b. Skewness = 3(Mean – Median) = $3(M\ M_d)$

c. Skewness = $(Q_3 - M_d) - (M_d - Q_1)$
$= Q_3 + Q_1 - 2M_d$

For comparing two or more distributions for Skewness we compute the relative measures of Skewness, also commonly known as coefficients of Skewness which are pure numbers independent. *The following are the coefficients of Skewness which are commonly used:*

1. Karl Pearson's Coefficient of Skewness

This is given by the formula:

$$S_k = \frac{\text{Mean} - \text{Mode}}{s.d.}$$

$$= \frac{M - M_0}{s.d.} = \frac{M - (3M_d - 2M)}{s.d.}$$

$$= \frac{3(M - M_d)}{s.d.}$$

Remarks

1. Theoretically Skewness given by the above formula lies between the limits ± 3, but these limits are rarely attained in practice.
2. From above formula skewness is zero if $M = M_0 = M_d$. In other words, for a symmetrical distribution mean, mode and median coincide.
3. Since *s.d.* is always positive, we have

$$S_k > O, \text{ if } M > M_0$$

and $\quad Sk > O, \text{ if } M > M_d$

$\because \quad 3M_d = M_0 + 2M$

$\therefore \quad S_k > O, \text{ if } 3M_d > M_0 + 2M_0$

$\Rightarrow \quad S_k > O, \text{ if } 3M_d > 3M_0$

$\Rightarrow \quad S_k > O, \text{ if } M_d > M_0$

From above equations we conclude that

$$S_k > O, \text{ if } M > M_d > M_0$$

or $\quad S_k > O, \text{ if } M_0 > M_d > M$

Thus for a positively skewed distribution, the value of the mean is the greatest of the three measures and the value of mode is the least of the three measures.

If the distribution is negatively Skewed, the above inequality is reversed *i.e.*, the inequalities 'greater than' (*i.e.*, >) and 'less than' (*i.e.*, <) are inter changed thus:

$$S_k < O, \text{ if } M < M_d < M_0$$

or $\quad S_k < O, \text{ if } M_0 > M_d > M$

In other words, for a negatively skewed distributions, of the three measures of central tendency mean, median and mode, the mode has the maximum value and the mean has the least value.

2. Bowley's Coefficient of Skewness

Prof. A.L. Bowley's coefficient of Skewness is based on the quartiles and is given by:

$$S_k = \frac{(Q_3 - M_d) - (M_d - Q_1)}{(Q_3 - M_d) + (M_d - Q_1)}$$

$$\Rightarrow \quad S_k = \frac{Q_3 + Q_1 - 2M_d}{Q_3 - Q_1}$$

where

Q_3 = Upper Quartile

Q_1 = Lower Quartile

M_d = Median

3. Kelly's Measure of Skewness

This is given by the formula

$$S_k = (P_{90} - P_{50}) - (P_{50} - P_{10})$$

$$= P_{90} + P_{10} - 2P_{50}$$

But $P_{90} = D_9$ and $P_{10} = D_1$. Hence,

$$S_k = (D_9 - D_5) - (D_5 - D_1) \quad [\therefore P_{50} = D_5]$$

$$= D_9 + D_1 - 2D_5$$

But this is an absolute measure of Skewness. However, for practical purposes, we generally compute the coefficient of Skewness, which is given by:

$$S_k(\text{Kelly}) = \frac{(P_{90} - P_{50}) - (P_{50} - P_{10})}{(P_{90} - P_{50}) + (P_{50} - P_{10})}$$

$$= \frac{P_{90} + P_{10} - 2P_{50}}{P_{90} - P_{10}}$$

$$= \frac{D_9 + D_1 - 2D_5}{D_9 - D_1}$$

$$\because \quad D_5 = P_{50} = \text{Median}$$

$$\therefore \quad S_k(\text{Kelly}) = \frac{P_{90} + P_{10} - 2M_d}{P_{90} - P_{10}}$$

$$= \frac{D_9 + D_1 - 2M_d}{D_9 - D_1}$$

MOMENTS

Moment is a measure of a force with respect to its tendency to produce rotation. The notion of moments in statistics is analogus to that in mechanics. The strength of tendency depends on the amount of force and the distance from the origin of the point at which the force is exerted.

Moments are calculated with the help of arithmetic mean. Moment calculated from arithmetic mean are called 'central moments' or 'moments about the arithmetic mean.'

In the calculation of moments, it deviations are taken from mean the resulting moments are denoted by symbol μ (pronounced as *Mu*).

Moments about Mean

The rth moment of X about the mean $\overline{X}$, usually denoted by μ_r is defined as

$$\mu_r = \frac{1}{N}\Sigma f(X - \overline{X})^r$$

where

$$r = 0, 1, 2, 3, ...$$

putting $r = 0$, in above equation we get

$$\mu_0 = \frac{1}{N}\Sigma f(X-\overline{X})^0$$
$$= \frac{1}{N}\Sigma f = \frac{1}{N}.N$$
$$= 1$$

Putting $r = 1$ in above equation, we get

$$\mu_1 = \frac{1}{N}\Sigma f(X-\overline{X})^1 = 0$$

Because the algebraic sum of deviations of a given set of observations from their mean is zero. Thus the first moment about mean is always zero again taking $r = 2$ we get

$$\mu_2 = \frac{1}{N}\Sigma f(X-\overline{X})^2 = (s.d.)^2$$

Hence the second moment about mean gives the variance of the distribution.

Remark: The moments about mean are invariant under change of origin but not of scale.

Sheppard's Correction For Moments

This correction is valid only for symmetrical or slightly asymmetrical continuous distributions and can not be applied in the case of extremely asymmetrical (Skewed) distributions like J-shaped or inverted J-shaped or U-shaped distributions.

KURTOSIS

The 'kurtosis' is the property of 'peakedness' of a frequency distribution.

If the freequency curve has long tails and high peak we call it '*lepto Kurtic*' distribution. On the other hand, if the frequency curve has shot and thick tails and is flat topped we call it 'platy kurtic'. A 'mesokurtic distribution' describes the situation in between a lepto kurtic and platykurtic distribution'. Diagrammatically these distributions will be as follows:

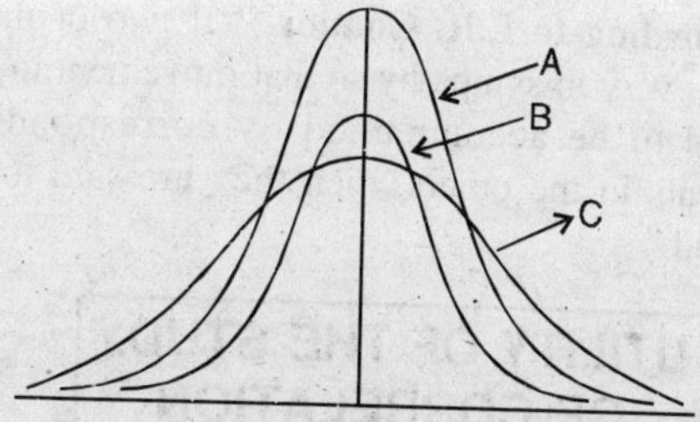

Fig.

Curve of type B which is neither flat nor peaked is known as Normal curve and shape of its hump is accepted as a standard one. Curve with humps of the form of normal curve are said to have normal kurtosis and are termed as *mesokurtic*. The curves of the type A, which are more peaked than the normal curve are known as *lepto kurtic* and are said to lack kurtosis or to have negative kurtosis. On the other hand, curves of the type C, which are flatter than the normal curve are called platy kurtic and they are said to possess kurtosis in excess or have positive kurtosis.

Measurement of Kurtosis

Karl Pearson gave the following formula for the measurment of kurtosis:

$$\beta_2 = \frac{\mu_4}{\mu_2^2} = \frac{\mu_4}{\sigma^4}$$

where

β_2 = Measure of Kurtosis

μ_4 = Fourth moment of Dispersion

μ_2 = Second moment of Dispersion

σ = Standard Deviation

if $\beta_2 = 3$, the curve is *mesokurtic*

if $\beta_2 > 3$, the curve is *Lepto Kurtic*

if $\beta_2 < 3$, the curve is *Platy Kurtic*

CORRELATION

MEANING OF CORRELATION

The study of relationship between two or more variables is the most important in life. It is a common knowledge that change in are variable will affect the other. For example, when the price of a commodity increases, its demand decreases and on the other hand, when the price of a commodity decreases, its demand increases. The statistical device with the help of which relationships between two or more than two variables are studied is called correlation.

According to L.R. Connor, "If two or more quantities vary in sympathy so that movement in the one tend to be accompanied by corresponding movements in the others, then they are said to be correlated."

UTILITY OF THE STUDY OF CORRELATION

1. With the help of correlation we can measure the degree of relationship existing between the variables.
2. Correlation analysis contribute to the economic behaviour, aids in locating the critically important variable and on which other depend.

POSITIVE AND NEGATIVE CORRELATION

A. Positive Correlation: If both the variables move in the same direction, correlation is said to be positive.

Some examples of series of positive correlation are:

a. Heights and weights.

b. The family income and expenditure on luxury items.

c. Price and supply of a commodity and so on.

B. Nagative Correlation: If both the variables move in opposite direction, the correlations is said to be negative.

Some examples of negative correlation are:

a. Price and demand of a commodity.

b. Volume and pressure of a perfect goes.

c. Sale of woollen garments and the day temperature, and so on.

LINEAR AND NON-LINEAR CORRELATION

The correlation between two variables is said to be linear if corresponding to a unit change in one variable, there is a constant change in the other variable over the entire range of the values. For example, let us consider the following data:

X	1	2	3	4	5
Y	5	7	9	11	13

Thus for a unit change in the value of X, there is a constant change in the corresponding values of Y (2 Units). Mathematically, above data can be expressed by the equation.

$$Y = 2X + 3$$

In general two variables X and Y are said to be linearly related, if these exists a relationship of the form

$$Y = a + bX \qquad \ldots(1)$$

between than. But we know that (1) is the equation of a straight line with slope *'b'* and which an intercept *'a'* on the Y-axis. Hence, if the values of the two variables are plotted as points in XY-plane, we shall get a straight line.

The relationship between two variables is said to be *Non-linear or curvilinear* if corresponding to a unit change in one variable, the other variable does not change at a constant rate but at fluctuating rate. In such cases, if the data are plotted on the XY-plane we do not get a straight line curve mathematically speaking, the correlation is said to be non-linear it the slope of the plotted curve is not constant such phenomena are common in the data relating to economics ans social sciencs.

Degree of Correlation

Degree	*Positive*	*Negative*
Perfect	+1	−1
High	Between + .75 and +1	Between − .75 and − 1
Moderate	Between + .50 and + .75	Between − .50 and −.75
Low	Between 0 and + .50	Between 0 and − .50
Absence	0	0

METHODS OF STUDYING CORRELATION

The commonly used methods for studying the correlation between two variables are:

1. Scatter Diagram Method
2. Karl Pearson's coefficient of correlation
3. Rank Correlation Method
4. Concurrent Deviations Method

Karl Pearson's Coefficient of Correlation

A mathematical method for measuring the intensity or the magnitude of linear relationship between two variables was suggested by *Karl Pearson,* a great British Bio-metriciam and statistician and is by for the most widely used method in practice.

Karl Pearson's coefficient of correlation is calculated by applying the following formula:

Ungrouped Data

When deviations are taken from an actual mean

$$r = \frac{\Sigma xy}{N.\sigma x\, \sigma y}$$

where

r = Karl Pearson's Coefficient of Correlation

$x = (x - \bar{x})$

$y = (y - \bar{y})$

σx = Standard Deviation of x series

σy = Standard Deviation of y series

N = Number of pairs of item

An alternate formula of the above is:

$$r = \frac{\Sigma xy}{\sqrt{\Sigma x^2 . \Sigma y^2}}$$

where

Σx^2 = Total of squares of deviations taken from an actual mean of X series

Σy^2 = Total of squares of deviations taken from an actual mean of Y - series

When deviations are taken from an assumed mean

$$r = \frac{N\Sigma dx.dy - (\Sigma dx)(\Sigma dy)}{\sqrt{[N\,\Sigma dx^2 - (\Sigma dx)^2][N\Sigma dy^2 - (\Sigma dy)^2]}}$$

where

dx = Deviations taken form an assumed mean of X variable (X – A)

dy = Deviations taken from an assumed mean of Y variable (Y – A)

Grouped Data

$$r = \frac{N.\Sigma dxdy - (\Sigma fdx)(\Sigma fdy)}{\sqrt{[N\Sigma fdx^2 - (\Sigma fdx)^2][N\Sigma fdy^2 - (\Sigma fdx)^2]}}$$

PROPERTIES OF CORRELATION COEFFICIENT

Property–1

Pearsonian correlation coefficient can not exceed 1 numerically. In other words, it lies between –1 and + 1. Symbolically,

$$-1 \le r \le 1$$

In other owrds, r = + 1 implies perfect positive correlation between the variables and r = – 1 implies perfect negative correlation between the variables.

Property–2

Correlation coefficient is independent of the change of origin and scale.

Property–3

Two independent variables are uncorrelated but the converse is not true.

Rank Correlation Method

Sometimes we come across statistical series in which the variables under consideration are not capable of quantitative measurement but can be arranged in serial order. This happens when we are dealing with qualitative characteristics scuh as honesty, beauty, character, morality, etc., which cannot be measured quantitatively but can be arranged serially. In such situations, Karl Pearson's coefficient of correlation cannot be used as such. *Charles Edward Spearman,* a British Psychologist, developed a formula in 1904 which consists in obtaining the correlation coefficient between the ranks of n individuals in the two attributes under study.

Suppose we want to find if two characteristics A, say, intelligence and B, say, beauty are related or not. Both the characteristics are in capable of quantitative measurement, but we can arrange a group of n individuals in order of merit (ranks) *w. r. t.* proficiency in the two characteristics. Let the random variables X and Y denote the ranks of the individuals in the characteristics A and B respectively. If we assume that there is no tie, *i.e.,* if no two individuals get the same rank in a characteristic then, obviously, X and Y assume numerical values ranking from 1 to n.

Spearman's rank correlation coefficient, is given by the formula

$$rk = 1 - \frac{\Sigma d^2}{n(n^2-1)}$$

where

d = Differences in ranks
n = Number of pairs of items

Remark

Spearman's rank correlation coefficient lies between – 1 and + 1, *i.e.*,

$$-1 \le rk \le 1$$

ASSUMPTIONS UNDERLYING KARL PEARSON'S CORRELATION COEFFICIENT

Pearsonian correlation coefficient r is based on the following assumptions:

(i) The variables X and Y under study are linearly related. In other words, the scatter diagram of the data will give a straight line curve.

(ii) Each of the variables is being affected by a large number of independent contributory causes of such a nature as to produce normal distribution.

(iii) The forces so operating on each of the variable series are not independent of each other but are related in a causal fashion.

PROBABLE ERROR

After computing the value of the correlation coefficient the next step is to find the extent to which it is dependable. Probable error of correlation coefficient, usually denoted by P.E. (r) is an old measure of testing the reliability of an observed value of correlation coefficient in so far as it depends upon the conditions of random sampling.

If r is the observed correlation coefficient in a sample of n pairs of observations then its standard error, usually denoted by

S.E. (r) is given by

$$\text{S.E.}\,(r) = \frac{1-r^2}{\sqrt{n}}$$

Probable error of the correlation coefficient is given by

$$\text{P.E.}\,(r) = 0.6745 \times \text{S.E.}\,(r)$$

$$= 0.6745\ \frac{1-r^2}{\sqrt{n}}$$

Reason for taking the factor 0.6745 is that in a normal distribution 50% of the observations lie in the range $M \pm 0.6745\,\sigma$, where M is the mean and σ is the S.D.

COEFFICIENT OF DETERMINATION

Coefficient of correlation between two variable series is a measure of linear relationship between them and indicates the amount of variation of one variable which is associated with or is accounted for by another variable. A more useful and readily comprehensible measure for this purpose is the coefficient of determination which gives the percentage variation in the dependent variable that is accounted for by the independent variable. In other words, the coefficient of determination gives the ratio of the explained variance to the determination is given by the square of the correlation coefficient, *i.e.*, r^2. Thus,

Coefficient of determination

$$= r^2 = \frac{\text{Explained Variance}}{\text{Total Variance}}$$

The coefficient of determination is a much useful and better measure for interpreting the value of r.

Coefficient of determination is always non-negative: and as such it does not tell us about the direction of the relationship (whether it is positive or negative) between the two series.

Coefficient of Non-Determination: The ratio of the unexplained variation to the to the total variation is called the coefficient of non-determination. It is usually denoted by K^2 and is given by the formula:

$$K^2 = \frac{\text{Un-explained Variance}}{\text{Total Variance}}$$

$$= 1 - \frac{\text{Explained Variance}}{\text{Total Variance}}$$

$$= 1 - r^2$$

Coefficient of Alienation: The coefficient of alienation is given by the square root of the coefficient of non-determination, *i.e.*, by K as given below

$$K = \pm\sqrt{1-r^2}$$

REGRESSION

Regression analysis, in the general sense, means the estimation or prediction of the unknown value of the variable from the known value of the other variable. It is one of the very important statistical tools which is extensively used in almost all sciences–natural; social and physical. It is specially used in business and economics to study the relationship between two or more variables that are related casually and for estimation of demand and supply curves. Cost functions, production and consumption functions, etc.

Prediction or estimation is one of the major problems in almost all spheres of human activity. The estimation or prediction of future production, consumption, prices, investments, sales, profits, income, etc., are of paramount importance to a businessman or economist. Regression analysis is one of the very scientific techniques for making such predictions. In the words of M.M. Blair "Regression analysis is a mathematical measure of the average relationship between two or more variables in terms of the original units of data."

In regression analysis there are two types of variables. The variable whose value is influenced or is to be predicted is called dependent variable and the variable which influences the values or is used for prediction, is called independent variable. In regression analysis independent variable is also known as regresser or predictor or explanator while the dependent variable is also known as regressed or explained variable.

LINES OF REGRESSION

Line of regression is the line which gives the best estimate of one variable for any given value of the other variable. In case of two variables x and y, we shall have two lines of regression, one of y on x and the other of x on y.

1. Line of Regression of y on x

Line of regression of y on x is the line which gives the best estimate for the value of y for any specified value of x. Hence, the equation of line of regression of y on x is

$$y = a + bx \text{ or } y - \bar{y} = r.\frac{\sigma y}{\sigma x}(x - \bar{x})$$

where

$\bar{x}$ = Arithmetic Mean of x - series

$\bar{y}$ = Arithmetic Mean of y - series

σx = Standard Deviation of x - series

σy = Standard Deviation of y - series

r = Coefficient of Correlation between two Variables x and y.

2. Line of Regression of x on y

Line of regression of x on y is the line which gives the best estimate for the value of x for any specified value of y.

Mathematically

$$x = \text{A} + \text{B}y \text{ or } x - \bar{x} = r.\frac{\sigma x}{\sigma y}(y - \bar{y})$$

Remarks

1. Both the lines of regression passes through the point $(\bar{x}, \bar{y})$. In other words, the mean values $(\bar{x}, \bar{y})$ can be obtained as the point of intersection of the two regression lines.
2. There are always two lines of regression. In a particular case of perfect correlation, positive or negative *i.e.,* $r = \pm 1$, the equation of line of regression of y on x becomes

$$y - \bar{y} = \pm\frac{\sigma y}{\sigma x}(x - \bar{x})$$

$$\Rightarrow \quad \frac{y - \bar{y}}{\sigma y} = \pm\left(\frac{x - \bar{x}}{\sigma x}\right) \quad \ldots(1)$$

Similarly, the equation of the line of regression of x on y becomes:

$$x - \bar{x} = \pm\frac{\sigma x}{\sigma y}(y - \bar{y})$$

$$\Rightarrow \quad \frac{y - \bar{y}}{\sigma y} = \pm\left(\frac{x - \bar{x}}{\sigma x}\right) \quad \ldots(2)$$

Both the equations are same.

Hence in case of perfect correlation ($r = \pm 1$) both the lines of regression coincide. Therefore, in general we always have two lines of regression except in the particular case of perfect correlation when both the lines coincide and we get only one line.

COEFFICIENTS OF REGRESSION

Let us consider the line of regression of y on x,

$$y = a + bc$$

The coefficient 'b' which is the slope of the line of regression of y on x is called the coefficient of regression of y on x. It represents the increment in the value of the dependent variable y for a unit change in the value of the independent variable x. In other words, it represents the rate of change of y *w.r.t.* x. For notational convenience, the slope b, *i.e.*, cofficient of regression of y on x is written as byx. Mathematically

$$byx = \frac{r\sigma y}{\sigma x}$$

similarly in the regression equation of x on y

$$x = A + By$$

the coefficient B represents the change in the value of dependent variable x for a unit change in the value of independent variable y and is called the coefficient of regression of x on y. For convenience, it is written as bxy.

$$bxy = \frac{r\sigma x}{\sigma y}$$

Remarks

1. Correlation coefficient between two variables x and y is a symmetrical function between x is y, *i.e.*, $rxy = ryx$. However, the regression coefficients are not symmetric functions of x and y, *i.e.*, $byx \neq bxy$.
2. Both the regression coefficients must have the same sign.
3. The sign of correlation coefficient is same as that of the regression coefficients. If regression coefficients are positive, r is positive and if regression coefficients are negative, r is negative.

THEOREMS ON REGRESSION COEFFICIENTS

Theorem–1

The correlation coefficient is the geometric mean of the regression.

$$r = \sqrt{byx.bxy}$$

Theorem–2

If one of the regression coefficients is greater than unity, the other must be less than unity:

Theorem–3

The arithmetic mean of the regression coefficients is greater than the correlation coefficient.

Theorem – 4

Regression coefficients are independent of change of origin but not of scale.

Correlation Analysis *Vs.* Regression Analysis

1. Correlation coefficient rxy is a relative measure of the linear relationship between x and y and is independent of the units of measurement. On the other hand, the regression coefficients are absolute measures representing the change in the value of the variable $y(x)$, for a unit change in the value of the variable $x(y)$.
2. Correlation analysis is confined only to the study of linear relationship between the variables and, therefore, has limited applications. Regression analysis has much wider applications as it studies linear as well as non-linear relationship between the variables.
3. Correlation need not imply cause and effect relationship between the variables under study. However, regression analysis clearly indicates the cause and effect relationship between the variables.

INDEX NUMBERS

MEANING

An index number is as its name suggests, an indicator of the general trend of a set of figures. Index numbers are devices for measuring the net amount of change in a group of related variables over a certain period of time. Index numbers are used to measure changes in industrial output, fluctuations in the level of business or variations in the size of agricultural output etc.

The important definitions of index numbers are given below:

According to Croxton and Cowden, "Index numbers are devices for measuring differences in the magnitude of a group of related variables."

According to Blair, "Index numbers are a specialised type of averages".

TYPES OF INDEX NUMBERS

1. Price Index Numbers
2. Quantity Index Numbers
3. Value Index Numbers

METHODS OF CONSTRUCTING INDEX NUMBERS

The various methods for constructing index numbers are given below:

1. *Fixed Base Method*

$$\text{Price Relatives (R)} = \frac{P_1}{P_0} \times 100$$

where

P_1 = Price of the current year
P_0 = Price of the base year

2. *Simple Aggregative Method*

$$P_{01} = \frac{\Sigma P_1}{\Sigma P_0} \times 100$$

where

P_{01} = Price index of the current year
ΣP_1 = Total of current year prices
ΣP_0 = Total of base year prices

3. *Simple Average of Price Relatives Methods*

$$P_{01} = \frac{\Sigma\left(\frac{P_1}{P_0} \times 100\right)}{N}$$

where N stands for number of items or commodities.

4. *Weighted Aggregate Method*

$$P_{01} = \frac{\Sigma WP_1}{\Sigma WP_0} \times 100$$

where w is the weight attached to a commodity.

By using different systems of weighting we get a number of formulas. Some of the important formulae are given below:

Laspeyre's Price Index or Base Year Method

Taking base year quantities as weights, *i.e.*, $w = q_0$ we get Laspeyre's Price Index given by:

$$P_{01} = \frac{\Sigma P_1 q_0}{\Sigma P_0 q_0} \times 100$$

where

P_1 = Current Year Price
q_0 = Base Year Quantity
P_0 = Base Year Price
q_1 = Current Year Quantity

This formula was devised by French Economist Laspeyre in 1871.

Paasche's Price Index

If we take current year quantities as weights we obtain Paasche's Price Index which is given by:

$$P_{01} = \frac{\Sigma P_1 q_1}{\Sigma P_0 q_0} \times 100$$

This formula was given by German statistician Paasche in 1874.

Dorbish - Bowley Price Index

This index is given by the arithmetic mean of Laspeyre's and Paasche's price index numbers and we have:

$$P_{01} = \frac{1}{2}\left[\frac{\Sigma P_1 q_0}{\Sigma P_0 q_0} + \frac{\Sigma P_1 q_1}{\Sigma P_0 q_1}\right] \times 100$$

This is also sometimes known as L - P formula.

Fisher's Price Index

Irving Fisher advocated the geometric mean of Laspeyre's and Paasche's price index numbers and is given by:

$$P_{0-1}\left[\frac{\Sigma P_1 q_0}{\Sigma P_0 q_0} \times \frac{\Sigma P_1 q_1}{\Sigma P_0 q_1}\right] \times 100$$

Fisher's price index is termed as an Ideal index since it satisfies time reversal and factor reversal tests for the consistency of index numbers.

Marshall Edgeworth Price Index

Taking the arithmetic cross of the quantities in the base year and the current year as weights *i.e.*,

$w = \dfrac{(q_1 + q_1)}{2}$, we obtain the Marshall-Edgeworth formula given by

$$P_{01} = \frac{\Sigma P_1 . \frac{(q_0 + q_1)}{2}}{\Sigma P_0 . \frac{(q_0 + q_1)}{2}} \times 100$$

$$= \frac{\Sigma P_1 (q_0 + q_1)}{\Sigma P_0 (q_0 + q_1)} \times 100$$

$$= \left[\frac{\Sigma P_1 q_0 + \Sigma P_1 q_1}{\Sigma P_0 q_0 + \Sigma P_0 q_0} \times 100\right]$$

Walsch's Price Index

Instead of taking the arithmetic mean of base year and current year quantities as weights, if we take their geometric mean, *i.e.*, $w = \sqrt{q_0 q_1}$, then we obtain Walsch Index given by the formula:

$$P_{01} = \frac{\Sigma P_1 \sqrt{q_0 q_1}}{\Sigma P_0 \sqrt{q_0 q_1}} \times 100$$

Kelly's Price Index or Fixed Weights Index

This formula, named after L. Kelly, requires the weights to be fixed for all periods and is also sometimes known as aggregative index with fixed weights and is given by the formula:

$$P_{01} = \frac{\Sigma P_1 q}{\Sigma P_0 q} \times 100$$

where the weights are the quantities *(q)* which may refer to some period (not necessarily the base year or the current year) and are kept constant for all periods.

Value Indices

Value index numbers are obtained on expressing the total value (or expenditure) in any given year as *a* percentage of the same in the base year symbolically, we write

$$V_{01} = \frac{\text{Total value in current year}}{\text{Total value in base year}} \times 100$$

$$\Rightarrow \quad V_{01} = \frac{\Sigma P_1 q_1}{\Sigma P_0 q_0} \times 100$$

Remarks

1. In general, Laspeyre's price index is greater than Paasche's price index. In other words, Laspeyre's price index has an upward bias in general, with rise in price.
   But if the correlation coefficients between the price relatives and quantity relatives is positive (a phenomenon which is rarely observed in economics), then Laspeyre's price index is less than Paasche's price index.
2. Fisher's ideal index number lies between Laspeyre's and Paasche's index numbers.

Proof : Let us consider two real positive numbers a and b such that $a > 0$.

Let $a > b$

$\Rightarrow a^2 < ab$ (multiplying by $a > 0$)

$\Rightarrow \quad a < \sqrt{ab}$ ... (1)

($\because a > 0$, negative sign is rejected)

Also $a < b$

$\Rightarrow ab < b^2$ (Multiplying by $b > 0$)

$\Rightarrow \quad \sqrt{ab} < b$ ... (2)

$(\because b > 0)$

Hence, from equation (1) and (2)

$$a < \sqrt{ab} < b$$

This, the geometric mean of two real positive numbers lies between them. Hence, Fisher's ideal index which is the geometric mean of Laspeyre's and Paasche's index numbers lies between them. More precisely,

if $P_{01}^{La} < P_{01}^{Pa}$

there $P_{01}^{La} < P_{01}^{F} < P_{01}^{pa}$

and if $P_{01}^{po} < P_{01}^{La}$

then $P_{01}^{pa} < P_{01}^{F} < P_{01}^{La}$

and if $P_{01}^{La} = P_{01}^{Pa}$

then $P_{01}^{Pa} = P_{01}^{La} = P_{01}^{F}$

3. *Marshall - Edgeworth index also lies between Laspeyre's and Paasche's indices. Rather we have*

if $P_{01}^{La} < P_{01}^{Pa}$

then $P_{01}^{La} < P_{01}^{F} < P_{01}^{ME} < P_{01}^{Pa}$

and if $P_{01}^{Pa} < P_{01}^{La}$

then $P_{01}^{Pa} < P_{01}^{F} < P_{01}^{ME} < P_{01}^{La}$

TESTS OF CONSISTENCY OF INDEX NUMBER FORMULA

1. Unit Test: This test requires that the index number formula should be independent of the units in which the prices or quantities of various commodities are quoted. All the formulae discussed above except the index number based on simple Aggregate of prices (Quantities) satisfy this test.

2. Time Reversal Test: The time reversal tests proposed by Prof. Irving Fisher requires the index number formula to possess time consistency by working both forward and back ward *w.r.t.* time.

In other words, if the index numbers are computed for the same data relating to two periods by the same formula but with the bases reversed, then the two index numbers so obtained should be the reciprocals of each other. Mathematically, we should have (omitting the factor 100),

$$P_{01} \times P_{10} = 1$$

or more generally

$$P_{ab} \times P_{ba} = 1$$

where

P_{ab} = Price index (without factor 100) for year '*b*' with year '*a*' as base

P_{ba} = Price index (without factor 100) for year '*a*' with year '*b*' as base

Time reversal test is satisfied by the following index number formulae:

(*i*) Marshall - Edgeworth formula
(*ii*) Fisher's ideal formula
(*iii*) Walsch formula
(*iv*) Kelly's fixed weight formula
(*v*) Simple aggregate index
(*vi*) Simple Geometric mean of Price Relatives formula
(*vii*) Weighted Geometric mean of Price Relatives formula with fixed weights

Remark

Laspeyre's and Paasche's index numbers do not satisfy this test.

Let us verify this test for Kelly's fixed weight formula. We have (without factor 100)

$$P_{10}^{k} = \frac{\Sigma WP_1}{\Sigma WP_0}$$

and $$P_{10}^{k} = \frac{\Sigma WP_0}{\Sigma WP_1}$$

$$\therefore P_{01}^{k} \times P_{10}^{k} = \frac{\Sigma WP_1}{\Sigma WP_0} \times \frac{\Sigma WP_0}{\Sigma WP_1} = 1$$

Hence Kelly's fixed weight formula satisfies time reversal test.

3. Factor Reversal Test: This is the second of the two important tests of consistency proposed by Prof. Irving Fisher. This implies that if the price and quantity indices are obtained for the same data same base and current periods and using the same formula, then their product (without the factor 100) should give the true value ratio, since price multiplied by quantity gives total value. Symbolically, we should have (without factor 100),

$$P_{01} \times Q_{01} = \frac{\Sigma P_1 q_1}{\Sigma P_0 q_0}$$

where

$\Sigma P_1 q_1$ and $\Sigma P_0 q_0$ denote the total value in the current and base year respectively.

Fisher's formula satisfies the factor reversal test. In fact Fisher's index is the only index satisfying this test and none of the formulae discussed above satisfies this test.

Remark: Since Fisher's index is the only index which satisfies both the time reversal and factor reversal tests, it is sometimes tremed as Fisher's Ideal Index.

4. Circular Test: Circular test, first suggested by Westergaard, is an extension of time reversal test for more than two periods and is based on the shiftability of the base period. This requires the index to work in a circular manner add this property enables us to find the index numbers from period to period without referring back to the original base each time. For, three periods *a, b, c,* the test requires:

$$P_{ab} \times P_{bc} \times P_{ca} = 1, \; a \neq b \neq c$$

or, $P_{01} \times P_{12} \times P_{20} = 1$

For instance

$$P_{01}^{La} \times P_{12}^{La} \times P_{20}^{La} = \frac{\Sigma p_1 q_0}{\Sigma p_0 q_0} \times \frac{\Sigma p_2 q_1}{\Sigma p_1 q_1} \times \frac{\Sigma p_0 q_2}{\Sigma p_2 q_2} \neq 1$$

Hence Laspeyre's index does not satisfy the circular test. Similarly, it can be verified that none of Pasche's, M - E's, Walsch's, and Fisher's indices satisfies this test. In fact, circular test is not satisfied by any of the weighted aggregative formula with changing weights, *i.e.,* if the weights used in the construction of index numbers P_{01}, P_{12} and P_{20} change. This test is satisfied only by the index number formulae based on:

(i) Simple geometric mean of the price relatives

(ii) Kelly's fixed base method

Remark: The circular test can be generalised to the case of more than three periods to give:

$$P_{01} \times P_{12} \times P_{23} \times .... \times P_{n,o} = 1$$

where the indices are, considered without the factor 400.

(i) Conversion of Fixed Base to Chain Base

Chain Index Number

$$= \frac{\text{Current year fixed base index No.}}{\text{Previous year fixed base index No.}} \times 100$$

(ii) Conversion of Chain Base to Fixed Base

Fixed Base Index Number

$$= \frac{\text{Current year's chain base index No.} \times \text{Previous year's fixed base index No.}}{100}$$

THEORY OF PROBABILITY

Meaning of Probability

In every day life we talk about probability of occurrence of various events. Whenever there is an element of uncertainty about the occurrence of some event one makes a probability statement. For example, the probability that India will win a cricket mach against West Indies is 30% or 0.30; the probability that it will rain tonight is 80% or 0.80, etc.

The concept of probability originally developed in the 17th century with the games of chance, like games of cards, tossing of coins and dies etc.

Let us illustrate the concept of probability with the help of the classical example of coin tossing experiment. Suppose a coin is tossed, what is the probability that it will turn up head? Perhaps the immediate answer it $\frac{1}{2}$, provided it is an ideal coin and it is not worn out or biased in any way. The argument will be that there are only two possible ways in which the coin can be tossed (either head or tail will turn up), and the coin being an ideal one both head and tail are equally likely. Therefore, the odds are fifty - fifty, *i.e.*, the probability of getting head is $\frac{1}{2}$ and so is the probability of getting tail. This is, in fact, the classical approach to obtain the probability of occurrence of an event.

According to La Place: "Probability is the ratio of favourable events to the total number of equally likely events."

Symbolically

$$P = \frac{\text{Number of favourable cases}}{\text{Total number of equally likely cases}}$$

where

P = Probability that the event will take place.

Similarly,

$$q = \frac{\text{Number of cases not favourable}}{\text{Total number of equally likely cases}}$$

In simple words, probability can be defined in the following manner:

The probability of the happening of any one of the several equally likely events is the ratio of the number of cases favourable to it to the total number of possible cases.

Mathematical Definition

If there are n mutually exclusive and equally likely cases and of these n cases, there are p cases favourable and q cases unfavourable to some event, then the probability of occurrence of the event is denoted by

$$P = \frac{p}{n}$$

The probability of non-occurrence of the event is denoted by

$$Q = \frac{q}{n}$$

where P = Chance of success
Q = Chance of failure

Mutually Exclusive Events

Two or more events are said to be mutually exclusive if the happening of any one of them excludes the happening of all others in the same experiment.

For example, in toss of a coin the events 'head' and 'tail' are mutually exclusive because if head comes, we cannot get tail and if tail comes we cannot get head.

Equally Likely Cases

The outcomes are said to be equally likely or equally probable if none of them is expected to occur in preference to other. Thus, in tossing of a coin, all the outcomes, namely, H and T are equally likely if the coin is unbiased.

Independent Events

Events are said to be independent of each other if happening of any one of there is not affected by and does not affect the happening of any one of others.

For example, in tossing of a die repeatedly the event of getting '5' in 1st throw is independent of getting '5' in second, third or subsequent throws.

Remark

The two events A and B are said to be disjoint or mutually exclusive if they cannot happen simultaneously *i.e.,* if their intersection is a null set. Thus, if A and B are disjoint events, then

$$A \cap B = \phi \Rightarrow P(A \cap B) = P(\Phi) = 0$$

Thus $P(A \cap B) = 0$, provides us with a criterion for finding if A and B are mutually exclusive.

Addition Rule of Probability

The probability of occurrence of at least one of the two events A and B is given by:

$$P(A \cup B) = P(A) + P(B) - P(A \cap B)$$

where

P (A) = Probability of occurrence of an event A

P (B) = Probability of occurrence of an event B

$P(A \cap B)$ = Probability of simultaneous occurrence of A and B

$P(A \cup B)$ = Probability of occurrence of at least one of the two events A and B

Addition Rule of Probability for Mutually Exclusive Events

If two events A and B are mutually exclusive (*i.e.,* only one of them can occur at a time) and P (A) and P (B) are the probabilities of occurrence of A and B, respectively; then

$$P(A \cup B) = P(A) + P(B)$$

Multiplication Rule of Probability

The probability of simultaneous happening of two events A and B is given by :

$$P(A \cap B) = P(A) \,.\, P(B/A); P(A) \neq 0$$

$$\text{or } P(B \cap A) = P(B) \,.\, P(A/B); P(B) \neq 0$$

where P (B/A) is the conditional probability of happening of B under the condition that A has happened and P (A/B) is the conditional probability of happening of A under the condition that B has happened.

Remark: *Multiplicative Rule for Independent Events.*

If A and B are independent so that the probability of occurrence or non-occurrence of A is not affected by the occurrence or non-occurrence of B, we have

$$P(A/B) = P(A) \text{ and } P(B/A) = P(B)$$

Hence

$$P(A \cap B) = P(A) . P(B)$$

Thus, the probability of simultaneous happening of two independent events is equal to the product of their individual probabilities.

Generalisation

The multiplication law of probability can be extended to more than two events. Thus, for three events A, B and C we have

$$P(A \cap B \cap C) = P(A). P(B/A) P(C/A \cap B)$$

In particular, if A, B and C are *independent events* then

$$P(A \cap B \cap C) = P(A) . P(B) . P(C)$$

i.e., the probability of the simultaneous happening of n independent events is equal to the product of their individual probabilities.

Theorem:

$$P(\overline{A}) = 1 - P(A)$$

where

$P(\overline{A})$ = Probability of event A does not happen

P (A) = Probability of event A happens

Theorem:

(i) $P(\overline{A} \cap B) = P(B) - P(A \cap B)$

where

$P(\overline{A} \cap B)$ = Probability of A does not happen but B happens

(ii) $P(A \cap \overline{B}) = P(A) - P(A \cap B)$

(iii) $P(\overline{A} \cap \overline{B}) = 1 - P(A \cup B)$

$$= 1 - [P(A) + P(B) - P(A \cap B)]$$

$$= 1 - P(A) - P(B) + P(A \cap B)]$$

where A and B are independent event.

$\because P(A \cap B) = P(A) . P(B)$

$$\therefore P(\overline{A} \cap \overline{B}) = 1 - P(A) - P(B) + P(A).P(B)$$

$$= 1 - P(A) - P(B) [1 - P(A)]$$

$$= [1 - P(A)] [1 - P(B)] = P(\overline{A}).P(\overline{B})$$

Mathematical Expectation

If x is a random variable which can assume any one of the values $x_1, x_2, \ldots x_n$ with respective probabilities $p_1, p_2 \ldots p_n$ there the mathematical expectation of x usually called the expected value of x and denoted by E (X) is defined as:

$$E(x) = p_1 x_1 + p_2 x_2 + \ldots + p_n x_n = \Sigma p.x$$

where

$$\Sigma p_i = p_1 + p_2 + \ldots . p_n = 1$$

More precisely, if x is a random variable with probability distribution $\{x, p(x)\}$, Hence

$$E(x) = \Sigma x . p(x)$$

Remark

Mathematical expectation of a random variable is nothing but its arithmetic mean.

Theorems on Expectation

Theorem-1

$$E(c) = C$$

where c is a constant

Proof: We have

$$E(c) = \text{Mean of } c$$

$$= \frac{c + c + c + \ldots . + c}{n} = \frac{nc}{n} = c$$

Theorem-2

$$E(cx) = C\,E(x)$$

where c is a constant

Theorem-3

$$E(ax \times b) = a\,E(x) + b$$

where a and b are constants.

Theorem-4. Addition Rule of Expectation

If X and Y are random variables then

$$E(X + Y) = E(X) + E(Y)$$

i.e., the expected value of the sum of two random variables is equal to the sum of their expected values.

Corollary

$$E(ax - by) = AE(X) + bE(Y)$$

where a and b are constants.

Theorem-5. Multiplication Rule of Expectation

If X and Y are independent random variables, then

$$E(XY) = E(X) . E(Y)$$

i.e., the expected value of the product of two independent random variables is equal to the product of their expected values.

BINOMIAL DISTRIBUTION

Suppose the variable under study is measured in such away that each observation can be classified into two categories. For example, if a coin is tossed, the result of each throw can be either a head or a tail. Similarly, if a die is thrown we may call getting 5 or 6 a 'success' and getting 1, 2, 3 or 4 a 'failure'. If data on income of households are collected, we may classify each household as 'Poor' or 'Not - Poor' on the basis of its income. For example, if the household monthly income is less than or equal to Rs. 500/- it may be classified as 'Poor' and if it is more than Rs.500/- we may call it 'Not - Poor.'

In Binomial Distribution, it is necessary that each observation is classified into only two categories.

For the sake of convenience we name there are two categories as 'success' and 'failure'.

In Binomial distribution, it is necessary that the probability of success and failure remains the same for each observation or in each trial. Thus, the probability of getting head (or tail) must remain the same in each toss; similarly, in case of the die throwing experiment the probability of success (*i.e.,* getting 5 or 6) must remain the same in each throw.

If the probability of success (or failure) changes from trial to trial or if the results of each trial are classified into more than two categories, then the Binomial distribution cannot be used.

Another condition underlying the Binomial distribution is that the trials (or individual observations) should be independent of each other

If n independent observations (or n independent trials) are made, the result of each trial is classified into two categories called 'success' and 'failure' and the probability of success is the same for each observation or in each trial, then the probability of getting x successes in n trials is equal to

$$\frac{n!}{x!(n-x)!} p^x q^{n-x}$$

where

p = probability of success in a single trial

q = probability of failure in a single trial.

and $p + q = 1$

For Binomial Distribution

1. *Mean* = np
2. *Variance* = $(\text{s.d.})^2 = npq$
3. *Third moments*

$$\mu_3 = npq(q-p)$$

4. *Fourth moments*

$$\mu_4 = npq[1 + 3pq(n-2)]$$

5. *Moment coefficient of Skewness is*

$$\beta_1 = \frac{(q-p)^2}{npq}$$

6. *Coefficient of Kurtosis is*

$$\beta_2 = 3 + \frac{1-6pq}{npq}$$

Remarks

1. Since q is the probability (of failure), we always have $0 < q < 1$.

$\therefore$ Variance = $np \times q < np$

$(\because 0 < q < 1)$

$\Rightarrow$ Variance < Mean

Hence for the Binomial distribution variance is less than mean.

2. Binomial distribution is symmetrical if $p = q$ $0.5 = \frac{1}{2}$. It is positively Skewed if $p < 0.5$ and negatively Skewed if $p > 0,5$.

POISSON DISTRIBUTION (AS A LIMITING CASE OF BINOMIAL DISTRIBUTION)

Poisson distribution was derived in1837 by *Simon D. Poisson.* Poisson distribution may be obtained as a limiting case of Binomial probability distribution under the following conditions:

(*i*) n, the number of trials is indefinitely large

(*ii*) p, the constant probability of success for each trial is indefinitely small *i.e.*, $p \to 0$.

(*iii*) $np = m$ is finite

Under the conditions given above the probability of getting x successes is

$$\frac{e^{-n}.m^x}{x!} \quad \ldots(i)$$

where $x = 0, 1, 2, 3$.........

m = mean = np

$e = 2.71828$

and $x! = x(x-1)(x-2)\ldots \times 3 \times 2 \times 1$.

Constants of Poisson Distribution

The mean of Poisson distribution

Mean = $m = np$

and the Variance = m = mean

Hence for the Poisson distribution with parameter m, we have

Mean = Variance = m

i.e., mean and variance are equal, each being equal to the parameter m.

Utility or Importance of Poisson Distribution

The conditions under which Poisson distribution is obtained as a limiting case of the Binomial distribution and also the conditions for the general model underlying. Poisson distribution suggest that Poisson distribution can be used to explain the behaviour of the discrete random variables where the probability of occurrence of the event is very small and the total number of possible cases is sufficiently large. We give below some practical situations where Poisson distribution can be used:

(*i*) Number of accidents taking place per day on a busy road.

(*ii*) The number of suicides reported in a particular day or the number of casualties due to a rare disease such as heart attack or cancer or snake bite in a year.

(*iii*) The number of defective material in a packing manufactured by a good concern.

(*iv*) To count the number of radioactive disintegrations of a radioactive element per unit of time.

NORMAL DISTRIBUTION

Normal distribution is one of the most important continuous theoretical distributions in statistics. Most of the data relating to economic and business statistics or even in social and physical sciences conform to this distribution.

Remark

If X is a random variable following normal distribution with mean m and standard deviation σ, then the random variable Z defined as follows:

$$Z = \frac{X - E(X)}{\sigma_x} = \frac{X - m}{\sigma}$$

is called the standard normal variate (S.N.V.).

The standard normal variate (S.N.V.) Z has mean 0 and standard deviation 1.

Properties of Normal Distribution

1. If the parameters m and σ^2 of the normal curve are specified, the normal curve is fully determined and we can draw it by obtaining the value of (y) corresponding to different values of x–the abscissa.

we note that the normal curve

$$y = \frac{1}{\sigma\sqrt{2\pi}} e^{-\frac{1}{2}\frac{(x-m)^2}{\sigma^2}}$$

is bell-shaped and it is symmetric about the straight line $x = m$.

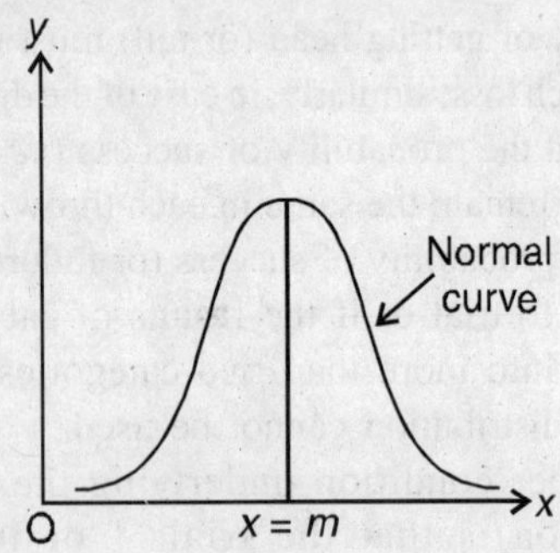

2. The normal curve tends to touch the x-axis only at infinity, *i.e.*, the x-axis is an 'asymptote' to the normal curve. It is a continuous curve stretching from $-\infty$ to $+\infty$.

3. Since the distribution is symmetrical, mean, median and mode coincide. Thus,

Mean = Median = Mode = m.

4. Since Mean = Median = m, the ordinate at $x = m$, divides the whole area into two equal parts. Further, since total area under normal curve is 1, the area to the right of the ordinate as well as to the left of the ordinate at $x = m$ is 0.5.

5. Also, by virtue of symmetry the quartiles are equidistant from median (m) *i.e.,*

$$Q_3 - M_d = M_d - Q_1 \Rightarrow Q_1 + Q_3 = 2M_d = 2M.$$

6. Since the distribution is symmetrical, the moment coefficient of Skewness is given by:

$$\beta_1 = 0.$$

7. The coefficient of Kurtosis is given by:

$$\beta_2 = 3.$$

8. No portion of the curve lies below the x-axis.

9. Theoretically, the range of the distribution is from $-\infty$ to ∞. But practically, Range = σ_{σ}.

10. Since the distribution is symmetrical, all moments of odd order about the mean are zero. Thus

$$\mu_1 = \mu_3 = \mu_5 = ... = 0.$$

11. X-axis is an asymptote to the curve, *i.e.,* for numerically large value of x (on either side of the point $x = m$), the curve becomes parallel, to the x-axis and is supposed to meet it at infinity.

12. Points of inflexion of the normal curve are at $x = m\ \sigma$ and $x = m - \sigma$.

At the point of inflexion the tangent changes its sign.

13. Area Property—One of the most fundamental properties of the normal probability curve is the area property. The area under the normal curve between the ordinates at $x = m - \sigma$ and $x = m + \sigma$ is 0.6826. In other words, the range $m \pm \sigma$ covers 68.26% of the observations.

The area under the normal probability curve between the ordinates at $x = m - 3\sigma$ and $x = m + 3\sigma$ is 0.9973 *i.e.,* the range $m \pm 3\sigma$ covers 99.73% of the observations. Hence, for practical purposes, the range $m \pm 3\sigma$ covers the entire area, which is 1.

Area Under Normal Curve

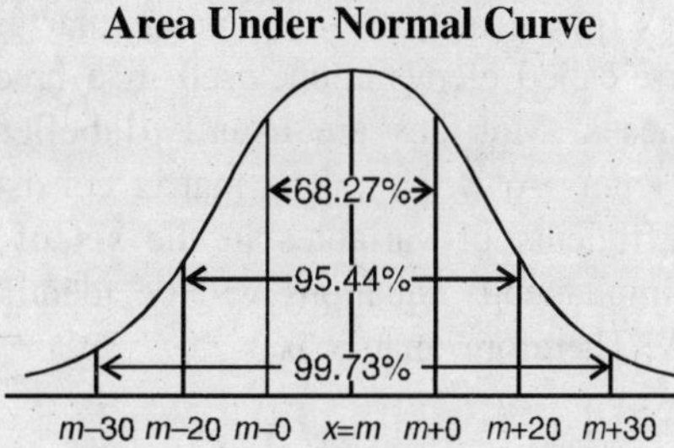

Business Mathematics

MATRICES AND DETERMINANTS

MATRIX

A matrix (plural matrices) is a rectangular array of numbers, called elements enclosed in a bracket or parentheses. Matrices are usually labelled with capital letters A, B, C, ... The matrix consisting of the coefficients of variables in the set of above three simultaneous equations will be identified by letter A. Therefore, matrix is

$$A = \begin{bmatrix} 4 & 2 & 3 \\ 3 & 3 & 2 \\ 4 & 3 & 4 \end{bmatrix} \text{ or } \begin{pmatrix} 4 & 2 & 3 \\ 3 & 3 & 2 \\ 4 & 3 & 4 \end{pmatrix}$$

Column 1 ↓ Column 2 ↓ Column 3 ↓

$$A = \begin{bmatrix} 4 & 2 & 3 \\ 3 & 3 & 2 \\ 4 & 3 & 4 \end{bmatrix} \begin{matrix} \leftarrow \text{Row 1} \\ \leftarrow \text{Row 2} \\ \leftarrow \text{Row 3} \end{matrix}$$

Types of Matrices

1. **Row and Column Matrices:** A matrix having only one row is called row matrix or a row vector, while the one having only one column is known as column matrix or column vector, *e.g.*,

   A = [2 7 6 0] is a 1 × 4 row matrix.

   $$B = \begin{bmatrix} 6 \\ -3 \\ 5 \end{bmatrix}$$ is a 3 × 1 column matrix.

2. **Null (or Zero) Matrix:** A matrix of order $m \times n$ each of whose element is 0, is called a null (or zero) matrix of order $m \times n$, *e.g.*,

   $$\begin{bmatrix} 0 & 0 & 0 \\ 0 & 0 & 0 \end{bmatrix}, \begin{bmatrix} 0 & 0 \\ 0 & 0 \\ 0 & 0 \end{bmatrix} \text{ and } [0\ 0] \text{ are null}$$

   matrices of order 2 × 3, 3 × 2 and 1 × 2 respectively.

3. **Square Matrix:** A matrix of order $n \times n$ for which $m = n$ (*i.e.,* the number of row equals the number of columns) is called a square matrix of order n or an n rowed square matrix.

4. **Diagonal Matrix:** A square matrix in which each one of the non-diagonal elements is 0 is called a diagonal matrix.

5. **Scalar Matrix:** A diagonal matrix in which all the diagonal elements are equal is called a scalar matrix. Thus, in a scalar matrix A = $[a_{ij}]_{n \times n}$, we have

   $$a_{ij} = \begin{cases} 0, \text{ when } i \neq j \\ k, \text{ when } i = j \end{cases}, \text{ where } k \text{ is any constant.}$$

6. **Unit Matrix:** A scalar matrix each of whose diagonal elements is unity is called a unit matrix or an identity matrix.

7. **Comparable Matrices:** Two matrices are said to be comparable, if they are of the same type, *e.g.*,

$\begin{bmatrix} 3 & -5 & 6 \\ 0 & 4 & 7 \end{bmatrix}$ and $\begin{bmatrix} 4 & 5 & 0 \\ 5 & 7 & -3 \end{bmatrix}$ are comparable matrices, each being of the type 2 × 3.

8. Equal Matrices: Two matrices A and B are said to be equal, written as A = B, if they are comparable and their corresponding elements are equal, *e.g.*,

$\begin{bmatrix} 2 & 1 & 4 \\ 3 & 2 & 5 \\ 5 & 0 & 9 \end{bmatrix}$ and $\begin{bmatrix} 2 & 1 & 4 \\ 3 & 2 & 6 \\ 5 & 0 & 9 \end{bmatrix}$ are clearly comparable but not equal, since they differ in correspondingly placed elements in second row and third column.

OPERATION OF MATRICES

Addition (or Subtraction) of Matrices

Two matrices are said to be conformable for addition (or subtraction) if they are comparable, *i.e.,* matrices must have the same number of rows and columns.

The sum (or difference) of matrices is obtained by adding (or subtracting) corresponding elements of the given matrix, *e.g.,* if

$$A = \begin{bmatrix} a_{11} & a_{12} & a_{13} \\ a_{21} & a_{22} & a_{23} \\ a_{31} & a_{32} & a_{33} \end{bmatrix}$$

and $$B = \begin{bmatrix} b_{11} & b_{12} & b_{13} \\ b_{21} & b_{22} & b_{23} \\ b_{31} & b_{32} & b_{33} \end{bmatrix}, \text{ then}$$

$$A + B = \begin{bmatrix} a_{11}+b_{11} & a_{12}+b_{12} & a_{13}+b_{13} \\ a_{21}+b_{21} & a_{22}+b_{22} & a_{23}+b_{23} \\ a_{31}+b_{31} & a_{32}+b_{32} & a_{33}+b_{33} \end{bmatrix}$$

and $$A - B = \begin{bmatrix} a_{11}-b_{11} & a_{12}-b_{12} & a_{13}-b_{13} \\ a_{21}-b_{21} & a_{22}-b_{22} & a_{23}-b_{23} \\ a_{31}-b_{31} & a_{32}-b_{32} & a_{33}-b_{33} \end{bmatrix}$$

Properties of Matrix Addition

If A, B and C are any three comparable matrices of the same dimensions, then

(*i*) A + B = B + A

(*ii*) (A + B) + C = A + (B + C)

(*iii*) *k* (A + B) = *k*A + *k*B

(*iv*) A + 0 = A = 0 + A

(*v*) A + (–A) = 0 = (–A) + A

(*vi*) A + C = B + C ⇒ A = B

Multiplication of Matrices

Let A be an $m \times p$ matrix and B be an $p \times n$ matrix. The product AB is an $m \times n$ matrix where each element is obtained by multiplying the *i*th row of A by the *j*th column of B and putting the result in the *i*th row and *j*th column of the product matrix AB.

It may be noted that two matrices can be multiplied *if and only if the number of columns of the first matrix equals the number of rows of the second.* (The resultant will be equal to the number of rows of the first matrix and the number of the columns of the second.)

Properties of Matrix Multiplication

1. The product of matrices is not, in general commutative, *i.e.,* if two matrices A, B are conformable for the product AB and BA, then in general AB ≠ BA.
2. Matrix multiplication is distributive *w.r.* to addition of matrices, *i.e.,* if A and B are conformal for the product AB, B and C are conformal for addition, then
   A (B + C) = AB + AC.
3. Matrix multiplication is associative, *i.e.,* if A and B are conformal for the product AB, and B & C are conformal for the product BC, then (AB) C = A (BC).
4. If A is $n \times m$ matrix and O is $m \times n$ matrix, then
   AO = O = OA.
5. Multiplication of a matrix by a unit Matrix. If A is square matrix of order $n \times n$ and I is the unit matrix of the same order, then
   AI = A = IA.
6. AB = 0 (null matrix) does not imply that
   A = 0 or B = 0 or both = 0.

Tranpose of a Matrix

The matrix of order $n \times m$ obtained by interchanging the rows and columns of an $m \times n$ matrix. The transpose matrix is denoted by A or A^t.

Properties of Transpose of a Matrix

1. Transpose of a sum (or difference) of two matrices is the sum (or difference) of their transposes, *i.e.,*
$$(A + B)' = A' + B'$$
2. The transpose of a transpose is the original matrix, *i.e.,*
$$(A')' = A$$
3. Transpose of a product of two matrices is the product of their transposes taken in reverse order. *i.e.,*
$$(AB)' = B'A'$$

DETERMINANTS

A determinant is a pure number associated with a square matrix. It is also a function called determinant function, which associates with a square matrix a real number called a determinant. The determinant A of a square matrix A can be depicted as:

A	→	|A|	=	determinant
square matrix		real number		of A

The determinant of the square matrix A is written as:

$$|A| \text{ or } \det A = \begin{vmatrix} a_{11} & a_{12} & \cdots & a_{1n} \\ a_{21} & a_{22} & \cdots & a_{2n} \\ \vdots & \vdots & & \vdots \\ a_{n1} & a_{n2} & \cdots & a_{mn} \end{vmatrix}$$

So a determinant is the pure number obtained by enclosing the elements of the square matrix A within two parallel straight lines (these two lines for a determinant are not indented at the end points as for a matrix).

Properties of Determinants

1. If the rows of a determinant are changed into columns and vice versa, the value of the determinant remains unchanged.
2. If any two adjacent rows (or columns) are interchanged, the value of the determinant so obtained is negative of the value of the original determinant.
3. If any two rows or any two columns of a determinant are identical, the value of the determinant is zero.
4. If the elements of any row or any column of a determinant is sum (difference) of two or more elements, then the determinant can be expressed as sum (difference) of two or more determinants.
5. If to each element of any row (or column) of a determinant are added or subtracted equi-multiples of the corresponding elements of one or more rows (columns), the value of the determinant remains unaltered.
6. If the elements of a row (or a column) of a determinant are multiplied by the same number *k*, value of determinant so obtained is *k* times the value of original determinant.

INVERSE OF A MATRIX

Minors and Cofactors of the Elements of a Determinant

The minor of an element a_{ij} of a determinant A is denoted by M_{ij} and is the determinant obtained from A by deleting the row and the column where a_{ij} occurs.

The cofactor of an element a_{ij} with minor M_{ij} is denoted by C_{ij} and is defined as

$$C_{ij} = \begin{cases} M_{ij}, & \text{if } i + j \text{ is even} \\ -M_{ij}, & \text{if } i + j \text{ is odd.} \end{cases}$$

Thus, cofactors are signed minors.

In the case of $\begin{vmatrix} a_{11} & a_{12} \\ a_{21} & a_{22} \end{vmatrix}$, we have

$M_{11} = a_{22}$, $M_{12} = a_{21}$, $M_{21} = a_{12}$, $M_{22} = a_{11}$

Also $C_{11} = a_{22}$, $C_{12} = -a_{21}$, $C_{21} = -a_{12}$, $C_{22} = a_{11}$

In the case of $\begin{vmatrix} a_{11} & a_{12} & a_{13} \\ a_{21} & a_{22} & a_{23} \\ a_{31} & a_{32} & a_{33} \end{vmatrix}$, we have

$$M_{11} = \begin{vmatrix} a_{22} & a_{23} \\ a_{32} & a_{33} \end{vmatrix}, \quad C_{11} = \begin{vmatrix} a_{22} & a_{23} \\ a_{32} & a_{33} \end{vmatrix};$$

$$M_{12} = \begin{vmatrix} a_{21} & a_{23} \\ a_{31} & a_{33} \end{vmatrix}, \quad C_{12} = -\begin{vmatrix} a_{21} & a_{23} \\ a_{31} & a_{33} \end{vmatrix};$$

$$M_{13} = \begin{vmatrix} a_{21} & a_{22} \\ a_{31} & a_{32} \end{vmatrix}, \quad C_{13} = \begin{vmatrix} a_{21} & a_{22} \\ a_{31} & a_{32} \end{vmatrix};$$

$$M_{21} = \begin{vmatrix} a_{12} & a_{13} \\ a_{32} & a_{33} \end{vmatrix}, \quad C_{21} = \begin{vmatrix} a_{12} & a_{13} \\ a_{32} & a_{33} \end{vmatrix}$$

and so on.

Adjoint of a Square Matrix

The transpose of the matrix got by replacing all the elements of a square matrix A by their corresponding cofactors in |A| is called the adjoint of A or adjugate of A and is denoted by Adj A.

Thus, $\text{AdjA} = A_c^t$

Note:

(*i*) Let $A = \begin{pmatrix} a & b \\ c & d \end{pmatrix}$ and $A_c = \begin{pmatrix} d & -c \\ -b & a \end{pmatrix}$

$$\therefore \text{Adj A} = A_c^t = \begin{pmatrix} d & -b \\ -c & a \end{pmatrix}$$

Thus the Adjoint of a 2 × 2 matrix $\begin{pmatrix} a & -b \\ -c & a \end{pmatrix}$.

(*ii*) AdjI = I, where I is the unit matrix

(*iii*) A(AdjA) = (AdjA) A = |A| I

(*iv*) Adj(AB) = (AdjB) (AdjA)

(*v*) If A is a square matrix of order 2, then |AdjA| = |A|

If A is a square matrix of order 3, then |AdjA| = $|A|^2$.

Inverse of a Non-Singular Matrix

The inverse of a non singular matrix. A is the matrix B such that AB = BA = I. B is then called the inverse of A and denoted by A^{-1}.

Note:

(*i*) A non-square matrix has no inverse.

(*ii*) The inverse of a square matrix A exists only when $|A| \neq 0$ that is, if A is a singular matrix then A^{-1} does not exist.

(*iii*) If B is the inverse of A then A is the inverse of B. That is $B = A^{-1} \Rightarrow A = B^{-1}$.

(*iv*) $A A^{-1} = I = A^{-1} A$.

(*v*) The inverse of a matrix, if it exists, is unique. That is, no matrix can have more than one inverse.

(*vi*) The order of the matrix A^{-1} will be the same as that of A.

(*vii*) $I^{-1} = I$.

(*viii*) $(AB)^{-1} = B^{-1} A^{-1}$, provided the inverses exist.

(*ix*) $A^2 = I$ implies $A^{-1} = A$.

(*x*) If AB = C then

(*a*) $A = CB^{-1}$

(*b*) $B = A^{-1}C$,

provided the inverses exist.

(*xi*) We have seen that

A(AdjA) = (AdjA)A = |A| I

$$\therefore A\frac{1}{|A|}(\text{AdjA}) = \frac{1}{|A|}(\text{AdjA})A = I$$

$(\because |A| \neq 0)$

This suggests that

$$A^{-1} = \frac{1}{|A|}(\text{AdjA}). \text{ That is, } A^{-1} = \frac{1}{|A|}A_c^t.$$

(*xii*) $(A^{-1})^{-1} = A$, provided the inverse exists.

Let $A = \begin{pmatrix} a & b \\ c & d \end{pmatrix}$ with $|A| = ad - bc \neq 0$

Now $A_c = \begin{pmatrix} d & -c \\ -b & a \end{pmatrix}$, $A_c^t = \begin{pmatrix} d & -b \\ -c & a \end{pmatrix}$

$$A^{-1} = \frac{1}{ad-bc}\begin{pmatrix} d & -b \\ -c & a \end{pmatrix}$$

Thus the inverse of a 2 × 2 matrix $\begin{pmatrix} a & b \\ c & d \end{pmatrix}$ can be written instantly as $\frac{1}{ad-bc}\begin{pmatrix} d & -b \\ -c & a \end{pmatrix}$ provided $ad - bc \neq 0$.

SYSTEM OF LINEAR EQUATIONS

Submatrices and Minors of a Matrix

Matrices obtained from a given matrix A by omitting some of its rows and columns are called submatrices of A.

e.g. If $A = \begin{pmatrix} 3 & 2 & 4 & 1 & 5 \\ 2 & 0 & 1 & -1 & 4 \\ 2 & 1 & 0 & 4 & 2 \\ 3 & 1 & 4 & 1 & 2 \end{pmatrix}$, some of the submatrices of A are:

$$\begin{pmatrix} 3 & 2 \\ 2 & 0 \end{pmatrix}, \begin{pmatrix} 3 & 5 \\ 2 & 4 \end{pmatrix}, \begin{pmatrix} 2 & 4 \\ 3 & 2 \end{pmatrix}, \begin{pmatrix} 1 & 4 \\ 0 & 2 \end{pmatrix},$$

$$\begin{pmatrix} 2 & 4 & 1 \\ 0 & 1 & -1 \end{pmatrix}, \begin{pmatrix} 0 & 1 & 4 \\ 1 & 0 & 2 \\ 1 & 4 & 2 \end{pmatrix}, \begin{pmatrix} 4 & 1 \\ 1 & -1 \\ 4 & 1 \end{pmatrix}$$

and $\begin{pmatrix} 3 & 2 & 4 & 5 \\ 2 & 0 & 1 & 4 \\ 3 & 1 & 4 & 2 \end{pmatrix}$.

The determinants of the square submatrices are called minors of the matrix.

Some of the minors of A are:

$$\begin{vmatrix} 2 & 4 \\ 0 & 1 \end{vmatrix}, \begin{vmatrix} 1 & 4 \\ 1 & 1 \end{vmatrix}, \begin{vmatrix} 3 & 2 \\ 2 & 0 \end{vmatrix}, \begin{vmatrix} 3 & 5 \\ 3 & 2 \end{vmatrix},$$

$$\begin{vmatrix} 3 & 4 & 1 \\ 2 & 1 & -1 \\ 2 & 0 & 4 \end{vmatrix} \text{ and } \begin{vmatrix} 1 & -1 & 4 \\ 0 & 4 & 2 \\ 4 & 1 & 2 \end{vmatrix}$$

Rank of Matrix

A positive integer 'r' is said to be the rank of a non-zero matrix A, denoted by $\rho(A)$, if

(*i*) there is at least one minor of A of order 'r' which is not zero, and

(*ii*) every minor of A of order greater than 'r' is zero.

Note:

(*i*) The rank of a matrix A is the order of the largest non-zero minor of A.

(*ii*) If A is a matrix of order $m \times n$ then $\rho(A) <$ minimum (m, n).

(*iii*) The rank of a zero matrix is taken to be 0.

(*iv*) For non-zero matrices, the least value of the rank is 1.

(*v*) The rank of a non-singular matrix of order $n \times n$ is n.

(*vi*) $\rho(A) = \rho(A^t)$.

(*vii*) $\rho(I_2) = 2, \rho(I_3) = 3$.

System of linear equations

A system of (simultaneous) equations in which the variables (*i.e.*, the unknowns) occur only in the first degree is said to be linear.

A system of linear equations can be represented in the form AX = B. For example, the equations $x - 3y + z = -1$, $2x + y - 4z = -1$, $6x - 7y + 8z = 7$ can be written in the matrix form as

$$\underset{A}{\begin{pmatrix} 1 & -3 & 1 \\ 2 & 1 & -4 \\ 6 & -7 & 8 \end{pmatrix}} \underset{X}{\begin{pmatrix} x \\ y \\ z \end{pmatrix}} = \underset{B}{\begin{pmatrix} -1 \\ -1 \\ 7 \end{pmatrix}}$$

14

A is called the coefficient matrix. If the matrix a is augmented with the column matrix B, at the end, we get the augmented matrix,

$$\begin{pmatrix} 1 & -3 & 1 & \vdots & -1 \\ 2 & 1 & -4 & \vdots & -1 \\ 6 & -7 & 8 & \vdots & 7 \end{pmatrix} \text{ denoted by (A, B)}$$

A system of (simultaneous) linear equations is said to be homogeneous if the constant term in each of the equations is zero. A system of linear homogeneous equations can be represented in the form AX = O. For example, the equations $3x + 4y - 2z = 0$, $5x + 2y = 0$, $3x - y + z = 0$ can be written in the matrix form as

$$\underset{A}{\begin{pmatrix} 3 & 4 & -2 \\ 5 & 2 & 0 \\ 3 & -1 & 1 \end{pmatrix}} \underset{X}{\begin{pmatrix} x \\ y \\ z \end{pmatrix}} = \underset{O}{\begin{pmatrix} 0 \\ 0 \\ 0 \end{pmatrix}}$$

Consistency of Equations

A system of equations is said to be consistent if it has at least one set of solution. Otherwise, it is said to be inconsistent.

Testing the Consistency of Equations by Rank Method

Consider the equations AX = B in 'n' unknowns

1. If $\rho(A, B) = \rho(A)$, then the equations are consistent.
2. If $\rho(A, B) \neq \rho(A)$, then the equations are inconsistent.

3. If $\rho(A, B) = \rho(A) = n$, then the equations are consistent and have unique solution.
4. If $\rho(A, B) = \rho(A) < n$, then the equations are consistent and have infinite sets of solution.

Consider the equations AX = 0 in 'n' unknowns

1. If $\rho(A) = n$ then equations have the trivial solution only.
2. If $\rho(A) < n$ then equations have the non-trivial solutions also.

SOLUTION OF LINEAR EQUATIONS

Solution by Matrix Method

When $|A| \neq 0$, the equations AX = B have the unique solution given by $X = A^{-1}B$.

Example 1: Solve using matrices the equations $2x - y = 3$, $5x + y = 4$.

Solution: The equations can be written in matrix form as

$$\begin{pmatrix} 2 & -1 \\ 5 & 1 \end{pmatrix}\begin{pmatrix} x \\ y \end{pmatrix} = \begin{pmatrix} 3 \\ 4 \end{pmatrix}$$

$$A \quad X = B$$

$$|A| = \begin{vmatrix} 2 & -1 \\ 5 & 1 \end{vmatrix} = 7$$

$\therefore$ The unique solution is given by

$$X = A^{-1}B$$

$$\Rightarrow \begin{pmatrix} x \\ y \end{pmatrix} = \frac{1}{7}\begin{pmatrix} 1 & 1 \\ -5 & 2 \end{pmatrix}\begin{pmatrix} 3 \\ 4 \end{pmatrix}$$

$$\Rightarrow \begin{pmatrix} x \\ y \end{pmatrix} = \frac{1}{7}\begin{pmatrix} 7 \\ -7 \end{pmatrix}$$

$$\Rightarrow \begin{pmatrix} x \\ y \end{pmatrix} = \begin{pmatrix} 1 \\ -1 \end{pmatrix} \qquad \therefore x = 1, y = -1$$

Solution by Determinant Method (Cramer's Rule)

Let the equations be

$$a_1x + b_1y + c_1z = d_1,$$
$$a_2x + b_2y + c_2z = d_2,$$
$$a_3x + b_3y + c_3z = d_3,$$

Let $\Delta = \begin{vmatrix} a_1 & b_1 & c_1 \\ a_2 & b_2 & c_2 \\ a_3 & b_3 & c_2 \end{vmatrix}$, $\Delta_x = \begin{vmatrix} d_1 & b_1 & c_1 \\ d_2 & b_2 & c_2 \\ d_3 & b_3 & c_3 \end{vmatrix}$

$\Delta_y = \begin{vmatrix} a_1 & d_1 & c_1 \\ a_2 & d_2 & c_2 \\ a_3 & d_3 & c_3 \end{vmatrix}$, $\Delta_z = \begin{vmatrix} a_1 & b_1 & d_1 \\ a_2 & b_2 & d_2 \\ a_3 & b_3 & d_3 \end{vmatrix}$.

when $\Delta \neq 0$, the unique solution is given by

$$x = \frac{\Delta_x}{\Delta},\ y = \frac{\Delta_y}{\Delta},\ z = \frac{\Delta_z}{\Delta}.$$

Example 2: Solve the equations

$$x + 2y + 5z = 23,$$
$$3x + 4z = 26,$$
$$6x + y + 7z = 47$$

by determinant method.

Solution: The equations are

$$x + 2y + 5z = 23$$
$$3x + y + 4z = 26$$
$$6x + y + 7z = 47$$

$$\Delta = \begin{vmatrix} 1 & 2 & 5 \\ 3 & 1 & 4 \\ 6 & 1 & 7 \end{vmatrix} = 6 \neq 0;$$

$$\Delta_x = \begin{vmatrix} 23 & 2 & 5 \\ 26 & 1 & 4 \\ 47 & 1 & 7 \end{vmatrix} = -24$$

$$\Delta_y = \begin{vmatrix} 1 & 23 & 5 \\ 3 & 26 & 4 \\ 6 & 47 & 7 \end{vmatrix} = -12;$$

$$\Delta_z = \begin{vmatrix} 1 & 2 & 23 \\ 3 & 1 & 26 \\ 6 & 1 & 47 \end{vmatrix} = -18$$

By Cramer's rule

$$\therefore x = \frac{\Delta_x}{\Delta} = \frac{-24}{-6} = 4 \ ; \ y = \frac{\Delta_y}{\Delta} = \frac{-12}{-6} = 2$$

$$z = \frac{\Delta_z}{\Delta} = \frac{-18}{-6} = 3 \ ; \ \Rightarrow x = 4, y = 2, z = 3.$$

Example 3: Solve the equations

$$2x - 3y - 1 = 0,$$
$$5x + 2y - 12 = 0$$

by Cramer's rule.

Solution: The equations are $2x - 3y = 1$, $5x + 2y = 12$

$$\Delta = \begin{vmatrix} 2 & -3 \\ 5 & 2 \end{vmatrix} = 19 \neq 0\,;$$

$$\Delta_x = \begin{vmatrix} 1 & -3 \\ 12 & 2 \end{vmatrix} = 38\,;$$

$$\Delta_y = \begin{vmatrix} 2 & 1 \\ 5 & 12 \end{vmatrix} = 19$$

By Cramer's rule

$$\therefore \quad x = \frac{\Delta_x}{\Delta} = \frac{38}{19} = 2, \quad y = \frac{\Delta_y}{\Delta} = \frac{19}{19} = 1$$

$\Rightarrow \quad x = 2,\ y = 1.$

LEONTIEF'S INPUT-OUTPUT MODEL

The production component of an economy may be thought of, as the composite of a number of industries. Each industry produces certain goods, part of which are used by the other industries as their input and the rest go to meet the demand of the consumption component of the economy, the consumers. Again, each industry for its production of goods, needs the products of other industries as input, apart from the primary input to be had from the environment. Thus industries, in general, are interdependent. *Input-output analysis* is the name given to a study of this interdependence of industries in any economy. The technique was first developed by W. Leontief in 1951. In simplest terms, the input-output model can be characterised as a description of an economy in which input equals output, *i.e.,* whatever is produced is always consumed.

Input-Output models are of two types

Closed input-output model: It is an input-output model in which the entire production is consumed by those participating in the production. The objective here is to find the relative income of each participant in the system.

Open input-output model: It is an input-output model in which some of the production is consumed by those participating in the production and the rest of production is consumed by external bodies such as households, government and so on. In this model we seek the amount of production needed to achieve a forecasted demand, when the amount of production needed to achieve a current demand is known.

The input-output model, due to Professor Leontief, makes some simplifying assumptions, which for all practical purposes, appear reasonable enough to do so. These are:

1. An economy is decomposed into n sectors (or industries) and each of these produces only one kind of product. Each of the sectors uses as input, the output of the other sectors.
2. The output of any industry becomes either the input of another industry or the final demand (or the final consumption).
3. In any productive process all inputs are used in fixed proportions and increase in input is in proportion with the level of output. Production takes place through processes with constant *technical coefficients*. The technical coefficient shows the number of units of any industry's output needed to produce one unit of another industry's output. In other words, it shows the amount of raw materials needed by an industry from any other industry to produce a certain product.
4. All transactions may be considered in terms of money values since money is a suitable common unit for aggregating inputs and outputs of industries. Quantities and prices can also be considered for transactions.
5. The economy is assumed to be in a state of dynamic equilibrium, *i.e.,* there is neither shortages nor surpluses of product under consideration. In other words, gross product of each sector is sufficient to meet the final demands as well as demands of other sectors. Let d_j ($j = 1, 2, ..., n$) be the final demand (in rupee value) for product produced by each of n sectors.

Remarks: It is important to note the following important points about input-output analysis:

(*i*) It studies the production structure of an economy on the basis of several production sectors of the economy.

(*ii*) It assumes the mutual interdependency of various production sectors of the economy.

(*iii*) It lays emphasis in working out certain technical coefficient which bring in the mathematical nature of the technique.

(*iv*) It is nothing more than finding the solution of a homogeneous (closed model) or non-homogeneous (open model) system of linear equations.

The input-output table displayed in the following table describes the independence of industries or the interrelationships between the industries and the final demand during some time period.

		To Consumer industries (Input) 1	2	3	...	n	Final demand	Total output
From Producer industries (output)	1	x_{11}	x_{12}	x_{13}	...	x_{1n}	F_1	x_1
	2	x_{21}	x_{22}	x_{23}	...	x_{2n}	F_2	x_2
	⋮	⋮	⋮	⋮	⋮	⋮	⋮	⋮
	n	x_{n1}	x_{n2}	x_{n3}	...	x_{nm}	F_n	x_n
Primary Inputs		l_1	l_2	l_3	...	l_n	—	
Total Input		x_1	x_2	x_3	...	x_n	—	

All entries in the above table are in appropriate units, say, in millions of rupees of output. Each industry appears in a row and column. The rows show the sales, called output, that each industry makes to the others. The columns show the purchases, called inputs, that each industry makes from the others. The two additional columns represents the final demand, showing the consumption by other agencies such as government (or in exports) and the total output.

Reading across Row 1, we find that of the total output of x_1 units worth of product of Industry 1, x_{11} went as input to Industry I itself (for internal use), x_{12} to Industry II, and so on and the remaining F_1 went direct to the consumer for final use. The other rows can be interpreted a similar fashion.

Reading down column 1, we find that in producing x_1 units worth of product, Industry 1 purchased x_{11} units worth from itself, x_{21} units worth from Industry 2 and so on. The other columns can be interpreted in the same way.

Input-output analysis allows us to estimate the total production of each industry if there is a change in final demand as long as the basic structure of the economy remains the same, *i.e.,* the amount of input required from each industry to produce one unit worth of output of a given industry must remain fixed.

Suppose that the value of final demand changes from F_1 to d_1 for Industry 1, F_2 to d_2 for Industry 2, and so on. To effect this change, one would like to estimate how much should each industry now produce?

The input requirements per unit worth of output for each industry can be obtained by setting:

$$\frac{x_{ij}}{x_j} = \frac{\text{Rupee value of the product of industry } i \text{ used by industry } j}{\text{Rupee value of the total product of industry } j}$$

= Rupee value of output of industry ith that jth industry must purchase to produce one rupee worth of its own product.

$= a_{ij}$ (say)

In other words :

$x_{ij} = a_{ij}\, x_j$ amounts to saying that sales of ith industry to jth industry are a constant proportion a_{ij} of the output of jth industry.

= Rupee value of the product of ith industry used by jth industry.

Coefficient Matrix: The constants a_{ij} introduced above are $n \times n$ in number. Arranged as a rectangular array, they give us the input-output coefficient matrix A

$$\text{where} \quad A = \begin{bmatrix} a_{11} & a_{12} & \cdots & a_{1n} \\ a_{21} & a_{22} & \cdots & a_{2n} \\ \vdots & \vdots & \vdots & \vdots \\ a_{n1} & a_{n2} & \cdots & a_{nn} \end{bmatrix}$$

The entries in the matrix A are called the input-output coefficients or technological coefficients. It may be noted that the technological coefficient a_{ij} represents the amount of input required from ith industry to produce 1 unit's worth of output of jth industry.

Final Demand Vector: Let $d_1, d_2, ..., d_n$ be the final demand in rupee value of the n products, then

$$\text{column vector } D = \begin{bmatrix} d_1 \\ d_2 \\ \vdots \\ d_n \end{bmatrix} \text{ is known as the final}$$

demand vector.

Gross output vector: If $x_1, x_2, ..., x_n$ is the gross output of the n industries, then the column vector

$$X = \begin{bmatrix} x_1 \\ x_2 \\ \vdots \\ x_n \end{bmatrix} \text{ is called the gross output vector.}$$

The Balance Equations: Under the condition of no surpluses and no shortages:

Internal consumption + Consumer demand = Total output.

$$\begin{aligned} a_{11}\, x_1 + a_{12}\, x_2 + \ldots + a_{1n}\, x_n + d_1 &= x_1 \\ a_{21}\, x_1 + a_{22}\, x_2 + \ldots + a_{2n}\, x_n + d_2 &= x_2 \\ \vdots \qquad\qquad & \quad \vdots \\ a_{n1}\, x_n + a_{n2}\, x_2 + \ldots + a_{nn} x_n + d_n &= x_n \end{aligned}$$

In matrix form :

$$\begin{bmatrix} x_1 \\ x_2 \\ \vdots \\ x_n \end{bmatrix} = \begin{bmatrix} a_{11} & a_{12} & \cdots & a_{1n} \\ a_{21} & a_{22} & \cdots & a_{2n} \\ \vdots & \vdots & \vdots & \vdots \\ a_{n1} & a_{n2} & \cdots & a_{nn} \end{bmatrix} \begin{bmatrix} x_1 \\ x_2 \\ \vdots \\ x_n \end{bmatrix} + \begin{bmatrix} d_1 \\ d_2 \\ \vdots \\ d_n \end{bmatrix}$$

$\Rightarrow$ X = AX + D or (I – A) X = D. The matrix I – A is called the Leontief matrix.

The solution: Since the n industries of the model are all distinct, (I – A) is non-singular. Thus the vector : X = $[I - A]^{-1}$ D gives the gross production level, which is just sufficient to meet the final demand, as well as the demand of all industries themselves.

The Transaction Matrix: The matrix $[I - A]^{-1}$ which provides a constant multiplier is known as transaction matrix. It may be noted that for that for different projected demand vectors, a simple multiplication would yield the gross output X.

Hawkins-Simon Conditions of Viability of the System:

The matrix [I – A]

$$= \begin{bmatrix} (1-a_{11}) & -a_{12} & \cdots & -a_{1n} \\ -a_{21} & (1-a_{22}) & \cdots & -a_{2n} \\ \vdots & \vdots & \vdots & \vdots \\ -a_{n1} & -a_{n2} & \cdots & (1-a_{nn}) \end{bmatrix}$$

should be such that

(*i*) the determinant of Leontief matrix [I – A] must always be positive, and

(*ii*) the diagonal elements $(1 - a_{11}), (1 - a_{22}), ..., (1 - a_{nn})$ should all be positive or in other words $a_{11}, a_{22}, ..., a_{nn}$ should all be less than one.

The above conditions were introduced by D. Hawkins and H.A. Simon to ensure that the system does not give negative outputs.

APPLICATIONS OF DIFFERENTIATION

FUNCTIONS IN ECONOMICS AND COMMERCE

Demand Function

Let q be the demand (quantity) of a commodity and p the price of that commodity. The demand function is defined as $q = f(p)$ where p and q are positive. Generally, p and q are inversely related.

Observe the graph of the demand function $q = f(p)$

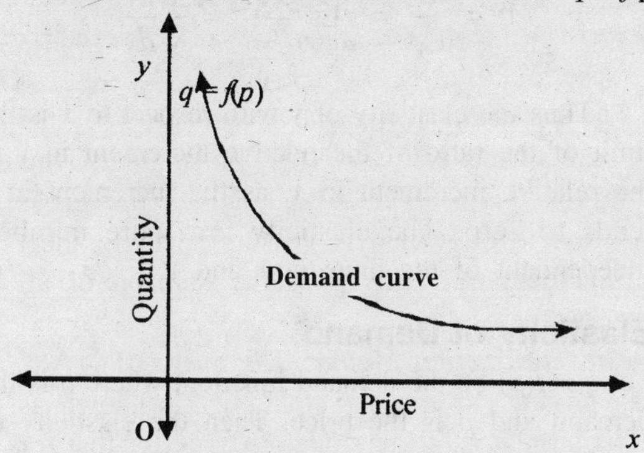

Following observations can be made from the graph (Fig.)

(*i*) only the first quadrant portion of the graph of the demand function is shown since p and q are positive.

(*ii*) slope of the demand curve is negative.

Supply Function

Let x denotes amount of a particular commodity that sellers offer in the market at various price p, then the supply function is given by $x = f(p)$ where x and p are positive.

Generally, x and p are directly related.

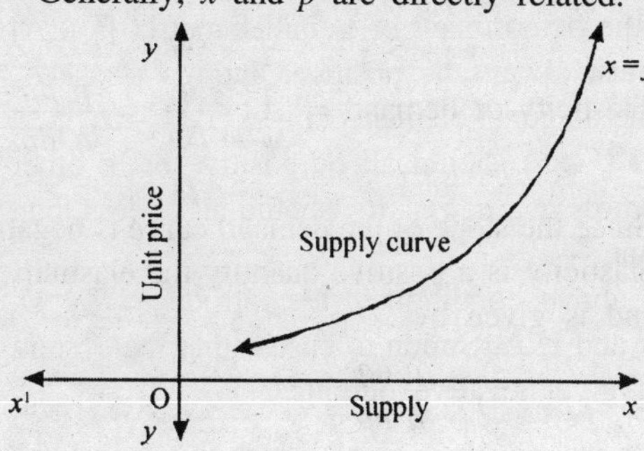

Observe the graph of the supply function, $x = f(p)$

Following observations can be made from the graph (Fig.)

(*i*) only the first quadrant portion of the graph of the supply function is shown since the function has meaning only for non-negative values of q and p.

(*ii*) slope of the supply function is positive.

Cost Function

Normally total cost consists of two parts.

(*i*) Variable cost and

(*ii*) Fixed cost.

Variable cost is a single-valued function of output, but fixed cost is independent of the level of output.

Let $f(x)$ be the variable cost and k be the fixed cost when the output is x units. The total cost function is defined as $C(x) = f(x) + k$, where x is positive.

Note that $f(x)$ does not contain constant term.

We define Average Cost (AC), Average Variable Cost (AVC), Average Fixed Cost (AFC), Marginal Cost (MC), and Marginal Average Cost (MAC) as follows.

(*i*) Average Cost (AC) $= \dfrac{f(x)+k}{x} = \dfrac{\text{Total Cost}}{\text{Output}}$

(*ii*) Average Variable Cost (AVC) $= \dfrac{f(x)}{x}$

$= \dfrac{\text{Variable Cost}}{\text{Output}}$

(*iii*) Average Fixed Cost (AFC) $= \dfrac{k}{x}$

$= \dfrac{\text{Fixed Cost}}{\text{Output}}$

(*iv*) Marginal Cost (MC) $= \dfrac{d}{dx}C(x) = C'(x)$

(*v*) Marginal Average Cost (MAC) $= \dfrac{d}{dx}(\text{AC})$

Note:
If C(x) is the total cost of producing x units of some product then its derivative C′(x) is the marginal cost which is the approximate cost of producing 1 more unit when the production level is x units. The graphical representation is shown here (Fig.).

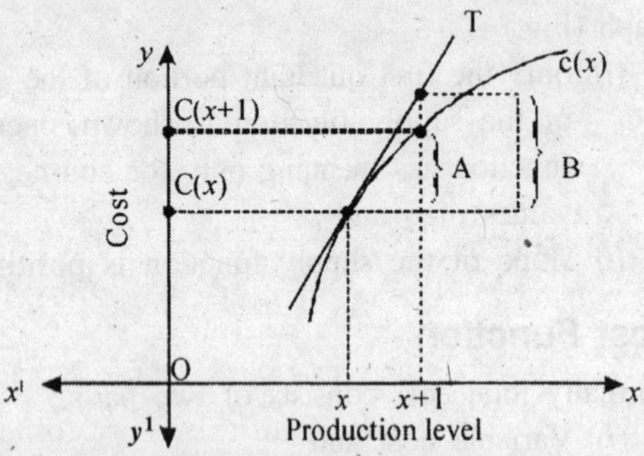

A = C(x + 1) – C(x)
B = C′(x) = Marginal Cost

Revenue Function

Let x units be sold at Rs. p per unit. Then the total revenue R(x) is defined as R(x) = px, where p and x are positive.

$$\text{Average revenue (AR)} = \frac{\text{total revenue}}{\text{quantity sold}} = \frac{px}{x} = p.$$

(*i.e.* Average revenue and price are the same)

$$\text{Marginal revenue (MR)} = \frac{d}{dx}(\text{R}) = \text{R}'(x)$$

Note:
If R(x) be the total revenue gained from selling x units of some product, then its derivative, R′(x) is the marginal revenue, which is approximate revenue gained from selling 1 more unit when the sales level is x units. The graphical representation is shown here (Fig.)

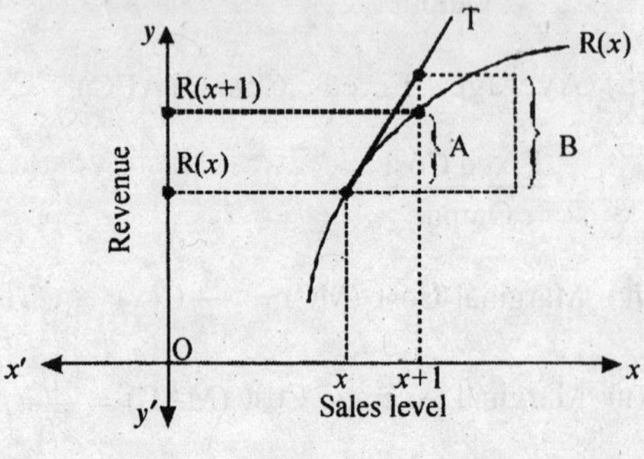

A = R(x + 1) – R(x)
B = R′(x) = marginal revenue

Profit Function

The profit function P(x) is defined as the difference between the total revenue and the total cost. *i.e.* P(x) = R(x) – C(x).

Elasticity

The elasticity of a function $y = f(x)$, with respect to x, is defined as

$$\eta = \frac{E_y}{E_x} = \underset{\Delta x \to 0}{\text{Lt}} \frac{\frac{\Delta y}{y}}{\frac{\Delta x}{x}} = \frac{x}{y}\frac{dy}{dx}$$

Thus the elasticity of y with respect to x is the limit of the ratio of the relative increment in y to the relative increment in x, as the increment in x tends to zero. The elasticity is a pure number, independent of the units in x and y.

Elasticity of Demand

Let $q = f(p)$ be the demand function, where q is the demand and p is the price. Then the elasticity of demand is $\eta_d = \frac{p}{q}\frac{dq}{dp}$ (Fig.)

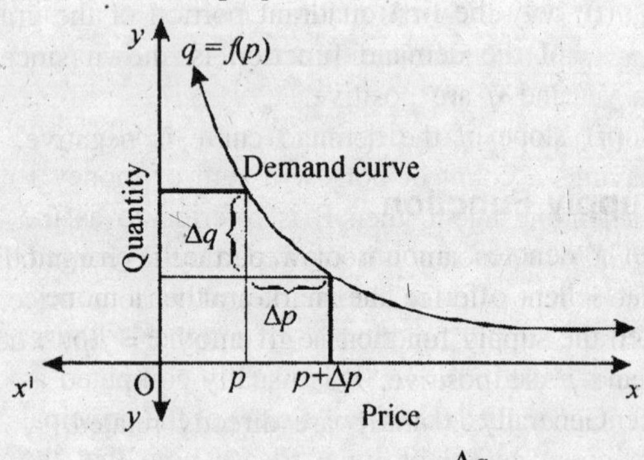

$$\text{Elasticity of demand} = \underset{\Delta p \to 0}{\text{Lt}} \frac{\frac{\Delta q}{q}}{\frac{\Delta p}{p}} = \frac{p}{q}\frac{dq}{dp}$$

Since the slope of the demand curve is negative and elasticity is a positive quantity the elasticity of demand is given by

$$\eta_d = \frac{p}{q}\frac{dq}{dp}$$

Equilibrium Price

The price at which quantity demanded is equal to quantity supplied is called equilibrium price.

Equilibrium Quantity

The quantity obtained by substituting the value of equilibrium price in any one of the given demand or supply functions is called equilibrium quantity.

Relation Between Marginal Revenue and Elasticity of Demand

Let q units be demanded at unit price p so that $p = f(q)$ where f is differentiable. The revenue is given by

$$R(q) = qp$$

$$R(q) = qf(q) \qquad [p = f(q)]$$

Marginal revenue is obtained by differentiating $R(q)$ with respect to q.

$$\therefore \; R'(q) = qf'(q) + f(q)$$

$$= q\frac{dp}{dq} + p \qquad \left[\because \frac{dp}{dq} = f'(q)\right]$$

$$R'(q) = p\left(1 + \frac{q}{p}\frac{dp}{dq}\right)$$

$$= p\left[1 + \frac{1}{\dfrac{p}{q}\dfrac{dq}{dp}}\right] = p\left[1 + \left\{\frac{1}{-\dfrac{p}{q}\dfrac{dq}{dp}}\right\}\right]$$

Since $\eta_d = \dfrac{p}{q}\dfrac{dq}{dp}$,

$$\text{Marginal Revenue} = R'(q) = p\left[1 - \frac{1}{\eta_d}\right].$$

MATHEMATICS OF FINANCE

SIMPLE INTEREST

Simple interest is generally used only on short-term notes—often of duration less than 1 year. The concept of simple interest, however, forms the basis of much of the rest of the material developed in this chapter, for which time periods may be much longer than a year.

Suppose a person deposits a sum of money P in a savings account or borrow a sum of money P from a lending agent, then P is referred to as the *principal.* When money is borrowed, a fee is charged. This fee is rent paid for the use of another's money, just as rent is paid for the use of another's house. The fee is called *interest.* It is usually computed as a percentage (called the *interest rate*) of the principal over a given period of time. Please note that the interest rate, unless otherwise stated, is an annual rate.

Simple Interest Formula

$$I = P \times r \times t,$$

where P = Principal

r = Annual simple interest rate (written as a decimal)

t = Time in years

Amount-Simple Interest

In general, if a principal P is borrowed at a rate r, then after t years the borrower will owe the lender an amount A that will include the principal P plus the interest I. Since P is the amount that is borrowed now and A is the amount that must be paid back in the future, P is often referred to as the *present value* and A as the future value.

$$A = P + Prt = P(1 + rt)$$

where P = Principal, or present value

r = Annual simple interest rate (written as a decimal)

t = Time in years

A = Amount, or future value

COMPOUND INTEREST

If at the end of a payment period, the interest due is reinvested at the same rate, then the interest as well as the original principal will earn interest during the next payment period. Interest paid on interest reinvested is called compound interest.

Amount-Compound Interest Formula

$$A = P(1 + i)^n, \; i = \frac{r}{m}, \text{ where}$$

r = Annual nominal rate
m = Number of compounding periods per year
i = Rate per compounding period
n = Total number of compounding periods
P = Principal or present value
A = Amount (or future value) at the end of n periods.

Continuous Compound Interest Formula

If a principal P is invested at an annual interest rate of r (expressed as a decimal) compounded continuously, then the amount of investment A after n years is given by :

$$A = Pe^{rn}$$

EFFECTIVE RATE

If principal P is invested at the annual (nominal) rate r compounded m times a year, then the effective rate r_e is given by:

$$r_e = \left(1+\frac{r}{m}\right)^m - 1$$

If interest is *compound continuously* at an annual interest rate r, then the effective rate is given in terms of the exponential function with base e by:

$r_e = e^r - 1$, where $e = 2.71828$

Force of Interest: The nominal rate r compound continuously and equivalent to a given effective rate, r_e is called the force of interest.

PRESENT (OR CAPITAL) VALUE

Present Value Formula

The present value of amount ₹ A, payable in n periods time subject to an interest rate 100 i% is given by:

$$P = \frac{A}{(1+i)^n} = S(1+i)^{-n}$$

where P = Present (or capital value)
A = Amount, due at the end of n period's time
i = interest (or discrete) rate of discount
n = number of time periods

The formula: $P = Ae^{-in}$ represents the present value of A due at the end of n years at the annual rate i compounded continuously.

Present Value of a Discount Rate

The present value of an obligation discounted as bank discount is given by:

$$P = A(1 - d)^n,$$

where d = the discount rate per period
A = the value of an obligation at the end of n periods
P = the present value of the obligation

Reducing Balance Depreciated Value

If book value B is subject to reducing balance depreciation at rate i% over n time periods, the depreciated value at the end of the nth time period is given by:

$$D = B(1 - i)^n,$$

where D = depreciated or scarp value at the end of the nth time period
B = Original book value
i = depreciation rate
n = number of time periods (normally years)

ANNUITY

Definition

An annuity is a sequence of a specific number of equal payments made at equally spaced times. The times at which payments are made are called payment dates and the interval between successive payment dates is the payment period (or payment interval) for the annuity. The time for the beginning of the first payment period to the end of the last period is called the term of the annuity.

Amount of an Annuity

The amount (or future) value of an ordinary annuity is the sum of the compound amounts of all the payments accumulated at the end of the term.

Future Value of an Annuity

The amount (or future value) S of an ordinary annuity of n payments of R rupees each, paid at the end of each investment period into an account that earns interest at the rate of i per period is given by:

$$S = R\left[\frac{(1+i)^n - 1}{i}\right] = R\, s_{\overline{n}|i}.$$

SINKING FUNDS

A sinking fund is a fund that is accumulated for the purpose of paying off a financial obligation at some future designated date.

Sinking Fund Payment

The periodic payment R required to a accumulate a sum of S rupees over n periods with interest charged at rate of i per period is given by:

$$S = R\left[\frac{(1+i)^n - 1}{r}\right]$$

$$\Rightarrow \qquad R = \frac{Sr}{[(1+i)^n - 1]}.$$

Present Value of a n Annuity

The present value (or capital value) of an ordinary annuity is the sum of the present values of all the payments.

The present value P of an ordinary annuity of n payments of R rupees each, paid at the end of each investment period into an account that earns interest at the rate of i per period is given by:

$$P = R\left[\frac{1-(1+i)^{-n}}{i}\right] = R\, a_{\overline{n}|i}.$$

Present Value When Interest is Compounded Continuously

The present value P of an annuity consisting of an income stream of ₹ R per year for n years at the rate of interest of 100 r% per annum compounded continuously is given by:

$$P = \int_0^n R e^{-rt}\, dt.$$

AMORTIZATION

A loan with a fixed rate of interest is said to be amortized if both principal and interest are paid by a sequence of equal payments made over equal periods of time.

Amortization Annuity Payments

The periodic payment R on a loan of P rupees to be amortized over n periods with interest charged at the rate of i per period is given by:

$$R = \frac{Pi}{[1-(1+i)^{-n}]}.$$

DEFERRED ANNUITY

It is an ordinary annuity in which the first payment is postponed until the expiration of a period of time equivalent to a certain number of payment intervals.

Amount of a Deferred Annuity

The amount of a deferred annuity of n payments, deferred m periods, is the value of the annuity at the end of its term. Thus, if a deferred annuity consists of n payments of ₹ R each, then the amount of this annuity is given by:

$$S = R\left[\frac{(1+i)^n - 1}{i}\right] = R\, s_{\overline{n}|i}.$$

PERPETUITY

Under the assumption that a company will never become bankrupt, the dividends on a share of its preferred stock may be thought of as a *perpetuity*. Clearly, one cannot speak of the amount of a perpetuity, it has, however, a definite present value.

Consider a perpetuity of ₹ R payable at the end of each interest period, the first payment due one period hence with money worth i per period. The *present value* of this perpetuity is given by:

$$x = R\,(1+i)^{-1} + R\,(1+i)^{-2} + R(1+i)^{-3} + \ldots$$

$$= \frac{R(1+i)}{[1-(1+i)^{-1}]} = \frac{R}{i},$$

which is the *cash equivalent* of an unlimited number of periodic payments of ₹ R each, the first being due one period hence.

Bond Price

The amount paid by the bondholder to the corporation at the time of the bond's original issuance, or the price at which the bond is traded between investors in bond markets after issuance. Bond prices are stated as a percentage of face amount. Thus, a price of 105 is equal to 105% of the face amount. When the bond price is higher than the face amount, the excess is referred to as a *bond premium*. If the price is lower than face amount, the difference is called a *bond discount.*

A bond is a contract between a borrower and a bondholder (or lender). Through this contract a borrower promises to pay a fixed stream of money at regular intervals of time until a certain maturity date. After this date, an amount equal to the face value of the bond is paid back to the bondholder.

Let F be the face value and V be the redemption value of a bond. Let r be the interest rate per period, and n be the number of interest periods from the date of purchase (assume to be an interest payment date). The purchase price of the bond is determined by the present value of the payments given by:

$$P = \frac{F}{1+i} + \frac{F}{(1+i)^2} + ... + \frac{F}{(1+i)^n} + \frac{V}{(1+i)^n}$$

where $i = \frac{r}{100}$

$$\Rightarrow \quad P = F\, r\, a_{\overline{n}|i} + V(1+i)^{-n}$$

From the above equations, we find that the worth or value of a bond is inversely related to the market rate of interest, *i.e.,* higher the market rate of interest the lower will be its value and vice-versa.

LINEAR PROGRAMMING

Linear Programming is a mathematical device developed by the mathematician **George Dantzing** is 1947 for planning the deversified activities of the U.S. Air Force connected with the problem of supplies to the forces. Linear or mathematical programming also known as activity analysis, has been further developed in its application to the economic theory of the firm, managerial economics, interregional trade, general equilibrium analysis, welfare economics and to development planning.

Meaning

It is mathematical technique for the analysis of optimum decisions subject to certain constraints in the form of linear in equalities. Mathematically speaking, it applies to those problems which require the solution of maximization or minimization problems subject to a system of linear inequalities stated in terms of certain variables. If x and y, the two variables, are the function of z, the value of z is maximized when any movement from that point results in a decreased value of z. The value of z is minimized when even a small movement results in an increased value of z. When cost and price per unit change with the size of output, the problem is not linear and if they do not change with output, the problem is linear. Linear programming may thus be defined as a method to decide the optimum combination of factors to produce a given output or the optimum combination of products to be produced by given plant and equipment.

Assumptions

The linear programming analysis of the firm is based upon the following assumptions:

1. The decision-making body is faced with certain constraints or resource restrictions. They may be credit, raw material and space constraints on its activities. Type of constraints infact depend upon the nature of problem. Mostly they are fixed factors in the production process.
2. It assumes a limited number of alternative production processes.
3. It assumes linear relations among the different variables which implies constant proportionality between inputs and output within a process.
4. Input-output prices and co-efficients are given and constant. They are known with certainty.
5. The assumption of additivity also under lies linear programming techniques which means

that the total resources used by all firms must equal the sum of resources used by each individual firm.

6. Linear programming techniques further assume continuity and divisibility in products and factors.
7. Institutional factors are also assumed to be constant.

Lastly, for programming a certain period is assumed. For convenience and more accurate results, the period is generally short, though longer periods are not ruled out.

PRINCIPLE OF SIMPLEX METHOD

'*Simplex Method*' was developed in 1957 by George B. Dantzig to solve complexities of linear programming problems.

The simplex method is applicable to any problem that can be formulated in terms of linear objective function subject to a set of linear constraints. There are no theoretical restrictions placed on the number of decision variables or constraints contained in a problem, as the simplex method, accompanied by the computational facility of a large computer, can solve linear programming problems with several thousand variables and several thousand constraints.

Computational procedure in the simplex method is based on the following fundamental property:

"*The optimal solution to a linear programming problem, if it exists, always occurs at one of the corner points of the feasible solution space.*"

The '*Simplex Algorithm*' is a systematic and efficient procedure for finding corner point solutions and taking them for optimality. The evaluation of corner points always starts at the point of origin (initial basic feasible solution) which is one of the corners of the feasible solution space. This solution is then tested for optimality, *i.e.,* it tests whether an improvement in the objective function is possible by moving to adjacent corner point of the feasible function space. This solution is then tested for optimality, *i.e.,* it tests whether an improvement in the objective function is possible by moving to adjacent corner point of the feasible solution space. If the improvement is possible then at a new corner point, the solution is again tested for optimality. This iterative search for a better corner point is repeated until an optimal solution, if it exists, is determined.

MULTIPLE CHOICE QUESTIONS

1. Find x and y if the matrix :

$$A = \frac{1}{3}\begin{bmatrix} 1 & 2 & 2 \\ 2 & 1 & -2 \\ x & 2 & y \end{bmatrix}$$ may satisfy the condition

$AA^t = I_3$.

A. 4, –2 B. –2, –4
C. –1, –2 D. –2, –1

2. Find the value of the determinant:

$$\begin{vmatrix} 13 & 16 & 19 \\ 14 & 17 & 20 \\ 15 & 18 & 21 \end{vmatrix}$$

A. 1 B. 0
C. 2 D. 4

3. Find the value of the determinant:

$$\Delta = \begin{vmatrix} 1 & 18 & 72 \\ 2 & 40 & 148 \\ 2 & 45 & 150 \end{vmatrix}$$

A. –8 B. 8
C. –12 D. 12

4. Find the adjoint of the matrix : $A = \begin{bmatrix} a & b \\ c & d \end{bmatrix}$.

A. $\begin{bmatrix} c & -b \\ -d & a \end{bmatrix}$ B. $\begin{bmatrix} d & -b \\ -c & a \end{bmatrix}$

C. $\begin{bmatrix} -b & -d \\ a & c \end{bmatrix}$ D. $\begin{bmatrix} a & -b \\ -c & d \end{bmatrix}$

5. Solve the following system of equations by inverting the appropriate matrix :

$10x_1 - 2x_2 = 8$ and $6x_1 + 3x_2 = 7$.

A. $\frac{38}{42}, \frac{22}{42}$ B. $\frac{22}{42}, \frac{38}{42}$

C. $\frac{24}{42}, \frac{32}{42}$ D. $\frac{26}{42}, \frac{32}{42}$

6. Solve the following system of equations by matrix inversion method :

$$2x + 8y + 5z = 5,$$
$$x + y + z = -2,$$
$$x + 2y - z = 2.$$

A. 1, –2, 3 B. 1, 2, –3
C. –3, 2, 1 D. –1, 2, –3

7. A company is considering which of the three methods of production it should use in producing three goods A, B and C. The amount of each good produced by each method is shown in the following matrix :

	A	B	C
Method 1	4	8	2
Method 2	5	7	1
Method 3	5	3	9

The matrix [10 4 6] represents the profit per unit for the goods A, B and C in that order. Using matrix multiplication, find which method maximizes total profit.

A. Method 1 B. Method 2
C. Method 3 D. All are equal

8. There are three electronic dealers in a pure competition market (*i.e.,* the prices of all the commodities are fixed) who sell Radios, Tape recorders and Television sets. If A sells weekly 48 radios, 20 tape recorders and 12 T.V. sets; B sells weekly 57 radios, 17 tape recorders and 15 T.V. sets; and C sells weekly 35 radios, 22 tape recorders and 18 T.V. sets, calculate their individual profits, if the net revenue on radio is ₹ 500, on tape recorder is ₹ 750 and on T.V. set is ₹ 2,500.

A. 60,000, 78,750, 79,000
B. 79,000, 78,750, 60,000
C. 78,750, 79,000, 60,000
D. 78,750, 60,000, 79,000

9. ABC manufacturer produces two types of products X and Y. Each product first processed in a machine M_1 and then sent to another machine M_2 for finishing. Each unit of × requires 20 minutes time in M_1 and 10 minutes time in M_2 whereas each unit of Y requires 10 minutes time in M_1 and 20 minutes time in M_2. The total time available in each machine is 600 minutes. Calculate the number of units of two types of products produced by constructing a matrix equation of the form AX = B and then solving it by the matrix inversion method.

A. 10, 30 B. 20, 20
C. 30, 10 D. 15, 25

10. The joint demand and supply functions of the two commodities are as under :

Commodity	Demand	Supply
X_1	$x_1 = 82 - 3p_1 + p_2$	$x_1 = 15p_1 - 5$
X_2	$x_2 = 92 + 2p_1 - 4p_2$	$x_2 = 32p_2 - 6$

Using matrix algebra, determine the equilibrium prices.

A. 3, 5 B. 4, 4
C. 5, 3 D. 2, 6

11. To control a crop disease it is necessary to use 8 units of chemical A, 14 units of chemical B and 13 units of chemical C. One barrel of spray P contains one unit of A, 2 units of B and 3 units of C. One barrel of spray Q contains 2 units of A, 3 units of B and 2 units of C. One barrel of spray R contains 1 unit of A, 2 units of B and 2 units of C. Find how many barrels of each spray be used to just meet the requiremet. (Solve by Matrix Algebra).

A. 2, 1, 3 B. 1, 2, 3
C. 3, 2, 1 D. 3, 1, 2

12. An amount of ₹ 6,50,000 is invested in three investments at rates of 6%, 8% and 9% per annum respectively. The total annual income is ₹ 48,000. The income from the third investment is ₹ 6,000 more than the income from the second investment. Using matrix algebra, determine the amount of each investment.

A. 3,00,000, 1,50,000, 2,00,000
B. 2,00,000, 3,00,000, 1,50,000
C. 1,50,000, 2,00,000, 3,00,000
D. 3,00,000, 2,00,000, 1,50,000

13. A mixture is to be made containing X kg of food A, Y kg of food B and Z kg of food C. The total weight of the mixture to be made is 5 kg. Food A contains 500 units of vitamin per kg and B & C contain 200 and 100 units respectively. The 5 kg mixture is to contain total of 1,500 units of vitamin. Foods 'A', 'B' and 'C' contains respectively 300, 600 and 700 calories per kg and 5 kg mixture is to contain a total of 2,500 calories. Derive a general solution for X and Y in terms of Z so that the 5 kg mixture contains the required 2,500 calories. If the variables X, Y and Z are not permitted to be negative, find the range of values that Z is restricted to.

A. (1, 2.5) B. (2, 3.5)
C. (1, 3.5) D. (0, 2.5)

14. An economy consists of two sectors—manufacturing and agriculture. To produce one unit of manufacturing output, 0.1 unit of manufacturing goods and 0.01 units of agriculture goods are required as inputs. One unit of agriculture output requires 40 units of manufacturing goods and nil unit of agricultural goods as inputs. A unit of manufacturing goods requires 4 man-hours of labour and a unit of agricultural output requires 100 man-hours of labour. Calculate the total labour requirement if 50 million units of manufacturing goods and 2 million units of agricultural good need to be produced for final consumption.

Supposing the wages rate as ₹ 10 per man-hour, calculate the equilibrium prices of manufacturing goods and agriculatural output.

A. 100, 5,000 B. 200, 5,000
C. 300, 5,000 D. 400, 5,000

15. Find maximum and minimum value of the function $y = x^3 - 3x - 1$.

A. 2, –2 B. –2, 1
C. 1, –1 D. –1, 1

16. The difference of two numbers is 100. The square of the larger one exceeds five times the square of the smaller one by an amount which is maximum. Find the numbers.

A. 25, 125 B. 125, 25
C. 45, 225 D. 45, 125

17. With fixed equipment the production function of a firm is given by :

$x = 50 + 0.5l^2 - 0.001l^3$ and the wage rate is ₹ 15. Find the marginal cost when $l = 150$.

A. 0.162 B. 0.172
C. 0.152 D. 0.182

18. At a certain factory, the total cost of manufacturing q units during daily production run is $C(q) = 0.2q^2 + q + 900$ rupees. From experience it has been determined that approximately $q(t) = t^2 + 100t$ units are manufactured during first t hours of production run. Compute the rate at which the total manufacturing cost is changing with respect to time 2 hours after production commences.

A. 8,590.4 B. 8,690.4
C. 8,490.4 D. 8,890.4

19. A monopolist's demand curve is : $p = 200 - 5q$. Find marginal revenue function. At what price is marginal revenue zero?

A. 200 B. 300
C. 100 D. 400

20. A manufacturing firm faces a demand schedule $p = 12{,}000 - 900x$ and its production function is $x = l^{1/3}$, where l is labour. Currently the firm employs 64 labourers. Find the marginal revenue product of labour.

A. 200 B. 300
C. 100 D. 400

21. If the consumption function is giveny by : $C = 8 + \frac{3Y}{4} - \frac{\sqrt{Y}}{3}$, determine the marginal propensity to consume and marginal propensity to save when Y = 25.

A. 0.254 B. 0.284
C. 0.244 D. 0.264

22. Find elasticity of supply for the supply function $x = 3p^2 + 7$, when $p = 5$.

A. 150/82 B. 82/150
C. 125/44 D. 44/125

23. The demand x as a function of income y is given by : $50x = 20 + 5y$. Obtain the expression for the income elasticity of demand and its value when $y = 400$.

A. 1,000/1,200 B. 2,000/2,020
C. 1,020/1,000 D. 2,020/2,000

24. A distributor of refrigerators has average monthly sales of 1,200 refrigerators, each selling for ₹ 18,000. From the past experience, the distributor knows that special month-long promotion will enable them to sell 150 additional refrigerators for each ₹ 1,000 decrease in price. What price should be charged for each refrigerator, during the month of promotion, in order to maximize revenue?

A. 13,000 B. 12,000
C. 11,000 D. 9,000

25. Find the profit maximizing output given the following revenue and cost functions :

$$R(q) = 1{,}000q - 2q^2$$

and $C(q) = q^3 - 59q^2 + 1{,}315q + 2{,}000$.

A. 15 B. 25
C. 35 D. 45

26. A manufacturer of men's shirts figures that his exclusive 'Executive' model will cost ₹ 5,000 for overhead plus ₹ 90 for each shirt made. The price he can get for the shirts depends on how exclusive they are. From experience, the Accounts Manager has estimated the following demand function : $p = 300 - 2\sqrt{q}$, where q is the number of shirts sold. How many shirts should the manufacturer produce in order to maximize his profit?

A. 4,200 B. 4,600
C. 4,500 D. 4,900

27. The proportion of people responding to an advertisement of a new product in a certain marketing area is given by $(1 - e^{-0.3t})$, where t is the number of days the advertisement runs. The marketing area contains 4,00,000 potential customers and each response to the advertisement results in an average profit of ₹ 2. The profit is exclusive of advertising cost. The fixed cost of producing the advertising is ₹ 30,000 and the variable cost is ₹ 4,000 for each day the advertisement runs. How many days should the advertisement run to maximize total net profit.

A. 11.5 B. 12.8
C. 13.6 D. 14.2

28. The total cost function of a product is given by :

$$C(x) = x^3 - 315x^2 + 27{,}000x + 20{,}000;$$

where x is the number of units produced. Determine the number of units that should be produced to minimize the total cost.

A. 350 B. 150
C. 450 D. 250

29. The marginal cost function of a manufacturer is given by : $MC = \frac{500x}{\sqrt{x^2+40}}$, where x is the number of units of a product in thousands. If x increases from 3,000 to 9,000 units, find the total increase in cost.

A. 2,000 B. 3,000
C. 4,000 D. 5,000

30. The function describing the marginal profit from producing and selling a product is : MP = $-6x + 750$, where x equals the number of units and MP is the marginal profit measured in rupees. When 100 units are produced and sold, total profit equals ₹ 25,000. Determine the total profit function.

A. $P(x) = -3x^2 + 750x - 20{,}000$
B. $P(x) = -2x^2 + 550x - 10{,}000$
C. $P(x) = -5x^2 + 750x - 20{,}000$
D. $P(x) = -x^2 + 750x - 20{,}000$

31. A small business is considering buying an energy saving device which will reduce its consumption of fuel. The device will cost ₹ 32,000. Engineering estimates suggest that savings from using the device will occur at a rate of $s(t)$ rupees per year, where $s(t) = 20{,}000\, e^{-0.5t}$ and t equals time measured in years. Determine how long will it take for the firm to recover the cost of device.

A. 4.22 B. 2.22
C. 1.22 D. 3.22

32. What ordinary simple interest rate is earned by a person who invests ₹ 1,200 and receives ₹ 1,240 at the end of 60 days?

A. 10% B. 12%
C. 20% D. 25%

33. A savings account opened 3 months ago now has a balance of ₹ 20,400. If the bank pays 8% simple interest, how much money was deposited?

A. 20,000 B. 25,000
C. 30,000 D. 50,000

34. How long will it take ₹ 12,000 to amount to ₹ 20,000 at 5% converted quarterly?

A. 10 years, 8 months
B. 8 years, 10 months
C. 5 years, 8 months
D. 8 years, 5 months

35. Find the compound interest on ₹ 6,950 for 3 years if interest is payable half yearly, the rate for the first two years being 6% p.a., and for the third year 9% p.a.

A. 1,689 B. 1,389
C. 1,489 D. 1,589

36. How many years will it take for money to double when interest is compounded annually at 7%?

A. 8.24 years B. 5.24 years
C. 10.24 years D. 7.24 years

37. If interest is compounded continuously, at what nominal rate will a principal of P triple in 12 years?

A. 5.15% B. 9.15%
C. 7.15% D. 8.15%

38. A money-lender changes 'interest' at the rate of 5 rupees per 100 rupees per quarter, payable in advance. What effective rate of interest does he charge per annum?

A. 22.7% B. 20.7%
C. 18.7% D. 21.7%

39. Find the effective rate equivalent to the nominal rate 7% converted (or compounded) continuously.

A. 8.3% B. 7.3%
C. 5.3% D. 6.3%

40. Find the force of interest corresponding to the effective rate 9%.
A. 8.61% B. 6.61%
C. 7.61% D. 5.61%

41. At the end of the year Mona Beverages Company must pay the Industrial Machinery Corporation ₹ 2,00,000 against the unpaid balance for the cost of new bottle sterilizing and filling machinery. If a bank pays 4 per cent per annum interest compounded quarterly on deposits, how much should the company deposit at the beginning of the year so that the accumulated amount on deposit will meet the company's obligation?
A. 19,22,960 B. 19,21,960
C. 19,19,960 D. 19,20,960

42. What is the present value of ₹ 10,000 due in 6 months and ₹ 20,000 due in 18 months if the interest rate is 8% compounded quarterly?
A. 27,371.1 B. 27,372.1
C. 27,370.1 D. 27,369.1

43. A person invests money in a bank paying interest 5% effective and plans to receive ₹ 5,000 in 5 years. What is the compound discount of this investment?
A. 1,081.4 B. 1,080.4
C. 1,082.4 D. 1,084.4

44. A machine, the life of which is estimated to be 15 years, costs ₹ 40,000. Calculate the scrap value at the end of its life, depreciation on the diminishing balance system being calculated at 10% per annum.
A. 8,220 B. 8,222
C. 8,226 D. 8,224

45. An item becomes depreciated in such a way that the value of the item at the end of any year is 90% of the value at the beginning of the year. The cost of the item is ₹ 20, and it was sold eventually as waste metal for ₹ 7.50. Obtain the number of years during which the item was in use.
A. 9.3 years B. 9.4 years
C. 9.2 years D. 9.0 years

46. Find the amount of an annuity of ₹ 7,000 payable at the end of each year for 7 years if money is worth 6% per annum compounded annually.
A. 58,750.87 B. 58,756.87
C. 58,250.87 D. 58,456.87

47. XYZ bank pays interest @ 8% per annum compounded semi-annually. If a person places ₹ 5,000 in the bank at the end of every 6 months, how much will be in his account after 5 years?
A. 60,040.53 B. 60,0.35.53
C. 60,030.53 D. 60,020.53

48. A company intends to create a sinking (or depreciation) fund to replace at the end of the 20th year assets costing ₹ 5,00,000. Calculate the amount to be retained out of profits every year if the interest rate is 5%.
A. 15,110 B. 15,115
C. 15,125 D. 15,105

49. X measures Wages in Rupees
A. Unit of its average is ₹ and unit of variance is ₹
B. Unit of its average is ₹ and unit of variance is ₹ square.
C. Unit of its average is ₹ but variance does not have any unit.
D. Unit of its average is ₹ but unit of variance is square not of ₹

50. In order to apply correctly the χ^2-test for goodness of fit, which of the following assumption is correct?
A. The observed and theoretical distribution contain the same number of elements
B. No expected frequency be less than five
C. The observed values are taken from a random sample
D. All of the above

51. If a boy cycles 8 km at the speed of 8 km per hour, and walks another 8 km at the speed of 2 km per hour. His average speed per hour is
A. 5 km B. $\frac{16}{5}$ km
C. 4 km D. 6 km

52. Two events are said to be independent, as per the theory of probability, if the occurrence of one

A. affects the probability of another
B. does not effect the probability of another
C. prevents the occurrence of another
D. makes the probability of occurrence of other as zero

53. The Fisher index number is

A. GM of Laspeyres and Paasche index numbers
B. AM of Laspeyres and Paasche index numbers
C. HM of Laspeyres and Paasche index numbers
D. GM of Laspeyres and Marshall-Edgeworth index numbers

54. Given the following numbers:
2, 8, 6, 5, 0, 9, 7, 11.
The product of their arithmetic and geometric means is

A. 64 B. 16
C. 0 D. 6

55. Given the following two regression equations
$y - 0.5 = \beta_1 x$
$x + 10 = \beta_2 y$
then the coefficient of correlation between x and y is

A. $\sqrt{\beta_1 \beta_2}$ B. $\sqrt{\beta_1 \beta_2} + 0.5$
C. $\sqrt{\beta_1 \beta_2} + 10.0$ D. $\sqrt{\beta_1 \beta_2}$

56. A commuter drives 10 miles on first day at a speed of 60 km/hour, the second day at 15 km/hour and third day 10 km/hour. The mean speed of the commuter is

A. 16.32 B. 42.50
C. 36.35 D. 22.10

57. The sum of squares of deviation of 20 observations from their mean is 720 and the mean is 60. The coefficient of vatriation is

A. 5% B. 10%
C. 15% D. 20%

58. If x is a random variable and 'a' and 'b' are constants, then Var $(ax + b)$ is

A. $(a + b)$ Var (x) B. $(a^2 + b^2)$ Var (x)
C. ab Var (x) D. a^2 Var (x)

59. The probability of drawing a 'spade' from a well shuffled packet of cards is

A. $\frac{1}{52}$ B. $\frac{4}{52}$
C. $\frac{1}{4}$ D. $\frac{2}{3}$

60. The coefficient of correlation between two series x and y is found to be 0.80. If all the values of x and y are reduced by 50 per cent, the correlation coefficient will be

A. 0.80 B. 0.40
C. 0.60 D. 0.20

61. For a Poisson's distribution with $n = 200$, $p = 0.02$, the mean is

A. 20 B. 40
C. 4 D. 10

62. The value of χ^2 in a 2 × 4 contingency table is computed as 4.0. The Null hypothesis that then no associationship will be accepted at 5% level of significance, if this computed value is less than or equal to the value of χ^2 from the table at ..... degrees of freedom.

A. 8 B. 6
C. 4 D. 3

63. The significance of the difference between two means of the populations, when σ^2 values are known and equal, is tested by

A. Z-test B. t-test
C. F-test D. χ^2-test

64. The portion of the total area covered in a normal curve under $\bar{x} \pm 2.54\,\sigma$ is

A. 85% B. 95%
C. 99% D. 90%

65. If A and B are dependent events, then

A. $P(A/B) = \frac{P(A) . P(B/A)}{P(A)}$

B. P(A/B) = P(A) . P(B/A)

C. P(A/B) = P(B) . P(A/B)

D. $P(A/B) = \frac{P(A) . P(B/A)}{P(A)}$

66. Arithmetic mean of earning of 42 workers in a factory is ₹ 1200 per month. On account of price rise, the workers managed to get 10% hike in their earnings. In addition to this, the management paid ₹ 100 per month to each employee as bonus. The arithmetic mean of total earning of the workers after these changes will be

A. ₹ 1300 B. ₹ 1320
C. ₹ 1420 D. ₹ 1510

67. If the Karl Pearson coefficient of correlation between x and y is 0.3, then the coefficient of correlation between $-x$ and $2y$ is

A. –0.6 B. –0.3
C. 0.3 D. 0.5

68. The arithmetic mean of series 'A' is twice that of series 'B' and the standard deviation of series 'B' is twice that of series 'A'. The coefficient of variation of series 'A' in relation to that of series 'B' will be

A. 1/4 B. 1/2
C. same D. twice

69. The sum of squared deviation is the least when taken from

A. mode B. median
C. arithmetic mean D. geometric mean

70. Suppose the average weight of 9 persons is 50 kg. Average weight of the first 5 persons is 45 kg, whereas average weight of the last 5 persons is 55 kg. Then the weight of the 5th member will be

A. 45.0 kg B. 47.5 kg
C. 50.0 kg D. 52.5 kg

71. Which one of the following statistical measures is NOT affected by extremely large or small values?

A. Median
B. Harmonic mean
C. Standard deviation
D. Coefficient of variation

72. Given is the following distribution of two variables x and y:

x :	1	2	3	4	5
y :	3	4	5	6	7

The standard deviation of y is

A. Same as standard deviation of x
B. (the standard deviation of x) × 2
C. (the standard deviation of x) + 2
D. (the standard deviation of x) – 2

73. The standard deviation of six numbers 3, 3, 3, 5, 5, 5 is

A. 1
B. 4
C. 0
D. Cannot be obtained since the unit of measurement is not given

74. If for a sample data: Mean < Median < Mode, then the distribution is

A. skewed to the right
B. symmetric
C. skewed to the left
D. neither symmetric nor skewwed

75. Let $x = \frac{9 - U}{3}$ and $y = V - 4$ and the correlation coefficient between U and V is – 0.93. Then the correlation coefficient between x and y will be

A. 0.093 B. –0.093
C. –0.93 D. cannot be derived

76. Which one of the following statements is NOT correct?

Fisher's index

A. lies between Laspeyre's index (L) and Paasche's index (P)
B. is the arithmetic mean of L and P
C. is the geometric mean of L and P
D. is equal to L or P if L = P

77. Consider the following statements:

1. Quartile deviation is more instructive range as it discards the dispersion of extreme items.
2. Coefficient of quartile deviation cannot be used to compare the degree of variations in different distributions.
3. There are 10 deciles for a series. Which of the above statements is/are correct?

A. 1, 2 and 3 B. 2 alone
C. 3 alone D. 1 alone

78. Which one of the following indices satisfies both time reversal and factor reversal tests?
A. Laspeyre's index B. Fisher's index
C. Paasche's index D. Keely's index

79. Given the following data—1, 2, 3, 4 and 100; the best measure of central tendency is the
A. arithmetic mean B. median
C. mode D. geometric mean

80. If for a given data, mode = 5, median = 15 and mean = 20, it means that the sample data is
A. skewed to the right
B. skewed to the left
C. symmetric
D. neither symmetric nor skewed

81. Consider the following statements:
1. Correlation analysis helps in determining the relationship between two or more variables—it does not tell us anything about the cause and effect relationship.
2. The ratio of explained variation to the total variation is called the coefficient of correlation.
3. Pearsonian coefficient always assumes linear relationship and is unduly effected by the extreme items.

Which of the above statements is/are correct?
A. 2 alone B. 1 and 2
C. 1 and 3 D. 2 and 3

82. The right-hand tail of a frequency distribution is found to the mirror image of the left-hand tail. The distribution is
A. positively skewed
B. negatively skewed
C. asymmetric
D. symmetric

83. From the cumulative frequency diagram which one of the following types of average can be estimated?
A. Geometric Mean B. Harmonic Mean
C. Median D. Mode

84. During one year the ratio of prices of two commodities is 3, whereas during the next year it is 2. For averaging these ratios
A. arithmetic mean is most appropriate
B. harmonic mean is most appropriate
C. geometric mean is most appropriate
D. all the three, arithmetic, harmonic and geometric means are equally appropriate

85. Consider the following statements:
1. Median is not useful while dealing with skewed distribution such as income distribution or price distribution.
2. Median can be determined graphically by drawing only one ogive.
3. Mode can be used to describe qualitative phenomenon.

Which of the above statements are correct?
A. 1 and 2 B. 1 and 3
C. 2 and 3 D. 1, 2 and 3

86. The following equation indicates the relationship among average median and mode:
A. Mode = 3 Median – 2 Mean
B. Mean = 2 Mode – 3 Median
C. Median = 3 Mean – 2 Mode
D. None of these

87. What is the median of 36, 72, 49, 45, 60, 33, 61, 72, 52?
A. 33 B. 52
C. 61 D. 60

88. In a moderately asymmetrical distribution.
A. A.M. > G.M > H.M
B. A.M. < G.M < H.M
C. A.M < G.M > H.M
D. None of these

89. The geometric mean of 8, 64 and 512 is
A. 194 B. 64
C. 16 D. None of these

90. The points of intersection of the 'less than' and the 'more than' ogives correspond to
A. mean B. median
C. geometric mean D. None of these

91. Histogram is useful to determine graphically the value of
A. arithmetic mean B. median
C. mode D. None of these

92. In a series of values if one value is zero, G.M. is

A. positive B. zero
C. indeterminate D. None of these

93. The sum of squared deviations is minimum when taken from
A. mean B. median
C. mode D. None of these

94. Coefficient of quartile deviation is calculated by the formula
A. $\frac{Q_3 + Q_1}{4}$ B. $\frac{Q_3 + Q_1}{2}$
C. $\frac{Q_3 - Q_1}{Q_3 + Q_1}$ D. $\frac{Q_3 + Q_1}{Q_3 - Q_1}$

95. Mean ± 3 σ covers
A. 99.37% items B. 90% items
C. 99.9% items D. 99.73% items

96. Quartile deviation is
A. $\frac{4}{5}\sigma$ B. $\frac{3}{2}\sigma$
C. $\frac{2}{3}\sigma$ D. $\frac{5}{4}\sigma$

97. Coefficient of variation is calculated by the formula
A. $\frac{\overline{x}}{\sigma} \times 100$ B. $\frac{\sigma}{\overline{x}} \times 100$
C. $\frac{\overline{x}}{\sigma}$ D. $\frac{\sigma}{\overline{x}}$

98. The measure of variation that is least effected by extreme observations is
A. Range
B. Mean deviation
C. Standard deviation
D. Quartile deviation

99. When coefficient of skewness is zero the distribution is
A. J-shaped B. U-shaped
C. Symmetrical D. L-shaped

100. When $\beta_2 < 3$ the distribution is
A. Leptokurtic B. Platykurtic
C. Mesokurtic D. None of these

101. The second moment about mean is
A. $\frac{\sum(x - \overline{x})^2}{N}$ B. $\frac{(x - \overline{x})^3}{N}$
C. $\frac{(x - \overline{x})^2}{N}$ D. None of these

102. In a negatively skewed distribution
A. Mode > Median > Mean
B. Median > Mode > Mean
C. Mode < Median < Mean
D. None of these

103. Karl Pearson's coefficient of skewness is... Bowley's coefficient of skewness for any skewed distribution.
A. equal to B. less than
C. greater than D. not related to

104. If a frequency distribution is positively skewed, the mean of the distribution is
A. greater than the mode
B. less than the mode
C. equal to the mode
D. None of these

105. When coefficient of skewness is negative
A. $Q_2 + Q_3 = 2Q_1$ B. $Q_3 + Q_1 < 2Q_2$
C. $Q_3 + Q_1 > 2Q_2$ D. $Q_3 + Q_2 < 2Q_1$

106. The coeficient of correlation is independent of change of
A. Origin B. Scale
C. Both A and B D. None of these

107. The coefficient of correlation
A. has no limits
B. can be less than one
C. can be more than one
D. varies between ± 1

108. Probable error is
A. 0.6745 S.E. B. 0.6457 S.E.
C. 0.6753 S.E. D. 0.7645 S.E.

109. Coefficient of determination is defined as
A. r^3 B. $1 - r^2$
C. $1 + r^2$ D. r^2

110. If sum of the product of deviations of x and y series from their means, *i.e.*, Σxy is zero, the coefficient of correlation shall be
A. +1 B. 0
C. –1 D. None of these

111. Mention the correct answers.
The ranks according to two attributes in a sample are given below:

R_1	1	2	3	4	5
R_2	5	4	3	2	1

The rank correlation between them is

A. 0 B. +1
C. −1 D. None of these

112. If both the regression coefficients are negative, the correlation coefficient would be...

A. negative B. positive
C. zero D. None of these

113. The under root of two... coefficients gives us the value of correlation coefficient.

A. regression B. S.E
C. S.D D. None of these

114. Both the regression coefficients cannot be

A. less than one B. greater than one
C. equal to one D. None of these

115. The regression lines cut each other at the point of

A. average of x and y
B. average of x only
C. average of y only
D. None of these

116. Regression coefficient is independent of change of

A. origin but not of scale
B. both origin and scale
C. scale but not of origin
D. none of these

117. There will be only one regression line in case of two variables if

A. $r = 0$ B. $r = \pm 1$
C. $r = 0.5$ D. None of these

118. When one regression coefficient is negative the other would be

A. negative B. positive
C. zero D. None of them

119. Where r is zero the regression lines but each other making an angle of

A. 45° B. 60°
C. 90° D. None of these

120. The farther the two regression lines cut each other

A. the greater will be the degree of correlation
B. the lesser will be degree of correlation
C. does not really matter
D. None of these

121. If with a rise of 10% in prices the wages are increased by 20%, the real wage increase is by

A. 10%
B. more than 10%
C. less than 10%
D. 20%

122. The circular test is satisfied when

A. $P_{12} \times P_{23} \times P_{31} = 0$
B. $P_{12} \times P_{32} \times P_{31} = 1$
C. $P_{12} \times P_{23} \times P_{31} = 1$
D. $P_{12} \times P_{23} \times P_{13} = 1$

123. Time reversal test is satisfied when

A. $P_{01} \times P_{10} = 0$ B. $P_{01} \times P_{10} = 1$
C. $P_{02} \times P_{10} > 1$ D. $P_{01} \times P_{10} < 1$

124. Fisher's ideal index is

A. arithmetic mean of Laspeyre's and Paasche's index
B. median of Laspeyre's and Paasche's index
C. geometric mean of Laspeyre's and Paasche's index
D. None of these

125. Laspeyre's index is based on

A. base year quantities
B. current year quantities
C. average of current and base year
D. None of these

126. A good index number is one that satisfies

A. Unit test
B. Time test
C. Time Reversal Test and Factor Reversal Test
D. None of these

127. Theoretically the best average in the construction of index number is

A. median B. geometric mean
C. mode D. arithmetic mean

128. Historically the first index was constructed in...

A. 1764 B. 1844
C. 1850 D. 1744

129. ... is known as the 'ideal' formula for constructing index numbers.
A. Fisher's Ideal Index
B. Laspeyre's Index
C. Paasche's Index
D. None of these

130. The most important factors causing seasonal variations are
A. growth of population
B. technological improvements
C. weather and social customs
D. change in fashions

131. The most widely used method of measuring seasonal variations is
A. Ratio-to-moving average method
B. Ratio-to-trend method
C. Link relative method
D. None of these

132. Cyclical fluctuations are caused by
A. Wars B. Earthquakes
C. Floods D. None of these

133. If E(X) is the mathematical expectation of the variable X and C is constant then E(CX) = ?
A. $E(c) + E(x)$ B. $E(c) \times E(x)$
C. $CE(x)$ D. None of these

134. $E(x + y) = ?$
A. $E(x) + E(y)$ B. $E(x) \times E(y)$
C. $E(x.y)$ D. None of these

135. If A and B are mutually exclusive events, P(AB) = ?
A. Zero B. P(A) + P(B)
C. P(A) D. None of these

136. The probability that the throw of two dice yields a total of 5 or 8 is...
A. 1/4 B. 1/5
C. 2/5 D. None of these

137. In case of conditional probability (A and B) = ?
A. P(B) × P(A/B) B. P(B) × P(A)
C. P(A) + P(B) D. None of these

138. If a card is drawn from a pack of cards the probability of getting either a king or a queen is...
A. 2/13 B. 5/15
C. 1/4 D. None of these

139. If an event cannot take place, probability will be
A. +1 B. –1
C. 0 D. None of these

140. Addition theorem states that if two events A and B are mutually exclusive the probability of occurrence of either A or B is given by:
A. P(A) + P(B) B. P(A) × P(B)
C. P(A) – P(B) D. None of these

141. If two events A and B are independent, the probability that they will both occur is given by:
A. P(A) + P(B)
B. P(A) × P(B)
C. P(A) – P(B)
D. P(A) + P(B) – P(AB)

142. If two events A and B are dependent, the conditional probability of B given A, *i.e.*, P(A/B) is calculated as:
A. P(AB)/P(B) B. P(A) / P(B)
C. P(AB) / P(A) D. P(A) / P(AB)

143. If two events A and B are dependent, the conditional probability of A given B, *i.e.*, P(A/B) is calculated as:
A. P(B/A)/P(AB) B. P(B)/P(A)
C. P(AB)/P(A) D. P(AB)/P(B)

144. ${}^5C_2$ is equal to
A. 20 B. 10
C. 30 D. 100

145. Two cards are drawn from a well-shuffled pack of 52 cards. Find the probability that they are both aces if the first is replaced.
A. $\frac{1}{169}$ B. $\frac{2}{52}$
C. $\frac{1}{221}$ D. None of these

146. The standard deviation of Binomial distribution is:
A. $\sqrt{npq}$ B. npq
C. $n^2p^2q^2$ D. np

147. The standard deviation of Poisson distribution is : (m = mean)

A. m B. $\sqrt{m}$

C. m^2 D. $1/\sqrt{m}$

148. In case of normal distribution $\bar{x} \pm 2\sigma$ covers

A. 95.45% B. 95.54%

C. 94.45% D. 99.73%

149. If in Binomial distribution mean is 10 and standard deviation 2, q will be

A. 0 B. 1

C. 0.4 D. 0.8

150. The normal distribution is an approximation to...

A. Binomial distribution

B. Poisson distribution

C. Both (A) and (B)

D. None of these

151. In a normal distribution the points of inflexion occur at...

A. $\bar{X} + \sigma$ B. $\bar{X} + 2\sigma$

C. $\bar{X} + 3\sigma$ D. None of these

152. The normal distribution with $x = 0$ and $\sigma = 1$ is known as.....

A. Standard normal distribution

B. Poisson distribution

C. Both A and B

D. None of these

153. The mean plus and minus 1.96 standard deviation includes... per cent of the items of normal distribution.

A. 75 B. 47.5

C. 74.5 D. None of these

154. ..... asserts that there is no true difference in the sample and the population in the particular matter under consideration.

A. Null hypothesis

B. Alternate hypothesis

C. Both A and B

D. None of these

155. ..... error is committed when the hypothesis is true but out test rejects it.

A. Type I B. Type II

C. Both A and B D. None of these

156. ..... errors are made when we accept a null hypothesis which is not true.

A. Type I B. Type II

C. Both A and B D. None of these

157. The standard deviation of sampling distribution is called...

A. Standard error B. Probable error

C. Both A and B D. None of these

158. Standard error of number of successes is given by:

A. $\sqrt{\frac{pq}{n}}$ B. $\sqrt{npq}$

C. npq D. n^2p^2

159. Large sample theory is applicable when:

A. N is > 30 B. N is < 30

C. N = 30 D. None of these

160. Student's 't' Distribution was discovered by:

A. Karl Pearson B. Laplace

C. Fisher D. Gosset

161. The difference of two means in case of small samples is tested by the formula:

A. $t = \frac{\bar{x}_1 - \bar{x}_2}{s}$

B. $t = \frac{\bar{x}_1 - \bar{x}_2}{s}\sqrt{\frac{n_1 + n_2}{n_1 - n_2}}$

C. $t = \frac{\bar{x}_1 - \bar{x}_2}{s}\sqrt{\frac{n_1 n_2}{n_1 + n_2}}$

D. None of these

162. While testing the significance of the difference of two sample means in case of small samples, the degrees of freedom is calculated by:

A. $\nu = n_1 + n_2 - 2$ B. $\nu = n_1 + n_2 - 1$

C. $\nu = n_1 - n_2 - 2$ D. $\nu = n_1 - n_2 + 2$

163. Which one of the following average can be computed from a cumulative frequency curve?

A. Geometric Mean B. Harmonic Mean

C. Mode D. Median

164. If the standard deviation of a variable x is s and if $y = a + bs$, where a and b are constants, the standard deviation of y would be

A. $a + bs$ B. bs

C. $\sqrt{b}.s$ D. b^2s

165. Which one of the following statistical measures is based on all observations?

A. Quartile Deviation
B. Harmonic Mean
C. Range
D. Mode

166. Consider the following measures:

1. Correlation coefficient
2. Covariance
3. Coefficient of variation
4. Index number

Which of these are unit-free?

A. 1 and 2 B. 1 and 3
C. 2 and 4 D. 1, 3 and 4

167. If r is the correlation coefficients between the two variables, then

A. $0 \le r \le 1$ B. $-1 \le r \le 0$
C. $-1 \le r \le 1$ D. $1 \le r \le 2$

168. If all values of a variable are multiplied by a given number, which one of the following will NOT be affected?

A. Mean
B. Median
C. Range
D. Coefficient of variation

169. Dispersions are NOT calculated about

A. Mean B. Median
C. Mode D. Geometric Mean

170. The price index that uses base year quantities as weights is called

A. Passche's index
B. Laspeyere's index
C. Fisher's ideal index
D. Wholesale price index

171. **Assertion (A):** Variance is always greater than the standard deviation.

Reason (R): Variance is the square of the standard deviation.

A. Both (A) and (R) are individually true and (R) is the correct explanation of (A)
B. Both (A) and (R) are individually true but (R) is not the correct explanation of (A)
C. (A) is true but (R) is false
D. (A) is false but (R) is true

172. Formula of linear correlation coefficient (r_{yx}) is:

A. $r_{yx} = \dfrac{b_{yx} + b_{xy}}{2}$

B. $r_{yx} = \sqrt{b_{yx} . b_{xy}}$

C. $r_{yx} = \dfrac{2}{\left(\dfrac{1}{b_{yx}} + \dfrac{1}{b_{xy}}\right)}$

D. $r_{yx} = \dfrac{W_1 . b_{yx} + W_2 . b_{yx}}{W_1 + W_2}$

173. The weighted mean of first n natural numbers whose weights are equal to the squares of corresponding numbers is

A. $\dfrac{n+1}{2}$ B. $\dfrac{3n(n+1)}{2(2n+1)}$

C. $\dfrac{(n+1)(2n+1)}{6}$ D. $\dfrac{n(n+1)}{2}$

174. The arithmetic mean of 9 observations is 100 and that of 6 is 80, the combined mean of all the 15 observations will be

A. 100 B. 80
C. 90 D. 92

175. If the difference between mean and mode is 63 the difference between mean and median is

A. 18 B. 24
C. 22 D. 21

176. The standard deviation of first n natural numbers is

A. $\dfrac{n(n+1)(2n+1)}{6}$ B. $\dfrac{n^2-1}{12}$

C. $\sqrt{\left(\dfrac{n^2-1}{12}\right)}$ D. None of these

177. Mean deviation of the series a, $a + d$, $a + 2d$, $a + 2nd$ from its mean is

A. $\dfrac{(n+1)d}{(2n+1)}$ B. $\dfrac{nd}{2n+1}$

C. $\dfrac{n(n+1)d}{(2n+1)}$ D. $\dfrac{(2n+1)d}{n(n+1)}$

178. A sample of 35 observations has the mean 80 and S.D. as 4. A second sample of 65 observations from the same population has mean 70 and S.D. 3. The S.D. of the combined sample is

A. 5.85 B. 5.58
C. 34.2 D. None of these

179. The mean and S.D. of the marks of 200 candidates were found to be 40 and 15 respectively. Later, it was discovered that a score 40 was wrongly read as 50. The correct mean and S.D. respectively are

A. 14.98, 39.95 B. 39.95, 14.98
C. 39.95, 224.5 D. None of these

180. The coefficient of correlation between two variables x and y is 0.5, their covariance is 16 and S.D. of x is 4, then the S.D. of y is

A. 4 B. 8
C. 16 D. 64

181. For the observations
{(1, 2), (2, 5), (3, 7), (4, 8), (5, 10)},
Karl Pearson's coefficient of correlation is given by

A. 0.75 B. 0.85
C. 0.52 D. 0.985

182. Two random variables have the least square regression lines $3x + 2y = 26$ and $6x + y = 331$. The coefficient of correlation between x and y is given by

A. – 0.5 B. 0.5
C. 0.25 D. None of these

183. The average age of 20 students in a class is 15 yr. If the teacher's age is included, the average increase by one. What is the teacher's age?

A. 30 yr B. 21 yr
C. 42 yr D. 36 yr

184. If the monthly expenditure pattern of a person who earns a monthly salary of ₹ 15000 is represented in a pie diagram, then the sector angle of an item on transport expenses measures 15°. What is his monthly expenditure on transport?

A. ₹ 450 B. ₹ 625
C. ₹ 675 D. Insufficient data

185. What is the standard deviation of numbers 7, 9, 11, 13 and 15?

A. 2.2 B. 2.4
C. 2.6 D. 2.8

186. Consider the two series of observations A and B as follows

Series A	1019	1008	1015	1006	1002
Series B	1.9	0.8	1.5	0.6	0.2

If the standard deviation of the series A is $\sqrt{38}$, then what is the standard deviation of the series B?

A. 3.8 B. $\sqrt{0.38}$
C. 0.38 D. $\sqrt{38}$

187. Following tables gives the mean and variance of monthly demand for four products A, B, C and D in a super market

Product	A	B	C	D
Mean demand	60	90	80	120
Variance	12	25	36	16

For which product the demand is consistent?

A. Product A B. Product B
C. Product C D. Product D

188. What is the mean deviation of the data 2, 9, 3, 6, 9, 4?

A. 2.23 B. 2.57
C. 3.23 D. 3.57

189. The two lines of regression are $8x - 10y = 66$ and $40x - 18y = 214$ and variance of x series is 9. What is the standard deviation of y series?

A. 3 B. 4
C. 6 D. 9

190. Two dice are thrown simultaneously. The probability of obtaining a total score of 5 is

A. 1/18 B. 1/12
C. 1/9 D. None of these

191. The probability that a leap year selected at random contain 53 Sundays is

A. 7/366 B. 26/183
C. 1/7 D. 2/7

192. A card is drawn at random from a pack of 100 cards numbered 1 to 100. The probability of drawing a number, which is a square, is

A. 1/5 B. 2/5
C. 1/10 D. None of these

193. One of the two exclusive events must occur the chance of one is 2/3 of the other, then odds in favour of the other are

A. 1 : 3 B. 3 : 1
C. 2 : 3 D. 3 : 2

194. Twelve coupons are numbered from 1 to 12. Six coupons are selected at random one at a time with replacement. The probability that the largest number appearing on a selected coupon is less than or equal to 8, is

A. $(2/3)^6$ B. $(7/12)^6$
C. 1/33 D. None of these

195. A bag contains 3 red, 4 white and 5 blue balls. All balls are different. Two balls are drawn at random. The probability that they are of different colours is

A. 47/66 B. 10/33
C. 5/22 D. None of these

196. The probabilities of three mutually exclusive events A, B and C are given by 2/3, 1/4 and 1/6 respectively. The statement

A. is true
B. is false
C. Nothing can be said
D. Could be either

197. A five digit number is formed by the digits 1, 2, 3, 4, 5, 6 and 8. The probability that the number has even digit at both ends is

A. 2/7 B. 3/7
C. 4/7 D. None of these

198. From a pack of playing cards, three cards are drawn successively with replacement. The probability of selecting 2 aces and one king is

A. $1/\{(13)^2 \times 17\}$ B. $1/(13)^3$
C. $3/(13)^3$ D. None of these

199. A father has 3 children with at least one boy. The probability that he has 2 boys and one girl is

A. 1/4 B. 3/7
C. 1/3 D. None of these

200. The probability that an event A happens in one trial of an experiment is 0.7. Three independent trails of the experiment are performed. The probability that the event A happens atleast once is

A. 0.657 B. 0.973
C. 0.189 D. None of these

201. Two players toss 4 coins each. The probability that they both obtain the same number of heads is

A. $\frac{5}{256}$ B. $\frac{1}{16}$
C. $\frac{35}{128}$ D. None of these

202. Let A and B be two events such that P(A) = 0.4, P(B) = 0.3 and $P(A \cup B) = 0.7$. Then

A. A and B are independent
B. A and B are exhaustive
C. A and B are mutually exclusive
D. None of these

203. A dice and two coins are tossed. The probability that both the coins show heads and the dice shows 1 or 2, is

A. 7/12 B. 4/7
C. 1/12 D. None of these

204. A six faced dice is so biased that it is twice as likely to show an even number as an odd number when thrown. It is thrown twice. The probability that the sum of two numbers shown is even is

A. 5/9 B. 4/9
C. 2/3 D. 1/3

205. Host, his wife and 8 guests are to be seated on a round dining table at random. The probability that the host and his wife sit together is

A. 1/9 B. 2/9
C. 1/5 D. 1/10

206. The letters of the word ALLAHABAD are arranged at random. The probability that in the word so formed, all similar letters are found together, is

A. 1/63 B. 16/17
C. 5!/9! D. None of these

207. The probability that a certain beginner at golf gets good shot if he uses the correct club is 1/3 and the probability of a good shot with an incorrect club is 1/4. In his bag, there are 5 different clubs only one of which is correct for the shot in question. If he chooses a club at random and takes a stroke, the probability that he gets a good shot is

A. 1/3 B. 1/12
C. 4/15 D. 7/12

208. 100 boys are randomly divided into two subgroups containing 50 boys each. The probability that the two tallest boys are in different groups is

A. 50/99 B. 49/99
C. 25/99 D. None of these

209. On a toss of two dice, A throws a total of 5. Then the probability that he will throw another 5 before he throws 7 is

A. 2/5 B. 2/45
C. 1/81 D. 1/9

210. In a box containing 100 bulbs, 10 are defective. The probability that out of a sample of 5 bulbs none is defective is

A. $1/10^5$ B. $(9/10)^5$
C. ${}^{90}C_5/{}^{100}C_5$ D. None of these

211. A pack of cards contains 4 aces, 4 kings, 4 queens and 4 jacks. Two cards are drawn at random. The probability that at least one of them is an ace is

A. 1/5 B. 3/16
C. 9/20 D. 1/9

212. A speaks truth 60% times and B speaks truth 70% times. The probability that they say same thing while describing a single event is

A. 0.42 B. 0.46
C. 0.54 D. 0.12

213. Three six faced dice are tossed together, then probability that exactly two of the three numbers are equal to

A. 120/216 B. 126/216
C. 96/216 D. 90/216

214. A bag contain 10 mangoes out of which 4 are rotten, two mangoes are taken out together. If one of them is found to be good, the probability that other is also good is

A. 5/18 B. 8/15
C. 5/13 D. 2/3

215. An unbiased die is tossed until a number greater than 4 appears. The probability that an even number of tosses is needed is

A. 1/2 B. 2/5
C. 1/5 D. 2/3

ANSWERS

1	2	3	4	5	6	7	8	9	10
D	B	C	B	A	C	C	A	B	C
11	**12**	**13**	**14**	**15**	**16**	**17**	**18**	**19**	**20**
B	A	D	A	C	B	D	A	C	C
21	**22**	**23**	**24**	**25**	**26**	**27**	**28**	**29**	**30**
B	A	B	A	C	D	C	B	A	A
31	**32**	**33**	**34**	**35**	**36**	**37**	**38**	**39**	**40**
D	C	A	A	D	C	B	A	B	A
41	**42**	**43**	**44**	**45**	**46**	**47**	**48**	**49**	**50**
B	A	C	D	A	B	C	D	C	D
51	**52**	**53**	**54**	**55**	**56**	**57**	**58**	**59**	**60**
B	B	A	C	A	A	B	A	B	A
61	**62**	**63**	**64**	**65**	**66**	**67**	**68**	**69**	**70**
C	D	D	C	C	C	C	A	C	C

71	72	73	74	75	76	77	78	79	80
A	A	A	C	C	B	C	B	D	A
81	**82**	**83**	**84**	**85**	**86**	**87**	**88**	**89**	**90**
C	B	C	C	B	A	B	A	B	B
91	**92**	**93**	**94**	**95**	**96**	**97**	**98**	**99**	**100**
C	B	A	C	D	C	B	B	C	B
101	**102**	**103**	**104**	**105**	**106**	**107**	**108**	**109**	**110**
A	A	D	A	A	A	D	A	D	B
111	**112**	**113**	**114**	**115**	**116**	**117**	**118**	**119**	**120**
C	A	A	B	A	A	B	A	D	B
121	**122**	**123**	**124**	**125**	**126**	**127**	**128**	**129**	**130**
C	C	B	C	A	C	B	A	A	C
131	**132**	**133**	**134**	**135**	**136**	**137**	**138**	**139**	**140**
A	D	C	A	A	A	A	A	C	A
141	**142**	**143**	**144**	**145**	**146**	**147**	**148**	**149**	**150**
B	C	D	B	A	A	B	A	C	A
151	**152**	**153**	**154**	**155**	**156**	**157**	**158**	**159**	**160**
A	A	D	A	A	B	A	B	A	D
161	**162**	**163**	**164**	**165**	**166**	**167**	**168**	**169**	**170**
C	A	D	B	B	D	C	D	D	B
171	**172**	**173**	**174**	**175**	**176**	**177**	**178**	**179**	**180**
A	B	B	D	D	C	C	A	B	B
181	**182**	**183**	**184**	**185**	**186**	**187**	**188**	**189**	**190**
D	A	D	B	D	B	D	B	B	C
191	**192**	**193**	**194**	**195**	**196**	**197**	**198**	**199**	**200**
D	C	D	A	A	B	A	C	B	B
201	**202**	**203**	**204**	**205**	**206**	**207**	**208**	**209**	**210**
C	C	C	A	B	A	C	A	A	C
211	**212**	**213**	**214**	**215**					
C	C	D	C	B					

SOME SELECTED EXPLANATIONS

1. $AA^t = \frac{1}{9}\begin{bmatrix} 1 & 2 & 2 \\ 2 & 1 & -2 \\ x & 2 & y \end{bmatrix} \times \begin{bmatrix} 1 & 2 & x \\ 2 & 1 & 2 \\ 2 & -2 & y \end{bmatrix}$

$= \frac{1}{9}\begin{bmatrix} 9 & 0 & x+4+2y \\ 0 & 9 & 2x+2-2y \\ x+4+2y & 2x+2-2y & x^2+4+y^2 \end{bmatrix}$

Since $AA^t = I$, it follows that

$\frac{1}{9}(x+4+2y) = 0 \Rightarrow x + 2y = -4$ ...(1)

$\frac{1}{9}(2x+2-2y) = 0 \Rightarrow x - y = -1$ ...(2)

$\frac{1}{9}(x^2+4+y^2) = 1 \Rightarrow x^2 + y^2 = 5$ ...(3)

Solving (1) and (2), we get

$x = -2, y = -1.$

2. Let the given determinant be denoted by Δ. Then

$$\Delta = \begin{vmatrix} 13 & 3 & 3 \\ 14 & 3 & 3 \\ 15 & 3 & 3 \end{vmatrix}$$

(Operate $C_2' \to C_2 - C_1$ and $C_3' \to C_3 - C_2$]

= 0 (since two columns are identical)

3. Let the given determinant be denoted by Δ.

$$\Delta = \begin{vmatrix} 1 & 18 & 72 \\ 0 & 4 & 4 \\ 0 & 5 & 2 \end{vmatrix}$$

[Operate $R_2' \to R_2 - 2R_1$ and $R_3' \to R_3 - R_2$]

$$= \begin{vmatrix} 4 & 4 \\ 5 & 2 \end{vmatrix} \text{ (Expanding by first column)}$$

$= 8 - 20 = -12.$

4. In the determinant |A|, the cofactors of *a, b, c* and *d* are respectively *d, –c, –b* and *a*. Hence the matrix of cofactors of elements of A is :

$$C = \begin{bmatrix} d & -c \\ -b & a \end{bmatrix} \text{ and adj } A = C^t = \begin{bmatrix} d & -b \\ -c & a \end{bmatrix}.$$

5. The given equations can be written in the matrix notations as :

$$AX = B \qquad ...(1)$$

where $A = \begin{bmatrix} 10 & -2 \\ 6 & 3 \end{bmatrix}$,

$X = \begin{bmatrix} x_1 \\ x_2 \end{bmatrix}$, $B = \begin{bmatrix} 8 \\ 7 \end{bmatrix}$

We have $|A| = \begin{bmatrix} 10 & -2 \\ 6 & 3 \end{bmatrix}$

$= 10 \times 3 - 6 \times (-2) = 42$

Since $|A| \neq 0$, A is non-singular. Hence A^{-1} exists and the solution of (1) is given by:

$$X = A^{-1}B \qquad ...(2)$$

The matrix C of factors of the elements of A is given by :

$$C = \begin{bmatrix} 3 & -6 \\ 2 & 10 \end{bmatrix}$$

$$\therefore \text{ adj } A = C^t = \begin{bmatrix} 3 & 2 \\ -6 & 10 \end{bmatrix}$$

and $A^{-1} = \frac{\text{adj}A}{|A|} = \begin{bmatrix} 3/42 & 2/42 \\ -6/42 & 10/42 \end{bmatrix}$

Now, substituting in (2), we get

$$\begin{bmatrix} x_1 \\ x_2 \end{bmatrix} = \begin{bmatrix} 3/42 & 2/42 \\ -6/42 & 10/42 \end{bmatrix}\begin{bmatrix} 8 \\ 7 \end{bmatrix} = \begin{bmatrix} 38/42 \\ 22/42 \end{bmatrix}.$$

Hence $x_1 = \frac{38}{42}$ and $x_2 = \frac{22}{42}$.

6. The given system of equations in matrix form may be represented by

$$\begin{bmatrix} 2 & 8 & 5 \\ 1 & 1 & 1 \\ 1 & 2 & -1 \end{bmatrix}\begin{bmatrix} x \\ y \\ z \end{bmatrix} = \begin{bmatrix} 5 \\ -2 \\ 2 \end{bmatrix} \text{ or more precisely}$$

AX = B,

where $A = \begin{bmatrix} 2 & 8 & 5 \\ 1 & 1 & 1 \\ 1 & 2 & -1 \end{bmatrix}$,

$X = \begin{bmatrix} x \\ y \\ z \end{bmatrix}$ and $B = \begin{bmatrix} 5 \\ -2 \\ 2 \end{bmatrix}$

Now $|A| = \begin{bmatrix} 2 & 8 & 5 \\ 1 & 1 & 1 \\ 1 & 2 & -1 \end{bmatrix}$

$= 2(-1-2) -8(-1-1) + 5(2-1) = 15$

Since $|A| \neq 0$, A^{-1} exists

$$\begin{bmatrix} x \\ y \\ z \end{bmatrix} = A^{-1}\begin{bmatrix} 5 \\ -2 \\ 2 \end{bmatrix}$$

It can be easily verified that

$$\therefore \text{ adj } A = \begin{bmatrix} -3 & 18 & 3 \\ 2 & -7 & 3 \\ 1 & 4 & -6 \end{bmatrix} \text{ so that } A^{-1}$$

$$= \frac{\text{adj}A}{|A|} = \begin{bmatrix} -\frac{1}{5} & \frac{6}{5} & \frac{1}{5} \\ \frac{2}{15} & -\frac{7}{15} & \frac{1}{5} \\ -\frac{1}{15} & \frac{4}{15} & -\frac{2}{5} \end{bmatrix}$$

$$\begin{bmatrix} x \\ y \\ z \end{bmatrix} = \frac{1}{15}\begin{bmatrix} -\frac{1}{5} & \frac{6}{5} & \frac{1}{5} \\ \frac{2}{15} & -\frac{7}{15} & \frac{1}{5} \\ -\frac{1}{15} & \frac{4}{15} & -\frac{2}{5} \end{bmatrix}\begin{bmatrix} 5 \\ -2 \\ 2 \end{bmatrix}$$

$$= \begin{bmatrix} -3 \\ 2 \\ -1 \end{bmatrix}$$

Hence the solution is :

$x = -3$, $y = 2$, and $z = -1$.

7. Let

$$G = \begin{matrix} \text{Method 1} \\ \text{Method 2} \\ \text{Method 3} \end{matrix}\overset{\begin{matrix} A & B & C \end{matrix}}{\begin{bmatrix} 4 & 8 & 2 \\ 5 & 7 & 1 \\ 5 & 3 & 9 \end{bmatrix}_{3\times3}};$$

$$P = \begin{matrix} A \\ B \\ C \end{matrix}\overset{\text{Profit}}{\begin{bmatrix} 10 \\ 4 \\ 6 \end{bmatrix}_{3\times1}}.$$

Total profits under the three methods are given by :

$$GP = \begin{matrix} \text{Method 1} \\ \text{Method 2} \\ \text{Method 3} \end{matrix}\overset{\begin{matrix} A & B & C \end{matrix}}{\begin{bmatrix} 4 & 8 & 2 \\ 5 & 7 & 1 \\ 5 & 3 & 9 \end{bmatrix}_{3\times3}} \times \begin{matrix} A \\ B \\ C \end{matrix}\overset{\text{Profit}}{\begin{bmatrix} 10 \\ 4 \\ 6 \end{bmatrix}_{3\times1}}$$

$$= \begin{matrix} \text{Method 1} \\ \text{Method 2} \\ \text{Method 3} \end{matrix}\overset{\text{Profit}}{\begin{bmatrix} 84 \\ 84 \\ 116 \end{bmatrix}}$$

Hence 'method 3' maximizes total profit.

8. The sales of 3 dealers can be arranged in the 3×3 matrix form as follows :

$$P = \begin{matrix} A \\ B \\ C \end{matrix}\overset{\begin{matrix} R & T.R. & T.V. \end{matrix}}{\begin{bmatrix} 48 & 20 & 12 \\ 57 & 17 & 15 \\ 35 & 22 & 18 \end{bmatrix}}$$

and the profits on each article can be put in the 3×1 column matrix as shown below:

$$Q = \begin{matrix} R \\ T.R. \\ T.V. \end{matrix}\begin{bmatrix} 500 \\ 750 \\ 2500 \end{bmatrix}$$

∴ The total profit of each of the dealer is an element of the 3×1 product matrix :

$$PQ = \begin{bmatrix} 48 & 20 & 12 \\ 57 & 17 & 15 \\ 35 & 22 & 18 \end{bmatrix}\begin{bmatrix} 500 \\ 750 \\ 2500 \end{bmatrix}$$

$$= \begin{bmatrix} 48\times500+20\times750+12\times2500 \\ 57\times500+17\times750+15\times2500 \\ 35\times500+22\times750+18\times2500 \end{bmatrix}$$

$$= \begin{bmatrix} 69{,}000 \\ 78{,}750 \\ 79{,}000 \end{bmatrix}$$

Hence A's profit is ₹ 60,000; B's profit is ₹ 78,750 and C's profit is ₹ 79,000.

9. The data of the problem is summarised in the following table.

	Machine (Time in minutes) M_1	M_2
Product X	20	10
Product Y	10	20
Total time available	600	600

Let x and y be the number of units of product X and Y manufactured respectively. Then the problem can be expressed in a matrix equation form as follow:

$$\begin{bmatrix} 20 & 10 \\ 10 & 20 \end{bmatrix}\begin{bmatrix} x \\ y \end{bmatrix} = \begin{bmatrix} 600 \\ 600 \end{bmatrix} \text{ or equivalently}$$

$$AX = B,$$

where $A = \begin{bmatrix} 20 & 10 \\ 10 & 20 \end{bmatrix}$, $X = \begin{bmatrix} x \\ y \end{bmatrix}$

and $B = \begin{bmatrix} 600 \\ 600 \end{bmatrix}$

Since $|A| = \begin{bmatrix} 20 & 10 \\ 10 & 20 \end{bmatrix} = 300 \neq 0$, A^{-1} exists so that unique solution of AX = B is given by :

$$X = A^{-1} B = \left\{ \frac{1}{|A|} \cdot \text{adj } A \right\} B \qquad ...(i)$$

It can be easily verified that:

$$\text{adj } A = \begin{bmatrix} 20 & -10 \\ -10 & 20 \end{bmatrix}$$

Substituting in (*i*), we obtain

$$\begin{bmatrix} x \\ y \end{bmatrix} = \frac{1}{300} \begin{bmatrix} 20 & -10 \\ -10 & 20 \end{bmatrix} \begin{bmatrix} 600 \\ 600 \end{bmatrix}$$

$$= \frac{1}{300} \begin{bmatrix} 600 \\ 600 \end{bmatrix} = \begin{bmatrix} 2 \\ 2 \end{bmatrix}$$

$\therefore \quad x = 20,\ y = 20.$

Hence the manufacturer should produce 20 units each of products X and Y respectively.

10. Since under equilibrium conditions, Demand = Supply :

$$82 - 3p_1 + p_2 = 15p_1 - 5$$

$$\Rightarrow \quad 18p_1 - p_2 = 87 \qquad ...(1)$$

$$92 + 2p_1 - 4p_2 = 32p_2 - 6$$

$$\Rightarrow \quad -2p_1 + 36p_2 = 98 \qquad ...(2)$$

Rewriting the equations in matrix form as follows :

$$\begin{bmatrix} 18 & -1 \\ -2 & 36 \end{bmatrix} \begin{bmatrix} p_1 \\ p_2 \end{bmatrix} = \begin{bmatrix} 87 \\ 98 \end{bmatrix} \text{ or equivalently}$$

$$AX = B \qquad ...(3)$$

Also $|A| = 646 \neq 0$ and $\text{adj } A = \begin{bmatrix} 36 & 1 \\ 2 & 18 \end{bmatrix}$.

Since $|A| \neq 0$, A^{-1} exists and the solution is given by $X = A^{-1}B$.

$$\begin{bmatrix} p_1 \\ p_2 \end{bmatrix} = \begin{bmatrix} 18 & -1 \\ -2 & 36 \end{bmatrix}^{-1} \begin{bmatrix} 87 \\ 98 \end{bmatrix}$$

$$= \frac{1}{646} \begin{bmatrix} 36 & 1 \\ 2 & 18 \end{bmatrix} \begin{bmatrix} 87 \\ 98 \end{bmatrix} = \begin{bmatrix} 5 \\ 3 \end{bmatrix}$$

Hence, $p_1 = 5$ and $p_2 = 3$ are the required equilibrium prices.

11. Let *x* barrels of spray P, *y* barrels of spray Q and *z* barrels of spray R be used to just meet the requirements. Then according to the given data :

$$x + 2y + z = 8$$

$$2x + 3y + 2z = 14$$

$$3x + 2y + 2z = 13$$

The above system of equations can be expressed in the matrix form as :

$$\begin{bmatrix} 1 & 2 & 1 \\ 2 & 3 & 2 \\ 3 & 3 & 2 \end{bmatrix} \begin{bmatrix} x \\ y \\ z \end{bmatrix} = \begin{bmatrix} 8 \\ 14 \\ 13 \end{bmatrix} \text{ or equivalently}$$

$$AX = B$$

Since $|A| = 1 \neq 0$, A^{-1} exists and the solution is given by $X = A^{-1} B$.

It can be easily verified that :

$$A^{-1} = \begin{bmatrix} 2 & -2 & 1 \\ 2 & -1 & 0 \\ -5 & 4 & -1 \end{bmatrix}$$

Hence the solution of the given system of equations is given by :

$$\begin{bmatrix} x \\ y \\ z \end{bmatrix} = \begin{bmatrix} 2 & -2 & 1 \\ 2 & -1 & 0 \\ -5 & 4 & -1 \end{bmatrix} \begin{bmatrix} 8 \\ 14 \\ 13 \end{bmatrix} = \begin{bmatrix} 1 \\ 2 \\ 3 \end{bmatrix}$$

$\Rightarrow \quad x = 1,\ y = 2$ and $z = 3$.

Thus 1 barrel of P, 2 barrels of Q and 3 barrels of R must be used to just meet the requirements.

12. Let *x*, *y* and *z* represent the investment at the rate of interest of 6%, 8% and 9% per annum respectively. Then according to the given data, we have

$$x + y + z = 6{,}50{,}000$$

$$0.06x + 0.08y + 0.09z = 48{,}000$$

$$\Rightarrow \quad 6x + 8y + 9z = 48{,}00{,}000$$

$$0.09z = 0.08y + 6{,}000$$

$$\Rightarrow \quad -8y + 9z = 6{,}00{,}000$$

The above system of equations can be written in the matrix form as :

$$\begin{bmatrix} 1 & 1 & 1 \\ 6 & 8 & 9 \\ 0 & -8 & 9 \end{bmatrix}\begin{bmatrix} x \\ y \\ z \end{bmatrix} = \begin{bmatrix} 6,50,000 \\ 48,00,000 \\ 6,00,000 \end{bmatrix}$$

or equivalently AX = B

Since |A| = 42 ≠ 0, A^{-1} exists so that unique solution of AX = B is given by X = A^{-1} B. It can be easily verified that :

$$A^{-1} = \frac{\text{adj}\,A}{|A|} = \frac{1}{42}\begin{bmatrix} 144 & -17 & 1 \\ -54 & 9 & -3 \\ -48 & 8 & 2 \end{bmatrix}.$$

Substituting in (*), we get

$$\begin{bmatrix} x \\ y \\ z \end{bmatrix} = \frac{1}{42}\begin{bmatrix} 144 & -17 & 1 \\ -54 & 9 & -3 \\ -48 & 8 & 2 \end{bmatrix}\begin{bmatrix} 6,50,000 \\ 48,00,000 \\ 6,00,000 \end{bmatrix}$$

$$= \frac{1}{42}\begin{bmatrix} 1,26,00,000 \\ 63,00,000 \\ 84,00,000 \end{bmatrix} = \begin{bmatrix} 3,00,000 \\ 1,50,000 \\ 2,00,000 \end{bmatrix}$$

Hence x = ₹ 3,00,000; y = ₹ 1,50,000 and z = ₹ 2,00,000.

13. Let x, y and z denote the units of foods I, II and III respectively. Then using the given data, we obtain the following set of simultaneous linear equations:

$$x + y + z = 5$$
$$500x + 200y + 100z = 1,500$$
$$\Rightarrow \quad 5x + 2y + z = 15$$
$$300x + 600y + 700z = 2,500$$
$$\Rightarrow \quad 3z + 6y + 7z = 25$$

The above system of equations in matrix from, can be written as follows :

$$\begin{bmatrix} 1 & 1 & 1 \\ 5 & 2 & 1 \\ 3 & 6 & 7 \end{bmatrix}\begin{bmatrix} x \\ y \\ z \end{bmatrix} = \begin{bmatrix} 5 \\ 15 \\ 25 \end{bmatrix} \text{ or equivalently}$$

AX = B

Since |A| = 0, A^{-1} does not exist and the solution of AX = B is not unique. Now we shall solve the above system of equations by writing augmented matrix and using the concept of row operations.

The augmented matrix is :

$$[A \mid B] = \begin{bmatrix} 1 & 1 & 1 \\ 5 & 2 & 1 \\ 3 & 6 & 7 \end{bmatrix}\begin{bmatrix} 5 \\ 15 \\ 25 \end{bmatrix}$$

$$\sim \left[\begin{array}{ccc|c} 1 & 1 & 1 & 5 \\ 0 & -3 & -4 & -10 \\ 0 & 3 & 4 & 10 \end{array}\right]$$

[Operate $R_2' \to R_2' - 5R_1$ and $R_3' \to R_3 - 3R_1$]

$$\sim \left[\begin{array}{ccc|c} 1 & 1 & 1 & 5 \\ 0 & -3 & 1 & -10 \\ 0 & 0 & 0 & 10 \end{array}\right]$$

[Operate, $R_3' \to R_2 + R_3$]

$$\therefore \quad x + y + z = 5 \quad \text{...(1)}$$
$$-3y - 4z = -10 \quad \text{...(2)}$$

Solving (1) and (2), we get

$$3x + 3y + 3z = 15 \quad \text{...(3)}$$
$$3y + 4z = 10 \quad \text{...(4)}$$

Subtracting (4) from (3), we obtain

$$3x - z = 5 \Rightarrow x = \frac{5+z}{3} \geq 0, \text{ or } z \geq -5$$

and $$y = \frac{10-4z}{3} \geq 0 \text{ or } z \leq 2.5$$

Since z cannot take negative values, its range should be (0, 2.5) kg.

14. Let A be the technology matrix. Then A is given by $A = \begin{bmatrix} 0.1 & 40 \\ 0.01 & 0 \end{bmatrix}$

Let $X = \begin{bmatrix} x \\ y \end{bmatrix}$ be the output required to meet the final demand $D = \begin{bmatrix} 50 \\ 2 \end{bmatrix}$.

Then X is given by : X = $[I - A]^{-1}$ D

Now $I - A = \begin{bmatrix} 0.9 & -40 \\ -0.01 & 1 \end{bmatrix}$

$\Rightarrow \quad |I - A| = 0.9 - 0.4 = 0.5 \neq 0$

$\therefore \quad X = [I - A]^{-1} D$

$$= \frac{1}{0.5}\begin{bmatrix} 1 & 40 \\ 0.01 & 0.9 \end{bmatrix}\begin{bmatrix} 50 \\ 2 \end{bmatrix} = \begin{bmatrix} 260 \\ 4.6 \end{bmatrix}$$

Hence the gross output of two sectors—manufacturing and agriculture, for a given final demands, are 260 and 4.6 million units respectively.

Total labour requirement $= [4 \quad 100]\begin{bmatrix} 260 \\ 4.6 \end{bmatrix}$

$= [1{,}500]$

Thus, total labour requirement is 1,500 million man-hours. Equilibrium prices are given by :

$$\begin{bmatrix} p_1 \\ p_2 \end{bmatrix} = [(I - A)^{-1}]' \begin{bmatrix} l_1 w \\ l_2 w \end{bmatrix}$$

$$= \frac{1}{0.5}\begin{bmatrix} 1 & 0.01 \\ 40 & 0.9 \end{bmatrix}\begin{bmatrix} 40 \\ 1{,}000 \end{bmatrix} = \begin{bmatrix} 100 \\ 5{,}000 \end{bmatrix}$$

Thus, the equilibrium prices for two sectors are ₹ 100 and ₹ 5,000 respectively.

15. $\frac{dy}{dx} = 3x^2 - 3$ and $\frac{d^2y}{dx^2} = 6x$

First order condition for maxima/minima is :

$\frac{dy}{dx} = 0 \Rightarrow 3x^2 - 3 = 0$ or $x = \pm 1$.

Second order condition requires $\frac{d^2y}{dx^2} < 0$ for maxima and $\frac{d^2y}{dx^2} > 0$ for minima. Now at $x = 1$, $\frac{d^2y}{dx^2} = 6 > 0$ and at $x = -1$, $\frac{d^2y}{dx^2} = -6 < 0$.

$\therefore$ Maxima occurs at $x = -1$ and minima occurs at $x = 1$.

Hence maximum $y = (-1)^3 - 3(-1) - 1 = 1$ and minimum $y = (1)^3 - 3(1) - 1 = -1$.

16. Let the numbers be x and y and that $x > y$. By given data :

$$x - y = 100 \qquad \text{...(1)}$$

and $x^2 - 5y^2$ is maximum

Let $S = x^2 - 5y^2 = x^2 - 5(x - 100)^2 = -4x^2 + 1{,}000x - 50{,}000$.

Since S is given to be maximum, $dS/dx = 0$ and $d^2S/dx^2 < 0$ for the roots of $dS/dx = 0$.

Now $\frac{dS}{dx} = 0 \Rightarrow -8x + 1{,}000 = 0$,

i.e., $x = 125$

and $\frac{d^2S}{dx^2} = -8$, which remains negative for $x = 125$.

Since when $x = 125$, $y = 125 - 100 = 25$. Hence the required numbers are 125 and 25.

17. Here $\quad \frac{dx}{dl} = l - 0.003l^2$

and variable cost,

$$v = wl = 15l$$

$$MC = \frac{dv}{dx} = \frac{dv}{dl}\cdot\frac{dl}{dx} = \frac{15}{l - 0.003l^2}$$

When $\quad l = 150$,

$$MC = \frac{15}{150 - 67.5} = 0.182.$$

18. Here, $\frac{dC}{dq} = \frac{d}{dq}(0.2q^2 + q + 900) = 0.4q + 1$

and $\frac{dq}{dt} = \frac{d}{dt}(t^2 + 100t) = 2t + 100$

Now $\frac{dC}{dt} = \frac{dC}{dq}\cdot\frac{dq}{dt} = (0.4q + 1)(2t + 100)$

When $t = 2$, $q = 4 + 200 = 204$.

$\therefore \quad \frac{dC}{dt} = [0.4\,(204) + 1]\,(104) =$ ₹ 8,590.4.

19. Let a be the output so that the price p and the revenue R are :

$$p = 200 - 5q \text{ and } R = q(200 - 5q)$$
$$= 200q - 5q^2$$

Now $MR = \frac{d}{dq}(200q - 5q^2)$

$$= 200 - 10q \qquad \text{...(1)}$$

Also $AR = \frac{R}{q} = 200 - 5q \qquad \text{...(2)}$

Differentiating *w.r.t.* q, we get

Slope of $MR = \frac{d}{dq}(200 - 10q) = -10 \quad \text{...(3)}$

Slope of $AR = \frac{d}{dq}(200 - 5q) = -5 \quad \text{...(4)}$

Thus both the slopes are negative and slope of MR = 2 (slope of AR) ...(5)
Again marginal revenue, MR is zero if $200 - 10q = 0 \Rightarrow q = 20$ and $q = 200 - 100 = 100$.
Hence marginal revenue is zero, when $p = 100$. ...(6)

20. Total revenue = R = $p.x. = 12000x - 900x^2$, where $x = l^{1/3}$.
The marginal revenue product is given by the change in total revenue due to an additional unit of labour, *i.e.,*

$$MRP_1 = \frac{dR}{dl} = \frac{dR}{dx}\cdot\frac{dx}{dl}$$

$$= (12{,}000 - 1{,}800l^{1/3}).\frac{1}{3}l^{-2/3}$$

$$= \frac{4{,}000}{l^{2/3}} - \frac{1{,}800}{3l^{1/3}}$$

$$= \frac{4{,}000}{16} - \frac{1{,}800}{12} = 100.$$

21. Marginal propensity to consume = $\frac{dC}{dY}$ = $\frac{3}{4} - \frac{1}{6}\cdot\frac{1}{\sqrt{Y}}$.
When Y = 25,

$$\frac{dC}{dY} = \frac{3}{4} - \frac{1}{6}\cdot\frac{1}{\sqrt{125}} = \frac{43}{60} \simeq 0.716$$

The marginal propensity to save when Y = 25 is : Y – 0.716 = 0.284.

22. Differentiating, we get $x = 3p^2 + 7$ *w.r.t.* p, we get $\frac{dx}{dp} = 6p$

$$\therefore \quad \eta_s = \frac{p}{x}\cdot\frac{dx}{dp} = \frac{p}{3p^2+7}\cdot(6p) = \frac{6p^2}{3p^2+7}$$

When $p = 5$,

$$\eta_s = \frac{6(5)^2}{\{3(5)^2+7\}} = \frac{150}{82}.$$

23. Now $\eta_y = \frac{y}{x}\cdot\frac{dx}{dy} = \frac{y}{\{(20+5y)/50\}}\cdot\left(\frac{1}{10}\right)$

$$= \frac{5y}{20+5y}$$

When $y = 400$,

$$\eta_y = \frac{5\times 400}{20+5\times 400} = \frac{2{,}000}{2{,}020}.$$

24. Let x be the number of refrigerators in excess of 150 and R be the revenue of the distributor during the month of promotion. Then price charged per refregerator is given by :

$$p = 18{,}000 - \frac{1{,}000}{150}(x - 1{,}200)$$

$$= 26{,}000 - \frac{20}{3}x$$

Total revenue, $R = px = 26{,}000x - \frac{20}{3}x^2$

For maximum revenue $\frac{dR}{dx} = 0$ and $\frac{dR}{dx^2} < 0$.

Now $\frac{dR}{dx} = 26{,}000 - \frac{40}{3}x = 0 \Rightarrow x = 19{,}500$

and $\frac{d^2R}{dx^2} = -\frac{40}{3} < 0$ for all x.

$\therefore$ Maximum revenue is obtained when price charged for each refrigerator during the month of sales promotion is :

$$p = 26{,}000 - \frac{20}{3}\times 19{,}500 = ₹\ 13{,}000.$$

25. The profit function P(q) is given by :

$$P(q) = R(q) - C(q)$$
$$= (1{,}000q - 2q^2) - (q^3 - 59q^2 + 1{,}315q + 2{,}000)$$

First-order condition for maximum profit is :

$$\frac{dP}{dx} = 0 \Rightarrow 1000 - 4q - 3q^2 + 118q - 1{,}315 = 0 \text{ or } q^2 - 38q + 105 = 0$$

$$\Rightarrow q = \frac{38 \pm \sqrt{(38)^2 - 4\times 1\times 105}}{2} = 35 \text{ or } 3$$

Second-order condition for maximum profit requires $\frac{d^2P}{dx^2} < 0$.

At $q = 3$, $\frac{d^2P}{dq^2} = [-6q + 114]_{q=3}$

$$= -6 \times 3 + 114 > 0$$

and at $q = 35$, $\frac{d^2P}{dq^2} = -6 \times 35 + 114 < 0$

Hence the profit is maximum when the output level is 35 units.

26. From the given information, we have

Cost function : $C(q) = 5{,}000 + 90q$

Revenue function :

$$R(q) = (300 - 2\sqrt{q})q = 300q - 2q^{3/2}$$

Profit function:

$$P(q) = R(q) - C(q) = 210q - 2q^{3/2} - 5{,}000$$

First order condition for maximum profit is :

$$\frac{dP}{dq} = 0 \Rightarrow 210 - 3\sqrt{q} = 0 \text{ or } \sqrt{q} = 70, \textit{ i.e.,}$$

$q = 4{,}900$

Second-order condition for maximum profit requires $\frac{d^2P}{dq^2} < 0$.

Now $\frac{d^2P}{dq^2} = -\frac{3}{2\sqrt{q}} < 0$, when $q = 4{,}900$

Thus profit is maximum when manufacturer produces 4,900 shirts. At a production level of 4,900; total profit

$$P = 210 \times 4{,}900 - 2 \times (4{,}900)^{3/2} - 5{,}000$$
$$= 10{,}29{,}000 - 2 \times (70)^3 - 5{,}000$$
$$= ₹\ 3{,}38{,}000$$

Please note that if 4,900 shirts are sold, then they will be sold at a price of

$$P = 300 - 2 \times 70 = ₹\ 160 \text{ each.}$$

27. Let the advertisement run t days. Then net profit is given by :

$$4{,}00{,}000\ (1 - e^{-0.3t})\ 2 - (30{,}000 + 4{,}000t)$$
$= y$, say

First-order condition for maximum profit is :

$$\frac{dy}{dt} = 0 \Rightarrow 24{,}000\ e^{-0.3t} - 4{,}000 = 0$$

or $e^{-0.3t} = 60$

$$t = \frac{\log t}{0.3 \log e} = \frac{1.7782}{0.1303} = 13.6 \text{ days.}$$

Second-order condition for maximum profit requires $\frac{d^2y}{dt^2} < 0$.

Now $\frac{d^2y}{dt^2} = -7200\ e^{-0.3t} < 0$, for $t = 13.6$

Hence $t^* = 13.6$, *i.e.*, the advertisement should run for 13.6 days to earn maximum profit.

28. Differentiating $C(x) = x^3 - 315x^2 + 27{,}000x + 20{,}000$ *w.r.t.* x, we get

$$\frac{dC}{dx} = 3x^2 - 630x + 27{,}000$$

and $\frac{d^2C}{dx^2} = 6x - 630$

First-order condition for minimum cost is :

$$\frac{dC}{dx} = 0 \Rightarrow 3x^2 - 630x + 27{,}000 = 0$$

$\Rightarrow$ $x = 150$ or 60

Second-order condition for minimum cost requires $\frac{d^2C}{dx^2} > 0$.

Now $\frac{d^2C}{dx^2} = 6x - 630$ which is

$$\begin{cases} > 0, \text{ when } x = 150 \\ < 0, \text{ when } x = 60 \end{cases}$$

$\therefore$ Minimum cost occurs when $x^* = 150$.

Hence 150 units should be produced to minimize the total cost.

29. We have to find total increase in cost when x increases from 3,000 to 9,000 *i.e.,* we have to find

$$C(9) - C(3) = \int_3^9 \frac{dC}{dx}dx = \int_3^9 \frac{500x}{\sqrt{x^2+40}}dx$$

$$= 250\int_{49}^{121} \frac{1}{\sqrt{t}}dt,$$

where $x^2 + 40 = t$

$$= \left|250\, 2\sqrt{t}\right|_{49}^{121} = 500\left(\sqrt{121} - \sqrt{49}\right) = ₹\ 2{,}000.$$

30. To determine the total profit function, we must first find the antiderivative of the marginal profit function, or

$$P(x) = \int(-6x + 750)dx = -3x^2 + 750x + k \quad ...(*)$$

Given that $C(100) = 25{,}000$; we can solve for the value of k, which happens to represent the fixed cost.

$$25{,}000 = -3(100)^2 + 750(100) + k$$
$$\Rightarrow \quad k = -20{,}000$$

The specific function representing the total profit of producing the product is given by :

$$P(x) = -3x^2 + 750x - 20{,}000.$$

31. Since the rate of savings is given by $S(t) = 20{,}000\, e^{-0.5t}$ and the cost of device is estimated to be ₹ 32,000, therefore if it takes x years to recover the cost of device, then

$$\int_0^n 20{,}000\, e^{-0.5t}\, dt = 32{,}000$$

$$\Rightarrow \quad 20{,}000 \left| \frac{e^{-0.5t}}{-0.5} \right|_0^n = 32{,}000$$

$\Rightarrow -40{,}000\ (e^{-0.5n} - 1) = 32{,}000$

or $1 - e^{-0.5n} = 0.8$, *i.e.*, $e^{0.5n} = 5$

Taking logarithms on both sides, we obtain

$0.5n \log e = \log 5$

$$\therefore\ n = \frac{\log 5}{0.5 \log e} = \frac{0.6990}{0.4343} \times 2 = 3.22 \text{ years.}$$

32. We know $I = Prt \Rightarrow r = I/Pt$

Here $I = 1{,}240 - 1{,}200 = 40$,

$$P = 1{,}200,\ t = \frac{60}{360} = \frac{1}{6}.$$

$$\therefore \quad r = \frac{40}{1{,}200 \times (1/6)} = \frac{40}{200} = 0.20 \text{ or } 20\%.$$

33. We know $A = P(1 + rt)$

$$\Rightarrow \quad P = \frac{A}{1 + rt}.$$ Here we are given :

$$A = 20{,}400;\ r = 0.08 \text{ and } t = \frac{3}{12}.$$

$$\therefore \quad P = \frac{20{,}400}{1 + (0.08)(3/12)} = ₹\ 20{,}000.$$

34. Substituting $P = 12{,}000$; $A = 20{,}000$; $i = \frac{r}{m} = \frac{0.05}{4} = 0.0125$ in the formula:

$A = P(1 + i)^n$, we get $(1.0125)^n = 5/3$

$\Rightarrow n \log 1.0125 = \log 5 - \log 3$

$$\therefore\ n = \frac{0.6990 - 0.4771}{0.0052} = 42.67$$

quarterly periods or 10 years 8 months.

35. Substituting $P = 6{,}950$; $i = \frac{r}{m} = \frac{0.06}{2} = 0.03$ in the formula $A = P(1 + i)^n$,

$$A = 6{,}950\ (1.03)^4.$$

Taking logarithms of each sides, we obtain

$$\log A = \log 6{,}950 + 4 \log 1.03$$
$$= 3.8420 + 4\ (0.0128)$$
$$= 3.8420 + 0.0512 = 3.8932$$
$$\therefore \quad A = \text{Antilog}\ (3.8932) = 7{,}820,$$

which is the principal for the third year.

$$\text{Again, } A = 7{,}820\left(1 + \frac{0.09}{2}\right)^{2\times1} = 7{,}820(1.045)^2$$

∴ Taking logarithms of each sides, we get

$$\log A = \log 7{,}820 + 2 \log 1.045$$
$$= 3.8932 + 2 \times 0.0191$$
$$= 3.8932 + 0.0382 = 3.9314$$
$$\therefore \quad A = \text{Antilog}\ (3.9314) = 8{,}539$$

Hence, C.I. = 8,539 – 6,950 = ₹ 1,589.

36. Let the number of years to double the principal P be n.

Then by using the formula $A = P(1 + r)^n$, we obtain

$$2P = P\left(1 + \frac{7}{100}\right)^n \Rightarrow 2 = (1.07)^n$$

or $\log 2 = n \log 1.07$

$$\therefore \quad n = \frac{\log 2}{\log 1.06} = \frac{0.3010}{0.0294} = 10.24 \text{ years.}$$

37. The nominal or annual rate, r, compounded continuously must be such as to satisfy the equation : $3P = Pe^{12r} \Rightarrow e^{12r} = 3$

$12r \log e = \log 3$ or $12r\ (0.4343) = 0.4771$

$$\therefore\ r = \frac{0.4771}{12(0.4343)} = \frac{0.4771}{5.2116} = 0.091546$$

Hence the nominal rate of interest compounded continuously is 9.15%.

38. Since the money-lender charges interest at the rate of ₹ 5 per ₹ 100 per quarter, payable in advance, ₹ 5 may be treated as interest on ₹ 95 for one month. Consequently, interest rate per month is $i = \frac{5}{95}$ or $\frac{1}{19}$. Thus the effective rate of interest is 100 r_e% per annum and is given by :

$$r_e = \left(1+\frac{1}{19}\right)^4 - 1 = \left(\frac{20}{19}\right)^4 - 1$$

$$\Rightarrow \quad 1 + r_e = \left(\frac{20}{19}\right)^4.$$

Taking logarithm of each sides, we obtain

$\log (1 + r_e) = 4 (\log 20 - \log 19)$
$= 4 (1.3010 - 1.2788) = 0.0888$

$\therefore \quad 1 + r_e = \text{Antilog } (0.0888) = 1.227$

$\Rightarrow \quad r_e = 0.227.$

Hence the effective rate of interest is 100 r_e% = 22.7%.

39. Substituting $r = 0.07$ in the formula $r_e = e^r - 1$, we obtain

$$r_e = e^{0.07} - 1 \text{ or } r_e + 1 = e^{0.07}$$

Taking the logarithms of each sides, we get

$\log (r_e + 1) = 0.07 \log e = 0.07 (0.4343)$
$= 0.030401$

$\therefore \quad r_e + 1 = \text{Antilog } (0.030401) = 1.073$

Hence the effective rate of interest is 100 r_e% = 7.3%.

40. Substituting $r_e = 0.09$ in $r_e = e^r - 1$, we get $0.09 = e^r - 1 \Rightarrow e^r = 1.09$ or $r \log e = \log 1.09$

$$\therefore \quad r = \frac{\log 1.09}{\log e} = \frac{0.0374}{0.4343} = 0.08611$$

Hence the force of interest is 8.61%. In other words 8.61% compounded continuously and 9% effective are equivalent rates.

41. Substituting A = ₹ 2,00,000, $i = \frac{0.04}{4} = 0.01$ and $n = 4$, in $P = A(1 + i)^{-n}$, we have

$$P = \frac{2,00,000}{(1+0.01)^4} = \frac{2,00,000}{(1.01)^4} = \frac{2,00,000}{1.0406}$$

$\approx$ ₹ 19,21,960.

42. Here P_1 = Present value of ₹ 10,000

$= 10,000 (1 + 0.02)^{-2}$

$= 10,000 (0.96116878) =$ ₹ 9611.7

P_2 = Present value of ₹ 20,000

$= 20,000 (1 + 0.02)^{-6}$

$= 20,000 (0.88797138) =$ ₹ 17759.4

Hence $P = P_1 + P_2 = 9,611.7 + 17,759.4$

= ₹ 27,371.1

43. Substituting S = 5,000; $i = 0.05$ & $n = 5$ in the formula : $P = A(1 + i)^{-n}$, we get

$P = 5,000 (1 + 0.05)^{-5} = 5,000 (1.05)^{-5}$

$= 5,000 (0.783527) =$ ₹ 3,917.6

Thus, compound discount = A – P = 5,000 – 3,917.6 = ₹ 1,082.4.

44. The scrap value of the machine is given by :

$D = B (1 - i)^n$, where B = 40,000;

$i = 0.10$ and $n = 15$.

$\therefore D = 40,000 (1 - 0.10)^{15} = 40,000 (90/100)^{15}$

Taking logarithm of each sides, we obtain

$\log D = \log 40,000 + 15 (\log 90 - \log 100)$

$= 4.6021 + 15 (1.9542 - 2)$

$= 4.6021 - 0.687 = 3.9151$

Hence D = Antilog (3.9151) = ₹ 8224.

45. The scrap value of the item is given by : $D = B(1 - i)^n$, where B = 20, D = 7.5,

$$d = \frac{10}{100} = \frac{1}{10} n = ?$$

$$\text{Now} \quad 7.5 = 20\left(1+\frac{1}{10}\right)^n = 20\left(\frac{9}{10}\right)^n$$

$$\Rightarrow \left(\frac{9}{10}\right)^n = \frac{7.5}{20}$$

Taking logarithm of each sides, we get

$n (\log 9 - \log 10) = \log 7.5 - \log 20$

$\Rightarrow n (0.9542 - 1) = 0.8751 - 1.3010$

$\Rightarrow \quad n \times -0.0458 = -0.4259$

$$\therefore \quad n = \frac{-0.4259}{-0.0458} = \frac{4259}{458} = 9.3 \text{ years.}$$

47. This is an ordinary annuity consisting of 10 payments of ₹ 5,000 each, interest being 0.04 per period. Thus the required amount in the account is given by :

$$S = R\left[\frac{(1+i)^n - 1}{0.04}\right];$$

where R = 5,000, $n = 10$ and $i = \frac{0.08}{2} = 0.04$.

$$\therefore \quad S = 5,000\left[\frac{(1.04)^{10} - 1}{i}\right]$$

$= 1,25,000 [(1.04)^{10} - 1]$

$= 1,25,000 [(\text{Antilog } 10 \log 1.04) - 1]$

= 1,25,000 [(Antilog 10 × 0.0170) – 1]
= 1,25,000 [(Antilog 0.17) – 1]
= 1,25,000 (1.479 – 1) = ₹ 59.875.

Aliter: Using the formula, S = R $s_{\overline{n}|i}$; where R = 5,000; $i = \frac{0.08}{2}$, $n = 10$, we obtain

S = 5,000 $s_{\overline{10}|0.04}$, where $s_{\overline{10}|0.04}$ = 12.006107

Hence, the required amount
= 5,000 × 12.006107 = ₹ 60,030.535.

48. Using the formula $S = R\left[\frac{(1+i)^n - 1}{i}\right]$; where S = 5,00,000; $n = 20$, $r = \frac{5}{100}$ or 0.05, we obtain

Let	$x = (1.05)^{20}$
	$\log x = 20 \log 1.05$
	$= 20 \times 0.0212 = 0.4240$
Thus	x = Antilog (0.4240)
	= 2.655

$$5{,}00{,}000 = \frac{R}{0.05}(2.655 - 1)$$

$$\therefore \quad R = \frac{5{,}00{,}000 \times 0.05}{1.655} = ₹\ 15{,}105.$$

173. $\bar{x} = \left(1\Big/\sum_{k=1}^{n} k^2\right).\sum_{1}^{n} k.k^2$

$$= \frac{n^2(n+1)^2.6}{4.n(n+1)(2n+1)} = \frac{3}{2}\frac{n(n+1)}{(2n+1)}.$$

174. $\bar{x} = \frac{9\times 100 + 6\times 80}{9+6} = 92.$

175. By the result mode = 3 median – 2 mean assuming mean > med > mode
mean – mode = 3 (mean – median)
∴ 63 = 3 (mean – median)
i.e., mean – median = 21.

176. $\sigma = \sqrt{\left[\frac{\Sigma x^2}{n} - \left(\frac{\Sigma x}{n}\right)^2\right]}$

$$= \sqrt{\left\{\frac{n(n+1)(2n+1)}{6n} - \frac{n^2(n+1)^2}{4n^2}\right\}}$$

$$= \sqrt{\left\{\frac{n^2-1}{12}\right\}}.$$

177. $\bar{x} = \frac{\frac{2n+1}{2}.[a + a + 2nd]}{(2n+1)} = a + nd$

$\Sigma\,|\,x - \bar{x}\,| = 2d\,[1 + 2 + ... + n] = n\,(n+1)d$

$\therefore \quad$ M.D. $= \frac{n(n+1)d}{2n+1}$.

180. $r = \frac{\text{cov.}(x,y)}{\sigma_x \sigma_y} \Rightarrow \sigma_y = \frac{\text{cov.}(x,y)}{r.\sigma_x} = \frac{16}{(0.5)\times 4} = 8.$

182. Equations of regression lines are
$3x + 2y = 26$ ...(1)
and $6x + y = 331$ ...(2)
(1) can be rewritten as

$$x = -\frac{2}{3}y + \frac{26}{3} \text{ or } y = -\frac{3}{2}x + 13$$

and (2) can be rewritten as
$x = (1/16)y + 31/6$ or y –6x + 31

Since b_{xy}, $b_{yx} \le 1$, we have
$b_{yx} = 3/2$ and $b_{xy} = -1/6$
∴ $r^2 = (-3/2)\,(-1/6) = 1/4$

Since $b_{xy} < 0$, $r < 0$ so $r - 1/2 = -0.5$.

183. Let the teacher's age is x year.

$$\therefore \quad 15 + 1 = \frac{20\times 15 + x}{21}$$

⇒ 16 × 21 = 300 + x
⇒ x = 336 – 300 = 36 yr.

184. Since, monthly salary = ₹ 15000
and sector angle of expenses = 15°

$$\therefore \text{ Amount} = \frac{15°}{360°}\times 15000 = ₹\,625.$$

187. Since, coefficient of variance $= \frac{\text{SD}}{\text{Mean}} \times 100$

Coefficient of variance A $= \frac{\sqrt{12}}{60}\times 100 = 57\%$

Coefficient of variance B $= \frac{\sqrt{25}}{90}\times 100 = 5.5\%$

Coefficient of variance C = $\frac{\sqrt{36}}{80} \times 100 = 7.5\%$

Coefficient of variance D = $\frac{\sqrt{16}}{120} \times 100 = 3.3\%$

Hence, we see that minimum coefficient of variance is D, product is consistent.

189. The regression coefficient y on x on the line

$8x - 10y = 66, b_{yx} = \frac{4}{5}$

The regression coefficient x on y on the line

$40x - 18y = 214, b_{yx} = \frac{9}{20}$

$\Rightarrow \quad r^2 = \frac{36}{100} \quad \Rightarrow \quad r = 0.6$

$\Rightarrow \quad b_{yx} = \frac{r\sigma_y}{\sigma_x} \quad \Rightarrow \quad \sigma_y = \frac{\frac{4}{5} \times 3}{0.6}$

$\Rightarrow \quad \sigma_y = \frac{12}{3} = 4.$

190. Total ways = 6 × 6 = 36
Total 5 can be obtained in the following 4 ways
1 + 4, 2 + 3, 3 + 2, 4 + 1
∴ Required probability = 4/36 = 1/9.

191. Leap year consists of 366 days, *i.e.,* 52 weeks having 52 Sundays and 2 days. These two days can be as follows.
Sun and Mon, Mon and Tues, Tues and Wed, Wed and Thrus, Thurs and Fri, Fri and Sat, Sat and Sun.
Out of these seven events, Sunday occurs in 2 events.
∴ Required probability =2/7.

192. Total number of ways = ${}^{100}C_1 = 100$
Favourable numbers are $1^2, 2^2, ..., 10^2$.
Therefore favourable ways = 10
∴ Probability = 10/100 = 1/10.

193. Let P(B) = x, P(A) = $2x/3$
P(A) + P(B) ⇒ $x + 2x/3 = 1 \Rightarrow 5x/3 = 1$
⇒ $x = 3/5$
P(A) = 2/5, P(B) = 3/5

Odds in favours of B = $\frac{3/5}{1-3/5} = \frac{3}{2}$.

194. Probability of a coupon selected with any number from 1 to 8 = 8/12.
In six trails:
P (number from 1 to 8) = $(8/12)^6$
or P = $(2/3)^6$.

195. We have the following pattern:
I red, white $\quad P_I = 3 \times 4/{}^{12}C_2$
II red, blue $\quad P_{II} = 3 \times 5/{}^{12}C_2$
III blue, white $P_{III} = 4 \times 5/{}^{12}C_2$
Since all these cases are exclusive, so the required probability = $(12 + 15 + 20)/{}^{12}C_2$
$= (47 \times 2)/(12 \times 11) = 47/66.$

196. Since the events A, B and C are mutually exclusive, we have

$P(A \cup B \cup C) = \frac{2}{3} + \frac{1}{4} + \frac{1}{6} = \frac{13}{12} > 1,$

which is not possible.
Hence the statement is false.

197. Total number of 5 digit numbers obtained by the digits 1, 2, 3, 4, 5, 6 and 8.
$= {}^7P_5 = 7.6.5.4.3 = 2520$
There are 4 even digits (2, 4, 6 and 8).
∴ 2 even digits can be selected in
${}^4C_2 = 6$ ways
∴ The two ends can be filled in
2 × 6 = 12 ways
Remaining 3 places from remaining 5 digits can be filled in ${}^5P_3 = 60$ ways.

Hence the required probability = $\frac{12 \times 60}{2520} = \frac{2}{7}$.

198. $P(\text{ace}) = \frac{4}{52} = \frac{1}{13}$

$P(\text{king}) = \frac{4}{52} = \frac{1}{13}$

P (2 aces and one king)

$= {}^3C_2 \cdot \left(\frac{1}{13}\right)^2 \left(\frac{1}{13}\right) = \frac{3}{(13)^3}.$

202. $P(A \cap B) = P(A) + P(B) - P(A \cup B)$
$= 0.4 + 0.3 - 0.7 = 0$
∴ $P(A \cap B) \neq P(A)\,P(B)$ so A and B are not independent.
{Since $P(A \cap B) \neq 1$, A and B are not exhaustive.}
$P(A \cap B) = 0$ gives A and B are mutually exclusive.

203. Probability of getting head on a coin = 1/2.
Probability of getting 1 or 2 on a dice = 2/6.

∴ Probability of getting heads on both coin and 1 or 2 on dice is $1/2 \times 1/2 \times 2/6 = 1/12$.

204. Let probability of getting an odd number be p, then the probability of getting an even number is $2p$. Then probability of getting any face is $3.2p + 3.p = 1 \Rightarrow p = 1/9$. Now sum of the two numbers is even if both are even or both are odd.

$$\therefore \text{ Probability} = 3.\frac{2}{9}.3.\frac{2}{9} + 3.\frac{1}{9}.3.\frac{1}{9}$$

$$= \frac{4}{9} + \frac{1}{9} = \frac{5}{9}.$$

205. Favourable ways = 2!.8!.

Total ways of arrangement of 10 persons $= (10 - 1)! = 9!$

$$\therefore \quad P = \frac{2!8!}{9!} = \frac{2}{9}.$$

206. Total ways of arranging letters of words

$$\text{ALLAHABAD} = \frac{9!}{4!2!}$$

Favourable ways = 4!.2!.5!

$$\therefore \quad p = \frac{4!2!5!4!2!}{9!} = \frac{1}{63}.$$

207. P (getting correct club) = 1/5

∴ P (hitting good shot by this correct club) $= 1/3 \times 1/5 = 1/15$

P (getting wrong club) = 4/5

P (hitting good shot with wrong club) $= 4/5 \times 1/4 = 1/5$

∴ P (hitting good shot) = 1/15 + 1/5 = 4/15.

208. Leaving two tallest boys the remaining 98 boys can be divided into two equal groups containing 49 boys each in 98!/(49!)(49!).2 ways. Two tallest boys can be distributed in two groups (one in each) in 2 ways.

$$\therefore \text{ Favourable ways} = \frac{98!.2}{(49)!(49)!.2} \quad ...(1)$$

Also 100 boys can be distributed in 2 equal groups of 50 each in

$$\frac{100!}{50!.50!.2} \text{ ways} \quad ...(2)$$

Hence, the required probability.

$$= \frac{98! \cdot 2}{49!\,49! \cdot 2} \div \frac{100!}{50!\,50! \cdot 2} = 50/99.$$

209. Let P(A) be probability of throwing that 5 and P(B) the probability of throwing total 7.

∴ P(A) = 4/36 = 1/9, P(B) = 6/36 = 1/6

P(A or B) = 5/18 as $A \cap B = \phi$

P(C) P(neither A nor B) = 13/18

∴ P(5 before 7)

$$= \frac{1}{9} + \frac{13}{18} \times \frac{1}{9} + \frac{15}{18} \times \frac{13}{18} \times \frac{1}{9} \ldots \infty$$

$$= \frac{1}{9}\left[\frac{1}{1-(13/18)}\right] = 2/5.$$

210. Favourable ways of selecting 5 non-defective bulbs = ${}^{90}C_5$.

Total no. of ways of selection = ${}^{100}C_5$

$$\therefore \text{ P (non-defective bulbs)} = \frac{{}^{90}C_5}{{}^{100}C_5}.$$

211. $$\text{P (both are ace)} = \frac{4}{16} \times \frac{3}{15} = \frac{1}{20}$$

$$\text{P (one is ace)} = \frac{1}{4}.\frac{12}{15} + \frac{12}{16}.\frac{4}{15} = \frac{2}{5}$$

$$\therefore \text{ P (at least one is ace)} = \frac{1}{20} + \frac{2}{5} = \frac{9}{20}.$$

212. P(A speaks truth) = 3/5, $P(\bar{A}) = 2/5$

P (B speaks truth) = 7/10, $P(\bar{B}) = 3/10$

P (both speak truth) = (3/5).(7/10) = 21/50

P (both speak false) = (2/5).(3/10) = 6/50

P (both say same thing) = 21/50 + 6/50 = 27/50 = 0.54.

214. Let A be event that the first one of the two selected mangoes is good and B is the event that other one is also good. We have to find P(B/A).

$$P(B/A) = \frac{P(A \cap B)}{A(A)} = \frac{O(A \cap B)}{O(A)}$$

$$= \frac{{}^6C_2}{{}^6C_2 + {}^6C_1.{}^4C_1} = \frac{5}{13}.$$

215. Probability of getting greater than 4 from a unbiased die = 1/3.

Probability (greater than 4 on 2nd, 4th, 6th, ... throw)

$$= \frac{2}{3}.\frac{1}{3} + \left(\frac{2}{3}\right)^3.\frac{1}{3} + \left(\frac{2}{3}\right)^5.\frac{1}{3} + \ldots = \frac{2/9}{1-4/9} = 2/5.$$

BUSINESS ORGANIZATION, MANAGEMENT, BUSINESS LAW, COMPANY LAW & INCOME TAX LAW

Business Organization

Business

Business may be defined as an activity involving regular production or purchase of goods and services for sale, transfer and exchange with an object of earning profit.

Classification of Business Activities

We can classify business as Industry and Commerce.

Industry

Industry primarily refers to all such business activities concerned with production/raising or processing of goods and services. It processes raw materials or semi-finished goods into finished goods. Extracting raw materials from earth's surface, manufacturing goods and commodities, producing crops, fish, flowers, etc., constructing buildings, dams, roads etc. are all examples of industry.

Commerce

All goods and services produced are to be made available by those who need them. This involves a number of additional activities. For example when somebody produces bread, he has to make it available at convenient locations at right time. This involves activities like making people aware about the product, storing the product at right places, arranging retail outlets, packaging the product, transportation of the product, selling the product and so on. All these activities taken together are known as Commerce. It provides the necessary link between producers and consumers of goods and services and facilitates the purchase and sale of goods and services. In fact, it performs all functions, that are essential for maintaining a smooth and uninterrupted flow of goods and services to the customers. Thus, commerce involves:

(a) Buying and selling of goods and services; and

(b) Activities essential for the smooth and uninterrupted flow of goods and services from the point of production to the point of consumption.

The first activity, that is, purchase and sale of goods and services is termed as Trade, and the second activity i.e., the activities that ensure smooth flow of goods to customers are known as 'Auxiliaries to trade' or 'Aids to trade'. Thus, commerce is classified as:

(1) Trade; and

(2) Auxiliaries to trade.

Electronic Commerce

Commerce involves buying and selling and support services like transport, insurance, banking, communication etc. When all these activities are undertaken using information and communication technologies, it is termed as Electronic Commerce or e-Commerce. In other words, e-Commerce refers to the process of conducting business with the help of electronic devices using the computer and interconnected telecommunication network. Here, offer for sale and its acceptance are made electronically through Internet.

It does not require physical interaction between the parties concerned. It is also known as 'on-line trading', 'on-line shopping' and 'e-shopping'.

e-Commerce takes place between companies i.e., business to business (B2B), between companies and their customers (B2C), and customer to customer (C2C).

B2B refers to interactions between a manufacturer and a supplier of materials and services, or between a manufacturer and a wholesaler, or between a wholesaler and a retailer. A network of computers is used for making enquiries seeking or placing orders, communicating supply of goods, making payments, and so on.

B2C, as the name implies, have business firms (manufacturer or retailers) at one end and its consumers on the other. It enables a business firm to be in touch with its customers on round the clock basis. It involves a wide range of marketing activities including promotion, seeking orders, intimating supply and so on.

C2C usually involves consumers at both ends dealing in goods for which there is no established market mechanism as is the case with used books and household equipments.

Outsourcing of Services

Outsourcing is a management strategy by which an organisation contracts out its major non-core functions to specialised service providers with a view to benefit from their expertise, efficiency and cost effectiveness, and allow managers to concentrate on their core activities. The Information Technology (IT) is one area in which this approach is growing fast, and in recent years, outsourcing the operation of IT systems has been supplemented by a move to outsourcing the whole business processes such as payroll processing, cheque processing, etc. This is known as BPO (Business Process Outsourcing).

Entrepreneurship

Entrepreneur is a person who tries to do something new, visualises a business opportunity, organises the necessary resources for setting up the business and bears the risk involved. Thus, an entrepreneur may be termed as an innovator, an organiser and a risk bearer.

The term 'entrepreneurship' refers to the functions performed by an entrepreneur. It is the process involving various actions to be undertaken by the entrepreneur in establishing a new enterprise. In fact, what an entrepreneur does is regarded as entrepreneurship.

Qualities of Successful Entrepreneur

(a) Initiative
(b) Wide Knowledge
(c) Willingness to assume risk
(d) Open mind and optimistic outlook
(e) Adaptability
(f) Self-confidence
(g) Leadership Qualities
(h) Orientation towards hard work

Functions of an Entrepreneur

The functions of an entrepreneur can be summarised as follows:

(a) Conception of an idea
(b) Promotion
(c) Innovation
(d) Bearer of risks and uncertainty
(e) Arranging necessary capital
(f) Staffing

Business Organisation

To carry out any business and achieve its objective of earning profit it is required to bring together all the resources and put them into action in a systematic way, and coordinate and control these activities properly. This arrangement is known as business organisation.

Forms of Business Organisation

A business organisation usually takes the following forms in India:

(1) Sole proprietorship
(2) Partnership
(3) Joint Hindu Family
(4) Cooperative Society
(5) Joint Stock Company

Sole Proprietorship

The term 'sole' means single and 'proprietorship' means 'ownership'. So, only one person is the owner of the business organisation. This means, that a form of business organisation in which a single individual owns and manages the business, takes the profits and bears the losses, is known as sole proprietorship form of business organisation.

Characteristics of Sole Proprietorship form of Business Organisation

(a) Single Ownership
(b) No Separation of Ownership and Management
(c) Less Legal Formalities
(d) No Separate Entity
(e) No Sharing of Profit and Loss
(f) Unlimited Liability
(g) One-man Control

Partnership

'Partnership' is an association of two or more persons who pool their financial and managerial resources and agree to carry on a business, and share its profit. The persons who form a partnership are individually known as partners and collectively a firm or partnership firm.

Partnership form of business organisation in India is governed by the Indian Partnership Act, 1932 which defines partnership as "the relation between persons who have agreed to share the profits of the business carried on by all or any of them acting for all".

Characteristics of Partnership form of Business Organisation

(a) Two or More Persons
(b) Contractual Relationship
(c) Sharing Profits and Business
(d) Existence of Lawful Business
(e) Principal Agent Relationship
(f) Principal Agent Relationship
(g) Voluntary Registration

Types of Partners

(A) **Based on the extent of participation** in the day-to-day management of the firm partners can be classified as 'Active Partners' and 'Sleeping Partners'.

(B) **Based on sharing of profits,** the partners may be classified as 'Nominal Partners' and 'Partners in Profits'.

(C) **Based on Liability,** the partners can be classified as 'Limited Partners' and 'General Partners'. The liability of limited partners is limited to the extent of their capital contribution. The partners having unlimited liability are called as general partners or partners with unlimited liability.

(D) **Based on the behaviour and conduct exhibited,** there are two more types of partners besides the ones discussed above. These are (a) Partner by Estoppel; and (b) Partner by Holding out. A person who behaves in the public in such a way as to give an impression that he/she is a partner of the firm, is called 'partner by estoppel'. Such partners are not entitled to share the profits of the firm, but are fully liable if some body suffers because of his/her false representation. Similarly, if a partner or partnership firm declares that a particular person is a partner of their firm, and such a person does not disclaim it, then he/she is known as 'partner by Holding out'.

Formation of Partnership form of Business Organisation

The following steps are to be taken in order to form a partnership firm:

(a) Minimum two members are required to form a partnership. The maximum limit is ten in banking and 20 in other businesses.
(b) Select the like-minded persons keeping in view the nature and objectives of the business.
(c) There must be an agreement among the partners to carry on the business and share the profits and losses. This agreement must preferably be in writing and duly signed by all the partners. The agreement, i.e., the partnership deed must contain the following:
  (i) Name of the firm
  (ii) Nature of the business
  (iii) Names and addresses of partners
  (iv) Location of business
  (v) Duration of partnership, if decided
  (vi) Amount of capital to be contributed by each partner
  (vii) Profit and loss sharing ratio
  (viii) Duties, powers and obligations of partners.
  (ix) Salaries and withdrawals of the partners
  (x) Preparation of accounts and their auditing.
  (xi) Procedure for dissolution of the firm etc.
  (xii) Procedure for settlement of disputes

(d) The partners should get their firm registered with the Registrar of Firms of the concerned state. Although registration is not compulsory, but to avoid the consequences of non-registration, it is advisable to get it registered when it is setup or at any time during its existence.

Dissolution of Partnership Firm

Dissolution of partnership firm means putting an end to the relationship among the partners. This may be of two types: they are

(a) Dissolution of firm

(b) Dissolution of partnership

(a) Dissolution of firm

Dissolution of firm means dissolution of partnership. On dissolution of firm, partnership business comes to an end. Its assets are realised and the creditors are paid off. The business cannot be continued after dissolution of partnership firm.

(b) Dissolution of partnership

Dissolution of partnership means the termination of the original partnership agreement. A partnership is dissolved by insolvency, retirement, expiry or completion of the term of partnership. The business will continue after dissolution of partnership.

The various circumstances leading to dissolution of partnership firm can be summarised by taking the first letters used in the term "Dissolution".

D – Death of partner
I – Incapacity of a partner
S – Stipulated period of partnership completed in the case of particular partnership
S – Serious misconduct of a partner
O – Object is completed (Particular partnership)
L – Lunacy of a partner
U – Unavoidable continuous loss
T – Transfer of interest of the firm
I – Insolvency of a partner
O – Objectionable unlawful objectives
N – Notice of dissolution by a partner.

Modes of dissolution of Partnership

1. Dissolution by Agreement

2. Compulsory Dissolution

3. Dissolution on the happening of certain contingencies: A partnership may be dissolved on the happening of the following contingencies:

(a) Death of a partner.

(b) Expiry of the time, if partnership is for a fixed period.

(c) Completion of the venture for which the firm was formed.

(d) Adjudication of a partner as an insolvent.

4. Dissolution by notice of partnership-at-will

5. Dissolution through Court

Joint Hindu Family form of Business Organisation

The Joint Hindu Family (JHF) business is a form of business organisation run by Hindu Undivided Family (HUF), where the family members of three successive generations own the business jointly. The head of the family known as Karta manages the business. The other members are called co-parceners and all of them have equal ownership right over the properties of the business.

The membership of the JHF is acquired by virtue of birth in the same family. There is no restriction for minors to become the members of the business. As per Dayabhaga system of Hindu Law, both male and female members are the joint owners. But Mitakashara system of Hindu Law says only male members of the family can become the coparceners. While the Dayabhaga system is applicable to the state of West Bengal, Mitakshara system of Hindu Law is applicable to the rest of the country.

Formation of JHF form of Business Organisation

A Joint Hindu Family business is formed as per the provision of Hindu law. It comes into existence on the death of the person who established the business. His successor automatically become the coparceners if they decide to continue it as a joint family business. The children become its members by birth. The senior most member of the family will become the Karta of the business. No legal formalities are required for its establishment. But it has to be registered with the Income tax department to avail the tax concessions involved.

Cooperative Society

The term cooperation is derived from the Latin word 'co-operari', where the word 'co' means 'with' and 'operari' mean 'to work'. Thus, the term cooperation means working together. So those who want to work together with some common economic objectives can form a society, which is termed as cooperative society.

The Section 4 of the Indian Cooperative Societies Act 1912 defines Cooperative Society as "a society, which has its objectives for the promotion of economic interests of its members in accordance with cooperative principles."

Characteristics of Cooperative Society

(*a*) **Voluntary Association**

(*b*) **Open Membership**

(*c*) **Number of Members:** A minimum of 10 members are required to form a cooperative society. In case of multi-state cooperative societies the minimum number of members should be 50 from each state in case the members are individuals. The Cooperative Society Act does not specify the maximum number of members for any cooperative society.

(*d*) **Registration of the Society:** In India, cooperative societies are registered under the Cooperative Societies Act 1912 or under the State Cooperative Societies Act. The Multi-state Cooperative Societies are registered under the Multi-state Cooperative Societies Act 2002. Once registered, the society becomes a separate legal entity and attain certain characteristics.

(*e*) **State Control:** Since registration of cooperative societies is compulsory, every cooperative society comes under the control and supervision of the government.

(*f*) **Return on Capital Investment:** The members get return on their capital investment in the form of dividend.

(*g*) **Distribution of Surplus:** After giving a limited dividend to the members of the society, the surplus profit is distributed in the form of bonus, keeping aside a certain percentage as reserve and for general welfare of the society.

Types of Cooperative Societies

(a) Consumers' Cooperative Societies
(b) Producers' Cooperative Societies
(c) Marketing Cooperative Societies
(d) Housing Cooperative Societies
(e) Farming Cooperative Societies
(f) Credit Cooperative Societies

Joint Stock Company

A Joint Stock Company or simply a company is a voluntary association of persons generally formed for undertaking some big business activity. It is established by law and can be dissolved by law. The company has a separate legal existence so that even if its members die, the company remains in existence. Its members contribute money for some **common purpose.** The money so contributed constitutes the **capital** of the company. The capital of the company is divided into small units called **shares**. Since members invest their money by purchasing the shares of the company, they are known as **shareholders** and the capital of the company is known as **share capital**.

In India, the joint stock companies are governed by the Companies Act, 1956. According to the Act, a company means 'a company formed and registered under this Act or an existing company'. An existing company means a company formed and registered under any of the previous Companies Acts. This definition is not exhaustive enough to reveal the basic features of the company. However, based on the definition given in the previous Companies Act and various judicial decisions, it can be defined as 'an artificial person created by law, having a separate legal entity, with a perpetual succession'.

Characteristics of Joint Stock Company

(a) Artificial Person: A joint stock company is an artificial person in the sense that it is created by law and does not possess physical attributes of a natural person. It cannot eat or walk, smile or marry, read or write. However, it has a legal status like a natural person.

(b) Formation: The formation of a joint stock company is time consuming and it involves preparation of several documents and compliance of several legal requirements before it starts its operation. A company comes into existence only when it is registered under the Indian Companies Act.

(c) Separate Legal Entity: Being an artificial person, a company exists independent of its members. It can make contracts, purchase and sell things, employ people and conduct any lawful business in its own name. It can sue and can be sued in the court of law. A shareholder cannot be held responsible for the acts of the company.

(d) Common Seal: Since a company has no physical existence, it must act through its Board of Directors. But all contracts entered by them shall have to be under the common seal of the company. This common seal is the official signature of the company. Any document with the common seal and duly signed by an officer of the company is binding on the company.

(e) Perpetual Existence: The company enjoys continuous existence. Death, lunacy, insolvency or retirement of the members does not affect the life of the company. It goes on forever. Since it is created by law, it can only be dissolved by law.

(f) Limited Liability of Members: The company form of business is able to attract large number of people to invest their money in shares because it offers them the facility of limited risk and liability. The liability of a member is limited to the extent of the amount of shares he holds.

(g) Transferability of Shares: The members of the company (Public company) are free to transfer the shares held by them to others as and when they like. They do not need the consent of other shareholders to transfer their shares.

(h) Membership: To form a joint stock company, a minimum of two members are required in case it is private limited company and seven members in case of public limited company. The maximum limit is fifty incase of private limited company. There is no maximum limit of membership for a public limited company.

(i) Democratic Management: You know that people of different categories and areas contribute towards the capital of a company. So, it is not possible for them to look after the day-to-day management of the company. They may take part in deciding the general policies of the company but the day-to-day affairs of the company are managed by their elected representatives, called Directors.

KINDS OF COMPANIES

Statutory Companies

Companies established by Special Acts of Parliament or State Legislatures are called statutory companies.

Registered Companies

Companies which are registered under The Companies Act, 1956 are called registered companies.

Holding and Subsidiary Companies

A company becomes a holding company of another

(i) if it can appoint or remove all or majority of the directors of the latter company or

(ii) if it holds more than 50% of the equity share capital of the latter or

(iii) if it can exercise more than 50% of the total voting power of the latter.

The other company which is so controlled is called subsidiary company.

Government Companies

A Government company is one in which not less than 51% of the paid up capital is held by the Central Government or by any one or more State Governments or partly by the Central Governments and partly by one or more State Governments.

Public Limited Companies

The public is invited to subscribe to the shares of the company usually by issuing a prospectus. Shares are easily transferable. Minimum number of persons is seven and there is no limit to the maximum number of shareholders. The company's name must end with the word 'Limited'.

Private Limited Companies

A private limited company is a company which has a minimum paid up capital of rupees one lakh or such higher paid up capital, as may be prescribed.

The Articles of Association may prescribe the following:

(i) Restricts the right to transfer the shares, if any.

(ii) limits the number of its members to 50 not including its present or past employee-members

(iii) prohibits any invitation to the public to subscribe to any shares in or debentures of the company.

The name of the company must end with the words " Private Limited".

Stages in the Formation of a Joint Stock Company

It is very easy to establish a sole proprietorship business or a partnership firm as there are a few regulations to meet. But for the establishment of a company, a lot of formalities are to be complied with. The registration of the company is mandatory before starting its operation. The formation of a company, right from the origin of idea to establish a company goes through four different stages, like:

Stage –I Promotion

Stage- II Incorporation

Stage- III Raising of Capital

Stage- IV Commencement of Business

Important Documents Prepared While Forming a Company

There are three basic documents which are prepared and filed with the Registrar during the formation of a company. These are:

(1) Memorandum of Association (MOA)

(2) Articles of Association (AOA)

(3) Prospectus

Out of these three documents, MOA and AOA are filed with the Registrar of Companies before the registration along with other supporting documents while asking for certificate of incorporation. The prospectus is issued to the public at the time of subscription to capital.

Public Enterprises

The business units owned, managed and controlled by the central, state or local government are termed as public sector enterprises or public enterprises. These are also known as public sector undertakings. A pubic sector enterprise may be defined as any commercial or industrial undertaking owned and managed by the government with a view to maximise social welfare and uphold the public interest.

Public enterprises consist of nationalised private sector enterprises, such as, banks, Life Insurance Corporation of India and the new enterprises set up by the government such as Hindustan Machine Tools(HMT), Gas Authority of India (GAIL), State Trading Corporation (STC) etc.

Characteristics of Public Enterprises

(a) Government Ownership and Management

(b) Financed from Government Funds

(c) Public Welfare

(d) Public Utility Services

(e) Public Accountability

(f) Excessive Formalities

Forms of Organisation of Public Enterprises

There are three different forms of organisation used for the public sector enterprises in India. These are (1) Departmental Undertaking; (2) Statutory (or Public) Corporation and (3) Government Company.

Departmental Undertaking form of organisation is primarily used for provision of essential services such as railways, postal services, broadcasting etc. Such organisations function under the overall control of a ministry of the Government and are financed and controlled in the same way as any other government department.

Statutory Corporation (or public corporation) refers to a corporate body created by the Parliament or State Legislature by a special Act which defines its powers, functions and pattern of management. Statutory corporation is also known as public corporation. Its capital is wholly provided by the government. Examples of such organisations are Life Insurance Corporation of India, State Trading Corporation etc.

Government Company refers to the company in which 51 per cent or more of the paid up capital is held by the government. It is registered under the Companies Act and is fully governed by the provisions of the Act. Most business units owned and managed by government fall in this category.

Management

Management refers to the process of using men, money, machines, material and processes through proper direction, coordination and integration of several activities so as to produce desired results and attain predetermined goals. In other words, management consists of a series of activities classified into various functions like planning, organising, staffing, directing and controlling.

Characteristics of Management

The various characteristics of management are:

(a) Management is universal
(b) Management is goal directed
(c) Management is a continuous process
(d) Management is intangible
(e) Management is multi-disciplinary
(f) Management is a social process
(g) Management is situational

Nature of Management

The nature of management can be better appreciated by looking at it

1. as a process
2. as a discipline
3. as a group of individuals
4. as a profession, and
5. as a science as well as an art.

FUNCTIONS OF MANAGEMENT

(a) Planning

Planning is deciding in advance what is to be done, when it is to be done, how it is to be done. It is basically concerned with the selection of goals to be achieved and determining the effective course of action from among the various alternatives. This involves forecasting, establishing targets, developing the policies and programming and scheduling the action, procedure, etc., Thus, planning requires decisions to be made on what should be done, how it should be done, who will do it, where it will be done, and why it is to be done. The essential part of planning consists of setting goals and programmes of activities.

(b) Organising

After the plans have been drawn, management has to organise the activities, and physical resources of the firm to carry out the selected programmes successfully. It also involves determining the authority and responsibility relationships among functions, departments and personnel at various levels to ensure smooth and effective function together in accomplishing the objective. Thus, the organising function of management is primarily concerned with identifying the tasks involved and grouping them into units and departments, and defining the duties and responsibilities of people in different positions within each department for well coordinated and cooperative effort in the organisation.

(c) Staffing

Staffing is concerned with employing people for the various activities to be performed. The objective of staffing is to ensure that suitable people have been appointed for different positions. It includes the functions of recruitment, training and development, placement and remuneration, and performance appraisal of the employees.

(d) Directing

The directing function of management includes guiding the subordinates, supervising their performance, communicating effectively and motivating them. A manager should be a good leader. He should be able to command and issue instruction without arousing any resentment among the subordinates. He should keep a watch on the performance of his subordinates and help them out whenever they come across any difficulty. The communication system, i.e., exchange of information should take place regularly for building common understanding and clarity. The managers should also understand the needs of subordinates and inspire them to do their best and encourage initiative and creativity.

(e) Controlling

This function of management consists of the steps taken to ensure that the performance of work is in accordance with the plans. It involves establishing performance standards and measuring the actual performance with the standards set. If differences are noticed, corrective steps are taken which may include revision of standards, regulate operations, remove deficiencies and improve performance.

(f) Co-ordinating

Management has to ensure that all the activities contribute to the achievement of the objectives of the business as a whole. This requires integration of activities and synchronisation of efforts. The heads of different departments should not treat each other as competitors but should work as organs of one body. As the proper functioning of every organ of a human body is important for a healthy body, the work of every department is important for the organisation as a whole. Managers should, therefore, see that everybody in the organisation understands its objectives and works in co-operation with others to achieve these objectives. This function of management is called co-ordination. It consists of harmonising group effort so as to achieve common objectives.

VARIOUS APPROACHES TO MANAGEMENT PHILOSOPHY

Scientific Management

Frederick Winslow Taylor (1856-1915) is the father of scientific management. He exerted great influence on the development of management thought through his experiments and writings. During a career spanning 26 years, he arranged a series of experiments in three companies: Midvale Steel, Simonds Rolling Machine and Bethlehem Steel.

1. Time and motion study: Since Taylor had been an operator himself; he knew how piecework workers used to hold back production to one-third its level. The workers feared that their employers would cut their piece rate as soon as there was a rise in production. The real trouble, Taylor thought, was that no one knew how much work was reasonable for a man to do. Therefore, he established the time and motion study.

2. Differential payment: Taylor had founded the differential piecework system and the related incentives with production. Under this plan, a worker received a low piece rate if he produced the standard number of pieces and a high rate if he surpassed the standard. Taylor also comprehended that the attraction of a new high piece rate would encourage the workers to increase production.

3. Drastic reorganisation of supervision: Taylor developed two new concepts: (i) Division of planning and doing and (ii) Functional foremanship. In those days, it was customary for each worker to plan his own work. The worker himself used to select his tools and decide the sequence of performance of operations. The foreman essentially told the worker what jobs were to be performed, not how they were to be performed. Taylor suggested that the work should be designed by a foreman and not by the worker. He stated that there were distinctive functions involved in doing any kind of job and that each of the foremen should give orders to the worker in his specialised field.

4. Scientific recruitment and training: Taylor also gave importance to the scientific selection and development of the worker. He said that the management should develop and train every worker in order to bring out his best output and to enable him to perform a superior, more interesting and profitable class of work than he has done in the past.

5. Intimate and friendly cooperation between the management and workers: Taylor said that, "a complete mental revolution" on the part of management and labour was necessary to make the organisation successful. Rather than argue over profits, they should both try to increase production. Consequently, profits will also increase manifold, which will leave no room for further disagreements. Taylor realised that both, the management and labour, had a common interest in maximising production.

Contributions of Scientific Management

Firstly, through the time and motion studies we understand that the tools and physical activity concerned in a job can be made better balanced and organised. Secondly, scientific management discovered how important scientific selection of workers was and comprehended that without capability and training, a person cannot be expected to do his job properly. Finally, the significance that scientific management gave to work design encouraged managers to seek the 'one best way' of doing a job. Thus, scientific management has developed a rational approach to solve the organisation's problems and contributed a great deal to the professionalism of management.

Administrative Management

While Taylor is considered the father of scientific management, Henri Fayol (1841-1925) is considered as the father of the administrative management theory, with a focus on the development of broad administrative principles applicable to general and higher managerial levels.

Fayol opined that all actions of business enterprises could be divided into six groups: technical, commercial, financial, accounting, security and administrative or managerial. Fayol's primary focus was on this last managerial activity because he felt that managerial skills had been the most neglected aspect of business operations. He explained management in terms of five functions: planning, organising, commanding, coordinating and controlling.

Fayol's 14 principles of management are as under:

- Division of work
- Authority and responsibility
- Discipline
- Unity of command
- Unity of direction
- Subordination of individual interest to general interest
- Remuneration
- Centralisation
- Scalar chain
- Order
- Equity
- Stability of tenure of personnel
- Initiative
- Esprit de Corps

MATHEMATICAL AND BEHAVIOURAL SERIAL SCHOOLS OF MANAGEMENT

Behavioural Approach

This approach is an enhanced and more developed version of the human relations approach to management. Douglas McGregor, Abraham Maslow, Kurt Lewin, Chester Barnard, Mary Parker Follett, George Romans, Rensis Likert, Chris Argyris and Warren Bennis are some of the foremost behavioural scientists who made significant contributions to the development of the behavioural approach to management. These scientists were more rigorously trained in various social sciences (such as psychology, sociology and anthropology). They use more sophisticated research methods.

Behavioural scientists consider organisations as groups of individuals with objectives. They have, conducted extensive studies of human groups—large and small. They have studied the problems relating to groups, process, and group cohesiveness and so on. Behavioural scientists have completed vast studies on leadership. To behavioural scientists, the realistic model of human motivation is complex. This model suggests that different people react differently to the same situation or react the same way to different situations. The manager should alter and customise his approach to control people according to their individual needs.

The behavioural approach to organisational differences and change is quite practical. It recognises that (a) conflict is inevitable and sometimes is even desirable and should be faced with understanding and determination, (b) every organisational change involves technological and social aspects, also it is generally the social aspect of a change that people resist.

Management School of Thought

A new school of thought known as the management process school came into existence, which drew motivation from Fayol. According to Harold Koontz and Cyril O'Donnell, "Management is a dynamic process of performing the functions of planning, organising, staffing, directing and controlling". They also believe that these functions and the principles on which they are based have general or universal applicability. Managers, whether they are managing directors or supervisors, perform the same functions of planning and control, although the degree of complexity may differ. Similarly, management functions are not confined to business enterprises alone but are applicable to all organisations wherever group accomplishment and enterprise is involved. Management theory is not culture-bound but is adaptable and flexible from one environment to another.

The Human Relations Movement

Managers face many problems because employees do not follow predetermined and balanced patterns of behaviour. Thus, there is an increase in interest to help managers deal more effectively with the 'people side' of their organisations. The original inspiration for the movement, however, came from the Hawthorne experiments, which were done by Prof. Elton Mayo and his colleagues at the Western Electric Company's plant in Cicero, Illinois from 1927 to 1932.

Mathematical/Quantitative Approach

1. Management science and MIS: Management science (also called operations research) uses mathematical and statistical approaches to solve management problems. It originated during World War II, as strategists tried to apply scientific knowledge and methods to the complex problems of war. Industry began to apply management science after the war. George Dantzig developed linear programming, an algebraic method to determine the optimal allocation of scarce resources. Other tools used in industry include inventory control theory, goal programming, queuing models and simulation. The advent of the computer made many management science tools and concepts more practical and applicable for the industry. Increasingly, management science and management information systems (MIS) are interconnected. MIS focuses on providing needed information to managers in a useful format and at the proper time. Decision support systems (DSS) attempts to integrate decision models, data and the decision maker into a system that supports better management decisions.

2. Production and operations management: This school focuses on the operation and control of the production process that transforms resources into finished goods and services. It has its roots in scientific management but it developed into an identifiable area of management study after World War II. It uses many tools of management science.

Operations management emphasises the productivity and quality of both manufacturing and service organisations. W. Edwards Deming exerted tremendous influence in shaping modern ideas about improving productivity and quality. Foremost areas of study within operations management include capacity-planning, facilities location, facilities layout, materials requirement planning, scheduling, purchasing and inventory control, quality control, computer integrated manufacturing, just-in-time inventory systems and flexible manufacturing systems.

Systems Approach

A recurrent drawback of the classical, behavioural and quantitative schools is that they lay more emphasis on one aspect of the organisation at the expense of another.

However, it is difficult to know which aspect is most functional, constructive and appropriate in a given situation. What is needed is a singular expansive, detailed, conceptual framework that can help a manager diagnose a problem and decide which tool or combination of tools will accomplish the task best. The systems approach helps in obtaining an integrated approach to management problems. Some important contributors of the systems approach are Chester Barnard, George Homans, Philip Selznick and Herbert Simon. The following are the key concepts of this approach:

A system is a set of interdependent parts, which together form a unitary whole that performs some function. An organisation is also a system composed of four interdependent parts, namely, task, structure, people and technology.

Features of Systems Approach

1. An organisation comprises of many sub-systems.
2. All the sub-systems are inter-related.
3. The sub-parts should be studied in their inter-relationships rather than in isolation.
4. The organisation provides a demarcating line that separates it from other systems. It determines the internal and external parts.
5. The organisation is responsive to environmental effect. It is vulnerable to the changes in environment.
6. An organsiation is a system consisting of many interrelated and interdependent parts or sub-systems. These elements are then arranged in an orderly fashion.
7. As a system, an organisation draws inputs (energy, information, materials, etc) from its environment. It transforms these inputs and returns the output into the environment in the form of goods and services.
8. Every system is a part of a super system.
9. Organisation is an open system and it interacts with its environment. It is also a dynamic system as the equilibrium in it is always changing.
10. Management is expected to regulate and adjust the system to secure better performance.
11. Management is multidisciplinary as it draws and integrates knowledge from various disciplines.

Contingency Approach

According to this approach, management values and concepts of various schools have no universal applications. In other words, there is no optimal or single best way of doing things under all conditions. Methods and techniques, which are highly effective in one situation, may not work in other situations. Results differ because situations differ.

Accordingly, the contingency approach suggests that the task of managers is to try to identify which technique will best contribute to the attainment of management goals in a particular situation. Thus, managers have to employ a sort of situational sensitivity and practical selectivity.

Features of Contingency Approach

1. Management is externally situational: the conditions of the situation will determine which techniques and control system should be designed to fit the particular situation.
2. Management is entirely situational.
3. There is no best way of doing anything.
4. One needs to adapt himself to the circumstances.
5. It is a kind of "if" "then" approach.
6. It is practically suited.
7. Management policies and procedures should respond to environment.
8. Managers should understand that there is no best way of managing. It dispels the universal validity of principles.

PLANNING

Planning is a systematic way of deciding about and doing things in a purposeful manner. In the context of business organisations and their management it may be defined as the process of setting future objectives and deciding on the ways and means of achieving them. In the words of M.E. Hurley "planning is deciding in advance what is to be done in future. It involves the selection of objectives, policies, procedures and programmes from among the alternatives".

Importance of Planning

Planning is the most important of all the management functions. Some of the features of planning are as follows:

(a) Planning reduces uncertainty, risk and confusion in operation.
(b) Planning guides the decision making by the managers.
(c) Planning helps in achieving coordination and facilitates control.
(d) Planning with an element of flexibility makes the organisation adaptable.
(e) Planning leads to economy and efficiency in operations.
(f) Planning begins with the determination of objectives and directed towards their achievement.

The Planning Process/Steps in Planning

Planning in organisation follows a step-by-step process without which it may be difficult to build up proper plans and ensure their implementation. Such steps are as follows:

1. Establishment of Objectives
2. Making Assumptions (establishing premises) about the External and Internal Conditions
3. Development of Alternative Courses of Action
4. Evaluation of Alternatives
5. Selecting the Appropriate Course of Action
6. Arranging for implementation

ORGANISING

Organising is the next important function of management after the planning. Organising refers to the process of :

- Identifying and grouping the work to be performed.
- Defining and determining responsibility and authority for each job position.
- Establishing relationship among various job positions.
- Determining detailed rules and regulations of working for individuals and groups in organisation.

Process of Organising

The process of organising consists of the following steps:

1. Identification of activities
2. Grouping of activities
3. Assignment of Responsibilities
4. Granting authority
5. Establishing relationship

Formal and Informal Organisation

Formal organisation refers to the officially established pattern of relationship among departments, divisions and individuals to achieve well-defined goals and is a consciously designed structure of roles. In other words, formal organisation clearly spells what a person has to do, from whom he has to take orders and what rules, policies and work procedures are to be followed. Thus, it is a system of well-defined jobs, each bearing a definitive measure of authority, responsibility and accountability. This promotes order and facilitates planning and controlling functions.

Informal organisations on the other hand, refers to relationship between individuals in the organisation based on personal attitudes, likes and dislikes and originates to meet their social and emotional needs and develops spontaneously. It represents natural grouping of people in work situation and is supplementary to formal organisation as it serves the needs not satisfied by formal organisation. The formal organisation does not provide opportunity to members to exchange personal views and experiences and so they interact informally to fulfill such interest and needs. In fact, informal organisation comes into being because of the limitations of the formal structure and both are interlinked. However, they differ in respect of their origin, purpose, structure, authority, channels of communication and behaviour of members.

Delegation

In organisations, it is difficult on the part of a manager to complete all the jobs assigned to him. He thus, can take help from others by asking them to do some of the work in a formal way. It means, he can assign some of the work to his subordinates and give them authority to carry on the work and at the same time make them accountable. For example, a production manager may have the target to produce 1000 units in a weeks time. He can distribute his work to three of his subordinates to produce 250 units each and keep 250 units for self to produce. And then he must also give them enough authority to use organisational resources to produce. By doing so he also makes his subordinates answerable to him for non-performance.

This active process of entrustment of a part of work or responsibility and authority to another and the creation of accountability for performance is known as delegation. Thus, there are three elements of delegation as follows:

1. Assignment of Responsibility
2. Granting Authority
3. Creating Accountability

Decentralisation

Decentralisation refers to a systematic effort to delegate authority at all levels of management and in all departments. This shifts the power of decision making to lower level under a well considered plan. Decentralisation has number of benefits. Firstly, it reduces the workload of the top level management. Secondly, it motivates the employees and gives them more autonomy. It promotes initiative and creativity. It also helps employees to take quick and appropriate decisions. In the process the top management is freed from the routine jobs and it enables them to concentrate on crucial areas and plan for growth.

Distinction Between Delegations and Decentralisation

Decentralisation is not same as delegation. The points of differences are:

- While delegation is the process of assigning responsibility and authority and thereby creating accountability; decentralisation is the ultimate outcome of planned delegation.
- Delegation of authority takes place between the manager and his subordinates while decentralisation involves the entire organisation, and is between top management and divisions/departments.
- Delegation is done to speed up the work and is essential in trace; while decentralisation is optional and is usually done in large scale organisations.
- In case of delegation the responsibility and authority delegated may be withdrawn by the delegator; which is not so easy in case of decentralisation.

Authority Relationship

When a person is given certain duties to perform, he must be given necessary authority to carry on the activity successfully. Otherwise, he will not able to do the work. Similarly, in an organisation every member must have some sort of authority while performing individual job. In other words, there must be an authority relationship among the staff members. Thus, on the basis of nature, authority may be of three types:

(a) Line authority
(b) Staff authority and
(c) Functional authority

Line Authority

Line authority is the authority of a manager over his immediate subordinates. For example, the chief manager has line authority over production manager and the production manager has line authority over managers of workshops. Line authority is the right of a manager to issue order and to see that these orders are carried out.

Staff Authority

When the work of line managers increases, staff officers are appointed to help them. The job of staff officers is to give advice, information, suggestion and guidance. Staff officers can only advice. Their advice can be accepted or rejected by line managers. So staff authority refers to the responsibility and authority of providing advice and services to the line managers.

Functional Authority

Functional authority is similar to line authority, but it is exercised over a person who is not the immediate subordinate of a manager.

STAFFING

Staffing refers to the managerial function of employing and developing human resources for carrying out the various managerial and non-managerial activities in an organisation. This involves determining the manpower requirement, and the methods of recruiting, selecting, training and developing the people for various positions created in the organisation. This, in fact happens to be a continuous process because the organisation's need to retain and update its personnel is a never ending exercise.

It may be noted that staffing function is an integral part of human resource management and, in its wider sense, also includes the activities of determining the remuneration of workers, appraising their performance, and deciding on their promotion, transfers, etc.

Process of Staffing

The process of staffing starts with ascertaining the required number of various categories of employees for the organisation. This is known as manpower planning. It decides the kinds of staff and the number of staff required for the organisation. This is done through several methods like job analysis, workload analysis, etc. The next thing to be done in the staffing process is the recruitment exercise, i.e., finding out the available manpower from internal and external sources. The next step is to select the right person from the available manpower through tests and interviews and make appointments. This is followed by their placement on the jobs and necessary introduction of the work environment and the rules of compensation, promotion, transfer etc. Thus, the various steps involved in the process of staffing are as follows:

(a) Manpower Planning
(b) Job Analysis
(c) Recruitment
(d) Selection
(e) Placement
(f) Induction
(g) Training and Development
(h) Performance Appraisal
(i) Compensation
(j) Promotion and Transfer

DIRECTING

Directing is concerned with instructing, guiding, supervising and inspiring people in the organisation to achieve its objectives. It is the process of telling people what to do and seeing that they do it in the best possible manner. The directing function thus, involves:

- telling people what is to be done and explaining to them how to do it;
- issuing instructions and orders to subordinates to carryout their assignments as scheduled;
- supervising their activities;
- inspiring them to meet the manager's expectation and contribute towards the achievement of organisational objectives; and
- providing leadership.

Elements in Directing

Communication, Supervision, Motivation and Leadership are the four essential elements of directing. In the subsequent sections we shall discuss about the nature and significance of each of these components.

COMMUNICATION

Communication is a basic organisational function, which refers to the process by which a person (known as sender) transmits information or messages to another person (known as receiver). The purpose of communication in organisations is to convey orders, instructions, or information so as to bring desired changes in the performance and or the attitude of employees. In an organisation, supervisors transmit information to subordinates. Proper communication results in clarity and securing the cooperation of subordinates. Faulty communication may create problems due to misunderstanding between the superior and subordinates. The subordinates must correctly understand the message conveyed to them. Thus, in communication:

- there are two parties, one is known as the sender and the other is known as receiver;
- there is a message sent by the sender to the receiver; and
- the receiver receives the message and understands it.

Communication does not always flow from supervisor to subordinate. It can also be from a subordinate to a supervisor. For example, subordinates can pass information to the supervisor about the faults/problems at the assembly line. Thus, it is a two way process.

Elements of Communication Process: Communication, being a process must have some elements to complete the process. The elements of communication are given below:

1. Sender
2. Message
3. Encoding
4. Channel
5. Receiver
6. Decoding
7. Feedback

Types of Communication

Formal and Informal Communication

The path through which information flows is called channel of communication. The paths of communication which are based on relationship establish formally by management are the formal channels. For example, the General Manager communicates a decision to the production manager who may then issue orders or instructions to the foremen.

Communication, which takes place on the basis of informal or social relations among staff, is called informal communication. For example, any sharing of information between a production supervisor and an accountant, as they happen to be friends or so. Mostly informal channels are used due to friendly interaction of members of an organisation. In fact, it may be purely personal or related to organisational matters. The informal path of communication is also known as **Grapevine.**

Table : Differences Between Formal Communication and Informal Communication

Formal Communication	Informal Communication
1. It is based on formal organisational relationships.	It emerges out of social interactions among the people.
2. The channels of communication are prescribed.	Channels of communication depend on individuals' relationships.
3. It is rigid as deviations are not allowed.	It is quite flexible because nothing is prescribed.
4. The speed of message travel is slow because of formalisation.	Message travels faster.
5. Chances of message distortion are low.	Message are often distorted.
6. It is treated as authentic.	It is not authentic even if the message is correct.

Upward, Downward, Horizontal and Diagonal Communication

On the basis of the flow or direction of communication in organisations, it can be classified as upward, downward, horizontal or diagonal. When employees make any request, appeal, report, suggest or communicate ideas to the superior, the flow of communication is **upward** i.e., from bottom to top. For instance, when a typist drops a suggestion in the suggestion box, or a foreman reports breakdown of machinery to the factory manager, the flow of communication is upward. Upward communication encourages employees to participate actively in the operations of their department.

When communication is made from superiors down the hierarchy it is called a downward communication. For instance, when superiors issue orders and instructions to subordinates, it is known as downward communication. When the General Manager orders supervisors to work overtime, the flow of communication is downward i.e., from top to bottom. Similarly, communication of work assignments, notices, requests for performance, etc. through bulletin boards, memos, reports, speeches, meetings, etc, are all forms of downward communication.

Communication can also be amongst members at the same level in the organisation. For instance, production manager may communicate the production plan to the sales manager.

This is known as **horizontal flow of communication**. Here, the communication is among people of the same rank and status.

When communication is made between people who are neither in the same department nor at the same level of organisational hierarchy, it is called **diagonal communication**.

Barriers in Communication

The problem of communication arises because there are various obstacles which may entirely prevent a communication, filter part of it out, or give it incorrect meaning. These obstacles are known as communication barriers.

Semantic Barriers: Semantics is the science of meaning, as contrasted with phonetics, the science of sounds. All communications are symbolic, that is, these use symbols (words, pictures, action, etc.) that suggest certain meanings. Semantic barriers arise from limitations in the symbols with which we communicate. Following types of semantic barriers are more prominent:

1. Symbols with Different Meanings
2. Badly Expressed Message
3. Faulty Translations
4. Unclarified Assumptions
5. Specialist's Language

Emotional or Psychological Barriers

Emotional or psychological factors are the prime barriers in interpersonal communication. Some emotional barriers are as follows:

1. Premature Evaluation
2. Inattention
3. Loss by Transmission and Poor Retention
4. Undue Reliance on the Written Word
5. Distrust of communicator
6. Failure to communicate

Organisational Barriers

An organisation being a deliberate creation for the attainment of certain specified objectives; day-to-day happenings within it require being regulated in such a manner that they contribute to attain these objectives in the most efficient manner. Major organisational barriers may be as follows:

1. Organisational Policy
2. Organisational Rules and Regulations
3. Status Relationships
4. Complexity in Organisational Structure
5. Organisational Facilities

Personal Barriers

1. Attitudes of Superiors
2. Fear of Challenges to Authority
3. Insistence on Proper Channel
4. Lack of Confidence in Subordinates
5. Ignoring Communication
6. Lack of Time
7. Lack of Awareness

SUPERVISION

After the employees have been instructed regarding what they have to do and how to do, it is the duty of the manager to see that they perform the work as per instructions. This is known as **supervision**. Managers play the role of supervisors and ensure that the work is done as per the instructions and the plans. Supervisors clarify all instructions and guide employees to work as a team in co-operation with others.

MOTIVATION

Motivation is one of the important elements of directing. Issuance of proper instructions or orders does not necessarily ensure that they will be properly carried out. It requires manager to inspire or induce the employees to act and get the expected result. This is called motivation. It is a force that inspires a person at work to intensify his willingness to use the best of his capability for achievement of specific objectives. It may be in the form of incentives like financial (such as bonus, commission etc.) or, non-financial (such as appreciation, growth etc.), or it could be positive or negative. Basically, motivation is directed towards goals and prompt people to act.

The following are the features of motivation:

- Motivation is an act of managers
- Motivation is a continuous process
- Motivation can be positive or negative
- Motivation is goal oriented
- Motivation is complex in nature
- Motivation is an art
- Motivation is system-oriented
- Motivation is different from job satisfaction

Motivational Factors

There are several factors that motivate a person to work. The motivational factors can be broadly divided into two groups:

I. Monetary Factors:

- Salaries or wages
- Bonus
- Incentives

II. Non-Monetary Factors:

- Status or job title
- Appreciation and recognition
- Delegation of authority
- Working conditions
- Job security
- Job enrichment
- Workers participation

Need and Importance of Motivation

Motivation offers several importance to the organization and to the employees:

- Higher efficiency
- Reduce absenteeism
- Reduces employee turn over
- Improves a corporate image
- Good relations
- Improved morale
- Reduced wastages and breakages
- Reduced accidents
- Facilitates initiative and innovation

Motivational Theories

Maslow's-Hierarchy of Needs Theory:

This theory was proposed by Abraham Maslow and is based on the assumption that people are motivated by a series of five universal needs. These needs are ranked, according to the order in which they influence human behaviour, in hierarchical fashion.

- **Physiological needs** are deemed to be the lowest-level needs. These needs include the needs such as food and water.
- **Safety needs** — the needs for shelter and security — become the motivators of human behavior.
- **Social needs** include the need for belongingness and love.
- After social needs have been satisfied, **ego and esteem needs** become the motivating needs.
- The highest need in Maslow's hierarchy is that of **self-actualization**; the need for self-realization, continuous self-development, and the process of becoming all that a person is capable of becoming.

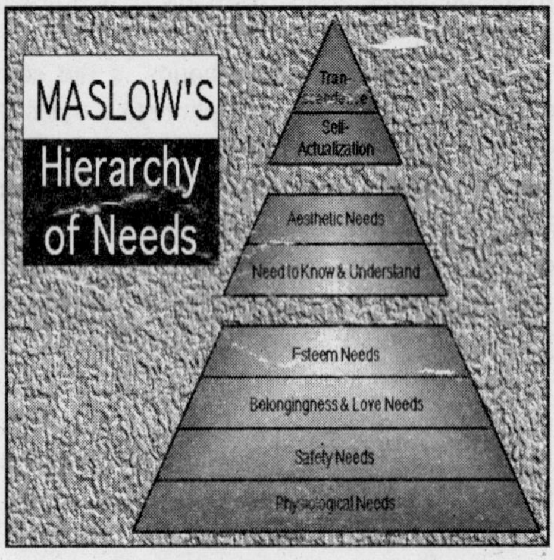

Alderfer's Hierarchy of Motivational Needs

Clayton Alderfer reworked Maslow's Need Hierarchy to align it more closely with empirical research. Alderfer's theory is called the **ERG theory** — **E**xistence, **R**elatedness, and **G**rowth.

1. Existence refers to our concern with basic material existence requirements; what Maslow called physiological and safety needs.
2. Relatedness refers to the desire we have for maintaining interpersonal relationships; similar to Maslow's social/love need, and the external component of his esteem need.
3. Growth refers to an intrinsic desire for personal development; the intrinsic component of Maslow's esteem need, and self-actualization

Alderfer's ERG theory differs from Maslow's Need Hierarchy insofar as ERG theory demonstrates that more than one need may be operative at the same time. ERG theory does not assume a rigid hierarchy where a lower need must be substantially satisfied before one can move on.

Alderfer also deals with frustration-regression. That is, if a higher-order need is frustrated, an individual then seeks to increase the satisfaction of a lower-order need.

In summary, ERG theory argues, like Maslow, that satisfied lower-order needs lead to the desire to satisfy higher-order needs; but multiple needs can be operating as motivators at the same time, and frustration in attempting to satisfy a higher- level need can result in regression to a lower-level need.

Two-factor Theory

Herzberg's Two Factor Theory, also known as the **Motivation-Hygiene Theory**, was derived from a study designed to test the concept that people have two sets of needs:

1. their needs as animals to avoid pain
2. their needs as humans to grow psychologically

Herzberg's study consisted of a series of interviews that sought to elicit responses to the questions:

(1) Recall a time when you felt exceptionally good about your job. Why did you feel that way about the job? Did this feeling affect your job performance in any way? Did this feeling have an impact on your personal relationships or your well-being?

(2) Recall a time on the job that resulted in negative feelings? Describe the sequence of events that resulted in these negative feelings.

Research Results: it appeared from the research, that the things making people happy on the job and those making them unhappy had two separate themes.

1. Satisfaction (Motivation): Five factors stood out as strong determiners of job satisfaction:

- achievement
- recognition
- work itself
- responsibility
- advancement

2. Dissatisfaction (Hygiene): The determinants of job dissatisfaction were found to be:

- company policy
- administrative policies
- supervision
- salary
- interpersonal relations
- working conditions

According to Herzberg, the factors leading to job satisfaction are separate and distinct form those that lead to job dissatisfaction. Therefore, managers who seek to eliminate factors that can create job dissatisfaction may bring about peace but not necessarily motivation. They will be placating their workforce rather than motivating them. As a result, conditions surrounding the job such as quality of supervision, pay, company policies, physical working conditions relations with others and job security were characterized by Herzberg as hygiene factors, when they're adequate, people will not be dissatisfied; neither will they be satisfied. If we want to motivate people on their jobs, Herzberg suggested emphasizing factors associated with the work itself or to outcomes directly derived form it, such as promotional opportunities, opportunities for personal growth, recognition, responsibility and achievement. These are the characteristics that people find intrinsically rewarding.

Expectancy Theory

In recent years, probably the most popular motivational theory has been the Expectancy Theory (also known as the Valence-Instrumentality-Expectancy Theory). Although there are a number of theories found with this general title, they all have their roots in Victor Vroom's 1964 work on motivation. The key elements to this theory are referred to as Expectancy (E), Instrumentality (I), and Valence (V).

Vroom suggests that an employee's beliefs about Expectancy, Instrumentality, and Valence interact psychologically to create a motivational force such that the employee acts in ways that bring pleasure and avoid pain.

McClelland's Theory of Needs

According to David McClelland, regardless of culture or gender, people are driven by three motives:

- achievement,
- affiliation and
- influence.

Since McClelland's first experiments, over 1,000 studies relevant to achievement motivation have been conducted. These studies strongly support the theory.

Achievement: The need for achievement is characterized by the wish to take responsibility for finding solutions to problems, master complex tasks, set goals, get feedback on level of success.

Affiliation: The need for affiliation is characterized by a desire to belong, an enjoyment of teamwork, a concern about interpersonal relationships, and a need to reduce uncertainty.

Power: The need for power is characterized by a drive to control and influence others, a need to win arguments, a need to persuade and prevail According to McClelland, the presence of these motives or drives in an individual indicates a predisposition to behave in certain ways. Therefore, from a manager's perspective, recognizing which need is dominant in any particular individual affects the way in which that person can be motivated.

Theory of "X" and Theory of "Y"

Douglas McGregor observed two diametrically opposing view points of managers about their employees, one is negative called "Theory of X" and one is positive called "Theory of Y".

(a) Theory of X: Following are the assumptions of managers who believe in the "Theory of X" in regard to their employees:

- Employees dislike work; if possible avoid the same
- Employees must be coerced, controlled or threatened to do the work
- Employees avoid responsibilities and seek formal direction
- Most employees consider security of job, most important of all other factors in the job and have very little ambition

(b) Theory of Y: Following are the assumptions of managers who believe in the "Theory of Y" in regard to their employees.

- Employees love work as play or rest
- Employees are self-directed and self-controlled and committed to the organizational objectives
- Employees accept and seek responsibilities
- Innovative spirit is not confined to managers alone, some employees also possess it.

LEADERSHIP

Leadership is the process, which influences the people and inspires them to willingly accomplish the organisational objectives. The main purpose of managerial leadership is to get willing cooperation of the workgroup in pursuit of the goals.

Importance of Leadership

The objectives of any organisation can only be fulfilled if its employees are working towards accomplishment of such objectives. To make people work in the desired manner, proper instructions and guidance are necessary. And this direction process becomes effective when the persons who give such direction have leadership qualities. Leadership is essential in functioning of any organisation and its importance and benefits are varied. Some of these importances are:

- leadership improves the performance of the employees. Leaders can motivate the followers to work and thereby increase their performance level.
- with continuous support and guidance, leaders are able to build confidence among the followers, thereby increasing speed and accuracy and decreasing wastage.
- with friendly and cooperative efforts the leader is able to build employees' morale which in turn contribute to higher productivity.

Leadership Qualities

In order to be successful, a leader must possess certain qualities. A good leader should be professionally competent, intelligent, analytical and he/she should have a sense of fair play, including honesty, sincerity, integrity, and sense of responsibility. He must possess initiative, perseverance, be diligent and realistic in his outlook. He must also be able to communicate his subordinates effectively. Human relation skills are a must for any leader.

Earlier, it was believed that the success or effectiveness of a leader depends upon his personal traits or characteristics, like physical appearance, intelligence, self-confidence, alertness, and initiative. This is no longer regarded as a correct approach. It has been established on the basis of experiments that the success or effectiveness of a person as a leader depends upon his behaviour pattern or leadership style in relation to the followers.

George R. Terry (Principles of Management) gives the following characteristics to a good leader:

- Energy
- Emotional stability
- Knowledge of human relations
- Empathy
- Objectivity
- Personal motivation
- Communication skill
- Teaching ability
- Social skill
- Technical competence

Viscount Slim gives the following six characteristics of leadership, which he considers common in a civil or military environment:

- Courage
- Will power
- Judgment
- Flexibility
- Knowledge
- Integrity

According to **Chester Barnard**, the qualities of a good leader are:

- Vitality and endurance
- Decisiveness
- Persuasiveness
- Stability in behaviour
- Intellectual ability
- Knowledge

Historical Evolution of Leadership

1776 - Adam Smith - A Wealth of Nations

- exchange will not occur voluntarily unless both people benefit.
- "I will follow you as long as I get some benefit in return."

1807 - Hegel - first book on leadership

- focused primarily on leadership as it related to the political process.

1847 - Thomas Carlyle - "Great Man Theory"

- the capacity for leadership is inherent – that great leaders are born, not made.
- only those men who are blessed with heroic qualities could ever emerge as leaders.
- portrays great leaders as heroic, mythic, and destined to rise to leadership when needed.

1910-1920 - first research on leadership conducted

- gave rise to **trait theories** - natural born leaders possess certain physical traits and personality characteristics which differentiate them from non-leaders.
- Similar in some ways to "Great Man" theory.
- People inherit certain qualities and traits that make them better suited to leadership.
- Trait theories often identify particular personality or behavioral characteristics shared by leaders.

1947-Jenkins - review of traits of military leaders

- concluded that traits were important but that the situation determined which traits were important and that expertise in the business at hand separated leaders from followers.

1948-Stogdil - review of traits of non-military leaders

- found that most important trait to possess was the trait most closely related to the task at hand.
- Max Weber - **charismatic leadership**
- descendant of thought from Hegel
- leaders emerge in a time of crisis due to their inherent charisma.

Situational Theory

Stogdil - proposed that leadership is a matter of situational demands emergence of a leader is a result of time, place, and circumstance

Behavioural Theories

The behavioral theorists identified determinants of leadership so that people could be trained to be leaders. They developed training programs to change managers' leadership behaviours and assumed that the best styles of leadership could be learned.

Path-Goal Theory – Robert House

- the successful leader shows followers the rewards available by meeting a goal and illustrates the path (behaviours) by which rewards may be obtained.

Contingency Theory – Fiedler

- dominated much of research in 1970's.
- suggested that there are two types of leaders - those who focus on tasks and those who focus on relationships.
- situation will determine which type of leader will be most effective.

Behavioural Theories

The behavioural theorists identified determinants of leadership so that people could be trained to be leaders. They developed training programs to change managers' leadership behaviours and assumed that the best styles of leadership could be learned.

Path-Goal Theory – Robert House

- the successful leader shows followers the rewards available by meeting a goal and illustrates the path (behaviors) by which rewards may be obtained.

Contingency Theory – Fiedler

- dominated much of research in 1970's.
- suggested that there are two types of leaders - those who focus on tasks and those who focus on relationships.
- situation will determine which type of leader will be most effective.

Leader-Participation Model - Vroom, Yetton, & Jago

- provides a set of sequential rules to determine the extent to which followers participate in the decision making process in different situations.

Process Theories

(a) Transformational Leadership—James MacGregor Burns

- leader asks followers to put aside personal interests for the good of the group
- leaders focuses on followers' needs and input in order to transform everyone into a leader by empowering and motivating them.

(b) Relational Model of Leadership—Komives, Lucas, & McMahon

- leadership is a relational process designed to accomplish a common goal to benefit all.
- leader must be inclusive, empowering, purposeful, ethical, and process-oriented to bind group together and achieve goal.

(c) Servant Leadership Theory—Robert Greenleaf

- successful leaders influence others as a result of dedicating their lives to serving others - individuals, groups, and organizations.

(d) Social Change Model of Leadership

- leadership is a process by which individuals and groups work toward the common goal of improving the quality of life for all by developing and promoting seven basic values.

Transactional Leadership

The transactional leader works through creating clear structures whereby it is clear what is required of their subordinates, and the rewards that they get for following orders. Punishments are not always mentioned, but they are also well-understood and formal systems of discipline are usually in place.

The early stage of Transactional Leadership is in negotiating the contract whereby the subordinate is given a salary and other benefits, and the company (and by implication the subordinate's manager) gets authority over the subordinate.

When the Transactional Leader allocates work to a subordinate, they are considered to be fully responsible for it, whether or not they have the resources or capability to carry it out. When things go wrong, then the subordinate is considered to be personally at fault, and is punished for their failure (just as they are rewarded for succeeding).

The transactional leader often uses management by exception, working on the principle that if something is operating to defined (and hence expected) performance then it does not need attention. Exceptions to expectation require praise and reward for exceeding expectation, whilst some kind of corrective action is applied for performance below expectation.

Whereas Transformational Leadership has more of a 'selling' style, Transactional Leadership, once the contract is in place, takes a 'telling' style.

The Managerial Grid

The dimensions identified at the University of Michigan provided the basis for the development of the managerial grid model developed by Robert Blake and Jane Mouton.

It identifies five various leadership styles that represent different combinations of concern for people and concern for production. Managers who scored high on both these dimensions simultaneously (labeled team management) performed the best. The five leadership styles of the managerial grid include impoverished, country club, produce or perish, middle-of-the road, and team.

CO-ORDINATION AND CONTROLLING

Co-ordination

In every organisation, different types of work are performed by various groups and no single group can be expected to achieve the goals of the organisation as a whole. Hence, it becomes essential that the activities of different work groups and departments should be harmonised. This function of management is known as 'co-ordination'. It ensures unity of action among individuals, work groups and departments, and brings harmony in carrying out the different activities and functions so as to achieve the organisational goals efficiently. Coordination is the orderly arrangement of individual and group efforts to provide unity of action in the pursuit of a common goal. In other words, coordination involves synchronisation of different activities and efforts of the various units of an organisation so that the planned objectives may be achieved with minimum conflict.

Controlling

Managerial planning results in the framing of objectives and laying down of targets. To achieve the objectives, a proper organisational structure is designed; people are assigned the various tasks; and are directed to perform their respective jobs. The actual performance is then assessed from time to time to ensure that what is achieved is in conformity with the plans and targets. This exactly is the controlling function. Thus, controlling as a function of management refers to the evaluation of actual performance of work against planned or standard performance and taking the corrective action, if necessary.

According to Henri Fayol, "Control consists in verifying whether everything occurs in conformity with the plan adopted, the instructions issued and principles established."

Planning and controlling are closely related and depend upon each other. Controlling depends upon planning because planning provides the targets or standards against which actual performance can be compared. Controlling, on the other hand, appraises planning.

It brings out the shortcomings of planning and helps to improve upon the plans.

Thus, controlling involves

(i) knowing the nature, quantum and time frame of the work;

(ii) comparing the performance with the plan;

(iii) analysing deviation, if any;

(iv) taking corrective steps; and

(v) suggesting revision of plans, if necessary.

Characteristics of Control

The following are the basic characteristics of control:

1. Planning is the basis of control
2. Control is a continuous process
3. Control is all pervasive
4. Action is the essence of control
5. Control is forward looking

Business Law

A. INDIAN CONTRACT ACT, 1872

Nature and Kinds of Contract

Definition of Contract

A contract is an agreement made between two or more parties which the law will enforce. According to Sec. 2(*h*), a contract is an agreement enforceable by law. An agreement comes into existence by the process of offer by one party and its unqualified acceptance by the other party.

The parties who enter into an agreement must agree upon the subject matter in the same sense and at the same time, *i.e.,* there must be consensus and idem. An agreement may be a social agreement or a legal agreement. A social agreement is that which does not give rise to legal consequences. In case of its breach the parties cannot go to the law court to enforce a right. A legal agreement is that which gives rise to legal consequences and remedies in the law court in case of its breach.

Essential of Contract

1. There must be an agree. This involves two parties, one party making the offer and the other party accepting it.
2. The parties must intend to create legal relationship.
3. The parties must be capable of entering into an agreement as regards age and understanding.
4. The agreement must be supported by consideration on both sides.
5. The consent of the parties must be free and genuine.
6. The object of the agreement must be lawful.
7. The terms of the agreement must be certain and capable of performance.
8. The agreement must not have been expressly declared as void.

Classification of Contracts

Void agreement—an agreement not enforceable by law (Sec. 2(*g*)].

Void contract—a contract which ceases to be enforceable by law [Sec. 2(*f*)].

Voidable contract—a contract which is enforceable by law at the option of one party thereto, but not at the option of the other [Sec. 2(*i*)].

Illegal Agreement—an agreement which involves the transgression of some rule of basic public policy and is criminal in nature or immoral. It is not only void as between the immediate parties but it also taints the collateral transactions with illegality.

Implied Contract—a contract which is inferred from the circumstances of the case or from the conduct of the parties.

Express Contract—a contract is which the terms are stated in words (written or spoken) by the parties.

Quasi-Contract—an obligation created by law, regardless of agreement.

Executed Contract—a contract which is wholly performed by both the parties.

Executory Contract—a contract in which the promises of both the parties have yet to be performed.

Partly executory, partly executed—a contract in which one party has performed his obligation, but the other party has yet to perform his obligation.

Unilateral Contract—a contract in which only one party has yet to perform his obligation.

Bilateral Contract—a contract in which both the parties have yet to perform their obligations.

Offer and Acceptance Offer

An offer is an undertaking by the offer or to be contractually bound in the event of a proper acceptance of the offer by the offeree. It may be made by express words spoken or written, or it may be implied when it is inferred from the conduct of the offeror or from the circumstances of the case. It is specific when it is made to a particular person and general when it is made to the world at large. In the former case, it is called a specific offer; in the later case, it is called a general offer.

Legal Rules as to Offer

1. It must be intended to create legal relations.
2. It must be certain.
3. It must be distinguished from :
   (a) a declaration of intention and
   (b) and invitation to make offer
4. It must be communicated to the offeree.
5. It must be made with a view to obtaining the essent of the offeree.
6. It must not contain a term non-compliance of which would amount to acceptance.
7. A statement of price is not an offer.

Lapse of Offer

An offer lapse or comes to an end—

1. By communication of notice of termination of offer to the offeree.
2. By lapse of the specified or reasonable time.
3. By death of insanity of the offeror.
4. By a counter offer. Counter offer is an offer to the original offer.
5. By not being accepted according to the prescribed or usual mode.
6. By non-fulfillment of a condition precedent.

Communication of Offer, Acceptance and Revocation

The communication of a proposal (offer) is complete when it comes to the knowledge of the person to whom it is made. The communication of an acceptance is complete—as against the proposer when it is put into a course of transmission to him, so as to be out of the power of the acceptor; as against the acceptor, when it comes to the knowledge of the proposer. The communication of a revocation is complete as against the person who makes it, when it is put into a course of transmission to the person to whom it is made so as to be out of the power of the person who makes it; as against the person to whom it is made, when it comes to his knowledge (Sec. 4)

Special Terms of Offer

These must be brought to the notice of the other party before the acceptance of the offer, otherwise the acceptor will not be bound by such terms. Where the acceptor knows that there are same special terms, and his attention is drawn to them, he is bound by them if he accepts the offer.

Contract by Telephone or Telex

It has the same effect as an oral agreement entered into between the parties when they are face to face.

Acceptance

Legal Rules as to Acceptance

1. It must be absolute and unqualified.
2. It must be communicated to the offeror.
3. It must be according to the prescribed or usual mode.
4. It must be given within the prescribed or reasonable time.
5. It must show an intention to fulfill the promise.
6. It cannot procede the offer.
7. It must be given by the specific person to whom the offer is made. If the offer is general, it may be accepted by any person.
8. It must be given before the offer lapses.
9. Mental acceptance is no acceptance.

Effect of Silence on Acceptance

The acceptance of an offer cannot be implied from the silence of the offeree unless the offeree has by his previous conduct indicated that his silence means that he accepts.

Acceptance Subject to Contract

An acceptance subject to contract means that the parties do not intend to be bound until a formal contract is prepared and signed by them.

Agreement to Agree in Future

If the parties have not agreed upon the terms of their agreement but have agreed to agree in future, there is no contract.

Consideration

Consideration means *something in return.* It is the price for which the promise of the other is bought. It must result in a benefit to the promisor and/or a deteriment to the promisee or both. Sec. 2(*d*) defines it as follows: "When at the desire, of the promisor, the promisee or any other person has done or abstained from doing, or does or abstains from doing something, such act or abstinence or promise is called a consideration for the promise."

Legal Rules as to Consideratin

1. It is essential to support every contract. **2.** It must move at the desire of the promisor. **3.** It may move from the promisee or any other person. **4.** It may be past, present or future. **5.** It need not be adequate. **6.** It must be real and not illusory. **7.** It must not be something which the promisor is already legally or contractually bound to do. **8.** It must not be illegal, immoral or opposed to public policy.

Stranger to Contract

The general rule is that a stranger to a contract cannot sue. But he may sue where—**1.** A trust or charge is created in some specific immovable property in favour of him. **2.** A provision is made in a marriage settlement, partition or family arrangement for his benefit. **3.** There is an acknowledgement of a liability by the promisor or the promisor constitutes himself as agent. **4.** He is the assignee of rights and benefits under a contract not involving personal skill. **5.** He enters into a contract through an agent; and **6.** There are convenants running with the land.

An Agreement made without Consideration is Void (Sec. 25)

The following are the exceptions to this rule, *i.e.,* no consideration is required in case of **1.** A written and registered agreement based on natural love and affection between parties standing in a near relation to each other [Sec. 25 (1)]; **2.** A promise to compensate, wholly or in part, a person who has already voluntarily done something for the promisor [Sec. 25(2)]; **3.** A promise by a debtor to pay a time-barred debt if it is made in writing and is signed by the debtor or by his agent [Sec. 25 (3)]; **4.** An agency (Sec. 185); **5.** A completed gift (Expl. 1 to Sec. 25).

Capacity to Contract

Every person is competent to contract who is of the age of majority according to the law to which he is subject, and who is of sound mind, and is not disqualified from contracting by any law to which he is subject (Sec. 11).

1. Minor

A minor is a person who has not completed eighteen years of age. But where a guardian has been appointed to a minor under the Guardians and Wards Act or where a minor is under the guardianship of the Court of Wards, he attains majority at the age of twenty one. The position as regards his agreements is as follows:

1. His agreement is altogether void and inoperative. **2.** He can be a promisee or a beneficiary in a contract. **3.** His estate is liable for the necessary goods supplied or necessary services rendered to him or to anyone whom he is legally bound to support or for money lent to him to buy necessaries. **4.** He may enter into contracts of apprenticeship, service, education and instruction provided these are beneficial to him. **5.** He can be an agent. **6.** He cannot be a partner. But he can be admitted to the benefits of an already existing partnership with the consent of the other partners. **7.** If he has received any benefit under a void agreement, he cannot be asked to compensate or pay for it. **8.** The court never orders specific performance of his agreements. **9.** He can always plead minority and is not estopped from doing so even when he enters into an agreement by falsely misrepresenting his age. **10.** He cannot be adjudged insolvent.

2. Persons of Unsound Mind

Lunatics. A lunatic can enter into a contract when he is of sound mind.

Idiots. An agreement of an idiot like that of a minor is altogether void.

Drunken or intoxicated persons. Their position is similar to that of lunatics.

These persons, like a minor, are liable for necessaries supplied to them or their minor dependants.

3. Other Persons

Alien enemies. During the war an Indian citizen cannot enter into a contract with an alien enemy. Contracts made before the war are either suspended or dissolved.

Foreign sovereigns and accredited representatives of a foreign state. They can enter into contracts and enforce these contracts in our Courts. But they cannot be sued in our Courts without the prior sanction of the Central Government.

Corporations. The contractual capacity of a statutory corporation is limited by the Statute governing it. As regards a company registered under the Companies Act, 1956, its contractual capacity is regulated by its Memorandum of Association and the Companies Act, 1956.

Insolvents. When a debtor is adjudged insolvent he is deprived of his power to leal in his property divisible among his creditors.

Convicts. A convict when undergoing imprisonment is incapable of entering into a contract.

Free Consent

All agreements are contract if they are made by the free consent of the parties. Two or more persons are said to consent when they agree upon the same thing in the same sense [Sec. 13] consent is said to be free when it is not caused by; *(i)* coercion or *(ii)* undue influence, or *(iii)* fraud, or *(iv)* misrepresentation, or *(v)* mistake subject to the provisions of Sec. 20, 21 and 22.

Effect of Agreement Without Free Consent

When consent to an agreement is caused by coercion, fraud, misrepresentation, or undue influence, the agreement is a contract voidable at the option of the party whose consent was so caused (Secs. 19 and 19-A).

Coercion

"Coercion" is the committing or threatening to commit any act forbidden by the Indian Penal Code, 1860 or the unlawful detaining, or threatening to detain, any property, to the prejudice of any person whatever, with the intention of causing any person to enter into an agreement (Sec. 15).

A threat to commit suicide amounts to coercion.

Undue Influence

A contract is said to be induced by "undue influence" where the relations subsisting between the parties are such that one of the parties is in a position to dominate the will of the other, and uses that position to obtain an unfair advantage over the other. A person is deemed to be in a position to dominate the will of another where he—*(a)* holds real or apparent authority over the other, or *(b)* stands in a fiduciary relation to the other; or *(c)* makes a contract with a person whose mental capacity is temporarily or permanently affected by reason of age, illness or mental or bodily distress. Where a person who is in a position to dominate the will of another, enters into a contract with him, and the transaction appears to be *unconscionable*, the burden of proving that such contract was not induced by undue influence lies upon the person in a position to dominate the will of the other (Sec. 16).

Relationships which raise presumption of undue influence : **1.** parent and child, **2.** trustee and beneficiary, **3.** religious guru and disciple. **4.** guardian and ward, **5.** solicitor and client, **6.** doctor and patient, and **7.** fiance and fiancee.

No presumption of undue influence in the following cases : **1.** husband and wife, **2.** landlord and tenant, **3.** creditor and debtor.

Misrepresentation and Fraud

"Misrepresentation" is a mis-statement of a material fact made innocently with an honest belief as to its truth or non-disclosure of a material fact, without any intent to deceive the other party.

"Fraud" exists when it is shown that a false representation has been made, **1.** knowingly, or **2.** without belief in its truth, or **3.** recklessly, not caring whether it is true or false, and **4.** the maker intends the other party to act upon it. It also exists when there is a concealment of a material fact.

Mistake

Mistake is erroneous belief about something. It may be a **1.** mistake of law, or **2.** mistake of fact.

1. *Mistake of law* : It may be a **(I)** mistake of law of the country, or **(II)** mistake of law of a foreign country. The general rule as regards mistake of law of the country is that ignorance of law is no excuse. Mistake of law of a foreign country is regarded as a mistake of fact.

2. *Mistake of fact* : It may be a **(I)** *Bilateral mistake.* Where *both* the parties to an agreement are under a mistake as to a matter of fact essential to the agreement, the agreement is void (Sec. 20).

Mistake of fact (bilateral mistake) may relate to :

(a) Subject-matter : Mistake of fact regarding subject-matter may relate to existence of the subject-matter; *(ii)* price of the subject-matter; *(iii)* quantity of the subject-matter; *(iv)* identity of the subject-matter; *(v)* quality of the subject-matter, or *(vi)* title to the subject-matter.

(b) Possibility of performance : Mistake of fact may also relate to *(i)* physical, or *(ii)* legal, impossibility of performance.

In both these cases, the agreement is void.

(II) *Unilateral mistake* : Where only *one* of the parties is under a mistake as to a matter of fact, the contract is not voidable (Sec. 22). There are however two exceptions to this rule.

(i) Identity of the person contracted with : If A intends to enter into a contract with B, C cannot give himself any right in respect of the contract by accepting the offer. In such a case the contract is void.

(ii) Nature of contract : Where a person is made to enter into a contract through the inducement of another but through no fault of his own, there is a mistake as to the nature of the contract, and the contract is void.

Legality of Object

An agreement is a contract if it is made for a lawful consideration and with a lawful object (Sec. 10).

Every agreement of which the object or consideration is unlawful is void. The consideration or object of an agreement is unlawful if—it is forbidden by law; or it is fraudulent; or involves or implies injury to the person or property of another; or the Court regards it as immoral, or opposed to public policy (Sec. 23).

Effects of Illegality

No action is allowed on an illegal agreement. This rule is based on the following two maxims : **1.** No action arises from a base cause. **2.** Where there is equal guilt, the defendant is in a better position.

The effects of illegality are summed up as follows: ***(i)*** The collateral transactions to an illegal agreement also become tainted with illegality. ***(ii)*** No action can be taken for the *(a)* recovery of money paid or property transferred under an illegal agreement, and *(b)* breach of an illegal agreement.

Agreements Opposed to Public Policy

An agreement is said to be opposed to public policy when it is injurious to the welfare of the society or it tends to be harmful to the public interest. The following agreements are, or have been held to be, opposed to public policy:

1. Agreements of trading with enemy. **2.** Agreement to commit a crime. **3.** Agreements interfering with administration of justic. These include *(a)* agreements for stifling prosecution and *(b)* agreements which interfere with the course of justice. **4.** Agreements in restraint of legal proceedings. These include *(a)* agreements to oust the jurisdiction of Courts, and *(b)* agreements to vary periods of limitation. **5.** Agreements for the sale of public offices. **6.** Agreements tending to create interest opposed to duty. **7.** Agreements in restraint of parental rights. **8.** Agreements restricting personal liberty. **9.** Agreements in restraint of marriage. **10.** Marriage brokerage agreements. **11.** Agreements interfering with marital duties. **12.** Agreements in fraud of creditors or revenue authorities. **13.** Agreements in restraint of trade. An agreement in restraint of trade is one which restrains a person from freely exercising his trade, business or profession. Every agreement, by which anyone is restrained from exercising a lawful profession, trade or business of any kind is, to that extent, void (Sec. 27). Exceptions are made.

In case of agreements for sale of goodwill and partners' agreements provided the restraint is reasonable.

Void Agreements

A void agreement is one which is not enforceable by law (Sec. 2(*g*)].

The following agreements have been expressly declared to be void :

1. Agreements made by incompetent persons (Sec. 11). **2.** Agreements made under a mutual mistake of fact (Sec. 20). **3.** Agreements the consideration or object of which is unlawful (Sec. 23). **4.** Agreements the consideration or object of which unlawful in part (Sec. 24). **5.** Agreements made without consideration (Sec. 25). **6.** Agreements in restraint of marriage (Sec. 26). **7.** Agreements in restraint of trade (Sec. 27). **8.** Agreements in restraint of legal proceedings (Sec. 28). **9.** Agreements the meaning of which is uncertain (Sec. 29). **10.** Agreements by way of wager (Sec. 30). **11.** Agreements contingent on impossible events (Sec. 36). **12.** Agreements to do impossible acts (Sec. 56).

Wagering agreements

A wagering agreement is an agreement to pay money or money's worth on the happening or non-happening of a specified uncertain event. Wagering agreements are void in India. In the States of Maharashtra and Gujarat, however, they have been declared to be illegal. The collateral transactions to such wagering agreements in the States of Maharashtra and Gujarat also become illegal. In the rest of India collateral transactions are valid.

Uncertain Agreements

Agreements the meaning of which is not certain, or capable of being made certain, are void.

Restitution

It means return of the benefit received from the plaintiff under a void contract. The principle of restitution is that the defendant who has been unjustly enriched at the expense of the plaintiff is required to make restitution to the plaintiff.

Contingent Contract

A contingent contract is a contract to do or not to do something. If some event, collateral to such contract, does or does not happen.

Characteristics of contingent contract

1. Its performance depends upon the happening or non-happening in future of some event.
2. The event must be uncertain.
3. The uncertain future event must be collateral to the contract.

Rules regarding contingent contracts

1. If a contingent contract is to be performed if an uncertain future event happens, it cannot be enforced until the event has happened. If it is to be performed if a particular event does not happen, its performance can be enforced if the event becomes impossible.
2. If a contingent contract depends for its performance on doing of an act by the promisor, the contract becomes void where the promisor makes the performance impossible.
3. If a contingent contract contemplates doing of a thing if a specified event happens within a fixed time, it becomes void if the event does not happen within that time.
4. If a contingent contract contemplates to do anything if an impossible event happens, it is void.

Performance of Contract

The parties to a contract must either *perform* or *offer to perform* their respective promises.

Attempted performance or tender : Attempted performance or tender is an offer of performance by the promisor in accordance with the terms of the contract. If the promisee does not accept performance, the promisor is not responsible for non-performance, nor does he thereby lose his rights under the contract. Thus a tender is equivalent to actual performance. The tender, in order to have this effect, must be uncondi-tional, of the whole quantity contracted for, at the proper time, place and in the manner specified; and, where these are not specified, it must be made in a reasonable manner.

Reciprocal Promises

Promises which form the consideration or part of the consideration for each other are called 'reciprocal promises'.

Rules regarding performance of reciprocal promises. **1.** When reciprocal promises have to be simultaneously performed the promisor is not bound to perform, unless the promisee is ready and willing to perform his promise. **2.** The reciprocal promises must be performed in the order fixed by the contract. **3.** Where the nature of reciprocal promises is such that one cannot be performed unless the other party performs his promise in the first place, then if the latter fails to perform he cannot claim performance from the other, but must make compensation to the first party for his loss.

By whom must contract be performed

1. *By promisor himself*—if that was the intention of the parties, *i.e.,* where personal consideration is the foundation of the contract.
2. *By agent*—where personal consideration is not the foundation of the contract.
3. *By legal representatives*—in case of death of the promisor.
4. *By joint promisors*—when two or more persons/have made a joint promise, then unless a contrary intention appears from the contract, all such persons must jointly fulfil the promise. If any of them dies, his legal representative must, jointly with the surviving promisors, fulfil the promise. If all the promisors die, the legal representa-tives of all of them must fulfil the promise jointly.

Who can Demand Performance?

It is only the promisee, and in case of his death, his legal representatives, who can demand performance.

When a person has made a promise to several persons, then, unless a contrary intention appears from the contract, the right to claim performance rests with all of them. When one of the promisees dies, it rests with his legal representatives jointly with the surviving promisees. When all the promisees die, it rests with their legal representatives jointly.

Time and Place of Performance

Time and place of performance of a contract are matters to be determined by agreement between the parties themselves. Where no time for performance is specified, the promisor must perform the promise within a reasonable time. If no time and place is fixed for the performance of the promise, the promisor must apply to the promisee to fix the day and time for performance.

Time as the Essence of Contract

Time for the performance of a contract may be fixed in the contract itself. In that case the contract must be performed *within* that time when time is of the essence of the contract. The general rule is that *in commercial contracts time is of the essence of contract.* In other contracts stipulations as to time are, in the absence of an express or implied evidence to the contrary, presumed not to be of the essence of the contract.

Appropriation of Payments

The debtor has, at the time of payment, right of choice of appropriating the payment; in default of the debtor, the creditor has the right to appropriate; in default of either, the law will allow appropriation of debts in order of time.

Rule in Clayton's Case

Where the parties have a current account between them, appropriation impliedly takes place in the order in which the receipts and payments take place and are entered in the account. The first item on the debit side of the account is discharged or reduced by the first item on the credit side.

Assignment of contract

Assignment of a contract means transfer of contractual rights and liabilities under the contract to a third party. It may take place by—

1. *Act of the parties* : This is subject to the following rules:

(*i*) Contracts involving personal skill or ability or other personal qualifications cannot be assigned.

(*ii*) A promisor cannot assign his liabilities or obligations under a contract.

(*iii*) The rights and benefits under a contract may be assigned if the obligation under the contract is not of a personal nature.

(*iv*) An actionable claim can always be assigned but the assignment to be complete and effectual must be effected by an instrument in writing. Notice of such assignment must also be given to the debtor.

2. *Operation of law* : This takes place in case of death or insolvency of a party to the contract.

Discharge of Contract

A contract is said to be discharged when the obligations created by it come to an end. The various modes of discharge of a contract are as follows :

1. Discharge by Performance

Discharge of a contract by performance takes place when the parties to the contract fulfil their obligations arising under the contract within the time and in the manner prescribed. The performance may be *(i)* actual performance, or *(ii)* attempted performance.

2. Discharge by Agreement or Consent

A contract rests on the agreement of the parties. As it is agreement which binds them, so by their agreement or consent they may be discharged.

The discharge by consent may be express or implied. Discharge by implied consent takes place by—*(a) Novation, i.e.,* when a new contract is substituted for an existing one, either between the same parties or between one of the parties and a third party. *(b) Alternation, i.e.,* when one or more of the terms of the contract is/are altered by the mutual consent of the parties to the contract. *(c) Rescission, i.e.,* when all or some of the terms of the contract are cancelled. *(d) Remission, i.e.,* acceptance of a lesser fulfillment of the promise made. *(e) Waiver* which means intentional relinquishment or giving up of a right by a party entitled thereto under a contract. *(f) Merger, i.e.,* when an inferior right accruing to a party under a contract merges into a superior right accruing to the same party under a new contract.

3. Discharge by Impossibility

Impossibility of performance may be—

Initial impossibility : An agreement to do an act impossible in itself is void.

Supervening impossibility : Impossibility which arises subsequent to the formation of a contract (which could be performed at the time when the contract was entered into) is called subsequent or supervening impossibility. The cases covered by supervening impossibility include; *(a)* Destruction of subject-matter of contract; *(b)* Non-existence or non-occurrence of a particular state of things; *(c)* Death or incapacity for personal service; *(d)* Change of law or stepping in of a person with statutory authority; *(e)* Outbreak of war. The contract is descharged in these cases.

The following cases are not covered by supervening impossibility; *(a)* Difficulty of performance; *(b)* Commercial impossibility; *(c)* Failure of a third person on whose work the promisor relied; *(d)* Strikes, lock-outs and civil disturbances; *(e)* Failure of one of the objects. The contract is not discharged in these cases.

4. Discharge by Lapse of Time

If a contract is not performed within the period of limitation and if no action is taken by the promisee in a Law Court, the contract is discharged.

5. Discharge by operation of law

This includes discharge by *(a)* death, *(b)* merger, *(c)* inolvency, *(d)* unauthorised alternation of the terms of a written agreement, and *(e)* rights and liabilities becoming vested in the same person.

6. Discharge by Breach of Contract

If a party breaks his obligation which the contract imposes, there takes place breach of contract. Breach of contract may be **(*i*)** actual breach, or **(*ii*)** anticipatory breach.

(*i*) *Actual breach of contract* may occur *(a)* at the time when the performance is due, or *(b)* during the performance of the contract.

(*ii*) *Anticipatory breach of contract occurs* when a party repudiates his liability or obligation under the contract before the time for performance arrives.

Remedies for Breach of Contract

In case of breach of a contract, the injured party has one or more of the following remedies :

1. Rescission

When there is breach of a contract by a party, the injured party may sue to treat the contract as rescinded. He is also absolved of all his obligations under the contract.

2. Damages

Damages are monetary compensation awarded to the injured party by Court for the loss or injury suflered by him. The foundation of modern law of damages, both in India and England, is to be found in the judgment in the case of *Hadley* vs. *Baxendale.* Sec. 73 of the Indian Contract Act which deals with"compensation for loss or damage caused by breach of contract" is based on the judgment in the case of *Hadley* v. *Baxendale*. Damages may be of four types:

(*i*) *Ordinary damages* : These are damages which actually arise in the usual course of things from the breach of a contract.

(*ii*) *Special damages* : Damages which may reasonably be supposed to have been in the contemplation of both the parties at the time when they made the contract as the probable result of the breach of it, are known as special damages and may be recovered.

(*iii*) *Vindictive or exemplary damages* : These damages are allowed in case of the breach of a contract to marry or dishonour of a cheque by a banker wrongfully.

(*iv*) *Nominal damages* : Where the injured party has not suffered any loss by reason of the breach of a contract, the Court may award a very nominal sum as damages.

Liquidated damages and penalty

'Liquidated damages' represent a sum, fixed or ascertained by the parties in the contract, which is *a fair and genuine preestimate* of the probable loss that might ensue as a result of the breach. A 'penalty' is a sum named in the contract at the time of its formation, which is disproportionate to the damage likely to accrue as a result of the breach. The Courts in India allow only 'reasonable compensation'.

3. Quantum meruit

A right to sue on a *quantum meruit* (as much as earned) arises where a contract, partly performed by one party, has become discharged by the breach of the contract by the other party. This right is founded on an implied promise by the other party arising from the acceptance of a benefit by that/party.

4. Specific performance

In certain cases the Court may direct the party in breach of a contract to actually carry out the promise, exactly according to the terms of the contract. This is called specific performance of the contract.

5. Injunction

It is a mode of securing the specific performance of the negative terms of a contract.

Quasi Contract

In certain cases the law imposes an obligation and allows an action to be brought on it as if it arose out of an agreement, though none was present in fact. Such cases, strictly speaking, are not contracts, but the law recognises them as "certain relations resembling those created by contracts". In English Law, such relations are called quasi-contracts.

Quasi-contracts rest on the ground of equity that a person shall not be allowed to enrich himself unjustly at the expense of another.

Secs. 68 to 72 deal with the following quasi-contracts :

1. Claim for necessaries supplied to a person incapable of contracting or on his account (Sec. 68).
2. Reimbursement of a person paying money due by another in payment of which he is interested (Sec. 69).
3. Obligation of a person enjoying benefit of a non-gratuitous act (Sec. 70).
4. Responsibility of finder of goods (Sec. 71)
5. Liability of person to whom money is paid or thing delivered by mistake or under coercion (Sec. 72).

Quantum Meruit

This means "as much as is earned".

Indemnity and Gurantee

Contract of Indemnity

A contract by which one party promises to save the other from loss caused to him by the conduct of the promisor himself, or by the conduct of any other person, is called a 'contract of indemnity' (Sec. 124). The person who promises to make good the loss is called the *indemnified* (promisor) and the person whose loss is to be made good is called the *indemnified* (promisee) or *indemnity-holder.*

A contract of indemnity is a species of the general contract. It must as such have all the essential elements of a valid contract. It may be *express* or *implied.*

Contract of Guarantee

A 'contract of guarantee' is a contract to perform the promise, or discharge the liability, of a third person in case of his default. The person who gives the guarantee is called the '*surety*', the person in respect of whose default the guarantee is given is called the '*principal debtor*', and the person to whom the guarantee is given is called the '*creditor*'. A guarantee may be either oral or written (Sec. 126).

A contract of guarantee must have all the essential elements of a valid contract. But the principal debtor may be a person suffering from incapacity to contract and it is not necessary that the contract must necessarily result in some benefit to the surely himself.

Kinds of guarantee : A guarantee may be given **1.** for the payment of a debt, or **2.** for the payment of the price of the goods sold on credit, or **3.** for the good conduct or honesty of a person employed in a particular office, in which case the guarantee is called a 'fidelity guarantee'. A guarantee may also be a *specific* or *simple* guarantee (which extends to a *single transaction*) or a *continuing* guarantee which extends to a *series of transactions* (Sec. 129).

Nature of surety's liability : The liability of the surety is *co-extensive* with that of the principal debtor, unless it is otherwise provided by the contract (Sec. 128).

Rights of Surety

1. *As against the creditor* : (*i*) Before payment of the principle debt, a surety can file a suit for declaration that the principal debtor shall be the person liable to pay the amount. (*ii*) On payment of the principal debt, the surety steps into the shoes of the creditor, *i.e.,* he is entitled to be placed in the position of the creditor.

2. *As against the debtor* : The surety, upon payment or performance of all that he is liable for, is inversted with all the rights which the creditor had against the principal debtor (Sec. 140). He is also entitled to recover from the principal debtor whatever sum he has rightfully paid under the guarantee, but no sums which he has paid wrongfully (Sec. 145).

3. *As against the co-sureties* : The co-sureties are, in the absence of any agreement to the contrary, liable to contribute equally (Sec. 146). If they are bound in different sums, they are liable to pay equally as for as the limits of their respective obligations permit (Sec. 147). As between co-sureties, there is *equality of burden and benefit.*

Discharge of Surety

A surety is discharged from liability :

1. *By revocation* : This includes revocation by (*i*) surety by giving a notice (Sec. 130), (*ii*) death of surety (Sec. 131), and (*iii*) novation (Sec. 62).

2. *By conduct of creditor* : This covers cases of (*i*) variance in terms of contract (Sec. 133), (*ii*) release or discharge of principal debtor (Sec. 134), (*iii*) compounding by creditor with principal debtor (Sec. 135), (*iv*) creditor's act or omission impairing surety's eventual remedy (Sec. 139), and (*v*) loss of security (Sec. 141)

3. *By invalidation of contract* : This includes guarantee (*i*) obtained by misrepresentation (Sec. 142) or concealment (Sec. 143), (*ii*) given on a condition that the creditor shall not act upon it until a co-surety joins the surety and the co-surety does not join (Sec. 144). A surety is also discharged where there is failure of consideration.

Bailment and Pledge

Bailment

A 'bailment' is the *delivery of goods* by one person to another for some *purpose,* upon a contract, that they shall, when the purpose is accomplished, be *returned* or otherwise *disposed* of according to the directions of the person delivering them. The person delivering the goods is called the '*bailor*' and the person to whom they are delivered is called the 'bailee' (Sec. 148).

Requisites of bailment : 1. Contract. **2.** Delivery of possession of goods for some purpose. **3.** Return of goods when the purpose is accomplished.

Classification of Bailments

Bailments may be for the **1.** exclusive benefit of the bailor, or **2.** exclusive benefit of the bailee, or **3.** mutual benefit of the bailor and the bailee. Bailments may also be classified into (*i*) gratuitous bailment, and (*ii*) non-gratuitous bailment or bailment for reward.

Duties of Bailee

1. To take care of the goods bailed. **2.** Not to make any unauthorised use of the goods. **3.** Not to mix the goods bailed with his own goods. **4.** Not to set up an adverse title. **5.** To return any accretion to the goods. **6.** To return the goods.

Duties of Bailor

1. To disclose known faults. **2.** To bear extraordinary expenses of bailment. **3.** To receive back the goods. **4.** To indemnify bailee.

Law relating to lien : Lien means the right of a person to retain possession of goods of another until some debt or claim of the person in possession is settled. A lien may be *(a)* a particular lien, or *(b)* a general lien. A *particular lien is* one which is available to the bailee against only those goods in respect of which he has rendered any service involving the exercise of labour or skill. A *general lien* means the right to retain all the goods or any property of the bailor which is in possession of the bailee until all the claims of the bailee are satisfied. This is a right to retain the property of another for a general balance of account.

Termination of Bailment

A contract of bailment is terminated —**1.** On the expiry of the peroid. **2.** On the achievement of the object. **3.** On the inconsistent use of goods bailed. A gratuitous bailment can be terminated by the bailor at any time even though the bailment was for a specified time or purpose provided the loss accruing to the bailee from such premature termination does not exceed the benefit he has derived out of the bailment.

Pledge

The *bailment* of goods *as security for payment of a debt or performance of a promise is called 'pledge'*. The bailor is, in this case, called the '*pawnor*' or '*pledger*' and the bailee is called the '*pawnee*' or '*pledge*' (Sec. 172).

Rights of Pawnee

1. Right to retain goods for debt, interest and expenses, and for subsequent advances. **2.** Right to extraordinary expenses. **3.** Right against true owner when the pawnor's title is defective. **4.** Rights where pawnor makes default—*(a)* suit against the pawnor. *(b)* Retention of the goods as a collateral security. *(c)* Suit for the sale of the goods pledged. *(d)* Right of sale. *(e)* Right to recover deficiency on sale.

Pledge by non-owners

The general rule is that it is the owner who can ordinarily create a valid pledge. But in the following cases pledge even by a non-owner is valid :

1. Pledge by mercantile agent. **2.** Pledge by seller or buyer in possession after sale. **3.** Pledge by a person having limited interest. **4.** Pledge by a co-owner in possession. **5.** Pledge by a person in possession under a voidable contract.

Contract of Agency

An 'agent' is a person employed *to do any act for another* or to represent another in dealings with third persons. The person for whom such act is done, or who is so represented, is called the '*principal*'(Sec. 182).

Rules of Agency

(a) Whatever a person competent to contract may do himself, he may do through an agent. *(b)* He, who does through another, does by himself.

The acts of an agent, therefore, are the acts of the principal. This is of course subject to certain conditions.

Who can employ an agent?

Any person who is of the age of majority according to the law to which he is subject, and who is of sound mind, may employ an agent (Sec. 183).

Creation of Agency

The relationship of principal and agent may be created by—

1. *Express agreement, i.e.,* by word of mouth or by an agreement in writing.
2. *Implied agreement i.e.,* by inference from the circumstances of the case. Implied agency includes :
   - (i) *Agency by estoppel or holding out, i.e.,* when a person, by his conduct or by statement, leads wilfully another person to believe that a certain person is his agent, he is estopped from denying subsequently that, that person is not his agent.
   - (ii) *Agency by necessity, i.e.,* when a person acts in some emergency as agent for another without requiring the consent of that other person.
   - (iii) *Ratification, i.e.,* when a person subsequently accepts the act of the agent done without his consent. *Ratification is tantamount to prior authority*. It relates back to the date when the act was done by the agent.

Rights and Duties of Agent

Rights of Agents

1. Right of retainer. **2.** Right to receive remuneration. **3.** Right of lien. **4.** Right of indemnification. **5.** Right of compensation. **6.** Right of stoppage in transit.

Duties of Agent

1. To carry out work undertaken according to instructions. **2.** To carry out the work with reasonable care, skill and diligence. **3.** To render accounts to the principal. **4.** To communicate with the principal in case of difficulty. **5.** Not to deal on his own account. **6.** To pay sums received for the principal. **7.** To protect and preserve the interests of the principal in case of his death or insolvency. **8.** Not to use information obtained in the course of agency against the principal. **9.** Not to make secret profit from agency. **10.** Not to set up an adverse title. **11.** Not to put himself in a position where his interest and duty conflict. **12.** Not to delegate authority.

Relation of Principal with Third Parties

Agent's authority : The authority of an agent means his capacity to bind the principal. This authority may be actual authority or ostensible authority.

Actual authority is the authority conferred on an agent by the principal. It may be expressed or implied (Sec. 186). An agent having authority to do an act has authority to do every lawful thing which is necessary in order to do such act (Sec. 188).

Ostensible or apparent authority is the authority of an agent as it appears to others.

Delegation of Authority

The general rule is that an agent cannot delegate his authority to another, *i.e.,* he cannot appoint a sub-agent.

Sub-agent. A 'sub-agent' is a person employed by, an acting under the control of, the original agent in the business of the agency (Sec. 191). A sub-agent, therefore, is the agent of the original agent. The relation of the sub-agent to the original agent is, as between themselves, that of agent and principal.

Substituted agent : A substituted agent is a person who is named by the agent, holding an express or implied authority from the principal, to act for the principal. He is the agent of the principal, though he is named at the request of the principal, by the agent (Sec. 194).

Position of Principal and Agent in Relation to Third Parties

1. *Named principal* : Where the agent contracts as agent for a named principal, the principal is *(a)* liable for the acts of the agent with third persons provided the acts are done within the *scope of his authority and in the course fo his employment* as an agent, *(b)* liable for the misrepresentations made or frauds committed by the agent in the course of employment, *(c)* bound by the notice given to or information obtained by the agent in the course of the business of the principal and for admissions made by the agent.

2. *Unnamed principal* : The principal is liable for the contracts of the agent, unless there is a trade custom, or a term, express or implied, to the effect which makes the agent personally liable. The legal position is the same as where the principal is named.

3. *Undisclosed principal* : The agent is bound by the contract. He may be sued on it and he has the right to sue the third party. The principal too has the right to intervene and assert his position as an undisclosed party to the contract.

Personal Liability of Agent

An agent is personally liable where **1.** the contract expressly provides; **2.** he acts for a foreign principal; **3.** he acts for a concealed principal; **4.** he acts for a principal who cannot be sued; **5.** he signs a contract in his own name; **6.** he acts for a principal not in existence; **7.** there is breach of warranty; **8.** he receives or pays money by mistake or fraud; **9.** his authority is coupled with interest; **10.** the trade usage or custom makes him personally liable.

Termination of Agency

An agency is terminated *(i)* by the principal revoking agent's authority: or *(ii)* by the agent renouncing the business of the agency; or *(iii)* by the business of the agency being completed; or *(iv)* by either the principal or agent dying or becoming of unsound mind; or *(v)* when the principal is adjudicated an insolvent under the provisions of any Act for the time being in force for the relief of insolvent debtors (Sec. 201).

Irrevocable agency : When an agency cannot be put an end to, it is said to be an irrevocable agency. An agency is irrevocable where **1.** it is coupled with interest, **2.** the agent has incurred a personal liability. **3.** the agent has partly exercised the authority.

B. SALE OF GOODS ACT, 1930

Sale of Goods

Contract of Sale

A contract of sale of goods is a contract whereby the seller *transfers* or *agrees to transfer* the property in goods to the buyer for a price (Sec. 4).

Sale and Agreement to Sell

Where under a contract of sale the property in the goods is transferred from the seller to the buyer, the contract is called a sale, but where the transfer of the property in the goods is to take place at a future time or subject to some condition therafter to be fulfilled the contract is called an agreement to sell. An agreement to sell becomes a sale when the time elapses or the conditions are fulfilled subject to which the property in the goods is to be transferred.

Contract of Sale how Made

A contract of sale is made by an offer to buy or sell goods for a price and the acceptance of such offer. It may provide for the immediate delivery of the goods or immediate payment of the price or both, or for the delivery or payment by instalments or that the delivery or payment or both shall be postponed. It may be made in writing or by word of mouth or partly in writing and partly by word of mouth, or may be implied from the conduct of the parties (Sec. 5).

Subject-matter of Sale

'Good' form the subject of a contract of sale. They mean *every kind of movable property* other than actionable claims and money, and include stock and shares, growing crops, grass and things attached to or forming part of the land which are agreed to be severed before sale or under the contract of sale [Sec. 2(7)] Goods may be : **1.** *Existing goods, i.e.,* goods which are owned and possessed by the seller at the time of sale. These goods may be specific ascertained or unascertained. **2.** *Future goods, i.e.,* goods which the seller does not possess at the time of the contract and which will be acquired, manufactured or produced by him at some future date. **3.** *Contingent goods i.e.,* goods the acquisition of which by the seller depends upon a contingency which may or may not happen.

Price : The price in a contract of sale must be expressed in money. It **1.** may be fixed by the contract itself, or **2.** may be left to be fixed in an agreed manner, or **3.** may be determined from the course of dealing between the parties. Where the price is not determined in accordance with these provisions, the buyer must pay the seller a reasonable price (Sec. 9).

Conditions and Warranties

A stipulation in a contract of sale with reference to goods which are the subject thereof may be a *condition* or a *warranty* [Sec. 12(1)]. A condition is a stipulation *essential to the main purpose* of the contract. Its breach gives a right to the buyer to treat the contract as repudiated [Sec. 12(2)]. A warranty is a stipulation *collateral* to the main purpose of the contract. Its breach gives rise to a claim for damages but not a right to reject the goods and treat the contract as repudiated [Sec. 12(3)].

Express and Implied Conditions and Warranties

In a contract of sale, conditions and warranties may be *express* or *implied*. Express conditions and warranties are those which are agreed upon between the parties at the time of the contract. Implied conditions and warranties are those which are implied by law unless the parties stipulated to the contrary.

Implied conditions

1. *Condition as to title :* In a contract of sale there is an implied condition on the part of the seller that *(a)* in the case of a sale, he has a right to sell the goods, and *(b)* in the case of an agreement to sell, he will have a right to sell the goods at the time when the property is to pass [Sec. 14(1)].

2. *Sale by description* : Where there is a contract for the sale of goods by description, there is an implied condition that the goods shall correspond with the description. If the sale is by sample as well as by description, the goods shall correspond both with the sample and the description (Sec. 15).

3. *Condition as to quality or fitness* : The condition as to quality or fitness is implied where *(a)* the goods sold are such as the seller deals in the ordinary course of his business; *(b)* the buyer relies on the seller's skill or judgment as to the fitness of the goods for any particular purpose; and *(c)* the buyer expressly or impliedly makes known to the seller that he wants the goods for that particular purpose [Sec. 16 (1)].

4. *Condition as to merchantability* : Where goods are bought by description from a seller who deals in goods of that description (whether he is the manufacturer or producer or not), there is an implied condition that the goods shall be of merchantable quality [Sec. 16(2)].

5. *Condition implied by custom* : An implied condition as to quality or fitness for a particular purpose may be annexed by the usage of trade [Sec. 16(3)].

6. *Sale by sample* : In the case of a contract for sale by sample there is an implied condition *(a)* that the bulk shall correspond with the sample in quality; *(b)* that the buyer shall have a reasonable opportunity of comparing the bulk with the sample; and *(c)* that the goods shall be free from any defect, rendering them unmerchantable, which would not be apparent on a reasonable examination of the sample (Sec. 17).

7. *Condition as to wholesomeness* : In case of eatables and provisions, there is an implied condition that the goods shall be wholesome and fit for human consumption.

Implied Warranties

In a contract of sale, unless there is a contrary intention, there is an implied warranty that **1.** the buyer shall have and enjoy *quiet possession* of the goods [Sec. 14(*b*)], and **2.** the goods are free from any change or encumbrance in favour of any third party [Sec. 14(*c*)].

Caveat emptor : This means "let the buyer beware". The doctrine of *caveat emptor* does not apply—**1.** In case of implied conditions and warranties; **2.** When the buyer intimates the purpose to the seller and depends upon his skill or judgment; **3.** When there is a usage of trade; **4.** When there is a fraud by the seller.

Transfer of Property

It is important to know the precise moment of time at which the property in goods passes from the seller to the buyer for the following reasons:

1. *Risk follows ownership* whether delivery has been made or not and whether price has been paid or not. This is, however, subject to agreement between the parties.
2. When the goods are damaged or destroyed by the action of the third parties, it is the owner of the goods who can take action against them.
3. In the event of insolvency of either the seller or the buyer, the question whether the Official Receiver or Assignee can take over the goods or not depends on whether the property in the goods has passed from the seller to the buyer.
4. The seller can sue for the price, unless otherwise agreed, only if the goods have become the property of the buyer.

Transfer of Property

The primary rules for ascertaining when the property in goods passes to the buyer are as follows:

1. Where there is a contract for the sale of unascertained goods, no property in the goods is transferred to the buyer unless and until the goods are ascertained (Sec. 18).

2. Where there is a contract for the sale of specific or ascertained goods, the property in them is transferred to the buyer at such time as the parties to the contract *intend* it to be transferred. For the purpose of ascertaining the intention of the parties, regard shall be had to the terms of the contract, the conduct of the parties and the circumstances of the case (Sec. 19). Where the intention of the parties cannot be ascertained, the following rules shall apply :

(*i*) *Specific goods* : In case of a contract for the sale of specific goods *(a)* in a deliverable state, if the contract is unconditional, property passes as soon as the contract is entered into (Sec. 20), *(b)* if the seller has to do something to put them in a deliverable state, property passes only when such thing is done and notice thereof is given to the buyer (Sec. 21), *(c)* in a deliverable state if the seller has to do something for the purpose of ascertaining the price, property will pass only when such act is done and notice thereof is given to the buyer (Sec. 22).

(*ii*) *Unascertained goods* : In case of unascertained or future goods sold by description, property passes only when goods according to the description are unconditionally appropriated to the contract and the buyer is given a notice thereof. Delivery to a carrier (the seller not reserving right of disposal, Sec. 25) amounts to an unconditional appropriation (Sec. 23).

(*iii*) *Goods sent on approval* : In case of goods delivered to a buyer on approval or 'on sale or return' property passes when he signifies his approval or acceptance or when he does some act adopting the transaction. If he retains the goods without giving notice of rejection, property passes when the time agreed for returning the goods expires or after a reasonable time has expired (Sec. 24).

Sale by non-owners

The general rule of law is that only the owner of the goods or any person specifically authorised by him can sell the goods. If any other person sells them, the title of the buyer will, not be better than that of the seller.

Exceptions : The following are the exceptions to the above rule : **1.** Sale by a mercantile agent. **2.** Sale under the implied authority of woner or title by estoppel. **3.** Sale by one of several joint woners. **4.** Sale by a person in possession of goods under a voidable contract. **5.** Sale by a seller in possession after sale. **6.** Sale by a buyer in possession after having bought or agreed to buy. **7.** Sale by an unpaid seller.

In all these cases, the person selling the goods must be in possession of the goods with the consent of the seller and the buyer must act *bona fide*.

Performance of Contract

It is the duty of the seller to deliver the goods and of the buyer to accept and pay for them in accordance with the terms of the contract of sale.

Delivery of goods : Delivery means voluntary transfer of possession of goods from the seller to the buyer. It may be *(i)* actual, *(ii)* symbolic, or *(iii)* constructive. But it must be according to the rules as given below :

Rules as to delivery. 1. Unless otherwise agreed, delivery of the goods and payment of the price are concurrent conditions. **2.** A delivery of part of the goods, in progress, of the delivery of whole, amounts to, for the purpose of passing the property in such goods, as a delivery of the whole. **3.** Apart from any express contract, the seller of goods is not bound to deliver them until the buyer applies for delivery. **4.** The place of delivery is the place at which they are at the time of the sale. **5.** If the goods are in possession of a third party, there is no delivery until such third party acknowledges to the buyer that he holds the goods on his behalf. **6.** Where the seller is bound to send the goods to the buyer but no time for sending them is fixed, they must be sent within a reasonable time. **7.** Expenses of making delivery are borns by the seller and expenses of obtaining delivery by the buyer. **8.** If the seller sends to the buyer a larger or a smaller quantity of goods than he ordered, the buyer may *(a)* reject the whole, or *(b)* accept the whole, or *(c)* accept the quantity he ordered and reject the rest. **9.** If the seller delivers, with the goods ordered, goods of a wrong description, the buyer may accept the goods ordered and reject the rest or reject the whole. **10.** Unless otherwise agreed, the goods are not to be delivered by instalments.

Rights of an Unpaid Seller

A seller of goods is deemed to be an unpaid seller **1.** when the whole of the price has not been paid or tendered; **2.** when a bill of exchange or other negotiable instrument has been received as a conditional payment, and the condition on which it was received has not been fulfilled by reason of the dishonour of the instrument, or otherwise (Sec. 45). An unpaid seller has the rights—

1. As against the goods : *(a)* *Right of lien* : It is available to the unpaid seller when *(i)* the goods have been sold without any stipulation as to credit; *(ii)* the goods have been sold on credit, but the term of the credit has expired; *(iii)* the buyer becomes insolvent (Sec. 47).

(b) *Right of stoppage in transit* : When the buyer of goods becomes insolvent the unpaid seller who has parted with the possession of the goods has the right of stopping them in transit. The seller may resume possession of the goods, as long as they are in the course of transit and may retain them until payment or tender of the price (Sce. 50). The unpaid seller may exercise this right of stoppage in transit either by taking actual possession of the goods, or by giving notice of his claim to the carrier or other bailee in whose possession the goods are.

(c) *Right of re-sale* : The unpaid seller can re-sell the goods *(i)* where the goods are of a perishable nature; *(ii)* where he has exercised his right of lien or stoppage in transit and given notice to the buyer of his intention to re-sell the goods and the buyer has not within a reasonable time paid the price; and *(iii)* where the seller expressly reserves a right of re-sale in case the buyer should make default (Sec. 54).

Right of Withholding Delivery

Where the property in goods has not passed to the buyer, the unpaid seller has, in addition to his other remedies, a right of withholding delivery similar to and co-extensive with his rights of lien and stoppage in transit where the property has passed to the buyer [Sec. 46 (2)].

2. As against the buyer personally : *(a) Suit for price* : Where under a contract of sale the property in the goods has passed to the buyer and the buyer wrongfully neglects or refuses to pay for the goods according to the terms of the contract, the seller may sue him for the price of the goods (Sec. 55).

(b) Damages for non-acceptance : Where the buyer wrongfully neglects or refuses to pay for the goods, the seller may sue him for damages for non-acceptance (Sec. 56).

(c) Repudiation of contract before due date : Where the buyer in a contract of sale repudiates the contract before the date of delivery, the seller may either treat the contract as subsisting and wait till the date of delivery, or he may treat the contract as rescinded and sue for damages for the breach (Sec. 60).

(d) Suit for interest : The seller can recover interest on price from the date on which the payment became due, if there is a special agreement to that effect.

Auction Sale

A sale by auction is a public sale where different intending buyers try to outbid each other. The goods are ultimately sold to the highest bidder. The law on auction sales is contained is Sec. 64 of the Sale of Goods Act.

C. PARTNERSHIP ACT, 1932

Definition Nature of Partnership

Partnership is the relation between persons who have agreed to share the profits of a business carried on by all or any of them acting for all (Sec. 4).

Characteristics of Partnership

1. Association of two or more persons. **2.** Agreement. **3.** Business. **4.** Sharing of profits of the business. **5.** Mutual agency.

Partners, Firm and Firm Name

Persons who have entered into partnership with one another are called individually *partners* and collectively a *firm.* The name under which their business is carried on is called the *firm name.* The partners may carry on business under any name and style. But the name should not resemble the name of any existing firm and it should not show or imply the parronage of the Government.

Law of partnership is an extension of the law of agency.

Partnership and Firm

Partnership is merely an abstract legal relationship between partners. A firm is a collective name for all the partners. Partnership is an abstract thing; a firm is a concrete thing.

Formation of Partnership

Partnership is a special type of contract. As such all the essential elements of a valid contract must be present. But a minor may be admitted to the benefits of partnership with the consent of all the partners for the time being, and no consideration is required to create partnership.

Duration of Partnership

A partnership may be for a *fixed period of time.* Where no provision is made by the partners for the duration of the partnership, it is *partnership-at-will.* When a person becomes a partner with another person or persons in a particular adventure or undertaking, it is *a particular partnership.*

Test of Partnership

In order to determine the existence of partnership between a group of persons, one has look to the agreement between them. If there is no agreement, we shall have to refer to Sec. 6. In determining whether a group of persons is or is not a firm, or whether a person is or not a partner in a firm, regard shall be had to the *real relation* between the parties as shown by all relevant facts taken together. The sharing of profits or of gross returns arising from property by persons holding a joint or common interest in that property does not of itself make such persons partners. Again the receipt by a person of a share of the profits of a business does not of itself make him a partner with the persons carrying on the business. The business. The test of partnership is *mutual agency* and not necessarily the sharing of profits or the contribution of capital or the holding of a particular property jointly.

Registration of Firms

The Partnership Act does not provide for the compulsory registration of firms. But by creating certain disabilities from which an unregistered firm suffers, the law has made the registration of firms compulsory.

Effects of non-registration

1. A partner of an unregistered firm cannot file a suit against the firm or any partner thereof for the purpose of enforcing a right arising from a contract or a right conferred by the Partnership Act, **2.** No suit can be filed on behalf of an unregistered firm against any third party for the purpose of enforcing a right arising from a contract. **3.** An unregistered firm cannot claim a set-off exceeding Rs. 100.

Procedure for registration : The registration of a firm may be effected any time by filing an application in the form of a statement giving the necessary details with the Registrar of Firms of the area. The application for registration should be accompanied by the prescribed registration fee. When the Registrar is satisfied that the provisions as laid down in the Act have been duly complied with, he records an entry of the statement in the Register of Firms, and files the statement. He then issues a certificate of registration.

Relation of Partner

Relation of Partners to one Another

The relations of the partners to one another are usually governed by the agreement among them. Where there is no specific agreement, their relations to one another are governed by Secs. 9 to 17 of the Partnership Act.

Rights of a Partner

Subject to the agreement between the partners, a partner, has the right

1. to take part in the conduct of the business of the firm,
2. to be consulted,
3. of access to accounts and books,
4. to share in the profits of the business,
5. to interest on capital (only if there is an agreement),
6. to interest on advances at 6 per cent per annum,
7. to be indemnified where he incurs liability in the ordinary course of business of the firm,
8. to have the use of partnership property for the purposes of the business of the firm,
9. to retire,
10. not to be expelled

Further as agent of the firm, he has the right to act in an emergency to protect the firm from loss.

Duties of a Partners

1. To observe good faith. **2.** To indemnify for fraud. **3.** To attend diligently to the business of the firm. **4.** Not to claim any remuneration. **5.** To share losses. **6.** To indemnify for willful neglect. **7.** To hold and use property of the firm for the firm. **8.** To account for personal profits. **9.** To account for profits in competing business. **10.** To act within authority. **11.** To be liable jointly and severally. **12.** Not to assign his rights.

Relations of Partners to Third Parties

Every partner is the agent of the firm for the purposes of the business of the firm (Sec. 18).

Authority of a partner : The authority of a partner means the right of a partner to bind the firm by his acts. This authority of a partner to bind the firm may be an *express* authority or *implied* authority. Where, there is no partnership agreement or where the agreement is silent. Sec. 19 (1) provides that the act of a partner, which is done to carry on, in the usual way, business of the kind carried on by the firm, binds the firm. This authority of a partner is called his *implied authority.*

No implied authority : In the absence of any usage or custom of trade to the contrary, the implied authority of a partner *does not empower* him to—

(a) submit a dispute relating to the business of the firm to arbitration;

(b) open a baking account on behalf of the firm in his own name;

(c) compromise or relinquish any claim or portion of claim by the firm;
(d) withdraw a suit or proceeding filed on behalf of the firm;
(e) admit any liability in a suit or proceeding against the firm;
(f) acquire immovable property on behalf of the firm;
(g) transfer immovable property belonging to the firm;
(h) enter into partnership on behalf of the firm [Sec. 19(2)].

A partner can do any of the above things if—

1. he has specific or express authority of the partners; or
2. the usage or custom of trade permits him.

Types of Partners

1. *Actual partner, i.e.,* one who becomes a partner by an agreement and is actively engaged in the conduct of the business of partnership.
2. *Sleeping partner, i.e.,* one who does not take an active part in the conduct of the business of the firm. He is, however, liable for the debts of the firm.
3. *Nominal partner, i.e.,* one who lends his name to the firm, without having any real interest in it. He is, however, liable to outsiders for the debts of the firm.
4. *Partner in profits only. i.e.,* one who gets a share in profits only and is not to contribute towards losses. He is, however, liable to outsiders for the debts of the firm.
5. *Partner by estoppel or holding out.* Anyone who by words spoken or written or by conduct prepresents himself, or knowingly permits himself to be represented to be a partner in a firm, is liable as a partner in that firm to anyone who has on the faith of any such representation given credit to the firm, whether the person representing himself or represented to be a partner does or does not know that the representation has reached the person so giving credit.
6. *Minor partner.* With the consent of all the partners for the time being, a minor may be admitted to the benefits of partnership. A minor partner has a right to such share of the property and of the profits of the firm as may have been agreed upon. He has also a right to have access to and to inspect and, copy any of the accounts, but not the books, of the firm. His liability is, however, confined only the extent of his share in the profits and property of the firm. He may, at any time within six months of his attaining majority, give public notice that he has elected to *(a)* become, or *(b)* not to become a partner in the firm. If he fails to give a public notice, he is deemed to have become a partner in the firm on the expiry of the said six months.

Reconstitution of a Firm

1. *Introduction of a new partner* (Sec. 31) : Subject to contract between the partners, on person can be introduced as a partner into a firm without the consent of all the existing partners. An incoming partner is not liable for any act of the firm done prior to his admission.

2. *Retirement of a partner* (Sec. 32) : A partner may retire from a firm with the consent of all the other partners. Where the partnership is at will, a partner may retire by giving notice in writing to all the other partners of his intention to retire.

3. *Explusion of partner* (Sec. 38) : A majority of partners can expel a partner only if such power is conferred by contract between the partners, and the power is exercised *bonafide* by the majority of partners.

4. *Insolvency of a partner* (Sec. 34) : Where a partner in a firm is adjudicated insolvent, he ceases to be a partner on the date on which the order of adjudication is made, whether or not the firm is thereby dissolved.

5. *Death of a partner* [Sec. 42*(c)*] : Subject to contract between the partners, a firm is dissolved by the death fo a partner.

Dissolution of Firm

The *dissolution of partnership* between all the partners of a firm is called the *dissolution of the firm* (Sec. 39). Dissolution of firm means complete breakdown of the relation of partnership between all the partners. If this breakdown of partnership relation is between a few and not all the partners, this amounts to dissolution of partnership which simply involves only a change in the relation of the partners.

Dissolution of a firm may be voluntary or without the order of Court, or it may take place by the order of Court.

Dissolution without the Order of Court

This takes place in the following ways :

1. *Dissolution by agreement* (Sec. 40). A firm may be dissolved *(i)* with the consent of all the partners, or *(ii)* in accordance with a contract between the partners.

2. *Compulsory dissolution* (Sec. 41). A firm is compulsorily dissolved *(a)* when all the partners or all the partners but one are adjudicated insolvent. *(b)* on the happening of any event which makes it unlawful for the business of the firm to be carried on, or for the partners to carry it on in partnership.

3. *Dissolution on the happening of certain contingencies* (Sec. 42). Subject to contract between the partners, a firm is dissolved *(a)* it constituted for a fixed term, by the expiry of that term; *(b)* if constituted to carry out one or more adventures or undertakings, by the completion thereof; *(c)* by the death of a partner; and *(d)* by the adjudication of a partner as an insolvent.

4. *Dissolution by notice of partnership-at-will* (Sec. 43). Where a partnership is at will, the firm may be dissolved by any partner by giving a notice in writing to all the other partners of his intention to dissolve the firm.

Dissolution by the Court (Sec. 44)

At the suit of a partner, the Court may dissolve a firm on any of the folloiwng grounds, viz., *(a)* Insanity of a partner, *(b)* Permanent incapacity of a partner, *(c)* Misconduct of a partner, *(d)* Persistent breach of agreement by a partner, *(e)* Transfer of interest by a partner, *(f)* Business working at a loss, *(g)* Any other ground which the Court deems just and equitable.

Rights and Liabilities of Partners on Dissolution

Rights : On the dissolution of a firm, a partner has the right to **1.** have the business of the firm would up and the debts of the firm settled out of the property of the firm; **2.** share in the profits of the firm earned after dissolution; **3.** have the premium returned on premature dissolution; **4.** restrain the use of firm name or property by any partner for his own benefit.

In case the partnership is rescinded on the ground of fraud or misrepresentation, the partner has the right of *(a)* lien on the surplus assets, *(b)* subrogation, and *(c)* indemnification.

Liabilities : If a public notice is not given of the dissolution of a firm the partners continue to be liable to third parties for any act done by any of them after dissolution. After the dissolution of the firm, the partners continue to be liable for acts done to wind up the affairs of the firm and to complete transactions begun but unfinished at the time of the dissolution.

D. NEGOTIABLE INSTRUMENT ACT, 1881

Negotiable Instruments

Definition : A negotiable instrument is one the property in which is acquired by anyone who takes it *bona fide* and for value, notwithstanding any defect of title in the person from whom he took it—*Justice Willis.*

The law relating to negotiable instruments is contained in the Negotiable Instruments Act, 1881, which deals with promissory notes, bill of exchange and cheques, as also *hundis* (bills of exchange in vernacular language).

Characteristics of a Negotiable Instrument

1. The property in a negotiable, instrument passes from one person to another by a simple process, *i.e.,* by mere *delivery* if it is payable to bearer, and by *indorsement* and *delivery* if it is payable to order.

2. The holder in due course (one who acquires the instrument in good faith and for consideration) gets it *free from all defects.*
3. He can sue upon the instrument in his own name.
4. The transferee of the instrument need not give notice of transfer to the party liable to pay.
5. Consideration is presumed to have been given for the instrument.

Presumptions

The Act lays down a number of presumptions in favour of negotiable instruments. These presumptions are as to *(a)* consideration, *(b)* date, *(c)* time of acceptance, *(d)* time of transfer, *(e)* order of indorsements, *(f)* stamp, *(g)* holder in due course, and *(h)* proof of protest.

Types of negotiable instruments : Negotiable instruments may be—

1. Negotiable by Statute, or
2. Negotiable by custom or usage.

Notes, Bills & Cheques

Promissory Note

A 'promissory note' is an instrument in writing (note being a bank note or a currency note) containing an unconditional undertaking signed by the maker, to pay a certain sum of money only to, or to the order of a certain person, or to the bearer of the instrument (Sec. 4). The person who makes the promissory note is called the *maker;* the person to whom the payment is to be made is called the *payee*.

Its essentials : **1.** It must be in writing. **2.** It must contain an express undertaking or promise to pay. **3.** The promise to pay should be unconditional. **4.** It must be signed by the maker. **5.** The parties, *i.e.,* the maker and the payee, must be certain. **6.** The sum payable must be certain. **7.** It must contain a promise to pay money. **8.** A bank note or a currency note is not a promissory note.

Bill of Exchange

A bill of exchange is an instrument in writing containing an unconditional order, signed by the maker, directing a certain person to pay a certain sum of money only to, or to the order of, a certain person, or to the bearer of the instrument (Sec. 5). The person who makes the bill is called the *drawer*. The person who is directed to pay is called the *drawee*. The person to whom the payment is to be made is called the *payee*.

Cheque

A cheque is a bill of exchange drawn on a specified banker and payable on demand (Sec. 6). It is a species of a bill of exchange with two additional qualification, *viz.,(i)* it is always drawn on a specified banker, and *(ii)* it is always payable on demand.

Crossing of cheque : When a cheque bears across its face two parallel transverse lines, the cheque is said to be crossed. The payment of a crossed cheque can be obtained only through another banker. The crossing may be general, special, or restrictive. In case of 'not negotiable crossing' the title of the transferee cannot be better than that of the transferor.

A cheque may be crossed by the drawer of the holder, or the banker.

Classification of Negotiable Instruments

Bearer and order instruments : A negotiable instrument is *payable to bearer (i)* when it is expressed to be so payable, or *(ii)* when the only or last indorsement on the instrument is an indorsement in blank.

A negotiable instrument is *payable to order (i)* when it is expressed to be so payable, or *(ii)* when it is expressed to be payable to a particular person, and does not contain words prohibiting or restricting it transfer (Explanation 1 to Sec. 13).

Inland and Foreign Instrument

A promissory note, bill of exchange, or cheque drawn or made in India and made payable in India, or drawn upon any person resident in India, is deemed to be an *inland* instrument (Sec. 11).

All instruments which are not inland instruments are deemed to be *foreign* instruments (Sec. 12).

Demand and Time Instruments

A promissory note or bill of exchange is payable on demand *(a)* when it is expressed to be payable 'on demand' or 'at sight' or 'on presentment'. or *(b)* when no time for payment is specified in it. A cheque is always payable on demand.

A bill or note is a time instrument if it is stated to be payable *(a)* at a fixed period after its date, or *(b)* at a fixed period after sight, or *(c)* on or at a fixed period after an event which is certain to happen.

Accommodation bill is a bill drawn, accepted or indorsed *without* any consideration.

Ambiguous instrument is an instrument which owing to its faulty drafting can be interpreted either as a promissory note or a bill or exchange.

Inchoate instrument is an instrument which is incomplete in some respect.

Bill in sets is a bill of exchange drawn in parts generally three. Each part, known as *via*, is sent separately.

Maturity and Days of Grace

When a promissory note or bill of exchnge is payable after a specified period, the date on which it falls due, known as date of maturity, has to be calculated. Every instrument payable otherwise than 'on demand' is entitled to three days of grace.

Payment in Due Course

It means payment in accordance with the apparent tenor of the instrument in good faith and without negligence to any person in possession thereof under circumstances which do not afford a reasonable ground for believing that he is not entitled to receive payment of the amount therein mentioned (Sec. 10).

Parties to a Negotiable Instrument

Capacity of Parties

The capacity of a person to incur liability as a party to a promissory note, bill of exchange or cheque is *co-extensive* with his capacity to contract.

Minor

A minor may draw, indorse, deliver and negotiate a negotiable instrument so as to bind all parties except himself, that is, he may operate as a channel to convey title and liability but not to criginate it.

Person of Unsound Mind

Bills and notes drawn or made by a person of unsound mind are void as against him (though the other parties continue to be liable) if at the time of the execution of such instruments, he is not capable of forming a rational judgment.

Corporation

A corporation, being an artificial person, can exercise only those powers which its Memorandum or Articles confer on it. A trading company has implied power, and a non-trading company must take express power, to draw, make, indorse, accept negotiable instruments.

Agent

An agent who signs a negotiable instrument for his principal may bind his principal provided **1.** he signs the principal's name or states on the face of the instrument that he signs as agent, and **2.** he acts within the scope of his authority.

Partner

In a trading firm each partner has implied authority to bind his co-partners by drawing indorsing accepting or negotiating bills, notes and cheques.

Parties to Negotiable Instruments

Parties to a Promissory Note

1. Maker, **2.** Payee, **3.** Holder, **4.** Indorser, **5.** Indorsee.

Parties to a Bill of Exchange

1. Drawer, **2.** Drawee, **3.** Acceptor, **4.** Payee, **5.** Holder, **6.** Indorser, **7.** Indorsee, **8.** Drawee in case of need, **9.** Acceptor for honour.

Parties to a Cheque

1. Drawer, **2.** Drawee, **3.** Payee, **4.** Holder, **5.** Indorser, **6.** indorsee.

Holder in Due Course

"Holder in due course" means any person who for consideration became the possessor of a promissory note, bill of exchange or cheque, if payable to bearer, or the payee or indorsee thereof if payable to order, before the amount mentioned in it became payable, and without having sufficient cause to believe that any defect existed in the title of the person from whom he derived his title (Sec. 9).

Privileges of a Holder in Due Course

1. A holder in due course can fill in an inchoate stamped instrument for any amount provided the stamp is sufficient to cover the amount. (Sec. 20).
2. Every prior party to a negotiable instrument is liable thereon to a holder in due course until the instrument is duly satisfied (Sec. 36).
3. If a bill or note is negotiated to a holder in due course, the other parties to the bill or note cannot avoid liability on the ground that the delivery of the instrument was conditional or for a special purpose only (Sec. 46).
4. Once a negotiable instrument passes through the hands of a holder in due course, it gets cleansed of all its defects (Sec. 53).
5. The defences on the part of a person liable on a negotiable instrument that it has been lost, or obtained from him by means of an offence, or fraud or unlawful consideration, cannot be setup againt a holder in due course (Sec. 58).
6. The law presumes that every holder is a holder in due course, although the presumption is rebuttable (Sec. 118).
7. In a suit on a negotiable instrument by a holder in due course, the validity of the instrument as orginally made or drawn cannot be denied (Sec. 120).
8. No indorser of a negotiable instrument is, in a suit thereon by a subsequent holder, permitted to deny the signature or capacity to contract of any prior party to the instrument (Sec. 121).

Negotiation

When a promissory note, bill of exchange, or cheque is *transferred* to any person, so as to constitute that person the *holder* thereof, the instrument is said to be negotiated (Sec. 14). There are two methods of negotiation:

1. *Negotiation by delivery* : If an instrument is payable to bearer, it is negotiable by *delivery* thereof (Sec. 47).

2. *Negotiation by indorsement and delivery* : If an instrument is payable to order, it is negotiable by the holder by *indorsement* and *delivery* thereof (Sec. 48).

The negotiation of an instrument should be distinguished from transfer by assignment.

Indorsement

It means *writing of a person's name* on an instrument for the purpose of negotiation. The person who indorses the instrument is called the '*indorser*', and the person to whom it is indorsed is called the '*indorsee*'.

Types of Indorsement

An indorsement may be **1.** blank or general, **2.** special or full, **3.** restrictive, **4.** partial, or **5.** conditional or qualified.

1. *Blank or general indorsement* : A blank indorsement is effected by the simple signature of the *indorser* on the face or back of the instrument. It specifies no indorsee and the instrument in consequence becomes payable to bearer.

2. *Full or special indorsement* : If the indorser signs his name and adds a direction to pay the amount mentioned in the instrument to, or to the order of, a specified person, the indorsement is said to be full.

3. *Restrictive indorsement* : An indorsement is said to be restrictive when it prohibits further negotiation of the instrument.

4. *Partial indorsement* : When an indorsement purports to transfer to the indorsee a part of the amount only, the indorsement is said to be partial. A partial indorsement does not operate as a negotiation of the instrument.

5. *Conditional or qualified indorsement* : An indorsement is conditional or qualified, if it limits or negatives the liability of the indorser.

Negotiation Back

If an indorser, after he has negotiated an instrument, again becomes its holder before its maturity, the instrument is said to be negotiated back. In such a case all the intermediate parties are absolved of their liability.

Instruments Obtained by Unlawful Means

Stolen and Lost Instruments

A person who steals or finds a lost negotiable instrument does not acquire a title to the instrument as against the rightful owner. He cannot enforce payment on it against any party thereto. If he obtains payment on it, he is liable to the true owner. If the bill or note is payable to bearer, he can negotiate it to a *bona fide* transferee for value who acquires a good title to it. But if the bill or note is payable to order, and the thief or finder forges the indorsement of the rightful owner, even a *bona fide* transferee for value does not acquire a title to it.

Instruments Obtained by Fraud

If a negotiable instrument is obtained by fraud, the person defrauding is not entitled to recover anything. But the defence of fraud cannot in general be set up against a holder in due course.

Forged Instruments

Forgery is the fraudulent making or alternation of a negotiable instrument to the prejudice of another man's rights. If any of the signatures on the instrument is forged, the signature in question is wholly inoperative and no person, even if acting in good faith, can acquire rights under the instrument.

Negotiable Instruments and Consideration

The rules as to consideration applicable to negotiable instruments are as follows:

1. Until the contrary is proved, it is presumed that every negotiable instrument was made or drawn for consideration.
2. The defence of absence or failure of consideration is available only between parties in immediate relationship with each other. It is not available against a holder in due course or a person deriving title from him.

Presentment of a Negotiable Instrument

Presentment means showing a negotiable instrument to the drawee, acceptor, or maker for **1.** acceptance, or **2.** sight, or **3.** payment.

1. Presentment for Acceptance

It is only bills of exchange of payable after sight that needs to be presented for acceptance. The acceptance of a bill is the *signification* by the drawee of his assent to the order of the drawer that he will pay the bill at the appropriate time.

The liability of the drawee does not arise untill he has accepted the bill

A bill payable on demand or at sight, or on a certain fixed date, need not be presented for acceptance unless it is specifically agreed that such a bill is to be presented for acceptance. But presentment for acceptance is obligatory in case of a bill payable some period after sight or after presentment or when there is an express stipulation in the bill that it shall be presented for acceptance.

Modes of Acceptance

An acceptance may be general or qualified.

General acceptance : The acceptance is general when the drawee, while accepting the bill, *does not attach any condition* or qualification to it.

Qualified accceptance : The acceptance is qualified when it is given *subject to some condition* or qualification. The holder may refuse to take the qualified acceptance, and treat the bill or dishonoured by non-acceptance. But if he takes it he does so tat his own risk and discharges all parties prior to himself unless he obtains their consent to such acceptance.

Presentment for Acceptance to Whom

Presentment for acceptance may be made—**1.** To the drawee or his duly authorised agent. **2.** To his legal representative if the drawee has died. **3.** To his assignee, if the drawee has been declared insolvent. **4.** To all the drawees, if there are several drawees unless they are partners or agents of one another. **5.** To drawee in case of need.

Presentment for acceptance excused : Presentment for acceptance is excused where **1.** the drawee is a fictitious or incompetent person, **2.** he cannot, after reasonable search, be found, **3.** he is dead or insolvent, **4.** although the presentment has been irregular, acceptance has been refused on some other ground.

Acceptor for honour : Normally a stranger to a bill cannot accept it, but he may, with the consent of the holder, accept the bill in place of the drawee, for the honour of some party liable on the bill. Such an acceptor is known as acceptor for honour.

2. Presentment for Sight

A promissory note payable after sight must be presented to the maker for sight to determine its maturity, during business hours, and on a business day. If the maker cannot be found, after a reasonable search, presentment is excused and the note may be treated as dishonoured (Sec. 62).

3. Presentment for Payment

Promissory notes, bills of exchange and cheques must be presented for payment to the maker, acceptor or drawee thereof respectively, by or on behalf of the holder. If default is made, the parties other than the parties primarily liable are discharged of their liability (Sec. 64).

Presentment for payment must be made during the usual hours of business. It must be made—*(a)* at the place of payment specified in the instrument; *(b)* if no place is specified, at the place of business or residence; *(c)* in any other case, wherever the party liable to pay can be found.

Presentment for payment to whom : Presentment for payment must be made—*(a)* to the drawee, maker or acceptor, as the case may be *(b)* where the drawee, maker or acceptor has died, to his representative; *(c)* where he has been declared insolvent, to his assignce. Delay in presentment for payment is excused if it is caused by circumstances beyond the control of the holder.

Presentment for payment is not necessary— *(a)* where it is intentionally prevented by the maker, drawee or acceptor, or *(b)* where the business of the maker, drawee or acceptor is closed or he cannot after due search be found, or there is no person at the place of payment, or *(c)* where there is a promise to pay not withstanding non-presentment, or *(d)* where presentment is expressly or impliedly waived, or *(d)* where the bill is dishonoured by non-acceptance, or *(f)* where the drawee is a fictitious person, or *(g)* where the presentment becomes impossible.

Payment for honour : Just as a bill may be accepted for the honour of a party to the bill, it may also be paid for the honour of a party liable to pay the bill.

Dishonour of Negotiable Instrument

A bill may be dishonoured by *(a)* non-acceptance, or by *(b)* non-payment. A promissory note or cheque can be dishonoured only by non-payment.

Notice of Dishonour

When a negotiable instrument is dishonoured, the holder must give a notice of dishonour to all the parties whom he wants to make liable on the instrument. If he fails to do so, except in cases when notice of dishonour may be excused, all the prior parties liable thereon are discharged of their liability (Sec. 93).

Notice by whom : Notice of dishonour may be given by the holder or by any of the parties to the instrument to the prior parties (Sec. 93).

Notice to whom : Notice of dishonour must be given to all the prior parties whom the holder seeks to make liable. Such notice need not be given to the maker of a note, acceptor of a bill or drawee of a cheque (Sec. 93).

From of notice : The notice of dishonour may be oral or in writing and may be sent by post. It may be in any form but it must inform the party to whom it is given that the instrument has been dishonoured. It must be given within a reasonable time at the place of business or residence of the party for whom it is intended (Sec. 94).

Notice of dishonour unnecessary (Sec. 98) : No notice of dishonour is necessary—*(a)* when it is dispensed with by the party entitled thereto; *(b)* to charge the drawer, when he has countermanded payment; *(c)* when the party charged could not suffer damage for want of notice; *(d)* when the party entitled to notice cannot after due search be found; *(e)* to charge the drawer when the acceptor is also a drawer; *(f)* in the case of a promissory note which is not negotiable; and *(g)* when the party entitled to notice promises to pay unconditionally.

Noting and Protesting

Noting : Noting means the recording of the fact of dishonour by a Notary Public on a dishonoured bill, or upon a paper attached thereto, or partly upon each (Sec. 99).

Protest : When a promissory note or bill of exchange has ben dishonoured by non-acceptance or non-payment, the holder may, within a reasonable time, cause such dishonour to be noted and certified by a Notary Public. Such formal certificate by the Notary Public is called 'protest' (See. 100).

Rules as to Compensation

The compensation payable in case of dishonour of a negotiable instrument inculdes, besides the principal amount and interest due, all proper expenses for noting, protesting or for exchange. An indorser who has paid the amount on the instrument is entitled to the amount paid with interest at the rate of 18 per cent per annum from the date of payment until tender or realisation of the instrument and all proper expenses caused by the dishonour. Further the party entitled to compensation may draw a bill on any party liable to compensate him. Such a bill is referred to as a 're-draft'. The 're-draft' must be accompained by the dishonoured bill and its protest, if any (Sec. 117).

Discharge of a Negotiable Instrument

An instrument is said to be discharged when all rights of action under it are completely extinguished and when it ceases to be negotiable. If one or more of the parties (excepting the party who is ultimately liable to pay) is discharged from liability, the instrument continues to be negotiable and the other parties continue to be liable on it.

An instrument is discharged—**1.** By payment in due course, **2.** By maker or acceptor becoming the holder, **3.** By express waiver, **4.** By cancellation. It may also be discharged like a contract for the payment of money.

A party to a negotiable instrument may be discharged from liability—**1.** By cancellation, **2.** By release, **3.** By allowing drawee more than 48 hours, **4.** By delay in presentment of a cheque, **5.** By material alternation, **6.** By operation of law which includes discharge by—*(a)* an order of Insolvency Court, *(b)* merger, *(c)* lapse of time, **7.** By payment of altered instrument.

Hundis

A *hundi* is an indigenous negotiable instrument written in a vernachular language and is subject to local usages and customs.

A *hundi* may be a *darshani hundi* or or a *muddati* or *miadi hundi.* The former is payable at sight whereas the latter is payable after a specified period. It may also be **1.** a *shah jog hundi* which is payable only to a *shah, i.e.,* a prespectable person, or **2.** a *nam jog hundi* which is payable to or to the order of the person named in the *hundi,* or **3.** a *dhani jog hundi* which is payable to the bearer, or **4.** a *firman jog hundi* which is payable to order, or **5.** a jawabee hundi in which case the persson receiving the amount of the hundi has to send a *jawab* to the remitter of money, or **6.** a *jokhami hundi* which is a combination of a bill of exchange and an insurance policy.

Company Law*

Introduction

A company, in common parlance, means a group of persons associated together for the attainment of a common end, social or economic. It has "no strictly technical or legal meaning."

According to sec. 3 (1) (ii) of the Companies Act, 1956 a company means a company formed and registered under the Companies Act, 1956 or any of the preceding Acts. Thus, a Company comes into existence only by registration under the Act, which can be termed as incorporation.

Kinds of Companies

Classification on the Basis of Liability

1. Companies with limited liability

(a) Companies limited by shares: Where the liability of the members of a company is limited to the amount unpaid on the shares, such a company is known as a company limited by shares

(b) Companies limited by guarantee: Where the liability of the members of a company is limited to a fixed amount which the members undertake to contribute to the assets of the company in the event of its being wound up, the company is called a company limited by guarantee.

2. Unlimited companies: A company without limited liability is known as an unlimited company. In case of such a company, every member is liable for the debts of the company.

Classification on the Basis of Number of Members

1. Private company: a private company is normally what the Americans call a 'close corporation'. According to Section 3(1), a private company means a company which has a minimum paid-up capital of Rs. 1,00,000 or such higher paid-up capital as may be prescribed, and by its Articles—

(i) restricts the right to transfer its shares, if any. The restriction is meant to preserve the private character of the company

(ii) limits the number of its members to 50 not including its employee-members

(iii) prohibits any invitation to the public to subscribe for any shares in, or debentures of, the company

(iv) prohibits any invitation or acceptance of deposits from persons other than its members, directors or their relatives.

Every private company, existing on the commencement of the Companies (Amendment) Act, 2000, with a paid-up capital of less than Rs. 1,00,000 shall, within a period of 2 years from such date of commencement, enhance its paid up capital to Rs. 1,00,000.

2. Public company: A public company means a company which—

(i) has a minimum paid-up capital of Rs. 5 lakh or such higher paid-up capital, as may be prescribed

(ii) is a private company which is a subsidiary of a company which is not a private company.

Every public company, existing on the commencement of the Companies (Amendment) Act, 2000, with a paid-up capital of less than Rs. 5,00,000 shall, within a period of 2 years from such date of commencement, enhance its paid up capital to Rs. 5,00,000.

* For Amendment see the section Highlights of New Companies Act 2013 & The Companies (Amendment) Act 2015.

Classification on the Basis of Control

1. Holding Company-Section 4(4): A company is known as the holding company of another company if is has control over that other company.

2. Subsidiary Company-Section 4(1): A company is known as a subsidiary of another company when control is exercised by the latter (called holding company) over the former called a subsidiary company.

A company is deemed to be a subsidiary of another company when—

(i) where the company controls the composition of Board of Directors of the subsidiary company.

(ii) where the company holds more than half the nominal value of equity share capital of another company.

(iii) where a company is subsidiary of another company, which is itself is subsidiary of the controlling company.

Classification on the Basis of Ownership

1. Government company: A Government company means any company in which not less than 51 % of the paid-up share capital is held by—

(i) the Central government

(ii) any State government or governments

(iii) partly by the Central government and partly by one or more State governments.

2. Non-government company

Foreign company: It means any company incorporated outside India which has an established place of business in India. **(Section 591(1))**

Rules Applicable by Government Companies

1. Appointment of auditor and audit reports-Section 619

2. Annual report to be placed before Parliament-Section 619

3. Provisions of Section 619 to apply to certain companies: The provisions of Section 619 shall apply to a company in which not less than 51% of the paid-up capital is held jointly by Government, Government companies and public financial corporations.

4. Certain provisions of the Companies Act do not apply-Section 620: The Central Government may, by notification in the Official Gazette, direct that any of the provisions of the Companies Act (other than Sections 618, 619), specified in the notification—

(a) shall not apply to any Government company,

(b) shall apply to any Government company, with such exceptions, modifications and adaptations, as may be specified in the notification.

Procedure for Registration of a Company

Section 33 of the Companies Act deals with registration of a company. To obtain registration an application has to be filed to the Registrar of Companies. The application must be accompanied by the following documents:

1. Memorandum of Association.
2. Articles of Association, if necessary.
3. A copy of the agreement, if any, which the company proposes to enter into with any individual for his appointment as the managing or the whole-time director or the manager.
4. A declaration that all the requirements of the Act have been complied with.

Articles are compulsory only for unlimited companies, companies limited by guarantee and private companies limited by shares(Section 26). The declaration must be signed by an advocate of the SC, or of a HC, or an attorney or a pleader entitled to appear before a HC, or any proposed director, manager or secretary of the company or by a secretary or chartered accountant who is in whole time practice in India [Section 33(2)].

Section 12, which states the mode of forming an incorporated company, enables any seven persons (two for private company) to associate for any lawful purpose and to get themselves incorporated into a company with or without limited liability. They can do so by subscribing their names to a memorandum of association and by complying with other documents.

If the Registrar finds the documents to be satisfactory, he registers them and enters the name of the company in the Register of Companies and issues a certificate called the Certificate of Incorporation. Certificate of Incorporation brings the company into existence as a legal person. It is the conclusive evidence that all the requirements under the Act in respect of registration and matters precedent and incidental thereto have been complied with and that the association is a company authorized to be registered and duly registered under the Act.

Clauses of Memorandum of Association

Memorandum of association is divided into 5 clauses:

1. Name clause
2. Registered office clause
3. Objects clause
4. Liability clause and
5. Capital clause

Name Clause

The first clause states the name of the proposed company. The name of a corporation is the symbol of its personal existence. The name should not be, in the opinion of the Central Government, undesirable. Generally it is so when it is identical with or too nearly resembles the name of another company. If the company is with "limited liability" the last word of the name should be "limited" and in case of a private company "private limited". The Central Government may permit a company to drop the word 'limited' from its name, if

(a) the company is formed for the promotion of arts, commerce, religion, science, charity or any other useful object.

(b) the company is to apply its income in promoting its objects and prohibits the payment of dividend to its members.

The name of a company must be painted outside of every place where the company carries on business and printed on every business document and official letter of the company. Misdescription entails personal liability(section 147).

Registered Office Clause

The second clause of the memorandum must specify the State in which the registered office of the company shall be situated (section 146). Within 30 days of incorporation or commencement of business, whichever is earlier, the exact place where the registered office is to be located must be decided and sent to the Registrar for recording of the same.

Objects Clause

The third clause states the objects of the proposed company. The objects clause s divided into two sub-clauses (section 13):

(a) *Main objects clause*: states the main objects to be pursued by the company and the objects incidental or ancillary to the main objects.

(b) *Other objects*: states any other objects which are not included in the main objects clause.

The essence of this clause is that the investors must be informed of the objects of the company in which their money is going to be employed and the creditors must feel protected when they know the assets are being used for the authorized objects.

Liability Clause

The fourth clause states the nature of liability the members incur. The clause will state whether the liability of the members shall be limited by shares or by guarantee or unlimited.

Capital Clause

The last clause states the amount of capital with which the company is proposed to be registered and the kinds, number and value of shares into which the capital is to be divided.

After the Companies (Amendment) Act, 2000, the minimum paid up capital of a public company must be five lakh rupees or more and one lakh or more for a private company.

Procedure for Alteration of Memorandum of Association

Alteration of Name (Section 21)

A company may change its name at any time by passing a special resolution and with the prior approval of the Central Government. Where a company has been registered with a name which is undesirable, the same may be changed by an ordinary resolution and with the prior approval of the Central Government. In such a case the central Government may also within 12 months of registration direct the company to rectify its name and the company must change the name within 3 months from the date of direction unless the time is extended. The new name would also require the prior approval of the Central Government The British Diabetic Society was compelled to change its name to something that would not impinge the goodwill of the British Diabetic Association ***(British Diabetic Association vs. The Diabetic Society).***

When a company changes its name, the Registrar of Companies has to enter the new name in the register and a new certificate of incorporation must be issued with necessary alterations.

However, it should be noted that no approval will be required if the change consists merely addition or deletion of the word "private" consequent on the conversion of a public company into a private company or vice versa.

Effect of such change: The old name of the company will stand abolished and the new name will come into existence from the date of passing such resolution. However, it does not affect the rights and obligations of the company (section 23).

Alteration of Registered Office Clause (Section 17)

Shifting of registered office from one State to another is a complicated affair. For this purpose, section 17 requires—

(a) A special resolution of the company.

(b) The sanction of the Company Law Board.

The Board can confirm the alteration only if the shifting of the registered office from one state to another is necessary for any purposes detailed in section 17(1).

Alteration of Objects (Section 17)

A company may alter its objects with the passing of a special resolution. The confirmation of the Company Law Board is not required for this purpose. An alteration of the objects is allowed only for the purposes mentioned in section 17(1).

Registration of Alteration (Sec. 18)

In case of alteration of objects, a copy of the resolution should be filed with the Registrar of Companies within one month from the date of resolution. In the case of inter-state shifting of the registered office a certified copy of the Board's order and a printed copy of the altered memorandum must be filed with the Registrar within three months of the Board's order. Within one month the Registrar will certify the registration. Alteration takes effect when it is so registered.

Articles of Association

Introduction

Articles of Association is the second important document, which in case of some companies, has to be registered along with the memorandum. As per section 26, companies which must have articles are:

(1) Unlimited companies;

(2) Companies limited by guarantee;

(3) Private companies limited by shares.

This document contains rules, regulations and bye-laws for the general administration of the company. Schedule I of the Act sets out tables of model forms of articles for different companies.

Contents

Articles of Association may prescribe such regulations for the company as the subscribers to the memorandum deem expedient. The Act gives the subscribers a free hand. Any stipulations as to the relation between the company and its members or members inter se may be inserted in the articles. But everything stated therein is subject to the Companies Act. Usually, articles contain provisions relating to the following matters:

1. Share capital, rights of shareholders, share certificates, payment of commission
2. Lien on shares
3. Call on shares
4. Transfer of shares
5. Transmission of shares
6. Forfeiture of shares
7. Conversion of shares into stock
8. Share warrants
9. Alteration of capital

10. General meetings and proceedings there at
11. Voting rights of members, voting and poll, proxies
12. Directors, their appointment, remuneration, qualifications, powers and proceedings of Board of Directors
13. Manager
14. Secretary
15. Dividends and reserves
16. Accounts, audit and borrowing power
17. Capitalization of profits
18. Winding up

Alteration of Articles (Sec 31)

Section 31 empowers every company to alter its articles at any time with the authority of a special resolution of the company and filing copy with the Registrar. Since it is a statutory power a company will not be deprived of the power of alteration by a contract with anyone.

The power of alteration of articles conferred by section 31 is almost absolute. It is subject only to two restrictions—

It must not be in contravention with the provisions of the Act.

It is subject to the conditions contained in the memorandum of association.

The proviso to sub-section (1) says that an alteration which has the effect of converting a public company into a private company would not have any effect unless it is approved by the Central Government.

Alteration against memorandum: In ***Hutton vs. Scarborough Cliff Hotel Co***, a resolution was passed in a general meeting of a company altered the articles by inserting the power to issue preference shares which did not exist in the memorandum. It was held inoperative. However, after ***Andrews vs. Gas Meter Co Ltd*** this view has been changed where a company was allowed by changing articles to issue preference shares when its memorandum was silent on the point. The power of alteration of art is subject only to what is clearly prohibited by the memorandum, expressly or impliedly.

Alteration in breach of contract: A company may change its articles even if the alteration would operate as a breach of contract. If the contract is wholly dependant on the articles, the company would not be liable in damages if it commits breach by changing articles. But if the contract is independent of the articles, the company will be liable in damages if it commits breach by changing articles. Thus in ***Southern Foundries Ltd vs. Shirlaw***, where a Managing Director was appointed for a term of ten years, but was removed earlier under the new articles on amalgamation with another company, the company was held liable for breach of contract.

Alteration as fraud on minority shareholders: An alteration must not constitute a fraud on the minority. It should not be an attempt to deprive the company or its minority shareholders of something that in equity belongs to them.

Alteration increasing liability of members: No alteration can require a person to purchase more shares in the company or to increase his liability in any manner except with his consent in writing.

Thus, the power of alteration should be exercised in absolute good faith in the interest of the company.

Prospectus

Definition

Section 2(36)—" Any document described or issued as a prospectus and includes any notice, circular, advertisement, or other document inviting deposits from the public or inviting offers from the public for the subscription or purchase of any share in, or debentures of, a corporate body."

In simple words, any document inviting deposits from the public or inviting offers from the public for the subscription of shares or debentures of a company is a prospectus.

Contents

"The Companies Act contains a comprehensive set of regulations intended to protect the investing public from victimization". The intention of the Legislature in making these regulations, is "to secure the fullest disclosure of material and essential particulars and lay the same in full view of all the intending purchasers of shares"

The relevant rules and regulations are-

1. Every prospects must be dated (section 55)
2. A copy of the prospectus must be registered with the Registrar and this fact must be stated on the face of the prospectus. The Registrar can refuse to register a prospectus which does not comply with the disclosure requirements. (Section 60). The prospectus must be issued within 90 days of its registration.
3. If the prospectus includes a statement purporting to be made by an expert, consent in writing of that expert must be obtained and this fact must be stated in the prospectus. (Section 58). The expert should be unconnected with the formation or management of the company. (Section 57). Section 59 provides that the expression "expert" includes an engineer, a valuer, an accountant and any other person whose profession gives authority to a statement made by him. Thus the expert becomes a party to the prospectus and liable for untrue statements, if any.
4. Section 56 requires every prospectus to disclose the matters specified in Schedule II of the Act. The information required to be disclosed refers to the objects of the company, details as to shares, managerial personnel, minimum subscription, underwriting, preliminary expenses, material contracts, etc.
5. Lastly, the "golden rule" – the public is at the mercy of the company's promoters. Everything must, therefore, be stated with strict and scrupulous accuracy"

Promoters

A promoter is a person who does the necessary preliminary work incidental to the formation of a company. It is a compendious term used for a person who undertakes, does and goes through all the necessary and incidental preliminaries, keeping in view the object, to bring into existence an incorporated company.

Chronologically, the first persons who control a company's affairs are its promoters.

Functions

1. The promoter of a company decides its name and ascertains that it will be accepted by the Registrar of Companies.
2. He settles the details of the company's Memorandum and Articles, the nominations of directors, solicitors, bankers, auditors and secretary and the registered office of the company.
3. He arranges for the printing of the Memorandum and Articles, the registration of the company, the issue of prospectus, where a public issue is necessary

He is responsible for bringing the company into existence for the object which he has in view.

Remuneration

A promoter has no right to get compensation from the company for his services in promoting the company unless there is a contract to that effect. In practice, a promoter takes remuneration for his services in one of the following ways—

1. He my sell his own property at a profit to the company for cash or fully-paid shares provided he makes a disclosure to this effect
2. He may be given an option to buy a certain number of shares in the company at par.
3. He may take a commission on the shares sold.
4. He may be paid a lump sum by the company.

Directors' Powers, Duties and Position

A company in the eyes of the law is an artificial person. It has no physical existence. It has neither soul nor a body of its own. As such, it cannot act in its own person.

The directors are the brain of a company. They occupy a pivotal position in the structure of the company. They are in fact the mainspring of the company.

Definition

'Director' includes any person occupying the position of director, by whatever name called. The important factor to determine whether a person is or not a director is to refer to the nature of the office and its duties. Thus a director may be defined as a person having control over the direction, conduct, management or superintendence of the affairs of the company.

Only individuals can be directors: No body corporate, association or firm can be appointed director of a company. Only an individual can be so appointed.

Powers of Directors

General Powers of the Board (Section 291)

The powers of the Board of directors are co-extensive with those of the company. This proposition is, however, subject to two conditions:

First, the Board shall not do any act which is to be done by the company in general meeting.

Second, the Board shall exercise its powers subject to the provisions contained in the Companies Act, or in the Memorandum or the Articles of the company or in any regulations made by the company in general meeting.

Powers to be exercised at Board meetings (Section 292)

The Board of directors of a company shall exercise the following powers on behalf of the company by means of resolutions passed at the meetings of the Board, viz, the power to—

(a) make calls on shareholders in respect of money unpaid on their shares
(b) issue debentures
(c) borrow money otherwise than on debentures
(d) invest the funds of the company
(e) make loans

Powers to be exercised with the approval of company in general meeting

(a) sale or lease of the company's undertaking
(b) extension of the time for payment of a debt due by a director
(c) investment of compensation received on acquisition of the company's assets in securities other than trust securities
(d) borrowing of money beyond the paid-up capital of the company
(e) contributions to any charitable fund beyond Rs.50,000 in one financial year or 5% of the average et profits during the preceding three financial years, whichever is greater.

Duties of the Directors

1. Fiduciary duties: As fiduciaries, the directors must—

(a) exercise their powers honestly and bona fide for the benefit of the company as a whole; and
(b) not place themselves in a position in which there is a conflict between their duties to the company and their personal interests. They must not make any secret profit out of their position. If they do, they have to account for it to the company.

2. Duties of care, skill and diligence: Directors should carry out their duties with reasonable care and exercise such degree of skill and diligence as is reasonably expected of persons of their knowledge and status. He is not bound to bring any special qualifications to his office.

Standard of care: The standard of care, skill and diligence depends upon the nature of the company's business and circumstances of the case. They are various standards of the care depending upon:

(a) the type and nature of work
(b) division of powers between directors and other officers
(c) general usages and customs in that type of business; and
(d) whether directors work gratuitously or remuneratively

3. Duty to disclose interest: Where a director is personally interested in a transaction of the company, he is required to disclose his interest to the board. An interested director is neither to vote on the matter of his interest nor his presence shall count for the purposes of quorum.

4. Duty to attend board meetings: The Act only says that the office of a director is automatically vacated if he fails to attend three consecutive meetings of the board or all meetings for a period of 3 months, whichever is longer. Moreover, a director's habitual absence may become evidence of negligence.

5. Duty not to delegate: A director should not delegate his functions to another person. But delegation of functions may be made to the extent to which it is authorized by the Act or the constitution of the company.

Quorum (Section 174)

'Quorum' means the minimum number of members who must be present in order to constitute a valid meeting and transact busies thereat. The quorum is generally fixed by the Articles. If the Articles of a company do not provide for a large quorum, the following rules apply:

1. Quorum for public company—5 members personally present
   Quorum for other companies—2
   For the purpose of quorum a person may be counted as 2 or more members if he holds shares in different capacities.
2. If within half an hour a quorum is not present, the meeting, if called upon the requisition of members, shall stand dissolved. In any other case, it shall stand adjourned to the same day, place and time in the next week. The Board of Directors may adjourn the meeting to be convened on any particular day, time and place to be fixed on the date of the meeting itself or at least before the commencement of the same in the next week. Where the Board of directors fails to do so, the meeting stands statutorily adjourned to the same day in the next week.

The Articles may provide for a large quorum: The Articles cannot provide for a quorum smaller than the statutory minimum. For the purpose of quorum, only members present in person and not proxies are to be counted.

When quorum should be present: Article 49(1) of Table A requires the quorum to be present at the time when the meeting proceeds to transact business. It need not be present throughout or at the time of taking vote on any resolution.

Dividends

One of the main objects of commercial enterprises is to earn profits which are disturbed among shareholders by way of 'dividend'. In commercial usage, 'dividend' is the share of the Company profits distributed among the members. Under Section 2(14A) of the Companies Act, 1956, 'dividend' includes any interim dividend.

Rules Regarding Dividend

1. Resolution at the annual general meetings: The dividend is declared by a company by a resolution passed at the annual general meetings. The Board of directors determines the rate of dividend. The rate determined by the Board is to be sanctioned by the members of the company in general meeting. The members may reduce the rate recommended by the Board but they cannot increase it.

2. Payment of dividend in proportion to paid up capital (Section 93): A company may, if authorized by its Articles, pay dividends in proportion to the amount paid up on each share. In the absence of such a clause in the Articles, members are entitled to dividend in proportion to the nominal value of the shares and not in proportion to the amounts paid thereon.

3. Dividend to be paid only out of profits (Section 205): The dividend can be declared or paid by a company for any financial year only—

(a) out of profits of the company for that year arrived at after providing for depreciation in the manner laid down in the Act, or
(b) out of the profits of the company for any previous financial year or years arrived at after providing for depreciation and remaining undistributed, or
(c) out of both, or
(d) out of moneys provided by the Central Government or a State Government for the payment of dividend in pursuance of a guarantee given by the Governmnet

4. Unpaid dividend to be transferred to special dividend account-(Section 205-A): Where a dividend has been declared by a company but has not been paid to or claimed by any shareholder within a period of 30 days from the date of declaration, the company shall, within 7 days from the date of expiry of the 30 days, transfer the unpaid or unclaimed dividend to a special account with any scheduled bank to be called "unpaid dividend account of….company limited/company private limited"

5. If any amount remains unpaid or unclaimed for 7 years from the date of such transfer, it should be transferred to "Investor Education & Protection Fund"

6. Dividend to be paid to the registered shareholder-Section 206: The dividend shall be paid only to

(a) to the registered shareholder or to his order or to his bankers,

(b) in case a share warrant has been issued, to the bearer of such warrant or to his bankers.

7. Penalty for defaulting directors-Section 207: Every director, who is knowingly a party to the default, is punishable with simple imprisonment up to 3 years and liable to a fine of Rs. 1000 for every day during which such default continues and the company shall be liable to pay interest @ 18% p.a during the period of default.

Debentures

The most usual form of borrowing by a company is by the issue of debentures. According to Section 2(12), 'debenture' includes debenture stock, bonds and any other securities of a company, whether constituting a charge on the assets of the company or not. Section 2(12) however does not explain as to what a debenture really is.

'Debenture' means a document which either creates a debt or acknowledges it.

Kinds of debentures

Classification according to negotiability

1. Bearer debentures/unregistered debentures: These debentures are payable to the bearer. These are regarded as negotiable instruments and are transferable by delivery and a bona fide transferee for value is not affected by the defect in the title of the prior holder.

2. Registered debentures: These are debentures which are payable to the registered holders. A holder is one whose name appears both on the debenture certificate and in the company's register of debentures.

Classification according to security

1. Secured debentures: Debentures which create some charge on the property of the company are known as secured debentures. The charge may be a fixed charge or floating charge.

2. Unsecured or naked debentures: Debentures which do not create any charge on the assets of the company are known as unsecured debentures. The holders of these debentures like ordinary unsecured creditors may sue the company for recovery of debt.

Classification according to permanence

1. Redeemable debentures: Debentures are usually issued on the condition that they shall be redeemed after a certain period. Such debentures are known as redeemable debentures. They may be re-issued after redemption in accordance with the provisions of Section 121.

2. Irredeemable or perpetual debentures: When debentures are irredeemable, they are called perpetual debentures.

Classification according to convertibility

1. Convertible debentures: These debentures give an option to the holders to convert them into preference or equity shares at stated rates of exchange, after a certain period.

2. Non-convertible debentures: These debentures do not give any option to their holders to convert them into preference or equity shares. They are to be duly paid as and when they mature.

Classification according to priority

1. First debentures: these are the debentures which are to be repaid in priority to other debentures which may be subsequently issued.

2. Second debentures: these are the debentures which are to be paid after the 'first debentures' have been redeemed.

Floating Charge

A floating charge is an equitable charge which is created on some class of property which is constantly changing, e.g, a charge on stock-in-trade, trade debtors, etc. The company can deal in such property in the normal course of its business until the charge becomes fixed on the happening of an event. The main idea behind floating charge is to allow the company to carry on its business in the ordinary course as if no charge had been created.

Debentures usually create a floating charge on the assets of a company.

Share Capital

Share capital means the capital raised by a company by the issue of shares. The capital of a company may be of two kinds:

1. Equity share capital—

(i) with voting rights

(ii) with differential rights as to dividend, voting or otherwise in accordance with such rules and subject to such conditions as may be prescribed.

Shares with differential rights: It means a share that is issued with differential rights in accordance with the provisions of Section 86.

2. Preference share capital: It means, in the case of a company limited by shares, that part of the capital of the company which carries a preferential right as to—

(a) payment of dividend during the lifetime of the company

(b) repayment of capital on winding up

Equity share capital means, with reference to a company limited by shares, all share capital which is not preference share capital. In other words it is capital which does not carry preferential right as to-

(a) payment of dividend

(b) repayment of capital on winding up.

Called-up capital: This is that part of the issued capital which has been called up on the shares.

Paid-up capital: This is that part of the issued capital which has been paid up by the shareholders or which is credited as paid-up on the shares.

Uncalled capital: This is the remainder of the issued capital which has not yet been called.

Reserve capital: This is that part of the uncalled capital of a company which can be called only in the event of its winding up.

Authorized or nominal capital: This is the nominal value of the shares which a company is authorized to issue by its Memorandum of Association.

Issued or subscribed capital: Issued capital is the nominal value of the shares which are offered to the public for subscription.

Bonus Shares

'Bonus' is something given in addition to what is usually or strictly due. It comes to shareholders in addition to what they get in the form of dividend. It may also be paid—

1. in case the company has surplus cash and has no use for it, or
2. by making partly paid shares as fully paid. Normally bonus is paid to the shareholders in the form of fully paid shares free of cost. This augments the resources and earning capacity of the company.

A company may be following a conservative policy of not disturbing all the profits every year accumulate large reserves over time. If the Articles so permit, it may convert a part of these reverses into share capital by issuing fully paid bonus shares to the existing shareholders. This is called capitalization of profits.

Issue of bonus shares results in capitalization of profits and reserves of the company.

Allotment of Shares

The capital of company is divided into certain indivisible units of a fixed amount. These units are called shares. 'Share' means share in the share capital of a company.

A share has been defined as "an interest having a money value and made up of diverse rights specified under the Articles of Association"- ***Commr. of Income Tax vs. Standard Vaççum Oil Co. Ltd***

A share is evidenced by a share certificate. A share certificate is issued by a company under its common seal.

Each share is to be distinguished by appropriate number **(Section 83).** Each share in a company having share capital is distinguished by its appropriate number.

General Principles

An effective allotment has to comply with the requirements of the law of contract relating to acceptance of an offer.

1. Allotment by proper authority: An allotment must be made by a resolution of the board of directors. "Allotment is a duty primarily falling upon the directors.", and this duty cannot be delegated except in accordance with the provisions of the articles.

2. Within reasonable time: Allotment must be made within a reasonable period of time, otherwise the application lapses. What is reasonable time must remain a question of fact in each case. The interval of about six months between application and allotment has been held to be reasonable. On the expiry of reasonable time Section 6 of the Contract Act applies and the application must be deemed to have been revoked.

3. Must be communicated: The allotment must be communicated to the applicant. Posting of a properly addressed and stamped letter of allotment is a sufficient communication even if the letter is delayed or lost in the course of post. ***Household Fire & Carriage Accident Insurance Co. vs. Grant*** is the leading authority.

4. Absolute and unconditional: Allotment must be absolute and in accordance with the terms and conditions of the applicant, if any. Thus where a person applied for 400 shares on the condition that he would be appointed cashier of a new branch of the company. He was not bound by any allotment unless he was so appointed.

A condition which is to operate subsequently to allotment will not affect its validity. An applicant to whom shares were allotted on the condition that he would pay for them only when the company paid dividends was held to be bound even though the company had gone into liquidation before paying any dividend.

The applicant must promptly reject the allotment when shares have been allotted to him without his condition being fulfilled. An acquiescence on his part would amount to a waiver of the condition.

Reduction of capital with the consent of the court

1. It may extinguish or reduce the liability on any of its shares in respect of share capital not paid-up
2. It may, either with or without extinguishing or reducing liability on any of its shares, cancel any paid-up share capital which is lost, or is unrepresented by available assets.
3. It may, either with or without extinguishing or reducing liability on any of its shares, pay off any paid-up share capital which is in excess of the wants of the company.

Procedure for reduction of share capital

1. Special resolution-Section 100: A company shall first pass a special resolution for reduction of capital. Power to reduce capital must be granted in the Articles of the company. If the Articles do not grant such power, they may be altered by a special resolution giving such power.

2. Application to the Court-Section 101: The company shall then apply to the Court by petition for an order confirming the reduction.

3. Registration of order of Court with Registrar-Section 103: The order of the Court confirming the reduction shall be produced before the Registrar and a certified copy thereof shall be filed with him for registration. With such a copy shall also be filed a minute, showing with respect to the share capital of the company as altered by the order.

Reduction of capital without the sanction of the Court

1. Forfeiture of shares: The company may, if authorized by its Articles, forfeit shares for non-payment of calls. This results in reduction of capital if the forfeited shares are not re-issued

2. Surrender of shares: The company may accept surrender of partly paid shares to save it from going through the formalities of forfeiture.

3. Cancellation of shares: The company may, if so authorized by its Articles, cancel shares which have not been taken or agreed to be taken by any person and diminish the amount of its share capital by the amount of the shares so cancelled.

4. Purchase of the shares by the company under Section 402(b): The Court may order the purchase of the shares of any members of the company by the company.

5. Redemption of redeemable shares: The company may redeem redeemable preference shares in accordance with the provisions of Section 80.

6. Buy-back of shares: A company may purchase its own shares, subject to fulfillment of conditions laid down in Section 79-A (2), purchase its own shares.

Income Tax Law

BASIC CONCEPTS

What is an Assessment Year [Sec.2(9)]

"Assessment year" means the period starting from April 1 and ending on Marh 31 of the next year.

What is a Preview Year [Sec. 3]

Income earned in a year is taxable in the next year. The year in which income is earned is known as previous year.

Who are Included in "Person" [Sec. 2(31)]

The term "person" includes:

(a) an individual
(b) a Hindu undivided family
(c) a company
(d) a firm
(e) an association of persons or a body of individuals, whether incorported or not
(f) a local authority; and
(g) every artificial juridical person not falling within any of the preciding categories.

These seven categories of persons chargeable to tax under the Act.

Who is Regarded as Assessee [Sec. 2(7)]

"Assessee" means a person by whom income tax or any other sum of money is payable under the Act.

THE PROCEDURE FOR CHARGING TAX

- Annual tax
- Tax rate of assessment year
- Rates fixed by finance Act
- Tax on person
- Tax on total income
- Provision as on April 1 of the assessment year.

What is 'Income'

The term, "Income" connotes a periodical monetary return coming in with some sort of regularity or expected regularity from definite sources.

Income may be received in cash or in kind. When income is received in kind, its valuation is to be made according to the rules prescribed in the income tax rules. If, However, there is no prescribed rule, valuation thereof is made on the basis of market value.

What is Gross total income

As per Section 14, income is computed under the following five heads:

1. Salaries
2. Income from house property
3. Profit and gains of business or profession
4. Capital gains
5. Income from other sources.

The aggregate income under these heads is termed as ''gross total income''. In other words, gross total income means total income computed in accordance with the provisions of the Act before making any deduction under section 80CCC to 80U.

WHAT IS AMALGAMATION

For a merger to qualify as an "amalgamation" for the purpose of the income tax Act, it has to satisfy the following conditions:

(a) All the properties of the amalgamating company immediately before the amalgamation should become the property of the amalgamated company by virtue of the amalgamation;

(b) All liabilities of the amalgamating company immediately before the amalgamation should become the liabilities of the amalgamated company by virtue of the amalgamation; and

(c) Shareholders holding not less than three fourths in value of the shares in the amalgamating company should become shareholders of the amalgamated company by virtue of the amalgamation.

RESIDENCE AND TAX LIABILITY

Tax liability on an assessee depends in his residential status. For instance, whether an income, accrued to an individual outside India, is taxable in India depends upon the residential status of the individual. Similarly, whether an income earned by a foreign national in India is taxable in India, depends on the residential status of the individual, rather than on his citizenship. Therefore, the determination of the residential status of a person is very significant in order to find out his tax liability.

The following norms one has to keep in mind while deciding residential status of an assess:

DIFFERENT TAXABLE ENTITIES

All taxable entities are divided in the following categories for the purpose of determining residential status:

1. An Individual
2. A Hindu undivided family
3. A firm or an association of persons
4. A joint stock company, and
5. Every other person.

Different Residential Status

An assessee is either : *(a)* resident in India or *(b)* non-resident in India. However, a resident individual or a Hindu undivided family has to be *(a)* resident and ordinarily resident, or *(b)* resident but not ordinarily resident. Therefore, an individual and a Hindu undivided family can either be :

(a) resident and ordinarily resident in India or

(b) resident but not ordinarily resident in India or

(c) non-resident in India

All other assessee (*viz.*, a firm, an association of persons, a joint stock company and every other person) can either be:

(a) resident in India, or

(b) non-resident in India

Residential Status for Previous Year

Residential status of an assessee is to be determined in respect of each previous year as it may vary from previous year to previous year.

Different residential status for different previous year in same assessment year not possible

If a person is resident in a previous year relevant to an assessment year in respect of any source of income, he shall be deemed to be resident in India in the previous year (s) relevant to the same assessment year in respect of each of his other sources of income.

Different residential status for different assessment year

An assessee may enjoy different residential status for different assessment years.

Resident in India and Abroad

It is not necessary that a person who is a resident in India, cannot become "resident" in other country for the same assessment year. A person may be resident in two (or more) countries at the same time. It is, therefore, not necessary that a person who is resident in India will be non-resident in all other countries for the same assessment year.

Onus of Proof

Whether an assessee is a resident or a non-resident is a question of fact and it is the duty of assessee to place all relevant facts before the income tax authorities.

Determination of Residential Status of an Individual

An individual may be *(a)* resident and ordinarily resident in India, *(b)* resident but not ordinarily resident in India or *(c)* non-resident in India.

Resident and ordinarily resident [Sec. 6(1), 6(6)(*a*)]

To find out whether an individual is "resident and ordinarily resident" in India, one has to proceed as follows:

Step 1: First find out whether such individual is "resident" in India.

Step 2 : If such individual is "resident" in India, then find out whether he is "ordinarily resident" in India. However, if such individual is a "non-resident" in India, then no further investigation is necessary.

Basic Conditions to Test as to When an Individual is Resident in India

Under Section 6(1) an individual is said to be resident in India is any previous year, if the satisfies at least one of the following basic conditions :

(*a*) he is in India in the previous year for a period of 182 days or more; or

(*b*) he is in India for a period of 60 days or more during the previous year and 365 days or more during 4 years immediately preceding the previous year.

Exceptions : The aforesaid rule of residence is subject to the following exceptions :

1. By virtue of Explanation *(a)* to section 6(1) the period of "60 days" referred to in *(b)* above has been extended as follows:

Assess-ment years	*Who can take the benefit of extented period*	*Extended period*
1990-91	An Indian citizen who leaves India during the previous year for the purpose of employment outside India or an Indian citizen who leaves India during the previous year as a member of the crew of an Indian.	182 days

2. By virtue of explanation *(b)*, the period of "60 days" referred to in *(b)* above has been extended as follows in the case of a person who comes on a visit to India—

Assess-ment years	*Who can take the benefit of extented period*	*Extended period*
1995-96 onwards	Indian citizen or a person of Indian origin	182 days
1990-91 to 1994-95	Indian citizen or a person of Indian origin	150 days

A person is deemed to be of Indian origin if he, or either of his parents or any of his grand-parents, was born in undivided India.

Additional conditions to test as to when a resident individual is ordinarily resident in India

Under section 6(6), a resident individual is treated as "resident and ordinarily resident" in India if he satisfies the following two additional conditions—

(i) he has been resident in India in at least 9 out of 10 previous years immediately preceding the relevant previous year; and

(ii) he has been in India for a period of 730 days or more during 7 years immediately preceding the relevant previous year.

In brief it can be said that an individual becomes resident and ordinarily resident in India if he satisfies at least one of the basic conditions [*i.e., (a)* or *(b)*] and the two additional conditions [*i.e., (a)* or *(ii)*].

Resident But Not Ordinarily Resident [Sec. 6(1), 6(*a*)]

An individual who satisfies at least one of the basic conditions [*i.e.,* condition *(a)* or *(b)*] but does not satisfy the two additional conditions [*i.e.,* conditions *(i)* and *(ii)* mentioned above] is treated as a resident but not ordinarily resident in India.

Non-Resident : An individual is a non-resident in India if he satisfies none of the basic conditions [*i.e.,* condition *(a)* or *(b)* mentioned above]. In the case of non-resident additional conditions [*i.e., (i)* and *(ii)* mentioned above] are not relevant.

Determination of residential status of a Hindu undivided family [Sec. 6(2)]

A Hindu undivided family is either resident in India or-resident in India. A resident Hindu undivided family is either ordinarily resident or not ordinarily resident.

When a Hindu undivided family is resident or non-resident

A Hindu undivided family is said to be resident in India if control and management of its affairs is wholly or partly situated in India. A Hindu undivided family is non-resident in India if control and management of its affairs is wholly situated outside India.

When a resident Hindu undivided family is ordinarily resident in India

A resident Hindu undivided family is our ordinarily resident in India if Karta or manager of the family satisfies the following two additional conditions as laid down by section 6(6)*(b)* :

(a) he has been resident in India in at least 9 out of 10 previous years immediately preceding the relevant; previous year; and

(b) he has been present in India for a period of 730 days or more during 7 years immediately preceding the previous year.

Determination of Residential Status of Firm and Association of Persons [Sec. 6(4)]

A partnership firm and an association of persons are said to be resident in India if control and management of their affairs are situated wholly outside India.

What is Control and Management

While in the case of a firm, control and management is vested in partners, in case of an association of persons it is vested in principle officer. Control and management means de facto control and management is usually situate at a place where the head, the seat and the directing power are situated.

Determination of Residential Status of a Company [Sec. 6(3)]

An Indian company is always resident in India. A foreign company is resident in India only if, during the previous year control and management of its affairs is situated wholly in India. However, a foreign company is treated as non-resident if, during the previous year, control and management of its affairs is either whooly or partly situated out of India.

Determination of Residential Status of Every Other Person [Sec. 6(4)]

Every other person is resident in India if control and management of his affairs is, wholly or partly, situated within India during the relevant previous year. On the other hand, every other person is non-resident in India if control and management of its affairs is wholly situated outside India.

Relationship Between Residential Status and Tax Liability [Sec. 5]

Under the Act, liability of tax on a tax payer depends on his residential status and also on the place and time of accrual of receipt of income.

Liability of tax in the Case of a Resident and Ordinarily Resident Assessee [Sec. 5(1)]

A resident and ordinarily resident in India is assessable to tax in respect of:

(a) income which is received or deemed to be received in India in the previous year by or non his behalf;

(b) income which accrues or arises or is deemed to accrue or arise to him during the previous year; and

(c) income which accrues or arises to him outside India during the relevant previous year.

Liability of Tax in the Case of a Resident But Not Ordinarily Resident Assessee [Sec. 5(1)]

The liability to tax of a resident but not ordinarily resident is the same as in the case of a resident and ordinarily resident. However, in case of a resident but not ordinarily resident, income is not liable to tax in India unless

(a) income is received or deemed to be received in India.

(b) income is accrued or deemed to be accrued in India, or

(c) business is controlled from a place within India or profession is set up in India.

If, therefore, follows that in the case of a resident and not ordinarily resident assessee, income is not chargeable to tax if it satisfies all the followings:

(a) income is neither received nor deemed to be received in India;

(b) it is neither accrued nor deemed to be accrued in India; and

(c) it is derived from a business controlled or profession set up outside India.

Liability of Tax in the Case of a Non-Resident [Sec. 5(2)]

Non-resident is liable to tax in respect of income received or deemed to be received in India by or on his behalf and accrues or arises or is deemed to accrue or arise in India during the previous year.

Other Points Relating to Tax Liability

The following points merit consideration in order to understand tax liability explaned :

- Total income of an assessee is to be computed in accordance with the provisions of the income-tax Act. For instance, a receipt may be income in a commercial sense but may not be taxable if it is exempt under section 10 or if it is deductible under section 80CCC to 80U
- The source of income is not relevant in order to determine its chargeability.

Heads of Income

As per section 14, income of a person is computed under the following five heads:

1. Salaries
2. Income from house property
3. Profits and gains of business or profession
4. Capital Gains
5. Income from other sources.

Multiple Choice Questions

1. Which of the following is not the characteristic of sole proprietorship
A. Single ownership
B. One man control
C. Whole profit to proprietorship
D. Non-flexibility

2. What is the advantage of sole proprietorship
A. Small capital
B. Hasty decision
C. Limited capital
D. Limited managerial ability

3. The agreement of partnership
A. Must be oral
B. Must be in writing
C. Must be writing in the stamp paper
D. Can be either oral or in writing

4. Partnership may come into existence
A. By the operation of law
B. By an express agreement
C. By an express or implied agreement
D. By inheritance of property

5. Management of a Jointstock company is entrusted to.
A. The Registrar of companies
B. The Board of Directors
C. The shareholder
D. The debenture holders

6. Registration is compulsory in the case of
A. A Sole trader
B. A partnership
C. A joint stock company
D. A joint hindu family business

7. In a co-operative society
A. One share one vote principle is followed
B. One man one vote principle is followed
C. A member must have 2 votes
D. Shares are transferable.

8. Co-operative society can be started
A. Only in villages
B. In towns and villages
C. Only in cities
D. Only in State headquarters

9. The most suitable form of organisation for operating defence industries is
A. Government Company
B. Public corporation
C. Departmental organisation
D. Board organization

10. The share capital of the government company must not be less than
A. 75% B. 60%
C. 95% D. 51%

11. A multinational company is also known as
A. Global giant
B. Partnership
C. Co-operative society
D. Public corporation

12. Membership by birth is main feature in
A. Sole trader
B. Joint Hindu family business
C. Co-operative society
D. Partnership

13. Sole trading business can be started by:
A. At least two persons

B. At least seven persons
C. Any one person
D. None of these

14. The liability of a soletrader is:
A. Limited only to his investment in the business
B. Limited to total property of the business
C. Unlimited
D. None of these

15. Sole proprietorship is suitable for:
A. Large scale concerns
B. Medium scale concerns
C. Small scale concerns
D. None of these

16. Decision-making process in soletrading business is:
A. Quick
B. Slow
C. Neither quick nor slow
D. None of these

17: A soletrader:
A. Cannot keep his business secrets
B. Can keep his business secrets
C. None of the above
D. None of these

18. A partnership is formed by
A. Agreement
B. Relationship among persons
C. The direction of government
D. None of these

19. The basis of partnership is
A. Utmost good faith
B. Money available for investment
C. Desire to work together
D. None of these

20. A partnership firm may be registered under
A. 1949 Act B. 1956 Act
C. 1932 Act D. None of these

21. Registration of partnership is
A. compulsory B. optional
C. not necessary D. None of these

22. In partnership there exists a relationship of
A. principal and agent
B. owner and servant
C. employer and employee.

23. Registration of a joint stock company is
A. compulsory
B. optional
C. compulsory for public limited companies and optional for private limited companies
D. optional for public limited companies and compulsory for private limited companies

24. The minimum number of members for a public limited company is
A. 2 B. 3
C. 7 D. 10

25. The liability of shareholders of a private limited company is limited to
A. the paid up value of the shares
B. amount remaining unpaid on the shares
C. the extent of private assets
D. amount called up

26. A private limited company can commence business
A. immediately on receiving the certificate of incorporation
B. only after the certificate of commencement of business is received
C. on getting name approval from the Registrar
D. on filing all the documents necessary for formation with the Registrar

27. The existence of a company comes to a close
A. on the death of all its promoters
B. on death of all the directors of the Board
C. on transfer of shares by most of its original members
D. none of the above

28. Table A of the Companies Act is a
A. model minutes book
B. model form of balance sheet
C. model of Articles of Association
D. model of memorandum of association

29. Which of the following documents define the scope of a company's activities?
A. Momorandum of Association

B. Articles of Association
C. Prospectus
D. Statutory Declaration

30. Which of the following is created by a Special Act of Parliament or in State Assemblies?
A. Chartered company
B. Foreign company
C. Government company
D. Statutory company

31. Which of the following companies must file with the Registrar a statement in lieu of prospectus?
A. a public limited company which raises funds from the public through issue of shares
B. a public limited company which has made arrangement for racing its capital from directors and their relatives
C. a private limited company
D. all of them

32. The minimum subscription specified in the prospectus must be received within
A. 90 days B. 120 days
C. 130 days D. 60 days

33. A preference share has priority in
A. dividend only
B. only in return of capital at the time of winding up
C. voting rights
D. both dividend and return of capital on winding up

34. Shares can be forfeited for
A. non-payment of any debt due to the company
B. not attending three annual general meetings consecutively
C. for non payment of call money
D. for violent activities at the annual general meetings

35. Where the shares are issued at a discount and the nominal value of share is Rs.100, the maximum discount that can be allowed is
A. Rs. 5 B. Rs. 10
C. Rs. 20 D. Rs. 15

36. Debenture holders of a company are its
A. Creditors B. Members
C. Credit customers D. Borrowers

37. Debenture holders are entitled to receive interest in the following circumstances
A. when there are profits
B. when shareholders also get dividend
C. every year irrespective of loss
D. all the above

38. First directors are appointed by
A. members in statutory meeting
B. members in the first Annual General meeting
C. by being named in the Articles of Association
D. Registrar of Companies

39. A director is acting as
A. agent of the company
B. trustee of the company
C. chief executive officer of the company
D. all of these

40. A person can hold directorship of not more than ________ public limited companies
A. 10 B. 15
C. 20 D. limitless

41. The value of qualification shares of a director in a public limited company shall not exceed
A. Rs. 5000 B. Rs. 5,00,000
C. Rs. 50,000 D. Rs. 500

42. The overall maximum managerial remuneration in a public limited company shall not exceed
A. 11% of net profits
B. 11% of paid up capital and free reserves
C. 5% of net profits
D. 5% of paid up capital and free reserves

43. A company secretary is appointed by
A. Government
B. The Institute of Company Secretaries of India
C. The Board of Directors
D. Shareholders in Annual General Meetings

44. A company should compulsorily appoint a qualified company secretary, having a paid up capital of more than

A. Rs. 5 Lakh B. Rs.50 Lakh
C. Rs.25 Lakh D. Rs.15 Lakh

45. Which of the following must hold a statutory meeting ?
A. Statutory Companies
B. Private Limited Companies
C. Public Limited Companies
D. Chartered Companies

46. The interval between two annual general meetings shall not exceed
A. 15 months B. 12 months
C. 18 months D. 20 months

47. Which of the following business is not transacted at the Annual General Meeting
A. appointment of auditors
B. issue of debentures
C. appointment of directors in place of those retiring
D. declaration of dividend

48. The first issues are floated in
A. Primary market
B. Secondary market
C. Commodity market
D. Regulated market

49. The popular method of sale of new shares in India is
A. Public issue B. Offer for sale
C. Managing brokers D. Underwriting

50. Stock exchanges deal in
A. Goods
B. Services
C. Financial securities
D. Country's currency

51. Number of recognised stock exchange in India
A. 2 B. 23
C. 22 D. 24

52. Stock exchange allow trading in
A. All types of shares of any company
B. Bonds issued by the Government
C. Listed securities
D. Unlisted securities

53. Jobbers transact in a stock exchange
A. For their clients
B. For their own transactions
C. For other brokers
D. For other members

54. A pessimistic speculator is
A. Stag B. Bear
C. Bull D. Lame duck

55. An optimistic speculator is
A. Bull B. Bear
C. Stag D. Lame duck

56. Securities Contract Regulation Act was passed in
A. 1952 B. 1956
C. 1964 D. 1966

57. SEBI is formed as per
A. Securities contract (Regulation) Act
B. Securities and Exchange Board of India Act
C. Companies Act
D. Indian constitution

58. A bull operator believes in
A. Increase in prices
B. Decrease in prices
C. Stability in prices
D. No change in prices

59. Stock exchange .... speculation in shares
A. Does not allow B. discourage
C. encourage D. prohibits

60. A cautious speculator is known as
A. Stag B. Bull
C. Lame duck D. Bear

61. A stock exchange is a place to
A. Exchange one security for another
B. Buy and sell financial securities
C. Float new shares
D. Buy and sell stock of goods.

62. SEBI has the following number of members including chairman.
A. 5 B. 7
C. 6 D. 8

63. Dividend is declared in a co-operative store to its members.
A. Share capital
B. Number of shares purchased
C. Amount of patronage given
D. None of the above

64. The basic objective of a co-operative society is.
A. Earn profit
B. Organise some essential service for the benefit of its member
C. Organize essential services to the community.
D. Arrange for enough of quality goods for the community

65. In a co-operative society, the shares of a member
A. Can be transferred
B. Can be repaid
C. Cannot be transferred
D. None of the above

66. Maximum membership in a co-operative society is
A. 50 B. 60
C. 100 D. Unlimited

67. A co-operative super market supplies
A. Credit B. service
C. Goods D. Cash

68. Consumers co-operation was first successful in
A. England B. USA
C. Swiss D. India

69. Minority interest can be protected in
A. Sole trader
B. Partnership
C. Co-operative societies
D. Public Company

70. Central Co-operative bank is established at
A. Villages B. Districts
C. State head quarters D. Urban areas

71. Government companies are registered under
A. Special statute of Government
B. Companies Act, 1956
C. Royal charter
D. Order of the Government

72. In a public corporation the management has
A. Limited freedom
B. No freedom of action
C. Controlled freedom
D. Unrestricted freedom of action.

73. For the efficient working of state enterprise the form of organisation generally considered suitable is
A. Departmental organisation
B. Public corporation
C. Government company
D. None of these

74. Public can also subscribe to the share capital of
A. Public corporation
B. Departmental undertaking
C. Government company
D. None of these

75. In a government company the share capital of the government must not be less than
A. 51% B. 60%
C. 75% D. 90%

76. Commerce is related to ________
A. Production of goods
B. Exchange of goods
C. Providing occupation
D. Providing services

77. Commerce is the branch of ________
A. Trade B. Banking
C. Industries D. Economics

78. The primary object of business is ________
A. To earn profit
B. To help its employees
C. To help society
D. To help Traders

79. Industries which are engaged in the conversion of raw materials into finished products.
A. Construction Industries
B. Genetic Industries
C. Manufacturing Industries
D. Extractive Industries

80. Goods are to be taken from the place of production to the place of consumption
A. Time utility B. Place Utility
C. Form Utility D. Service Utility

81. Which one of the following orders indicates the correct logical order of managerial functions?
A. Organising, planning, directing, staffing, coordination and control.
B. Planning, organising, staffing, directing, coordination and control.
C. Planning, directing, organising, staffing, control and coordination.
D. Organising, planning, staffing, directing, control and coordination.

82. Planning refers to
A. Looking backward
B. Looking forward
C. Looking forward and backward
D. Looking and actual performance to decide action to be taken.

83. Management by exception introduces
A. selective, responsibility oriented reporting.
B. reporting of significant variances.
C. requirement of full reports on performance
D. computation of actuals in different spheres of performance.

84. Which one of the following is not related to the trait theory of leadership?
A. Physical factors such as height
B. Intelligence and extroversion
C. Self confidence and ambition
D. Training and experience of employees

85. Span of control means that
A. an organisation consists of various departments.
B. each person's authority is clearly defined.
C. every subordinate has one superior
D. a manager can supervise only a limited number of subordinates.

86. MBO is a technique which requires that the objectives of the enterprise.
A. be written and defined in board terms.
B. lay down the time period for achieving the results.
C. include a plan of action for achieving the desired results.
D. be defined in terms of measurable results

87. "Human Relating Approach" to management was origined by
A. Henery Fayol B. Winslow Taylor
C. Elton Mayo D. Peter F.Drucker.

88. 'Unity of command' principle of effective direction means
A. Subordinates should be responsible to one superior.
B. Boosting the morale of the subordinates.
C. decreasing the productivity of subordinates.
D. All of these.

89. In line organisation
A. the organisation is divided according to the skill required to perform a work.
B. the organisation is divided according to the type of work involve.
C. the authority flows from the man at the top to the lowest man vertically.
D. each worker serves a number of supervisors.

90. The function of 'staff' in 'line and staff' organisation is to
A. take advice form the line
B. advice the line
C. hold authority and responsibility
D. fix responsibility for performance of tasks in a definite manner upon certain individuals.

91. Control function of management implies
A. to bring harmony in various activities.
B. to keep the work force content
C. taking corrective course of action.
D. to provide sufficient finance.

92. Delegation can be
A. upward B. downward
C. side ward D. all of these

93. 'Theory X' and 'Theory Y' is given by
A. Maslow B. Herzberg
C. Mc Gregor D. Norman

94. The Need – Hirearchy Theory of Motivation is given by

A. Maslow B. Herzberg
C. Vroom D. Mc Gregor

95. Maslow's Need – Hirearchy Theory of Motivation has classified the human needs into five categories as follows :

I. Safety needs
II. Esteem needs
III. Social needs
IV. Physiological needs
V. Self – actualisation needs

What is the sequence of domination of these needs?

A. I, IV, III, II, V B. IV, I, III, II, V
C. V, III, II, IV, I D. IV, I, III, II, V

96. Under Expectancy Theory of Motivation, increase in motivation results when

A. Valence increases
B. Valence decreases
C. No effect on valence
D. None of these

97. Which one of the following is a motivating factor as per Herzberg's Theory?

A. Salary and allowances
B. Job design
C. Working conditions
D. None of these

98. "Grapevine" is a term used in relation to

A. formal communication
B. informal communication
C. both formal and informal communications
D. this term is not used in relation to communication

99. "Perceived equity in reward results in satisfaction". Which one of the following motivation theories take this into account?

A. Porter and Lowler model
B. Victor Vroom's Expectancy model.
C. F.W. Taylor's incentive scheme
D. Herzberg's Two-factor theory.

100. Which among the following are sub systems of business firms

A. Production system
B. Finance system
C. Research a development system
D. All of the above

101. In management principles, grid refers to

A. Diverse managerial styles
B. Coordination
C. Communication
D. Motivation

102. Hawthorne studies have underlined the significance of which of the following?

A. System approach to management
B. Contingency approach to management
C. Modern approach to management
D. Human relations approach to management

103. Which one of the following is the most important function of a manager?

A. Communication B. Directing
C. Supervising D. Decision making

104. The term "organisational climate" best represents

A. human environment prevailing in an organisation.
B. union – management relations with an organization.
C. problems introduced by faulty organisational structure.
D. Socio - cultural environment in an organization

105. Job evaluation is carried on mainly for

A. identifying geographical locational factors of business enterprise.
B. promoting job satisfaction
C. simplifying wage administration.
D. meeting competition effectively

106. To indicate the functions of management, the catch word POSDCORB was coined by

A. Luther Gulik B. Henri Fayol
C. Ernest Dale D. None of the above

107. Registered companies are the companies which are incorporated

A. By a royal character.
B. By a special Act of Parliament.
C. Under the companies Act, 1956.
D. By a special Act of Legislative Assembly.

108. A private company can commence business.
A. Immediately after its incorporation.
B. After it is able to raise minimum subscription.
C. After it gets certificate to commence business.
D. After it gets permission from the registered of companies to commence business.

109. A public company can be converted into a private company by passing
A. A special resolution to after the aricles to include the restrictions on private companies.
B. An ordinary resolution.
C. A special resolution to alter the articles and obtaining the approval of the company of the Central Government.
D. By passing a special resolution and obtaining the approval of the company law Board.

110. The secretary of a company may be
A. Any individual, firm or body corporate
B. Only an individual
C. Only a body corporate
D. Only a firm

111. A company may change its name by passing
A. A special resolution.
B. An ordinary equal resolution.
C. A special as well as an ordinary resolution as the case may be.
D. An unanimous resolution of the Board of Directors.

112. The altered memorandum must be filed with the Registrar within
A. 1 month of the company Law Board order
B. 2 months of the company Law Board order
C. 3 months of the company Law Board order
D. 4 months of the company Law Board order

113. If the Articles of a company conflict with the memorandum
A. The articles shall prevail
B. The memorandum shall prevail
C. The director will resolve the conflict
D. The court will resolve the conflict

114. Doctrine of constructive notice means
A. Notice of altreration of objects clause to the Registrar
B. Notice of change of name to members
C. Notice to outsides dealing with the company as to contents of memorandum and articles
D. Notice to public as to issue of prospectus

115. Table A given in schedule I to the companies Act, 1956 gives the model
A. Memorandum of Association
B. Articles of Association
C. Share Transfer Form
D. Prospectus

116. A prospectus is a document.
A. Filed by a company with the Registrar before its incorporation
B. Issued by a company inviting deposits from the public
C. Which governs the relationship of a company with the creditors dealing with the company
D. None of these

117. Share capital of a company means
A. Equity share capital
B. Preference share capital
C. Equity and preference share capital
D. Equity and preference share capital and debentures

118. Rights shares mean shares which are
A. Issued by a newly formed company
B. Legally issued to the public
C. Offered to existing share holders
D. Issued to the Central Government on conversion of debentures into shares.

119. The terms "members" and "share holders" are used interchangeably in the case of
A. A company limited by shares
B. A company limited by guarantee
C. A companylimited by guarantee and having a share capital
D. An unlimited company

120. Equity shareholders of a company are
A. Creditors of the company
B. Owners of the company
C. Customers of the company
D. None of these

121. Preference shareholders of a company are
A. Creditors of the company
B. Owners of the company
C. Customers of the company
D. None of these

122. Public limited companies cannot issue
A. Equity shares
B. Preference shares
C. Debentures shares
D. Deffered shares

123. Dividend declared by a company
A. May be paid in cash
B. May be paid in cash or in kind
C. Must be paid in cash only
D. May be paid in any form

124. A statutory meeting is required to be held by
A. All companies
B. Only private companies
C. Only public companies
D. Only Government companies

125. The first annual general meeting of a company must be held within
A. 1 year of its incorporation
B. 15 months of its incorporation
C. 18 months of its incorporation
D. 2 years of its incorporation

126. Proxy is appointed by a shareholder to
A. Vote at meeting of the shareholders
B. Speak at a meeting of the shareholders
C. Speak and vote at a meeting of the share holders
D. Attend the meeting without the right to vote or to speak

127. The quorum for a Board meeting is
A. One half of the total strength of the Board or 2 directors which ever is less
B. One third of its strength
C. One half of its strength
D. One third of its strength or 2 directors which ever is higher

128. Under the companies Act, 1956, the 'financial year' of a company
A. Must be exactly 12 months
B. Must not be less than 12 months
C. May be more or less than a calendar year but it shall not exceed 15 months
D. May be more or less than a celender year , but it shall not exceed 20 months

129. A 'blue chip' security is one which
A. Gives assured high returns.
B. Almost every investor is willing to buy.
C. Offers the highest liquidity and sells always much above par.
D. Is issued by the reputed and profit making companies.

130. The power to make calls on shares can be exercised by the.
A. Shareholders of the company in general meeting
B. Company secretary on his own
C. Board of Directors of the company
D. Managing director of the company

131. The annual general meeting can be called by the
A. Company secretary
B. Board of directors
C. Managing director
D. Non – executive director of the company

132. The company secretary is the agent of the
A. Managing director
B. Shareholders
C. Board of directors
D. Promoters

133. Right share are the shares
A. Issued to the director of the company
B. First offered to the debentures holders
C. First offered to the existing sharesholders
D. Issued by a newly formed company

134. Under the Indian companies Act 1956, a person can be a director in
A. 7 companies
B. 10 companies
C. 20 companies
D. 25 companies

135. Partnership is a form of business organisation in which business debts can be recovered from

A. The managing partners
B. All the managers and partners
C. The firm and the managers
D. The firm and all the partners

136. A company is called an artificial person because
A. It does not have the shape of a normal man
B. It can not be sued in the sort of law
C. It is invisible and intangible
D. It exists only in contemplation of law

137. The first directors of a public company are appointed by the
A. Public B. Shareholders
C. Promoters D. Government

138. Which one of the following is a conclusive proof of the existence of a company?
A. Certifcate of incorporation
B. Certificate of commencement of business
C. Filing of registration papers duly stamped with the registrar of the companies
D. Share certificate

139. According to the companies Act, account books of a company are to be reserved for the proced- ing
A. Six years B. Eight years
C. Five years D. Nine years

140. The source of rules relating to internal manage- ment of a company is known from
A. Memorandum of Association
B. Prospectus
C. Articles of Assosiation
D. Fundamental Rules

141. When a company exceeds the power granted to it by its memorandum of Association, it is called
A. Intravires B. Ultra vires
C. Lien D. Mutatis mutandis

142. Which one of the following statement is not correct in respect of private limited companies?
A. Number of members is limted to 50
B. Operations are restricted to a particular state
C. Invitation to public for subscription to capital is prohibited
D. Transfer of shares is restricted

143. A company needs to issue prospectus
A. For every public issue
B. For every public issue as well as rights issue
C. For every public issue, rights issue and bonus shares
D. For every public issue if it is a private limited company

144. Registration of Articles of Association is optional in the case of
A. Unlimited company
B. Private company limited by shares
C. Company limited by guarentee
D. Pulic company limited by shares

145. Power to use official seal of a company outside India is to be authorised by
A. Articles of Association
B. Memorandum of Association
C. Both Memorandum and Articles of Association
D. Central Government

146. 'Body corporate' under the companies Act, 1956 includes
A. Cooperative Society
B. Company incorporated outside India
C. Corporation sole
D. Any other body corporate, not being a company, which the Central Government may specify

147. A person shall not be appointed as Director if he is found to be of unsound mind by
A. The company
B. The company court
C. A court of competent jurisdiction and the finding is in force
D. The shareholders

148. Dumping is an example of
A. Monopolistic practice in international trade
B. Monopoly in international trade
C. Oligopoly in international trade
D. Perfect competition in international trade

149. The Board of Directors can not appoint
A. Additional directors.
B. Alternate directors.
C. Directors in casual vacancy
D. Directors under Section 408 of the companies Act, 1956

150. "Arbitrage" means
A. A business arrangement by which a share broker tries to take advantage of difference in 'spot' and 'futures' prices of a share
B. A business arrangement in which a share broker tries to take advantage of difference in prices between two Stock Exchange centres on a particular share.
C. An arbitration proceedings that is invoked by either the buyer or the seller when the order party is unable to meet its commitment
D. A compromise arrangement by which the transaction is postponed to the next settlement date.

151. Which one of the following is Not an advantage of the incorporation of a company?
A. Perpetual seccession
B. Limited liability of members
C. Capital contributions forming part of the joint stock of the company
D. Freedom to do any business

152. The liability of the Karta in a Joint Hindu family is
A. Limited to his interest in the joint family
B. Unlimited
C. Limited to the entire property of the family
D. Limited to the private properties of all the members

153. Competition Act, 2002 has replaced the
A. Company Act
B. FERA Act
C. MRTP Act
D. None of these

154. 'Fishing Culture' is classified in
A. Extractive Industry
B. Genetic Industry
C. Construction Industry
D. None of these

155. Which of the following is not an economic activity?
A. A doctor practising
B. A lawyer practising law
C. A professional cricketer playing cricket
D. A student playing cricket

156. The agreement of partnership.
A. must be in oral
B. must be in writing
C. can be either oral or in writing
D. must be in writing on a stamp paper

157. Partnership may come into existence
A. by the opration of law
B. by an express agreement only
C. by an express or implied agreement only
D. by inheritance of property

158. Dissolution of firm takes place
A. by the death or insolvency of anyone partner
B. the retirement of any one partner
C. by the expiry of the term
D. by the insolvency of all but one partner

159. The term, 'capitalisation' is used in relation to
A. sole-proprietorship
B. partnership
C. joint stock companies
D. co-operative societies

160. Watered capital means
A. over- capitalistation
B. under capitalistation
C. excessive capital
D. part of the capital not reprensented by assets.

161. Over capitalisation may be remedied by
A. increasing the number of equity shares
B. increasing the per value of shares
C. issuing additional preference shares
D. redemption of debentures

162. Under Capitalisation can be remedied by
A. isssue of bonus shares
B. redemption of preference shares
C. redemption of debentures
D. reduction of interest of debentures

163. Capital gearing means
A. proper capitalisation
B. watered capital
C. fixation of a proper ratio between two or more types of securities
D. trading on equity

164. Underwriters are persons who
A. purchase the shares and debentures of a company
B. work as agents of the company for the sale of shares and debentures
C. manage the issue of shares and debentures
D. undertake to buy those shares and debentures not subscribed for by the public

165. The first stock exchange was set up in India in
A. Kolkata B. Mumbai
C. Delhi D. Chennai

166. The first stock exchange was set up in India in
A. 1887 B. 1905
C. 1908 D. 1923

167. Cantango charge is paid by a
A. bull speculator to bear speculator
B. bear speculator to bull speculator
C. lame duck to bull speculator
D. bull to lame duck speculator

168. Stock exchange deals with the
A. second hand securities
B. issues of equity shares
C. issue of preference shares
D. issue of debentures

169. Cartel is a type of
A. horizontal combination
B. vertical combination
C. allied combination
D. mixed combination

170. Entrepot trade means
A. import trade
B. export trade
C. foreign trade
D. goods imported for re-export

171. A letter of credit means
A. a letter sent by importer to exporter sanctioning credit deal.
B. a letter sent by exporter to importer sanctioning credit deal.
C. a letter containing conditions of credit purchase or sale.
D. a bank agreeing to accept and pay on due date.

172. Mate's receipt is issued by
A. the exporter
B. the importer
C. the captain of the ship or his assistant
D. the bank

173. The principle of subrogation applies to.
A. all types of insurance.
B. fire insurance only.
C. marine insurance only.
D. fire and marine insurance.

174. Combination of printing and dyeing companies is a type of.
A. vertical combination.
B. horizontal combination
C. circular combination.
D. allied combination.

175. EXIM bank can be described as a.
A. non-banking financial company
B. commercial bank
C. non-banking non-financial company
D. schedule bank.

176. Who among the following is not a speculator in stock exchange?
A. Broker B. Bull
C. Bear D. Stag

177. The gilt edged market refers to the market for
A. industrial securities
B. Govt. and semi-govt securities
C. shares and debentures
D. public limited company securities.

178. "Causa promia" implies that the loss must arise from
A. the nearest place.
B. an assertainable place source.
C. the cause insured against.
D. unforeseen source.

179. Trading on equity takes place
A. when capital other than that of equity share holders is also employed
B. only when equity capital is employed.
C. only when debentures funds are employed
D. when profits are ploughed back.

180. Vertical combination helps to
A. achieve economy by combination allied activities.
B. survive during the times of depression
C. fight a common enemy
D. add new product lines

181. "Bill of loading" is issued by
A. Indian commercial bank
B. foreign bank
C. shipping company
D. exporters

182. A mixed marine policy means
A. combination of fire and marine losses coverage
B. combination of voyage and time policies
C. combination of all types of risk on the sea
D. combination of export credit insurance and marine insurance.

183. The term duty draw-back means
A. higher rate of import duty
B. refund of import duty for the exporters
C. handicap in the matter of export
D. refund of export duty for exporters

184. A partner under his 'Implied Authority' can
A. enter into partnership with others on behalf of the firm.
B. submit dispute relating to the business of the firm for arbitration.
C. defend any suit filed against the firm .
D. withdraw any suit or proceedings filed on behalf of the firm .

185. E Commerce can be of following types
A. B 2 B B. B 2 C
C. B 2 A D. All of these

186. 'Matrix organisation' refers to a form of
A. organisation where authority and responsibility coexist.
B. organisation in which two or more basic types of departmentation are combined
C. mathematical arrangement of events in columns and rows
D. organisation where mathemetical simulation issued.

187. LIBOR refers to
A. liberalised system of foreign exchange transfer between Banks.
B. inter-bank lending rate for Eurodollars at London.
C. lowest rate of interest at which banks in London lend pound sterling.
D. lowest rate of interest prescribed by the Reserve Bank of India.

188. Which of the following is false? An offer to be valid must:
A. Intend to create legal relations.
B. Have certain & unambiguous terms.
C. Contain a term the non-compliance of which would amount to acceptance.
D. Be communicated to the person to whom it is made.

189. Which of the following statement is true?
A. Consideration must result in a benefit to both parties.
B. Past consideration is no consideration in India.
C. Consideration must be adequate.
D. Consideration must be something, which a promisor is not already bound to do.

190. Which of the following is not an exception to the rule – No Consideration, No Contract?
A. Compensation for involuntary services.
B. Love & Affection.
C. Contract of Agency.
D. Gift.

191. A minor's liability for 'necessaries' supplied to him;
A. Arises after he attains majority age.
B. Is against only minor's property.
C. Does not arise at all.
D. Arises if minor gives a promise for it.

192. An agreement is void if it is opposed to public policy. Which of the following is not covered by heads of public policy?
A. Trading with an enemy.
B. Trafficking in public offices.
C. Marriage brokerage contracts.
D. Contracts to do impossible acts.

193. Which of the following persons can perform the contract?
A. Promisor alone.
B. Legal representatives of promisor.
C. Agent of the promisor.
D. All of these.

194. A, B and C jointly promised to pay Rs. 60,000 to D. Before performance of the contract, C dies. Here, the contract
A. becomes void on C's death.
B. should be performed by A and B along with C's legal representatives.
C. should be performed by A and B alone.
D. should be renewed between A, B and D.

195. Generally, which of the following damages are not recoverable?
A. Ordinary damages B. Special damages.
C. Remote damages D. Nominal damages

196. A mistake as to a law not in force in India has the same effect as:
A. mistake of fact
B. mistake of Indian law
C. fraud
D. misrepresentation

197. The term "goods" under Sale of Goods Act, 1930 does not include
A. goodwill B. actionable claims
C. stocks and shares D. harvested crops

198. Which of the following is not an implied condition in a contract of sale?
A. Condition as to title.
B. Condition as to description.
C. Condition as to free from encumbrance.
D. Condition as to sample.

199. Which of the following is not a form of delivery?
A. Constructive delivery.
B. Structured delivery.
C. Actual delivery.
D. Symbolic delivery.

200. Mercantile Agent is having an authority to
A. sell or consign goods.
B. raise money on the security of goods.
C. sell or buy goods.
D. any of the above.

201. Doctrine of Caveat Emptor means
A. let the seller beware.
B. let the buyer beware.
C. let the creditor beware.
D. none of the above.

202. The most important element in partnership is:
A. Business
B. Sharing of Profits
C. Agreement
D. Business to be carried on by all or any of them acting for all.

203. In the absence of agreement to the contrary all partners are:
A. Not entitled to share profits
B. Entitled to share in capital ratio.
C. Entitled to share in proportion to their ages.
D. Entitled to share profits equally.

204. Active partner is one who:
A. Takes part in the business of the firm
B. Actively participates in co-curricular activities
C. Actively shares the profits
D. Makes a show of authority

205. On dissolution the partners remain liable to till
A. Accounts are settled
B. Partners dues are paid off
C. Public notice is given
D. The registrar strikes off the name

206. Which of the following statements, about the registration of firm, is not true:
A. It must be done at the time of its formation.
B. It may be done at the time of formation.

C. It may be done before filing a suit against third party.
D. It may be done at any time after its formation.

207. An agreement which is enforceable by law at the option of one or more of the parties thereon but not at the option of the other or others is a ___________
A. Valid Contract B. Void Contract
C. Voidable Contract D. Illegal Contract

208. When the consent of a party is not free, the contract is ___________
A. Void B. Voidable
C. Valid D. Illegal

209. Ordinarily, a minor's agreement is ___________
A. Void ab initio B. Voidable
C. Valid D. Unlawful

210. The threat to commit suicide amounts to ___________
A. Coercion
B. Undue Influence
C. Misrepresentation
D. Fraud

211. An agreement the object or consideration of which is unlawful, is ___________
A. Void B. Valid
C. Voidable D. Contingent

212. A contingent contract is ___________
A. Void B. Voidable
C. Valid D. Illegal

213. A agrees to sell his car worth Rs. 100,000 to B for Rs. 20,000 only, and A's consent was obtained by coercion. Here, the agreement is ___________
A. void B. valid
C. voidable D. unlawful

214. A agrees to pay Rs. 5 lakhs to B if he (B) procures an employment for A in Income Tax Department. This agreement is ___________
A. void B. valid
C. voidable D. contingent

215. Agreement-the meaning of which is uncertain is ___________
A. Valid B. Void
C. Voidable D. Illegal

216. A contract for the sale of "future goods" is ___________
A. sale
B. agreement to sell
C. void
D. hire-purchase contract

217. A stipulation which is collateral to the main purpose of the contract, and if proves false, gives the buyer only a right to claim damages, is known as ___________
A. conditions B. guarantee.
C. warranty D. none of these

218. Goods which are in existence at the time of the Contract of Sale is known as___________
A. present Goods
B. existing Goods
C. specific Goods
D. none of the above

219. Selection of goods with the intention of using them in performance of the contract and with the mutual consent of the seller and the buyer is known as ___________
A. distribution B. appropriation
C. amortization D. storage

220. An auction sale is complete on the ___________
A. delivery of goods
B. payment of price
C. fall of hammer
D. none of the above

221. If A agrees to deliver 100 kg of sugar to B in exchange of 15 mts of cloth, then it is___________
A. Contract of sale B. Agreement to sell
C. Sale on Approval D. Barter

222. A partner can retire on___________
A. Reaching the age of superannuation
B. On the balance in the capital account reaching a certain amount
C. In accordance with the Partnership Deed
D. On the condition of his nominee becoming a partner

223. Death of partner has the effect of________
A. Dissolving the firm
B. Result in continuance of the business of the firm
C. His heirs joining the firm
D. Computation of profits upto the date of death.

224. Registration of a firm is__________
A. Compulsory
B. Optional
C. Occasional
D. None of the above

225. The reconstitution of the firm takes place in case of ________
A. Admission of a partner
B. Retirement of a partner
C. Expulsion or death of a partner
D. All of the above

226. G paid Rs.1,00,000 to H to influence the head of the Government Organisation in order to provide him some employment. On his failure to provide the job, G sued H for recovery of the amount. Which of the following is correct?
A. The contract is valid and G can recover the amount from H.
B. The contract is void as it is opposed to public policy and G cannot recover.
C. G can recover the amount with interest.
D. G can recover the amount of Rs.1,00,000 and damages.

227. A sold a tin of disinfectant powder to K without warning knowing fully that if the tin was not opened with care, it will likely to cause injury. K was injured while opening the tin. Which of the following statement(s) is/are correct?
A. A is not liable to K under the Doctrine of caveat emptor.
B. A is liable for the damages.
C. A has no duty to disclose the facts to K.
D. The buyer has the responsibility to enquire about all the things before purchasing the goods.

228. The law of contract in India is contained in
A. Indian Contract Act, 1862
B. Indian Contract Act, 1962
C. Indian Contract Act, 1872
D. Indian Contract Act, 1972

229. A void agreement is one which is
A. Valid but not enforceable
B. Enforceable at the option of both the parties.
C. Enforceable at the option of one party
D. Not enforceable in a court of law.

230. Which of the following is false? An acceptance:
A. Must be communicated.
B. Must be absolute and unconditional.
C. Must be accepted by a person having authority to accept.
D. May be presumed from silence of offeree.

231. A proposal when accepted becomes a
A. Promise B. Contract
C. Offer D. Acceptance

232. Which of the following statement is false? Consideration:
A. Must move at the desire of the promisor.
B. May move from any person.
C. Must be illusory.
D. Must be of some value.

233. Which of the following statement is true?
A. A contract with a minor is voidable at the option of the minor.
B. An agreement with a minor can be ratified after he attains majority.
C. A person who is usually of an unsound mind cannot enter into contract even when he is of a sound mind.
D. A person who is usually of a sound mind cannot enter into contract when he is of unsound mind.

234. Which of the following statement is true?
A. A threat to commit suicide does not amount to coercion.
B. Undue influence involves use of physical pressure.
C. Ignorance of law is no excuse.
D. Silence always amounts to fraud.

235. On the valid performance of the contractual obligations by the parties, the contract
A. is discharged
B. becomes enforceable
C. becomes void
D. none of these

236. A contract is discharged by rescission which means the
A. change in one or more terms of the contract.
B. acceptance of lesser performance.
C. abandonment of rights by a party.
D. cancellation of the existing contract.

237. The Sale of Goods Act, 1930 deals with
A. sale B. mortgage
C. pledge D. all of the above

238. Which one of the following is/are document of title to goods?
A. railway receipt.
B. wharfinger's certificate.
C. warehouse keeper's certificate.
D. all of the above

239. Which one of the following is not true?
A. Document showing title is different from document of title.
B. Bill of lading is a document of title to goods.
C. Specific goods can be identified and agreed upon at the time of the contract of Sale.
D. None of the above.

240. In which form of the contract, the property in the goods passes to the buyer immediately:
A. agreement to sell.
B. hire purchase.
C. sale
D. installment to sell.

241. Which one of the following is not an implied warranty?
A. Warranty as to undisturbed possession.
B. Warranty as to existence of encumbrance.
C. Disclosure of dangerous nature of goods.
D. Warranty as to quality or fitness by usage of trade.

242. A firm is the name of:
A. The Partners
B. The minors in the firm.
C. The business under which the firm carries on business
D. The collective name under which it caries on business.

243. A partnership at will is one:
A. which does not have any deed
B. which does not have any partner
C. which does not provide for how long the business will continue
D. which cannot be dissolved.

244. Every partner has the right to:
A. Take part in the business of the firm
B. To share exclusive profits
C. To use the property of the firm for personal purposes
D. Pay taxes

245. Which of the following is not disability of an unregistered firm?
A. It cannot file a suit against third parties
B. Its partners cannot file a suit against a firm.
C. It cannot claim a set-off exceeding Rs. 100.
D. It cannot be sued by a third party.

246. Which of the following is not the right of a partner i.e., which he cannot claim as a matter of right?
A. Right to take part in business.
B. Right to have access to account books.
C. Right to share profits.
D. Right to receive remuneration.

247. In case of illegal agreements, the collateral agreements are ___________ .
A. Valid B. Void
C. Voidable D. None of these

248. Consent is not said to be free when it is caused by ___________
A. Coercion B. Undue Influence
C. Fraud D. All of these

249. Moral pressure is involved in the case of ___________

A. Coercion.
B. Undue Influence.
C. Misrepresentation.
D. Fraud.

250. Sometimes, a party is entitled to claim compensation in proportion to the work done by him. It is possible by a suit for ________
A. damages B. injunction
C. quantum meruit D. none of these

251. A contract dependent on the happening or non-happening of future uncertain event, is a ________
A. Uncertain contract.
B. Contingent contract.
C. Void contract.
D. Voidable contract.

252. A agrees to pay Rs. One lakh to B if he brings on earth a star from sky. This is a contingent contract and ________.
A. Illegal B. Valid
C. Voidable D. Void

253. As a general rule, an agreement made without consideration is ________
A. void B. voidable
C. valid D. unlawful

254. An agreement made with free consent to which the consideration is lawful but inadequate, is ________.
A. void B. valid
C. voidable D. unlawful

255. A contract with the minor, which is beneficial for him, is ________
A. void ab initio B. voidable
C. valid D. illegal

256. A stipulation in a contract of sale of goods whose violation by seller gives a right of rescission to buyer, is called ________
A. Guarantee B. Warranty
C. Condition D. Term

257. The essence of a right of lien is to ______
A. deliver the goods
B. retain the possession
C. regain the possession
D. none of the above

258. If a seller handed over the keys of a warehouse containing the goods to the buyer results in ________
A. constructive delivery
B. actual delivery
C. symbolic delivery
D. none of the above

259. A agrees to deliver his old car valued at Rs. 80,000 to B, a car dealer, in exchange for a new car, and agrees to pay the difference in cash it is ________
A. Contract of sale B. Agreement to sell
C. Exchange D. Barter

260. A contact for the sale of goods which provide that the property would pass to the buyer on full payment of price and execution of sale deed, is known as ________
A. sale
B. agreement to Sell
C. hire-purchase Agreement
D. sale of approval

261. Voluntary transfer of possession by one person to another is popularly known as ________
A. Transfer B. Possession
C. Delivery D. None of the above

262. A partner can be expelled if ________
A. Such expulsion is in good faith
B. The majority of the partner agree on such expulsion
C. The expelled partner is given an opportunity to start a business competing with that of the firm
D. Compensation is paid

263. A new partner can be admitted in the firm with the consent of ________
A. All the partners
B. Simple majority of partners
C. Special majority of partners
D. New partner only

264. A partner may retire from an existing firm ________
A. with consent of all partners
B. as per express agreement

C. by written notice in partnership at will
D. all of the above

265 A partnership firm is compulsorily dissolved where ___________
A. All partners have become insolvent
B. Firm's business has become unlawful
C. The fixed term has expired
D. In cases (A) and (B) only.

266. Ram, Rohit and Kiran jointly borrowed Rs.2,00,000 from Rahim by executing a promissory note. Rohit and Kiran are not traceable. Rahim wants to recover the entire amount from Ram. Ram objected this move by saying he is liable to pay 1/3 of the debt only. Which of the following statement(s) is correct?
A. Rahim can recover the entire amount from Ram.
B. Rahim can only recover 1/3 of Rs. 2,00,000 from Ram.
C. Rahim cannot recover any amount from Ram.
D. The promissory note is not executable against Ram as Rohit and Kiran are not traceable.

267. X agrees with Y to carry passengers by taxi from Delhi to Gurgaon on the following terms, namely, Y is to pay X Rs. 100 per mile per annum, and X and Y are to share the costs of repairing and replacement of the cars, and to divide equally between them the proceeds of fares received from passengers. Choose the correct alternative.
A. X and Y are partners
B. X and Y are cab owners
C. X and Y are co-owners
D. Can't be decided

268. Which of the following statement is true?
A. An agreement is an unaccepted proposal.
B. An agreement enforceable by law is a contract.
C. An agreement can only consist of an offer.
D. An agreement can only consist of an acceptance.

269 An offer may lapse by:
A. Revocation
B. Counter Offer
C. Rejection of Offer by Offeree
D. All of these

270. Consideration must move at the desire of
A. Promisor
B. Promisee
C. Any other person
D. Any of these

271. Which of the following statements is not true about minor's position in a firm?
A. He cannot become a partner in an existing firm.
B. He can become a partner in an existing firm.
C. He can be admitted only to the benefits of any existing firm.
D. He can become partner on becoming a major.

272. A contract is discharged by novation which means the
A. cancellation of the existing contract.
B. change in one or more terms of the contract.
C. substitution of existing contract for a new one.
D. none of these.

273. When prior to the due date of performance, the promisor absolutely refuses to perform the contract, it is known as
A. abandonment of contract.
B. remission of contract.
C. actual breach of contract.
D. anticipatory breach of contract.

274. In case of breach of contract, which of the following remedy is available to the aggrieved party?
A. Suit for rescission.
B. Suit for damages.
C. Suit for specific performance.
D. All of these.

275. A voidable contract is one which
A. can be enforced at the option of aggrieved party

B. can be enforced at the option of both the parties
C. cannot be enforced in a court of law
D. courts prohibit.

276. A agrees to sell his car worth Rs. 100,000 to B for Rs. 20,000 only, and A's consent was obtained by coercion. Here, the agreement is
A. void B. valid
C. voidable D. unlawful

277. The term "goods" under Sale of Goods Act, 1930 does not include
A. goodwill
B. actionable claims
C. stocks and shares
D. harvested crops

278. Which of the following is not an implied condition in a contract of sale?
A. Condition as to title.
B. Condition as to description.
C. Condition as to free from encumbrance.
D. Condition as to sample.

279. Which of the following is not a form of delivery?
A. Constructive delivery.
B. Structured delivery.
C. Actual delivery.
D. Symbolic delivery.

280. Goods which are in existence at the time of the Contract of Sale is known as
A. present Goods B. existing Goods
C. specific Goods D. none of the above

281. The doctrine of Caveat Emptor does not apply, when
A. the goods are bought by sample.
B. the goods are bought by sample as well as description.
C. the goods are purchased under its brand name.
D. all of the above.

282 If X commissioned Y, an artist, to paint a portrait of A for 200 dollars & Y uses his own canvas & paint then it is
A. Contract of sale.
B. Contract of work & materials.
C. Sale on approval.
D. Hire-Purchase agreement.

283. The most important element in partnership is:
A. Business
B. Sharing of Profits
C. Agreement
D. Business to be carried on by all or any of them acting for all.

284. On dissolution the partners remain liable to till
A. Accounts are settled
B. Partners dues are paid off
C. Public notice is given
D. The registrar strikes off the name

285. Which of the following acts are not included in the implied authority of a partner?
A. To buy or sell goods on accounts of partners.
B. To borrow money for the purposes of firm.
C. To enter into partnership on behalf of firm.
D. To engage a lawyer to defend actions against firm.

286. After retirement from firm, which of the following partners is not liable by holding out, even if the public notice of retirement is not given?
A. Active partner
B. Sleeping partner
C. Representative of deceased partner
D. Both B and C

287. An agreement enforceable by law is a ______.
A. Promise B. Contract
C. Obligation D. Lawful Promise

288. A wrong representation when made without any intention to deceive the other party amounts to __________.
A. Coercion B. Undue Influence
C. Misrepresentation D. Fraud

289. When the consent of a party is obtained by coercion undue influence, fraud or misrepresentation, the contract is________.
A. void B. voidable
C. valid D. illegal

290. A threatens to kill B if he does not agree to sell his scooter to him for Rs. 1000 only. Here Bs consent is obtained by ________.
A. undue influence B. fraud
C. coercion D. none of these

291. Where the consent of both the parties is given by mistake, the contract is ________
A. void B. valid
C. voidable D. illegal

292. A mistake as to a law not in force in India has the same effect as ________.
A. mistake of fact
B. mistake of Indian law
C. fraud
D. misrepresentation

293. An agreement, which prevents a person from carrying a lawful business, is ________.
A. Valid B. Void
C. Voidable D. Contingent

294. A agrees to sell his car to B at a price which B may be able to pay. This agreement is ________.
A. void B. valid
C. voidable D. contingent

295. An agreement to pay money or money's worth on the happening or non-happening of a specified uncertain event is a ________.
A. wagering agreement
B. contingent contract
C. quasi contract
D. uncertain agreement.

296. Agreement-the meaning of which is uncertain is ________.
A. Valid B. Void
C. Voidable D. Illegal

297. The goods are at the risk of a party who has the ________.
A. Ownership of goods
B. Possession of goods
C. Custody of goods
D. both B and C

298. In case of unconditional contract of sale, the property passes to the buyer at the time of making the contract. For this rule to apply, the goods must be ________
A. specific
B. in a deliverable state
C. physically transferred to buyer
D. both A and B

299. In case of sale of unascertained goods, the ownership is transferred to the buyer when the goods are ________.
A. ascertained
B. appropriated to the contract
C. weighed and measured
D. both A and B

300. In case of sale on approval, the ownership is transferred to the buyer when he ________.
A. accepts the goods
B. adopts the transaction
C. fails to return goods
D. in all the above cases.

301. The bidder at an auction sale can withdraw his bid ________.
A. any time during auction
B. before fall of hammer
C. before payment of price
D. cannot withdraw at all.

302. A partner can retire on ________
A. Reaching the age of superannuation
B. On the balance in the capital account reaching a certain amount
C. In accordance with the Partnership Deed
D. On the condition of his nominee becoming a partner

303. Death of partner has the effect of ________
A. Dissolving the firm
B. Result in continuance of the business of the firm
C. His heirs joining the firm
D. Computation of profits upto the date of death

304. The reconstitution of the firm takes place in case of ________
A. Admission of a partner
B. Retirement of a partner
C. Expulsion or death of a partner
D. All of the above

305. A partner may be expelled from the firm on the fulfillment of the condition that the expulsion power is exercised ________.

A. As given by express contract
B. By majority of partners
C. In absolute good faith
D. All of the above.

306 A contracts with B to buy a necklace, believing it is made of pearls whereas in fact it is made of imitation pearls of no value. B knows that A is mistaken and takes no steps to correct the error. Now A wants to cancel the contract on the basis of fraud. Which of the following statement is correct?

A. A can cancel the contract alleging fraud.
B. A cannot cancel the contract.
C. A can cancel the contract alleging undue influence.
D. A can claim damages.

307. A timber merchant agreed to supply best teak at a certain agreed price to a builder. Later the merchant supplied timber which was identified as ordinary class of timber and demanded the payment from the builder. Which of the following statements is/are true?

A. Builder can reject the goods and can claim damages.
B. Builder has to accept the goods.
C. Builder has to pay the price by taking delivery of teak wood.
D. Timber merchant cannot plead the doctrine of caveat emptor.

308. Cross Offers means

A. Exchanging identical offers by two parties in ignorance.
B. Offer made to the public in general.
C. Offer allowed to remain open for acceptance over a period of time.
D. Offer made to a definite person.

309. Valid Contract:

A. In case of this collateral agreements are void.
B. Not enforceable in a court of law.
C. An agreement enforceable by law at the option of one or more of the parties thereon but not at the option of the other or others.
D. Enforceable at the option of both the parties.

310. Which of the following is a requirement for misrepresentation to exist?

A. Misrepresentation should relate to a material fact.
B. The person making a misrepresentation should not believe it to be true.
C. It must be made with an intention to deceive the other party.
D. All of the above.

311. Which of the following agreements is void?

A. Agreements made under the unilateral mistake of fact.
B. Agreements made under the bilateral mistake of fact.
C. Agreements made under the influence of fraud.
D. Contingent agreement.

312. Which of the following offers constitute a valid offer?

A. An auctioneer displays a TV. set before a gathering in an auction sale.
B. Ram who is in possession of three cars purchased in different years says 'I will sell you a car'.
C. A says to B, "Will you purchase my motor cycle for Rs. 20,000?
D. All of the above.

313. Which of the following statements is true?

A. Even if a proposal is not accepted properly it becomes a valid contract.
B. The agreements which are against the public policy can be enforced if the parties are willing to contract.
C. A contract can consist of an offer or an acceptance only.
D. Two are more persons are said to consent when they agree upon the same thing in the same sense.

314. Contract caused by which of the following is void?

A. Fraud
B. Misrepresentation
C. Coercion
D. Bilateral Mistake

315 Suppose the time fixed for performance of the contract has expired but the time is not essential. What is the remedy of the promisee in the circumstances?
A. Can rescind the contract
B. To claim compensation
C. No remedy available
D. Can't be determined

316. What is legal terminology for the doing or not doing of something which the promisor desires to be done or not done?
A. Desires B. Wishes
C. Consideration D. Promise

317. Goods must be the same as wanted by the seller. This is
A. Condition as to description
B. Condition as to sample
C. Condition as to wholesomeness
D. Condition as to title

318. Goods dependant upon certain events which may or may not happen.
A. Unascertained goods
B. Future goods
C. Contingent Goods
D. Existing Goods

319. Which of the following is a not document of title to goods?
A. Bill of Lading B. Railway Receipt
C. Dock Warrant D. Performa invoice

320. The term 'goods' for the purpose of Sale of Goods Act, includes
A. Money
B. Actionable claims
C. Growing crops, grass
D. None of these

321. In which of the following cases, the unpaid seller loses his right of lien?
A. Delivery of goods to buyer.
B. Delivery of goods to carrier.
C. Tender of price by buyer.
D. All of these.

322. In case of sale of standing trees, the property passes to the buyer when trees are
A. Felled and ascertained.
B. Not felled but earmarked.
C. Counted and ascertained.
D. Both B and C

323. Partnership
A. Arises by operation of law.
B. Comes into existence only after registration.
C. Can arise by agreement or otherwise.
D. Arise by way of an agreement only.

324. X and Y agree to work together as carpenters but X shall receive all profit and shall pay wages to Y. The relation between X and Y is that
A. Partners B. Carpenters
C. Labourers D. Master-Servant

325. Which of the following is an essential feature of partnership?
A. Registration.
B. Test of Mutual Agency.
C. Separate Legal Entity.
D. All of the above.

326. Which of the following acts are not included in the implied authority of a partner?
A. To buy or sell goods on accounts of partners.
B. To borrow money for the purposes of firm.
C. To enter into partnership on behalf of firm.
D. To engage a lawyer to defend actions against firm.

327. Implied contract, even if not in writing or express words, is perfectly ________ if other conditions are satisfied
A. Void B. Valid
C. Voidable D. Illegal

328. R, an optical surgeon, employs S as the assistant for a term of three years and S agrees not to practice as a surgeon during this period. This contract is ________
A. Valid B. Void
C. Voidable D. Illegal

329. _______ consideration is no consideration in England.
A. Past B. Present
C. Future D. Past and Present

330. A agrees to pay Rs. 500 to B if it rains, and B promises to pay a like amount to A if it does not rain, this agreement is called ________.
A. Quasi Contract
B. Contingent Contract
C. Wagering Agreement
D. Voidable Contract

331. When the offeree offers to qualified acceptance of the offer subject to modifications and variations he is said to have made a ___________.
A. Standing, open or continuing offer
B. Counter Offer
C. Cross Offers
D. Special Offer

332. When after the formation of a valid contract, an event happens which makes the performance of contract impossible, and then the contract becomes ___________.
A. Void B. Voidable
C. Valid D. Illegal

333. Where the performance of a promise by one party depends on the prior performance of promise by the other party, such reciprocal promises fall under the category of ___________.
A. Mutual and concurrent
B. Conditional and dependent
C. Mutual and independent
D. Can't be determined

334. The basis of 'quasi contractual relations' is the __________.
A. Existence of a valid contract between the parties
B. Prevention of unjust enrichment at the expense of others
C. Provisions contained in Section 10 of the Contract Act
D. Existence of a voidable contract between the parties

335. A agrees to pay Rs. 1000 to B if a certain ship returns within a year. However, the ship sinks within the year. In this case, the contract becomes ___________
A. Valid B. Void
C. Voidable D. Illegal

336. Where an agreement consists of two parts once legal and the other illegal, and the legal part is separable from the illegal one, such legal part is _________.
A. Void B. Valid
C. Voidable D. Illegal

337. The Sale of Goods Act, 1930 came into force on ___________.
A. 15th March, 1930 B. 1st July, 1930
C. 30th July, 1930 D. 30th June, 1930

338. Contract of Sale is _______________.
A. Executory Contract
B. Executed Contract
C. Executory Contract or Executed Contract
D. None of the above

339. Where in an auction sale, the seller appoints more than one bidder, the sale is _________.
A. Void B. Illegal
C. Conditional D. Voidable

340. Where the goods are delivered to a carrier or wharfinger for the purpose of transmission to the buyer, the delivery is ___________.
A. Invalid and ineffective
B. Valid and effective
C. Conditional
D. None of these

341. The property in the goods means the ______.
A. Possession of goods
B. Custody of goods
C. Ownership of goods
D. Both A and B

342. Untill goods are ascertained there is merely ___________.
A. An agreement to sell
B. A breach of warranty
C. A breach of condition
D. All the above

343. The rights of an agent against the principal are the following __________.

A. Right of indemnification
B. Right to compensation
C. Right of stoppage in transit
D. All of the above

344. Discharge by mutual agreement may involve____________.
A. Novation B. Recission
C. Alteration D. All of the above

345. A enquires from B, "Will you purchase my cow for $ 100?" B replies, "I shall purchase your cow for $ 100 provided you purchase my parrot for $ 120." In this case ________.
A. B has accepted the offer of A
B. B has made a counter offer to A
C. A is bound by the actions of B
D. B cannot make such an offer

346. A sold 1000 tins of oil to B without appropriating any particular oil to the contract. B sold 600 tins out it to C and gave delivery order addressed to A. C lodged the delivery order with A requesting him to "await" his orders. Meanwhile, B became insolvent and thus A became the unpaid seller.
A. A can exercise his right of lien and refuse to make delivery to C.
B. A cannot exercise his right of lien and refuse to make delivery to C.
C. C has claim over the goods in possession of A.
D. None of the above.

347. X fraudulently induced Y to enter into partnership with him and Y pays a premium of Rs.5,000/- to A. Within three months the firm incurs liabilities to the extent of Rs.10,000/-. On discovering the fraud, Y files a suit for the rescission of the contract creating partnership and contract is rescinded. The creditors of the firm also levy attachment on Y who pays Rs.3,000/- to them as well. Which of the following is correct?
A. Y can obtain a decree for Rs.8000/- against A.
B. Y can obtain a decree for Rs.5000/- against A.
C. Y can obtain a decree for Rs.3000/- against A.
D. Y cannot obtain a decree for either Rs.5,000/- or Rs.3,000/- or Rs.8000/- against.

348. A mate's receipt
A. Is a document of title to goods.
B. Is an acknowledgement for the receipt of goods.
C. Both the above.
D. None of the above.

349. Each partner is a principal as well as an agent of other partners.
A. The above statement is correct.
B. The above statement is not correct in case of unregistered partnerships.
C. The above statement is incorrect.
D. The above statement is correct only in case of registered partnerships.

350. A contract was entered before 1st September, 1872 is governed by The Indian Contract Act, 1872
A. Yes if the contract was entered in Indian soil.
B. Yes if there was performance of the contract on or after 1st September 1872.
C. No as the act does not apply retrospectively.
D. No as there was no performance on or after 1st September 1872.

351. A share in a partnership:
A. Can be transferred in accordance with the terms and conditions contained in the partnership deed.
B. Can be transferred only if all the partners agree for such transfer
C. Cannot be transferred at all.
D. Can be transferred through the recognized stock exchanges.

352. Which of the following is not correct?
A. Joint Hindu Family is governed by law relating to registration of agreements.
B. Joint Hindu Family is governed by Hindu Law.

C. Joint Hindu Family is governed by the Civil Procedure Code.
D. Both A & C

353. In case of sale
A. Property in goods passes to the buyer.
B. Risk in the goods passes to the buyer.
C. Both the above.
D. None of the above.

354. Which one of the following is not a contract?
A. A engages B for a certain work and promises to pay such remuneration as shall be fixed by C. B does the work.
B. A and B promise to marry each other.
C. A takes a seat in a public vehicle.
D. A invites B to a card party. B accepts the invitation.

355. Which of the statement is incorrect?
A. All illegal agreements are void but all void agreements are not necessary illegal.
B. A voidable contract is not voidable at the option of the aggrieved party.
C. Contracts that are immoral or opposed to public policy are illegal in nature.
D. All of the above.

356. The difference between contingent contract and wagering agreements are as follows:
A. A wagering agreement consists of reciprocal promises whereas a contingent contract may not contain reciprocal promises.
B. In a wagering agreement the uncertain event is the sole determining factor while in a contingent contract the event is only collateral.
C. A wagering agreement is void whereas a contingent contract is valid.
D. All of the above.

357. An agreement made without consideration is valid under Section 25 of The Indian Contract Act, 1872 if
A. The agreement is expresses in writing.
B. The agreement is made on account of natural love and affection or the parties to the agreement stand in a near relation to each other.
C. The document is registered under the law for the time being in force for registration of such document.
D. All of the above.

358. Which of the following is not correct?
A. Minor can always plead minority.
B. Minor is liable for necessaries supplied to him.
C. Minor is a person who has not completed 18 years of age.
D. Minor can be a beneficiary.

359. Which of the following is not correct?
A. Consideration must be at the desire of the promisor.
B. Consideration may be past, present or future.
C. Consideration need not be adequate, but should be real and supported by free consent.
D. Consideration should be always monetary.

360. Novation means
A. Substituting a new contract for the old one.
B. Cancellation of the old contract.
C. Modifying or altering the terms of contract such that it has the effect of substituting a new contract for the old one.
D. Dispensing away the performance of the promise made by the other party.

ANSWERS

1	2	3	4	5	6	7	8	9	10
D	C	C	B	B	C	B	B	C	D
11	**12**	**13**	**14**	**15**	**16**	**17**	**18**	**19**	**20**
A	B	C	C	C	A	B	A	A	C

21	22	23	24	25	26	27	28	29	30
B	A	A	C	B	A	D	C	A	D
31	**32**	**33**	**34**	**35**	**36**	**37**	**38**	**39**	**40**
B	A	D	C	B	A	D	C	D	B
41	**42**	**43**	**44**	**45**	**46**	**47**	**48**	**49**	**50**
A	A	C	B	C	A	B	A	A	C
51	**52**	**53**	**54**	**55**	**56**	**57**	**58**	**59**	**60**
B	C	B	B	A	B	B	A	C	A
61	**62**	**63**	**64**	**65**	**66**	**67**	**68**	**69**	**70**
B	C	C	B	B	D	C	A	C	B
71	**72**	**73**	**74**	**75**	**76**	**77**	**78**	**79**	**80**
B	C	B	C	A	B	D	A	C	B
81	**82**	**83**	**84**	**85**	**86**	**87**	**88**	**89**	**90**
B	D	B	D	D	D	C	A	C	B
91	**92**	**93**	**94**	**95**	**96**	**97**	**98**	**99**	**100**
A	B	B	A	D	A	C	B	A	D
101	**102**	**103**	**104**	**105**	**106**	**107**	**108**	**109**	**110**
C	D	B	A	C	A	C	A	C	B
111	**112**	**113**	**114**	**115**	**116**	**117**	**118**	**119**	**120**
A	C	B	C	B	B	C	C	A	B
121	**122**	**123**	**124**	**125**	**126**	**127**	**128**	**129**	**130**
D	D	C	C	C	A	D	C	D	C
131	**132**	**133**	**134**	**135**	**136**	**137**	**138**	**139**	**140**
B	C	C	C	D	D	C	A	B	C
141	**142**	**143**	**144**	**145**	**146**	**147**	**148**	**149**	**150**
B	D	A	D	A	B	C	A	D	B
151	**152**	**153**	**154**	**155**	**156**	**157**	**158**	**159**	**160**
D	B	C	B	D	C	C	D	C	D
161	**162**	**163**	**164**	**165**	**166**	**167**	**168**	**169**	**170**
D	A	D	D	B	A	A	A	A	D
171	**172**	**173**	**174**	**175**	**176**	**177**	**178**	**179**	**180**
A	C	D	C	A	A	B	C	A	A
181	**182**	**183**	**184**	**185**	**186**	**187**	**188**	**189**	**190**
C	B	B	C	D	B	C	C	D	A
191	**192**	**193**	**194**	**195**	**196**	**197**	**198**	**199**	**200**
B	D	D	B	C	A	B	C	B	D
201	**202**	**203**	**204**	**205**	**206**	**207**	**208**	**209**	**210**
B	D	D	A	C	A	C	B	A	A

211	212	213	214	215	216	217	218	219	220
A	C	C	A	B	B	C	B	B	C
221	222	223	224	225	226	227	228	229	230
D	C	A	B	D	B	B	C	D	D
231	232	233	234	235	236	237	238	239	240
A	C	D	C	A	D	A	D	D	C
241	242	243	244	245	246	247	248	249	250
B	D	C	A	D	D	B	D	B	C
251	252	253	254	255	256	257	258	259	260
B	D	A	B	C	C	B	C	A	B
261	262	263	264	265	266	267	268	269	270
C	A	A	D	D	A	A	B	D	A
271	272	273	274	275	276	277	278	279	280
B	C	D	D	A	C	B	C	B	B
281	282	283	284	285	286	287	288	289	290
D	B	D	C	C	D	B	C	B	C
291	292	293	294	295	296	297	298	299	300
A	A	B	A	A	B	A	D	D	D
301	302	303	304	305	306	307	308	309	310
B	C	A	D	D	B	A	A	D	A
311	312	313	314	315	316	317	318	319	320
B	C	D	D	B	C	A	C	D	C
321	322	323	324	325	326	327	328	329	330
D	C	D	D	B	C	B	A	A	C
331	332	333	334	335	336	337	338	339	340
B	A	B	B	B	B	B	C	D	B
341	342	343	344	345	346	347	348	349	350
C	A	D	D	B	A	A	B	A	C
351	352	353	354	355	356	357	358	359	360
B	D	C	D	B	D	D	B	D	A

HIGHLIGHTS OF COMPANIES ACT, 2013

INTRODUCTION

Background

Companies Bill, 2012 was passed by the Lok Sabha on 18th December, 2012 and by the Rajya Sabha on 8th August, 2013. On receiving the assent of the Hon'ble President of India on August 29, 2013, it was notified on **August 30, 2013** as the Companies Act, 2013.

It may be noted that **only Section 1** of the Companies Act, 2013 has come into force with effect from 30th August, 2013. As far as the remaining provisions of this Act is concerned, they shall come into force on such date as the **Central Government (Ministry of Corporate Affairs)** may, by notification in the Official Gazette, appoint and different dates may be appointed for bringing into force different provisions of the Companies Act, 2013. For instance, Central Government has made, **98 Sections and part thereof** of the Companies Act, 2013, **effective from 12th September, 2013.**

Thus, Companies Act, 2013 is all set to replace the existing 56 year old company law, i.e., Companies Act, 1956, very soon. It moves from the regime of control to that of liberalisation or self-regulation.

Structure of the Act

The Companies Act, 2013 has **470 Sections (covered in 29 Chapters) and 7 Schedules** as against 658 Sections (covered in 13 Parts) and 15 Schedules of the Companies Act, 1956.

It may be noted that the number of Sections has been drastically reduced, but at the same time the Central Government has been empowered, in number of Sections, to prescribe various aspects in the form of **Rules,** thereby recognizing the more importance of **delegated legislation.** It can be said Companies Act, 2013 has been structured on **skeleton approach.** This has been done for ensuring that the law remains relevant at all times in the changing economic environment.

Applicability of the Act

Section 1 provides that the Companies Act, 2013 applies on whole of India.

Companies Act, 1956 also applies on whole of India. However, proviso to Section 1(3) of the Companies Act, 1956 empowers the Central Government to modify the provisions of the Act, while applying this Act on the State of Nagaland. Similarly, Sections 620B and 620C of the Companies Act, 1956 empowers the Central Government to, modify, or exempt from, the provisions of the Act, while applying this Act on the States of Goa, Daman, Diu and Jammu & Kashmir respectively. These kinds of powers of the Central Government have been taken away by the Companies Act, 2013.

Thus, the 2013 Act puts an end to the power of the Central Government under the 1956 Act to exempt companies from provisions of Companies Act based on regional considerations.

IMPORTANT HIGHLIGHTS

Following are the important highlights of Companies Act, 2013 :

Preliminary

- New definitions have been introduced, some of which are auditing standards, associate company, CEO, CFO, control, employee stock option, financial statement, global depository receipt, Indian depository receipt, independent director, interested director, key managerial personnel, promoter, one person company, small company, turnover, voting right, etc.
- Number of existing definitions have been modified, for example, definitions of abridged prospectus, body corporate, director, expert, managing director, officer in default, etc.
- Definition of private company changed - the limit on maximum number of members increased from 50 to 200.
- The concept of One Person Company introduced. It will be a private limited company.
- The concept of Small Company introduced. It will be subject to lesser stringent regulatory framework.

Capital Raising

- Money raised through a prospectus cannot be used for dealing in equity shares of another company. If a company changes terms of the prospectus or objects for which money is raised, it shall provide dissenting shareholders an exit opportunity.
- Shares, other than Sweat Equity Shares, cannot be issued at a discount. It means the practice of issuing shares at a discount with the approval of CLB, as provided in Section 79 of Companies Act, 1956, has been discontinued.
- Public companies can accept deposit from public on complying with certain conditions like credit rating.

Management & Administration

- All companies to follow uniform financial year, running from April to March. Exceptions to be made only for certain companies with the approval of NCLT.
- First Annual General Meeting of the Company shall be held within 9 months from the closure of its first financial year instead of 18 months from the date of incorporation, as provided in the Companies Act, 1956.
- Quorum of general meeting for a **public company** will now depend upon the numbers of the company. For companies with up to 1000 members, 5 members personally present; for companies with members more than 1000 but up to 5000, 15 members personally present; and for companies with more than 5000 members, 30 members personally present, shall be the quorum. The Companies Act, 1956 prescribes a fixed quorum of 5 members personally present.
- Postal Ballot to be applicable to all the companies, whether listed or unlisted.
- The National Advisory Committee on Accounting Standards renamed as The National Financial Reporting Authority (NFRA).

Auditors & Financial Statements

- Every company is required at its first annual general meeting (AGM) to appoint an individual or a firm as an auditor. The auditor shall hold office from the conclusion of that meeting till the conclusion of its 6th AGM and thereafter till the conclusion of every 6th meeting. The appointment of the auditor is to be ratified at every AGM.
- Individual auditors are to be compulsorily rotated every 5 years and audit firm every 10 years in listed companies & certain other classes of companies, as may be prescribed.
- A company's auditor shall not provide, directly or indirectly, the specified services to the company, its holding and subsidiary company.

Directors

- Prescribed class or classes of companies are required to appoint at least one woman director **(Woman Director).**
- At least one director should be a person who has stayed in India for a total period of not less than 182 days in the previous calendar year **(Resident Director).**
- At least one-third of the total number of director of a listed public company should be independent directors. Government may prescribe requirement of Independent Directors for certain unlisted public companies also.
- Liability of independent directors and non-executive directors not being promoter or key managerial personnel to be limited.
- A person can hold directorship of up to 20 companies, of which not more than 10 can be public companies.
- Companies can have maximum of 15 directors. More can be appointed after passing a special resolution.

Governance

- Companies with more than 1,000 shareholders, debenture-holders, and any other security holders at any time during a financial year to constitute a Stakeholder's Relationship Committee, with a non-executive director as a chairperson.
- The provisions on inter-corporate loans and investment (372A of Companies Act, 1956) extended to include loan and investment to any person.
- A company cannot, unless otherwise prescribed, make investment through more than 2 layers of investment companies.
- No central government approval required for entering into any related party transactions.
- No central government approval required for appointment of any director or any other person to any office or place of profit in the company or its subsidiary.
- The Act makes provision for cross border amalgamation between Indian Companies and companies incorporated in the jurisdictions of such countries as may be notified from time to time by the central government.
- The authority CLB is being replaced by National Company Law Tribunal (NCLT).

Miscellaneous

- The Act provides provisions related to Corporate Social Responsibility (CSR).
- The Act provides for class action suit by specified number of members or depositors against the company except the banking company, which is prevalent in developed countries.
- Where any valuation is required to made of any property, stocks, shares, debentures, securities or goodwill or any other assets or net worth of a company or its liabilities under the Act, it shall be valued by a registered valuer.

CONCEPTS OMITTED

Major Omission/Deletions

S.No.	Section of Companies Act, 1956	Provisions of the Companies Act, 1956 which have been deleted in the Companies Act, 2013
1.	43A	Private company to become public company in certain cases.
2.	44	Filing of Prospectus or statement in lieu of prospectus by private company on ceasing to be private company.
3.	58AA	The provisions of section 58AA relating to acceptance of deposits from small depositors and intimation of default in repayment of deposits thereof has been dropped.
4.	58AAA	Section 58AAA which makes any offence connected with or arising out of acceptance of deposits u/s 58A or 58AA as cognizable has been done away with.
5.	120	The concept of perpetual debentures has been omitted.
6.	121	The concept of re-issue of redeemed debentures has been omitted.
7.	153A	Appointment of public trustee.
8.	165	Statutory meeting and statutory report of company.
9.	224A	Auditor not to be appointed except with the approval of the company by special resolution in certain cases.
10.	233A	Power of Central Government to direct special audit in certain cases.
11.	258	Right of company to increase or reduce the number of directors.
12.	270	Time within which share qualification is to be obtained and maximum amount thereof.
13.	294AA	Power of Central Government to prohibit the appointment of sole selling agents in certain cases.
14.	417	Employees' securities to be deposited in post office/savings bank or Scheduled Bank.

IMPORTANT POINTS OF COMPANIES ACT 2013

New Concepts and Definitions

2013 Act has introduced several new concepts and definitions. Few of them which we believe to be the most crucial are analyzed below:

Companies

- **One Person Company:** 2013 Act now allows one person to form a company vis-à-vis the earlier position where a minimum of two persons were required to form a company (private). This new concept will be beneficial as entrepreneurs will be able to singly set up a corporate entity, restrict the liability of business and reduce compliances. Further, it will now be easier for foreign companies to set up wholly owned private subsidiaries in India, as it will not require divesting any part of stake in such subsidiaries to its group or subsidiary companies unlike under the 1956 Act wherein such divestment was required to meet the minimum two person rule to set up a company. [Section 2(62) and Section 3(1)(c)].
- **Small Company:** 2013 Act introduces this new concept of a small company, which means a company other than a public company having paid up share capital not exceeding INR 50,00,000 (or such higher amount as may be prescribed which shall not be more than INR 5,00,00,000) or turnover of which as per its last profit and loss account does not exceed INR 2,00,00,000 (or such higher amount as may be prescribed which shall not be more than INR 20,00,00,000). However, this section of small company will not be applicable to (a) holding or subsidiary company; (b) company registered under Section 8 of 2013 Act (i.e. companies form with the charitable object); or (c) company or a body corporate formed under the special Act. [Section 2(85)].
- **Dormant Company:** 2013 Act now allows a company to be formed and classified as a dormant company

for holding assets or intellectual property subject to the company not having any significant accounting transaction. Further, an inactive company can also make an application to the Registrar in such manner as may be prescribed for obtaining the status of a dormant company. [Section 455]

- **Associate Company:** 2013 Act now defines the much controversial Associate Company to mean a company which has 'Significant Influence' over the other company and which is not a subsidiary company but includes a joint venture company. Further it has been explained that 'Significant Influence' shall mean control of at least having 20% of total share capital or control of the business decision under an agreement. [Section 2(6)]
- **Private Company:** 2013 Act has now increased the total limit of number of members / shareholders in private company from 50 to 200. [Section 2(68)(ii)]
- **Investments Companies:** 2013 Act provides that any company (unless otherwise prescribed) shall not make investment through more than two layers of investment companies. However, this section has not been made applicable to a company acquiring any other company incorporated outside India, if such other company has investment subsidiaries beyond two layers as per the laws of such country. This Section may considerably restrict the flexibility of Indian companies in structuring their transactions. [Section 186]

Object Clause : 1956 Act required the object clause (which is stated in the memorandum of association of a company) to be classified into (a) main object; (b) objects incidental or ancillary to the attainment of the main objects; and (c) other objects of the company. The reason for having such classification in the object clause was to restrict the company from commencing any other business unless it complies with certain requirements. However, this requirement of such classification has been done away with by the 2013 Act, i.e. all objects will now be the main objects of the company. [Section 4(1)]

Key Managerial Personnel (KMP): KMP is commonly used in investment agreements and now finds a place in the 2013 Act. KMP includes (a) Managing Director (MD) or Chief Executive Officer (CEO); (b) Whole time director; (c) Chief Financial Officer (CFO); (d) Company Secretary (CS) and; (e) such other officer as may be prescribed. 2013 Act requires certain companies to appoint KMPs which will be notified in the Rules. [Section 2(51)]

Promoter: The term Promoter was not defined in the 1956 Act. However, it was extensively used through company law. 2013 Act now specifically defines Promoter, which includes (a) a person who has been named as such in the prospectus or is identified as such in the annual return; or (b) who has control over the affairs of the company (other than in a professional capacity), as a shareholder or a director or otherwise; or (c) in accordance with whose advice or directions the Board is accustomed to Act. [Section 2(69)]

Class Action Suits: 2013 Act introduces the western concept of class action suits which allows requisite number of members, depositors or any class of them file a suit against the company, its directors, auditors and/or other experts or consultants or advisors, if they believe that affairs of the company are conducted in a manner prejudice to the company or its members or depositors. [Section 245]

Buy back of Securities: 2013 Act provides that no buy back will be done by a company within one year from date of closure of previous buy back. Based on this provision, each company will now require having a cooling off period of one year between the two buy backs. Further, if a company has defaulted in repayment of its loans, deposits or interests payable then the company shall compulsorily have to wait for a period of three years after repayment of all such outstanding amount and rectifying such breach. [Section 68]

Management and Administration

2013 Act provides detailed role of the management by incorporating sections enunciating powers, duties and responsibilities of board of directors, KMP, etc. Following are some of the important changes in the 2013 Act vis-à-vis 1956 Act:

Directors

- **Maximum Number of Directors:** The maximum number of directors for a public company has been increased from 12 to 15. In case, the company desires to further increase the board size, it may do so by passing a special resolution. The requirement of taking permission of the Central Government as provided in 1956 Act is done away within 2013 Act. [Section 149(1)]
- **Number of Directorships:** A person cannot be a director (including alternate director) in more than 20 companies out of which he or she cannot be a director of more than 10 public companies. 2013 Act now restricts over all directorship of any individual as compared to 1956 Act which allowed 15 directorships of any person in a public company and any number of directorships in a private company. [Section 165]

- **Resident Director:** At least one director of the company is required to fulfill the residency test i.e. stay for not less than 182 days in India in the previous calendar year. [Section 149(3)]
- **Woman Director:** Certain class of the companies (which will be notified in the Rules) must have at least one woman director on the board. [Section 149(1)]
- **Small Shareholder Director:** A listed company may have one director elected by small shareholders. Small shareholder means a shareholder holding shares of nominal value of not more than INR 20,000 or such other sum as may be prescribed.
- **Independent Directors:** To align the company law with Clause 49 of Equity Listing Agreement **(Clause 49),** 2013 Act has introduced the concept of Independent Directors. In this respect, few of our general observations are as follows:

(a) The term independent director has been defined with certain prescribed qualification and disqualification. [Section 149(6)]

(b) Every listed company is required to have at-least one-third of the total number of directors as independent directors. Independent directors shall be entitled to sitting fees, commission from the profit and reimbursement of expenses. However, they will not be entitled to stock options. [Section 149(9)]

(c) The appointment of the independent director shall be approved by the members in a general meeting and they will not be required to retire by rotation. [Section 149(13)]

(d) An independent director can hold the office for consecutive two terms of five years each following which there should be three years break before he or she is reappointed as an independent director. [Section 149(11)]

(e) Nominee director shall not be considered as an independent director. [Section 149(6)]

(f) While the intention of 2013 Act is to align itself with Clause 49, there are few aspects which are different. All listed companies will now have to comply with Clause 49 and 2013 Act which will make the compliance process more cumbersome.

(g) Independent director shall only be liable for such act of omission, commission by a company which had occurred with his or her knowledge, attributable through Board processes, and with his/her consent or connivance or where he or she had not acted diligently. [Section 149(12)]

Duties of the Director: 2013 Act attempts to codify the duties of directors, including but not limited to the following, they are required to (a) act in good faith and in the best interest of the company; (b) not to have direct or indirect conflict of interest with the interest of the company; and (c) exercise duties with diligence and reasonable care and declares that it would be punishable offence to commit a breach of those duties. The liability of the director in default for contravention, for which no specific penalty is prescribed, has been increased from INR 50,000 to INR 500,000. [Section 166)]

Board Meetings:

- The first board meeting is required to be held within 30 days of incorporation of a company and a minimum of four meetings are required to be held every year in such a manner that there are not more than 120 days between two meetings. [Section 173 (1)]
- A notice of minimum seven days is required to be given for convening a board meeting. The company can hold board meetings at a shorter notice to transact urgent business subject an independent director, if any shall be present in the meeting. In case of absence of independent directors from such a meeting, the decisions taken at such a meeting shall be circulated to all the directors and shall be final only upon the ratification thereof by at least one independent director, if any. [Section 173 (3)]
- The board meeting can be attended by the directors through video conferencing or other audio-visual modes, and such presence will be counted as quorum for the meeting, subject to the condition that they can be recorded and stored. [Section 173 (2)]

Committees: Besides the Audit Committee, the 2013 Act requires listed and such other class of companies as may be prescribed to form Nomination and Remuneration Committee, Corporate Social Responsibility Committee and Stakeholders Relationship Committee. [Section 178]

Corporate Social Responsibility (CSR)

The Ministry of Corporate Affair had introduced CSR Voluntary Guidelines in 2009. These guidelines are now part of the 2013 Act and mandates following companies with the CSR activities:

Every company having net worth of INR 500,00,00,000 or more, or turnover of INR 1000,00,00,000 or more or a net profit of INR 5,00,00,000 or more during any financial year shall constitute a CSR Committee of the Board consisting of three or more directors, out of which at least one director shall be an independent director.

CSR Committee shall formulate the policy for activities specified in Schedule VII of the 2013 Act which broadly includes (a) eradicating extreme hunger and poverty; (b) promotion of education; (c) promoting gender equality and empowering women; (d) reducing child mortality and improving maternal health; (e) combating human immunodeficiency virus, acquired immune deficiency syndrome, malaria and other diseases; (f) ensuring environmental sustainability; (g) employment enhancing vocational skills; (h) social business projects; (i) contribution to the Prime Minister's National Relief Fund or any other fund set up by the Central Government or the State Governments for socio-economic development and relief and funds for the welfare of the Scheduled Castes, the Scheduled Tribes, other backward classes, minorities and women; (j) such other matters as may be prescribed.

2013 Act mandates companies to spent at least two percent of the average net-profits of immediately preceding three years on CSR activities, and if not spent, an explanation with the reasons thereof shall be required to be given in the Director's Report. [Section 135]

Shareholders Meeting

Notice: A notice of clear 21 days is required to be given to each shareholder. 2013 Act now permits notice to be sent through electronic mode and should also be given to all the directors.

Quorum: 2013 Act has revised the quorum requirement for a general meeting of public company. The new requirements are broadly linked to the total number of shareholders of the particular company. Quorum for the meeting will be as follows:

Public Company

(a) Five members personally present shall be the quorum for the meeting, if the total number of members does not exceed 1000;

(b) 15 members personally present shall be the quorum for the meeting, if the total number of members are up to 5000; and

(c) 30 members personally present shall be the quorum for the meeting, if the total number of members exceeds 5000. [Section 103]

Private Company: Two members personally present shall form the quorum for the meeting.

Electronic Voting: Central Government shall prescribe class or classes of companies and the manner in which members may exercise his/her rights to vote by electronic means. [Section 108]

Demand for Poll: A member having not less than 1/10th of the total voting power or holding shares of an aggregate of not less than INR 500,000 can demand poll. Further, 2013 Act removes the distinction between the private or public company in terms of eligibility of members for making demand for poll. [Section 109]

Postal Ballot: Unlike 1956 Act wherein postal ballot was only applicable to listed companies, it appears that 2013 Act has extended postal ballot requirement to all the companies which includes pubic unlisted and private companies as well. Central Government has yet to provide what specific items would require members' resolutions passed through postal ballot. [Section 110]

Mergers and Amalgamation

2013 Act introduces some new provisions with regard to mergers and acquisitions, apart from incorporating changes to the existing provisions in the 1956 Act. The objective of bringing these changes is to simplify the procedures involved and ensure higher standards of accountability. Some of the key new provisions in this respect are:

Holding and subsidiary: A fast track procedure has been introduced for merger and amalgamation of holding company and its fully owned subsidiary. An approval of the court is not required as long as the Registrar of Companies **(ROC)** and official liquidator have no objection and the Central Government has granted its consent. [Section 233]

Cross Border Mergers: 1956 Act did not permit Indian companies to merge with foreign companies. 2013 Act now allows Indian companies to merge with foreign companies subject to an approval of the Reserve Bank of India and foreign company being incorporated in the jurisdiction notified by Central Government. [Section 234]

Listed to Unlisted: In the event of an arrangement between a listed transferor company and an unlisted transferee company, 2013 Act now permits for the (subject to consent of the tribunal) unlisted company to stay unlisted until it becomes listed. Further, if the shareholders of the transferor company decide to exit, the exit price cannot be less than the price as provided under Securities Exchange Board of India Regulations.

Squeeze out of minority shareholding: 2013 Act now allows 90% majority shareholders of a company to squeeze out the minority shareholders at a price determined on the bases of value determined by the registered valuer. [Section 236]

Audit and Auditors

With the background of Satyam corporate scandal in India, 2013 Act extensively enhances accountability of the auditors. The key changes in this respect are as follows:

Appointment of Auditors: Auditors will now be appointed for a term of five years. However, their term will be ratified at each annual general meeting. [Section 139(1)]

Mandatory Rotation: Auditors for listed companies (and other class(es) of companies as may be prescribed) are now required to mandatorily rotate their auditors – every five years in case of the appointment of an individual as auditor and every 10 years in case of appointment of an audit firm with a uniform cooling off period of five years in both cases. Further, firms with common partners in the outgoing audit firm will also be ineligible for appointment as auditor during the cooling off period. [Section 139(3)]

Non-audit Service: Any services to be rendered by an auditor of a company should be approved by the Audit Committee or the board of the company. Additionally, the auditor is restricted directly or indirectly from providing certain specific services, which include (a) accounting and book keeping services; (b) internal audit; (c) design and implementation of any financial information system; (d) actuarial services; (e) investment advisory services; (f) investment banking services; (g) rendering of outsourced financial services; (h) management services, and any other services which may be prescribed. [Section 144].

Secretarial Audit: 2013 Act provides for a mandatory requirement to have secretarial audit which is required to form a part of the director's report for all listed companies and other classes of companies that may be prescribed. [Section 204]

Financial Statement and Dividend

Financial Year: Under the 1956 Act, companies were permitted to decide their own financial year. 2013 Act has taken away this liberty and requires all the companies to have a financial year ending as on the 31st of March. If any company desires to follow a different financial year because the holding company or subsidiary company requires following of different financial year for consolidation of its accounts, it will have to make an application to Tribunal. Tribunal, if satisfied, shall grant such an exemption. [Section 2(41)]

Consolidated Statement: 2013 Act requires consolidation of certain financial statements of any company having subsidiary, associate or joint venture company to prepare and present in addition to stand alone financial statements.

Dividend: Unlike the 1956 Act, the 2013 Act does not require certain percentage of profit to be transferred to the reserves before declaring the dividend. Further, a company which has incurred any loss during the current financial year upto to the end of the quarter immediately preceding the date of declaration of interim dividend, shall not be required to declare such interim dividend at a rate higher than the average dividends declared by the company during the immediately preceding three financial years. [Section 123]

Regulators

National Company Law Tribunal (NCLT or Tribunal): 2013 Act provides for constitution of Tribunal and Appellate Tribunal with the objective of facilitating expeditious disposal of proceedings. All the matters, issues and disputes falling within the ambit of 2013 Act will now be referred to NCLT. Appeal would lie before the Appellate Tribunal and thereafter can be challenged before the Supreme Court. High Courts will now have no jurisdiction in matters related to company law. [Section 407 to 434]

National Financial Reporting Authority (NFRA): 2013 Act also provides for constitution of NFRA which will substitute the National Advisory Committee on Accounting and Auditing Standards. NFRA will supervise and regulate the activities of auditors and companies and see that they are in compliance with accounting and auditing standards. [Section 132]

Serious Fraud Investigation Office (SFIO): SFIO is an expert body established by Central Government in 2003 as a special organization to examine serious cases of fraud and scams received from MCA. The body was formed to carry out investigations under the provisions of the 1956 Act and was formed in light of the rise in white collar crimes and stock market scams. 2013 Act now itself incorporates within its folds the mandate for setting up an investigative body and recognizes the already existing SFIO as the investigative body. [Section 211]

Revival and Rehabilitation of Sick Company

The existing provisions for revival and rehabilitation of sick companies have been substantially altered. 2013 Act now permits 'any' company and not just an 'industrial' company to be declared as sick company and avail benefits of this scheme.

The determination of whether a company is a sick company or not has moved from the concept of 'erosion of net worth' to 'inability to pay debt'. If a company fails to repay its debt within 30 days from receipt of a demand from the secured creditor representing 50% or more in value of the outstanding debt of the company, the company would be considered as a sick company.

A secured creditor whose debt has not been repaid can apply to the Tribunal for declaration of the company to be sick. If the said company is unable to provide a scheme to the Tribunal for its revival, an interim administrator may be appointed by the Tribunal to take over the management of the sick company. The Tribunal may consider various options for the revival of the sick company including its acquisition by a solvent company, restructuring of its assets, etc. If the Tribunal is satisfied that revival is not possible, it will pass an order for winding up of the company. [Chapter XIX]

Winding-up

1956 Act provided three modes of winding-up of a company i.e. (a) Compulsory Winding-up ordered by the court; (b) Voluntary Winding-up by members; and (c) Winding-up under supervision of the court. 2013 Act now prescribes only two modes i.e. (a) Winding-up by the Tribunal and (b) Voluntary Winding-up. Further, 2013 Act does not acknowledge the distinction between member voluntary winding-up and creditor voluntary winding-up vis-à-vis the position in the 1956 Act.

2013 Act adds following new grounds for winding-up of a company by NCLT:

- If the company has acted against the interests of the sovereignty and integrity of India, the security of the State, friendly relations with foreign States, public order, decency or morality;
- If order has been made by NCTL under Chapter XIX (Revival and Rehabilitation of Sick Companies);
- If on an application made by the ROC or any other person authorised by the Central Government by notification under 2013 Act and NCLT is of the opinion that the affairs of a company have been conducted in a fraudulent manner or the company was formed for fraudulent and unlawful purpose or the persons concerned in the formation or management of its affairs have been guilty of fraud, misfeasance or misconduct in connection therewith and that it is proper that the company be wound-up;
- If the company has made a default in filing with the ROC its financial statements or annual returns for immediately preceding five consecutive financial years; or
- If NCLT is of the opinion that it is just and equitable that the company should be wound-up. [Section 270 to 365]

The Companies (Amendment) Act, 2015

The Companies (Amendment) Bill, 2014, a bill to amend the Companies Act, 2013 ("**Act**"), has now been passed by both the houses of the Parliament and has received the assent of the President of India on May 25, 2015 making it the Companies (Amendment) Act, 2015 ("**Amendment Act**"). The provisions of the Amendment Act have come into force from May 29, 2015.

ANALYSIS AND IMPACT OF THE KEY AMENDMENTS

I. Related Party Transactions ("RPTs")

Section 297 of the erstwhile Companies Act, 1956 set out the requirement for procuring Central Government approval for RPTs while the Act required a special resolution for RPTs where a shareholder who was a related party was not allowed to vote on such special resolution. Now, the Amendment Act further relaxes this provision and allows companies to enter into RPTs after passing an ordinary resolution for the same. This will enable group companies in transacting *inter se* business. Further, the requirement of shareholder's approval in case of RPT between holding company and wholly owned subsidiary ("**WOS**") has been dispensed with. This exception was earlier present under the Companies (Meetings of Board and its Powers) Rules, 2014 ("**Rules**") and now has been incorporated in the substantive law itself.

II. Omnibus approval for RPTs

In addition to the amendment of allowing companies to undertake RPTs through an ordinary resolution, the Amendment Act amends Section 177 whereby a new proviso to Section 177 (4) has been inserted which reads as follows *"provided that the Audit Committee may make omnibus approval for related party transactions proposed to be entered into by the company, subject to such conditions as may be prescribed."* Thus, for ease in doing business, now the audit committee will be empowered to give omnibus approvals for related party transactions to be entered into by the company.

This amendment seems to be in line with the provisions of the recently amended Clause 49 of the Listing Agreement as regards omnibus approval of related party transactions by the audit committee constituted under the Board of the company. This amendment may also result in defeating the principles of healthy corporate governance practices to be followed by companies whereby they are required to inform the shareholder of all pertinent details in relation to a related party transaction so as to enable him to take an informed decision. The conditions for the omnibus approval are yet to be notified and are expected to bring in more clarity on the subject.

III. Minimum Capital Requirement

The requirement for having a minimum paid-up capital of ₹ 1,00,000 for private limited companies and ₹ 5,00,000 for public limited companies has now been done away with. This amendment is expected to reduce registration costs for incorporation of new companies. However, the minimum capital requirements generally acted as filters and, to an extent, ensured the formation of companies for bonafide and genuine purposes. This amendment may now encourage formation of bogus shell companies.

IV. Loan to WOS

Section 185 of Act prohibits a company from:

(i) advancing any loan, including a loan represented by a book debt, to its director or to any other person in whom the said director is interested; and/or

(ii) giving any guarantee or providing any security in connection with any loan taken by the director or any other person in whom the director is interested.

Transactions in the nature of loans and guarantees between a holding company and its WOS were exempted from the applicability of Section 185. This exemption was already provided for in the Rules and now it has been incorporated in the substantive law itself.

V. Restriction on inspection of Board Resolutions

Section 117 of the Act required a company to file certain specified resolutions with the Registrar of Companies and permitted public inspection of such resolutions, thus raising concerns of breach of confidentiality. This provision under the Act was not well received by the stakeholders. The Amendment Act now inserts a new proviso to clause (g) of Section 117 of the Act, which states that *"provided that no person shall be entitled under section 399 to inspect or obtain copies of such resolutions"* thus ensuring confidentiality of such resolutions.

VI. Common Seal

The Amendment Act has omitted the words 'and a common seal' appearing under Section 9 of the Act which means it shall not be mandatory for a company to have a common seal. This is not a major change yet it is a welcome change. In the era of digital signatures and documents being maintained in the electronic form, common seal was an obsolete requirement of the law.

VII. Deposits

Section 76(A) has been inserted by the Amendment Act whereby a minimum penalty of ₹ 1 Crore is sought to be imposed on companies which *"accept or invite or allow or cause any other person to accept or invite on its behalf"* deposit in contravention of provisions of Section 73 of the Act or *"fails to repay the deposit and interest thereon"*. This insertion seeks to protect the interests of the funds of the investors and imposes a harsh fine and punishment on the company as well as every other officer who is in default in relation to such non-compliance.

VIII. No dividend, without depreciation

The Companies (Declaration and Payment of Dividend) Rules, 2014 were amended by the Companies (Declaration and Payment of Dividend) Amendment Rules, 2014 whereby companies were prohibited from declaring dividend unless the previous year or years' losses and unabsorbed depreciation which had not been provided for by the company were set off against current year's profits. This provision has been incorporated in the substantive law by amendment of Section 123 of the Act. This is a welcome move for ensuring financial health of a company.

IX. Fraud Reporting-threshold limits

The Act required an auditor, who believes that an offence involving a fraud is being or has been committed in a company, to report the same to the Central Government. The existing Section 143 (12) has been substituted by a new clause which stipulates that if the auditor, during the course of his audit, discovers or suspects a fraud, he has to report it to the Central Government when the amount of the fraud crosses the threshold limit to be prescribed by the Central Government and in respect of other frauds/suspected frauds below the threshold limit, the same needs to be reported by the auditor to the audit committee constituted under the Board of the company and in cases where the company does not have an audit committee, the same may be reported to the Board of the company. Whether or not the amendment is a welcome change can be more affirmatively ascertained upon notification of the threshold limits.

X. Special Courts

The Amendment Act amends the provisions of Section 435 whereby the Special Courts constituted under the Act shall try only those offences which are punishable by an imprisonment of two years or more. All other offences may be tried by the Metropolitan Magistrate or Judicial Magistrate First Class.

XI. Bail restrictions to apply only for offence relating to fraud

Section 212 of the Act specified the offences under specific Sections of the Act which attracted the punishment for fraud under Section 447 and which were to be cognizable offences and in respect of which, bail restrictions as specified in Section 212 (6) (i) and (ii) would apply. The Amendment Act now widens the ambit of Section 212 to remove the specific list of offences and specifies that any offence which falls within the definition of 'fraud' under Section 447 shall be considered as a cognizable offence and the bail restrictions as specified in Section 212 (6) (i) and (ii) would apply to any such offence.

SECTION-WISE SUMMARY OF AMENDMENTS

SECTION	EARLIER PROVISION	PROVISIONS AFTER AMENDMENT
2 (68)	Private Company required "Minimum Paid up Share Capital of ₹ 100,000"	No requirement of Minimum Paid Up Capital.
2 (71)	Public Company required "Minimum Paid up Share Capital of ₹ 500,000"	No requirement of Minimum Paid Up Capital.
9, 12 and 223	Affixation of Common Seal is Mandatory	Use of Common Seal is now optional. (Not Mandatory)
11	Commencement of Business	No requirement of Commencement of Business Certificate. Such section shall be omitted.
22	Execution of Bills of Exchange	Use of Common Seal is now optional. (Not Mandatory)If company doesn't have common seal the authorization under sub section (2) of Section 22 shall be made by two directors or by a director and the Company Secretary, wherever the company has appointed a Company Secretary.
46	Issue of Share Certificate(46(1): A share certificate issue under the common seal of Company{Clause substituted)	Use of Common Seal is now optional. (Not Mandatory) If company doesn't have common seal then signed by two Directors or by a director and Company secretary (if any)
76A	This was not in the Act.	New Section 76A inserted after Section 76 for punishment for deposits accepted in violation of the provisions of the said Act.
117(3)(g)	Public can inspect the form MGT-14 filed by the Companies as per section 179(3) for the Board Resolution.	Public can't inspects form MGT-14 filed for the purposes mention in section 179(3). {MGT-14 (filed for purpose of Section 179(3), Board Resolution) will not available for public inspection on MCA portal.}
123(1)	This was not in the Act.	After the third proviso of 123(1), the following proviso is inserted. Proviso, No company shall declare dividend unless carried over previous losses and depreciation not provided in previous year or years are set off against profit of the company for the current year.

SECTION	EARLIER PROVISION	PROVISIONS AFTER AMENDMENT
124(6)	Unpaid or unclaimed dividend has been transferred under sub-section (5) Substituted	(i) For the words, brackets and figure "unpaid or unclaimed dividend has been transferred under sub-section (5) shall also be", the words "dividend has not been paid or claimed for seven consecutive years or more (ii) After the proviso, the following explanation shall be inserted", namely: — "Explanation— In case any dividend is paid or claimed for any year during the said period of seven consecutive years, the share shall not be transferred to Investor Education and Protection Fund."
134(3)	Not Earlier in the Act.	After Clause "c" following clause (ca) is inserted: Details in respect of frauds reported by auditors under sub-section (12) of section 143 **"other than those which are reportable to the Central Government"**
143(12)	The Act requires that if the auditor of a company has reason to believe that an offence of fraud has been committed against the company, by its employees, he must report the matter to the central government within a time period and in a manner prescribed.	Notwithstanding anything contained in this section, if any auditor of a company in the course of the performance of his duties as auditor, has reason to believe that an offence of fraud involving such amount or amounts as may be prescribed, is being or has been committed in the company by its officers or employees, the auditor shall report the matter to the central government within such time and in such manner as may be prescribed: Provided that in case of a fraud involving lesser than the specified amount, the auditor shall report the matter to the audit committee constituted under section 177 or to the Board in other cases within such time and in such manner as may be prescribed: Provided further that the companies whose auditors have reported frauds under subsection 12 to the Audit Committee or the Board but not reported to the Central Government, shall disclosed details about such frauds in the Board Report in such manner as may be prescribed.
117(4)(iv)	Every Audit Committee shall act in accordance with the terms of reference specified in writing by the Board which shall inter alia include (iv) approval or any subsequent modification of transaction of the Company with Related Party.	After 117(4)(iv) following proviso added: Provided that the Audit Committee may make omnibus approval for related party transaction proposed to be entered into by the company subject to such conditions as may be prescribed.
185	Not Earlier in the Act. Bare Act Language of Section 185(1)(b) : A company which in the ordinary course of its business provides loans or gives guarantees or securities for the due repayment of any loan and	After clause (b) Sub Section (1) of Section 185 following clause and proviso added: (c) Any loan made by a Holding Company to its Wholly own Subsidiary Company or any guarantee given or security provided by a Holding Company in respect of any loan made to its wholly own subsidiary

SECTION	EARLIER PROVISION	PROVISIONS AFTER AMENDMENT
	in respect of such loan an interest in charged at a rate not less than the bank rate declared by the RBI.	Company, (d) Any guarantee given or security provided by a Holding Company in respect of Loan made by any Bank or financial institution to its subsidiary Company provided that the loan made under clauses (c) and (d) are utilized by the subsidiary company for its **principal business activity.**
188(1)	Earlier Special Resolution was required.(As per the previous system, the companies with a paid up capital of Rs 10 crore or more were required to get shareholders' nod through a special resolution in case of related party transactions)	For the word "Special Resolution" the word "Resolution" is substituted under the Act. Now Ordinary resolution will work.
188(1)	Not Earlier in the Act.	Not required to follow provision of Section 188. After the third proviso of Section 188(1) the following proviso inserted: Provided also that the requirement of passing the resolution under the first proviso shall not be applicable for transactions entered between a holding company and its wholly owned subsidiary whose accounts are consolidated with such holding company and have been placed before the shareholders for their approval.
212(6)	Investigation into affairs of Company by Serious Fraud Investigation Office. Here, provided Bail restriction for many sections.	The bail restrictions to apply only for offence relating to fraud u/s 447.
419(4)	In Section 419(4) winding up was mentioned.	The word WINDING UP shall be omitted.
435	Establishment of Special Courts. The Central Govt. may for the purpose of providing speedy (Trial of offences under this Act), established or designate as many Special Courts as may be necessary.	For the Words "Trial of Offences under This Act", The words "Trial of offences punishable under this Act with imprisonment with 2 years or more" is substituted. After Sub Clause (1) the following proviso is inserted: "Provided that all other offences shall be tried, as the case may be by a metropolitan Magistrate or a Judicial Magistrate of the first class having jurisdiction to try any offence under this Act or under any pervious Company Law.
436	Offence Triable by special courts Section 436(1)(a)	For the words "all offences under this Act", the words, brackets and figures "all offences specified under sub-section (1) of section 435" shall be substituted Section 435(1) given below.
462	Sub-section {2,3 and 4 of Section 462) shall be substituted.	Substituted language of Section 462(2),(3) and (4).

HIGHLIGHTS OF COMPANIES (Amendment) ACT, 2017

Companies (Amendment) Bill, 2017 was introduced in Lok Sabha on March 16, 2016 then the Bill was referred to the Standing Committee on Finance on 12 April, 2016 and Committee after hearing the views of different representatives and professionals adopted its report on 30th November, 2016.

- Lok Sabha passed this bill on July 27, 2017,
- Rajya Sabha passed this bill on December 19, 2017
- Received assent of President of India on the January 3rd, 2018 and it was published in the "Official Gazette of India" on the same date i.e., WEDNESDAY, JANUARY, 3, 2018, and the Bill becomes the Companies (Amendment) Act, 2017 from this date and is applicable from the same date.

The Companies (Amendment) Act, 2017 introduces several amendments to the Companies Act 2013, realigning provisions to improve corporate governance and ease of doing business in India while continuing to strengthen compliance and investor protection. This is the second round of amendments made to the Companies Act, 2013, with the first are being made in 2015.

The major amendments include simplification of the private placement process, rationalization of provisions related to loan to directors, omission of provisions relating to forward dealing and insider trading, doing away with the requirement of approval of the Central Government for managerial remuneration above prescribed limits, aligning disclosure requirements in the prospectus with the regulations to be made by SEBI, providing for maintenance of register of significant beneficial owners and filing of returns in this regard to the ROC and removal of requirement for annual ratification of appointment or continuance of auditor.

The major official amendments subsequently introduced include continuing with the provisions relating to layers of subsidiaries, continuing with the earlier provisions with respect of memorandum, making offence for contravention of provisions relating to deposits as non-compoundable, requiring attaching of financial statement of associate companies, stringent additional fees of ₹ 100 per day in case of delay in filing of annual return and financial statement etc.

The Companies (Amendment) Act, 2017. Key Changes and Highlights

S. No.	Section	AMENDMENT
1.	Section 2(6)- Definition of 'associate company'	• Change in explanation of the term 'significant influence' under the definition of Associate Company has been proposed. Significant influence is proposed to mean control of at least 20% of the voting power or control or participation in business decision under an agreement. Currently the Act provides for control of at least 20% total share capital.
		• Further the term 'Joint Venture' has also been defined to mean a joint arrangement whereby the parties that have joint control of the arrangement have rights to the net assets of the arrangement.
2.	Section 2(28)- Definition of 'cost accountant'	Change in definition of 'cost accountant' is proposed. "Cost Accountant" means a person who is a member of the Institute of Cost and Works Accountants of India and who holds a valid certificate of practice.
3.	Section 2(30)- Definition of 'Debenture'	Under the definition of the term "debenture", it is proposed to exclude instruments referred to in Chapter III-D of the Reserve Bank of India Act 1934 and such other instruments prescribed by the Central Government in consultation with the RBI.
4.	Section 2(41)- Definition of 'Financial year'	It is proposed that associate company of a company incorporated outside India can also apply to the Tribunal for a different financial year.

S. No.	Section	AMENDMENT
5.	Section 2(46)- Definition of 'Holding Company'	It is proposed that for the purpose of definition of the term 'holding company', the expression "company" will include any body corporate.
6.	Section 2(49)- Definition of 'Interested director'	It is proposed to delete the definition of the term 'Interested director'.
7.	Section 2(51)- Definition of 'Key Managerial Personnel'	Under the definition of the term "Key Managerial Personnel", such other officer not more than one level below the directors who is in whole time employment and designated as KMP by the Board, is proposed to be included.
8.	Section 2(57)- Definition of 'net worth'	It is proposed to include the debit or credit balance of profit and loss account in the calculation of net worth.
9.	Section 2(71)- Definition of 'public company'	Including the word 'and' in the definition for more clarity is proposed to clarify that a public company must satisfy both the conditions mentioned in the subsection.
10.	Section 2(72)- Definition of 'public financial institution'	It is proposed that the Central Government may notify other institution which has been established or constituted by or under any Central or State Act other than the Companies Act, 2013 or previous Company Law after consultation with the RBI as "public financial institution".
11.	Section 2(76)- Definition of 'Related Party'	Following two amendments are proposed: • Instead of only a company, anybody corporate which is holding, subsidiary or an associate company of such company or a subsidiary of a holding company to which it is also a subsidiary or an investing company or venture of the Company, shall be considered as a related party. • "An investing company or the venturer of the company" will mean a body corporate whose investment in the company would result in the company becoming an associate company of the body corporate.
12.	Section 2(85)- Definition of 'small company'	• It is proposed to increase the maximum paid-up share capital amount which can be prescribed for the purpose of determining a company as a small company from five crore rupees to ten crore rupees and prescribed turnover amount from twenty crore rupees to one hundred crore rupees. • Further turnover should be as per profit and loss account for the immediately preceding financial year and not as per its last financial year.
13.	Section 2(87)- Definition of 'subsidiary company'	It is proposed that a company will be treated as subsidiary in case the holding company exercises or controls more than one-half of the total voting power either at its own or together with one or more of its subsidiary companies. Currently the Act provides for exercise or control of more than half of the total share capital.

S. No.	Section	AMENDMENT
14.	Section 2(91)-Definition of 'Turnover'	It is proposed to change the definition of turnover to mean the gross amount of revenue recognised in the profit and loss account from the sale, supply, or distribution of goods or on account of services rendered, or both, by a company during a financial year.
15.	Section 3A-Members severally liable certain cases	It is proposed to insert a new section regarding liability of members in case number of members is reduced from statutory minimum, i.e. seven in the case of public company or two in case of a private company. This section was there in the Companies Act 1956 but was missing from the Companies Act 2013.
16.	Section 4-Memorandum	• It is proposed that in case of incorporation, name reserved by the RoC shall be valid for 20 days from date of the approval or such other period as may be prescribed instead of 60 days from the date of application, as currently provided;
		• in case of change in name by an existing company, name reserved by the RoC shall be valid for 60 days from the date of approval.
17.	Section 7-Incorporation of company	At the time of incorporation of the company, declaration by each subscriber will be required to be attached instead of an affidavit, as currently provided.
18.	Section 12-Registered office of company	• It is proposed that the company shall within 30 of its incorporation have registered office instead of current requirement to have registered office on and from the fifteenth day of its incorporation.
		• It is proposed that notice of every change of the situation of the registered office, shall be given to the Registrar within 30 days instead of 15 days, as currently provided.
19.	Section 21-Authentication of documents, proceedings and contracts	Apart from KMP and any officer of the company, it is proposed that an employee can also be authorized to authenticate documents on behalf of the company.
20.	Section 26-Matters to be stated in Prospectus	Instead of detailed list of contents of the Prospectus, it is proposed that the prospectus shall state such information and set out such reports on financial information as may be specified by SEBI in consultation with the Central Government. Till the time SEBI specifies the information and reports on financial information, the regulations made by it under the SEBI Act, 1992, in respect of such financial information or reports on financial information shall apply.
21.	Section 35-Civil liability for Misstatements in prospectus	It is proposed to amend section 35 of the Act to relieve the Director, promoter etc. from any civil liability if such person(s) has relied on a misleading statement made by an expert and he had reasonable ground to believe and did up to the time of the issue of the prospectus believe, that the person making the statement was competent to make it and that the said person had given the consent required and had not withdrawn it.

S. No.	Section	AMENDMENT
22.	Section 42-Private placement	Though the entire section is proposed to be substituted but major changes proposed are: – • Return of allotment has to be filed within 15 days instead of 30 days.
		• Money received under the private placement shall not be utilized unless the return of allotment is filed with the ROC.
		• Private Placement offer letter shall not contain any right of renunciation.
23.	Section 47-Voting rights	Since a member who is a related party cannot vote on a resolution to be passed under section 188 of the Companies Act 2013, it is proposed to clarify that the right of every member holding equity shares to vote on all resolutions placed before the meeting would be subject to sub-section (1) of section 188 of the Act.
24.	Section 53-Prohibition on issue of shares at discount	• It is proposed to replace the words "discounted price" with the word "discount".
		• Further it is proposed to allow companies to issue shares at a discount to its creditors when its debt is converted into shares in pursuance of any statutory resolution plan or debt restructuring scheme in accordance with any guidelines or directions or regulations specified by Reserve Bank of India under the Banking Regulation Act, 1949 or the Reserve Bank of India Act 1934.
25.	Section 54-Issue of Sweat Equity Shares	It is proposed to allow issue of sweat equity shares at any time after registration of the company. Currently such shares can be issued only after the expiry of one year from the date of commencement of business.
26.	Section 62-Further issue of share capital	• It is proposed to bring the requirement of compliance with section 42 in respect of the preferential offer in the section itself. Currently the applicability of section 42 is provided by the rules.
		• It is proposed that right issue offer letter can be sent through courier also.
27.	Section 73-Prohibition on acceptance of deposits from public	• It is proposed that an amount being not less than 20% of the amount of deposits, maturing during the following financial year be deposited on or before the 30th day of April each year and kept in a scheduled bank in a separate bank account to be called deposit repayment reserve account. Currently at least 15% of such amount is required to be deposited and that is also of amount of deposits maturing during a financial year and the financial year next following.
		• Further it is proposed to omit the requirement of providing deposit insurance.
		• It is also proposed that companies which had defaulted in repayment of deposits, can also accept deposits after a period of 5 years from the date of making good the default.

S. No.	Section	AMENDMENT
28.	Section 74-Repayment of Deposits, etc., accepted before commencement of this act	Where any amount of deposit or part thereof or interest thereof remains unpaid on the commencement of the Companies Act 2013, it is proposed that such amount shall be repaid within 3 years from the date of commencement or before the expiry of the period for which the deposit was accepted, whichever is earlier. Currently the amount was to be repaid within 1 year or before the expiry of the period for which the deposit was accepted, whichever is earlier.
29.	Section 76A-Punishment for Contravention of Section 73 or Section 76	• It is proposed to change the penalty from a fine not less than rupees one crore to rupees one crore or twice the amount of deposits accepted by the company, whichever is lower.
		• Further it is proposed that an officer of the company who is in default shall be punishable with imprisonment and fine. Earlier it was imprisonment or fine. In the process, the offence has been made non-compoundable.
30.	Section 77-Duty to register charges, etc.	It is proposed that this section shall not apply to certain charges, as may be prescribed by the Central Government in consultation with the Reserve Bank of India.
31.	Section 78-Application for Registration of charge	It is proposed that the person in whose favour the charge has been created can file the charge on the expiry of 30 days from the creation of charge where a company fails to file so. Currently the charge holder can register the charge only in case the company fails to do so within the period specified under section 77, which is 300 days.
32.	Section 82-Company to report satisfaction of charge	Timeline for filing of satisfaction of charge is proposed to be increased to 300 days on payment of additional fee.
33.	Section 89-Declaration in respect of beneficial interest in any share	As per the current law, return of beneficial interest declaration can also be filed on payment of additional fee within 270 days from the date by which it should have been filed. It is proposed to do away with the time limit of 270 days and the return can be filed at any time on payment of prescribed additional fee. For the purpose of declaration of beneficial interest, it is proposed that beneficial interest in a share includes, directly or indirectly, through any contract, arrangement or otherwise, the right or entitlement of a person alone or together with any other person to—
		• exercise or cause to be exercised any or all of the rights attached to such share; or
		• receive or participate in any dividend or other distribution in respect of such share.
34.	Section 90-Investigation of beneficial ownership of shares in certain cases	The provisions are proposed to be revamped. Key changes proposed are as under: • Every individual, who acting alone or together, or through one or more persons or trust, including a trust and persons resident outside India, holds beneficial interests, of not less than twenty-five per cent. or such

S. No.	Section	AMENDMENT
		other percentage as may be prescribed, in shares of a company or the right to exercise, or the actual exercising of significant influence or control as defined in clause (27) of section 2, over the company shall make a declaration to the company. The Central Government may however, prescribe class(es) of persons who shall not be required to make declaration.
		• Every company shall maintain a register of the interest declared by individuals as aforesaid and such register shall be open to inspection of members.
		• Every company shall file a return of significant beneficial owners of the company and changes therein with the Registrar.
		• Obligation is cast on the company to give notice, in the prescribed manner, to any person whom the company knows or has reasonable cause to believe to be a significant beneficial owner of the company who is not registered as a significant beneficial owner with the company as required under this section.
		• In case information asked is not provided, the Company shall apply to the Tribunal for an order directing that the shares in question be subject to restrictions with regard to transfer of interest, suspension of all rights attached to the shares.
		• Stringent penalties have been provided for default of this section including liability for fraud u/s 447.
35.	Section 92-Annual Return	• It is proposed to omit the requirement of MGT-9 i.e. extract of annual return to form part of the Board's Report. Instead, the copy of annual return shall be uploaded on the website of the company, if any, and its link shall be disclosed in the Board's report.
		• The Central Government may prescribe abridged form of annual return for One Person Company ('OPC'), Small Company and such other class or classes of companies as may be prescribed.
		• It is also proposed to omit the requirement related to disclosing indebtedness and details with respect to name, address, country of incorporation etc. of FII in the annual return of the company.
		• Time limit of 270 days within which annual return could be filed on payment of additional fee has been done away with. It is proposed that a company can file the annual return with ROC at any time on payment of prescribed additional fee.
36.	Section 93-Return to be filed with Registrar in case Promoters' stake changes	It is proposed to omit section 93 relating to return to be filed with respect to changes in promoters' and top ten shareholders' stake.
37.	Section 94-Place of keeping and inspection of	• It is proposed to omit the requirement of filing of special resolution in advance with the Registrar of Companies for keeping of the registers and returns at a place other than the registered office of the company.

S. No.	Section	AMENDMENT
	registers, returns, etc.	• Further it is proposed that certain prescribed particulars in the return, register or index referred to in this section shall not be available for inspection or for taking extracts or copies.
38.	Section 96- Annual General Meeting	It is proposed that Annual General Meeting ('AGM') of unlisted company may be held at anyplace in India if consent is given is writing or by electronic mode by all the members in advance.
39.	Section 100- Calling of Extraordinary General Meeting	It is proposed that Extraordinary General Meeting ('EGM') of wholly owned subsidiary of a company incorporated outside India can be held outside India. A company other than wholly owned subsidiary of a company incorporated outside India must hold EGM at a place within India.
40.	Section 101- Notice of meeting	• It is proposed that a general meeting may be held at a shorter notice if in case of an Annual General Meeting consent in writing or by electronic mode is given by not less than 95% of the members entitled to vote and in case of other general meetings consent is given by majority in number of members entitled to vote and who represent not less than 95% of paid-up share capital (in case of company having share capital) or total voting power exercisable at the meeting (in case of company not having share capital).
		• Where any member of a company is entitled to vote only on some resolution or resolutions to be moved at a meeting and not on the others, then his vote with respect to shorter notice shall only be counted for the purpose of the resolution on which he can vote.
		• Currently for calling both AGM and EGM at shorter notice, consent of 95% of members entitled to vote at the meeting is required.
41.	Section 110- Postal Ballot	It is proposed to allow companies which are mandatorily required to provide electronic voting facility, to transact items in general which, which are mandatorily required to be transacted through postal ballot.
42.	Section 117- Resolutions and Agreements to be filed	• It is proposed to provide exemption to banking companies from filing resolutions with respect to grant of loans, giving of guarantee or providing of security in respect of loans in the ordinary course of its business.
		• It is proposed to omit clause (e) of sub-section (3) of the section as the requirement under the clause is already covered in clause (a).
		• The minimum fine for non-filing under this section for company and officer in default is proposed to be reduced from rupees five lakh to one lakh rupees and from rupees one lakh to rupees fifty thousand.
		• Time limit of 270 days within which resolutions and agreements could be filed on payment of additional fee has been done away with. It is proposed that a company can file the resolutions and agreements with ROC at any time on payment of prescribed additional fee.

S. No.	Section	AMENDMENT
43.	Section 121- Report on annual general meeting	Time limit of 270 days within which report on annual general meeting could be filed on payment of additional fee has been done away with. It is proposed that a company can file the report on annual general meeting with ROC at any time on payment of prescribed additional fee.
44.	Section 123- Declaration of dividend	• It is proposed that in computing profits any amount representing unrealized gains, notional gains or revaluation of assets and any change in carrying of an asset or of a liability on measurement of the asset or the liability at fair value shall be excluded
		• In the case of inadequate or absence of profits, dividend can be declared out of accumulated profits earned by the company in previous years and transferred by the company to free reserves (instead of reserves).
		• It is also proposed that the Board of Directors of a company may declare interim dividend during any financial year or at any time during the period from closure of financial year till holding of the annual general meeting out of the surplus in the profit and loss account or out of profits of the financial year for which such interim dividend is sought to be declared or out of profits generated in the financial year till the quarter preceding the date of declaration of the interim dividend. In case the company has incurred loss during the current financial year up to the end of the quarter immediately preceding the date of declaration of interim dividend, such interim dividend shall not be declared at a rate higher than the average dividends declared by the company during immediately preceding three financial years.
45.	Section 129- Financial Statement	• The explanation providing that subsidiary includes associate company and joint venture has been deleted. The section has been amended to provide for consolidation of the accounts of associate companies in addition to its subsidiaries in the same form and manner as that of its own in accordance with applicable accounting standards.
		• The company shall also attach along with its financial statement, a separate statement containing the salient features of the subsidiary and associate companies.
46.	Section 130- Reopening of accounts on court's or tribunal's orders	• It is proposed that in addition to authorities already specified, any other person concerned shall be given notice before passing an order for re-opening of accounts and the court or the Tribunal shall also take into consideration the representations made by the other person.
		• It is also proposed that order for reopening of accounts can be made upto eight financial years preceding the current financial year unless there is a specific direction under section 128(5) from the Central Government that the books of accounts may be kept for longer period in which case the books of account may be ordered to be reopened for a longer period
47.	Section 132- Constitution of National Financial Reporting Authority	• It is proposed to reduce the minimum fine in respect of professional or other misconduct from ten lakh rupees to five lakh rupees.
		• It is proposed to omit the provisions regarding constitution of separate Appellate Authority under this section and appeal against any order of NFRA shall lie before the National Company Law Appellate Tribunal in the prescribed manner.

S. No.	Section	AMENDMENT
48.	Section 134- Financial Statement, Board's report, etc.	• It is proposed that CEO whether appointed as a Director or not, will sign the financial statement, in case there is no chairperson of the Company. Currently CEO is required to sign, only if he is also acting as a director.
		• In case of Board report, it is proposed that disclosures which have been provided in the financial statement shall not be required to be reproduced in the report again.
		• It is proposed that in place of extract of the annual return, only the web address, if any, where annual return has been placed shall be mentioned.
		• It is proposed that instead of exact text of the policies, key feature of policies along with its web link shall be disclosed in Board report.
		• In respect to performance evaluation, it is proposed to omit the responsibility of the Board for carrying the performance evaluation of Board, Directors and Committee. It is now required to include in the Board's report of listed companies and other prescribed public companies that annual evaluation of the performance of the Board, its Committees and of individual directors has been made.
		• Central Government may prescribe abridged Board Report for small and one person companies.
49.	Section 135- Corporate Social Responsibility	• Eligibility criteria for the purpose of constituting the corporate social responsibility committee and incurring expenditure towards CSR is proposed to be calculated based on immediately preceding financial year. Currently this eligibility is decided based on preceding three financial years.
		• Further it is proposed that where a company is not required to appoint an independent director, it shall have in its Corporate Social Responsibility Committee two or more directors.
		• It also proposed to empower the Central Government to prescribe sums which shall not be included for calculating 'net profit' of a company under section 135.
50.	Section 136- Right of member to copies of audited financial statement	• It is proposed that copies of audited financial statements and other documents can be sent at shorter notice if it is so agreed by members- (a) holding, if the company has a share capital, majority in number entitled to vote and who represent not less than ninety-five per cent of such part of the paid-up share capital of the company as gives a right to vote at the meeting; or (b) having, if the company has no share capital, not less than ninety-five per cent of the total voting power exercisable at the meeting.
		• It is proposed that only listed companies shall place on its website, if any the separate audited accounts of its subsidiary or subsidiaries. Currently all companies required to comply this.
		• If the foreign subsidiary is statutorily required to prepare consolidated financial statement under any law of the country of its incorporation, it is proposed that the requirement of posting audited accounts of subsidiary shall be met if consolidated financial statement of such foreign subsidiary is placed on the website of the listed company.

S. No.	Section	AMENDMENT
		• If the foreign subsidiary is not required to get its financial statement audited, it is proposed that the holding listed company may place such unaudited financial statement on its website and where such financial statement is in a language other than English, a translated copy of the financial statement in English shall also be placed on the website.
		• It is proposed that every company having a subsidiary or subsidiaries shall provide a copy of separate audited or unaudited financial statements, as the case may be, as prepared in respect of each of its subsidiary to any member who asks for it.
51.	Section 137- Copy of Financial Statement to be filed with Registrar	• It is proposed to allow the filing of unaudited financial statements of foreign subsidiary which is not required to get its accounts audited along with a declaration to that effect.
		• Time limit of 270 days within which financial statement could be filed on payment of additional fee has been done away with under all the sub-sections. It is proposed that a company can file the financial statement with ROC at any time on payment of prescribed additional fee.
52.	Section 139-Appointment of Auditors	It is proposed to omit the requirement related to ratification of appointment of auditors by members at every annual general meeting.
53.	Section 140-Removal, Resignation of Auditor and giving of special notice	It is proposed to reduce the fine in case of failure to file resignation by auditor in Form ADT-3 to fifty thousand rupees or the remuneration of auditor whichever is less.
54.	Section 141- Eligibility, Qualification and Disqualifications of Auditors	It is proposed that a person who, directly or indirectly, renders any service referred to in section 144 to the company or its holding company or its subsidiary company will not be eligible for appointment as Auditor. Currently the restriction is only on the person, whose subsidiary, associate company or any other form of entity is engaged as on the date of appointment in consulting and specialized services as provided in section 144.
55.	Section 143- Powers and duties of auditors and auditing standards	• It is proposed to cover associate companies along with subsidiary companies with respect to right of auditors to have access to accounts and records.
		• The auditor's report is to include whether internal financial controls with reference to financial statement are in place and not in respect of internal financial control system.
56.	Section 147- Punishment for contravention	• The maximum fine which can be imposed on an auditor has been revised from rupees five lakh to rupees five lakh or four times the remuneration of the auditor, whichever is less. If the auditor has contravened provisions knowingly or wilfully with the intention to deceive the company etc., the amount of fine has been reduced to minimum of fifty thousand rupees but which may extend to twenty-five lakh rupees or eight times the remuneration of the auditor, whichever is less.

S. No.	Section	AMENDMENT
		• It is proposed to restrict the liability of auditor who is convicted of any default, to pay the damages to any person for loss arising out of incorrect or misleading statements made in the audit report, to only members and creditors of the company. Currently the Auditor is liable to pay damages to any person concerned.
		• It is proposed that criminal liability of an audit firm, in respect of liability other than fine, the concerned partner or partners, who acted in a fraudulent manner or abetted or, as the case may be, colluded in any fraud shall only be liable. Currently the criminal liability is of the partner or partners concerned of the audit firm and the firm, jointly and severally.
57.	Section 148-Central Government to specify audit of items of Cost in respect of Certain Companies	It is proposed to substitute the words 'cost accountant in practice' with the words 'cost accountant' and also to substitute the words 'Institute of Cost and Works Accountants of India' with the words 'Institute of Cost.
58.	Section 149-Company to have Board of Directors	• It is proposed that 182 days for determining whether a director is resident in India shall be computed with reference to the financial year. Currently it is calculated in reference to previous calendar year.
		• Further it is proposed that in case of new companies, the requirement of period of 182 days shall apply proportionately at the end of the financial year in which it is incorporated.
		• In the definition of Independent Director, the words 'pecuniary interest' is proposed to be substituted by pecuniary relationship, other than remuneration as such director or having transaction not exceeding ten per cent, of his total income or such amount as may be prescribed.
		• While determining the eligibility for appointment as Independent director, it is proposed to extend the restriction related to pecuniary relationships with respect to relative of a director to include the following: (i) is holding any security of or interest in the company, its holding, subsidiary or associate company during the two immediately preceding financial years or during the current financial year. Provided that the relative may hold security or interest in the company of face value not exceeding fifty lakh rupees or two per cent of the paid-up capital of the company, its holding, subsidiary or associate company or such higher sum as may be prescribed; (ii) is indebted to the company, its holding, subsidiary or associate company or their promoters, or directors, in excess of such amount as may be prescribed during the two immediately preceding financial years or during the current financial year; (iii) has given a guarantee or provided any security in connection with the indebtedness of any third person to the company, its holding, subsidiary or associate company or their promoters, or directors of such holding company, for such amount as may be prescribed during the two immediately preceding financial years or during the current financial year; or

S. No.	Section	AMENDMENT
		(iv) has any other pecuniary transaction or relationship with the company, or its subsidiary, or its holding or associate company amounting to two per cent or more of its gross turnover or total income singly or in combination with the transactions referred to in subclause (i), (ii) or (iii) above.
		• It is proposed to allow the appointment of person as an independent director, whose relative is an employee during the three financial years immediately preceding the financial year, in which the person is proposed to be appointed as Independent Director.
59.	Section 152-Appointment of directors	It is proposed to make necessary provisions to provide that in addition to DIN, a director may hold any other identification as may be prescribed by the Central Government under section 153.
60.	Section 153-Application for allotment of Director Identification Number	It is proposed to empower the Central Government to recognize any other identification number to be treated as director identification number. It is expected that Central Government will notify either PAN or Aadhar as DIN.
61.	Section 157-Company to inform Director Identification Number to Registrar	Time limit of 270 days within which a company could furnish DIN of all its directors on payment of additional fee has been done away with. It is proposed that a company can furnish DIN of all directors to ROC at any time on payment of prescribed additional fee.
62.	Section 160-Right of persons other than retiring directors to stand for directorship	It is proposed that the requirement of deposit of rupees one lakh with respect to nomination of directors shall not be applicable in case of appointment of independent directors or directors nominated by nomination and remuneration committee or a director recommended by the Board of Directors of the Company, in the case of a company not required to constitute Nomination and Remuneration Committee.
63.	Section 161-Appointment of Additional director, Alternate director and Nominee director	• It is proposed to restrict a person from being appointed as an alternate director if he is holding directorship in the same company.
		• It is also proposed that all companies including a private company may fill up the causal vacancy by the board and casual vacancy filled by the Board shall be subsequently approved in the immediate next general meeting.
64.	Section 164-Disqualifications for appointment of director	• It is proposed that when a director is appointed in company which is in default of filing of financial statements or annual return or repayment of deposits or pay interest or redemption of debentures or payment of interest thereon or payment of dividend then such director shall not incur the disqualification for a period of six months from the date of his appointment. It is also proposed to be clarified that disqualification arising due to conviction by court or order passed by court or tribunal or conviction related to section 188, shall continue to exist even if appeal or petition has been filed against the order of conviction or disqualification.

S. No.	Section	AMENDMENT
65.	Section 165-Number of Directorship	It is proposed that the directorship in a dormant company shall not be included in the limit of directorships of 20 companies.
66.	Section 167-Vacation of office of director	• It is proposed that in case a director incurs any of disqualifications under section 164 (2) due to default of filing of financial statements or annual return or repayment of deposits or pay interest or redemption of debentures or payment of interest thereon or payment of dividend, then he shall vacate office in all the companies other than the company which is in default.
		• It is also proposed that the director will not vacate office in certain cases where an appeal is preferred.
67.	Section 168-Resignation of director	It is proposed to make filing of Form DIR-11 regarding forwarding of copy of resignation by director to the Registrar optional.
68.	Section 173-Meetings of Board	It is proposed to allow participation of directors on restricted items at Board meetings through video conferencing or other audio-visual means if there is quorum through physical presence of directors.
69.	Section 177-Audit Committee	• It is proposed that instead of every listed company, every listed public company shall constitute an audit committee.
		• It is proposed that related party transactions other than those prescribed under section 188, if not approved by Audit committee, will require the approval of Board of Directors.
		• In case any transaction involving any amount not exceeding one crore rupees is entered into by a director or officer of the company without obtaining the approval of the Audit Committee and it is not ratified by the Audit Committee within three months from the date of the transaction, such transaction shall be voidable at the option of the Audit Committee and if the transaction is with the related party to any director or is authorised by any other director, the director concerned shall indemnify the company against any loss incurred by it.
		• It is also proposed that approval of audit committee with respect to transactions between a holding company and its wholly owned subsidiary company will only be required, if the transactions falls under section 188.
70.	Section 178-Nomination and remuneration Committee and Stakeholders Relationship Committee	• It is proposed that instead of every listed company, every listed public company shall constitute a Nomination and Remuneration Committee ('NRC').
		• It is proposed that committee will specify methodology for effective evaluation of performance of Board and committees and individual directors either by the Board, NRC or an independent external agency and NRC can review the implementation of evaluation system.
		• It is further proposed that instead of disclosing the policy in the Board's report, such policy shall be placed on the website of the company, if any and only the salient features of the policy and the changes therein need to be disclosed in the Board's report.

S. No.	Section	AMENDMENT
71.	Section 180- Restrictions on powers of board	It is proposed to include securities premium along with paid-up share capital and free reserves for calculation of maximum limits on borrowing powers of the Board.
72.	Section 184- Disclosure of interest by directors	• It is proposed to omit the minimum penalty with respect to failure by directors to disclose interest.
		• It is also proposed to exempt body corporate where any director or two or more of them holds or hold not more than 2% of the paid-up share capital, from the purview of section 184.
73.	Section 185- Loan to directors, etc.	A completely new section 185 is proposed. Some of the key changes are: • Complete restriction on providing loan, guarantee or security in connection with loan to any director, director of the holding company or any partner or relative of any such director or any firm in which any such director or relative in a partner.
		• Loan to following parties is allowed subject to special resolution of shareholders and certain other prescribed conditions (i) any private company of which any such director is a director or member; (ii) any body corporate at a general meeting of which not less than twenty-five per cent of the total voting power may be exercised or controlled by any such director, or by two or more such directors, together; or (iii) any body corporate, the Board of directors, managing director or manager, whereof is accustomed to act in accordance with the directions or instructions of the Board, or of any director or directors, of the lending company. Currently transactions with aforesaid categories is prohibited • Current exemption provided under section 185(1) continues to remain except that when company which in the ordinary course of its business provides loans or gives guarantees or securities for the due repayment of any loan and in respect of such loans an interest is charged at a rate not less than the rate of prevailing yield of one year, three year, five year or ten year Government security closest to the tenure of the loan. The rate of interest is clarified
		• It is also proposed to penalize defaulting officer in the company along with the company and director or the other person to whom any loan is advanced or guarantee or security is given.
74.	Section 186- Loan and Investment by company	• It also proposed to exclude employees from the ambit of this section.
		• It is proposed that shareholders' approval will not be required where a loan or guarantee is given or where a security has been provided by a company to its wholly owned subsidiary company or a joint venture company, or acquisition is made by a holding company, by way of subscription, purchase or otherwise of, the securities of its wholly owned subsidiary company.

S. No.	Section	AMENDMENT
75.	Section 188-Related Party Transactions	• It is proposed that the requirement related to restriction on voting by relatives in the general meeting shall not apply to a company in which ninety per cent or more members in numbers are relatives of promoters or related parties.
		• It is also proposed to provide that non-ratification of transaction shall be voidable at the option of the Board or shareholders, as the case may be. This amendment aims at bringing clarity since currently though ratification is allowed both by Board or Shareholders but transaction was only voidable at the option of the Board.
76.	Section 194-Prohibition on Forward dealings in securities of company by director or Key Managerial Personnel	It is proposed to omit this section.
77.	Section 195-Prohibition on Insider trading of securities	It is proposed to omit this section.
78.	Section 196-Appointment of Managing Director, Wholetime director or Manager	• It is proposed that a person beyond the age of seventy years can be appointed as managing director or whole time director or manager even when such appointment has not been approved by special resolution provided that the resolution for such appointment is passed with votes cast in favour of the motion exceed the votes, if any, cast against the motion and the Central Government is satisfied, on an application made by the Board, that such appointment is most beneficial to the company, the appointment of the person who has attained the age of seventy years may be made.
		• Further it is proposed that in respect of appointment of managing director, whole time director or manager, approval of Central Government shall only be required in case the appointment is not in accordance with the matters specified in Part I of Schedule V.
79.	Section 197-Overall maximum managerial remuneration and managerial remuneration in case of absence or inadequacy of profits	• It is proposed that the approval of the Central Government shall not be required at the time of the payment of remuneration exceeding 11% of the net profits of the company.
		• It is proposed that company with the approval of shareholders by way of special resolution can pay the remuneration in excess of individual limits provided for payment of remuneration to executive or non-executive directors. Further where the company has defaulted in payment of dues to any bank or public financial institution or non-convertible debenture holders or any other secured creditor, the prior approval of the bank or public financial institution concerned or the non-convertible debenture holders or other secured creditor, as the case may be, shall be obtained by the company before obtaining the approval in the general meeting. Currently requirement is of ordinary resolution and no provision is there for approval of financial institutions etc.

S. No.	Section	AMENDMENT
		• It is also proposed that in case of loss or inadequacy of profits, remuneration can only be paid in accordance with Schedule V. This is very important amendment because currently in case where remuneration is not paid in accordance with Schedule V, then approval of Central Government can be obtained but by way of amendment, the provision of approval is proposed to be omitted.
		• It is also proposed to provide relief to director to refund the excess remuneration received by providing a timeline of two years or such lesser period as may be allowed by the company. Further until such sum is refunded, the director shall hold it in trust for the company. Consequently it is proposed to delete the provisions related to waiver of excess remuneration paid to directors with the approval of Central Government.
		• It is also proposed to make a provision which empowers the Company to waive the recovery of excess remuneration paid to directors provided approval of company by special resolution within two years from the date the sum becomes refundable is obtained. Further where any term loan of any bank or public financial institution is subsisting or the company has defaulted in payment of dues to any bank or public financial institution or non-convertible debenture holders or any other secured creditor, the prior approval of the bank or public financial institution concerned or the non-convertible debenture holders or other secured creditor, as the case may be, shall be obtained by the company before obtaining the approval in the general meeting.
		• It is also proposed that the auditor of the company shall, in his report under section 143, make a statement as to whether the remuneration paid by the company to its directors is in accordance with the provisions of this section, whether remuneration paid to any director is in excess of the limit laid down under this section and give such other details as may be prescribed.
		• It is also proposed to provide relief to the company whose application is pending for approval before the Central Government under section 197 by making a provision under which on and from the commencement of the Companies (Amendment) Act, 2017, any application made to the Central Government under the provisions of this section as it stood before such commencement, which is pending with that Government shall abate, and the company shall, within one year of such commencement, obtain the approval in accordance with the provisions of this section, as so amended.
80.	Section 198-Calculation of profits	It is proposed that credit for profit arising by way of premium on shares or debentures of the company which are issued or sold by an investment company as referred to in clause (a) of the explanation to section 186 shall be allowed as credit to the profit and loss account. Currently such credit is not allowed in case of all companies including investment companies. • It is also proposed that at the time of calculation of profits, credit shall not be given for any amount representing unrealized gains, notional gains or revaluation of assets.
		• It is further proposed that sums related to excess of expenditure over income, which had arisen in computing the net profits in accordance with this section in any year, in so far as such excess has not been deducted in any subsequent year preceding the year in respect of which the net profits have to be ascertained, shall be allowed as a deduction.

S. No.	Section	AMENDMENT
81.	Section 200-Central Government or company to fix limits with regard to remuneration	It is proposed to omit the power of the Central Government to fix the remuneration within the limits specified in the Act, at such amount or percentage of profits as it may deems fit.
82.	Section 201-Forms of, and procedure in relation to, certain applications	It is proposed to amend the section as a consequential change to amendment in section 196.
83.	Section 216-Investigation of ownership of company	It is proposed to empower the Central Government to appoint inspectors for determining true persons who have or had beneficial interest in shares of a company or who are or have been beneficial owners or significant beneficial owner of the company.
84.	Section 223-Inspector's report	It is proposed that a copy of inspectors report shall be made available only to members, creditors or any other person whose interest is likely to be affected, on their request. Currently any person can request for the copy.
85.	Section 236-Purchase of Minority Shareholding	It is proposed to substitute the words 'transferor company' with the words 'company whose shares are being transferred' for providing clarity in sub-sections (4), (5) and (6).
86.	Section 247-Valuation by Registered Valuers	It is proposed to dilute the restriction on appointment of a registered valuer by providing that registered valuer can be appointed for valuation of an asset in which he has a direct or indirect interest or becomes so interested during a period of three years prior to appointment as valuer or three years after valuation of assets. Currently restriction on appointment of registered valuer for undertaking valuation of any assets in which he has a direct or indirect interest or becomes so interested is without any limitation on time.
87.	Section 366-Companies capable of being registered	It is proposed to allow conversions of partnership firms, LLP, etc. with two or more partners into private companies. Currently they must have seven partners.
88.	Section 374-Obligations of companies registering under this Part	It is proposed to bring the clarity that upon registration as a company under the Part-I of Chapter-XXI, a limited liability partnership incorporated under the Limited Liability Partnership Act, 2008 shall be deemed to have been dissolved under that Act without any further act or deed.
89.	Section 379-Application of Act to foreign companies	• It is proposed to bring clarity with respect to applicability of provisions of the Act to foreign companies by providing that sections 380 to 386 and 392 and 393 shall apply to foreign companies. • It is also proposed to empower the Central Government to exempt any class of foreign companies from complying with the aforesaid provisions.

S. No.	Section	AMENDMENT
90.	Section 384-Debentures, Annual Return, Registration of charges, books of account and their Inspection	It is proposed to amend the section for providing applicability of section 135 on foreign companies.
91.	Section 391-Application of sections 34 to 36 and Chapter XX	It is proposed that the provisions relating to winding up contained in Chapter XX shall apply for closure of place of business of a foreign company in India as if it were a company incorporated in India in case such foreign company has raised monies through offer or issue of securities which have not been repaid or redeemed. In other words, if a foreign company has not raised monies, the provisions relating to winding up will not be applicable.
92.	Section 403-Fee for Filings, etc.	• It is proposed that only document, fact or information required to be submitted under section 92 (Annual Return) or 137 (Copy of financial statement to be filed with registrar) may be submitted, after expiry of the period so provided in those sections, on payment of such additional fee as may be prescribed which shall not be less than ₹ 100 per day and different amounts may be prescribed for different classes of companies.
		• Further it is proposed that where the document, fact or information, in cases other than sections 92 or 137, is not submitted, within the period provided in the relevant section, it may, without prejudice to any other legal action or liability under this Act, be submitted, filed, registered or recorded, on payment of such additional fee as may be prescribed and different fees may be prescribed for different classes of companies.
		• It is also proposed that where there is default on two or more occasions in submitting, filing, registering or recording of the document, fact or information, it may, without prejudice to any other legal action or liability under this Act, be submitted, filed, registered or recorded, on payment of a higher additional fee, as may be prescribed and which shall not be lesser than twice the additional fee provided under the first or the second proviso as applicable.
		• Further it is proposed that where a company fails or commits any default to submit, file, register or record any document, fact or information before the expiry of the period specified in the relevant section, the company and the officers of the company who are in default, shall, without prejudice to the liability for the payment of fee and additional fee, be liable for the penalty or punishment provided under this Act for such failure or default.
93.	Section 406-Power to modify act in its application to 'Nidhis'	• It is proposed to provide that Nidhi" or "Mutual Benefit Society" means a company which the Central Government may, by notification in the Official Gazette, declare to be a Nidhi or Mutual Benefit Society, as the case may be. Currently mutual benefit society is not covered.
		• Further exhaustive definition of Nidhi company has been deleted and it is left to the Government to declare a company to be a Nidhi or Mutual Benefit Society by notification in the Official Gazette.
		• It is also proposed to modify the requirements relating to laying of copy of exemption notification before both Houses of Parliament.

S. No.	Section	AMENDMENT
94.	Section 409-Qualification of President and Members of Tribunal	Following changes are proposed with respect to eligibility for technical members with respect to the constitution of the National Company Law Tribunal: • Instead of Joint Secretary to the Government of India, person who has been holding the rank of Secretary or Additional Secretary to the Government of India, will be eligible.
		• A person of proven ability, integrity and standing having special knowledge and professional experience of not less than fifteen years in industrial finance, industrial management, industrial reconstruction, investment and accountancy will be eligible. Expertise in other disciplines like law, labour laws, and disciplines related to management, conduct of affairs, revival, rehabilitation and winding-up of companies are proposed to be deleted.
95.	Section 410-Constitution of Appellate Tribunal	In addition to the order of the Tribunal, it is proposed to bring out the order of the National Financial Reporting Authority also for appeal before the National Company Law Appellate Tribunal.
96.	Section 411-Qualifications of Chairperson and Members of Appellate Tribunal	Eligibility for appointment as Technical member is proposed to be brought in sync with the amendment proposed in section 409.
97.	Section 412-Selection of Members of Tribunal and Appellate Tribunal	It is proposed to align with Supreme Court directions with respect to constitution of Selection Committee.
98.	Section 435-Establishment of Special Courts	• It is proposed to authorize Central Government to establish Special Courts for the purpose of speedy trials of offences under the Act. Currently Special Court can be established for trying offences punishable with imprisonment of two years or more.
		• The constitution of Special Court has been changed and will depend upon the nature of offence.
99.	Section 438-Application of Code to proceedings before Special Court	It is proposed to amend section 438 of the Act as a consequence of amendments to section 435.
100.	Section 439-Offences to be non-cognizable	It is proposed to include member along with shareholders in respect of complaint with respect to taking cognizance of offences under the Act by the Court.
101.	Section 440-Transitional provisions	It is proposed to provide that till the time a Special Court is established, the trial of offences shall be continued with Court of Session or Court of Metropolitan Magistrate or a Judicial Magistrate of the First Class.
102.	Section 441-Compounding of certain offences	It is proposed to enable the Tribunal to compound offences punishable with fine only as well as offences punishable with fine or imprisonment. The provision has now been brought in line with section 621A of the 1956 Act.

S. No.	Section	AMENDMENT
103.	Section 446A-Factors for determining level of punishment	It is proposed to insert a new section providing for the following factors which the court or special court will consider while determining level of punishment: (a) Size of the company; (b) Nature of business carried on by the company; (c) Injury to public interest; (d) Nature of the default; and (e) Repetition of the default.
104.	Section 446B-Lesser penalties for One Person Companies or small companies	It is proposed to provide relief to OPC and Small Co., in case of failure to comply with the provisions of sub-section (5) of section 92 (Annual Return), clause (c) of sub-section (2) of section 117 (Resolutions and agreements to be filed), sub-section (3) of section 137 (Copy of financial statement to be filed with Registrar). In case of default, such company and officer in default of such company shall be punishable with fine or imprisonment or fine and imprisonment, as the case may be, which shall not be more than one-half of the fine or imprisonment or fine and imprisonment, as the case may be, of the minimum or maximum fine or imprisonment or fine and imprisonment, as the case may be, specified in such sections.
105.	Section 447-Punishment for Fraud	• It is proposed that only person guilty of fraud involving an amount of at least ten lakh rupees or one per cent of the turnover of the company, whichever is lower shall be punishable with imprisonment for a term which shall not be less than 6 months but which may extend to ten years and shall also be liable to a fine which shall not less than the amount involved in the fraud but which may extend to three times the amount involved in the fraud.
		• Further that where the fraud involves an amount less than ten lakh rupees or one per cent of the turnover of the company, whichever is lower and does not involve public interest,. any person guilty of such fraud shall be punishable with imprisonment for a term which may extend to five years or with fine which may extend to twenty lakh rupees or with both.
106.	Section 458 Delegation by Central Government of its powers and functions	Consequent upon omission of sections 194 (Forward dealings) and 195 (Insider trading), the proviso to sub-section (1) of section 458 is proposed to be omitted.

●●●